| Presidential Terms | Judicial Decisions | Constitutionally Significant Events |
|---|---|---|
| Cleveland (1885–1889) | | Samuel Gompers organizes the American Federation of Labor (1886); creation of the Interstate Commerce Commission (1887). |
| B. Harrison (1889–1893) | | |
| Cleveland (1893–1897) | United States v. E. C. Knight Co. (1895)<br>Pollock v. Farmers' Loan & Trust Co. (1895) | |
| McKinley (1897–1901) | Plessy v. Ferguson (1896) | War with Spain (1898); acquisition of territories previously belonging to Spain; McKinley assassinated (1901). |
| T. Roosevelt (1901–1909) | Champion v. Ames (1903)<br>McCray v. United States (1904)<br>Lochner v. New York (1905) | Rise of Progressivism; muckraking era; "Brandeis brief." |
| Taft (1909–1913) | | |
| Wilson (1913–1921) | Hammer v. Dagenhart (1918)<br>Schenck v. United States (1919)<br>Missouri v. Holland (1920) | Establishment of the Federal Reserve System (1913); 16th and 17th Amendments (1913); World War I (U.S. involvement, 1917–1918); 18th Amendment (1919) ushers in the Prohibition era; 19th Amendment (1920); "Palmer raids" (1919–1920). |
| Harding (1921–1923) | Stafford v. Wallace (1922) | |
| Coolidge (1923–1929) | Gitlow v. New York (1925)<br>Whitney v. California (1927)<br>Olmstead v. United States (1928) | |
| Hoover (1929–1933) | Powell v. Alabama (1932) | Onset of Great Depression (1929); Senate rejects nomination of Judge John Parker to the Supreme Court; 20th Amendment (1933). |
| F. Roosevelt (1933–1945) | Nebbia v. New York (1934)<br>Home Bldg. & Loan Assoc. v. Blaisdell (1934)<br>United States v. Butler (1936)<br>Carter v. Carter Coal Co. (1936)<br>N.L.R.B. v. Jones & Laughlin (1937)<br>West Coast Hotel v. Parrish (1937)<br>Palko v. Connecticut (1937)<br>Minersville School District v. Gobitis (1940)<br>Wickard v. Filburn (1941)<br>West Virginia Board of Education v. Barnette (1943)<br>Korematsu v. United States (1944) | New Deal agenda begins to go to Congress; 21st Amendment (1933) ends Prohibition.<br><br>Court-packing fight (1937). Supreme Court's "switch-in-time."<br><br><br><br>World War II (U.S. involvement, 1941–1945). U.S. drops two atomic bombs on Japan (1945). |
| Truman (1945–1953) | Southern Pacific v. Arizona (1945)<br>Adamson v. California (1947)<br>Dennis v. United States (1951)<br>Youngstown v. Sawyer (1952) | Cold War begins (1946); Employment Act of 1946; Americans for Democratic Action organized (1947); Democratic National Convention adopts strong civil rights plank (1948); modern civil rights movement develops; NATO established (1949); Korean War (1950–1953); height of influence of Senator Joseph McCarthy (1950–1954); 22nd Amendment (1951). |
| Eisenhower (1953–1961) | Brown v. Board of Education (I) (1954)<br>Bolling v. Sharpe (1954)<br>Brown v. Board of Education (II) (1955)<br>Watkins v. United States (1957)<br>Cooper v. Aaron (1958)<br>Barenblatt v. United States (1959) | Civil rights movement intensifies in the wake of the Court's school integration decisions in 1954 and 1955; massive resistance to school integration begins in some southern states.<br><br>Congress enacts the first civil rights law since 1875 (1957). |

FOURTEENTH EDITION

# AMERICAN CONSTITUTIONAL LAW

## INTRODUCTORY ESSAYS AND SELECTED CASES

**Alpheus Thomas Mason**
*Late of Princeton University*

**Donald Grier Stephenson, Jr.**
*Franklin and Marshall College*

PEARSON
Prentice
Hall

UPPER SADDLE RIVER, NEW JERSEY 07458

*Library of Congress Cataloging-in-Publication Data*

MASON, ALPHEUS THOMAS, [date].
 American constitutional law: introductory essays and selected cases / Alpheus Thomas
Mason, Donald Grier Stephenson, Jr.—14th ed.
  p. cm.
 Includes bibliographical references and index.
 ISBN 0-13-117437-1
 1. Constitutional law—United States—Cases I. Stephenson, D. Grier. II. Title.
KF4549.M3 2005
342.73—dc22

Editorial Director: *Charlyce Jones Owen*
Acquisitions Editor: *Glenn Johnston*
Assistant Editor: *John Ragozzine*
Editorial Assistant: *Suzanne Remore*
Editorial/Production Supervision: *Edie Riker*
Prepress and Manufacturing Buyer: *Sherry Lewis*
Marketing Manager: *Kara Kindstrom*
Marketing Assistant: *Jennifer Lang*
Cover Designer: *Bruce Kenselaar*
Cover Photo: *Cass Gilbert/Corbis Digital Stock*
Cover Art Director: *Jayne Conte*

> ### *In memory of*
> ### *William M. Beaney*
> ### *(1918–2003)*
> ### *and in honor of the arrival of*
> ### *Mason Allan Stephenson*

Pearson Education LTD.
Pearson Education Singapore, Pte. Ltd
Pearson Education, Canada, Ltd
Pearson Education—Japan
Pearson Education Australia PTY, Limited

Pearson Education North Asia Ltd
Pearson Educación de Mexico, S.A. de C.V.
Pearson Education Malaysia, Pte. Ltd
Pearson Education, Upper Saddle River, NJ

10 9 8 7 6 5 4 3 2 1

ISBN 0-13-117437-1

# Contents

**CHAPTER THREE**

# CONGRESS AND THE PRESIDENT  80

**CHAPTER FOUR**

## FEDERALISM  132

**CHAPTER FIVE**

## THE ELECTORAL PROCESS  181

## CHAPTER TEN

# CRIMINAL JUSTICE  399

## CHAPTER THIRTEEN

# PRIVACY 579

## CHAPTER FOURTEEN

# EQUAL PROTECTION OF THE LAWS 618

# *Preface*

The devastating terrorist attacks on September 11, 2001, and the U.S. government's responses to them and to terrorism generally, have brought to the forefront the recurring tension in American constitutional law between security and freedom. Understandably, Americans demand security. Yet the nation that is defended is defined by its devotion to individual liberty and constitutional limitations. This tension is reflected throughout this book in many ways and is expressly addressed in a new concluding Chapter Fifteen, Epilogue: Security and Freedom in Wartime. This is a subject that most Americans have thought little about in decades.

The tension rekindled by the terrorist attacks came only nine months after the extended and chaotic finish to the presidential election of 2000, that, in *Bush* v. *Gore,* was itself a reminder of the Supreme Court's central place in American government. That development in turn must be considered alongside two other facts: First, on a substantial number of major constitutional issues in recent terms, the Court has split 5 to 4, or 6 to 3. Second, as of early 2004, the bench remains among the most stable in history. At no time since 1869, when Congress last set the Court's roster at nine, have so many years passed without a vacancy. Moreover, excepting only the period 1812–1823, the years since Justice Harry Blackmun's retirement and Justice Stephen Breyer's arrival in 1994 mark the longest stretch of stability in membership in Court history. Given that, on average, a vacancy has usually occurred about once every two years since 1790, the person elected president in 2004 may have an inordinate influence on the make-up of the Court and therefore on American constitutional law. With that prospect in mind, the Introduction retains its distinctive focus on institutional development and the politics of judicial selection.

The Court marked the end of calendar 2003 with yet another reminder of the impact that it can have on American politics. Just in time for the presidential campaign season of 2004, *McConnell* v. *Federal Election Commission* narrowly resolved most constitutional doubts in favor of the comprehensive and far-reaching provisions of the Bipartisan Campaign Reform Act of 2002, Congress's most significant overhaul of campaign finance legislation since 1974.

This edition, following the pattern set in earlier ones, is rooted in the conviction that constitutional law is an intricate blend of politics, history, and competing values. Even though judicial decisions are couched in the language and method used by lawyers, constitutional cases are therefore proper turf for students of politics and government. This is because the judiciary is the place where law and politics meet.

Accordingly, the book emphasizes the ongoing importance of constitutional interpretation. Interpretation represents choices made about the meaning of the Constitution. These choices in turn affect the operation of the political system, they help to define individual rights and freedoms, and they influence the quality of life that Americans enjoy. Constitutional interpretation has thus made the justices participants in the governing process. Their decisions embody selections among hard (and consequential) alternatives, rather than the easy dictates of a cold mechanical process. The book invites students to become party to the dialogue that the Court has maintained with the American people for over two centuries, a dialogue that reflects a historic attraction to, and suspicion of, majority rule—on the part of both the people and the Court.

Aside from the new Chapter Fifteen, noted above, readers familiar with the previous edition will notice one additional change in the organization of the fourteenth edition. Presentation of the Bill of Rights and criminal justice issues, previously combined in a single chapter, are now developed in two: Chapter Nine (Nationalization of the Bill of Rights) and Chapter Ten (Criminal Justice). Moreover, Chapter Nine continues the discussion, begun in Chapter Eight, of the various uses the Court has made of due process of law.

Readers of *American Constitutional Law* are encouraged to visit the book's Web site: **www.prenhall.com/mason**. The site complements the fourteenth edition and facilitates teaching and learning in at least three ways: (1) The site contains important decisions handed down after this edition went to press, which are edited in the same manner as cases excerpted in the book. (2) The site retains cases from the twelfth and thirteenth editions that were displaced by new material and so may be used as a case archive. Faculty designing syllabi thus have a larger number of edited cases from which to choose. (3) Finally, the site contains useful noncase material as well as links to other Court-related sites.

A distinctive feature of the book remains the essay preceding the cases in each chapter. These essays supply the historical and political contexts and trace the meandering thread of constitutional doctrine across major decisions. The case excerpts that follow—essential for learning and in depicting constitutional interpretation at work—are as generous as space allows. As shown in the Contents, cases in each chapter are now grouped by subtopic within that chapter, loosely corresponding to the organization of the essay itself.

New material in both essays and cases reflects recent developments, especially from the 2002–2003 term: in Chapter Three, a summary of events leading to the war in Iraq and the protracted occupation; in Chapter Five, recent developments in campaign finance regulation; in Chapter Ten, decisions on electronic surveillance, arrests, drug testing, and capital punishment; in Chapter Eleven, rulings on cross-burning, access to the public forum, and child pornography; in Chapter Twelve, the Court's first pronouncement on school vouchers; in Chapter Thirteen, reconsideration of government's authority to regulate sexual privacy; in Chapter Fourteen, the first holdings in a quarter century on affirmative action in the context of university admissions; and, in Chapter Fifteen, the tension between freedom and security in wartime, especially in the context of the war on terrorism in the wake of the September 11 attacks.

Emphasis on constitutional interpretation has shaped the pedagogical design of the book. To assist newcomers to constitutional law in the task of learning to read cases, Chapter One offers suggestions on "Reading a Supreme Court Decision." The same chapter contains lists of Court-related publications as well as the abundant

Court-related resources available on the Internet. Relevant to both essays and cases, and intended to aid discussion and further study, are a list of key terms and queries following the essay in each chapter. Each term is boldfaced and defined in the chapter and relates to the cases that follow. And the lists of selected readings following each essay have been reworked and updated.

Throughout, names of cases discussed in the essays that are also reprinted in the book appear in boldface italics. Each case headnote features the voting alignment for that case. The few footnotes scattered about are numbered consecutively by chapter. In every instance, footnotes and other explanatory material appearing within excerpted opinions are the Court's, unless specially marked "—ED." as having been inserted for this book. The endpapers display a table on American constitutional development, which also serves as a chronology of all cases reprinted in the book. Citations to cases referenced in the essays may be found in the Index of Cases. In the Appendix, Tables 1 and 2 show appointments to the Court by natural or discrete Court periods and by president and party affiliation as well.

Through the years since publication of the first edition of *American Constitutional Law* in 1954, general readers, faculty, and students have contributed to its betterment. Their suggestions, reflected in both deletions and additions, indicate the measure of my indebtedness. I am especially grateful to those scholars who thoroughly reviewed the thirteenth edition and made recommendations for the fourteenth. These include Jim R. Alexander of Texas Woman's University, Richard A. Glenn of Millersville University of Pennsylvania, Peter G. Renstrom of Western Michigan University, and John W. Winkle III of the University of Mississippi. Other helpful suggestions came from Robert G. Seddig of Allegheny College, James F. Van Orden of the University of North Carolina Law School, and John R. Vile of Middle Tennessee State University. Thanks are also due to my students, past and present, in Government 314 and 315 at Franklin and Marshall College, especially to Matthew Batzel, Wallace Eisenhauer, and Forrest Watson who helped in ways both seen and unseen.

As always, deserving of much credit for their wisdom, guidance, and forbearance are the many people at Prentice Hall who have supported this book. In particular, my thanks go to editor John Ragozzine in the political science division, to production editor Edie Riker, and to copy editor Serena Hoffman.

Gratitude is owed also to family—especially to Ellen, my wife and best friend for more than 36 years. Her love, encouragement, and patience have been invaluable.

Finally, this Preface must end on a sad note. While working on the revisions, I learned of the passing of William M. Beaney, in Denver, Colorado, on July 20, 2003. Through more than a half century of teaching at Princeton University and the University of Denver Law School, including service as dean at the latter, he enriched the minds and lives of thousands of students. Those familiar with the history of this book will instantly recall his role. Through the first six editions (1954–1978), he was co-author with Alpheus Mason. When I was asked to do the revisions for the seventh edition (1983), our three names appeared together as co-authors. Although Professor Beaney had no direct hand in subsequent editions, much of his imprint from the first six remains, especially in Chapters One and Ten. The presence of his name on the dedication page reflects the debt I owe to him as teacher, counselor, and friend.

Questions, suggestions, and comments about the book are welcomed via e-mail: grier.stephenson@fandm.edu.

*D. G. S., Jr.*

# INTRODUCTION

# *A Political Supreme Court*

*There are two parties in the United States, most decidedly opposed to each other as to the rights, powers and province of the judiciary. . . . One party almost claims infallibility for the judges, and would hedge them round about in such a manner that they cannot be reached by popular opinion at all, and . . . the other would subject them to the vacillations of popular prejudice and seemingly require it of them to define and administer the law, and interpret the Constitution, according to the real or apparent expediency of things.*

—NILES' WEEKLY REGISTER (1822)

It was one of George Washington's first concerns as president: Who would sit on the Supreme Court of the United States? "Impressed with a conviction that the true administration of justice is the firmest pillar of good government," he wrote future Attorney General Edmund Randolph in 1789, "I have considered the first arrangement of the judicial department as essential to the happiness of our country and the stability of its political system." Under the Articles of Confederation, which the recently ratified Constitution replaced, there had been no national judiciary. The Court's role in the new political system was unclear, but Washington realized the impact the Court might have in the young Republic. This required, he told Randolph, "the selection of the fittest characters to expound the laws and dispense justice. . . ." As he selected the six justices Congress had authorized, Washington also made sure that each section of the nation was represented and that the six were strong supporters of the new Constitution.

The first session of the newly constituted Supreme Court was scheduled for February 1, 1790, in the Exchange Building at the foot of Broad Street in New York City. The occasion was inauspicious. Only three of the six justices were present, so the Court adjourned until February 2. By then a fourth justice had arrived. In contrast to the black robes worn today, the justices were dressed in black and red gowns.

A newspaper account of the day reported, "As no business appeared to require immediate notice, the Court was adjourned."

Against the background of the Court's beginnings in 1790, anyone embarking on the study of constitutional law today is aided by an appreciation of three points. First, the justices have had an impact on American life that can scarcely be exaggerated. This reality is made possible by, and is bound up with, democratic politics and a written Constitution. Students of political science therefore pay attention to Supreme Court decisions because they matter. As Washington anticipated, what the Court does—or does not do—affects the allocation of power. Second, the Court of Washington's time was not the Court of today. Like Congress and the presidency, it has changed markedly as an institution. Third, even though people frequently think of the Court as being "above" politics, it is not. From the outset, the membership of the Supreme Court has consisted of politicians (all justices have had some experience in public affairs, and many were active in partisan politics before going on the bench) appointed by politicians (presidents) and confirmed by politicians (senators). Moreover, the Court's decisions have given the justices a hand in governing the nation. That fact alone makes the Court political.

This introductory chapter considers these points in turn. Later chapters will explore the organization and jurisdiction of the federal courts and many of the constitutional issues that have bedeviled the justices and the nation for more than two centuries.

## CONSTITUTIONAL INTERPRETATION AND POLITICAL CHOICE

"[W]e must never forget that it is a *constitution*[1] we are expounding." With this commanding reminder, Chief Justice John Marshall interrupted a closely reasoned argument in ***McCulloch* v. *Maryland*** (1819).[2] He did not pause to spell out what he had in mind. His meaning emerged from other passages in the opinion.

As Chapter Four will show, Marshall found in the Constitution a deep reservoir of congressional power and a subordinate place for the states in the federal system. Even without express authorization in the Constitution, Congress could charter a national bank. Furthermore, Maryland and other states could not tax it. The Supreme Court, as expounder of the Constitution, would correspondingly have a narrow but nonetheless important role, guarding national over state interests. The results of *McCulloch* have been far-reaching.

In *McCulloch* Marshall made **constitutional law.**[3] Constitutional law or jurisprudence consists of the prevailing meaning of the Constitution as found mainly in decisions by the U.S. Supreme Court. As law, these decisions are "legal," to be sure, but the law they announce is not ordinary law. Because it deals with fundamental matters such as the organization of government and the authority of officials over the lives of citizens, constitutional law is a very special kind of law, fusing politics, history, and political philosophy. This art of interpreting the Constitution is a lawyer's art only in the narrow sense that justices of the Supreme Court have been

---

[1] Throughout the book, emphasis within quotations is in the original, unless otherwise indicated.
[2] Boldface italic type is used throughout to indicate those cases reprinted in the book.
[3] Key terms, boldfaced at the point in each essay where they are first explained, also appear in a list at the end of each chapter essay.

lawyers. But they have had to be more than mere legal technicians. Supreme Court justices succeed as credible constitutional authorities to the degree that they are persuasive that it is the Constitution, not their individual preferences, that speaks.

A theme of this book is the continuing importance of constitutional interpretation. After 200 years, the Constitution is far more than a historic relic on display for tourists visiting the National Archives in Washington. The Constitution is the vital foundation of our political system. Broad or narrow, the prevailing interpretation of the Constitution at different times has been a major influence on the kind of nation and society Americans have enjoyed. Interpretation requires choice and is always the product of contending values. Some of these ideas promote centralized power; others, control by the states. Some enlarge or diminish the influence of one branch of the national government in relation to another. Some expand individual liberties; others expand the powers of government, state and national, at the expense of the individual. Still others allow government to protect minorities from majorities.

**Constitutional interpretation** occurs when the Supreme Court and other courts decide cases that require judges to give meaning to particular words and passages in the Constitution. **Cases** are disputes handled by a court. They may pit one individual against another, the government against an individual or corporation, and so forth. Cases are thus the raw material of the judicial process. Although many cases do not involve conflicting interpretations of the Constitution, those that do enable courts to apply the nation's fundamental law—largely crafted for an agrarian society near the end of the eighteenth century—to the needs of a technological nation in the twenty-first century.

The justices long ago established the Supreme Court as the oracle of the Constitution through the power of **judicial review:** the authority to set aside laws passed by Congress and the state legislatures as being contrary to the Constitution. Accordingly, judicial review is law steeped in politics. The development of judicial review has meant that two branches of the national government—Congress and the presidency—are preoccupied with partisan pressures. The third branch—the judiciary—is preoccupied with constitutional principles packed with political significance. Constitutional interpretation is political in the broadest sense because it makes courts, especially the Supreme Court, participants in the process of government. American courts are therefore distinctive because they routinely speak the language of the fundamental values of the political system.

## A CHANGING JUDICIARY

Understanding constitutional law today is helped by an awareness of the Court's institutional development.

**BEGINNINGS.** The Court's first decade was characterized by obscurity, weakness, and uncertainty. To a degree, each was both a cause and an effect of a high turnover in membership, an absence of effective leadership, and relatively few cases to decide. After George Washington filled the six positions Congress had authorized, he and his successor, John Adams, encountered eight vacancies between 1790 and 1800. Moreover, the Court had three chief justices during the same period (John Jay, John Rutledge, and Oliver Ellsworth). By contrast, of the thirteen chiefs since 1800, only two (Harlan Fiske Stone and Fred M. Vinson) served for fewer than eight years.

For some early jurists, other positions were more appealing. Washington's first choice for one of the initial appointments in 1789 was Robert Harrison. Five days after his confirmation by the Senate he was selected chancellor of Maryland, a position he preferred to the seat on the Supreme Court. Without having attended a single session of the Court, John Rutledge resigned as associate justice in 1791 to become chief justice of South Carolina. He would later return when Washington handed him a **recess appointment** to be the second chief justice, a nomination the Senate rejected a few months later. (A recess appointment allows the president to fill a vacancy when the Senate is not in session. The appointment expires at the end of the next session unless the Senate has acted on the nomination.) Chief Justice Jay did not attend a session of the Court after 1793; accepted a diplomatic mission to England in 1794, which led to an accord that today bears his name; and resigned in 1795 to become governor of New York. Departing Treasury Secretary Alexander Hamilton then turned down Washington's offer of the chief justiceship so he could resume law practice in New York. Today, presidents are rarely rebuffed by prospective nominees. Moreover, a justice's tenure is usually long, with both the average and median length of service for justices appointed since 1900 equaling nearly four presidential terms.

Detracting from the attractiveness of the high bench in the early years was the **circuit riding** Congress imposed on the justices, a duty not finally eliminated until 1891. In addition to sitting collectively as the Supreme Court, justices sat as judges of the circuit courts, one of the two types of lower federal courts established by the Judiciary Act of 1789. Though the act provided for three types of courts (district courts, circuit courts, and the Supreme Court), it authorized the appointment of judges only for the district courts and the Supreme Court. Except for a brief period in 1801–1802, no separate circuit judgeships existed until 1855 (for California) and then in 1869 for the rest of the nation. Each circuit court was at first staffed by two justices (a number soon reduced to one) and one district judge. As a result, the early justices spent far more time holding circuit court than they did sitting on the Supreme Court. Nonetheless, though small in number, some of the Court's decisions in this first decade were instrumental in laying the foundations of an enlarged judicial power that emerged in the nineteenth century.

Whether a justice traveled by carriage or by boat, riding circuit was onerous. The rigors must have tested devotion to Court and country. Not only were the distances long, but each justice paid his expenses out of his own salary. Accommodations were rarely ideal. Justice Cushing once found himself with twelve other lodgers in a single room, and Justice Iredell reported encountering, unexpectedly, "a bed fellow of the wrong sort." While crossing the frozen Susquehanna River at Havre de Grace, Maryland, Justice Chase fell through the ice and almost drowned.

**THE COURT COMES OF AGE.** Although the Supreme Court had three chief justices in its first decade, the combined service of the next three chief justices (John Marshall, Roger Taney, and Salmon Chase) totaled 72 years. As an institution of American government, the Supreme Court owes much to John Marshall, sometimes called "the Great Chief Justice" as if no other occupant of that office could ever be his equal. Appointed in the last days of John Adams's term after former Chief Justice Jay had refused reappointment (in declining, Jay wrote Adams that the Court "would not obtain the energy, weight and dignity which are essential to its affording due support to the National Government"), Marshall served 34 years, longer than any other chief.

Marshall dominated the Court like no chief justice before or since, making the Court the institution Jay had doubted it could become. Some of the factors that contributed to Marshall's influence were his personality and political acumen, the issues embedded within the cases the Court decided, and his determination to use the federal judiciary as a means to reinforce constitutional principles he thought vital to the advancement of the nation. In addition, circumstances of life in Washington—the justices resided and took their meals at the same boardinghouse and traveled together across town to the small courtroom in the Capitol basement—made it easier for a strong-willed individual like Marshall to influence his colleagues. Marshall also ended the practice of **seriatim opinions** inherited from English courts whereby each judge gave his view of the case. Henceforth, the Court would speak with one voice—the opinion of the Court—and the voice was usually Marshall's.

**JUDICIAL BUSINESS IN THE NINETEENTH CENTURY.** Despite Marshall's deserved reputation in constitutional law, the bulk of the Court's work in his time and for years afterward was nonconstitutional in nature. Private law cases vastly outnumbered public law cases. In fact, of the 1,121 cases the Court decided during Marshall's tenure between 1801 and 1835, only 76 raised federal constitutional issues. The majority involved admiralty and maritime issues (these cases were numerous given the fact that most of the nation's commerce before the Civil War was waterborne), common-law matters, and diversity disputes. (Created by the Judiciary Act of 1789, **diversity jurisdiction** allows federal courts to hear some suits involving ordinary matters of state law when the parties are citizens of different states.) In 1825 for example, there were no constitutional cases decided at all, and 54 percent of the docket involved admiralty, common-law, and diversity matters. As late as 1875, such cases consumed 45 percent of the docket; constitutional cases amounted to but 6 percent of the total. The Court of the nineteenth century was still largely a tribunal for the final settlement of disputes between individual parties. Its role as policymaker was decidedly secondary.

Though secondary, policymaking was hardly unimportant. Congress recognized as much in a series of statutes that altered the number of justices. Between 1789 and 1869, Congress changed the number of justices from six to five, five to six, six to seven, seven to nine, nine to ten, ten to seven, and seven to nine (the number authorized today)—each time partly with an eye toward influencing the Court's constitutional decisions.

**THE MODERN COURT.** The federal judiciary underwent important structural changes beginning in the late nineteenth century. By the 1880s it had a case backlog of several years. A cartoon of the day depicted the justices wading about their courtroom in a sea of briefs and other documents, pleading for relief, but a docket in arrears was not simply the product of an expanding population. Congress had gradually enlarged the jurisdiction of the federal courts, meaning that a greater variety of questions confronted the justices. Through its cases, the Court could hardly escape embroiling itself in virtually every political movement of the day. Swollen dockets prompted Congress to act. First, in 1891 Congress authorized intermediate appellate courts called circuit courts of appeals. For the first time, the federal judiciary had appellate tribunals below the Supreme Court. For most cases, the old circuit courts had not been appellate tribunals; a case began in either the district or circuit court depending on the subject matter. The old circuit courts were soon merged into the district courts. Circuit riding by the justices, already reduced substantially in the latter half of the nineteenth century, came to an end (ironically just as interstate rail transportation had become faster, more reliable, and more comfortable).

Second, the 1891 statute introduced some certiorari, or discretionary, jurisdiction for the Court. This meant that there were fewer categories of cases the justices were legally obliged to hear and that the new courts of appeals became the courts of last resort for many cases.

Third, as a result of intense lobbying by Chief Justice William Howard Taft (the only president to have become chief justice), Congress in 1925 passed the Judges Bill, which expanded discretionary jurisdiction even further. Now, the Court was in control of most of its docket, not only in terms of the number of cases it would decide each year but also, for the most part, of the issues it would confront. Taft's political talents left another institutional legacy: the Supreme Court Building. With construction finished in 1935, five years after Taft's death, the justices finally had a home of their own.

Today, in contrast to the docket in the nineteenth century, public law consumes the Court's time. Roughly half of the Court's business now consists of constitutional cases, with statutory interpretation accounting for almost all of the rest. Moving beyond its dispute-resolution role, the Court has become mainly a maker of public policy for uniform application across the nation.

## APPOINTMENT POLITICS, 1968–1984

The Constitution entrusts the selection of Supreme Court justices, as well as judges of the lower federal courts, to both the president and the Senate. The choice of the former requires the consent of the latter. Senatorial approval is usually forthcoming, but not always. Through early 2004, 108 individuals have served on the Court. Of all the nominations presidents have submitted to the Senate, 25 have failed to pass, all but six in the nineteenth century. Several confirmed persons have declined to sit. By contrast, the Senate has blocked only nine nominations to the Cabinet since 1789. In exercising their constitutional obligation to give "advice and consent," senators ordinarily employ greater scrutiny and more independence with the review of justices than with heads of executive departments. Enhanced attention to the former is explained by the Court's place in the political system, life tenure for justices, and the fact that the Court, unlike the Cabinet, is not part of the executive branch.

Most senatorial scrutiny today occurs during hearings before the Judiciary Committee at which the nominee testifies. For most of American history, however, Supreme Court nominees did not appear before the committee to answer questions. The first was Harlan F. Stone in 1925, who did so only after his nomination by President Calvin Coolidge ran into difficulty. The second was Felix Frankfurter in 1939, who agreed to appear only when supporters informed him that he would probably be rejected if he did not. Such appearances did not become the rule until after 1954. Ever since, all nominees have been expected to appear, although concerns persist over the propriety of questions that senators ask and what obligation the nominee has to answer them.

"The good that Presidents do is often interred with their Administrations," *The Nation* editorialized in 1939. "It is their choice of Supreme Court Justices that lives after them." Although the separate institutions mandated by the Constitution make possible the Court's considerable independence from outside political pressure, three factors thrust the Court into the partisan life of the nation: the role of interpretation the Constitution allows, the significance of the decisions the justices render, and the method of judicial selection the Constitution imposes. Little wonder the appointment of justices is of paramount concern to presidents, senators, and citizens alike, as events since 1968 illustrate.

**FROM WARREN TO BURGER.** On June 26, 1968, President Lyndon Johnson announced Chief Justice Earl Warren's intention to resign. Appointment of a chief justice is a rare occurrence. There have been 43 presidents, counting Grover Cleveland's separated presidencies twice, but only 16 chief justices. During the 34 years John Marshall sat in the Court's center chair, there were six presidents. The contrast is significant substantively as well as statistically, a fact that prompted President John Quincy Adams to rate the office of chief justice as "more important than that of President." Chief justice since 1953, Warren's tenure had been one of the most active and remarkable in American history. By one count, in the approximately 150 years before Warren's appointment, the Court had overruled 88 of its precedents. In Warren's 16 years it added another 45 to the list. Hardly an aspect of life had gone untouched by landmark decisions on race discrimination, legislative apportionment, and the Bill of Rights. The **Warren Court** initiated a revolution that is measured by President Dwight Eisenhower's latter-day lament over Warren's appointment: "The biggest damn fool mistake I ever made."

On June 27, President Johnson nominated Associate Justice Abe Fortas, a close friend, to succeed the controversial chief. Accusing President Johnson of "cronyism," opposition formed immediately. Fortas was charged with various improprieties, including participation in White House strategy conferences on the Vietnam War and acceptance of high lecture fees raised by wealthy business executives who happened to be clients of Fortas's former law partner, Paul Porter. After four days of deliberation, the Senate voted 45–43 on October 1 to cut off debate, well shy of the margin necessary to end the anti-Fortas filibuster. Two days later, the ill-fated justice withdrew his name. For the first time, nomination of a Supreme Court justice had been blocked by a Senate filibuster.

It remains unclear why Johnson refused to submit another name to the Senate. The lame-duck president left this high-level appointment to President Richard M. Nixon, whose 1968 campaign for the White House had been in part a campaign against the Warren Court. President Nixon's first step toward fulfilling his 1968 campaign promise to strengthen the "peace forces as against the criminal forces of the country" was the selection of Warren Earl Burger, 61, chief judge of the U.S. Court of Appeals for the District of Columbia Circuit. Burger's confirmation came 18 days later on June 9, 1969, by a vote of 74–3.

**FORTAS RESIGNS.** In the spring of 1969, *Life* magazine revealed that Justice Fortas had received a yearly $20,000 fee from the Family Foundation of Louis Wolfson, then serving a prison term for selling unregistered stock. Once again the judicial fat was in the political fire. Fortas's resignation on May 16, 1969, the first by a justice because of public criticism, opened the way for Nixon's nomination of Clement F. Haynsworth, Jr., chief judge of the Court of Appeals for the Fourth Circuit. Because Haynsworth had taken a restrictive view of school desegregation and had been insensitive to proprieties in ways that involved finance and conflict of interest, the Senate, still in Democratic hands, in a surprise vote rejected the president's nominee 55–45.

Rejection of Haynsworth strengthened Nixon's determination to "pack" the Court with "strict constructionists." His next nominee, G. Harrold Carswell, had served seven years as a federal district judge in Florida and six months on the Court of Appeals for the Fifth Circuit. In 1948, he had said, "I yield to no man as a fellow candidate [he was then running for political office] or as a fellow citizen in the firm, vigorous belief in the principles of White Supremacy, and I shall always be so governed." Quite apart from Judge Carswell's avowed racism (which he now disavowed), critics charged that President Nixon's nominee was mediocre. Accepting the criticism, Nebraska Senator Roman Hruska tried to convert it into an asset: "Even if he is mediocre, there are a lot of mediocre judges and people and lawyers. They are entitled to a little representation, aren't they, and a little chance? We can't have all Brandeises, Cardozos and Frankfurters and stuff like that there."

Carswell was rejected 51–45. Not since the second presidency of Grover Cleveland in 1893 and 1894 had the Senate refused to accept two nominees for the same Supreme Court vacancy. Nixon's third choice was Chief Justice Burger's longtime Minnesota friend, Harry A. Blackmun of the Court of Appeals for the Eighth Circuit. Blackmun aroused little opposition and was promptly confirmed 94–0 and sworn in on June 9, 1970.

**POWELL, REHNQUIST, AND STEVENS.** In the fall of 1970, President Nixon was still determined to appoint a southerner to the Supreme Court. The most likely spot to be vacated was that occupied by 84-year-old Justice Hugo Black. Asked for his reaction, Black replied, "I think it would be nice to have another Southerner up here." The Alabaman had moved into third place in length of service. The longevity goal was in sight, but fate defeated its realization. In September 1971, Justices Black and John Harlan, both ailing, resigned within days of each other. Black fell eight months shy of Justice Stephen J. Field's record of 34½ years.

Nixon now had an opportunity no president had experienced since 1940—that of simultaneously filling two Supreme Court vacancies. His choices were Lewis F. Powell, Jr., 64, a distinguished Richmond lawyer, and William H. Rehnquist, 47, law clerk, 1952–1953, to the late Justice Robert H. Jackson, and since 1969 assistant attorney general in charge of the Justice Department's Office of Legal Counsel.

Powell, arousing little or no objection, was confirmed 89–1 on December 6. Rehnquist ran into stormy waters. Among other things, critics charged that he had advocated curtailment of defendants' rights in criminal cases, use of electronic surveillance, preventive detention, and "no knock" police entry. He had proclaimed virtually unlimited war power for the president and sanctioned mass arrest of demonstrators against the Vietnam War. Confronted with these barbed attacks, Rehnquist told the Judiciary Committee: "My fundamental commitment, if I am confirmed, will be to totally disregard my own personal belief." Rehnquist received Senate approval on December 10, 1971, 68–26. Powell was sworn in on January 6, 1972, and Rehnquist on January 7.

On New Year's Eve 1974, Justice William O. Douglas suffered a stroke. Although seriously disabled, Douglas was reluctant to retire. "Even if I'm only half alive," he remarked, "I can still cast a liberal vote." But some of his colleagues questioned whether he should be casting any votes at all. "I should like to register my protest," Justice Byron White wrote Chief Justice Burger on October 20, 1975 (with copies to the other justices), "against the decision of the Court not to assign the writing of any opinions to Mr. Justice Douglas. . . . [T]here are one or more Justices who are doubtful about the competence of Mr. Justice Douglas that they would not join any opinion purportedly authored by him. At the very least, they would not hand down any judgment arrived at by a 5–4 vote where Mr. Justice Douglas is in the majority. . . . That decision, made in the absence of Mr. Justice Douglas, was supported by seven Justices. It is clear that the ground for the action was the assumed incompetence of the justice." White then reminded the Brethren that "nowhere" does the Constitution provide "that a Justice's colleagues may deprive him of his office by refusing to permit him to function as a Justice. . . . If the Court is convinced that Justice Douglas should not continue to function as a Justice, the Court should say so publicly and invite Congress to take appropriate action."

Raised again was the thorny question of how to remove an incapacitated Supreme Court justice. The Constitution supplies no answer, but history does. On more than one occasion, the power of persuasion exerted on a faltering justice by colleagues has proved effective. In 1869, Justice Field convinced Justice Grier that he was too ill to continue. Later, according to one account, when Justice Field became incapacitated, the first Justice Harlan asked his colleague whether he remembered urging Grier to retire. "Yes," Field snapped, "and a dirtier day's work I never did in my life." After Justice McKenna's all too obvious demonstration of mental slowdown in the 1920s, Chief Justice Taft persuaded him to retire. Justice Holmes, older than McKenna, then a bystander, was sure he would be "intellectually honest in judging my condition and my product." But the 90-year-old justice gave up in 1932 only after Chief Justice Hughes requested him to do so. Ignoring or eluding pressure from whatever source, Douglas reached his own decision to leave the Court on November 12, almost a year after he was stricken. He had served 36 years, surpassing the record long held by Justice Field.

For Douglas's seat President Ford nominated John Paul Stevens, a 55-year-old appeals court judge from the Seventh Circuit. After graduating first in his class at Northwestern University Law School, he had served two years as Justice Wiley Rutledge's law clerk. The Senate quickly confirmed him 98–0; on December 19, 1975, Stevens was sworn in.

**THE FIRST WOMAN JUSTICE.** The judiciary figured prominently in the presidential campaign of 1980. Five years had passed without a Supreme Court vacancy on a bench where more than half the justices were above 70 years of age. Moreover, the Court only seven years before had injected itself into the most divisive of contemporary moral issues by declaring abortion to be a constitutional right. Three Nixon appointees had voted with the majority, and one of them—Blackmun—had written the majority opinion. This case alone was reminder enough that Republican presidents Eisenhower, Nixon, and Ford had not been notably adept in picking nominees who accorded with their political views. Warren, Brennan, Blackmun, and Stevens had all proved to be "surprises" in various ways, lending credence to President Truman's lament: "Packing the Supreme Court simply can't be done. I've tried and it won't work." This time, conservative Republicans wanted to try harder.

The Republican platform therefore called for judges "who respect traditional family values and the sanctity of innocent human life." The second part was a code word for opposition to abortion. Denounced by the National Organization for Women for "medieval stances on women's issues," Ronald Reagan confounded the campaign by promising to name a woman to fill one of "the first Supreme Court vacancies in my administration."

As president, Reagan soon had his chance. At age 66, Potter Stewart, appointed by President Eisenhower in 1958 and long regarded as a "swing vote" among the justices, announced his retirement on June 18, 1981. Reagan's choice for a successor was Sandra Day O'Connor, 51, of the Arizona Court of Appeals. A law student with Justice Rehnquist at Stanford University (he finished first, she third, in the class of 1952), not only was O'Connor to be the first woman to sit on the High Court, she was the first since Brennan to have had experience on a state bench. Moreover, she was the first since Justice Harold Burton, Stewart's predecessor, to have served as a state legislator. Criticized by some for injecting gender into justice, Reagan's fulfillment of a campaign pledge placed him squarely in an established tradition in which other presidents considered region, religion, and race in making appointments to the Court. Despite concerns of right-to-life groups that she was "unsound" on abortion, the Senate, under Republican control for the first time since 1955, confirmed her 99–0 on September 21.

With the approach of the 1984 presidential race, the Court's future again became an issue. Some saw the coming election as a referendum on the Constitution. The High Bench was the second oldest in history, just behind the "Nine Old Men" of Franklin Roosevelt's first term in the 1930s. Reagan's opponents feared appointees who would not be merely conservative but potentially radical, discarding settled constitutional doctrine. Yet, in headline-generating remarks, Justice Rehnquist tried to minimize the impact of any president on the Court: "Presidents who wish to pack the Supreme Court, like murder suspects in a detective novel, must have both motive and opportunity." Even with both, "a number of factors militate against a president having anything more than partial success." Chief among them was that neither presidents nor nominees "are usually vouchsafed the foresight to see what the great issues of 10 or 15 years hence are to be."

## APPOINTMENT POLITICS, 1984–1992

On June 17, 1986, President Reagan announced Chief Justice Burger's retirement and his intention to nominate Rehnquist as chief justice. Rehnquist would become only the third chief to have been selected from the Court itself.

At age 78, Burger had served longer than any other chief justice nominated in the twentieth century. Although Nixon named Burger to the Court in 1969 to fulfill a campaign pledge against judicial activism, the Court during Burger's time did not overturn outright a single major decision of the activist Warren Court (1953–1969). The persistence of the Warren Court's jurisprudence was all the more remarkable when it is remembered that by 1986, only three members of the Warren Court were still serving, and of the three only two (Justices Brennan and Marshall) had been closely identified with the Warren Court's major accomplishments. Although some of the Warren Court's landmark rulings on criminal procedure were restricted—most notably the exclusionary rule (see Chapter Ten)—the Burger Court practiced its own kind of judicial activism, especially with respect to racial and sexual equality, abortion, and other privacy issues (see Chapters Thirteen and Fourteen). With the possible exception of William Howard Taft, Burger was the most active chief justice outside the Supreme Court. He treated his office like a pulpit from which to campaign energetically for changes in legal education, professional standards for bench and bar, criminal sanctions, prisons, and the administration of justice.

Also on June 17, 1986, Reagan nominated Antonin Scalia, 50, of the Court of Appeals for the District of Columbia Circuit as associate justice. Scalia would become the first Italian American to serve on the nation's highest court. A summa cum laude graduate of Georgetown University in 1957, he received his legal training at Harvard, where he was an editor of the *Law Review*. He was an assistant attorney general in the U.S. Department of Justice between 1974 and 1977 and had taught at several law schools before his appointment to the court of appeals in 1982. Like Rehnquist, he was widely regarded as a politically conservative legal thinker.

**Whose Supreme Court Is It?** From the outset the Rehnquist nomination encountered intense opposition, even though Republicans still controlled the Senate. If the president took a nominee's views into account, should not the Senate do the same? Preferring to forget their party's opposition to Abe Fortas in 1965 and

1968, Republican leaders wanted to limit the Senate to a consideration of character and merit, but some Democrats seemed intent on ensuring a coordinate role for the Senate. "The framers envisioned a major role for the Senate in the appointment of judges," argued Senator Edward Kennedy. "It is historical nonsense to suggest that all the Senate has to do is to check the nominee's I.Q., be sure he has a law degree and no arrests, and rubber stamp the President's choice." If Rehnquist's vision of the Constitution was properly the Senate's concern, how much should it matter? Neither the Constitution nor Senate tradition offered a conclusive answer.

Rehnquist's nomination was unusual because it offered a rare second chance to vote on the results of a justice's career, not just on its prospects. With characteristic bluntness, Kennedy charged that the nominee was "too extreme on race, too extreme on women's rights, too extreme on freedom of speech, too extreme on separation of church and state, too extreme to be Chief Justice." Yet some senators instead directed questions to other, perhaps surrogate, issues that cast doubt on Rehnquist's fitness to serve—a "Rehnquisition," Senator Orrin Hatch called it. As a Republican activist in Phoenix, Arizona, in 1962 and 1964, Rehnquist was supposed to have intimidated voters. He denied the charges. In a deed for a house Rehnquist had purchased in Vermont in 1974, a 1933 covenant (now legally unenforceable) barred sale or lease to a person of "the Hebrew race." Rehnquist explained that he was unaware of the existence of the restriction and promised that he would have the offensive language removed.

A third charge turned on the propriety of Rehnquist's participation in a free-speech case in 1972, *Laird* v. *Tatum,* which dismissed 5 to 4 a suit challenging surveillance by the army of domestic political groups. In October 1972, Rehnquist issued a 16-page opinion [Memorandum on Motion to Recuse, 409 U.S. 824 (1972)], explaining that as an assistant attorney general he had not taken part in the government's case and that he did not know much about the evidence. Now opponents claimed that Rehnquist knew more than he admitted in 1972. On August 12, Rehnquist responded to questions from Senator Charles Mathias, writing that he had "no recollection of any participation in the formulation of policy" on the surveillance.

Hearings by the Judiciary Committee on the Rehnquist nomination consumed four days, and Senate floor debate five. Confirmation, 65–33, came on September 17. Not since 1836, when the Senate confirmed Roger Taney, had a nominee for chief justice been approved by a ratio of less than 2–1.

Perhaps because the Senate's scrutiny of Rehnquist was so intense, Scalia's nomination generated only mild turbulence. The Judiciary Committee's hearings on Judge Scalia lasted only two days. Floor debate did not exceed five minutes. Following the vote on Rehnquist, the Senate confirmed Scalia, 98–0.

**THE BORK DEBACLE.** At the end of Rehnquist's first term as chief, Justice Lewis Powell announced his retirement. For several years Powell had been in a pivotal position on the Court, especially in abortion, privacy, church-state, and affirmative action cases. Reagan now had a chance to advance his social agenda judicially, much of which had been rebuffed by Congress: prayer in the schools, restrictions on abortions, and limits on affirmative action.

Reagan's announcement on July 1, 1987, was no surprise. At his side was Robert H. Bork, 60, who had been passed over in favor of Scalia the year before. Since 1982 Bork had been a judge on the Court of Appeals for the District of Columbia Circuit. From 1962 to 1981 he had been a member of the faculty at Yale Law School, taking time out from 1973 to 1977 to serve as solicitor general. It was as the third-ranking official in the Department of Justice that Bork found himself caught up in the "Saturday Night Massacre" on October 20, 1973, in the Watergate affair. Refusing to obey President Nixon's order to fire special prosecutor Archibald Cox, Attorney General Elliot Richardson and Deputy Attorney General William Ruckelshaus had resigned. As the ranking officer in the department, Bork carried out the president's command. Some senators still considered Bork's actions legally and ethically dubious.

He was also a prolific writer. Not since Felix Frankfurter's appointment in 1939 had the Senate considered a Supreme Court nominee with so many publications. Of particular interest was a 1971 article in the *Indiana Law Journal* that, among other things, called into question the constitutional underpinnings of **Griswold v. Connecticut,** the landmark 1965 ruling on a right of privacy and birth control. If *Griswold* rested on dubious ground, so did **Roe v. Wade,** the 1973 abortion rights decision (see Chapter Thirteen).

Bork's nomination was therefore guaranteed to be rancorous. The midterm elections in 1986 had converted a 53–47 Republican majority in the Senate into a 54–46 Democratic one. Joseph Biden, not Strom Thurmond, chaired the Senate Judiciary Committee. Two of the Democrats on the committee (Biden and Paul Simon) were running for president. Moreover, Reagan himself was politically weaker in mid-1987 than in mid-1986. Intervening were revelations of the Iran-contra affair, which had shaken public confidence in the administration.

Before the Judiciary Committee began its record-setting 12 days of hearings on the nomination on September 15 (Bork would testify and be questioned on five of those days), the battle lines had already been drawn. Hesitation expressed in 1986 over close scrutiny of a nominee's judicial philosophy vanished. Some Democrats, including Biden, let it be known well before the hearings started that they would vote against the nomination. The nomination had hardly been announced before Senator Kennedy fired one of the opening shots. "Robert Bork's America is a land in which women would be forced into back alley abortions, blacks would sit at segregated lunch counters, rogue police could break down citizens' doors in midnight raids, school children could not be taught about evolution, writers and artists could be censored at the whim of government, and the doors of the federal courts would be shut on the fingers of millions of citizens for whom the judiciary is—and is often the only—protector of the individual rights that are the heart of our democracy." Bork's supporters had gravely underestimated the nature and extent of the opposition. Democrats like Kennedy succeeded in demonizing Bork before he could define himself.

Cooperating with Democrats in the Senate was the Leadership Conference on Civil Rights, an umbrella organization of nearly 200 groups. It coordinated a massive public relations drive to galvanize public opposition. Nearly 2,000 law school professors (about 40 percent of all law faculty in the nation) signed a petition urging rejection, as compared to only 300 who publicly opposed Carswell in 1970. The American Civil Liberties Union repealed a 50-year-old rule so that it could take a public stance against the nomination. Direct mail, television and newspaper advertisements, and other techniques of modern interest-group politics for the first time were aimed squarely against a Supreme Court nominee. Not since Woodrow Wilson nominated Louis Brandeis in 1916 had a confirmation battle become so vitriolic. On October 23, Judge Bork's Senate opponents prevailed, 58–42, a larger negative vote than either Haynsworth or Carswell endured.

In place of Bork, President Reagan's advisers recommended a conservative without a paper trail. Senate Minority Leader Robert Dole advised anyone with ambitions to sit on the Supreme Court not to "write a word. I would hide in the closet until I was nominated."

On October 29, Reagan selected Douglas H. Ginsburg, one of Bork's colleagues on the District of Columbia Circuit, but senators never got a chance to query Ginsburg. Problems surfaced almost instantly. As an official in the Justice Department, he had handled a major case regarding the cable television industry while owning $140,000 worth of stock in a Canadian cable company. Then Ginsburg acknowledged that he had used marijuana as a student in the 1960s and more recently as a member of the Harvard law faculty in the 1970s. On November 7, the nomination went up in a puff of smoke as he withdrew his name from consideration.

Not since 1970 had a president had to make a third nomination to fill a single vacancy. Time was critical. Reagan was nearing the start of his last year in office. "Lame-duck" talk abounded. Like Johnson with Fortas in 1968, the vacancy might carry over to his successor in 1989. On November 10, Reagan made his next move, nominating long-time acquaintance Anthony M. Kennedy, 51, who had been a judge on the Ninth Circuit Court of Appeals since leaving private practice in 1975. Kennedy had been Chief of Staff Howard Baker's first choice after Bork's defeat, when Attorney General Edwin Meese convinced the president to pick Ginsburg. Democrats could find little wrong with the nominee. An hour's debate in the Senate on February 3, 1988, preceded the vote to confirm, 97–0. Anthony Kennedy was sworn in on February 18 as the Court's 104th justice, ending a seven-month struggle over Justice Powell's successor.

The fight to replace Powell has had consequences apart from Kennedy's career on the Court. The tentative senatorial probing of ideology in the nominations of Rehnquist and Scalia in 1986 gave way to searching scrutiny in 1987. The Senate firmly reestablished the precedent that judicial philosophy is relevant and important. One of President Reagan's contributions to American government was no doubt unintended: He helped to make the Senate a more equal partner in shaping the Supreme Court.

**END OF THE BRENNAN ERA.** On the evening of July 20, 1990, Justice William J. Brennan, Jr., sent a note to the White House informing President George H. W. Bush that he would step down from the bench. The most senior justice in age (84) and in length of service (34 years), Brennan had suffered a mild stroke several days after the Court's term ended on June 27. With four years of experience on the New Jersey Supreme Court, Brennan's career on the High Court began in 1956 when President Eisenhower offered him a recess appointment after Justice Sherman Minton retired. Senator Joseph McCarthy of Wisconsin cast the only negative vote when the Senate confirmed him in early 1957. Brennan's contribution to American constitutional law was substantial. Since the 1960s, Brennan had been leader of the Court's liberal bloc. He was one of the driving forces behind the Court's major decisions on subjects as varied as racial justice, affirmative action, criminal procedure, access to the courts, privacy and abortion, religious freedom, free speech and press, and legislative districting.

Bush faced a Senate firmly in Democratic hands. Moreover, he had recently suffered political embarrassment after reversing his "read my lips" pledge of "no new taxes." He needed Democratic support in breaking an impasse on the budget, and his high public approval ratings had fallen precipitously. In short, the president was in no position to force a contentious nominee on the Senate. Within 72 hours of Brennan's retirement, Bush picked David H. Souter, the first justice to be appointed from New Hampshire since Levi Woodbury in 1845 and the first bachelor since Frank Murphy in 1940. Only three months before Bush's announcement, the Senate had unanimously confirmed Souter for a seat on the United States Court of Appeals for the First Circuit. A Rhodes Scholar, Souter was a close friend and political protégé of New Hampshire's Senator Warren Rudman and had been state attorney general and a trial judge before Governor John Sununu (later Bush's chief of staff) placed him on the New Hampshire Supreme Court in 1983. Yet this background yielded few clues to his thinking on the most divisive federal constitutional issues. For Alabama's Senator Howell Heflin, Souter was "the stealth candidate." On national television Justice Thurgood Marshall harrumphed, "Never heard of him." The contrast with what had abundantly been known about Bork was stunning, deliberately so in the opinion of suspicious senators. Many forgot that Brennan himself had seemed rather obscure upon his appointment in 1956.

Bush disavowed the use of "any litmus test" on abortion or on any other specific matter. Was Bush heeding Abraham Lincoln's advice? Presented with the opportunity to name Roger Taney's successor as chief justice in 1864, Lincoln advised, "We cannot ask a man what he will do, and if we should, and he should answer us, we should despise him for it. Therefore, we must take a man whose opinions are known."

Members of the Senate Judiciary Committee unabashedly asked the questions President Bush had not, making it clear that abortion was the ever-present issue at the hearings. Democrats especially wanted to satisfy themselves that Souter passed the "not Bork" test. They fretted that Justice Kennedy's nomination had moved through the Senate virtually unopposed in the wake of the rejection of Bork. They remembered Bork's retort after Kennedy's first full term that the new justice had voted in accordance with his own views in every case, save one. While Souter spoke to some issues, he remained silent on the abortion right. His reticence made it difficult for opponents to mobilize the kind of interest-group opposition that had worked so well in stopping Bork. On October 2, the Senate voted overwhelmingly (90–9) to confirm Souter as the 105th justice, barely two weeks after his 51st birthday.

The appointment again demonstrated how both the president and senators have an interest in the views of the nominee. Yet Souter presented a dilemma. When the accessible record of nominees leaves their constitutional values shrouded in mystery, should they be expected publicly to lay bare their positions on current constitutional controversies? If they do, has their independence as justices been compromised? If they do not, does the Senate's approval amount to informed consent?

**THE THOMAS MAELSTROM.** Souter's first term marked Thurgood Marshall's last. On June 27, 1991, five days shy of his 83rd birthday, Justice Marshall, citing the physical toll taken by age and ill health, sent President Bush his notice of retirement. "What's wrong with me?" he responded to a reporter, "I'm old! I'm getting old and coming apart." Despite his age, the announcement took some by surprise. Only recently, Marshall had been characteristically defiant about stepping down. "I have a lifetime appointment, and I intend to serve it." His attitude seemed not to have changed from the day in 1970 when President Nixon, upon learning that Marshall was ill with pneumonia at Bethesda Naval Hospital, asked to see his medical records. Marshall let the records be sent, but not before scrawling on the folder in large print, "NOT YET."

Marshall occupies a unique place in Supreme Court history. Not only was he the first black justice, but in a way equaled by few, he helped to shape constitutional law off the Court as well as on the bench. His appointment by President Johnson in 1967 (Johnson had named him solicitor general just two years earlier) was as much recognition of what he had accomplished as it was an expectation of what he would do as a justice. From 1938 until his appointment by President Kennedy in 1961 to the Court of Appeals for the Second Circuit, he was one of the leaders in efforts by the Legal Defense Fund of the National Association for the Advancement of Colored People (NAACP) to use the judiciary as a vehicle to combat racial discrimination. He argued 32 cases before the Supreme Court and won 29, including ***Brown v. Board of Education*** in 1954, reprinted in Chapter Fourteen. As a justice he remained a tenacious advocate of civil rights.

The irony created by Marshall's departure escaped few. As an outspoken opponent of racial quotas, would the president name a black person to the bench? The suspense was short-lived. On July 1, Bush turned to Clarence Thomas, 43, of the U.S. Court of Appeals for the District of Columbia Circuit. A 1971 graduate of Holy Cross with a law degree from Yale, Thomas had been an assistant attorney general in Missouri and a lawyer for the Monsanto Company before going to work for Senator John Danforth from 1979 to 1981. He was assistant secretary for civil rights in the Department of Education in 1981 and 1982 and then chaired the Equal Employment Opportunity Commission (EEOC) until his appeals court appointment in 1990.

Although an African American like Marshall, the contrast between the two was striking. True, both had been reared in a racially segregated environment, but Marshall came from a middle-class Maryland home. Thomas had been born into abject poverty in the tiny coastal plain community of Pin Point, Georgia, and was deserted by his father at the age of two. More significant, Thomas rejected much of what Marshall had strived for. He had questioned the wisdom of busing to achieve racial integration and opposed preferences for racial minorities, among other things. During the five days Thomas appeared before the Senate Judiciary Committee in September, Democrats especially pressed him to reveal his position on abortion. Although acknowledging the existence of a constitutional right to privacy, Thomas rebuffed their entreaties, asserting that he had not formed an opinion on the subject and claiming that he could not maintain his impartiality as a judge if he had. He wanted to avoid testimony that would give senators reason to reject him. The Souter approach had been to come across as a compassionate person but to leave senators in doubt on constitutional particulars. Robert Bork, after all, gave forthright answers and was rejected.

Objections to what Thomas's constitutional values might be and concern over his qualifications, however, led to a 7–7 split when members of the Judiciary Committee voted on September 27. One Democrat, Senator DeConcini, joined the six Republicans in support of the nomination, which thus went to the Senate floor without a recommendation. Press accounts predicted that Thomas would be approved easily in a vote scheduled for October 8.

Events suddenly took an unexpected turn when a leak to the press during the weekend of October 5 placed the nomination in doubt. Several weeks before the committee's vote, Professor Anita F. Hill of the University of Oklahoma School of Law had notified the committee's staff, in confidence, that Thomas had sexually harassed her in 1981–1983 while she was his assistant, first at the Department of Education and later at the Equal Employment Opportunity Commission. Some members of the committee were aware of Hill's accusations prior to their vote on September 27. Thanks to the leak, virtually the entire nation knew about them.

Now senators were themselves on trial for failing to take sexual harassment seriously. Accordingly, they sent the nomination back to the Judiciary Committee. What followed was a television spectacle that left few satisfied: 28 hours of additional hearings marked by lurid details, bitter charges and countercharges, and equally bitter denials and counterdenials. Thomas told the committee that he was the victim of a "high-tech lynching for uppity blacks." Likened by some to a morality play or a psychodrama, the acrimonious hearings drew a larger viewing audience than the National League and American League playoffs going on at the same time.

The charges were grave and were potentially fatal. Thomas had headed the agency responsible for enforcing the law against sexual harassment. Moreover, the charges undercut his principal strength. Without a record of legal scholarship or extensive judicial service, the merits of the nomination had rested all along on character—precisely what Hill called into question. On October 15, such doubts helped to make the Senate's vote to confirm, 52–48, one of the closest on record for a successful Supreme Court nominee. Only the approval of Stanley Matthews by a vote of 24–23 in 1881 had generated a higher percentage of negative votes.

Thomas took the constitutional oath at a public ceremony at the White House on October 18, and the chief justice administered the judicial oath in a private ceremony at the Court on October 23. Not since the controversy over membership in the Ku Klux Klan enveloped Hugo Black shortly after his confirmation in 1937 had a justice begun his tenure under such a cloud of suspicion.

## THE CLINTON YEARS

In appointing Thomas, the elder Bush never anticipated the catalytic effects of the confirmation proceedings. The hearings gave high visibility to sexual harassment in the workplace, which in the 1992 election became one of several factors leading to increased participation by women candidates, contributors, and voters. Even in the presidential race, where economic matters were dominant, the Supreme Court was not far from the center of the campaign. Bush and Bill Clinton differed on several important constitutional issues, but on none was the difference any sharper than abortion. During his campaign for the Democratic nomination, Clinton warned of the consequences for reproductive freedom if Bush were reelected: The "constitutional right to choose is hanging by a thread. We are only one justice away from an outright reversal of *Roe*. This is one of the things this Presidential election is about." Bush's position was plainly on the other side: "I am prolife," he declared.

**APPOINTMENTS.** Clinton's inauguration as the 42nd president was soon followed by news of an impending vacancy on the Supreme Court, as Justice Byron White on March 19, 1993, announced his intention to retire. Placed on the Court in 1962 by President John Kennedy, White was by 1993 the sole justice to have been nominated by a Democrat. Nonetheless, he voted against abortion rights in every case decided by the Court, in favor of most laws that arguably supported religion, and usually with the government in criminal justice matters. Although he opposed racial and gender discrimination, his vote in affirmative action cases was unpredictable. The length of his judicial career was itself a lesson in constitutional change. Some of the issues that occupied the Court's time near the end of his tenure were not even on the docket in the early 1960s. Similarly, some highly visible issues in White's first year on the Court had all but disappeared by his last.

During the campaign Clinton had indicated a preference for Supreme Court nominees with stature in public life who had run for election, not just those with prior judicial service. (Excepting only White and Rehnquist, the justices in 1993 had all come to the Court with at least some prior judicial experience. Only O'Connor had ever faced the voters in an election.) Clinton thought that the Court in previous decades had benefitted from the presence of persons such as Chief Justice Warren, who had never been a judge but who was governor of California from 1942 until 1953. Clinton therefore suggested someone with the right credentials: Governor Mario Cuomo of New York.

Cuomo quickly removed himself from consideration, however. Among the reported front-runners the president then considered were his Interior Secretary, Bruce Babbitt—who, as governor of Arizona in the 1970s, had named Sandra Day O'Connor to that state's Court of Appeals—and federal appeals Judge Stephen Breyer. However, Clinton dropped Babbitt's name from the list, reportedly because he was "too valuable" at Interior. Breyer's fortunes fell when a meeting with Clinton did not go well. On June 14, Clinton revealed his choice: Ruth Bader Ginsburg, 60, of the Court of Appeals for the District of Columbia Circuit, one of President Carter's last nominations to the federal bench in 1980.

Upon confirmation to the Supreme Court, she became the first Jewish justice since Abe Fortas resigned in 1969 and the first native New Yorker to sit on the Court since Benjamin Cardozo died in 1938. Ginsburg had been turned down for a Supreme Court clerkship in 1960 by Justice Frankfurter, who explained to her Harvard professor that he "just wasn't ready to hire a woman." Ginsburg had never held public office, but she had been in public life. As founder and director of the Women's Rights Project of the American Civil Liberties Union, she had participated in 35 cases in the Supreme Court, had argued six, and had won five, including **Frontiero v. Richardson** (see Chapter Fourteen). Of recent justices, only Thurgood Marshall had come to the Court with similar experience in the creative use of constitutional law to right social wrongs.

Ironically, Ginsburg had been critical of *Roe* v. *Wade*. Although favoring a woman's right to abortion, she had suggested in a lecture[4] at New York University in March that the right might more properly rest on equal protection, not privacy, doctrine. That is, "disadvantageous treatment of a woman because of her pregnancy and reproductive choice is a paradigm case of discrimination on the basis of sex." *Roe* may even have been untimely, she mused, because state legislatures had begun to loosen restrictions on abortions in the early 1970s. Had *Roe* been more limited in its scope, it might have "invited . . . dialogue with legislators," thus continuing the trend. Instead, the decision provoked a backlash and "prolonged divisiveness."

Ginsburg's record invited questions but spawned few doubts about her confirmation when the Senate Judiciary Committee convened for four days of hearings on July 20. Cautious in discussing most issues except abortion, Ginsburg appeared to be a person of politically liberal views with a sense of limits to judicial power. On August 3, the Senate approved her nomination by a vote of 96–3; on August 10 she took the constitutional and judicial oaths as the Court's 107th justice. The occasion was noteworthy. For the first time a nominee to the Supreme Court had been forthright in presenting her views on abortion and had been confirmed.

In the public's mind, no justice has been more closely linked with abortion than Harry A. Blackmun, author of the Court's opinion in *Roe* v. *Wade*. On April 6, 1994, Blackmun, age 85, announced his forthcoming retirement. Although 20 justices (including White) since 1789 had served longer than Blackmun's 24 years, only two were older at the time they left the Court. Widely expected to practice judicial restraint and to harbor conservative judicial values when appointed, Blackmun soon

---

[4]Her lecture was published as "Speaking in a Judicial Voice," 67 *New York University Law Review* 1185 (1992).

left the reservation. Insisting at retirement that the Court, not he, had changed, he was only partly correct. He had changed as well. At the hearings on his nomination in 1970, for example, senators queried him on only a single specific constitutional issue: capital punishment. His position then on that question was the exact opposite of his position two decades later. While he still sided with the government on Fourth Amendment issues, in nearly every other category of constitutional law he had become by 1991 the Court's most consistently liberal voice.

Speculation focused immediately on outgoing Senate Majority Leader George Mitchell as a successor. Mitchell, who also had experience as a federal judge in Maine, was not only politically liberal; as a politician of national stature, he seemed made to order for Clinton. Equally important, like Ginsburg, he seemed highly confirmable. Within a week, however, Mitchell removed himself from consideration, leaving the spurned president to cast about for other candidates that included previous runners-up Babbitt and Breyer plus Richard S. Arnold of Arkansas, a federal appeals judge from Blackmun's old circuit. Having called for a nominee who possessed a "big heart," the president on May 13 revealed his choice: Boston's Judge Stephen Gerald Breyer, 55, of the Court of Appeals for the First Circuit. Clinton's announcement was unprecedented. He publicly agonized over his decision, discussed reasons why he could not offer the seat to Babbitt or Arnold, and left the impression that Breyer was third best.

Breyer clerked for Justice Arthur Goldberg in 1964–1965, worked on the Watergate prosecution team, taught at Harvard Law School, and was chief counsel to the Senate Judiciary Committee before Carter named him to the federal bench in 1980. With legal interests in administrative law and regulation and a reputation for assessing laws by their effects, Breyer was well-known and highly regarded by both Democrats and Republicans in the Senate, and so encountered only minor resistance. On July 12, hearings convened for four days with confirmation, 87–9, following on July 29. Unwilling to wait for swearing-in ceremonies at the White House, Breyer and his wife drove to the Rehnquists' vacation home in Greensboro, Vermont, where the Chief Justice administered both oaths to the 108th justice on August 3. With the addition of Breyer, when the Court convened on October 3, the bench contained two Jewish justices for the first time since 1938.

**IMPEACHMENT.** In 1997 Breyer and Ginsburg joined the other seven justices in ***Clinton v. Jones,*** holding that a sitting president was suable for actions arising from his unofficial conduct—in this instance, alleged sexual harassment of Paula Jones that preceded Clinton's presidency (see Chapter Three). A civil deposition by President Clinton followed on January 17, 1998, in which Clinton denied that he had had a sexual relationship with White House intern Monica Lewinsky. As the Jones lawsuit was winding down, a criminal investigation of the president by the Office of Independent Counsel—begun in 1994 to review a questionable land deal in Arkansas and later expanded to other matters—was moving ahead under the direction of former U.S. solicitor general and federal appeals judge Kenneth W. Starr. (Ironically, this was possible only because the statute authorizing an independent counsel, allowed to expire during the Bush administration, had been revived by a Democratic Congress and signed into law by Clinton.) On August 17, 1998, Clinton testified by videotape to a federal grand jury impaneled by Starr and admitted certain details of a relationship with Lewinsky from late 1995 through early 1997 that he had previously denied.

In September Starr submitted a report to Congress (in Republican hands since January 1995), asserting, among other things, that Clinton had perjured himself in both his deposition and grand jury testimony about the nature of his relationship with Lewinsky. On December 19, 1998, the House of Representatives, in a highly partisan atmosphere, impeached the president on two counts: for making false statements to the grand jury (by a vote of 228–206), and for obstruction of justice in trying to cover up the former (221–212). On January 7, 1999, Chief Justice Rehnquist entered the Senate chamber in a role filled by only one other chief justice—presiding officer for a trial of the president of the United States. It had been 131 years since Chief Justice Salmon P. Chase presided at the trial of President Andrew Johnson. On February 12, by votes falling well short of the required two-thirds, the Senate acquitted Clinton, concluding that neither count one (45–55) nor count two (50–50) amounted to the "Treason, Bribery, or other high Crimes and Misdemeanors" that Article II, section 4 in the Constitution specifies as removable behavior.

Though secure in office, Clinton was dogged by the Lewinsky affair through the rest of his term. He had settled the Jones lawsuit out of court in November 1998 with a payment of $850,000, but the president was held in contempt on April 12, 1999, by Chief Judge Susan Webber Wright of the U.S. District Court for the Eastern District of Arkansas, for whose court Clinton had given the 1998 Jones deposition. "[T]here simply is no escaping the fact that the President deliberately violated this court's discovery orders and thereby undermined the integrity of the judicial system" by his "falsehoods" in the deposition, she wrote. On July 29, she ordered the president to pay reimbursement of $1,200 to her court and $89,484.05 to counsel for Jones (*Jones* v. *Clinton I* and *II,* 1999). Wright referred the matter to the Professional Conduct Committee of the Arkansas Supreme Court for proceedings on revocation of Clinton's license to practice law.

On January 19, 2001—his last full day in office—Clinton reached agreement with Independent Counsel Robert Ray allowing him to avoid the possibility of indictment in exchange for admitting that "certain of my responses to questions about Ms. Lewinsky were false." Moreover, the president agreed to surrender his law license for five years, to pay a fine of $25,000 to the Arkansas Bar Association, and not to seek reimbursement of any legal fees from a federal court, as the independent counsel statute entitled him to do as someone who was investigated but not indicted.

## THE BUSH PRESIDENCY

As Democratic and Republican nominees Al Gore and George W. Bush campaigned for the presidency in the fall of 2000, both acknowledged that the future direction of the Supreme Court might well rest in the outcome of the election. This seemed true for two reasons. First, on a series of salient "hot-button" constitutional issues ranging from abortion and affirmative action to federalism and religious liberty, the Court at the start of the new century was divided 5 to 4 or 6 to 3. (Several of these important decisions are reprinted in this book.) Second, the membership of the Court remained unchanged since Breyer's arrival in 1994. This fact was unique. Since 1869, when Congress set the Court's roster at the current complement of nine justices, there had been no other period of at least six years without the retirement or death of a justice.

In 2004, as George W. Bush entered the final year of his term, however, the membership of the Court remained as he had found it on January 20, 2001. That fact did not mean that the politics of judicial selection had taken a vacation, in particular with nominees to the courts of appeals. An ideological and political war with no end in sight had been raging between the White House and Senate Democrats over who becomes a judge. Even after Republicans gained a one-vote majority in the Senate in the 2002 midterm elections, Democrats deployed or threatened to deploy the filibuster against certain nominees favorably reported by the Judiciary Committee. Most notably, on September 4, 2003, Justice Department attorney Miguel Estrada, whom Bush probably wanted to groom for the Supreme Court as the first Hispanic justice, asked the president to withdraw his name after his nomination to the court of appeals for the District of Columbia Circuit had languished in the Senate for nearly two years. Observers thought such combat might be merely a dress rehearsal in preparation for the next Supreme Court vacancy, whenever that occasion arises. What is certain is that the occasion will arise, assuring once again a debate over the future of the Supreme Court in the presidential elections of 2004 and beyond.

## KEY TERMS

constitutional law
constitutional
   interpretation
cases

judicial review
recess appointment
circuit riding

seriatim opinions
diversity jurisdiction
Warren Court

## QUERIES

**1.** A long-running debate asks whether prior judicial experience makes one better qualified for the Supreme Court. Of the Court's roster in 2003, only one justice (Rehnquist) arrived on the bench with no previous service as a judge. By contrast, of the Court's roster 40 years earlier, six justices had no prior judicial experience. Justice Frankfurter flatly declared in 1957 that "the correlation between prior judicial experience and fitness for the Supreme Court is zero." What qualifications should a president consider when selecting a justice?

**2.** All nominees to the Supreme Court in the past half century have appeared before the Senate Judiciary Committee. Is this a desirable practice? If so, are there questions that senators should (and should not) ask? Are there questions that nominees should (and should not) answer?

**3.** Is there an acceptable way to combine both judicial independence (now made possible partly by life tenure) with political accountability? One proposal calls for a constitutional amendment to fix a term of 14 years for Supreme Court justices and other federal judges. In the fourteenth year, the president in office could choose to reappoint, or not, the individual for another term of 14 years. As with the initial appointment, reappointment would be subject to approval by the Senate. What are the strengths and weaknesses of this proposal?

**4.** Some Supreme Court nominations in recent decades have been highly controversial. Others have aroused little controversy and have moved through the Senate with little or no opposition. What factors seem to account for the difference?

## SELECTED READINGS ON FEDERAL JUDICIAL APPOINTMENTS

ABRAHAM, HENRY J. *Justices, Presidents, and Senators: A History of the U.S. Supreme Court Appointments from Washington to Clinton.* Lanham, Md.: Rowman & Littlefield, 2000.

BRONNER, ETHAN. *Battle for Justice: How the Bork Nomination Shook America.* New York: Doubleday, 1990.

CARTER, STEPHEN L. *The Confirmation Mess.* New York: Basic Books, 1994.

DANELSKI, DAVID J. *A Supreme Court Justice Is Appointed.* New York: Random House, 1964.

FRANK, JOHN P. *Clement Haynsworth, the Senate, and the Supreme Court.* Charlottesville: University Press of Virginia, 1991.

GOLDMAN, SHELDON. *Picking Federal Judges.* New Haven, Conn.: Yale University Press, 1997.

MALTESE, JOHN A. *The Selling of Supreme Court Nominees.* Baltimore, Md.: Johns Hopkins University Press, 1995.

MASSARO, JOHN. *Supremely Political: The Role of Ideology and Presidential Management in Unsuccessful Supreme Court Nominations.* Albany: State University of New York Press, 1990.

SILVERSTEIN, MARK. *Judicious Choices: The New Politics of Supreme Court Confirmations.* New York: Norton, 1994.

YALOF, DAVID ALISTAIR. *Pursuit of Justices: Presidential Politics and the Selection of Supreme Court Nominees.* Chicago: University of Chicago Press, 1999.

## SELECTED READINGS ON THE SUPREME COURT

ABRAHAM, HENRY J., and BARBARA A. PERRY. *Freedom and the Court,* 8th ed. Lawrence: University Press of Kansas, 2003.

EPSTEIN, LEE, and JACK KNIGHT. *The Choices Justices Make.* Washington, D.C.: CQ Press, 1998.

GARRATY, JOHN, ed. *Quarrels That Have Shaped the Constitution,* rev. ed. New York: Harper & Row, 1987.

JACKSON, ROBERT H. *The Struggle for Judicial Supremacy.* New York: Knopf, 1941.

JOHNSON, HERBERT, gen. ed. *Chief Justiceships of the United States Supreme Court.* Columbia: University of South Carolina Press, 1995–. Volumes to date include: WILLIAM R. CASTO, *The Supreme Court in the Early Republic: The Chief Justiceships of John Jay and Oliver Ellsworth* (1995); HERBERT A. JOHNSON, *The Chief Justiceship of John Marshall, 1801–1835* (1997); JAMES W. ELY, JR., *The Chief Justiceship of Melville W. Fuller, 1888–1910* (1995); WALTER F. PRATT, JR., *The Supreme Court under Edward Douglass White, 1910–1921* (1999); MELVIN I. UROFSKY, *Division and Discord: The Supreme Court under Stone and Vinson, 1941–1953* (1997); EARL M. MALTZ, *The Chief Justiceship of Warren Burger, 1969–1986* (2000).

KELLY, ALFRED H., WINFRED A. HARBISON, and HERMAN BELZ. *The American Constitution,* 7th ed., 2 vols. New York: Norton, 1997.

McCLOSKEY, ROBERT G. *The American Supreme Court,* 3d ed. Chicago: University of Chicago Press, 2000.

MASON, ALPHEUS T. *The Supreme Court from Taft to Burger*. Baton Rouge: Louisiana State University Press, 1979.

MURPHY, WALTER F. *Elements of Judicial Strategy*. Chicago: University of Chicago Press, 1964.

O'BRIEN, DAVID M. *Storm Center,* 6th ed. New York: Norton, 2002.

POWE, LUCAS A., JR. *The Warren Court and American Politics*. Cambridge, Mass.: Harvard University Press, 2000.

RENSTROM, PETER G., gen. ed. *Supreme Court Handbooks Series*. Santa Barbara, Calif.: ABC-CLIO, 2000–. Volumes to date include: TINSLEY E. YARBROUGH, *The Burger Court* (2000); PETER G. RENSTROM, *The Stone Court* (2001) and *The Taft Court* (2003); MELVIN I. UROFSKY, *The Warren Court* (2001); MICHAEL E. PARRISH, *The Hughes Court* (2002); JAMES W. ELY, JR., *The Fuller Court* (2003); TIMOTHY S. HUEBNER, *The Taney Court* (2003); DONALD GRIER STEPHENSON, JR., *The Waite Court* (2003).

STEPHENSON, DONALD GRIER, JR. *Campaigns and the Court: The U.S. Supreme Court in Presidential Elections*. New York: Columbia University Press, 1999.

———, ed. *An Essential Safeguard: Essays on the United States Supreme Court and Its Justices*. Westport, Conn.: Greenwood, 1991. (Includes essays by Henry J. Abraham, William M. Beaney, Jesse H. Choper, Rex E. Lee, Walter F. Murphy, Martin Shapiro, James F. Simon, and Harold J. Spaeth.)

WARD, ARTEMUS. *Deciding to Leave: The Politics of Retirement from the United States Supreme Court*. Albany: State University of New York Press, 2003.

WARREN, CHARLES. *The Supreme Court in United States History,* 2 vols. Boston: Little, Brown, 1926.

WIECEK, WILLIAM M. *Liberty Under Law*. Baltimore, Md.: Johns Hopkins University Press, 1988.

YARBROUGH, TINSLEY. *The Rehnquist Court and the Constitution*. New York: Oxford University Press, 2000.

## SELECTED BIOGRAPHIES

ARKES, HADLEY. *The Return of George Sutherland*. Princeton, N.J.: Princeton University Press, 1994.

CRAY, ED. *Chief Justice: A Biography of Earl Warren*. New York: Simon & Schuster, 1997.

DUNNE, GERALD T. *Hugo Black and the Judicial Revolution*. New York: Simon & Schuster, 1978.

FAIRMAN, CHARLES. *Mr. Justice Miller and the Supreme Court, 1862–1890*. Cambridge, Mass.: Harvard University Press, 1939.

HOBSON, CHARLES F. *The Great Chief Justice: John Marshall and the Rule of Law*. Lawrence: University Press of Kansas, 1996.

JEFFRIES, JOHN C., JR. *Justice Lewis F. Powell, Jr.* New York: Macmillan, 1994.

KENS, PAUL. *Justice Stephen Field*. Lawrence: University Press of Kansas, 1997.

MAGRATH, C. PETER. *Morrison R. Waite*. New York: Macmillan, 1963.

MASON, ALPHEUS THOMAS. *Brandeis: A Free Man's Life*. New York: Viking, 1946.

———. *Harlan Fiske Stone: Pillar of the Law*. New York: Viking, 1956.

———. *William Howard Taft: Chief Justice*. New York: Simon & Schuster, 1964.

MORGAN, DONALD G. *Justice William Johnson: The First Dissenter.* Columbia: University of South Carolina Press, 1954.

MURPHY, BRUCE ALLEN. *Wild Bill: The Legend and Life of William O. Douglas.* New York: Random House, 2003.

NEWMYER, R. KENT. *John Marshall and the Heroic Age of the Supreme Court.* Baton Rouge: Louisiana State University Press, 2001.

NIVEN, JOHN. *Salmon P. Chase.* New York: Oxford University Press, 1995.

SMITH, JEAN EDWARD. *John Marshall: Definer of a Nation.* New York: Henry Holt, 1996.

STRUM, PHILIPPA. *Louis D. Brandeis.* Cambridge, Mass.: Harvard University Press, 1984.

SWISHER, CARL B. *Roger B. Taney.* Washington, D.C.: Brookings Institution, 1935.

TUSHNET, MARK V. *Making Civil Rights Law: Thurgood Marshall and the Supreme Court,* 2 vols. New York: Oxford University Press, 1994, 1996.

WHITE, G. EDWARD. *Justice Oliver Wendell Holmes.* New York: Oxford University Press, 1993.

YARBROUGH, TINSLEY E. *John Marshall Harlan: Great Dissenter of the Warren Court.* New York: Oxford University Press, 1992.

———. *Judicial Enigma: The First Justice Harlan.* New York: Oxford University Press, 1995.

# CHAPTER ONE

# *Jurisdiction and Organization of the Federal Courts*

*[R]eversal by a higher court is not proof that justice is thereby better done. There is no doubt that if there were a super-Supreme Court, a substantial proportion of our reversals of state courts would also be reversed. We are not final because we are infallible, but we are infallible only because we are final.*

—JUSTICE ROBERT H. JACKSON (1953)

American constitutional law represents only a tiny fraction of the entire corpus of the law. Routine litigation between private parties seldom falls into the category of "cases" to which the judicial power of the Supreme Court extends. Even cases involving constitutional questions may be sidestepped. The Supreme Court of the United States is not "a super legal aid bureau."

This chapter presents certain rules and procedures guiding the justices in choosing the cases they will decide and sketches the major steps leading to a decision. The rules governing jurisdiction and standing to sue vest in the justices' considerable discretionary power. The justices control their workload by selecting the cases that demand attention at the highest level. In the governing process, the Supreme Court has an important, if circumscribed, role to play.

## THE JUDICIAL POWER

The Constitution in Article III makes possible the resolution of certain legal disputes in national, as opposed to state, courts. One significant difference between American government under the Articles of Confederation and the Constitution was the provision in the latter for a system of national courts. Under the Articles, there was not even a Supreme Court.

**FIFTY-ONE JUDICIAL SYSTEMS.** Civilian courts in the United States comprise 51 separate judicial systems: the court systems of the 50 states and the courts of the national government. The latter are commonly referred to, somewhat misleadingly, as **federal courts** and draw their authority from the Constitution and acts of Congress. **State courts** receive their authority from the constitutions and statutes of their respective states. This dual system of federal and state courts means that almost everyone in any of the 50 states is simultaneously within the **jurisdiction,** or reach, of two judicial systems, one state and the other federal. Jurisdiction refers to the authority a court has to decide a case. The term has two basic dimensions: who and what. The first identifies the parties who may take a case into a particular court. The second refers to the subject matter the parties may raise in their case.

According to Article III, federal judicial power extends to: (1) cases arising under the Constitution, the laws of the United States, and treaties made under the authority of the United States; (2) admiralty and maritime cases; (3) controversies between two or more states; (4) controversies to which the United States is a party, even where the other party is a state; (5) suits between citizens of different states; and (6) cases begun by a state against a citizen of another state or against another country. (As explained in Chapter Four, the Eleventh Amendment modified Article III to bar suits brought against a state by a citizen of another state or country.) The Constitution vests this judicial power of the United States in "one Supreme Court and in such inferior courts as the Congress may from time to time ordain and establish." This provision is not self-executing, and Congress at the outset of the government in 1789 created a system of lower federal courts in addition to the Supreme Court. As currently organized, this system consists of: (1) a court of appeals for each of the 11 judicial circuits, plus one for the District of Columbia; (2) district courts, of which there are now 91 (89 in the 50 states, plus one in the District of Columbia and one in Puerto Rico); and (3) other courts, such as the Court of Appeals for the Federal Circuit. (See Figure 1.1 on page 26.)

The Supreme Court, courts of appeals, and the district courts within the 50 states, District of Columbia, and Puerto Rico are known as constitutional, or **Article III courts.** Their judges are appointed by the president, confirmed by the Senate, and enjoy the constitutional assurances of tenure "during good behavior" (effectively lifetime appointment) and no reduction in salary. Specialized courts such as the Court of Federal Claims or the Court of Appeals for the Armed Forces are legislative, or **Article I courts,** meaning that they were created by Congress in furtherance of a power granted by Article I. In contrast to Article III courts, Congress has full power over the salaries and tenure of judges of these Article I legislative courts and may assign administrative or legislative duties to them. The district courts in the territories of Guam, Northern Mariana Islands, and the Virgin Islands are also Article I courts. The distinction between Article III and Article I judges has real operational significance. In *Nguyen* v. *United States* (2003), the Supreme Court vacated two judgments of the Ninth Circuit Court of Appeals because the panel of three judges included the chief judge of the District Court of the Northern Mariana Islands (an Article I judge) who was sitting by designation with the Article III appeals court judges.

**JURISDICTION OF THE DISTRICT COURTS.** The district courts are the trial courts of the federal judicial system (see Figure 1.2 on page 27). Their original jurisdiction includes cases that raise a federal question and cases that involve more than $75,000 where the parties are citizens of different states. (A court has **original jurisdiction** when a case begins or originates there, **appellate jurisdiction** when a

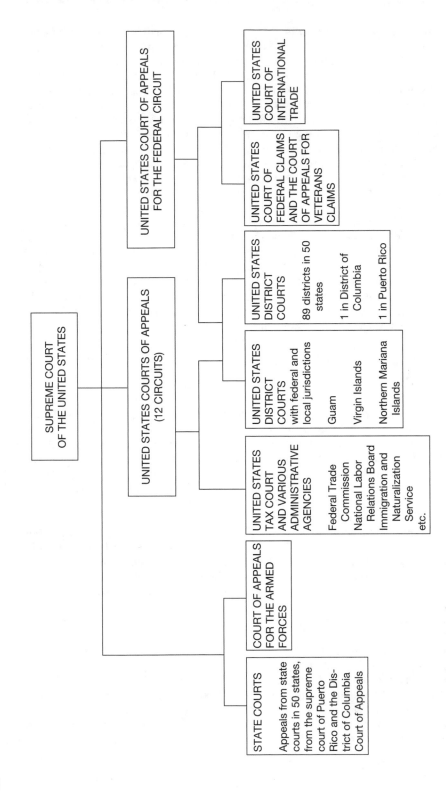

**FIGURE 1.1  The National Court System**
Cases in the federal courts usually originate in the district courts. Cases in state courts may qualify for review by the U.S. Supreme Court if they raise a federal question.

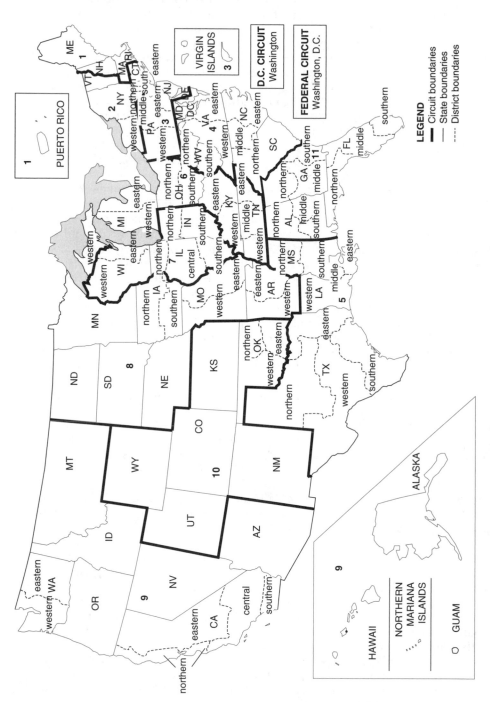

**FIGURE 1.2  Geographic Boundaries of the U.S. Courts of Appeals and U.S. District Courts**

This map shows how the 94 U.S. District Courts and the 13 U.S. Courts of Appeals exist with the court systems of the 50 states and the District of Columbia. The District Courts include 89 divided among the 50 states, plus one each for the District of Columbia, Guam, Puerto Rico, Northern Mariana Islands, and the Virgin Islands.

case involves review of the decision of a lower court. A **federal question** is one that involves the meaning and/or application of the Constitution, a statute, or a treaty of the United States.) Two wholly independent bases of jurisdiction are thus provided: The first is defined by the nature of the question, and the second (**diversity jurisdiction**) by the citizenship of the parties and the amount at stake. Diversity jurisdiction allows cases presenting issues normally heard in state court to be tried in federal court. District courts also have supervisory powers over bankruptcy courts within each district and appellate jurisdiction with respect to a few classes of cases tried before U.S. **magistrate judges.** These judicial officers issue search warrants, conduct arraignments of persons charged with federal crimes, and perform other duties assigned by their district court. The U.S. District Court for the District of Columbia has a special responsibility in reviewing changes in local electoral practices in certain states under the Voting Rights Act. (See Chapter Five.)

JURISDICTION OF THE COURTS OF APPEALS. Congress has given the courts of appeals jurisdiction in appeals taken from the district courts within their respective circuits, from judgments of the Tax Court, and from the rulings of particular administrative and regulatory agencies such as the National Labor Relations Board and the Securities and Exchange Commission. In addition, courts of appeals may review cases from the district courts in the territories. (For example, Guam and the Northern Mariana Islands are part of the Ninth Circuit.) The Court of Appeals for the Federal Circuit has a more specialized jurisdiction. Unlike the other 12, it hears appeals in patent, trademark, and copyright cases and in certain administrative law matters from district courts in all circuits as well as from the Court of Federal Claims, Court of International Trade, Court of Appeals for Veterans Claims, and specified administrative bodies.

JURISDICTION OF THE SUPREME COURT. The Supreme Court's jurisdiction is in two parts: original and appellate. The Court's original jurisdiction is specified in Article III and can be neither diminished nor enlarged by Congress. It includes four kinds of disputes: (1) cases between one of the states and the national government; (2) cases between two or more states; (3) cases involving foreign ambassadors, ministers, or consuls; and (4) cases begun by a state against a citizen of another state or against another country. Only controversies between states qualify today exclusively as original cases in the Supreme Court. For the others, Congress has given concurrent jurisdiction to the lower federal courts. As a result, almost all of the Court's cases come from its appellate jurisdiction.

According to Article III, the Supreme Court has appellate jurisdiction "in all other cases both . . . as to law and fact, with such exceptions, and under such regulations as the Congress shall make." Congress, in other words, decides which categories of cases in the lower courts qualify for review by the Supreme Court. Not until 1889, for example, was there a right of appeal to the Supreme Court in some federal criminal cases. Perhaps Congress could even deprive the Court of all appellate review and make final the decisions of lower courts. An extreme example occurred in 1869 when Congress, fearing that the Court would invalidate the Reconstruction Acts, hastily withdrew the Court's jurisdiction under the Habeas Corpus Act of 1867. The Court thus became powerless to pass on a case in which argument had been heard (**Ex parte** *McCardle,* in Chapter Two).

The major change in the appellate jurisdiction of the Supreme Court since 1789 has been in the proportion of cases qualifying for obligatory, as opposed to discretionary, review. Although the Judiciary Act of 1789 allowed Supreme Court review of certain cases from the state and lower federal courts by way of a writ of error, it was not until 1891, with passage of the Circuit Courts of Appeals Act, that the justices gained some discretion over the cases they would decide.

The Judges Act of 1925 further reduced the mandatory jurisdiction. As a result, most cases raising a federal question reached the Court on **certiorari** (Latin for "to make sure"). Review in this category was plainly discretionary. The justices could select for decision those cases they considered most worthy of their time. A smaller number of cases came to the Court on **appeal.** As with the old writ of error, these cases qualified by statute for obligatory review, without regard to the importance of the issue raised or its impact on the government or the general public. By the mid-1980s, the appeal category of the Court's appellate docket accounted for only 5 percent of the total filings but a full one-third of the cases the Court decided on the merits.

In 1988 Congress enacted a major overhaul of the Supreme Court's jurisdiction. With the start of the October 1988 term, the Court's appellate jurisdiction became almost entirely discretionary, meaning that nearly every case now comes to the Court on certiorari. The mandatory appeal category has been virtually abolished, except for decisions by three-judge district courts (required by Congress in a few instances), which reach the Supreme Court on **direct appeal,** bypassing the courts of appeals.

**SELF-IMPOSED LIMITATIONS ON JUDICIAL POWER.** In many cases where the federal courts, including the Supreme Court, would appear to have jurisdiction, one or more other requirements may prevent a court from accepting and deciding the case. Some of these self-denying ordinances were set forth by Justice Brandeis, concurring, in *Ashwander* v. *TVA* (1936). Summarized briefly, these so-called **Ashwander rules** provide that:

1. The Court will not issue a constitutional ruling in a friendly, nonadversary proceeding.
2. The Court will not anticipate a question of constitutional law in advance of the necessity for deciding it.
3. The Court will not formulate a rule of law broader than the facts of the case require.
4. If possible, the Court will dispose of a case on nonconstitutional grounds.
5. The Court will not pass upon the validity of a statute on complaint of one who fails to show injury to person or property.
6. The Court will not pass upon the constitutionality of a statute at the instance of one who has accepted its benefits.
7. Whenever possible, the court will construe statutes so as to avoid a constitutional issue.

Specifically, before a federal court will accept jurisdiction, there must be an actual **case or controversy,** in the language of Article III. That is, the conflict must be real, touching the parties who have adverse interests. This case or controversy requirement means, therefore, that a case must present a live dispute. In *DeFunis* v. *Odegaard* (1974), for example, the Court held that a suit brought by a white law student, challenging a racially preferential admissions program at the University of Washington, was moot. Although the case had attracted national attention, the majority concluded that since DeFunis had already been admitted to law school by court order and was about to graduate, he had suffered no injury.

Similarly, a case must be "ripe for review." The **ripeness** requirement injects an element of timing in order to avoid premature adjudication. A controversy must have reached a certain stage of maturity before the Court will engage it.

The case or controversy requirement also means that the federal courts, unlike the courts of some states, will not render an **advisory opinion**—a statement about a hypothetical situation or a statement indicating how a court would rule were litigation to develop. This policy originated in 1793. Responding to a request from President Washington and Secretary of State Thomas Jefferson, the justices declined to offer their views on "the construction of treaties, laws of nations and laws of the land, which the Secretary said were often presented under circumstances which 'do not give a cognizance of them to the tribunals of the country.'"

Closely related to the case or controversy stipulation is the rule requiring "standing to sue." **Standing** focuses attention on whether the litigant is the proper party to bring a lawsuit, not whether the issue itself is appropriate for courts to decide. Standing is a threshold question, for without it, litigants do not get to press the merits or substance of their dispute. In federal litigation, standing consists of three elements: (1) the plaintiff must have suffered an "injury in fact" (an invasion of a legally protected interest that is "concrete and particularized" and is "actual or imminent"); (2) a "causal connection" must exist between the injury and the conduct complained of; and (3) it must be "likely," and not merely "speculative," that the injury will be redressed by a favorable decision (*Lujan* v. *Defenders of Wildlife,* 1992).

For example, *Frothingham* v. *Mellon* (1923) held that a federal taxpayer could not challenge the Federal Maternity Act because the taxpayer's interest was minute and indeterminable. In spite of this decision, the Court in 1968 conceded standing to a federal taxpayer who sought to challenge an alleged breach of the First Amendment's establishment-of-religion clause through federal expenditures under a 1965 act for textbooks and instructional costs in sectarian schools (*Flast* v. *Cohen*). The Court distinguished this situation from the typical taxpayer suit by viewing the establishment clause itself as a limitation on the taxing and spending power of Congress; hence taxpayers could urge more than their general interest in the expenditure of federal funds. Yet in 1982, the Court denied standing in a case where surplus government property had been transferred to a sectarian school (*Valley Forge Christian College* v. *Americans United for Separation of Church and State*). The majority regarded the transfer as an executive action under the property clause of Article IV, not congressional action under the taxing and spending clause, as had been the case in *Flast.* So the easier standing rules of *Flast* did not apply.

Absence of a live controversy, ripeness, standing, or jurisdiction makes a case **nonjusticiable,** or inappropriate for settlement by a court. Justiciability in turn merges into the **political question doctrine** (discussed more fully in Chapter Two). A political question is one that the Court believes should be decided by the "political branches" of the government—Congress or the presidency. Today, political questions include certain foreign-policy matters, the Constitution's stipulation of a "republican form of government" for every state, and the ratification of constitutional amendments. At one time legislative apportionment and districting were deemed "political" and hence out of judicial bounds.

Contrary views pervade these self-denials, and the justices differ markedly in defining their role. **Judicial activists** (those more eager to intervene and to substitute their views for those of other policymakers) tend to gloss over such matters as "technical." **Judicial restraintists** (those inclined to defer to decisions made elsewhere in the political system) can frequently avoid a decision on the merits by insisting that a litigant has run afoul of one or more rules.

## SUPREME COURT DECISION MAKING

Article III of the Constitution establishes "the judicial power of the United States" in "one Supreme Court." Initially staffed by six justices, since 1869 the Supreme Court's size has been set by Congress at nine—eight associate justices and the Chief Justice

**Table 1.1  Caseload in the United States Supreme Court, 1930–2003**

| Term | Total Cases on Docket | Cases Decided with Opinion* |
|---|---|---|
| 1929–1930 | 981 | 156 |
| 1939–1940 | 1,078 | 151 |
| 1949–1950 | 1,441 | 122 |
| 1959–1960 | 2,143 | 132 |
| 1969–1970 | 4,172 | 126 |
| 1979–1980 | 4,781 | 155 |
| 1989–1990 | 5,746 | 146 |
| 1990–1991 | 6,316 | 125 |
| 1994–1995 | 8,100 | 94 |
| 1999–2000 | 8,445 | 81 |
| 2002–2003 | 9,406 | 84 |

*Data include all cases submitted to oral argument and disposed of by a signed or per curiam opinion; the number of such opinions filed each term may be slightly lower because a single opinion may dispose of more than one case.

of the United States. Also by statute, the Court's annual term opens on the first Monday in October and concludes when the justices have disposed of all argued cases, usually in late June or very early July.

ACCESS TO THE SUPREME COURT. Having a case decided by a state or lower federal court by no means assures the losing litigant of review eventually by the United States Supreme Court. The justices reject many more cases for review than they decide—indeed, so many more that most of what the Supreme Court does is to say "no." In recent terms, the justices have annually denied review in over 7,000 cases and have given plenary treatment (consisting of oral argument and a signed opinion, as explained below) to fewer than 100. Another several dozen other cases may be decided summarily. About 1,100 cases may be carried over for action the following term. Indeed, despite an enlarged docket, the number of decided cases has actually fallen. (See Table 1.1.) Moreover, prisoner appeals, most of which are assigned to the "miscellaneous" docket for indigents (where fees and other requirements are waived), are routinely granted review at a far lower rate than cases on the "paid" docket. For example, only 19 of 6,958 were granted review and decided (plenarily or summarily) from the former category in 2001–2002, as compared with 139 of the 2,210 paid cases.

THE JUSTICES AT WORK. The actual work of the Supreme Court proceeds through five stages: agenda setting, briefs on the merits, oral argument, conference, opinions and decision.

(1) *Agenda Setting.* Petitions for review from litigants and their counsel who lost in the court below arrive in the form of documents called **briefs** that demonstrate why the Court should accept the case for decision. Litigants and their counsel who won in the court below file briefs in opposition, explaining why the Court should not grant review. A minimum of four justices must vote to accept the case. This is the so-called **rule of four.** Deciding what to decide is therefore an important stage in the judicial process. At this and other stages in Supreme Court decision making, the United States government is represented by the **solicitor general,** the

third-ranking official in the Department of Justice. Thus, when an agency of the national government such as the Federal Election Commission has lost a case in a court of appeals, it is the solicitor general who makes the call whether to seek review in the Supreme Court.

When the justices meet in conference to act on petitions for review, the chief justice uses a "discuss list." This is a timesaving device. Any justice may add a case to the discuss list, but unless a case makes the list—and over 70 percent do not—review is automatically denied, without discussion. If the Court grants review, the case moves to the steps explained below. If the Court denies review, the case is ordinarily at an end. The decision of "the court below"—the last court to render a decision in the case—stands.

Mystery surrounds selection of cases because the justices only very rarely publish their reasons favoring a grant or denying of review. Yet experience suggests that the presence of one or more of the following factors increases the likelihood that the justices will accept a case: (a) the United States is a party to the case and requests review; (b) courts of appeals have issued conflicting decisions on the question; (c) the issue is one some justices are eager to engage; (d) the court below has made a decision clearly at odds with established Supreme Court interpretation of a law or constitutional provision; (e) the case is not "fact-bound"—that is, of primary interest only to the parties to the case; and (f) the case raises an issue of overriding importance to the nation.

(2) *Briefs on the Merits.* Once the justices have accepted a case, opposing counsel submit yet another round of briefs. Like briefs seeking or opposing review, length has been limited since 1980 to a maximum of 50 pages each. These briefs focus not on why the Court should hear the case, but on the substantive issues the case presents. Sometimes the Court will have specified in its grant of review that it wants to limit consideration to a single question. Persons, governments, and organizations interested in, but not parties to, a case may file their own briefs as **amici curiae,** or "friends of the Court." (Less frequently, an amicus may have already submitted a brief during stage one, thus alerting the Court to the national importance of a case.) Nongovernmental entities filing an amicus brief must obtain the permission of the opposing parties, although the Court itself may grant permission if a litigant refuses. The solicitor general and state attorneys general may file amici briefs without seeking permission.

(3) *Oral Argument.* In addition to reading the printed briefs submitted by counsel, the Court listens to **oral argument.** During the chief justiceship of John Marshall (1801–1835), arguments were well nigh interminable. Daniel Webster, a leading attorney of that day, used to run on for days. In 1849, the Court reduced the time for oral argument to two hours: one for each side. Opposing counsel now divide an hour between themselves, with additional time allotted only in exceptional circumstances. From October until the end of April, Mondays, Tuesdays, and Wednesdays of two consecutive weeks are set aside for oral argument, with at least two weeks following being reserved for the preparation of opinions. The justices hear arguments on those days from 10:00 A.M. until 3:00 P.M., with an hour recess at noon for lunch. This stage of the decision-making process gives the justices an opportunity to ask questions to clear up uncertainties or other matters that they may have noticed in the briefs. For even seasoned attorneys, the experience can be like a grueling oral examination.

Oral arguments are open to the public, but most seating in the small courtroom is on a first-come, first-served basis. The Marshal makes an audio recording of arguments, but no cameras are permitted in the courtroom. As of late 2002, the Court abandoned its curious policy of prohibiting ordinary spectators from making written notes in the courtroom. (Attorneys and journalists had always been allowed to do so.) But the policy against slouching, placing one's arm along the top of a bench, or nodding off—applied to all visitors—remains and is strictly enforced. Probably in no other place in official Washington is decorum so highly prized.

(4) *Conference.* Wednesday and Friday are **conference** days—the time set apart primarily for confidential discussion and decision of cases argued during the week. "As soon as we come off the bench Wednesday afternoon . . . ," Chief Justice Rehnquist has explained,

> we go into private "conference" in a room adjoining the chambers of the Chief Justice. At our Wednesday afternoon meeting we deliberate and vote on the . . . cases which we heard argued the preceding Monday. The Chief Justice begins the discussion of each case with a summary of the facts, his analysis of the law, and an announcement of his proposed vote (that is, whether to affirm, reverse, modify, etc.). The discussion then passes to the senior Associate Justice who does likewise. It then goes on down the line to the junior Associate Justice. When the discussion of one case is concluded, the discussion of the next one is immediately taken up, until all the argued cases on the agenda for that particular Conference have been disposed of.

In cases of greatest importance, discussion may take place at more than one conference before the justices are prepared to reach a decision. All cases are decided by majority vote, a fact that gives meaning to the question Justice Brennan used to pose to his new clerks each year: "What is the most important rule around here?" he would ask. After they offered various, but incorrect, responses, Brennan would say, "It's the 'rule of five.' You need five votes to get anything done."

(5) *Opinions and Decisions.* On Monday after a two-week argument session, the chief justice circulates an assignment list to the justices. If the chief justice is in the majority, he assigns the task of writing the opinion for the Court; if not, the senior associate justice in the majority makes the assignment. Preparation of the majority opinion requires much give and take, with an opinion going through as many as a dozen drafts. The goal is an **opinion of the Court,** representing the consensus of the majority, not merely the views of the writer, that explains and applies the legal principles applicable to that case. In situations where a majority of the justices are unable to agree on a single opinion, a **plurality opinion** announces the "judgment of the Court" (the outcome of the case) and explains the views of the plurality. The justices' positions are fluid. Up to the moment—weeks or months after the opinion writing began—the writer announces the decision in open Court, the justices are free to change their votes.

In contrast to a norm of consensus in the nineteenth century and early twentieth century Supreme Court that discouraged published dissents (even when justices disagreed with a decision), in only about a quarter of the decisions each term today is the Court unanimous. In the rest dissenters file one or more opinions explaining their differences with the majority. According to Chief Justice Hughes, a **dissent** is "an appeal to the brooding spirit of the law, to the intelligence of a future day, when a later decision may possibly correct the error into which the dissenting judge believes the court to have been betrayed." Justices may also write a **concurring opinion** to indicate their acceptance of the majority decision but either an unwillingness to adopt all the reasoning contained in the opinion of the Court or a desire to say something additional.

Throughout this decision-making process, justices are assisted by their **law clerks.** Congress authorized the first clerk or "secretary" (as the position was first labeled) in 1886. Today, most justices annually employ four clerks, each a recent law school graduate usually with experience clerking on a lower federal court. In addition with one aide to chambers (formerly called a messenger) and two secretaries for each justice (the Chief enjoys a somewhat larger staff), the Court, as Justice Powell once remarked, resembles a collection of "nine small, independent law firms." Increased reliance by most members of the Court on their clerks—the "junior Supreme Court" in Justice Douglas's words—both in making recommendations on which cases to accept for review and in writing opinions calls into question the observation made long ago by Justice Brandeis that "the Justices . . . are almost the only people in Washington who do their own work." Yet by congressional or White House standards, the Court's support staff remains small. "[I]ndividual justices still continue to do a great deal more of their 'own work,'" Chief Justice Rehnquist insists, "than do their counterparts in the other branches of the federal government."

## SOURCE MATERIALS

Within just the past decade, the Internet has transformed study of the judiciary. Today, with a computer properly connected, even someone in a remote location has easy access to many resources previously available only at law or other research libraries. What follows is a listing and annotation of essential source materials in both print and electronic form.

**SUPREME COURT DECISIONS.** The reported decisions and opinions of the Supreme Court form the basic material for the study of constitutional law. They appear in several printed editions and formats and are accessible on the Internet.

(1) *United States Reports.* This is the official edition published by the Government Printing Office. Until 1875, the reports were cited according to the name of the Reporter of Decisions, with the reporter's name usually abbreviated. Beginning with volume 91 in 1875, the reports have been cited only by volume and page number and the designation "U.S." For example, a case cited as 444 U.S. 130 is located in volume 444 of the *U.S. Reports,* beginning on page 130.

| | |
|---|---|
| 1789–1800 Dallas | (1–4 Dall., 1–4 U.S.) |
| 1801–1815 Cranch | (1–9 Cr., 5–13 U.S.) |
| 1816–1827 Wheaton | (1–12 Wheat., 14–25 U.S.) |
| 1828–1842 Peters | (1–16 Pet., 26–41 U.S.) |
| 1843–1860 Howard | (1–24 How., 42–65 U.S.) |
| 1861–1862 Black | (1–2 Bl., 66–67 U.S.) |
| 1863–1874 Wallace | (1–23 Wall., 68–90 U.S.) |
| 1875– | (91–U.S.) |

(2) *United States Supreme Court Reports, Lawyers' Edition* (until 1996 published by Lawyers' Cooperative Publishing Company; now published by Lexis-Nexis). The

advantage of this complete edition lies in the inclusion of summaries of briefs of counsel plus notes and annotations on various topics of constitutional law. *Lawyers' Edition* is cited as L.Ed. (96 L.Ed. 954). Decisions since 1956 appear in a second series (118 L.Ed. 2d 293).

(3) *Supreme Court Reporter* (until 1996 published by West Publishing Company; now published by West Group). This is similar in concept to *Lawyers' Edition* but includes only decisions since 1882. Thus for cases in volumes 1–105 U.S., one must consult one of the other editions. It is cited as S.Ct. (58 S.Ct. 166).

(4) *United States Law Week* (published by the Bureau of National Affairs, another commercial publisher). This is a looseleaf service, one advantage of which is that decisions are published within a day of their release at the Court. Thus, decisions appear in *Law Week* well before even the advance issues distributed by the two other commercial publishers listed above (and long before the government's). *Law Week* also keeps track of all cases on the Supreme Court's docket, whether ultimately accepted for decision or not, and publishes timely excerpts from oral arguments in selected cases throughout the Court's term. It is cited as U.S.L.W. (71 U.S.L.W. 4263).

(5) Electronic access. Supreme Court decisions are accessible through Westlaw and Lexis-Nexis (available through many college and university libraries or by subscription), on CD-ROM, and at various Internet sites. At present, the sites listed below are available at no charge. Be advised that any Internet address is subject to change.

(a) The LII and Hermes: The Legal Information Institute and Project Hermes provide decisions since May 1990 through Cornell University. Decisions are ordinarily accessible within hours of their announcement by the Supreme Court. Several hundred selected decisions prior to 1990 are available from LII at the second address.

http://supct.law.cornell.edu/supct/
http://supct.law.cornell.edu/supct/cases/name.htm

(b) FindLaw: FindLaw Internet Legal Resources includes decisions since 1791.

http://www.findlaw.com/casecode/supreme.html

(c) The U.S. Supreme Court: This official site contains the current docket, calendar, court rules, transcripts of oral arguments (posted within 15 days after the close of the particular argument session), decisions, orders, press releases, and some speeches by the justices.

http://www.supremecourtus.gov/index.html

(6) Case record. The record of each decided case includes briefs of counsel, oral argument, proceedings in lower courts, and exhibits. Unfortunately, these are not nearly so widely available as the Supreme Court decisions themselves. University Publications of America publishes *Landmark Briefs and Arguments of the Supreme Court of the United States: Constitutional Law*. With new volumes added annually, this set contains the complete extant record of major constitutional decisions of the Supreme Court, beginning in 1793, including many of the cases selected for this book. Briefs in recent cases are available online through FindLaw:

http://supreme.findlaw.com/supreme_court/resources.html. Briefs filed by the solicitor general may be accessed at http://www.usdoj.gov/osg.

**LOWER FEDERAL COURT DECISIONS.** Decisions by the lower federal courts are published by West Group. Decisions of the courts of appeals appear in *Federal Reporter* in 300 numbered volumes, subsequently numbered in a second, and now a third, series; they are cited as F., F. 2d, or F. 3d. Selected decisions of the district courts appear in *Federal Supplement,* cited as F. Supp., or F. Supp. 2d. Most recent rulings by appeals and district courts are available online at FindLaw: www.findlaw.com/casecode/cases.html, and at the Federal Judiciary Home Page: http://www.uscourts.gov/.

**STATE COURT DECISIONS.** The decisions of the highest state courts are published separately by either the state or a commercial publisher. A sectional reporter system, which combines selected decisions of the courts of several states in one publication, is also available in most law libraries. Some state court decisions are accessible through FindLaw: http://www.findlaw.com/11stategov/. The National Center for State Courts maintains a directory of state court sites: http://www.ncsconline.org/.

**MISCELLANEOUS JUDICIAL RESOURCES ONLINE.** In addition to sites that make judicial decisions available, other Internet locations contain a variety of materials related to the courts.

(1) Oyez Oyez Oyez: The Supreme Court Resource at Northwestern University holds digital sound recordings of oral arguments at the Supreme Court in selected cases since 1956.

http://oyez.nwu.edu/

(2) The Federal Judicial Center: Of particular interest is the "History of the Federal Judiciary." This online reference contains a biographical database of federal judges since 1789, histories of the federal courts, and historical documents related to the judicial branch of government.

http://www.fjc.gov

(3) The Federal Judiciary Home Page: Maintained by the Administrative Office of U.S. Courts, the site provides the text of both current and back issues of *The Third Branch* newsletter, various reports and other publications, and press releases.

http://www.uscourts.gov

(4) *The Law and Politics Book Review*: Produced by the Law and Courts Section of the American Political Science Association, this electronic journal is the best single source for timely reviews of recent books on constitutional law, the Supreme Court, and the judicial process generally.

http://www.bsos.umd.edu/gvpt/lpbr

(5) LAWlink: Maintained by the American Bar Association, this is a depository of links to dozens of law and law-related sites.

http://www.abanet.org/lawlink/

(6) Federal Court Locator: Maintained by the Villanova University School of Law, the site provides a comprehensive list of federal court Web sites and resources.

http://vls.law.vill.edu/Locator/fedcourt.html

**LEGISLATIVE AND ADMINISTRATIVE MATERIALS.** Acts of Congress may be found chronologically arranged in *United States Statutes at Large,* of which a new volume appears annually, and, for statutes currently in effect, are available in an analytical form in the *United States Code* (Government Printing Office), *United States Code Annotated* (West Group), and *United States Code Service* (Lexis-Nexis). The *U.S. Code* is accessible online:

http://www.access.gpo.gov/congress/cong013.html

Debates in Congress are available under the following titles and have been officially published since 1873: *Annals of Congress,* 1789–1824; *Register of Debates in Congress,* 1824–1837; *Congressional Globe,* 1833–1873; *Congressional Record,* 1873–. Text of the *Congressional Record* (as well as bills), beginning with the 101st Congress in 1989, is available online at http://thomas.loc.gov. The Library of Congress is gradually placing earlier congressional materials online at http://www.loc.gov.

Executive orders and proposed administrative rules and orders are published chronologically in the *Federal Register;* regulations in force are presented analytically in the *Code of Federal Regulations.* These publications are accessible online at http://www.access.gpo.gov/nara/cfr/index.html. Administrative and congressional activity is followed by *Congressional Quarterly Weekly Report* (published by Congressional Quarterly, Inc.) and by *National Journal* (published by Government Research Corp.).

**GENERAL REFERENCE WORKS.** Bibliographic sources include the massive set compiled by Kermit L. Hall, *A Comprehensive Bibliography of American Constitutional and Legal History, 1896–1979,* 5 vols. (Millwood, N.Y.: Kraus International Publications, 1984), and Fenton S. Martin and Robert U. Goehlert, *The U.S. Supreme Court: A Bibliography* (Washington, D.C.: Congressional Quarterly Press, 1990). More concise is D. Grier Stephenson, Jr., *The Supreme Court and the American Republic: An Annotated Bibliography* (New York: Garland Publishing, 1981). The latter volume includes a guide to the location of the papers of Supreme Court justices.

Study of individual justices is aided by Linda A. Blandford and Patricia Russell Evans, eds., *Supreme Court of the United States 1789–1980: An Index to Opinions Arranged by Justice,* 2 vols. (Millwood, N.Y.: Kraus International Publications, 1983). A supplement covering the years 1981–1991 was issued by the same publisher in 1994. Biographical essays are contained in Leon Friedman and Fred L. Israel, *The Justices of the United States Supreme Court 1789–1995,* rev. ed., 5 vols. (New York: Chelsea House, 1995). Briefer treatments appear in Clare Cushman, ed., *The Supreme Court Justices; Illustrated Biographies, 1789–1993,* 2d ed. (Washington, D.C.: Congressional Quarterly, 1996), and in Melvin I. Urofsky, ed., *The Supreme Court Justices: A Biographical Dictionary* (New York: Garland Publishing, 1994).

General information on many aspects of the work of the Supreme Court is contained in Kermit L. Hall, ed., *The Oxford Companion to the Supreme Court of the United States,* and *The Oxford Guide to United States Supreme Court Decisions* (New York: Oxford University Press, 1992 and 1999); Lee Epstein et al., *The Supreme Court Compendium,* 3d ed. (Washington, D.C.: Congressional Quarterly, 2003); and Congressional Quarterly's *Guide to the U.S. Supreme Court,* 2 vols., 4th ed. (2004). *The Constitution of the United States: Analysis and Interpretation,* originally authored by Edward S. Corwin and subsequently maintained by the Congressional Research Service, is accessible online at http://www.loc.gov/law/guide/usconst.html. Other resources include Sue Davis and J. W. Peltason, *Understanding the Constitution,* 16th ed. (Belmont, Calif.: Wadsworth, 2004), and Robert J. Janosik, ed., *Encyclopedia of the American Judicial System,* 3 vols. (New York: Macmillan, 1987).

## READING A SUPREME COURT DECISION

Every discipline has its own literature, and the literature of the study of the Constitution includes judicial opinions. It is essential, therefore, to acquire a talent for reading cases because they represent the medium through which a court speaks. Students of the Court will find it helpful to take careful notes in the form of an outline on the cases they read. Making the outline is called **briefing a case.** Thorough case briefing consists of a summary of at least four elements.

LITIGANTS AND THE FACTS. Always located at the beginning, the name or title identifies the parties to the case called the litigants. The name of the person or entity bringing the case to the Supreme Court appears first; the party being brought to the Court is listed second. The *v.* stands for "versus" or "against." In cases that reach the Supreme Court on certiorari (as almost all now do) the **petitioner** brings the case against the **respondent.** In cases on appeal, the **appellant** brings the case against the **appellee.** Cases are real, not hypothetical, controversies between parties. The issues of a case arise from circumstances or events that have prompted one or both parties to seek redress or resolution in court. The facts of a case may or may not be in dispute, but they are always a factor in how cases are decided.

QUESTION(S). The facts of a case present one or more issues or questions for decision. Most of a judicial opinion is an effort to answer those questions. Although even a relatively simple case may generate many questions, counsel in the Supreme Court seek review only of those of the gravest importance—to the parties involved and to the nation. Ordinarily, the Supreme Court decides questions of law, not fact. In reviewing a criminal conviction, for instance, the Court is rarely concerned with a defendant's actual guilt or innocence. Rather, the justices focus on procedural issues, such as the admissibility of evidence or the lawfulness of an arrest.

DECISION. The answers to the questions that arise from the facts of a case lead to a decision. This is the result or outcome of a case. For example, a government agency has, or has not, exceeded its authority under the law or the Constitution. Typically in the Supreme Court, decisions take the form of **affirming** (accepting) or **reversing** (rejecting and setting aside) the judgment of the court below. When reversing, the justices will often **remand** (send back) a case to the lower court for action "consistent with" the Court's decision.

REASONING OF THE OPINIONS. As explained in a previous section, the goal of the Court's decision-making process is a statement reflecting the consensus of a majority of the justices. This statement is the opinion of the Court—also called the majority opinion—that explains why a certain question requires a certain answer. An exercise in persuasion, the majority opinion attempts to justify the decision the Court has reached. Concurring and dissenting opinions should also be examined closely because they may shed light on what has been decided. Dissenting opinions attempt to highlight weaknesses in the majority's reasoning. Concurring opinions may indicate the limits to a line of reasoning beyond which certain members of the majority are unwilling to go. Both may highlight legal trends. Moreover, awareness of the votes of individual justices can alert the reader to shifts in a justice's position. Throughout this book, the headnote for each excerpted case displays the voting alignment.

## KEY TERMS

federal courts
state courts
jurisdiction
Article III courts
Article I courts
original jurisdiction
appellate jurisdiction
federal question
diversity jurisdiction
magistrate judges
certiorari
appeal
direct appeal
Ashwander rules

case or controversy
ripeness
advisory opinion
standing
nonjusticiable
political question
   doctrine
judicial activists
judicial restraintists
briefs
rule of four
solicitor general
amicus curiae
oral argument

conference
opinion of the Court
plurality opinion
dissent
concurring opinion
law clerks
briefing a case
petitioner
respondent
appellant
appellee
affirming
reversing
remand

## QUERIES

**1.** Review Table 1.1 on page 31. What do the data suggest about the importance of state and lower federal courts in helping to shape American constitutional law?

**2.** How can "threshold questions" such as standing be crucial in the outcome of a constitutional case?

**3.** Between 1800 and the 1940s, nonunanimous Supreme Court decisions were the exception, not the rule. Rarely did a published dissent appear in as many as 25 percent of the cases, and the dissent rate usually hovered near 10 percent. The pattern in the past 60 years has been sharply different. Nonunanimous decisions are the rule, not the exception. Published dissents routinely appear in at least half the decisions. What factors might account for this change? Is the Court helped or hurt by dissenting opinions?

**4.** Fred Graham, former Supreme Court reporter for *The New York Times* and CBS News and a founder of Court TV, has said, "The only groups who don't appear on television are the Supreme Court and the Mafia." Although the Court's argument sessions are open to the public, the justices resolutely refuse to allow oral arguments to be telecast at all. Moreover, few justices grant interviews to journalists, and when they do they rarely speak about specific cases. Should oral arguments be telecast in the same way that the House and Senate allow televised coverage of their floor proceedings? Would the Court appear less mysterious to the public if the justices sought publicity like other officials in Washington? Would increased exposure negatively affect the Court?

## SELECTED READINGS

BARROW, DEBORAH J., GARY ZUK, and GERARD S. GRYSKI. *The Federal Judiciary and Institutional Change.* Ann Arbor: University of Michigan Press, 1996.

EPSTEIN, LEE, JEFFREY A. SEGAL, and HAROLD J. SPAETH. "The Norm of Consensus on the U.S. Supreme Court." 45 *American Journal of Political Science* 362 (2001).

FRANKFURTER, FELIX, and J. M. LANDIS. *The Business of the Supreme Court.* New York: Macmillan, 1928.

PERRY, H. W., JR. *Deciding to Decide: Agenda Setting in the United States Supreme Court.* Cambridge, Mass.: Harvard University Press, 1991.

ROWLAND, C. K., and ROBERT A. CARP. *Politics and Judgment in Federal District Courts.* Lawrence: University Press of Kansas, 1996.

SALOKAR, REBECCA MAE. *The Solicitor General: The Politics of Law.* Philadelphia, Pa.: Temple University Press, 1992.

SONGER, DONALD R., REGINALD S. SHEEHAN, and SUSAN B. HAIRE. *Continuity and Change on the United States Courts of Appeals.* Ann Arbor: University of Michigan Press, 2000.

STERN, ROBERT L., ed. *Supreme Court Practice,* 8th ed. Washington, D.C.: BNA Books, 2002.

# CHAPTER TWO

# *The Constitution, the Supreme Court, and Judicial Review*

*Judicial review represents an attempt by American Democracy to cover its bet.*
—Professor Edward S. Corwin (1942)

The Constitution of 1787 and its 27 amendments can be read in about half an hour. One could memorize the written document word for word and still know little or nothing of its meaning. The reason is that the body of rules known as constitutional law consists primarily of decisions and opinions of the United States Supreme Court—the gloss that the justices have spread on the formal document. Charles Warren asked us not to forget that "however the Court may interpret the provisions of the Constitution, it is still the Constitution which is law and not decisions of the Court." But Charles Evans Hughes bluntly asserted that "The Constitution is what the Judges say it is." Furthermore, recurrent declarations of reverence for "our Ark of Covenant," as Chief Justice Taft called the Constitution, stand in sharp contrast to the reality that most Americans do not adequately understand the Constitution. Popular perceptions about the Constitution are frequently at odds with the document itself, making the American Constitution in its broadest sense greater than the sum of its parts. Myth wars with fact both within and without the Court.

## GRANTING AND LIMITING POWER

In the United States the Constitution alone is supreme. All agencies of government stand in the relationship of creator to creatures. There is, Woodrow Wilson observed, "no sovereign government in America." But Wilson was not blind to the fact that government means action. "Power belongs to government, is lodged in organs of initiative; control belongs to the community, is lodged with the voters"—and the courts.

**CONSTITUTIONALISM.** American **constitutionalism**—the belief in limiting government power by a written charter—deals with the problem James Madison posed in *The Federalist,* No. 51: "In framing a government which is to be administered by men over men, the great difficulty lies in this: you must first enable the government to control the governed; and in the next place oblige it to control itself." To achieve those twin objectives, the Constitution both grants and limits power; yet in ways both obvious and subtle, the Constitution appears to be more an instrument of rights and limitations than of powers. Certain things Congress is expressly forbidden to do. It may not pass an ex post facto law or a bill of attainder; it may not tax exports from any state; and it may not—except in great emergencies—suspend the writ of habeas corpus. The Bill of Rights (Amendments I through VIII) contains a longer list of things government is powerless to do. (Most restrictions imposed by the Bill of Rights on the national government have now been "incorporated" into the Fourteenth Amendment as limits on the states, as Chapter Nine explains.) State governments are likewise forbidden to do specific things. Article I, Section 10, declares that a state may not enact ex post facto laws, impair the obligation of contracts, coin money, emit bills of credit, or enter into any treaty or alliance with a foreign state. Chief Justice Marshall called parts of this section, the only one in the original Constitution limiting state power, "a bill of rights for the people of the states." Nonetheless, the Constitution provides no definition of either powers or limitations, nor does the Constitution state how its words are to be interpreted.

**SEPARATION AND SHARING OF POWERS.** Government is also circumscribed in less specific ways. The Constitution divides power, even as it confers it. Congress is endowed with "legislative" power; it may not, therefore (except as a result of a specific grant or by implication), exercise executive or judicial power. The same restrictions apply to the other branches of the national government: The terms *judicial power* and *executive power,* like *legislative power,* have a technical meaning. In the exercise of their respective functions, neither Congress, president, nor judiciary may, under the principle of **separation of powers,** encroach on fields allocated to the other branches of government. Instead of requiring that the departments be kept absolutely separate and distinct, however, the Constitution mingles their functions. Congress is granted legislative power, but the grant is not exclusive. Lawmaking is shared by the president through the veto. The appointing authority is vested in the president, but for many appointments the Senate must give its advice and consent.

**FEDERALISM.** The second power-limiting principle, **federalism,** means a constitutional system in which two authorities, each having a complete government system, exist in the same territory and act on the same people. In its American manifestation, federalism is a complicated arrangement whereby the national government exercises enumerated, implied, and inherent powers, with all others being "reserved to the States respectively, or to the people." Each government is supreme within its own sphere; neither is supreme within the sphere of the other. Federalism, like separation of powers and checks and balances, is a means of obliging government to control itself. None of these limiting principles is spelled out; they are either implicit in the organization and structure of the Constitution, or as with judicial review, deducible from "the theory of our government."

James Madison and other Founders generally called this intricate system **free government.** The power surrendered by the people is first divided "vertically" between two distinct governments (the national government and the states), and then the portion allotted to each is subdivided "horizontally" among distinct and separate departments. Hence, a double security is provided for the rights of the people. Distinct governments will exercise control over each other, and at the same time each will be checked by itself. "Vibrations of power" (the "genius" of free government, Alexander Hamilton called it) are inherent in this complexus of restraints. Just how such controls were to be enforced the Constitution does not specify.

## THE DOCTRINE OF JUDICIAL REVIEW

For correctives against abuse of power, Americans have not been content to rely on **political checks** such as public opinion and the ballot box. The essential safeguards in most free societies, they have not sufficed here. In America, government is kept within bounds, not only by the electoral process but also through separation of powers, federalism, and (as an adjunct to all these) **judicial review**—the authority of courts to set aside actions of another branch of government which, in the judges' view, conflict with the Constitution.

**THE FRAMERS.** The **supremacy clause** in Article VI of the Constitution declares that the Constitution (along with treaties and federal statutes) is "the supreme law of the land." This principle is essential to the operation of the federal system and makes explicit the doctrine that national law will prevail in situations where it conflicts with state law. The framers, however, left unanswered the question of who or what was to sustain this supremacy. Moreover, their Constitution did not expressly contain a method for resolving disputes concerning the constitutionality of specific acts of Congress. In the Philadelphia Convention debates of 1787, it was suggested that each house of Congress might, when in doubt, call on the judges for an opinion concerning the validity of national legislation. Madison declared that a "law violating a constitution established by the people themselves would be considered by the judges as null and void." It was repeatedly urged that Supreme Court justices be joined with the executive in a council of revision and be empowered to veto congressional legislation. Certain delegates objected to this proposal, contending that the justices would have this power anyway in cases properly before them. Any such provision, they argued, would give the Court a double check. It would compromise "the impartiality of the Court by making them go on record before they were called in due course, to give . . . their exposition of the laws, which involved a power of deciding on their constitutionality." Other members of the Convention, though not denying that the Court could exercise such power, asserted that it would violate the principle of separation of powers and have the effect, as Elbridge Gerry remarked, of "making statesmen of judges." In the end the power of judicial review was not expressly authorized.

Professor Edward Corwin suggested that for the Constitution's framers, judicial review rested "upon certain general principles [government under law, separation of powers, federalism, Bill of Rights] which, in their estimation, made specific provision for it unnecessary." Indeed, James Wilson, Oliver Ellsworth, and John Marshall, all destined for appointment to the Supreme Court, subscribed to the doctrine of judicial review in their respective state ratifying conventions. As Ellsworth of Connecticut declared on January 17, 1788,

> If the United States go beyond their powers, if they make a law which the constitution does not authorize, it is void; and the judicial power, the national judges, who, to secure their impartiality, are to be made independent, will declare it to be void. On the

other hand, if the States go beyond their limits, if they make a law which is an usurpation upon the general government, the law is void; and upright independent judges will declare it so.

Robert Yates, Philadelphia Convention delegate from New York but a non-signer of the Constitution, probed these realities and predicted that judicial review, which he took for granted, would enable the justices "to mould the government into almost any shape they please. . . . Men placed in this situation will generally soon feel themselves independent of heaven itself."

Yates leveled a serious charge. To answer it, Hamilton argued in *The Federalist,* No. 78, that judicial review does not suppose "a superiority of the judicial to the legislative power. It only supposes that the power of the people (whose will the Constitution embodies) is superior to both." Thanks to judicial review, the "intentions of the people" would prevail over "the intentions of their agents." Hamilton, apparently realizing that such reasoning bordered on deception, went the whole way toward legerdemain: "It may be truly said that the judiciary has neither force nor will, but merely judgment." For Hamilton, judges claim no supremacy in exercising this high authority; they claim only to administer the public will. If an act of the legislature is held void, it is not because judges have any control over legislative power but because the act is forbidden by the Constitution and because the will of the people, which is declared supreme, is paramount to that of their representatives. Hence the ideal of a "government of laws and not of men." Hence also the intriguing paradox of judicial review: While wearing the magical habiliments of the law and speaking the language of the Constitution, Supreme Court justices take sides on vital social and political issues. This unstaged debate between Yates and Hamilton is excerpted in this chapter.

**THE WRITTEN AND UNWRITTEN CONSTITUTION.** The American Constitution, unlike the British, cannot be changed by an ordinary act of legislation; this is its distinctive feature, not that it is written. No constitution, including our own, is either altogether written or altogether unwritten. The British constitution, though supposedly made up of custom and tradition, is partly written: Magna Charta, Petition of Right, Bill of Rights, Act of Settlement, and Parliament Act of 1911 are written. In the Constitution, there is no mention of the president's cabinet and no reference to senatorial courtesy, to political parties, or to the national presidential nominating conventions. The electoral college is expressly provided for in the written Constitution; usage has discarded it as an independent decision-making body. Thus, the Constitution is only the original trunk, and important new branches have been added, through formal amendment, custom and usage, and above all, judicial interpretation. The American Constitution "in operation," Woodrow Wilson wrote, "is manifestly a very different thing from the Constitution of the books."

**FROM WILLIAM MARBURY TO DRED SCOTT.** Several weeks before Thomas Jefferson's inauguration as the third president in 1801, Congress—lame-duck and Federalist-dominated—passed the District of Columbia Act, which authorized the appointment of 42 new justices of the peace. Outgoing President Adams made the nominations and the Senate confirmed them, but in the waning hours of the administration, Chief Justice John Marshall, also serving as secretary of state, failed to deliver all of the commissions of office to the would-be justices of the peace. Upon assuming office on March 4, Jefferson held back delivery to some of Adams's appointees. Later that year, William Marbury and three others whom Adams had named filed suit in the Supreme Court against Secretary of State James Madison.

They wanted the Court to issue a **writ of mandamus,** commanding Madison to hand over the undelivered commissions. (A writ of mandamus is an order by a court to a public official directing performance of a ministerial, or nondiscretionary, act.)

When the Court heard argument in February 1803, it was apparent that the justices were in a predicament. Because of tense partisan differences between Federalists and Democratic-Republicans, Jefferson and Madison would probably disregard the writ. There would then be no one to enforce the order. Yet for the Court to rule that Marbury was not entitled to the judgeship would be an open and painful acknowledgment of weakness.

Marshall's opinion in *Marbury* v. *Madison* avoided both dangers and claimed power for the Court. He announced first that Marbury and the others were entitled to their jobs and that the Court in a proper case could direct a coordinate branch of government to comply with the law. However, the Court was powerless to act in this instance. Why? Section 13 of the Judiciary Act of 1789 had given the Court authority to issue writs of mandamus as part of the Court's original, as opposed to appellate, jurisdiction (see Chapter One). Marshall noted that the Court's original jurisdiction is spelled out in Article III, and Article III includes no reference to writs of mandamus. By enlarging the Court's original jurisdiction, Section 13 conflicted with the Constitution. Was the Court to apply an unconstitutional statute? To do so would make the statute (and Congress) superior to the Constitution. Section 13 was, therefore, void. Thus judicial review was a necessary adjunct to both a written Constitution and a government deriving its power from the people. Nor does judicial power, he maintained, give the Supreme Court any practical or real omnipotence. The Court merely exercised judicial power conferred by the Constitution and sustained by the principle of separation of powers. "It is, emphatically, the province and duty of the Judicial department to say what the law is." The effect, in theory, was not to elevate Court over legislature, but rather to make "the power of the people superior to both."

John Marshall did not "invent" judicial review. Aside from Hamilton's defense of it in 1788, several earlier Supreme Court decisions assumed this power, as had some state supreme courts. Nonetheless, *Marbury* may have been Marshall's most important contribution as chief justice. He was the first to articulate a defense of judicial review in a U.S. Supreme Court decision. Moreover, as much anyone, he "legalized" the Constitution, treating the nation's fundamental charter as *law:* a text whose meaning would be discerned in the process of deciding cases. That meaning, in turn, would resolve disputes over allocations of power. This transformation, however, did not take place overnight. Marshall's assertion and defense of judicial review in *Marbury* stated more possibility than reality. Still, it was in *Marbury* that the view of the Constitution as a juridical document began to take root.

Marshall's theory was not unanswerable, as Justice Gibson's trenchant criticism in *Eakin* v. *Raub* made clear 22 years later. "[T]o affirm that the judiciary has a right to judge of the existence of such collision [between the Constitution and a statute]," declared the Pennsylvania jurist, "is to take for granted the very thing to be proved." Nonetheless, in 1803, and for quite some time thereafter, *Marbury* aroused comment and criticism, not because the "great Chief Justice" asserted the power of judicial review, but because he went out of his way to read a lecture to President Jefferson and Secretary of State Madison concerning their official duties under the Constitution. Earlier, Jefferson and other Democratic-Republicans had severely criticized the Sedition Act of 1798 and incorporation of the national bank in 1791 as unconstitutional. Indeed, the principle of judicial review of congressional statutes was so widely accepted by 1830 that Gibson's opposition to it partly explained why he was passed over in favor of fellow Pennsylvanian Henry Baldwin when President Andrew Jackson picked a successor to Justice Bushrod Washington. Where the principle remained controversial was with Supreme Court review of *state* legislation, a practice which, ironically, Gibson accepted.

The "autocratic" potential of the judicial veto, at least in Marshall's time, was less onerous than is sometimes imagined. It was not until 1857 and the ill-fated decision in **Scott v. Sandford** that the second act of Congress ran afoul of the Constitution. Rejecting Marshall's view of a constitution intended to endure, Chief Justice Taney affirmed that the Constitution "speaks not only with the same words, but with the same meaning and intent" as when it came from the hands of the framers. Taney did not confine his opinion to the question of black citizenship and Dred Scott's right to bring suit in federal court but proceeded to discuss the extent of congressional power over the territories. Congress had no power to prohibit slavery in the territories, and therefore the Missouri Compromise of 1820 was invalid. In so doing, the Court declared as illegitimate the organizing principle of the new Republican party.

*Dred Scott* marked a major expansion of judicial review. Unlike the statute in *Marbury,* the invalidated act did not pertain to the Judicial Department nor contravene a seemingly unambiguous provision of the Constitution. Indeed, the Court ruled as it did even though the Constitution contained express authority in Article IV for Congress to legislate concerning "the Territory . . . belonging to the United States." By vetoing a major legislative policy, the bench forestalled future congressional efforts to deal with the foremost political issue of the day. *Dred Scott,* not *Marbury,* foreshadowed future controversies concerning the scope of judicial review. For Marshall's doctrine of national supremacy, Taney substituted judicial supremacy.

**SUPREME COURT REVIEW OF STATE COURT DECISIONS.** More important than judicial review of acts of Congress is the control federal courts exercise over state laws and court decisions. During the formative period of our history, it was of first importance to establish an effective barrier against state action hostile to the Constitution and the Union it created. Jefferson voiced the hope "that some peaceable means should be contrived for the federal head to enforce compliance on the part of the States." The Philadelphia Convention delegates, keenly aware of the necessity of establishing external control over state action, suggested various limitations. One proposal gave Congress a negative on state laws; another provided for federal appointment of state governors and gave the general government a negative on state acts. All these were rejected. In its final form "this Constitution," and the laws "made in pursuance thereof, and all treaties made, or which shall be made, under the authority of the United States," are declared by the supremacy clause in Article VI to be "the supreme law of the land; and the judges in every state are bound thereby, anything in the Constitution or laws of any State to the contrary notwithstanding." The first Congress, apparently believing that the purpose of the clause was to make the judiciary the final resort for all cases arising in the states, enacted **Section 25** of the Judiciary Act of 1789, authorizing the Supreme Court to pass on the validity of state legislation and to review decisions of state tribunals in cases where constitutional questions had been answered in favor of the state, or adversely to national power. Though Section 25 recognized the important role that state courts might play in interpreting and applying the Constitution, federal law, and treaties, it had the effect of strengthening national power by making explicit a function of the Supreme Court left to inference in the Constitution itself.

**Table 2.1  Statutes Invalidated by the U.S. Supreme Court**

| Period | Chief Justice | U.S. Statutes | State Statutes and Local Ordinances |
|---|---|---|---|
| 1789–1800 | Jay, Rutledge, Ellsworth | 0 | 0 |
| 1801–1835 | Marshall | 1 | 19 |
| 1836–1864 | Taney | 1 | 21 |
| 1864–1873 | Chase | 8 | 34 |
| 1874–1888 | Waite | 8 | 66 |
| 1888–1910 | Fuller | 14 | 91 |
| 1910–1921 | White | 12 | 175 |
| 1921–1930 | Taft | 12 | 138 |
| 1930–1941 | Hughes | 14 | 92 |
| 1941–1946 | Stone | 2 | 27 |
| 1946–1953 | Vinson | 1 | 47 |
| 1953–1969 | Warren | 23 | 188 |
| 1969–1986 | Burger | 32 | 308 |
| 1986– | Rehnquist | 35 | 142 |

Data include decisions through January 2004.

The number of congressional acts invalidated has been comparatively small (see Table 2.1), less than 170 not counting the potentially broad swath cut by ***Immigration and Naturalization Service v. Chadha*** (see Chapter Three) on legislative vetoes found in several hundred congressional statutes. Quite otherwise has been the effect of judicial review of state action. Since 1810, when the Court overturned the first state act on constitutional grounds in *Fletcher* v. *Peck,* 1,350 state laws and local ordinances have been struck down.

The tension between the doctrine of judicial review of congressional legislation and the need for effective government did not become a serious public issue until the last quarter of the nineteenth century. Prior to 1900 the Court had invoked its authority against Congress so sparingly that Justice Oliver Wendell Holmes could predict that "the United States would not come to an end if we lost our power to declare an Act of Congress void." But Holmes added, "I do think the Union would be imperiled if we could not make that declaration as to the laws of the several states. . . . [H]ow often a local policy prevails with those who are not trained to national views."

## CHECKS ON JUDICIAL POWER

Even though judicial review was already firmly a part of American government in the late 1800s, Justice Brewer maintained that judges "make no laws, establish no policy, never enter into the domain of popular action. They do not govern." "All the court does, or can do," Justice Roberts declared in 1936, "is to announce its considered judgment. . . . The only power it has, if such it may be called, is the power of judgment. This court neither approves nor condemns any legislative policy." Through the years, Supreme Court justices have continued to profess judicial impotence, but hardly ever without arousing incredulity. In its dual role of symbol and instrument of authority—temple and forum—the Supreme Court has always been confronted with the difficult task of reconciling the claim of judicial aloofness with the reality of personal discretion and political power. "We are not final because we are infallible, but we are infallible only because we are final," Justice Jackson observed with refreshing candor in 1953.

**EXTERNAL CHECKS.** Supreme Court justices are appointed for life—or during "good behavior." They may be impeached, but impeachment has proved in practice to be not even a "scarecrow," as Jefferson said. Nevertheless, the Court is subject to various direct and indirect controls. The dramatic repudiation of its own decisions in 1937, on the heels of President Roosevelt's audacious Court-packing plan, contradicted Justice Stone's self-effacing dictum that "the only check upon our own exercise of power is our own sense of self-restraint." Although Roosevelt's proposal failed of enactment, it was not without effect. Justice Roberts told a congressional committee in 1954 that he had been "fully conscious of the tremendous strain and threat to the existing court" (see Chapter Six). Decisions on constitutional issues may be changed by constitutional amendment, as in the Income Tax Case of 1895. Decisions involving statutory interpretation can be altered by an act of Congress, as was done by the Civil Rights Restoration Act of 1988, which overturned *Grove City College* v. *Bell* (1984). In *Grove City,* the Court had interpreted the Education Amendments of 1972 to require a cutoff of federal funds to a discriminatory program, but not to the whole institution. Clarifying the law in 1988, Congress left no doubt that it intended the cutoff of aid to be institution-wide, even if only a part of an institution was found not to be in compliance with the law.

The Constitution expressly gives Congress control over the Court's appellate jurisdiction. That is, Congress determines what categories of cases qualify for appeal to the High Court from state courts and lower federal courts. To prevent the Court from passing on the constitutionality of the Reconstruction Acts, Congress denied the Court's jurisdiction in a case then pending (**Ex parte *McCardle,*** 1869). Moreover, a president—if the opportunity presents itself—may change the voting balance within the Court through discerning appointments. Ours is "a government of laws and not of men" only in a qualified sense.

**THE POLITICAL QUESTION DOCTRINE.** One important historical check on judicial power has not been external, but one that the Court has placed upon itself. "If judges can open it [the Constitution] at all," Chief Justice Marshall asked in *Marbury* v. *Madison,* "what part of it are they forbidden to read or obey?" A self-disabling answer, at odds with Marshall's inference, was given in *Luther* v. *Borden* (1849), where Chief Justice Taney attempted for the first time to explain why a case raising a federal question might nonetheless be off limits to the federal courts. The litigation stemmed from the Dorr Rebellion of 1841–1842 in Rhode Island, which pitted rival factions against each other, each claiming to be the lawful government of the state. Luther was a participant in the rebellion against the state's old charter government; Borden was a member of the militia who had forcibly entered Luther's house under martial law. Article IV of the Constitution guarantees "to every State in this Union a Republican Form of government." Luther relied on the **guarantee** (or guaranty) **clause** to claim that the old charter government was not "Republican" and therefore illegitimate, making Borden's entry a trespass. In the Court's view, however, whether a state maintained a "Republican Form of government" lay "beyond [the judiciary's] appropriate sphere of action." The matter was "political" in that it must be determined not by the judiciary but either by Congress through its seating of representatives from the state or by presidential acts in response to requests for assistance in suppressing domestic violence. The Court was "not to involve itself in discussions which properly belong to other forums." This posture is called the **political question doctrine.** Seemingly a misnomer because it suggests that other decisions are not political, the term is used in a specific sense to designate a type of controversy which is nonjusticiable. A political question is an issue the resolution of which belongs to one of the "political" branches of government (executive and legislative) and is, for that reason, inappropriate for judicial decision.

Accordingly, most decisions made by Congress and the executive concerning the international relations of the United States are considered "political" and binding on the Court. Another political question is determination of whether a state has properly ratified a proposed constitutional amendment (*Coleman* v. *Miller,* 1939). The Court has also refused to decide whether use by a state of initiative and referendum is in conflict with the guarantee clause (*Pacific States Tel. & Tel. Co.* v. *Oregon,* 1912). And for years the Court declined to intervene in lawsuits challenging population imbalances in legislative districts (*Colegrove* v. *Green,* 1946). "It is hostile to a democratic system to involve the judiciary in the politics of the people," warned Justice Frankfurter. "And it is not less pernicious if such judicial intervention in an essentially political contest be dressed up in the abstract phrases of the law."

Ironically, the Court has come closest to articulating a formula identifying a political question in the act of deciding that legislative apportionment and districting are not out of judicial bounds. **Baker v. Carr** (in Chapter Five) held in 1962 that numerically unequal legislative districts may constitute a violation of the Fourteenth Amendment's equal protection clause and that federal courts could provide a remedy. The political question doctrine was no obstacle. "Prominent on the surface of any case held to involve a political question," explained Justice Brennan,

> is found a textually demonstrable constitutional commitment of the issue to a coordinate political department; or a lack of judicially discoverable and manageable standards for resolving it; or the impossibility of deciding without an initial policy determination of a kind clearly for nonjudicial discretion; or the impossibility of a court's undertaking independent resolution without expressing lack of the respect due coordinate branches of government; or an unusual need for unquestioning adherence to a political decision already made; or the potentiality of embarrassment from multifarious pronouncements by various departments on one question.

Even this taxonomy yields no touchstone for deciding precisely what is, and what is not, a political question. Justices disagree among themselves as to when this discretionary tool should be invoked. Some have favored use of this self-imposed limitation as a way of steering clear of "inconvenient" cases or those fraught with partisan controversy. Others have viewed it as a cowardly evasion of the Court's duty to provide peaceful solutions to any and all issues arising in a constitutional system.

## FINALITY OF SUPREME COURT DECISIONS

Closely related to external and internal checks on judicial power is the question of the finality of Supreme Court decisions. Is constitutional interpretation a uniquely judicial responsibility? To what degree are constitutional decisions by the Supreme Court binding on the rest of the political system?

Even though Jefferson often impugned his nemesis John Marshall for abusing judicial power—"a crafty chief judge, who sophisticates the law to his mind, by the turn of his own reasoning," the third president once said—Jefferson himself never denied the authority of the Supreme Court to pass on the validity of acts of Congress in the course of deciding cases. But he did deny that such a decision was binding on the president in the performance of his purely executive function. As Jefferson explained in 1804:

> The judges, believing the [Sedition] law constitutional, had a right to pass a sentence of fine and imprisonment, because that power was placed in their hands by the Constitution. But the Executive, believing the law to be unconstitutional, was bound to remit the execution of it, because that power has been confided to him by the Constitution. That instrument meant that its coordinate branches should be checks on each other. But the opinion which gives to the judges the right to decide what laws are constitutional, and what not, not only for themselves in their own sphere of action, but for the legislative and Executive also in their spheres, would make the Judiciary a despotic branch.

Jefferson accepted the finality of judicial decisions in cases where their effects were primarily on the judiciary, as in *Marbury;* he rejected their binding effect on coordinate branches of the government. Other presidents (notably Jackson, Lincoln, both Roosevelts, Nixon, Reagan, and Clinton) and Congress too have also on occasion refused to accept Supreme Court decisions as foreclosing further debate on the meaning of the Constitution. Their view is that all constitutional officers, not the justices alone, play a part in constitutional interpretation.

Is their position supported by the Constitution itself? Section 5 of the Fourteenth Amendment empowers Congress to "enforce, by appropriate legislation, the provisions of this article." Those "provisions" offer broad protections against infringement of individual rights by state governments that the Court has never defined in any fixed way. Relying on Section 5, one part of the Voting Rights Act of 1965 directed that no person be denied the right to vote because of an inability to read and write English if that person had completed the sixth grade in a Spanish-language school in Puerto Rico. The law effectively nullified New York's English-language literacy test, even though the Supreme Court had upheld the constitutionality of literacy tests against a challenge on Fourteenth Amendment grounds only six years earlier (*Lassiter* v. *Board of Elections*). In upholding the 1965 legislation, Justice Brennan declared in *Katzenbach* v. *Morgan* (1966) that Section 5 was "a positive grant of legislative power authorizing Congress to exercise its discretion in determining whether and what legislation is needed to secure the guarantees of the Fourteenth Amendment." Either Congress might have reasoned that enfranchised Puerto Ricans would now be able to fight discrimination or, Brennan continued, Congress might have concluded that the English-language literacy test itself violated the amendment, despite the Court's stated position to the contrary. The first basis was remedial; the second basis was declaratory, elevating Congress to the role of constitutional expositor within the Fourteenth Amendment domain.

Some commentators claimed that *Morgan* stood *Marbury* on its head. Justice Harlan declared later that "Congress' expression of [its] view . . . cannot displace the duty of this Court to make an independent determination whether Congress has exceeded its powers." To give Congress a free hand in construing the Fourteenth would contradict the "structure of the constitutional system itself" by allowing Congress effectively to amend the Constitution by a simple majority vote and the president's signature.

Controversy over Section 5 persists. Since 1940 the Supreme Court has agreed that the Fourteenth Amendment's due process clause "incorporates" within its meaning the First Amendment's guarantee of free exercise of religion. As will be explained further in Chapter Twelve, the Supreme Court in 1963 expanded the protections of the free exercise clause, requiring state and federal governments in many circumstances to grant religiously based exemptions in the application of otherwise valid laws that inhibited religious practice (**Sherbert v. Verner**). In 1990, however, the Court did a near about-face on its interpretation of the clause, announcing that when a law of general application conflicted with religious practice, the former would prevail (**Employment Division v. Smith**). In 1993 Congress responded with enactment of the **Religious Freedom Restoration Act** (RFRA), directing with its Section 5 powers that the free exercise clause meant what the Court deemed it to mean in 1963 (and arguably even more), not what the Court deemed it to mean in 1990.

A test of RFRA soon materialized, and in **City of Boerne v. Flores** the Court invalidated the statute 6 to 3. Laudable though its objectives were, Congress had exceeded its constitutional authority. Conspicuously, the dissenting opinions took issue less with the Court's conclusion about Congress and Section 5 and more with the 1990 decision shrinking the free exercise clause. As a result, congressional power under *Morgan* survives only insofar as it is remedial, not declaratory. Excerpts from *City of Boerne* precede an "unstaged debate" on the finality of Supreme Court decisions at the end of this chapter.

## APPROACHES TO CONSTITUTIONAL INTERPRETATION

A long-standing consensus that the Supreme Court is the chief, if not the only, expositor of the Constitution dissolves over the question of how judges are supposed to interpret the Constitution. The answer to this question partly determines the values the Constitution protects.

**WHAT IS "THE CONSTITUTION"?** There is first the matter of what is interpreted. To say that the answer is obvious, that the Court interprets the Constitution, merely presumes a consensus on what "the Constitution" includes. One might suppose that it includes at least the text of the document of 1787, as amended. But even such a conventional statement needs qualification. The Constitution may be less than the text. There are, after all, parts of the text (the privileges and immunities clause of the Fourteenth Amendment or the guarantee clause, for instance) that the Court has largely neglected or forsworn. Moreover, tension exists between some provisions of the text. Chapter Twelve, for example, grapples with how one satisfies fully both the safeguards of free exercise (freedom *for* religion) and nonestablishment (freedom *from* religion).

The Constitution may also encompass *more* than the document because judges may seek its meaning apart from the text itself. One justice may turn to the intent of those who drafted and ratified its provisions. Another might look to documents of the period that describe the kind of system the framers established. In speaking of "liberty" and the "consent of the governed," the Declaration of Independence certainly anticipated constitutional government to cure the evils of unchecked power.

Should custom count as part of the Constitution? "Long settled and established practice is a consideration of great weight in a proper interpretation of constitutional provisions," the Court noted in 1919. Similarly, in **Youngstown Sheet and**

*Tube Co.* **v.** *Sawyer* in 1952 (see Chapter Three), Justice Felix Frankfurter argued that "a systematic, unbroken, executive practice, long pursued in the knowledge of Congress and never before questioned, engaged in by Presidents who have also sworn to uphold the Constitution, making as it were such exercise of power part of the structure of our government, may be treated as a gloss on the 'executive power' vested in the President. . . ."

Sometimes interpretations of the Constitution become almost inseparable from the text. One thinks of judicial review itself, nowhere in the document expressly authorized for the Supreme Court, but widely regarded today as an essential component of the "judicial power."

Deciding what the Constitution includes is therefore an important starting point for interpretation. Then one must consider the method to be used. Four of the most common approaches judges employ in constitutional interpretation include clear meaning, adaptation, original intent, and structuralism. These methods, however, are not mutually exclusive categories. More than one may appear in a single opinion.

**CLEAR MEANING.** For some, constitutional interpretation is a mechanical process, much like the sales clerk measuring fabric. "When an act of Congress is appropriately challenged in the courts as not conforming to constitutional mandate," explained Justice Roberts in *United States* **v.** *Butler* (1936), "the judicial branch of the Government has only one duty—to lay the article of the Constitution which is invoked beside the statute which is challenged and to decide whether the latter squares with the former." (As will be seen in Chapter Seven, Justice Roberts seemed oblivious to the fact that three of his colleagues had performed this "squaring" and had reached the opposite conclusion.) Approached in this way, the Constitution speaks for itself; the words emit clear meaning. The judge's task is to point out what is plainly there. John Jay seemed to suggest as much at the New York ratifying convention. The meaning of the Constitution would involve "no sophistry, no construction, no false glosses, but simple inferences from the obvious operation of things." Of course, some parts of the Constitution do have a clear meaning. The president's term is four years, a senator's six. Yet these are rarely, if ever, involved in litigation. More common and more troublesome are the "commerce" that Article I empowers Congress to regulate (see Chapter Six) and the "speech" that the First Amendment protects (see Chapter Eleven).

**ADAPTATION.** Even judges who sometimes rest on the Constitution's clear meaning will also employ adaptation. The judge reasons from the Constitution by first identifying principles or values the Constitution contains, and then applying them to contemporary circumstances. As much as any other, this method enables the Court to accommodate the Constitution to situations and problems the framers did not foresee, yet it opens the Court to charges that it has engaged in "lawmaking." A variation on adaptation resembles *majoritarianism,* meaning that judges construe the Constitution's limits to permit most policies the dominant opinion of the day deems necessary or desirable.

**ORIGINAL INTENT.** Originalists look for what the framers of a constitutional provision meant. That meaning is the supreme will of the people, which is the only authority by which a judge may invalidate an action taken by the people's representatives. Anything else amounts to lawmaking by judges and is illegitimate. The method combines historicity with contemporary application: identifying how those who wrote (and perhaps those who ratified) the Constitution would resolve a contemporary question. For some advocates of original intent, such as former Judge Robert Bork, the absence of an ascertainable intent is not an invitation for judges to create one but a reason for them to defer to the elected branches so that the people's will might prevail.

As with other approaches, original intent is not without its difficulties. Aside from discerning intent, it is problematic to argue that intention should always be controlling when the framers themselves had mixed feelings on publication of the record of their work. The official *Journal* of the Convention, which was entrusted to George Washington at the close of business in 1787 but which contains only the barest account of what transpired, was not published until 1819—three decades after government under the Constitution began. Madison's notes, the single most complete record of the Convention, were not published until 1840, four years after his death. "As a guide in expounding and applying the provisions of the Constitution," Madison wrote Thomas Ritchie in 1821, "the debates and incidental decisions of the Convention can have no authoritative character.... [T]he legitimate meaning of the Instrument must be derived from the text itself; or if a key is to be sought elsewhere, it must be not in the opinions or intentions of the Body which planned & proposed the Constitution, but in the sense attached to it by the people in their respective State Conventions where it rec[eive]d all the authority which it possesses." The strengths and weaknesses of original intent are explored in the "unstaged debate" between Judge Bork and Professor Laurence Tribe later in this chapter.

**STRUCTURALISM.** Some cases are decided on principles drawn not so much from the words of single passages but from the design or framework the Constitution establishes or from the relation of one clause to another. Chief Justice Marshall's opinion in *Marbury* v. *Madison* is an example of structuralism at work. Examining the system of limited government created by the Constitution, Marshall found the basis of judicial review. Structuralism lies at the heart of separation-of-powers decisions like ***Morrison* v. *Olson*** (1988), in Chapter Three.

With any interpretative approach, judges have considerable leeway. Agreement on the method to be used by no means assures agreement on the outcome in individual cases. Because it is the Constitution that is being applied, judges do something more than merely interpret its written provisions. The justices not only formulate the principles that govern the federal system and the relations of Congress, Court, and president; they sit in judgment on the policy that controls the social and economic life of the nation. There are limits to judicial review, to be sure, but many seem largely self-imposed. "Government by judiciary" is no idle phrase when applied to the politics of the United States.

# JUDICIAL REVIEW—A DISTINCTIVELY AMERICAN CONTRIBUTION

The pervasiveness of judicial power is now one of the most conspicuous aspects of the American political system. It is hard to think of a feature of life left untouched by the Court's decrees. Its docket reads like a policy agenda for the nation. "The restraining power of the judiciary does not manifest its chief worth," Judge Cardozo observed, "in the few cases in which the legislature has gone beyond the lines that mark the limits of discretion." Its primary value has been in "making vocal and audible the ideals that might otherwise be silenced. . . ." Had this not been so, a document framed in the context of agrarianism, and largely unamended except by constitutional interpretation, could not serve the expanding needs of government in a complex technological society.

In the Virginia ratifying convention, John Marshall envisioned judicial review as an alternative to revolution. "What is the service or purpose of a judiciary but to execute the laws in a peaceful, orderly manner, without shedding blood, or creating a contest, or availing yourselves of force?" Madison reinforced Marshall: "A political system that does not provide for a peaceable and effectual decision of all controversies arising among the parties is not a Government, but a mere Treaty between independent nations, without any resort for terminating disputes but negotiations, and that failing, the sword." Failure to lodge this power in the federal judiciary, he added in 1832, "would be as much a mockery as a scabbard put into the hands of a soldier without a sword in it."

Applying standards drawn from the Constitution, the Court is the ultimate guardian of individual rights and governmental prerogative alike. "The people have seemed to feel that the Supreme Court, whatever its defects," Justice Jackson concluded, "is still the most detached, dispassionate, and trustworthy custodian that our system affords for the translation of abstract into concrete constitutional commands." It is, Woodrow Wilson observed, "the balance-wheel of our entire system." Thanks largely to the Supreme Court, the Constitution has been more than "a mere lawyer's document." It has been "a vehicle of the nation's life." The justices have become keepers of American constitutional values. That reality is both a source of, and limit on, their power.

## KEY TERMS

constitutionalism
separation of powers
federalism
free government
political checks

judicial review
supremacy clause
writ of mandamus
Section 25
guarantee clause

political question
   doctrine
Religious Freedom
   Restoration Act

## QUERIES

**1.** Was *Marbury* v. *Madison* a usurpation of power by the Supreme Court? Would the absence of judicial review "subvert the very foundations of all written constitutions"?

**2.** Several theories have dominated judicial discourse on constitutional interpretation. One holds that the "intention of the framers" is the sole guide. Another favors an adaptive approach. What problems will a judge probably encounter with each approach? With any of the approaches, do a judge's political values cease to be a factor in deciding a case?

**3.** Constitutional scholars widely regard *Dred Scott* not only as a consequential decision but also as the worst decision ever rendered by the Supreme Court. Why?

**4.** On what point are Robert Yates ("Letters of Brutus") and Alexander Hamilton (*The Federalist,* No. 78) in agreement? Where do they disagree? Does Yates overstate the dangers to popular government posed by judicial power? Does Hamilton understate them? Does the Constitution provide adequate safeguards against abuse of judicial power?

## SELECTED READINGS

CLINTON, ROBERT LOWRY. *Marbury v. Madison and Judicial Review.* Lawrence: University Press of Kansas, 1989.

CORWIN, EDWARD S. *The Doctrine of Judicial Review.* Gloucester, Mass.: Peter Smith, 1963; reissue of 1914 edition, published by Princeton University Press.

FEHRENBACHER, DON E. *The Dred Scott Case.* New York: Oxford University Press, 1978.

HOBSON, CHARLES F. "The Negative on State Laws: James Madison, the Constitution, and the Crisis of Republican Government." 36 *William and Mary Quarterly* (3d series) 215 (1979).

MALTZ, EARL M. *Rethinking Constitutional Law: Originalism, Interventionism, and the Politics of Judicial Review.* Lawrence: University Press of Kansas, 1994.

MASON, ALPHEUS T. *The Supreme Court: Palladium of Freedom.* Ann Arbor: University of Michigan Press, 1962.

NELSON, WILLIAM E. *Marbury v. Madison: The Origins and Legacy of Judicial Review.* Lawrence: University Press of Kansas, 2000.

SEDDIG, ROBERT G. "John Marshall and the Origins of Supreme Court Leadership." 36 *University of Pittsburgh Law Review* 785 (1975); reprinted in *Journal of Supreme Court History* 63 (1991).

SNOWISS, SYLVIA. *Judicial Review and the Law of the Constitution.* New Haven, Conn.: Yale University Press, 1990.

WOLFE, CHRISTOPHER. *The Rise of Modern Judicial Review.* New York: Basic Books, 1986.

# I. ESTABLISHING AND TESTING JUDICIAL REVIEW

## Unstaged Debate of 1788: *Robert Yates* v. *Alexander Hamilton*

### ROBERT YATES, *LETTERS OF BRUTUS*[1]

#### NO. XI
#### 31 JANUARY 1788

. . . Much has been said and written upon the subject of this new system on both sides, but I have not met with any writer, who has discussed the judicial powers with any degree of accuracy. . . . The real effect of this system of government will therefore be brought home to the feelings of the people through the medium of the judicial power. It is, moreover, of great importance, to examine with care the nature and extent of the judicial power, because those who are to be vested with it, are to be placed in a situation altogether unprecedented in a free country. They are to be rendered totally independent, both of the people and the legislature, both with respect to their offices and salaries. No errors they may commit can be corrected by any power above them, if any such power there be, nor can they be removed from office for making ever so many erroneous adjudications.

The only causes for which they can be displaced, is, conviction of treason, bribery, and high crimes and misdemeanors.

This part of the plan is so modelled, as to authorize the courts, not only to carry into execution the powers expressly given, but where these are wanting or ambiguously expressed, to supply what is wanting by their own decisions. . . .

They [the courts] will give the sense of every article of the constitution, that may from time to time come before them. And in their decisions they will not confine themselves to any fixed or established rules, but will determine, according to what appears to them, the reason and spirit of the constitution. The opinions of the supreme court, whatever they may be, will have the force of law, because there is no power provided in the constitution, that can correct their errors, or control their adjudications. From this court there is no appeal. And I conceive the legislature themselves, cannot set aside a judgment of this court, because they are authorized by the constitution to decide in the last resort. The legislature must be controlled by the constitution, and not the constitution by them. They have therefore no more right to set aside any judgment pronounced upon the construction of the constitution, than they have to take from the president, the chief command of the army and navy, and commit it to some other person. The reason is plain; the judicial and executive derive their authority from the same source, that the legislature do theirs; and therefore in all cases, where the constitution does not make the one responsible to, or controllable by the other, they are altogether independent of each other.

The judicial power will operate to effect, in the most certain, but yet silent and imperceptible manner, what is evidently the tendency of the constitution:—I mean, an entire subversion of the legislative, executive and judicial powers of the individual states. Every adjudication of the supreme court, on any question that may arise upon the nature and extent of the general government, will affect the limits of the state jurisdiction. In proportion as the former enlarge the exercise of their powers, will that of the latter be restricted.

That the judicial power of the United States, will lean strongly in favor of the general government, it will give such an explanation to the constitution, as will favour an extension of

---

[1] Published in the *New York Journal and Weekly Register,* Numbers 11 and 15. Reprinted in E. S. Corwin, *Court Over Constitution* (Princeton, N.J.: Princeton University Press, 1938), pp. 231–62. The full text of Numbers 11, 12, and 15 may also be found at www.prenhall.com/mason. It was common practice in the eighteenth and early nineteenth centuries for writers to adopt a signature ("Brutus" for Yates, or "Publius" for the authors of *The Federalist*) as a means to ensure temporary anonymity.

its jurisdiction, is very evident from a variety of considerations.

1st. The constitution itself strongly countenances such a mode of construction. Most of the articles in this system, which convey powers of any considerable importance, are conceived in general and indefinite terms, which are either equivocal, ambiguous, or which require long definitions to unfold the extent of their meaning. . . . The clause which vests the power to pass all laws which are proper and necessary, to carry the powers given into execution . . . leaves the legislature at liberty, to do every thing, which in their judgment is best. . .

2d. Not only will the constitution justify the courts in inclining to this mode of explaining it, but they will be interested in using this latitude of interpretation. Every body of men invested with office are tenacious of power; they feel interested, and hence it has become a kind of maxim, to hand down their offices, with all its rights and privileges, unimpaired to their successors; the same principle will influence them to extend their power, and increase their rights; this of itself will operate strongly upon the courts to give such a meaning to the constitution in all cases where it can possibly be done, as will enlarge the sphere of their own authority. . . .

3d. Because they will have precedent to plead, to justify them in it. It is well known, that the courts in England, have by their own authority, extended their jurisdiction far beyond the limits set them in their original institution, and by the laws of the land. . . .

This power in the judicial, will enable them to mold the government, into almost any shape they please. . . .

## NO. XV
## 20 MARCH 1788

I do not object to the judges holding their commissions during good behavior. I suppose it a proper provision provided they were made properly responsible. But I say, this system has followed the English government in this, while it has departed from almost every other principle of their jurisprudence, under the idea, of rendering the judges independent; which, in the British constitution, means no more than that they hold their places during good behavior, and have fixed salaries, they have made the judges independent, in the fullest sense of the word. There is no power above them, to control any of their decisions. There is no authority that can remove them, and they cannot be controlled by the laws of the legislature. In short, they are independent of the people, of the legislature, and of every power under heaven. Men placed in this situation will generally soon feel themselves independent of heaven itself. . . .

The supreme court then have a right, independent of the legislature, to give a construction of the constitution and every part of it, and there is no power provided in this system to correct their construction or do it away. If, therefore, the legislature pass any laws, inconsistent with the sense the judges put upon the constitution, they will declare it void; and therefore in this respect their power is superior to that of the legislature. . . .

Had the construction of the constitution been left with the legislature, they would have explained it at their peril; if they exceeded their powers, or sought to find, in the spirit of the constitution, more than was expressed in the letter, the people from whom they derived their power could remove them, and do themselves right; and indeed I can see no other remedy that the people can have against their rulers for encroachments of this nature. A constitution is a compact of a people with their rulers; if the rulers break the compact, the people have a right and ought to remove them and do themselves justice; but in order to enable them to do this with the greater facility, those whom the people choose at stated periods, should have the power in the last resort to determine the sense of the compact; if they determine contrary to the understanding of the people, an appeal will lie to the people at the period when the rulers are to be elected, and they will have it in their power to remedy the evil; but when this power is lodged in the hands of men independent of the people, and of their representatives, and who are not, constitutionally, accountable for their opinions, no way is left to control them but with a high hand and an outstretched arm.

## ALEXANDER HAMILTON'S REPLY TO BRUTUS: *THE FEDERALIST,* NO. 78[2]

We proceed now to an examination of the judiciary department of the proposed government. . . .

Whoever attentively considers the different departments of power must perceive, that, in a government in which they are separated from each other, the judiciary, from the nature of its functions, will always be the least dangerous to the political rights of the Constitution; because it will be least in a capacity to annoy or injure them. . . . The judiciary . . . has no influence over either the sword or the purse; no direction either of the strength or of the wealth of the society; and can take no active resolution whatever. It may truly be said to have neither FORCE nor WILL, but merely judgment; and must ultimately depend upon the aid of the executive arm even for the efficacy of its judgments.

This simple view of the matter suggests several important consequences. It proves incontestably, that the judiciary is beyond comparison the weakest of the three departments of power; that it can never attack with success either of the other two; and that all possible care is requisite to enable it to defend itself against their attacks. It equally proves, that though individual oppression may now and then proceed from the courts of justice, the general liberty of the people can never be endangered from that quarter; I mean so long as the judiciary remains truly distinct from both the legislature and the Executive. . . .

Some perplexity respecting the right of courts to pronounce legislative acts void, because contrary to the Constitution, has arisen from an imagination that the doctrine would imply a superiority of the judiciary to the legislative power. It is urged that the authority which can declare the acts of another void,

must necessarily be superior to the one whose acts may be declared void. As this doctrine is of great importance in all the American constitutions, a brief discussion of the ground on which it rests cannot be unacceptable.

There is no position which depends on clearer principles, than that every act of a delegated authority, contrary to the tenor of the commission under which it is exercised, is void. No legislative act, therefore, contrary to the Constitution, can be valid. To deny this, would be to affirm, that the deputy is greater than his principal; that the servant is above his master; that the representatives of the people are superior to the people themselves; that men acting by virtue of powers, may do not only what their powers do not authorize, but what they forbid.

If it be said that the legislative body are themselves the constitutional judges of their own powers, and that the construction they put upon them is conclusive upon the other departments, it may be answered, that this cannot be the natural presumption, where it is not to be collected from any particular provisions in the Constitution. It is not otherwise to be supposed, that the Constitution could intend to enable the representatives of the people to substitute their will to that of their constituents. It is far more rational to suppose, that the courts were designed to be an intermediate body between the people and the legislature, in order, among other things, to keep the latter within the limits assigned to their authority. The interpretation of the laws is the proper and peculiar province of the courts. A constitution is, in fact, and must be regarded by the judges, as a fundamental law. It therefore belongs to them to ascertain its meaning, as well as the meaning of any particular act proceeding from the legislative body. If there should happen to be an irreconcilable variance between the two, that which has the superior obligation and validity ought, of course, to be preferred; or, in other words, the Constitution ought to be preferred to the statute, the intention of the people to the intention of their agents.

Nor does this conclusion by any means suppose a superiority of the judicial to the

[2] Henry Cabot Lodge, ed., *The Federalist* (New York: Putnam, 1904).

legislative power. It only supposes that the power of the people is superior to both; and that where the will of the legislature, declared in its statutes, stands in opposition to that of the people, declared in the Constitution, the judges ought to be governed by the latter rather than the former. They ought to regulate their decisions by the fundamental laws, rather than by those which are not fundamental. . . .

If, then, the courts of justice are to be considered as the bulwarks of a limited Constitution against legislative encroachments, this consideration will afford a strong argument for the permanent tenure of judicial offices, since nothing will contribute so much as this to that independent spirit in the judges which must be essential to the faithful performance of so arduous a duty.

This independence of the judges is equally requisite to guard the Constitution and the rights of individuals from the effects of those ill humors, which the arts of designing men, or the influence of particular conjectures, sometimes disseminate among the people themselves, and which, though they speedily give place to better information, and more deliberate reflection, have a tendency, in the meantime, to occasion dangerous innovations in the government, and serious oppressions of the minor party in the community. . . .

But it is not with a view to infractions of the Constitution only, that the independence of the judges may be an essential safeguard against the effects of occasional ill humors in the society. These sometimes extend no farther than to the injury of the private rights of particular classes of citizens, by unjust and partial laws. Here also the firmness of the judicial magistracy is of vast importance in mitigating the severity and confining the operation of such laws. . . .

There is yet a further and a weightier reason for the permanency of the judicial offices, which is deducible from the nature of the qualifications they require. It has been frequently remarked, with great propriety, that a voluminous code of laws is one of the inconveniences necessarily connected with the advantages of a free government. To avoid an arbitrary discretion in the courts, it is indispensable that they should be bound down by strict rules and precedents, which serve to define and point out their duty in every particular case that comes before them; and it will readily be conceived from the variety of controversies which grow out of the folly and wickedness of mankind, that the records of those precedents must unavoidably swell to a very considerable bulk, and must demand long and laborious study to acquire a competent knowledge of them. Hence it is, that there can be but few men in the society who will have sufficient skill in the laws to qualify them for the stations of judges. And making the proper deductions for the ordinary depravity of human nature, the number must be still smaller of those who unite the requisite integrity with the requisite knowledge. These considerations apprise us, that the government can have no great option between fit character; and that a temporary duration in office, which would naturally discourage such characters from quitting a lucrative line of practice to accept a seat on the bench, would have a tendency to throw the administration of justice into hands less able, and less well qualified, to conduct it with utility and dignity. . . .

## *Marbury* v. *Madison*
## 5 U.S. (1 Cranch) 137, 2 L.Ed. 60 (1803)
### http://supct.law.cornell.edu/supct/cases/name.htm#Case_Name-M

Several weeks before the end of his term, President John Adams nominated William Marbury and others to be justices of the peace in the District of Columbia. Their nominations were confirmed and commissions signed by the president, but the secretary of state, John Marshall, had not delivered them by the time Thomas Jefferson became president on March 4, 1801. Jefferson's new secretary of state, James Madison, refused to deliver the commissions of Marbury and three others, claiming that delivery was necessary to complete the appointments. The four men asked the Supreme Court to issue a writ of mandamus ordering delivery under its original jurisdiction as authorized by Section 13 of the Judiciary Act of 1789. Mandamus was not sought from lower federal courts. Majority: Marshall, Chase, Paterson, Washington. Not participating: Cushing, Moore.

**The opinion of the court was delivered by the CHIEF JUSTICE [MARSHALL]. . . .**

The first object of inquiry is—Has the applicant a right to the commission he demands?. . .

It is . . . decidedly the opinion of the court, that when a commission has been signed by the president, the appointment is made; and that the commission is complete, when the seal of the United States has been affixed to it by the secretary of state. . . .

Mr. Marbury, then, since his commission was signed by the president, and sealed by the secretary of state, was appointed; and as the law creating the office, gave the officer a right to hold for five years, independent of the executive, the appointment was not revocable, but vested in the officer legal rights, which are protected by the laws of his country. To withhold his commission, therefore, is an act deemed by the court not warranted by law, but violative of a vested legal right.

This brings us to the second inquiry; which is: If he has a right, and that right has been violated, do the laws of this country afford him a remedy?. . .

The very essence of civil liberty certainly consists in the right of every individual to claim the protection of the laws, whenever he receives an injury. One of the first duties of government is to afford that protection. . . .

The government of the United States has been emphatically termed a government of laws, and not of men. It will certainly cease to deserve this high appellation, if the laws furnish no remedy for the violation of a vested legal right . . . .

By the constitution . . . , the president is invested with certain important political powers, in the exercise of which he is to use his own discretion, and is accountable only to his country in his political character, and to his own conscience. To aid him in the performance of these duties, he is authorized to appoint certain officers, who act by his authority, and in conformity with his orders. In such cases, their acts are his acts; and whatever opinion may be entertained of the manner in which executive discretion may be used, still there exists, and can exist, no power to control that discretion. The subjects are political; they respect the nation, not individual rights, and being entrusted to the executive, the decision of the executive is conclusive. . . .

The conclusion from this reasoning is, that where the heads of departments are the political or confidential agents of the executive, merely to execute the will of the president, or rather to act in cases in which the executive possesses a constitutional or legal discretion, nothing can be more perfectly clear, than that their acts are only politically examinable. But where a specific duty is assigned by law, and individual rights depend upon the performance of that duty, it seems equally clear, that the individual who considers himself injured, has a right to resort to the laws of his country for a remedy. . . .

The question whether a right has vested or not, is in its nature, judicial, and must be tried by the judicial authority. . . .

It is, then, the opinion of the Court: 1st. That . . . the appointment conferred on him a legal right to the office for the space of five years. 2d. That, having this legal title to the office, he has a consequent right to the commission; a refusal to deliver which is a plain violation of that right, for which the laws of his country afford him a remedy.

It remains to be inquired whether he is entitled to the remedy for which he applies [the writ of mandamus]. This depends on 1st. The nature of the writ applied for; and 2d. The power of this court.

1st . . . This, then, is a plain case for a *mandamus,* either to deliver the commission, or a copy of it from the record; and it only remains to be inquired, whether it can issue from this court.

The act to establish the judicial courts of the United States authorizes the supreme court "to issue writs of *mandamus,* in cases warranted by the principles and usages of law, to any courts appointed, or persons holding office, under the authority of the United States." . . . The constitution vests the whole judicial power of the United States in one supreme court, and such inferior courts as congress shall, from time to time, ordain and establish. This power is expressly extended to all cases arising under the laws of the United States; and consequently, in some form, may be exercised over the present case; because the right claimed is given by a law of the United States.

In the distribution of this power, it is declared, that "the supreme court shall have original jurisdiction, in all cases affecting ambassadors, other public ministers and consuls, and those in which a state shall be a party. In all other cases, the supreme court shall have appellate jurisdiction." . . . If it had been intended to leave it in the discretion of the legislature, to apportion the judicial power between the supreme and inferior courts, according to the will of that body, it would certainly have been useless to have proceeded further than to have defined the judicial power, and the tribunals in which it should be vested. The subsequent part of the section is mere surplusage—is entirely without meaning, if such is to be the construction. If congress remains at liberty to give this court appellate jurisdiction, where the constitution has declared their jurisdiction shall be original; and original jurisdiction where the constitution has declared it shall be appellate; the distribution of jurisdiction, made in the constitution, is form without substance. . . . To enable this court, then, to issue a *mandamus,* it must be shown to be an exercise of appellate jurisdiction, or to be necessary to enable them to exercise appellate jurisdiction. . . . It is the essential criterion of appellate jurisdiction, that it revises and corrects the proceedings in a cause already instituted, and does not create that cause. Although therefore, a *mandamus* may be directed to courts, yet to issue such a writ to an officer, for the delivery of a paper, is, in effect, the same as to sustain an original action for that paper, and therefore, seems not to belong to appellate, but to original jurisdiction. Neither is it necessary in such a case as this to enable the court to exercise its appellate jurisdiction. The authority, therefore, given to the supreme court, by the act establishing the judicial courts of the United States, to issue writs of *mandamus* to public officers, appears not to be warranted by the constitution; and it becomes necessary to inquire whether a jurisdiction so conferred can be exercised.

The question, whether an act, repugnant to the constitution, can become the law of the land, is a question deeply interesting to the United States: but, happily, not of an intricacy proportioned to its interest. It seems only necessary to recognize certain principles, supposed to have been long and well established, to decide it. That the people have an original right to establish, for their future government, such principles as, in their opinion, shall most conduce to their own happiness, is the basis on which the whole American fabric has been erected. The exercise of this original right is a very great exertion; nor can it, nor ought it, to be frequently repeated. The principles, therefore, so established, are deemed fundamental: and as the authority from which they proceed is supreme, and can seldom act, they are designed to be permanent.

This original and supreme will organizes the government, and assigns to different departments their respective powers. It may either stop here, or establish certain limits not to be transcended by those departments. The government of the United States is of the latter description. The powers of the legislature are defined and limited; and that those limits may not be mistaken, or forgotten, the constitution is written. To what purpose are powers limited, and to what purpose is that limitation committed to writing, if these limits may, at any time, be passed by those intended to be restrained? The distinction between a government with limited and unlimited powers is abolished, if those limits do not confine the persons on whom they are imposed, and if acts prohibited and acts allowed, are of equal obligation. It is a proposition too plain to be contested, that the constitution controls any legislative act repugnant to it; or, that the legislature may alter the constitution by an ordinary act.

Between these alternatives, there is no middle ground. The constitution is either a superior paramount law, unchangeable by ordinary means, or it is on a level with ordinary legislative acts, and, like other acts, is alterable when the legislature shall please to alter it. If the former part of the alternative be true, then a legislative act, contrary to the constitution, is not law; if the latter part be true, then written constitutions are absurd attempts, on the part of the people, to limit a power, in its own nature, illimitable.

Certainly, all those who have framed written constitutions contemplate them as forming the fundamental and paramount law of the nation, and consequently, the theory of every such government must be, that an act of the legislature, repugnant to the constitution, is void. This theory is essentially attached to a written constitution, and is, consequently, to be considered, by this court, as one of the fundamental principles of our society. It is not, therefore, to be lost sight of, in the further consideration of this subject.

If an act of the legislature, repugnant to the constitution, is void, does it, notwithstanding its invalidity, bind the courts, and oblige them to give it effect? Or, in other words, though it be not law, does it constitute a rule as operative as if it was a law? This would be to overthrow, in fact, what was established in theory; and would seem, at first view, an absurdity too gross to be insisted on. It shall, however, receive a more attentive consideration.

It is, emphatically, the province and duty of the judicial department, to say what the law is. Those who apply the rule to particular cases, must of necessity expound and interpret that rule. If two laws conflict with each other, the courts must decide on the operation of each. So, if a law be in opposition to the constitution; if both the law and the constitution apply to a particular case, so that the court must either decide that case, conformably to the law, disregarding the constitution; or conformably to the constitution, disregarding the law; the court must determine which of these conflicting rules governs the case: this is of the very essence of judicial duty. If then, the courts are to regard the constitution, and the constitution is superior to any ordinary act of the legislature, the constitution, and not such ordinary act, must govern the case to which they both apply.

Those, then, who controvert the principle, that the constitution is to be considered, in court, as a paramount law, are reduced to the necessity of maintaining that courts must close their eyes on the constitution, and see only the law. This doctrine would subvert the very foundation of all written constitutions. It would declare that an act which, according to the principles and theory of our government, is entirely void, is yet, in practice, completely obligatory. It would declare, that if the legislature shall do what is expressly forbidden, such act, notwithstanding the express prohibition, is in reality effectual. It would be giving to the legislature a practical and real omnipotence, with the same breath which professes to restrict their powers within narrow limits. It is prescribing limits, and declaring that those limits may be passed at pleasure. That it thus reduces to nothing, what we have deemed the greatest improvement on political institutions, a written constitution, would, of itself, be sufficient, in America, where written constitutions have been viewed with so much reverence, for rejecting the construction. But the peculiar expressions of the constitution of the United States furnish additional arguments in favor of its rejection. The judicial power of the United States is extended to all cases arising under the constitution. Could it be the intention of those who gave this power, to say, that in using it, the constitution should not be looked into? That a case arising under the constitution should be decided, without examining the instrument under which it arises? This is too extravagant to be maintained. In some cases, then, the constitution must be looked into by the judges. And if they can open it at all, what part of it are they forbidden to read or to obey?

There are many other parts of the constitution which serve to illustrate this subject. It is declared, that "no tax or duty shall be laid on articles exported from any state." Suppose, a duty on the export of cotton, of tobacco, or of flour; and a suit instituted to recover it. Ought judgment to be rendered in such a case? Ought the judges to close their eyes on the constitution, and only see the law?

The constitution declares "that no bill of attainder or *ex post facto* law shall be passed." If, however, such a bill should be passed, and a person should be prosecuted under it, must the court condemn to death those victims whom the constitution endeavors to preserve?

"No person," says the constitution, "shall be convicted of treason, unless on the testimony of two witnesses to the same overt act, or on confession in open court." Here, the language of the constitution is addressed especially to the courts. It prescribes, directly for them, a rule of evidence not to be departed from. If the legislature should change that rule, and declare one witness, or a confession out of court,

sufficient for conviction, must the constitutional principle yield to the legislative act?

From these, and many other selections which might be made, it is apparent, that the framers of the constitution contemplated that instrument as a rule for the government of courts, as well as of the legislature. Why otherwise does it direct the judges to take an oath to support it? This oath certainly applies, in an especial manner, to their conduct in their official character. How immoral to impose it on them, if they were to be used as the instruments, and the knowing instruments, for violating what they swear to support!

The oath of office, too, imposed by the legislature, is completely demonstrative of the legislative opinion on this subject. It is in these words: "I do solemnly swear, that I will administer justice, without respect to persons, and do equal right to the poor and to the rich; and that I will faithfully and impartially discharge all the duties incumbent on me as———according to the best of my abilities and understanding, agreeable to the constitution and laws of the United States." Why does a judge swear to discharge his duties agreeably to the constitution of the United States, if that constitution forms no rule for his government? If it is closed upon him, and cannot be inspected by him? If such be the real state of things, this is worse than solemn mockery. To prescribe, or to take this oath, becomes equally a crime.

It is also not entirely unworthy of observation, that in declaring what shall be the supreme law of the land, the constitution itself is first mentioned; and not the laws of the United States, generally, but those only which shall be made in pursuance of the constitution, have that rank.

Thus, the particular phraseology of the constitution of the United States confirms and strengthens the principle, supposed to be essential to all written constitutions, that a law repugnant to the constitution is void; and that courts, as well as other departments, are bound by that instrument.

*The rule must be discharged.*

## *Eakin* v. *Raub*
## 12 Sergeant & Rawle (Pennsylvania Supreme Court) 330 (1825)
## http://www.prenhall.com/mason

The dissenting opinion by Justice John Bannister Gibson of the Pennsylvania Supreme Court in this otherwise unimportant 1825 case is generally recognized as the most effective answer to Marshall's argument supporting judicial review. Gibson's opinion, Professor J. B. Thayer observed 68 years later, "is much the ablest discussion of the question [of judicial review] which I have ever seen, not excepting the judgment of Marshall in *Marbury* v. *Madison,* which as I venture to think has been overpraised." Gibson's bold argument was a probable factor in preventing his appointment to the U.S. Supreme Court on the death of Justice Washington in 1830. In 1845 Gibson recanted, because the legislature of Pennsylvania had "sanctioned the pretensions of the courts to deal freely with the acts of the legislature, and from experience of the necessity of the case" (see *Norris* v. *Clymer,* 2 Pa. 281). The former reference was to the state convention which produced the new constitution of 1838 that, by its silence on the subject, seemed to countenance judicial review. Gibson's second reference was to legislative intrusion into judicial matters.

GIBSON, J. . . .

I am aware, that a right [in the judiciary] to declare all unconstitutional acts void . . . is generally held as a professional dogma, but, I apprehend, rather as a matter of faith than of reason. I admit that I once embraced the same doctrine, but without examination, and I shall therefore state the arguments that impelled me to abandon it, with great respect for those by whom it is still maintained. But I may premise, that it is not a little remarkable, that although the right in question has all along been claimed by the judiciary, no judge has ventured to discuss it, except Chief Justice Marshall, and if the argument of a jurist so distinguished for the strength of his ratiocinative powers be found inconclusive, it may fairly be set down to the weakness of the position which he attempts to defend. . . .

I begin, then, by observing that in this country, the powers of the judiciary are divisible into those that are POLITICAL and those that are purely civil. Every power by which one organ of the government is enabled to control another, or to exert an influence over its acts, is a political power. . . .

The constitution and the right of the legislature to pass the act, may be in collision. But is that a legitimate subject for judicial determination? If it be, the judiciary must be a peculiar organ, to revise the proceedings of the legislature, and to correct its mistakes; and in what part of the constitution are we to look for this proud pre-eminence? Viewing the matter in the opposite direction, what would be thought of an act of assembly in which it should be declared that the supreme court had, in a particular case, put a wrong construction on the constitution of the United States, and that the judgment should therefore be reversed? It would doubtless be thought a usurpation of judicial power. But it is by no means clear, that to declare a law void which has been enacted according to the forms prescribed in the constitution, is not a usurpation of legislative power. . . . It is the business of the judiciary to interpret the laws, not scan the authority of the lawgiver; and without the latter, it cannot take cognizance of a collision between a law and the constitution. So that to affirm that the judiciary has a right to judge of the existence of such collision, is to take for granted the very thing to be proved.

But it has been said to be emphatically the business of the judiciary, to ascertain and pronounce what the law is; and that this necessarily involves a consideration of the constitution. It does so: but how far? If the judiciary will inquire into anything besides the form of enactment, where shall it stop?. . .

In theory, all the organs of the government are of equal capacity; or, if not equal, each must be supposed to have superior capacity only for those things which peculiarly belong to it; and as legislation peculiarly involves the consideration of those limitations which are put on the law-making power, and the interpretation of the laws when made, involves only the construction of the laws themselves, it follows that the construction of the constitution in this particular belongs to the legislature, which ought therefore to be taken to have superior capacity to judge of the constitutionality of its own acts. . . .

When the entire sovereignty was separated into its elementary parts, and distributed to the appropriate branches, all things incident to the exercise of its powers were committed to each branch exclusively. The negative which each part of the legislature may exercise, in regard to the acts of the other, was thought sufficient to prevent material infractions of the restraints which were put on the power of the whole; for, had it been intended to interpose the judiciary as an additional barrier, the matter would surely not have been left in doubt. The judges would not have been left to stand on the insecure and ever shifting ground of public opinion as to constructive powers; they would have been placed on the impregnable ground of an express grant. They would not have been compelled to resort to debates in the convention, or the opinion that was generally entertained at the time. . . .

The power is said to be restricted to cases that are free from doubt or difficulty. But the abstract existence of a power cannot depend on the clearness or obscurity of the case in which it is to be exercised; for that is a consideration that cannot present itself, before the question of the existence of the power shall have been determined; and, if its existence be conceded, no considerations of policy arising from the obscurity of the particular case, ought to influence the exercise of it. . . .

To say, therefore, that the power is to be exercised but in perfectly clear cases, is to

betray a doubt of the propriety of exercising it at all. Were the same caution used in judging of the existence of the power that is inculcated as to the exercise of it, the profession would perhaps arrive at a different conclusion. The grant of a power so extraordinary ought to appear so plain, that he who should run might read. . . .

What I have in view in this inquiry, is the supposed right of the judiciary to interfere, in cases where the constitution is to be carried into effect through the instrumentality of the legislature, and where that organ must necessarily first decide on the constitutionality of its own act. The oath to support the constitution is not peculiar to the judges, but is taken indiscriminately by every officer of the government, and is designed rather as a test of the political principles of the man, than to bind the officer in the discharge of his duty: otherwise it is difficult to determine what operation it is to have in the case of a recorder of deeds, for instance, who, in the execution of his office, has nothing to do with the constitution. But granting it to relate to the official conduct of the judge, as well as every other officer, and not to his political principles, still it must be understood in reference to supporting the constitution, only as far as that may be involved in his official duty; and, consequently, if his official duty does not comprehend an inquiry into the authority of the legislature, neither does his oath. . . .

But do not the judges do a positive act in violation of the constitution, when they give effect to an unconstitutional law? Not if the law has been passed according to the forms established in the constitution. The fallacy of the question is, in supposing that the judiciary adopts the acts of the legislature as its own. . . . The fault is imputable to the legislature, and on it the responsibility exclusively rests. . . .

But it has been said, that this construction would deprive the citizen of the advantages which are peculiar to a written constitution, by at once declaring the power of the legislature in practice to be illimitable. . . . But there is no magic or inherent power in parchment and ink, to command respect and protect principles from violation. In the business of government a recurrence to first principles answers the end of an observation at sea with a view to correct the dead reckoning; and for this purpose, a written constitution is an instrument of inestimable value. It is of inestimable value, also, in rendering its first principles familiar to the mass of people; for, after all, there is no effectual guard against legislative usurpation but public opinion, the force of which, in this country is inconceivably great. . . . Once let public opinion be so corrupt as to sanction every misconception of the constitution and abuse of power which the temptation of the moment may dictate, and the party which may happen to be predominant, will laugh at the puny efforts of a dependent power to arrest it in its course.

For these reasons, I am of [the] opinion that it rests with the people, in whom full and absolute sovereign power resides, to correct abuses in legislation, by instructing their representatives to repeal the obnoxious act. . . . It might, perhaps, have been better to vest the power in the judiciary; as it might be expected that its habits of deliberation, and the aid derived from the arguments of counsel, would more frequently lead to accurate conclusions. On the other hand, the judiciary is not infallible; and an error by it would admit of no remedy but a more distinct expression of the public will, through the extraordinary medium of a convention; whereas, an error by the legislature admits of a remedy by an exertion of the same will, in the ordinary exercise of the right of suffrage—a mode better calculated to attain the end, without popular excitement. . . .

But in regard to an act of [a state] assembly, which is found to be in collision with the constitution, laws, or treaties of the United States, I take the duty of the judiciary to be exactly the reverse. By becoming parties to the federal constitution, the states have agreed to several limitations of their individual sovereignty, to enforce which, it was thought to be absolutely necessary to prevent them from giving effect to laws in violation of those limitations, through the instrumentality of their own judges. Accordingly, it is declared in the sixth article and second section of the federal constitution, that, "This constitution, and the laws of the United States which shall be made in pursuance thereof, and all treaties made, or which shall be made under the authority of the United States, shall be the supreme law of the land; and the judges in every state shall be BOUND thereby: anything in the laws or constitution of any state to the contrary notwithstanding.". . .

## Scott v. Sandford
### 60 U.S. (19 Howard) 393, 15 L.Ed. 691 (1857)
### http://laws.findlaw.com/us/60/393.html

In 1834, Dr. John Emerson, an Army surgeon, took his slave Dred Scott from Missouri to Illinois, where slavery was forbidden. In 1836 Emerson took Scott to Fort Snelling in present-day Minnesota, well north of 36° 30′ in the old Louisiana territory, where slavery had been banned by the Missouri Compromise of 1820. In 1838 Emerson returned to Missouri with Scott. After Emerson died, a suit was brought in the Missouri courts against his widow, claiming that Scott's residence in free territory had made him a free person. The lower court held for Scott, but the state supreme court reversed in 1852. Whatever Scott's legal status outside Missouri, it concluded, he remained a slave under Missouri law. By this time Mrs. Emerson had married Dr. C. C. Chaffee, an abolitionist from Massachusetts. To reopen the case, and to shield both his reputation and the friendly nature of the litigation, he transferred ownership of

Scott to Mrs. Chaffee's brother, John Sanford, of New York. (In *Howard's Reports,* Sanford's name was incorrectly spelled "Sandford.") In 1853 Chaffee arranged for Roswell Field, an abolitionist attorney in St. Louis, to file suit on Scott's behalf against Sanford in the U.S. Circuit Court in Missouri. On a writ of error from an adverse judgment, Scott appealed to the Supreme Court. The justices twice heard arguments in the case, in February and December of 1856. The case came down on March 6, 1857, just two days after James Buchanan's inauguration. Strong pressures from all sides pushed the justices to accomplish judicially what the elected branches had been unable to resolve. "On the principles of the . . . decision depended . . . the destiny of this country," Alexander H. Stephens observed five months later on the assumption that the Court's ruling would be accepted nationwide. Each of the nine justices filed an opinion; Taney's and Curtis's are included here. Majority: Taney, Campbell, Catron, Daniel, Grier, Nelson, Wayne. Dissenting: Curtis, McLean. (Not all members of the majority agreed with Taney's disposition of all points in the case.)

## MR. CHIEF JUSTICE TANEY delivered the opinion of the Court. . . .

The question is simply this: Can a negro, whose ancestors were imported into this country, and sold as slaves, become a member of the political community formed and brought into existence by the Constitution of the United States, and as such become entitled to all the rights, and privileges, and immunities guarantied by that instrument to the citizen? One of which rights is the privilege of suing in a court of the United States in the cases specified in the Constitution.

We think . . . [the people of that race] . . . are not included, and were not intended to be included, under the words "citizens" in the Constitution, and can therefore claim none of the rights and privileges which that instrument provides for and secures to citizens of the United States. On the contrary, they were at that time considered as a subordinate and inferior class of beings, who had been subjugated by the dominant race, and, whether emancipated or not, yet remained subject to their authority, and had no rights or privileges but such as those who held the power and the Government might choose to grant them. . . .

The question then arises, whether the provisions of the Constitution, in relation to the personal rights and privileges to which the citizen of the State should be entitled, embraced the negro African race, at that time in this country, or who might afterwards be imported, who had then or should afterwards be made free in any State; and to put it in the power of a single State to make him a citizen of the United States, and endue him with the full rights of citizenship in every other State without their consent? Does the Constitution of the United States act upon him whenever he shall be made free under the laws of a State, and raised there to the rank of a citizen, and immediately clothe him with all the privileges of a citizen in every other State, and in its own courts?

The court thinks the affirmative of these propositions cannot be maintained. And if it cannot, the plaintiff in error could not be a citizen of the State of Missouri, within the meaning of the Constitution of the United States, and, consequently, was not entitled to sue in its courts. . . .

No one, we presume, supposes that any change in public opinion or feeling, in relation to this unfortunate race, in the civilized nations of Europe or in this country, should induce the court to give to the words of the Constitution a more liberal construction in their favor than they were intended to bear when the instrument was framed and adopted. Such an argument would be altogether inadmissible in any tribunal called on to interpret it. If any of its provisions are deemed unjust, there is a mode prescribed in the instrument itself by which it may be amended; but while it remains unaltered, it must be construed now as it was understood at the time of its adoption. It is not only the same in words, but the same in meaning, and delegates the same powers to the Government, and reserves and secures the same rights and privileges to the citizen; and as long as it continues to exist in its present form, it speaks not only in the same words, but with the same meaning and intent with which it spoke when it came from the hands of its framers, and was voted on and adopted by the people of the United States. Any other rule of construction would abrogate the judicial character of this court, and make it the mere reflex of the popular opinion of the day. . . .

What the construction was at that time, we think can hardly admit of doubt. We have the language of the Declaration of Independence and of the Articles of Confederation, in addition to the plain words of the Constitution itself; we have the legislation of the different States, before, about the time, and since, the Constitution was adopted; we have the legislation of Congress, from the time of its adoption to a recent period; and we have the constant and uniform action of the Executive Department, all concurring together, and leading to the same result. And if anything in relation to the construction of the Constitution can be regarded as settled, it is that which we now give to the word "citizen" and the word "people.". . .

The act of Congress, upon which the plaintiff relies, declares that slavery and involuntary servitude, except as a punishment for crime, shall be forever prohibited in all that part of the territory ceded by France, under the name of Louisiana, which lies north of thirty-six degrees thirty minutes north latitude, and not included within the limits of Missouri. And the . . . inquiry is whether Congress was authorized to pass this law under any of the powers granted to it by the Constitution; for if the authority is not given by that instrument, it is the duty of this court to declare it void and inoperative, and incapable of conferring freedom upon any one who is held as a slave under the laws of any one of the States.

The counsel for the plaintiff has laid much stress upon that article in the Constitution which confers on Congress the power "to dispose of and make all needful rules and regulations respecting the territory or other property belonging to the United States," but, in the judgment of the court, that provision has no bearing on the present controversy, and the power there given, whatever it may be, is confined, and was intended to be confined, to the territory which at that time belonged to, or was claimed by the United States, and was within their boundaries as settled by the treaty with Great Britain, and can have no influence upon a territory afterwards acquired from a foreign Government. It was a special provision for a known and particular territory, and to meet a present emergency, and nothing more.

. . . The powers of the Government and the rights and privileges of the citizen are regulated and plainly defined by the Constitution itself. And when the Territory becomes a part of the United States, the Federal Government enters into possession in the character impressed upon it by those who created it. It enters upon it with its powers over the citizen strictly defined, and limited by the Constitution, from which it derives its own existence, and by virtue of which alone it continues to exist and act as a Government and sovereignty. It has not power of any kind beyond it; and it cannot, when it enters a Territory of the United States, put off its character and assume discretionary or despotic powers which the Constitution has denied to it. It cannot create for itself a new character separated from the citizens of the United States, and the duties it owes them under the provisions of the Constitution. The Territory being a part of the United States, the Government and the citizen both enter it under the authority of the Constitution, with their respective rights defined and marked out; and the Federal Government can exercise no power over his person or property, beyond what that instrument confers, nor lawfully deny any right which it has reserved. . . .

An Act of Congress which deprives a citizen of the United States of his liberty or property, merely because he came himself or brought his property into a particular Territory of the United States, and who had committed no offense against the laws, could hardly be dignified with the name of due process of law. . . .

And if Congress itself cannot do this—if it is beyond the powers conferred on the Federal Government—it will be admitted . . . that it could not authorize a Territorial Government to exercise them. It could confer no power on any local Government, established by its authority, to violate the provisions of the Constitution. . . .

Upon these considerations, it is the opinion of the court that the act of Congress which prohibited a citizen from holding and owning property of this kind in the territory of the United States north of the line therein mentioned, is not warranted by the Constitution, and is therefore void; and that neither Dred Scott himself, nor any of his family, were made free by being carried into this territory; even if they had been carried there by the owner, with the intention of becoming a permanent resident. . . .

But there is another point in the case which depends on State power and State law. . . . [T]he principle on which it depends was decided in this court . . . in . . . *Strader* v. *Graham* [1851]. . . . In that case, the slaves had been taken from Kentucky to Ohio, with the consent of the owner, and afterwards brought back to Kentucky. And this court held that their status or condition, as free or slave, depended upon the laws of Kentucky, when they were brought back into that State, and not of Ohio; and that this court had no jurisdiction to revise the judgment of a State court upon its own laws. . . .

So in this case. As Scott was a slave when taken into the State of Illinois by his owner, and was there held as such, and brought back in that character, his status, as free or slave, depended on the laws of Missouri, not of Illinois. . . .

[I]t is the judgment of this court, that it appears by the record before us that the plaintiff in error is not a citizen of Missouri, in the sense in which that word is used in the Constitution; and that the Circuit Court . . . , for that reason, had no jurisdiction in the case, and could give no judgment in it. Its judgment for the defendant must, consequently, be reversed, and a mandate issued, directing the suit to be dismissed for want of jurisdiction.

### MR. JUSTICE CURTIS, joined by MR. JUSTICE McLEAN, dissenting. . . .

To determine whether any free persons, descended from Africans held in slavery, were citizens of the United States under the Confederation, and consequently at the time of the adoption of the Constitution of the United States, it is only necessary to know whether any such persons were citizens of either of the States under the Confederation, at the time of the adoption of the Constitution.

Of this there can be no doubt. At the time of the ratification of the Articles of Confederation, all free native-born inhabitants of the States of New Hampshire, Massachusetts, New York, New Jersey, and North Carolina, though descended from African slaves, were not only citizens of those States, but such of them as had the other necessary qualifications possessed the franchise of electors, on equal terms with other citizens. . . .

Having first decided that they were bound to consider the sufficiency of the plea to the jurisdiction of the Circuit Court, and having decided that this plea showed that the Circuit Court had no jurisdiction, and consequently that this is a case to which the judicial power of the United States does not extend, they have gone on to examine the merits of the case as they appeared on the trial before the court and jury, on the issues joined on the pleas in bar, and so have reached the question of the power of Congress to pass the act of 1820. On so grave a subject as this, I feel obliged to say that, in my opinion, such an exertion of judicial power transcends the limits of the authority of the court, as described by its repeated decisions and, as I understand, acknowledged in this opinion of the majority of the court. . . .

Nor, in my judgment, will the position, that a prohibition to bring slaves into a Territory deprives any one of his property without due process of law, bear examination. . . .

## II. EXTERNAL AND INTERNAL CHECKS ON JUDICIAL POWER

### Ex parte *McCardle*
### 74 U.S. (7 Wall.) 506, 19 L.Ed. 264 (1869)

http://laws.findlaw.com/us/74/506.html

During Reconstruction after the Civil War, a newspaper editor in Mississippi named William McCardle was jailed by a military commander for trial before a military commission for publishing "incendiary and libelous" articles. McCardle was a civilian and sought release on habeas corpus in the Circuit Court for the Southern District of Mississippi. After hearing his case the judge remanded McCardle to the custody of the military authorities. McCardle then took an appeal to the Supreme Court authorized by a statute passed by Congress in 1867. Following argument of his case in the Supreme Court and while the justices had it under advisement, Congress overrode President Andrew Johnson's veto and repealed the statute in 1868. The majority in Congress apparently feared that the constitutionality of much of its Reconstruction program was at stake in the litigation. Chief Justice Chase noted in his opinion that decision in the case had been delayed by his participation in the president's impeachment trial in the Senate. McCardle should be read in the light of Ex parte *Yerger* (1869) and *United States* v. *Klein* (1872). Majority: Chase, Clifford, Davis, Field, Grier, Miller, Nelson, Swayne.

**MR. CHIEF JUSTICE CHASE delivered the opinion of the Court. . . .**

The first question necessarily is that of jurisdiction; for, if the act of March, 1868, takes away the jurisdiction defined by the act of February, 1867, it is useless, if not improper, to enter into any discussion of other questions.

It is quite true, as was argued by the counsel for the petitioner, that the appellate jurisdiction of this court is not derived from acts of Congress. It is, strictly speaking, conferred by the Constitution. But it is conferred "with such exceptions and under such regulations as Congress shall make."

It is unnecessary to consider whether, if Congress had made no exceptions and no regulations, this court might not have exercised general appellate jurisdiction under rules prescribed by itself. For among the earliest acts of the first Congress, at its first session, was the act of September 24th, 1789, to establish the judicial courts of the United States. That act provided for the organization of this court, and prescribed regulations for the exercise of its jurisdiction.

The source of that jurisdiction, and the limitations of it by the Constitution, and by statute, have been on several occasions subjects of consideration here. . . .

The principle that the affirmation of appellate jurisdiction implies the negation of all such jurisdiction not affirmed having been thus established, it was an almost necessary consequence that acts of Congress, providing for the exercise of jurisdiction, should come to be spoken of as acts granting jurisdiction, and not as acts making exceptions to the constitutional grant of it.

The exception to appellate jurisdiction in the case before us, however, is not an inference from the affirmation of other appellate jurisdiction. It is made in terms. The provision of the act of 1867, affirming the appellate jurisdiction of this court in cases of habeas corpus is expressly repealed. It is hardly possible to imagine a plainer instance of positive exception.

We are not at liberty to inquire into the motives of the legislature. We can only examine into its power under the Constitution; and the power to make exceptions to the appellate jurisdiction of this court is given by express words.

What, then, is the effect of the repealing act upon the case before us? We cannot doubt as to this. Without jurisdiction the court cannot proceed at all in any cause. Jurisdiction is power to declare the law, and when it ceases to exist, the only function remaining to the court is that of announcing the fact and dismissing the cause. And this is not less clear upon authority than upon principle. . . .

It is quite clear, therefore, that this court cannot proceed to pronounce judgment in this case, for it has no longer jurisdiction of the appeal; and judicial duty is not less fitly performed by declining ungranted jurisdiction than in exercising firmly that which the Constitution and the laws confer.

Counsel seem to have supposed, if effect be given to the repealing act in question, that the whole appellate power of the court, in cases of habeas corpus, is denied. But this is an error. The act of 1868 does not except from that jurisdiction any cases but appeals from Circuit Courts under the act of 1867. It does not affect the jurisdiction which was previously exercised.

The appeal of the petitioner in this case must be dismissed for want of jurisdiction.

## *Baker* v. *Carr*
## 369 U.S. 186, 82 S.Ct. 691, 7 L.Ed. 2d 663 (1962)
## http://laws.findlaw.com/us/369/186.html

(This case is reprinted in Chapter Five, beginning on page 198.)

## III. FINALITY OF SUPREME COURT DECISIONS

## *City of Boerne* v. *Flores*
## 521 U.S. 507, 117 S.Ct. 2157, 138 L.Ed. 2d 624 (1997)
## http://laws.findlaw.com/us/521/507.html

The Catholic Archbishop of San Antonio applied for a building permit to enlarge a church in Boerne, Texas. When local officials denied the permit under a historic preservation ordinance, the Archbishop challenged the rejection as a violation of the Religious Freedom Restoration Act (RFRA) of 1993. Congress enacted RFRA in response to the Supreme Court's decision in *Employment Division* v. *Smith* (1990) (see Chapter Twelve). This decision upheld, against a challenge under the free exercise clause, the denial of unemployment benefits to members of the Native American Church who lost their jobs because of the ritual use of peyote in violation of an Oregon statute of general applicability banning the use of certain drugs, including peyote. Preferring the religion-friendly standard from earlier Supreme Court decisions

(*Sherbert* v. *Verner,* 1963; and *Wisconsin* v. *Yoder,* 1972) and relying on Section 5 of the Fourteenth Amendment, Congress prohibited any local, state, or federal government agency or official from "substantially burden[ing]" a person's exercise of religion even if the burden results from application of a law of general applicability, unless the government can demonstrate that the burden "(1) is in furtherance of a compelling governmental interest; and (2) is the least restrictive means of furthering that . . . interest." The U.S. District Court for the Western District of Texas concluded that by enacting RFRA, Congress exceeded the scope of its enforcement powers under the Fourteenth Amendment, but the Court of Appeals for the Fifth Circuit reversed. Majority: Kennedy, Rehnquist, Stevens, Scalia, Thomas, Ginsburg. Dissenting: O'Connor, Souter, Breyer.

## JUSTICE KENNEDY delivered the opinion of the Court. . . .

The case calls into question the authority of Congress to enact RFRA. We conclude the statute exceeds Congress' power. . . .

Under our Constitution, the Federal Government is one of enumerated powers. The judicial authority to determine the constitutionality of laws, in cases and controversies, is based on the premise that the "powers of the legislature are defined and limited; and that those limits may not be mistaken, or forgotten, the constitution is written.". . .

The parties disagree over whether RFRA is a proper exercise of Congress' § 5 power to enforce by "appropriate legislation" the constitutional guarantee that no State shall deprive any person of "life, liberty, or property, without due process of law" nor deny any person "equal protection of the laws."

In defense of the Act respondent contends, with support from the United States as amicus, that RFRA is permissible enforcement legislation. Congress, it is said, is only protecting by legislation one of the liberties guaranteed by the Fourteenth Amendment's Due Process Clause, the free exercise of religion, beyond what is necessary under *Smith*. It is said the congressional decision to dispense with proof of deliberate or overt discrimination and instead concentrate on a law's effects accords with the settled understanding that § 5 includes the power to enact legislation designed to prevent as well as remedy constitutional violations. It is further contended that Congress'

§ 5 power is not limited to remedial or preventive legislation.

All must acknowledge that § 5 is "a positive grant of legislative power" to Congress. . . .

Legislation which deters or remedies constitutional violations can fall within the sweep of Congress' enforcement power even if in the process it prohibits conduct which is not itself unconstitutional and intrudes into "legislative spheres of autonomy previously reserved to the States." For example, the Court upheld a suspension of literacy tests and similar voting requirements under Congress' parallel power to enforce the provisions of the Fifteenth Amendment, as a measure to combat racial discrimination in voting, despite the facial constitutionality of the tests under *Lassiter* v. *Northampton County Bd. of Elections* (1959). . . .

It is also true, however, that "[a]s broad as the congressional enforcement power is, it is not unlimited." In assessing the breadth of § 5's enforcement power, we begin with its text. Congress has been given the power "to enforce" the "provisions of this article." We agree with respondent, of course, that Congress can enact legislation under § 5 enforcing the constitutional right to the free exercise of religion. The "provisions of this article," to which § 5 refers, include the Due Process Clause of the Fourteenth Amendment. Congress' power to enforce the Free Exercise Clause follows from our holding in *Cantwell* v. *Connecticut* (1940), that the "fundamental concept of liberty embodied in [the Fourteenth Amendment's Due Process Clause] embraces the liberties guaranteed by the First Amendment.". . .

Congress' power under § 5, however, extends only to "enforc[ing]" the provisions of the Fourteenth Amendment. . . . The design of the Amendment and the text of § 5 are inconsistent with the suggestion that Congress has the power to decree the substance of the Fourteenth Amendment's restrictions on the States. Legislation which alters the meaning of the Free Exercise Clause cannot be said to be enforcing the Clause. Congress does not enforce a constitutional right by changing what the right is. . . . Were it not so, what Congress would be enforcing would no longer be, in any meaningful sense, the "provisions of [the Fourteenth Amendment]."

While the line between measures that remedy or prevent unconstitutional actions and measures that make a substantive change in the governing law is not easy to discern, and Congress must have wide latitude in determining where it lies, the distinction exists and must be observed. There must be a congruence and proportionality between the injury to be prevented or remedied and the means adopted to that end. . . .

The remedial and preventive nature of Congress' enforcement power, and the limitation inherent in the power, were confirmed in our earliest cases on the Fourteenth Amendment. . . .

Recent cases have continued to revolve around the question of whether § 5 legislation can be considered remedial . . . . In *South Carolina* v. *Katzenbach,* we emphasized that "[t]he constitutional propriety of [legislation adopted under the Enforcement Clause] must be judged with reference to the historical experience. . . it reflects." There we upheld various provisions of the Voting Rights Act of 1965, finding them to be "remedies aimed at areas where voting discrimination has been most flagrant.". . . The new, unprecedented remedies were deemed necessary given the ineffectiveness of the existing voting rights laws and the slow costly character of case-by-case litigation.

Any suggestion that Congress has a substantive, non-remedial power under the Fourteenth Amendment is not supported by our case law. In *Oregon* v. *Mitchell,* a majority of the Court concluded Congress had exceeded its enforcement powers by enacting legislation lowering the minimum age of voters from 21 to 18 in state and local elections. . . .

If Congress could define its own powers by altering the Fourteenth Amendment's meaning, no longer would the Constitution be "superior paramount law, unchangeable by ordinary means." It would be "on a level with ordinary legislative acts, and, like other acts, . . . alterable when the legislature shall please to alter it." Under this approach, it is difficult to conceive of a principle that would limit congressional power. Shifting legislative majorities could change the Constitution and effectively circumvent the difficult and detailed amendment process contained in Article V.

We now turn to consider whether RFRA can be considered enforcement legislation under § 5 of the Fourteenth Amendment.

Respondent contends that RFRA is a proper exercise of Congress' remedial or preventive power. The Act, it is said, is a reasonable means of protecting the free exercise of religion as defined by *Smith*. It prevents and remedies laws which are enacted with the unconstitutional object of targeting religious beliefs and practices. . . . To avoid the difficulty of proving such violations, it is said, Congress can simply invalidate any law which imposes a substantial burden on a religious practice unless it is justified by a compelling interest and is the least restrictive means of accomplishing that interest. If Congress can prohibit laws with discriminatory effects in order to prevent racial discrimination in violation of the Equal Protection Clause, then it can do the same, respondent argues, to promote religious liberty.

While preventive rules are sometimes appropriate remedial measures, there must be a congruence between the means used and the ends to be achieved. . . . Strong measures appropriate to address one harm may be an unwarranted response to another, lesser one.

A comparison between RFRA and the Voting Rights Act is instructive. In contrast to the record which confronted Congress and the judiciary in the voting rights cases, RFRA's legislative record lacks examples of modern instances of generally applicable laws passed because of religious bigotry. The history of persecution in this country detailed in the hearings mentions no episodes occurring in the past 40 years. . . .

Regardless of the state of the legislative record, RFRA cannot be considered remedial, preventive legislation, if those terms are to have any meaning. RFRA is so out of proportion to a supposed remedial or preventive object that it cannot be understood as responsive to, or designed to prevent, unconstitutional behavior. It appears, instead, to attempt a substantive change in constitutional protections. . . .

When the exercise of religion has been burdened in an incidental way by a law of general application, it does not follow that the persons affected have been burdened any more than other citizens, let alone burdened because of their religious beliefs. In addition, the Act imposes in every case a least restrictive means requirement—a requirement that was not used in the pre-*Smith* jurisprudence RFRA purported to codify—which also indicates that the legislation is broader than is appropriate if the goal is to prevent and remedy constitutional violations. . . .

Broad as the power of Congress is under the Enforcement Clause of the Fourteenth Amendment, RFRA contradicts vital principles necessary to maintain separation of powers and the federal balance. The judgment of the Court of Appeals sustaining the Act's constitutionality is reversed.

*It is so ordered.*

JUSTICE STEVENS, concurring . . . [omitted].
JUSTICE SCALIA, with whom JUSTICE STEVENS joins, concurring in part . . . [omitted].

**JUSTICE O'CONNOR, with whom JUSTICE BREYER joins in part, dissenting. . . .**

[I]f I agreed with the Court's standard in *Smith,* I would join the opinion. As the Court's careful and thorough historical analysis shows, Congress lacks the "power to decree the substance of the Fourteenth Amendment's restrictions on the States." Rather, its power under § 5 of the Fourteenth Amendment extends only to enforcing the Amendment's provisions. In short, Congress lacks the ability independently to define or expand the scope of constitutional rights by statute. . . . This recognition does not, of course, in any way diminish Congress' obligation to draw its own conclusions regarding the Constitution's meaning. Congress, no less than this Court, is called upon to consider the requirements of the Constitution and to act in accordance with its dictates. But when it enacts legislation in furtherance of its delegated powers, Congress must make its judgments consistent with this Court's exposition of the Constitution and with the limits placed on its legislative authority by provisions such as the Fourteenth Amendment.

The Court's analysis of whether RFRA is a constitutional exercise of Congress' § 5 power . . . is premised on the assumption that *Smith* correctly interprets the Free Exercise Clause. This is an assumption that I do not accept. . . . [T]he Free Exercise Clause is not simply an antidiscrimination principle that protects only against those laws that single out religious practice for unfavorable treatment. Rather, the Clause is best understood as an affirmative guarantee of the right to participate in religious practices and conduct without impermissible governmental interference, even when such conduct conflicts with a neutral, generally applicable law. . . .

JUSTICE SOUTER, dissenting . . . [omitted].
JUSTICE BREYER, dissenting . . . [omitted].

## Unstaged Debate: *Andrew Jackson, Abraham Lincoln, and Arkansas* v. *The Supreme Court*[3]

When Congress voted to recharter the Bank of the United States in 1832, President Andrew Jackson vetoed the bill in part because he thought it unconstitutional. The Supreme Court in *McCulloch* v. *Maryland* (1819), reprinted in Chapter Four, had upheld the constitutionality of the bank. Jackson's words in the first excerpt were drafted mainly by Roger Brooke Taney, whom Jackson soon appointed to succeed John Marshall as chief justice of the United States. It was the Taney Court's decision in *Scott* v. *Sandford* (1857) that Lincoln had in mind in the second excerpt. A century later *Cooper* v. *Aaron* grew out of official resistance in Little Rock, Arkansas, to the Supreme Court's 1954 school desegregation decision (*Brown* v. *Board of Education,* in Chapter Fourteen). The opinion is unusual in that all nine justices signed it. Note the reliance in *Cooper* on both the supremacy clause and *Marbury* v. *Madison.*

### PRESIDENT JACKSON VETOES THE BANK ACT (1832)

It is maintained by the advocates of the bank that its constitutionality in all its features ought to be considered as settled by precedent and by the decision of the Supreme Court. To this conclusion I can not assent.

If the opinion of the Supreme Court covered the whole ground of this act, it ought not to control the coordinate authorities of this Government. The Congress, the Executive, and the Court must each for itself be guided by its own opinion of the Constitution. Each public officer who takes an oath to support the Constitution swears that he will support it as he understands it, and not as it is understood by others. It is as much the duty of the House of Representatives, of the Senate, and of the President to decide upon the constitutionality of any bill or resolution which may be presented to them for passage or approval as it is of the supreme judges when it may be brought before them for judicial decision. The opinion of the judges has no more authority over Congress than the opinion of Congress has over the judges, and on that point the President is independent of both. The authority of the Supreme Court must not, therefore,

[3] The Jackson and Lincoln messages appear in James D. Richardson, ed., *A Compilation of the Messages and Papers of the Presidents* (Washington, D.C.: Bureau of National Literature and Art, 1908), Vol. 2, pp. 581–82, and Vol. 6, p. 9, respectively.

be permitted to control the Congress or the Executive when acting in their legislative capacities, but to have only such influence as the force of their reasoning may deserve.

### PRESIDENT LINCOLN DELIVERS HIS FIRST INAUGURAL ADDRESS (1861)

I do not forget the position assumed by some, that constitutional questions are to be decided by the Supreme Court; nor do I deny that such decisions must be binding in any case, upon the parties to a suit, as to the object of that suit, while they are also entitled to a very high respect and consideration, in all parallel cases, by all other departments of government. And while it is obviously possible that such decision may be erroneous in any given case, still the evil effect following it, being limited to that particular case, with the chance that it may be over-ruled, and never become a precedent for other cases, can better be borne than could the evils of a different practice. At the same time the candid citizen must confess that if the policy of the government, upon vital questions, affecting the whole people, is to be irrevocably fixed by decisions of the Supreme Court, the instant they are made, in ordinary litigation between parties, in personal actions, the people will have ceased, to be their own rulers, having to that extent, practically resigned their government, into the hands of that eminent tribunal. Nor is there, in this view, any assault upon the court, or the judges. It is a duty, from which they may not shrink, to decide cases properly brought before them; and it is no fault of theirs, if others seek to turn their decisions to political purposes.

## THE SUPREME COURT DECIDES
## *COOPER* v. *AARON*
## 358 U.S. 1, 78 S.Ct. 1401, 3 L.Ed. 2d 5 (1958)

http://laws.findlaw.com/us/358/1.html

**Opinion of the Court by the CHIEF JUSTICE, MR. JUSTICE BLACK, MR. JUSTICE FRANKFURTER, MR. JUSTICE DOUGLAS, MR. JUSTICE BURTON, MR. JUSTICE CLARK, MR. JUSTICE HARLAN, MR. JUSTICE BRENNAN, and MR. JUSTICE WHITTAKER.**

As this case reaches us it raises questions of the highest importance to the maintenance of our federal system of government. It necessarily involves a claim by the Governor and Legislature of a State that there is no duty on state officials to obey federal court orders resting on this Court's considered interpretation of the United States Constitution. Specifically it involves actions by the Governor and Legislature of Arkansas upon the premise that they are not bound by our holding in *Brown* v. *Board of Education.* . . .

What has been said, in the light of the facts developed, is enough to dispose of the case. However, we should answer the premise of the actions of the Governor and Legislature that they are not bound by our holding in the Brown case. It is necessary only to recall some basic constitutional propositions which are settled doctrine.

Article VI of the Constitution makes the Constitution the "supreme Law of the Land." In 1803, Chief Justice Marshall, speaking for a unanimous Court, referring to the Constitution as "the fundamental and paramount law of the nation," declared in the notable case of *Marbury* v. *Madison* . . . that "It is emphatically the province and duty of the judicial department to say what the law is." This decision declared the basic principle that the federal judiciary is supreme in the exposition of the law of the Constitution, and that principle has ever since been respected by this Court and the Country as a permanent and indispensable feature of our constitutional system. It follows that the interpretation of the Fourteenth Amendment enunciated by this Court in the Brown Case is the supreme law of the land, and Art. VI of the Constitution makes it of binding effect on the States "any Thing in the Constitution or Laws of any State to the Contrary notwithstanding." Every state legislator and executive and judicial officer is solemnly committed by oath taken pursuant to Art. VI, cl. 3 "to support this Constitution." Chief Justice Taney, speaking for a unanimous Court in 1859, said that this requirement reflected the framers' "anxiety to preserve it [the Constitution] in full force, in all its powers, and to guard against resistance to or evasion of its authority, on the part of a State. . . ."

No state legislator or executive or judicial officer can war against the Constitution without violating his undertaking to support it. Chief Justice Marshall spoke for a unanimous Court in saying that: "If the legislatures of the several states may, at will, annul the judgments of the courts of the United States, and destroy the rights acquired under those judgments, the constitution itself becomes a solemn mockery. . . ." A Governor who asserts a power to nullify a federal court order is similarly restrained. If he had such power, said Chief Justice Hughes, in 1932, also for a unanimous Court, "it is manifest that the fiat of a state Governor, and not the Constitution of the United States, would be the supreme law of the land; that the restrictions of the Federal Constitution upon the exercise of state power would be but impotent phrases. . . ."

## IV. APPROACHES TO CONSTITUTIONAL INTERPRETATION

## Unstaged Debate of 1986: *Judge Bork* v. *Professor Tribe*

At the time of this exchange, Robert Bork was a judge on the U.S. Court of Appeals for the District of Columbia Circuit, and Laurence Tribe was Tyler Professor of Constitutional Law at Harvard Law School. In 1987, the Senate rejected President Reagan's nomination of Judge Bork to the Supreme Court. Professor Tribe was one of those who testified at Senate hearings against the nomination.

### ROBERT H. BORK, "ORIGINAL INTENT AND THE CONSTITUTION," 7 *HUMANITIES* 22, 26–27 (FEB. 1986)

. . . The controversy [over original intent] swirls around the question whether judges, who undertake to strike down laws and executive actions in the name of the Constitution, must do so only in accordance with the intentions of those who wrote, proposed, and ratified the Constitution's various provisions. This philosophy of originalism comports with what most people assume judges are, and should be, doing. But it is not what most academic constitutional specialists want of judges and it is apparently not what some judges conceive their function to be. They have evolved a philosophy of non-originalism according to which judges should create individual rights that supersede democratic decisions. . . .

It is argued by some legal theorists that the Constitution's meaning should evolve and that the course of evolution should be determined by moral and political philosophy. It is not entirely clear why this method of changing the document's meaning, if it is legitimate, should be confined to individual freedoms. . . . It could as well be applied to the interpretation of the powers and structures of government laid out in the first three articles of the Constitution. That is rarely, if ever, proposed, probably because it would make embarrassingly clear that the professors are asking judges to remake our form of government. Yet one form of judicial creativity is no more illegitimate than the other. But the problem with the argument goes deeper. There is no single philosophy or method of philosophic reasoning upon which all Americans agree. . . .

Perhaps recognizing these difficulties, other constitutional theorists would have judges apply not philosophical analysis but something more akin to a sense, almost intuitive, of what "our evolving morality" demands at the moment. This idea rests upon the correct observation that a society's morality does evolve and that the American morality of today differs in a number of respects from the American morality of the late eighteenth century. All quite true, but inadequate to support the conclusion. The Constitution's guarantees—freedom of speech, press, and religion; freedom from unreasonable searches and seizures; freedom from required self-incrimination; and much more—remain highly relevant today. Any free society must respect them. No theorist, to my knowledge, suggests that, if American morality evolves so that these freedoms are disliked, judges should abandon them—yet that is what would seem to be required by this approach. Again, however, the trouble goes deeper. To the degree that the morality that is evolving deserves the name of "our morality," it will be embodied in legislation and executive action. There will be no need for judges to tell the society what the society's morality is. Judges who undertake to apply "our evolving morality" to invalidate democratically enacted law will, in truth, be enforcing their own morality upon the rest of us and calling it the Constitution.

These considerations seem to me to leave only the method of original intent as a legitimate means of applying the Constitution. Only that can give us law that is something other than, and superior to, the judge's will. It is objected that the process of discerning the Framers' intentions can be manipulated and that, in any event, it is impossible to know what the Framers would have done in specific cases. Those things are true and, if they are insuperable objections, the only conclusion left is that the Constitution can never be law and judicial review should be abandoned. The objections are by no means fatal, however.

Any system of argument which is complex and involves questions of degree and of judgment is manipulable. Certainly, it will be easier to detect manipulation of historical materials than of philosophic concepts or subjective estimates of contemporary morality. The only ultimate solution is the selection of intellectually honest judges.

The objection that we can never know what the Framers would have done about specific modern situations is entirely beside the point. The originalist attempts to discern the principles the Framers enacted, the values they sought to protect. All that the philosophy of original intention requires is that the text, structure, and history of the Constitution provide the judge not with a conclusion about a specific case but with a premise from which to begin reasoning about that case. For instance, while the Fourth Amendment, when framed, envisioned protection only against unwarranted searches and seizures by physical invasion, its intended prohibition of unreasonable intrusions by the state against the individual can certainly be applied in the context of electronic surveillance. . . .

Adherence to a philosophy of searching for original intent does not mean that judges will invariably decide cases the way the Framers would have, though many cases will be decided that way. At the very least, the originalist philosophy confines judges to areas the Framers assigned to them and reserves to democratic processes those areas of life the Framers placed there. That much is indispensable if judges are not to usurp the legitimate freedom of the people to govern themselves, and no philosophy other than that of original intent can provide that safeguard.

## LAURENCE H. TRIBE, "THE HOLY GRAIL OF ORIGINAL INTENT," 7 *HUMANITIES* 23–25 (FEB. 1986)

. . . In today's highly visible and notably politicized constitutional discourse, a particular version of "history"—what some confidently claim to know our country's Founders and our Constitution's Framers "originally intended"— is offered as the only relevant, and indeed the definitive, source of the true meaning of each provision in the constitutional text. But, by standing on its head Santayana's injunction that those who forget the past are condemned to repeat it, these new "originalists" are busily inventing a particular past that might dictate our constitutional future. In doing so, they are claiming for history a decisive authority that is incompatible with the limits of what we can know and false to the nature of the Constitution itself. . . .

To begin with, the very generality of many of the terms the Framers used—such as "liberty," "due process," and "equal protection"— strongly suggests an intent not to confine their meaning to the specific outcomes and contexts that occurred to those who first used them, but to invite the development of meanings in light of the needs and insights of succeeding generations. . . .

The originalists must accordingly persuade us that their own departure from that overarching original intent is justified—and that it may be coherently pursued despite the often conflicting things that the many who wrote, or voted to ratify, the Constitution's provisions had in mind. And they must, in addition, convince us that their program will succeed in its proclaimed objective of placing the interpretive enterprise beyond the reach of personal predilection and subjective judgment.

For my part, I gravely doubt that the program can come even close to succeeding. Consider the justices who wrote in *Dred Scott* that slaves are mere property, the justices who wrote in *Plessy* [v. *Ferguson,* 1896] that racial separation by law need not deny equality, and the justices who wrote in *Lochner* [v. *New York,* 1905] that laws regulating hours and wages invade "freedom of contract." All of them invoked "original intent" with considerable conviction and plausibility. . . . If one wants to say—as I do, and as . . . Judge Bork seem[s] to—that those cases were wrongly decided, one must do much better than the originalists have yet done to explain away the awkward facts of history that weighed in on the wrong side of those disputes. Nor can the program of the originalists avoid the charge of subjective and even politically motivated selectivity and manipulation when those who advocate it so readily support the constitutionality of eminently sensible and currently indispensable policies that would certainly have shocked those who framed the Constitution and the Bill of Rights—such as "stop and frisk" practices by police in urban areas, the extraction of coerced testimony in response to promises of immunity, and the authorization of police searches for mere evidence of crime as opposed to contraband. Finally, the originalist project can hardly succeed when even its most ardent proponents counsel that some constitutional decisions, even if originally wrong by their own test of the Framers' intent, have become so deeply rooted that it would be neither prudent nor necessary to roll back the clock. . . .

The major difference between those who insist that they are passively discerning and enforcing the specific intentions of the Framers, and those who concede that they are of necessity doing something more, is likely to come down to this: The originalists seek to deny their own responsibility for the choices they are making—and imposing upon the rest of us—whereas their opponents, for better or worse, accept such responsibility as inescapably theirs. . . .

To insist, as I would, that all judicial choices ought to be seriously constrained by constitutional text, structure, and tradition indeed requires one to confess that such choices are never merely the passive products of a single "original intent" existing in history and waiting to be discovered. The danger that judges might wield power in the name of the Constitution but in the service of nothing beyond their personal moral predilections is heightened, not reduced, by the habit of couching judicial determinations in the form of ineluctable readings of a purely external reality. However adorned by scholarly references to history, such claims are far less subject to meaningful dispute, and hence far less constrained by the requirements of persuasion, than are the more modest claims of those who admittedly base their constitutional arguments on a more eclectic, less determinate mix of appeals to language, precedent, and legal philosophy. . . . A candid avowal of the limits of originalism can open the process of constitutional interpretation to the full public debate without which it partakes only of miracle, mystery, and unquestioned authority.

# CHAPTER THREE

# *Congress and the President*

*The doctrine of the separation of powers was adopted by the Convention of 1787, not to promote efficiency but to preclude the exercise of arbitrary power. The purpose was, not to avoid friction, but, by means of the inevitable friction incident to the distribution of the governmental powers among three departments, to save the people from autocracy.*

—Justice Louis D. Brandeis (1926)

The principle of separation of powers, propounded by seventeenth- and eighteenth-century political philosophers Harrington, Locke, and Montesquieu, was a device for limiting government power by taking the ancient lawmaking power from the monarch and vesting it in a legislature. The American development of this doctrine went much further. In place of the traditional division into legislative and executive, the American colonies adopted a threefold division, elevating the judiciary to coequal position and putting all three under the rule of law established by a written constitution.

## SEPARATION OF POWERS

The federal Constitution contains no specific declaration concerning **separation of powers.** The principle is implicit in the organization of the first three articles: (1) "All legislative powers herein granted shall be vested in a Congress of the United States"; (2) "The executive power shall be vested in a President of the United States"; (3) "The judicial power shall be vested in one Supreme Court and in such inferior courts as the congress shall . . . ordain and establish." From this separation is derived the doctrine that certain functions, because of their essential nature, may properly be exercised by only a particular branch of the government; that such functions cannot be delegated to any other branch; and that one department may not interfere with another by usurping its powers or by supervising their exercise. Separation of powers was endorsed with virtual unanimity at the Convention of 1787. Inherited from Montesquieu, the concept is inspired by the conviction that "every man vested with power is apt to abuse it; and carry his authority as far as it will go." One objective of the Constitution, therefore, was to avoid the "accumulation of all powers, legislative, executive, and judiciary, in the same hands, whether of one, a few, or many, and whether hereditary, self-appointed, or elective." Such concentration declared James Madison in *The Federalist,* No. 47, "may justly be pronounced the very definition of tyranny."

**SHARING WITHIN SEPARATION.** Separation of powers, however, is a misnomer. No precise line is, or could be, drawn between the three branches of the national government. The Constitution separates organs of government; it fuses functions and powers. Because of frequently voiced criticism of the blending of executive, legislative, and judiciary in the proposed Constitution, Madison felt compelled to restate the traditional theory. The sharing of powers through the scheme of **checks and balances** was, he explained, a valuable additional restraint on government that complemented the principle of separation of powers. Not only did the blending of powers limit government itself, but it also provided weapons by which each branch could defend its position in the constitutional system. The president's veto, it was urged, protected him against legislative encroachments, and his power of appointment gave him influence against judicial assault. The Court had the power to pass on legislation and was protected by life tenure. The Congress could impeach a president and members of the Court. The national lawmakers controlled the purse on which both the other departments depended, the Senate passed on presidential appointments, and the Congress controlled the appellate jurisdiction of the Supreme Court. The legislature may exercise the executive power of pardon in the form of a grant of amnesty or immunity from prosecution. It may punish contempts and may provide in minute detail the rules of procedure to be followed by the courts. The power of Congress to control the issuance of injunctions by federal courts and to restrict their power to punish disobedience has also been sustained. Although the courts do not legislate in the strict sense of the word, their decisions may be regarded from a realistic point of view as a form of lawmaking. As upheld in *Morrison* **v.** *Olson* (1988) the courts, within limits, may exercise the executive power of appointment; and Congress may confer on them the power to suspend sentence, even though such power is legislative in nature. The president's power over foreign relations is such that the functions of advising and consenting to treaties and of "declaring" war, apparently entrusted by the Constitution to the legislature, have come largely under his control. Executive officers and administrative agencies also exercise functions that belong to other departments. Thus, independent regulatory commissions and the cabinet departments themselves exercise legislative and judicial powers through rule-making and adjudication.

**TWO APPROACHES.** In confronting a claim that a policy violates the principle of separation of powers, justices today tend to adopt one of two approaches. The first is tolerant of structural arrangements Congress deems to be in the public interest. It sees relationships among the branches as fluid. Because the Constitution already permits each branch to share some of the functions of the others, the words of the Constitution itself should not be read literally to preclude useful variations. The second finds within the Constitution a series of structural directives, which are not to be transgressed. In this approach, the Constitution purposely commands separate compartments, nearly hermetically sealed from each other. Exceptions include only those the Constitution itself allows.

## CONGRESS AND LAWMAKING

Created nearly full-blown by Article I, Congress is sometimes called "the first branch" or "the people's branch." Few legislative bodies elsewhere in the world possess greater authority over the lives, property, and happiness of a nation. Yet much of the policy leadership that many of the framers expected from Congress and that Congress exercised during most of the nineteenth century has shifted into the executive branch.

**DELEGATION.** In many cases, however, the statutes Congress passes cannot be so detailed as to contain every regulation and form of procedure by which the legislative policies set forth in them are to be carried out. The courts have consequently recognized that administrative officers must be permitted some discretion to determine when a given statute shall become operative and to fill in the details through appropriate regulations. This sharing of rule-making authority is called **delegation.** In such situations, Chief Justice Taft explained in *Hampton & Co.* v. *United States* (1928), Congress must "lay down by legislative act an *intelligible principle* to which the person or body authorized to [act] is directed to conform" [emphasis added].

Only twice has the Supreme Court invalidated a statute as an unconstitutional delegation of power to the executive, both in 1935. A provision of the National Industrial Recovery Act authorizing the president to prohibit the interstate shipment of oil produced or withdrawn in violation of state regulations was struck down in *Panama Refining Co.* v. *Ryan* (Hot Oil Case) because of the absence of guidance for the exercise of discretion. Then *Schechter Poultry Corp.* v. *United States* condemned the same statute's delegation to the president of code-approving authority. The president's discretion, the Court said, was "virtually unfettered," and Cardozo, in a concurring opinion, termed it "delegation run riot." Ordinarily, however, the Court regards even rather vague standards as sufficiently definite. *Yakus* v. *United States* (1944), for example, sustained wartime price-fixing authority to the Office of Price Administration, even though Congress's guidance to the regulators stipulated only that prices be "fair and equitable." *Whitman* v. *American Trucking Association* (2001) upheld the Environmental Protection Agency's National Air Quality Standards. The Clean Air Act directed the administrator of the EPA to set "ambient air quality standards the attainment and maintenance of which . . . , and allowing an adequate margin of safety, are requisite to protect the public health."

***Mistretta* v. *United States*** (1989), which challenged the constitutionality of the Sentencing Reform Act of 1984, illustrates allegations of improper delegation. The statute empowers the U.S. Sentencing Commission (an independent body lodged in the judicial branch) to promulgate binding guidelines for federal judges, including a range of determinate sentences for all categories of federal crimes and defendants. The majority "harbor[ed] no doubt" that the nondelegation principle had not been transgressed. It was "constitutionally sufficient if Congress clearly delineates the general policy, the public agency which is to apply it, and the boundaries of this delegated authority." For dissenting Justice Scalia, however, the majority missed the point. The commission was flawed because it existed only to make law, not to make law incidentally to carrying out executive or judicial functions. In short, it was a "junior-varsity Congress."

**LEGISLATIVE VETO.** The delegation cases point to the fact that much "legislation" today is not enacted by Congress but is promulgated by dozens of administrative agencies. "The rise of administrative bodies probably has been the most significant legal trend of the last century," observed Justice Jackson in 1952. "They have become a veritable fourth branch of the Government. . . ." To control these agencies, Congress wrote nearly 300 "veto" provisions into about 200 statutes between 1932 and 1983, with about half of those enacted after 1970. This **legislative veto** enabled Congress to have its cake and eat it too. Agencies could continue making rules, but Congress could set aside such regulations by a one-house, a two-house, or even a committee resolution. Of course, such "vetoes" were not subject to presidential vetoes, and here lay the rub. Congress seemed to be making law other than in the constitutionally prescribed fashion, as the Court held in ***Immigration and Naturalization Service* v. *Chadha*** (1983). Although generous in allowing delegated rule-making, the justices were unwilling to allow this method of controlling it. *Chadha* has frustrated Congress's efforts to keep control of the many agencies to which it has delegated rule-making authority. One response has been the Congressional Review Act of 1996 that requires agencies to send their final regulations to Congress for review 60 days before they take effect. A regulation is negated within the review period if Congress passes a joint resolution of disapproval and if the president signs it. The resolution is subject to presidential veto, which requires a two-thirds vote by both houses to override. As a result, agencies may still craft rules and regulations that could not garner a congressional majority. Through mid-2003, only one joint resolution of disapproval had been passed.

**THE SHORT-LIVED ITEM VETO.** When Congress passes a bill, the president must accept or reject the bill in its entirely. American presidents have lacked a power enjoyed by some state governors: the **item veto,** which allows an executive to cross out certain provisions *within* a bill. To be sure, a president could enjoy an item veto by way of constitutional amendment, but could Congress provide something akin to an item veto by statute? In 1996 Congress passed legislation allowing the president to cancel specific items within appropriations and tax bills within five days after signing the bill into law. Congress might reinsert the items by passing a "disapproval bill," but this would be subject to the president's regular veto, which could be overridden only by a two-thirds vote in both houses. Certain senators and representatives who believed the law unwisely strengthened the presidency at Congress's expense challenged the constitutionality of the item veto. In *Raines* v. *Byrd* (1997), the Supreme Court dismissed the suit because members of Congress had not "alleged a sufficiently concrete injury to have established Article III standing." Asserting an institutional injury as against the executive did not give them standing, for, individually, no member of Congress had been harmed by the law. Within two months of this decision, President Clinton canceled numerous items in bills passed by Congress, including provisions which would have benefitted two hospitals in New York City and a potato farmers' cooperative. With demonstrable individual injury, the aggrieved parties renewed the attack. Voting 6 to 3, the Court held in ***Clinton* v. *City of New York*** (1998) that the item veto act violated the Constitution. "If there is to be a new procedure in which the President will play a different role in determining the final text of what may 'become a law,'" wrote Justice Stevens, "such change must come not by legislation but through the amendment procedures set forth in Article V of the Constitution."

**INVESTIGATIONS.** A function of Congress vying in importance with lawmaking itself is investigation. Woodrow Wilson rated the "informing function" higher than that of legislation. "[T]he power of inquiry," maintained Justice Van Devanter in *McGrain* v. *Daugherty* (1927), "with process to enforce it—is an essential and appropriate auxiliary to the legislative function." In 1936 Senator Hugo L. Black, who the next year became a Supreme Court justice, referred to congressional investigations as "among the most useful and fruitful functions of the national legislature." Though derived immediately from the "necessary and proper" clause, the investigatory power is also grounded in the fact that Congress, like Parliament and the early state legislatures, is a deliberative body. Each house, separately or concurrently, may pass resolutions expressing its views on any subject it sees fit. To inform itself on matters likely to become subjects of legislation, Congress establishes committees that may **subpoena** witnesses (that is, compel their attendance) and take testimony. If witnesses refuse to cooperate, they may be punished for contempt. Such imprisonment, however, may not extend beyond the session of Congress in which the offense was committed, and any investigation must be related to a valid legislative purpose (*Kilbourn* v. *Thompson,* 1881).

During the Cold War, ***Watkins* v. *United States*** (1957) questioned the authority of either house to delve into the private lives of individuals—to "expose for the sake of exposure" or to deny freedom of speech or right of association. The 6–1 majority agreed that the power to conduct investigations "is inherent in the legislative process" but insisted that as a matter of due process of law all witnesses must be informed of the pertinency of the questions put to them. Accordingly, the Court overturned Watkins's conviction for contempt of Congress after the labor organizer refused to answer questions about the political views of associates. Reaction to the decision both in and out of Congress was hotly critical. Two years later, by construing *Watkins* narrowly, ***Barenblatt* v. *United States*** reached a different result. Five justices affirmed the conviction of a former Vassar College professor for failure to answer questions about past affiliation with the Communist Party.

**MEMBERSHIP AND PRIVILEGE.** On March 1, 1967, the House of Representatives voted to exclude recently reelected Congressman Adam Clayton Powell on the ground that he had misused public funds and was contemptuous of the New York courts and committees of Congress. By a vote of 7–1 (*Powell* v. *McCormack*), the Supreme Court held in 1969 that the House lacked power to exclude from its membership a person duly elected who meets the age, citizenship, and residence requirements specified in the Constitution. **Exclusion,** however, must not be confused with **expulsion.** The first refers to barring representatives from taking their seats; the second is a penalty for members judged by their colleagues to be guilty of extremely serious misconduct. In Chief Justice Warren's last major opinion, the Court reversed the opinion of Appeals Judge Warren E. Burger, the person nominated to succeed him. Invoking separation of powers, Burger had dismissed Powell's suit for reinstatement, contending that courts should not rule on a political issue fraught with possible conflict between Congress and courts. Warren disagreed: "A fundamental principle of our representative democracy is . . . 'that the people should choose whom they please to govern them. . . .' [T]his principle is undermined as much by limiting whom the people can elect as by limiting the franchise itself."

The Court has also declined to allow Congress to be the sole judge of the scope of the privilege enshrined in the **speech or debate clause** of the Constitution. The protection against being "questioned in any other Place" is a pillar of legislative independence. It extends "not only to a member but also to his aides insofar as the conduct of the latter would be a protected legislative act if performed by the member himself" (*Gravel* v. *United States,* 1972). Critical to the scope of the privilege is the definition of a "protected legislative act," by no means an all-inclusive term. Such protection extends to voting and preparing committee reports but not to newsletters and press releases, declared the Court in *Hutchinson* v. *Proxmire* (1979). Senator William Proxmire's "Golden Fleece of the Month Award" had ridiculed a researcher for studies done on animals. In a newsletter the senator claimed that the research had "made a monkey out of the American taxpayer." Without the protection of the speech or debate clause, the Court ruled that Proxmire could be sued for damages.

## THE PRESIDENT AND EXECUTIVE POWER

Addressing himself to the executive in *The Federalist,* No. 70, Alexander Hamilton rejected the widely held belief of his day that "a vigorous executive is inconsistent with the genius of republican government." On the contrary, he insisted,

> Energy in the Executive is a leading character in the definition of good government. It is essential to the protection of the community against foreign attacks; it is not less essential to the steady administration of the laws; to the protection of property against those irregular and high-handed combinations which sometimes interrupt the ordinary course of justice; to the security of liberty against the enterprises and assaults of ambition, of faction, and of anarchy. A feeble executive implies a feeble execution of the government. A feeble execution is but another phrase for a bad execution; and a government ill executed, whatever it may be in theory, must be, in practice, a bad government.

Members of the Convention of 1787 who feared that the president inevitably would succumb to an all-powerful legislature have proved to be poor prophets. Of the three branches of government, it is the presidency that has expanded most in power and in the number and variety of its activities. War, economic crisis, the increasing complexity of problems, and advances in communication have combined to thrust obligations on the executive not contemplated in an earlier age. While this swelling of executive authority is hardly unique to America, few, if any, chief executives of other democratic countries command a more impressive array of powers. "[T]he history of the presidency has been a history of aggrandizement," wrote Professor Edward Corwin in 1941. The president is both head of state and the political head of the government; he is responsible for executing the laws. He exercises the power to pardon, the power to appoint, the veto power, and extensive war powers, and directs foreign policy. Only since 1970 has Congress taken steps to reverse the trend toward presidential dominance.

**THEORIES OF PRESIDENTIAL POWER.** Three strikingly divergent views purport to describe the nature and scope of presidential power: the **constitutional theory,** the **stewardship theory,** and the **prerogative theory.** As William Howard Taft explained in his book, *Our Chief Magistrate and His Powers,* three years after leaving the White House, the constitutional theory holds that Article II contains an enumeration of executive powers and that the president must be prepared to justify all his actions on the basis of either enumerated or implied power. Theodore Roosevelt countered that the president is a "steward of the people," and is therefore under the duty to do "anything that the needs of the nation demanded unless such action was forbidden by the Constitution and the laws." Taft denounced Roosevelt's theory as calculated to make the president a "universal Providence." As chief justice, however, he indicated greater sympathy for it. Going beyond the first Roosevelt's stewardship theory, Franklin D. Roosevelt's concept of his duties conforms essentially to John Locke's description of "prerogative"—"the power to act according to discretion for the public good, without the prescription of the law and sometimes even against it." During his long incumbency, President Roosevelt often sacrificed constitutional and legal restrictions on the altar of "emergency" and a commanding public interest.

Parts of Justice Sutherland's opinion in ***United States v. Curtiss-Wright Export Corp.*** (1936) seem to justify "inherent" power, at least in foreign affairs, where the president speaks and acts for the nation. In the domestic sphere, however, this is a highly dubious rationale for presidential action, even in wartime, as ***Youngstown Sheet & Tube Co. v. Sawyer*** (1952) suggests. When the Steel Seizure Case was before the District Court, counsel for the United States, asked by the bench to specify the source of the president's power to seize the steel mills in peacetime, declared, "We base the President's power on Sections 1, 2, and 3 of Article II of the Constitution, and whatever inherent, implied or residual powers may flow therefrom." "So you contend the Executive has unlimited power in time of an emergency?" the judge inquired. Government counsel replied that the president "has the power to take such action as is necessary to meet the emergency" and indicated that the only limitations on executive power in an emergency are the ballot box and impeachment. In argument before the Supreme Court, however, government counsel stressed that the president's specific powers derived from the duty to execute the laws and as commander in chief.

**EXECUTIVE PRIVILEGE.** On July 24, 1974, ***United States v. Nixon*** held that the president himself must respond to a subpoena issued in connection with a pending trial of former government officials. Although expressly acknowledging **executive privilege** for the first time—the right of certain officials in the executive branch to refuse to appear before Congress and the courts and to provide requested documents—the justices ruled that neither the doctrine of separation of powers nor the need for confidentiality of executive communications barred the federal courts from access to White House audiotapes needed as evidence in a criminal case. In constitutional theory and political consequences, the decision remains among the most remarkable in the Court's history. Within days President Nixon complied, and the tapes linked him to a conspiracy to obstruct justice. On August 9, Nixon became the first president to leave office by resignation.

**APPOINTMENT AND REMOVAL OF OFFICERS.** The Constitution provides that the president "shall nominate and, by and with the advice and consent of the Senate, shall appoint ambassadors . . . judges of the Supreme Court, and all other officers of the United States, whose appointments are not herein otherwise provided for and which shall be established by law. . . ." The Constitution makes no provision for the removal of officers appointed under this clause, but the power of removal is generally regarded as a power derived from the power to appoint. Following the decision of *Myers* v. *United States* (1926), it was generally thought that the power of the president to remove officials appointed by him was plenary, free from any limitations by Congress. In that case the Court upheld Woodrow Wilson's removal of a presidentially appointed (and Senate-confirmed) postmaster, even though a statute allowed removal during the four-year term only with Senate approval. In 1935, however, the Court whittled down the broad rule, holding that the removal of officials from certain independent agencies, such as the Federal Trade Commission, could be limited to causes defined by Congress (*Humphrey's Executor* v. *United States*). The Court distinguished positions in the traditional executive departments, for whose administration the president assumed primary responsibility, from those in agencies established by Congress to carry out legislative policy essentially free from any executive influence other than that resulting from appointment.

Questions of appointment and removal and separation of powers combined in **Morrison v. Olson** (1988). The politically charged case challenged the provision in the Ethics in Government Act of 1978 for an **independent counsel** to investigate criminal wrongdoing by high officials in the executive branch. Under the terms of the statute, upon receiving information suggesting criminal conduct, the attorney general conducted a preliminary inquiry and then could refer the matter to a division of the Court of Appeals for the District of Columbia Circuit. This division appointed the independent counsel. Once named, the independent counsel could be removed only for cause, and the removal was subject to judicial review. The independent counsel possessed the full investigative and prosecutorial functions of the Department of Justice with respect to the matters within the scope of the referral. In essence Congress decreed that criminal investigation at the highest levels be done by an attorney not subject to routine control by the attorney general and the president.

Looking back to *Myers* (which recognized broad removal power) and to *Humphrey's Executor* (which narrowed the removal power), eight justices agreed that Congress could place the independent counsel under the terms of the latter. Counsel's independence from the executive branch, Chief Justice Rehnquist explained, did not impermissibly interfere "with the President's exercise of his constitutionally appointed functions." The Court faced two conflicting views of separation of powers. One allowed some blurring of distinctions among the branches in order to retain an additional check in the scheme of checks and balances. The other maintained the hierarchical integrity of a branch limited ultimately only by the people through the ballot box and Congress through impeachment. Choosing the first, the majority effected "a revolution in our constitutional jurisprudence," Justice Scalia charged in his lone dissent. To take away prosecutorial discretion from the president is "to remove the core of the prosecutorial function"—"a quintessentially executive function."

The statute was allowed to expire in December 1992. Retaining the basic features of the previous version, Congress revived the law in 1994 for a period of five years. In 1999, Republicans and Democrats alike allowed the statute to expire again. The attorney general, acting for the president, may still name a **special prosecutor** in circumstances that, before, might have called for an independent counsel. But a special prosecutor, like any other federal prosecutor, is not only appointed by, but serves at the pleasure of, the president.

**IMMUNITY.** If presidents may have the constitutionality of their policies challenged in court, under what circumstances may a president be subjected to personal lawsuits because of a disregard of legal and constitutional limits? In 1982 **Nixon v. Fitzgerald** bestowed on the president an **absolute immunity** (shared also by federal judges and prosecutors) from private lawsuit that extends to all acts within "the outer perimeter" of his official duties even where, as in this instance, the suit was not commenced until after Nixon resigned. The immunity is a "functionally mandated incident of his unique office," declared Justice Powell for a majority of five, "rooted in the constitutional tradition of the separation of powers and supported by the Nation's history." Other checks such as the impeachment remedy, the availability of congressional and public oversight, and concern for one's "place in history" would presumably suffice as guards against presidential wrongdoing. Presidential aides, however, do not enjoy the same unqualified protection. Instead, theirs is a good-faith or **qualified immunity,** shielding them from damage suits as long as their conduct does not violate "clearly established" statutory or constitutional rights of which a reasonable person would have known (*Harlow* v. *Fitzgerald,* 1982).

*Fitzgerald's* broad declaration of civil immunity, however, does not extend to a White House incumbent sued for actions predating his presidency. In 1997 ***Clinton v. Jones*** unanimously rejected President Clinton's request that litigation against him by Paula Jones for sexual harassment be postponed until completion of his second term. The suit grew out of events alleged to have occurred while Clinton was governor of Arkansas. *Jones* turned aside Clinton's argument that allowing the suit to proceed would breach separation of powers by placing the president's schedule in judicial hands. Emphasizing that a trial judge would be expected to be sensitive to competing demands on the president's time, the Court made clear the basis of the immunity recognized in *Fitzgerald.* The latter's immunity exists not because the president is "too busy" but because the threat of personal civil liability might inhibit a president from making crucial decisions. As explained in the introductory chapter, legal proceedings in the Jones suit following the Supreme Court's decision took an ironic turn. They became caught up in an investigation already underway by independent counsel Kenneth Starr, leading eventually to Clinton's impeachment by the House of Representatives in 1998 and his trial and acquittal in the Senate in 1999.

## FOREIGN POLICY AND NATIONAL SECURITY

Recent presidents have enjoyed considerably more independence in shaping foreign, as opposed to domestic, policy. When applied abroad, presidential power is limited by Congress only with some difficulty, mainly by congressional control of the purse, approval of trade agreements, and the power to investigate. Even with those restraints, however, the making of foreign and defense policy remains a shared responsibility.

**TREATIES.** Under the Constitution, the executive branch negotiates treaties, but all treaties must receive the consent of two-thirds of the Senate. Once approved, a treaty may then be the basis of implementing legislation that otherwise would not be within the power of Congress. This is the significance of ***Missouri* v. *Holland.*** Congress as well may by statute alter or negate the effect of a treaty on domestic law. However, the tendency of modern presidents has been to use **executive agreements** in place of treaties, thus freeing them from dependency on the Senate. Under *United States* v. *Belmont* (1937) and *United States* v. *Pink* (1942), such agreements have the same legal effect as treaties. Strengthening the president's hand in foreign policy is the theory of sovereignty set forth in Justice Sutherland's opinion in *Curtiss-Wright* and the great reservoir of inherent power possessed by the president as representative of the United States in dealing with other nations.

**MILITARY POWERS.** The power of the federal government over the armed forces of the nation is also divided between the president and Congress. The legislature is given the important powers to "declare war," to raise armies and provide a navy, and to make "rules for the government and regulation" of the armed forces. The president is designated commander in chief of the armed forces. He may issue regulations of his own and may take charge of all military operations in time of peace as well as in war.

The framers thus made war making a joint enterprise. At the urging of James Madison and Elbridge Gerry, the Convention changed the original phrase from "make war" to "declare war." In changing this language, the framers presumably intended to allow the president the authority to repel sudden attacks on the United States, its territories, or its armed forces. The commander-in-chief clause seems to have been designed not to alter this relationship nor to grant the president additional war-making powers. Rather, the clause established the principle of civilian control over the military. The president was to be, in Hamilton's words, "the first general and admiral." Presidents, however, have used their powers to control the armed forces to manipulate Congress and, to some extent, to preempt the war power itself. Technology has expanded the president's role and correspondingly curtailed the power of Congress. Only since 1970 have legislators attempted to regain their constitutional share of war making or war avoiding. Practice changes the working meaning of the Constitution.

Two contrasting approaches by presidents to the problem of waging war can be found in American history. Under Lincoln, Congress was ignored or asked to ratify executive actions already accomplished or under way. For example, on April 19, 1861, Lincoln ordered a blockade of Confederate ports; on July 13 Congress authorized the president to declare that a state of insurrection existed and on August 6 voted to ratify retroactively the military decisions that Lincoln had made. Claiming the president had acted unlawfully, owners of four vessels seized before July 13 sued to recover their property. Could the president impose a blockade without congressional authorization? Was an insurrection—the Lincoln administration refused to recognize the Confederacy as a separate country—a "war," to which the rules of prize applied? The Prize Cases (1863) upheld both Lincoln's theory of the war and his authority to act without Congress. The Court, Justice Grier explained for a majority of five, could not be asked "to affect a technical ignorance of the existence of a war, which all the world acknowledges to be the greatest civil war known in the history of the human race." In World Wars I and II, by contrast, Congress passed a vast number of general statutes of wide scope assigning to the president, or to persons designated by him, vast discretionary powers. The broadest of these delegations was upheld in *Bowles* v. *Willingham* (1944).

**VIETNAM AND THE WAR POWERS RESOLUTION.** In the face of rising public protest against the undeclared Vietnam war, Congress enacted (over President Nixon's veto) the **War Powers Resolution,** designed to curb presidential discretion in committing the armed forces of the nation to combat. The 1973 resolution was a far cry from the Gulf of Tonkin Resolution of 1964, passed early in the Vietnam conflict, which declared "that Congress approves and supports the determination of the President as commander-in-chief, to take all necessary measures to repel any armed attack against the forces of the United States and to prevent further aggression." President Lyndon Johnson viewed the Tonkin Resolution as the functional equivalent of a declaration of war.

In contrast, according to the War Powers Resolution, whenever military action takes place without prior congressional approval, the president is supposed to consult with Congress whenever possible before committing troops, and in any event he is supposed to inform Congress of what he has done within 48 hours. Unless Congress authorizes continued action, use of troops must cease after 60 days. Furthermore, by concurrent resolution (not subject to presidential veto) Congress may order the president to withdraw the troops from combat. *Chadha* casts doubt on the constitutionality of this legislative veto.

Experience since 1973 demonstrates that the War Powers Resolution is not itself a significant restraint on presidential power. Most presidents have considered the act unconstitutional and have generally failed to "invoke" the act by claiming the law does not apply to military operations they have initiated. They report to Congress "consistent with," not "pursuant to," the terms of the resolution. When presidents do turn to Congress for authorization to use force, it is more often because of the political support the authorization provides than any obligation to the War Powers Resolution itself. Moreover, Congress has yet to display sufficient political will to ensure compliance.

**IRAQ (I).** Iraq's invasion of Kuwait in August 1990 and the American response to it rekindled debate on the president's war powers. After President George H. W. Bush sent 230,000 military personnel to the Persian Gulf region, and after the United Nations Security Council imposed a number of economic sanctions and a blockade against Iraq, both houses of Congress in October passed resolutions supporting the action. On November 8, however, Bush ordered a doubling of U.S. military forces to provide an offensive capability. The Security Council then passed Resolution 678 on November 29 authorizing "all necessary means" to force Iraqi troops from Kuwait should they not withdraw by January 15, 1991. All along, the president claimed authority to launch an attack without congressional approval, so initially he did not request congressional approval, and Congress ventured to offer none. However, on January 8, 1991, Bush formally requested a congressional resolution authorizing the use of force, although he told reporters, "I don't think I need it." On January 12, after vigorous debate, the Senate and the House gave the president the approval he sought. The occasion was historic. It was the first time since World War II that Congress directly debated ahead of time the sending of thousands of American troops into combat. It was also the first request by a president for approval of the use of force since the Gulf of Tonkin Resolution in 1964. Did President Bush blink? In requesting the resolution, was he effectively acknowledging that he lacked constitutional authority to wage war against Iraq unless Congress first approved? Perhaps. Or perhaps Bush had requested only political support, not constitutional authority, recognizing that symbolically the vote placed him in a much stronger position.

**YUGOSLAVIA.** On March 24, 1999, at President Clinton's direction, U.S. military forces commenced NATO-coordinated air and cruise missile attacks on targets in Yugoslavia, in an effort to dislodge hostile troops from the province of Kosovo and to prevent atrocities. On March 26, Clinton reported the action to Congress "consistent with the War Powers Resolution," asserting that he had "taken these actions pursuant to [his] authority as Commander in Chief and Chief Executive." On April 28, Congress sent mixed signals as it voted on four measures related to the hostilities. The House voted 427 to 2 against a declaration of war, and divided 213 to 213 on an "authorization" of the air campaign. A resolution requiring an immediate end to U.S. participation failed to pass, but emergency funding was approved. On June 10, the Yugoslav government agreed to withdraw its forces from Kosovo and to allow deployment of NATO peacekeepers.

Some 60 days into the conflict, 31 members of Congress filed suit in district court seeking a declaratory judgment that the president's actions were unlawful under both the war powers clause of the Constitution and the War Powers Resolution. According to both the district court and, on appeal, the D.C. Circuit Court of Appeals, members of Congress lacked standing to contest Clinton's actions judicially. *Raines* v. *Byrd,* noted above in connection with the item veto, was controlling. Personal injury to members of Congress, not institutional injury, was required. Moreover Congress had a wide range of "self-help" measures at its disposal to stop the war (*Campbell* v. *Clinton,* 1999 and 2000). *Campbell's* application of *Raines* to war powers disputes between Congress and the president suggests that they may now be entirely nonjusticiable.

**THE WAR ON TERRORISM, AFGHANISTAN, AND IRAQ (II).** The terrorist attacks on the United States on September 11, 2001, profoundly changed America. Politically, the attacks transformed the presidency of George W. Bush. Constitutionally, they strengthened the executive branch, in the short term at least, because of large-scale military actions, passage of the Patriot Act, and a heightened sense of danger of other attacks that might be far worse than those of September 11. At the outset, perhaps due to the trauma of September 11, the military initiatives that ensued had a degree of formal congressional support that has been uncommon since the end of the Vietnam War. To be sure, there was skepticism aplenty about the wisdom of the Bush administration's military policy, but a minimum of doubt in Congress about its constitutional validity. Yet, among other costs, some civil liberties have been placed at risk. These concerns and the Patriot Act itself are addressed in Chapter Fifteen: "Security and Freedom in Wartime."

The foundation of the initial military response was laid on September 18, 2001, when Congress approved Senate Joint Resolution 23 (115 Stat. 2241), which was tantamount to a declaration of war on terrorists. With its words constituting "specific statutory authorization within the meaning of section 5 (b) of the War Powers Resolution,"

> the President is authorized to use all necessary and appropriate force against those nations, organizations, or persons he determines planned, authorized, committed, or aided the terrorist attacks that occurred on September 11, 2001, or harbored such organizations or persons, in order to prevent any future acts of international terrorism against the United States by such nations, organizations or persons.

An attack on Afghanistan commenced on October 8, followed by an invasion by American and British forces. The objective was to root out, disrupt, and destroy the al Quaeda terrorist network that was using Afghanistan as one of its bases of operation, to topple the terrorist-friendly Taliban government, and to replace it with one hostile to terrorism. Organized military resistance to the American-led coalition forces had dissolved by November 25. Several hundred Taliban and al Qaeda fighters who had been captured were later transferred for detention and questioning to the U.S. naval base at Guantanamo Bay, Cuba, where they remain.

In the summer of 2002, President Bush and his national security advisers became convinced that Iraq posed an imminent danger not only to the Persian Gulf region but to the United States. Although intermittently subjected to inspections by United Nations officials since the end of the first Iraq war, Iraq, it was feared, still possessed biological, chemical, and/or radiological weapons in violation of several Security Council resolutions and was prepared to transfer them to terrorists who would then attack the United States. What was needed was not merely a disarmed Iraq but a disarmed Iraq without its dictator—Saddam Hussein.

On October 16, Congress gave the president the statutory authority to move ahead. Noting that it constituted "specific statutory authorization within the meaning of section 5 (b) of the War Powers Resolution," House Joint Resolution 114 (116 Stat. 1498) authorized the president to use military force against Iraq if he concluded that

> (1) reliance by the United States on further diplomatic or other peaceful means alone either (a) will not adequately protect the national security of the United States against the continuing threat posed by Iraq, or (b) is not likely to lead to enforcement of all

relevant United Nations Security Council resolutions regarding Iraq; and (2) acting pursuant to this joint resolution is consistent with the United States and other countries continuing to take the necessary actions against international terrorists and terrorist organizations, including those nations, organizations, or persons who planned, authorized, committed or aided the terrorist attacks that occurred on September 11, 2001.

After lengthy, and often bitter, diplomatic efforts failed to obtain the blessing either of the United Nations or of most other major countries for an attack on Iraq at this time, the United States, joined by the United Kingdom and a handful of minor allies, again went to war. Air strikes opened the campaign on March 20, 2003, and were quickly followed by an invasion of ground troops. Three weeks later, U.S. forces were in Baghdad, and the Hussein regime had fallen. By May 1, resistance by organized Iraqi units had ended. A protracted and dangerous American-directed occupation of Iraq began.

The power to wage war thus remains constitutionally indeterminate. The president is under a positive obligation "to take care that the laws be faithfully executed." His power must be adapted to changed and changing conditions. But, in fulfilling this responsibility, he must also take into account those principles and provisions of the Constitution that restrict as well as enlarge his powers. Likewise, Congress's share in war making must be adapted to unforeseen developments. Otherwise, technological evolution will vastly alter the constitutional balance. The power of Congress in this sensitive area was not meant to cripple and impede; it was designed to produce a wiser course of action. Sound in 1787, it is no less so today.

## KEY TERMS

| | | |
|---|---|---|
| separation of powers | expulsion | special prosecutor |
| checks and balances | speech or debate clause | absolute immunity |
| delegation | constitutional theory | qualified immunity |
| legislative veto | stewardship theory | executive agreement |
| subpoena | prerogative theory | War Powers Resolution |
| item veto | executive privilege | |
| exclusion | independent counsel | |

## QUERIES

**1.** Consider *City of Boerne* v. *Flores* (1997) from Chapter Two alongside *Missouri* v. *Holland* below. Does the latter suggest a way by which the Religious Freedom Restoration Act might itself be restored? In "The Global Dimensions of RFRA," [14 *Constitutional Commentary* 33 (1997)], Gerald L. Neuman calls attention to the International Covenant on Civil and Political Rights (CCPR) to which the United States became a party in 1992. Among the provisions that member states agree to implement is Article 18, which offers protection, among other things, for one "to manifest his religion or belief in worship, observance, practice and teaching." Limitations on the right are to be permitted only where "necessary to protect public safety, order, health, or morals or the fundamental rights and freedoms of others."

**2.** Plainly, the Supreme Court's decision in *United States* v. *Nixon* was a defeat for President Nixon. Yet, was it also at least a partial victory for the presidency?

**3.** Writing three years after leaving the White House, President Harry Truman argued that "the President . . . must always act in a national emergency . . . [He] must be able to act at all times to meet any sudden threat to the nation's security." Did the majority in the Steel Seizure Case reject this position? What is the relevance of Truman's comment for the war on terrorism?

**4.** Does the aftermath of *Clinton* v. *Jones* carry its own refutation of one of the controlling assumptions behind the Court's categorical rejection of even temporary immunity for a president facing a civil suit for unofficial conduct? Tinsley Yarbrough notes that "those providing financial support and legal representation for [Jones] were staunch opponents of President Clinton's position on . . . controversial issues. . . . Presidential fears of civil liability in such cases would appear at least as likely to inhibit a president in the fearless and effective performance of his duties as a suit directed at official misconduct" [*The Rehnquist Court and the Constitution* (New York: Oxford University Press, 2000), p. 82].

## SELECTED READINGS

BARBER, S. A. *The Constitution and the Delegation of Congressional Power.* Chicago: University of Chicago Press, 1975.

BERGER, RAOUL. *Executive Privilege.* Cambridge, Mass.: Harvard University Press, 1974.

CORWIN, EDWARD S. *The President, Office and Powers,* 4th ed. New York: New York University Press, 1957.

CRAIG, BARBARA HINKSON. *Chadha.* New York: Oxford University Press, 1988.

FISHER, LOUIS. *Constitutional Conflicts Between Congress and the President,* 4th ed. Lawrence: University Press of Kansas, 1997.

———. *Congressional Abdication on War and Spending.* College Station: Texas A&M University Press, 2000.

HENKIN, LOUIS. *Foreign Affairs and the Constitution,* 2d ed. New York: Oxford University Press, 1997.

KORN, JESSICA. *The Power of Separation.* Princeton, N.J.: Princeton University Press, 1996.

LEHMAN, JOHN. *Making War: The Battle for Jurisdiction Between the President and Congress from the Time of the Barbary Pirates to Desert Storm.* New York: Scribner's, 1992.

MARCUS, MAEVA. *Truman and the Steel Seizure Case.* New York: Columbia University Press, 1977.

RANDALL, J. G. *Constitutional Problems Under Lincoln,* rev. ed. Urbana: University of Illinois Press, 1951.

# I. DELEGATION AND LAWMAKING

## *Mistretta v. United States*
### 488 U.S. 361, 109 S.Ct. 647, 102 L.Ed. 2d 714 (1989)
http://laws.findlaw.com/us/488/361.html

Because of serious disparities among sentences imposed by federal judges upon similarly situated offenders, Congress passed the Sentencing Reform Act of 1984, which, among other things, established the U.S. Sentencing Commission as an independent body in the Judicial Branch. The act empowered the commission to promulgate binding sentencing guidelines, including a range of determinate sentences for all categories of federal offenses and defendants according to specific and detailed factors.

On December 10, 1987, John Mistretta was indicted in the U.S. District Court for the Western District of Missouri on three counts centering on a sale of cocaine. Mistretta moved to have the promulgated guidelines declared unconstitutional on the grounds that the commission was constituted in violation of the principle of separation of powers and that Congress delegated excessive authority to the commission to create the guidelines. After the district court rejected Mistretta's argument, he pleaded guilty to one count of his indictment. The remaining counts were dropped. Mistretta then filed a notice of appeal to the Court of Appeals for the Eighth Circuit, and both Mistretta and the United States petitioned the U.S. Supreme Court for certiorari before judgment. Mistretta's attack on the commission and the guidelines was only one of many throughout the nation. Prior to the Supreme Court's decision in this case, some 150 district judges had declared the Sentencing Reform Act unconstitutional, and 115 district judges had upheld its constitutionality. The excerpts that follow are limited to passages dealing with delegation of power. Majority: Blackmun, Brennan, Kennedy, Marshall, O'Connor, Rehnquist, Stevens, White. Dissenting: Scalia.

**JUSTICE BLACKMUN delivered the opinion of the Court. . . .**

Petitioner argues that in delegating the power to promulgate sentencing guidelines for every federal criminal offense to an independent Sentencing Commission, Congress had granted the Commission excessive legislative discretion in violation of the constitutionally based nondelegation doctrine. We do not agree.

The nondelegation doctrine is rooted in the principle of separation of powers that underlies our tripartite system of government. The Constitution provides that "[a]ll legislative Powers herein granted shall be vested in a Congress of the United States," and we long have insisted that "the integrity and

maintenance of the system of government ordained by the Constitution," mandate that Congress generally cannot delegate its legislative power to another Branch. . . . So long as Congress "shall lay down by legislative act an intelligible principle to which the person or body authorized to [exercise the delegated authority] is directed to conform, such legislative action is not a forbidden delegation of legislative power."

Applying this "intelligible principle" test to congressional delegations, our jurisprudence has been driven by a practical understanding that in our increasingly complex society, replete with ever changing and more technical problems, Congress simply cannot do its job absent an ability to delegate power under broad general directives. . . . Accordingly, this

Court has deemed it "constitutionally sufficient if Congress clearly delineates the general policy, the public agency which is to apply it, and the boundaries of this delegated authority.". . .

In light of our approval of these broad delegations, we harbor no doubt that Congress' delegation of authority to the Sentencing Commission is sufficiently specific and detailed to meet constitutional requirements. . . .

To guide the Commission in its formulation of offense categories, Congress directed it to consider seven factors: the grade of the offense; the aggravating and mitigating circumstances of the crime; the nature and degree of the harm caused by the crime; the community view of the gravity of the offense; the public concern generated by the crime; the deterrent effect that a particular sentence may have on others; and the current incidence of the offense. Congress set forth 11 factors for the Commission to consider in establishing categories of defendants. . . .

We cannot dispute petitioner's contention that the Commission enjoys significant discretion in formulating guidelines. The Commission does have discretionary authority to determine the relative severity of federal crimes and to assess the relative weight of the offender characteristics that Congress listed for the Commission to consider. . . . The Commission also has significant discretion to determine which crimes have been punished too leniently, and which too severely. Congress has called upon the Commission to exercise its judgment about which types of crimes and which types of criminals are to be considered similar for the purposes of sentencing.

But our cases do not at all suggest that delegations of this type may not carry with them the need to exercise judgment on matters of policy. . . . In *Yakus* [v. *U.S.,* 1944], the Court laid down the applicable principle: . . . "Only if we could say that there is an absence of standards for the guidance of the Administrator's action, so that it would be impossible in a proper proceeding to ascertain whether the will of Congress has been obeyed, would we

be justified in overriding its choice of means for effecting its declared purpose."

Congress has met that standard here. . . .

Developing proportionate penalties for hundreds of different crimes by a virtually limitless array of offenders is precisely the sort of intricate, labor intensive task for which delegation to an expert body is especially appropriate. Although Congress has delegated significant discretion to the Commission to draw judgments from its analysis of existing sentencing practice and alternative sentencing models, "Congress is not confined to that method of executing its policy which involves the least possible delegation of discretion to administrative officers." We have no doubt that in the hands of the Commission "the criteria which Congress has supplied are wholly adequate for carrying out the general policy and purpose" of the Act. . . .

We conclude that in creating the Sentencing Commission—an unusual hybrid in structure and authority—Congress neither delegated excessive legislative power nor upset the constitutionally mandated balance of powers among the coordinate Branches. The Constitution's structural protections do not . . . prohibit Congress from calling upon the accumulated wisdom and experience of the Judicial Branch in creating policy on a matter uniquely within the ken of judges. Accordingly, we hold that the Act is constitutional.

The judgment of United States District Court for the Western District of Missouri is affirmed.

*It is so ordered.*

### JUSTICE SCALIA, dissenting. . . .

I dissent from today's decision because I can find no place within our constitutional system for an agency created by Congress to exercise no governmental power other than the making of laws. . . .

Precisely because the scope of delegation is largely uncontrollable by the courts, we must be particularly rigorous in preserving the Constitution's structural restrictions that deter excessive delegation. The major one, it seems to me, is that the power to make law cannot be exercised by anyone other than Congress, except in conjunction with the lawful exercise of executive or judicial power.

The whole theory of *lawful* congressional "delegation" is not that Congress is sometimes too busy or too divided and can therefore assign its responsibility of making law to someone else; but rather that a certain degree of discretion, and thus of lawmaking, *inheres* in most executive or judicial action, and it is up to Congress, by the relative specificity or generality of its statutory commands, to determine—up to a point—how small or how large that degree shall be. Thus, the courts could be given the power to say precisely what constitutes a "restraint of trade," or to adopt rules of procedure, or to prescribe by rule the manner in which their officers shall execute their judgments, because that "lawmaking" was ancillary to their exercise of judicial powers. And the Executive could be given the power to adopt policies and rules specifying in detail what radio and television licenses will be in the "public interest, convenience or necessity," because that was ancillary to exercise of its executive powers in granting and policing licenses and making a "fair and equitable allocation" of the electromagnetic spectrum. . . .

The focus of controversy, in the long line of our so-called excessive delegation cases, has been whether the *degree* of generality contained in the authorization for exercise of executive or judicial powers in a particular field is so unacceptably high as to *amount* to a delegation of legislative powers. I say "so-called excessive delegation" because although that convenient terminology is often used, what is really at issue is whether there has been *any* delegation of legislative power, which occurs (rarely) when Congress authorizes the exercise of executive or judicial power without adequate standards. Strictly speaking, there is *no* acceptable delegation of legislative power. . . . In the present case, however, a pure delegation of legislative power is precisely what we have before us. It is irrelevant whether the standards are adequate, because they are not standards related to the exercise of executive or judicial powers; they are, plainly and simply, standards for further legislation. . . .

By reason of today's decision, I anticipate that Congress will find delegation of its lawmaking powers much more attractive in the future. If rulemaking can be entirely unrelated to the exercise of judicial or executive powers, I foresee all manner of "expert" bodies, insulated from the political process, to which Congress will delegate various portions of its lawmaking responsibility. How tempting to create an expert Medical Commission (mostly MDs, with perhaps a few PhDs in moral philosophy) to dispose of such thorny, "no-win" political issues as the withholding of life-support systems in federally funded hospitals, or the use of fetal tissue for research. This is an undemocratic precedent that we set—not because of the scope of the delegated power, but because its recipient is not one of the three Branches of Government. The only governmental power the Commission possesses is the power to make law; and it is not the Congress. . . .

Today's decision follows the regrettable tendency of our recent separation-of-powers jurisprudence to treat the Constitution as though it were no more than a generalized prescription that the functions of the Branches should not be commingled too much—how much is too much to be determined, case-by-case, by this Court. The Constitution is not that. Rather, as its name suggests, it is a prescribed structure, a framework, for the conduct of government. . . .

I think the Court errs . . . because it fails to recognize that this case is . . . about the creation of a new branch altogether, a sort of junior-varsity Congress. It may well be that in some circumstances such a branch would be desirable; perhaps the agency before us here will prove to be so. But there are many desirable dispositions that do not accord with the constitutional structure we live under. And in the long run the improvisation of a constitutional structure on the basis of currently perceived utility will be disastrous.

## *Immigration and Naturalization Service* v. *Chadha*
## 462 U.S. 919, 103 S.Ct. 2764, 77 L.Ed. 2d 317 (1983)
http://laws.findlaw.com/us/462/919.html

Section 244(a)(1) of the Immigration and Nationality Act authorized the attorney general, in his discretion, to suspend the deportation of a deportable alien. Under Section 244(c)(1), the attorney general was required to report such suspension to Congress. Section 244(c)(2) of the act authorized either house of Congress by resolution to invalidate the suspension before the end of the session following the one during which the suspension occurred. The attorney general discharged his responsibilities through the Immigration and Naturalization Service (INS), part of the Department of Justice.

Jagdish Rai Chadha is an East Indian who was born in Kenya and who was lawfully admitted to the United States in 1966 on a nonimmigrant student visa. He remained in the United States after his visa had expired in 1972 and was soon ordered by the INS to show cause why he should not be deported. Chadha applied for suspension of the deportation order, and in 1974 an immigration judge, acting for the attorney general, ordered the suspension. On December 16, 1975, the House of Representatives exercised the veto authority reserved to it under Section 244(c)(2). Without action by either house of Congress, Chadha's status would have become that of permanent resident alien when Congress adjourned on December 19, 1975.

The immigration judge then reopened the deportation proceedings, but Chadha moved to block further action, arguing that Section 244(c)(2) violated the Constitution. The immigration judge ruled that he had no authority to question the constitutionality of the law and directed that Chadha be deported as the House had directed. Chadha appealed that order to the Board of Immigration Appeals, which upheld the immigration judge. Chadha next asked the Court of Appeals for the Ninth Circuit to review the deportation order. The INS joined Chadha in arguing that Section 244(c)(2) was unconstitutional. At this point, the court of appeals invited both the Senate and the House of Representatives to file briefs amici curiae. This invitation was important because the principal arguments in support of the validity of the legislative veto came from counsel representing the House and Senate. The court of appeals ruled in 1981 that the House of Representatives lacked constitutional authority to order Chadha's deportation. Majority: Burger, Blackmun, Brennan, Marshall, O'Connor, Powell, Stevens. Dissenting: White, Rehnquist.

**CHIEF JUSTICE BURGER delivered the opinion of the Court. . . .**

We turn now to the question whether action of one House of Congress under § 244(c)(2) violates strictures of the Constitution. . . .

Explicit and unambiguous provisions of the Constitution prescribe and define the respective functions of the Congress and of the Executive in the legislative process. Since the precise terms of those familiar provisions are critical to the resolution of this case, we set them out verbatim. Article I provides:

"All legislative Powers herein granted shall be vested in a Congress of the United States, which shall consist of a Senate *and* a House of Representatives." (Emphasis added [by Chief Justice].)

"Every Bill which shall have passed the House of Representatives and the Senate, *shall*, before it become a Law, be presented to the President of the United States; . . . " (Emphasis added [by the Chief Justice].)

"*Every* Order, Resolution, or Vote to which the Concurrence of the Senate and House of Representatives may be necessary (except on a question of Adjournment) *shall* be presented to the President of the United States; and before the Same shall take Effect, *shall* be approved by him, or being disapproved by him, shall be repassed by two thirds of the Senate and House of Representatives, according to the Rules and Limitations prescribed in the Case of a Bill." (Emphasis added [by the Chief Justice].)

The records of the Constitutional Convention reveal that the requirement that all legislation be presented to the President before becoming law was uniformly accepted by the Framers. Presentment to the President and the Presidential veto were considered so imperative that the draftsmen took special pains to assure that these requirements could not be circumvented. . . .

The bicameral requirement . . . was of scarcely less concern to the Framers than was the Presidential veto and indeed the two concepts are interdependent. By providing that no law could take effect without the concurrence of the prescribed majority of the Members of both Houses, the Framers reemphasized their belief, already remarked upon in connection with the Presentment Clauses, that legislation should not be enacted unless it has been carefully and fully considered by the Nation's elected officials. . . .

The Constitution sought to divide the delegated powers of the new federal government into three defined categories, legislative, executive and judicial, to assure, as nearly as possible, that each Branch of government would confine itself to its assigned responsibility. The hydraulic pressure inherent within each of the separate Branches to exceed the outer limits of its power, even to accomplish desirable objectives, must be resisted.

Although not "hermetically" sealed from one another, . . . the powers delegated to the three Branches are functionally identifiable. When any Branch acts, it is presumptively exercising the power the Constitution has delegated to it. . . .

Beginning with this presumption, we must nevertheless establish that the challenged action under § 244(c)(2) is of the kind to which the procedural requirements of Article. I, § 7 apply. Not every action taken by either House is subject to the bicameralism and presentment requirements of Article. I. . . . Whether actions taken by either House are, in law and fact, an exercise of legislative power depends not on their form but upon "whether they contain matter which is properly to be regarded as legislative in its character and effect.". . .

Examination of the action taken here by one House pursuant to § 244(c)(2) reveals that it was essentially legislative in purpose and effect. In purporting to exercise power . . . to "establish an uniform Rule of Naturalization," the House took action that had the purpose and effect of altering the legal rights, duties and relations of persons, including the Attorney General, Executive Branch officials and Chadha, all outside the legislative branch. . . .

The choices we discern as having been made in the Constitutional Convention impose burdens on governmental processes that often seem clumsy, inefficient, even unworkable, but those hard choices were consciously made by men who had lived under a form of government that permitted arbitrary governmental acts to go unchecked. There is no support in the Constitution or decisions of this Court for the proposition that the cumbersomeness and delays often encountered in complying with explicit Constitutional standards may be avoided, either by the Congress or by the President. . . . With all the obvious flaws of delay, untidiness, and potential for abuse, we have not yet found a better way to preserve freedom than by making the exercise of power subject to the carefully crafted restraints spelled out in the Constitution.

We hold that the Congressional veto provision in § 244(c)(2) is . . . unconstitutional. Accordingly, the judgment of the Court of Appeals is

*Affirmed.*

JUSTICE POWELL, concurring . . . [omitted].

**Justice White, dissenting.**

Today the Court not only invalidates § 244(c)(2) of the Immigration and Nationality Act, but also sounds the death knell for nearly 200 other statutory provisions in which Congress has reserved a "legislative veto." For this reason, the Court's decision is of surpassing importance. . . .

The prominence of the legislative veto mechanism in our contemporary political system and its importance to Congress can hardly be overstated. It has become a central means by which Congress secures the accountability of executive and independent agencies. Without the legislative veto, Congress is faced with a Hobson's choice: either to refrain from delegating the necessary authority, leaving itself with a hopeless task of writing laws with the requisite specificity to cover endless special circumstances across the entire policy landscape, or in the alternative, to abdicate its lawmaking function to the executive branch and independent agencies. To choose the former leaves major national problems unresolved; to opt for the latter risks unaccountable policymaking by those not elected to fill that role. Accordingly, over the past five decades, the legislative veto has been placed in nearly 200 statutes. The device is known in every field of governmental concern: reorganization, budgets, foreign affairs, war powers, and regulation of trade, safety, energy, the environment and the economy. . . .

The Court's holding today that all legislative-type action must be enacted through the lawmaking process ignores that legislative authority is routinely delegated to the Executive branch, to the independent regulatory agencies, and to private individuals and groups. . . .

The wisdom and the constitutionality of these broad delegations are matters that still have not been put to rest. But for present purposes, these cases establish that by virtue of congressional delegation, legislative power can be exercised by independent agencies and Executive departments without the passage of new legislation. . . . There is no question but that agency rulemaking is lawmaking in any functional or realistic sense of the term. . . .

If Congress may delegate lawmaking power to independent and executive agencies, it is most difficult to understand Article I as forbidding Congress from also reserving a check on legislative power for itself. Absent the veto, the agencies receiving delegations of legislative or quasi-legislative power may issue regulations having the force of law without bicameral approval and without the President's signature. It is thus not apparent why the reservation of a veto over the exercise of that legislative power must be subject to a more exacting test. . . .

The Court also takes no account of perhaps the most relevant consideration: However resolutions of disapproval under § 244(c)(2) are formally characterized, in reality, a departure from the status quo occurs only upon the concurrence of opinion among the House, Senate, and President. . . .

Section 244(a)(1) authorizes the Attorney General, in his discretion, to suspend the deportation of certain aliens who are otherwise deportable and, upon Congress' approval, to adjust their status to that of aliens lawfully admitted for permanent residence. . . . [T]he suspension proceeding "has two phases: a determination whether the statutory conditions have been met, which generally involves a question of law, and a determination whether relief shall be granted, which [ultimately] . . . is confided to the sound discretion of the Attorney General [and his delegates]." . . .

There is also a third phase to the process. Under § 244(c)(1) the Attorney General must report all such suspensions, with a detailed statement of facts and reasons, to the Congress. Either House may then act, in that session or the next, to block the suspension of deportation by passing a resolution of disapproval § 244(c)(2). Upon Congressional approval of the suspension—by its silence—the alien's permanent status is adjusted to that of a lawful resident alien. . . .

At all times, . . . a permanent change in a deportable alien's status could be accomplished only with the agreement of the Attorney General, the House, and the Senate. . . .

**Justice Rehnquist**, with whom **Justice White** joins, dissenting . . . [omitted].

## Clinton v. City of New York
### 524 U.S. 417, 118 S.Ct. 2091, 141 L.Ed. 2d 393 (1998)

http://laws.findlaw.com/us/524/417.html

In April 1996 Congress passed the Line Item Veto Act, to become effective on January 1, 1997. On January 2, six members of Congress who had voted against the law challenged its constitutionality in a suit filed in the United States District Court for the District of Columbia. The district court held the act unconstitutional, but on appeal the Supreme Court ruled that members of Congress lacked standing to sue because they had not "alleged a sufficiently concrete injury to have established Article III standing" (*Raines* v. *Byrd,* 1997). Within two months of this decision, President Clinton exercised his authority under the law to cancel one provision in the Balanced Budget Act of 1997 and two provisions in the Taxpayer Relief Act of 1997. Adversely affected by the president's actions, the City of New York, a hospital, two hospital associations, two unions representing health care employees, Snake River Potato Growers, Inc., and an individual farmer then challenged the Line Item Veto Act in the same district court. The district court again held the law invalid. Sections of the opinions below dealing with standing have been omitted. (Prior to the Supreme Court's decision in this case, President Clinton wielded his new statutory veto authority 82 times; Congress overrode 38 of the item vetoes early in 1998, and the president withdrew one veto. The remaining 43 vetoes involved $869 million in total spending.) Majority: Stevens, Ginsburg, Kennedy, Rehnquist, Souter, Thomas. Dissenting (with respect to the constitutionality of the act): Scalia, Breyer, O'Connor.

**JUSTICE STEVENS delivered the opinion of the Court. . . .**

We . . . agree that the cancellation procedures set forth in the Act violate the Presentment Clause of the Constitution. . . .

The Line Item Veto Act gives the President the power to "cancel in whole" three types of provisions that have been signed into law: "(1) any dollar amount of discretionary budget authority; (2) any item of new direct spending; or (3) any limited tax benefit." It is undisputed that the New York case involves an "item of new direct spending" and that the Snake River case involves a "limited tax benefit" as those terms are defined in the Act. It is also undisputed that each of those provisions had been signed into law pursuant to Article I, § 7, of the Constitution before it was canceled. . . .

A cancellation takes effect upon receipt by Congress of the special message from the President. If, however, a "disapproval bill" pertaining to a special message is enacted into law, the cancellations set forth in that message

become "null and void." The Act sets forth a detailed expedited procedure for the consideration of a "disapproval bill," but no such bill was passed for either of the cancellations involved in these cases.

A majority vote of both Houses is sufficient to enact a disapproval bill. The Act does not grant the President the authority to cancel a disapproval bill, but he does, of course, retain his constitutional authority to veto such a bill.

Thus, under the plain text of the statute, the two actions of the President that are challenged in these cases prevented one section of the Balanced Budget Act of 1997 and one section of the Taxpayer Relief Act of 1997 "from having legal force or effect." The remaining provisions of those statutes, with the exception of the second canceled item in the latter, continue to have the same force and effect as they had when signed into law.

In both legal and practical effect, the President has amended two Acts of Congress by repealing a portion of each. . . . There is no provision in the Constitution that authorizes the President to enact, to amend, or to repeal statutes.... [A]fter a bill has passed both Houses of Congress, but "before it become[s] a Law," it must be presented to the President. If he approves it, "he shall sign it, but if not he shall return it, with his Objections to that House in which it shall have originated, who shall enter the Objections at large on their Journal, and proceed to reconsider it." His "return" of a bill, which is usually described as a "veto," is subject to being overridden by a two-thirds vote in each House.

There are important differences between the President's "return" of a bill pursuant to Article I, § 7, and the exercise of the President's cancellation authority pursuant to the Line Item Veto Act. The constitutional return takes place *before* the bill becomes law; the statutory cancellation occurs *after* the bill becomes law. The constitutional return is of the entire bill; the statutory cancellation is of only a part. Although the Constitution expressly authorizes the President to play a role in the process of enacting statutes, it is silent on the subject of unilateral Presidential action that either repeals or amends parts of duly enacted statutes.

There are powerful reasons for construing constitutional silence on this profoundly important issue as equivalent to an express prohibition. The procedures governing the enactment of statutes set forth in the text of Article I were the product of the great debates and compromises that produced the Constitution itself.... Our first President understood the text of the Presentment Clause as requiring that he either "approve all the parts of a Bill, or reject it in toto."

What has emerged in these cases from the President's exercise of his statutory cancellation powers, however, are truncated versions of two bills that passed both Houses of Congress. They are not the product of the "finely wrought" procedure that the Framers designed....

The Government advances two related arguments to support its position that despite the unambiguous provisions of the Act, cancellations do not amend or repeal properly enacted statutes in violation of the Presentment Clause. First, relying primarily on *Field* v. *Clark* (1892),

the Government contends that the cancellations were merely exercises of discretionary authority granted to the President by the Balanced Budget Act and the Taxpayer Relief Act read in light of the previously enacted Line Item Veto Act. Second, the Government submits that the substance of the authority to cancel tax and spending items "is, in practical effect, no more and no less than the power to 'decline to spend' specified sums of money, or to 'decline to implement' specified tax measures." Neither argument is persuasive.

In *Field* v. *Clark,* the Court upheld the constitutionality of the Tariff Act of 1890. That statute contained a "free list" of almost 300 specific articles that were exempted from import duties "unless otherwise specially provided for in this act." Section 3 was a special provision that directed the President to suspend that exemption for sugar, molasses, coffee, tea, and hides "whenever, and so often" as he should be satisfied that any country producing and exporting those products imposed duties on the agricultural products of the United States that he deemed to be "reciprocally unequal and unreasonable...."

[T]he conclusion ... that the suspensions mandated by the Tariff Act were not exercises of legislative power does not undermine our opinion that cancellations pursuant to the Line Item Veto Act are the functional equivalent of partial repeals of Acts of Congress that fail to satisfy Article I, § 7.

Neither are we persuaded by the Government's contention that the President's authority to cancel new direct spending and tax benefit items is no greater than his traditional authority to decline to spend appropriated funds. The Government has reviewed in some detail the series of statutes in which Congress has given the Executive broad discretion over the expenditure of appropriated funds.... It is argued that the Line Item Veto Act merely confers comparable discretionary authority over the expenditure of appropriated funds. The critical difference between this statute and all of its predecessors, however, is that unlike any of them, this Act gives the President the unilateral power to change the text of duly enacted statutes. None of the Act's predecessors could even arguably have been construed to authorize such a change. . . .

[O]ur decision rests on the narrow ground that the procedures authorized by the Line Item Veto Act are not authorized by the Constitution. The Balanced Budget Act of 1997 is a 500-page document that became "Public Law 105-33" after three procedural steps were taken: (1) a bill containing its exact text was approved by a majority of the Members of the House of Representatives; (2) the Senate approved precisely the same text; and (3) that text was signed into law by the President. The Constitution explicitly requires that each of those three steps be taken before a bill may "become a law." If one paragraph of that text had been omitted at any one of those three stages, Public Law 105-33 would not have been validly enacted. If the Line Item Veto Act were valid, it would authorize the President to create a different law, one whose text was not voted on by either House of Congress or presented to the President for signature. Something that might be known as "Public Law 105-33 as modified by the President" may or may not be desirable, but it is surely not a document that may "become a law" pursuant to the procedures designed by the Framers of Article I, § 7, of the Constitution.

If there is to be a new procedure in which the President will play a different role in determining the final text of what may "become a law," such change must come not by legislation but through the amendment procedures set forth in Article V of the Constitution.

The judgment of the District Court is affirmed.

*It is so ordered.*

JUSTICE      KENNEDY,      concurring . . . [omitted].

**JUSTICE SCALIA, with whom JUSTICE O'CONNOR joins, and with whom JUSTICE BREYER joins in part, concurring in part and dissenting in part. . . .**

[U]nlike the Court I find the President's cancellation of spending items to be entirely in accord with the Constitution. . . .

The short of the matter is this: Had the Line Item Veto Act authorized the President to "decline to spend" any item of spending contained in the Balanced Budget Act of 1997, there is not the slightest doubt that authorization would have been constitutional. What the Line Item Veto Act does instead—authorizing the President to "cancel" an item of spending—is technically different. But the technical difference does not relate to the technicalities of the Presentment Clause, which have been fully complied with; and the doctrine of unconstitutional delegation, which is at issue here, is preeminently not a doctrine of technicalities. The title of the Line Item Veto Act, which was perhaps designed to simplify for public comprehension, or perhaps merely to comply with the terms of a campaign pledge, has succeeded in faking out the Supreme Court. The President's action it authorizes in fact is not a line item veto and . . . insofar as the substance of that action is concerned, it is no different from what Congress has permitted the President to do since the formation of the Union.

. . . Because I find no party before us who has standing to challenge the President's cancellation of § 968 of the Taxpayer Relief Act, I do not reach the question whether that violates the Constitution. . . .

**JUSTICE BREYER, with whom JUSTICE O'CONNOR and JUSTICE SCALIA join in part, dissenting. . . .**

In my view the Line Item Veto Act does not violate any specific textual constitutional command, nor does it violate any implicit Separation of Powers principle. Consequently, I believe that the Act is constitutional. . . .

The Court believes that the Act violates the literal text of the Constitution. A simple syllogism captures its basic reasoning: Major Premise: The Constitution sets forth an exclusive method for enacting, repealing, or amending laws. Minor Premise: The Act authorizes the President to "repea[l] or amen[d]" laws in a different way, namely by announcing a cancellation of a portion of a previously enacted law. Conclusion: The Act is inconsistent with the Constitution.

I find this syllogism unconvincing, however, because its Minor Premise is faulty. When the President "canceled" the two appropriation measures now before us, he did not repeal any law nor did he amend any law. He simply followed the law, leaving the statutes, as they are literally written, intact.

To understand why one cannot say, literally speaking, that the President has repealed or amended any law, imagine how the provisions of law before us might have been, but were not, written. Imagine that the canceled New York health care tax provision at issue here had instead said the following:

Section One. Taxes ... that were collected by the State of New York from a health care provider before June 1, 1997 and for which a waiver of provisions [requiring payment] have been sought ... are deemed to be permissible health care related taxes ... *provided however that the President may prevent the just mentioned provision from having legal force or effect if he determines x, y and z.* (Assume x, y and z to be the same determinations required by the Line Item Veto Act.) [Ellipses and italics in this paragraph are in the original.] Whatever a person might say, or think, about the constitutionality of this imaginary law, there is one thing the English language would prevent one from saying. One could not say that a President who "prevent[s]" the deeming language from "having legal force or effect," has either repealed or amended this particular hypothetical statute. Rather, the President has followed that law to the letter. He has exercised the power it explicitly delegates to him. He has executed the law, not repealed it.

It could make no significant difference to this linguistic point were the italicized proviso to appear, not as part of what I have called Section One, but, instead, at the bottom of the statute page, say referenced by an asterisk, with a statement that it applies to every spending provision in the act next to which a similar asterisk appears. And that being so, it could make no difference if that proviso appeared, instead, in a different, earlier-enacted law, along with legal language that makes it applicable to every future spending provision picked out according to a specified formula. ...

Because I disagree with the Court's holding of literal violation, I must consider whether the Act nonetheless violates Separation of Powers principles—principles that arise out of the Constitution's vesting of the "executive Power" in "a President," and "[a]ll legislative Powers" in "a Congress." There are three relevant Separation of Powers questions here: (1) Has Congress given the President the wrong kind of power, i.e., "non-Executive" power? (2) Has Congress given the President the power to "encroach" upon Congress' own constitutionally reserved territory? (3) Has Congress given the President too much power, violating the doctrine of "nondelegation"? ... [W]ith respect to this Act, the answer to all these questions is "no."

Viewed conceptually, the power the Act conveys is the right kind of power. It is "executive." As explained above, an exercise of that power "executes" the Act. Conceptually speaking, it closely resembles the kind of delegated authority—to spend or not to spend appropriations, to change or not to change tariff rates—that Congress has frequently granted the President, any differences being differences in degree, not kind. ...

[O]ne cannot say that the Act "encroaches" upon Congress' power, when Congress retained the power to insert, by simple majority, into any future appropriations bill, into any section of any such bill, or into any phrase of any section, a provision that says the Act will not apply. ... Where is the encroachment?

Nor can one say the Act's grant of power "aggrandizes" the Presidential office. The grant is limited to the context of the budget. It is limited to the power to spend, or not to spend, particular appropriated items, and the power to permit, or not to permit, specific limited exemptions from generally applicable tax law from taking effect. These powers, as I will explain in detail, resemble those the President has exercised in the past on other occasions. The delegation of those powers to the President may strengthen the Presidency, but any such change in Executive Branch authority seems minute when compared with the changes worked by delegations of other kinds of authority that the Court in the past has upheld. ...

The "nondelegation" doctrine represents an added constitutional check upon Congress' authority to delegate power to the Executive Branch. And it raises a more serious constitutional obstacle here. The Constitution permits Congress to "see[k] assistance from another branch" of Government, the "extent and character" of that assistance to be fixed "according to commonsense and the inherent necessities of the governmental co-ordination." But there are limits on the way in which Congress can obtain such assistance; it "cannot delegate any part of its legislative power except under the limitation of a prescribed standard." Or, in Chief Justice Taft's more familiar words, the Constitution permits only those delegations where Congress "shall lay down by legislative act an intelligible principle to which the person or body authorized to [act] is directed to conform."

The Act before us seeks to create such a principle in three ways. The first is procedural. The Act tells the President that, in "identifying dollar amounts [or] . . . items . . . for cancellation" (which I take to refer to his selection of the amounts or items he will "prevent from having legal force or effect"), he is to "consider," among other things, "the legislative history, construction, and purposes of the law which contains [those amounts or items, and] . . . any specific sources of information referenced in such law or . . . the best available information. . . ."

The second is purposive. The clear purpose behind the Act, confirmed by its legisla-tive history, is to promote "greater fiscal accountability" and to "eliminate wasteful federal spending and . . . special tax breaks."

The third is substantive. The President must determine that, to "prevent" the item or amount "from having legal force or effect" will "reduce the Federal budget deficit; . . . not impair any essential Government functions; and . . . not harm the national interest."

The resulting standards are broad. But this Court has upheld standards that are equally broad, or broader. . . . To the contrary, (a) the broadly phrased limitations in the Act, together with (b) its evident deficit reduction purpose, and (c) a procedure that guarantees Presidential awareness of the reasons for including a particular provision in a budget bill, taken together, guide the President's exercise of his discretionary powers. . . .

In sum, I recognize that the Act before us is novel. In a sense, it skirts a constitutional edge. But that edge has to do with means, not ends. The means chosen do not amount literally to the enactment, repeal, or amendment of a law. Nor, for that matter, do they amount literally to the "line item veto" that the Act's title announces. . . . They represent an experiment that may, or may not, help representative government work better. The Constitution, in my view, authorizes Congress and the President to try novel methods in this way. Consequently, with respect, I dissent.

## II. CONGRESSIONAL INVESTIGATIONS

### *Watkins* v. *United States*
### 354 U.S. 178, 77 S.Ct. 1173, 1 L.Ed. 2d 1273 (1957)
### http://laws.findlaw.com/us/354/178.html

The broad investigating power of Congress was upheld in *McGrain* v. *Daugherty* (1927), where the purpose was to obtain information about alleged wrongdoing by the attorney general and the Department of Justice. Increasingly in the period after World War II, Congress turned its attention to the activities within the United States of alleged members and officers of the Communist Party. Subpoenaed for a hearing before the House Committee on Un-American Activities on April 29, 1954, Watkins, a labor organizer, refused to answer on the ground that the questions were outside of the proper scope of the committee's activities and not relevant to its work. He was then convicted in U.S. district court under 2 U.S.C. 192, which makes it a misdemeanor for any person summoned as a witness by either House of Congress to refuse to answer any question "pertinent to the question under inquiry." Voting 2–1, the Court of Appeals for the District of Columbia reversed. Upon rehearing en banc, the full bench affirmed the conviction. Majority: Warren, Black, Brennan, Douglas, Frankfurter, Harlan. Dissenting: Clark. Not participating: Burton, Whittaker.

**MR. CHIEF JUSTICE WARREN delivered the opinion of the Court. . . .**

We start with several basic premises on which there is general agreement. The power of the Congress to conduct investigations is inherent in the legislative process. That power is broad. . . . But broad as is this power of inquiry, it is not unlimited. There is no general authority to expose the private affairs of individuals without justification in terms of the functions of the Congress. This was freely conceded by the Solicitor General in his argument of this case. . . .

It is unquestionably the duty of all citizens to cooperate with the Congress in its efforts to obtain the facts needed for intelligent legislative action. It is their unremitting obligation to respond to subpoenas, to respect the dignity of the Congress and its committees, and to testify fully with respect to matters within the province of proper investigation. This, of course, assumes that the constitutional rights of witnesses will be respected by the Congress as they are in a court of justice.

In the decade following World War II, there appeared a new kind of congressional inquiry unknown in prior periods of American history. Principally this was the result of the various investigations into the threat of subversion of the United States Government, but other subjects of congressional interest also contributed to the changed scene. This new phase of legislative inquiry involved a broad-scale intrusion into the lives and affairs of private citizens. It brought before the courts novel questions of the appropriate limits of congressional inquiry.

Prior cases . . . had defined the scope of investigative power in terms of the inherent limitations of the sources of that power. In the more recent cases, the emphasis shifted to problems of accommodating the interest of the Government with the rights and privileges of individuals. The central theme was the application of the Bill of Rights as a restraint upon the assertion of governmental power in this form.

It was during this period that the Fifth Amendment privilege against self-incrimination was frequently invoked and recognized as a legal limit upon the authority of a committee to require that a witness answer its questions. Some early doubts as to the applicability of the privilege before a legislative committee never matured. When the matter reached this Court, the Government did not challenge in any way that the Fifth Amendment protection was available to the witness, and such a challenge could not have prevailed. It confined its argument to the character of the answers sought and to the adequacy of the claim of privilege. . . .

A far more difficult task evolved from the claim by witnesses that the committees' interrogations were infringements upon the freedoms of the First Amendment. Clearly, an investigation is subject to the command that the Congress shall make no law abridging freedom of speech or press or assembly. While it is true that there is no statute to be reviewed, and that an investigation is not a law, nevertheless an investigation is part of lawmaking. It is justified solely as an adjunct to the legislative process. The First Amendment may be invoked against infringement of the protected freedoms by law or by lawmaking.

Abuses of the investigative process may imperceptibly lead to abridgement of protected freedoms. The mere summoning of a witness and compelling him to testify, against his will, about his beliefs, expressions or associations is a measure of governmental interference. And when those forced revelations concern matters that are unorthodox, unpopular, or even hateful to the general public, the reaction in the life of the witness may be disastrous. . . .

It is the responsibility of the Congress, in the first instance, to insure that compulsory process is used only in furtherance of a legislative purpose. That requires that the instructions to an investigating committee spell out that group's jurisdiction and purpose with sufficient particularity. Those instructions are embodied in the authorizing resolution. That document is the committee's charter. Broadly drafted and loosely worded, however, such resolutions can leave tremendous latitude to the discretion of investigators. The more vague the committee's charter is, the greater becomes the possibility that the committee's specific actions are not in conformity with the will of the parent House of Congress.

The authorizing resolution of the Un-American Activities Committee was adopted in 1938 when a select committee, under the chairmanship of Representative Dies, was created. Several years later, the Committee was made a standing organ of the House with the same mandate. It defines the Committee's authority as follows:

> The Committee on Un-American Activities, as a whole or by subcommittee, is authorized to make from time to time investigations of (i) the extent, character, and objects of un-American propaganda activities in the United States, (ii) the diffusion within the United States of subversive and un-American propaganda that is instigated from foreign countries or of a domestic origin and attacks the principle of the form of government as guaranteed by our Constitution, and (iii) all other questions in relation thereto that would aid Congress in any necessary remedial legislation. [Rule XI]

It would be difficult to imagine a less explicit authorizing resolution. Who can define the meaning of "un-American"? . . .

Plainly . . . committees are restricted to the missions delegated to them, i.e., to acquire certain data to be used by the House or the Senate in coping with a problem that falls within its legislative sphere. No witness can be compelled to make disclosures on matters outside that area. . . . When the definition of jurisdictional pertinency is as uncertain and wavering as in the case of the Un-American Activities Committee, it becomes extremely difficult for the Committee to limit its inquiries to statutory pertinency.

In fulfillment of their obligation under this statute, the courts must accord to the defendants every right which is guaranteed to defendants in all other criminal cases. Among these is the right to have available, through a sufficiently precise statute, information revealing the standard of criminality before the commission of the alleged offense. Applied to persons prosecuted under § 192, this raises a special problem in that the statute defines the crime as refusal to answer "any question pertinent to the question under inquiry." Part of the standard of criminality, therefore, is the pertinency of the questions propounded to the witness.

The problem attains proportion when viewed from the standpoint of the witness who appears before a congressional committee. He must decide at the time the questions are propounded whether or not to answer. . . .

It is obvious that a person compelled to make this choice is entitled to have knowledge of the subject to which the interrogation is deemed pertinent. That knowledge must be available with the same degree of explicitness and clarity that the Due Process Clause requires in the expression of any element of a criminal offense. The "vice of vagueness" must be avoided here as in all other crimes. There are several sources that can outline the "question under inquiry" in such a way that the rules against vagueness are satisfied. The authorizing resolution, the remarks of the chairman or members of the committee, or even the nature of the proceedings themselves might sometimes make the topic clear. This case demonstrates, however, that these sources often leave the matter in grave doubt. . . .

The conclusions which we have reached in this case will not prevent the Congress, through its committees, from obtaining any information it needs for the proper fulfillment of its role in our scheme of government. The legislature is free to determine the kinds of data that should be collected. It is only those investigations that are conducted by use of compulsory process that give rise to a need to protect the rights of individuals against illegal encroachment. . . . That is a small price to pay if it serves to uphold the principles of limited, constitutional government without constricting the power of the Congress to inform itself.

The judgment of the Court of Appeals is reversed, and the case is remanded to the District Court with instructions to dismiss the indictment.

*It is so ordered.*

MR. JUSTICE FRANKFURTER, concurring . . . [omitted].

**MR. JUSTICE CLARK, dissenting. . . .**

It may be that at times the House Committee on Un-American Activities has, as the Court says, "conceived of its task in the grand view of its name." And, perhaps, as the Court indicates, the rules of conduct placed upon the Committee by the House admit of individual abuse and unfairness. But that is none of our affair. So long as the object of a legislative inquiry is legitimate and the questions propounded are pertinent thereto, it is not for the courts to interfere with the committee system of inquiry. To hold otherwise would be an infringement on the power given the Congress to inform itself, and thus a trespass upon the fundamental American principle of separation of powers. The majority has substituted the judiciary as the grand inquisitor and supervisor of congressional investigations. It has never been so. . . .

## *Barenblatt v. United States*
### 360 U.S. 109, 79 S.Ct. 1081, 3 L.Ed. 2d 1115 (1959)
http://laws.findlaw.com/us/360/109.html

Lloyd Barenblatt, a former college teacher, was called as a witness before a subcommittee of the House Un-American Activities Committee investigating Communist infiltration in education. Disclaiming any reliance on the Fifth Amendment, he refused to answer questions regarding past affiliation with the Communist Party, contending that the subcommittee had no power to inquire into political beliefs and associations. The Supreme Court vacated his conviction for contempt of Congress under 2 U.S.C. 192 and remanded the case for reconsideration in light of the 1957 Watkins decision. The years 1957–1958 witnessed a flurry of anti-Court legislation introduced in Congress, the most since 1936–1937. Barenblatt's conviction was again upheld by the court of appeals. Majority: Harlan, Clark, Frankfurter, Stewart, Whittaker. Dissenting: Black, Brennan, Douglas, Warren.

### MR. JUSTICE HARLAN delivered the opinion of the Court.

Once more the Court is required to resolve the conflicting constitutional claims of congressional power and of an individual's right to resist its exercise. . . .

Broad as it is, the power is not, however, without limitations. Since Congress may only investigate into those areas in which it may potentially legislate or appropriate, it cannot inquire into matters which are within the exclusive province of one of the other branches of the Government. . . . And the Congress, in common with all branches of the Government, must exercise its powers subject to the limitations placed by the Constitution on governmental action, more particularly in the context of this case the relevant limitations of the Bill of Rights. . . .

In the present case congressional efforts to learn the extent of a nationwide, indeed worldwide, problem have brought one of its investigating committees into the field of education. Of course, broadly viewed, inquiries cannot be made into the teaching that is pursued in any of our educational institutions. When academic teaching-freedom and its corollary learning-freedom, so essential to the well-being of the Nation, are claimed, this Court will always be on the alert against intrusion by Congress into this constitutionally protected domain. But this does not mean that the Congress is precluded from interrogating a witness merely because he is a teacher. An educational institution is not a constitutional sanctuary from inquiry into matters that may otherwise be within the constitutional legislative domain merely for the reason that inquiry is made of someone within its walls. . . .

At the outset it should be noted that Rule XI authorized this Subcommittee to compel testimony within the framework of the investigative authority conferred on the Un-American Activities Committee. Petitioner contends that *Watkins* v. *United States* . . . nevertheless held the grant of this power in all circumstances ineffective because of the vagueness of Rule XI in delineating the Committee jurisdiction to which its exercise was to be appurtenant. . . .

The Watkins case cannot properly be read as standing for such a proposition. A principal contention in *Watkins* was that the refusals to answer were justified because the requirement . . . that the questions asked be "pertinent to the question under inquiry" had not been satisfied. . . . This Court reversed the conviction solely on that ground, holding that Watkins had not been adequately apprised of the subject matter of the Subcommittee's investigation or the pertinency thereto of the questions he refused to answer. . . . In so deciding the Court drew upon Rule XI only as one of the facets in the total *mise en scène* in its search for the "question under inquiry" in that particular investigation. . . . In short, while *Watkins* was critical of Rule XI, it did not involve the broad and inflexible holding petitioner now attributes to it. . . .

What we deal with here is whether petitioner was sufficiently apprised of "the topic under inquiry" thus authorized "and the connective reasoning whereby the precise questions asked related to it.". . . In light of this prepared memorandum of constitutional objectives there can be no doubt that this petitioner was well aware of the Subcommittee's authority and purpose to question him as it did. . . . In addition the other sources of this information which we recognized in *Watkins* . . . leave no room for a "pertinency" objection on this record. The subject matter of the inquiry had been identified at the commencement of the investigation as Communist infiltration into the field of education. . . .

The protections of the First Amendment, unlike a proper claim of the privilege against self-incrimination under the Fifth Amendment, do not afford a witness the right to resist inquiry in all circumstances. Where First Amendment rights are asserted to bar governmental interrogation, resolution of the issue always involves a balancing by the courts of the competing private and public interests at stake in the particular circumstances shown. These principles were recognized in the Watkins case. . . .

An investigation of advocacy or of preparation for overthrow certainly embraces the right to identify a witness as a member of the Communist Party . . . and to inquire into various manifestations of the Party's tenets. The strict requirements of a prosecution under the Smith Act . . . are not the measure of the permissible scope of a congressional investigation into "overthrow," for of necessity the investigatory process must proceed step by step. Nor can it fairly be concluded that this investigation was directed at controlling what is being taught at our universities rather than at overthrow. . . .

Nor can we accept the further contention that this investigation should not be deemed to have been in furtherance of a legislative purpose because the true objective of the Committee and of the Congress was purely "exposure." So long as Congress acts in pursuance of its constitutional power, the Judiciary lacks authority to intervene on the basis of the motives which spurred the exercise of that power. . . .

We conclude that the balance between the individual and the governmental interests here at stake must be struck in favor of the latter, and that therefore the provisions of the First Amendment have not been offended. . . .

*Affirmed.*

**MR. JUSTICE BLACK, with whom the CHIEF JUSTICE and MR. JUSTICE DOUGLAS concur, dissenting. . . .**

I do not agree that laws directly abridging First Amendment freedoms can be justified by a congressional or judicial balancing process. . . .

But even assuming what I cannot assume, that some balancing is proper in this case, I feel that the Court after stating the test ignores it completely. At most it balances the right of the Government to preserve itself, against Barenblatt's right to refrain from revealing Communist affiliations. Such a balance, however, mistakes the factors to be weighed. . . . [I]t completely leaves out the real interest in Barenblatt's silence, the interest of the people as a whole in being able to join organizations, advocate causes and make political "mistakes" without later being subjected to governmental penalties for having dared to think for themselves. . . . It is these interests of society, rather than Barenblatt's own right to silence, which I think the Court should put on the balance against the demands of the Government, if any balancing process is to be tolerated. . . .

MR. JUSTICE BRENNAN, dissenting . . . [omitted].

## III. PRESIDENTIAL PRIVILEGE AND IMMUNITY

### *United States* v. *Nixon*
### 418 U.S. 683, 94 S.Ct. 3090, 41 L.Ed. 2d 1039 (1974)
### http://laws.findlaw.com/us/418/683.html

Following the indictment of seven high-ranking officials—including former presidential assistants H. R. Haldeman and John Ehrlichman and former Attorney General John Mitchell—for conspiracy to defraud the U.S. government and obstruction of justice, the special prosecutor obtained a subpoena duces tecum directing President Richard M. Nixon to deliver to the trial judge certain tape recordings and memoranda of conversations held in the White House. (A subpoena duces tecum is a judicial order, requested by a party to a case, that compels a person in possession of items relevant to the litigation to produce them in court.) Nixon produced some of the subpoenaed material but withheld other portions, invoking executive privilege, which placed confidential presidential documents beyond judicial reach. The trial judge denied the president's claim, and he appealed to the court of appeals. The special prosecutor asked the Supreme Court to review the case before the court of appeals had passed judgment. The decision, rendered on July 24, led directly to Nixon's resignation from office on August 8, 1974. Majority: Burger, Blackmun, Brennan, Douglas, Marshall, Powell, Stewart, White. Not participating: Rehnquist.

## Mr. Chief Justice Burger delivered the opinion of the Court. . . .

We turn to the claim that the subpoena should be quashed because it demands "confidential conversations between a President and his close advisors that it would be inconsistent with the public interest to produce." . . . The first contention is a broad claim that the separation of powers doctrine precludes judicial review of a President's claim of privilege. The second contention is that if he does not prevail on the claim of absolute privilege, the court should hold as a matter of constitutional law that the privilege prevails over the subpoena duces tecum.

In the performance of assigned constitutional duties each branch of the Government must initially interpret the Constitution, and the interpretation of its powers by any branch is due great respect from the others. The President's counsel . . . reads the Constitution as providing an absolute privilege of confidentiality for all presidential communications. Many decisions of this Court, however, have unequivocally reaffirmed the holding of *Marbury* v. *Madison* that "it is emphatically the province and duty of the judicial department to say what the law is.". . .

No holding of the Court has defined the scope of judicial power specifically relating to the enforcement of a subpoena for confidential presidential communications for use in a criminal prosecution, but other exercises of power by the Executive Branch and the Legislative Branch have been found invalid as in conflict with the Constitution. Since this Court has consistently exercised the power to construe and delineate claims arising under express powers, it must follow that the Court has authority to interpret claims with respect to powers alleged to derive from enumerated powers.

In support of his claim of absolute privilege, the President's counsel urges two grounds, one of which is common to all governments and one of which is peculiar to our system of separation of powers. The first ground is the valid need for protection of communications between high government officials and those who advise and assist them in the performance of their manifold duties; the importance of this confidentiality is too plain to require further discussion. . . . Whatever the nature of the privilege of confidentiality of presidential communications in the exercise of Article II powers, the privilege can be said to derive from the supremacy of each branch within its own assigned area of constitutional duties. Certain powers and privileges flow from the nature of enumerated powers; the protection of the confidentiality of presidential communications has similar constitutional underpinnings.

The second ground asserted by the President's counsel in support of the claim of absolute privilege rests on the doctrine of separation of powers. Here it is argued that the independence of the Executive Branch within its own sphere . . . insulates a president from a judicial subpoena in an ongoing criminal prosecution, and thereby protects confidential presidential communications.

However, neither the doctrine of separation of powers, nor the need for confidentiality of high level communications, without more, can sustain an absolute, unqualified presidential privilege of immunity from judicial process under all circumstances. The President's need for complete candor and objectivity from advisers calls for great deference from the courts. However, when the privilege depends solely on the broad, undifferentiated claim of public interest in the confidentiality of such conversations, a confrontation with other values arises. Absent a claim of need to protect military, diplomatic or sensitive national security secrets, we find it difficult to accept the argument that even the very important interest in confidentiality of presidential communications is significantly diminished by production of such material for in camera inspection with all the protection that a district court will be obliged to provide.

The impediment that an absolute, unqualified privilege would place in the way of the primary constitutional duty of the Judicial Branch to do justice in criminal prosecutions would plainly conflict with the function of the courts under Article III. . . .

Since we conclude that the legitimate needs of the judicial process may outweigh presidential privilege, it is necessary to resolve those competing interests in a manner that preserves the essential functions of each branch. The right and indeed the duty to resolve that question does not free the judiciary from according high respect to the representations made on behalf of the President.

The expectation of a President to the confidentiality of his conversations and correspondence, like the claim of confidentiality of judicial deliberations, for example, has all the values to which we accord deference for the privacy of all citizens and added to those values the necessity for protection of the public interest in candid, objective, and even blunt or harsh opinions in presidential decision making. . . . The privilege is fundamental to the operation of government and inextricably rooted in the separation of powers under the Constitution. . . . We agree with Mr. Chief Justice Marshall's observation, therefore, that "in no case of this kind would a court be required to proceed against the President as against an ordinary individual" (*United States* v. *Burr,* 1807).

But this presumptive privilege must be considered in light of our historic commitment to the rule of law. This is nowhere more profoundly manifest than in our view that "the twofold aim of criminal justice is that guilt shall not escape or innocence suffer.". . . The

need to develop all relevant facts in the adversary system is both fundamental and comprehensive. . . . To ensure that justice is done, it is imperative to the function of courts that compulsory process be available for the production of evidence needed either by the prosecution or by the defense.

In this case the President challenges a subpoena served on him as a third party requiring the production of materials for use in a criminal prosecution on the claim that he has a privilege against disclosure of confidential communications. He does not place his claim of privilege on the ground they are military or diplomatic secrets. As to these areas of Article II duties, the courts have traditionally shown the utmost deference to presidential responsibilities. . . . No case of the Court . . . has extended this high degree of deference to a President's generalized interest in confidentiality. Nowhere in the Constitution . . . is there any explicit reference to a privilege of confidentiality, yet to the extent this interest relates to the effective discharge of a President's powers, it is constitutionally based.

The right to the production of all evidence at a criminal trial similarly has constitutional dimensions. The Sixth Amendment explicitly confers upon every defendant in a criminal trial the right "to be confronted with the witnesses against him" and "to have compulsory process for obtaining witnesses in his favor." Moreover, the Fifth Amendment also guarantees that no person shall be deprived of liberty without due process of law. It is the manifest duty of the courts to vindicate those guarantees and to accomplish that it is essential that all relevant and admissible evidence be produced. . . .

A President's acknowledged need for confidentiality in the communications of his office is general in nature, whereas the constitutional need for production of relevant evidence in a criminal proceeding is specific and central to the fair adjudication of a particular criminal case in the administration of justice. Without access to specific facts a criminal prosecution may be totally frustrated. . . .

We conclude that when the ground for asserting privilege as to subpoenaed materials sought for use in a criminal trial is based only on the generalized interest in confidentiality, it cannot prevail over the fundamental demands of due process of law in the fair administration of criminal justice. The generalized as-sertion of privilege must yield to the demonstrated, specific need for evidence in a pending criminal trial. . . .

*Affirmed.*

## Nixon v. Fitzgerald
### 457 U.S. 731, 102 S.Ct. 2690, 73 L.Ed. 2d 349 (1982)
http://laws.findlaw.com/us/457/731.html

Ernest Fitzgerald was employed as a civilian analyst by the Air Force. In testimony to Congress in 1968, he revealed anticipated cost overruns of $2 billion, as well as various technical difficulties, in construction of the C-5A transport plane. Hailed as a "whistle-blower" by Congress and the press, Fitzgerald lost his job in 1969, ostensibly in a departmental reorganization. The Civil Service Commission ruled that his dismissal violated government regulations. Fitzgerald filed a suit for damages in the U.S. District Court for the District of Columbia against various persons in the Department of Defense and the White House staff. In January 1973, President Richard Nixon publicly took responsibility for his discharge and in 1978 was named a defendant in the suit, but Nixon claimed an absolute immunity from civil suits stemming from official actions. In its decision, delayed until 1980 (six years after Nixon resigned the presidency) because of several intermediate rulings, the district court rejected Nixon's claim of immunity, and the Court of Appeals for the District of Columbia Circuit dismissed Nixon's appeal. Ironically, had Nixon lost his case in the Supreme Court, Fitzgerald's suit against him for damages would never have gone to trial. After Nixon petitioned the Court for review, he and Fitzgerald agreed to a settlement under the terms of which Nixon paid Fitzgerald $142,000, with an additional $28,000 to be paid in the event Nixon lost in the Supreme Court. Fitzgerald was rehired, with back pay, by the Air Force in June 1982. Justice Powell's opinion of the Court expressly reserved the question whether Congress might statutorily alter the president's immunity. Majority: Powell, Burger, O'Connor, Rehnquist, Stevens. Dissenting: White, Blackmun, Brennan, Marshall.

### JUSTICE POWELL delivered the opinion of the Court.

The plaintiff in this lawsuit seeks relief in civil damages from a former President of the United States. The claim rests on actions allegedly taken in the former President's official capacity during his tenure in office. The issue before us is the scope of the immunity possessed by the President of the United States. . . .

This Court consistently has recognized that government officials are entitled to some form of immunity from suits for civil damages. . . . [I]n *Butz* v. *Economou* (1978), . . . we considered for the first time the kind of immunity possessed by *federal* executive officials who are sued for constitutional violations. In *Butz* the Court rejected an argument, based on decisions involving federal officials charged with common-law torts, that all high federal officials have a right to absolute immunity from constitutional damages actions. Concluding that a blanket recognition of absolute immunity would be anomalous in light of the qualified immunity standard applied to state executive officials, we held that federal officials generally have the same qualified immunity possessed by state officials. . . . In so doing we reaffirmed our holdings that some officials, notably judges and prosecutors, "because of the special nature of their responsibilities," "require a full exemption from liability." In *Butz* itself we upheld a claim of absolute immunity for administrative officials engaged in functions analogous to those of judges and prosecutors. We also left open the question whether other federal officials could show that "public policy requires an exemption of that scope."

Here a former President asserts his immunity from civil damages claims of two kinds. He stands named as a defendant in a direct action under the Constitution and in two statutory actions under federal laws of general applicability. In neither case has Congress taken express legislative action to subject the President to civil liability for his official acts.

Applying the principles of our cases to claims of this kind, we hold that petitioner, as a former President of the United States, is entitled to absolute immunity from damages liability predicated on his official acts. We consider this immunity a functionally mandated incident of the President's unique office, rooted in the constitutional tradition of the separation of powers and supported by our history. . . .

In arguing that the President is entitled only to qualified immunity, the respondent relies on cases in which we have recognized immunity of this scope for governors and cabinet officers. We find these cases to be inapposite. The President's unique status under the Constitution distinguishes him from other executive officials.

Because of the singular importance of the President's duties, diversion of his energies by concern with private law suits would raise unique risks to the effective functioning of government. As is the case with prosecutors

and judges—for whom absolute immunity now is established—a President must concern himself with matters likely to "arouse the most intense feelings." Yet, as our decisions have recognized, it is in precisely such cases that there exists the greatest public interest in providing an official "the maximum ability to deal fearlessly and impartially with" the duties of his office. This concern is compelling where the officeholder must make the most sensitive and far-reaching decisions entrusted to any official under our constitutional system. Nor can the sheer prominence of the President's office be ignored. In view of the visibility of his office and the effect of his actions on countless people, the President would be an easily identifiable target for suits for civil damages. Cognizance of this personal vulnerability frequently could distract a President from his public duties, to the detriment of not only the President and his office but also the Nation that the Presidency was designed to serve. . . .

Under the Constitution and laws of the United States the President has discretionary responsibility in a broad variety of areas, many of them highly sensitive. In many cases it would be difficult to determine which of the President's innumerable "functions" encompassed a particular action. In this case, for example, respondent argues that he was dismissed in retaliation for his testimony to Congress—a violation of [federal law]. The Air Force, however, has claimed that the underlying reorganization was undertaken to promote efficiency. Assuming that petitioner Nixon ordered the reorganization in which respondent lost his job, an inquiry into the President's motives could not be avoided under the kind of "functional" theory asserted both by respondent and the dissent. Inquiries of this kind could be highly intrusive.

Here respondent argues that petitioner Nixon would have acted outside the outer perimeter of his duties by ordering the discharge of an employee who was lawfully entitled to retain his job in the absence of " 'such cause as will promote the efficiency of the service.' " Because Congress has granted this legislative protection, respondent argues, no federal official could, within the outer perimeter of his duties of office, cause Fitzgerald to be dismissed without satisfying this standard in prescribed statutory proceedings.

This construction would subject the President to trial on virtually every allegation that an action was unlawful, or was taken for a forbidden purpose. Adoption of this construction thus would deprive absolute immunity of its intended effect. It clearly is within the President's constitutional and statutory authority to prescribe the manner in which the Secretary will conduct the business of the Air Force. Because this mandate of office must include the authority to prescribe reorganizations and reductions in force, we conclude that petitioner's alleged wrongful acts lay well within the outer perimeter of his authority.

A rule of absolute immunity for the President will not leave the Nation without sufficient protection against misconduct on the part of the Chief Executive. There remains the constitutional remedy of impeachment. In addition, there are formal and informal checks on Presidential action that do not apply with equal force to other executive officials. The President is subjected to constant scrutiny by the press. Vigilant oversight by Congress also may serve to deter Presidential abuses of office, as well as to make credible the threat of impeachment. Other incentives to avoid misconduct may include a desire to earn reelection, the need to maintain prestige as an element of Presidential influence, and a President's traditional concern for his historical stature.

The existence of alternative remedies and deterrents establishes that absolute immunity will not place the President "above the law." For the President, as for judges and prosecutors, absolute immunity merely precludes a particular private remedy for alleged misconduct in order to advance compelling public ends.

For the reasons stated in this opinion, the decision of the Court of Appeals is reversed, and the case is remanded for action consistent with this opinion.

*So ordered.*

CHIEF JUSTICE BURGER, concurring . . . [omitted].

**JUSTICE WHITE, with whom JUSTICE BRENNAN, JUSTICE MARSHALL, and JUSTICE BLACKMUN join, dissenting. . . .**

Attaching absolute immunity to the Office of the President, rather than to particular activities that the President might perform, places the President above the law. It is a reversion to the old notion that the King can do no wrong. Until now, this concept had survived in this country only in the form of sovereign immunity. That doctrine forecloses suit against the Government itself and against Government officials, but only when the suit against the latter actually seeks relief against the sovereign. Suit against an officer, however, may be maintained where it seeks specific relief against him for conduct contrary to his statutory authority or to the Constitution. Now, however, the Court clothes the Office of the President with sovereign immunity, placing it beyond the law. . . .

Unfortunately, the Court now abandons basic principles that have been powerful guides to decision. It is particularly unfortunate since the judgment in this case has few, if any, indicia of a judicial decision; it is almost wholly a policy choice, a choice that is without substantial support and that in all events is ambiguous in its reach and import. . . . The Court casually, but candidly, abandons the functional approach to immunity that has run through all of our decisions. Indeed, the majority turns this rule on its head by declaring that because the functions of the President's office are so varied and diverse and some of them so profoundly important, the office is unique and must be clothed with officewide, absolute immunity. This is policy, not law, and in my view, very poor policy. . . .

I find it ironic, as well as tragic, that the Court would so casually discard its own role of assuring "the right of every individual to claim the protection of the laws," in the name of protecting the principle of separation of powers. Accordingly, I dissent.

JUSTICE BLACKMUN, with whom JUSTICE BRENNAN and JUSTICE MARSHALL join, dissenting . . . [omitted].

## Clinton v. Jones
## 520 U.S. 681, 117 S.Ct. 1636, 137 L.Ed. 2d 945 (1997)
http://laws.findlaw.com/us/520/681.html

The facts of this case are contained in the opinion below. Majority: Stevens, Rehnquist, O'Connor, Scalia, Kennedy, Souter, Thomas, Ginsburg, Breyer.

**JUSTICE STEVENS delivered the opinion of the Court.**

This case raises a constitutional and a prudential question concerning the Office of the President of the United States. Respondent, a private citizen, seeks to recover damages from the current occupant of that office based on actions allegedly taken before his term began. The President submits that in all but the most exceptional cases the Constitution requires federal courts to defer such litigation until his term ends and that, in any event, respect for the office warrants such a stay. Despite the force of the arguments supporting the President's submissions, we conclude that they must be rejected.

Petitioner, William Jefferson Clinton, was elected to the Presidency in 1992, and re-elected in 1996. His term of office expires on January 20, 2001. In 1991 he was the Governor of the State of Arkansas. Respondent, Paula Corbin Jones, is a resident of California. In 1991 she lived in Arkansas, and was an employee of the Arkansas Industrial Development Commission.

On May 6, 1994, she commenced this action in the United States District Court for the Eastern District of Arkansas by filing a complaint naming petitioner and Danny Ferguson, a former Arkansas State Police officer, as defendants. The complaint alleges two federal claims, and two state law claims over which the federal court has jurisdiction because of the diverse citizenship of the parties. As the case comes to us, we are required to assume the truth of the detailed—but as yet untested—factual allegations in the complaint.

Those allegations principally describe events that are said to have occurred on the afternoon of May 8, 1991, during an official conference held at the Excelsior Hotel in Little Rock, Arkansas. The Governor delivered a speech at the conference; respondent—working as a state employee—staffed the registration desk. She alleges that Ferguson persuaded her to leave her desk and to visit the Governor in a business suite at the hotel, where he made "abhorrent" sexual advances that she vehemently rejected. She further claims that her superiors at work subsequently dealt with her in a hostile and rude manner, and changed her duties to punish her for rejecting those advances. Finally, she alleges that after petitioner was elected President, Ferguson defamed her by making a statement to a reporter that implied she had accepted petitioner's alleged overtures, and that various persons authorized to speak for the President publicly branded her a liar by denying that the incident had occurred. . . .

In response to the complaint, petitioner promptly advised the District Court that he intended to file a motion to dismiss on grounds of Presidential immunity. . . .

The District Judge denied the motion to dismiss on immunity grounds and ruled that discovery in the case could go forward, but ordered any trial stayed until the end of petitioner's Presidency. Although she recognized that a "thin majority" in *Nixon* v. *Fitzgerald* (1982), had held that "the President has absolute immunity from civil damage actions arising out of the execution of official duties of office," she was not convinced that "a President has absolute immunity from civil causes of action arising prior to assuming the office." She was, however, persuaded by some of the reasoning in our opinion in *Fitzgerald* that deferring the trial if one were required would be appropriate. Relying in part on the fact that respondent had failed to bring her

complaint until two days before the 3-year period of limitations expired, she concluded that
the public interest in avoiding litigation that
might hamper the President in conducting the
duties of his office outweighed any demonstrated need for an immediate trial.

Both parties appealed. A divided panel of
the Court of Appeals affirmed the denial of the
motion to dismiss, but because it regarded the
order postponing the trial until the President
leaves office as the "functional equivalent" of
a grant of temporary immunity, it reversed
that order. Writing for the majority, Judge
Bowman explained that "the President, like all
other government officials, is subject to the
same laws that apply to all other members of
our society.". . . .

Petitioner's principal submission—that "in
all but the most exceptional cases," the
Constitution affords the President temporary
immunity from civil damages litigation arising
out of events that occurred before he took
office—cannot be sustained on the basis of
precedent. . . .

The principal rationale for affording certain
public servants immunity from suits for money
damages arising out of their official acts is inapplicable to unofficial conduct. In cases involving prosecutors, legislators, and judges
we have repeatedly explained that the immunity serves the public interest in enabling such
officials to perform their designated functions
effectively without fear that a particular decision may give rise to personal liability. . . . .
That rationale provided the principal basis for
our holding that a former President of the
United States was "entitled to absolute immunity from damages liability predicated on his
official acts." Our central concern was to avoid
rendering the President "unduly cautious in
the discharge of his official duties."

This reasoning provides no support for an
immunity for *unofficial* conduct. As we explained in *Fitzgerald,* "the sphere of protected
action must be related closely to the immunity's justifying purposes." Because of the
President's broad responsibilities, we recognized in that case an immunity from damages
claims arising out of official acts extending to
the "outer perimeter of his authority." But we

have never suggested that the President, or
any other official, has an immunity that extends beyond the scope of any action taken in
an official capacity. . . .

As our opinions have made clear, immunities are grounded in "the nature of the function performed, not the identity of the actor
who performed it."

Petitioner's effort to construct an immunity
from suit for unofficial acts grounded purely
in the identity of his office is unsupported by
precedent. . . .

Petitioner's strongest argument supporting
his immunity claim is based on the text and
structure of the Constitution. He does not contend that the occupant of the Office of the
President is "above the law," in the sense that
his conduct is entirely immune from judicial
scrutiny. The President argues merely for a
postponement of the judicial proceedings that
will determine whether he violated any law.
His argument is grounded in the character of
the office that was created by Article II of the
Constitution, and relies on separation of powers principles that have structured our constitutional arrangement since the founding.

As a starting premise, petitioner contends
that he occupies a unique office with powers
and responsibilities so vast and important that
the public interest demands that he devote his
undivided time and attention to his public duties. He submits that—given the nature of the
office—the doctrine of separation of powers
places limits on the authority of the Federal
Judiciary to interfere with the Executive
Branch that would be transgressed by allowing this action to proceed.

We have no dispute with the initial premise
of the argument. . . .

It does not follow, however, that separation
of powers principles would be violated by
allowing this action to proceed. . . .

Rather than arguing that the decision of the
case will produce either an aggrandizement of
judicial power or a narrowing of executive
power, petitioner contends that—as a by-
product of an otherwise traditional exercise of
judicial power—burdens will be placed on the
President that will hamper the performance of
his official duties. We have recognized that

"[e]ven when a branch does not arrogate power to itself . . . the separation-of-powers doctrine requires that a branch not impair another in the performance of its constitutional duties.". . . Petitioner's predictive judgment finds little support in either history or the relatively narrow compass of the issues raised in this particular case. As we have already noted, in the more than 200-year history of the Republic, only three sitting Presidents have been subjected to suits for their private actions. If the past is any indicator, it seems unlikely that a deluge of such litigation will ever engulf the Presidency. As for the case at hand, if properly managed by the District Court, it appears to us highly unlikely to occupy any substantial amount of petitioner's time.

Of greater significance, petitioner errs by presuming that interactions between the Judicial Branch and the Executive, even quite burdensome interactions, necessarily rise to the level of constitutionally forbidden impairment of the Executive's ability to perform its constitutionally mandated functions. . . .

First, we have long held that when the President takes official action, the Court has the authority to determine whether he has acted within the law. Perhaps the most dramatic example of such a case is our holding that President Truman exceeded his constitutional authority when he issued an order directing the Secretary of Commerce to take possession of and operate most of the Nation's steel mills in order to avert a national catastrophe. Despite the serious impact of that decision on the ability of the Executive Branch to accomplish its assigned mission, and the substantial time that the President must necessarily have devoted to the matter as a result of judicial involvement, we exercised our Article III jurisdiction to decide whether his official conduct conformed to the law. Our holding was an application of the principle established in *Marbury* v. *Madison,* that "[i]t is emphatically the province and duty of the judicial department to say what the law is."

Second, it is also settled that the President is subject to judicial process in appropriate circumstances. Although Thomas Jefferson apparently thought otherwise, Chief Justice Marshall, when presiding in the treason trial of Aaron Burr, ruled that a subpoena duces tecum could be directed to the President. We unequivocally and emphatically endorsed Marshall's position when we held that President Nixon was obligated to comply with a subpoena commanding him to produce certain tape recordings of his conversations with his aides. . . .

In sum, "[i]t is settled law that the separation-of-powers doctrine does not bar every exercise of jurisdiction over the President of the United States." If the Judiciary may severely burden the Executive Branch by reviewing the legality of the President's official conduct, and if it may direct appropriate process to the President himself, it must follow that the federal courts have power to determine the legality of his unofficial conduct. The burden on the President's time and energy that is a mere by-product of such review surely cannot be considered as onerous as the direct burden imposed by judicial review and the occasional invalidation of his official actions. We therefore hold that the doctrine of separation of powers does not require federal courts to stay all private actions against the President until he leaves office.

The reasons for rejecting such a categorical rule apply as well to a rule that would require a stay "in all but the most exceptional cases." Indeed, if the Framers of the Constitution had thought it necessary to protect the President from the burdens of private litigation, we think it far more likely that they would have adopted a categorical rule than a rule that required the President to litigate the question whether a specific case belonged in the "exceptional case" subcategory. In all events, the question whether a specific case should receive exceptional treatment is more appropriately the subject of the exercise of judicial discretion than an interpretation of the Constitution. . . .

Although we have rejected the argument that the potential burdens on the President violate separation-of-powers principles, those burdens are appropriate matters for the District Court to evaluate in its management of the case. The high respect that is owed to the office of the Chief Executive, though not justifying a rule of categorical immunity, is a matter that should inform the conduct of the entire proceeding, including the timing and scope of discovery.

Nevertheless, we are persuaded that it was an abuse of discretion for the District Court to defer the trial until after the President leaves office. Such a lengthy and categorical stay takes no account whatever of the respondent's interest in bringing the case to trial. The complaint was filed within the statutory limitations period—albeit near the end of that period—and delaying trial would increase the danger of prejudice resulting from the loss of evidence, including the inability of witnesses to recall specific facts, or the possible death of a party. . . .

We add a final comment on two matters that are discussed at length in the briefs: the risk that our decision will generate a large volume of politically motivated harassing and frivolous litigation, and the danger that national security concerns might prevent the President from explaining a legitimate need for a continuance.

We are not persuaded that either of these risks is serious. Most frivolous and vexatious litigation is terminated at the pleading stage or on summary judgment, with little if any personal involvement by the defendant. . . . History indicates that the likelihood that a significant number of such cases will be filed is remote. Although scheduling problems may arise, there is no reason to assume that the District Courts will be either unable to accommodate the President's needs or unfaithful to the tradition—especially in matters involving national security—of giving "the utmost deference to Presidential responsibilities." Several Presidents, including petitioner, have given testimony without jeopardizing the Nation's security. In short, we have confidence in the ability of our federal judges to deal with both of these concerns.

If Congress deems it appropriate to afford the President stronger protection, it may respond with appropriate legislation. . . .

The Federal District Court has jurisdiction to decide this case. Like every other citizen who properly invokes that jurisdiction, respondent has a right to an orderly disposition of her claims. Accordingly, the judgment of the Court of Appeals is affirmed.

*It is so ordered.*

JUSTICE BREYER, concurring in the judgment . . . [omitted].

## IV. APPOINTMENT AND REMOVAL

### *Morrison* v. *Olson*
### 487 U.S. 654, 108 S.Ct. 2597, 101 L.Ed. 2d 569 (1988)
### http://laws.findlaw.com/us/487/654.html

The Ethics in Government Act of 1978 provided for appointment of an independent counsel to investigate and, if appropriate, to prosecute high-ranking officials of the executive branch for violation of federal criminal laws. Once appointed, an independent counsel was removable only for cause. In 1985, after a three-year dispute between Congress and the Reagan administration over the Superfund law and the cleanup of toxic wastes, the House Judiciary Committee issued a report suggesting that Theodore Olson had given false and misleading testimony to the committee and that two others had wrongfully withheld documents from the committee. All three held important positions in the Department of Justice. Under the terms of the act, Attorney General Edwin Meese conducted a preliminary investigation and applied to the Special Division of the Court of Appeals for the District of Columbia Circuit for an independent counsel to investigate Olson alone. The Special Division designated Alexia Morrison as independent counsel. When a grand jury issued subpoenas to Olson and the others, they moved to quash the subpoenas on the grounds that the 1978 act was unconstitutional.

In 1987 the district court upheld the act. A divided court of appeals reversed in 1988, concluding, among other things, (1) that the act's restrictions on the attorney general's power to remove an independent counsel infringed the separation of powers, and (2) that the act violated the executive's duty to "take care that the Laws be faithfully executed." The excerpts below are limited to the Court's consideration of those two issues. (Four years after this case was decided, the independent counsel law was allowed to expire. Retaining the basic features of the previous version, Congress revived the statute in 1994 for a period of five years, but allowed it to expire again in 1999.) Majority: Rehnquist, Blackmun, Brennan, Marshall, O'Connor, Stevens, White. Dissenting: Scalia. Not participating: Kennedy.

**CHIEF JUSTICE REHNQUIST delivered the opinion of the Court.**

This case presents us with a challenge to the independent counsel provisions of the Ethics in Government Act of 1978. . . . We hold today that these provisions of the Act do not . . . impermissibly interfere with the President's authority under Article II in violation of the constitutional principle of separation of powers. . . .

Two related issues must be addressed: The first is whether the provision of the Act restricting the Attorney General's power to remove the independent counsel to only those instances in which he can show "good cause," taken by itself, impermissibly interferes with the President's exercise of his constitutionally appointed functions. The second is whether, taken as a whole, the Act violates the separation of powers by reducing the President's ability to control the prosecutorial powers wielded by the independent counsel.

Two Terms ago we had occasion to consider whether it was consistent with the separation of powers for Congress to pass a statute that authorized a government official who is removable only by Congress to participate in what we found to be "executive powers." We held in *Bowsher* [v. *Synar*] that "Congress cannot reserve for itself the power of removal of an officer charged with the execution of the

laws except by impeachment." A primary antecedent for this ruling was our 1925 decision in *Myers* v. *United States*. . . .

Unlike both *Bowsher* and *Myers*, this case does not involve an attempt by Congress itself to gain a role in the removal of executive officials other than its established powers of impeachment and conviction. . . . In our view, the removal provisions of the Act make this case more analogous to *Humphrey's Executor* v. *United States*. . . .

At the other end of the spectrum from *Myers*, the characterization of the agencies in *Humphrey's Executor* . . . as "quasi-legislative" or "quasi-judicial" in large part reflected our judgment that it was not essential to the President's proper execution of his Article II powers that these agencies be headed up by individuals who were removable at will. We do not mean to suggest that an analysis of the functions served by the officials at issue is irrelevant. But the real question is whether the removal restrictions are of such a nature that they impede the President's ability to perform his constitutional duty, and the functions of the officials in question must be analyzed in that light. . . .

The final question to be addressed is whether the Act taken as a whole, violates the principle of separation of powers by unduly interfering with the role of the Executive Branch. . . .

We observe first that this case does not involve an attempt by Congress to increase its own powers at the expense of the Executive Branch. . . .

Finally, we do not think that the Act "impermissibly undermine[s]" the powers of the Executive Branch, or "disrupts the proper balance between the coordinate branches [by] prevent[ing] the Executive Branch from accomplishing its constitutionally assigned functions." It is undeniable that the Act reduces the amount of control or supervision that the Attorney General and, through him, the President exercises over the investigation and prosecution of a certain class of alleged criminal activity. The Attorney General is not allowed to appoint the individual of his choice; he does not determine the counsel's jurisdiction; and his power to remove a counsel is limited. Nonetheless, the Act does give the Attorney General several means of supervising or controlling the prosecutorial powers that may be wielded by an independent counsel. Most importantly, the Attorney General retains the power to remove the counsel for "good cause," a power that we have already concluded provides the Executive with substantial ability to ensure that the laws are "faithfully executed" by an independent counsel. No independent counsel may be appointed without a specific request by the Attorney General, and the Attorney General's decision not to request appointment if he finds "no reasonable grounds to believe that further investigation is warranted" is committed to his unreviewable discretion. . . .

In sum, we conclude today that . . . the Act does not violate the separation of powers principle by impermissibly interfering with the functions of the Executive Branch. The decision of the Court of Appeals is therefore

*Reversed.*

### JUSTICE SCALIA, dissenting. . . .

The framers of the Federal Constitution . . . viewed the principle of separation of powers as the absolutely central guarantee of a just government. . . .

That is what this suit is about. Power. The allocation of power among Congress, the President and the courts in such fashion as to preserve the equilibrium the Constitution sought to establish—so that "a gradual concentration of the several powers in the same department" can effectively be resisted. Frequently an issue of this sort will come before the Court clad, so to speak, in sheep's clothing: the potential of the asserted principle to effect important change in the equilibrium of power is not immediately evident and must be discerned by a careful and perceptive analysis. But this wolf comes as a wolf. . . .

If to describe this case is not to decide it, the concept of a government of separate and coordinate powers no longer has meaning. . . .

The Court concedes that "[t]here is no real dispute that the functions performed by the independent counsel are 'executive,'" though it qualifies that concession by adding "in the sense that they are 'law enforcement' functions that typically have been undertaken by officials within the Executive Branch." The qualifier adds nothing but atmosphere. In what other sense can one identify "the executive Power" that is supposed to be vested in the President (unless it includes everything the Executive Branch is given to do) except by reference to what has always and everywhere—if conducted by Government at all—been conducted never by the legislature, never by the courts, and always by the executive. There is no possible doubt that the independent counsel's functions fit this description. She is vested with the "full power and independent authority to exercise all investigative and prosecutorial functions and powers of the Department of Justice [and] the Attorney General." Governmental investigation and prosecution of crimes is a quintessentially executive function.

As for the . . . question, whether the statute before us deprives the President of exclusive control over that quintessentially executive activity: The Court does not, and could not possibly, assert that it does not. That is indeed the whole object of the statute. Instead, the Court points out that the President, through his Attorney General, has at least some control. That concession is alone enough to invalidate the statute, but I cannot refrain from pointing out that the Court greatly exaggerates the extent of that "some" presidential control. "Most importan[t]" among these controls, the Court asserts, is the Attorney General's "power to remove the counsel for 'good cause.' " This is somewhat like referring to shackles as an effective means of locomotion. As we recognized in *Humphrey's Executor* . . . , limiting removal power to "good cause" is an impediment to, not an effective grant of, presidential control. We said that limitation was necessary with respect to members of the Federal Trade Commission, which we found to be "an agency of the legislative and judicial departments," and "wholly disconnected from the executive department," because "it is quite evident that one who holds his office only during the pleasure of another, cannot be depended upon to maintain an attitude of independence against the latter's will." What we in *Humphrey's Executor* found to be a means of eliminating presidential control, the Court today considers the "most importan[t]" means of assuring presidential control. Congress, of course, operated under no such illusion when it enacted this statute, describing the "good cause" limitation as "protecting the independent counsel's ability to act independently of the President's direct control" since it permits removal only for "misconduct.". . .

It is not for us to determine, and we have never presumed to determine, how much of the purely executive powers of government must be within the full control of the President. The Constitution prescribes that they all are. . . .

While the separation of powers may prevent us from righting every wrong, it does so in order to ensure that we do not lose liberty. The checks against any Branch's abuse of its exclusive powers are twofold: First, retaliation by one of the other Branch's use of its exclusive powers: Congress, for example, can impeach the Executive who willfully fails to enforce the laws; the Executive can decline to prosecute under unconstitutional statutes; and the courts can dismiss malicious prosecutions. Second, and ultimately, there is the political check that the people will replace those in the political branches . . . who are guilty of abuse. Political pressures produced special prosecutors—for Teapot Dome and for Watergate, for example—long before this statute created the independent counsel. . . .

Since our 1935 decision in *Humphrey's Executor* . . . which was considered by many at the time the product of an activist, anti–New Deal court bent on reducing the power of President Franklin Roosevelt—it has been established that the line of permissible restriction upon removal of principal officers lies at the point at which the powers exercised by those officers are no longer purely executive. . . . By its short-sighted action today, I fear the Court has permanently encumbered the Republic with an institution that will do it great harm.

Worse than what it has done, however, is the manner in which it has done it. A government of laws means a government of rules. Today's decision on the basic issue of fragmentation of executive power is ungoverned by rule, and hence ungoverned by law. . . . Taking all things into account, we conclude that the power taken away from the President here is not really *too* much. . . .

The ad hoc approach to constitutional adjudication has real attraction, even apart from its work-saving potential. It is guaranteed to produce a result, in every case, that will make a majority of the Court happy with the law. The law is, by definition, precisely what the majority thinks, taking all things into account, it ought to be. I prefer to rely upon the judgment of the wise men who constructed our system, and of the people who approved it, and of two centuries of history that have shown it to be sound. Like it or not, that judgment says, quite plainly, that "[t]he executive Power shall be vested in a President of the United States."

## V. FOREIGN POLICY AND NATIONAL SECURITY

### Ex Parte *Milligan*
### 71 U.S. (4 Wall.) 2, 18 L.Ed. 281 (1866)

http://supct.law.cornell.edu/supct/cases/name.htm#Case_Name-D-E

(This case is reprinted in Chapter Fifteen, beginning on page 648.)

### *Missouri* v. *Holland*
### 252 U.S. 416, 40 S.Ct. 382, 64 L.Ed. 641 (1920)

http://laws.findlaw.com/us/252/416.html

By a treaty of 1916, the United States and Great Britain undertook the regulation and protection of birds migrating between Canada and various parts of the United States. An act of 1918 gave effect to the treaty by establishing closed seasons and other rules. The state of Missouri sued to prevent a game warden of the United States from enforcing the act, and appealed from the district court's dismissal of the case. Majority: Holmes, Brandeis, Clarke, Day, McKenna, McReynolds, White. Dissenting: Pitney, Van Devanter.

**MR. JUSTICE HOLMES delivered the opinion of the Court. . . .**

The question raised is the general one whether the treaty and statute are void as an interference with the rights reserved to the States.

To answer this question it is not enough to refer to the Tenth Amendment, reserving the powers not delegated to the United States, because by Article II, § 2, the power to make treaties is delegated expressly, and by Article VI treaties made under the authority of the United States, along with the Constitution and laws of the United States made in pursuance thereof, are declared the supreme law of the land. If the treaty is valid there can be no dispute about the validity of the statute under Article I, § 8, as a necessary and proper means to execute the powers of the Government. The language of the Constitution as to the supremacy of treaties being general, the question before us is narrowed to an inquiry into the ground upon which the present supposed exception is placed.

It is said that a treaty cannot be valid if it infringes the Constitution, that there are limits, therefore, to the treaty-making power, and that one such limit is what an act of Congress could not do unaided, in derogation of the powers reserved to the States a treaty cannot do. An earlier act of Congress that attempted by itself and not in pursuance of a treaty to regulate the killing of migratory birds within the States had been held bad in the District Court. Those decisions were supported by arguments that migratory birds were owned by the States in their sovereign capacity for the benefit of their people and that . . . this control was one that Congress had no power to displace. The same argument is supposed to apply now with equal force.

. . . Acts of Congress are the supreme law of the land only when made in pursuance of the Constitution, while treaties are declared to be so when made under the authority of the United States. It is open to question whether the authority of the United States means more than the formal acts prescribed to make the convention. We do not mean to imply that there are no qualifications to the treaty-making power; but they must be ascertained in a different way. It is obvious that there may be matters of the sharpest exigency for the national well-being that an act of Congress could not deal with but that a treaty followed by such an act could, and it is not lightly to be assumed that, in matters requiring national action, "a power which must belong to and somewhere reside in every civilized government" is not to be found. . . . [W]hen we are dealing with words that also are a constituent act, like the Constitution of the United States, we must realize that they have called into life a being the development of which could not have been foreseen completely by the most gifted of its begetters. It was not enough for them to realize or to hope that they had created an organism; it has taken a century and has cost their successors much sweat and blood to prove that they created a nation. The case before us must be considered in the light of our whole experience and not merely in that of what was said a hundred years ago. The treaty in question does not contravene any prohibitory words to be found in the Constitution. The only question is whether it is forbidden by some invisible radiation from the general terms of the Tenth Amendment. We must consider what this country has become in deciding what that Amendment has reserved.

The State as we have intimated founds its claim of exclusive authority upon an assertion of title to migratory birds. . . . To put the claim of the State upon title is to lean upon a slender reed. Wild birds are not in the possession of anyone; and possession is the beginning of ownership. The whole foundation of the State's rights is the presence within their jurisdiction of birds that yesterday had not arrived, tomorrow may be in another State and in a week a thousand miles away. . . .

Here a national interest of very nearly the first magnitude is involved. It can be protected only by national action in concert with that of another power. The subject matter is only transitorily within the State and has no permanent habitat therein. But for the treaty and the statute there soon might be no birds for any powers to deal with. We see nothing in the constitution that compels the Government to sit by while a food supply is cut off and the protectors of our forests and our crops are destroyed. It is not sufficient to rely upon the States. The reliance is vain, and were it otherwise, the question is whether the United States is forbidden to act. We are of opinion that the treaty and statute must be upheld.

*Decree affirmed.*

Mr. Justice Van Devanter and Mr. Justice Pitney dissent [without opinion].

## United States v. Curtiss-Wright Export Corp.
### 299 U.S. 304, 57 S.Ct. 216, 81 L.Ed. 255 (1936)
#### http://laws.findlaw.com/us/299/304.html

This case grew out of the efforts of Congress to limit a war between Bolivia and Paraguay by granting to the president the power to prohibit the sale of arms and munitions to the warring nations. The defendant corporation, charged with conspiring to sell 15 machine guns to Bolivia, objected to the indictment on the ground that the delegation of power to the president was invalid. The district court sustained the demurrer. (A demurrer is the formal mode of disputing the sufficiency in law of the pleading of the other side, even if the facts are true.) Majority: Sutherland, Brandeis, Butler, Cardozo, Hughes, Roberts, Van Devanter. Dissenting: McReynolds. Not participating: Stone.

**MR. JUSTICE SUTHERLAND delivered the opinion of the Court. . . .**

Whether, if the Joint Resolution had related solely to internal affairs, it would be open to the challenge that it constituted an unlawful delegation of legislative power to the Executive, we find it unnecessary to determine. The whole aim of the resolution is to affect a situation entirely external to the United States, and falling within the category of foreign affairs. The determination which we are called to make, therefore, is whether the Joint Resolution . . . is vulnerable to attack under the rule that forbids a delegation of the lawmaking power. In other words, assuming (but not deciding) that the challenged delegation, if it were confined to internal affairs, would be invalid, may it nevertheless be sustained on the ground that its exclusive aim is to afford a remedy for a hurtful condition within foreign territory?

It will contribute to the elucidation of the question if we first consider the differences between the powers of the federal government in respect of foreign or external affairs and those in respect of domestic or internal affairs. . . .

The two classes of powers are different, both in respect of their origin and their nature. The broad statement that the federal government can exercise no powers except those specifically enumerated in the Constitution, and such implied powers as are necessary and proper to carry into effect the enumerated powers, is categorically true only in respect of our internal affairs. In that field, the primary purpose of the Constitution was to carve from the general mass of legislative powers then possessed by the states such portions as it was thought desirable to vest in the federal government leaving those not included in the enumeration still in the states. . . . That this doctrine applies only to powers which the states had is self-evident. And since the states severally never possessed international powers, such powers could not have been carved from the mass of state powers but obviously were transmitted to the United States from some other source. During the Colonial period, those powers were possessed exclusively by and were entirely under the control of the Crown.

By the Declaration of Independence, "the Representatives of the United States of America" declared the United (not the several) Colonies to be free and independent states, and as such to have "full Power to levy War, conclude Peace, contract Alliances, establish Commerce and to do all other Acts and Things which Independent States may of right do."

As a result of the separation from Great Britain by the colonies, acting as a unit, the powers of external sovereignty passed from the Crown not to the colonies severally, but to the colonies in their collective and corporate capacity as the United States of America. . . . When, therefore, the external sovereignty of Great Britain in respect of the colonies ceased, it immediately passed to the Union. . . . That fact was given practical application almost at once. The treaty of peace, made on September 3, 1783, was concluded between his Britannic Majesty and the "United States of America.". . .

The Union existed before the Constitution, which was ordained and established among other things to form "a more perfect Union." Prior to that event, it is clear that the Union declared by the Articles of Confederation to be "perpetual," was the sole possessor of external sovereignty, and in the Union it remained without change save in so far as the Constitution in express terms qualified its exercise. The Framers' Convention was called and exerted its powers upon the irrefutable postulate that though the states were several their people in respect of foreign affairs were one. . . .

It results that the investment of the federal government with the powers of external sovereignty did not depend upon the affirmative grants of the Constitution. The powers to declare and wage war, to conclude peace, to make treaties, to maintain diplomatic relations with other sovereignties, if they had never been mentioned in the Constitution, would have vested in the federal government as necessary concomitants of nationality. . . . As a member of the family of nations, the right and power of the United States in that field are equal to the right and power of the other members of the international family. Otherwise, the United States is not completely sovereign. . . .

Not only, as we have shown, is the federal power over external affairs in origin and essential character different from that over internal affairs, but participation in the exercise of the power is significantly limited. In this vast external realm, with its important, complicated, delicate and manifold problems, the President alone has the power to speak or listen as a representative of the nation. He makes treaties with the advice and consent of the Senate; but he alone negotiates. Into the field of negotiation the Senate cannot intrude; and Congress itself is powerless to invade it. . . .

It is important to bear in mind that we are here dealing not alone with an authority vested in the President by an exertion of legislative power, but with such an authority plus the very delicate, plenary and exclusive power of the President as the sole organ of the federal government in the field of international relations—a power which does not require as a basis for its exercise an act of Congress, but which, of course, like every other governmental power, must be exercised in subordination to the applicable provisions of the Constitution. It is quite apparent that if, in the maintenance of our international relations, embarrassment—perhaps serious embarrassment—is to be avoided and success

for our aims achieved, congressional legislation which is to be made effective through negotiation and inquiry within the international field must often accord to the President a degree of discretion and freedom from statutory restriction which would not be admissible were domestic affairs alone involved. . . . Indeed, so clearly is this true that the first President refused to accede to a request to lay before the House of Representatives the instructions, correspondence and documents relating to the negotiation of the Jay Treaty—a refusal the wisdom of which was recognized by the House itself and has never been doubted. . . .

Both upon principle and in accordance with precedent, we conclude there is sufficient warrant for the broad discretion vested in the President to determine whether the enforcement of the statute will have a beneficial effect upon the reestablishment of peace in the affected countries; whether he shall make proclamation to bring the resolution into operation; whether and when the resolution shall cease to operate and to make proclamation accordingly; and to prescribe limitations and exceptions to which the enforcement of the resolution shall be subject. . . .

*Reversed.*

## *Korematsu v. United States*
## 323 U.S. 214, 65 S.Ct. 193, 89 L.Ed. 194 (1944)
### http://laws.findlaw.com/us/323/214.html

(This case is reprinted in Chapter Fifteen, beginning on page 691.)

## *Youngstown Sheet & Tube Co. v. Sawyer*
## 343 U.S. 579, 72 S.Ct. 863, 96 L.Ed. 1153 (1952)
### http://laws.findlaw.com/us/343/579.html

Labor unrest in the steel industry that began in 1951 resulted in a 1952 presidential order authorizing the secretary of commerce to seize and operate steel mills. The order was not based on any statute but rather was premised on the national emergency created by the threatened strike in an industry vital to defense production during the Korean War. The steel companies obtained an injunction from a district court restraining Secretary of Commerce Sawyer, and a court of appeals decision stayed the injunction. Majority: Black, Burton, Clark, Douglas, Frankfurter, Jackson. Dissenting: Vinson, Minton, Reed.

## MR. JUSTICE BLACK delivered the opinion of the Court.

We are asked to decide whether the President was acting within his constitutional power when he issued an order directing the Secretary of Commerce to take possession of and operate most of the Nation's steel mills. The mill owners argue that the President's order amounts to law making, a legislative function which the Constitution has expressly confided to the Congress and not to the President. The Government's position is that the order was made on findings of the President that his action was necessary to avert a national catastrophe which would inevitably result from a stoppage of steel production, and that in meeting this grave emergency the President was acting within the aggregate of his constitutional powers as the Nation's Chief Executive and the Commander in Chief of the Armed Forces of the United States. . . .

The President's power, if any, to issue the order must stem either from an act of Congress or from the Constitution itself. There is no statute that expressly authorizes the President to take possession of property as he did here. Nor is there any act of Congress to which such a power can fairly be implied. Indeed, we do not understand the Government to rely on statutory authorization for this seizure. . . .

Moreover, the use of the seizure technique to solve labor disputes in order to prevent work stoppages was not only unauthorized by any congressional enactment; prior to this controversy, Congress had refused to adopt that method of settling labor disputes. When the Taft-Hartley Act was under consideration in 1947, Congress rejected an amendment which would have authorized such governmental seizures in case of emergency. . . .

It is clear that if the President had authority to issue the order he did, it must be found in some provision of the Constitution. And it is not claimed that express constitutional language grants this power to the President. The contention is that presidential power should be implied from the aggregate of his powers under the Constitution. Particular reliance is placed on provisions in Article II which say that "the executive Power shall be vested in a President. . . ."; that "he shall take Care that the Laws be faithfully executed"; and that he "shall be Commander in Chief of the Army and Navy of the United States."

The order cannot properly be sustained as an exercise of the President's military power as Commander in Chief of the Armed Forces. The Government attempts to do so by citing a number of cases upholding broad powers in military commanders engaged in day-to-day fighting in a theater of war. Such cases need not concern us here. Even though "theater of war" be an expanding concept, we cannot with faithfulness to our constitutional system hold that the Commander in Chief of the Armed Forces has the ultimate power as such to take possession of private property in order to keep labor disputes from stopping production. This is a job for the Nation's lawmakers, not for its military authorities.

Nor can the seizure order be sustained because of the several constitutional provisions that grant executive power to the President. In the framework of our Constitution, the President's power to see that the laws are faithfully executed refutes the idea that he is to be a lawmaker. The Constitution limits his functions in the lawmaking process to the recommending of laws he thinks wise and the vetoing of laws he thinks bad. And the Constitution is neither silent nor equivocal about who shall make laws which the President is to execute. . . .

The Founders of this Nation entrusted the lawmaking power to the Congress alone in both good and bad times. It would do no good to recall the historical events, the fears of power and the hopes for freedom that lay behind their choice. Such a review would but confirm our holding that this seizure order cannot stand.

The judgment of the District Court is

*Affirmed.*

## MR. JUSTICE FRANKFURTER, concurring. . . .

The Constitution is a framework for government. Therefore the way the framework has consistently operated fairly establishes that it has operated according to its true nature. Deeply embedded traditional ways of conducting government cannot supplant the Constitution or legislation, but they give meaning to the words of a text or supply them. It is an inadmissibly narrow conception of American constitutional law to confine it to the words of the Constitution and to disregard the gloss which life has written upon them. In short, a systematic, unbroken, executive practice, long pursued to the knowledge of the Congress and never before questioned, engaged in by Presidents who have also sworn to uphold the Constitution, making as it were such exercise of power part of the structure of our government, may be treated as a gloss on "executive Power" vested in the President by § 1 of Article II. . . .

Down to the World War II period . . . the record is barren of instances comparable to the one before us. . . . [T]he list of executive assertions of the power of seizure in circumstances comparable to the present reduces to three in the six-month period from June to December of 1941. . . . [I]t suffices to say that these three isolated instances do not add up, either in number, scope, duration or contemporaneous legal justification, to the kind of executive construction of the Constitution [claimed here]. Nor do they come to us sanctioned by long-continued acquiescence of Congress giving decisive weight to a construction by the Executive of its powers.

MR. JUSTICE DOUGLAS, concurring . . . [omitted].

## MR. JUSTICE JACKSON, concurring in the judgment and opinion of the Court. . . .

While the Constitution diffuses power the better to secure liberty, it also contemplates that practice will integrate the dispersed powers into a workable government. It enjoins upon its branches separateness but interdependence, autonomy but reciprocity. Presidential powers are not fixed but fluctuate, depending upon their disjunction or conjunction with those of Congress. We may well begin by a somewhat oversimplified grouping of practical situations in which a President may doubt, or others may challenge, his powers. . . .

(1) When the President acts pursuant to an express or implied authorization of Congress his authority is at its maximum, for it includes all that he possesses in his own right plus all that Congress can delegate. In these circumstances, and in these only, may he be said (for what it may be worth) to personify the federal sovereignty. . . . A seizure executed by the President pursuant to an Act of Congress would be supported by the strongest of presumptions and the widest latitude of judicial interpretation, and the burden of persuasion would rest heavily upon any who might attack it.

(2) When the President acts in absence of either a congressional grant or denial of authority, he can only rely upon his own independent powers, but there is a zone of twilight in which he and Congress may have concurrent authority, or in which its distribution is uncertain. Therefore, congressional inertia, indifference or quiescence may sometimes, at least as a practical matter, enable, if not invite, measures on independent presidential responsibility. In this area, any actual test of power is likely to depend on the imperatives of events and contemporary imponderables rather than on abstract theories of law.

(3) When the President takes measures incompatible with the expressed or implied will of Congress, his power is at its lowest ebb,

for then he can rely only upon his own constitutional powers minus any constitutional powers of Congress over the matter. Courts can sustain exclusive presidential control in such a case only by disabling the Congress from acting upon the subject. Presidential claim to a power at once so conclusive and preclusive must be scrutinized with caution, for what is at stake is the equilibrium established by our constitutional system.

Into which of these classifications does this executive seizure of the steel industry fit? It is eliminated from the first by admission, for it is conceded that no congressional authorization exists for this seizure. . . .

Can it then be defended under flexible tests available to the second category? It seems clearly eliminated from that class because Congress has not left seizure of private property an open field but has covered it by three statutory policies inconsistent with this seizure. In cases where the purpose is to supply needs of the Government itself, two courses are provided: one, seizure of a plant which fails to comply with obligatory orders placed by the Government, another, condemnation of facilities, including temporary use under the power of eminent domain. The third is applicable where it is the general economy of the country that is to be protected rather than exclusive governmental interests. None of these were invoked. . . .

The Solicitor General seeks the power of seizure in three clauses of the Executive Article, the first reading, "The executive Power shall be vested in a President of the United States of America." Lest I be thought to exaggerate, I quote the interpretation which his brief puts upon it: "In our view, this clause constitutes a grant of all the executive powers of which the Government is capable." If that be true, it is difficult to see why the forefathers bothered to add several specific items, including some trifling ones.

The example of such unlimited executive power that must have most impressed the forefathers was the prerogative exercised by George III, and the description of its evils in the Declaration of Independence leads me to doubt that they were creating their new Executive in his image. Continental European examples were no more appealing. And if we seek instruction from our own times, we can match it only from the executive powers in those governments we disparagingly describe as totalitarian. I cannot accept the view that this clause is a grant in bulk of all conceivable executive power but regard it as an allocation to the presidential office of the generic powers thereafter stated.

The clause on which the Government next relies is that "The President shall be Commander in Chief of the Army and Navy of the United States. . . ." These cryptic words have given rise to some of the most persistent controversies in our constitutional history. Of course, they imply something more than an empty title. But just what authority goes with the name has plagued presidential advisers who would not waive or narrow it by nonassertion yet cannot say where it begins or ends. It undoubtedly puts the Nation's armed forces under presidential command. Hence, this loose appellation is sometimes advanced as support for any presidential action, internal or external, involving use of force, the idea being that it vests power to do anything, anywhere, that can be done with an army or navy.

That seems to be the logic of an argument tendered at our bar—that the President having, on his own responsibility, sent American troops abroad derives from that act "affirmative power" to seize the means of producing a supply of steel for them. To quote, "Perhaps the most forceful illustration of the scope of presidential power in this connection is the fact that American troops in Korea, whose safety and effectiveness are so directly involved here, were sent to the field by an exercise of the President's constitutional powers." Thus, it is said he has invested himself with "war powers."

I cannot foresee all that it might entail if the Court should endorse this argument. Nothing in our Constitution is plainer than that declaration of a war is entrusted only to Congress. Of course, a state of war may in fact exist without a formal declaration. But no doctrine that the Court could promulgate would seem to me more sinister and alarming than that a President whose conduct of foreign affairs is so largely uncontrolled, and often even is unknown, can vastly enlarge his mastery over the internal affairs of the country by his own commitment of the Nation's armed forces to some foreign venture. . . .

The third clause in which the Solicitor General finds seizure powers is that "he shall take Care that the Laws be faithfully executed. . . ." That authority must be matched against words of the Fifth Amendment that "No person shall be . . . deprived of life, liberty or property, without due process of law. . . ."

One gives a governmental authority that reaches so far as there is law, the other gives a private right that shall go no farther. These signify about all there is of the principle that ours is a government of laws, not of men, and that we submit ourselves to rulers only if under rules.

The Solicitor General lastly grounds support of the seizure upon nebulous, inherent powers never expressly granted but said to have accrued to the office from the customs and claims of preceding administrations. The plea is for a resulting power to deal with a crisis or an emergency according to the necessities of the case, the unarticulated assumption being that necessity knows no law. . . .

Contemporary foreign experience may be inconclusive as to the wisdom of lodging emergency powers somewhere in a modern government. But it suggests that emergency powers are consistent with free government only when their control is lodged elsewhere than in the Executive who exercises them. That is the safeguard that would be nullified by our adoption of the "inherent powers" formula. . . .

In the practical working of our Government we already have evolved a technique within the framework of the Constitution by which normal executive powers may be considerably expanded to meet an emergency. Congress may and has granted extraordinary authorities which lie dormant in normal times but may be called into play by the Executive in war or upon proclamation of a national emergency. . . .

In view of the ease, expedition and safety with which Congress can grant and has granted large emergency powers, certainly ample to embrace this crisis, I am quite unimpressed with the argument that we should affirm possession of them without statute. Such power either has no beginning or it has no end. If it exists, it need submit to no legal restraint. I am not alarmed that it would plunge us straightaway into dictatorship, but it is at least a step in that wrong direction. . . .

The executive action we have here originates in the individual will of the President and represents an exercise of authority without law. No one, perhaps not even the President, knows the limits of the power he may seek to exert in this instance and the parties affected cannot learn the limit of their rights. We do not know today what powers over labor or property would be claimed to flow from Government possession if we should legalize it, what rights to compensation would be claimed or recognized, or on what contingency it would end. With all its defects, delays and inconveniences, men have discovered no technique for long preserving free government except that the Executive be under the law, and that the law be made by parliamentary deliberations.

Such institutions may be destined to pass away. But it is the duty of the Court to be last, not first, to give them up.

MR. JUSTICE BURTON, concurring . . . [omitted].

MR. JUSTICE CLARK, concurring . . . [omitted].

**MR. CHIEF JUSTICE VINSON, with whom MR. JUSTICE REED and MR. JUSTICE MINTON join, dissenting. . . .**

Those who suggest that this is a case involving extraordinary powers should be mindful that these are extraordinary times. A world not yet recovered from the devastation of World War II has been forced to face the threat of another and more terrifying global conflict. . . .

The steel mills were seized for a public use. The power of eminent domain, invoked in this case, is an essential attribute of sovereignty and has long been recognized as a power of the Federal Government. . . .

Admitting that the Government could seize the mills, plaintiffs claim that the implied power of eminent domain can be exercised only under an Act of Congress; under no circumstances, they say, can that power be exercised by the President unless he can point to an express provision in enabling legislation. This was the view adopted by the District Judge when he granted the preliminary injunction. Without an answer, without hearing evidence, he determined the issue on the basis of his "fixed conclusion . . . that defendant's acts are illegal" because the President's only course in the face of an emergency is to present the matter to Congress and await the final passage of legislation which will enable the Government to cope with threatened disaster.

Under this view, the President is left powerless at the very moment when the need for action may be most pressing and when no one, other than he, is immediately capable of action. Under this view, he is left powerless because a power not expressly given to Congress is nevertheless found to rest exclusively with Congress. . . .

A review of executive action demonstrates that our Presidents have on many occasions exhibited the leadership contemplated by the Framers when they made the President Commander in Chief, and imposed upon him the trust to "take care that the Laws be faithfully executed." With or without explicit statutory authorization, Presidents have at such times dealt with national emergencies by acting promptly and resolutely to enforce legislative programs, at least to save those programs until Congress could act. Congress and the courts have responded to such executive initiative with consistent approval. . . .

## United States v. United States District Court
### 407 U.S. 297, 92 S.Ct. 2125, 32 L.Ed. 2d 752 (1972)

http://laws.findlaw.com/us/407/297.html

(This case is reprinted in Chapter Fifteen, beginning on page 694.)

## War Powers Resolution
### 87 Stat. 555 (1973), 50 U.S.C. ch. 33

http://www4.law.cornell.edu/uscode/50/ch33.html#PC33

A peace accord to end American military involvement in Vietnam was signed in January 1973 following several years of domestic discontent over the nation's Indochina policy. After U.S. bombing of Cambodia, Congress passed the War Powers Resolution in the fall of 1973 in an attempt to provide a legal check on the president's authority to commit American forces abroad without congressional approval. President Richard Nixon vetoed the resolution on October 24, calling it both "dangerous" and "unconstitutional." By a vote of 284–135 (four more than the required two-thirds margin) in the House and 75–18 in the Senate, Congress overrode Nixon's veto on November 7. Nixon's political troubles over Watergate probably contributed to the successful congressional effort to thwart his veto.

*Resolved by the Senate and House of Representatives of the United States of America in Congress assembled, That:* . . .

Sec. 2. (c) The constitutional powers of the President as Commander-in-Chief to introduce United States Armed Forces into hostilities, or into situations where imminent involvement in hostilities is clearly indicated by the circumstances, are exercised only pursuant to (1) a declaration of war, (2) specific statutory authorization, or (3) a national emergency created by attack upon the United States, its territories or possessions, or its armed forces.

Sec. 3. The President in every possible instance shall consult with Congress before introducing United States Armed Forces into hostilities or into situations where imminent involvement in hostilities is clearly indicated by the circumstances, and after every such introduction shall consult regularly with the Congress until United States Armed Forces are no longer engaged in hostilities or have been removed from such situations.

Sec. 4. (a) In the absence of a declaration of war, in any case in which United States Armed Forces are introduced—

(1) into hostilities or into situations where imminent involvement in hostilities is clearly indicated by the circumstances;

(2) into the territory, airspace or waters of a foreign nation, while equipped for combat, except for deployments which relate solely to supply, replacement, repair, or training of such forces; or

(3) in numbers which substantially enlarge United States Armed Forces equipped for combat already located in a foreign nation;

The President shall submit within 48 hours to the Speaker of the House of Representatives and to the President pro tempore of the Senate a report, in writing, setting forth—

(A) the circumstances necessitating the introduction of United States Armed Forces;

(B) the constitutional and legislative authority under which such introduction took place; and

(C) the estimated scope and duration of the hostilities or involvement.

(b) The President shall provide such other information as the Congress may request in the fulfillment of its constitutional responsibilities with respect to committing the Nation to war and to the use of United States Armed Forces abroad.

(c) Whenever United States Armed Forces are introduced into hostilities or into any situation described in subsection (a) of this section, the President shall, so long as such armed forces continue to be engaged in such hostilities or situation, report to the Congress periodically on the status of such hostilities or situation as well as on the scope and duration of such hostilities or situation, but in no event shall he report to the Congress less often than once every six months.

Sec. 5. (a) Each report submitted pursuant to section 4(a)(1) shall be transmitted to the Speaker of the House of Representatives and to the President pro tempore of the Senate on the same calendar day. Each report so transmitted shall be referred to the Committee on Foreign Affairs of the House of Representatives and to the Committee on Foreign Relations of the Senate for appropriate action. . . .

(b) Within sixty calendar days after a report is submitted or is required to be submitted pursuant to section 4(a)(1), whichever is earlier, the President shall terminate any use of United States Armed Forces with respect to which such report was submitted (or required to be submitted), unless the Congress (1) has declared war or has enacted a specific authorization for such use of United States Armed Forces, (2) has extended by law such sixty-day period, or (3) is physically unable to meet as a result of an armed attack upon the United States. Such sixty-day period shall be extended for not more than an additional thirty days if the President determines and certifies to the Congress in writing that unavoidable military necessity respecting the safety of United States Armed Forces requires the continued use of such armed forces in the course of bringing about a prompt removal of such forces.

(c) Notwithstanding subsection (b), at any time that United States Armed Forces are engaged in hostilities outside the territory of the United States, its possessions and territories without a declaration of war or specific statutory authorization, such forces shall be removed by the President if the Congress so directs by concurrent resolution. . . .

# CHAPTER FOUR

# *Federalism*

*Federalism was our Nation's own discovery. The Framers split the atom of sovereignty. It was the genius of their idea that our citizens would have two political capacities, one state and one federal, each protected from incursion by the other. The resulting Constitution created a legal system unprecedented in form and design, establishing two orders of government, each with its own direct relationship, its own privity, its own set of mutual rights and obligations to the people who sustain it and are governed by it.*

—JUSTICE ANTHONY M. KENNEDY (1995)

Although many consider judicial review to be America's unique contribution to political science, federalism may continue to be of equal influence on other nations and of unending importance at home. Unfortunately for those who look upon federalism as the key to world or regional order under law, our history—unless one takes the long view—is not reassuring.

A distinguishing characteristic of American government is **federalism**—a dual system in which governmental powers are constitutionally distributed between central (national) and local (state) authorities. The reasons for the adoption of such an arrangement are both historical and rational. During the revolutionary period the states regarded themselves as independent sovereignties. Under the Articles of Confederation, little of their power over internal affairs was surrendered to the Continental Congress. In the face of proved inability of the Confederation to cope with the problems confronting it, local patriotism had to yield.

When the Constitutional Convention met, compromise between the advocates of a strong central government and supporters of states' rights was necessary. Federalism fitted into James Madison's basic requirement, reflecting his purpose, as stated in *The Federalist,* No. 51, to so contrive "the interior structure of the government as that its several constituent parts may, by their mutual relations, be the means of keeping each other in their proper places." Alexander Hamilton, in *The Federalist,* No. 23, listed four chief purposes to be served by union: common defense, public peace, regulation of commerce, and foreign relations. General agreement that these objectives required unified government drew together representatives of small and large states alike.

## SOURCES OF CONTENTION

One point on which the nationalists at the Philadelphia Convention remained firm was their determination that no precise line should be drawn dividing national power from state power. The powers of the national government were enumerated but not defined. Alert to possible inroads on the states, Hugh Williamson of North Carolina objected that the effect might be to "restrain the States from regulating their internal affairs." Elbridge Gerry of Massachusetts objected that indefinite power in the central authority might "enslave the States." Hamilton, Madison, and James Wilson would not budge, contending that a line dividing state and national power would unduly weaken national authority. "When we come near the line," Wilson explained, "it cannot be found. . . . A discretion must be left on one side or the other. . . . Will it not be most safely lodged on the side of the National Government? . . . What danger is there that the whole will unnecessarily sacrifice a part? But reverse the case, and leave the whole at the mercy of each part, and will not the general interest be continually sacrificed to local interests?" This avowal of national supremacy evoked from opponents of the Constitution an expected query: "[W]here is the bill of rights which shall check the power of this congress, which shall say, *thus far shall ye come and no farther?* The safety of the people depends on a bill of rights."

    **ORIGINS OF THE TENTH AMENDMENT.** In the First Congress, Madison and others made good on the promise they had made during the debates over ratification to make the addition of a bill of rights a priority for the new government. (Documents relating to the development of a bill of rights are reprinted in Chapter Nine.) **Antifederalists** (those who had opposed ratification in 1787–1788) had conjured up the image of the central government as a colossus, determined to swallow defenseless states. To quiet their fears, Madison included among the amendments submitted on June 8, 1789, the one that became the Tenth: "The powers not delegated to the United States by the Constitution, nor prohibited by it to the States, are reserved to the States respectively, or to the people."

    Madison was on record shortly before the Convention as having said that the states should be retained insofar as they could be "subordinately useful." Equally well-known was his early aversion to including a bill of rights. "It was obviously and self-evidently the case," he had insisted, "that every thing not granted is reserved." Now with an amendment on the floor, he resisted efforts to convert it into a substantive check on national power. "While I approve of these amendments [the Ninth and Tenth]," Madison tersely stated on August 15, "I should oppose the consideration at this time of such as are likely to change the principles of the government." And when, three days later, Thomas Tucker proposed to add the word *expressly* to the proposed Tenth Amendment, making it read, "the powers not expressly delegated to the United States by the Constitution," Madison objected. "It was impossible," he explained, "to confine a Government to the exercise of express powers; there must necessarily be admitted powers by implication." Tucker's motion was defeated. Gerry's effort of August 21, to get the word *expressly* inserted, suffered the same fate, the vote being 32–17. Madison's position on the floor of Congress about the Tenth Amendment bears out Chief Justice Marshall's later observation in ***McCulloch* v. *Maryland.*** It was designed "for the purpose of quieting excessive jealousy which had been excited."

The unavailing struggle to give meaning to the Tenth Amendment underscores the conclusion that for many Antifederalists, states' rights weighed more heavily than their concern for personal rights. This would explain why so many Antifederalists were disappointed with the amendments as they emerged from Congress. To William Grayson, the amendments were "so mutilated and gutted that in fact they are good for nothing. . . ." Richard Henry Lee still saw "the most essential danger" arising from the Constitution's "tendency to a consolidated government, instead of a union of Confederated States. . . ." Instead of "substantial amendments," complained South Carolina's Pierce Butler, here were a "few milk-and-water amendments . . . such as liberty of conscience, a free press, and one or two general things already well secured." Georgia's Congressman James Jackson agreed: The amendments were not worth "a pinch of salt." Antifederalists had failed to make the Tenth Amendment a limit on national power.

**TRUISM OR INDEPENDENT CHECK?** The distribution of powers agreed on in the Convention, and the reassurance given the states by the Tenth Amendment, did not preclude conflict. The struggle continued in politics and in the courts, and when prolonged debate and bitter controversy failed to yield a conclusive verdict, the contestants carried this baffling issue of political and constitutional theory to the battlefield in 1861 for settlement by the arbitrament of the sword. Even this holocaust was not conclusive.

The problem of determining the extent of national and state power and of resolving the conflicts between the two centers of authority was ultimately left to the Supreme Court, which has alternated between two ways of thinking about the Tenth Amendment. The one more favorable to national power envisions the Tenth as a "truism," as Justice Stone declared in 1941, meaning that what the states have not surrendered has been retained (*United States* v. *Darby*). Accordingly, states (and those interests dominant in state governments) are to look not to the Constitution but to the political process for protection against Congress. The other regards the amendment as a discrete barrier to national power, in addition to other limits that the Constitution imposes, that is judicially enforceable against Congress on behalf of the states.

## NATURE OF NATIONAL AUTHORITY

The authority of the central government in relation to state governments can be classified in several ways.

**DIMENSIONS OF NATIONAL POWER.** Of all the things governments in the United States may do, the powers of the national government are theoretically limited to those assigned to it by the Constitution, expressly or by implication, and are therefore **delegated powers.** This is the premise of the Tenth Amendment. From a national perspective, states therefore possess what remains. These **reserved powers** in turn are a function of state law and may vary from state to state. As a second dimension, the national government may use any and all means to give effect to any power specifically granted. This doctrine of **implied powers** finds its textual basis in Congress's authority to make all laws "necessary and proper" for carrying into execution what are called **express powers,** those powers specifically delegated to it (Art. 1, Sec. 8, Cl. 18). No new or additional powers are granted by the **necessary and proper clause** (also called the "elastic clause"); it merely gives the federal government a choice of means as it operates within the limited sphere of its activity. As an extension of implied powers, **resulting powers** derive from the mass of delegated powers or from a group of them. Such powers include taking of property by eminent domain for a purpose not specified in the Constitution, carrying into effect treaties entered into by the United States, and making paper money legal tender in payment of public and private debts (*Juilliard* v. *Greenman,* 1884). The **supremacy clause** (Art. VI, Para. 2), the keystone of the federal system, supplies a third dimension of national power. It indicates that if the legitimate powers of state and nation conflict, those of the national government shall prevail.

Thus national power is of three dimensions: (1) the enumeration in which the grant of power is couched, (2) the discretionary choice of means that Congress has for carrying its enumerated powers into execution, and (3) the fact of supremacy. Under this three-dimensional theory of national authority, no subject matter whatever is withdrawn from control or regulation by the United States simply because it also lies within the usual domain of state power.

**CONCURRENT AND EXCLUSIVE POWERS.** The powers of the national government may also be classified as **concurrent** or **exclusive.** A concurrent power refers to an authority shared by both state and national governments, such as taxation or operating a court system. States may legislate in such instances provided they do not conflict with valid national laws or purposes. In contrast, under the following conditions, powers delegated to Congress by the Constitution are exclusive and therefore are denied to the states:

1. Where the right to exercise the power is made exclusive by express provision of the Constitution. Article I, for example, gives Congress exclusive power over the District of Columbia and over property purchased from a state with the consent of the legislature.
2. Where one section of the Constitution grants an express power to Congress and another section prohibits the states from exercising a similar power. For example, Congress is given the power to coin money (Art. I, Sec. 8, Cl. 5), and the states are expressly prohibited from exercising such power (Art. I, Sec. 10, Cl. 1).
3. Where the power granted to Congress, though not in terms exclusive, is such that the exercise of a similar power by the states would be utterly incompatible with national power. In ***Cooley*** v. ***Board of Wardens*** (1851) (see Chapter Six), the Court admitted the existence of a concurrent power to control interstate commerce but limited state power to matters of local concern. Where the subject matter is national in scope and requires uniform legislative treatment, such as the federal government alone can provide, the power of Congress is exclusive. "Exclusive" is here used in a special sense, since the disability of the states arises not from the Constitution but from the nature of the subject matter to which the power is applied. Such power has been termed "latent concurrent power" since Congress may consent to its exercise by the state.

**PREEMPTION.** Concurrent powers are fruitful sources of friction between national and state authority. The supremacy clause in Article VI means that state statutes and constitutional provisions must give way when they conflict with the Constitution, treaties, and valid laws of the United States. The latter preempt or supersede the former. What is the outcome when state and national governments choose to legislate on the same topic without enacting conflicting laws? Sometimes

Congress explicitly recognizes a concurrent state interest and so approves complementary state statutes. At other times, Congress explicitly rules out a role for the states. A more difficult issue arises when state policies do not conflict and there is no expressed congressional intent to welcome or to displace action by the states.

In *Pennsylvania* v. *Nelson* (1956), for example, the Court confronted a state statute criminalizing sedition against the United States. In the Smith Act of 1940 (see Chapter Eleven) Congress had prohibited the same thing. In holding that the Smith Act preempted the Pennsylvania law, Chief Justice Warren noted three conditions that suggest supersession: First, the scheme of federal regulation is "so pervasive as to make reasonable the inference that Congress left no room for the states to supplement it. . . ." Second, the national interest is so dominant on a subject that the federal system must "be assumed to preclude enforcement of state laws on the same subject." Third, there is a danger of conflict between state and federal enforcement efforts. The presence of the three conditions in *Nelson* meant that Congress had chosen to "occupy the field."

Foreign policy and concern for human rights may pose a **preemption** question too. In 1996 Massachusetts passed a law effectively barring American or foreign companies operating in Myanmar from doing business with state agencies. Myanmar was then ruled by a military dictatorship. Three months later Congress banned new investment by American firms in Myanmar and gave the president discretion to lift the sanctions, to suspend them, or to impose new ones as circumstances required. Even though Congress did not expressly rule out sanctions imposed by state governments, the Supreme Court held unanimously that national policy preempted the more stringent state law because the latter undermined the president's role in foreign relations. Congress had implicitly chosen to occupy the field. "It is implausible to think," declared Justice Souter, "that Congress would have gone to such lengths to empower the President if it had been willing to compromise his effectiveness by deference to every provision of state statute or local ordinance that might, if enforced, blunt the consequences of discretionary presidential action" (*Crosby* v. *National Foreign Trade Council,* 2000).

**JUDICIAL FEDERALISM.** The fact that much of the Supreme Court's docket each term consists of cases from state courts is another reason why the justices are active players in the game of federalism. Interaction between state and federal courts is called **judicial federalism.** One of its dimensions involves Supreme Court review of state court decisions, which arguably rest on a state, not on the national, constitution.

As explained in Chapter One, the Court may sit in judgment on the decisions of the highest court of each state when federal questions are involved. A case raises a **federal question** when a provision of the U.S. Constitution, a treaty, or a national statute is at issue. Once a federal question is present, the Supreme Court becomes the ultimate arbiter of its resolution. This rule encourages uniformity among the states. In contrast, the absence of a federal question encourages diverse policies because there is no judicial mechanism for imposing uniform rules of law on the states. In such situations resolution of an issue rests with the individual states.

What happens when a state court gives greater protection to a right found in both state and federal constitutions and rests its decision on the former? Noninterference by the Supreme Court in such situations allows states to expand liberties that have parallel protections in both constitutions. The Supreme Court, however, will not accept a state court's interpretation of the federal Constitution at variance with its own, even if the state's decision is more protective of individual liberty.

In *Michigan* v. *Long* (1983), the Supreme Court of Michigan decided that police had infringed Long's rights when making a search of his car. But which rights? Those protected by the Fourth Amendment in the United States Constitution, or those in parallel provisions in the Michigan constitution? Prior to this case, the Supreme Court presumed that state court decisions rested on an "adequate and independent state ground" unless the party bringing the case could persuade the justices to the contrary. But in *Long*, the Court changed its mind. According to Justice O'Connor, when

> a state court decision fairly appears to rest primarily on federal law, or to be interwoven with the federal law, and when the adequacy and independence of any possible state law ground is not clear from the face of the opinion, we will accept . . . that the state court decided the case the way it did because it believed that federal law required it to do so.

To be served, O'Connor said, were the twin goals of allowing states to develop their own jurisprudence "unimpeded by federal interference" and preserving "the integrity of federal law." Accordingly, "[i]f the state court decision indicates clearly and expressly that it is alternatively based on bona fide separate, adequate, and independent grounds, we, of course, will not undertake to review the decision." Her statement means that state courts not only must provide a rationale that disavows reliance on federal law but also must satisfy a majority of the Court that this reliance is "bona fide." Adding "separate" to "adequate" and "independent" makes it much easier for the Court to review any state court decision that makes so much as a passing reference to federal law or the Constitution.

## CONCEPTS OF FEDERALISM

As was inevitable, the formal distribution of powers between the national government and the states proved to be a subject of diverse interpretations. The fault line along which supporters and opponents of the Constitution had divided in 1787–1788 carried over into debates within the new government over how national authority would be construed. On one side were advocates of national supremacy; on the other were advocates of dual federalism. Echoes of this nineteenth-century verbal combat reverberate today.

**NATIONAL SUPREMACY: LEGACY OF CHIEF JUSTICE JOHN MARSHALL.** As John Adams left the presidency in early 1801, he installed John Marshall, an ardent nationalist and a Virginian, as chief justice. Marshall read into our constitutional law a concept of federalism that magnified national at the expense of state power. Important precedents existed to aid his labors. Besides the House of Representatives debates out of which the Tenth Amendment emerged, there was the 1793 case of ***Chisholm* v. *Georgia*** in which state sovereignty pretensions were denied by a vote of 4–1.

The Court's decision holding the state of Georgia amenable to the jurisdiction of the national judiciary and suable by a citizen of another state in the federal courts was one of the first instances in which the Court gave meaning to the text of the Constitution. However, the ruling provoked speedy and largely unfavorable reaction and prompted immediate steps toward constitutional amendment. On January 8, 1798, three years before Marshall was appointed chief justice, the Eleventh Amendment became a part of the Constitution, overturning *Chisholm*. Yet one element of this case should not be overlooked: Nearly a decade before Chief Justice Marshall's assertion of judicial review in **Marbury v. Madison** (reprinted in Chapter Two), the Court's interpretation of the Constitution was apparently equated with the document itself.

Marshall's tenure (1801–1835), covering a period in which his political enemies dominated the political branches of the government, made his fervent nationalism stand out even more dramatically than if he had represented merely the judicial element in a broad nationalist movement. It was not until 1819, however, that the chief justice found himself face-to-face with the dreaded issue of "clashing sovereignties" in **McCulloch v. Maryland.** The state of Maryland levied a tax on the Second Bank of the United States, raising questions not only about the powers of Congress to charter a bank but also about the place of the states in the federal system. For Marshall, the necessary and proper clause gave Congress a discretionary choice of means in implementing granted powers, and the Tenth Amendment in no way limited this freedom of selection. As a result Congress possessed not only those powers expressly granted by the Constitution but an indefinite number of others as well, unless prohibited by the Constitution. Moreover, the breadth that the Constitution allowed in a choice of means was largely a matter for Congress, not the judiciary, to decide. Thus, Marshall established not only the proposition that national powers must be liberally construed but also the equally decisive principle that the Tenth Amendment does not create in the states an independent limitation on such authority. In reply to the argument that the taxing power was reserved to the states by the Tenth Amendment, and hence could operate even against a legitimate national instrumentality, Marshall went out of his way to deny state power to tax national instrumentalities. A part of the union could not be allowed to cripple the whole.

Two years later, in **Cohens v. Virginia** (1821), the chief justice refuted the argument that in all cases "arising" in their courts, state judges had final authority to interpret the Constitution and the U.S. laws and treaties made under its authority. "The American States," he said, "as well as the American People, have believed a close and firm Union to be essential to their liberty, and to their happiness." As a consequence the people had surrendered portions of state sovereignty to the national government. The supremacy clause and the principle of judicial review required that final decisions on constitutional issues "arising" in state courts be made only by the Supreme Court. Otherwise the Constitution would have different meanings from state to state.

Marshall biographer Albert J. Beveridge described the chief justice's opinion as "one of the strongest and most enduring strands of that mighty cable woven to hold the American people together as a united and imperishable nation." Thomas Jefferson condemned it as indicating judicial determination "to undermine the foundations of our confederated fabric." Denouncing the justices as a "subtle corps of sappers and miners constantly working underground," Jefferson charged that they had transformed the federal system into "a general and supreme one alone."

Marshall's doctrine of **national supremacy** built on the proposition that the central government and states confront each other in the relationship of superior and subordinate. If the exercise of Congress's enumerated powers be legitimate, the fact that their exercise encroaches on the states' traditional authority is of no significance. Moreover, the Court's duty is not to preserve state sovereignty but to protect national power against state encroachments. The Court functions not as an umpire but as an agency of national authority. For Marshall, as for Madison in 1788, the principal danger of the federal system lay in erosive state action. Effective political limitations, such as a Senate elected by state legislators, existed against national efforts to impinge on state power, but only the Supreme Court could peacefully restrain state action from infringing on the authority of the national government.

**DUAL FEDERALISM: LEGACY OF CHIEF JUSTICE ROGER B. TANEY.** Marshall's doctrine of federalism did not go unchallenged. His successor, Roger B. Taney of Maryland, strove valiantly during his long tenure (1836–1864) to redefine federalism in terms more favorable to state power.

The concept of federalism common to Marshall's critics insisted that the Constitution was a compact of sovereign states, not an ordinance of the people. The national government and the states faced each other as equals across a precise constitutional line defining their respective jurisdictions. This concept of nation-state equality had been the basis of Virginia's anarchical arguments in *Cohens* v. *Virginia.*

Accepting the basic creed of nation-state equality, the Taney Court stripped it of its anarchic implications. Within the powers reserved by the Tenth Amendment, the states were sovereign, but final authority to determine the scope of state powers rested with the national judiciary, an arbitrator standing aloof from the sovereign pretensions of both nation and states. "This judicial power," Taney wrote in *Ableman* v. *Booth* (1859), "was justly regarded as indispensable, not merely to maintain the supremacy of the laws of the United States, but also to guard the states from any encroachment upon their reserved rights by the general government. . . . So long . . . as this Constitution shall endure, this tribunal must exist with it, deciding in the peaceful forum of judicial proceeding the angry and irritating controversies between sovereignties, which in other countries have been determined by the arbitrament of force." For Marshall's concept of national supremacy, the Taney Court substituted a theory of federal equilibrium, later called "dual sovereignty" or **dual federalism.** Yet Marshall and Taney were agreed on one essential point: The Supreme Court provided a forum for keeping conflict within peaceful bounds.

**CONSEQUENCES FOR PUBLIC POLICY.** Marshall headed the Court for 34 years, Taney for 28, leaving two theories of federalism succeeding justices were free to apply as their inclinations or needs of the time dictated. Particularly in the period from the end of the Civil War to 1937, Taney's dual federalism had considerable impact on national policy. In ***Texas* v. *White*** (1869), as the Court acknowledged national power and congressional discretion in setting Reconstruction policy in the states of the late Confederacy, Chief Justice Chase observed that the Constitution "in all its provisions, looks to an indestructible Union, composed of indestructible states." The sentence was not mere rhetoric. Initially, it was said that the powers of the national government were "enumerated," those of the states "reserved." In the hands of others, Taney's federalism allowed this order of things to change, turning the Tenth Amendment upside down and denying Congress a discretionary choice of means for carrying its enumerated powers into execution. As Chapters Six and Seven will show, the justices ruled on occasion that there were certain subject matters especially regarding economic and social regulation that were "expressly" reserved to the states, and, therefore, beyond national control. Thus, the states enjoyed their own enumerated powers in certain areas, not by the Constitution but by judicial mandate. The effect was to eliminate the second dimension of national power. Since 1937 the Supreme Court has adhered generally to a national supremacy view of federalism. But as explained below, dual federalism has reappeared in a few contexts in recent years.

Taney's passionate concern for states' rights should not, however, obscure the fact that in his day the state **police power** (see Chapter Eight) was the only practical tool at hand to cope with the pressing problems of the day. Taney called it "the power to govern men and things. . . ." It consisted of that mass of regulatory authority that the states had not surrendered to the central government under the Constitution. In a period in which the national government was not yet prepared to deal realistically with economic and social problems, the theory of national supremacy had the effect of posing the unexercised commerce power of Congress or the contract clause as barriers to any government action. Taney's dual federalism in the years before the Civil War enabled states to deal experimentally with problems that the national government would not begin to face until another half century had elapsed.

**INTERGOVERNMENTAL IMMUNITY.** In addition to the express limitations and prohibitions on national and state power contained in the Constitution, the Court has developed other limitations stemming from federalism itself. Maintenance of a political system in which two sovereignties must operate side by side led to the adoption of the doctrine that neither government may interfere with the government functions of the other, nor with the agencies and officials through which those functions are executed.

This doctrine of **governmental immunity** had its inception in *McCulloch* v. *Maryland*. On the premise that "the power to tax involves the power to destroy," Chief Justice Marshall declared, "The states have no power, by taxation or otherwise, to retard, impede, burden, or in any manner control the operations of the constitutional laws enacted by Congress to carry into execution the powers vested in the general government." Marshall's immunity doctrine was based on his theory of national supremacy. Regarded in this light, it is consistent with his attitude toward the role of the central government in a federal system. Accordingly, he denied emphatically the proposition that "every argument which would sustain the right of the general government to tax banks chartered by the states will equally sustain the right of the state to tax banks chartered by the general government." "The difference," he explained, "is that which always exists, and always must exist, between the action of the whole on the part, and the part on the whole—between the laws of a government declared to be supreme, and those of a government, which, when in opposition to those laws, is not supreme."

In *Collector* v. *Day* (1871), ruling that the salaries of state court judges were immune from a national income tax, the justices established the doctrine of **reciprocal immunity,** based on the theory of the equality of national and state authority under the federal system. If states could not tax the national government, the national government could not tax the states. In time, both governments were denied fruitful sources of taxation. *Graves* v. *New York* (1939) overruled *Day* so far as it recognized "an implied constitutional immunity from income taxation of salaries of officers or employees of the national or state government or their instrumentalities." The immunity doctrine as to the states had been qualified even earlier in *South Carolina* v. *United States* (1905), which upheld a federal tax on South Carolina's liquor-dispensing business. In *New York* v. *United States* (1946), the Court refused to distinguish South Carolina's traffic in liquor from New York's traffic in mineral water.

The Court made further inroads on the reciprocal immunity doctrine in *South Carolina* v. *Baker* (1988), which expressly overruled *Pollock* v. *Farmers' Loan & Trust Co.* (first hearing, 1895). *Pollock* held that interest earned from municipal bonds was immune from federal taxation. In upholding a 1982 tax which removed the federal income tax exemption from interest earned on bearer (as opposed to registered) municipal bonds, the Court explained in *Baker* that the sources of state and federal immunity were different: "the state immunity arises from the constitutional structure and a concern for protecting state sovereignty, whereas the federal immunity arises from the Supremacy Clause." The states, therefore, "can never tax the United States directly, but can tax any private parties with whom it does business, even though the financial burden falls on the United States, as long as the tax does not discriminate against the United States or those with whom it deals. . . . The rule with respect to state tax immunity is essentially the same . . . except that at least some nondiscriminatory federal taxes can be collected directly from the States even though a parallel state tax could not be collected directly from the Federal Government." So the issue whether a nondiscriminatory federal tax might violate state tax immunity does not even arise today, unless the federal government seeks to collect the tax directly from a state.

**COOPERATIVE FEDERALISM.** Cooperation—not courtroom combat—more often characterizes the many manifestations of federalism today. Federalism not only shapes American politics but dictates the way many national policies are both developed and implemented. The national government may appropriate funds for such state activities as education, road building, and unemployment relief. It may grant such funds to the states on condition that a like amount or a specified proportion be raised by them for similar purposes, or on condition that the funds be spent in ways specified by federal law. Changing views on the proper roles of nation and states amply demonstrate that federalism is now, as always, in flux. What presidents, governors, and members of Congress and state legislatures have to say about their respective responsibilities remains as important as are judicial decisions in deciding what federalism, American-style, means.

# THE RETURN OF DUAL FEDERALISM

As Chapter Six explains, the Constitutional Revolution of 1937 reestablished Marshall's doctrine of national supremacy as the guiding principle of American federalism. The view that the Tenth Amendment no longer served as an independent limit on national power marked the end of an era. It also seemed to mark the demise of dual federalism. The Supreme Court seemed unimpressed by arguments that an act of Congress could be invalid because it intruded into matters ordinarily of concern to state governments.

Recently, however, the federalism wars have resumed in earnest, with a series of victories for dual federalism since 1992 in two types of cases, usually by votes of 5 to 4. First, a statute might be found unconstitutional either because Congress exceeded the scope of one of its powers or because the exercise of a legitimate power unduly infringed on matters traditionally belonging to state governments. Second, an act might be unconstitutional because it allowed individuals to sue unconsenting state governments to assert rights that Congress had created. The first involves the Tenth Amendment, and the other involves the Eleventh. With both, some justices believe that political checks alone are inadequate safeguards of federalism and need to be supplemented with judicial checks.

**THE TENTH AMENDMENT REVIVED.** Led by Rehnquist, five justices declared in *National League of Cities* v. *Usery* (1976) that Congress could not extend the minimum wage and maximum hours provisions of the Fair Labor Standards Act to employees of states and their political subdivisions. To do so was to regulate "the States as states." The majority recognized

> limits upon the power of Congress to override state sovereignty, even when exercising its otherwise plenary powers to tax or to regulate commerce. . . . [T]here are attributes of sovereignty attaching to every state government which may not be impaired by Congress, not because Congress may lack an affirmative grant of legislative authority to reach the matter, but because the Constitution prohibits it from exercising the authority in that manner.

In a series of cases testing *National League of Cities,* the Court upheld the challenged statute each time. Still, the 1976 decision meant that virtually every congressional statute when applied to states was a candidate for constitutional attack before the Supreme Court. By 1985, the Court remained sharply divided between those whose fealty lay with Marshall's national supremacy and those who would breathe new life into the Tenth Amendment as a substantive check on congressional power.

In ***Garcia* v. *San Antonio Metropolitan Transit Authority*** (1985), the *National League of Cities* dissenters prevailed. At issue was whether Congress could subject SAMTA to the minimum wage and overtime requirements of the Fair Labor Standards Act. Justice Blackmun, himself a reluctant member of the *National League of Cities* majority, announced for a majority of five that "the attempt to draw the boundaries of state regulatory immunity in terms of 'traditional governmental function' is not only unworkable but is inconsistent with established principles of federalism. . . . That case, accordingly, is overruled." Reaffirmed was a view of the Tenth Amendment in which constitutional limits on Congress are structural, not substantive—that states must find their protection from congressional regulation through the national political process, "not through judicially defined spheres of unregulable state activity."

Only three members of the Garcia majority remained on the bench in 1992. The shift in personnel partly explains *New York* v. *United States,* in which six justices invalidated a key provision of the Low-Level Radioactive Waste Policy Amendments Act of 1985—a congressional device to persuade states to provide for disposal of certain radioactive wastes generated within their borders. The act contained three categories of incentives: monetary, access, and ownership. The first stipulated that noncomplying states would have to take title to the waste or forfeit incentive payments they had already received from the Department of Energy. The second imposed escalating surcharges for noncompliance leading to a denial of access to established disposal facilities. The third required states unable or unwilling to provide for disposal of all low-level waste by January 1, 1996, to "take title to the waste," to take possession of it, and to assume liability for all damages incurred by producers of the waste.

The Court unanimously upheld the first two sets of incentives. Six justices, however, concluded that the take-title provision was defective. Justice O'Connor explained that the Tenth Amendment requires the Court to determine whether an aspect of state sovereignty is protected by a constitutional limitation on congressional authority. While Congress could encourage states to regulate in certain ways through, for example, the granting and withholding of funds, Congress could not give states a "choice" between accepting ownership of the waste or following Congress's dictates for its disposal. Standing alone, the directive to take title and the order to regulate were beyond Congress's lawmaking powers.

In contrast, when faced with the constitutionality of state-imposed limits on the number of terms that a member of the U.S. House of Representatives might serve—that is, a state policy altering the nationally prescribed requirements for public office—the Court voted 5 to 4 against the state position (***U.S. Term Limits, Inc.* v. *Thornton,*** 1995). "[W]e conclude," wrote Justice Stevens, "that the power to add qualifications is not within the 'original powers' of the States by the Tenth Amendment." Moreover, "even if States possessed some original power in this area, . . . the Framers intended the Constitution to be the exclusive source of qualifications for members. . . ." Advocates of term limits would have to resort to constitutional amendment.

Dual federalist thinking reemerged in *Printz* v. *United States* (1997), which struck down, 5 to 4, a section of the 1993 Brady gun control law that required state officials to conduct background checks of prospective purchasers of handguns. This was an interim arrangement, pending operation of a national database that would allow gun dealers to conduct instant background checks on their own. Although Congress possesses authority under the commerce clause to regulate the firearms trade, the Court reasoned that the Tenth Amendment stands as an independent check on the manner in which that regulation may proceed. Opposing opinions echoed visions of federalism reminiscent of debates from the nineteenth and early twentieth centuries. National and state governments are coequal sovereigns. State officers can no more be required to administer federal laws than national officers could "be impressed into service for the execution of state laws," maintained Justice Scalia. There "is not a clause, sentence, or paragraph in the entire text of the Constitution," retorted Justice Stevens, "that supports the proposition that a local police officer can ignore a command by Congress" under one of its constitutional powers.

If laws challenged in *National League of Cities* and the take-title and Brady gun law cases were defective because of their impact on state government, the civil remedy provision of the Violence Against Women Act would seem at first glance to have raised few constitutional eyebrows. Enacted by Congress in 1994, this law allowed victims of gender-motivated violence to sue their attackers for damages in federal court. The collective view from the states seemed to be that the law was needed. Attorneys general from 38 states had urged its enactment. When challenged in the Supreme Court, the governments of 36 states joined a brief urging that the law be sustained, with only Alabama asking that the law be struck down. But five justices voted to strike it down, finding it constitutionally sustainable neither as an exercise of Congress's power to regulate interstate commerce nor as an exercise of Congress's power to enforce the provisions of the Fourteenth Amendment (***United States* v. *Morrison,*** 2000). The "irony of these cases," declared Justice Souter in dissent, is "that the States will be forced to enjoy the new federalism whether they want it or not."

At one level, the decision seemed to be a replay of ***United States* v. *Lopez*** (1995) (reprinted in Chapter Six), when, for the first time since 1936, the Court invalidated an act of Congress—the Gun-Free School Zones Act—as being beyond the scope of the power to regulate interstate commerce. But there is an important distinction between *Lopez* and *Morrison.* In the former, Congress had not demonstrated a clear nexus or connection between firearms in or near schools and interstate commerce, and the Court majority was unwilling to defer to Congress absent such substantiation. But in *Morrison,* the record contained ample congressional documentation describing the impact of gender-motivated violence on its victims and their families and its effects on interstate commerce. "If accepted," maintained Chief Justice Rehnquist in an attempt to distinguish the national commerce power from a national and nearly boundless police power, "petitioners' reasoning would allow Congress to regulate any crime as long as the nationwide, aggregated impact of that crime has substantial effects on employment, production, transit, or consumption." Because most violence has traditionally been within the jurisdiction of the states, it was the Court's duty to draw the line between what could properly be the subject of national regulation and what could not. "The Constitution requires a distinction between what is truly national and what is truly local."

**ELEVENTH AMENDMENT LIMITATIONS.** "The judicial power of the United States shall not be construed to extend to any suit . . . commenced or prosecuted against one of the United States by Citizens of another State, or by Citizens or Subjects of any Foreign States," declares the Eleventh Amendment. As noted, this amendment was the nation's response to *Chisholm* v. *Georgia* (1793), which allowed a citizen of South Carolina to sue the state of Georgia in the federal courts. Much interpretation of this amendment deals with technicalities of federal jurisdiction and so lies outside the scope of this book. But some recent rulings illustrate that the amendment has also been a battleground in the federalism wars, shielding state governments from congressional authority.

A background summary should demonstrate why the amendment is important in understanding federalism today. In 1890 *Hans* v. *Louisiana* went beyond the actual language of the amendment by barring a suit in federal court by a citizen of Louisiana against the state of Louisiana after the latter failed to pay interest on its bonds. The Court concluded that the principle of **sovereign immunity**—that a state cannot be sued without its consent—was an implied limitation on the jurisdiction of the federal courts outlined in Article III. As a result the federal courts were off-limits to suits against states by citizens and noncitizens alike. Later cases, however, greatly diminished this immunity. Ex parte *Young* (1908) held that state officials, as distinguished from the state itself, were subject to suits brought in federal court. *Fitzpatrick* v. *Bitzer* (1976) allowed Congress to negate or abrogate a state's Eleventh Amendment immunity in a suit for damages because of Congress's authority under section 5 of the Fourteenth Amendment (ratified 70 years after the Eleventh Amendment) "to enforce, by appropriate legislation, the provisions of the" amendment. Similarly, *Pennsylvania* v. *Union Gas Co.* (1989) allowed suits against states for monetary damages on the basis of Congress's powers under Article I. Viewing the political process as the primary safeguard of federalism, as in *Garcia,* the Court reasoned that a clear statement in a statute of an intention to abrogate state immunity was an adequate check on congressional overreaching.

This theory was abruptly rejected seven years later in *Seminole Tribe* v. *Florida* (1996). The Court overruled *Union Gas* and denied that Congress could abrogate a state's immunity from suit in federal court under its Article I powers, with or without a clear intention to do so. "The majority's opinion," explained Justice Stevens in dissent, ". . . prevents Congress from providing a federal forum for a broad range of actions against States, from . . . copyright and patent law to those concerning bankruptcy, environmental law, and the regulation of our vast national economy."

The Court's interest in augmenting political safeguards with judicial checks continued in *Alden* v. *Maine* (1999). The Fair Labor Standards Act allowed aggrieved state workers to sue their employer in state court for violating the law's overtime provisions. Because Maine had not consented to the suit, the Court reasoned that Congress could not compel the state courts to accept the suit. "[T]he sovereign immunity of the States neither derives from nor is limited by the terms of the Eleventh Amendment," declared Justice Kennedy. Rather, the immunity "is a fundamental aspect of the sovereignty which the States enjoyed before the ratification of the Constitution, and which they retain today . . . except as altered by the plan of the Convention or certain constitutional Amendments." Because the Eleventh Amendment confirmed but did not establish state immunity, "it follows that the scope of the States' immunity from suit is demarcated not by the text of the Amendment alone but by fundamental postulates implicit in the constitutional design." Just as *Seminole Tribe* closed the federal courts to suits against states when Congress acted on its Article I powers, *Alden* blocked them from the courts of unconsenting states.

One term later, the same five justices comprising the majority in *Seminole Tribe* and *Alden* restricted Congress's authority under the Fourteenth Amendment to abrogate state immunity. **Kimel v. Florida Board of Regents** held that Congress could not force states to submit to suits for monetary damages in federal courts brought by employees under the Age Discrimination in Employment Act. In reasoning similar to that followed in **City of Bourne v. Flores** (reprinted in Chapter Two), the Court found that the ADEA was not "appropriate legislation" under section 5 of the amendment because its protections against age discrimination went far beyond what the Court had held the amendment required. Similarly, *Board of Trustees* v. *Garrett* (2001) barred lawsuits against the state by Alabama state employees under the Americans with Disabilities Act. When Congress protects a class of people beyond the precise scope of the rights enshrined in section one of the Fourteenth Amendment, there must be both "congruence and proportionality between the injury to be prevented or remedied and the means adopted to that end," a condition Congress failed to satisfy. The ADA's legislative record failed "to show that Congress identified a history and pattern of irrational employment discrimination by the States against the disabled."

In holding that state employees may recover money damages in federal court because of a state's failure to comply with the Family and Medical Leave Act of 1993, *Nevada Dept. of Human Resources* v. *Hibbs* (2003) is the principal exception to this line of recent decisions. Because of evidence of a long history of gender discrimination by the states in their administration of leave benefits, six justices agreed that application of the FMLA to the states was appropriately prophylactic under section 5, rather than a substantive redefinition by Congress of a state's constitutional obligations.

Cumulatively, decisions to date invoking dual federalism have not tied the hands of the national government to such a degree as to provoke a confrontation between the Congress and the president on one side, and the Court on the other, as happened in 1937. Moreover, the current trend may be reversed when one or two new justices are appointed. Yet these recent cases are symbolic warning shots, even if they have been fired by slender majorities. As it gives renewed emphasis to dual federalism, the bench seems less willing than at any time since 1937 to defer to Congress on matters of national versus state power. This judicial insistence that Congress be more mindful of the place of the states in the constitutional order may prove to be one of those quiet developments that has long-range effects on American government.

## KEY TERMS

federalism
Antifederalists
delegated powers
reserved powers
implied powers
express powers
necessary and proper
    clause

resulting powers
supremacy clause
concurrent powers
exclusive powers
preemption
judicial federalism
federal question
national supremacy

dual federalism
police power
governmental immunity
reciprocal immunity
sovereign immunity

## QUERIES

**1.** The Supreme Court's decisions in both *McCulloch* and *Cohens* were highly controversial in their day. Yet, in the first, the Court agreed only to accept an institution that Congress had already established; in the second, Virginia actually won on the merits. Why then would certain political groups have found Marshall's opinions in these cases unsettling?

**2.** "Whatever the judicial role," wrote Justice Kennedy in his concurring opinion in *United States* v. *Lopez* (see Chapter Six), "it is axiomatic that Congress does have substantial discretion and control over the federal balance.... The political branches of the Government must fulfill this grave constitutional obligation if democratic liberty and the federalism that secures it are to endure. At the same time, the absence of structural mechanisms to require those officials to undertake this principled task, and the momentary political convenience often attendant upon their failure to do so, argue against a complete renunciation of the judicial role." Does this passage offer insight into the reasons why some members of the Court believe that political checks to safeguard federalism must be augmented with judicial checks?

**3.** What is the significance of the Seventeenth Amendment (1913) for the debate over political versus judicial checks on Congress? Does its presence in the Constitution support or undercut Justice Kennedy's statement in question 2?

**4.** Review Robert Yates's "Letters of Brutus" in Chapter Two. Does *Chisholm* v. *Georgia* confirm or refute his forebodings about the Supreme Court?

## SELECTED READINGS

BEER, SAMUEL H. *To Make a Nation: The Rediscovery of American Federalism.* Cambridge, Mass.: Harvard University Press, 1993.

FINO, SUSAN P. *The Role of State Supreme Courts in the New Judicial Federalism.* Westport, Conn.: Greenwood, 1987.

HYMAN, HAROLD M. *The Reconstruction Justice of Salmon P. Chase: In re Turner and Texas v. White.* Lawrence: University Press of Kansas, 1997.

LOFGREN, CHARLES A. "The Origins of the Tenth Amendment." In Ronald K. L. Collins, ed. *Constitutional Government in America.* Durham, N.C.: Carolina Academic Press, 1980.

LUCE, W. RAY. *Cohens v. Virginia* (1821). New York: Garland, 1990.

MASON, ALPHEUS T. *The States Rights Debate.* New York: Oxford University Press, 1972.

MATHIS, DOYLE. "Chisholm v. Georgia: Background and Settlement." 54 *Journal of American History* 19 (1967).

NAGEL, ROBERT F. *The Implosion of American Federalism.* New York: Oxford University Press, 2001.

SCHMIDHAUSER, JOHN R. *The Supreme Court as Final Arbiter in Federal–State Relations, 1789–1957.* Chapel Hill: University of North Carolina Press, 1958.

WALKER, DAVID B. *The Rebirth of Federalism,* 2d ed. Chatham, N.J.: Chatham House, 2000.

## I. DEFINING THE NATURE OF THE UNION

### Chisholm v. Georgia
### 2 U.S. (2 Dall.) 419, 1 L.Ed. 440 (1793)

http://supct.law.cornell.edu/supct/cases/name.htm#Case_Name-C

On October 31, 1777, the Executive Council of Georgia authorized State Commissioners Thomas Stone and Edward Davies to purchase much-needed supplies from Robert Farquhar, a Charleston, South Carolina, merchant. For his merchandise, Stone and Davies agreed to pay Farquhar $169,613.33 in Continental Currency or in indigo at Carolina prices, if currency was not available. Farquhar never received payment. His claims were still unsatisfied when he was hit by the boom of a pilot boat headed for Savannah. A short time after his death, Alexander Chisholm, a Charleston merchant, was qualified as Farquhar's executor and began to press for payment of Farquhar's claim. When Georgia refused to pay, the executor brought suit against the state in the U.S. Circuit Court for the District of Georgia. Alleging its sovereign and independent status under the federal Constitution, Georgia answered that it could not be made a party to any suit by a South Carolina citizen. Judges James Iredell and Nathaniel Pendleton upheld, for different reasons, Georgia's objections.

In 1792, Chisholm filed suit in the Supreme Court, but Georgia failed to respond. "Any person having authority to speak for the State of Georgia is required to come forth and appear accordingly," the Court directed. When Georgia persisted in its refusal, the case again was postponed until February 4, 1793. No one appeared, and the justices issued another invitation. Still nothing happened, and the decision came down February 19, 1793. In the face of assurances made by Hamilton, Madison, and Marshall during the ratification debates that a state could not, without its consent, be made a defendant in the federal courts by a citizen of another state, the Court took jurisdiction and decided against the state.

The negative reaction was strong and prompt. A House resolution calling for amendment to the Constitution was filed the day of the decision, followed the next day by a supportive Senate resolution. The Eleventh Amendment was proposed by Congress on March 4, 1794, and ratification was completed in 11 months. Official announcement of ratification was not made until January 8, 1798, when President John Adams in a message to Congress declared that it "may now be deemed to be a part of the Constitution." Majority: Wilson, Blair, Cushing, Jay. Dissenting: Iredell.

**WILSON, JUSTICE:**

This is a case of uncommon magnitude. One of the parties to it is a state; certainly respectable, claiming to be sovereign. The question to be determined is whether this state, so respectable, and whose claim soars so high, is amenable to the jurisdiction of the supreme court of the United States? This question, important in itself, will depend on others, more important still; and, may, perhaps, be ultimately resolved into one, no less radical than this—"do the people of the United States form a nation?"...

To the Constitution of the United States the term sovereign is totally unknown. There is but one place where it could have been used with propriety. But, even in that place it would not, perhaps, have comported with the delicacy of those who ordained and established that constitution. They might have announced themselves "sovereign" people of the United States: But serenely conscious of the fact, they avoided the ostentatious declaration. . . .

With the strictest propriety, therefore, classical and political, our national scene opens with the most magnificent object which the nation could present. "The people of the United States" are the first personages introduced. Who were those people? They were the citizens of thirteen states, each of which had a separate constitution and government, and all of which were connected together by articles of confederation. . . .

The question now opens fairly to our view, could the people of those states, among whom were those of Georgia, bind those states, and Georgia, among the others, by the legislative, executive, and judicial power so vested? If the principles on which I have founded myself are just and true, this question must, unavoidably, receive an affirmative answer. . . .

The next question under this head is—Has the constitution done so? Did those people mean to exercise this, their undoubted power? These questions may be resolved, either by fair and conclusive deductions, or by direct and explicit declarations. In order, ultimately, to discover, whether the people of the United States intended to bind those states by the judicial power vested by the national constitution, a previous inquiry will naturally be: Did those people intend to bind those states by the legislative power vested by that constitution? The articles of confederation, it is well known, did not operate upon individual citizens, but operated only upon states. This defect was remedied by the national constitution, which, as all allow, has an operation on individual citizens. But if an opinion, which some seem to entertain, be just; the defect remedied, on one side, was balanced by a defect introduced on the other: for they seem to think, that the present constitution operates only on individual citizens, and not on states. This opinion, however, appears to be altogether unfounded. When certain laws of the states are declared to be "subject to the revision and control of the congress"; it cannot, surely be contended, that the legislative

power of the national government was meant to have no operation on the several states. The fact, uncontrovertibly established in one instance, proves the principle in all other instances, to which the facts will be found to apply. We may then infer, that the people of the United States intended to bind the several states, by the legislative power of the national government. . . .

But, in my opinion, this doctrine rests not upon the legitimate result of fair and conclusive deduction from the constitution; it is confirmed, beyond all doubt, by the direct and explicit declaration of the constitution itself. "The judicial power of the United States shall extend to controversies between two States." Two States are supposed to have a controversy between them; this controversy is supposed to be brought before those vested with the judicial power of the United States; can the most consummate degree of professional ingenuity devise a mode by which this "controversy between two States" can be brought before a court of law, and yet neither of those States be a defendant? "The judicial power of the United States shall extend to controversies between a State and citizens of another State." Could the strictest legal language; could even that language which is peculiarly appropriated to an art, deemed by a great master to be one of the most honorable, laudable, and profitable things in our law; could this strict and appropriate language describe with more precise accuracy the cause now pending before the tribunal? Causes, and not parties to causes, are weighed by justice in her equal scales; on the former, solely, her attention is fixed; to the latter she is, as she is painted, blind. . . .

JAY, CHIEF JUSTICE . . . [omitted]
CUSHING, JUSTICE . . . [omitted]
BLAIR, JUSTICE . . . [omitted]

**IREDELL, JUSTICE: [Dissenting]**

A general question of great importance here occurs. What controversy of a civil nature can be maintained against a state by an individual? The framers of the constitution, I presume, must have meant one of two things—Either, 1. In the conveyance of that part of the judicial power which did not relate to the execution of the other authorities of the general government . . . to refer to antecedent laws for the construction of the general words they use: or, 2. To enable congress in all such cases to pass all such laws as they might deem necessary and proper to carry the purposes of this constitution into full effect, either absolutely at their discretion, or, at least, in cases where prior laws were deficient for such purposes, if any such deficiency existed.

The attorney-general has indeed suggested another construction, a construction, I confess, that I never heard of before, nor can I now consider it grounded on any solid foundation, though it appeared to me to be the basis of the attorney-general's argument. His construction I take to be this: "That the moment a supreme court is formed, it is to exercise all the judicial power vested in it by the constitution, by its own authority, whether the legislature has prescribed methods of doing so, or not." My conception of the constitution is entirely different. I conceive, that all the courts of the United States must receive, not merely their organization as to the number of judges of which they are to consist; but all their authority, as to the manner of their proceeding, from the legislature only. . . .

## McCulloch v. Maryland
## 17 U.S. (4 Wheat.) 316, 4 L.Ed. 579 (1819)

### http://laws.findlaw.com/us/17/316.html

> This famous case resulted from the attempt of the Maryland legislature in 1818 to tax banks and bank branches not chartered by the state legislature. James McCulloch, cashier of the Baltimore branch of the Second Bank of the United States, against which the law was directed, failed to pay the $15,000 annual fee or comply with the alternative requirement by affixing tax stamps to the bank notes issued. McCulloch brought a writ of error against the Court of Appeals of the State of Maryland, which had upheld a lower court judgment against him. Majority: Marshall, Duvall, Johnson, Livingston, Story, Todd, Washington.

**MARSHALL, CHIEF JUSTICE, delivered the opinion of the Court.**

In the case now to be determined, the defendant, a sovereign state, denies the obligation of a law enacted by the legislature of the Union; and the plaintiff, on his part, contests the validity of an act which has been passed by the legislature of that state. . . . No tribunal can approach such a question without a deep sense of its importance, and of the awful responsibility involved in its decision. But it must be decided peacefully, or remain a source of hostile legislation, perhaps of hostility of a still more serious nature; and if it is to be so decided, by this tribunal alone can the decision be made. On the supreme court of the United States has the constitution of our country devolved this important duty.

The first question made in the case is, has congress power to incorporate a bank?. . .

In discussing this question, the counsel for the state of Maryland have deemed it of some importance, in the construction of the constitution, to consider that instrument not as emanating from the people, but as the act of sovereign and independent states. The powers of the general government, it has been said, are delegated by the states, who alone are truly sovereign; and must be exercised in subordination to the states, who alone possess supreme dominion. It would be difficult to sustain this proposition. The convention which framed the constitution was, indeed, elected by the state legislatures. But the instrument, when it came from their hands, was a mere proposal, without obligation. . . . It was reported to the then existing congress of the United States, with a request that it might "be submitted to a convention of delegates, chosen in each state by the people thereof, under the recommendation of its legislature, for their assent and ratification." This mode of proceeding was adopted; and by the convention, by congress, and by the state legislatures, the instrument was submitted to the people. They acted upon it, in the only manner in which they can act safely, effectively, and wisely, on such a subject by assembling in convention. It is true, they assembled in their several states; and where else should they have assembled? No political dreamer was ever wild enough to think of breaking down the lines which separate the states, and of compounding the American people into one common mass. Of consequence, when they act, they act in their states. But the measures they adopt do not, on that account, cease to be the measures of the people themselves, or become the measures of the state governments.

From these conventions the constitution derives its whole authority. The government proceeds directly from the people; is "ordained and established" in the name of the people; and is declared to be ordained, "in order to form a more perfect union, establish justice, insure domestic tranquillity, and secure the blessings of liberty, to themselves and to their posterity." The assent of the States, in their sovereign capacity, is implied in calling a convention, and thus submitting that instrument to the people. . . .

This government is acknowledged by all to be one of enumerated powers. . . . [T]hat principle is now universally admitted. But the question respecting the extent of the powers actually granted, is perpetually arising, and will probably continue to arise, as long as our system shall exist. In discussing these questions, the conflicting powers of the general and state governments must be brought into view, and the supremacy of their respective laws, when they are in opposition, must be settled.

If any one proposition could command the universal assent of mankind, we might expect that it would be this—that the government of the Union, though limited in its powers, is supreme within its sphere of action. This would seem to result, necessarily, from its nature. It is the government of all; its powers are delegated by all; it represents all, and acts for all. Though any one state may be willing to control its operations, no state is willing to allow others to control them. The nation, on those subjects on which it can act, must necessarily bind its component parts. But this question is not left to mere reason: the people have, in express terms, decided it, by saying, "this constitution, and the laws of the United States, which shall be made in pursuance thereof," "shall be the supreme law of the land," and by requiring that the members of the state legislatures, and the officers of the executive and judicial departments of the states, shall take the oath of fidelity to it. The government of the United States, then, though limited in its powers, is supreme; and its laws, when made in pursuance of the constitution, form the supreme law of the land, "anything in the constitution or laws of any state, to the contrary notwithstanding."

Among the enumerated powers, we do not find that of establishing a bank or creating a corporation. But there is no phrase in the instrument which, like the articles of confederation, excludes incidental or implied powers; and which requires that everything granted shall be expressly and minutely described. Even the 10th amendment, which was framed for the purpose of quieting the excessive jealousies which had been excited, omits the word "expressly," and declares only that the powers "not delegated to the United States, nor prohibited to the states, are reserved to the states or to the people;" thus leaving the question, whether the particular power which may become the subject of contest, has been delegated to the one government, or prohibited to the other, to depend on a fair construction of the whole instrument. The men who drew and adopted this amendment had experienced the embarrassments resulting from the insertion of this word in the articles of confederation, and probably omitted it, to avoid those embarrassments. A constitution, to contain an accurate detail of all the subdivisions of which its great powers will admit, and of all the means by which they may be carried into execution, would partake of the prolixity of a legal code, and could scarcely be embraced by the human mind. It would, probably, never be understood by the public. Its nature, therefore, requires, that only its great outlines should be marked, its important objects designated, and the minor ingredients which compose those objects, be deduced from the nature of the objects themselves. That this idea was entertained by the framers of the American constitution, is not only to be inferred from the nature of the instrument, but from the language. Why else were some of the limitations, found in the 9th section of the 1st article, introduced? It is also, in some degree, warranted, by their having omitted to use any restrictive term which might prevent its receiving a fair and just interpretation. In considering this question, then, we must never forget, that it is a *constitution* we are expounding.

Although, among the enumerated powers of government, we do not find the word "bank," or "incorporation," we find the great powers, to lay and collect taxes; to borrow money; to regulate commerce; to declare and conduct war; and to raise and support armies and navies. The sword and the purse, all the external relations, and no inconsiderable portion of the industry of the nation, are intrusted to its government. It can never be pretended, that these vast powers draw after them others of inferior importance, merely because they are inferior. Such an idea can never be advanced. But it may with great reason be contended, that a government, intrusted with such ample powers, on the due execution of which the happiness and prosperity of the nation so vitally depends, must also be intrusted with ample means for their execution. The power being given, it is the interest of the nation to facilitate its execution. It can never be their interest, and cannot be presumed to have been their intention, to clog and

embarrass its execution, by withholding the most appropriate means. Throughout this vast republic, from the St. Croix to the Gulf of Mexico, from the Atlantic to the Pacific, revenue is to be collected and expended, armies are to be marched and supported. The exigencies of the nation may require, that the treasure raised in the north should be transported to the south, that raised in the east, conveyed to the west, or that this order should be reversed. Is that construction of the constitution to be preferred, which would render these operations difficult, hazardous, and expensive? Can we adopt that construction (unless the words imperiously require it), which would impute to the framers of that instrument, when granting these powers for the public good, the intention of impeding their exercise by withholding a choice of means?. . .

But the constitution of the United States has not left the right of congress to employ the necessary means, for the execution of the powers conferred on the government, to general reasoning. To its enumeration of powers is added, that of making "all laws which shall be necessary and proper, for carrying into execution the foregoing powers, and all other powers vested by this constitution, in the government of the United States, or in any department thereof.". . .

But the argument on which most reliance is placed, is drawn from the peculiar language of this clause. Congress is not empowered by it to make all laws, which may have relation to the powers conferred on the government, but only such as may be "necessary and proper" for carrying them into execution. The word "necessary" is considered as controlling the whole sentence, and as limiting the right to pass laws for the execution of the granted powers, to such as are indispensable, and without which the power would be nugatory. That it excludes the choice of means, and leaves to Congress, in each case, that only which is most direct and simple.

Is it true, that this is the sense in which the word "necessary" is always used? Does it always import an absolute physical necessity, so strong, that one thing, to which another may be termed necessary, cannot exist without that other? We think it does not. If reference be had to its use, in the common affairs of the world, or in approved authors, we find that it frequently imports no more than that one thing is convenient, or useful, or essential to another. To employ the means necessary to an end, is generally understood as employing any means calculated to produce the end, and not as being confined to those single means, without which the end would be entirely unattainable. . . .

This provision is made in a constitution, intended to endure for ages to come, and consequently to be adapted to the various *crises* of human affairs. To have prescribed the means by which government should, in all future times, execute its powers, would have been to change, entirely, the character of the instrument, and give it the properties of a legal code. It would have been an unwise attempt to provide, by immutable rules, for exigencies which, if foreseen at all, must have been seen dimly, and which can be best provided for as they occur. To have declared, that the best means shall not be used, but those alone, without which the power given would be nugatory, would have been to deprive the legislature of the capacity to avail itself of experience, to exercise its reason, and to accommodate its legislation to circumstances. If we apply this principle of construction to any of the powers of the government, we shall find it so pernicious in its operation that we shall be compelled to discard it. . . .

But the argument which most conclusively demonstrates the error of the construction contended for by the counsel for the state of Maryland, is founded on the intention of the convention, as manifested in the whole clause. . . . That this could not be intended is, we should think, had it not been already controverted, too apparent for controversy.

We think so for the following reasons: 1st. The clause is placed among the powers of congress, not among the limitations on those powers. 2d. Its terms purport to enlarge, not to diminish the powers vested in the government. It purports to be an additional power, not a restriction on those already granted. No reason has been, or can be assigned, for thus concealing an intention to narrow the discretion of the national legislature, under words which purport to enlarge it. The framers of the constitution wished its adoption, and well knew that it would be endangered by its strength, not by its weakness. Had they been capable of using language which would convey to the eye one idea, and, after deep reflection, impress on the mind, another, they would rather have disguised the grant of power, than its limitation. If then, their intention had been, by this clause, to restrain the free use of means which might otherwise have been implied, that intention would have been inserted in another place, and would have been expressed in terms resembling these. "In carrying into execution the foregoing powers and all others," &c., "no laws shall be passed but such as are necessary and proper.". . .

We admit, as all must admit, that the powers of the government are limited, and that its limits are not to be transcended. But we think the sound construction of the constitution must allow to the national legislature that discretion, with respect to the means by which the powers it confers are to be carried into execution, which will enable that body to perform the high duties assigned to it, in the manner most beneficial to the people. Let the end be legitimate, let it be within the scope of the constitution, and all means which are appropriate, which are plainly adapted to that end, which are not prohibited, but consistent with the letter and spirit of the constitution, are constitutional. . . .

It being the opinion of the court, that the act incorporating the bank is constitutional; and that the power of establishing a branch in the state of Maryland might be properly exercised by the bank itself, we proceed to inquire—

Whether the state of Maryland may, without violating the constitution, tax that branch? That the power of taxation is . . . retained by the states; . . . that it is to be concurrently exercised by the two governments are truths which have never been denied. But such is the paramount character of the constitution, that its capacity to withdraw any subject from the action of even this power, is admitted. . . .

On this ground, the counsel for the bank place its claim to be exempted from the power of a state to tax its operations. There is no express provision for the case, but the claim has been sustained on a principle which so entirely pervades the constitution . . . as to be incapable of being separated from it, without rending it into shreds. This great principle is, that the constitution and the laws made in pursuance thereof are supreme; that they control the constitution and laws of the respective states, and cannot be controlled by them. From this, which may be almost termed an axiom, other propositions are deduced as corollaries, on the truth or error of which, and on their application to this case, the cause has been supposed to depend. These are, 1st: That a power to create implies a power to preserve: 2d. That a power to destroy, if wielded by a different hand, is hostile to, and incompatible with, these powers to create and preserve: 3d. That where this repugnancy exists, that authority which is supreme must control, not yield to that over which it is supreme. . . .

The sovereignty of a state extends to everything which exists by its own authority, or is introduced by its permission; but does it extend to those means which are employed by Congress to carry into execution—powers conferred on that body by the people of the United States? We think it demonstrable that it does not. Those powers are not given by the people of a single state. They are given by the people of the United States, to a government whose laws, made in pursuance of the constitution, are declared to be supreme. Consequently, the people of a single state cannot confer a sovereignty which will extend over them.

If we measure the power of taxation residing in a state, by the extent of sovereignty which the people of a single state possess, and can confer on its government, we have an intelligible standard, applicable to every case to which the power may be applied. We have a principle which leaves the power of taxing the people and property of a state unimpaired; which leaves to a state the command of all its resources, and which places beyond its reach, all those powers which are conferred by the people of the United States

on the government of the Union, and all those means which are given for the purpose of carrying those powers into execution. We have a principle which is safe for the states, and safe for the Union. We are relieved, as we ought to be, from clashing sovereignty; from interfering powers; from a repugnancy between a right in one government to pull down, what there is an acknowledged right in another to build up; from the incompatibility of a right in one government to destroy, what there is an acknowledged right in another to build up; from the incompatibility of a right in one government to destroy, what there is a right in another to preserve. We are not driven to the perplexing inquiry, so unfit for the judicial department, what degree of taxation is a legitimate use, and what degree may amount to the abuse of the power. The attempt to use it on the means employed by the government of the Union, in pursuance of the constitution, is itself an abuse, because it is the usurpation of a power, which the people of a single state cannot give. We find, then, on just theory, a total failure of this original right to tax the means employed by the government of the Union, for the execution of its powers. The right never existed, and the question whether it has been surrendered, cannot arise.

But, waiving this theory for the present, let us resume the inquiry, whether this power can be exercised by the respective states, consistently with a fair construction of the constitution? That the power to tax involves the power to destroy; that the power to destroy may defeat and render useless the power to create; that there is a plain repugnancy in conferring on one government a power to control the constitutional measures of another, which other, with respect to those very measures, is declared to be supreme over that which exerts the control, are propositions not to be denied. But all inconsistencies are to be reconciled by the magic of the word confidence. Taxation, it is said, does not necessarily and unavoidably destroy. To carry it to the excess of destruction, would be an abuse, to presume which, would banish that confidence which is essential to all government. But is this a case of confidence? Would the people of any one state trust those of another with a power to control the most significant operations of their state government? We know they would not. Why, then, should we suppose, that the people of any one state should be willing to trust those of another with a power to control the operations of a government to which they have confided their most important and most valuable interests? In the legislature of the Union alone, all are represented. The legislature of the Union alone, therefore, can be trusted by the people with the power of controlling measures which concern all, in the confidence that it will not be abused. This, then is not a case of confidence, and we must consider it as it really is.

If we apply the principle for which the state of Maryland contends, to the constitution generally, we shall find it capable of changing totally the character of that instrument. We shall find it capable of arresting all the measures of the government, and of prostrating it at the foot of the states. The American people have declared their constitution and the laws made in pursuance thereof, to be supreme; but this principle would transfer the supremacy, in fact, to the states. If the states may tax one instrument, employed by the government in the execution of its powers, they may tax any and every other instrument. They may tax the mail; they may tax the mint; they may tax patent rights; they may tax the papers of the custom-house; they may tax judicial process; they may tax all the means employed by the government, to an excess which would defeat all the ends of government. This was not intended by the American people. They did not design to make their government dependent on the states. . . .

The question is, in truth, a question of supremacy, and if the right of the states to tax the means employed by the general government be conceded, the declaration that the constitution, and the laws made in pursuance thereof, shall be the supreme law of the land, is empty and unmeaning declamation. . . .

It has also been insisted, that, as the power of taxation in the general and state governments is acknowledged to be concurrent, every argument which would sustain the right of the general government to tax banks chartered by the states, will equally sustain the rights of the states to tax banks chartered by the general government. But the two cases are not the same reason. The people of all the states have created the general government, and have conferred upon it the general power of taxation. The people of all the states, and the states themselves, are represented in congress, and, by their representatives, exercise this power. When they tax the chartered institutions of the states, they tax their constituents; and these taxes must be uniform. But when a state taxes the operations of the government of the United States, it acts upon institutions created, not by their own constituents, but by people over whom they claim no control. It acts upon the measures of a government created by others as well as themselves, for the benefit of others in common with themselves. The difference is that which always exists, and always must exist, between the action of the whole on a part, and the action of a part on the whole—between the laws of a government declared to be supreme, and those of a government which, when in opposition to those laws, is not supreme. . . . The court has bestowed on this subject its most deliberate consideration. The result is a conviction that the states have no power, by taxation or otherwise, to retard, impede, burden, or in any manner control, the operations of the constitutional laws enacted by congress to carry into execution the powers vested in the general government. This is, we think, the unavoidable consequence of that supremacy which the constitution has declared. We are unanimously of opinion, that the law passed by the legislature of Maryland, imposing a tax on the Bank of the United States, is unconstitutional and void. . . .

## Cohens v. Virginia
## 19 U.S. (6 Wheat.) 264, 5 L.Ed. 257 (1821)
http://laws.findlaw.com/us/19/264.html

In 1802 Congress authorized the District of Columbia to conduct a lottery. P. J. and M. J. Cohen, agents of the Jacob I. Cohen and Brother Lottery Office in Baltimore, Maryland, sold District lottery tickets in Norfolk, Virginia, but were arrested and convicted under a state law of 1819 that banned the sale of all lottery tickets not approved by the state legislature. Virginia legislators justified the restriction as a means of discouraging the export of capital to finance public improvements elsewhere at a time of financial exigencies at home. According to W. Ray Luce's book *Cohens v. Virginia (1821),* the case may have been arranged. The Supreme Court docketed the Cohens' appeal before their case came to trial in Norfolk's borough court, as if the case had already been decided and any possible appeal in the Virginia courts rejected. The portion of the opinion that follows pertains solely to the question of jurisdiction. Majority: Marshall, Duvall, Johnson, Livingston, Story, Todd. Not participating: Washington.

### MR. CHIEF JUSTICE MARSHALL delivered the opinion of the Court. . . .

Judgment was rendered against the defendants; and the court in which it was rendered being the highest court of the state in which the cause was cognizable, the record has been brought into this court by a writ of error.

The defendant in error moves to dismiss this writ, for want of jurisdiction.

In support of this motion, three points have been made, and argued with the ability which the importance of the question merits. These points are—

1st. That a state is a defendant.

2nd. That no writ of error lies from this court to a state court. [Point 3 has been omitted.]

The questions presented to the court by the two first points made at the bar are of great magnitude, and may truly be said vitally to affect the Union. They exclude the inquiry whether the constitution and laws of the United States have been violated by the judgment which the plaintiffs in error seek to review; and maintain that, admitting such violation, it is not in the power of the government to apply a corrective. They maintain that the nation does not possess a department capable of restraining, peaceably, and by authority of law, any attempts which may be made, by a part, against the legitimate powers of the whole; and that the government is reduced to the alternative of submitting to such attempts, or of resisting them by force. They maintain that the constitution of the United States has provided no tribunal for the final construction of itself, or of the laws or treaties of the nation; but that this power may be exercised in the last resort by the courts of every state of the Union. That the constitution, laws and treaties may receive as many constructions as there are states; and that this is not a mischief, or, if a mischief is irremediable. . . .

1st. The first question to be considered is, whether the jurisdiction of this court is excluded by the character of the parties, one of them being a state, and the other a citizen of that state?. . .

The American states, as well as the American people, have believed a close and firm Union to be essential to their liberty and to their happiness. They have been taught by experience, that this Union cannot exist without a government for the whole; and they have been taught by the same experience that this government would be a mere shadow, that must disappoint all their hopes, unless invested with large portions of that sovereignty which belongs to independent states. Under the influence of this opinion, and thus instructed by experience, the American people, in the conventions of their respective states, adopted the present constitution.

If it could be doubted whether, from its nature, it were not supreme in all cases where it is empowered to act, that doubt would be removed by the declaration that "this constitution, and the laws of the United States which shall be made in pursuance thereof and all treaties made, or which shall be made, under the authority of the United States, shall be the supreme law of the land; and the judges in every state shall be bound thereby, anything in the constitution or laws of any state to the contrary notwithstanding."

This is the authoritative language of the American people; and, if gentlemen please, of the American states. It marks with lines too strong to be mistaken, the characteristic distinction between the government of the Union and those of the states. The general government, though limited as to its objects, is supreme with respect to those objects. This principle is a part of the constitution; and if there be any who deny its necessity, none can deny its authority.

To this supreme government ample powers are confided; and if it were possible to doubt the great purposes for which they were so confided, the people of the United States have declared that they are given "in order to form a more perfect union, establish justice, insure domestic tranquility, provide for the common defense, promote the general welfare, and secure the blessings of liberty to themselves and their posterity."

With the ample powers confided to this supreme government, for these interesting purposes, are connected many express and important limitations on the sovereignty of the states, which are made for the same purposes. The powers of the Union on the great subjects of war, peace, and commerce, and on many others, are in themselves limitations of the sovereignty of the states; but in addition to these, the sovereignty of the states is surrendered in many instances where the surrender can only operate to the benefit of the people, and where, perhaps, no other power is con-

ferred on congress than a conservative power to maintain the principles established in the constitution. The maintenance of these principles in their purity is certainly among the great duties of the government. One of the instruments by which this duty may be peaceably performed is the judicial department. It is authorized to decide all cases, of every description, arising under the constitution or laws of the United States. From this general grant of jurisdiction, no exception is made of those cases in which a state may be a party. When we consider the situation of the government of the Union and of a state, in relation to each other; the nature of our constitution; the subordination of the state governments to that constitution; the great purpose for which jurisdiction over all cases arising under the constitution and laws of the United States, is confided to the judicial department; are we at liberty to insert in this general grant, an exception of those cases in which a state may be a party? Will the spirit of the constitution justify this attempt to control its words? We think it will not. We think a case arising under the constitution or laws of the United States, is cognizable in the courts of the Union, whoever may be the parties of that case. . . .

One of the express objects, then, for which the judicial department was established, is the decision of controversies between states, and between a state and individuals. The mere circumstance, that a state is a party, gives jurisdiction to the court. How, then, can it be contended, that the very same instrument, in the very same section, should be so construed, as that this same circumstance should withdraw a case from the jurisdiction of the court, where the constitution or laws of the United States are supposed to have been violated?. . .

The mischievous consequences of the construction contended for on the part of Virginia, are also entitled to great consideration. It would prostrate, it has been said, the government and its laws at the feet of every state in the Union. And would not this be its effect? What power of the government could be executed by its own means, in any state disposed to resist its execution by a course of legislation? The laws must be executed by individuals acting within the several states. If these individuals may be exposed to penalties, and if the courts of the Union cannot correct the judgments by which these penalties may be enforced, the course of the government may be . . . arrested by the will of one of its members. Each member will possess a veto on the will of the whole. . . .

These collisions may take place in times of no extraordinary commotion. But a constitution is framed for ages to come, and is designed to approach immortality as nearly as human institutions can approach it. Its course cannot always be tranquil. It is exposed to storms and tempests, and its framers must be unwise statesmen indeed, if they have not provided it, as far as its nature will permit, with the means of self-preservation from the perils it may be destined to encounter. No government ought to be so defective in its organization, as not to contain within itself the means of securing the execution of its own laws against other dangers than those which occur every day. Courts of justice are the means most usually employed; and it is reasonable to expect that a government should repose on its own courts, rather than on others. There is certainly nothing in the circumstances under which our constitution was formed; nothing in the history of the times, which would justify the opinion that the confidence reposed in the states was so implicit as to leave in them and their tribunals the power of resisting or defeating, in the form of law, the legitimate measures of the Union. . . .

If jurisdiction depended entirely on the character of the parties, and was not given where the parties have not an original right to come into court, that part of the 2d section of the 3d article, which extends the judicial power to all cases arising under the constitution and laws of the United States, would be surplusage. It is to give jurisdiction where the character of the parties would not give it, that this very important part of the clause was inserted. . . .

It is most true, that this court will not take jurisdiction if it should not; but it is equally true, that it must take jurisdiction, if it should. The judiciary cannot, as the legislature may, avoid a measure, because it approaches the confines of the constitution. We cannot pass it by, because it is doubtful. With whatever doubts, with whatever difficulties, a case may be attended, we must decide it, if it be brought before us. We have no more right to decline the exercise of jurisdiction which is given, than to usurp that which is not given. The one or the other would be treason to the constitution. Questions may occur, which we would gladly avoid; but we cannot avoid them. All we can do is, to exercise our best judgment, and conscientiously to perform our duty. In doing this, on the present occasion, we find this tribunal invested with appellate jurisdiction in all cases arising under the constitution and laws of the United States. We find no exception to this grant, and we cannot insert one. . . .

This leads to a consideration of the 11th amendment. It is in these words: "The judicial power of the United States shall not be construed to extend to any suit in law or equity commenced or prosecuted against one of the United States, by citizens of another state, or by citizens or subjects of any foreign state." It is a part of our history, that, at the adoption of the constitution, all the states were greatly indebted; and the apprehension that these debts might be prosecuted in the federal courts, formed a very serious objection to that instrument. Suits were instituted; and the court maintained its jurisdiction. The alarm was general; and, to quiet the apprehensions that were so extensively entertained, this amendment was proposed in Congress, and adopted by the state legislatures. That its motive was not to maintain the sovereignty of a state from the degradation supposed to attend a compulsory appearance before the tribunal of the nation, may be inferred from the terms of the amendment. It does not comprehend controversies between two or more states, or between a state and a foreign state. The jurisdiction of the court still extends to these cases; and in these a state may still be sued. We must ascribe the amendment, then, to some other cause than the dignity of a state. There is no difficulty in finding this cause. Those who were inhibited from commencing a suit against a state, or from prosecuting one which might be commenced before the adoption of the amendment, were persons who might probably be its creditors. There was not much reason to fear that foreign or sister states would be creditors to any considerable amount, and there was reason to retain the jurisdiction of the court in those cases, because it might be essential to the preservation of peace. The amendment, therefore, extended to suits commenced or prosecuted by individuals, but not to those brought by states. . . .

Under the Judiciary Act, the effect of a writ of error is simply to bring the record into court, and submit the judgment of the inferior tribunal to reexamination. It does not in any manner act upon the parties; it acts only on the record. It removes the record into the supervising tribunal. Where, then, a state obtains a judgment against an individual, and the court rendering such judgment overrules a defense set up under the constitution or laws of the United States, the transfer of this record into the supreme court for the sole purpose of inquiring whether the judgment violates the constitution of the United States, can, with no propriety, we think, be denominated a suit commenced or prosecuted against the state whose judgment is so far reexamined. Nothing is demanded from the state. No claim against it of any description is asserted or prosecuted. The party is not to be restored to the possession of anything. Essentially, it is an appeal on a single point; and the defendant who appeals from a judgment rendered against him, is never said to commence or prosecute a suit against the plaintiff who has obtained the judgment. . . .

It is, then, the opinion of the court, that the defendant who removes a judgment rendered against him by a state court into this court, for the purpose of reexamining the question, whether that judgment be in violation of the constitution or laws of the United States, does not commence or prosecute a suit against the state. . . .

2d. The second objection to the jurisdiction of the court is, that its appellate power cannot be exercised, in any case, over the judgment of a state court. . . .

America has chosen to be, in many respects, and to many purposes, a nation; and for all these purposes, her government is complete; to all these objects it is competent. The people have declared, that in the exercise of all powers given for these objects, it is supreme. It can, then, in effecting these objects, legitimately control all individuals or governments within the American territory. The constitution and laws of a state, so far as they are repugnant to the constitution and laws of the United States, are absolutely void. These states are constituent parts of the United States; they are members of one great empire—for some purposes sovereign, for some purposes subordinate.

In a government so constituted, is it unreasonable, that the judicial power should be competent to give efficacy to the constitutional laws of the legislature? That department can decide on the validity of the constitution or law of a state, if it be repugnant to the constitution or to a law of the United States. Is it unreasonable, that it should also be empowered to decide on the judgment of a state tribunal enforcing such unconstitutional law? . . .

The propriety of entrusting the construction of the constitution, and laws made in pursuance thereof, to the judiciary of the Union has not, we believe, as yet, been drawn into question. It seems to be a corollary from this political axiom, that the federal courts should either possess exclusive jurisdiction in such cases, or a power to revise the judgment rendered in them, by the state tribunals. If the federal and state courts have concurrent jurisdiction in all cases arising under the constitution, laws, and treaties of the United States; and if a case of this description brought in a state court cannot be removed before judgment, nor revised after judgment, then the construction of the constitution, laws, and treaties of the United States is not confided particularly to their judicial department, but is confided equally to that department and to the state courts, however they may be constituted. "Thirteen independent courts," says a very celebrated statesman (and we have now more than twenty such courts), "of final jurisdiction over the same causes, arising upon the same laws, is a hydra in government, from which nothing but contradiction and confusion can proceed."

Dismissing the unpleasant suggestion, that any motives which may not be fairly avowed, or which ought not to exist, can ever influence a state or its courts, the necessity of uniformity, as well as correctness in expounding the constitution and laws of the United States, would itself suggest the propriety of vesting in some single tribunal the power of deciding, in the last resort, all cases in which they are involved. . . . [T]he words of the constitution . . . give to the supreme court appellate jurisdiction in all cases arising under the constitution, laws, and treaties of the United States. The words are broad enough to comprehend all cases of this description, in whatever court they may be decided. . . .

Let the nature and objects of our Union be considered; let the great fundamental principles, on which the fabric stands, be examined; and we think, the result must be, that there is nothing so extravagantly absurd, in giving to the court of the nation the power of revising the decisions of local tribunals, on questions which affect the nation, as to require the words which import this power should be restricted by a forced construction. . . .

[On the merits of the case, the Supreme Court upheld the convictions, declaring that the federal lottery law afforded no immunity to prosecution outside the District of Columbia.—ED.]

*Judgment affirmed.*

## *Texas* v. *White*
## 74 U.S. (7 Wall.) 700, 19 L.Ed. 227 (1869)
## http://laws.findlaw.com/us/74/700.html

In 1851 Congress provided that $10 million in U.S. bonds should be transferred to the state of Texas, payable to the state or bearer and redeemable in 1864. In receiving the bonds, the Texas legislature stipulated that endorsement by the governor of the state was necessary to make any of the bonds valid in the hands of individual holders. After Texas became part of the Confederate States of America, the Texas legislature repealed this act in 1862 and authorized use of the bonds for war supplies. In 1866 the Reconstruction government in Texas sought to block payment to George White and others out of state who now held the bonds. The defense interposed was that the Supreme Court lacked jurisdiction to entertain this original action because the plaintiff (Texas) was not a state of the Union—that it had seceded in 1861 and had not been restored as a full-fledged member of the Union. In response Chief Justice Chase simultaneously espoused Lincoln's theory (that secession was illegal, that the Union was perpetual, and that the rebellion had temporarily suspended Texas's rights as a member of the Union) and, without passing on the validity of any particular Reconstruction statute, acknowledged Congress's authority to maintain provisional governments in the southern states. Majority: Chase, Clifford, Davis, Field, Nelson. Dissenting: Grier, Miller, Swayne.

**THE CHIEF JUSTICE [CHASE] delivered the opinion of the Court. . . .**

Texas took part, with the other Confederate States, in the war of the rebellion. . . . During the whole of that war there was no governor, or judge, or any other State official in Texas, who recognized the National authority. Nor was any officer of the United States permitted to exercise any authority whatever under the

National government within the limits of the State, except under the immediate protection of the National military forces.

Did Texas, in consequence of these acts, cease to be a State? Or, if not, did the State cease to be a member of the Union?

It is needless to discuss, at length, the question whether the right of a State to withdraw from the Union for any cause, regarded by herself as sufficient, is consistent with the Constitution of the United States.

The Union of the States never was a purely artificial and arbitrary relation. It began among the Colonies, and grew out of common origin, mutual sympathies, kindred principles, similar interests, and geographical relations. It was confirmed and strengthened by the necessities of war, and received definite form, and character, and sanction from the Articles of Confederation. By these the Union was solemnly declared to "be perpetual." And when these Articles were found to be inadequate to the exigencies of the country, the Constitution was ordained "to form a more perfect Union." It is difficult to convey the idea of indissoluble unity more clearly than by these words. What can be indissoluble if a perpetual Union, made more perfect, is not?

But the perpetuity and indissolubility of the Union, by no means implies the loss of distinct and individual existence, or of the right of self-government by the States. Under the Articles of Confederation, each State retained its sovereignty, freedom, and independence, and every power, jurisdiction, and right not expressly delegated to the United States. Under the Constitution, though the powers of the States were much restricted, still, all powers not delegated to the United States, nor prohibited to the States, are reserved to the States respectively, or to the people. . . . Not only therefore can there be no loss of separate and independent autonomy to the States, through their union under the Constitution, but it may be not unreasonably said the preservation of the States, and the maintenance of their governments, are as much within the design and care of the Constitution as the preservation of the Union and the maintenance of the National government. The Constitution, in all

its provisions, looks to an indestructible Union, composed of indestructible States.

When, therefore, Texas became one of the United States, she entered into an indissoluble relation. All the obligations of perpetual union and all the guarantes of republican government in the Union, attached at once to the State. The act which consummated her admission into the Union was something more than a compact; it was the incorporation of a new member into the political body. And it was final. The union between Texas and the other States was as complete, as perpetual, and as indissoluble as the union between the original States. There was no place for reconsideration, or revocation, except through revolution, or through consent of the States.

Considered therefore as transactions under the Constitution, the ordinance of secession, adopted by the convention and ratified by a majority of the citizens of Texas, and all the acts of her legislature intended to give effect to that ordinance, were absolutely null. They were utterly without operation in law. The obligations of the State, as a member of the Union, and of every citizen of the State, as a citizen of the United States, remained perfect and unimpaired. It certainly follows that the State did not cease to be a State, nor her citizens to be citizens of the Union. If this were otherwise, the State must have become foreign, and her citizens foreigners. The war must have ceased to be a war for the suppression of rebellion, and must have become a war of conquest and subjugation.

Our conclusion therefore is, that Texas continued to be a State, and a State of the Union, notwithstanding the transactions to which we have referred. And this conclusion, in our judgment, is not in conflict with any act or declaration of any department of the National government, but entirely in accordance with the whole series of such acts and declarations, since the first outbreak of rebellion.

But in order to the exercise, by a State, of the right to sue in this court, there needs to be a State government, competent to represent the State in its relations with the National government, so far at least as the institution and prosecution of a suit is concerned. . . .

All admit that, during this condition of civil war, the rights of the State as a member, and her people as citizens of the Union, were suspended. The government and the citizens of the State, refusing to recognize their constitutional obligations, assumed the character of enemies, and incurred the consequences of rebellion.

These new relations imposed new duties upon the United States. The first was that of suppressing the rebellion. The next was that of re-establishing the broken relations of the State with the Union. The first of these duties having been performed, the next necessarily engaged the attention of the National government. . . .

There being then no government in Texas in constitutional relations with the Union, it became the duty of the United States to provide for the restoration of such a government. But the restoration of the government which existed before the rebellion, without a new election of officers, was obviously impossible; and before any such election could be properly held, it was necessary that the old constitution should receive such amendments as would conform its provisions to the new conditions created by emancipation, and afford adequate security to the people of the State.

In the exercise of the power conferred by the guaranty clause, as in the exercise of every other constitutional power, a discretion in the choice of means is necessarily allowed. It is essential only that the means must be necessary and proper for carrying into execution the power conferred, through the restoration of the State to its constitutional relations, under a republican form of government, and that no acts be done, and no authority exerted, which is either prohibited or unsanctioned by the Constitution. . . .

Nothing in the case before us requires the court to pronounce judgment upon the constitutionality of any particular provision of these acts.

But it is important to observe that these acts themselves show that the governments, which had been established and had been in actual operation under executive direction, were recognized by Congress as provisional, as existing, and as capable of continuance. . . .

[The right of Texas to bring suit was affirmed and a decree issued enjoining White and others from setting up any claim to the bonds.—ED.]

### MR. JUSTICE GRIER, dissenting. . . .

The original jurisdiction of this court can be invoked only by one of the United States. The Territories have no such right conferred on them by the Constitution, nor have the Indian tribes who are under the protection of the military authorities of the government.

Is Texas one of these United States? Or was she such at the time the bill was filed, or since?

This is to be decided as a political fact, not as a legal fiction. This court is bound to know and notice the public history of the nation.

If I regard the truth of history for the last eight years, I cannot discover the State of Texas as one of these United States. . . .

[Justices Swayne and Miller joined Justice Grier "as to the incapacity of the State of Texas, in her present condition, to maintain an original suit in this court."—ED.]

## II. NATIONAL SUPREMACY V. DUAL FEDERALISM IN THE MODERN ERA

### *Garcia* v. *San Antonio Metropolitan Transit Authority*
### 469 U.S. 528, 105 S.Ct. 1005, 83 L.Ed. 2d 1016 (1985)
http://laws.findlaw.com/us/469/528.html

San Antonio Metropolitan Transit Authority (SAMTA) operates a public mass-transit system in San Antonio, Texas, and the surrounding area. In 1976 the Supreme Court in *National League of Cities* v. *Usery* invalidated the extension of the maximum hours and minimum wage provisions of the Fair Labor Standards Act (FLSA) to most state and municipal employees. The transit authority informed its employees that this decision relieved it of overtime pay obligations. In 1979, the Wage and Hour Administration of the Department of Labor informed SAMTA that its operations were nonetheless covered by the FLSA. The authority then asked the U.S. District Court for the Western District of Texas for a declaratory judgment that the 1976 decision precluded application of the FLSA's overtime requirements to its operations. At the same time, Joe Garcia and several other SAMTA employees filed suit against SAMTA in district court for overtime pay under the FLSA. In 1981, the district court ruled that, under *National League of Cities,* SAMTA was immune from the requirements of the FLSA. The Secretary of Labor and Garcia appealed directly to the Supreme Court. While the San Antonio case was in progress, the Supreme Court held in *Transportation Union* v. *Long Island Rail Road Co.* (1982) that commuter rail service provided by a state-owned entity did not constitute a "traditional governmental function" and so did not qualify for immunity under *National League of Cities.* The Court vacated the district court's judgment in the SAMTA case for further consideration in light of *Long Island Rail Road.* On remand, the district court maintained its original view and decided in favor of SAMTA. Majority: Blackmun, Brennan, Marshall, Stevens, White. Dissenting: Powell, Burger, O'Connor, Rehnquist.

**JUSTICE BLACKMUN delivered the opinion of the Court.**

We revisit in these cases an issue raised in *National League of Cities* v. *Usery.* . . . In that litigation, this Court, by a sharply divided vote, ruled that the Commerce Clause does not empower Congress to enforce the minimum-wage and overtime provisions of the Fair Labor Standards Act (FLSA) against the States "in areas of traditional governmental functions.". . . Although National League of Cities supplied some examples of "traditional governmental functions," it did not offer a general explanation of how a "traditional" function is to be distinguished from a "nontraditional" one. Since then, federal and state courts have struggled with the task, thus imposed, of identifying a tra-

ditional function for purposes of state immunity under the Commerce Clause. . . .

Our examination of this "function" standard applied in these and other cases over the last eight years now persuades us that the attempt to draw the boundaries of state regulatory immunity in terms of "traditional governmental function" is not only unworkable but is inconsistent with established principles of federalism and, indeed, with those very federalism principles on which *National League of Cities* purported to rest. That case, accordingly, is overruled. . . .

We therefore now reject, as unsound in principle and unworkable in practice, a rule of state immunity from federal regulation that turns on a judicial appraisal of whether a particular governmental function is "integral" or "traditional." Any such rule leads to inconsistent results at the same time that it disserves principles of democratic self-governance, and it breeds inconsistency precisely because it is divorced from those principles. If there are to be limits on the Federal Government's power to interfere with state functions—as undoubtedly there are—we must look elsewhere to find them. We accordingly return to the underlying issue that confronted this Court in *National League of Cities*—the manner in which the Constitution insulates States from the reach of Congress' power under the Commerce Clause.

The central theme of *National League of Cities* was that the States occupy a special position in our constitutional system and that the scope of Congress' authority under the Commerce Clause must reflect that position. . . .

What has proved problematic is not the perception that the Constitution's federal structure imposes limitations on the Commerce Clause, but rather the nature and content of those limitations. . . .

We doubt that courts ultimately can identify principled constitutional limitations on the scope of Congress' Commerce Clause powers over the States merely by relying on *a priori* definitions of state sovereignty. In part, this is because of the elusiveness of objective criteria for "fundamental" elements of state sovereignty, a problem we have witnessed in the search for "traditional governmental functions." There is, however, a more fundamental reason: the sovereignty of the States is limited by the Constitution itself. A variety of sovereign powers, for example, are withdrawn from the States by Article I, § 10. Section 8 of the same Article works an equally sharp contraction of state sovereignty by authorizing Congress to exercise a wide range of legislative powers and (in conjunction with the Supremacy Clause of Article VI) to displace contrary state legislation. . . . By providing for final review of questions of federal law in this Court, Article III curtails the sovereign power of the States' judiciaries to make authoritative determinations of law. . . .

As a result, to say that the Constitution assumes the continued role of the States is to say little about the nature of that role. . . . With rare exceptions, like the guarantee, in Article IV, § 3, of state territorial integrity, the Constitution does not carve out express elements of state sovereignty that Congress may not employ its delegated powers to displace. . . . [A]nd the fact that the States remain sovereign as to all powers not vested in Congress or denied them by the Constitution offers no guidance about where the frontier between state and federal power lies. . . . [W]e have no license to employ freestanding conceptions of state sovereignty when measuring congressional authority under the Commerce Clause. . . .

In short, the Framers chose to rely on a federal system in which special restraints on federal power over the States inhered principally in the workings of the National Government itself, rather than in discrete limitations on the objects of federal authority. State sovereign interests, then, are more properly protected by procedural safeguards inherent in the structure of the federal system than by judicially created limitations on federal power.

Insofar as the present cases are concerned, then, we need go no further than to state that we perceive nothing in the overtime and minimum-wage requirements of the FLSA, as applied to SAMTA, that is destructive of state sovereignty or violative of any constitutional provision. SAMTA faces nothing more than the same minimum-wage and overtime obligations that hundreds of thousands of other employers, public as well as private, have to meet. . . .

Of course, we continue to recognize that the States occupy a special and specific position in our constitutional system and that the scope of Congress' authority under the Commerce Clause must reflect that position. But the principal and basic limit on the federal commerce power is that inherent in all congressional action—the built-in restraints that our system provides through state participation in federal governmental action. The political process ensures that laws that unduly burden the States will not be promulgated. In the factual setting of these cases the internal safeguards of the political process have performed as intended. . . .

Though the separate concurrence [by Justice Blackmun—Ed.] providing the fifth vote in *National League of Cities* was "not untroubled by certain possible implications" of the decision . . . the Court in that case attempted to articulate affirmative limits on the Commerce Clause power in terms of core governmental functions and fundamental attributes of state sovereignty. But the model of democratic decisionmaking the Court there identified underestimated, in our view, the solicitude of the national political process for the continued vitality of the States. Attempts by other courts since then to draw guidance from this model have proved it both impracticable and doctrinally barren. In sum, in *National League of Cities* the Court tried to repair what did not need repair.

We do not lightly overrule recent precedent. We have not hesitated, however, when it has become apparent that a prior decision has departed from a proper understanding of congressional power under the Commerce Clause. . . . Due respect for the reach of congressional power within the federal system mandates that we do so now.

. . . The judgment of the District Court is reversed, and these cases are remanded to that court for further proceedings consistent with this opinion.

*It is so ordered.*

**JUSTICE POWELL, with whom THE CHIEF JUSTICE, JUSTICE REHNQUIST, and JUSTICE O'CONNOR join, dissenting. . . .**

Despite some genuflecting in the Court's opinion to the concept of federalism, today's decision effectively reduces the Tenth Amendment to meaningless rhetoric when Congress acts pursuant to the Commerce Clause.

. . . [T]he extent to which the States may exercise their authority, when Congress purports to act under the Commerce Clause, henceforth is to be determined from time to time by political decisions made by members of the federal government, decisions the Court says will not be subject to judicial review. I note that it does not seem to have occurred to the Court that it—an unelected majority of five Justices—today rejects almost 200 years of the understanding of

the constitutional status of federalism. In doing so, there is only a single passing reference to the Tenth Amendment. Nor is so much as a dictum of any court cited in support of the view that the role of the States in the federal system may depend upon the grace of elected federal officials, rather than on the Constitution as interpreted by this Court. . . .

Far from being "unsound in principle" . . . judicial enforcement of the Tenth Amendment is essential to maintaining the federal system so carefully designed by the Framers and adopted in the Constitution. . . .

Thus, the harm to the States that results from federal overreaching under the Commerce Clause is not simply a matter of dollars and cents. . . . Rather, by usurping functions traditionally performed by the States, federal overreaching under the Commerce Clause undermines the constitutionally mandated balance of power between the States and the federal government, a balance designed to protect our fundamental liberties. . . .

JUSTICE REHNQUIST, dissenting . . . [omitted].

**JUSTICE O'CONNOR, with whom JUSTICE POWELL and JUSTICE REHNQUIST join, dissenting. . . .**

Due to the emergence of an integrated and industrialized national economy, this Court has been required to examine and review a breath-taking expansion of the powers of Congress. In doing so the Court correctly perceived that the Framers of our Constitution intended Congress to have sufficient power to address national problems. But the Framers were not single-minded. The Constitution is animated by an array of intentions. . . . Just as surely as the Framers envisioned a National Government capable of solving national problems, they also envisioned a republic whose vitality was assured by the diffusion of power not only among the branches of the Federal Government, but also between the Federal Government and the States. . . . In the 18th century these intentions did not conflict because technology had not yet converted every local problem into a national one. A conflict has now emerged, and the Court today retreats rather than reconciles the Constitution's dual concerns for federalism and an effective commerce power. . . .

Incidental to this expansion of the commerce power, Congress has been given an ability it lacked prior to the emergence of an integrated national economy. Because virtually every *state* activity, like virtually every activity of a private individual, arguably "affects" interstate commerce, Congress can now supplant the States from the significant sphere of activities envisioned for them by the Framers. It is in this context that recent changes in the workings of Congress, such as the direct election of Senators and the expanded influence of national interest groups . . . become relevant. These changes may well have lessened the weight Congress gives to the legitimate interests of States as States. As a result, there is now a real risk that Congress will gradually erase the diffusion of power between state

and nation on which the Framers based their faith in the efficiency and vitality of our Republic. . . .

It is worth recalling the cited passage in *McCulloch* v. *Maryland* . . . that lies at the source of the recent expansion of the commerce power. "Let the end be legitimate, let it be within the scope of the constitution," Chief Justice Marshall said, "and all means which are appropriate, which are plainly adapted to that end, which are not prohibited, but consist with the letter *and spirit* of the constitution, are constitutional" (emphasis added [by Justice O'Connor]). The *spirit* of the Tenth Amendment, of course, is that the States will retain their integrity in a system in which the laws of the United States are nevertheless supreme. . . .

This . . . requires the Court to enforce affirmative limits on federal regulation of the States to complement the judicially crafted expansion of the interstate commerce power. . . .

## *U.S. Term Limits, Inc.* v. *Thornton*
### 514 U.S. 779, 115 S.Ct. 1842, 131 L.Ed. 2d 881 (1995)
### http://laws.findlaw.com/us/514/779.html

Joining 21 other states, voters in Arkansas in 1992 amended the state constitution to impose term limits on their legislators. Section 3 of Amendment 73 prohibited the name of an otherwise eligible candidate from appearing on the general election ballot: (1) for the U.S. House of Representatives if the candidate had been elected to the House to three or more terms; and (2) for the U.S. Senate if the candidate had been elected to the Senate to two or more terms. Two legal challenges to the amendment emerged. One involved a national advocacy group and Ray Thornton (by 1995 a six-term member of the U.S. House of Representatives from Arkansas); the other involved Bobbie Hill (past president of the League of Women Voters of Arkansas, on behalf of herself and other voters) and Arkansas attorney general Winston Bryant. In both cases, the state supreme court held that Section 3 violated Article I of the U.S. Constitution. Docketed first at the U.S. Supreme Court, Thornton's case became the name by which this landmark decision is known. While states remain free to impose term limits on state officials, and while candidates and officials at any level of government may informally "term-limit" themselves, the Supreme Court's decision soon squelched the movement to impose term limits on national legislators. The excerpts that follow are greatly compressed; Justice Thomas's dissent alone reached 88 pages. Majority: Stevens, Breyer, Ginsburg, Kennedy, Souter. Dissenting: Thomas, O'Connor, Rehnquist, Scalia.

**JUSTICE STEVENS delivered the opinion of the Court. . . .**

Today's cases present a challenge to an amendment to the Arkansas State Constitution that prohibits the name of an otherwise-eligible candidate for Congress from appearing on the general election ballot if that candidate has already served three terms in the House of Representatives or two terms in the Senate. The Arkansas Supreme Court held that the amendment violates the Federal Constitution. We agree with that holding. Such a state-imposed restriction is contrary to the "fundamental principle of our representative democracy," embodied in the Constitution, that "the people should choose whom they please to govern them." Allowing individual States to adopt their own qualifications for congressional service would be inconsistent with the Framers' vision of a uniform National Legislature representing the people of the United States. If the qualifications set forth in the text of the Constitution are to be changed, that text must be amended. . . .

[T]he constitutionality of Amendment 73 depends critically on the resolution of two distinct issues. The first is whether the Constitution forbids States from adding to or altering the qualifications specifically enumerated in the Constitution. The second is, if the Constitution does so forbid, whether the fact that Amendment 73 is formulated as a ballot access restriction rather than as an outright disqualification is of constitutional significance. Our resolution of these issues draws upon our prior resolution of a related but distinct issue: whether Congress has the power to add to or alter the qualifications of its Members.

Twenty-six years ago, in *Powell* v. *McCormack* (1969), we reviewed the history and text of the Qualifications Clauses in a case involving an attempted exclusion of a duly elected Member of Congress. The principal issue was whether the power granted to each House in Art. I, § 5, to judge the "Qualifications of its own Members" includes the power to impose qualifications other than those set forth in the text of the Constitution. In an opinion by Chief Justice Warren for eight Members of the Court, we held that it does not. . . . [The Court reviews *Powell* at length and reaffirms its holding.]

Petitioners argue that the Constitution contains no express prohibition against state-added qualifications, and that Amendment 73 is therefore an appropriate exercise of a State's reserved power to place additional restrictions on the choices that its own voters may make. We disagree for two independent reasons. First, we conclude that the power to add qualifications is not within the "original powers" of the States, and thus is not reserved to the States by the Tenth Amendment. Second, even if States possessed some original power in this area, we conclude that the Framers intended the Constitution to be the exclusive source of qualifications for members of Congress, and that the Framers thereby "divested" States of any power to add qualifications. . . .

Contrary to petitioners' assertions, the power to add qualifications is not part of the original powers of sovereignty that the Tenth Amendment reserved to the States. Petitioners' Tenth Amendment argument misconceives the nature of the right at issue because that Amendment could only "reserve" that which existed before. . . .

With respect to setting qualifications for service in Congress, no such right existed before the Constitution was ratified. The contrary argument overlooks the revolutionary character of the government that the Framers conceived. Prior to the adoption of the Constitution, the States had joined together under the Articles of Confederation. In that system, "the States retained most of their sovereignty, like independent nations bound together only by treaties." After the Constitutional Convention convened, the Framers were presented with, and eventually adopted a variation of, "a plan not merely to amend the Articles of Confederation but to create an entirely new National Government with a National Executive, National Judiciary, and a National Legislature." In adopting that plan, the Framers envisioned a uniform national system, rejecting the notion that the Nation was a collection of States, and instead creating a direct link between the National Government and the people of the United States. . . . In that National Government, representatives owe primary allegiance not to the people of a State, but to the people of the Nation. . . .

In short, as the Framers recognized, electing representatives to the National Legislature was a new right, arising from the Constitution itself. The Tenth Amendment thus provides no basis for concluding that the States possess reserved power to add qualifications to those that are fixed in the Constitution. Instead, any state power to set the qualifications for membership in Congress must derive not from the reserved powers of state sovereignty, but rather from the delegated powers of national sovereignty. In the absence of any constitutional delegation to the States of power to add qualifications to those enumerated in the Constitution, such a power does not exist.

Even if we believed that States possessed as part of their original powers some control over congressional qualifications, the text and structure of the Constitution, the relevant historical materials, and, most importantly, the "basic principles of our democratic system" all demonstrate that the Qualifications Clauses were intended to preclude the States from exercising any such power and to fix as exclusive the qualifications in the Constitution. . . .

[S]tate-imposed restrictions, unlike the congressionally imposed restrictions at issue in *Powell,* violate a . . . basic principle: that the right to choose representatives belongs not to the States, but to the people. . . . Thus the Framers, in perhaps their most important contribution, conceived of a Federal Government directly responsible to the people, possessed of direct power over the people, and chosen directly, not by States, but by the people. The Framers implemented this ideal most clearly in the provision, extant from the beginning of the Republic, that calls for the Members of the House of Representatives to be "chosen every second Year by the People of the several States." Following the adoption of the 17th Amendment in 1913, this ideal was extended to elections for the Senate. The Congress of the United States, therefore, is not a confederation of nations in which separate sovereigns are represented by appointed delegates, but

is instead a body composed of representatives of the people. . . .

Permitting individual States to formulate diverse qualifications for their representatives would result in a patchwork of state qualifications, undermining the uniformity and the national character that the Framers envisioned and sought to ensure. . . . Such a patchwork would also sever the direct link that the Framers found so critical between the National Government and the people of the United States. . . .

Petitioners argue that, even if States may not add qualifications, Amendment 73 is constitutional because it is not such a qualification, and because Amendment 73 is a permissible exercise of state power to regulate the "Times, Places and Manner of Holding Elections." We reject these contentions. . . .

In our view, Amendment 73 is an indirect attempt to accomplish what the Constitution prohibits Arkansas from accomplishing directly. . . . There is no hint that § 3 was intended to have any other purpose. . . .

The merits of term limits, or "rotation," have been the subject of debate since the formation of our Constitution, when the Framers unanimously rejected a proposal to add such limits to the Constitution. The cogent arguments on both sides of the question that were articulated during the process of ratification largely retain their force today. Over half the States have adopted measures that impose such limits on some offices either directly or indirectly, and the Nation as a whole, notably by constitutional amendment, has imposed a limit on the number of terms that the President may serve. Term limits, like any other qualification for office, unquestionably restrict the ability of voters to vote for whom they wish. On the other hand, such limits may provide for the infusion of fresh ideas and new perspectives, and may decrease the likelihood that representatives will lose touch with their constituents. It is not our province to resolve this longstanding debate.

We are, however, firmly convinced that allowing the several States to adopt term limits for congressional service would effect a fundamental change in the constitutional framework. Any such change must come not by legislation adopted either by Congress or by an individual State, but rather—as have other important changes in the electoral process—through the Amendment procedures set forth in Article V. . . .

The judgment is affirmed.

*It is so ordered.*

Justice Kennedy, concurring . . . [omitted].

## Justice Thomas, with whom The Chief Justice, Justice O'Connor, and Justice Scalia join, dissenting.

It is ironic that the Court bases today's decision on the right of the people to "choose whom they please to govern them." Under our Constitution, there is only one State whose people have the right to "choose whom they please" to represent Arkansas in Congress. The Court holds, however, that neither the elected legislature of that State nor the people themselves (acting by ballot initiative) may prescribe any qualifications for those representatives. The majority therefore defends the right of the people of Arkansas to "choose whom they please to govern them" by invalidating a provision that won nearly 60% of the votes cast in a direct election and that carried every congressional district in the State.

I dissent. Nothing in the Constitution deprives the people of each State of the power to prescribe eligibility requirements for the candidates who seek to represent them in Congress. The Constitution is simply silent on this question. And where the Constitution is silent, it raises no bar to action by the States or the people.

Because the majority fundamentally misunderstands the notion of "reserved" powers, I start with some first principles. Contrary to the majority's suggestion, the people of the States need not point to any affirmative grant of power in the Constitution in order to prescribe qualifications for their representatives in Congress, or to authorize their elected state legislators to do so.

Our system of government rests on one overriding principle: all power stems from the consent of the people. To phrase the principle in this way, however, is to be imprecise about something important to the notion of "reserved" powers. The ultimate source of the Constitution's authority is the consent of the people of each individual State, not the consent of the undifferentiated people of the Nation as a whole. . . .

When they adopted the Federal Constitution, of course, the people of each State surrendered some of their authority to the United States (and hence to entities accountable to the people of other States as well as to themselves). They affirmatively deprived their States of certain powers, and they affirmatively conferred certain powers upon the Federal Government. Because the people of the several States are the only true source of power, however, the Federal Government enjoys no authority beyond what the Constitution confers: the Federal Government's powers are limited and enumerated. . . .

In each State, the remainder of the people's powers . . . are either delegated to the state government or retained by the people. The Federal Constitution does not specify which of these two possibilities obtains; it is up to the various state constitutions to declare which powers the people of each State have delegated to their state government. As far as the Federal Constitution is concerned, then, the States can exercise all powers that the Constitution does not withhold from them. The Federal Government and the States thus face different default rules: where the Constitution is silent about the exercise of a particular power—that is, where the Constitution does not speak either expressly or by necessary implication—the Federal Government lacks that power and the States enjoy it.

These basic principles are enshrined in the Tenth Amendment, which declares that all powers neither delegated to the Federal Government nor prohibited to the States "are reserved to the States respectively, or to the people." With this careful last phrase, the Amendment avoids taking any position on the division of power between the state governments and the people of the States: it is up to the people of each State to determine which "reserved" powers their state government may exercise. But the Amendment does make clear that powers reside at the state level except where the Constitution removes them from that level. All powers that the Constitution neither delegates to the Federal Government nor prohibits to the States are controlled by the people of each State. . . .

The majority's essential logic is that the state governments could not "reserve" any powers that they did not control at the time the Constitution was drafted. But it was not the state governments that were doing the reserving. The Constitution derives its authority instead from the consent of the people of the States. Given the fundamental principle that all governmental powers stem from the people of the States, it would simply be incoherent to assert that the people of the States could not reserve any powers that they had not previously controlled.

The Tenth Amendment's use of the word "reserved" does not help the majority's position. If someone says that the power to use a particular facility is reserved to some group, he is not saying anything about whether that group has previously used the facility. He is merely saying that the people who control the facility have designated that group as the entity with authority to use it. The Tenth Amendment is similar: the people of the States, from whom all governmental powers stem, have specified that all powers not prohibited to the States by the Federal Constitution are reserved "to the States respectively, or to the people.". . .

The majority settles on "the Qualifications Clauses" as the constitutional provisions that Amendment 73 violates. Because I do not read those provisions to impose any unstated prohibitions on the States, it is unnecessary for me to decide whether the majority is correct to identify Arkansas' ballot-access restriction with laws fixing true term limits or otherwise prescribing "qualifications" for congressional office. . . . [T]he Qualifications Clauses are merely straightforward recitations of the minimum eligibility requirements that the Framers thought it essential for every Member of Congress to meet. They restrict state power only in that they prevent the States from abolishing all eligibility requirements for membership in Congress. . . .

It is radical enough for the majority to hold that the Constitution implicitly precludes the people of the States from prescribing any eligibility requirements for the congressional candidates who seek their votes. This holding, after all, does not stop with negating the term limits that many States have seen fit to impose on their Senators and Representatives. Today's decision also means that no State may disqualify congressional candidates whom a court has found to be mentally incompetent, who are currently in prison, or who have past vote-fraud convictions. Likewise, after today's decision, the people of each State must leave open the possibility that they will trust someone with their vote in Congress even though they do not trust him with a vote in the election for Congress. . . .

## United States v. Morrison
### 529 U.S. 598, 120 S.Ct. 1740, 146 L.Ed. 2d 658 (2000)

http://laws.findlaw.com/us/529/598.html

Christy Brzonkala enrolled at Virginia Polytechnic Institute (Virginia Tech) in the fall of 1994 where she met respondents Antonio Morrison and James Crawford, who were also students and members of the varsity football team. In a complaint filed under Virginia Tech's sexual assault policy, Brzonkala alleged that, within 30 minutes of meeting Morrison and Crawford, they assaulted and repeatedly raped her. After the attack, Morrison allegedly told her, "You better not have any . . . diseases." In the months following the rape, Morrison also allegedly announced in the dormitory's dining room that he "like[d] to get girls drunk and. . . ." "[T]he omitted portions, quoted verbatim in the briefs on file with this Court," explained Chief Justice Rehnquist, "consist of boasting, debased remarks about what Morrison would do to women, vulgar remarks that cannot fail to shock and offend." After a complex series of proceedings at the university failed to result in punishment for Morrison and Crawford, and after learning from a newspaper that Morrison would be returning to campus in the fall of 1995, Brzonkala withdrew from school and filed suit under 42 U.S.C. § 13981 (*Brzonkala* v. *Morrison*). This provision of the Violence Against Women Act of 1994 provided a federal civil remedy for victims of gender-motivated violence, including situations where alleged acts did not result in criminal charges, prosecution, or conviction. The United States District Court for the Western District of Virginia held that Congress lacked authority to enact § 13981 under either the commerce clause or section 5 of the Fourteenth Amendment. A divided panel of the Court of Appeals for the Fourth Circuit reversed the District Court, but on rehearing en banc, a majority of the appeals court upheld the district court. Majority: Rehnquist, O'Connor, Scalia, Kennedy, Thomas. Dissenting: Souter, Stevens, Ginsburg, Breyer.

**CHIEF JUSTICE REHNQUIST delivered the opinion of the Court. . . .**

Section 13981 was part of the Violence Against Women Act of 1994. It states that "[a]ll persons within the United States shall have the right to be free from crimes of violence motivated by gender." To enforce that right, subsection (c) declares: "A person . . . who commits a crime of violence motivated by gender and thus deprives another of the right declared in subsection (b) of this section shall be liable to the party injured, in an action for the recovery of compensatory and punitive damages, injunctive and declaratory relief, and such other relief as a court may deem appropriate."

Congress explicitly identified the sources of federal authority on which it relied in enacting § 13981. It said that a "federal civil rights cause of action" is established "[p]ursuant to the affirmative power of Congress . . . under section 5 of the Fourteenth Amendment to the Constitution, as well as under section 8 of Article I of the Constitution." We address Congress' authority to enact this remedy under each of these constitutional provisions in turn. . . .

As we observed in [*United States* v.] *Lopez*, modern Commerce Clause jurisprudence has "identified three broad categories of activity that Congress may regulate under its commerce power." "First, Congress may regulate the use of the channels of interstate commerce." "Second, Congress is empowered to regulate and protect the instrumentalities of interstate commerce, or persons or things in interstate commerce, even though the threat may come only from intrastate activities." "Finally, Congress' commerce authority includes the power to regulate those activities having a substantial relation to interstate commerce, . . . i.e., those activities that substantially affect interstate commerce."

Petitioners do not contend that these cases fall within either of the first two of these categories of Commerce Clause regulation. They seek to sustain § 13981 as a regulation of activity that substantially affects interstate commerce. . . .

Since *Lopez* most recently canvassed and clarified our case law governing this third category of Commerce Clause regulation, it provides the proper framework for conducting the required analysis of § 13981. In *Lopez*, we held that the Gun-Free School Zones Act of 1990, § 922(q), which made it a federal crime to knowingly possess a firearm in a school zone, exceeded Congress' authority under the Commerce Clause. Several significant considerations contributed to our decision.

First, we observed that § 922(q) was "a criminal statute that by its terms has nothing to do with 'commerce' or any sort of economic enterprise, however broadly one might define those terms.". . . [A] fair reading of *Lopez* shows that the noneconomic, criminal nature of the conduct at issue was central to our decision in that case. . . .

The second consideration that we found important in analyzing § 922(q) was that the statute contained "no express jurisdictional element which might limit its reach to a discrete set of firearm possessions that additionally have an explicit connection with or effect on interstate commerce.". . .

Third, we noted that neither § 922(q) "'nor its legislative history contain[s] express congressional findings regarding the effects upon interstate commerce of gun possession in a school zone.'". . .

Finally, our decision in *Lopez* rested in part on the fact that the link between gun possession and a substantial effect on interstate commerce was attenuated. . . .

With these principles underlying our Commerce Clause jurisprudence as reference points, the proper resolution of the present cases is clear. Gender-motivated crimes of violence are not, in any sense of the phrase, economic activity. While we need not adopt a categorical rule against aggregating the effects of any noneconomic activity in order to decide these cases, thus far in our Nation's history our cases have upheld Commerce Clause regulation of intrastate activity only where that activity is economic in nature.

Like the Gun-Free School Zones Act at issue in *Lopez,* § 13981 contains no jurisdictional element establishing that the federal cause of action is in pursuance of Congress' power to regulate interstate commerce. . . .

In contrast with the lack of congressional findings that we faced in *Lopez,* § 13981 is supported by numerous findings regarding the serious impact that gender-motivated violence has on victims and their families. But the existence of congressional findings is not suffi-

cient, by itself, to sustain the constitutionality of Commerce Clause legislation. . . .

Congress found that gender-motivated violence affects interstate commerce "by deterring potential victims from traveling interstate, from engaging in employment in interstate business, and from transacting with business, and in places involved in interstate commerce; . . . by diminishing national productivity, increasing medical and other costs, and decreasing the supply of and the demand for interstate products." Given these findings and petitioners' arguments, the concern that we expressed in *Lopez* that Congress might use the Commerce Clause to completely obliterate the Constitution's distinction between national and local authority seems well founded. The reasoning that petitioners advance seeks to follow the but-for causal chain from the initial occurrence of violent crime (the suppression of which has always been the prime object of the States' police power) to every attenuated effect upon interstate commerce. If accepted, petitioners' reasoning would allow Congress to regulate any crime as long as the nationwide, aggregated impact of that crime has substantial effects on employment, production, transit, or consumption. . . .

Petitioners' reasoning, moreover, will not limit Congress to regulating violence but may, as we suggested in *Lopez,* be applied equally as well to family law and other areas of traditional state regulation since the aggregate effect of marriage, divorce, and childrearing on the national economy is undoubtedly significant. Congress may have recognized this specter when it expressly precluded § 13981 from being used in the family law context. . . .

We accordingly reject the argument that Congress may regulate noneconomic, violent criminal conduct based solely on that conduct's aggregate effect on interstate commerce. The Constitution requires a distinction between what is truly national and what is truly local. . . .

Because we conclude that the Commerce Clause does not provide Congress with authority to enact § 13981, we address petitioners' alternative argument that the section's civil remedy should be upheld as an exercise of Congress' remedial power under § 5 of the Fourteenth Amendment. . . .

The principles governing an analysis of congressional legislation under § 5 are well settled. Section 5 states that Congress may "'enforce,' by 'appropriate legislation' the constitutional guarantee that no State shall deprive any person of 'life, liberty or property, without due process of law,' nor deny any person 'equal protection of the laws.'" Section 5 is "a positive grant of legislative power" that includes authority to "prohibit conduct which is not itself unconstitutional and [to] intrud[e] into 'legislative spheres of autonomy previously reserved to the States.'" . . .

Petitioners' § 5 argument is founded on an assertion that there is pervasive bias in various state justice systems against victims of gender-motivated violence. This assertion is supported by a voluminous congressional record. Specifically, Congress received evidence that many participants in state justice systems are perpetuating an array of erroneous stereotypes and assumptions. . . . Petitioners contend that this bias denies victims of gender-motivated violence the equal protection of the laws and that Congress therefore acted appropriately in enacting a private civil remedy against the perpetrators of gender-motivated violence to both remedy the States' bias and deter future instances of discrimination in the state courts. . . .

However, the language and purpose of the Fourteenth Amendment place certain limitations on the manner in which Congress may attack discriminatory conduct. These limitations are necessary to prevent the Fourteenth Amendment from obliterating the Framers' carefully crafted balance of power between the States and the National Government. . . . Foremost among these limitations is the time-honored principle that the Fourteenth Amendment, by its very terms, prohibits only state action. . . .

[P]rophylactic legislation under § 5 must have a "'congruence and proportionality between the injury to be prevented or remedied and the means adopted to that end.'" Section 13981 is not aimed at proscribing discrimination by officials which the Fourteenth Amendment might not itself proscribe; it is directed not at any State or state actor, but at individuals who have committed criminal acts motivated by gender bias. . . .

For these reasons, we conclude that Congress' power under § 5 does not extend to the enactment of § 13981.

Petitioner Brzonkala's complaint alleges that she was the victim of a brutal assault. But Congress' effort in § 13981 to provide a federal civil remedy can be sustained neither under the Commerce Clause nor under § 5 of the Fourteenth Amendment. If the allegations here are true, no civilized system of justice could fail to provide her a remedy for the conduct of respondent Morrison. But under our federal system that remedy must be provided by the Commonwealth of Virginia, and not by the United States. The judgment of the Court of Appeals is

*Affirmed.*

JUSTICE THOMAS, concurring . . . [omitted].

**JUSTICE SOUTER, with whom JUSTICES STEVENS, GINSBURG, and BREYER, join, dissenting.**

The Court says both that it leaves Commerce Clause precedent undisturbed and that the Civil Rights Remedy of the Violence Against Women Act of 1994 exceeds Congress's power under that Clause. I find the claims irreconcilable and respectfully dissent.

Our cases, which remain at least nominally undisturbed, stand for the following propositions. Congress has the power to legislate with regard to activity that, in the aggregate, has a substantial effect on interstate commerce. The fact of such a substantial effect is not an issue for the courts in the first instance, but for the Congress, whose institutional capacity for gathering evidence and taking testimony far exceeds ours. By passing legislation, Congress indicates its conclusion, whether explicitly or not, that facts support its exercise of the commerce power. The business of the courts is to review the congressional assessment, not for soundness but simply for the rationality of concluding that a jurisdictional basis exists in fact. Any explicit findings that Congress chooses to make, though not dispositive of the question of rationality, may advance judicial review by identifying factual authority on which Congress relied. Applying those propositions in these cases can lead to only one conclusion.

One obvious difference from *Lopez* is the mountain of data assembled by Congress, here showing the effects of violence against women on interstate commerce. Passage of the Act in 1994 was preceded by four years of hearings, which included testimony from physicians and law professors; from survivors of rape and domestic violence; and from representatives of state law enforcement and private business. The record includes reports on gender bias from task forces in 21 States, and we have the benefit of specific factual findings in the eight separate Reports issued by Congress and its committees over the long course leading to enactment. . . .

Congress found that "crimes of violence motivated by gender have a substantial adverse effect on interstate commerce, by deterring potential victims from traveling interstate, from engaging in employment in interstate business, and from transacting with business, and in places involved, in interstate commerce . . . [,] by diminishing national productivity, increasing medical and other costs, and decreasing the supply of and the demand for interstate products. . . ." [T]he sufficiency of the evidence before Congress to provide a rational basis for the finding cannot seriously be questioned. . . .

The fact that the Act does not pass muster before the Court today is therefore proof, to a degree that *Lopez* was not, that the Court's nominal adherence to the substantial effects test is merely that. Although a new jurisprudence has not emerged with any distinctness, it is clear that some congressional conclusions about obviously substantial, cumulative effects on commerce are being assigned lesser values than the once-stable doctrine would assign them. . . .

Thus the elusive heart of the majority's analysis in these cases is its statement that Congress's findings of fact are "weakened" by the presence of a disfavored "method of reasoning." This seems to suggest that the "substantial effects" analysis is not a factual enquiry, for Congress in the first instance with subsequent judicial review looking only to the rationality of the congressional conclusion, but one of a rather different sort, dependent upon a uniquely judicial competence.

This new characterization of substantial effects has no support in our cases (the self-fulfilling prophecies of *Lopez* aside), least of all those the majority cites. Perhaps this explains why the majority is not content to rest on its cited precedent but claims a textual justification for moving toward its new system of congressional deference subject to selective discounts. Thus it purports to rely on the sensible and traditional understanding that the listing in the Constitution of some powers implies the exclusion of others unmentioned. . . . It follows, for the majority, not only that there must be some limits to "commerce," but that some particular subjects arguably within the commerce power can be identified in advance as excluded, on the basis of characteristics other than their commercial effects. Such exclusions come into sight when the activity regulated is not itself commercial or when the States have traditionally addressed it in the exercise of the general police power, conferred under the state constitutions but never extended to Congress under the Constitution of the Nation.

The premise that the enumeration of powers implies that other powers are withheld is sound; the conclusion that some particular categories of subject matter are therefore presumptively beyond the reach of the commerce power is, however, a non sequitur. . . .

[F]or significant periods of our history, the Court has defined the commerce power as plenary, unsusceptible to categorical exclusions, and this was the view expressed throughout the latter part of the 20th century in the substantial effects test. These two conceptions of the commerce power, plenary and categorically limited, are in fact old rivals, and today's revival of their competition summons up familiar history. . . .

Since adherence to these formalistically contrived confines of commerce power in large measure provoked the judicial crisis of

1937, one might reasonably have doubted that Members of this Court would ever again toy with a return to the days before *NLRB* v. *Jones & Laughlin Steel Corp.,* which brought the earlier and nearly disastrous experiment to an end. And yet today's decision can only be seen as a step toward recapturing the prior mistakes. . . .

Why is the majority tempted to reject the lesson so painfully learned in 1937? . . .

[T]he answer is not that the majority fails to see causal connections in an integrated economic world. The answer is that in the minds of the majority there is a new animating theory that makes categorical formalism seem useful again. Just as the old formalism had value in the service of an economic conception, the new one is useful in serving a conception of federalism. It is the instrument by which assertions of national power are to be limited in favor of preserving a supposedly discernible, proper sphere of state autonomy to legislate or refrain from legislating as the individual States see fit. . . .

The objection to reviving traditional state spheres of action as a consideration in commerce analysis, however, not only rests on the portent of incoherence, but is compounded by a further defect just as fundamental. The defect, in essence, is the majority's rejection of the Founders' considered judgment that politics, not judicial review, should mediate between state and national interests as the strength and legislative jurisdiction of the National Government inevitably increased through the expected growth of the national economy. Whereas today's majority takes a

leaf from the book of the old judicial economists in saying that the Court should somehow draw the line to keep the federal relationship in a proper balance, Madison, Wilson, and Marshall understood the Constitution very differently.

Politics as the moderator of the congressional employment of the commerce power was the theme many years later in *Wickard.* . . .

Amendments that alter the balance of power between the National and State Governments, like the Fourteenth, or that change the way the States are represented within the Federal Government, like the Seventeenth, are not rips in the fabric of the Framers' Constitution, inviting judicial repairs. The Seventeenth Amendment may indeed have lessened the enthusiasm of the Senate to represent the States as discrete sovereignties, but the Amendment did not convert the judiciary into an alternate shield against the commerce power. . . .

The facts that cannot be ignored today are the facts of integrated national commerce and a political relationship between States and Nation much affected by their respective treasuries and constitutional modifications adopted by the people. The federalism of some earlier time is no more adequate to account for those facts today than the theory of laissez-faire was able to govern the national economy 70 years ago.

JUSTICE BREYER, with whom JUSTICE STEVENS joins and with whom JUSTICES GINSBURG and BREYER join in part, dissenting . . . [omitted].

## *Kimel v. Florida Board of Regents*
## 528 U.S. 62, 120 S.Ct. 631, 145 L.Ed. 2d 522 (2000)
### http://laws.findlaw.com/us/528/62.html

> The Age Discrimination in Employment Act of 1967 makes it unlawful for an employer "to fail or refuse to hire or to discharge any individual or otherwise discriminate against any individual [over 40 years of age] . . . because of such individual's age." In 1974 Congress extended the ADEA to include state and local governments.

In 1995 J. Daniel Kimel, Jr., and other current and former faculty and librarians of Florida State University sued the Florida Board of Regents in the United States District Court for the Northern District of Florida, alleging that a failure to allocate funds to provide for previously agreed-upon adjustments to salaries had a disparate impact on the salaries of older employees. Rejecting a motion by the Regents that the Eleventh Amendment shielded them from the suit, the District Court held that Congress in the ADEA had expressed its intent to abrogate the states' Eleventh Amendment immunity and that the ADEA was appropriate legislation under the Fourteenth Amendment. Consolidating Kimel's case with a similar case from Alabama and another one from Florida, the Eleventh Circuit Court of Appeals reversed the district court, 2–1. One judge found no congressional intention in the ADEA to abrogate state immunity, and the other believed that Congress lacked authority under the Fourteenth Amendment to do so. Majority: O'Connor, Rehnquist, Scalia, Kennedy, Thomas. Dissenting: Stevens, Souter, Ginsburg, and Breyer.

### JUSTICE O'CONNOR delivered the opinion of the Court. . . .

Although today's cases concern suits brought by citizens against their own States, this Court has long "'understood the Eleventh Amendment to stand not so much for what it says, but for the presupposition . . . which it confirms.'" Accordingly, for over a century now, we have made clear that the Constitution does not provide for federal jurisdiction over suits against nonconsenting States. Petitioners nevertheless contend that the States of Alabama and Florida must defend the present suits on the merits because Congress abrogated their Eleventh Amendment immunity in the ADEA. To determine whether petitioners are correct, we must resolve two predicate questions: first, whether Congress unequivocally expressed its intent to abrogate that immunity; and second, if it did, whether Congress acted pursuant to a valid grant of constitutional authority. . . .

[Justice O'Connor concludes that] Congress unequivocally expressed its intent to abrogate the States' Eleventh Amendment immunity. . . .

This is not the first time we have considered the constitutional validity of the 1974 extension of the ADEA to state and local governments. In *EEOC* v. *Wyoming* (1983), we held that the ADEA constitutes a valid exercise of Congress' power "[t]o regulate Commerce . . . among the several States," and that the Act did not transgress any external restraints imposed on the commerce power by the Tenth Amendment. Because we found the ADEA valid under Congress' Commerce Clause power, we concluded that it was unnecessary to determine whether the Act also could be supported by Congress' power under § 5 of the Fourteenth Amendment. Resolution of today's cases requires us to decide that question.

In *Seminole Tribe* [*of Florida* v. *Florida* (1996)], we held that Congress lacks power under Article I to abrogate the States' sovereign immunity. "Even when the Constitution vests in Congress complete lawmaking authority over a particular area, the Eleventh Amendment prevents congressional authorization of suits by private parties against unconsenting States.". . . Under our firmly established precedent then, if the ADEA rests solely on Congress' Article I commerce power, the private petitioners in today's cases cannot maintain their suits against their state employers.

Justice Stevens disputes that well-established precedent again. In *Alden* [v. *Maine* (1999)], we explained that, "[a]lthough the sovereign immunity of the States derives at least in part from the common-law tradition, the structure and history of the Constitution make clear that the immunity exists today by constitutional design.". . . Indeed, the present dissenters' refusal to accept the validity and natural import of decisions like *Hans* [v. *Louisiana*, (1890)], rendered over a full century ago by this Court, makes it difficult to engage in additional meaningful debate on the place of state sovereign immunity in the Constitution. Today we adhere to our holding in *Seminole Tribe:* Congress' powers under Article I of the Constitution do not include the power to subject States to suit at the hands of private individuals.

Section 5 of the Fourteenth Amendment, however, does grant Congress the authority to abrogate the States' sovereign immunity. In *Fitzpatrick* v. *Bitzer* (1976), we recognized that "the Eleventh Amendment, and the principle of state sovereignty which it embodies, are necessarily limited by the enforcement provisions of § 5 of the Fourteenth Amendment." . . . Accordingly, the private petitioners in these cases may maintain their ADEA suits against the States of Alabama and Florida if, and only if, the ADEA is appropriate legislation under § 5. . . .

As we recognized most recently in *City of Boerne* v. *Flores* (1997), . . . "It is for Congress in the first instance to 'determin[e] whether and what legislation is needed to secure the guarantees of the Fourteenth Amendment,' and its conclusions are entitled to much deference." Congress' § 5 power is not confined to the enactment of legislation that merely parrots the precise wording of the Fourteenth Amendment. Rather, Congress' power "to enforce" the Amendment includes the authority both to remedy and to deter violation of rights guaranteed thereunder by prohibiting a somewhat broader swath of conduct, including that which is not itself forbidden by the Amendment's text.

Nevertheless, we have also recognized that the same language that serves as the basis for the affirmative grant of congressional power also serves to limit that power. For example, Congress cannot "decree the substance of the Fourteenth Amendment's restrictions on the States. . . . It has been given the power 'to enforce,' not the power to determine what constitutes a constitutional violation." The ultimate interpretation and determination of the Fourteenth Amendment's substantive meaning remains the province of the Judicial Branch. In *City of Boerne,* we noted that the determina-

tion whether purportedly prophylactic legislation constitutes appropriate remedial legislation, or instead effects a substantive redefinition of the Fourteenth Amendment right at issue, is often difficult. The line between the two is a fine one. Accordingly, recognizing that "Congress must have wide latitude in determining where [that line] lies," we held that "[t]here must be a congruence and proportionality between the injury to be prevented or remedied and the means adopted to that end."

Applying the . . . test in these cases, we conclude that the ADEA is not "appropriate legislation" under § 5. . . . Initially, the substantive requirements the ADEA imposes on state and local governments are disproportionate to any unconstitutional conduct that conceivably could be targeted by the Act. . . .

States may discriminate on the basis of age without offending the Fourteenth Amendment if the age classification in question is rationally related to a legitimate state interest. The rationality commanded by the Equal Protection Clause does not require States to match age distinctions and the legitimate interests they serve with razorlike precision. . . . Under the Fourteenth Amendment, a State may rely on age as a proxy for other qualities, abilities, or characteristics that are relevant to the State's legitimate interests. The Constitution does not preclude reliance on such generalizations. That age proves to be an inaccurate proxy in any individual case is irrelevant. . . . Finally, because an age classification is presumptively rational, the individual challenging its constitutionality bears the burden of proving that the "facts on which the classification is apparently based could not reasonably be conceived to be true by the governmental decisionmaker." . . .

Judged against the backdrop of our equal protection jurisprudence, it is clear that the ADEA is "so out of proportion to a supposed remedial or preventive object that it cannot be understood as responsive to, or designed to prevent, unconstitutional behavior." The Act, through its broad restriction on the use of age as a discriminating factor, prohibits substantially more state employment decisions and practices than would likely be held unconstitutional under the applicable equal protection, rational basis standard. The ADEA makes unlawful, in the employment context, all "discriminat[ion] against any individual . . . because of such individual's age." . . .

That the ADEA prohibits very little conduct likely to be held unconstitutional, while significant, does not alone provide the answer to our § 5 inquiry. . . . [W]e have never held that § 5 precludes Congress from enacting reasonably prophylactic legislation. Our task is to determine whether the ADEA is in fact just such an appropriate remedy or, instead, merely an attempt to substantively redefine the States' legal obligations with respect to age discrimination. . . .

Our examination of the ADEA's legislative record confirms that Congress' 1974 extension of the Act to the States was an unwarranted response to a perhaps inconsequential problem. Congress never identified any pattern of age discrimination by the States, much less any discrimination whatsoever that rose to the level of constitutional violation. . . .

A review of the ADEA's legislative record as a whole, then, reveals that Congress had virtually no reason to believe that state and local governments were unconstitutionally discriminating against their employees on the basis of age. Although that lack of support is not determinative of the § 5 inquiry, Congress' failure to uncover any significant pattern of unconstitutional discrimination here confirms that Congress had no reason to believe that broad prophylactic legislation was necessary in this field. . . . [W]e hold that the ADEA is not a valid exercise of Congress' power under § 5 of the Fourteenth Amendment. The ADEA's purported abrogation of the States' sovereign immunity is accordingly invalid.

Our decision today does not signal the end of the line for employees who find themselves subject to age discrimination at the hands of their state employers. We hold only that, in the ADEA, Congress did not validly abrogate the States' sovereign immunity to suits by private individuals. State employees are protected by state age discrimination statutes, and may recover money damages from their state employers, in almost every State of

the Union. Those avenues of relief remain available today, just as they were before this decision.

Because the ADEA does not validly abrogate the States' sovereign immunity, however, the present suits must be dismissed. Accordingly, the judgment of the Court of Appeals is affirmed.

*It is so ordered.*

**JUSTICE STEVENS, with whom JUSTICE SOUTER, JUSTICE GINSBURG, and JUSTICE BREYER join, dissenting in part and concurring in part.**

Congress' power to regulate the American economy includes the power to regulate both the public and the private sectors of the labor market. Federal rules outlawing discrimination in the workplace, like the regulation of wages and hours or health and safety standards, may be enforced against public as well as private employers. In my opinion, Congress' power to authorize federal remedies against state agencies that violate federal statutory obligations is coextensive with its power to impose those obligations on the States in the first place. Neither the Eleventh Amendment nor the doctrine of sovereign immunity places any limit on that power.

The application of the ancient judge-made doctrine of sovereign immunity in cases like these is supposedly justified as a freestanding limit on congressional authority, a limit necessary to protect States' "dignity and respect" from impairment by the National Government. The Framers did not, however, select the Judicial Branch as the constitutional guardian of those state interests. Rather, the Framers designed important structural safeguards to ensure that when the National Government enacted substantive law (and provided for its enforcement), the normal operation of the legislative process itself would adequately defend state interests from undue infringement.

It is the Framers' compromise giving each State equal representation in the Senate that provides the principal structural protection for the sovereignty of the several States. The composition of the Senate was originally determined by the legislatures of the States, which would guarantee that their interests could not be ignored by Congress. The Framers also directed that the House be composed of Representatives selected by voters in the several States, the consequence of which is that "the states are the strategic yardsticks for the measurement of interest and opinion, the special centers of political activity, the separate geographical determinants of national as well as local politics."

Whenever Congress passes a statute, it does so against the background of state law already in place; the propriety of taking national action is thus measured by the metric of the existing state norms that Congress seeks to supplement or supplant. The persuasiveness of any justification for overcoming legislative inertia and taking national action, either creating new federal obligations or providing for their enforcement, must necessarily be judged in reference to state interests, as expressed in existing state laws. The precise scope of federal laws, of course, can be shaped with nuanced attention to state interests. The Congress also has the authority to grant or withhold jurisdiction in lower federal courts. The burden of being haled into a federal forum for the enforcement of federal law, thus, can be expanded or contracted as Congress deems proper, which decision, like all other legislative acts, necessarily contemplates state interests. Thus, Congress can use its broad range of flexible legislative tools to approach the delicate issue of how to balance local and national interests in the most responsive and careful manner. It is quite evident, therefore, that the Framers did not view this Court as the ultimate guardian of the States' interest in protecting their own sovereignty from impairment by "burdensome" federal laws.

Federalism concerns do make it appropriate for Congress to speak clearly when it regulates state action. But when it does so, as it has in these cases, we can safely presume that the burdens the statute imposes on the sovereignty of the several States were taken into account during the deliberative process leading to the enactment of the measure. Those burdens necessarily include the cost of defending against enforcement proceedings and paying whatever penalties might be incurred for violating the statute. In my judgment, the question whether those enforcement proceedings should be conducted exclusively by federal agencies, or may be brought by private parties as well, is a matter of policy for Congress to decide. In either event, once Congress has made its policy choice, the sovereignty concerns of the several States are satisfied, and the federal interest in evenhanded enforcement of federal law, explicitly endorsed in Article VI of the Constitution, does not countenance further limitations. There is not a word in the text of the Constitution supporting the Court's conclusion that the judge-made doctrine of sovereign immunity limits Congress' power to authorize private parties, as well as federal agencies, to enforce federal law against the States. The importance of respecting the Framers' decision to assign the business of lawmaking to the Congress dictates firm resistance to the present majority's repeated substitution of its own views of federalism for those expressed in statutes enacted by the Congress and signed by the President.

The Eleventh Amendment simply does not support the Court's view. As has been stated before, the Amendment only places a textual limitation on the diversity jurisdiction of the federal courts. Because the Amendment is a part of the Constitution, I have never understood how its limitation on the diversity jurisdiction of federal courts defined in Article III could be "abrogated" by an Act of Congress. Here, however, private petitioners did not invoke the federal courts' diversity jurisdiction; they are citizens of the same State as the defendants and they are asserting claims that arise under federal law. Thus, today's decision (relying as it does on *Seminole Tribe*) rests entirely on a novel judicial interpretation of the doctrine of sovereign immunity, which the Court treats as though it were a constitutional precept. It is nevertheless clear to me that if Congress has the power to create the federal rights that these petitioners are asserting, it must also have the power to give the federal courts jurisdiction to remedy violations of those rights, even if it is necessary to "abrogate" the Court's Eleventh Amendment" version of the common-law defense of sovereign immunity to do so. That is the essence of the Court's holding in *Pennsylvania* v. *Union Gas Co.* (1989).

I remain convinced that *Union Gas* was correctly decided and that the decision of five Justices in *Seminole Tribe* to overrule that case was profoundly misguided. Despite my respect for stare decisis, I am unwilling to accept *Seminole Tribe* as controlling precedent. First and foremost, the reasoning of that opinion is so profoundly mistaken and so fundamentally inconsistent with the Framers' conception of the constitutional order that it has forsaken any claim to the usual deference or respect owed to decisions of this Court. Stare decisis, furthermore, has less force in the area of constitutional law. And in this instance, it is but a hollow pretense for any State to seek refuge in stare decisis' protection of reliance interests. It cannot be credibly maintained that a State's ordering of its affairs with respect to potential liability under federal law

requires adherence to *Seminole Tribe,* as that decision leaves open a State's liability upon enforcement of federal law by federal agencies. . . . Further, *Seminole Tribe* is a case that will unquestionably have serious ramifications in future cases; indeed, it has already had such an effect, as in the Court's decision today and in the equally misguided opinion of *Alden* v. *Maine.* Further still, the Seminole Tribe decision unnecessarily forces the Court to resolve vexing questions of constitutional law respecting Congress' § 5 authority. Finally, by its own repeated overruling of earlier precedent, the majority has itself discounted the importance of stare decisis in this area of the law. Th[is] kind of judicial activism . . . represents such a radical departure from the proper role of this Court that it should be opposed whenever the opportunity arises. . . .

[Justice Stevens concurred with the majority's conclusion that Congress intended to subject states to suits by private parties under the ADEA.—ED.]

JUSTICE THOMAS, with whom JUSTICE KENNEDY joins, concurring in part and dissenting in part . . . [omitted].

# CHAPTER FIVE

# *The Electoral Process*

*The conception of political equality from the Declaration of Independence, to Lincoln's Gettysburg Address, to the Fifteenth, Seventeenth, and Nineteenth Amendments can mean only one thing—one person, one vote.*

—Justice William O. Douglas (1963)

Preceding chapters illustrate the commonplace observation that the Supreme Court is a political institution. Being political does not mean that the justices routinely campaign for their favorite candidates or run for office themselves, although nineteenth-century American history offers examples of both. (Even in the twentieth century, Justice Charles Evans Hughes left the bench to run for president in 1916—he lost—, and Justice William O. Douglas had presidential aspirations in the 1940s and early 1950s.) Indeed justices and other federal judges today are expected to be "above politics" in that they are not supposed to take sides publicly in elections.

But the Court is political in at least four respects. First, as each of the following chapters demonstrates, its decisions shape public policy by deciding what government—national, state, or local—may or may not do. Second, decisions clarify the boundaries of political authority, focusing less on *what* may be done than on *who* may do it or *how* it may be done. As shown in Chapter Three, the Steel Seizure case of 1952 turned not on whether government could cope with labor disruptions but on whether President Truman had exceeded his authority and intruded into Congress's lawmaking domain. The Legislative Veto case of 1983 did not question government's authority to deport a particular individual but instead challenged the device by which Congress had ordered deportation. Third, the Court itself may become an issue in presidential elections, as has happened 12 times since 1800 because of unpopular decisions. Campaigns in the last quarter century would have taken a different shape without the Supreme Court's 1973 abortion decision, for instance. So in these ways, the Court has been political from practically the beginning.

Finally, the justices may affect the electoral process itself, as has happened in cases on voting rights, districting, or campaign contributions, and certainly in the disputed Florida vote count in the 2000 presidential election. This electoral dimension of constitutional law is the subject of this chapter. It is a significant part of the Court's work because of the role that political parties and elections play in the life of the nation. It is through the electoral process that "We the people" attempt to control government by choosing those who will govern. Because judges help to determine the ground rules of politics, decisions on the electoral process affect the acquisition and allocation of power in the most fundamental sense.

## VOTING

One could write a history of American politics by studying efforts to extend the vote, or **franchise.** The Constitution of 1787 left voting qualifications entirely in the hands of the states, with the result that most Americans—women, blacks, and some white adult males—were initially kept from the ballot box. By the 1820s the national trend was to chip away at those restrictions, first with removal of property qualifications for voting, followed by the Fifteenth, Nineteenth, and Twenty-sixth Amendments in 1870, 1920, and 1971 that dealt with race, gender, and age, respectively. With race however, many years would pass before the promise of the Fifteenth Amendment was realized.

**THE WHITE PRIMARY.** After the Civil War, national legislation implementing the Fourteenth and Fifteenth Amendments was only occasionally invoked successfully to protect the right of African-Americans to vote in congressional elections (Ex parte *Yarbrough,* 1884), as some states employed ingenious means to sidestep the Constitution. In *Guinn* v. *United States* (1915), the Court invalidated one of these racially discriminatory devices called a **grandfather clause.** It exempted from a literacy test for voting all persons and their lineal descendants who had voted on or before January 1, 1866, a date that excluded virtually every black. *Guinn* stood in sharp contrast to *Giles* v. *Harris* (1903), in which the Court confessed judicial impotence: Remedying a voter registration system designed to perpetuate white supremacy was beyond the Court's capacity, especially when the discrimination was as widespread as all acknowledged it to be.

Despite a few decisions like *Guinn,* however, some states remained intent on disfranchising blacks. For one thing, the Supreme Court held in *Newberry* v. *United States* (1921) that party primaries were not "elections" in the constitutional sense; clearly, if blacks could be excluded from primaries in one-party states, their political influence would evaporate. Nevertheless, the equal protection clause of the Fourteenth Amendment was successfully invoked both against a state law setting up a **white primary** for the Texas Democratic Party (*Nixon* v. *Herndon,* 1927) and against a similar resolution by the Democratic State Executive Committee acting under authority of statute (*Nixon* v. *Condon,* 1932). (The equal protection clause is covered more fully in Chapter Fourteen.) But in *Grovey* v. *Townsend* (1935), a resolution forbidding black participation adopted by the state convention of the Democratic Party was held to be private action and therefore not within the protective range of the Constitution. Moreover, along with the white primary, states had already adopted the literacy test, **poll tax** (payment of which was required to maintain voter eligibility), and similar gimmicks to prevent blacks (and some whites as well) from voting.

The story was not, however, to end on this note. In 1941 the Court held that the right to vote in a primary election in a one-party state, in this instance Louisiana, where the primary was a step in the election of members of Congress, was a right or privilege secured by the Constitution because the actions at the primary were officially accepted by the state. Hence, the failure of state officials, acting under "color" of state law, to count ballots properly was a violation of the provision of the U.S. Criminal Code that prohibited such "state" action (*United States* v. *Classic*). Then *Smith* v. *Allwright* (1944) overruled *Grovey* v. *Townsend* and held that the right to vote guaranteed by the Fifteenth Amendment applied to primaries as well as general elections. Later efforts by Texas to evade the principle of that case by accepting the candidates of the Jaybird Party, a Democratic political organization that conducted an unofficial primary in which blacks could not vote, were similarly deemed invalid (*Terry* v. *Adams,* 1953).

In an entirely different setting a half century later, the Court found a Fifteenth Amendment violation where ancestry was a proxy for race. Hawaii's Office of Hawaiian Affairs, headed by nine trustees, administers programs that benefit persons with Hawaiian ancestors—those living on the islands before 1778. Only persons of Hawaiian ancestry defined in this way were allowed to vote for the trustees. In the Court's view, this ancestrally linked restriction on the franchise implicated the same concerns as would a classification specifying a particular race by name and so amounted to a race-based voting qualification (*Rice* v. *Cayetano,* 2000).

**THE VOTING RIGHTS ACT.** Courtroom victories over the white primary, however, did little to overcome the more subtle ways in which African Americans could be kept from the polls. Much of the delay in implementing the landmark school integration decision of 1954 (***Brown v. Board of Education***), for example, stemmed from the political powerlessness of those who had the most to gain from the ruling (see Chapter Fourteen). As always, effective access to the ballot box was an important condition for equality under the law. Indeed, loss of the vote a half century earlier had helped to make possible the rigid and pervasive system of legalized segregation attacked in *Brown* and other cases.

Black organizations and their white allies became increasingly aware of the hitherto undeveloped potential of the black vote in the South. In 1961 only one in four eligible persons was registered. Further measures were therefore sought to achieve a dramatic increase in electoral strength. Adoption of the Twenty-fourth Amendment (1964), prohibiting use of a poll tax in federal elections, was a notable success. The poll tax as a requirement in state elections was invalidated in *Harper* v. *Virginia Board of Elections* (1966), as the Court emphasized the economic (not racial) discrimination inherent in the $1.50 tax. "To introduce wealth or payment of a fee as a measure of a voter's qualifications is to introduce a capricious or irrelevant factor. The degree of discrimination is irrelevant." Almost 30 years earlier the Court had upheld the tax (*Breedlove* v. *Suttles,* 1937).

The **Voting Rights Act** of 1965 remains the most important voter legislation ever enacted by Congress. Its measures (such as a ban on literacy tests) were extreme, but so were the evils it sought to correct. The act, upheld in *South Carolina* v. *Katzenbach* (1966), has had a far-reaching impact. By 1967, black voter registration had doubled in Georgia, nearly tripled in Alabama, and jumped almost 800 percent in Mississippi. In the South today, blacks vote in percentages that almost equal those for whites.

Three sections of the 1965 act merit attention here. Section 2 repeats the Fifteenth Amendment's prohibition against racial discrimination in voting and applies throughout the United States. An amendment to section 2 in 1982 expressly prohibits voting regulations that *result* in a denial of the right to vote on account of race. A violation of section 2 occurs when the "totality of circumstances" reveals that minority voters have less opportunity than others to elect officials "of their choice." Section 4 sets up a triggering mechanism for determining which parts of the country (mostly in the South) are subject to Section 5. Section 5 requires that any change in a "standard, practice, or procedure with respect to voting" can take effect only after being cleared by the attorney general or by the U.S. District Court for the District of Columbia. The Supreme Court has interpreted "standard, practice, or procedure" to include any changes in a locale's electoral system. This preclearance requirement is satisfied only if the jurisdiction proposing the change can demonstrate that the change neither has the purpose nor will have the effect of "denying or abridging the right to vote on account of race or color." Black voting strength, therefore, cannot be weakened or diluted by a change in local election practices. For example, the Supreme Court decided that Section 5 is violated if a city covered by the act enlarges its boundaries in such a way that blacks become a smaller percentage of the voting population (*Rome* v. *United States,* 1980).

Thus, **retrogression**—being worse off than before—is ordinarily dispositive for Section 5 violations. "[T]he purpose of § 5 has always been to insure that no voting-procedure changes would be made that would lead to a retrogression in the position of racial minorities with respect to their effective exercise of the electoral franchise" (*Beer* v. *United States,* 1976). According to *Georgia* v. *Ashcroft* (2003), section 5 allows states to risk having fewer minority representatives in order to achieve greater overall representation of a minority group by increasing the number of representatives sympathetic to the interests of minority voters through the creation of "influence" or "coalitional" districts. Even in situations where a discriminatory intent might be evident, section 5 "prevents nothing but backsliding," declared Justice Scalia in a Louisiana case challenging voting districts for school board members (*Reno* v. *Bossier Parish School Board,* 2000). This decision altered an approach to preclearance that the Department of Justice had used for 30 years and is in harmony with the Court's current attitude regarding creation of majority-minority districts, discussed later in this chapter.

**THE FLORIDA ELECTION CASE.** Florida became a battleground after Election Day 2000 even though all agreed that, nationally, Democratic presidential candidate Albert Gore had a lead in the popular vote total of several hundred thousand over Republican candidate George W. Bush. But that national margin made no difference. What mattered was the popular vote *in Florida,* because Florida's 25 electoral votes would decide whether Bush or Gore became the 43rd president.

Some ballots could not be read by the machines because some voters who used punch cards did not completely puncture the card, or, if they did, left a piece of paper (a chad) dangling, or left only an impression. The same thing had happened at other times in Florida, but the margins were not as close and the stakes were not as high. Trailing by only 537 votes (out of about six million cast), Gore wanted those uncounted ballots read by hand, as allowed by law. Bush feared that any hand count to determine the intention of the voter would inject enough subjectivity into the process to cost him the election.

The U.S. Supreme Court first stopped a hand recount ordered by the Florida Supreme Court and then ruled in **Bush v. Gore** that hand-counting could not proceed without uniform standards to determine the intent of the voter. With voting by the Electoral College just days away, five justices concluded that no constitutionally acceptable hand-counting was possible. Otherwise, citing the legislative districting cases (discussed below), they reasoned that one person's ballot might be treated differently from another's. This unprecedented decision may have an impact far beyond the presidential election of 2000. The Court established a rule that could affect voting procedures and recounts anywhere in the United States. The case lent irony to Chief Justice Waite's 1877 aphorism that "[f]or protection against abuses by legislatures, the people must resort to the polls, not to the courts."

## REPRESENTATION

When Earl Warren retired as chief justice in 1969, journalists asked him to identify his major contribution. The question was potentially difficult because between 1953 and 1969 the Warren Court, with revolutionary effects, had erected landmark decisions across the landscape of American constitutional law. Yet his apparently surprising answer was categorical: the redistricting cases. Why? The right to vote freely and equitably for the candidates of one's choice is the essence of democracy. Untrammeled exercise of this right is essential to the preservation of all others—"the bedrock of our political system," he called it.

**ENTERING THE POLITICAL THICKET.** Chapter Two introduced the **political question doctrine,** which holds that the resolution of certain disputes lies not with the judiciary but with one or both of the "political" branches of government. One of the most important fields in which the Court once invoked this self-imposed limitation is **legislative districting,** the drawing of geographical boundaries within states to determine representation in state legislatures and the U.S. House of Representatives. (**Legislative apportionment** refers generally to the distribution of seats in a legislative body, and specifically to the allocation of U.S. House seats among the states following each decennial census. According to *Dept. of Commerce* v. *U.S. House of Representatives* [1999], this apportionment must be based upon an actual count, not sampling techniques.)

In *Colegrove* v. *Green* (1946), Justice Frankfurter termed legislative districting as "peculiarly political" and "therefore not meet for judicial determination." Voters seeking relief from Illinois's numerically skewed congressional districts were told to turn to the state legislature or Congress, not to the Court. "Courts ought not to enter this 'political thicket,'" Frankfurter warned. "It is hostile to a democratic system to involve the judiciary in the politics of the people. . . . The remedy for unfairness in districting is to secure state legislatures that will apportion properly, or to invoke the ample powers of Congress." Congress, however, had lately been silent on the subject. Although a statute in 1842 required each state with more than one representative to employ single-member districts "composed of contiguous territory," and statutes in 1901 and 1911 mandated "compact" congressional districts (to rein in rampant gerrymandering), the apportionment act of 1929 left out any requirements for compact, contiguous, or equally populated districts. As the years went by, populations of House districts across the nation grew increasingly imbalanced.

In contrast to *Colegrove, Gomillion* v. *Lightfoot* (1960) hinted that a federal judicial remedy might indeed be available. Involved was an Alabama law that redrew the boundaries of the city of Tuskegee from a simple square into a 28-sided monster. The result was to remove from the city all but a handful of black voters, while leaving white voters unaffected. Justice Frankfurter, in spite of his position in *Colegrove* about political questions, declared that the Fifteenth Amendment guarantee against racial discrimination in voting justified judicial action. Left unanswered was the question whether the Fourteenth Amendment's equal protection clause might offer a judicial remedy for nonracial discrimination, based on urban versus suburban or rural residence.

An affirmative answer came in ***Baker* v. *Carr*** (1962). Finding no obstacle in the political question doctrine, Justice Brennan ruled that unequal legislative districts presented a valid question under the equal protection clause and that federal courts were empowered to provide a remedy.

**ONE PERSON, ONE VOTE.** In making belated entrance into this political thicket, *Baker* neglected (or refused) to lay down guidelines by which a valid districting plan could be distinguished from an invalid plan. That came the next year, in *Gray* v. *Sanders* (1963), in which the Court, applying the **one-person-one-vote** principle, invalidated the Georgia county unit system of primary elections for statewide offices that greatly disfavored urban counties. A candidate could win the popular vote but lose the election. Said Justice Douglas, "Once the geographical unit for which a representative is to be chosen is designated, all who participate in the election are to have an equal vote—whatever their race, whatever their sex, whatever their occupation, whatever their income, and wherever their home may be in that geographical unit. This is required by the equal protection clause of the Fourteenth Amendment."

In 1964, *Wesberry* v. *Sanders* extended the same principle to congressional districts, holding that the Constitution had the "plain objective of making equal representation for equal numbers of people the fundamental goal for the House of Representatives." "As nearly as practicable," the Court declared, "one man's vote in a congressional election is to be worth as much as another's." The conclusion of the three-round contest, set in motion by *Baker* v. *Carr,* came in ***Reynolds* v. *Sims.*** By applying the now familiar principle of one-person-one-vote, the justices challenged the legitimacy of at least 40 state legislatures by mandating numerically equal districts for both legislative chambers. Since 1964, the justices have applied the one-person-one-vote principle in a variety of redistricting cases. Only in the most unusual situations, and then only if congressional districts are not at issue, will the Court make an exception to its rule of numerical equality.

**GERRYMANDERING.** In 1986 the Court ventured further into the political thicket. In a challenge to a districting plan for the Indiana legislature, the Court concluded in ***Davis* v. *Bandemer*** that partisan **gerrymandering** presented a justiciable issue under the equal protection clause. Democrats claimed that Republicans had unfairly (and unconstitutionally) advantaged themselves in drawing state legislative district lines after the 1980 census. Yet only two justices found a constitutional defect in the Indiana plan. For future cases, the Court announced a standard much less precise than one-person-one-vote, which made it difficult to show a constitutional violation: "Unconstitutional discrimination occurs only when the electoral system is arranged in a manner that will consistently degrade a voter's or a group of voters' influence on the political process as a whole." Left in doubt was the kind of evidence and the period of time required to prove an unconstitutional gerrymander.

Complicating any such litigation is the redistricting that occurs after each decennial census.

**MAJORITY-MINORITY DISTRICTS.** Legislative districting to enhance the representation of racial minorities has also given rise to constitutional disputes. When states attempt to boost the representation of racial minorities by drawing district lines to create one or more districts where a racial minority is in the majority, white voters have complained that such race-based districting violates the Fourteenth Amendment. Moreover, some political leaders find **majority-minority districts** of dubious value because, in a system of single-member districts, they concentrate minority voters in a few districts, thereby reducing the influence of those voters statewide. In some southern states, for example, majority-minority districts have had the effect of increasing the number of white Republicans elected to Congress, all the while decreasing the number of white Democratic representatives and increasing the number of African-American or Latino Democratic representatives.

In the first benign race-conscious districting case to reach the Supreme Court, the justices turned back a challenge to a New York plan that split a Hasidic Jewish community among several state legislative districts in order to increase black representation (*United Jewish Organizations* v. *Carey,* 1977). The case signaled that such steps were not only appropriate under the Voting Rights Act but were permitted by the Constitution.

After the 1990 census the North Carolina legislature created two black-majority congressional districts, the first and the twelfth, but this time the Court adopted a skeptical posture. District 1 seemed crudely drawn, and critics ridiculed it as resembling a "Rorschach ink-blot test." District 12 meandered along Interstate 85 dividing counties and towns en route, its shape also hinting that it was drawn primarily with racial objectives in mind. Without saying outright that either district 12 or 1 violated the equal protection clause, five justices nonetheless declared that the petitioners had a valid "cause of action" and remanded the case so that the district court could determine whether the districts amounted to a racial gerrymander (*Shaw* v. *Reno,* 1993). The district court then concluded that the state's plan was race-based but satisfied strict judicial scrutiny by being narrowly tailored to further a compelling interest in complying with the Voting Rights Act. The Supreme Court reversed definitively with respect to district 12. District 1 had been dropped from the litigation because the white voters who mounted the original challenge had since moved out of the district. (*Shaw* v. *Hunt,* 1996). The plan was precluded by *Miller* **v.** *Johnson* (1995), which had invalidated a Georgia congressional arrangement that created three majority-minority districts, at least one of which seemed explainable only on the basis of race (see Figure 5.1). Left unanswered in *Miller* was: (1) how courts in other situations were to determine the relative weight of factors accounting for a districting plan; (2) whether race-based districting in compliance with Section 5 was sufficiently "compelling" to pass scrutiny under the equal protection clause; and (3) whether nonracial variables might yield a constitutionally acceptable majority-minority district.

The 2000 census had barely been completed when the battle over North Carolina's district 12, launched after the 1990 census, ended in *Hunt [Easley]* **v.** *Cromartie* (2001), where the Court found the now-reshaped district 12 constitutionally acceptable. Five justices agreed with the district court that the district was created largely for partisan, and not racial, reasons; therefore, it was judged by the less demanding Fourteenth Amendment standard applied to nonracial gerrymanders.

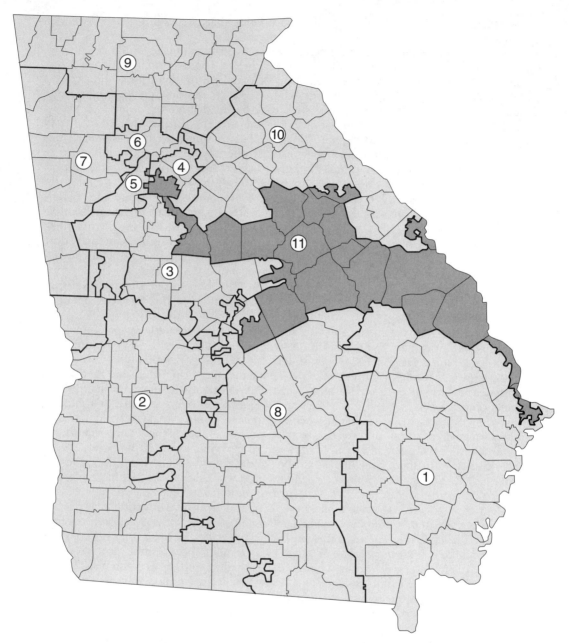

**FIGURE 5.1   Georgia Congressional Districting Plan Attacked in *Miller* v. *Johnson*.**

It remains to be seen whether the Court's razor-thin majority against most race-based districting holds, and if so, whether states seeking to enhance minority representation may meet the inevitable challenges by drawing districts with more conventional shapes. It also remains to be seen whether, because African-Americans are among the most reliable Democratic voters, *Cromartie* will now allow *party* to be a proxy for *race* in the effort to increase minority representation.

# PARTY POLITICS AND CAMPAIGNS

Campaigns and elections are democracy's battlegrounds. Political parties are the organizations created for the purpose of choosing candidates, mobilizing supporters, and running campaigns in order to win elections and to enact the values of their coalitions into law. A political party is thus a private group that performs very public functions. Understandably, therefore, conflicts may arise between the party's right to define itself and to carry on its business and the government's interest in how officials are elected and how campaigns are conducted. As explained in Chapter Eleven, at least since 1957 the Court has held that the First Amendment implicitly protects a freedom of association, but like other constitutional rights, this freedom is not absolute.

**PRIMARIES AND ELECTIONS.** As noted, the Court ruled decades ago that the public functions of parties in nominating candidates amount to "state action," meaning that exclusion of black voters by some state Democratic parties (the white primary) violates the Fifteenth Amendment. On other questions, however, party preferences have prevailed. *Tashjian* v. *Connecticut* (1986) overturned a state law requiring that party primaries be "closed" rather than "open." Connecticut Republicans, knowing they were a minority, thought they could attract independent voters in the general election by allowing them to vote in the primary. Relying on associational rights, the Court held that parties, not state legislatures, should determine who participates in party affairs.

This view seemed to explain the outcome in ***California Democratic Party v. Jones*** (2000), which invalidated an initiative-imposed system of blanket primaries in place of the closed primaries mandated by the rules of four parties in the state. (In a **blanket primary,** voters may select a candidate from any party for each office.) Against the asserted public interest—presumably served by blanket primaries—in increasing voter turnout by assuring candidates less extreme, more centrist, and therefore more representative of the population at large, the parties argued successfully that freedom of association allowed them to decide who their nominees (and hence what their messages) would be.

Whether in primaries or elections, may government restrict what candidates say as they campaign for office? This was the question posed by ***Republican Party of Minnesota*** v. ***White*** (2002). Unlike federal judges who are all appointed, most state judges are elected. For several decades, judicial elections in many states have been conducted under rules which prohibit candidates from discussing certain subjects. With far-reaching implications for judicial selection procedures and campaigns, the Court announced in *White* that such restrictions violate the First Amendment's protection of freedom of speech.

**CAMPAIGN FINANCE.** "There are two things that are important in politics," Republican strategist Mark Hanna is supposed to have said more than a century ago. "The first is money, and I can't remember what the second one is." Restrictions on the source, amount, and use of campaign funds implicate the First Amendment rights of free speech and association because candidates and parties, as well as other political groups, require money to build their organizations and to convey their messages to voters. Money is, in short, a proxy for speech. This view lay at the heart of *Buckley* v. *Valeo* (1976), which reviewed at length the constitutionality of the **Federal Election Campaign Act** (FECA), amended in 1974 to reduce the influence of "big money" in national elections. The objective of FECA was to minimize corruption or the appearance of corruption in federal elections. In a **per curiam** opinion and in five separate opinions that consumed almost 300 pages in the *United States Reports,* the Court made an important constitutional distinction between *contributions* and *expenditures:* Limitations on the former were less harmful to speech than limitations on the latter. Furthermore, large contributions seemed more easily linked to corruption or to the appearance of corruption. The result was a bench more willing to accept restrictions on contributions than on expenditures. (Per curiam means "by the court" and is a designation the Supreme Court uses for unsigned opinions. A per curiam opinion may indicate that the Court is only applying "settled law" or may be used in situations, as in *Buckley,* where no majority opinion was practical.) Accordingly, the Court disallowed provisions of FECA that put a limit of $50,000 on the use by a presidential candidate of his own or his immediate family's money, as well as a limit on "independent spending" by individuals and groups on behalf of a candidate in a federal election. Endorsed, however, were ceilings on contributions of $1,000 and $5,000 per election from individuals and groups, respectively, to candidates seeking federal office. Also upheld was a conditional scheme of public financing for presidential races (on a matching basis in primaries and caucuses and with full funding in the general election), in return for which candidates agreed to abide by spending limits.

Spending on advertising by independent political action committees (PACs) and party groups plays an important role in federal elections. Prior to 1985, when a presidential candidate accepted public financing, FECA made it a criminal offense for independent political committees to spend more than $1,000 on a candidate's behalf. *Buckley* had held in 1976 that Congress could not constitutionally limit independent expenditures in presidential campaigns generally. Unclear was whether Congress could limit independent expenditures when the candidates had accepted federal funding. *Federal Election Commission* v. *National Conservative Political Action Committee* (1985) declared that independent expenditures "produce speech at the core of the First Amendment" and, finding no corruption or appearance of corruption in the practice, invalidated the spending limitation.

*Colorado Republican Federal Campaign Committee* v. *FEC* (1996) (*Colorado I*) went far toward removing remaining legal limitations on expenditures by anyone on behalf of a candidate's own organization. At issue was a provision of FECA that imposed dollar limits upon "coordinated expenditures"—that is, money spent by a political party "in connection with the general election campaign of a [congressional] candidate." In the Court's view, party spending was not presumptively coordinated, as the government maintained; "independent" party expenditures were entitled to full First Amendment protection. As long as a state party developed its media campaign independently of, and not pursuant to, any understanding with the party's nominee, limits on spending by the party violated the Constitution. **Federal Election Commission v. Colorado Republican Federal Campaign Committee** (2001) (*Colorado II*) answered a question *Colorado I* had not: If the First Amendment bars limits on a party's independent expenditures on behalf of one of its candidates, does it also bar limits on expenditures that are coordinated with the candidate's campaign? Phrased differently, were such coordinated expenditures more like ordinary campaign expenditures (where the Court has been hostile to regulation) or more like contributions to the candidate (where the Court has accepted limits)? For five justices, coordinated expenditures were more like the latter; otherwise, contribution limits themselves might be circumvented.

Campaign finance issues remain litigious. In 2002 Congress enacted the most sweeping changes to FECA in more than a quarter century. Aside from raising the limit for individual contributions to $2,000 per election (and $25,000 per year to national parties) and indexing those amounts for inflation, the **Bipartisan Campaign Reform Act** (BCRA) bans all "**soft money**" (unregulated) contributions to national party organizations. (In the 2000 elections, Republicans raised $250 million in soft money, and the Democrats raised $245 million.) Annual contributions to state and local party organizations are capped at $10,000. Moreover, "issue ads" or "electioneering communications" that are broadcast or telecast and that refer to a specific candidate may not be run 30 days before a primary or 60 days before a general election unless they are funded by a party's or a group's "**hard money**" (regulated) contributions.

Dividing as it had in *Colorado II,* the Supreme Court upheld almost all provisions of BCRA in ***McConnell* v. *Federal Election Commission*** (2003), including the soft money ban and the restriction on electioneering communications, in a decision that matched *Buckley* in length. Yet as the majority opinion observed, BCRA will hardly be Congress's last word on campaign finance regulation. Parties and groups remain hard at work to learn how to turn BCRA to their advantage and to discover ways around limitations they dislike. Moreover, rules crafted by the FEC to implement BCRA's many-faceted restrictions are themselves sure to become grist for the judicial mill in future litigation.

**PATRONAGE.** The Constitution has brought the Court closer to the day-to-day world of American politics in other ways. *Elrod* v. *Burns* (1976) invalidated "a practice as old as the Republic, a practice which has contributed significantly to the democratization of American politics," said Justice Powell in dissent. At issue was patronage—in particular, discharging employees not on civil service because of their party affiliation. Burns and others were employees of the sheriff's department in Cook County, Illinois. They were also Republicans. Elrod was the newly elected sheriff and a Democrat. The Court resisted the argument that judicial intervention would badly weaken the party system. Besides, "any contribution of patronage dismissals to the democratic process does not suffice to override their severe encroachment on First Amendment freedoms." Covered by this decision were "nonpolicy making, nonconfidential government employees." As clarified somewhat by *Branti* v. *Finkel* (1980), one's party affiliation can be a condition for continued employment only if "that party affiliation is an appropriate requirement for the effective performance of the public office involved." In 1990 *Rutan* v. *Republican Party of Illinois* applied this reasoning to patronage hiring. These decisions in turn led to *O'Hare Truck Services, Inc.* v. *Northlake* (1996), in which a tow truck operator who provided services on call for this Illinois city claimed that he had been dropped from the rotation list because he declined to contribute to the mayor's campaign. In the Court's view the First Amendment protection against patronage firing extended to public contractors as well.

These decisions, and others sure to come, make clear that the Supreme Court will continue to be involved in the partisan and electoral life of the nation.

## KEY TERMS

franchise
grandfather clause
white primary
poll tax
Voting Rights Act
retrogression
political question
    doctrine

legislative districting
legislative apportionment
one-person-one-vote
gerrymandering
majority-minority districts
blanket primary
Federal Election
    Campaign Act

per curiam
Bipartisan Campaign
    Reform Act
soft money
hard money

## QUERIES

**1.** In *Reynolds* v. *Sims* (1964), Justice Stewart agreed with the majority that the badly skewed Alabama legislature violated the Constitution. Yet he refused to accept the majority's automatic application of one-person-one-vote as the constitutionally required standard in all redistricting cases. Explain.

**2.** Is there merit to the argument that the single-member district (the most common basis of representation in the United States) unavoidably injects discrimination into representation on city councils and in state legislatures and the U.S. House of Representatives?

**3.** According to Justice Ginsburg's dissent in *Miller* v. *Johnson* (1995), the majority effectively invalidated any district drawn for the purpose of keeping a particular ethnic group together. Is her conclusion correct?

**4.** In his separate opinion in *Colorado Republican Federal Campaign Committee* v. *FEC* (1996) (*Colorado I*), Justice Thomas claimed that the distinction between contributions and expenditures, on which *Buckley* v. *Valeo* rested, lacked constitutional significance.

> Contributions and expenditures both involve core First Amendment expression because they further the "[d]iscussion of public issues and debate on the qualifications of candidates . . . integral to the operation of the system of government established by our Constitution." When an individual donates money to a candidate or to a partisan organization, he enhances the donee's ability to communicate a message and thereby adds to political debate, just as when that individual communicates the message himself. Indeed, the individual may add more to political discourse by giving rather than spending, if the donee is able to put the funds to more productive use than can the individual. The contribution of funds to a candidate or to a political group thus fosters the "free discussion of governmental affairs."

Do you agree?

## SELECTED READINGS

CANNON, DAVID T., ed. *Race, Redistricting and Representation*. Chicago: University of Chicago Press, 1999.

CORTNER, RICHARD C. *The Apportionment Cases*. Knoxville: University of Tennessee Press, 1970.

DAVIDSON, CHANDLER, and BERNARD GROFMAN, eds. *Quiet Revolution in the South: The Impact of the Voting Rights Act, 1965–1990*. Princeton, N.J.: Princeton University Press, 1994.

GUINIER, LANI. *The Tyranny of the Majority: Fundamental Fairness in Representative Democracy*. New York: Free Press, 1994.

HANSON, ROYCE. *The Political Thicket*. Upper Saddle River, N.J.: Prentice Hall, 1966.

SCHER, RICHARD K., JON L. MILLS, and JOHN J. HOTALING. *Voting Rights and Democracy: The Law and Politics of Districting*. Chicago: Nelson-Hall, 1997.

KEYSSAR, ALEXANDER. *The Right to Vote: The Contested History of Democracy in the United States*. New York: Basic Books, 2000.

2 2

22222222222222 2

2222 22 22222222222222

SLABACH, FREDERICK G., ed. *The Constitution and Campaign Finance Reform.* Durham, N.C.: Carolina Academic Press, 1998.

THERNSTRONE, ABIGAIL M. *Whose Votes Count: Affirmative Action and Minority Voting Rights.* Cambridge, Mass.: Harvard University Press, 1987.

WROTH, L. KINVIN. "Election Contests and the Electoral Vote." 65 *Dickinson Law Review* 321 (1961).

YARBROUGH, TINSLEY E. *Race and Redistricting: The* Shaw-Cromartie *Cases.* Lawrence: University Press of Kansas, 2002.

## I. VOTING

### *Bush* v. *Gore*
### 531 U.S. 98, 121 S.Ct. 525, 148 L.Ed. 2d 388 (2000)
http://laws.findlaw.com/us/531/98.html

> This remarkable litigation involving the extended presidential election of 2000 was twice before the U. S. Supreme Court in less than two weeks. At its conclusion, the Court effectively handed the White House to Republican candidate Governor George W. Bush. Some essential facts appear in the per curiam opinion below. The Supreme Court heard oral arguments in *Bush I* on the morning of December 1, and in *Bush II* on the morning of December 11, and in record-setting time, rendered its decision on the night of December 12. Twenty-four hours later, Democratic candidate Vice President Albert Gore, Jr., conceded the election to Bush. Florida's 25 electoral votes gave Bush a total of 271, one more than the required minimum, to Gore's 267. Unofficial tallies in mid-December placed Gore's nation-wide lead in popular votes at approximately 338,000, out of more than 104 million cast. (The official tally, not available until weeks later, sets Gore's plurality at 540,520.)
>
> In *Bush I*, the petition for certiorari posed three questions. Two dealt with Article II and 3 U.S.C. § 5; the third raised the equal protection issue. In its reply brief, Gore's legal team deflected the third question, and it was excluded from the U.S. Supreme Court's grant of review and the oral argument on December 1. Ironically, with even less time in which to conduct the manual recounts, the equal protection issue resurfaced the following week in *Bush* v. *Gore* (*Bush II*) and proved dispositive. Majority: Rehnquist, O'Connor, Scalia, Kennedy, Thomas. Dissenting: Stevens, Souter, Ginsburg, Breyer.

PER CURIAM. . . .

On November 8, 2000, the day following the Presidential election, the Florida Division of Elections reported that petitioner, Governor Bush, had received 2,909,135 votes, and respondent, Vice President Gore, had received 2,907,351 votes, a margin of 1,784 for Governor Bush. Because Governor Bush's margin of victory was less than "one-half of a percent . . . of the votes cast," an automatic machine recount was conducted under § 102.141(4) of the [Florida] election code, the results of which showed Governor Bush still winning the race but by a diminished margin. Vice President Gore then sought manual recounts in Volusia, Palm Beach, Broward, and Miami-Dade Counties, pursuant to Florida's election protest provisions. A dispute arose concerning the deadline for local county canvassing boards to submit their returns to the Secretary of State. The

Secretary declined to waive the November 14 deadline imposed by statute. The Florida Supreme Court, however, set the deadline at November 26. We granted certiorari and vacated the Florida Supreme Court's decision, finding considerable uncertainty as to the grounds on which it was based [*Bush* v. *Palm Beach County Canvassing Board* (*Bush I*)]. On December 11, the Florida Supreme Court issued a decision on remand reinstating that date.

On November 26, the Florida Elections Canvassing Commission certified the results of the election and declared Governor Bush the winner of Florida's 25 electoral votes. On November 27, Vice President Gore . . . filed a complaint in Leon County Circuit Court contesting the certification. He sought relief pursuant to § 102.168(3)(c), which provides that "[r]eceipt of a number of illegal votes or rejection of a number of legal votes sufficient to change or place in doubt the result of the election" shall be grounds for a contest. The Circuit Court denied relief, stating that Vice President Gore failed to meet his burden of proof. . . .

Accepting jurisdiction, the Florida Supreme Court . . . held that the Circuit Court had been correct to reject Vice President Gore's challenge to the results certified in Nassau County and his challenge to the Palm Beach County Canvassing Board's determination that 3,300 ballots cast in that county were not, in the statutory phrase, "legal votes." . . .

The Supreme Court held that Vice President Gore had satisfied his burden of proof under § 102.168(3)(c) with respect to his challenge to Miami-Dade County's failure to tabulate, by manual count, 9,000 ballots on which the machines had failed to detect a vote for President ("undervotes"). Noting the closeness of the election, the Court explained that "[o]n this record, there can be no question that there are legal votes within the 9,000 uncounted votes sufficient to place the results of this election in doubt." A "legal vote," as determined by the Supreme Court, is "one in which there is a 'clear indication of the intent of the voter.'" The court therefore ordered a hand recount of the 9,000 ballots in Miami-Dade County. Observing that the contest provisions vest broad discretion in the circuit judge to "provide any relief appropriate under such circumstances," the Supreme Court further held that the Circuit Court could order "the Supervisor of Elections and the Canvassing Boards, as well as the necessary public officials, in all counties that have not conducted a manual recount or tabulation of the undervotes . . . to do so forthwith, said tabulation to take place in the individual counties where the ballots are located." . . .

The petition [in *Bush* v. *Gore* (*Bush II*)] presents the following questions: whether the Florida Supreme Court established new standards for resolving Presidential election contests, thereby violating Art. II, § 1, cl. 2, of the United States Constitution and failing to comply with 3 U.S.C. § 5 and whether the use of standardless manual recounts violates the Equal Protection and Due Process Clauses. With respect to the equal protection question,

we find a violation of the Equal Protection Clause. . . .

The individual citizen has no federal constitutional right to vote for electors for the President of the United States unless and until the state legislature chooses a statewide election as the means to implement its power to appoint members of the Electoral College. . . . [I]t may, if it so chooses, select the electors itself, which indeed was the manner used by State legislatures in several States for many years after the Framing of our Constitution. History has now favored the voter, and in each of the several States the citizens themselves vote for Presidential electors. When the state legislature vests the right to vote for President in its people, the right to vote as the legislature has prescribed is fundamental; and one source of its fundamental nature lies in the equal weight accorded to each vote and the equal dignity owed to each voter. . . .

The right to vote is protected in more than the initial allocation of the franchise. Equal protection applies as well to the manner of its exercise. Having once granted the right to vote on equal terms, the State may not, by later arbitrary and disparate treatment, value one person's vote over that of another. . . .

There is no difference between the two sides of the present controversy on these basic propositions. . . . The question before us, however, is whether the recount procedures the Florida Supreme Court has adopted are consistent with its obligation to avoid arbitrary and disparate treatment of the members of its electorate.

Much of the controversy seems to revolve around ballot cards designed to be perforated by a stylus but which, either through error or deliberate omission, have not been perforated with sufficient precision for a machine to count them. In some cases a piece of the card—a chad—is hanging, say by two corners. In other cases there is no separation at all, just an indentation.

The Florida Supreme Court has ordered that the intent of the voter be discerned from such ballots. For purposes of resolving the equal protection challenge, it is not necessary to decide whether the Florida Supreme Court had the authority under the legislative scheme for resolving election disputes to define what a legal vote is and to mandate a manual recount implementing that definition. The recount mechanisms implemented in response to the decisions of the Florida Supreme Court do not satisfy the minimum requirement for non-arbitrary treatment of voters necessary to secure the fundamental right. Florida's basic command for the count of legally cast votes is to consider the "intent of the voter." This is unobjectionable as an abstract proposition and a starting principle. The problem inheres in the absence of specific standards to ensure its equal application. The formulation of uniform rules to determine intent based on these recurring circumstances is practicable and, we conclude, necessary. . . .

The question before the Court is not whether local entities, in the exercise of their expertise, may develop different systems for implementing elections. Instead, we are presented with a situation where a state court with the power to assure uniformity has ordered a statewide recount with minimal procedural safeguards. . . . Given the Court's assessment that the recount process underway was probably being conducted in an unconstitutional manner, the Court stayed the order directing the recount so it could hear this case and render an expedited decision. The contest provision, as it was mandated by the State Supreme Court, is not well calculated to sustain the confidence that all citizens must have in the outcome of elections. The State has not shown that its procedures include the necessary safeguards. . . .

Upon due consideration of the difficulties identified to this point, it is obvious that the recount cannot be conducted in compliance with the requirements of equal protection and due process without substantial additional work. . . .

The Supreme Court of Florida has said that the legislature intended the State's electors to "participat[e] fully in the federal electoral process," as provided in 3 U.S.C. § 5. That statute, in turn, requires that any controversy or contest that is designed to lead to a conclusive selection of electors be completed by December 12. That date is upon us, and there is no recount procedure in place under the State Supreme Court's order that comports with minimal constitutional standards. Because it is evident that any recount seeking to meet the December 12 date will be unconstitutional for the reasons we have discussed, we reverse the judgment of the Supreme Court of Florida ordering a recount to proceed. . . .

*It is so ordered.*

### CHIEF JUSTICE REHNQUIST, with whom JUSTICE SCALIA and JUSTICE THOMAS join, concurring. . . .

In *McPherson* v. *Blacker* (1892), we explained that Art. II, § 1, cl. 2, "convey[s] the broadest power of determination" and "leaves it to the legislature exclusively to define the method" of appointment. A significant departure from the legislative scheme for appointing Presidential electors presents a federal constitutional question.

3 U.S.C. § 5 informs our application of Art. II, § 1, cl. 2, to the Florida statutory scheme, which, as the Florida Supreme Court acknowledged, took that statute into account. Section 5 provides that the State's selection of electors "shall be conclusive, and shall govern in the counting of the electoral votes" if the electors are chosen under laws enacted prior to election day, and if the selection process is completed six days prior to the meeting of the electoral college. . . . If we are to respect the legislature's Article II powers, therefore, we must ensure that postelection state-court actions do not frustrate the legislative desire to attain the "safe harbor" provided by § 5. . . .

The scope and nature of the remedy ordered by the Florida Supreme Court jeopardizes the "legislative wish" to take advantage of the safe harbor provided by 3 U.S.C. § 5. . . . This was done in a search for elusive—perhaps delusive—certainty as to the exact count of 6 million votes. But no one claims that these ballots have not previously been tabulated; they were initially read by voting machines at the time of the election, and thereafter reread by virtue of Florida's automatic recount provision. . . . It significantly departed from the statutory framework in place on November 7, and authorized open-ended further proceedings which could not be completed by December 12, thereby preventing a final determination by that date. . . .

### JUSTICE STEVENS, with whom JUSTICE GINSBURG and JUSTICE BREYER join, dissenting. . .

The federal questions that ultimately emerged in this case are not substantial. . . .

It hardly needs stating that Congress, pursuant to 3 U.S.C. § 5 did not impose any affirmative duties upon the States that their governmental branches could "violate." Rather, § 5 provides a safe harbor for States to select electors in contested elections "by judicial or other methods" established by laws prior to the election day. Section 5, like Article II, assumes the involvement of the state judiciary in interpreting state election laws and resolving election disputes under those laws. Neither § 5 nor Article II grants federal judges any special authority to substitute their views for those of the state judiciary on matters of state law. . . .

Even assuming that aspects of the remedial scheme might ultimately be found to violate the Equal Protection Clause, I could not subscribe to the majority's disposition of the case. . . .

In the interest of finality, however, the majority effectively orders the disenfranchisement of an unknown number of voters whose ballots reveal their intent—and are therefore legal votes under state law—but were for some reason rejected by ballot-counting machines. It does so on the basis of the deadlines set forth in Title 3 of the United States Code. But . . . those provisions merely provide rules of decision for Congress to follow when selecting among conflicting slates of electors. They do not prohibit a State from counting what the majority concedes to be legal votes until a bona fide winner is determined. Indeed, in 1960, Hawaii appointed two slates of electors and Congress chose to count the one appointed on January 4, 1961, well after the Title 3 deadlines. Thus, nothing prevents the majority, even if it properly found an

equal protection violation, from ordering relief appropriate to remedy that violation without depriving Florida voters of their right to have their votes counted. . . .

What must underlie petitioners' entire federal assault on the Florida election procedures is an unstated lack of confidence in the impartiality and capacity of the state judges who would make the critical decisions if the vote count were to proceed. Otherwise, their position is wholly without merit. . . . Time will one day heal the wound to that confidence that will be inflicted by today's decision. One thing, however, is certain. Although we may never know with complete certainty the identity of the winner of this year's Presidential election, the identity of the loser is perfectly clear. It is the Nation's confidence in the judge as an impartial guardian of the rule of law.

JUSTICE SOUTER, with whom JUSTICE BREYER joins and with whom JUSTICE STEVENS and JUSTICE GINSBURG join in part, dissenting . . . [omitted].

### JUSTICE GINSBURG, with whom JUSTICE STEVENS joins, and with whom JUSTICE SOUTER and JUSTICE BREYER join in part, dissenting. . . .

Were the other members of this Court as mindful as they generally are of our system of dual sovereignty, they would affirm the judgment of the Florida Supreme Court. . . .

[T]he Court's conclusion that a constitutionally adequate recount is impractical is a prophecy the Court's own judgment will not allow to be tested. Such an untested prophecy should not decide the Presidency of the United States.

### JUSTICE BREYER, with whom JUSTICE STEVENS, JUSTICE SOUTER, and JUSTICE GINSBURG join in part, dissenting. . . .

[T]here is no justification for the majority's remedy, which is simply to reverse the lower court and halt the recount entirely. An appropriate remedy would be, instead, to remand this case with instructions that, even at this late date, would permit the Florida Supreme Court to require recounting all undercounted votes in Florida ... and to do so in accordance with a single-uniform substandard. The majority justifies stopping the recount entirely on the ground that there is no more time. ... But the majority reaches this conclusion in the absence of any record evidence that the recount could not have been completed in the time allowed by the Florida Supreme Court. The majority finds facts outside of the record on matters that state courts are in a far better position to address. Of course, it is too late for any such recount to take place by December 12, the date by which election disputes must be decided if a State is to take advantage of the safe harbor provisions of 3 U.S.C. § 5. Whether there is time to conduct a recount prior to December 18, when the electors are scheduled to meet, is a matter for the state courts to determine. And whether, under Florida law, Florida could or could not take further action is obviously a matter for Florida courts, not this Court, to decide. By halting the manual recount, and thus ensuring that the uncounted legal votes will not be counted under any standard, this Court crafts a remedy out of proportion to the asserted harm. ...

## II. REPRESENTATION

### Baker v. Carr
### 369 U.S. 186, 82 S.Ct. 691, 7 L.Ed. 2d 663 (1962)
### http://laws.findlaw.com/us/369/186.html

Appellants brought suit in U.S. District Court in Tennessee, objecting to a 1901 Tennessee statute that apportioned seats for the state's 95 counties in the General Assembly. They claimed that the legislature's failure subsequently to redistrict the seats to take account of substantial growth and redistribution of the state's population debased their votes and thus denied them equal protection of the laws guaranteed by the Fourteenth Amendment. The facts showed that districts containing 37 percent of Tennessee's population elected 20 of the 33 senators; districts containing 40 percent of the population elected 63 of the 99 representatives. The district court ruled that it lacked jurisdiction of the subject matter. Majority: Brennan, Black, Clark, Douglas, Stewart, Warren. Dissenting: Frankfurter, Harlan. Not participating: Whittaker.

**MR. JUSTICE BRENNAN delivered the opinion of the Court. . . .**

The complaint alleges that the 1901 statute effects an apportionment that deprives the appellants of the equal protection of the laws in violation of the Fourteenth Amendment. . . .

We hold that the appellants do have standing to maintain this suit. Our decisions plainly support this conclusion. Many of the cases have assumed rather than articulated the premise in deciding the merits of similar claims.

And *Colegrove* v. *Green* . . . squarely held that voters who allege facts showing disadvantage to themselves as individuals have standing to sue. [A footnote points out that the concurring opinion of Justice Rutledge and Justice Black's dissenting opinion held there was standing, and expressed doubt whether Justice Frankfurter's opinion intimated lack of it.] . . .

We hold that the claim pleaded here neither rests upon nor implicates the Guaranty Clause and that its justiciability is therefore not foreclosed by our decisions of cases involving that clause. The District Court misinterpreted *Colegrove* and other decisions of this Court on which it relied. Appellants' claim that they are being denied equal protection is justiciable, and if "discrimination is sufficiently shown, the right to relief under the equal protection clause is not diminished by the fact that the discrimination relates to political rights." . . . To show why we reject the argument based on the Guaranty Clause, we must examine the authorities under it. But because there appears to be some uncertainty as to why those cases did present political questions, and specifically as to whether this apportionment case is like those cases, we deem it necessary first to consider the contours of the "political question" doctrine. . . . [The opinion considers foreign relations, "durations of hostilities," validity of enactments of constitutional amendments, and the status of Indian tribes.]

Prominent on the surface of any case held to involve a political question is found a textually demonstrable constitutional commitment of the issue to a coordinate political department; or a lack of judicially discoverable and manageable standards for resolving it; or the impossibility of deciding without an initial policy determination of a kind clearly for non-judicial discretion; or the impossibility of a court's undertaking independent resolution without expressing lack of the respect due coordinate branches of government; or an unusual need for unquestioning adherence to a political decision already made; or the potentiality of embarrassment from multifarious pronouncements by various departments on one question.

Unless one of these formulations is inextricable from the case at bar, there should be no dismissal for nonjusticiability on the ground of a political question's presence. The doctrine of which we treat is one of "political questions," not one of "political cases." The courts cannot reject as "no lawsuit" a bona fide controversy as to whether some action denominated "political" exceeds constitutional authority. . . .

Several factors were thought by the Court in *Luther* [v. *Borden*] to make the question there "political": the commitment to the other branches of the decision as to which is the lawful state government; the unambiguous action by the President, in recognizing the charter government as the lawful authority; the need for finality in the executive's decision; and the lack of criteria by which a court could determine which form of government was republican.

But the only significance that *Luther* could have for our immediate purposes is in its holding that the Guaranty Clause is not a repository of judicially manageable standards which a court could utilize independently in order to identify a State's lawful government. The Court has since refused to resort to the Guaranty Clause—which alone had been invoked for the purpose—as the source of a constitutional standard for invalidating state action. . . .

We come, finally, to the ultimate inquiry whether our precedents as to what constitutes a nonjusticiable "political question" bring the case before us under the umbrella of that doctrine. A natural beginning is to note whether any of the common characteristics which we have been able to identify and label descriptively are present. We find none: The question here is the consistency of state action with the Federal Constitution. We have no question decided, or to be decided, by a political branch of government coequal with this Court. Nor do we risk embarrassment of our government abroad, or grave disturbance at home if we take issue with Tennessee as to the constitutionality of her action here challenged. Nor need the appellants, in order to succeed in this action, ask the Court to enter upon policy determinations for which judicially manageable standards are lacking. Judicial standards under the Equal Protection Clause are well developed and familiar, and it has been open to courts since the enactment of the Fourteenth Amendment to determine, if on the particular facts they review, that a discrimination reflects no policy, but simply arbitrary and capricious action. . . .

We conclude then that the nonjusticiability of claims resting on the Guaranty Clause which arises from their embodiment of questions that were thought "political," can have no bearing upon the justiciability of the equal protection claim presented in this case. Finally, we emphasize that it is the involvement in Guaranty Clause claims of the elements thought to define "political questions," and no other feature, which could render them nonjusticiable. Specifically, we have said that such claims are not held nonjusticiable because they touch matters of state governmental organization. . . .

Article I, Sections 2, 4, and 5 and Amendment 14, Section 2 relate only to congressional elections and obviously do not govern apportionment of state legislatures. However, our decisions in favor of justiciability even in light of those provisions plainly afford no support for the District Court's conclusion that the subject matter of this controversy presents a political question. Indeed, the refusal to award relief in *Colegrove* resulted only from the controlling view of a want of equity. . . .

We conclude that the complaint's allegations of a denial of equal protection present a justiciable constitutional cause of action upon which appellants are entitled to a trial and a decision. The right asserted is within the reach of judicial protection under the Fourteenth Amendment.

The judgment of the District Court is reversed and the cause is remanded for further proceedings consistent with this opinion.

*Reversed and remanded.*

MR. JUSTICE DOUGLAS, concurring . . . [omitted].

## MR. JUSTICE CLARK, concurring. . . .

Although I find the Tennessee apportionment statute offends the Equal Protection Clause, I would not consider intervention by this Court into so delicate a field if there were any other relief available to the people of Tennessee. But the majority of the people of Tennessee have no "practical opportunities for exerting their political weight at the polls" to correct the existing "invidious discrimination." Tennessee has no initiative and referendum. I have searched diligently for other "practical opportunities" present under the law. I find

none other than through the federal courts. . . . It is said that there is recourse in Congress and perhaps that may be, but from a practical standpoint this is without substance. To date Congress has never undertaken such a task in any State. We therefore must conclude that the people of Tennessee are stymied and without judicial intervention will be saddled with the present discrimination in the affairs of their state government. . . .

MR. JUSTICE STEWART, concurring . . . [omitted].

## MR. JUSTICE FRANKFURTER, with whom MR. JUSTICE HARLAN joins, dissenting.

The Court today reverses a uniform course of decision established by a dozen cases, including one by which the very claim now sustained was unanimously rejected only five years ago. . . . Such a massive repudiation of the experience of our whole past in asserting destructively novel judicial power demands a detailed analysis of the role of this Court in our constitutional scheme. Disregard of inherent limits in the effective exercise of the Court's "judicial Power" not only presages the futility of judicial intervention in the essentially political conflict of forces by which the relation between population and representation has time out of mind been and now is determined. It may well impair the Court's position as the ultimate organ of "the supreme Law of the Land" in that vast range of legal problems, often strongly entangled in popular feeling, on which this Court must pronounce. The Court's authority—possessed neither of the purse nor the sword—ultimately rests on sustained public confidence in its moral sanction. Such feeling must be nourished by the Court's complete detachment, in fact and in appearance, from political entanglements and by abstention from injecting itself into the clash of political forces in political settlements. . . .

For this Court to direct the District Court to enforce a claim to which the Court has over the years consistently found itself required to deny legal enforcement and at the same time to find it necessary to withhold any guidance to the lower court how to enforce this turnabout, new legal claim, manifests an odd—indeed an esoteric—conception of judicial propriety. . . .

Even assuming the indispensable intellectual disinterestedness on the part of judges in such matters, they do not have accepted legal standards or criteria or even reliable analogies to draw upon for making judicial judgments. To charge courts with the task of accommodating the incommensurable factors of policy that underlie these mathematical puzzles is to attribute, however flatteringly, omnicompetence to judges. . . .

We are soothingly told at the bar of this Court that we need not worry about the kind of remedy a court could effectively fashion once the abstract constitutional right to have courts pass on a statewide system of electoral districting is recognized as a matter of judicial rhetoric, because legislatures would heed the Court's admonition. This is not only an euphoric hope. It implies a sorry confession of judicial impotence in place of a frank acknowledgment that there is not under our Constitution a judicial remedy for every political mischief, for every undesirable exercise of legislative power. The Framers carefully and with deliberate forethought refused so to enthrone the judiciary. In this situation, as in others of like nature, appeal for relief does not belong here. Appeal must be to an informed, civically militant electorate. In a democratic society like ours, relief must come through an aroused popular conscience that sears the conscience of the people's representatives. In any event there is nothing judicially more unseemly nor more self-defeating than for this Court to make interrorem pronouncements, to indulge in merely empty rhetoric, sounding a word of promise to the ear, sure to be disappointing to the hope. . . .

What, then, is this question of legislative apportionment? Appellants invoke the right to vote and to have their votes counted. But they are permitted to vote and their votes are counted. They go to the polls, they cast their ballots, they send their representatives to the state councils. Their complaint is simply that the representatives are not sufficiently numerous or powerful—in short, that Tennessee has adopted a basis of representation with which they are dissatisfied. Talk of "debasement" or "dilution" is circular talk. One cannot speak of "debasement" or "dilution" of the value of a vote until there is first defined a standard of reference as to what a vote should be worth. What is actually asked of the Court in this case is to choose among competing bases of representation—ultimately, really, among competing theories of political philosophy—in order to establish an appropriate frame of government for the State of Tennessee and thereby for all the States of the Union. . . .

What Tennessee illustrates is an old and still widespread method of representation—representation by local geographical division, only in part respective of population—in preference to others, others, forsooth, more appealing. Appellants contest this choice and seek to make this Court the arbiter of the disagreement. They would make the Equal Protection Clause the charter of adjudication, asserting that the equality which it guarantees comports, if not the assurance of equal weight to every voter's vote, at least the basic conception that representation ought to be proportionate to population, a standard by reference to which the reasonableness of apportionment plans may be judged.

To find such a political conception legally enforceable in the broad and unspecific guarantee of equal protection is to rewrite the Constitution. . . .

Mr. Justice Harlan, with whom Mr. Justice Frankfurter joins, dissenting . . . [omitted].

## Reynolds v. Sims
### 377 U.S. 533, 84 S.Ct. 1362, 12 L.Ed. 2d 506 (1964)
http://laws.findlaw.com/us/377/533.html

The climax of a series of cases involving challenges to state apportionment arrangements came in 1964, when the Court invalidated the legislative apportionments of Alabama, Colorado, Delaware, Maryland, New York, and Virginia. Challenged specifically in Alabama were three distinct apportionment schemes: the existing plan, a proposed plan, and a "stand-by" plan. All contained population variations ranging, at the least, from 31,175 to 634,854 for the 35-member state senate, and from 20,000 to 52,000 for the 106-member house. A three-judge panel of the U.S. District Court for the Middle District of Alabama found each plan constitutionally deficient. The majority opinion in *Reynolds* v. *Sims* (the Alabama case) sets forth the basic principles applied in each of the six cases. Majority: Warren, Black, Brennan, Clark, Douglas, Goldberg, Stewart, White. Dissenting: Harlan. Justice Stewart, joined by Justice Clark, dissented in the New York and Colorado cases, although both were in the majority in *Reynolds*. Stewart's opinion from the New York and Colorado cases is reprinted here following Justice Harlan's dissent.

**MR. CHIEF JUSTICE WARREN delivered the opinion of the Court. . . .**

Plaintiffs below alleged that the last apportionment of the Alabama Legislature was based on the 1900 federal census, despite the requirement of the State Constitution that the legislature be reapportioned decennially. They asserted that, since the population growth in the State from 1900 to 1960 had been uneven, Jefferson and other counties were now victims of serious discrimination with respect to the allocation of legislative representation. . . .

Legislators represent people, not trees or acres. Legislators are elected by voters, not farms or cities or economic interests. As long as ours is a representative form of government, and our legislatures are those instruments of government elected directly by and directly representative of the people, the right to elect legislators in a free and unimpaired fashion is a bedrock of our political system. It could hardly be gainsaid that a constitutional claim had been asserted by an allegation that certain otherwise qualified voters had been entirely prohibited from voting for members of their state legislature. And, if a State should provide that the votes of citizens in one part of the State should be given two times, or five times, or 10 times the weight of votes of citizens in another part of the State, it could hardly be contended that the right to vote of those residing in the disfavored areas had not been effectively diluted. It would appear extraordinary to suggest that a state could be constitutionally permitted to enact a law providing that certain of the state's voters could vote two, five, or 10 times for their legislative representatives, while voters living elsewhere could vote only once. And it is inconceivable that a state law to the effect that, in counting votes for legislators, the votes of citizens in one part of the State would be multiplied by two, five or 10, while the votes of persons in another area would be counted only at face value, could be constitutionally sustainable. Of course, the effect of state legislative districting schemes which give the same number of representatives to unequal numbers of constituents is identical. . . .

Logically, in a society that is ostensibly grounded on representative government, it would seem reasonable that a majority of the people of the State could elect a majority of that State's legislators. To conclude differently, and to sanction minority control of state legislative bodies, would appear to deny majority rights in a way that far surpasses any possible denial of minority rights that might otherwise be thought to result. Since legislatures are responsible for enacting laws by which all citizens are to be governed, they should be bodies which are collectively responsive to the popular will. And the concept of equal protection has been traditionally viewed as requiring the uniform treatment of persons standing in the same relation to the governmental action questioned or challenged. With respect to the allocation of legislative representation, all voters, as citizens of a State, stand in the same relation regardless of where they live. Any suggested criteria for the differentiation of citizens are insufficient to justify any discrimination, as to the weight of their votes, unless relevant to the permissible purposes of legislative apportionment. Since the achieving of fair and effective representation for all citizens is concededly the basic aim of legislative apportionment, we conclude that the Equal Protection Clause guarantees the opportunity for equal participation by all voters in the election of state legislators. . . .

To the extent that a citizen's right to vote is debased, he is that much less a citizen. The fact that an individual lives here or there is not a legitimate reason for overweighting or diluting the efficacy of his vote. The complexions of societies and civilizations change, often with amazing rapidity. A nation once primarily rural in character becomes predominantly urban. Representation schemes once fair and equitable become archaic and outdated. But the basic principle of representative government remains, and must remain, unchanged—the weight of a citizen's vote cannot be made to depend on where he lives. Population is, of necessity, the starting point for consideration and the controlling criterion for judgment in legislative apportionment controversies. A citizen, a qualified voter, is no more nor no less so because he lives in the city or on the farm. This is the clear and strong command of our Constitution's Equal Protection Clause. This is an essential part of the concept of a government of laws and not men. This is at the heart of Lincoln's vision of "government of the people, by the people, [and] for the people." The Equal Protection Clause demands no less than substantially

equal state legislative representation for all citizens, of all places as well as of all races.

We hold that, as a basic constitutional standard, the Equal Protection Clause requires that the seats in both houses of a bicameral state legislature must be apportioned on a population basis. Simply stated, an individual's right to vote for state legislators is unconstitutionally impaired when its weight is in a substantial fashion diluted when compared with votes of citizens living in other parts of the State. Since, under neither the existing apportionment provisions nor under either of the proposed plans was either of the houses of the Alabama Legislature apportioned on a population basis, the District Court correctly held that all three of these schemes were constitutionally invalid. . . .

Much has been written since our decision in *Baker* v. *Carr* about the applicability of the so-called federal analogy to state legislative apportionment arrangements. After considering the matter, the court below concluded that no conceivable analogy could be drawn between the federal scheme and the apportionment of seats in the Alabama Legislature under the proposed constitutional amendment. We agree with the District Court and find the federal analogy inapposite and irrelevant to state legislative districting schemes. Attempted reliance on the federal analogy often appears to be little more than an after-the-fact rationalization offered in defense of maladjusted state apportionment arrangements. The original constitutions of 36 of our States provided that representation in both houses of the state legislatures would be based completely, or predominantly, on population. And the Founding Fathers clearly had no intention of establishing a pattern or model for the apportionment of seats in state legislatures when the system of representation in the Federal Congress was adopted. Demonstrative of this is the fact that the Northwest Ordinance, adopted in the same year, 1787, as the Federal Constitution, provided for the apportionment of seats in territorial legislatures solely on the basis of population.

The system of representation in the two Houses of the Federal Congress is one ingrained in our Constitution, as part of the law of the land. It is one conceived out of compromise and concession indispensable to the establishment of our federal republic. Arising from unique historical circumstances, it is based on the consideration that in establishing our type of federalism a group of formerly independent States bound themselves together under one national government. . . .

We do not believe that the concept of bicameralism is rendered anachronistic and meaningless when the predominant basis of representation in the two state legislative bodies is required to be the same—population. A prime reason for bicameralism, modernly considered, is to insure mature and deliberate consideration of, and to prevent precipitate action on, proposed legislative measures. Simply because the controlling criterion for apportioning representation is required to be the same in both houses does not mean that there will be no differences in the composition and complexion of the two bodies. Different constituencies can be represented in the two houses. One body could be composed of single-member districts while the other could have at least some multimember districts. The length of terms of the legislators in the separate bodies could differ. The numerical size of the two bodies could be made to differ, even significantly, and the geographical size of districts from which legislators are elected could also be made to differ. . . . [T]hese and other factors could be, and are presently in many States, utilized to engender differing complexions and collective attitudes in the two bodies of a state legislature, although both are apportioned substantially on a population basis. . . .

[W]e affirm the judgment below and remand the cases for further proceedings consistent with the views stated in this opinion.

*It is so ordered.*

### MR. JUSTICE HARLAN, dissenting. . . .

These decisions also cut deeply into the fabric of our federalism. What must follow from them may eventually appear to be the product of State Legislatures. Nevertheless, no thinking person can fail to recognize that the aftermath of these cases, however desirable it may be thought in itself, will have been achieved at the cost of a radical alteration in the relationship between the States and the Federal Government, more particularly the Federal Judiciary. Only one who has an overbearing impatience with the federal system and its political processes will believe that the cost was not too high or was inevitable.

. . . [T]hese decisions give support to a current mistaken view of the Constitution and the constitutional function of this Court. This view, in a nutshell, is that every major social ill in this country can find its cure in some constitutional "principle," and that this Court should "take the lead" in promoting reform when other branches of government fail to act. The Constitution is not a panacea for every blot upon the public welfare, nor should this Court, ordained as a judicial body, be thought of as a general haven for reform movements. The Constitution is an instrument of government, fundamental to which is the premise that in a diffusion of governmental authority lies the greatest promise that this Nation will realize liberty for all its citizens. This Court, limited in function in accordance with that premise, does not serve its high purpose when it exceeds its authority, even to satisfy justified impatience with the slow workings of the political process. For when, in the name of constitutional interpretation, the Court adds something to the Constitution that was deliberately excluded from it, the Court in reality substitutes its view of what should be so for the amending process. . . .

### MR. JUSTICE STEWART, whom MR. JUSTICE CLARK joins, dissenting [in the New York and Colorado cases]. . . .

Simply stated, the question is to what degree, if at all, the Equal Protection Clause of the Fourteenth Amendment limits each sovereign State's freedom to establish appropriate electoral constituencies from which representatives to the State's bicameral legislative assembly are to be chosen. The Court's answer is a blunt one, and, I think, woefully wrong. The Equal

Protection Clause, said the Court, "requires that the seats in both houses of a bicameral state legislature must be apportioned on a population basis." . . .

With all respect, I think that this is not correct, simply as a matter of fact. It has been unanswerably demonstrated before now that this "was not the colonial system, it was not the system chosen for the national government by the Constitution, it was not the system exclusively or even predominantly practiced by the States at the time of adoption of the Fourteenth Amendment, it is not predominantly practiced by the States today." . . .

The Court's draconian pronouncement, which makes unconstitutional the legislatures of most of the 50 States, finds no support in the words of the Constitution, in any prior decision of this Court, or in the 175-year political history of our Federal Union. With all respect, I am convinced these decisions mark a long step backward into that unhappy era when a majority of the members of this Court were thought by many to have convinced themselves and each other that the demands of the Constitution were to be measured not by what it says, but by their own notions of wise political theory. . . .

What the Court has done is to convert a particular political philosophy into a constitutional rule, binding upon each of the 50 States, from Maine to Hawaii, from Alaska to Texas, without regard and without respect for the many individualized and differentiated characteristics stemming from each State's distinct history, distinct geography, distinct distribution of population, and distinct political heritage. My own understanding of the various theories of representative government is that no one theory has ever commanded unanimous assent among political scientists, historians, or others who have considered the problem. But even if it were thought that the rule announced today by the Court is, as a matter of political theory, the most desirable general rule which can be devised as a basis for the make-up of the representative assembly of a typical State, I could not join in the fabrication of a constitutional mandate which imports and forever freezes one theory of political thought into our Constitution, and forever denies to every State any

opportunity for enlightened and progressive innovation in the design of its democratic institutions, so as to accommodate within a system of representative government the interests and aspirations of diverse groups of people, without subjecting any group or class to absolute domination by a geographically concentrated or highly organized majority.

Representative government is a process of accommodating group interests through democratic institutional arrangements. Its function is to channel the numerous opinions, interests, and abilities of the people of a State into the making of the State's public policy. Appropriate legislative apportionment, therefore, should ideally be designed to insure effective representation in the State's legislature, in cooperation with other organs of political power, of the various groups and interests making up the electorate. In practice, of course, this ideal is approximated in the particular apportionment system of any State by a realistic accommodation of the diverse and often conflicting political forces operating within the State. . . .

The Court today declines to give any recognition to these considerations and countless others, tangible and intangible, in holding unconstitutional the particular systems of legislative apportionment which these States have chosen. Instead, the Court says that the requirements of the Equal Protection Clause can be met in any State only by the uncritical, simplistic, and heavy-handed application of sixth-grade arithmetic.

But legislators do not represent faceless numbers. They represent people, or, more accurately, a majority of the voters in their districts—people with identifiable needs and interests which require legislative representation, and which can often be related to the geographical areas in which these people live. The very fact of geographic districting, the constitutional validity of which the Court does not question, carries with it an acceptance of the idea of legislative representation of regional needs and interests. Yet if geographical residence is irrelevant, as the Court suggests, and the goal is solely that of equally "weighted" votes, I do not understand why the Court's constitutional rule does not require the abolition of districts and the holding of all elections at large. . . .

I think that the Equal Protection Clause demands but two basic attributes of any plan of state legislative apportionment. First, it demands that, in the light of the State's own characteristics and needs, the plan must be a rational one. Secondly, it demands that the plan must be such as not to permit the systematic frustration of the will of a majority of the electorate of the State. I think it is apparent that any plan of legislative apportionment which could be shown to reflect no policy, but simply arbitrary and capricious action or inaction, and that any plan which could be shown systematically to prevent ultimate effective majority rule, would be invalid under accepted Equal Protection Clause standards. But, beyond this, I think there is nothing in the Federal Constitution to prevent a State from choosing any electoral legislative structure it thinks best suited to the interests, temper, and customs of its people. . . .

## *Davis* v. *Bandemer*
## 478 U.S. 109, 106 S.Ct. 2797, 92 L.Ed. 2d 85 (1986)
### http://laws.findlaw.com/us/478/109.html

> The Indiana legislature comprises a 100-member House and a 50-member Senate. House members serve two-year terms, with elections for all seats every two years. Senators serve four-year terms, with half of the seats up for election every two years. Senators are elected from single-member districts; representatives are elected from a mixture of single-member and multimember districts. Following the 1981 reapportionment based on 1980 census figures, Bandemer and others filed suit in U.S. District Court for the Southern District of Indiana, claiming that the 1981 reapportionment plan was a political gerrymander intended to disadvantage Democrats and so was a violation of the equal protection clause. Before the case went to trial, elections under the new plan were held in November 1982. Democratic candidates for the House received 51.9 percent of the votes cast statewide but only 43 of the 100 seats to be filled. Democratic candidates for the Senate received 53.1 percent of the votes cast statewide, and 13 of the 25 Democratic candidates were elected. In Marion and Allen Counties, both divided into multimember House districts, Democratic candidates received 46.6 percent of the vote but won only 3 of the 21 seats at stake. Relying primarily on these data, the district court invalidated the 1981 reapportionment plan and ordered the legislature to prepare a new plan. In the opinions that follow, note that six of the nine justices concluded that political gerrymanders presented a justiciable question, even though there was no "opinion of the Court." Majority: White, Blackmun, Brennan, Burger, Marshall, O'Connor, Rehnquist. Dissenting: Powell, Stevens.

**JUSTICE WHITE announced the judgment of the Court and delivered an opinion in which JUSTICES BRENNAN, MARSHALL, and BLACKMUN joined. . . .**

We address first the question whether this case presents a justiciable controversy or a nonjusticiable political question. . . .

The outlines of the political question doctrine were described and to a large extent defined in *Baker* v. *Carr*. . . .

This analysis applies equally to the question now before us. Disposition of this question does not involve us in a matter more properly decided by a coequal branch of our Government. There is no risk of foreign or domestic disturbance, and in light of our cases since *Baker* we are not persuaded that there are no judicially discernible and manageable standards by which political gerrymander cases are to be decided. . . .

Having determined that the political gerrymandering claim in this case is justiciable, we turn to the question whether the District Court erred in holding that appellees had alleged and proved a violation of the Equal Protection Clause. . . .

[W]e are confident that if the law challenged here had discriminatory effects on Democrats, this record would support a finding that the discrimination was intentional. Thus, we decline to overturn the District Court's finding of discriminatory intent as clearly erroneous. . . .

We do not accept, however, the District Court's legal and factual bases for concluding that the 1981 Act visited a sufficiently adverse effect on the appellees' constitutionally protected rights to make out a violation of the Equal Protection Clause. The District Court held that because any apportionment scheme that purposely prevents proportional representation is unconstitutional, Democratic voters need only show that their proportionate voting influence has been adversely affected. . . . Our cases, however, clearly foreclose any claim that the Constitution requires proportional representation or that legislatures in reapportioning must draw district lines to come as near as possible to allocating seats to the contending parties in proportion to what their anticipated statewide vote will be. . . .

[T]he mere fact that a particular apportionment scheme makes it more difficult for a particular group in a particular district to elect the representatives of its choice does not render that scheme constitutionally infirm. This conviction, in turn, stems from a perception that the power to influence the political process is not limited to winning elections. An individual or a group of individuals who votes for a losing candidate is usually deemed to be adequately represented by the winning candidate and to have as much opportunity to influence that candidate as other voters in the district.

We cannot presume in such a situation, without actual proof to the contrary, that the candidate elected will entirely ignore the interests of those voters. This is true even in a safe district where the losing group loses election after election. Thus, a group's electoral power is not unconstitutionally diminished by the simple fact of an apportionment scheme that makes winning elections more difficult, and a failure of proportional representation alone does not constitute impermissible discrimination under the Equal Protection Clause. . . .

Rather, unconstitutional discrimination occurs only when the electoral system is arranged in a manner that will consistently degrade a voter's or a group of voters' influence on the political process as a whole. . . .

Based on these views, we would reject the District Court's apparent holding that any interference with an opportunity to elect a representative of one's choice would be sufficient to allege or make out an equal protection violation, unless justified by some acceptable state interest that the State would be required to demonstrate. In addition to being contrary to the above-described conception of an unconstitutional political gerrymander, such a low threshold for legal action would invite attack on all or almost all reapportionment statutes. District-based elections hardly ever produce a perfect fit between votes and representation. The one-person, one-vote imperative often mandates departure from this result as does the no-retrogression rule required by § 5 of the Voting Rights Act. Inviting attack on minor departures from some supposed norm would too much embroil the judiciary in second-guessing what has consistently been referred to as a political task for the legislature, a task that should not be monitored too closely unless the express or tacit goal is to effect its removal from legislative halls. We decline to take a major step toward that end, which would be so much at odds with our history and experience. . . .

The District Court's findings do not satisfy this threshold condition to stating and proving a cause of action. In reaching its conclusion, the District Court relied primarily on the results of the 1982 elections. . . .

Relying on a single election to prove unconstitutional discrimination is unsatisfactory. . . . Rather, we have required that there be proof that the complaining minority "had less opportunity . . . to participate in the political processes and to elect legislators of their choice." . . .

We recognize that our own view may be difficult of application. Determining when an electoral system has been "arranged in a manner that will consistently degrade a voter's or a group of voters' influence on the political process as a whole" . . . is of necessity a difficult inquiry. Nevertheless, we believe that it recognizes the delicacy of intruding on this most political of legislative functions and is at the same time consistent with our prior cases regarding individual multimember districts, which have formulated a parallel standard.

In sum, we hold that political gerrymandering cases are properly justiciable under the Equal Protection Clause. We also conclude, however, that a threshold showing of discriminatory vote dilution is required for a prima facie case of an equal protection violation. In this case, the findings made by the District Court of an adverse effect on the appellees do not surmount the threshold requirement. Consequently, the judgment of the District Court is *Reversed*.

CHIEF JUSTICE BURGER, concurring . . . [omitted].

### JUSTICE O'CONNOR, with whom THE CHIEF JUSTICE and JUSTICE REHNQUIST join, concurring in the judgment.

Today the Court holds that claims of political gerrymandering lodged by members of one of the political parties that make up our two-party system are justiciable under the Equal Protection Clause of the Fourteenth Amendment. Nothing in our precedents compels us to take this step, and there is every reason not to do so. I would hold that the partisan gerrymandering claims of major political parties raise a nonjusticiable political question that the judiciary should leave to the legislative branch

as the Framers of the Constitution unquestionably intended. Accordingly, I would reverse the District Court's judgment on the grounds that appellees' claim is nonjusticiable. . . .

[T]he legislative business of apportionment is fundamentally a political affair, and challenges to the manner in which an apportionment has been carried out—by the very parties that are responsible for this process—present a political question in the truest sense of the term.

To turn these matters over to the federal judiciary is to inject the courts into the most heated partisan issues. . . . I do not believe, and the Court offers not a shred of evidence to suggest, that the Framers of the Constitution intended the judicial power to encompass the making of such fundamental choices about how this Nation is to be governed. Nor do I believe that the proportional representation towards which the Court's expansion of equal protection doctrine will lead is consistent with our history, our traditions, or our political institutions. . . .

The standard the plurality proposes exemplifies the intractable difficulties in deriving a judicially manageable standard from the Equal Protection Clause for adjudicating political gerrymandering claims. The plurality rejects any standard that would require drawing "district lines to come as near as possible to allocating seats to the contending parties in proportion to what their anticipated statewide vote will be," . . . and states that "unconstitutional discrimination occurs only when the electoral system is arranged in a manner that will consistently degrade a voter's or a group of voters' influence on the political process as a whole." . . . In my view, this standard will over time either prove unmanageable and arbitrary or else evolve towards some loose form of proportionality. . . . Either outcome would be calamitous for the federal courts, for the States, and for our two-party system.

Vote dilution analysis is far less manageable when extended to major political parties than if confined to racial minority groups. First, an increase in the number of competing claims to equal group representation will make judicial review of apportionment vastly more complex. Designing an apportionment plan that does not impair or degrade the voting strength of several groups is more difficult than designing a plan that does not have such an effect on one group for the simple reason that, as the number of criteria the plan must meet increases, the number of solutions that will satisfy those criteria will decrease. Even where it is not impossible to reconcile the competing claims of political, racial, and other groups, the predictable result will be greater judicial intrusion into the apportionment process.

Second, while membership in a racial group is an immutable characteristic, voters can—and often do—move from one party to the other or support candidates from both parties. Consequently, the difficulty of measuring voting strength is heightened in the case of a major political party. It is difficult enough to measure "a voter's or a group of voters' influence on the political process as a whole" . . . when the group is a racial minority in a particular district or community. When the group is a major political party the difficulty is greater, and the constitutional basis for intervening far more tenuous.

Moreover, any such intervention is likely to move in the direction of proportional representation for political parties. . . .

I would avoid the difficulties generated by the plurality's efforts to confine the effects of a generalized group's right to equal representation by not recognizing such a right in the first instance. To allow district courts to strike down apportionment plans on the basis of their prognostications as to the outcome of future elections or future apportionments invites "findings" on matters as to which neither judges nor anyone else can have any confidence. Once it is conceded that "a group's electoral power is not unconstitutionally diminished by the simple fact of an apportionment scheme that makes winning elections more difficult" . . . the virtual impossibility of reliably predicting how difficult it will be to win an election in 2, or 4, or 10 years should, in my view, weigh in favor of holding such challenges nonjusticiable. Racial gerrymandering should remain justiciable, for the harms it

engenders run counter to the central thrust of the Fourteenth Amendment. But no such justification can be given for judicial intervention on behalf of mainstream political parties, and the risks such intervention poses to our political institutions are unacceptable. "Political affiliation is the keystone of the political trade. Race, ideally, is not." . . .

**Justice Powell, with whom Justice Stevens joins, concurring in part and dissenting in part. . . .**

The Equal Protection Clause guarantees citizens that their state will govern them impartially. . . . In the context of redistricting, that guarantee is of critical importance because the franchise provides most citizens their only voice in the legislative process. . . . Since the contours of a voting district powerfully may affect citizens' ability to exercise influence through their vote, district lines should be determined in accordance with neutral and legitimate criteria. When deciding where those lines will fall, the state should treat its voters as standing in the same position, regardless of their political beliefs or party affiliation. . . .

In light of the foregoing principles, I believe that the plurality's opinion is seriously flawed in several respects. First, apparently to avoid the forceful evidence that some district lines indisputably were designed to and did discriminate against Democrats, the plurality describes appellees' claim as alleging that "Democratic voters over the State as a whole, not Democratic voters in particular districts, have been subjected to unconstitutional discrimination." . . . This characterization is not inconsistent with appellees' proof, and the District Court's finding, of statewide discriminatory effect resulting from "individual districting" that "exemplif[ies] this discrimination." . . . If Democratic voters in a number of critical districts are the focus of unconstitutional discrimination, as the District Court found, the effect of that discrimination will be felt over the State as a whole.

The plurality also erroneously characterizes the harm members of the losing party suffer as a group when they are deprived, through deliberate and arbitrary distortion of district boundaries, of the opportunity to elect representatives of their choosing. It may be, as the plurality suggests, that representation will not "entirely ignore the interests" of opposition voters. . . . But it defies political reality to suppose that members of a losing party have as much political influence over state government as do members of the victorious party. Even the most conscientious state legislators do not disregard opportunities to reward persons or groups who were active supporters in their election campaigns. Similarly, no one doubts that partisan considerations play a major role in the passage of legislation and the appointment of state officers. Not surprisingly, therefore, the District Court expressly found that "[c]ontrol of the General Assembly is crucial" to members of the major political parties in Indiana. . . . In light of those findings, I cannot accept the plurality's apparent conclusion that loss of this "crucial" position is constitutionally insignificant as long as the losers are not "entirely ignored" by the winners. . . .

The final and most basic flaw in the plurality's opinion is its failure to enunciate any standard that affords guidance to legislatures and courts. Legislators and judges are left to wonder whether compliance with "one person, one vote" completely insulates a partisan gerrymander from constitutional scrutiny, or whether a fairer but as yet undefined standard applies. The failure to articulate clear doctrine in this area places the plurality in the curious position of inviting further litigation even as it appears to signal the "constitutional green light" to would-be gerrymanderers. . . .

## Miller v. Johnson
### 515 U.S. 900, 115 S.Ct. 2475, 132 L.Ed. 2d 762 (1995)
### http://laws.findlaw.com/us/515/900.html

In 1972 Georgia gained its first African American member of Congress since Reconstruction, and redistricting after the 1980 census created the state's first majority-minority district. Under the 1990 census, Georgia's population (27 percent of which is black) entitled the state to an additional representative in Congress. The state's General Assembly approved a districting plan that contained three majority-minority districts after the Justice Department refused to preclear, under § 5 of the Voting Rights Act, two earlier plans that each contained only two majority-black districts. Elections held in November 1992 resulted in the election of black representatives from all three majority-minority districts. In 1994 five white voters in the new Eleventh District challenged the constitutionality of their district on the ground that it was a racial gerrymander in violation of the equal protection clause as interpreted in *Shaw v. Reno* (1993). A three-judge panel of the U.S. District Court for the Southern District of Georgia agreed, holding that the state legislature's purpose, as well as the district's irregular borders, showed that race was the overriding and predominant force in the districting determination. The lower court assumed that compliance with the Voting Rights Act would be a compelling interest, but found that the plan was not narrowly tailored to meet that interest because the law did not require three majority-minority districts.

After the Supreme Court's decision reprinted below, the Georgia legislature did not reach agreement on a revised plan by the October 15, 1995, deadline imposed by the district court. The district court then redrew the boundaries of the state's 11 congressional districts, leaving only the one majority-minority district, which roughly corresponded to the district that had been created after the 1980 census. In the November 1996 elections, the black incumbents who had represented the formerly majority-minority districts won reelection to the U.S. House of Representatives, as did the incumbent from the surviving majority-minority district. In 1997, the Supreme Court upheld the districting plan used in the 1996 elections (*Abrams* v. *Johnson*). Majority: Kennedy, Rehnquist, O'Connor, Scalia, Thomas. Dissenting: Stevens, Souter, Ginsburg, Breyer.

## JUSTICE KENNEDY delivered the opinion of the Court. . . .

The Equal Protection Clause's . . . central mandate is racial neutrality in governmental decisionmaking. . . . Laws classifying citizens on the basis of race cannot be upheld unless they are narrowly tailored to achieving a compelling state interest. . . .

In *Shaw* v. *Reno* we recognized that these equal protection principles govern a State's drawing of congressional districts, though, as our cautious approach there discloses, application of these principles to electoral districting is a most delicate task. . . .

This case requires us to apply the principles articulated in *Shaw* to the most recent congressional redistricting plan enacted by the State of Georgia.

In 1965, the Attorney General designated Georgia a covered jurisdiction under § 4(b) of the Voting Rights Act. In consequence, § 5 of the Act requires Georgia to obtain either administrative preclearance by the Attorney General or approval by the United States District Court for the District of Columbia of any change in a "standard, practice, or procedure with respect to voting" made after November 1, 1964. The preclearance mechanism applies to congressional redistricting plans, and requires that the proposed change "not have the purpose and will not have the effect of denying or abridging the right to vote on account of race or color." "[T]he purpose of § 5 has always been to insure that no voting-procedure changes would be made that would lead to a retrogression in the position of racial minorities with respect to their effective exercise of the electoral franchise." . . .

Twice spurned [by the Justice Department], the General Assembly set out to create three majority-minority districts to gain preclearance. Using the A[merican] C[ivil] L[iberties] U[nion]'s "max-black" plan as its benchmark, the General Assembly enacted a plan that "bore all the signs of [the Justice Department's] involvement. . . ." The new plan . . . connect[ed] the black neighborhoods of metropolitan Atlanta and the poor black populace of coastal Chatham County, though 260 miles apart in distance and worlds apart in culture. . . . [T]he social, political and economic makeup of the Eleventh District tells a tale of disparity, not community. . . .

[Appellants] contend that evidence of a legislature's deliberate classification of voters on the basis of race cannot alone suffice to state a claim under *Shaw*. They argue that, regardless of the legislature's purposes, a plaintiff must demonstrate that a district's shape is so bizarre that it is unexplainable other than on the basis of race, and that appellees failed to make that showing here. Appellants' conception of the constitutional violation misapprehends our holding in Shaw. . . .

Our observation in *Shaw* of the consequences of racial stereotyping was not meant to suggest that a district must be bizarre on its face before there is a constitutional violation. . . . Shape is relevant not because bizarreness is . . . the constitutional wrong . . . , but because it may be persuasive circumstantial evidence that race for its own sake, and not other districting principles, was the legislature's dominant and controlling rationale in drawing its district lines. The logical implication, as courts applying *Shaw* have recognized, is that parties may rely on evidence other than bizarreness to establish race-based districting. . . .

In sum, we make clear that parties alleging that a State has assigned voters on the basis of race are neither confined in their proof to evidence regarding the district's geometry and makeup nor required to make a threshold showing of bizarreness. Today's case requires us further to consider the requirements of the proof necessary to sustain this equal protection challenge.

Federal court review of districting legislation represents a serious intrusion on the most vital of local functions. . . . Redistricting legislatures will, for example, almost always be aware of racial demographics; but it does not follow that race predominates in the redistricting process. . . . The distinction between being aware of racial considerations and being motivated by them may be difficult to make. This evidentiary difficulty, together with the sensitive nature of redistricting and the presumption of good faith that must be accorded legislative enactments, requires courts to exercise extraordinary caution in adjudicating claims that a state has drawn district lines on the basis of race. The plaintiff's burden is to show, either through circumstantial evidence of a district's shape and demographics or more direct evidence going to legislative purpose, that race was the predominant factor motivating the legislature's decision to place a significant number of voters within or without a particular district. To make this showing, a plaintiff must prove that the legislature subordinated traditional race-neutral districting principles, including but not limited to compactness, contiguity, respect for political subdivisions or communities defined by actual shared interests, to racial considerations. Where these or other race-neutral considerations are the basis for redistricting legislation, and are not subordinated to race, a state can "defeat a claim that a district has been gerrymandered on racial lines." . . .

In our view, the District Court applied the correct analysis, and its finding that race was the predominant factor motivating the drawing of the Eleventh District was not clearly erroneous. The court found it was "exceedingly obvious" from the shape of the Eleventh District, together with the relevant racial demographics, that the drawing of narrow land bridges to incorporate within the district outlying appendages containing nearly 80% of the district's total black population was a deliberate attempt to bring black populations into the district. . . .

As a result, Georgia's congressional redistricting plan cannot be upheld unless it satisfies strict scrutiny, our most rigorous and exacting standard of constitutional review.

To satisfy strict scrutiny, the State must demonstrate that its districting legislation is narrowly tailored to achieve a compelling interest. . . . The State does not argue, however, that it created the Eleventh District to remedy past discrimination, and with good reason: there is little doubt that the State's true interest in designing the Eleventh District was creating a third majority-black district to satisfy the Justice Department's preclearance demands. . . . Whether or not in some cases compliance with the Voting Rights Act, standing alone, can provide a compelling interest independent of any interest in remedying past discrimination, it cannot do so here. . . . The congressional plan challenged here was not required by the Voting Rights Act under a correct reading of the statute. . . .

Georgia's drawing of the Eleventh District was not required under the Act because there was no reasonable basis to believe that Georgia's earlier enacted plans violated § 5. . . . Georgia's first and second proposed plans increased the number of majority-black districts from 1 out of 10 (10%) to 2 out of 11 (18.18%). These plans were "ameliorative" and could not have violated § 5's nonretrogression principle. Acknowledging as much, the United States . . . [objects] that Georgia failed to proffer a nondiscriminatory purpose for its refusal in the first two submissions to take the steps necessary to create a third majority-minority district.

The Government's position is insupportable. . . . The State's policy of adhering to other districting principles instead of creating as many majority-minority districts as possible does not support an inference that the plan "so discriminates on the basis of race or color as to violate the Constitution," and thus cannot provide any basis under § 5 for the Justice Department's objection.

"[T]he purpose of § 5 has always been to insure that no voting-procedure changes would be made that would lead to a retrogression in the position of racial minorities with respect to their effective exercise of the electoral franchise." The Justice Department's maximization policy seems quite far removed from this purpose. We are especially reluctant to conclude that § 5 justifies that policy given the serious constitutional concerns it raises. . . .

The Voting Rights Act, and its grant of authority to the federal courts to uncover official efforts to abridge minorities' right to vote, has been of vital importance in eradicating invidious discrimination from the electoral process and enhancing the legitimacy of our political institutions. Only if our political system and our society cleanse themselves of that discrimination will all members of the polity share an equal opportunity to gain public office regardless of race. . . . It takes a shortsighted and unauthorized view of the Voting Rights Act to invoke that statute, which has played a decisive role in redressing some of our worst forms of discrimination, to demand the very racial stereotyping the Fourteenth Amendment forbids.

The judgment of the District Court is affirmed, and the case is remanded for further proceedings consistent with this decision.

*It is so ordered.*

JUSTICE O'CONNOR, concurring . . . [omitted].

JUSTICE STEVENS, dissenting . . . [omitted].

## JUSTICE GINSBURG, with whom JUSTICES STEVENS and BREYER join, and with whom JUSTICE SOUTER joins in part, dissenting. . . .

[T]he fact that the Georgia General Assembly took account of race in drawing district lines—a fact not in dispute—does not render the State's plan invalid. To offend the Equal Protection Clause, all agree, the legislature had to do more than consider race. How much more, is the issue that divides the Court today. . . .

The record before us does not show that race . . . overwhelmed traditional districting practices in Georgia. Although the Georgia General Assembly prominently considered race in shaping the Eleventh District, race did not crowd out all other factors. . . .

In contrast to the snake-like North Carolina district inspected in *Shaw,* Georgia's Eleventh District is hardly "bizarre," "extremely irregular," or "irrational on its face." . . .

Along with attention to size, shape, and political subdivisions, the Court recognizes as an appropriate districting principle, "respect for . . . communities defined by actual shared interests." The Court finds no community here, however, because a report in the record showed "fractured political, social, and economic interests within the Eleventh District's black population."

But ethnicity itself can tie people together, as volumes of social science literature have documented—even people with divergent economic interests. . . .

To accommodate the reality of ethnic bonds, legislatures have long drawn voting districts along ethnic lines. Our Nation's cities are full of districts identified by their ethnic character—Chinese, Irish, Italian, Jewish, Polish, Russian, for example. . . . The creation of ethnic districts reflecting felt identity is not ordinarily viewed as offensive or demeaning to those included in the delineation. . . .

In adopting districting plans, . . . States do not treat people as individuals. Apportionment schemes, by their very nature, assemble people in groups. States do not assign voters to districts based on merit or achievement, standards States might use in hiring employees or engaging contractors. Rather, legislators classify voters in groups—by economic, geographical, political, or social characteristics—and then "reconcile the competing claims of [these] groups."

That ethnicity defines some of these groups is a political reality. Until now, no constitutional infirmity has been seen in districting Irish or Italian voters together, for example, so long as the delineation does not abandon familiar apportionment practices. If Chinese-Americans and Russian-Americans may seek and secure group recognition in the delineation of voting districts, then African-Americans should not be dissimilarly treated.

Otherwise, in the name of equal protection, we would shut out "the very minority group whose history in the United States gave birth to the Equal Protection Clause."

Under the Court's approach, judicial review of the same intensity, i.e., strict scrutiny, is in order once it is determined that an apportionment is predominantly motivated by race. It matters not at all, in this new regime, whether the apportionment dilutes or enhances minority voting strength. As very recently observed, however, "[t]here is no moral or constitutional equivalence between a policy that is designed to perpetuate a caste system and one that seeks to eradicate racial subordination."

Special circumstances justify vigilant judicial inspection to protect minority voters—circumstances that do not apply to majority voters. . . . The majority, by definition, encounters no such blockage. White voters in Georgia do not lack means to exert strong pressure on their state legislators. The force of their numbers is itself a powerful determiner of what the legislature will do that does not coincide with perceived majority interests. . . .

The Court's disposition renders redistricting perilous work for state legislatures. . . . Only after litigation—under either the Voting Rights Act, the Court's new *Miller* standard, or both—will States now be assured that plans conscious of race are safe. . . . This enlargement of the judicial role is unwarranted. . . . Accordingly, I dissent.

## *Hunt [Easley]* v. *Cromartie*
### 532 U.S. 234, 121 S.Ct. 1452, 149 L.Ed. 2d 430 (2001)
http://laws.findlaw.com/us/532/234.html

This case is the conclusion to legal challenges to North Carolina's 1992 congressional redistricting plan. As a result of the 1990 census, the state was entitled to a twelfth seat in the U.S. House of Representatives. The first redistricting plan adopted by the state General Assembly had one district in the northeastern part of the state with a majority of African-American voters. (No African-American had been elected from the state to the U.S. House of Representatives since 1901.) Acting under the pre-clearance provisions of § 5 of the Voting Rights Act, the Justice Department insisted on two such districts. The state legislature revised the redistricting plan to comply, although both districts were oddly shaped. District 1 in the eastern part of the state was said to resemble a "bug splattered on a windshield." District 12 in the central region stretched for 160 miles along the Interstate 85 corridor. Five state residents then brought suit claiming that both districts amounted to racial gerrymanders in violation of the equal protection clause of the Fourteenth Amendment. In 1992 a three-judge panel of the U.S. District Court for the Eastern District of North Carolina dismissed the suit because of the absence of a cognizable claim under the Constitution. On appeal in *Shaw* v. *Hunt* (1993), the Supreme Court recognized, 5 to 4, a Fourteenth Amendment right for voters to live in a district that had not been drawn primarily on the basis of race, even where (as here) the legislature's intent was to enhance minority representation. The Court then remanded the case to see whether either district was constitutionally flawed. After the district court upheld the plan, the Supreme Court, citing *Miller* v. *Johnson* (1995) as authority, concluded, 5 to 4, in *Shaw* v. *Hunt* (1996) that district 12 was a "predominantly racial" gerrymander and so violated the Fourteenth Amendment; District 1 had been dropped from the litigation because the white voters who mounted the original challenge had since moved out of the district.

The remaining facts appear in Justice Breyer's opinion below. Cases involving voting rights disputes are among the handful of cases today that are decided by a panel of three judges at the district court level. Review of such a decision goes directly to the Supreme Court, by-passing a court of appeals. Majority: Breyer, Ginsburg, O'Connor, Souter, Stevens. Dissenting: Thomas, Kennedy, Rehnquist, Scalia.

**JUSTICE BREYER delivered the opinion of the Court.**

In this appeal, we review a three-judge District Court's determination that North Carolina's legislature used race as the "predominant factor" in drawing its 12th Congressional District's 1997 boundaries. The court's findings, in our view, are clearly erroneous. We therefore reverse its conclusion that the State violated the Equal Protection Clause.

This "racial districting" litigation is before us for the fourth time. Our first two holdings addressed North Carolina's former Congressional District 12, one of two North Carolina congressional districts drawn in 1992 that contained a majority of African-American voters. See *Shaw* v. *Reno* (*Shaw I*); *Shaw* v. *Hunt* (*Shaw II*). . . .

Our third holding focused on a new District 12, the boundaries of which the legislature had redrawn in 1997. A three-judge District Court, with one judge dissenting, had granted summary judgment in favor of those challenging the district's boundaries. The court found that the legislature again had "used criteria . . . that are facially race driven," in violation of the Equal Protection Clause. . . .

This Court reversed (*Hunt* v. *Cromartie*, 1999). We agreed with the District Court that the new district's shape, the way in which it split towns and counties, and its heavily African-American voting population all helped the plaintiffs' case. But neither that evidence by itself, nor when coupled with the evidence of Democratic registration, was sufficient to show, on summary judgment, the unconstitutional race-based objective that plaintiffs claimed. That is because there was a genuine issue of material fact as to whether the evidence also was consistent with a constitutional political objective, namely, the creation of a safe Democratic seat. . . .

On remand, the . . . three-judge District Court . . . again held (over a dissent) that the legislature had unconstitutionally drawn District 12's new 1997 boundaries. It found that the legislature had tried "(1) [to] cur[e] the [previous district's] constitutional defects" while also "(2) drawing the plan to maintain the existing partisan balance in the State's congressional delegation." It added that to "achieve the second goal," the legislature "drew the new plan (1) to avoid placing two incumbents in the same district and (2) to preserve the partisan core of the existing districts." The court concluded that the "plan as enacted largely reflects these directives." But the court also found "as a matter of fact that the General Assembly . . . used criteria . . . that are facially race driven" without any compelling justification for doing so. . . .

We noted probable jurisdiction. And we now reverse.

The issue in this case is evidentiary. We must determine whether there is adequate support for the District Court's key findings, particularly the ultimate finding that the legislature's motive was predominantly racial, not political. In making this determination, we are aware that, under *Shaw I* and later cases, the burden of proof on the plaintiffs (who attack the district) is a "demanding one." The Court has specified that those who claim that a legislature has improperly used race as a criterion, in order, for example, to create a majority-minority district, must show at a minimum that the "legislature subordinated traditional race-neutral districting principles . . . to racial considerations." . . .

The Court also has made clear that the underlying districting decision is one that ordinarily falls within a legislature's sphere of competence. Hence, the legislature "must have discretion to exercise the political judgment necessary to balance competing interests," and courts must "exercise *extraordinary caution* in adjudicating claims that a State has drawn district lines on the basis of race" (emphasis added [by Justice Breyer]). Caution is especially appropriate in this case, where the State has articulated a legitimate political explanation for its districting decision, and the voting population is one in which race and political affiliation are highly correlated. . . .

The critical District Court determination—the matter for which we remanded this litigation—consists of the finding that race rather than politics predominantly explains District 12's 1997 boundaries. . . .

The District Court primarily based its "race, not politics," conclusion upon its finding that "the legislators excluded many heavily-Democratic precincts from District 12, even when those precincts immediately border the Twelfth and would have established a far more compact district." . . . This finding, however . . . rests solely upon evidence that the legislature excluded heavily white precincts with high Democratic Party registration, while including heavily African-American precincts with equivalent, or lower, Democratic Party registration. Indeed, the District Court cites at length figures showing that the legislature included "several precincts with racial compositions of 40 to 100 percent African-American," while excluding certain adjacent precincts "with less than 35 percent African-American population" but which contain between 54% and 76% registered Democrats. As we said before, the problem with this evidence is that it focuses upon party registration, not upon voting behavior. And we previously found the same evidence . . . inadequate because registration figures do not accurately predict preference at the polls. . . .

A legislature trying to secure a safe Democratic seat is interested in Democratic voting behavior. Hence, a legislature may, by placing reliable Democratic precincts within a district without regard to race, end up with a district containing more heavily African-American precincts, but the reasons would be political rather than racial. . . .

We concede the record contains a modicum of evidence offering support for the District Court's conclusion. . . . The evidence taken together, however, does not show that racial considerations predominated in the drawing of District 12's boundaries. That is because race in this case correlates closely with political behavior. The basic question is whether the legislature drew District 12's boundaries because of race rather than because of political behavior (coupled with traditional, nonracial districting considerations). . . .

We can put the matter more generally as follows: In a case such as this one where majority-minority districts (or the approximate equivalent) are at issue and where racial identification correlates highly with political affiliation, the party attacking the legislatively drawn boundaries must show at the least that the legislature could have achieved its legitimate political objectives in alternative ways that are comparably consistent with traditional districting principles. That party must also show that those districting alternatives would have brought about significantly greater racial balance. Appellees failed to make any such showing here. We conclude that the District Court's contrary findings are clearly erroneous. . . .

The judgment of the District Court is

*Reversed.*

### JUSTICE THOMAS, with whom THE CHIEF JUSTICE, JUSTICE SCALIA, and JUSTICE KENNEDY join, dissenting. . . .

Because I do not believe the court below committed clear error, I respectfully dissent.

The District Court's conclusion that race was the predominant factor motivating the North Carolina Legislature is a factual finding. . . . Accordingly, we should not overturn the District Court's determination unless it is clearly erroneous. . . .

The Court does cite cases that address the correct standard of review, and does couch its conclusion in "clearly erroneous" terms. But these incantations of the correct standard are empty gestures, contradicted by the Court's conclusion that it must engage in "extensive review." In several ways, the Court ignores its role as a reviewing court and engages in its own factfinding enterprise. First, the Court suggests that there is some significance to the absence of an intermediate court in this action. This cannot be a legitimate consideration. If it were legitimate, we would have mentioned it in prior redistricting cases. After all, in *Miller* and *Shaw,* we also did not have the benefit of intermediate appellate review. . . .

Finally, perhaps the best evidence that the Court has emptied clear error review of meaningful content in the redistricting context (and the strongest testament to the fact that the District Court was dealing with a complex fact pattern) is the Court's foray into the minutiae of the record. . . .

Reviewing for clear error, I cannot say that the District Court's view of the evidence was impermissible. First, the court relied on objective measures of compactness, which show that District 12 is the most geographically scattered district in North Carolina, to support its conclusion that the district's design was not dictated by traditional districting concerns. . . .

Second, the court relied on the expert opinion of Dr. Weber, who interpreted statistical data to conclude that there were Democratic precincts with low black populations excluded from District 12, which would have created a more compact district had they been included. And contrary to the Court's assertion, Dr. Weber did not merely examine the registration data in reaching his conclusions. . . .

If I were the District Court, I might have reached the same conclusion that the Court does, that "[t]he evidence taken together . . . does not show that racial considerations predominated in the drawing of District 12's boundaries." But I am not the trier of fact, and it is not my role to weigh evidence in the first instance. The only question that this Court should decide is whether the District Court's finding of racial predominance was clearly erroneous. In light of the direct evidence of racial motive and the inferences that may be drawn from the circumstantial evidence, I am satisfied that the District Court's finding was permissible, even if not compelled by the record.

## III. PARTY POLITICS AND CAMPAIGNS

### *California Democratic Party* v. *Jones*
### 530 U.S. 567, 120 S.Ct. 2402, 147 L.Ed. 2d 502 (2000)
### http://laws.findlaw.com/us/530/567.html

In 1996 voters in California approved Proposition 198 that converted closed party primaries to blanket primaries. Under the closed primary, voters received a ballot limited to candidates of their own party. Democratic voters picked among Democratic candidates, and Republican voters picked among Republican candidates. In the blanket primary, every voter's ballot listed every candidate regardless of party affiliation and allowed voters to choose among them. Thus, a voter might vote for a Democrat for governor and a Republican for state senate. The candidate of each party who won the greatest number of votes for a particular office became that party's candidate in the ensuing general election. The state Democratic, Republican, Libertarian, and Peace and Freedom parties filed suit against California Secretary of State Bill Jones in the U.S. District Court for the Eastern District of California, asserting that the blanket primary violated their First Amendment freedom of association. Rejecting this claim, the district court concluded that the burden on the parties' right of association was not severe and was justified by the state's interest in "enhanc[ing] the democratic nature of the election process and the representative-ness of elected officials." The Court of Appeals for the Ninth Circuit affirmed. Majority: Scalia, Rehnquist, O'Connor, Kennedy, Thomas, Souter, Breyer. Dissenting: Stevens, Ginsburg.

### JUSTICE SCALIA delivered the opinion of the Court.

This case presents the question whether the State of California may, consistent with the First Amendment to the United States Constitution, use a so-called "blanket" primary to determine a political party's nominee for the general election. . . .

Respondents rest their defense of the blanket primary upon the proposition that primaries play an integral role in citizens' selection of public officials. As a consequence, they contend, primaries are public rather than private proceedings, and the States may and must play a role in ensuring that they serve the public interest. Proposition 198, respondents conclude, is simply a rather pedestrian example of a State's regulating its system of elections.

We have recognized, of course, that States have a major role to play in structuring and monitoring the election process, including primaries. . . .

What we have not held, however, is that the processes by which political parties select their nominees are, as respondents would have it, wholly public affairs that States may regulate freely. . . . In this regard, respondents' reliance on *Smith* v. *Allwright* (1944) and *Terry* v. *Adams* (1953) is misplaced. In *Allwright,* we invalidated the Texas Democratic Party's rule limiting participation in its primary to whites; in *Terry,* we invalidated the same rule promulgated by the Jaybird Democratic Association, a "self-governing voluntary club." These cases held only that, when a State prescribes an election process that gives a special role to political parties, it "endorses, adopts and enforces the discrimination against Negroes," that the parties (or, in the case of the Jaybird Democratic Association, organizations that are "part and parcel" of the parties) bring into the process— so that the parties' discriminatory action becomes state action under the Fifteenth Amendment. . . . They do not stand for the proposition that party affairs are public affairs, free of First Amendment protections—and our later holdings make that entirely clear.

Representative democracy in any populous unit of governance is unimaginable without the ability of citizens to band together in promoting among the electorate candidates who espouse their political views. The formation of national political parties was almost concurrent with the formation of the Republic itself. . . .

In no area is the political association's right to exclude more important than in the process of selecting its nominee. That process often determines the party's positions on the most significant public policy issues of the day, and even when those positions are predetermined it is the nominee who becomes the party's ambassador to the general electorate in winning it over to the party's views. . . .

Proposition 198 forces political parties to associate with—to have their nominees, and hence their positions, determined by—those who, at best, have refused to affiliate with the party, and, at worst, have expressly affiliated with a rival. In this respect, it is qualitatively different from a closed primary. Under that system, even when it is made quite easy for a voter to change his party affiliation the day of the primary, and thus, in some sense, to "cross over," at least he must formally become a member of the party; and once he does so, he is limited to voting for candidates of that party.

The evidence in this case demonstrates that under California's blanket primary system, the prospect of having a party's nominee determined by adherents of an opposing party is far from remote—indeed, it is a clear and present danger. For example, in one 1997 survey of California voters 37 percent of Republicans said that they planned to vote in the 1998 Democratic gubernatorial primary, and 20 percent of Democrats said they planned to vote in the 1998 Republican United States Senate primary. . . .

The record also supports the obvious proposition that these substantial numbers of voters who help select the nominees of parties they have chosen not to join often have policy views that diverge from those of the party faithful. . . .

In any event, the deleterious effects of Proposition 198 are not limited to altering the identity of the nominee. Even when the person favored by a majority of the party members prevails, he will have prevailed by taking somewhat different positions—and, should he be elected, will continue to take somewhat different positions in order to be renominated. As respondents' own expert concluded, "[t]he policy positions of Members of Congress elected from blanket primary states are . . . more moderate, both in an absolute sense and relative to the other party, and so are more reflective of the preferences of the mass of voters at the center of the ideological spectrum." It is unnecessary to cumulate evidence of this phenomenon, since, after all, the whole purpose of Proposition 198 was to favor nominees with "moderate" positions. It encourages candidates—and officeholders who hope to be renominated—to curry favor with persons whose views are more "centrist" than those of the party base. In effect, Proposition 198 has simply moved the general election one step earlier in the process, at the expense of the parties' ability to perform the "basic function" of choosing their own leaders. . . .

In sum, Proposition 198 forces petitioners to adulterate their candidate-selection process—the "basic function of a political party"—by opening it up to persons wholly unaffiliated with the party. Such forced association has the likely outcome—indeed, in this case the intended outcome—of changing the parties' message. We can think of no heavier burden on a political party's associational freedom. Proposition 198 is therefore unconstitutional unless it is narrowly tailored to serve a compelling state interest . . . It is to that question which we now turn.

Respondents proffer seven state interests they claim are compelling. Two of them—producing elected officials who better represent the electorate and expanding candidate debate beyond the scope of partisan concerns—are simply circumlocution for producing nominees and nominee positions other than those the parties would choose if left to their own devices. Indeed, respondents admit as much. . . . And in explaining their desire to increase debate, respondents claim that a blanket primary forces parties to reconsider long standing positions since it "compels [their] candidates to appeal to a larger segment of the electorate." Both of these supposed interests, therefore, reduce to nothing more than a stark repudiation of freedom of political association: Parties should not be free to select their own nominees because those nominees, and the positions taken by those nominees, will not be congenial to the majority.

Respondents' third asserted compelling interest is that the blanket primary is the only way to ensure that disenfranchised persons enjoy the right to an effective vote. By "disenfranchised," respondents do not mean those who cannot vote; they mean simply independents and members of the minority party in "safe" districts. These persons are disenfranchised, according to respondents, because under a closed primary they are unable to participate in what amounts to the determinative election—the majority party's primary; the only way to ensure they have an "effective" vote is to force the party to open its primary to them. . . . We have said, however, that a "nonmember's desire to participate in the party's affairs is overborne by the countervailing and legitimate right of the party to determine its own membership qualifications." . . . Moreover, even if it were accurate to describe the plight of the non-party-member in a safe district as "disenfranchisement," Proposition 198 is not needed to solve the problem. The voter who feels himself disenfranchised should simply join the party. . . .

Respondents' remaining four asserted state interests—promoting fairness, affording voters greater choice, increasing voter participation, and protecting privacy—are not, like the others, automatically out of the running; but neither are they, in the circumstances of this case, compelling. . . .

Finally, we may observe that even if all these state interests were compelling ones, Proposition 198 is not a narrowly tailored means of furthering them. Respondents could protect them all by resorting to a nonpartisan blanket primary. Generally speaking, under such a system, the State determines what qualifications it requires for a candidate to have a place on the primary ballot—which may include nomination by established parties and voter-petition requirements for independent candidates. Each voter, regardless of party affiliation, may then vote for any candidate, and the top two vote getters (or however many the State prescribes) then move on to the general election. This system has all the characteristics of the partisan blanket primary, save the constitutionally crucial one: Primary voters are not choosing a party's nominee. . . .

The burden Proposition 198 places on petitioners' rights of political association is both severe and unnecessary. The judgment for the Court of Appeals for the Ninth Circuit is reversed.

*It is so ordered.*

JUSTICE   KENNEDY,   concurring   . . . [omitted].

### JUSTICE STEVENS, with whom JUSTICE GINSBURG joins in part, dissenting.

Today the Court construes the First Amendment as a limitation on a State's power to broaden voter participation in elections conducted by the State. The Court's holding is novel and, in my judgment, plainly wrong. I am convinced that California's adoption of a blanket primary pursuant to Proposition 198 does not violate the First Amendment, and that its use in primary elections for state offices is therefore valid. . . .

A State's power to determine how its officials are to be elected is a quintessential attribute of sovereignty. This case is about the State of California's power to decide who may vote in an election conducted, and paid for, by the State. . . .

In my view, principles of federalism require us to respect the policy choice made by the State's voters in approving Proposition 198.

The blanket primary system instituted by Proposition 198 does not abridge "the ability of citizens to band together in promoting among the electorate candidates who espouse their political views." The Court's contrary conclusion rests on the premise that a political party's freedom of expressive association includes a "right not to associate," which in turn includes a right to exclude voters unaffiliated with the party from participating in the selection of that party's nominee in a primary election. In drawing this conclusion, however, the Court blurs two distinctions that are critical: (1) the distinction between a private organization's right to define itself and its messages, on the one hand, and the State's right to define the obligations of citizens and organizations performing public functions, on the other; and (2) the distinction between laws that abridge participation in the political process and those that encourage such participation.

When a political party defines the organization and composition of its governing units, when it decides what candidates to endorse, and when it decides whether and how to communicate those endorsements to the public, it is engaged in the kind of private expressive associational activity that the First Amendment protects. . . .

[H]owever, the associational rights of political parties are neither absolute nor as comprehensive as the rights enjoyed by wholly private associations. . . . The reason a State may impose this significant restriction on a party's associational freedoms is that both the general election and the primary are quintessential forms of state action. It is because the primary is state action that an organization—whether it calls itself a political party or just a "Jaybird" association—may not deny non-Caucasians the right to participate in the selection of its nominees. The Court is quite right in stating that those cases "do not stand for the proposition that party affairs are [wholly] public affairs, free of First Amendment protections." They do, however, stand for the proposition that primary elections, unlike most "party affairs," are state action. The protections that the First

Amendment affords to the "internal processes" of a political party do not encompass a right to exclude nonmembers from voting in a state-required, state-financed primary election.

The so-called "right not to associate" that the Court relies upon, then, is simply inapplicable to participation in a state election. A political party, like any other association, may refuse to allow non-members to participate in the party's decisions when it is conducting its own affairs; California's blanket primary system does not infringe this principle. But an election, unlike a convention or caucus, is a public affair. . . .

It is noteworthy that the bylaws of each of the political parties that are petitioners in this case unequivocally state that participation in partisan primary elections is to be limited to registered members of the party only. Under the Court's reasoning, it would seem to follow that conducting anything but a closed partisan primary in the face of such bylaws would necessarily burden the parties' " 'freedom to identify the people who constitute the association.' " Given that open primaries are supported by essentially the same state interests that the Court disparages today and are not as "narrow" as nonpartisan primaries, there is surely a danger that open primaries will fare no better against a First Amendment challenge than blanket primaries have. . . .

[In the remainder of his opinion Justice Stevens suggests that application of California's blanket primary to U.S. senators and representatives arguably violates the clause of Article I, Section 4, in that it was imposed by the electorate not by the state legislature. "Because the point was neither raised by the parties nor discussed by the courts below, I reserve judgment on it."]

## Republican Party of Minnesota v. White
## 536 U.S. 765, 122 S.Ct. 2528, 153 L.Ed. 2d 694 (2002)

http://laws.findlaw.com/us/536/765.html

A canon of judicial conduct adopted by the Minnesota Supreme Court prohibited a "candidate for a judicial office" from "announc[ing] his or her views on disputed legal or political issues." In 1996 petitioner Gregory Wersal withdrew from the election for the state supreme court after an accusation was made that he had violated the rule. While running for associate justice of that court again in 1998, Wersal and others filed suit seeking a declaration that the announce clause violated the First Amendment and an injunction against its enforcement. In 1999 the U.S. District Court for the District of Minnesota granted White and other respondent officials summary judgment, a ruling that the U.S. Court of Appeals for the Eighth Circuit affirmed in 2001. Majority: Scalia, Kennedy, O'Connor, Rehnquist, Thomas. Dissenting: Stevens, Breyer, Ginsburg, Souter.

**JUSTICE SCALIA delivered the opinion of the Court.**

The question presented in this case is whether the First Amendment permits the Minnesota Supreme Court to prohibit candidates for judicial election in that State from announcing their views on disputed legal and political issues.

Since Minnesota's admission to the Union in 1858, the State's Constitution has provided for the selection of all state judges by popular election. Since 1912, those elections have been nonpartisan. Since 1974, they have been subject to a legal restriction which states that a "candidate for a judicial office, including an incumbent judge," shall not "announce his or her views on disputed legal or political issues." This prohibition, promulgated by the Minnesota Supreme Court and based on Canon 7(B) of the 1972 American Bar Association (ABA) Model Code of Judicial Conduct, is known as the "announce clause." Incumbent judges who violate it are subject to discipline, including removal, censure, civil penalties, and suspension without pay. Lawyers who run for judicial office also must comply with the announce clause. . . . Those who violate it are subject to, *inter alia,* disbarment, suspension, and probation. . . .

Before considering the constitutionality of the announce clause, we must be clear about its meaning. Its text says that a candidate for judicial office shall not "announce his or her views on disputed legal or political issues." We know that "announc[ing] . . . views" on an issue covers much more than *promising* to decide an issue a particular way. The prohibition extends to the candidate's mere statement of his current position, even if he does not bind himself to maintain that position after election. All the parties agree this is the case, because the Minnesota Code contains a so-called "pledges or promises" clause, which *separately* prohibits judicial candidates from making "pledges or promises of conduct in office other than the faithful and impartial performance of the duties of the office"—a prohibition that is not challenged here and on which we express no view.

There are, however, some limitations that the Minnesota Supreme Court has placed upon the scope of the announce clause that are not (to put it politely) immediately apparent from its text. The statements that formed the basis of the complaint against Wersal in 1996 included criticism of past decisions of the Minnesota Supreme Court. One piece of campaign literature stated that "[t]he Minnesota Supreme Court has issued decisions which are marked by their disregard for the Legislature and a lack of common sense." It went on to criticize a decision excluding from

evidence confessions by criminal defendants that were not tape-recorded, asking "[s]hould we conclude that because the Supreme Court does not trust police, it allows confessed criminals to go free?" It criticized a decision striking down a state law restricting welfare benefits, asserting that "[i]t's the Legislature which should set our spending policies." . . . Although one would think that all of these statements touched on disputed legal or political issues, they did not (or at least do not now) fall within the scope of the announce clause. The Judicial Board issued an opinion stating that judicial candidates may criticize past decisions, and the Lawyers Board refused to discipline Wersal for the foregoing statements because, in part, it thought they did not violate the announce clause. The Eighth Circuit relied on the Judicial Board's opinion in upholding the announce clause, and the Minnesota Supreme Court recently embraced the Eighth Circuit's interpretation.

There are yet further limitations upon the apparent plain meaning of the announce clause: In light of the constitutional concerns, the District Court construed the clause to reach only disputed issues that are likely to come before the candidate if he is elected judge. The Eighth Circuit accepted this limiting interpretation by the District Court, and in addition construed the clause to allow general discussions of case law and judicial philosophy. The Supreme Court of Minnesota adopted these interpretations as well when it ordered enforcement of the announce clause in accordance with the Eighth Circuit's opinion.

It seems to us, however, that—like the text of the announce clause itself—these limitations upon the text of the announce clause are not all that they appear to be. First, respondents acknowledged at oral argument that statements critical of past judicial decisions are *not* permissible if the candidate also states that he is against *stare decisis*. Thus, candidates must choose between stating their views critical of past decisions and stating their views in opposition to *stare decisis*. Or, to look at it more concretely, they may state their view that prior decisions were erroneous only if they do not assert that they, if elected, have any power to eliminate erroneous decisions. Second, limiting the scope of the clause to issues likely to come before a court is not much of a limitation at all. . . . Quite obviously, they will be those legal or political disputes that are the proper (or by past decisions have been made the improper) business of the state courts. And within that relevant category, "[t]here is almost no legal or political issue that is unlikely to come before a judge of an American court, state or federal, of general jurisdiction." Third, construing the clause to allow "general" discussions of case law and judicial philosophy turns out to be of little help in an election campaign. At oral argument, respondents gave, as an example of this exception, that a candidate is free to assert that he is a " 'strict constructionist.' " But that, like most other philosophical generalities, has little meaningful content for the electorate unless it is exemplified by application to a particular issue of construction likely to come before a court. . . . Without such application to real-life issues, all candidates can claim to be "strict constructionists" with equal (and unhelpful) plausibility.

In any event, it is clear that the announce clause prohibits a judicial candidate from stating his views on any specific nonfanciful legal question within the province of the court for which he is running, except in the context of discussing past decisions—and in the latter context as well, if he expresses the view that he is not bound by *stare decisis.*

Respondents contend that this still leaves plenty of topics for discussion on the campaign trail. . . . Indeed, the Judicial Board has printed a list of preapproved questions which judicial candidates are allowed to answer. These include how the candidate feels about cameras in the courtroom, how he would go about reducing the caseload, how the costs of judicial administration can be reduced, and how he proposes to ensure that minorities and women are treated more fairly by the court system. Whether this list of preapproved subjects, and other topics not prohibited by the announce clause, adequately fulfill the First Amendment's guarantee of freedom of speech is the question to which we now turn.

As the Court of Appeals recognized, the announce clause both prohibits speech on the basis of its content and burdens a category of speech that is "at the core of our First Amendment freedoms"—speech about the qualifications of candidates for public office. The Court of Appeals concluded that the proper test to be applied to determine the constitutionality of such a restriction is what our cases have called strict scrutiny; the parties do not dispute that this is correct. Under the strict-scrutiny test, respondents have the burden to prove that the announce clause is (1) narrowly tailored, to serve (2) a compelling state interest. In order for respondents to show that the announce clause is narrowly tailored, they must demonstrate that it does not "unnecessarily circumscrib[e] protected expression."

The Court of Appeals concluded that respondents had established two interests as sufficiently compelling to justify the announce clause: preserving the impartiality of the state judiciary and preserving the appearance of the impartiality of the state judiciary. Respondents reassert these two interests before us, arguing that the first is compelling because it protects the due process rights of litigants, and that the second is compelling because it preserves public confidence in the judiciary. Respondents are rather vague, however, about what they mean by "impartiality." . . . Clarity on this point is essential before we can decide whether impartiality is indeed a compelling state interest, and, if so, whether the announce clause is narrowly tailored to achieve it.

One meaning of "impartiality" in the judicial context—and of course its root meaning—is the lack of bias for or against either *party* to the proceeding. Impartiality in this sense assures equal application of the law. That is, it guarantees a party that the judge who hears his case will apply the law to him in the same way he applies it to any other party. This is the traditional sense in which the term is used. . . .

We think it plain that the announce clause is not narrowly tailored to serve impartiality (or the appearance of impartiality) in this sense. Indeed, the clause is barely tailored to serve that interest *at all,* inasmuch as it does not restrict speech for or against particular *parties,* but rather speech for or against particular *issues.* To be sure, when a case arises that turns on a legal issue on which the judge (as a candidate) had taken a particular stand, the party taking the opposite stand is likely to lose. But not because of any bias against that party, or favoritism toward the other party. *Any* party taking that position is just as likely to lose. The judge is applying the law (as he sees it) evenhandedly.

It is perhaps possible to use the term "impartiality" in the judicial context (though this is certainly not a common usage) to mean lack of preconception in favor of or against a particular *legal view.* This sort of impartiality would be concerned, not with guaranteeing litigants equal application of the law, but rather with guaranteeing them an equal chance to persuade the court on the legal points in their case. Impartiality in this sense may well be an interest served by the announce clause, but it is not a *compelling* state interest, as strict scrutiny requires. A judge's lack of predisposition regarding the relevant legal issues in a case has never been thought a necessary component of equal justice, and with good reason. For one thing, it is virtually impossible to find a judge who does not have preconceptions about the law.... Indeed, even if it were possible to select judges who did not have preconceived views on legal issues, it would hardly be desirable to do so. "Proof that a Justice's mind at the time he joined the Court was a complete *tabula rasa* in the area of constitutional adjudication would be evidence of lack of qualification, not lack of bias." ... And since avoiding judicial preconceptions on legal issues is neither possible nor desirable, pretending otherwise by attempting to preserve the "appearance" of that type of impartiality can hardly be a compelling state interest either.

A third possible meaning of "impartiality" (again not a common one) might be described as openmindedness. This quality in a judge demands, not that he have no preconceptions on legal issues, but that he be willing to consider views that oppose his preconceptions, and re-

main open to persuasion, when the issues arise in a pending case. This sort of impartiality seeks to guarantee each litigant, not an *equal* chance to win the legal points in the case, but at least *some* chance of doing so. ...

Respondents argue that the announce clause serves the interest in openmindedness, or at least in the appearance of openmindedness, because it relieves a judge from pressure to rule a certain way in order to maintain consistency with statements the judge has previously made. The problem is, however, that statements in election campaigns are such an infinitesimal portion of the public commitments to legal positions that judges (or judges-to-be) undertake, that this object of the prohibition is implausible. Before they arrive on the bench (whether by election or otherwise) judges have often committed themselves on legal issues that they must later rule upon.... More common still is a judge's confronting a legal issue on which he has expressed an opinion while on the bench. Most frequently, of course, that prior expression will have occurred in ruling on an earlier case. But judges often state their views on disputed legal issues outside the context of adjudication—in classes that they conduct, and in books and speeches.... That is quite incompatible with the notion that the need for openmindedness (or for the appearance of openmindedness) lies behind the prohibition at issue here.

The short of the matter is this: In Minnesota, a candidate for judicial office may not say "I think it is constitutional for the legislature to prohibit same-sex marriages." He may say the very same thing, however, up until the very day before he declares himself a candidate, and may say it repeatedly (until litigation is pending) after he is elected. As a means of pursuing the objective of open-mindedness that respondents now articulate, the announce clause is so woefully underinclusive as to render belief in that purpose a challenge to the credulous. ...

To sustain the announce clause, the Eighth Circuit relied heavily on the fact that a pervasive practice of prohibiting judicial candidates from discussing disputed legal and political issues developed during the last half of the 20th century. It is true that a "universal and long-established" tradition of prohibiting certain conduct creates "a strong presumption" that the prohibition is constitutional. . . . The practice of prohibiting speech by judicial candidates on disputed issues, however, is neither long nor universal. . . .

We know of no restrictions upon statements that could be made by judicial candidates (including judges) throughout the 19th and the first quarter of the 20th century. Indeed, judicial elections were generally partisan during this period, the movement toward nonpartisan judicial elections not even beginning until the 1870's. Thus, not only were judicial candidates (including judges) discussing disputed legal and political issues on the campaign trail, but they were touting party affiliations and angling for party nominations all the while. . . .

There is an obvious tension between the article of Minnesota's popularly approved Constitution which provides that judges shall be elected, and the Minnesota Supreme Court's announce clause which places most subjects of interest to the voters off limits. . . .

The Minnesota Supreme Court's canon of judicial conduct prohibiting candidates for judicial election from announcing their views on disputed legal and political issues violates the First Amendment. Accordingly, we reverse the grant of summary judgment to respondents and remand the case for proceedings consistent with this opinion.

*It is so ordered.*

Justice O'Connor, concurring . . . [omitted].

Justice Kennedy, concurring . . . [omitted].

**Justice Stevens, with whom Justice Souter, Justice Ginsburg, and Justice Breyer join, dissenting. . . .**

By obscuring the fundamental distinction between campaigns for the judiciary and the political branches, and by failing to recognize the difference between statements made in articles or opinions and those made on the campaign trail, the Court defies any sensible notion of the judicial office and the importance of impartiality in that context.

The Court's disposition rests on two seriously flawed premises—an inaccurate appraisal of the importance of judicial independence and impartiality, and an assumption that judicial candidates should have the same freedom "'to express themselves on matters of current public importance'" as do all other elected officials. Elected judges, no less than appointed judges, occupy an office of trust that is fundamentally different from that occupied by policymaking officials. Although the fact that they must stand for election makes their job more difficult than that of the tenured judge, that fact does not lessen their duty to respect essential attributes of the judicial office that have been embedded in Anglo-American law for centuries.

There is a critical difference between the work of the judge and the work of other public officials. In a democracy, issues of policy are properly decided by majority vote; it is the business of legislators and executives to be popular. But in litigation, issues of law or fact should not be determined by popular vote; it is the business of judges to be indifferent to unpopularity. . . .

[T]he elected judge, like the lifetime appointee, does not serve a constituency while holding that office. He has a duty to uphold the law and to follow the dictates of the Constitution. If he is not a judge on the highest court in the State, he has an obligation to follow the precedent of that court, not his personal views or public opinion polls. He may make common law, but judged on the merits of individual cases, not as a mandate from the voters.

By recognizing a conflict between the demands of electoral politics and the distinct characteristics of the judiciary, we do not have to put States to an all or nothing choice of abandoning judicial elections or having elections in which anything goes. As a practical matter, we cannot know for sure whether an elected judge's decisions are based on his interpretation of the law or political expediency.

In the absence of reliable evidence one way or the other, a State may reasonably presume that elected judges are motivated by the highest aspirations of their office. But we do know that a judicial candidate, who announces his views in the context of a campaign, is effectively telling the electorate: "Vote for me because I believe X, and I will judge cases accordingly." Once elected, he may feel free to disregard his campaign statements, but that does not change the fact that the judge announced his position on an issue likely to come before him *as a reason to vote for him*. Minnesota has a compelling interest in sanctioning such statements.

A candidate for judicial office who goes beyond the expression of "general observation about the law . . . in order to obtain favorable consideration" of his candidacy, demonstrates either a lack of impartiality or a lack of understanding of the importance of maintaining public confidence in the impartiality of the judiciary. It is only by failing to recognize the distinction, . . . between statements made during a campaign or confirmation hearing and those made before announcing one's candidacy, that the Court is able to conclude: "[S]ince avoiding judicial preconceptions on legal issues is neither possible nor desirable, pretending otherwise by attempting to preserve the 'appearance' of that type of impartiality can hardly be a compelling state interest either."

Even when "impartiality" is defined in its narrowest sense to embrace only "the lack of bias for or against either *party* to the proceeding," the announce clause serves that interest. Expressions that stress a candidate's unbroken record of affirming convictions for rape, for example, imply a bias in favor of a particular litigant (the prosecutor) and against a class of litigants (defendants in rape cases). Contrary to the Court's reasoning in its first attempt to define impartiality, an interpretation of the announce clause that prohibits such statements serves the State's interest in maintaining both the appearance of this form of impartiality and its actuality.

When the Court evaluates the importance of impartiality in its broadest sense, which it describes as "the interest in openmindedness, or at least in the appearance of openmindedness," it concludes that the announce clause is "so woefully underinclusive as to render belief in that purpose a challenge to the credulous." It is underinclusive, in the Court's view, because campaign statements are an infinitesimal portion of the public commitments to legal positions that candidates make during their professional careers. It is not, however, the number of legal views that a candidate may have formed or discussed in his prior career that is significant. Rather, it is the ability both to reevaluate them in the light of an adversarial presentation, and to apply the governing rule of law even when inconsistent with those views, that characterize judicial openmindedness. . . .

[T]he very purpose of most statements prohibited by the announce clause is to convey the message that the candidate's mind is not open on a particular issue. The lawyer who writes an article advocating harsher penalties for polluters surely does not commit to that position to the same degree as the candidate who says "vote for me because I believe all polluters deserve harsher penalties." At the very least, such statements obscure the appearance of openmindedness. More importantly, like the reasoning in the Court's opinion, they create the false impression that the standards for the election of political candidates apply equally to candidates for judicial office. . . .

[T]he judicial reputation for impartiality and openmindedness is compromised by electioneering that emphasizes the candidate's personal predilections rather than his qualifications for judicial office. . . .

The disposition of this case on the flawed premise that the criteria for the election to judicial office should mirror the rules applicable to political elections is profoundly misguided. I therefore respectfully dissent.

Justice Ginsburg, with whom Justice Stevens, Justice Souter, and Justice Breyer join, dissenting . . . [omitted].

## Federal Election Commission v. Colorado Republican Federal Campaign Committee
## 533 U.S. 431, 121 S.Ct. 2351, 150 L.Ed. 2d 461 (2001)

http://laws.findlaw.com/us/533/431.html

Among other restrictions, the Federal Election Campaign Act limits expenditures by party committees on behalf of senatorial candidates to the greater of $20,000 (adjusted for inflation), or two cents multiplied by the voting age population of the state in which the election is held. The same limits apply to campaigns for House seats in states with only one representative. For other states, the limit on party expenditures in House campaigns is $10,000, preadjusted. As adjusted, these limits in Senate races in 2000 ranged from $67,560 to $1,636,438; House limits ranged from $33,780 to $67,560. A 1996 decision by the Supreme Court struck down these limits as applied to expenditures *independent* of a candidate's campaign. On remand, the U.S. district court in Colorado invalidated the limits as applied to *coordinated* expenditures, and the U.S. Court of Appeals for the Tenth Circuit affirmed. Majority: Souter, Stevens, O'Connor, Ginsburg, Breyer. Dissenting: Thomas, Rehnquist, Scalia, Kennedy.

**JUSTICE SOUTER delivered the opinion of the Court.**

In *Colorado Republican Federal Campaign Comm.* v. *Federal Election Comm'n.,* (*Colorado I*) (1996), we held that spending limits set by the Federal Election Campaign Act were unconstitutional as applied to the Colorado Republican Party's independent expenditures in connection with a senatorial campaign. We remanded for consideration of the party's claim that all limits on expenditures by a political party in connection with congressional campaigns are facially unconstitutional and thus unenforceable even as to spending coordinated with a candidate. Today we reject that facial challenge to the limits on parties' coordinated expenditures. . . .

Spending for political ends and contributing to political candidates both fall within the First Amendment's protection of speech and political association. But ever since we first reviewed the 1971 Act [in *Buckley* v. *Valeo* (1976)], we have understood that limits on political expenditures deserve closer scrutiny than restrictions on political contributions. Restraints on expenditures generally curb more expressive and associational activity than limits on contributions do. A further reason for the distinction is that limits on contributions

are more clearly justified by a link to political corruption than limits on other kinds of unlimited political spending are (corruption being understood not only as *quid pro quo* agreements, but also as undue influence on an officerholder's judgment, and the appearance of such influence). . . . Given these differences, we have routinely struck down limitations on independent expenditures by candidates, other individuals, and groups, . . . while repeatedly upholding contribution limits. . . .

The First Amendment line between spending and donating is easy to draw when it falls between independent expenditures by individuals or political action committees (PACs) without any candidate's approval (or wink or nod), and contributions in the form of cash gifts to candidates. But facts speak less clearly once the independence of the spending cannot be taken for granted, and money spent by an individual or PAC according to an arrangement with a candidate is therefore harder to classify. As already seen, Congress drew a functional, not a formal, line between contributions and expenditures when it provided that coordinated expenditures by individuals and nonparty groups are subject to the Act's contribution limits. In *Buckley*, the Court acknowledged Congress's functional classification, and observed that treating coordinated expenditures as contributions "prevent[s] attempts to circumvent the Act through pre-arranged or coordinated expenditures amounting to disguised contributions." *Buckley,* in fact, enhanced the significance of this functional treatment by striking down independent expenditure limits on First Amendment grounds while upholding limitations on contributions (by individuals and nonparty groups), as defined to include coordinated expenditures. . . .

The Party's argument that its coordinated spending, like its independent spending, should be left free from restriction under the *Buckley* line of cases boils down to this: [B]ecause a party's most important speech is aimed at electing candidates and is itself expressed through those candidates, any limit on party support for a candidate imposes a unique First Amendment burden. The point of organizing a party, the argument goes, is to run a successful candidate who shares the party's policy goals. Therefore, while a campaign contribution is only one of several ways that individuals and nonparty groups speak and associate politically, financial support of candidates is essential to the nature of political parties as we know them. And coordination with a candidate is a party's natural way of operating, not merely an option that can easily be avoided. . . .

The Government's argument for treating coordinated spending like contributions goes back to *Buckley.* There, the rationale for endorsing Congress's equation of coordinated expenditures and contributions was that the equation "prevent[s] attempts to circumvent the Act through prearranged or coordinated expenditures amounting to disguised contributions." The idea was that coordinated expenditures are as useful to the candidate as cash, and that such "disguised contributions" might be given "as a *quid pro quo* for improper commitments from the candidate" (in contrast to independent expenditures, which are poor sources of leverage for a spender because they might be duplicative or counterproductive from a candidate's point of view). In effect, therefore, *Buckley* subjected limits on coordinated expenditures by individuals and nonparty groups to the same scrutiny it applied to limits on their cash contributions. The standard of scrutiny requires the limit to be " 'closely drawn' to match a 'sufficiently important interest,' . . . though the dollar amount of the limit need not be 'fine tun[ed],' "

The Government develops this rationale a step further in applying it here. Coordinated spending by a party should be limited not only because it is like a party contribution, but for a further reason. A party's right to make unlimited expenditures coordinated with a candidate would induce individual and other nonparty contributors to give to the party in order to finance coordinated spending for a favored candidate beyond the contribution limits binding on them. The Government points out that a degree of circumvention is occurring under present law (which allows unlimited independent spending and some coordinated spending). Individuals and nonparty groups who have reached the limit of direct contributions to a candidate give to a party with the understanding that the contribution to the party will produce increased party spending for the candidate's benefit. The Government argues that if coordinated spending were unlimited, circumvention would increase: [B]ecause coordinated spending is as effective as direct contributions in supporting a candidate, an increased opportunity for coordinated spending would aggravate the use of a party to funnel money to a candidate from individuals and nonparty groups, who would thus bypass the contribution limits that *Buckley* upheld. . . .

The assertion that the party is so joined at the hip to candidates that most of its spending must necessarily be coordinated spending is a statement at odds with the history of nearly 30 years under the Act. It is well to remember that ever since the Act was amended in 1974, coordinated spending by a party committee in a given race has been limited by the provision challenged here (or its predecessor). It was not until 1996 and the decision in *Colorado I* that any spending was allowed above that amount, and since then only independent spending has been unlimited. As a consequence, the Party's claim that coordinated spending beyond the limit imposed by the Act is essential to its very function as a party amounts implicitly to saying that for almost three decades political parties have not been functional or have been functioning in systematic violation of the law. The Party, of course, does not in terms make either statement, and we cannot accept either implication. . . .

There is a different weakness in the seemingly unexceptionable premise that parties are organized for the purpose of electing candidates, so that imposing on the way parties serve that function is uniquely burdensome. The fault here is not so much metaphysics as myopia, a refusal to see how the power of money actually works in the political structure.

When we look directly at a party's function in getting and spending money, it would ignore reality to think that the party role is adequately described by speaking generally of electing particular candidates. The money parties spend comes from contributors with their own personal interests. PACs, for example, are frequent party contributors who (according to one of the Party's own experts) "do not pursue the same objectives in electoral politics," that parties do. . . . In fact, many PACs naturally express their narrow interests by contributing to both parties during the same electoral cycle, and sometimes even directly to two competing candidates in the same election. Parties are thus necessarily the instruments of some contributors whose object is not to support the party's message or to elect party candidates across the board, but rather to support a specific candidate for the sake of a position on one, narrow issue, or even to support any candidate who will be obliged to the contributors. . . .

Parties thus perform functions more complex than simply electing candidates; whether they like it or not, they act as agents for spending on behalf of those who seek to produce obligated officeholders. It is this party role, which functionally unites parties with other self-interested political actors, that the Party Expenditure Provision targets. This party role, accordingly, provides good reason to view limits on coordinated spending by parties through the same lens applied to such spending by donors, like PACs, that can use parties as conduits for contributions meant to place candidates under obligation.

Insofar as the Party suggests that its strong working relationship with candidates and its unique ability to speak in coordination with them should be taken into account in the First Amendment analysis, we agree. . . .

It does not, however, follow from a party's efficiency in getting large sums and spending intelligently that limits on a party's coordinated spending should be scrutinized under an unusually high standard, and in fact any argument from sophistication and power would cut both ways. . . . If the coordinated spending of other, less efficient and perhaps less practiced political actors can be limited consistently with the Constitution, why would the Constitution forbid regulation aimed at a party whose very efficiency in channeling benefits to candidates threatens to undermine the contribution (and hence coordinated spending) limits to which those others are unquestionably subject? . . .

The Party's arguments for being treated differently from other political actors subject to limitation on political spending under the Act do not pan out. . . .

We accordingly apply to a party's coordinated spending limitation the same scrutiny we have applied to the other political actors, that is, scrutiny appropriate for a contribution limit, enquiring whether the restriction is "closely drawn" to match what we have recognized as the "sufficiently important" government interest in combating political corruption. . . .

Since there is no recent experience with unlimited coordinated spending, the question is whether experience under the present law confirms a serious threat of abuse from the unlimited coordinated party spending as the Government contends. It clearly does. Despite years of enforcement of the challenged limits, substantial evidence demonstrates how candidates, donors, and parties test the limits of the current law, and it shows beyond serious doubt how contribution limits would be eroded if inducement to circumvent them were enhanced by declaring parties' coordinated spending wide open.

Under the Act, a donor is limited to $2,000 in contributions to one candidate in a given election cycle. The same donor may give as much as another $20,000 each year to a national party committee supporting the candidate. What a realist would expect to occur has occurred. Donors give to the party with the tacit understanding that the favored candidate will benefit. . . .

If suddenly every dollar of spending could be coordinated with the candidate, the inducement to circumvent would almost certainly intensify. Indeed, if a candidate could be assured that donations through a party could result in funds passed through to him for spending on virtually identical items as his own campaign funds, a candidate enjoying the patronage of affluent contributors would have a strong incentive not merely to direct donors to his party, but to promote circumvention as a step toward reducing the number of donors requiring time-consuming cultivation. If a candidate could arrange for a party committee to foot his bills, to be paid with $20,000 contributions to the party by his supporters, the number of donors necessary to raise $1,000,000 could be reduced from 500 (at $2,000 per cycle) to 46 (at $2,000 to the candidate and $20,000 to the party, without regard to donations outside the election year). . . .

There is no significant functional difference between a party's coordinated expenditure and a direct party contribution to the candidate, and there is good reason to expect that a party's right of unlimited coordinated spending would attract increased contributions to parties to finance exactly that kind of spending. Coordinated expenditures of money donated to a party are tailor-made to undermine contribution limits. Therefore the choice here is not, as in *Buckley* and *Colorado I,* between a limit on pure contributions and pure expenditures. The choice is between limiting contributions and limiting expenditures whose special value as expenditures is also the source of their power to corrupt. Congress is entitled to its choice.

We hold that a party's coordinated expenditures, unlike expenditures truly independent, may be restricted to minimize circumvention of contribution limits. We therefore reject the Party's facial challenge and, accordingly,

reverse the judgment of the United States Court of Appeals for the Tenth Circuit.

*It is so ordered.*

**JUSTICE THOMAS, with whom JUSTICE SCALIA and JUSTICE KENNEDY join, and with whom THE CHIEF JUSTICE joins in part, dissenting.**

The Party Expenditure Provision severely limits the amount of money that a national or state committee of a political party can spend in coordination with its own candidate for the Senate or House of Representatives. Because this provision sweeps too broadly, interferes with the party-candidate relationship, and has not been proved necessary to combat corruption, I respectfully dissent.

As an initial matter, I continue to believe that *Buckley* should be overruled. . . . I remain baffled that this Court has extended the most generous First Amendment safeguards to filing lawsuits, wearing profane jackets, and exhibiting drive-in movies with nudity, but has offered only tepid protection to the core speech and associational rights that our Founders sought to defend.

In this case, the Government does not attempt to argue that the Party Expenditure Provision satisfies strict scrutiny. . . . Nor could it. [T]he campaign financing law at issue fails strict scrutiny.

We need not, however, overrule *Buckley* and apply strict scrutiny in order to hold the Party Expenditure Provision unconstitutional. Even under *Buckley,* which described the requisite scrutiny as "exacting" and "rigorous," the regulation cannot pass constitutional muster. In practice, *Buckley* scrutiny has meant that restrictions on contributions by individuals and political committees do not violate the First Amendment so long as they are "closely drawn" to match a "sufficiently important" government interest. . . .

The Court notes this existing rationale and attempts simply to treat coordinated expenditures by political parties as equivalent to contributions by individuals and political committees. Thus, at least implicitly, the Court draws two conclusions: coordinated expenditures are no different from contributions, and political parties are no different from individuals and political committees. Both conclusions are flawed. . . .

Even if I were to ignore the breadth of the statutory text, and to assume that all coordinated expenditures are functionally equivalent to contributions, I still would strike down the Party Expenditure Provision. The source of the "contribution" at issue is a political party, not an individual or a political committee, as in *Buckley*. . . . Restricting contributions by individuals and political committees may, under *Buckley*, entail only a "marginal restriction," but the same cannot be said about limitations on political parties. Political parties and their candidates are "inextricably intertwined" in the conduct of an election. A party nominates its candidate; a candidate often is identified by party affiliation throughout the election and on the ballot; and a party's public image is largely defined by what its candidates say and do. . . .

The Court nevertheless concludes that these concerns of inhibiting party speech are rendered "implausible" by the nearly 30 years of history in which coordinated spending has been statutorily limited. . . . I find more convincing, and more relevant, the record evidence that the parties have developed, which indicates that parties have suffered as a result of the Party Expenditure Provision. Second, we have never before upheld a limitation on speech simply because speakers have coped with the limitation for 30 years. . . . And finally, if the passage of time were relevant to the constitutional inquiry, I would wonder why the Court adopted a "30-year" rule rather than the possible countervailing "200-year" rule. For nearly 200 years, this country had congressional elections without limitations on coordinated expenditures by political parties. Nowhere does the Court suggest that these elections were not "functional," or that they were marred by corruption. . . .

But even if I were to view parties' coordinated expenditures as akin to contributions by individuals and political committees, I still would hold the Party Expenditure Provision constitutionally invalid. . . . In this case, there is no question that the Government has asserted a sufficient interest, that of preventing corruption. . . . The question is whether the Government has demonstrated both that coordinated expenditures by parties give rise to corruption and that the restriction is "closely drawn" to curb this corruption. I believe it has not. . . .

Even if the Government had presented evidence that the Party Expenditure Provision affects corruption, the statute still would be unconstitutional, because there are better tailored alternatives for addressing the corruption. In addition to bribery laws and disclosure laws, the Government has two options that would not entail the restriction of political parties' First Amendment rights. First, the Government could enforce the earmarking rule under which contributions that "are in any way earmarked or otherwise directed through an intermediary or conduit to [a] candidate" are treated as contributions to the candidate. Vigilant enforcement of this provision is a precise response to the Court's circumvention concerns. If a donor contributes $2,000 to a candidate (the maximum donation in an election cycle), he cannot direct the political party to funnel another dime to the candidate without confronting the Federal Election Campaign Act's civil and criminal penalties. . . .

[T]here is a second, well-tailored option for combating corruption that does not entail the reduction of parties' First Amendment freedoms. The heart of the Court's circumvention argument is that, whereas individuals can donate only $2,000 to a candidate in a given election cycle, they can donate $20,000 to the national committees of a political party, an amount that is allegedly large enough to corrupt the candidate. If indeed $20,000 is enough to corrupt a candidate (an assumption that seems implausible on its face and is, in any event, unsupported by any evidence), the proper response is to lower the cap. That way, the speech restriction is directed at the source of the alleged corruption—the individual donor—and not the party. . . .

In my view, it makes no sense to contravene a political party's core First Amendment rights because of what a third party might unlawfully try to do. Instead of broadly restricting political parties' speech, the Government should have pursued better-tailored alternatives for combating the alleged corruption.

## McConnell v. Federal Election Commission
### 72 U.S.L.W. 4015, 124 S.Ct. 619, 157 L.Ed. 2d 491 (2003)

http://supct.law.cornell.edu/supct/html/02-1674.ZS.html

The Bipartisan Campaign Reform Act of 2002 (BCRA) is the most far-reaching campaign finance legislation passed by Congress since the 1974 amendments to the Federal Election Campaign Act (FECA). BCRA's Title I bans "soft money" contributions to political parties. Title II prohibits certain "issue ads," funded from a corporation's, a union's, or nonprofit corporation's general treasury that appear on a broadcast, cable, or satellite channel within 30 days of a primary or 60 days of an election in which candidates for federal office are on the ballot. Three additional titles impose additional regulations or otherwise make changes in existing law. Soon after the legislation became law, twelve suits challenging the constitutionality of various parts of the act, on First Amendment and other grounds, were filed in the United States District Court for the District of Columbia. On May 1, 2003, a three-judge panel held some parts of BCRA unconstitutional and upheld others. On direct appeal, the Supreme Court heard an extraordinary four hours of oral arguments in a special session on September 8. Its decision on December 10 upheld all but two parts of the act: a requirement in § 213 that political parties choose between coordinating campaign activities with their House and Senate candidates and operating entirely independently of them, and a ban in § 318 on campaign contributions from minors. In addition the Court construed the limitation on issue ads in § 316 to exclude nonprofit entities that are so-called *MCFL* corporations. [Derived from *FEC* v. *Massachusetts Citizens for Life* (1986), such organizations are formed for the express purpose of promoting political ideas, have no shareholders, and are neither established by a business corporation or labor union nor accept contributions from them.] The excerpts below from the 119-page majority opinion and from Justice Kennedy's 59-page dissent address only Titles I and II. Majority (on the main provisions of Titles I and II): Stevens, O'Connor, Breyer, Ginsburg, Souter. Dissenting: Kennedy, Rehnquist, Scalia, Thomas.

**JUSTICE STEVENS and JUSTICE O'CONNOR delivered the opinion of the Court. . . .**

Three important developments in the years after our decision in *Buckley* [v. *Valeo*, 1976) persuaded Congress that further legislation was necessary to regulate the role that corporations, unions, and wealthy contributors play in the electoral process. As a preface to our discussion of the specific provisions of BCRA, we comment briefly on the increased importance of "soft money," the proliferation of "issue ads," and the disturbing findings of a Senate investigation into campaign practices related to the 1996 federal elections.

Under FECA, "contributions" must be made with funds that are subject to the Act's disclosure requirements and source and amount limitations. Such funds are known as "federal" or "hard" money. FECA defines the term "contribution," however, to include only the gift or advance of anything of value "made by any person for the purpose of influencing any election for *Federal* office" (emphasis added [by the Court]). Donations made solely for the purpose of influencing state or local elections are therefore unaffected by FECA's requirements and prohibitions. As a result, prior to the enactment of BCRA, federal law permitted corporations and unions, as well as individuals who had already made the maximum permissible contributions to federal candidates, to contribute "nonfederal money"—also known as "soft money"—to political parties for activities intended to influence state or local elections.

Shortly after *Buckley* was decided, questions arose concerning the treatment of contributions intended to influence both federal and state elections. . . . [T]he FEC ruled that political parties could fund mixed-purpose activities—including get-out-the-vote drives and generic party advertising—in part with soft money. In 1995 the FEC concluded that the parties could also use soft money to defray the costs of "legislative advocacy media advertisements," even if the ads mentioned the name of a federal candidate, so long as they did not expressly advocate the candidate's election or defeat.

As the permissible uses of soft money expanded, the amount of soft money raised and spent by the national political parties increased exponentially. . . . The national parties transferred large amounts of their soft money to the state parties, which were allowed to use a larger percentage of soft money to finance mixed-purpose activities under FEC rules. In the year 2000, for example, the national parties diverted $280 million—more than half of their soft money—to state parties. . . .

The solicitation, transfer, and use of soft money thus enabled parties and candidates to circumvent FECA's limitations on the source and amount of contributions in connection with federal elections.

In *Buckley* we construed FECA's disclosure and reporting requirements, as well as its expenditure limitations, "to reach only funds used for communications that expressly advocate the election or defeat of a clearly identified candidate." As a result of that strict reading of the statute, the use or omission of "magic words" such as "Elect John Smith" or "Vote Against Jane Doe" marked a bright statutory line separating "express advocacy" from "issue advocacy." Express advocacy was subject to FECA's limitations and could be financed only using hard money. The political parties, in other words, could not use soft money to sponsor ads that used any magic words, and corporations and unions could not fund such ads out of their general treasuries. So-called issue ads, on the other hand, not only could be financed with soft money, but could be aired without disclosing the identity of, or any other information about, their sponsors.

While the distinction between "issue" and express advocacy seemed neat in theory, the

two categories of advertisements proved functionally identical in important respects. . . . Little difference existed, for example, between an ad that urged viewers to "vote against Jane Doe" and one that condemned Jane Doe's record on a particular issue before exhorting viewers to "call Jane Doe and tell her what you think." . . .

In 1998 the Senate Committee on Governmental Affairs issued a six-volume report summarizing the results of an extensive investigation into the campaign practices in the 1996 federal elections. . . . The committee's principal findings relating to Democratic Party fundraising were set forth in the majority's report, while the minority report primarily described Republican practices. The two reports reached consensus, however, on certain central propositions. They agreed that the "soft money loophole" had led to a "meltdown" of the campaign finance system that had been intended "to keep corporate, union and large individual contributions from influencing the electoral process." . . .

## [TITLE I]

Title I is Congress' effort to plug the soft-money loophole. The cornerstone of Title I is new FECA § 323(a), which prohibits national party committees and their agents from soliciting, receiving, directing, or spending any soft money. In short, § 323(a) takes national parties out of the soft-money business. . . .

In *Buckley* and subsequent cases, we have subjected restrictions on campaign expenditures to closer scrutiny than limits on campaign contributions. In these cases we have recognized that contribution limits, unlike limits on expenditures, "entai[l] only a marginal restriction upon the contributor's ability to engage in free communication." . . .

Our treatment of contribution restrictions reflects more than the limited burdens they impose on First Amendment freedoms. It also reflects the importance of the interests that underlie contribution limits—interests in preventing "both the actual corruption threatened by large financial contributions and the eroding of public confidence in the electoral process through the appearance of corruption." . . .

For that reason, when reviewing Congress' decision to enact contribution limits, "there is no place for a strong presumption against constitutionality, of the sort often thought to accompany the words 'strict scrutiny.'" The less rigorous standard of review we have applied to contribution limits (*Buckley's* "closely drawn" scrutiny) shows proper deference to Congress' ability to weigh competing constitutional interests in an area in which it enjoys particular expertise. It also provides Congress with sufficient room to anticipate and respond to concerns about circumvention of regulations designed to protect the integrity of the political process. . . .

Like the contribution limits we upheld in *Buckley*, § 323's restrictions have only a marginal impact on the ability of contributors, candidates, officeholders, and parties to engage in effective political speech. Complex as its provisions may be, § 323, in the main, . . . merely subjects a greater percentage of contributions to parties and candidates to FECA's source and amount limitations. . . .

The question for present purposes is whether large *soft-money* contributions to national party committees have a corrupting influence or give rise to the appearance of corruption. Both common sense and the ample record in these cases confirm Congress' belief that they do. . . .

Particularly telling is the fact that, in 1996 and 2000, more than half of the top 50 soft-money donors gave substantial sums to *both* major national parties, leaving room for no other conclusion but that these donors were seeking influence, or avoiding retaliation, rather than promoting any particular ideology. . . .

Just as troubling to a functioning democracy as classic *quid pro quo* corruption is the danger that officeholders will decide issues not on the merits or the desires of their constituencies, but according to the wishes of those who have made large financial contributions valued by the officeholder. Even if it occurs only occasionally, the potential for such undue influence is manifest. And unlike straight cash-for-votes transactions, such corruption is neither easily detected nor practical to criminalize. The best means of prevention is to identify and to remove the temptation. . . .

In constructing a coherent scheme of campaign finance regulation, Congress recognized that, given the close ties between federal candidates and state party committees, BCRA's restrictions on national committee activity would rapidly become ineffective if state and local committees remained available as a conduit for soft-money donations. Section 323(b) is designed to foreclose wholesale evasion of § 323(a)'s anticorruption measures by sharply curbing state committees' ability to use large soft-money contributions to influence federal elections. The core of § 323(b) is a straightforward contribution regulation: It prevents donors from contributing nonfederal funds to state and local party committees to help finance "Federal election activity." The term "Federal election activity" encompasses four distinct categories of electioneering: (1) voter registration activity during the 120 days preceding a regularly scheduled federal election; (2) voter identification, get-out-the-vote (GOTV), and generic campaign activity that is "conducted in connection with an election in which a candidate for Federal office appears on the ballot"; (3) any "public communication" that "refers to a clearly identified candidate for Federal office" and "promotes," "supports," "attacks," or "opposes" a candidate for that office; and (4) the services provided by a state committee employee who dedicates more than 25 percent of his or her time to "activities in connection with a Federal election." . . . All activities that fall within the statutory definition must be funded with hard money. . . .

[I]n addressing the problem of soft-money contributions to state committees, Congress both drew a conclusion and made a prediction. Its conclusion, based on the evidence before it, was that the corrupting influence of soft money does not insinuate itself into the political process solely through national party committees. Rather, state committees function as an alternate avenue for precisely the same corrupting forces. . . .

Congress also made a prediction. Having been taught the hard lesson of circumvention by the entire history of campaign finance regulation, Congress knew that soft-money donors would react to § 323(a) by scrambling to find another way to purchase influence. . . .

Finally, plaintiffs argue that Title I violates the equal protection component of the Due Process Clause of the Fifth Amendment because it discriminates against political parties in favor of special interest groups such as the National Rifle Association (NRA), American Civil Liberties Union (ACLU), and Sierra Club. . . . BCRA imposes numerous restrictions on the fundraising abilities of political parties, of which the soft-money ban is only the most prominent. Interest groups, however, remain free to raise soft money to fund voter registration, GOTV activities, mailings, and broadcast advertising (other than electioneering communications). We conclude that this disparate treatment does not offend the Constitution.

As an initial matter, we note that BCRA actually favors political parties in many ways. Most obviously, party committees are entitled to receive individual contributions that substantially exceed FECA's limits on contributions to nonparty political committees; individuals can give $25,000 to political party committees whereas they can give a maximum of $5,000 to nonparty political committees. . . .

More importantly, however, Congress is fully entitled to consider the real-world differences between political parties and interest groups when crafting a system of campaign finance regulation. Interest groups do not select slates of candidates for elections. Interest groups do not determine who will serve on legislative committees, elect congressional leadership, or organize legislative caucuses. Political parties have influence and power in the legislature that vastly exceeds that of any interest group. As a result, it is hardly surprising that party affiliation is the primary way by which voters identify candidates, or that parties in turn have special access to and relationships with federal officeholders. Congress' efforts at campaign finance regulation may account for these salient differences. . . . We therefore reject those arguments. . . .

### [Title II]

The first section of Title II, § 201 . . . coins a new term, "electioneering communication," to replace the narrowing construction of FECA's disclosure provisions adopted by this Court in

*Buckley.* . . . [T]hat construction limited the coverage of FECA's disclosure requirement to communications expressly advocating the election or defeat of particular candidates. By contrast, the term "electioneering communication" is not so limited, but is defined to encompass any "broadcast, cable, or satellite communication" that

"(I)   refers to a clearly identified candidate for Federal office;
"(II)  is made within—
   "(aa) 60 days before a general, special, or runoff election for the office sought by the candidate; or
   "(bb) 30 days before a primary or preference election, or a convention or caucus of a political party that has authority to nominate a candidate, for the office sought by the candidate; and
"(III) in the case of a communication which refers to a candidate other than President or Vice President, is targeted to the relevant electorate."

New FECA § 304(f)(3)(C) further provides that a communication is " 'targeted to the relevant electorate' " if it "can be received by 50,000 or more persons" in the district or State the candidate seeks to represent. . . . [FECA § 304(f)(3)(B) excludes from the definition of electioneering communications any "communication appearing in a news story, commentary, or editorial distributed through the facilities of any broadcasting station, unless such facilities are owned or controlled by any political party, political committee, or candidate."—ED.]

The major premise of plaintiffs' challenge to BCRA's use of the term "electioneering communication" is that *Buckley* drew a constitutionally mandated line between express advocacy and so-called issue advocacy, and that speakers possess an inviolable First Amendment right to engage in the latter category of speech. . . .

That position misapprehends our prior decisions. . . .

Nor are we persuaded, independent of our precedents, that the First Amendment erects a rigid barrier between express advocacy and so-called issue advocacy. That notion cannot be squared with our longstanding recognition that the presence or absence of magic words cannot meaningfully distinguish electioneering speech from a true issue ad. . . .

*Buckley*'s express advocacy line, in short, has not aided the legislative effort to combat real or apparent corruption, and Congress enacted BCRA to correct the flaws it found in the existing system.

Finally we observe that new FECA § 304(f)(3)'s definition of "electioneering communication" raises none of the vagueness concerns that drove our analysis in *Buckley*. . . . Thus, the constitutional objection that persuaded the Court in *Buckley* to limit FECA's reach to express advocacy is simply inapposite here. . . .

Thus, under BCRA, corporations and unions may not use their general treasury funds to finance electioneering communications, but they remain free to organize and administer segregated funds, or PACs, for that purpose. Because corporations can still fund electioneering communications with PAC money, it is "simply wrong" to view the provision as a "complete ban" on expression rather than a regulation. . . .

[I]ssue ads broadcast during the 30- and 60-day periods preceding federal primary and general elections are the functional equivalent of express advocacy. The justifications for the regulation of express advocacy apply equally to ads aired during those periods if the ads are intended to influence the voters' decisions and have that effect. . . . [I]n the future corporations and unions may finance genuine issue ads during those time frames by simply avoiding any specific reference to federal candidates, or in doubtful cases by paying for the ad from a segregated fund.

We are therefore not persuaded that plaintiffs have carried their heavy burden of proving that amended FECA § 316(b)(2) is overbroad. . . .

Many years ago we observed that "[t]o say that Congress is without power to pass appropriate legislation to safeguard . . . an election from the improper use of money to influence the result is to deny to the nation in a vital particular the power of self protection." We abide by that conviction in considering Congress' most recent effort to confine the ill effects of aggregated wealth on our political system. We are under no illusion that BCRA will be the last congressional statement on the matter. Money, like water, will always find an outlet. What problems will arise, and how Congress will respond, are concerns for another day. In the main we uphold BCRA's two principal, complementary features: the control of soft money and the regulation of electioneering communications. Accordingly, we affirm in part and reverse in part the District Court's judgment with respect to Titles I and II.

*It is so ordered.*

THE CHIEF JUSTICE, concurring in part and dissenting in part . . . [omitted].

**JUSTICE KENNEDY, with whom THE CHIEF JUSTICE joins and with whom JUSTICE SCALIA and JUSTICE THOMAS join, concurring in part and dissenting in part. . . .**

Until today's consolidated cases, the Court has accepted but two principles to use in determining the validity of campaign finance restrictions. First is the anticorruption rationale. The principal concern, of course, is the agreement for a *quid pro quo* between officeholders (or candidates) and those who would seek to influence them. The Court has said the interest in preventing corruption allows limitations on receipt of the *quid* by a candidate or officeholder, regardless of who gives it or of the intent of the donor or officeholder. Second, the Court has analyzed laws that classify on the basis of the speaker's corporate or union identity under the corporate speech rationale. The Court has said that the willing adoption of the entity form by corporations and unions justifies regulating them differently: Their ability to give candidates *quids* may be subject not only to limits but also to outright bans; their electoral speech may likewise be curtailed.

The Court ignores these constitutional bounds and in effect interprets the anticorruption rationale to allow regulation not just of "actual or apparent *quid pro quo* arrangements," but of any conduct that wins goodwill from or influences a Member of Congress. . . . The very aim of *Buckley*'s standard . . . was to define undue influence by reference to the presence of *quid pro quo* involving the officeholder. The Court, in contrast, concludes that access, without more, proves influence is undue. Access, in the Court's view, has the same legal ramifications as actual or apparent corruption of officeholders. This new definition of corruption sweeps away all protections for speech that lie in its path.

Access in itself, however, shows only that in a general sense an officeholder favors someone or that someone has influence on the officeholder. There is no basis, in law or in fact, to say favoritism or influence in general is the same as corrupt favoritism or influence in particular. By equating vague and generic claims of favoritism or influence with actual or apparent corruption, the Court adopts a definition of corruption that dismantles basic First Amendment rules, permits Congress to suppress speech in the absence of a *quid pro quo* threat, and moves beyond the rationale that is *Buckley*'s very foundation.

The generic favoritism or influence theory articulated by the Court is at odds with standard First Amendment analyses because it is unbounded and susceptible to no limiting principle. Any given action might be favored by any given person, so by the Court's reasoning political loyalty of the purest sort can be prohibited. There is no remaining principled method for inquiring whether a campaign finance regulation does in fact regulate corruption in a serious and meaningful way. We are left to defer to a congressional conclusion that certain conduct creates favoritism or influence.

Though the majority cites common sense as the foundation for its definition of corruption, in the context of the real world only a single definition of corruption has been found to identify political corruption successfully and to distinguish good political responsiveness from bad—that is *quid pro quo*. Favoritism and influence are not, as the Government's theory suggests, avoidable in representative politics. It is in the nature of an elected representative to favor certain policies, and, by necessary corollary, to favor the voters and contributors who support those policies. It is well understood that a substantial and legitimate reason, if not the only reason, to cast a vote for, or to make a contribution to, one candidate over another is that the candidate will respond by producing those political outcomes the supporter favors. Democracy is premised on responsiveness. *Quid pro quo* corruption has been, until now, the only agreed upon conduct that represents the bad form of responsiveness and presents a justiciable standard with a relatively clear limiting principle: Bad responsiveness may be demonstrated by pointing to a relationship between an official and a *quid*. . . .

From that it follows that the Court today should not ask, as it does, whether some persons, even Members of Congress, conclusorily assert that the regulated conduct appears corrupt to them. Following *Buckley,* it should instead inquire whether the conduct now prohibited inherently poses a real or substantive *quid pro quo* danger, so that its regulation will stem the appearance of *quid pro quo* corruption. . . .

[I]ndependent party activity, which by definition includes independent receipt and spending of soft money, lacks a possibility for *quid pro quo* corruption of federal officeholders. This must be all the more true of a party's independent receipt and spending of soft money donations neither directed to nor solicited by a candidate. . . .

Few interferences with the speech, association, and free expression of our people are greater than attempts by Congress to say which groups can or cannot advocate a cause, or how they must do it. . . .

The majority permits a new and serious intrusion on speech when it upholds § 203, the key provision in Title II that prohibits corporations and labor unions from using money from their general treasury to fund electioneering communications. . . .

The Government and the majority are right about one thing: The express-advocacy requirement, with its list of magic words, is easy to circumvent. The Government seizes on this observation to defend § 203, arguing it will prevent what it calls "sham issue ads" that are really to the same effect as their more express counterparts. What the Court and the Government call sham, however, are the ads speakers find most effective. . . . It is a measure of the Government's disdain for protected speech that it would label as a sham the mode of communication sophisticated speakers choose because it is the most powerful. . . .

The Government is unwilling to characterize § 203 as a ban, citing the possibility of funding electioneering communications out of a separate segregated fund. This option, though, does not alter the categorical nature of the prohibition on the corporation. . . . What the law allows—permitting the corporation "to serve as the founder and treasurer of a different association of individuals that can endorse or oppose political candidates"—"is not speech by the corporation."

Our cases recognize the practical difficulties corporations face when they are limited to communicating through PACs. . . .

These regulations are more than minor clerical requirements. Rather, they create major disincentives for speech, with the effect falling most heavily on smaller entities that often have the most difficulty bearing the costs of compliance. Even worse, for an organization that has not yet set up a PAC, spontaneous speech that "refers to a clearly identified candidate for Federal office" becomes impossible, even if the group's vital interests are threatened by a piece of legislation pending before Congress on the eve of a federal election. . . .

Even if the newly formed PACs manage to attract members and disseminate their messages against these heavy odds, they have been forced to assume a false identity while doing so. As the American Civil Liberties Union (ACLU) points out, political committees are regulated in minute detail because their primary purpose is to influence federal elections. "The ACLU and thousands of other organizations like it," however, "are not created for this purpose and therefore should not be required to operate as if they were." . . .

The majority can articulate no compelling justification for imposing this scheme of compulsory ventriloquism. . . .

[S]uppose a few Senators want to show their constituents in the logging industry how much they care about working families and propose a law, 60 days before the election, that would harm the environment by allowing logging in national forests. Under § 203, a nonprofit environmental group would be unable to run an ad referring to these Senators in their districts. The suggestion that the group could form and fund a PAC in the short time required for effective participation in the political debate is fanciful. For reasons already discussed, moreover, an ad hoc PAC would not be as effective as the environmental group itself in gaining credibility with the public. Never before in our history has the Court upheld a law that suppresses speech to this extent. . . .

The First Amendment commands that Congress "shall make no law . . . abridging the freedom of speech." The command cannot be read to allow Congress to provide for the imprisonment of those who attempt to establish new political parties and alter the civic discourse. Our pluralistic society is filled with voices expressing new and different viewpoints, speaking through modes and mechanisms that must be allowed to change in response to the demands of an interested public. As communities have grown and technology has evolved, concerted speech not only has become more effective than a single voice but also has become the natural preference and efficacious choice for many Americans. The Court, upholding multiple laws that suppress both spontaneous and concerted speech, leaves us less free than before. Today's decision breaks faith with our tradition of robust and unfettered debate.

For the foregoing reasons, with respect, I dissent from the Court's decision upholding the main features of Titles I and II.

Justice Scalia, concurring in part and dissenting in part . . . [omitted].

Justice Thomas, concurring in part and dissenting in part . . . [omitted].

# CHAPTER SIX

# *The Commerce Clause*

*The desire of the Forefathers to federalize regulation of foreign and interstate commerce stands in sharp contrast to their jealous preservation of the State's power over its internal affairs. No other federal power was so universally assumed to be necessary. No other state power was so readily relinquished.*

—JUSTICE ROBERT H. JACKSON (1949)

Section 8 of Article I of the Constitution declares, "The Congress shall have Power. . . . To regulate Commerce with foreign Nations, and among the several States, and with the Indian Tribes. . . ." These 21 words have long been among the most important in the nation's fundamental charter, for both Congress and the states as well. This is because the commerce clause has two dimensions. In its active mode, it empowers Congress; in its dormant or negative mode, it is a self-executing limitation on the states, even in the absence of any legislation by Congress.

As a grant of authority to Congress, the commerce clause did not become a constitutional battleground until the late 1800s, when a truly national economy, tied together by the railroads, developed. Then, two major questions arose. First, what was the "commerce" that Congress was authorized to regulate? Second, what was the extent of the commerce power? Could the commerce power touch matters and relationships traditionally regarded as local in nature and within the purview of the states? Answers to these questions have greatly affected national policy for over a century.

Yet, as important as congressional enactments may be, most legislation in the United States comes from state and local governments. These laws are examples of the **police power**—that general, residual, and regulatory authority retained by the states under the Constitution. Is such legislation valid when it regulates commerce "among the several States" or in some way affects commerce? Such questions engage the commerce clause in its dormant or negative dimension and date from the earliest years of the Republic. "The simple fact," Justice Kennedy has explained, "was that in the early years of the Republic, Congress seldom perceived the necessity to exercise its power in circumstances where its authority would be called into question. The Court's initial task, therefore, was to elaborate the theories that would permit the States to act where Congress had not done so."

## VIEWS OF THE FRAMERS

Removal of trade restrictions imposed by the states was a moving cause of the Convention of 1787. For protection against these burdens, James Madison, as a member of the Continental Congress, had advocated general authority over commerce. Later on he was conspicuous among those who set in motion the sequence of events leading to the successful meeting at Philadelphia.

**THE CONSTITUTIONAL CONVENTION.** There seems to be no doubt that the commerce clause was inserted in the Constitution primarily to prevent the states from interfering with the freedom of commercial intercourse. Yet all the plans offered by the Convention apparently also envisioned a positive power in the national government to regulate commerce, and subsequent developments converted this clause into a significant source of national authority. Was this the intention of those who framed the Constitution? The record of the Convention of 1787 affords no conclusive answer.

On September 15, 1787, Madison commented on the question whether, under Article I, Section 10, a tonnage tax could be levied by the states for purposes of clearing and dredging harbors. "It depends on the extent of the commerce power. These terms—to regulate commerce—are vague but seem to exclude this power of the states. [Madison] was more and more convinced that the regulation of commerce was in its nature indivisible and ought to be wholly under one authority." Immediately following this statement, Roger Sherman of Connecticut observed, "The Power of the United States to regulate trade, being Supreme, can control interferences of the State regulations where such interferences happen; so that there is no danger to be apprehended from a concurrent jurisdiction." Had this issue "been clearly posed and unequivocally settled," Albert S. Abel commented, "it must perhaps have eliminated decades of judicial groping and guessing; on the other hand it might have broken up the convention."

Nonetheless, certain inferences about the nature and scope of the commerce power may be drawn from changes the Convention made in the wording of the commerce clause itself. In the Pinckney Plan the word *exclusive* was used before *power*. Draft VII of the Committee of Detail used *exclusive*, but in Draft IX it was deleted and reported out in its present form. No evidence has been presented concerning the significance of this deletion. *Exclusive* is used as a description of congressional power only in Clause 17 (laws for the District of Columbia). Even the power of Congress to declare war is not stated to be "exclusive," but Article I, Section 10, explicitly limits state action. The only restriction on states of a commercial nature forbids duty on imports (or exports), except for the amount necessary to meet inspection costs. This seems to suggest freedom of the states to pass other laws regulating or affecting commerce.

**THE RATIFICATION DEBATES.** Because of the motives of the speakers during the heated debates surrounding ratification of the Constitution, contemporary opinion on the meaning of the clause is no sure guide. Those opposed to the new Constitution stressed its centralizing tendencies in lurid colors; supporters, on the other hand, minimized the significance of the commerce power. James McHenry of the Maryland delegation said, "We almost shuddered at the fate of commerce of Maryland should we be unable to make any change in this extraordinary power." In the Virginia ratifying convention, Edmund Randolph agreed that the broad power over commerce was a sine qua non of the Union, and yet he favored a two-thirds vote by Congress for national commerce acts. Richard Henry Lee, also of Virginia, voiced a widespread fear that the clause would be used to discriminate against southern states by the establishment of northern monopolies.

The skillful writers of that campaign document *The Federalist* employed their usual tactics. They made clear the dangers of not giving a broad power over commerce to the general government but blurred the precise limits of national power. "The competitions of commerce would be another fruitful source of contention," Alexander Hamilton stated in No. 7. "Each state or separate confederacy would pursue a system of commercial policy peculiar to itself. . . . The infraction of these [state] regulations on one side, the efforts to prevent and repel them on the other, would naturally lead to outrages, and these to reprisals and war." In No. 42 Madison glossed over the nature of the commerce power by discussing it chiefly as a supplement to the power over foreign commerce and by stressing the unfairness of permitting coastal states to levy a toll on states in the interior. In No. 45 Madison again hinted that the commerce power would be exercised chiefly on foreign commerce.

In 1829, after the "Father of the Constitution" had become a proponent of states' rights, Madison wrote to J. C. Cabell that the power to regulate commerce was designed to prevent abuses by the states rather than for positive purposes of the national government: "[I]t is very certain that it . . . was intended as a negative and preventive provision against injustice among the States themselves, rather than as a power to be used for the positive purposes of the General Government, in which alone, however, the remedial power could be lodged."

## THE MARSHALL DOCTRINE

The intriguing question of the meaning of the commerce clause was first presented to the Court in 1824. The Marshall Court's experience demonstrated that the commerce clause would be a battleground between believers in state prerogatives and supporters of a strong national presence. Under what circumstances could a state policy be struck down as violative of the national Constitution?

**THE STEAMBOAT CASE.** *Gibbons v. Ogden* involved the steamboat monopoly which the New York legislature had granted to Robert Livingston and Robert Fulton, their heirs, and others, granting them an exclusive right to operate steamboats in the state's waters. Ex-governor Ogden of New Jersey held a license under the monopoly to operate a steam-powered ferry between New York and New Jersey. Gibbons, who possessed a "coasting license" under a congressional statute but no license from the monopoly, operated boats on the same route in competition with Ogden. Chancellor Kent of the New York court upheld the monopoly and maintained that Congress had no direct jurisdiction over internal commerce or waters. Daniel Webster, arguing for Gibbons on appeal to the Supreme Court, asserted that Congress alone could regulate "high branches" of commerce. Counsel for the monopoly claimed that a concurrent power existed whenever such a power was not clearly denied by the Constitution. Webster's prophetic construction of commerce as comprehending "almost all the business and intercourse of life" was countered by the definition of commerce as "the transportation and sale of commodities." Both sides agreed that if an actual collision of state and national power occurred the latter must prevail, but counsel for the monopoly held that state power gave way only to the extent needed to give effect to the federal law. Accordingly, navigation on state waters remained under state control.

Chief Justice Marshall could have resolved the case simply by finding that both state and nation had acted within their powers, but because the state law conflicted with the federal licensing act, it must give way. He chose instead to examine the nature of the commerce power before finding the existence of a conflict. Commerce was more than traffic; "it is intercourse," and comprehended navigation. He reiterated the point that commerce "among" the states cannot stop at state lines but "may be introduced into the interior." The power to regulate was "complete in itself, may be exercised to its utmost extent, and acknowledges no limitations, other than are prescribed in the Constitution." Though the states retained authority to enact inspection, pilotage, and health laws, even here Congress could enter the field if it chose.

In a separate opinion, Justice William Johnson went beyond Marshall and took an exclusive view of the commerce clause. Even in the absence of the licensing act, the state monopoly must give way. For Johnson, the national commerce power embraced *all* power enjoyed by the states over commerce before the Constitution. It was a grant of the whole power, carrying the whole domain exclusively into the hands of the national government.

With the exception of monopolists and southern slave owners who feared the consequence of a broad definition of national power over commerce, public opinion welcomed the rebuke the decision gave holders of special privilege. Following the decision, the number of steamboats plying in and out of New York harbor increased in one year from 6 to 43.

**DEFINING STATE AUTHORITY.** Though Marshall described the subject matter of commerce and national power to regulate it in the most sweeping terms, he did not overlook the tremendous power reserved to the states. But on what authority would state policy rest?

Marshall's view on this question comes out most clearly in *Willson* v. *Black Bird Creek Marsh Co.* (1829). The Delaware legislature had authorized the firm to build a dam across the creek for the purpose of reclaiming marshland. Willson, who owned a sloop licensed under federal authority, broke through the dam and continued to navigate the creek. The company sued for trespass. Upholding the Delaware act, Marshall explained,

> The act of assembly by which the plaintiffs were authorized to construct their dam, shows plainly that this is *one of those many creeks,* passing through a deep, level marsh, adjoining the Delaware, up which the tide flows for some distance. The value of the property on its banks must be enhanced by excluding the water from the marsh, and the *health of the inhabitants probably improved.* Measures calculated to produce these objects, provided they do not come into collision with the powers of the general government, are undoubtedly within those which are reserved to the states. . . .
>
> The counsel for the plaintiffs in error insist that it comes in conflict with the power of the United States "to regulate commerce . . . among the several states." If Congress had passed any act which bore upon the case; any act in execution of the power to regulate commerce, the object of which was to control state legislation over *those small navigable creeks* into which the tide flows, and *which abound throughout the lower country of the middle and southern states,* we should feel not much difficulty in saying that a state law coming in conflict with such act would be void. But Congress has passed no such act. . . .

We do not think, that the act empowering the Black Bird Creek Marsh company to place a dam across the creek, can, *under all the circumstances of the case,* be considered as repugnant to the power to regulate commerce in its dormant state, or as being in conflict with any law passed on the subject. [Italics added.]

Marshall was at pains to show the bearing of the dam on land values and the health of the community. As a health measure, enacted under police power, the act was valid until it collided with national authority. He passed over the fact that the sloop in question was federally licensed—the vital consideration in *Gibbons.* Moreover, for the first time Marshall expressly acknowledged the **dormant commerce power,** to refer to the restraint the commerce clause imposes on the states even in the absence of national legislation.

## THE DOCTRINE OF THE TANEY COURT

Roger B. Taney became chief justice after Marshall. During his tenure (1836–1864), the Court squarely faced the question Marshall had pointedly sidestepped in *Gibbons:* May the states regulate commerce in the absence of federal regulation? The **concurrent commerce doctrine** would answer that question in the affirmative. The **exclusive commerce doctrine** would dictate otherwise. The importance of the answer cannot be overstressed. Congress was not likely to react positively during this period. Thus invalidation of state laws regulating commerce meant that commerce was likely to be free from all regulation.

**THE MUDDLE OF COMMERCE.** In *New York* v. *Miln* (1837), the Taney Court issued a confused set of opinions that upheld as a police-power regulation a state act requiring the ship's master on incoming vessels to furnish information concerning his passengers. Justice Thompson, originally assigned the task of writing the opinion, treated the law as a police measure and permissible—in the absence of national action. Because four members of the Court balked at Thompson's analysis, Justice Barbour wrote an opinion holding the state law valid purely as a police measure, but added gratuitous comments that persons were not "subjects of commerce," a pronouncement highly pleasing to the slave states.

In 1847, the even more confused opinions in the License Cases revealed the Court's apparent inability to settle on any one view of the commerce power. Even though the Court unanimously upheld the state laws in question that regulated imported liquor, it was difficult to understand why. Taney and at least three other justices reasoned that Congress's power over commerce was not exclusive. Others insisted that the laws affected only internal commerce and derived from the state police power, and so were not regulations of commerce "among the states."

In the Passenger Cases (1849), argued on three different occasions over a four-year period, litigants challenged state taxes on passengers on incoming vessels. Daniel Webster, who as counsel opposed the laws, feared the absence of a "strong and leading mind" on the Court. Martin Van Buren, for the states, stressed the popular support for the acts and state sovereignty. Webster won a 5–4 decision. Each of the five justices stated his views in such a way, however, that the reporter of decisions could enter as a headnote only that the act was invalid. Three of the four dissenters wrote separate opinions. Taney held that since states could expel undesirable immigrants, they could reject them in the first place, and he cited *New York* v. *Miln* to show that persons were not "subjects of commerce." The majority split—two justices ruling congressional power over foreign commerce to be exclusive, three holding that this was unnecessary for the decision because the state act conflicted with existing national legislation. For those hoping for clarity on the commerce power, disappointment and frustration understandably greeted the decision.

**THE COOLEY DOCTRINE.** The law was in this muddle when President Millard Fillmore appointed Benjamin R. Curtis to the Court in 1851. A brilliant Massachusetts lawyer, Curtis was destined to be the mediator between the tenuous coalitions and the effective medium through whom a compromise was reached. The famous case of *Cooley* **v.** *Board of Wardens* (1851) upheld a state pilotage fee against the charge that it conflicted with the national commerce power. Complicating the situation was a congressional act of 1789 stating that pilots should be regulated in conformity "with such laws as the states may hereafter enact . . . until further legislative provision shall be made by Congress." Combining elements of the "exclusive" and "concurrent" doctrines, Curtis fashioned a new formula of **selective exclusiveness.** His middle ground was this: Subjects national in scope required uniform regulation that only Congress could provide, and in the absence of such legislation the states could not act. As to subjects of a local character, not requiring uniform legislation, states could legislate (according to Curtis) until Congress, by acting on the same subject, displaced the state law. Where national and state laws were in conflict, the federal rule would prevail.

The opinions delivered during the Marshall and Taney courts contained plenty of ammunition for those advocating or opposing commercial regulation by either state or nation. For future courts, substantial difficulties existed, despite the formula fashioned by the **Cooley doctrine.** How was one to decide whether a subject matter required a national (or uniform) regulation? Was inaction by Congress the same as a declaration that the desired uniformity was no regulation? In the absence of a need for uniform regulation, would any state regulation be acceptable? Answers to these and other questions were left to the future.

## STATES AND THE COMMERCE CLAUSE TODAY

As inspired by the Cooley doctrine, the Court's first duty in the absence of congressional legislation has been to determine the nature of the subject matter regulated. Does the state policy disrupt a desired uniformity? If it requires national regulation (or an absence of regulation), state action is foreclosed. If the subject matter permits local regulation, two questions remain: First, does the state law discriminate against interstate commerce and in favor of local commerce? Second, does the act, although nondiscriminatory, place an unreasonable burden on interstate commerce? Socioeconomic fact and theory, flavored by judicial bias, have entered inevitably into the attempts to answer these questions.

**THREE VIEWS OF STATE REGULATION.** Over a half century ago, three basic positions crystallized as the Court attempted to answer these questions. Then as now, all justices were opposed to **protectionism:** No state could discriminate against interstate commerce to gain for itself a commercial advantage over its neighbors. A few justices believed that was all the commerce clause in its dormant state was meant to prevent. A second group preferred a balancing-of-interests or cost-benefits rule when faced with state legislation that was not protectionist but that arguably burdened interstate commerce. This is illustrated by *Southern Pacific Co.* **v.** *Arizona* (1945), where the Court had to decide whether a state limit on the length of interstate and intrastate trains could stand. In such situations the need for the regulation is weighed against its costs to determine whether the burden imposed is undue. Incantation of worthy purposes alone will not suffice to save a state statute from challenge under the commerce clause. A third group found the first two positions equally objectionable. Neither gave due weight to a danger the commerce clause was designed to avert—**balkanization**—which would permit individual states to raise barriers to commerce. According to this view, even in the absence of congressional legislation, the commerce clause of its own force prohibited states from doing anything to burden, obstruct, hinder, or restrain interstate commerce. Furthermore, it was the duty of the Supreme Court to guard national commerce from such local encroachments.

It has been the second position, sometimes veering toward the third, that has most often been reflected in Court decisions in recent decades. As Justice Stewart restated the balancing test in 1970,

> Where the statute regulates even-handedly to effectuate a legitimate local public interest, and its effects on interstate commerce are only incidental, it will be upheld unless the burden imposed on such commerce is clearly excessive in relation to the putative local benefits. If a legitimate local purpose is found, then the question becomes one of degree. And the extent of the burden that will be tolerated will of course depend on the nature of the local interest involved, and on whether it could be promoted as well with a lesser impact on interstate activities (*Pike* v. *Bruce Church, Inc.*).

This view continues to be reflected in decisions involving the many ways state laws arguably affect commerce.

**TRANSPORTATION.** Initially, the Court was rather generous in upholding state acts regulating motor transportation, such as the licensing of vehicles (*Buck* v. *Kuykendall,* 1925). In 1938 *South Carolina* v. *Barnwell* approved a statute barring from state roads trucks with loads over 20,000 pounds and widths exceeding 90 inches. In the absence of congressional legislation it was deemed reasonable to protect roads built and maintained by the state, especially since no discrimination or attempt to burden interstate commerce had been shown. In such situations today, the bench is inclined toward the balancing-of-interests approach reflected in Justice Stone's opinion in the Arizona Train Limit Case, and exhibits less deference to, and more skepticism of, state restrictions. In truck-length cases, for example, the Court has ruled that state bans on 65-foot double trailers, especially where neighboring states permit them on the highways, violate the commerce clause (*Raymond Motor Transportation, Inc.* v. *Rice,* 1978; *Kassel* v. *Consolidated Freightways Corp.,* 1981). As Justice Powell maintained in *Kassel,* "[T]he incantation of a purpose to promote the public health or safety does not insulate a state law from Commerce Clause attack. Regulations designed for that salutary purpose nevertheless may further the purpose so marginally, and interfere with commerce so substantially, as to be invalid. . . ." The judicial task in these cases is at heart both empirical and political—a weighing of one value against another.[1]

---

[1] The junior author of this book once received a close-up demonstration of what was at work. Before *Kassel* came down, Justice Harry Blackmun and Mrs. Blackmun had been guests on campus. It fell to me to drive them back to their home in Arlington, Virginia. On Interstate 83 in southern Pennsylvania, Justice Blackmun leaned forward from the back seat and asked me to pass as many trucks as I could at varying speeds. He then made notes on the type of truck, my speed, and the length of time required to pass safely.

**QUALITY OF LIFE.** State and local regulations to protect the environment or to improve the quality of life also meet challenges under the commerce clause. In *Burbank* v. *Lockheed Air Terminal* (1973), the Court struck down an ordinance banning takeoffs and landings by certain jet aircraft at an airport during late-night hours. Although finding no express preemption by national statutes, Justice Douglas for the Court found an implied one: "If we were to uphold the Burbank ordinance and a significant number of municipalities followed suit, it is obvious that fractionalized control of the timing of takeoffs and landings would severely limit the flexibility of the FAA in controlling air traffic flow. The difficulties of scheduling flights to avoid congestion and the concomitant decrease in safety would be compounded."

Similarly, trash disposal implicates the commerce clause. In 1978 a seven-member majority overturned a New Jersey statute prohibiting the importation of most "solid or liquid waste which originated or was collected outside the territorial limits of the State" (***Philadelphia* v. *New Jersey.***) The laudable intent of the law was to prevent the state from becoming a dumping ground for New York and Pennsylvania, but the constitutionally impermissible effect of the law was "to saddle those outside the State with the entire burden of slowing the flow of refuse into New Jersey's remaining landfill sites."

Garbage is commerce not because of its own worth but because of the fact that the one who possesses garbage must pay to get rid of it. There is business in trash. Both the generation of solid waste and the cost of landfill capacity have moved local governments to spend considerable amounts of money on trash control systems, as happened in the Town of Clarkstown, New York, which authorized a private company to build a solid waste transfer facility. To finance the plant, the town adopted a flow control ordinance that required trash to be processed at that facility before being shipped from the locale. In *C&A Carbone* v. *Clarkstown* (1994), however, six justices cited *Philadelphia* v. *New Jersey* and ruled that such ordinances discriminate against interstate commerce. Acknowledging that the town intended to use processing fees to amortize the cost of the facility, Justice Kennedy explained that the requirement "attains this goal by depriving competitors, including out-of-state firms, of access to a local market. . . . The Commerce Clause preserves a national market free from local legislation that discriminates in favor of local interests."

**STATES AS MARKET PARTICIPANTS.** Would the outcome in the Carbone case have been different had Clarkstown owned and operated the transfer facility? Perhaps. This is because of a distinction the Court has drawn between the state as **market participant** and the state as **market regulator.** The strictures of the dormant commerce clause do not apply to the former in the same way they do to the latter.

***Reeves, Inc.* v. *Stake*** (1980) illustrates the distinction. Here the justices examined the sales policies of a state-owned cement plant where, after a cut in production, the state chose to supply in-state customers first. As a result, an out-of-state concrete business had to reduce its own production by 76 percent. For the majority, Justice Blackmun drew on a novel distinction the Court first employed in *Hughes* v. *Alexandria Scrap Corp.* (1976) between the state as participant or actor in the market and the state as regulator of the market. Admittedly, the state could not have passed a law requiring firms to supply in-state customers at the expense of those out-of-state, but as operator of the plant, it was free to do exactly that. Because the state was acting in the role of the former, there was no violation of the commerce clause even though the state's policy clearly placed out-of-state buyers at a disadvantage.

The participant/regulator distinction was important in *South-Central Timber Development, Inc.* v. *Wunnicke* (1984). Alaska's Department of Natural Resources required that timber cut from state lands be partially processed within the state before being shipped out of state. Yet the Court held that Alaska could not rely on the market participant doctrine to immunize its downstream regulation of where the timber would have its first processing because the state, albeit a seller of timber, was not a participant in the timber processing market. Reaffirmed was the view that the commerce clause precludes a state's giving in-state businesses a preferred right of access to its natural resources or to products derived from those resources.

**A Continuing Judicial Role.** From this chapter thus far, certain conclusions can be drawn. First, the dormant commerce clause has not been used to frustrate state legislation, simply because one might argue that a national rule would be more efficient or desirable. Second, decisions have in fact permitted the erection of what amount to modest trade barriers (motor carrier limitations, taxes, inspection laws, safety laws). Third, Congress for many reasons has not chosen to regulate all subjects that lie within the reach of its commerce power, and so much has been left to the states. Fourth, cases testing state power under the commerce clause unavoidably require the exercise of judicial discretion and remain a staple of the Court's docket.

Throughout, the Supreme Court has undertaken the role of guardian of the national market against efforts to re-erect the type of trade barriers that marked the preconstitutional era. The commerce clause in its twin dimensions has not only been a "prolific source of conflict" between state interests and national prerogatives but, as the remainder of this chapter will show, an equally "prolific source of national power."

## THE NATIONAL COMMERCE POWER: COMPETING VISIONS

In the post-Civil War period, state legislatures were under pressure to solve the problems arising from a burgeoning industrialism and an economy that was becoming truly national for the first time. And until the 1880s, regulation—if it was to come at all—would largely be state regulation. However, once Congress began to enact economic legislation of its own, the commerce clause in its active mode became a persistent constitutional issue.

**The Wabash and Sugar Trust Cases.** It was state regulation of railroads that focused judicial attention on problems that could arise in the absence of congressional action. Initially the Court allowed states to set rates that railroads could charge, even though this regulation had an indirect effect on interstate commerce. However, as state after state adopted its own system of rate regulation, the Court later changed its mind. The facts in the Wabash case (*Wabash, St. Louis & Pacific Ry. Co.* v. *Illinois,* 1886) illustrated the quandary. The railroad charged 15 cents per hundred pounds from Peoria, Illinois, and 25 cents per hundred pounds from Gilman, Illinois, on shipments of similar chattels to New York City. Because Gilman was 86 miles closer to New York, the two rates ran afoul of an Illinois statute banning long-short haul rate discrimination. With most of the distance for each shipment lying outside Illinois, the state was in effect regulating interstate commerce.

The majority in *Wabash* found the state law an invalid intrusion on the national commerce power. "This is commerce of national character," Justice Miller said, "and national regulation is required." *Wabash* was significant in helping to bring about a climate of opinion favorable to national regulation of interstate railroad rates through passage of the Interstate Commerce Act the following year. This 1887 law established the Interstate Commerce Commission, the second permanent federal regulatory agency created by Congress with broad quasi-legislative, executive, and judicial powers.

Three years later, passage of the Sherman Anti-Trust Act showed that Congress was prepared to use its commerce power to accomplish purposes far beyond anything hitherto attempted. The rationale of the act was that certain combinations and conspiracies in businesses that had the effect of restraining or monopolizing interstate commerce should be prohibited. Difficult questions arose at the very outset, however, concerning the applicability of the law to industrial and commercial firms, because Congress could outlaw monopolistic practices only in businesses that engaged in commerce "among the states." In *United States* **v.** *E. C. Knight Co.* (the Sugar Trust Case, 1895), the Court held that a monopoly in the production of refined sugar was exempt from the Sherman Act. To Chief Justice Fuller, commerce meant primarily sale and distribution—the physical movement of goods following manufacture. The effect of contracts and combinations to control manufacture, "however inevitable and whatever its extent," would be "indirect," the chief justice believed, and therefore beyond congressional reach. Fuller thus made use of a distinction that would persist for some years in the jurisprudence of the commerce clause: **direct versus indirect effects,** with only the former being subject to national regulation. Yet, because he recognized that goods are manufactured *only* because they can be sold and that manufacture and commerce are interrelated, he was much disturbed by the implications of an integrated national economy for federal power. It is no surprise, therefore, that *Fuller* echoed Justice L.Q.C. Lamar's admonition from *Kidd* v. *Pearson* (1888): "No distinction is more popular to the common mind . . . than that between manufactures and commerce. . . . If it is held that [commerce] includes the regulation of all such manufactures as are intended to be the subject of commercial transactions in the future, . . . Congress would be invested, to the exclusion of the States, with the power to regulate, not only manufacture, but also agriculture, horticulture, stock raising, domestic fisheries, mining—in short, every branch of human industry."

In 1904, however (*Northern Securities Co.* v. *United States*), the Court allowed application of the Sherman Act to a scheme by which a holding company had been established to hold the stock of competing interstate railroads, thus eliminating competition between them. In another broad interpretation of the commerce power (*Swift* v. *United States,* 1905), a combination of meat packers was held unlawful under the act, on the ground that their activities, though geographically "local," were important incidents in a "current of commerce." The Sugar Trust Case seemed seriously undermined.

**A NATIONAL POLICE POWER?** A series of cases between 1903 and World War I clearly established the principle that the commerce power could also be used as a device for accomplishing purely social goals, apart from regulating commercial activities of large corporations. These decisions meant that Congress in effect possessed a **national police power,** alongside the police power ("the power to govern men and things," Chief Justice Taney once called it) the states had always enjoyed. (See Chapter Eight for a discussion of the development of the state police power.)

In the first case (*Champion* v. *Ames,* 1903), the Court sustained a federal act prohibiting the interstate shipment of lottery tickets. Alongside the majority's frequent references to the evil nature of these tickets, Chief Justice Fuller's dissent pointed out that the evil began only with their illegal use at the point of destination.

Besides, "[t]o hold that Congress has general police power would be to hold that it may accomplish objects not intrusted to the General Government, and to defeat the operation of the Tenth Amendment." On grounds similar to those in the Lottery Case, the Pure Food and Drug Act withstood attack in 1911 (*Hipolite Egg Co.* v. *United States*). *Hoke* v. *United States* (1913) approved the Mann Act, making it a felony to transport a woman from one state to another for immoral purposes. In *Houston, E. & W. Texas Ry. Co.* v. *United States* (the Shreveport Case), the Court upheld in 1914 an Interstate Commerce Commission order fixing intrastate railroad rates because of their effect on interstate commerce, echoing Marshall's view that the national commerce power extends to all commerce that "affects more than one state." The inference was that local practices were within the reach of national power if they affected commerce.

The pattern then became confused. **Hammer v. Dagenhart** (1918) adhered to the Sugar Trust Case by distinguishing between commerce and manufacturing, as the Court invalidated the Keating-Owen Child Labor Act of 1916. Considered a triumph of the Progressive era, it prohibited the transportation in interstate commerce of products produced by child labor (age 16 in mines, age 14 in factories, or more than 48 hours a week for the age group 14–16 years). Justice Day, for the Court, characterized the precedents involving lotteries, food, and prostitution as attempts to regulate where transportation was used to accomplish harmful results; production and its incidents, on the other hand, were (in Day's mind) local matters, and the items produced by child labor were not harmful in themselves. As Chapter Seven explains, Congress then tried an alternate attack on child labor in 1919 relying on the taxing power, but the Court invalidated that law as well, 8–1 (*Bailey* v. *Drexel Furniture Co.*, 1922).

Other cases seemed to indicate once again that the Court might be prepared to accept a broad construction of the commerce power. **Stafford v. Wallace** (1992) upheld the Packers and Stockyards Act of 1921, which was aimed at harmful trade practices in the Chicago meatpacking industry. Chief Justice Taft reasoned that although in a geographic sense the packers were conducting a local business, in an economic sense their activities were only an incident in a continuing interstate market from ranches to dinner tables. Following the same line of reasoning, *Brooks* v. *United States* (1925) sustained the National Motor Theft Act, making it a crime to transport or conceal a stolen automobile. These decisions stood in contrast to cases like *Dagenhart* and seemed to portend a return to the broad doctrines of Chief Justice Marshall.

## CONSTITUTIONAL CRISIS

Franklin D. Roosevelt was inaugurated president in 1933 in the depths of the Great Depression. His administration achieved rapid passage in Congress of a series of measures designed to aid economic recovery. The first phase of FDR's domestic reform program (called the **New Deal**) involved agricultural and business regulation, price stabilization, public works, and banking and finance regulation. Prominent legislation included the National Industrial Recovery Act (NIRA) and the Agricultural Adjustment Act (AAA), both enacted in 1933. The second phase began in 1935 and emphasized social and economic legislation—such as the Social Security Act of 1935 and the Fair Labor Standards Act of 1938—to benefit working people directly and in the long term. What would be the constitutional fate of these bold programs? The Court, after all, had at hand two viable lines of precedent. There were the doctrines established by John Marshall, which had inspired decisions such as *Stafford* v. *Wallace*. Alternatively, there were the restrictive interpretations of the Sugar Trust Case and *Hammer* v. *Dagenhart*.

**THE NEW DEAL IN COURT.** The first New Deal reform measure reached the Supreme Bench for argument in December 1934 under circumstances that did not augur well for the validity of executive orders issued under NIRA. The Panama Refining Company had challenged the act's prohibition against shipment of "hot oil" (that exceeding state allowances) across state lines. Early in the argument government counsel disclosed that criminal penalties attaching to the violation of the relevant code provisions had been inadvertently omitted from the executive order. Judicial curiosity was immediately aroused, and concern deepened when opposing counsel bitterly complained that his client had been arrested, indicted, and held several days in jail for violating this nonexistent "law." With these points against it, the government was at a disadvantage in pressing its argument that Congress could constitutionally empower the president in his discretion to ban hot oil from interstate commerce. Eight justices held Section 9(c) of the NIRA invalid as an unconstitutional delegation of legislative power to the chief executive (*Panama Refining Co.* v. *Ryan,* 1935). Congress, they said, established no "primary standard," thus leaving "the matter to the President without standard or rule, to be dealt with as he pleased."

Before the dust thrown up by the hot oil decision had settled, the Court made headlines again in its 5–4 decision scuttling the recently enacted railroad retirement scheme, which required carriers to subscribe to a pension plan (*Railroad Retirement Board* v. *Alton R. R. Co.,* 1935). For the majority, Justice Roberts ridiculed the statute. Brushing the legislation aside as based on "the contentment and satisfaction theory" of social progress, he inquired, "Is it not apparent that they [pensions] are really and essentially related solely to the social welfare of the worker, and therefore remote from any regulation of commerce as such?" Congress might, he agreed, require outright dismissal of all aged workers, but it could not give them pensions. If superannuation is a danger, Roberts argued in effect, the commerce clause authorizes compulsory retirement—without a pension. Congressional effort to compel railroads to pension off older workers failed for lack of any perceived relation between the pensioning system and the efficiency or safety of the national rail network.

Taken together, the Panama Refining and the Railroad Retirement cases forecast the New Deal's doom. The blow fell on May 27, 1935, "Black Monday," when NIRA (symbolized by the Blue Eagle) was guillotined out of the recovery program (*Schechter Poultry Co.* v. *United States*). The Schechter brothers, wholesale poultry dealers in Brooklyn, New York, were charged with violating NIRA's Live Poultry Code by ignoring minimum wage and maximum hour requirements, by giving special treatment to preferred customers, and by selling an "unfit chicken" to a butcher. The Court, speaking through Chief Justice Hughes, found the act deficient as an unconstitutional delegation of legislative power. Moreover, government counsel conceded that congressional authority to regulate the Schechter business had to be based on the commerce clause, but the Court held the defendants' business was neither interstate commerce in itself nor closely enough connected with it to "affect" such commerce.

In May of the following year, the justices ruled 6–3 that Congress had exceeded its authority in enacting the Guffey-Snyder Bituminous Coal Conservation Act (***Carter* v. *Carter Coal Co.,*** 1936). Through a complex system of wage and price controls administered by a commission, the statute attempted to provide remedies for the notoriously distressed soft coal industry. The situation was so urgent and the benefits of the legislation so evident that President Roosevelt had taken the unusual step of asking the congressional subcommittee, while the coal act was pending, not to "permit doubts as to constitutionality, however reasonable," to block the suggested legislation. The Court, however, was not prepared to set aside such doubts. "[I]t is of vital moment," Justice Sutherland said for the majority, "that, in order to preserve the fixed balance intended by the Constitution, the powers of the general government be not so extended as to embrace any not within the express terms of the several grants or the implications necessary to be drawn therefrom." Sutherland's opinion was clear-cut and unequivocal on the nature of the distinction between direct and indirect effects. "The local character of mining, of manufacturing, and of crop growing is a fact, and remains a fact, whatever may be done with the products," Sutherland said. Going back to Chief Justice Fuller's opinion in the Sugar Trust Case and paraphrasing his words, Sutherland declared, "Such effect as they [working conditions] may have upon commerce, however extensive it may be, is secondary and indirect. An increase in the greatness of the effect adds to its importance. It does not alter its character." Dual federalism (see Chapter Four) remained an independent check on the extent of Congress's power under the commerce clause.

As far as the commerce power was concerned, the Court by 1936 had adopted the view that certain subjects were local in nature and beyond the power of Congress, even though they required national or uniform regulations if they were to be regulated at all. On the other hand, effective state-by-state regulation was clearly impossible; even if it were attempted it might, if any state regulation were found to have any substantial effect on interstate commerce, run afoul of the dormant commerce power. The Court thus had narrowed the commerce doctrines of Marshall by withdrawing from congressional power certain subject matters, such as production, agriculture, and the employer-employee relationship. In effect, the Court had created a category other than those enumerated in the Cooley Case: objects that could not in practice be regulated by either government—a "twilight zone." As Justice Stone wrote to his sister at the end of the Court's term in June 1936, "we seem to have tied Uncle Sam up in a hard knot." Indeed, in the years 1934–1936 the Supreme Court in 12 decisions had declared unconstitutional all or part of 11 New Deal measures.[2] And these decisions were made by a bench without a single Roosevelt appointee. None of the "nine old men" (as some journalists called them) opted to retire during FDR's first term.

**THE COURT-PACKING THREAT.** By the summer of 1936 it looked as if the Court had put the New Deal firmly on the rack of unconstitutionality, rendering government impotent. The entire legislative program overwhelmingly approved by the American people at the polls in 1932, 1934, and 1936 was, as Assistant Attorney General Robert Jackson said, in danger of being lost in "a maze of constitutional metaphors."

President Roosevelt had several options. He and Congress might limit the jurisdiction of the Supreme Court, sponsor constitutional amendments limiting the

---

[2] Economy Act of 1933 in *Lynch* v. *United States* (1934); Agricultural Adjustment Act of 1933 in *United States* v. *Butler* (1936); Joint Resolution of June 5, 1933, in *Perry* v. *United States* (1935); National Industrial Recovery Act of 1933 in *Schechter Poultry Corp.* v. *United States* (1935) and *Panama Refining Co.* v. *Ryan* (1935); Independent Offices Appropriation Act of 1933 in *Booth* v. *United States* (1934); 1933 Amendments to Home Owners' Loan Act in *Hopkins Savings Assn.* v. *Cleary* (1935); 1934 Amendments to Bankruptcy Act of 1898 in *Ashton* v. *Cameron County Dist.* (1936); Railroad Retirement Act of 1934 in *Railroad Retirement Board* v. *Alton R. Co.* (1935); Frazier-Lemke Act of 1934 in *Louisville Bank* v. *Radford* (1935); AAA Amendments of 1935 in *Rickert Rice Mills* v. *Fontenot* (1936); Bituminous Coal Conservation Act in *Carter* v. *Carter Coal Co.* (1936).

Court's power or reversing its rulings, or increase the number of judges to override the present majority. Though many members of Congress urged that something be done, they were uncertain what to do, not quite sure whether the trouble was the fault of the Constitution or of judges. The president and his party were uncertain, too, at least on the most feasible remedy politically. The Democratic Party platform in 1936 said, "If these problems [social and economic] cannot be effectively solved by legislation within the Constitution, we shall seek such clarifying amendments as [we] . . . shall find necessary, in order adequately to regulate commerce, protect public health and safety and safeguard economic liberty. Thus we propose to maintain the letter and spirit of the Constitution." Throughout the campaign Democratic orators muted the discord, giving no hint that Roosevelt would, if reelected, wage all-out war on the judiciary.

FDR awaited the propitious moment. With Roosevelt's carrying 46 of the 48 states, the November election had, as one newspaper said, yielded "a roar in which cheers for the Supreme Court were drowned out." Congressional opinion also appeared overtly hostile to the Court. Yet even in the face of his overwhelming electoral triumph, the president could not be sure that the Court would give ground. Did not the traditional theory insist that the justices are, and must be, immune to election returns? Unwilling to take chances, the president, on February 5, 1937, sent to Congress his message proposing a drastic shake-up in the judiciary. Supreme Court justices past the age of 70 would have six months in which to retire. A justice who failed to retire within the appointed time could continue in office, but the chief executive would appoint an additional justice, up to a maximum bench of 15 justices—presumably younger and better able to carry the heavy load. Because there were six justices in this category, Roosevelt would have been able to make that number of appointments at once. In presenting his proposal the president gave no hint of wishing to stem the tide of anti-New Deal decisions. He tendered the hemlock cup to the elderly jurists on the elevated ground that they slowed the efficient dispatch of judicial business.

From the very start, the **Court-packing plan** ran into terrific opposition, even though Democrats in the new 75th Congress enjoyed their largest majorities of the twentieth century and Republicans had nearly become an endangered species. Overnight, Supreme Court justices were again pictured as demigods, weighing public policy in the delicate scales of the law. "Constitutionality" was talked about as if it were a tangible fact, undeviating and precise, not merely the current judicial theory of what ought and what ought not to be done. The same members of Congress who, before the president's message, had demanded the scalps of reactionary justices were "shocked beyond measure" and turned on Roosevelt in an attitude of anguished surprise. Closing ranks with bar associations, newspapers lined up almost solidly against Court packing. The idea implicit in Roosevelt's scheme, that the Court may change its interpretation in such a way as to sustain legislative power to meet national needs, was called as "false in theory, as it would be ruinous in practice." Throughout the ensuing months debate waxed furiously. Clergy, educators, business leaders, and lawyers trekked to Washington and testified for or against the plan. Said Walter Lippmann, "No issue so great or so deep has been raised in America since secession."

Everyone who could read knew that the justices were not the vestal virgins of the Constitution. Yet through the years, and despite increasing evidence that judicial interpretation and not fundamental law shackled the power to govern, the American people had come to regard the Court as the symbol of their freedom. Tarnished though the symbol was, it made, like the English monarchy, for national stability and poise in crisis; moreover, like its English counterpart, the Supreme Court commanded the loyalty of the citizenry, providing perhaps an impregnable barrier against tyrannical government. "The President wants to control the Supreme Court" was hammered home incessantly. If the plan were accepted, the anti–New Deal press averred, nothing would stand between Roosevelt and the absolute dictatorship of the United States.

Quick to sense that his initial approach had been a major blunder, FDR moved closer to the real issue on March 4, when he likened the judiciary to an unruly horse on the government gang plough, unwilling to pull with its teammates, the executive and Congress. As he saw it now, the crucial question was not whether the Court had kept up with its calendar but whether it had kept up with the country. But the president's false assertion that the judges lagged in their work had blurred the issue, diverting public attention so completely that his later effort to face the difficulty squarely never quite succeeded.

In a nationwide Fireside Chat on March 9, the president threw off the cloak of sophistry and frankly explained: "The Court has been acting not as a judicial body, but as a policymaking body. . . . That is not only my accusation, it is the accusation of most distinguished Justices of the present Supreme Court. . . . In holding the AAA unconstitutional, Justice Stone said of the majority opinion that it was 'a tortured construction of the Constitution' and two other Justices agreed with him. In the case holding the New York Minimum Wage Law unconstitutional [*Morehead* v. *New York* ex rel. *Tipaldo,* 1936], Justice Stone said that the majority were actually reading into the Constitution their own 'personal economic predilections' . . . and two other justices agreed with him."

**COUNTERATTACK.** A vigorous campaign against the president's bill was being waged in the Senate under the leadership of Senator Burton K. Wheeler. White House advisor Tom Corcoran tried vainly to dissuade the Montana Democrat from making a fight; the president himself told Wheeler of the futility of opposing a measure certain to pass in any event. "A liberal cause," Wheeler explained bluntly, "was never won by stacking a deck of cards, by stuffing a ballot box or packing a Court."

Meanwhile, those able to make the most realistic estimate of the condition of the Court's docket—the justices themselves—maintained a discreet silence. Finally, Senator Wheeler nervously sought an interview with Justice Brandeis who, with Stone and Cardozo, belonged to the trio of justices most inclined to uphold New Deal legislation. Much to his surprise he found Brandeis cooperative. "Why don't you call on the Chief Justice?" Brandeis suggested. "But I don't know the Chief Justice," the Montana senator hesitated. "Well," said Brandeis, somewhat impatiently, "the Chief Justice knows you and knows what you are doing."

This was late Friday afternoon, March 19, 1937. The next day Senator Wheeler went to see Chief Justice Hughes. The senator wanted to know from the justices themselves whether the president's oft-repeated allegations about the back-logged docket, lack of efficiency, and so on had any basis in fact. As Brandeis had indicated, the chief justice was not only enlisted but enthusiastic. Though Wheeler had not reached him until Saturday, March 20, Hughes was able somehow to prepare a long and closely reasoned document for the senator's use the following Monday, March 22. "The baby is born," he said with a broad smile, as he put the letter into Wheeler's hand late Sunday afternoon.

Hughes's letter not only scotched the president's charge that the "old men" were not abreast of their docket but also revealed its composer as a canny dialectician. Though carefully refraining from open opposition to the plan, the letter suggested that the president's idea of an enlarged Court and the hearing of cases in divisions might run counter to the constitutional provision for "one Supreme Court." It was extraordinary enough, some of his colleagues thought, for a justice to go out of his way to meet constitutional issues unnecessary for deciding a case; Hughes went further and handed down an advisory opinion on a burning political issue. Hughes also conveyed the erroneous impression that the entire Court had been consulted and endorsed his statement.

The chief justice's letter, combined with the Court's forthcoming about-face, put a fatal crimp in the president's scheme. Then, Justice Van Devanter—one of the New Deal's archenemies—announced his retirement on May 18, ensuring Roosevelt his first opportunity to make an appointment to the Court. (The Supreme Court Retirement Act, signed into law on March 1, 1937, allowed justices to retire at the age of 70 with full salary.) Roosevelt's plan might no longer be needed. "Why run for a train after you've caught it?" asked Senator (and future justice) James F. Byrnes.

On June 14, the Senate Judiciary Committee voted 10 to 8 against the president's bill. On July 14, Senator Joseph T. Robinson of Arkansas, the bill's floor leader, died unexpectedly. Ironically, Robinson was thought by many to have been promised Van Devanter's seat, which Roosevelt eventually handed to New Deal stalwart Senator Hugo L. Black of Alabama on the night of August 11. Finally, in an act that was almost anticlimactic, the full Senate voted 70–20 on July 22 to recommit the bill to committee, thus sealing the plan's fate.

The Court's victory was not, however, unmixed. Roosevelt's plan was defeated, but without the appointment of a single new justice, he extracted from the embattled bench decisions favorable to the New Deal. "In politics the black-robed reactionary Justices had won over the master liberal politician of their day," opined future Justice Robert Jackson. "In law the President defeated the recalcitrant Justices in their own Court." Even as the fight raged about them, the justices had begun destruction of their most recent handiwork.

**A Switch in Time.** The major issue facing Court and country in the spring of 1937 was posed by the National Labor Relations Act (also known as the Wagner Act). Passed in 1935, the statute was the most encompassing labor legislation ever enacted by Congress. The law established the National Labor Relations Board with authority to oversee all interstate labor affairs. It defined unfair labor practices and gave unions considerable protection against management. Would the justices turn their backs on the Schechter and Carter Coal rulings and permit the national government to substitute law for naked force in labor relations? In the heat of the court fight, industrial peace—or war—seemed to hang in the balance. Then, on April 12, 1937, Chief Justice Hughes put forward a broad and encompassing definition of interstate commerce and conceded to Congress the power to protect the lifelines of the national economy from private industrial warfare (***NLRB v. Jones & Laughlin Steel Corp.***).

Arguments that had proved effective in *Schechter* and *Carter Coal* cases now availed nothing, even though the Court's membership had not changed. "Those cases," the chief justice commented summarily, "are not controlling here." They were not controlling because he now chose to consider the distinction between direct and indirect effects as one of degree rather than kind. Because interstate commerce was now seen as a "practical conception," interference with that commerce "must be appraised by a judgment that does not ignore actual experience." Therefore, it was "idle to say" that interference by strikes or other labor disturbances "would be indirect or remote. It is obvious that it would be immediate and might be catastrophic." "We are asked to shut our eyes to the plainest facts of our national life," the chief justice continued, "and to deal with the question of direct and indirect effects in an intellectual vacuum."

Moreover, the chief justice's sweeping doctrine did not apply solely to large-scale industries, such as steel. On the same day, the Court applied the same doctrine to two smaller concerns, a trailer company and a men's clothing manufacturer (*NLRB* v. *Freuhauf Trailer Co., NLRB* v. *Friedman–Harry Marks Clothing Co.*). By a vote of 5–4 each time, this major New Deal enactment was sustained. The **Constitutional Revolution of 1937** was under way. The effects of FDR's assault on the Court went far beyond a string of pro–New Deal rulings. Had there been nothing more than this, the confrontation of 1937 would be important but hardly epochal. Instead, the event marked a constitutional divide.

## THE COMMERCE POWER REBORN

*United States* v. *Darby* (1941) unanimously upheld the Fair Labor Standards Act (FLSA), which fixed minimum wages and maximum hours for producers of goods shipped in interstate commerce and which banned the interstate shipment of goods manufactured under substandard conditions or by children. In his opinion, Justice Stone included this significant comment: "The motive and purpose of a regulation of interstate commerce are matters for the legislative judgment upon the exercise of which the Constitution places no restriction and over which the Courts are given no control." *Hammer* v. *Dagenhart* was overruled. **Wickard v. Filburn** (1942) marked just how far the Court had come since 1936 by upholding the marketing provisions of the Agricultural Adjustment Act of 1938 as applied to wheat grown for home consumption. *Filburn* and *Darby* were light-years removed from *Carter Coal*.

The commerce power had been reborn in three important respects: The Court accepted a greatly enlarged definition of "commerce." Second, the Court accepted Congress's judgment as to those conditions that "affected" commerce. Third, the Tenth Amendment (hitherto the guardian of state prerogatives) furnished no independent limitation on Congress, even if the national statute interfered with matters historically within the purview of the states. Was there now any commerce-related activity beyond the reach of congressional power?

**Expanded Applications.** Decisions sustaining the 1964 Civil Rights Act illustrate the post–New Deal conception of the commerce to which congressional power extends. **Heart of Atlanta Motel v. United States** and **Katzenbach v. McClung** (1964) approved the application of Title II of the act barring racial discrimination not only to a private establishment serving interstate travelers (*Atlanta Motel*) but also to Ollie's Barbeque, a restaurant in Birmingham that served mainly a local clientele and purchased all of its supplies in-state (*McClung*). Ollie's was nonetheless deemed part of interstate commerce because half of the food it served had previously "moved" in commerce between the states. "The absence of direct evidence connecting discriminatory restaurant service with the flow of interstate food," observed Justice Clark, "is not . . . a crucial matter." The significance of such deference to Congress became manifest in *Daniel* v. *Paul* (1969), where a recreational facility near Little Rock, Arkansas, was found to be a "public accommodation" affecting commerce and within the reach of the 1964 law. The entire 232-acre establishment with its golf, swimming, dancing, and other activities was held to be within the act's provisions because three of the four items sold at the snack bar had originated outside of the state.

**Revolution or Counterrevolution?** So far as the commerce power is concerned, the Constitutional Revolution of 1937 thus appears as much as a counterrevolution as a revolution. From 1890 to 1936, when the Court began to develop a series of implied limitations on the exercise of the commerce power, it was not doing so in response to any rule of law announced by the Marshall or Taney Court. Marshall, although not denying the power of the states to regulate certain local matters, defined the commerce power broadly and preferred political, not judicial, checks on its exercise. Taney's Court, although more generous to local regulation in the absence of federal legislation, made it clear that Congress's power was broad and to the extent exercised would be upheld, and that the Court would undertake to determine the validity of state acts by measuring the need for uniform regulation in each case. The Court, in other words, would play the difficult role of ascertaining the limits of state power over commerce until Congress should act. In the period 1890–1936, the Court inverted the role of the Taney Court. At one time it would use the commerce power to frustrate state acts where they interfered with national commerce; but at other times it would imply limits on the national power to regulate certain aspects of commerce by evolving rules denying to mining, agriculture, and manufacturing any relationship with interstate commerce.

Yet as generous as the Marshall and Taney courts were in construing Congress's power under the commerce clause, it is also important to remember that Congress made little use of that authority prior to the Civil War. Judicial limitations on the national commerce power emerged after Congress began to make full use of the authority it presumably had.

If one is inclined to protest that the Founders never dreamed of AAA, FLSA, and NLRA, the answer is that of course they did not. This argument, it might be pointed out, could be used to reject the great bulk of modern state and national regulatory acts. But as Marshall said in *McCulloch* v. *Maryland* (1819), "This provision [necessary and proper clause] is made in a constitution, intended to endure for ages to come, and consequently, to be adapted to the various *crises* of human affairs." In the light of this philosophy, the growth of national power through the commerce clause can be described as the necessary response by government to economic and social change. So when those adversely affected by regulation clamor "back to the Constitution," the question becomes, back to which constitution—that of 1787, as interpreted by John Marshall, or that of 1890–1936?

## A RETURN TO LIMITATIONS

In 1995, for the first time since 1936, the Court struck down an act of Congress on commerce grounds alone. Falling victim in **United States v. Lopez** was the Gun-Free School Zones Act of 1990, which made it a federal crime to possess a firearm within 1,000 feet of a school. Although the government's brief argued that the presence of guns in or near schools adversely affected education, among other things, and that in turn adversely affected interstate commerce, Congress had not made this link to commerce explicit as part of its "findings" when passing the law. Commentators wondered whether *Lopez* was merely a reprimand to Congress for being legislatively sloppy. For some it was only a directive to "go back and do it right"—to substantiate connections with commerce. If so, then *Lopez* was no more than a blip. For others, *Lopez* more significantly signaled a more exacting judicial scrutiny. If the Lopez majority believed that firearms possession near a schoolhouse could in no way be sufficiently tied to commerce to bring it within the reach of congressional power, then the statute would be invalid even if Congress had tried to demonstrate a nexus between guns near schools and commerce. Judicial skepticism would take the place of the customary deference to congressional findings.

That the Court had altered its posture toward the commerce clause became plainly evident in 2000 when the same five justices of the Lopez majority struck down a provision of the Violence Against Women Act in **United States v. Morrison.** Enacted by Congress in 1994, this law allowed victims of gender-motivated violence to sue their attackers for damages in federal court. In contrast to the Gun-Free School Zones Act, the record contained ample congressional documentation describing the impact of gender-motivated violence on its victims and their families and its effects on interstate commerce. But the Court found the law constitutionally unsustainable under the commerce clause. "If accepted," maintained Chief Justice Rehnquist, attempting to prevent the commerce power from transforming itself into a general national police power, "petitioners' reasoning would allow Congress to regulate any crime as long as the nationwide, aggregated impact of that crime has substantial effects on employment, production, transit, or consumption." Because most violence has traditionally been within the jurisdiction of the states, it was the Court's duty to draw the line between what could properly be the subject of national regulation and what could not. "The Constitution requires a distinction between what is truly national and what is truly local," the chief justice declared, echoing Chief Justice Fuller's premise in the Sugar Trust Case. (Because *Morrison* involves the Fourteenth Amendment as well as the commerce clause, the case is reprinted in Chapter Four.)

With inevitable changes in the Court's membership, the coming years will demonstrate whether the commerce clause has truly entered a new era of interpretation. We shall soon see whether *Lopez* and *Morrison,* both decided by a margin of one vote, are merely minor exceptions to an otherwise practically boundless commerce power or the foundation of a new regime of limitations.

## KEY TERMS

police power
dormant commerce
  power
concurrent commerce
  doctrine
exclusive commerce
  doctrine
selective exclusiveness

Cooley doctrine
protectionism
balkanization
market participant
market regulator
direct versus indirect
  effects

national police
  power
New Deal
Court-packing plan
Constitutional Revolution
  of 1937

## QUERIES

**1.** What questions, left unresolved by *Gibbons* v. *Ogden,* did *Cooley* v. *Board of Wardens* attempt to resolve?

**2.** Concurring in *Bendix Autolite Corp.* v. *Midwesco Enterprises* (1988), Justice Scalia announced that he favored abandoning the "balancing" involved in dormant commerce clause cases,

> leav[ing] essentially legislative judgments to Congress. . . . [A] state statute is invalid under the Commerce Clause if, and only if, it accords discriminatory treatment to interstate commerce in a respect not required to achieve a lawful state purpose. When such a validating purpose exists, it is for Congress and not us to determine it is not significant enough to justify the burden on [commerce].

What would be the probable effect on national commerce were the Court to adopt Scalia's view?

**3.** In the Court-packing struggle of 1937, both sides won; both sides lost. Explain.

**4.** Consider these sentences from Justice Kennedy's concurring opinion in *United States* v. *Lopez*.

> Congress can regulate in the commercial sphere on the assumption that we have a single market and a unified purpose to build a stable national economy. . . . [U]nlike the earlier cases to come before the Court here neither the actors nor their conduct have a commercial character, and neither the purposes nor the design of the statute have an evident commercial nexus. . . . In a sense any conduct in this interdependent world of ours has an ultimate commercial origin or consequence, but we have not yet said the commerce power may reach so far.

Does Kennedy accurately point to the gravamen or defect in the Gun Free School Zones Act that led the Court to decide as it did? May the same assessment fairly be applied to the Violence Against Women Act at issue in *United States* v. *Morrison?*

## SELECTED READINGS

BENSON, PAUL R., JR. *The Supreme Court and the Commerce Clause, 1937–1970.* Cambridge, Mass.: Dunellen, 1970.

CORTNER, RICHARD C. *The Arizona Train Limit Case.* Tucson: University of Arizona Press, 1970.

————. *Civil Rights and Public Accommodations: The Heart of Atlanta and McClung Cases.* Lawrence: University Press of Kansas, 2001.

————. *The Jones & Laughlin Case.* New York: Knopf, 1970.

CORWIN, EDWARD S. *The Commerce Power Versus States Rights.* Princeton, N.J.: Princeton University Press, 1936.

————. *Constitutional Revolution, Ltd.* Westport, Conn.: Greenwood, 1977 (reissue of the 1941 edition).

CUSHMAN, BARRY. *Rethinking the New Deal Court.* New York: Oxford University Press, 1998.

FARBER, DANIEL A. "State Regulation and the Dormant Commerce Clause." 3 *Constitutional Commentary* 395 (1986).

FRANKFURTER, FELIX. *The Commerce Clause Under Marshall, Taney and Waite.* Chapel Hill: University of North Carolina Press, 1937.

*Reorganization of the Federal Judiciary.* Hearings by the Senate Judiciary Committee on S. 1392, March 10–April 23, 1937; 6 parts, 75th Congress, 1st session, 1937. Washington, D.C.: Government Printing Office, 1937.

STEPHENSON, DONALD GRIER, JR. *Campaigns and the Court: The United States Supreme Court in Presidential Elections,* Chapter 6. New York: Columbia University Press, 1999.

WHITE, G. EDWARD. *The Constitution and the New Deal.* Cambridge, Mass.: Harvard University Press, 2000.

WOOD, STEPHEN B. *Constitutional Politics in the Progressive Era: Child Labor and the Law.* Chicago: University of Chicago Press, 1968.

# I. DEFINING THE COMMERCE POWER

## *Gibbons* v. *Ogden*
## 22 U.S. (9 Wheat.) 1, 6 L.Ed. 23 (1824)

http://supct.law.cornell.edu/supct/cases/name.htm#Case_Name-F-G

In 1811 the state of New York granted the fifth in a series of monopolies to jurist and diplomat Robert Livingston and steamboat pioneer Robert Fulton to operate steamboats on the waterways of New York. The monopoly required all persons navigating by steam in New York to obtain a license from Livingston and Fulton, their heirs or assigns. Any unlicensed vessel, "together with the engine, tackle and apparel thereof," would be forfeited to them. Ex-governor Aaron Ogden of New Jersey operated a licensed steam-powered ferry between New York and New Jersey. In 1818 his former associate Thomas Gibbons, who held a "coasting license" under a 1793 act of Congress but no license under the New York monopoly, began to run boats along the same route in competition with Ogden. Ogden brought action in the New York Court of Chancery in 1819 to stop his rival. Chancellor James Kent ruled for Ogden, holding that the congressional statute was not in conflict with the New York monopoly and conferred no right on Gibbons to navigate on New York waters. The New York Court of Errors affirmed in 1820, and Gibbons appealed. This dispute gave rise to the first important case in the Supreme Court concerning the meaning of the commerce clause. Writing a century after the decision, Albert J. Beveridge found that Marshall's opinion "has done more to knit the American people into an indivisible Nation than any other one force in our history, excepting only war." Majority: Marshall, Duvall, Johnson, Story, Todd, Washington. Not participating: Thompson.

**MARSHALL, CH. J., delivered the opinion of the Court. . . .**

This instrument [the Constitution] contains an enumeration of powers expressly granted by the people to their government. It has been said, that these powers ought to be construed strictly. But why ought they to be so construed? Is there one sentence in the constitution which gives countenance to this rule? In the last of the enumerated powers, that which grants, expressly, the means for carrying all others into execution, congress is authorized "to make all laws which shall be necessary and proper" for the purpose. But this limitation on the means which may be used, is not extended to the powers which are conferred; nor is there one sentence in the constitution, which has been pointed out by the gentlemen of the bar, or which we have been able to discern, that prescribes this rule. We do not, therefore, think ourselves justified in adopting it. What do gentlemen mean, by a strict construction? If they contend only against that enlarged construction, which would extend words beyond their natural and obvious import, we might question the application of the term, but should not controvert the principle. If they contend for that narrow construction which, in support of some theory not to be found in the constitution, would deny to the government those powers which the words of the grant, as usually understood, import, and which are consistent with the general views and objects of the instrument—for that narrow construction, which would cripple the government, and render it unequal to the objects for which it is declared to be instituted, and to which the powers given, as fairly understood, render it competent—then we cannot perceive the propriety of this strict construction, nor adopt it as the rule by which the constitution is to be expounded. As men whose intentions require no concealment, generally employ the words which most directly and aptly express the ideas they intend to convey, the enlightened patriots who framed our constitution, and the people who adopted it, must be understood to have employed words in their natural sense, and to have intended what they have said. If, from the imperfection of human language, there should be serious doubts respecting the extent of any given power, it is a well settled rule, that the objects for which it was given, especially, when those objects are expressed in the instrument itself, should have great influence in the construction. . . . We know of no rule for construing the extent of such powers, other than is given by the language of the instrument which confers them, taken in connection with the purposes for which they were conferred.

The words are: "Congress shall have power to regulate commerce with foreign nations, and among the several states, and with the Indian tribes." The subject to be regulated is commerce; and our constitution being, as was aptly said at the bar, one of enumeration, and not of definition, to ascertain the extent of the power, it becomes necessary to settle the meaning of the word. The counsel for the appellee would limit it to traffic, to buying and selling, or the interchange of commodities, and do not admit that it comprehends navigation. This would restrict a general term, applicable to many objects, to one of its significations. Commerce, undoubtedly, is traffic, but it is something more—it is intercourse. It describes the commercial intercourse between nations, and parts of nations, in all its branches, and is regulated by prescribing rules for carrying on that intercourse. The mind can scarcely conceive a system for regulating commerce between nations which shall exclude all laws concerning navigation, which shall be silent on the admission of the vessels of the one nation into the ports of the other, and confined to prescribing rules for the conduct of individuals, in the actual employment of buying and selling or of barter. If commerce does not include navigation, the government of the Union has no direct power over that subject, and can make no law prescribing what shall constitute American vessels, or requiring that they shall be navi-

gated by American seamen. Yet this power has been exercised from the commencement of the government, has been exercised with the consent of all, and has been understood by all to be a commercial regulation. All America understands, and has uniformly understood, the word "commerce," to comprehend navigation. It was so understood, and must have been so understood, when the constitution was framed. The power over commerce, including navigation, was one of the primary objects for which the people of America adopted their government, and must have been contemplated in forming it. The convention must have used the word in that sense, because all have understood it in that sense; and the attempt to restrict it comes too late. If the opinion that "commerce," as the word is used in the constitution, comprehends navigation also, requires any additional confirmation, that additional confirmation is, we think, furnished by the words of the instrument itself. It is a rule of construction, acknowledged by all, that the exceptions from a power mark its extent: for it would be absurd, as well as useless, to except from a granted power, that which was not granted—that which the words of the grant could not comprehend. If, then, there are in the constitution plain exceptions from the power over navigation, plain inhibitions to the exercise of that power in a particular way, it is a proof that those who made these exceptions, and prescribed these inhibitions, understood the power to which they applied as being granted. The 9th section of the last article declares, that "no preference shall be given, by any regulation of commerce or revenue, to the ports of one state over those of another." This clause cannot be understood as applicable to those laws only which are passed for the purposes of revenue, because it is expressly applied to commercial regulations; and the most obvious preference which can be given to one port over another, in regulating commerce, relates to navigation. But the subsequent part of the sentence is still more explicit. It is, "nor shall vessels bound to or from one state, be obliged to enter, clear or pay duties in another." These words have a direct reference to navigation. . . .

The word used in the constitution, then, comprehends, and has been always understood to comprehend, navigation within its meaning; and a power to regulate navigation, is as expressly granted, as if that term had been added to the word "commerce." To what commerce does this power extend? The constitution informs us, to commerce "with foreign nations, and among the several states, and with the Indian tribes." It has, we believe, been universally admitted, that these words comprehend every species of commercial intercourse between the United States and foreign nations. No sort of trade can be carried on between this country and any other, to which this power does not extend. It has been truly said, that commerce, as the word is used in the constitution, is a unit, every part of which is indicated by the term. . . .

But, in regulating commerce with foreign nations, the power of congress does not stop at the jurisdictional lines of the several states. It would be a very useless power, if it could not pass those lines. The commerce of the United States with foreign nations is that of the whole United States; every district has a right to participate in it. The deep streams which penetrate our country in every direction pass through the interior of almost every state in the Union, and furnish the means of exercising this right. If congress has the power to regulate it, that power must be exercised whenever the subject exists. If it exists within the states, if a foreign voyage may commence or terminate at a port within a state, then the power of congress may be exercised within a state.

This principle is, if possible, still more clear, when applied to commerce "among the several states." They either join each other, in which case they are separated by a mathematical line, or they are remote from each other, in which case other states lie between them. What is commerce "among" them; and how is it to be conducted? Can a trading expedition between two adjoining states, commence and terminate outside of each? And if the trading intercourse be between two states remote from each other, must it not commence in one, terminate in the other, and probably pass

through a third? Commerce among the states must of necessity, be commerce with the states. In the regulation of trade with the Indian tribes, the action of the law, especially, when the constitution was made, was chiefly within a state. The power of congress, then, whatever it may be, must be exercised within the territorial jurisdiction of the several states. The sense of the nation on this subject, is unequivocally manifested by the provisions made in the laws for transporting goods, by land, between Baltimore and Providence, between New York and Philadelphia, and between Philadelphia and Baltimore.

We are now arrived at the inquiry—what is this power? It is the power to regulate; that is, to prescribe the rule by which commerce is to be governed. This power, like all others vested in congress, is complete in itself, may be exercised to its utmost extent, and acknowledges no limitations, other than are prescribed in the constitution. These are expressed in plain terms, and do not affect the questions which arise in this case, or which have been discussed at the bar. If, as has always been understood, the sovereignty of congress, though limited to specified objects, is plenary as to those objects, the power over commerce with foreign nations, and among the several states, is vested in congress as absolutely as it would be in a single government, having in its constitution the same restrictions on the exercise of the power as are found in the constitution of the United States. The wisdom and the discretion of congress, their identity with the people, and the influence which their constituents possess at elections, are, in this, as in many other instances, as that, for example, of declaring war, the sole restraints on which they have relied, to secure them from its abuse. They are the restraints on which the people must often rely solely, in all representative governments. . . .

But it has been urged, with great earnestness, that although the power of congress to regulate commerce with foreign nations, and among the several states, be co-extensive with the subject itself, and have no other limits than are prescribed in the constitution, yet the states may severally exercise the same power within their respective jurisdictions. In support of this argument, it is said that they possessed it as an inseparable attribute of sovereignty before the formation of the constitution, and still retain it, except so far as they have surrendered it by that instrument; that this principle results from the nature of the government, and is secured by the tenth amendment; that an affirmative grant of power is not exclusive, unless in its own nature it be such that the continued exercise of it by the former possessor is inconsistent with the grant, and that this is not of that description. The appellant conceding these postulates, except the last, contends that full power to regulate a particular subject implies the whole power, and leaves no residuum; that a grant of the whole is incompatible with the existence of a right in another to any part of it. . . .

The grant of the power to lay and collect taxes is, like the power to regulate commerce, made in general terms, and has never been understood to interfere with the exercise of the same power by the states; and hence has been drawn an argument which has been applied to the question under consideration. But the two grants are not, it is conceived, similar in their terms or their nature. Although many of the powers formerly exercised by the states are transferred to the government of the Union, yet the state governments remain, and constitute a most important part of our system. The power of taxation is indispensable to their existence, and is a power which, in its own nature, is capable of residing in, and being exercised by, different authorities at the same time. We are accustomed to see it placed, for different purposes, in different hands. Taxation is the simple operation of taking small portions from a perpetually accumulating mass, susceptible of almost infinite division; and a power in one to take what is necessary for certain purposes, is not in its nature incompatible with a power in another to take what is necessary for other purposes. Congress is authorized to lay and collect taxes, etc., to pay the debts, and provide for the common defense and general welfare of the United States. This does not interfere with the power of the states to tax for the

support of their own governments; nor is the exercise of that power by the states an exercise of any portion of the power that is granted to the United States. In imposing taxes for state purposes, they are not doing what congress is empowered to do. Congress is not empowered to tax for those purposes which are within the exclusive province of the States. When, then, each government exercises the power of taxation, neither is exercising the power of the other. But when a state proceeds to regulate commerce with foreign nations, or among the several states, it is exercising the very power that is granted to congress, and is doing the very thing which congress is authorized to do. There is no analogy then, between the power of taxation and the power of regulating commerce. . . .

But the inspection laws are said to be regulations of commerce, and are certainly recognized in the constitution as being passed in the exercise of a power remaining with the states.

That inspection laws may have a remote and considerable influence on commerce, will not be denied; but that a power to regulate commerce is the source from which the right to pass them is derived, cannot be admitted. The object of inspection laws, is to improve the quality of articles produced by the labor of a country; to fit them for exportation; or it may be, for domestic use. They act upon the subject, before it becomes an article of foreign commerce, or of commerce among the states, and prepare it for that purpose. They form a portion of that immense mass of legislation, which embraces everything within the territory of a state, not surrendered to a general government; all of which can be most advantageously exercised by the states themselves. Inspection laws, quarantine laws, health laws of every description, as well as laws for regulating the internal commerce of a state, and those which respect turnpike roads, ferries, etc., are component parts of this mass.

No direct general power over these objects is granted to congress, and, consequently, they remain subject to state legislation. If the legislative power of the Union can reach them, it must be, where the power is expressly given for a special purpose, or is clearly incidental to some power which is expressly given. It is obvious, that the government of the Union, in the exercise of its express powers, that, for example, of regulating commerce with foreign nations and among the states, may use means that may also be employed by a state, in the exercise of its acknowledged powers; that, for example, of regulating commerce within the state. If congress licenses vessels to sail from one port to another, in the same state, the act is supposed to be, necessarily, incidental to the power expressly granted to congress, and implies no claim of a direct power to regulate the purely internal commerce of a state, or to act directly on its system of police. So, if a state, in passing laws on subjects acknowledged to be within its control, and with a view to those subjects, shall adopt a measure of the same character with one which congress may adopt, it does not derive its authority from the particular power which has been granted, but from some other which remains with the state. . . .

Since, however, in exercising the power of regulating their own purely internal affairs, whether of trading or police, the states may sometimes enact laws, the validity of which depends on their [not] interfering with, and being contrary to, an act of congress passed in pursuance of the constitution, the court will enter upon the inquiry whether the laws of New York, as expounded by the highest tribunal of that state, have, in their application to this case, come into collision with an act of congress, and deprived a citizen of a right to which that act entitles him. Should this collision exist, it will be immaterial whether those laws were passed in virtue of a concurrent power "to regulate commerce with foreign nations and among the several States," or, in virtue of a power to regulate their domestic trade and police. In one case and the other, the acts of New York must yield to the law of congress, and the decision sustaining the privilege they confer, against a right given by a law of the Union, must be erroneous. . . .

In argument, however, it has been contended, that if a law passed by a state, in the exercise of its acknowledged sovereignty comes into conflict with a law passed by con-

gress in pursuance of the constitution, they affect the subject, and each other, like equal opposing powers.

But the framers of our constitution foresaw this state of things, and provided for it, by declaring the supremacy not only of itself, but of the laws made in pursuance of it. The nullity of any act, inconsistent with the constitution, is produced by the declaration, that the constitution is the supreme law. . . . In every such case, the act of congress, or the treaty, is supreme; and the law of the state, though enacted in the exercise of powers not controverted, must yield to it. . . .

Powerful and ingenious minds, taking, as postulates, that the powers expressly granted to the government of the Union are to be contracted, by construction, into the narrowest possible compass, and that the original powers of the States are retained, if any possible construction will retain them, may, by a course of well digested, but refined and metaphysical reasoning, founded on these premises, explain away the constitution of our country, and leave it a magnificent structure indeed, to look at, but totally unfit for use. They may so entangle and perplex the understanding, as to obscure principles which were before thought quite plain, and induce doubts where, if the mind were to pursue its own course, none would be perceived. In such a case, it is peculiarly necessary to recur to safe and fundamental principles to sustain those principles, and, when sustained, to make them the tests of the arguments to be examined.

### JOHNSON, JUSTICE. . . .

Power to regulate foreign commerce, is given in the same words, and in the same breath, as it were, with that over the commerce of the states and with the Indian tribes. But the power to regulate foreign commerce is necessarily exclusive. The states are unknown to foreign nations; their sovereignty exists only with relation to each other and the general government. . . .

It is impossible, with the views which I entertain of the principle on which the commercial privileges of the people of the United

States among themselves, rests [sic], to concur in the view which this court takes of the effect of the coasting license in this cause. I do not regard it as the foundation of the right set up in behalf of the appellant. If there was any one object riding over every other in the adoption of the constitution, it was to keep the commercial intercourse among the states free from all invidious and partial restraints.

And I cannot overcome the conviction, that if the licensing act was repealed tomorrow, the rights of the appellant to a reversal of the decision complained of, would be as strong as it is under this license. . . .

This court doth further direct, order and decree, that the bill of the said Aaron Ogden be dismissed, and the same is hereby dismissed accordingly.

## *Cooley* v. *Board of Wardens*
## 53 U.S. (12 How.) 299, 13 L.Ed. 996 (1851)

### http://supct.law.cornell.edu/supct/cases/name.htm#Case_Name-C

A Pennsylvania pilotage law of 1803 required vessels leaving the port of Philadelphia to pay one-half of the standard pilotage fee for use of the Society for the Relief of Distressed and Decayed Pilots, their Widows and Children, if a local pilot were not hired. An act of the United States of 1789 declared that existing state pilotage acts should continue in effect. Cooley, the consignee of two vessels outward-bound from Philadelphia, refused to pay the fee. From adverse judgments in the state courts, he brought writs of error. Majority: Curtis, Catron, Daniel, Grier, Nelson, Taney. Dissenting: McLean, Wayne. Not participating: McKinley.

### Mr. Justice Curtis delivered the opinion of the Court. . . .

It remains to consider the objection that it [the state act] is repugnant to the third clause of the eighth section of the first article. "The Congress shall have power to regulate commerce with foreign nations and among the several states, and with the Indian tribes."

That the power to regulate commerce includes the regulation of navigation, we consider settled. . . .

The act of 1789 . . . already referred to, contains a clear legislative exposition of the Constitution by the first Congress, to the effect that the power to regulate pilots was conferred on Congress by the Constitution. . . . And a majority of the court are of opinion that a regulation of pilots is a regulation of commerce, within the grant to Congress of the commercial power, contained in the third clause of the eighth section of the first article of the Constitution.

It becomes necessary, therefore, to consider whether this law of Pennsylvania, being a regulation of commerce, is valid.

The act of Congress of the 7th of August, 1789, sec. 4, is as follows:

> That all pilots in the bays, inlets, rivers, harbors, and ports of the United States shall continue to be regulated in conformity with the existing laws of the states, respectively wherein such pilots may be, or with such laws as the states may respectively hereafter enact for the purpose, until further legislative provision shall be made by Congress.

If the law of Pennsylvania, now in question, had been in existence at the date of this act of Congress, we might hold it to have been adopted by Congress, and thus made a law of the United States, and so valid. Because this act does, in effect, give the force of an act of Congress, to the then existing state laws on this subject, so long as they should continue unrepealed by the state which enacted them.

But the law on which these actions are founded was not enacted till 1803. What effect then can be attributed to so much of the act of 1789, as declares, that pilots shall continue to be regulated in conformity "with such laws as the states may respectively hereafter enact for the purpose, until further legislative provision shall be made by Congress"?

If the states were divested of the power to legislate on this subject by the grant of the commercial power to Congress, it is plain this act could not confer upon them power thus to legislate. If the Constitution excluded the states from making any law regulating commerce, certainly Congress cannot regrant, or in any manner reconvey to the states that power. And yet this act of 1789 gives its sanction only to laws enacted by the States. This necessarily implies a constitutional power to legislate; for only a rule created by the sovereign power of a state acting in its legislative capacity, can be deemed a law enacted by a state; and if the state has so limited its sovereign power that it no longer extends to a particular subject, manifestly it cannot, in any proper sense, be said to enact law thereon. Entertaining these views, we are brought directly and unavoidably to the consideration of the question, whether the grant of the commercial power to Congress, did per se deprive the states of all power to regulate pilots. This question has never been decided by this court, nor, in our judgment, has any case depending upon all the considerations which must govern this one, come before this court. The grant of commercial power to Congress does not contain any terms which expressly exclude the states from exercising an authority over its subject matter. If they are excluded, it must be because the nature of the power, thus granted to Congress, requires that a similar authority should not exist in the states. . . .

Now the power to regulate commerce embraces a vast field, containing not only many, but exceedingly various subjects, quite unlike in their nature; some imperatively demanding a single uniform rule, operating equally on the commerce of the United States in every port; and some, like the subject now in question, as imperatively demanding that diversity which alone can meet the local necessities of navigation.

Either absolutely to affirm, or deny that the nature of this power requires exclusive legislation by Congress, is to lose sight of the nature of the subjects of this power, and to assert concerning all of them, what is really applicable but to a part. Whatever subjects of this power are in their nature national, or admit only of one uniform system, or plan of regulation, may justly be said to be of such a nature as to require exclusive legislation by Congress. That this cannot be affirmed of laws for the regulation of pilots and pilotage is plain. The act of 1789 contains a clear and authoritative declaration by the first Congress that the nature of this subject is such that until Congress should find it necessary to exert its power, it should be left to the legislation of the states; that it is local and not national; that it is likely to be the best provided for, not by one system, or plan or regulation but by as many as the legislative discretion of the several states should deem applicable to the local peculiarities of the ports within their limits.

Viewed in this light, so much of this act of 1789 as declares that pilots shall continue to be regulated "by such laws as the states may respectively hereafter enact for that purpose," instead of being held to be inoperative, as an attempt to confer on the states a power to legislate, of which the Constitution had deprived them, is allowed an appropriate and important signification. It manifests the understanding of Congress, at the outset of the government, that the nature of this subject is not such as to require its exclusive legislation. . . .

It is the opinion of a majority of the court that the mere grant to Congress of the power to regulate commerce did not deprive the states of power to regulate pilots, and that although Congress has legislated on this subject, its legislation manifests an intention, with a single exception not to regulate this subject, but to leave its regulation to the several states.

To these precise questions, which are all we are called on to decide, this opinion must be understood to be confined. It does not extend to the question what other subjects, under the commercial power, are within the exclusive control of Congress, or may be regulated by the states in the absence of all congressional legislation; nor to the general question, how far any regulation of a subject by Congress, may be deemed to operate as an exclusion of all legislation by the states upon the same subject. . . . We go no further. . . .

We are of opinion that this state law was enacted by virtue of a power, residing in the state to legislate; that it is not in conflict with any law of Congress; that it does not interfere with any system which Congress has established by making regulations, or by intentionally leaving individuals to their own unrestricted action: that this law is therefore valid, and the judgment of the Supreme Court of Pennsylvania in each case must be affirmed.

MR. JUSTICE DANIEL, concurring in the judgment . . . [omitted].

MR. JUSTICE MCLEAN, dissenting . . . [omitted].

MR. JUSTICE WAYNE dissented [without opinion].

## II. STATES AND THE COMMERCE POWER

### Southern Pacific Co. v. Arizona
### 325 U.S. 761, 65 S.Ct. 1515, 89 L.Ed. 1915 (1945)

http://laws.findlaw.com/us/325/761.html

The Arizona Train Limit Law of 1912 made it unlawful to operate within the state a railroad train of more than 14 passenger or 70 freight cars. In 1940, when the state sought to collect penalties for violations of the act, the appellant company objected, claiming that the act was unconstitutional. The Supreme Court of Arizona upheld the constitutionality of the law, and the company appealed. Majority: Stone, Frankfurter, Jackson, Murphy, Reed, Roberts, Rutledge. Dissenting: Black, Douglas.

**MR. CHIEF JUSTICE STONE delivered the opinion of the Court. . . .**

We are . . . brought to appellant's contention, that the state statute contravenes the commerce clause of the Federal Constitution.

Although the commerce clause conferred on the national government power to regulate commerce, its possession of the power does not exclude all state power of regulation. Ever since *Willson* v. *Black Bird Creek Marsh Co.* and *Cooley* v. *Wardens* . . . it has been recognized that, in the absence of conflicting legislation by Congress, there is a residuum of power in the state to make laws governing matters of local concern which nevertheless in some measure affect interstate commerce or even, to some extent, regulate it. . . . Thus the states may regulate matters which, because of their number and diversity, may never be adequately dealt with by Congress. . . . When the regulation of matters of local concern is local in character and effect, and its impact on the national commerce does not seriously interfere with its operation, and the consequent incentive to deal with them nationally is slight, such regulation has been generally held to be within state authority. . . .

But ever since *Gibbons* v. *Ogden* . . . the states have not been deemed to have authority to impede substantially the free flow of commerce from state to state, or to regulate those phases of the national commerce which, because of the need of national uniformity, demand that their regulation, if any, be prescribed by a single authority. . . .

For a hundred years it has been accepted constitutional doctrine that the commerce clause, without the aid of Congressional legislation, thus affords some protection from state legislation inimical to the national commerce, and that in such cases, where Congress has not acted, this Court, and not the state legislature, is under the commerce clause the final arbiter of the competing demands of state and national interests. . . .

Congress has undoubted power to redefine the distribution of power over interstate commerce. It may either permit the states to regulate the commerce in a manner which would otherwise not be permissible . . . or exclude state regulation even of matters of peculiarly local concern which nevertheless affect interstate commerce. . . .

But in general Congress has left it to the courts to formulate the rules thus interpreting the commerce clause in its application, doubtless because it has appreciated the destructive consequences to the commerce of the nation if their protection were withdrawn and has been aware that in their application state laws will not be invalidated without the support of relevant factual material which will "afford a sure basis" for an informed judgment. . . . Hence the matters for ultimate determination here are the nature and extent of the burden which the state regulation of interstate trains, adopted as a safety measure, imposes on interstate commerce, and whether the relative weights of the state and national interests involved are such as to make inapplicable the rule, generally observed, that the free flow of interstate commerce and its freedom from local restraints in matters requiring uniformity of regulation are interests safeguarded by the commerce clause from state interference. . . .

The findings show that the operation of long trains, that is trains of more than fourteen passenger and more than seventy freight cars, is standard practice over the main lines of the railroads of the United States, and that, if the length of trains is to be regulated at all, national

uniformity in the regulation adopted, such as only Congress can prescribe, is practically indispensable to the operation of an efficient and economical national railway system. . . .

The unchallenged findings leave no doubt that the Arizona Train Limit Law imposes a serious burden on the interstate commerce conducted by appellant. It materially impedes the movement of appellant's interstate trains through that state and interposes a substantial obstruction to the national policy proclaimed by Congress, to promote adequate, economical and efficient railway transportation service. . . . Enforcement of the law in Arizona, while train lengths remain unregulated or are regulated by varying standards in other states, must inevitably result in an impairment of uniformity of efficient railroad operation because the railroads are subjected to regulation which is not uniform in its application. Compliance with a state statute limiting train lengths requires interstate trains of a length lawful in other states to be broken up and reconstituted as they enter each state according as it may impose varying limitations upon train lengths. The alternative is for the carrier to conform to the lowest train limit restriction of any of the states through which its trains pass, whose laws thus control the carriers' operations both within and without the regulating state. . . .

The trial court found that the Arizona law had no reasonable relation to safety, and made train operation more dangerous. Examination of the evidence and the detailed findings makes it clear that this conclusion was rested on facts found which indicate that such increased danger of accident and personal injury as may result from the greater length of trains is more than offset by the increase in the number of accidents resulting from the larger number of trains when train lengths are reduced. In considering the effect of the statute as a safety measure, therefore, the factor of controlling significance for present purposes is not whether there is basis for the conclusion of the Arizona Supreme Court that the increase in length of trains beyond the statutory maximum has an adverse effect upon safety of operation. The decisive question is whether in the circumstances the total effect of the law as a safety measure in reducing accidents and casualties is so slight or problematical as not to outweigh the national interest in keeping interstate commerce free from interferences which seriously impede it and subject it to local regulation which does not have a uniform effect on the interstate train journey which it interrupts. . . .

We think, as the trial court found, that the Arizona Train Limit Law, viewed as a safety measure, affords at most slight and dubious advantage, if any, over unregulated train lengths, because it results in an increase in the number of trains and train operations and the consequent increase in train accidents of a character generally more severe than those due to slack action. Its undoubted effect on the commerce is the regulation, without securing uniformity, of the length of trains operated in interstate commerce, which lack is itself a primary cause of preventing the free flow of commerce by delaying it and by substantially increasing its cost and impairing its efficiency. In these respects the case differs from those where a state, by regulatory measures affecting the commerce, has removed or reduced safety hazards without substantial interference with the interstate movement of trains. . . .

Appellees especially rely on the full train crew cases, . . . and also on *South Carolina* v. *Barnwell Bros.,* as supporting the state's authority to regulate the length of interstate trains. While the full train crew laws undoubtedly placed an added financial burden on the railroads in order to serve a local interest, they did not obstruct interstate transportation or seriously impede it. . . .

*Barnwell Bros.* was concerned with the power of the state to regulate the weight and width of motor cars passing interstate over its highways, a legislative field over which the state has a far more extensive control than over interstate railroads. In that case . . . we were at pains to point out that there are few subjects of state regulation affecting interstate commerce which are so peculiarly of local concern as is the use of the state's highways. Unlike the railroads local highways are built, owned and maintained by the state or its municipal subdivisions. The state is responsible for their safe and economical administration. Regulations affecting the safety of their use must be applied alike to intrastate and interstate traffic. The fact that they affect alike shippers in interstate and intrastate commerce in great numbers, within as well as without the state, is a safeguard against regulatory abuses. Their regulation is akin to quarantine measures, game laws, and like local regulations of rivers, harbors, piers, and docks, with respect to which the state has exceptional scope for the exercise of its regulatory power, and which, Congress not acting, have been sustained even though they materially interfere with interstate commerce.

The contrast between the present regulation and the full train crew laws in point of their effects on the commerce, and the like contrast with the highway safety regulations, in point of the nature of the subject of regulation and the state's interest in it, illustrate and emphasize the considerations which enter into a determination of the relative weights of state and national interests where state regulation affecting commerce is attempted. Here examination of all the relevant factors makes it plain that the state interest is outweighed by the interest of the Nation in an adequate, economical and efficient railway transportation service, which must prevail.

*Reversed.*

Mr. Justice Rutledge concurs in the result.

### Mr. Justice Black, dissenting. . . .

I think that legislatures, to the exclusion of courts, have the constitutional power to enact laws limiting train lengths, for the purpose of reducing injuries brought about by "slack movements." Their power is not less because a requirement of short trains might increase grade crossing accidents. This latter fact raises an entirely different element of danger which is itself subject to legislative regulation. For legislatures may, if necessary, require railroads to take appropriate steps to reduce the likelihood of injuries at grade crossings. . . . And the fact that grade-crossing improvements may be expensive is no sufficient reason to say that an unconstitutional "burden" is put upon a railroad even though it be an interstate road. . . .

There have been many sharp divisions of this Court concerning its authority, in the absence of congressional enactment, to invalidate state laws as violating the Commerce Clause. . . . That discussion need not be renewed here, because even the broadest exponents of judicial power in this field have not heretofore expressed doubt as to a state's power, absent a paramount congressional declaration, to regulate interstate trains in the interest of safety. . . .

This record in its entirety leaves me with no doubt whatever that many employees have been seriously injured and killed in the past, and that many more are likely to be so in the future, because of "slack movement" in trains. Everyday knowledge as well as direct evidence presented at the various hearings, substantiates the report of the Senate Committee that danger from slack movement is greater in long trains than in short trains. It may be that offsetting dangers are possible in the operation of short trains. The balancing of these probabilities, however, is not in my judgment a matter for judicial determination, but one which calls for legislative consideration. Representatives elected by the people to make their laws, rather than judges appointed to interpret those laws, can best determine the policies which govern the people. That at least is the basic principle on which our democratic society rests. I would affirm the judgment of the Supreme Court of Arizona.

MR. JUSTICE DOUGLAS, dissenting . . . [omitted].

## Philadelphia v. New Jersey
## 437 U.S. 617, 98 S.Ct. 2531, 57 L.Ed. 2d 475 (1978)
## http://laws.findlaw.com/us/437/617.html

A 1974 New Jersey law (referred to in the following opinions as chapter 363) provided, "No person shall bring into this State any solid or liquid waste which originated or was collected outside the territorial limits of the State, except garbage to be fed to swine in the State . . . until the commissioner [of the state Department of Environmental Protection] shall determine that such action can be permitted without endangering the public health, safety and welfare and has promulgated regulations permitting and regulating the treatment and disposal of such waste in this State." As authorized, the commissioner issued regulations permitting four categories of waste to enter the state, mainly for recycling and reprocessing. The city of Philadelphia, other out-of-state cities, and private landfills—all affected by the statute—challenged the law mainly on commerce clause grounds. Majority: Stewart, Blackmun, Brennan, Marshall, Powell, Stevens, White. Dissenting: Rehnquist, Burger.

**MR. JUSTICE STEWART delivered the opinion of the Court. . . .**

The crucial inquiry . . . must be directed to determining whether ch. 363 is basically a protectionist measure, or whether it can fairly be viewed as a law directed to legitimate local concerns, with effects upon interstate commerce that are only incidental.

The purpose of ch. 363 is set out in the statute itself as follows:

The Legislature finds and determines that . . . the volume of solid and liquid waste continues to rapidly increase, that the treatment and disposal of these wastes continues to pose an even greater threat to the quality of the environment of New Jersey, that the available and appropriate landfill sites within the State are being diminished, that the environment continues to be threatened by the treatment and disposal of waste which originated or was collected outside the State and that the public health, safety and welfare require that the treatment and disposal within this State of all wastes generated outside of the State be prohibited.

The New Jersey Supreme Court accepted this statement of the state legislature's purpose. The state court additionally found that New Jersey's existing landfill sites will be exhausted within a few years; that to go on using these sites or to develop new ones will take a heavy environmental toll, both from pollution and from loss of scarce open lands; that new techniques to divert waste from landfills to other methods of disposal and resource recovery processes are under development, but that these changes will require time; and finally, that "the extension of the lifespan of existing landfills, resulting from the exclusion of out-of-state waste, may be of crucial importance in preventing further virgin wetlands or other undeveloped lands from being devoted to landfill purposes." Based on these findings, the court concluded that ch. 363 was designed to protect not the State's economy, but its environment, and that its substantial benefits outweigh its "slight" burden on interstate commerce.

The appellants strenuously contend that ch. 363, "while outwardly cloaked 'in the currently fashionable garb of environmental protection' . . . is actually no more than a legislative effort to suppress competition and stabilize the cost of solid waste disposal for New Jersey residents. . . ."

This dispute about ultimate legislative purpose need not be resolved, because its resolution would not be relevant to the constitutional issue to be decided in this case. Contrary to the evident assumption of the state court and the parties, the evil of protectionism can reside in legislative means as well as legislative ends. Thus, it does not matter

whether the ultimate aim of ch. 363 is to reduce the waste disposal costs of New Jersey residents or to save remaining open lands from pollution, for we assume New Jersey has every right to protect its residents' pocketbooks as well as their environment. And it may be assumed as well that New Jersey may pursue those ends by slowing the flow of all waste into the State's remaining landfills, even though interstate commerce may incidentally be affected. But whatever New Jersey's ultimate purpose, it may not be accomplished by discriminating against articles of commerce coming from outside the State unless there is some reason, apart from their origin, to treat them differently. Both on its face and in its plain effect, ch. 363 violates this principle of nondiscrimination. . . .

The New Jersey law at issue in this case falls squarely within the area that the Commerce Clause puts off-limits to state regulation. On its face, it imposes on out-of-state commercial interests the full burden of conserving the State's remaining landfill space. It is true that in our previous cases the scarce natural resource was itself the article of commerce, whereas here the scarce resource and the article of commerce are distinct. But that difference is without consequence. In both instances, the State has overtly moved to slow or freeze the flow of commerce for protectionist reasons. It does not matter that the State has shut the article of commerce inside the State in one case and outside the State in the other. What is crucial is the attempt by one State to isolate itself from a problem common to many by erecting a barrier against the movement of interstate trade. . . .

It is true that certain quarantine laws have not been considered forbidden protectionist measures, even though they were directed against out-of-state commerce. . . . But those quarantine laws banned the importation of articles such as diseased livestock that required destruction as soon as possible because their very movement risked contagion and other evils. Those laws thus did not discriminate against interstate commerce as such, but simply prevented traffic in noxious articles, whatever their origin.

The New Jersey statute is not such a quarantine law. There has been no claim here that the very movement of waste into or through New Jersey endangers health, or that waste must be disposed of as soon and as close to its point of generation as possible. The harms caused by waste are said to arise after its disposal in landfill sites, and at that point, as New Jersey concedes, there is no basis to distinguish out-of-state waste from domestic waste. If one is inherently harmful, so is the other. Yet New Jersey has banned the former while leaving its landfill sites open to the latter. The New Jersey law blocks the importation of waste in an obvious effort to saddle those outside the State with the entire burden of slowing the flow of refuse into New Jersey's remaining landfill sites. That legislative effort is clearly impermissible under the Commerce Clause of the Constitution.

Today, cities in Pennsylvania and New York find it expedient or necessary to send their waste into New Jersey for disposal, and New Jersey claims the right to close its borders to such traffic. Tomorrow, cities in New Jersey may find it expedient or necessary to send their waste into Pennsylvania or New York for disposal, and those States might then claim the right to close their borders. The Commerce Clause will protect New Jersey in the future, just as it protects her neighbors now, from efforts by one State to isolate itself in the stream of interstate commerce from a problem shared by all.

*The judgment is reversed.*

### Mr. Justice Rehnquist, with whom The Chief Justice joins, dissenting. . . .

The Court recognizes that States can prohibit the importation of items "which, on account of their existing condition, would bring in and spread disease, pestilence, and death, such as rags or other substances infected with the germs of yellow fever or the virus of smallpox, or cattle or meat or other provisions that are diseased or decayed, or otherwise, from their condition and quality, unfit for human use or consumption."

In my opinion, these cases are dispositive of the present one. Under them, New Jersey may require germ-infected rags or diseased meat to be disposed of as best as possible within the State, but at the same time prohibit the importation of such items for disposal at the facilities that are set up within New Jersey for disposal of such material generated within the State. The physical fact of life that New Jersey must somehow dispose of its own noxious items does not mean that it must serve as a depository for those of every other State. Similarly, New Jersey should be free under our past precedents to prohibit the importation of solid waste because of the health and safety problems that such waste poses to its citizens. The fact that New Jersey continues to, and indeed must continue to, dispose of its own solid waste does not mean that New Jersey may not prohibit the importation of even more solid waste into the State. I simply see no way to distinguish solid waste, on the record of this case, from germ-infected rags, diseased meat, and other noxious items.

The Court's effort to distinguish these prior cases is unconvincing. It first asserts that the quarantine laws which have previously been upheld "ban the importation of articles such as diseased livestock that required destruction as soon as possible because their very movement risked contagion and other evils." According to the Court, the New Jersey law is distinguishable from these other laws, and invalid, because the concern of New Jersey is not with the movement of solid waste but of the present inability to safely dispose of it once it reaches its destination. But I think it far from clear that the State's law has as limited a focus as the Court imputes to it: Solid waste which is a health hazard when it reaches its destination may in all likelihood be an equally great health hazard in transit. . . .

Second, the Court implies that the challenged laws must be invalidated because New Jersey has left its landfills open to domestic waste. But, as the Court notes, this Court has repeatedly upheld quarantine laws "even though they appear to single out interstate commerce for special treatment." The fact that

New Jersey has left its landfill sites open for domestic waste does not, of course, mean that solid waste is not innately harmful. Nor does it mean that New Jersey prohibits importation of solid waste for reasons other than the health and safety of its population. New Jersey must out of sheer necessity treat and dispose of its solid waste in some fashion, just as it must treat New Jersey cattle suffering from hoof-and-mouth disease. It does not follow that New Jersey must, under the Commerce Clause, accept solid waste or diseased cattle from outside its borders and thereby exacerbate its problems. . . .

## Reeves, Inc. v. Stake
### 447 U.S. 429, 100 S.Ct. 2271, 65 L.Ed. 2d 244 (1980)
http://laws.findlaw.com/us/447/429.html

For many years the state of South Dakota has operated a cement plant. Between 1970 and 1977, some 40 percent of the plant's production was shipped to buyers outside the state. Reeves, Inc., a ready-mix concrete distributor in Wyoming, from 1958 until 1978 obtained 95 percent of its cement from the state-owned plant in South Dakota. In 1978, various difficulties at the cement plant forced a cut in production. The State Cement Commission chose to supply all South Dakota customers first and to honor other contract commitments. Being out of state and lacking a long-term contract, Reeves was unable to purchase any more cement and was obliged to reduce its own concrete production by 76 percent when no other adequate suppliers could be found. Reeves then sued the commission in district court, which "reasoned that South Dakota's 'hoarding' was inimical to the national free market envisioned by the Commerce Clause." The Court of Appeals for the Eighth Circuit reversed. Justice Blackmun's majority opinion and Justice Powell's dissent, reprinted below, refer to *Hughes* v. *Alexandria Scrap Corp.* (1976). In that case Maryland offered a bounty for every Maryland-titled junk car converted into scrap. Documentation requirements were more exacting for out-of-state processors, making it less profitable for suppliers to transfer vehicles outside Maryland. Thus, in-state processors of junk cars were favored over those out of state. Upholding the policy, the Court declared, "Nothing in the purposes animating the Commerce Clause prohibits a State, in the absence of congressional action, from participating in the market and exercising the right to favor its own citizens over others." In *Alexandria Scrap,* Justice Powell wrote the opinion of the Court, and Justices Brennan, White, and Marshall dissented. Majority in *Reeves:* Blackmun, Burger, Marshall, Rehnquist, Stewart. Dissenting: Powell, Brennan, Stevens, White.

**MR. JUSTICE BLACKMUN delivered the opinion of the Court. . . .**

The basic distinction drawn in *Alexandria Scrap* between States as market participants and States as market regulators makes good sense and sound law. As that case explains, the Commerce Clause responds principally to state taxes and regulatory measures impeding free private trade in the national marketplace. . . . There is no indication of a constitutional plan to limit the ability of the States themselves to operate freely in the free market. . . .

Moreover, state proprietary activities may be, and often are, burdened with the same restrictions imposed on private market participants. Evenhandedness suggests that, when acting as proprietors, States should similarly share existing freedoms from federal constraints, including the inherent limits of the Commerce Clause. . . . Finally, as this case illustrates, the competing considerations in cases involving state proprietary action often will be subtle, complex, politically charged, and difficult to assess under traditional Commerce Clause analysis. Given these factors, *Alexandria Scrap* wisely recognizes that, as a rule, the adjustment of interests in this context is a task better suited for Congress than this Court.

South Dakota, as a seller of cement, unquestionably fits the "market participant" label more comfortably than a State acting to subsidize local scrap processors. Thus, the general rule of *Alexandria Scrap* plainly applies here. . . .

In finding a Commerce Clause violation, the District Court emphasized "that the Commission . . . made an election to become part of the interstate commerce system." . . . The gist of this reasoning, repeated by petitioner here, is that one good turn deserves another. Having long exploited the interstate market, South Dakota should not be permitted to withdraw from it when a shortage arises. This argument is not persuasive. It is somewhat self-serving to say that South Dakota has "exploited" the interstate market. An equally fair characterization is that neighboring States have long benefited from South Dakota's foresight and industry. . . .

Our rejection of petitioner's market-exploitation theory fundamentally refocuses analysis. It means that to reverse we would have to void a South Dakota "residents only" policy even if it had been enforced from the plant's very first days. Such a holding, however, would interfere significantly with a State's ability to structure relations exclusively with its own citizens. It would also threaten the future fashioning of effective and creative programs for solving local problems and distributing government largesse. . . . A healthy regard for federalism and good government renders us reluctant to risk these results. . . .

Undaunted by these considerations, petitioner advances four more arguments for reversal:

First, petitioner protests that South Dakota's preference for its residents responds solely to the "non-governmental objective" of protectionism. . . . Therefore, petitioner argues the policy is *per se* invalid. . . .

We find the label "protectionism" of little help in this context. The State's refusal to sell to buyers other than South Dakotans is "protectionist" only in the sense that it limits benefits generated by a state program to those who fund the state treasury and whom the State was created to serve. Petitioner's argument apparently also would characterize as "protectionist" rules restricting to state residents the enjoyment of state educational institutions, energy generated by a state-run plant, police and fire protection, and agricultural improvement and business development programs. Such policies, while perhaps "protectionist" in a loose sense, reflect the essential and patently unobjectionable purpose of state government—to serve the citizens of the State.

Second, petitioner echoes the District Court's warning.

> If a state in this union, were allowed to hoard its commodities or resources for the use of their own residents only, a drastic situation might evolve. For example, Pennsylvania or Wyoming might keep their coal, the northwest its timber, and the mining states their minerals. The result being that embargo may be retaliated by embargo and commerce would be halted at state lines. . . .

This argument, although rooted in the core purpose of the Commerce Clause, does not fit the present facts. Cement is not a natural resource, like coal, timber, wild game, or minerals. . . . It is the end-product of a complex process whereby a costly physical plant and human labor act on raw materials. South Dakota has not sought to limit access to the State's limestone or other materials used to make cement. Nor has it restricted the ability of private firms or sister States to set up plants within its borders. . . .

Third, it is suggested that the South Dakota program is infirm because it places South Dakota suppliers of ready-mix concrete at a competitive advantage in the out-of-state market; Wyoming suppliers, such as petitioner, have little chance against South Dakota suppliers who can purchase cement from the State's plant and freely sell beyond South Dakota's borders.

The force of this argument is seriously diminished, if not eliminated, by several considerations. The argument necessarily implies that the South Dakota scheme would be unobjectionable if sales in other States were totally barred. It therefore proves too much, for it would tolerate even a greater measure of protectionism and stifling of interstate commerce than the challenged system allows. . . . Finally, the competitive plight of out-of-state ready-mix suppliers cannot be laid solely at the feet of South Dakota. It is attributable as well to their own States' not providing or attracting alternative sources of supply and to the suppliers' own failure to guard against shortages by executing long-term supply contracts with the South Dakota plant.

In its last argument, petitioner urges that, had South Dakota not acted, free market forces would have generated an appropriate level of supply at free market prices for all buyers in the region. Having replaced free market forces, South Dakota should be forced to replicate how the free market would have operated under prevailing conditions.

This argument appears to us to be simplistic and speculative. The very reason South Dakota built its plant was because the free market had failed adequately to supply the region with cement. . . .

We conclude, then, that the arguments for invalidating South Dakota's resident-preference program are weak at best. Whatever residual force inheres in them is more than offset by countervailing considerations of policy and fairness. Reversal would discourage similar state projects, even though this project demonstrably has served the needs of state residents and has helped the entire region for more than a half century. Reversal also would rob South Dakota of the intended benefit of its foresight, risk, and industry. Under these circumstances, there is no reason to depart from the general rule of *Alexandria Scrap*.

The judgment of the United States Court of Appeals is affirmed.

*It is so ordered.*

**Mr. Justice Powell, with whom Mr. Justice Brennan, Mr. Justice White and Mr. Justice Stevens join, dissenting. . . .**

The Commerce Clause would bar legislation imposing on private parties the type of restraint on commerce adopted by South Dakota. . . . Conversely, a private business constitutionally could adopt a marketing policy that excluded customers who come from another State. This case falls between those polar situations. The State, through its Commission, engages in a commercial enterprise and restricts its own interstate distribution. The question is whether the Commission's policy should be treated like state regulation of private parties or like the marketing policy of a private business.

The application of the Commerce Clause to this case should turn on the nature of the governmental activity involved. If a public enterprise undertakes an "integral operatio[n] in areas of traditional governmental functions" . . . the Commerce Clause is not directly relevant. If, however, the State enters the private market and operates a commercial enterprise for the advantage of its private citizens, it may not evade the constitutional policy against economic balkanization.

This distinction derives from the power of governments to supply their own needs . . . and from the purpose of the Commerce Clause itself, which is designed to protect "the natural functioning of the interstate market." . . . In procuring goods and services for the operation of government, a State may act without regard to the private marketplace and remove itself from the reach of the Commerce Clause. . . . But when a State itself becomes a participant in the private market for other purposes, the Constitution forbids actions that would impede the flow of interstate commerce. These categories recognize no more than the "constitutional line between the State as Government and the State as trader."

The threshold issue is whether South Dakota has undertaken integral government operations in an area of traditional governmental functions, or whether it has participated in the marketplace as a private firm. If the latter characterization applies, we also must determine whether the State Commission's marketing policy burdens the flow of interstate trade. This analysis highlights the differences between the state action here and that before the Court in *Alexandria Scrap.* . . .

*Alexandria Scrap* determined that Maryland's bounty program constituted direct state participation in the market for automobile hulks. . . . But the critical question—the second step in the opinion's analysis—was whether the bounty program constituted an impermissible burden on interstate commerce. Recognizing that the case did not fit neatly into conventional Commerce Clause theory . . . we found no burden on commerce. . . .

Unlike the market subsidies at issue in *Alexandria Scrap,* the marketing policy of the South Dakota Cement Commission has cut off interstate trade. . . . The effect on interstate trade is the same as if the state legislature had imposed the policy on private cement producers. The Commerce Clause prohibits this severe restraint on commerce. . . .

The creation of a free national economy was a major goal of the States when they resolved to unite under the Federal Constitution. The decision today cannot be reconciled with that purpose.

## III. COMPETING VISIONS OF CONGRESS'S COMMERCE POWER

### *United States* v. *E. C. Knight Co.*
### 156 U.S. 1, 15 S.Ct. 249, 39 L.Ed. 325 (1895)
### http://laws.findlaw.com/us/156/1.html

The American Sugar Refining Company, which controlled the bulk of sugar-refining capacity in the United States, attempted to attain an almost complete monopoly by purchasing control of the E. C. Knight Company and three other companies, which together produced about one-third of the national output. Alleging that the defendant companies (American Sugar, E. C. Knight, and three others) had entered into contracts that constituted combinations in restraint of trade, and that these companies had conspired to restrain trade, both contrary to the Sherman Anti-Trust Act of 1890, the government sought to obtain a court order canceling the various agreements. The lower federal courts refused to grant this relief on the ground that the combination or conspiracy involved in this case pertained to manufacturing and not to interstate commerce. Majority: Fuller, Brewer, Brown, Field, Gray, Jackson, Shiras, White. Dissenting: Harlan.

**MR. CHIEF JUSTICE FULLER . . .
delivered the opinion of the Court. . . .**

The fundamental question is, whether conceding that the existence of a monopoly in manufacture is established by the evidence, that monopoly can be directly suppressed under the act of Congress in the mode attempted by this bill.

It cannot be denied that the power of a state to protect the lives, health, and property of its citizens, and to preserve good order and the public morals, "the power to govern men and things within the limits of its dominion," is a power originally and always belonging to the States, not surrendered by them to the general government, nor directly restrained by the Constitution of the United States, and essentially exclusive. The relief of the citizens of each State from the burden of monopoly and the evils resulting from the restraint of trade among such citizens was left with the States to deal with, and this court has recognized their possession of that power even to the extent of holding that an employment or business carried on by private individuals, when it becomes a matter of such public interest and importance as to create a common charge or burden upon the citizen; in other words, when it becomes a practical monopoly, to which the citizen is compelled to resort and by means of which a tribute can be exacted from the community, is subject to regulation by state legislative power. On the other hand, the power of Congress to regulate commerce among the several States is also exclusive. The Constitution does not provide that interstate commerce shall be free, but, by the grant of this exclusive power to regulate it, it was left free except as Congress might impose restraints. . . . That which belongs to commerce is within the jurisdiction of the United States, but that which does not belong to commerce is within the jurisdiction of the police power of the State. . . .

The argument is that the power to control the manufacture of refined sugar is a monopoly over a necessary of life, to the enjoyment of which by a large part of the population of the United States interstate commerce is indispensable, and that, therefore, the general government in the exercise of the power to regulate commerce may repress such monopoly directly and set aside the instruments which have created it. But this argument cannot be confined to necessaries of life merely, and must include all articles of general consumption. Doubtless the power to control the manufacture of a given thing involves in a certain sense the control of its disposition, but this is a secondary and not the primary sense; and although the exercise of that power may result in bringing the operation of commerce into play, it does not control it, and affects it only incidentally and indirectly. Commerce succeeds to manufacture, and is not a part of it. The power to regulate commerce is the power to prescribe the rule by which commerce shall be governed, and is a power independent of

the power to suppress monopoly. But it may operate in repression of monopoly whenever that comes within the rules by which commerce is governed or whenever the transaction is itself a monopoly of commerce. . . .

It is vital that the independence of the commercial power and of the police power, and the delimitation between them, however sometimes perplexing, should always be recognized and observed, for while the one furnishes the strongest bond of union, the other is essential to the preservation of the autonomy of the States as required by our dual form of government; and acknowledged evils, however grave and urgent they may appear to be, had better be borne, than the risk be run, in the effort to suppress them, of more serious consequences by resort to expedients of even doubtful constitutionality. . . .

Slight reflection will show that if the national power extends to all contracts and combinations in manufacture, agriculture, mining, and other productive industries, whose ultimate result may affect external commerce, comparatively little of business operations and affairs would be left for state control.

It was in the light of well-settled principles that the act of July 2, 1890, was framed. Congress did not attempt thereby to assert the power to deal with monopoly directly as such. . . . [W]hat the law struck at was combinations, contracts, and conspiracies to monopolize trade and commerce among the several States or with foreign nations; but the contracts and acts of the defendants related exclusively to the acquisition of the Philadelphia refineries and the business of sugar refining in Pennsylvania, and bore no direct relation to commerce between the States or with foreign nations. . . .

*Decree affirmed.*

### MR. JUSTICE HARLAN, dissenting. . . .

If this combination, so far as its operations necessarily or directly affect interstate commerce, cannot be restrained or suppressed under some power granted to Congress, it will be cause for regret that the patriotic statesmen who framed the Constitution did not foresee the necessity of investing the national government with power to deal with gigantic monopolies holding in their grasp, and injuriously controlling in their own interest, the entire trade among the States in food products that are essential to the comfort of every household in the land. . . .

The power of Congress covers and protects the absolute freedom of such intercourse and trade among the States as may or must succeed manufacture and precede transportation from the place of purchase. This would seem to be conceded; for, the court in the present case expressly declares that "contracts to buy, sell, or exchange goods to be transported among the several States, the transportation and its instrumentalities, and articles bought, sold, or exchanged for the purpose of such transit among the States, or put in the way of transit, may be regulated, but this is because they form part of interstate trade or commerce." Here is a direct admission—one which the settled doctrines of this court justify—that contracts to buy and the purchasing of goods to be transported from one State to another, and transportation, with its instru-

mentalities, are all parts of interstate trade or commerce. Each part of such trade is then under the protection of Congress. And yet, by the opinion and judgment in this case, if I do not misapprehend them, Congress is without power to protect the commercial intercourse that such purchasing necessarily involves against the restraints and burdens arising from the existence of combinations that meet purchasers, from whatever State they come, with the threat—for it is nothing more or less than a threat—that they shall not purchase what they desire to purchase, except at the prices fixed by such combinations. . . .

The common government of all the people is the only one that can adequately deal with a matter which directly and injuriously affects the entire commerce of the country, which concerns equally all the people of the Union, and which, it must be confessed, cannot be adequately controlled by any one State. Its authority should not be so weakened by construction that it cannot reach and eradicate evils that, beyond all question, tend to defeat an object which that government is entitled, by the Constitution, to accomplish. . . .

## *Champion* v. *Ames* (The Lottery Case)
## 188 U.S. 321, 23 S.Ct. 321, 47 L.Ed. 492 (1903)
### http://laws.findlaw.com/us/188/321.html

An act of Congress of 1895 made it an offense to send or conspire to send lottery tickets in interstate commerce. The defendants, who were convicted under the statute, appealed from a circuit court order dismissing a writ of habeas corpus. Majority: Harlan, Brown, Holmes, McKenna, White. Dissenting: Fuller, Brewer, Peckham, Shiras.

**MR. JUSTICE HARLAN . . . delivered the opinion of the Court.**

The appellant insists that the carrying of lottery tickets from one State to another State by an express company engaged in carrying freight and packages, from State to State, although such tickets may be contained in a box or package, does not constitute, and cannot by

any act of Congress be legally made to constitute, commerce among the states within the meaning of the . . . Constitution of the United States . . . ; consequently, that Congress cannot make it an offense to cause such tickets to be carried from one State to another. . . .

What is the import of the word "commerce" as used in the Constitution? It is not defined by that instrument. Undoubtedly, the carrying from one State to another by independent carriers of things or commodities that are ordinary subjects of traffic, and which have in themselves a recognized value in money, constitutes interstate commerce. But does not commerce among the several States include something more? Does not the carrying from one State to another, by independent carriers, of lottery tickets that entitle the holder to the payment of a certain amount of money therein specified, also constitute commerce among the States? . . .

The cases cited . . . show that commerce among the States embraces navigation, intercourse, communication, traffic, the transit of persons, and the transmission of messages by telegraph. They also show that the power to regulate commerce among the several States is vested in Congress as absolutely as it would be in a single government, having in its constitution the same restrictions on the exercise of the power as are found in the Constitution of the United States; that such power is plenary, complete in itself, and may be exerted by Congress to its utmost extent, subject only to such limitations as the Constitution imposes upon the exercise of the powers granted by it; and that in determining the character of the regulations to be adopted Congress has a large discretion which is not to be controlled by the courts, simply because, in their opinion, such regulations may not be the best or most effective that could be employed.

We come then to inquire whether there is any solid foundation upon which to rest the contention that Congress may not regulate the carrying of lottery tickets from one State to another, at least by corporations or companies whose business it is, for hire, to carry tangible property from one State to another. . . .

We are of opinion that lottery tickets are subjects of traffic, and therefore are subjects of commerce, and the regulation of the carriage of such tickets from State to State, at least by independent carriers, is a regulation of commerce among the several States.

But it is said that the statute in question does not regulate the carrying of lottery tickets from State to State, but by punishing those who cause them to be so carried Congress in effect prohibits such carrying; that in respect of the carrying from one State to another of articles or things that are, in fact, or according to usage in business, the subjects of commerce, the authority given Congress was not to *prohibit,* but only to *regulate.* . . .

If a State, when considering legislation for the suppression of lotteries within its own limits, may properly take into view the evils that inhere in the raising of money, in that mode, why may not Congress, invested with the power to regulate commerce among the several States, provide that such commerce shall not be polluted by the carrying of lottery tickets from one State to another? In this connection it must not be forgotten that the power of Congress to regulate commerce among the States is plenary, is complete in itself, and is subject to no limitations except such as may be found in the Constitution. What provision in that instrument can be regarded as limiting the exercise of the power granted? . . .

If it be said that the act of 1895 is inconsistent with the Tenth Amendment, reserving to the States respectively, or to the people, the powers not delegated to the United States, the answer is that the power to regulate commerce among the States has been expressly delegated to Congress. . . .

We should hesitate long before adjudging that an evil of such appalling character, carried on through interstate commerce, cannot be met and crushed by the only power competent to that end. . . .

It is said, however, that if, in order to suppress lotteries carried on through interstate commerce, Congress may exclude lottery tickets from such commerce, that principle leads necessarily to the conclusion that Congress may arbitrarily exclude from commerce among the States any article, commodity, or thing, of whatever kind or nature, or however useful or valuable, which it may choose, no matter with what motive, to declare shall not be carried from one State to another. It will be time enough to consider the constitutionality of such legislation when we must do so. The present case does not require the court to declare the full extent of the power that Congress may exercise in the regulation of commerce among the States. We may, however, repeat, in this connection, what the court has heretofore said, that the power of Congress to regulate commerce among the States, although plenary, cannot be deemed arbitrary, since it is subject to such limitations or restrictions as are prescribed by the Constitution. . . .

*Affirmed.*

## MR. CHIEF JUSTICE FULLER . . . dissenting: . . .

The power of the State to impose restraints and burdens on persons and property in conservation and promotion of the public health, good order, and prosperity is a power originally and always belonging to the States, not surrendered by them to the general government, nor directly restrained by the Constitution of the United States, and essentially exclusive, and the suppression of lotteries as a harmful business falls within this power, commonly called, of police. . . .

It is urged, however, that because Congress is empowered to regulate commerce between the several States, it, therefore, may suppress lotteries by prohibiting the carriage of lottery matter. Congress may, indeed, make all laws necessary and proper for carrying the powers granted to it into execution, and doubtless an act prohibiting the carriage of lottery matter would be necessary and proper to the execution of a power to suppress lotteries; but that power belongs to the States and not to Congress. To hold that Congress has general police power would be to hold that it may accomplish objects not intrusted to the General Government, and to defeat the operation of the Tenth Amendment. . . .

To say that the mere carrying of an article which is not an article of commerce in and of itself nevertheless becomes such the moment it is to be transported from one State to another, is to transform a non-commercial article into one simply because it is transported. I cannot conceive that any such result can properly follow. . . .

This in effect breaks down all the differences between that which is, and that which is not, an article of commerce, and the necessary consequence is to take from the States all jurisdiction over the subject so far as interstate communication is concerned. It is a long step in the direction of wiping out all traces of state lines, and the creation of a centralized Government. . . .

The power to prohibit the transportation of diseased animals and infected goods over railroads or on steamboats is an entirely different thing, for they would be in themselves injurious to the transaction of interstate commerce, and, moreover, are essentially commercial in their nature. And the exclusion of diseased persons rests on different ground, for nobody would pretend that persons could be kept off the trains because they were going from one state to another to engage in the lottery business. However enticing that business may be, we do not understand how these pieces of paper themselves can communicate bad principles by contact. . . .

I regard this decision as inconsistent with the views of the framers of the Constitution, and of Marshall, its great expounder. Our form of government may remain notwithstanding legislation or decision, but, as long ago observed, it is with governments, as with religions, the form may survive the substance of the faith.

In my opinion the act in question in the particular under consideration is invalid, and the judgments below ought to be reversed, and my brothers Brewer, Shiras and Peckham concur in this dissent.

## Hammer v. Dagenhart
### 247 U.S. 251, 38 S.Ct. 529, 62 L.Ed. 1101 (1918)
http://laws.findlaw.com/us/247/251.html

> The Keating-Owen Child Labor Act of 1916 forbade the shipment in interstate commerce of products of child labor. A father of two minor children who worked in a cotton mill in Charlotte, North Carolina, obtained an injunction from the U.S. District Court for the Western District of North Carolina against enforcement of the act, on the ground that it was unconstitutional. Majority: Day, McReynolds, Pitney, Van Devanter, White. Dissenting: Holmes, Brandeis, Clarke, McKenna.

**MR. JUSTICE DAY delivered the opinion of the Court. . . .**

The controlling question for decision is: Is it within the authority of Congress in regulating commerce among the States to prohibit the transportation in interstate commerce of manufactured goods, the product of a factory in which, within thirty days prior to their removal therefrom, children under the age of fourteen have been employed or permitted to work, or children between the ages of fourteen and sixteen years have been employed or permitted to work more than eight hours in any day, or more than six days in any week, or after the hour of 7 o'clock p.m. or before the hour of 6 o'clock a.m.?

The power essential to the passage of this act, the Government contends, is found in the commerce clause of the Constitution which authorizes Congress to regulate commerce with foreign nations and among the States. . . .

[I]t is insisted that adjudged cases in this court establish the doctrine that the power to regulate given to Congress incidentally includes the authority to prohibit the movement of ordinary commodities and therefore that the subject is not open for discussion. The cases demonstrate the contrary. They rest upon the character of the particular subjects dealt with and the fact that the scope of governmental authority, state or national, possessed over them is such that the authority to prohibit is as to them but the exertion of the power to regulate. . . .

In each of these instances the use of interstate transportation was necessary to the accomplishment of harmful results. In other words, although the power over interstate transportation was to regulate, that could only be accomplished by prohibiting the use of the facilities of interstate commerce to effect the evil intended.

This element is wanting in the present case. The thing intended to be accomplished by this statute is the denial of the facilities of interstate commerce to those manufacturers in the States who employ children within the prohibited ages. The act in its effect does not regulate transportation among the States, but aims to standardize the ages at which children may be employed in mining and manufacturing within the States. The goods shipped are of themselves harmless. The act permits them to be freely shipped after thirty days from the time of their removal from the factory. When offered for shipment, and before transportation begins, the labor of their production is over, and the mere fact that they were intended for interstate commerce transportation does not make their production subject to federal control under the commerce power. . . .

That there should be limitations upon the right to employ children in mines and factories in the interest of their own and the public welfare, all will admit. That such employment is generally deemed to require regulation is shown by the fact that the brief of counsel states that every State in the Union has a law upon the subject, limiting the right to thus employ children. In North Carolina, the State wherein is located the factory in which the employment was had in the present case, no child under twelve years of age is permitted to work.

It may be desirable that such laws be uniform, but our Federal Government is one of enumerated powers. . . .

In interpreting the Constitution it must never be forgotten that the nation is made up of States to which are entrusted the powers of local government. And to them and to the people the powers not expressly [sic] delegated to the national government are reserved. . . . Thus the act in a twofold sense is repugnant to the Constitution. It not only transcends the authority delegated to Congress over commerce but also exerts a power as to a purely local matter to which the federal authority does not extend. The far-reaching result of upholding the act cannot be more plainly indicated than by pointing out that if Congress can thus regulate matters entrusted to local authority by prohibition of the movement of commodities in interstate commerce, all freedom of commerce will be at an end, and the power of the states over local matters may be eliminated, and thus our system of government be practically destroyed.

For these reasons we hold that this law exceeds the constitutional authority of Congress. It follows that the decree of the District Court must be

*Affirmed.*

### MR. JUSTICE HOLMES, dissenting. . . .

The first step in my argument is to make plain what no one is likely to dispute—that the statute in question is within the power expressly given to Congress if considered only as to its immediate effects and that if invalid it is so only upon some collateral ground. The statute confines itself to prohibiting the carriage of certain goods in interstate or foreign commerce. Congress is given power to regulate such commerce in unqualified terms. It would not be argued today that the power to regulate does not include the power to prohibit. Regulation means the prohibition of something, and when interstate commerce is the matter to be regulated I cannot doubt that the regulation may prohibit any part of such commerce that Congress sees fit to forbid. At all events it is established by the Lottery Case

and others that have followed it that a law is not beyond the regulative power of Congress merely because it prohibits certain transportation out and out. . . . So I repeat that this statute in its immediate operation is clearly within the Congress's constitutional power.

The question then is narrowed to whether the exercise of its otherwise constitutional power by Congress can be pronounced unconstitutional because of its possible reaction upon the conduct of the States in a matter upon which I have admitted that they are free from direct control. I should have thought that that matter had been disposed of so fully as to leave no room for doubt. I should have thought that the most conspicuous decisions of this Court had made it clear that the power to regulate commerce and other constitutional powers could not be cut down or qualified by the fact that it might interfere with the carrying out of the domestic policy of any State. . . .

The notion that prohibition is any less prohibition when applied to things now thought evil I do not understand. But if there is any matter upon which civilized countries have agreed—far more unanimously than they have with regard to intoxicants and some other matters over which this country is now emotionally aroused—it is the evil of premature and excessive child labor. I should have thought that if we were to introduce our own moral conceptions where in my opinion they do not belong, this was preeminently a case for upholding the exercise of all its powers by the United States.

But I had thought that the propriety of the exercise of a power admitted to exist in some cases was for the consideration of Congress alone and that this Court always had disavowed the right to intrude its judgment upon questions of policy or morals. It is not for this Court to pronounce when prohibition is necessary to regulation if it ever may be necessary—to say that it is permissible as against strong drink but not as against the product of ruined lives.

The act does not meddle with anything belonging to the States. They may regulate their internal affairs and their domestic commerce as they like. But when they seek to send their products across the state line they are no longer within their rights. If there were no Constitution and no Congress their power to cross the line would depend upon their neighbors. Under the Constitution such commerce belongs not to the States but to Congress to regulate. . . .

MR. JUSTICE MCKENNA, MR. JUSTICE BRANDEIS and MR. JUSTICE CLARKE concur in this opinion.

## Stafford v. Wallace
## 258 U.S. 495, 42 S.Ct. 397, 66 L.Ed. 735 (1922)

http://laws.findlaw.com/us/258/495.html

> The Packers and Stockyards Act of 1921 imposed regulations on stockyard sales of livestock and other practices involving meat products that took place between the two legs of an interstate journey. Stafford unsuccessfully sought an injunction against enforcement of the act. Majority: Taft, Brandeis, Clarke, Holmes, McKenna, Pitney, Van Devanter. Dissenting: McReynolds. Not participating: Day.

**MR. CHIEF JUSTICE TAFT . . . delivered the opinion of the Court. . . .**

The Packers and Stockyards Act of 1921 seeks to regulate the business of the packers done in interstate commerce and forbids them to engage in unfair, discriminatory or deceptive practices in such commerce, or to subject any person to unreasonable prejudice therein, or to do any of a number of acts to control prices or establish a monopoly in the business. . . .

The object to be secured by the act is the free and unburdened flow of live stock from the ranges and farms of the West and the Southwest through the great stockyards and slaughtering centers on the borders of that region, and thence in the form of meat products to the consuming cities of the country in the Middle West and East, or, still as live stock, to the feeding places and fattening farms in the Middle West or East for further preparation for the market.

The chief evil feared is the monopoly of the packers, enabling them unduly and arbitrarily to lower prices to the shipper who sells, and unduly and arbitrarily to increase the price to the consumer who buys. Congress thought that the power to maintain this monopoly was aided by control of the stockyards. Another evil which it sought to provide against by the act, was exorbitant charges, duplication of commissions, deceptive practices in respect of prices, in the passage of the live stock through the stockyards, all made possible by collusion between the stockyards management and the commission men, on the one hand, and the packers and dealers on the other.

The stockyards are not a place of rest or final destination. Thousands of head of live stock arrive daily by carload and trainload lots, and must be promptly sold and disposed of and moved out to give place to the constantly flowing traffic that presses behind. The stockyards are but a throat through which the current flows, and the transactions which occur therein are only incident to this current from the West to the East, and from one State to another. Such transactions cannot be separated from the movement to which they contribute and necessarily take on its character. . . . The stockyards and the sales are necessary factors in the middle of this current of commerce.

The act, therefore, treats the various stockyards of the country as great national public utilities to promote the flow of commerce from the ranges and farms of the West to the consumers in the East. It assumes that they conduct a business affected by a public use of a national character and subject to national regulation. That it is a business within the power of regulation by legislative action needs no discussion. That has been settled since the case of *Munn* v. *Illinois*. . . . Nor is there any doubt that in the receipt of live stock by rail and in their delivery by rail the stockyards are an interstate commerce agency. . . . The only question here is whether the business done in the stockyards between the receipt of the live stock in the yards and the shipment of them therefrom is a part of interstate commerce, or is so associated with it as to bring it within the power of national regulation. A similar question has been before this court and had great consideration in *Swift & Co.* v. *United States*. The judgment in that case gives a clear and comprehensive exposition which leaves to us in this case little but the obvious application of the principles there declared. . . .

The application of the commerce clause of the Constitution in the Swift Case was the result of the natural development of interstate commerce under modern conditions. It was the inevitable recognition of the great central fact that such streams of commerce from one part of the country to another which are ever flowing are in their very essence the commerce among the States and with foreign nations which historically it was one of the chief purposes of the Constitution to bring under national protection and control. This court declined to defeat this purpose in respect of such a stream and take it out of complete national regulation by a nice and technical inquiry into the non-interstate character of some of its necessary incidents and facilities when considered alone and without reference to their association with the movement of which they were an essential but subordinate part. . . .

If Congress could provide for punishment or restraint of such conspiracies after their formation through the Anti-Trust Law as in the Swift Case, certainly it may provide regulation to prevent their formation. The reasonable fear by Congress that such acts, usually lawful and affecting only intrastate commerce when considered alone, will probably and more or less constantly be used in conspiracies against interstate commerce or constitute a direct and undue burden on it, expressed in this remedial legislation, serves the same purpose as the intent charged in the *Swift* indictment to bring acts of a similar character into the current of interstate commerce for federal restraint. Whatever amounts to more or less constant practice, and threatens to obstruct or unduly to burden the freedom of interstate commerce is within the regulatory power of Congress under the commerce clause, and it is primarily for Congress to consider and decide the fact of danger and meet it. This court will certainly not substitute its judgment for that of Congress in such a matter unless the relation of the subject to interstate commerce and its effect upon it are clearly nonexistent. . . .

The orders of the District Court refusing the interlocutory injunctions are

*Affirmed.*

MR. JUSTICE MCREYNOLDS dissents [without opinion].

# IV. THE NEW DEAL IN COURT

## *Carter* v. *Carter Coal Co.*
### 298 U.S. 238, 56 S.Ct. 855, 80 L.Ed. 1160 (1936)
### http://laws.findlaw.com/us/298/238.html

In the Bituminous Coal Conservation Act of 1935, Congress attempted to stabilize the production and marketing of coal. The law provided for a National Bituminous Coal Commission with general supervisory powers over the industry through a

Bituminous Coal Code. In each of 23 districts, boards were to be given the power to fix minimum coal prices. National hours of labor and district minimum wage agreements were to be effective when the producers of two-thirds of the annual tonnage and representatives of more than one-half of the employed workers agreed to terms. A labor board in the Department of Labor was given the duty of protecting the collective bargaining process and adjudicating labor disputes. Producers were to be induced to accept these codes by a tax provision that allowed 90 percent of a tax of 15 percent on sales at the mines to be refunded to those producers who accepted the code provisions. Four cases involving suits to bar payment of the tax and acceptance of the code were consolidated on certiorari from circuit courts of appeals and from district courts. A majority of the Supreme Court held the delegation of code-drafting power to a part of the producers and workers to be invalid. The following excerpts from the opinion deal with whether federal regulation of mining activities was permissible under the commerce clause. Majority: Sutherland, Butler, Hughes, McReynolds, Roberts, Van Devanter. Dissenting: Cardozo, Brandeis, Stone.

## MR. JUSTICE SUTHERLAND delivered the opinion of the Court. . . .

The general rule with regard to the respective powers of the national and the state governments under the Constitution is not in doubt. The States were before the Constitution; and, consequently, their legislative powers antedated the Constitution. Those who framed and those who adopted that instrument meant to carve from the general mass of legislative powers, then possessed by the States, only such portions as it was thought wise to confer upon the federal government; and in order that there should be no uncertainty in respect of what was taken and what was left, the national powers of legislation were not aggregated but enumerated—with the result that what was not embraced by the enumeration remained vested in the States without change or impairment. . . . While the States are not sovereign in the true sense of that term, but only quasi-sovereign, yet in respect of all powers reserved to them they are supreme—"as independent of the general government as that government within its sphere is independent of the States." And since every addition to the national legislative power to some extent detracts from or invades the power of the States, it is of vital moment that, in order to preserve the fixed balance intended by the Constitution, the powers of the general government be not so extended as to embrace any not within the express terms of the several grants or implications necessarily to be drawn therefrom. It is no longer open to question that the general government, unlike the States . . . possesses no inherent power in respect of the internal affairs of the States; and emphatically not with regard to legislation. . . .

Every journey to a forbidden end begins with the first step; and the danger of such a step by the federal government in the direction of taking over the powers of the states is that the end of the journey may find the states so despoiled of their powers, or—what may amount to the same thing—so relieved of the responsibilities which possession of the powers necessarily enjoins, as to reduce them to little more than geographical subdivisions of the national domain. It is safe to say that if, when the Constitution was under consideration, it had been thought that any such danger lurked behind its plain words, it would never have been ratified. . . .

Since the validity of the act depends upon whether it is a regulation of interstate commerce, the nature and extent of the power conferred upon Congress by the commerce clause becomes the determinative question in this branch of the case. . . . We first inquire, then—What is commerce? The term, as this court many times has said, is one of extensive import. No all-embracing definition has ever been formulated. The question is to be approached both affirmatively and negatively—

that is to say, from the points of view as to what it includes and what it excludes. . . .

That commodities produced or manufactured within a State are intended to be sold or transported outside the State does not render their production or manufacture subject to federal regulation under the commerce clause. . . .

We have seen that the word "commerce" is the equivalent of the phrase "intercourse for the purposes of trade." Plainly, the incidents leading up to and culminating in the mining of coal do not constitute such intercourse. The employment of men, the fixing of their wages, hours of labor, and working conditions, the bargaining in respect of these things—whether carried on separately or collectively—each and all constitute intercourse for the purposes of production, not of trade. The latter is a thing apart from the relation of employer and employee, which in all producing occupations is purely local in character. Extraction of coal from the mine is the aim and the completed result of local activities. Commerce in the coal mined is not brought into being by force of these activities, but by negotiations, agreements and circumstances entirely apart from production. Mining brings the subject matter of commerce into existence. Commerce disposes of it.

A consideration of the foregoing . . . renders inescapable the conclusion that the effect of the labor provisions of the act, including those in respect of minimum wages, wage agreements, collective bargaining, and the Labor Board and its powers, primarily falls upon production and not upon commerce; and confirms the further resulting conclusion that production is a purely local activity. It follows that none of these essential antecedents of production constitutes a transaction in or forms any part of interstate commerce. . . .

But § 1 (the preamble) of the act now under review declares that all production and distribution of bituminous coal "bear upon and directly affect its interstate commerce"; and that regulation thereof is imperative for the protection of such commerce. The contention of the government is that the labor provisions of the act may be sustained in that way.

That the production of every commodity intended for interstate sale and transportation has some effect upon interstate commerce may be, if it has not already been, freely granted: and we are brought to the final and decisive inquiry, whether here that effect is direct, as the "preamble" recites, or indirect. The distinction is not formal, but substantial in the highest degree as we pointed out in the Schechter case. . . . "If the commerce clause were construed," we there said, "to reach all enterprises and transactions which could be said to have an indirect effect upon interstate commerce, the federal authority would embrace practically all the activities of the people and the authority of the State over its domestic concerns would exist only by sufferance of the federal government. Indeed, on such a theory, even the development of the State's commercial facilities would be subject to federal control." It was also pointed out . . . "that the distinction between direct and indirect effects of intrastate transactions upon interstate commerce must be recognized as a fundamental one, essential to the maintenance of our constitutional system."

Whether the effect of a given activity or condition is direct or indirect is not always easy to determine. The word "direct" implies that the activity or condition invoked or blamed shall operate proximately—not mediately, remotely, or collaterally—to produce the effect. It connotes the absence of an efficient intervening agency or condition. And the extent of the effect bears no logical relation to its character. The distinction between a direct and an indirect effect turns, not upon the magnitude of either the cause or the effect, but entirely upon the manner in which the effect has been brought about. If the production by one man of a single ton of coal intended for interstate sale and shipment, and actually so sold and shipped, affects interstate commerce indirectly, the effect does not become direct by multiplying the tonnage, or increasing the number of men employed, or adding to the expense or complexities of the business, or by all combined. It is quite true that rules of law are sometimes qualified by considerations of degree, as the government argues. But the matter of degree has no bearing upon the question here, since that question is not— What is the extent of the local activity or condition, or the extent of the effect produced upon interstate commerce? but—What is the relation between the activity or condition and the effect?

Much stress is put upon the evils which come from the struggle between employers and employees over the matter of wages, working conditions, the right of collective bargaining, etc., and the resulting strikes, curtailment, and irregularity of production and effect on prices; and it is insisted that interstate commerce is greatly affected thereby. But, in addition to what has just been said, the conclusive answer is that the evils are all local evils over which the federal government has no legislative control. The relation of employer and employee is a local relation. . . . Such effect as they may have upon commerce, however extensive it may be, is secondary and indirect. An increase in the greatness of the effect adds to its importance. It does not alter its character. . . .

The government's contentions in defense of the labor provisions are really disposed of adversely by our decision in the Schechter Case. The only perceptible difference between that case and this is that in the Schechter Case the federal power was asserted with respect to commodities which had come to rest after their interstate transportation; while here, the case deals with commodities at rest before interstate commerce has begun. That difference is without significance. The federal regulatory power ceases when interstate commercial intercourse ends; and, correlatively, the power does not attach until interstate commercial intercourse begins . . . [A]fter calling attention to the fact that if the commerce clause could be construed to reach transactions having an indirect effect upon interstate commerce, the federal authority would embrace practically all the activities of the people, and the authority of the state over its domestic concerns would exist only by sufferance of the federal government, we said: "Indeed, on such a theory, even the development of the state's commercial facilities would be subject to federal control." And again, after pointing out that hours and wages have no direct relation to interstate

commerce and that if the federal government had power to determine the wages and hours of employees in the internal commerce of a state because of their relation to cost and prices and their indirect effect upon interstate commerce, we said "All the processes of production and distribution that enter into cost could likewise be controlled. If the cost of doing an intrastate business is in itself the permitted object of federal control, the extent of the regulation of cost would be a question of discretion and not of power." A reading of the entire opinion makes clear, what we now declare, that the want of power on the part of the federal government is the same whether the wages, hours of service, and working conditions, and the bargaining about them, are related to production before interstate commerce has begun, or to sale and distribution after it has ended. . . .

The decrees in Nos. 636, 649, and 650 must be reversed and the causes remanded for further consideration in conformity with this opinion. The decree in No. 651 will be affirmed.

*It is so ordered.*

### MR. JUSTICE CARDOZO, dissenting. . . .

I am satisfied that the Act is within the power of the central government in so far as it provides for minimum and maximum prices upon sales of bituminous coal in the transactions of interstate commerce and in those of intrastate commerce where interstate commerce is directly or intimately affected. . . .

[S]o far as the Act is directed to interstate transactions, . . . sales made in such conditions constitute interstate commerce, and do not merely "affect" it. . . . To regulate the price for such transactions is to regulate commerce itself, and not alone its antecedent conditions or its ultimate consequences. The very act of sale is limited and governed. Prices in interstate transactions may not be regulated by the States. They must therefore be subject to the power of the nation unless they are to be withdrawn altogether from governmental supervision. . . . If such a vacuum were permitted, many a public evil incidental to interstate transactions would be left without a remedy. . . .

Regulation of prices being an exercise of the commerce power in respect of interstate transactions, the question remains whether it comes within that power as applied to intrastate sales where interstate prices are directly or intimately affected. Mining and agriculture and manufacture are not interstate commerce considered by themselves, yet their relation to that commerce may be such that for the protection of the one there is need to regulate the other. . . . Sometimes it is said that the relation must be "direct" to bring that power into play. In many circumstances such a description will be sufficiently precise to meet the needs of the occasion. But a great principle of constitutional law is not susceptible of comprehensive statement in an adjective. The underlying thought is merely this, that "the law is not indifferent to considerations of degree." . . . It cannot be indifferent to them without an expansion of the commerce clause that would absorb or imperil the reserved powers of the States. At times, as in the case cited, the

waves of causation will have radiated so far that their undulatory motion, if discernible at all, will be too faint or obscure, too broken by crosscurrents, to be heeded by the law. In such circumstances the holding is not directed at prices or wages considered in the abstract, but at prices or wages in particular conditions. The relation may be tenuous or the opposite according to the facts. Always the setting of the facts is to be viewed if one would know the closeness of the tie. Perhaps, if one group of adjectives is to be chosen in preference to another, "intimate" and "remote" will be found to be as good as any. At all events, "direct" and "indirect," even if accepted as sufficient, must not be read too narrowly. . . . A survey of the cases shows that the words have been interpreted with suppleness of adaptation and flexibility of meaning. The power is as broad as the need that evokes it. . . .

I am authorized to state that MR. JUSTICE BRANDEIS and MR. JUSTICE STONE join in this opinion.

## *National Labor Relations Board* v. *Jones & Laughlin Steel Corporation*
## 301 U.S. 1, 57 S.Ct. 615, 81 L.Ed. 893 (1937)
### http://laws.findlaw.com/us/301/1.html

The National Labor Relations Act of 1935 protects the right of workers to organize and to encourage collective bargaining procedures. In this case the National Labor Relations Board ordered the steel company to cease and desist from certain "unfair labor practices." When the corporation failed to comply, the NLRB unsuccessfully petitioned the circuit court of appeals (as provided in the act) to enforce the board's order. Majority: Hughes, Brandeis, Cardozo, Roberts, Stone. Dissenting: McReynolds, Butler, Sutherland, Van Devanter.

**MR. CHIEF JUSTICE HUGHES delivered the opinion of the Court. . . .**

The Act is challenged in its entirety as an attempt to regulate all industry, thus invading the reserved powers of the States over their local concerns. . . .

If this conception of terms, intent and consequent inseparability were sound, the Act

would necessarily fall by reason of the limitation upon the federal power which inheres in the constitutional grant, as well as because of the explicit reservation of the Tenth Amendment. . . . The authority of the federal government may not be pushed to such an extreme as to destroy the distinction, which the commerce clause itself establishes, between commerce "among the several States" and the internal concerns of a State. That distinction between what is national and what is local in the activities of commerce is vital to the maintenance of our federal system. . . .

We think it clear that the National Labor Relations Act may be construed so as to operate within the sphere of constitutional authority. The jurisdiction conferred upon the Board, and invoked in this instance, is found in § 10(a), which provides: "Sec. 10(a). The Board is empowered, as hereinafter provided, to prevent any person from engaging in any unfair labor practice (listed in § 8) affecting commerce."

The critical words of this provision, prescribing the limits of the Board's authority in dealing with the labor practices, are "affecting commerce." . . .

There can be no question that the commerce thus contemplated by the Act (aside from that within a Territory or the District of Columbia) is interstate and foreign commerce in the constitutional sense. The Act also defines the term "affecting commerce" (§ 2(6)):

"The term 'affecting commerce' means in commerce, or burdening or obstructing commerce or the free flow of commerce, or having led or tending to lead to a labor dispute burdening or obstructing commerce or the free flow of commerce."

This definition is one of exclusion as well as inclusion. The grant of authority to the Board does not purport to extend to the relationship between all industrial employees and employers. Its terms do not impose collective bargaining upon all industry regardless of effects upon interstate or foreign commerce. It purports to reach only what may be deemed to burden or obstruct that commerce and, thus qualified, it must be construed as contemplating the exercise of control within constitutional bounds. . . .

Respondent says that whatever may be said of employees engaged in interstate commerce, the industrial relations and activities in the manufacturing department of respondent's enterprise are not subject to federal regulation. The argument rests upon the proposition that manufacturing in itself is not commerce. . . .

Reference is made to our decision sustaining the Packers and Stockyards Act. . . . The Court found that the stockyards were but a "throat" through which the current of commerce flowed and the transactions which there occurred could not be separated from that movement. . . .

Respondent contends that the instant case presents material distinction. Respondent says that the Aliquippa plant is extensive in size and represents a large investment in buildings, machinery and equipment. The raw materials which are brought to the plant are delayed for long periods and, after being subjected to manufacturing processes "are changed substantially as to character, utility and value." . . .

We do not find it necessary to determine whether these features of defendant's business dispose of the asserted analogy to the "stream of commerce" cases. The instances in which that metaphor has been used are but particular, and not exclusive, illustrations of the protective power which the Government invokes in support of the present Act. The congressional authority to protect interstate commerce from burdens and obstructions is not limited to transactions which can be deemed to be an essential part of a "flow" of interstate or foreign commerce. Burdens and obstructions may be due to injurious action springing from other sources. The fundamental principle is that the power to regulate commerce is the power to enact "all appropriate legislation" for "its protection and advancement." . . . That power is plenary and may be exerted to protect interstate commerce "no matter what the source of the dangers which threaten it." . . . Although activities may be intrastate in character when separately considered, if they have such a close and substantial relation to interstate commerce that their control is essential or appropriate to protect that commerce from burdens and obstructions, Congress cannot be denied the power to exercise that control. . . . Undoubtedly the scope of this power must be considered in the light of our dual system of government and may not be extended so as to embrace effects upon interstate commerce so indirect and remote that to embrace them, in view of our complex society, would effectually obliterate the distinction between what is national and what is local and create a completely centralized government.... The question is necessarily one of degree....

It is thus apparent that the fact that the employees here concerned were engaged in production is not determinative. The question remains as to the effect upon interstate commerce of the labor practice involved. In the Schechter case, we found that the effect there was so remote as to be beyond the federal power. To find "immediacy or directness" there was to find it "almost everywhere," a result inconsistent with the maintenance of our federal system. In the Carter case, the Court was of the opinion that the provisions of the statute relating to production were invalid upon several grounds—that there was improper delegation of legislative power, and that the requirements not only went beyond any sustainable measure of protection of interstate commerce but were also inconsistent with due process. These cases are not controlling here.

Giving full weight to respondent's contention with respect to a break in the complete continuity of the "stream of commerce" by reason of respondent's manufacturing operations, the fact remains that the stoppage of those operations by industrial strife would have a most serious effect upon interstate commerce. In view of respondent's farflung activities, it is idle to say that the effect would be indirect or remote. It is obvious that it would be immediate and might be catastrophic. We are asked to shut our eyes to the plainest facts of our national life and to deal with the question of direct and indirect effects in an intellectual vacuum. Because there may be but indirect and remote effects upon interstate commerce in connection with a host of local enterprises throughout the country, it does not follow that other industrial activities do not have such a close and intimate relation to interstate commerce as to make the presence of industrial strife a matter of the most urgent national concern. When industries organize themselves on a national scale, making their relation to interstate commerce the dominant factor in their activities, how can it be maintained that their industrial labor relations constitute a forbidden field into which Congress may not enter when it is necessary to protect interstate commerce from the paralyzing consequences of industrial war? We have often said that interstate commerce itself is a practical conception. It is equally true that interferences with that commerce must be appraised by a judgment that does not ignore actual experience....

Our conclusion is that the order of the Board was within its competency and that the Act is valid as here applied. The judgment of the Circuit Court of Appeals is reversed and the case is remanded for further proceedings in conformity with this opinion.

*Reversed.*

### MR. JUSTICE MCREYNOLDS, dissenting.

MR. JUSTICE VAN DEVANTER, MR. JUSTICE SUTHERLAND, MR. JUSTICE BUTLER and I are unable to agree with the decisions just announced....

The Court as we think departs from well-established principles followed in *Schechter Poultry Corp.* v. *United States* . . . and *Carter* v. *Carter Coal Co.* . . . . Every consideration brought forward to uphold the Act before us was applicable to support the Acts held unconstitutional in cases decided within two years. And the lower courts rightly deemed them controlling. . . .

Any effect on interstate commerce by the discharge of employees shown here, would be indirect and remote in the highest degree, as consideration of the facts will show. In No. 419 (*NLRB* v. *Jones & Laughlin.*) ten men out of ten thousand were discharged; in the other cases only a few. The immediate effect in the factory may be to create discontent among all those employed and a strike may follow, which, in turn, may result in reducing production, which ultimately may reduce the volume of goods moving in interstate commerce. By this chain of indirect and progressively remote events we finally reach the evil with which it is said the legislation under consideration undertakes to deal. A more remote and indirect interference with interstate commerce or a more definite invasion of the powers reserved to the States is difficult, if not impossible, to imagine. The constitution still recognizes the existence of States with indestructible powers; the Tenth Amendment was supposed to put them beyond controversy.

## V. CONTEMPORARY VIEWS OF THE COMMERCE POWER

### *Wickard* v. *Filburn*
### 317 U.S. 111, 63 S.Ct. 82, 87 L.Ed. 122 (1942)
http://laws.findlaw.com/us/317/111.html

The Agricultural Adjustment Act of 1938 was passed by Congress in an effort to stabilize agricultural production. The basic scheme as applied to wheat involved an annual proclamation by the secretary of agriculture of a national acreage allotment,
which was then apportioned to states and eventually passed on in the form of quotas
to individual farmers. Penalties were imposed for production in excess of an agreed-
upon quota. Ohio farmer Roscoe Filburn planted wheat each year to feed his livestock and poultry. He accepted an allotment of 11.1 acres, but actually planted
23 acres and grew 239 bushels in excess of his quota. Filburn resisted payment of the
penalty and obtained an injunction in the U.S. District Court for the Southern District
of Ohio against Secretary of Agriculture Claude R. Wickard and other officials.
Majority: Jackson, Black, Douglas, Frankfurter, Murphy, Reed, Roberts, Stone.

**MR. JUSTICE JACKSON delivered the
opinion of the Court. . . .**

It is argued that under the Commerce
Clause . . . Congress does not possess the
power it has in this instance sought to exercise. The question would merit little consideration . . . except for the fact that this Act
extends federal regulation to production not
intended in any part for commerce but wholly
for consumption on the farm. . . .

Appellee says that this is a regulation of
production and consumption of wheat. Such
activities are, he urges, beyond the reach of
Congressional power under the Commerce
Clause, since they are local in character, and
their effects upon interstate commerce are at
most "indirect." In answer the Government argues that the statute regulates neither production nor consumption, but only marketing;
and, in the alternative, that if the Act does go
beyond the regulation of marketing it is
sustainable as a "necessary and proper" implementation of the power of Congress over interstate commerce. . . .

We believe that a review of the course of
decision under the Commerce Clause will
make plain . . . that questions of the power of
Congress are not to be decided by reference
to any formula which would give controlling

force to nomenclature such as "production"
and "indirect" and foreclose consideration of
the actual effects of the activity in question
upon interstate commerce. . . .

The Court's recognition of the relevance of
the economic effects in the application of the
Commerce Clause . . . has made the mechanical application of legal formulas no longer feasible. Once an economic measure of the reach
of the power granted to Congress in the Commerce Clause is accepted, questions of federal
power cannot be decided simply by finding
the activity in question to be "production" nor
can consideration of its economic effects be
foreclosed by calling them "indirect." . . .

Whether the subject of the regulation in
question was "production," "consumption," or
"marketing" is, therefore, not material for purposes of deciding the question of federal
power before us. That an activity is of local
character may help in a doubtful case to determine whether Congress intended to reach
it. The same consideration might help in determining whether in the absence of Congressional action it would be permissible for the
state to exert its power on the subject matter,
even though in so doing it to some degree
affected interstate commerce. But even if appellant's activity be local and though it may
not be regarded as commerce, it may still,

whatever its nature, be reached by Congress if it exerts a substantial economic effect on interstate commerce and this irrespective of whether such effect is what might at some earlier time have been defined as "direct" or "indirect." . . .

The effect of consumption of home-grown wheat on interstate commerce is due to the fact that it constitutes the most variable factor in the disappearance of the wheat crop. Consumption on the farm where grown appears to vary in an amount greater than 10 percent of average production. The total amount of wheat consumed as food varies but relatively little, and use as seed is relatively constant. . . .

It is well established by decisions of this Court that the power to regulate commerce includes the power to regulate the prices at which commodities in that commerce are dealt in and practices affecting such prices. One of the primary purposes of the Act in question was to increase the market price of wheat and to that end to limit the volume thereof that could affect the market. It can hardly be denied that a factor of such volume and variability as home-consumed wheat would have a substantial influence on price and market conditions. This may arise because being in marketable condition such home-grown wheat overhangs the market and if induced by rising prices tends to flow into the market and check price increases. But if we assume that it is never marketed, it supplies a need of the man who grew it which would otherwise be reflected by purchases in the open market. Home-grown wheat in this sense competes with wheat in commerce. The stimulation of commerce is a use of a regulatory function quite as definitely as prohibitions or restrictions thereon. This record leaves us in no doubt that Congress may properly have considered that wheat consumed on the farm where grown if wholly outside the scheme of regulation would have a substantial effect in defeating and obstructing its purpose to stimulate trade therein at increased prices.

It is said, however, that this Act, forcing some farmers into the market to buy what they could provide for themselves, is an unfair promotion of the markets and prices of specializing wheat growers. It is of the essence of regulation that it lays a restraining hand on the self-interest of the regulated and that advantages from the regulation commonly fall to others. The conflicts of economic interest between the regulated and those who advantage by it are wisely left under our system to resolution by the Congress under its more flexible and responsible legislative process. Such conflicts rarely lend themselves to judicial determination. And with the wisdom, workability, or fairness, of the plan of regulation we have nothing to do. . . .

*Reversed.*

## Heart of Atlanta Motel v. United States
### 379 U.S. 241, 85 S.Ct. 348, 13 L.Ed. 2d 258 (1964)
http://laws.findlaw.com/us/379/241.html

## Katzenbach v. McClung
### 379 U.S. 294, 85 S.Ct. 377, 13 L.Ed. 2d 290 (1964)
http://laws.findlaw.com/us/379/294.html

In the Civil Rights Act of 1964, Congress sought, among other purposes, to eliminate racial discrimination in hotels, motels, restaurants, and similar places of public accommodation, basing its action on the commerce clause as well as on the equal protection clause and section 5 of the Fourteenth Amendment. In *Atlanta Motel,* the act was applied to a business where 75 percent of the guests were from out of state. In contrast, *McClung* began not at the federal government's initiative but as an action against the attorney general by the owner of Ollie's Barbeque in Birmingham, Alabama, who wanted to avoid being lumped with national restaurant and motel chains. Ollie McClung challenged the provision banning discrimination in any restaurant that "serves or offers to serve interstate travelers or a substantial portion of the food which it serves . . . has moved in commerce." Even though Ollie's was a homespun eatery, well removed from major highways and the airport, approximately half the food served, though purchased within Alabama, had "moved" in commerce. The motel appealed from a district court injunction against its refusal to accept black lodgers, and the attorney general appealed in *McClung* from a district court holding that the act could not be applied to the restaurant. Although Justices Douglas and Goldberg would have upheld the act under the Fourteenth Amendment as well as the commerce clause, the majority rested its decision on the commerce clause. A brief excerpt from Justice Clark's opinion for the Court in *Atlanta Motel* is followed by a somewhat longer extract from his opinion in *McClung*. Majority: Clark, Black, Brennan, Douglas, Goldberg, Harlan, Stewart, Warren, White.

## MR. JUSTICE CLARK delivered the opinion of the Court. . . . (*Atlanta Motel*)

It is admitted that the operation of the motel brings it within the provisions of § 201(a) of the Act and that appellant refused to provide lodging for transient Negroes because of their race or color and that it intends to continue that policy unless restrained. . . .

The determinative test of the exercise of power by the Congress under the Commerce Clause is simply whether the activity sought to be regulated is "commerce which concerns more than one state" and has a real and substantial relation to the national interest. . . .

It is said that the operation of the motel here is of a purely local character. But, assuming this to be true, "if it is interstate commerce that feels the pinch, it does not matter how local the operation that applies the squeeze." . . .

The power of Congress to promote interstate commerce also includes the power to regulate the local incidents thereof, including local activities in both the States of origin and destination, which might have a substantial and harmful effect upon that commerce. One need only examine the evidence which we have discussed above to see that Congress may—as it has—prohibit racial discrimination

by motels serving travelers, however "local" their operations may appear. . . .

*Affirmed.*

## MR. JUSTICE CLARK delivered the opinion of the Court. . . . (*McClung*)

The activities that are beyond the reach of Congress are "those which are completely within a particular State, which do not affect other States, and with which it is not necessary to interfere, for the purpose of executing some of the general powers of the government." . . . This rule is as good today as it was when Chief Justice Marshall laid it down almost a century and a half ago.

This Court has held time and again that this power extends to activities of retail establishments, including restaurants, which directly or indirectly burden or obstruct interstate commerce. . . .

Here, as there, Congress has determined for itself that refusals of service to Negroes have imposed burdens both upon the interstate flow of food and upon the movement of products generally. Of course, the mere fact that Congress has said when particular activity shall be deemed to affect commerce does not preclude further examination by this Court. But where we find that the legislators, in light of the facts and testimony before them, have a rational basis for finding a chosen regulatory scheme necessary to the protection of commerce, our investigation is at an end. . . .

Confronted as we are with the facts laid before Congress, we must conclude that it had a rational basis for finding that racial discrimination in restaurants had a direct and adverse effect on the free flow of interstate commerce. . . .

The absence of direct evidence connecting discriminatory restaurant service with the flow of interstate food, a factor on which the appellees place much reliance, is not, given the evidence as to the effect of such practices on other aspects of commerce, a crucial matter.

The power of Congress in this field is broad and sweeping; where it keeps within its sphere and violates no express constitutional limita-

tion it has been the rule of this Court, going back almost to the founding days of the Republic, not to interfere. The Civil Rights Act of 1964, as here applied, we find to be plainly appropriate in the resolution of what the Congress found to be a national commercial problem of the first magnitude. We find it in no violation of any express limitations of the Constitution and we therefore declare it valid.

The judgment is therefore

*Reversed.*

Mr. Justice Black, concurring . . . [omitted].

Mr. Justice Douglas, concurring . . . [omitted].

Mr. Justice Goldberg, concurring . . . [omitted].

## *United States* v. *Lopez*
## 514 U.S. 549, 115 S.Ct. 1624, 131 L.Ed. 2d 626 (1995)
### http://laws.findlaw.com/us/514/549.html

In the Gun-Free School Zones Act of 1990, referred to below as § 922(q), Congress made it a federal crime "for any individual knowingly to possess a firearm at a . . . public, parochial or private school" or "within a distance of 1,000 feet from the grounds of a . . . school." On March 12, 1992, Alfonso Lopez, Jr., was found carrying a concealed .38 caliber handgun and five bullets at Edison High School in San Antonio, Texas, where he was a senior. He was arrested under a Texas law that banned possession of a firearm on school premises. On March 13, the state dismissed charges after federal agents charged Lopez with violation of the Gun-Free School Zones Act. Over an objection that the federal statute violated the Constitution, the U.S. District Court for the Western District of Texas found Lopez guilty at a bench trial and sentenced him to six months' imprisonment and two years' supervised release. The Court of Appeals for the Fifth Circuit reversed, holding that § 922(q) was "invalid as beyond the power of Congress under the Commerce Clause." Majority: Rehnquist, Kennedy, O'Connor, Scalia, Thomas. Dissenting: Breyer, Ginsburg, Souter, Stevens.

**Chief Justice Rehnquist delivered the opinion of the Court. . . .**

We start with first principles. The Constitution creates a Federal Government of enumerated powers. . . .

[*NLRB* v.] *Jones & Laughlin Steel*, [*United States* v.] *Darby*, and *Wickard* [v. *Filburn*] ushered in an era of Commerce Clause jurisprudence that greatly expanded the previously defined authority of Congress under that Clause. In part, this was a recognition of the great changes that had occurred in the way business was carried on in this country. Enterprises that had once been local or at most regional in nature had become national in scope. But the doctrinal change also reflected a view that earlier Commerce Clause cases artificially had constrained the authority of Congress to regulate interstate commerce.

But even these modern-era precedents which have expanded congressional power under the Commerce Clause confirm that this power is subject to outer limits. . . .

Consistent with this structure, we have identified three broad categories of activity that Congress may regulate under its commerce power. First, Congress may regulate the use of the channels of interstate commerce. . . . Second, Congress is empowered to regulate and protect the instrumentalities of interstate commerce, or persons or things in interstate commerce, even though the threat may come only from intrastate activities. . . . Finally, Congress' commerce authority includes the power to regulate those activities having a substantial relation to interstate commerce, i.e., those activities that substantially affect interstate commerce.

Within this final category, admittedly, our case law has not been clear whether an activity must "affect" or "substantially affect" interstate commerce in order to be within Congress' power to regulate it under the Commerce Clause. . . . We conclude, consistent with the great weight of our case law, that the proper test requires an analysis of whether the regulated activity "substantially affects" interstate commerce.

We now turn to consider the power of Congress, in the light of this framework, to enact § 922(q). The first two categories of authority may be quickly disposed of: § 922(q) is not a regulation of the use of the channels of interstate commerce, nor is it an attempt to prohibit the interstate transportation of a commodity through the channels of commerce; nor can § 922(q) be justified as a regulation by which Congress has sought to protect an instrumentality of interstate commerce or a thing in interstate commerce. Thus, if § 922(q)

is to be sustained, it must be under the third category as a regulation of an activity that substantially affects interstate commerce. . . .

Section 922(q) is a criminal statute that by its terms has nothing to do with "commerce" or any sort of economic enterprise, however broadly one might define those terms. Section 922(q) is not an essential part of a larger regulation of economic activity, in which the regulatory scheme could be undercut unless the intrastate activity were regulated. It cannot, therefore, be sustained under our cases upholding regulations of activities that arise out of or are connected with a commercial transaction, which viewed in the aggregate, substantially affects interstate commerce.

Second, § 922(q) contains no jurisdictional element which would ensure, through case-by-case inquiry, that the firearm possession in question affects interstate commerce. . . .

Although as part of our independent evaluation of constitutionality under the Commerce Clause we of course consider legislative findings, and indeed even congressional committee findings, regarding effect on interstate commerce, the Government concedes that "[n]either the statute nor its legislative history contain[s] express congressional findings regarding the effects upon interstate commerce of gun possession in a school zone." We agree with the Government that Congress normally is not required to make formal findings as to the substantial burdens that an activity has on interstate commerce. . . . But to the extent that congressional findings would enable us to evaluate the legislative judgment that the activity in question substantially affected interstate commerce, even though no such substantial effect was visible to the naked eye, they are lacking here. . . .

The Government's essential contention, in fine, is that we may determine here that § 922(q) is valid because possession of a firearm in a local school zone does indeed substantially affect interstate commerce. The Government argues that possession of a firearm in a school zone may result in violent crime and that violent crime can be expected to affect the functioning of the national economy in two ways. First, the costs of violent crime are substantial, and, through the mechanism of insurance, those costs are spread throughout the population. Second, violent crime reduces the willingness of individuals to travel to areas within the country that are perceived to be unsafe. The Government also argues that the presence of guns in schools poses a substantial threat to the educational process by threatening the learning environment. A handicapped educational process, in turn, will result in a less productive citizenry. That, in turn, would have an adverse effect on the Nation's economic well-being. As a result, the Government argues that Congress could rationally have concluded that § 922(q) substantially affects interstate commerce.

We pause to consider the implications of the Government's arguments. The Government admits, under its "costs of crime" reasoning, that Congress could regulate not only all violent crime, but all activities that might lead to violent crime, regardless of how tenuously they relate to interstate commerce. Similarly, under the Government's "national productivity" reasoning, Congress could regulate any activity that it found was related to the economic productivity of individual citizens: family law (including marriage, divorce, and child custody), for example. Under the theories that the Government presents in support of § 922(q), it is difficult to perceive any limitation on federal power, even in areas such as criminal law enforcement or education where States historically have been sovereign. Thus, if we were to accept the Government's arguments, we are hard-pressed to posit any activity by an individual that Congress is without power to regulate.

Although JUSTICE BREYER argues that acceptance of the Government's rationales would not authorize a general federal police power, he is unable to identify any activity that the States may regulate but Congress may not. . . .

JUSTICE BREYER focuses, for the most part, on the threat that firearm possession in and near schools poses to the educational process and the potential economic consequences flowing from that threat. Specifically, the dissent reasons that (1) gun-related violence is a serious problem; (2) that problem, in turn, has an adverse effect on classroom learning; and (3) that adverse effect on classroom learning, in turn, represents a substantial threat to trade and commerce. This analysis would be equally applicable, if not more so, to subjects such as family law and direct regulation of education.

For instance, if Congress can, pursuant to its Commerce Clause power, regulate activities that adversely affect the learning environment, then, *a fortiori,* it also can regulate the educational process directly. Congress could determine that a school's curriculum has a "significant" effect on the extent of classroom learning. As a result, Congress could mandate a federal curriculum for local elementary and secondary schools because what is taught in local schools has a significant "effect on classroom learning," and that, in turn, has a substantial effect on interstate commerce. . . .

To uphold the Government's contentions here, we would have to pile inference upon inference in a manner that would bid fair to convert congressional authority under the Commerce Clause to a general police power of the sort retained by the States. Admittedly, some of our prior cases have taken long steps down that road, giving great deference to congressional action. The broad language in these opinions has suggested the possibility of additional expansion, but we decline here to proceed any further. To do so would require us to conclude that the Constitution's enumeration of powers does not presuppose something not enumerated, and that there never will be a distinction between what is truly national and what is truly local. This we are unwilling to do.

For the foregoing reasons the judgment of the Court of Appeals is

*Affirmed.*

JUSTICE KENNEDY, with whom JUSTICE O'CONNOR joins, concurring . . . [omitted].

JUSTICE THOMAS, concurring . . . [omitted].

JUSTICE STEVENS, dissenting . . . [omitted].

JUSTICE SOUTER, dissenting . . . [omitted].

**JUSTICE BREYER, with whom JUSTICE STEVENS, JUSTICE SOUTER, and JUSTICE GINSBURG join, dissenting. . . .**

In my view, the statute falls well within the scope of the commerce power as this Court has understood that power over the last half-century.

In reaching this conclusion, I apply three basic principles of Commerce Clause interpretation. First, the power to "regulate Commerce . . . among the several States" encompasses the power to regulate local activities insofar as they significantly affect interstate commerce. . . .

Second, in determining whether a local activity will likely have a significant effect upon interstate commerce, a court must consider, not the effect of an individual act (a single instance of gun possession), but rather the cumulative effect of all similar instances (i.e., the effect of all guns possessed in or near schools). . . .

Third, the Constitution requires us to judge the connection between a regulated activity and interstate commerce, not directly, but at one remove. Courts must give Congress a degree of leeway in determining the existence of a significant factual connection between the regulated activity and interstate commerce— both because the Constitution delegates the commerce power directly to Congress and because the determination requires an empirical judgment of a kind that a legislature is more likely than a court to make with accuracy. The traditional words "rational basis" capture this leeway. Thus, the specific question before us, as the Court recognizes, is not whether the "regulated activity sufficiently affected interstate commerce," but, rather, whether Congress could have had "a rational basis" for so concluding. . . .

Applying these principles to the case at hand, we must ask whether Congress could have . . . found that "violent crime in school zones," through its effect on the "quality of education," significantly (or substantially) affects "interstate" or "foreign commerce"? As long as one views the commerce connection, not as a "technical legal conception," but as "a practical one," the answer to this question must be yes.

Numerous reports and studies—generated both inside and outside government—make clear that Congress could reasonably have found the empirical connection that its law, implicitly or explicitly, asserts. . . .

Having found that guns in schools significantly undermine the quality of education in our Nation's classrooms, Congress could also have found, given the effect of education upon interstate and foreign commerce, that gun-related violence in and around schools is a commercial, as well as a human, problem. Education, although far more than a matter of economics, has long been inextricably intertwined with the Nation's economy. . . .

The economic links I have just sketched seem fairly obvious. Why then is it not equally obvious, in light of those links, that a widespread, serious, and substantial physical threat to teaching and learning also substantially threatens the commerce to which that teaching and learning is inextricably tied? That is to say, guns in the hands of six percent of inner-city high school students and gun-related violence throughout a city's schools must threaten the trade and commerce that those schools support. The only question, then, is whether the latter threat is (to use the majority's terminology) "substantial." And, the evidence of (1) the extent of the gun-related violence problem, (2) the extent of the resulting negative effect on classroom learning, and (3) the extent of the consequent negative commercial effects, when taken together, indicate a threat to trade and commerce that is "substantial." At the very least, Congress could rationally have concluded that the links are "substantial."

Specifically, Congress could have found that gun-related violence near the classroom poses a serious economic threat (1) to consequently inadequately educated workers who must endure low paying jobs, and (2) to communities and businesses that might (in today's "information society") otherwise gain, from a well-educated work force, an important commercial advantage, of a kind that location near a railhead or harbor provided in the past. Congress might also have found these threats to be no different in kind from other threats that this Court has found within the commerce power, such as the threat that loan sharking poses to the "funds" of "numerous localities," and that unfair labor practices pose to instrumentalities of commerce. As I have pointed out, Congress has written that "the occurrence of violent crime in school zones" has brought about a "decline in the quality of education" that "has an adverse impact on interstate commerce and the foreign commerce of the United States." The violence-related facts, the educational facts, and the economic facts, taken together, make this conclusion rational. And, because under our case law the sufficiency of the constitutionally necessary Commerce Clause link between a crime of violence and interstate commerce turns simply upon size or degree, those same facts make the statute constitutional. . . .

In sum, a holding that the particular statute before us falls within the commerce power would not expand the scope of that Clause. Rather, it simply would apply pre-existing law to changing economic circumstances. . . .

## *United States* v. *Morrison*
**529 U.S. 598, 120 S.Ct. 1740, 146 L.Ed. 2d 658 (2000)**
**http://laws.findlaw.com/us/529/598.html**

(This case is reprinted in Chapter Four beginning on page 170.)

# CHAPTER SEVEN

# *National Taxing and Spending Power*

*Taxes are what we pay for civilized society. . . .*

—JUSTICE OLIVER WENDELL HOLMES (1927)

**G**overnment, like individual citizens, must have regular income to pay bills and maintain credit. Government programs cost money, whether in building aircraft carriers, sponsoring cancer research, or maintaining national parks. Moreover, government must have coercive power to collect taxes. No government can carry on effectively if it has to depend, as did the Congress under the **Articles of Confederation,** on what amounted to voluntary contributions. Indeed, the principal weakness of the central government under the Articles was absence of power to levy taxes. National expenditures were defrayed out of a common treasury, supplied by the states in proportion to the occupied land in each state, and upon requisition by Congress. The states reserved the right to levy taxes for this purpose and were usually delinquent in making payments.

Therefore, it is not surprising that, although members of the federal Convention were sharply divided on many issues, they were almost unanimous in their insistence that Congress should have broad power to tax and spend. Heading the list of enumerated powers in Article I, Section 8, stands the provision that Congress shall have power "to lay and collect taxes, duties, imposts and excises, to pay the debts and provide for the common defense and general welfare of the United States."

It would be difficult to fashion more sweeping language. In the exercise of its taxing and spending power, the national government acts directly on individual citizens and their property as though there were no states. Nor are there any limits (apart from those imposed on Congress at the ballot box) on the amount Congress may attempt to collect through taxation. The only limitations on the taxing power are those that the Supreme Court has established and those that the Constitution specifically provides in Article I. Section 9 specifically bars a preference to one state's ports over another's and forbids a tax on exports (a concession made in 1787 to southern exporters). These provisions have occasioned no difficulties. Yet the Court's interpretation of the stipulation on direct taxes in the same section led to a constitutional amendment.

## DIRECT AND INDIRECT TAXES

The Constitution declares that taxes are of two kinds and sets forth briefly the rules by which Congress may use each. Article I, Section 9, declares that **direct taxes** shall be levied according to the rule of apportionment among the several states on the basis of census enumeration or population. **Indirect taxes** shall be levied according to the rule of uniformity, which means geographical uniformity, as *Knowlton* v. *Moore* (1900) made clear. That is to say, a tax must be laid at the same rate and on the same basis in all parts of the United States. The meaning of indirect taxes, which include all excises and duties, has rarely troubled the Court, but the definition of direct taxes has proved troublesome.

**VIEWS OF THE FRAMERS.** James Madison's notes from the federal Convention throw no light on the mystery of what is a direct tax. The single entry on this question runs, "Mr. Davie of North Carolina rose to ask the meaning of the direct taxes. Mr. King said he did not know." Like so many other terms in the Constitution, the meaning of direct taxes had to be spelled out by judicial construction.

The Court first addressed the subject in 1796 in ***Hylton* v. *United States,*** where a federal tax on carriages was held to be an indirect tax and therefore not subject to apportionment. The Court's ruling was based first on the nature of the carriage tax, which it considered a levy on the privilege of using carriages and, second, on the impossibility of fairly apportioning a tax of this kind because the ratio of carriages to population was obviously not the same in each state. The justices agreed that the only direct taxes were capitation and land taxes, and these categories remained frozen for a century.

**THE INCOME TAX CASE.** Believing that the Court would adhere to this definition, Congress levied an income tax during the Civil War. It was challenged unsuccessfully in *Springer* v. *United States* (1881), a precedent that stood until the 1890s, when Congress enacted another income tax law, levied, as the Civil War tax had been, as if it were indirect. This time, in ***Pollock* v. *Farmers' Loan & Trust Co.,*** the Court changed its mind, boldly rewriting the definition of direct taxes given in *Hylton,* thus correcting, by a margin of one vote, "a century of error." In his brief attacking the validity of the income tax (on the theory that it was direct and had to be apportioned), Joseph H. Choate, one of the leaders of the American bar, referred to the tax in caustic terms—he called it "communism," "socialism," and "populism." Adopting Choate's sulphurous language, Justice Field in a concurring opinion warned, "The present assault upon capital is but the beginning . . . the stepping stone to others . . . till our political contests will become a war of the poor against the rich." He insisted that this kind of class struggle had to be stopped. The dissenting judges decried in equally fervent language what they deemed a disastrous blow to congressional power and an unwarranted expansion of judicial review.

The immediate effect of this decision was to add income taxes to the category of direct taxes, and because it was not feasible to apportion income taxes, Congress was deprived of this fruitful source of revenue for nearly 20 years. To correct this situation, Congress and the states resorted finally to the cumbersome formal amending process, which in 1913 resulted in the Sixteenth Amendment: "The Congress shall have power to lay and collect taxes on incomes, from whatever source derived, without apportionment among the several states, and without regard to any census or enumeration."

Even this seemingly comprehensive language, however, was not allowed to mean all that it seemed to say. By judicial construction, the amendment was held to mean only that income taxes need not be apportioned and was not interpreted as authorizing taxes on all incomes. The salaries of federal judges, the Court ruled in 1920 in *Evans* v. *Gore,* were still exempt from the income tax. However, without any revision of the Sixteenth Amendment, *Evans* was overruled in 1939 by *O'Malley* v. *Woodrough*. As Justice Frankfurter observed, "To suggest that it [a nondiscriminatory income tax] makes inroads upon the independence of judges . . . by making them bear their aliquot share of the cost of maintaining the government is to trivialize the great historic experience on which the framers based the safeguards of Article 3, Section 1."

## REGULATION THROUGH TAXATION

In addition to express limitations, the Supreme Court developed two others through interpretation. The first is the doctrine of reciprocal immunity of the state and national governments from taxation by the other (a subject covered in Chapter Four). The second is the **independent constitutional bar** (or external check) that the Court has constructed when Congress has arguably used its taxing or spending power to accomplish an objective forbidden by the Constitution. This second limitation typically arises in the context of **regulatory taxation.** As a check on national power, both today are mere shadows of their former selves.

While the most obvious and normal purpose of taxation is the raising of revenue, this is not taxation's only legitimate purpose. A protective tariff, for example, exists not to enrich the federal treasury but to shield an industry or a commodity from foreign competition. Taxes on certain tobacco products enrich the treasury but are also designed to discourage their use, especially among younger smokers, by making cigarettes very expensive. Whether a tax is primarily for revenue or regulation is frequently a difficult question, a matter of degree, for strictly speaking, no tax is or can be solely a revenue measure.

**ENUMERATED AND UNENUMERATED POWERS.** One aspect of this question has been definitely settled. Congress may use its taxing power primarily for purposes of regulation, or even destruction, when the tax serves to aid Congress in exercising one of its other **enumerated,** or delegated, **powers,** such as regulating interstate commerce, controlling the currency, or maintaining a postal service. An illustrative case is *Veazie Bank* v. *Fenno* (1869), involving an act of Congress that placed a 10 percent tax on state bank notes to protect the notes of the new national banks from the state banks' competition. The tax was of course destructive, as it was intended to be; yet the Court upheld it on the ground that Congress could have achieved the same end by absolute prohibition of state bank notes under the currency power.

A more controversial question remains: May Congress use a tax primarily as a regulatory device, that is, to enforce some social or economic policy, when no enumerated power of Congress can be invoked in justification? For a long period the Court's answers to this question wavered between a clear yes and an equally clear no.

An important affirmative case is **_McCray_ v. _United States_** (1904), which concerned the validity of a **destructive tax** on oleomargarine artificially colored to resemble butter. That the primary purpose of the tax was regulation and not revenue was clear from the much higher tax on colored oleomargarine (ten cents per pound), as compared to the uncolored product (1/4 cent per pound). Yet the Court held that because Congress had virtually unlimited discretion in the selection of the objects of taxation, it was not part of the judicial function to explore congressional motives. Under this judicial hands-off policy, Congress proceeded to regulate by taxation the manufacture of phosphorus matches and narcotics and the retail sale of certain firearms. The McCray doctrine came close to making the question of the validity of destructive and regulatory taxation a political question.

In due course, the Court evolved a more effective technique for imposing limitations on the destructive use of the federal taxing power for social and economic regulation. The change came in 1922 in _Bailey_ v. _Drexel Furniture Co.,_ which involved the constitutionality of a 10 percent federal tax on the net income of any employer of child labor, regardless of the number of children employed. In addition, the act set up an elaborate code for regulating each employer's conduct, a matter over which Congress admittedly had no direct control. Speaking through Chief Justice Taft, an all but unanimous Court condemned the act primarily because it was a "penalty" and not a tax, and secondarily because by regulating production the act invaded the reserved powers of the states. (Four years earlier in **_Hammer_ v. _Dagenhart_,** reprinted in Chapter Six, the Court invalidated a child labor law Congress had passed under its commerce power.)

**Taxing, Spending, and the General Welfare.** In 1935–1936, when taxation provisions of President Franklin Roosevelt's New Deal programs were tested, two lines of precedents were thus available. If the Court chose to sustain a measure under the taxing power, it could employ the generous principle of _McCray_. If, on the other hand, the Court chose to set aside the legislation, it could look on the tax—as Chief Justice Taft did in _Drexel Furniture_—as a "penalty," a form of "regulation," an invasion of domain reserved to the states.

One of the planks in the platform on which FDR was elected in 1932 was his solemn vow to restore agricultural prosperity. The Agricultural Adjustment Act of 1933 (AAA) levied a processing tax on basic commodities such as wheat, corn, and cotton. From the funds thus accumulated, money was paid out to farmers as "inducement" to reduce acreage. Popular with both farmers and their suppliers, it was a self-financing scheme to subsidize farmers as the protective tariff had long subsidized industry. And it was effective, transferring millions of dollars from the non-agricultural sector of the economy into farming.

Despite high expectations, the program became shrouded in doubt when the Supreme Court considered a challenge to the law in December 1935 in **_United States_ v. _Butler_.** Attacking the act's constitutionality at oral argument in the newly finished Supreme Court Building was Philadelphia's most eminent lawyer, George Wharton Pepper. Perfectly cast for the role, Pepper observed, "I have tried very hard to argue this case calmly and dispassionately, because it seems to me that this is the best way in which an advocate can discharge his duty to this Court. But I do not want Your Honors to think my feelings are not involved and that my emotions are not deeply stirred. Indeed, may it please Your Honors, I believe I am standing here today to plead the cause of the America I have loved; and I pray Almighty God that not in my time may 'the land of the regimented' be accepted as a worthy substitute for 'the land of the free.'" For Pepper, economic dogma, no less than congressional taxing power, was at stake.

The former senator's prayer was soon answered. Within a month the Court announced its decision. According to Justice Owen J. Roberts, Pepper's former student at the University of Pennsylvania Law School, the processing tax could not be upheld as a tax. "The word has never been thought to connote the expropriation of money from one group for the benefit of another." If valid, the exaction could be supported only as an exercise of the disputed power to tax and spend for the general welfare. The Court was thus face to face with an unresolved issue dating from George Washington's first term.

Was the authorization in Section 8 of Article I to tax and spend in providing for the general welfare a substantive, independent power, as Alexander Hamilton maintained at the founding? Or was it no power at all, but rather an appendage of Congress's other enumerated powers, as Madison contended? Through many administrations, regardless of party, appropriations of money had been made to accomplish purposes not identified with those that Congress is authorized to promote under its other powers. Hamilton had upheld this view in his famous *Report on Manufactures* (1791), and Justice Roberts emphatically embraced it. No sooner had he adopted the **Hamiltonian theory,** however, than Roberts proceeded to enforce, for all practical purposes, the narrow **Madisonian theory** he had just repudiated. Congress might appropriate money for an objective designated as the general welfare, but it could attach no terms or conditions to the use of funds so appropriated unless such terms or conditions were themselves authorized by another specific congressional grant. Federal money might be spent for the broad purposes outlined by Hamilton, but Congress could control the expenditure only if the objectives were within the narrow scope Madison gave the general welfare clause.

Probing congressional motives, Justice Roberts discovered that this was not a tax at all but payment of benefits to farmers to induce (or coerce) them into curtailing agricultural production. Congress, he said, had no power to regulate production. The tax was thus in effect an ingeniously disguised regulation, an invalid invasion of the reserved domain of the states. "It is an established principle," he concluded, "that the attainment of a prohibited end may not be accomplished under the pretext of the exertion of powers which are granted."

Having chosen to adopt a narrow construction of the taxing power in *Butler,* the Court reverted to the more generous rule of *McCray* two years later, when *Steward Machine Co.* v. *Davis* (1937) upheld the unemployment compensation component of the landmark Social Security Act of 1935. Justice Cardozo set forth a strongly nationalistic theory of legislative power which declared that Congress has full power to tax and spend for the general welfare. For five justices, the Tenth Amendment was no barrier to the payroll tax at issue. On the same day, seven justices upheld the payroll tax dedicated to funding benefits for the elderly against a challenge, among others, that it also contravened the Tenth Amendment. The discretion to define the general welfare, Cardozo wrote, "is not confided to the courts. The discretion belongs to Congress, unless the choice is clearly wrong, a display of arbitrary power, not an exercise of judgment" (*Helvering* v. *Davis*). Reflecting the "revolution" of 1937, both opinions represented a significant shift in constitutional interpretation and in the Court's view of the federal system.

## REGULATION THROUGH SPENDING

In the years since the New Deal legislation of the 1930s, Congress has employed its spending power to achieve various policy objectives by allocating billions of dollars in grants to state and local governments, private organizations, and even individuals. These grants routinely come with a variety of conditions attached. Constitutional questions arise when Congress attempts through such **conditional spending** to accomplish indirectly what the Constitution might not allow it to do directly.

**ALCOHOL.** The 1980s witnessed efforts by Congress to cope with alcohol-related traffic accidents by imposing indirectly a national drinking age through conditional spending. The National Minimum Drinking Age Amendment of 1982 directed the secretary of transportation to withhold 5 percent of allotted federal highway funds from states with a legal drinking age under 21. Justice Roberts in *Butler* had relied on the Tenth Amendment to block indirect federal regulation of agriculture. Now South Dakota contended that the Twenty-first Amendment, which not only ended Prohibition but affirmed state control over the sale and use of alcoholic beverages, limited this new use of the spending power. *South Dakota v. Dole* (1987) rejected the state's claim. Although seven justices left open the question whether Congress could legislate a national drinking age directly, they had little doubt about its authority to do so by way of disbursement of funds. In her dissent, Justice O'Connor paid special attention to Roberts's reasoning in *Butler*. "The immense size and power of the Government of the United States ought not obscure its fundamental character. It remains a Government of enumerated powers."

In 2000, the drinking age decision was authority for congressional legislation directing each state to set a 0.08 percent blood-alcohol level to combat drunken driving. (At the time, 31 states used the less stringent limit of 0.1 percent.) States not complying by 2004 lose 2 percent of their federal highway trust funds, with the penalty increasing to 8 percent in 2007.

**CIVIL LIBERTIES.** What happens when conditional spending appears to collide with a protection in the Bill of Rights or the Fourteenth Amendment? An act of Congress declares that no federal funds can be spent in programs where abortion is part of family planning. In 1988 the Department of Health and Human Services issued regulations under the statute barring employees at clinics receiving federal funds from counseling pregnant women about the availability of abortion. *Rust* v. *Sullivan* (1991) upheld the gag rule against an attack on privacy and First Amendment free speech grounds. Yet First Amendment interests prevailed in *Legal Services Corp.* v. *Valazquez* (2001), which struck down Congress's 1996 ban on LSC funding of any local organization that represented clients in courtroom challenges to welfare laws.

*National Endowment for the Arts v. Finley* (1998) posed perhaps an equally difficult question. At issue were congressionally mandated standards for the National Endowment for the Arts in awarding grants. Aside from judging applicants by criteria of "artistic excellence and artistic merit," Congress directed the NEA to "tak[e] into consideration general standards of decency and respect for the diverse beliefs and values of the American public." The language on decency and beliefs had been added after public outcry over several exhibits where their creators had received NEA support. Four performance artists brought suit, claiming that Congress had engaged in viewpoint discrimination in violation of the First Amendment and that the language was unconstitutionally vague. All members of the Court agreed that no one could be criminally punished for displaying "indecent" art, but in upholding the statute eight justices were less demanding when government acted not as regulator, but as a patron, subsidizer, or consumer of art. Congress's broad powers to spend continue to raise questions under the Constitution.


## KEY TERMS

Articles of Confederation

direct taxes

indirect taxes

independent
   constitutional bar

regulatory taxation

enumerated powers

destructive tax

Hamiltonian theory

Madisonian theory

conditional spending


## QUERIES

**1.** In what way does *Hylton* v. *United States* anticipate Chapter Two's *Marbury* v. *Madison?*

**2.** Review the materials in Chapter Four discussing the revival of dual federalism in some recent Supreme Court decisions. In what way was dual federalism a factor in Justice Roberts's opinion in *United States* v. *Butler?*

**3.** In light of *South Dakota* v. *Dole,* are there any remaining judicial checks to augment the purely political checks on congressional spending power in relation to the states?

**4.** In evaluating Congress's powers under the spending clause, what difference does it make whether the Court prefers the Hamiltonian or Madisonian theory?


## SELECTED READINGS

CORWIN, EDWARD S. "The Spending Power of Congress." 36 *Harvard Law Review* 548 (1923).

EPSTEIN, RICHARD A. "Foreword: Unconstitutional Conditions, State Power, and the Limits of Consent." 102 *Harvard Law Review* 4 (1988).

KADEN, LEWIS B. "Politics, Money, and State Sovereignty: The Judicial Role." 79 *Columbia Law Review* 847 (1979).

LAWSON, J. F. *The General Welfare Clause.* Washington D.C.: J. F. Lawson, 1926.

LUND, NELSON. "Congressional Power over Taxation and Commerce: The Supreme Court's Lost Chance to Devise a Consistent Doctrine." 18 *Texas Tech Law Review* 729 (1987).

MCCOY, THOMAS R., and BARRY FRIEDMAN. "Conditional Spending: Federalism's Trojan Horse." 1988 *Supreme Court Review* 85.

MOORE, W. S., and RUDOLF G. PENNER, eds. *The Constitution and the Budget.* Washington, D.C.: American Enterprise Institute, 1980.

STANLEY, ROBERT. *Dimensions of Law in the Service of Order: Origins of the Federal Income Tax, 1861–1913.* New York: Oxford University Press, 1993.

WITTE, JOHN F. *The Politics and Development of the Federal Income Tax.* Madison: University of Wisconsin Press, 1985.

# I. DIRECT AND INDIRECT TAXES

## *Hylton v. United States*
## 3 U.S. (3 Dall.) 171, 1 L.Ed. 556 (1796)
### http://laws.findlaw.com/us/3/171.html

Daniel Hylton claimed that a congressional act of 1794 levying a tax of $16 on each carriage was a direct tax and must be laid in proportion to the census. With an ownership of 125 carriages, Hylton obtained review of an adverse judgment in the U.S. circuit court in Virginia. Majority: Chase, Iredell, Paterson, Wilson. Not participating: Ellsworth, Cushing.

CHASE, JUSTICE.

By the case stated, only one question is submitted to the opinion of this court— whether the law of Congress of the 5th of June 1794, entitled, "An act to lay duties upon carriages for the conveyance of persons," is unconstitutional and void?

The principles laid down, to prove the above law void, are these: that a tax on carriages is a direct tax, and, therefore, by the constitution, must be laid according to the census, directed by the constitution to be taken, to ascertain the number of representatives from each state. And that the tax in question on carriages is not laid by that rule of apportionment, but by the rule of uniformity, prescribed by the constitution in the case of duties, imposts and excises; and a tax on carriages is not within either of those descriptions. . . .

I think, an annual tax on carriages, for the conveyance of persons, may be considered as within the power granted to congress to lay duties. . . .

I am inclined to think but of this I do not give a judicial opinion, that the direct taxes contemplated by the constitution, are only two, to wit, a capitation or poll tax, simply, without regard to property, profession or any other circumstance; and a tax on land. I doubt, whether a tax, by a general assessment of personal property, within the United States, is included within the term direct tax. . . .

PATERSON, JUSTICE. . . .

I never entertained a doubt that the principal, I will not say, the only, objects, that the framers of the constitution contemplated, as falling within the rules of apportionment, were a capitation tax and a tax on land. Local considerations, and the particular circumstances, and relative situation of the states, naturally lead to this view of the subject. The provision was made in favor of the southern states; they possessed a large number of slaves; they had extensive tracts of territory, thinly settled, and not very productive. A majority of the states had but few slaves, and several of them a limited territory, well settled, and in a high state of cultivation. The southern states, if no provision had been introduced in the constitution, would have been wholly at the mercy of the other states. Congress in such case, might tax slaves, at discretion or arbitrarily, and land in every part of the Union, after the same rate or measure: so much a head in the first instance, and so much an acre, in the second. To guard them against imposition, in these particulars, was the reason of introducing the clause in the constitution, which directs that representatives and direct taxes shall be apportioned among the states, according to their respective numbers. . . .

IREDELL, JUSTICE. . . .

As all direct taxes must be apportioned, it is evident, that the constitution contemplated none as direct, but such as could be apportioned. If this cannot be apportioned, it is, therefore, not a direct tax in the sense of the constitution.

That this tax cannot be apportioned, is evident. Suppose, ten dollars contemplated as a tax on each chariot, or post chaise, in the United States, and the number of both in all the United States be computed at 105, the number of representatives in congress.

This would produce in the whole . . . . $1,050.00

The share of Virginia being 19/105 parts,
    would be . . . . . . . . . . . . . . . . . . . . . 190.00

The share of Connecticut being 7/105 parts,
    would be . . . . .. . . . . . . . . . . . . . . . . 70.00

Then suppose Virginia had 50 carriages,
    Connecticut 2,

The share of Virginia being $190, this must,
    of course, be collected from the owners
    of carriages, and there would, therefore,
    be collected from each carriage . . . . . . . 3.80

The share of Connecticut being $70,
    each carriage would pay . . . . . . . . . . . 35.00

If any state had no carriages, there could be no apportionment at all. This mode is too manifestly absurd to be supported, and has not even been attempted in debate. . . .

WILSON, JUSTICE.— . . . [omitted].

BY THE COURT.—Let the judgment of the circuit court be affirmed.

## Pollock v. Farmers' Loan & Trust Company
### 158 U.S. 601, 15 S.Ct. 673, 39 L.Ed. 1108 (1895) (Rehearing)
http://laws.findlaw.com/us/158/601.html

> In 1894 Congress imposed a tax of 2 percent on income above $4,000 derived from various classes of property as well as that resulting from personal services. In the first decision (April 1895) involving the act, the Court, with Justice Howell Jackson absent, declared the act invalid insofar as it was applied to the income from real estate and the interest on municipal bonds. The Court was evenly divided on other questions presented. In May 1895, the Court decided the remaining questions on a rehearing after the terminally ill Jackson made a special trip to Washington. Jackson's vote to uphold the tax meant that one of the other justices changed sides. Majority: Fuller, Brewer, Field, Gray, Shiras. Dissenting: Harlan, Brown, Jackson, White.

**MR. CHIEF JUSTICE FULLER delivered the opinion of the Court. . . .**

The Constitution divided Federal taxation into two great classes, the class of direct taxes and the class of duties, imposts, and excises, and prescribed two rules which qualified the grant of power as to each class.

The power to lay direct taxes, apportioned among the several States in proportion to their representation in the popular branch of Congress, a representation based on population as ascertained by the census, was plenary and absolute, but to lay direct taxes without apportionment was forbidden. The power to lay duties, imposts, and excises was subject to the qualification that the imposition must be uniform throughout the United States.

Our previous decision was confined to the consideration of the validity of the tax on the income from real estate, and on the income from municipal bonds. . . .

We are now permitted to broaden the field of inquiry, and determine to which of the two great classes a tax upon a person's entire income, whether derived from rents, or products, or otherwise, of real estate, or from bonds, stocks or other forms of personal property, belongs; and we are unable to conclude that the enforced subtraction from the yield of all the owner's real or personal property, in the manner prescribed, is so different from a tax upon the property itself, that it is not a direct, but an indirect tax. . . .

We know of no reason for holding otherwise than that the words "direct taxes" on the one hand, and "duties, imposts, and excises" on the other, were used in the Constitution in their natural and obvious sense, nor, in arriving at what those terms embrace, do we perceive any ground for enlarging them beyond, or narrowing them within, their natural and obvious import at the time the Constitution was framed and ratified. . . .

The reasons for the clauses of the Constitution in respect of direct taxation are not far to seek. The States, respectively, possessed plenary powers of taxation. . . . They retained the power of direct taxation, and to that they looked as their chief resource; but even in respect of that, they granted the concurrent power, and if the tax were placed by both governments on the same subject, the claim of the United States had preference. Therefore, they did not grant the power of direct taxation without regard to their own condition and resources as States; but they granted the power of apportioned direct taxation, a power just as efficacious to serve the needs of the general government, but securing to the States the opportunity to pay the amount apportioned, and to recoup from their own citizens in the most feasible way, and in harmony with their systems of local self-government. . . .

It is said that a tax on the whole income of property is not a direct tax in the meaning of the Constitution, but a duty, and, as a duty, leviable without apportionment, whether direct or indirect. We do not think so. Direct taxation was not restricted in one breath, and the restriction blown to the winds in another. . . .

Whatever the speculative views of political economists or revenue reformers may be, can it be properly held that the Constitution, taken in its plain and obvious sense, and with due regard to the circumstances attending the formation of the government, authorizes a general unapportioned tax on the products of the farm and the rents of real estate, although imposed merely because of ownership and with no possible means of escape from payment, as belonging to a totally different class from that which includes the property from which the income proceeds?

There can be only one answer, unless the constitutional restriction is to be treated as utterly illusory and futile, and the object of its framers defeated. We find it impossible to hold that a fundamental requisition, deemed so important as to be enforced by two provisions, one affirmative and one negative, can be refined away by forced distinctions between that which gives value to property and the property itself.

Nor can we perceive any ground why the same reasoning does not apply to capital in personalty held for the purpose of income or ordinarily yielding income, and to the income therefrom. All the real estate of the country, and all its invested personal property, are open to the direct operation of the taxing power if an apportionment be made according to the Constitution. The Constitution does not say that no direct tax shall be laid by apportionment on any other property than land; on the contrary, it forbids all unapportioned direct taxes; and we know of no warrant for excepting personal property from the exercise of the power, or any reason why an apportioned direct tax cannot be laid and assessed. . . .

We have considered the act only in respect of the tax on income derived from real estate, and from invested personal property, and have not commented on so much of it as bears on gains or profits from business, privileges, or employments, in view of the instances in which taxation on business, privileges, or employments has assumed the guise of an excise tax and been sustained as such.

Being of opinion that so much of the sections of this law as lays a tax on income from real and personal property is invalid, we are brought to the question of the effect of that conclusion upon these sections as a whole.

It is elementary that the same statute may be in part constitutional and in part unconstitutional, and if the parts are wholly independent of each other, that which is constitutional may stand while that which is unconstitutional will be rejected. And in the case before us there is no question as to validity of this act, except sections twenty-seven to thirty-seven inclusive, which relate to the subject which has been under discussion; and as to them we think that the rule laid down by Chief Justice Shaw [of the Massachusetts Supreme Court] in *Warren* v. *Charlestown* is applicable, that if the different parts "are so mutually connected with and dependent on each other, as conditions, considerations or compensations for each other, as to warrant the belief that the legislature intended them as a whole, and that, if all could not be carried into effect, the legislature would not pass the residue independently, and some parts are unconstitutional, all the provisions which are thus dependent, conditional or connected, must fall with them." . . .

Our conclusions may, therefore, be summed up as follows:

*First.* We adhere to the opinion already announced, that, taxes on real estate being indisputably direct taxes, taxes on the rents or incomes of real estate are equally direct taxes.

*Second.* We are of opinion that taxes on personal property, or on the income of personal property, are likewise direct taxes.

*Third.* The tax imposed by sections twenty-seven to thirty-seven, inclusive, of the act of 1894, so far as it falls on the income of real estate and of personal property, being a direct tax within the meaning of the Constitution, and, therefore, unconstitutional and void because not apportioned according to representation, all those sections, constituting one entire scheme of taxation, are necessarily invalid.

*The decrees hereinbefore entered in this court will be vacated; the decrees below will be reversed, and the case remanded, with instructions to grant the relief prayed.*

### MR. JUSTICE HARLAN dissenting. . . .

In my judgment a tax on income derived from real property ought not to be, and until now has never been, regarded by any court as a direct tax on such property within the meaning of the Constitution. As the great mass of lands in most of the States do not bring any rents, and as incomes from rents vary in different States, such a tax cannot possibly be apportioned among the States on the basis merely of numbers with any approach to equality of right among taxpayers, any more than a tax on carriages or other personal property could be so apportioned. And, in view of former adjudications, beginning with the Hylton case and ending with the Springer case, a decision now that a tax on income from real property can be laid and collected only by apportioning the same among the States, on the basis of numbers, may, not improperly, be regarded as a judicial revolution, that may sow the seeds of hate and distrust among the people of different sections of our common country. . . .

In my judgment—to say nothing of the disregard of the former adjudications of this court, and of the settled practice of the government—this decision may well excite the gravest apprehensions. It strikes at the very foundations of national authority, in that it denies to the general government a power which is, or may become, vital to the very existence and preservation of the Union in a national emergency, such as that of war with a great commercial nation, during which the collection of all duties upon imports will cease or be materially diminished. It tends to reestablish that condition of helplessness in which Congress found itself during the period of the Articles of Confederation, when it was without authority by laws operating directly upon individuals, to lay and collect, through its own agents, taxes sufficient to pay the debts and defray the expenses of government, but was dependent, in all such matters, upon the good will of the States, and their promptness in meeting requisitions made upon them by Congress.

Why do I say that the decision just rendered impairs or menaces the national authority? The reason is so apparent that it need only be stated. In its practical operation this decision withdraws from national taxation not only all incomes derived from real estate, but tangible personal property, *invested* personal property, bonds, stocks, investments of all kinds, and the income that may be derived from such property. This results from the fact that by the decision of the court, all such personal property and all incomes from real estate and personal property are placed beyond national taxation otherwise than by *apportionment* among the States *on the basis* simply *of population*. No such apportionment can possibly be made without doing gross injustice to the many for the benefit of the favored few in particular States. Any attempt upon the part of Congress to apportion among the States, upon the basis simply of their population, taxation of personal property or of incomes, would tend to arouse such indignation among the freemen of America that it would never be repeated. When therefore, this court adjudges, as it does now adjudge, that Congress cannot impose a duty or tax upon personal property, or upon income arising either from rents of real estate or from personal property, including invested personal property, bonds, stocks, and investments of all kinds, except by apportioning the sum to be so raised among the States according to population, it *practically* decides that, *without an amendment of the Constitution*—two-thirds of both Houses of Congress and three-fourths of the States concurring—such property and incomes can never be made to contribute to the support of the national government. . . .

Mr. Justice Brown, dissenting . . . [omitted].

Mr. Justice Jackson, dissenting . . . [omitted].

### Mr. Justice White, dissenting. . . .

[The decision] takes invested wealth and reads it into the Constitution as a favored and protected class of property, which cannot be taxed without apportionment, whilst it leaves the occupation of the minister, the doctor, the professor, the lawyer, . . . the merchant, the mechanic, and all other forms of industry upon which the prosperity of a people must depend, subject to taxation without that condition. A rule which works out this result, which . . . stultifies the Constitution by making it an instrument of the most grievous wrong, should not be adopted, especially when, in order to do so, the decisions of this court, the opinions of the law writers and publicists, tradition, practice, and the settled policy of the government must be overthrown. . . .

## II. REGULATION THROUGH TAXATION

### *McCray v. United States*
### 195 U.S. 27, 24 S.Ct. 769, 49 L.Ed. 78 (1904)
### http://laws.findlaw.com/us/195/27.html

The Oleomargarine Act, passed by Congress in 1886 and amended in 1902, levied a tax of one-quarter cent per pound on uncolored oleomargarine and ten cents per pound on oleomargarine colored yellow. (The tax was not removed until 1950.) McCray, a licensed dealer, failed to pay the higher tax in making sales of the colored product and was fined. Majority: White, Brewer, Day, Harlan, Holmes, McKenna. Dissenting: Fuller, Brown, Peckham.

### Mr. Justice White . . . delivered the opinion of the court. . . .

That the acts in question on their face impose excise taxes which Congress had the power to levy is so completely established as to require only statement. . . .

It is, however, argued if a lawful power may be exerted for an unlawful purpose, and thus by abusing the power it may be made to accomplish a result not intended by the Constitution, all limitations of power must disappear, and the grave function lodged in the judiciary, to confine all the departments within the authority conferred by the Constitution, will be of no avail. This, when reduced to its last analysis, comes to this, that, because a particular department of the government may exert its lawful powers with the object or motive of reaching an end not justified, therefore it becomes the duty of the judiciary to restrain the exercise of a lawful power wherever it seems to the judicial mind that such lawful power has been abused. But this reduces itself to the contention that, under our constitutional system, the abuse by one department of the government of its lawful powers is to be corrected by the abuse of its powers by another department. . . .

It is, of course, true, as suggested, that if there be no authority in the judiciary to restrain a lawful exercise of power by another department of the government, where a wrong motive or purpose has impelled to the exertion of the power, that abuses of a power conferred may be temporarily effectual. The remedy for this, however, lies, not in the abuse by the judicial authority of its functions, but in the people, upon whom, after all, under our institutions, reliance must be placed for the correction of abuses committed in the exercise of a lawful power. . . .

It being thus demonstrated that the motive or purpose of Congress in adopting the acts in question may not be inquired into, we are brought to consider the contentions relied upon to show that the acts assailed were beyond the power of Congress, putting entirely out of view all considerations based upon purpose or motive. . . .

Since . . . the taxing power conferred by the Constitution knows no limits except those expressly stated in that instrument, it must follow, if a tax be within the lawful power, the exertion of that power may not be judicially restrained because of the results to arise from its exercise. . . .

Whilst undoubtedly both the Fifth and Tenth Amendments qualify, in so far as they are applicable, all the provisions of the Constitution, nothing in those amendments operates to take away the grant of power to tax conferred by the Constitution upon Congress. The contention on this subject rests upon the theory that the purpose and motive of Congress in exercising its undoubted powers may be inquired into by the courts, and the proposition is therefore disposed of by what has been said on that subject.

The right of Congress to tax within its delegated powers being unrestrained, except as limited by the Constitution, it was within the authority conferred on Congress to select the objects upon which an excise should be laid. It therefore follows that, in exerting its power, no want of due process of law could possibly result, because that body chose to impose an excise on artificially colored oleomargarine and not upon natural butter artificially colored. The judicial power may not usurp the functions of the legislative in order to control that branch of the government in the performance of its lawful duties. . . .

Let us concede that if a case was presented where the abuse of the taxing power was so extreme as to be beyond the principles which we have previously stated, and where it was plain to the judicial mind that the power had been called into play not for revenue but solely for the purpose of destroying rights which could not be rightfully destroyed consistently with the principles of freedom and justice upon which the Constitution rests, that it would be the duty of the courts to say that such an arbitrary act was not merely an abuse of a delegated power, but was the exercise of an authority not conferred. This concession, however, like the one previously made, must be without influence upon the decision of this case for the reasons previously stated: that is, that the manufacture of artificially colored oleomargarine may be prohibited by a free government without a violation of fundamental rights.

*Affirmed.*

THE CHIEF JUSTICE, MR. JUSTICE BROWN, and MR. JUSTICE PECKHAM dissent [without opinion].

# III. REGULATION THROUGH SPENDING

## United States v. Butler
## 297 U.S. 1, 56 S.Ct. 312, 80 L.Ed. 477 (1936)
http://laws.findlaw.com/us/297/1.html

> As a major part of President Roosevelt's New Deal, Congress enacted the Agricultural Adjustment Act in 1933 to benefit farm producers by raising commodity prices and assuring farmers purchasing power comparable to their position in 1909–1914. In order to bring supply in line with demand, the government made payments to farmers in return for their promise to reduce crop acreage. To finance the program, a processing tax was levied on the first processor of the commodity involved. In the first year of the program, more than 40 million acres were taken out of cultivation, and payments to farmers totaled several hundred million dollars. Butler, the receiver for a processor, refused to pay the tax. The district court ordered it paid, but the court of appeals reversed. With *Carter* v. *Carter Coal Co.*, decided two months later, this decision helped to precipitate the Court-packing fight of 1937 (see Chapter Six). Majority: Roberts, Butler, Hughes, McReynolds, Sutherland, Van Devanter. Dissenting: Stone, Brandeis, Cardozo.

**MR. JUSTICE ROBERTS delivered the opinion of the Court. . . .**

There should be no misunderstanding as to the function of this court in such a case. It is sometimes said that the court assumes a power to overrule or control the action of the people's representatives. This is a misconception. . . . When an act of Congress is appropriately challenged in the courts as not conforming to the constitutional mandate, the judicial branch of the Government has only one duty—to lay the article of the Constitution which is invoked beside the statute which is challenged and to decide whether the latter squares with the former. All the court does, or can do, is to announce its considered judgment upon the question. The only power it has, if such it may be called, is the power of judgment. This court neither approves nor condemns any legislative policy. Its delicate and difficult office is to ascertain and declare whether the legislation is in accordance with, or in contravention of, the provisions of the Constitution; and having done that, its duty ends. . . .

The clause thought to authorize the legislation . . . confers upon the Congress power "to

lay and collect Taxes, Duties, Imposts and Excises, to pay the Debts and provide for the common Defense and general Welfare of the United States. . . ." It is not contended that this provision grants power to regulate agricultural production upon the theory that such legislation would promote the general welfare. The government concedes that the phrase "to provide for the general welfare" qualifies the power "to lay and collect taxes." The view that the clause grants power to provide for the general welfare, independently of the taxing power, has never been authoritatively accepted. Mr. Justice Story points out that, if it were adopted, "it is obvious that under color of the generality of the words, to 'provide for the common defence and general welfare,' the government of the United States is, in reality, a government of general and unlimited powers, notwithstanding the subsequent enumeration of specific powers." The true construction undoubtedly is that the only thing granted is the power to tax for the purpose of providing funds for payment for the nation's debts and making provision for the general welfare.

Nevertheless, the Government asserts that warrant is found in this clause for the adoption of the Agricultural Adjustment Act. The argument is that Congress may appropriate and authorize the spending of moneys for the "general welfare"; that the phrase should be liberally construed to cover anything conducive to national welfare; that decision as to what will promote such welfare rests with Congress alone, and the courts may not review its determination; and, finally, that the appropriation under attack was in fact for the general welfare of the United States.

The Congress is expressly empowered to lay taxes to provide for the general welfare. . . .

Since the foundation of the nation, sharp differences of opinion have persisted as to the true interpretation of the phrase. Madison asserted it amounted to no more than a reference to the other powers enumerated in the subsequent clauses of the same section; that, as the United States is a government of limited and enumerated powers, the grant of power to tax and spend for the general national welfare must be confined to the enumerated legislative fields committed to the Congress. In this view the phrase is mere tautology, for taxation and appropriation are or may be necessary incidents of the exercise of any of the enumerated legislative powers. Hamilton, on the other hand, maintained the clause confers a power separate and distinct from those later enumerated, is not restricted in meaning by the grant of them, and Congress consequently has a substantive power to tax and to appropriate, limited only by the requirement that it shall be exercised to provide for the general welfare of the United States. Each contention has had the support of those whose views are entitled to weight. This court has noticed the question, but has never found it necessary to decide which is the true construction. Mr. Justice Story, in his Commentaries, espouses the Hamiltonian position. We shall not review the writings of public men and commentators or discuss the legislative practice. Study of all these leads us to conclude that the reading advocated by Mr. Justice Story is the correct one. While, therefore, the power to tax is not unlimited, its confines are set in the clause which confers it and not in those of Section 8 which bestow and define the leg-

islative powers of the Congress. It results that the power of Congress to authorize expenditure of public moneys for public purposes is not limited by the direct grants of legislative power found in the Constitution.

But the adoption of the broader construction leaves the power to spend subject to limitations. . . .

Story says that if the tax be not proposed for the common defence or general welfare, but for other objects wholly extraneous, it would be wholly indefensible upon constitutional principles. And he makes it clear that the powers of taxation and appropriation extend only to matters of national, as distinguished from local welfare. . . .

We are not now required to ascertain the scope of the phrase "general welfare of the United States" or to determine whether an appropriation in aid of agriculture falls within it. Wholly apart from that question, another principle embedded in our Constitution prohibits the enforcement of the Agricultural Adjustment Act. The act invades the reserved rights of the states. It is a statutory plan to regulate and control agricultural production, a matter beyond the powers delegated to the federal government. The tax, the appropriation of the funds raised, and the direction for their disbursement, are but parts of the plan. They are but means to an unconstitutional end.

From the accepted doctrine that the United States is a government of delegated powers, it follows that those not expressly granted, or reasonably to be implied from such as are conferred, are reserved to the states or to the people. To forestall any suggestion to the contrary, the Tenth Amendment was adopted. The same proposition, otherwise stated, is that powers not granted are prohibited. None to regulate agricultural production is given, and therefore legislation by Congress for that purpose is forbidden. . . .

If the act before us is a proper exercise of the federal taxing power, evidently the regulation of all industry throughout the United States may be accomplished by similar exercises of the same power. . . .

Until recently no suggestion of the existence of any such power in the federal government has been advanced. The expressions of the framers of the Constitution, the decisions of this court interpreting that instrument and the writings of great commentators will be searched in vain for any suggestion that there exists in the clause under discussion or elsewhere in the Constitution, the authority whereby every provision and every fair implication from that instrument may be subverted, the independence of the individual states obliterated, and the United States converted into a central government exercising uncontrolled police power in every state of the Union, superseding all local control or regulation of the affairs or concerns of the states. . . .

*Affirmed.*

### MR. JUSTICE STONE, dissenting. . . .

The power of courts to declare a statute unconstitutional is subject to two guiding principles of decision which ought never to be absent from judicial consciousness. One is that courts are concerned only with the power to enact statutes, not with their wisdom. The other is that while unconstitutional exercise of power by the executive and legislative branches of the government is subject to judicial restraint, the only check upon our own exercise of power is our own sense of self-restraint. For the removal of unwise laws from the statute books appeal lies not to the courts but to the ballot and to the processes of democratic government. . . .

The spending power of Congress is in addition to the legislative power and not subordinate to it. This independent grant of the power of the purse, and its very nature, involving in its exercise the duty to insure expenditure within the granted power presuppose freedom of selection among diverse ends and aims, and the capacity to impose such conditions as will render the choice effective. It is a contradiction in terms to say that there is power to spend for the national welfare, while rejecting any power to impose conditions reasonably adapted to

the attainment of the end which alone would justify the expenditure.

The limitation now sanctioned must lead to absurd consequences. The government may give seeds to farmers, but may not condition the gift upon their being planted in places where they are most needed or even planted at all. . . . It may give money to sufferers from earthquake, fire, tornado, pestilence or flood, but may not impose conditions—health precautions designed to prevent the spread of disease, or induce the movement of population to safer or more sanitary areas. All that, because it is purchased regulation infringing state powers, must be left for the states, who are unable or unwilling to supply the necessary relief. . . .

The suggestions that [the power of the purse] must now be curtailed by judicial fiat because it may be abused by unwise use hardly rises to the dignity of the arguments. So may judicial power be abused. "The power to tax is the power to destroy," but we do not, for that reason, doubt its existence, or hold that its efficacy is to be restricted by its incidental or collateral effects upon the states. . . .

A tortured construction of the Constitution is not to be justified by recourse to extreme examples of reckless congressional spending which might occur if courts could not prevent expenditures which, even if they could be thought to effect any national purpose, would be possible only by action of a legislature lost to all sense of public responsibility. Such suppositions are addressed to the mind accustomed to believe that it is the business of courts to sit in judgment on the wisdom of legislative action. Courts are not the only agency of government that must be assumed to have capacity to govern. Congress and the courts both unhappily may falter or be mistaken in the performance of their constitutional duty. But interpretation of our great charter of government which proceeds on any assumption that the responsibility for the preservation of our institutions is the exclusive concern of any one of the three branches of government, or that it alone can save them from destruction is far more likely, in the long run, "to obliterate the constituent members" of "an indestructible union of indestructible states" than the frank recognition that language, even of a constitution, may mean what it says: that the power to tax and spend

includes the power to relieve a nationwide economic maladjustment by conditional gifts of money.

Mr. Justice Brandeis and Mr. Justice Cardozo joined in this opinion.

## *South Dakota* v. *Dole*
## 483 U.S. 203, 107 S.Ct. 2793, 97 L.Ed. 2d 171 (1987)

http://laws.findlaw.com/us/483/203.html

> In 1984 Congress enacted the National Minimum Drinking Age Amendment, referred to in the following opinions as § 158. It directed the department of transportation to withhold 5 percent of federal highway funds from states "in which the purchase or public possession of any alcoholic beverage by a person who is less than twenty-one years of age is lawful." At the time South Dakota permitted persons 19 years of age or older to purchase beer containing 3.2 percent alcohol. The state sued Transportation Secretary Elizabeth Dole in U.S. district court, asserting that the law exceeded Congress's spending power and that it violated the Twenty-first Amendment. The district court rejected South Dakota's claims, and the Court of Appeals for the Eighth Circuit affirmed. Majority: Rehnquist, Blackmun, Marshall, Powell, Scalia, Stevens, White. Dissenting: Brennan, O'Connor.

**Chief Justice Rehnquist delivered the opinion of the Court. . . .**

Despite the extended treatment of the question by the parties . . . we need not decide in this case whether [the Twenty-first] Amendment would prohibit an attempt by Congress to legislate directly a national minimum drinking age. Here, Congress has acted indirectly under its spending power to encourage uniformity in the States' drinking ages. As we explain below, we find this legislative effort within constitutional bounds even if Congress may not regulate drinking ages directly. . . .

The spending power is of course not unlimited, but is instead subject to several general restrictions articulated in our cases. The first of these limitations is derived from the language of the Constitution itself: the exercise of the spending power must be in pursuit of "the general welfare." In considering whether a particular expenditure is intended

to serve general public purposes, courts should defer substantially to the judgment of Congress. Second, we have required that if Congress desires to condition the States' receipt of federal funds, it "must do so unambiguously . . . enabl[ing] the States to exercise their choice knowingly, cognizant of the consequences of their participation." Third, our cases have suggested (without significant elaboration) that conditions on federal grants might be illegitimate if they are unrelated "to the federal interest in particular national projects or programs." . . . Finally, we have noted that other constitutional provisions may provide an independent bar to the conditional grant of federal funds. . . .

South Dakota does not seriously claim that § 158 is inconsistent with any of the first three restrictions mentioned above.

[T]he basic point of disagreement between the parties—is whether the Twenty-first Amendment constitutes an "independent constitutional bar" to the conditional grant of federal funds. Petitioner, relying on its view that the Twenty-first Amendment prohibits direct regulation of drinking ages by Congress, asserts that "Congress may not use the spending power to regulate that which it is prohibited from regulating directly under the Twenty-first Amendment." But our cases show that this "independent constitutional bar" limitation on the spending power is not of the kind petitioner suggests. *United States* v. *Butler,* for example, established that the constitutional limitations on Congress when exercising its spending power are less exacting than those on its authority to regulate directly.

We have also held that a perceived Tenth Amendment limitation on congressional regulation of state affairs did not concomitantly limit the range of conditions legitimately placed on federal grants. . . .

These cases establish that the "independent constitutional bar" limitation on the spending power is not, as petitioner suggests, a prohibition on the indirect achievement of objectives which Congress is not empowered to achieve directly. Instead, we think that the language in our earlier opinions stands for the unexceptionable proposition that the power may not be used to induce the States to engage in activities that would themselves be unconstitutional. Thus, for example, a grant of federal funds conditioned on invidiously discriminatory state action or the infliction of cruel and unusual punishment would be an illegitimate exercise of the Congress' broad spending power. But no such claim can be or is made here. Were South Dakota to succumb to the blandishments offered by Congress and raise its drinking age to 21, the State's action in so doing would not violate the constitutional rights of anyone.

Our decisions have recognized that in some circumstances the financial inducement offered by Congress might be so coercive as to pass the point at which "pressure turns into compulsion." Here, however, Congress has directed only that a State desiring to establish a minimum drinking age lower than 21 lose a relatively small percentage of certain federal highway funds. Petitioner contends that the coercive nature of this program is evident

from the degree of success it has achieved. We cannot conclude, however, that a conditional grant of federal money of this sort is unconstitutional simply by reason of its success in achieving the congressional objective.

When we consider, for a moment, that all South Dakota would lose if she adheres to her chosen course as to a suitable minimum drinking age is 5% of the funds otherwise obtainable under specified highway grant programs, the argument as to coercion is shown to be more rhetoric than fact. . . .

Accordingly, the judgment of the Court of Appeals is

*Affirmed.*

JUSTICE BRENNAN, dissenting . . . [omitted].

## JUSTICE O'CONNOR, dissenting. . . .

[T]he Court's application of the requirement that the condition imposed be reasonably related to the purpose for which the funds are expended, is cursory and unconvincing. We have repeatedly said that Congress may condition grants under the Spending Power only in ways reasonably related to the purpose of the federal program. . . .

[T]he Court asserts the reasonableness of the relationship between the supposed purpose of the expenditure—"safe interstate travel"—and the drinking age condition. The Court reasons that Congress wishes that the roads it builds may be used safely, that drunk drivers threaten highway safety, and that young people are more likely to drive while under the influence of alcohol under existing law than would be the case if there were a uniform national drinking age of 21. It hardly needs saying, however, that if the purpose of § 158 is to deter drunken driving, it is far too over- and under-inclusive. It is over-inclusive because it stops teenagers from drinking even when they are not about to drive on interstate highways. It is under-inclusive because teenagers pose only a small part of the drunken driving problem in this Nation. . . .

There is a clear place at which the Court can draw the line between permissible and impermissible conditions on federal grants. It is the line identified in the Brief for the National Conference of State Legislatures as *Amici Curiae:*

> Congress has the power to *spend* for the general welfare, it has the power to *legislate* only for delegated purposes. . . .
>
> The appropriate inquiry, then, is whether the spending requirement or prohibition is a condition on a grant or whether it is regulation. The difference turns on whether the requirement specifies in some way how the money should be spent, so that Congress' intent in making the grant will be effectuated. Congress has no power under the Spending Clause to impose requirements on a grant that go beyond specifying how the money should be spent. A requirement that is not such a specification is not a condition, but a regulation, which is valid only if it falls within one of Congress' delegated regulatory powers.

This approach harks back to *United States* v. *Butler,* the last case in which this Court struck down an Act of Congress as beyond the authority granted by the Spending Clause. There the Court wrote that "[t]here is an obvious difference between a statute stating the conditions upon which moneys shall be expended and one effective only upon assumption of a contractual obligation to submit to a regulation which otherwise could not be enforced." The Butler Court saw the Agricultural Adjustment Act for what it was—an exercise of regulatory, not spending, power. The error in *Butler* was not the Court's conclusion that the Act was essentially regulatory, but rather its crabbed view of the extent of Congress' regulatory power under the Commerce Clause. . . .

While *Butler's* authority is questionable insofar as it assumes that Congress has no regulatory power over farm production, its discussion of the Spending Power and its description of both the power's breadth and its limitations remains sound. The Court's decision in *Butler* also properly recognizes the gravity of the task of appropriately limiting the Spending Power. If the Spending Power is to be limited only by Congress' notion of the general welfare, the reality, given the vast financial resources of the Federal Government, is that the Spending Clause gives "power to the Congress to tear down the barriers, to invade the states' jurisdiction, and to become a parliament of the whole people, subject to no restrictions save such as are self-imposed." This, of course, as *Butler* held, was not the Framers' plan and it is not the meaning of the Spending Clause.

Of the other possible sources of congressional authority for regulating the sale of liquor only the Commerce Power comes to mind. But in my view, the regulation of the age of the purchasers of liquor, just as the regulation of the price at which liquor may be sold, falls squarely within the scope of those powers reserved to the States by the Twenty-first Amendment. . . . Accordingly, Congress simply lacks power under the Commerce Clause to displace state regulation of this kind.

The immense size and power of the Government of the United States ought not obscure its fundamental character. It remains a Government of enumerated powers. . . .

## National Endowment for the Arts v. Finley
## 524 U.S. 569, 118 S.Ct. 2168, 141 L.Ed. 2d 500 (1998)
### http://laws.findlaw.com/us/524/569.html

> In 1990 Congress amended the National Foundation on the Arts and the Humanities Act, directing in § 954(d)(1) of Title 20 of the U.S. Code that the Chair of the National Endowment for the Arts "shall ensure" that "artistic excellence and artistic merit are the criteria by which applications are judged, taking into consideration general

standards of decency and respect for the diverse beliefs and values of the American public." These changes were prompted by public outcry over several artistic projects that had benefited from NEA funding. Of particular concern were exhibits of Robert Mapplethorpe's works that included homo-erotic photography and of Andres Serrano's "Piss Christ" that featured a photograph of a crucifix immersed in the artist's urine. The amendment represented a compromise in Congress on whether and how to impose greater public control over the grants selection process at the NEA.

Karen Finley and three other performance artists had applications pending at the NEA in 1990.[1] When their requests for funds were denied, they filed suit in the United States District Court for the Central District of California, claiming that the NEA had rejected their applications on political grounds. Once the 1990 amendments became law, the National Association of Artists' Organizations joined the four individuals in an amended complaint in the district court, alleging that § 954(d)(1) on its face violated the free speech clause of the First Amendment and the due process clause of the Fifth Amendment. In 1992, the district court found both arguments persuasive and enjoined the NEA from enforcing § 954(d)(1). In 1996 a divided three-judge panel of the Ninth Circuit Court of Appeals affirmed. Majority: O'Connor, Breyer, Ginsburg, Kennedy, Rehnquist, Scalia, Stevens, Thomas. Dissenting: Souter.

## JUSTICE O'CONNOR delivered the opinion of the Court. . . .

Respondents raise a facial constitutional challenge to § 954(d)(1), and consequently they confront "a heavy burden" in advancing their claim. . . . To prevail, respondents must demonstrate a substantial risk that application of the provision will lead to the suppression of speech.

Respondents argue that the provision is a paradigmatic example of viewpoint discrimi-

nation because it rejects any artistic speech that either fails to respect mainstream values or offends standards of decency. The premise . . . is that § 954(d)(1) constrains the agency's ability to fund certain categories of artistic expression. The NEA, however, reads the provision as merely hortatory, and contends that it stops well short of an absolute restriction. Section 954(d)(1) adds "considerations" to the grant-making process; it does not preclude awards to projects that might be deemed "indecent" or "disrespectful," nor place conditions on grants, or even specify that those factors must be given any particular weight in reviewing an application. Indeed, the agency asserts that it has adequately implemented § 954(d)(1) merely by ensuring the representation of various backgrounds and points of view on the advisory panels that analyze grant applications. . . . It is clear . . . that the text of § 954(d)(1) imposes no categorical requirement. . . .

Furthermore, like the plain language of § 954(d), the political context surrounding the adoption of the "decency and respect" clause is inconsistent with respondents' assertion that the provision compels the NEA to deny funding on the basis of viewpoint discriminatory criteria. The legislation was a bipartisan proposal introduced as a counterweight to amendments aimed at eliminating the NEA's

---

[1] The works for which the four individuals sought funding have been described by one article as follows: "Finley's controversial show, 'We Keep Our Victims Ready,' contains three segments. In the second segment, Finley visually recounts a sexual assault by stripping to the waist and smearing chocolate on her breasts and by using profanity to describe the assault. Holly Hughes' monologue 'World Without End' is a somewhat graphic recollection of the artist's realization of her lesbianism and reminiscence of her mother's sexuality. John Fleck, in his stage performance 'Blessed Are All the Little Fishes,' confronts alcoholism and Catholicism. . . . Fleck appears dressed as a mermaid, urinates on the stage and creates an altar out of a toilet bowl by putting a photograph of Jesus Christ on the lid. Tim Miller derives his performance 'Some Golden States' from childhood experiences, from his life as a homosexual, and from the constant threat of AIDS. Miller uses vegetables in his performances to represent sexual symbols." Note, 48 *Washington & Lee Law Review* 1545, 1546, n. 2 (1991) (citations omitted).

funding or substantially constraining its grant-making authority. . . .

That § 954(d)(1) admonishes the NEA merely to take "decency and respect" into consideration, and that the legislation was aimed at reforming procedures rather than precluding speech, undercut respondents' argument that the provision inevitably will be utilized as a tool for invidious viewpoint discrimination. . . .

In contrast, the "decency and respect" criteria do not silence speakers by expressly "threaten[ing] censorship of ideas." Thus, we do not perceive a realistic danger that § 954(d)(1) will compromise First Amendment values. As respondents' own arguments demonstrate, the considerations that the provision introduces, by their nature, do not engender the kind of directed viewpoint discrimination that would prompt this Court to invalidate a statute on its face. Respondents assert, for example, that "[o]ne would be hard-pressed to find two people in the United States who could agree on what the 'diverse beliefs and values of the American public' are, much less on whether a particular work of art 'respects' them"; and they claim that "'[d]ecency' is likely to mean something very different to a septuagenarian in Tuscaloosa and a teenager in Las Vegas." . . . Accordingly, the provision does not introduce considerations that, in practice, would effectively preclude or punish the expression of particular views. . . .

Respondents' claim that the provision is facially unconstitutional may be reduced to the argument that the criteria in § 954(d)(1) are sufficiently subjective that the agency could utilize them to engage in viewpoint discrimination. Given the varied interpretations of the criteria and the vague exhortation to "take them into consideration," it seems unlikely that this provision will introduce any greater element of selectivity than the determination of "artistic excellence" itself. And we are reluctant, in any event, to invalidate legislation "on the basis of its hypothetical application to situations not before the Court." . . .

Any content-based considerations that may be taken into account in the grant-making process are a consequence of the nature of arts funding. The NEA has limited resources and it must deny the majority of the grant applications that it receives, including many that propose "artistically excellent" projects. The agency may decide to fund particular projects for a wide variety of reasons, "such as the technical proficiency of the artist, the creativity of the work, the anticipated public interest in or appreciation of the work, the work's contemporary relevance, its educational value, its suitability for or appeal to special audiences (such as children or the disabled), its service to a rural or isolated community, or even simply that the work could increase public knowledge of an art form." As the dissent below noted, it would be "impossible to have a highly selective grant program without denying money to a large amount of constitutionally protected expression." . . .

Respondent's reliance on our decision in *Rosenberger* v. *Rector* (1995) is therefore misplaced. In *Rosenberger,* a public university declined to authorize disbursements from its Student Activities Fund to finance the printing of a Christian student newspaper. We held that by subsidizing the Student Activities Fund, the University had created a limited public forum, from which it impermissibly excluded all publications with religious editorial viewpoints. Although the scarcity of NEA funding does not distinguish this case from *Rosenberger,* the competitive process according to which the grants are allocated does. In the context of arts funding, in contrast to many other subsidies, the Government does not indiscriminately "encourage a diversity of views from private speakers." The NEA's mandate is to make aesthetic judgments, and the inherently content-based "excellence" threshold for NEA support sets it apart from the subsidy at issue in *Rosenberger*—which was available to all student organizations that were "'related to the educational purpose of the University,'"—and from comparably objective decisions on allocating public benefits, such as access to a school auditorium or a municipal theater. . . .

Finally, although the First Amendment certainly has application in the subsidy context, we note that the Government may allocate competitive funding according to criteria that would be impermissible were direct regulation of speech or a criminal penalty at stake. So long as legislation does not infringe on other constitutionally protected rights, Congress has wide latitude to set spending priorities. . . . In doing so, "the Government has not discriminated on the basis of viewpoint; it has merely chosen to fund one activity to the exclusion of the other." . . .

The lower courts also erred in invalidating § 954(d)(1) as unconstitutionally vague. Under the First and Fifth Amendments, speakers are protected from arbitrary and discriminatory enforcement of vague standards. The terms of the provision are undeniably opaque, and if they appeared in a criminal statute or regulatory scheme, they could raise substantial vagueness concerns. It is unlikely, however, that speakers will be compelled to steer too far clear of any "forbidden area" in the context of grants of this nature. . . . We recognize, as a practical matter, that artists may conform their speech to what they believe to be the decision-making criteria in order to acquire funding. . . . But when the Government is acting as patron rather than as sovereign, the consequences of imprecision are not constitutionally severe.

In the context of selective subsidies, it is not always feasible for Congress to legislate with clarity. Indeed, if this statute is unconstitutionally vague, then so too are all government programs awarding scholarships and grants on the basis of subjective criteria such as "excellence." To accept respondents' vagueness argument would be to call into question the constitutionality of these valuable government programs and countless others like them.

Section 954(d)(1) merely adds some imprecise considerations to an already subjective selection process. It does not, on its face, impermissibly infringe on First or Fifth Amendment rights. Accordingly, the judgment of the Court of Appeals is reversed and the case is remanded for further proceedings consistent with this opinion.

*It is so ordered.*

**JUSTICE SCALIA, with whom JUSTICE THOMAS joins, concurring in the judgment. . . .**

It is the very business of government to favor and disfavor points of view on (in modern times, at least) innumerable subjects. . . . And it makes not a bit of difference, insofar as either common sense or the Constitution is concerned, whether these officials further their (and, in a democracy, our) favored point of view by achieving it directly (having government-employed artists paint pictures . . . or government-employed doctors perform abortions); or by advocating it officially (establishing an Office of Art Appreciation . . . or an Office of Voluntary Population Control); or by giving money to others who achieve or advocate it (funding private art classes . . . or Planned Parenthood). . . . *Rosenberger* . . . found the viewpoint discrimination unconstitutional, not because funding of "private" speech was involved, but because the government had established a limited public forum—to which the NEA's granting of highly selective (if not highly discriminatory) awards bears no resemblance.

The nub of the difference between me and the Court is that I regard the distinction between "abridging" speech and funding it as a fundamental divide, on this side of which the First Amendment is inapplicable. . . . Finally, what is true of the First Amendment is also true of the constitutional rule against vague legislation: it has no application to funding. Insofar as it bears upon First Amendment concerns, the vagueness doctrine addresses the problems from government regulation of expressive conduct. . . . I cannot refrain from observing, however, that if the vagueness doctrine were applicable, the agency charged with making grants under a statutory standard of "artistic excellence"—and which has itself thought that standard met by everything from the playing of a Beethoven symphony to a depiction of a crucifix immersed in urine—would be of more dubious constitutional validity than the "decency" and "respect" limitations that respondents (who demand to be judged on the same strict standard of "artistic excellence") have the humorlessness to call too vague. . . .

## JUSTICE SOUTER, dissenting. . . .

The decency and respect proviso mandates viewpoint based decisions in the disbursement of government subsidies, and the Government has wholly failed to explain why the statute should be afforded an exemption from the fundamental rule of the First Amendment that viewpoint discrimination in the exercise of public authority over expressive activity is unconstitutional. The Court's conclusions that the proviso is not viewpoint based, that it is not a regulation, and that the NEA may permissibly engage in viewpoint-based discrimination, are all patently mistaken.

"If there is a bedrock principle underlying the First Amendment, it is that the government may not prohibit the expression of an idea simply because society finds the idea itself offensive or disagreeable." . . .

When called upon to vindicate this ideal, we characteristically begin by asking "whether the government has adopted a regulation of speech because of disagreement with the message it conveys. The government's purpose is the controlling consideration." The answer in this case is damning. One need do nothing more than read the text of the statute to conclude that Congress's purpose in imposing the decency and respect criteria was to prevent the funding of art that conveys an offensive message; the decency and respect provision on its face is quintessentially viewpoint based, and quotations from the Congressional Record merely confirm the obvious legislative purpose. In the words of a cosponsor of the bill that enacted the proviso, "[w]orks which deeply offend the sensibilities of significant portions of the public ought not to be supported with public funds." . . .

[A] statute disfavoring speech that fails to respect America's "diverse beliefs and values" is the very model of viewpoint discrimination; it penalizes any view disrespectful to any belief or value espoused by someone in the American populace. Boiled down to its practical essence, the limitation obviously means that art that disrespects the ideology, opinions, or convictions of a significant segment of the American public is to be disfavored, whereas art that reinforces those values is not. After all, the whole point of the proviso was to make sure that works like Serrano's ostensibly blasphemous portrayal of Jesus would not be funded, while a reverent treatment, conventionally respectful of Christian sensibilities, would not run afoul of the law. Nothing could be more viewpoint based than that. . . .

A[nother] try at avoiding constitutional problems is the Court's disclaimer of any constitutional issue here because "[s]ection 954(d)(1) adds 'considerations' to the grant making process; it does not preclude awards to projects that might be deemed 'indecent' or 'disrespectful,' nor place conditions on grants, or even specify that those factors must be given any particular weight in reviewing an application." Since "§ 954(d)(1) admonishes the NEA merely to take 'decency and respect' into consideration," not to make funding decisions specifically on those grounds, the Court sees no constitutional difficulty.

That is not a fair reading. Just as the statute cannot be read as anything but viewpoint based, or as requiring nothing more than diverse review panels, it cannot be read as tolerating awards to spread indecency or disrespect, so long as the review panel, the National Council on the Arts, and the Chairperson have given some thought to the offending qualities and decided to underwrite them anyway. That, after all, is presumably just what prompted the congressional outrage in the first place, and there was nothing naive about the Representative who said he voted for the bill because it does "not tolerate wasting Federal funds for sexually explicit photographs [or] sacrilegious works."

A second basic strand in the Court's treatment of today's question, and the heart of JUSTICE SCALIA's, in effect assumes that whether or not the statute mandates viewpoint discrimination, there is no constitutional issue here because government art subsidies fall within a zone of activity free from First Amendment restraints. The Government calls attention to the roles of government-as-speaker and government-as-buyer, in which the government is of course entitled to engage in viewpoint discrimination: if the Food and Drug Administration launches an advertising campaign on the subject of smoking, it may condemn the habit without also having to show a cowboy taking a puff on the opposite page; and if the Secretary of Defense wishes to buy a portrait to decorate the Pentagon, he is free to prefer George Washington over George the Third.

The Government freely admits, however, that it neither speaks through the expression subsidized by the NEA, nor buys anything for itself with its NEA grants. On the contrary, the Government acts as a patron, financially underwriting the production of art by private artists and impresarios for independent consumption. Accordingly, the Government would have us liberate government-as-patron from First Amendment strictures not by placing it squarely within the categories of government-as-buyer or government-as-speaker, but by recognizing a new category by analogy to those accepted ones. The analogy is, however, a very poor fit, and this patronage falls embarrassingly on the wrong side of the line between government-as-buyer or -speaker and government-as-regulator-of-private-speech. . . .

Our most thorough statement of these principles is found in the recent case of *Rosenberger,* . . . which held that the University of Virginia could not discriminate on viewpoint in underwriting the speech of student-run publications. . . . When the government acts as patron, subsidizing the expression of others, it may not prefer one lawfully stated view over another. *Rosenberger* controls here. The NEA, like the student activities fund in *Rosenberger,* is a subsidy scheme created to encourage expression of a diversity of views from private speakers. . . .

Since the decency and respect proviso of § 954(d)(1) is substantially overbroad and carries with it a significant power to chill artistic production and display, it should be struck down on its face. . . .

# CHAPTER EIGHT

# *Property Rights and the Development of Due Process*

*That government can scarcely be deemed to be free where the rights of property are left solely dependent upon the will of a legislative body without any restraint. The fundamental maxims of a free government seem to require that the rights of personal liberty and private property should be sacred.*

—JUSTICE JOSEPH STORY (1829)

Chapters Six and Seven were concerned partly with national power—the power of Congress to regulate commerce and to tax and spend. Out of the Court's interpretation of national power emerged one of the first great antinomies of constitutional law—national supremacy versus dual federalism. By 1937 the Court had largely resolved that conflict in favor of national power.

This chapter features another major **antinomy,** or conflict between doctrines—**vested rights** versus state **police power.** The first emphasizes the sanctity of private property and demands that legislation not unduly or unreasonably restrict rights of ownership. The second includes the authority states retain to promote health, safety, and the general welfare. In *Brown* v. *Maryland* (1827) Chief Justice Marshall spoke of the police power as *residual,* comprising what remained of a state's authority beyond the other great prerogatives of eminent domain and taxation. Insistence on vested rights at the expense of the police power eventually pushed the Court in the 1930s to a radical restatement of its role. The chapter concludes with a review of that shift, Fifth Amendment "takings," and the "new property."

Prominent throughout is the ongoing debate about the proper adjustment of competing claims involving the police power, individual rights, and the constitutional limitations on that power. As much as in any other area of constitutional law, this debate reflects not just opposing views on what the proper adjustment should be but opposing views on the Court's place in the political system. So, the chapter displays a debate over judicial review itself, anticipating the later controversy over abortion and the Court's development of a constitutional right of privacy (see Chapter Thirteen).

## THE DOCTRINE OF VESTED RIGHTS

The struggle between vested rights and police power is a variant of the earlier conflict between theories of natural rights, on the one hand, and the principle of legislative supremacy, on the other. On this side of the Atlantic, these two doctrines represent the reaction on each other of the prerevolutionary contest between the natural rights of the colonists and parliamentary supremacy. The same phenomenon was manifest after 1776 in the efforts by state legislative majorities to regulate the property and contract rights of individual citizens.

Of the two doctrines, that of vested rights is of earlier origin, being rooted in the notion that property is the basic social institution—the guardian of every other right. The term connotes a way of thinking that emphasizes protection of a person's property from interference by other individuals or even by the government except under specified conditions. Antedating civil society itself, property fixes the limits within which even supreme legislative authority may properly operate. Indeed, the main function of government, its raison d'être, is to protect property. "The right of acquiring and possessing property and having it protected," Justice Paterson wrote in an early circuit court opinion, "is one of the natural inherent and unalienable rights of man. Men have a sense of property: Property is necessary to their subsistence, and correspondent to their natural wants and desires; its security was one of the objects that induced them to unite in society. No man would become a member of a community in which he could not enjoy the fruits of his honest labor and industry. The preservation of property, then, is a primary object of the social compact" (*Van Horne's Lessee* v. *Dorrance,* 1795).

**AT THE CONVENTION.** Among the major causes of the federal Convention of 1787 was the claimed injustice of state laws concerning property, calling into question a fundamental principle of republican government: that the majority could be trusted to safeguard both the public good and private rights. That point was illustrated by the colloquy that occurred in the early days of the Philadelphia Convention between Roger Sherman of Connecticut and James Madison of Virginia. Sherman enumerated the objects of the Convention as defense against foreign danger and internal disputes and the need for a central authority to make treaties with foreign nations and to regulate foreign commerce. Madison agreed that these objects were important but insisted on combining with them "the necessity of providing more effectually for the security of private rights and the steady dispensation of justice within the states." "Interferences with these," Madison added, "were evils which had, more perhaps than anything else, produced this convention."

What Madison had in mind was state legislation on behalf of the debt-burdened but politically dominant small-farmer class, led by such rabble-rousers as Daniel Shays in Massachusetts. They sought special legislation to alter the legal rights of designated parties; intervention by state legislatures in private controversies pending in, or already decided by, the courts; and legislation setting aside judgments, granting new hearings, voiding valid wills, or validating void wills. Those who wished to see the menace of special legislation and state legislative supremacy abated, those who felt the need for outside protection of the rights of property and of contract, naturally supported the movement afoot for a constitutional convention.

But how were the framers to secure such protection? Various measures were proposed, but every motion looking to the imposition of a property qualification for suffrage or officeholding failed. The suggestion that the Senate be organized to shield property was also defeated. Even the difficult and delicate matter of suffrage was ultimately left to the states. As the Constitution came from the hands of the framers, it contained only one brief clause that might afford vested rights protection against state legislative majorities—Article I, Section 10: "No State shall . . . pass any . . . ex post facto law or laws impairing the obligation of contracts. . . ."

THE COURT'S RESPONSE. When it was construed in *Calder* **v.** *Bull,* even this clause was given a very narrow construction. Confining the application of **ex post facto laws** to retroactive penal legislation, the Court held that it was not "inserted to secure the citizen in his private rights of either property or contracts," thus creating a wide breach in the constitutional protection afforded civil rights. Justice Chase seemed nearly apologetic, suggesting that legislation adversely affecting vested rights might be set aside as violation of natural law. "There are certain vital principles," Chase observed, "in our free republican governments which will determine and overrule an apparent and flagrant abuse of legislative power. An act of the legislature (for I cannot call it a law) contrary to the great principles of the social compact cannot be considered a rightful exercise of the legislative authority."

But Justice Iredell questioned whether natural law could be judicially applied to limit legislative power. He characterized such talk as the plaything of "some speculative jurists" and said that if the Constitution itself imposed no checks on legislative power, "whatever the legislature chose to enact would be lawfully enacted, and the judicial power could never interpose to pronounce it void." "The ideas of natural justice are regulated by no fixed standard," Iredell commented. "The ablest and purest of men have differed upon the subject, and all that the Court could properly say in such an event would be that the legislature . . . had passed an act which, in the opinion of the judges, was inconsistent with abstract principles of justice."

Which of these views on the scope of judicial power has prevailed? In appearance Iredell's, but a century later, Chase's views were for all practical purposes triumphant. By 1890 the Court achieved, under the due process clause of the Fourteenth Amendment, the very power to supervise and control legislative action in relation to abstract principles of justice against which Iredell had so strongly protested.

## EXPANSION OF THE CONTRACT CLAUSE

The Marshall Court had its first opportunity to examine the contract clause in *Fletcher* v. *Peck.* "Marshall," Professor Edward Corwin observed, found here "a task of restoration awaiting him in that great field of Constitutional Law which defines state power in relation to private rights." Alexander Hamilton had laid solid foundations for an effective national government; no such preliminary work had been done in the task now confronting the chief justice. Indeed, *Calder* v. *Bull* presented a well-nigh insuperable barrier.

THE YAZOO LAND CASE. *Fletcher* v. *Peck* illustrates the speculative spirit rife in America at the close of the 1700s. Land companies found Georgia an especially inviting field. Between 1789 and 1795 speculators badgered the Georgia legislators without success. Finally, however, on January 7, 1795, the governor of Georgia signed a bill granting the greater part of what is now Alabama and Mississippi to four groups of purchasers, known as the Yazoo Land Companies, at 1½ cents per acre. The "purchasers" included men of national reputation and local politicians (all but one member of the Georgia legislature who voted for the act held shares in one or more of the companies). Indignation ran high, and in 1796 a new legislature repealed the land-grab act. By the time of repeal, some of the lands had passed into the hands of purchasers, mostly Boston capitalists, who in turn sold extensively to investors in New England and the Middle Atlantic states.

Contending that the repeal act of 1796 could not constitutionally divest them of their titles, these innocent purchasers decided to test their rights in federal court. The case, an "arranged" suit, first came before the Supreme Court in the 1809 term; it was reargued the next year, and a decision was rendered on March 16, 1810. Sustaining the contention of the Yazoo claimants in the first decision by the Court invalidating a state statute on constitutional grounds, Chief Justice Marshall held that the 1796 repeal act was an unconstitutional impairment of the obligation of a contract. At the outset Marshall suggested that the rescinding act of the Georgia legislature was void as a violation of vested rights and hence contrary to the underlying principles of society and government. But apparently realizing that a decision based on such flimsy ground would be less secure than one grounded in the Constitution, he turned to the **contract clause.** In doing this, he was confronted with two difficulties: First, the sort of contract the framers had in mind must have been executory—a contract in which the obligation of performance is still to be discharged. Marshall got around this by saying that every grant is attended by an implied contract on the part of the grantor not to reassert his or her right to the thing granted. Therefore, the clause covered executed contracts in which performance has been fulfilled as well as executory contracts.

The greater difficulty was that the contract before the Court was public, not private. In private contracts it is easy enough to distinguish the contract as an agreement between the parties from the obligation that comes from the law and holds the parties to their agreement. Who, in this case, was to hold Georgia to its engagement? Certainly not Georgia, which had passed the rescinding act, nor the Georgia state court. Marshall escaped the dilemma by ruling that Georgia's obligation was moral and that this moral injunction had been elevated to legal status by Article I, Section 10—"a Bill of Rights for the people of each State," Marshall called it. But the chief justice was uncertain at the very end. The last paragraph of his opinion states that Georgia was restrained from passing the rescinding act "either by general principles that are common to our free institutions, or by particular provisions of the Constitution."

**FILLING THE BREACH.** Relying as it did on the contract clause, *Fletcher* went a long way toward bridging the gap opened by *Calder* v. *Bull* in the constitutional protection of private rights. But since Marshall's ruling was somewhat ambiguous, there remained the question of whether the clause safeguarded corporate charters as well as public grants against legislative interference. In 1819, by his opinion in **_Dartmouth College_ v. _Woodward_,** Marshall filled in the breach Justice Chase had created in the constitutional protection of vested rights.

The college's original charter was granted by the King of England. Parliament could have destroyed it at any time before 1776, and before 1788 the state of New Hampshire could have wiped it out. After that year, Marshall held that it must continue in perpetuity. His opinion adds up to these propositions: The college was not public, but a "private eleemosynary institution"; its charter was the outgrowth of a contract between the original donors and the Crown; the trustees represented the interest of the donors; the Constitution protects this representative interest. Marshall agonized at only one point. The requirement of the contract clause was admittedly designed to protect those having a vested beneficial interest. No one then living, not even the trustees, had any such interest in Dartmouth College. But Marshall held that the case came within the spirit, if not the words, of the Constitution.

The nub of Marshall's decision is the proposition that any ambiguity in a charter must be construed in favor of the adventurers and against the state. With perpetuity thus implied, the college charter was placed beyond the reach of the legislature. By that same token, the charters of profit-seeking corporations were likewise beyond the control of legislative majorities. In short, the doctrine of vested rights, heretofore having no safeguard except the principles of natural law, now enjoyed the solid protection of a specific provision of the Constitution—the impairment-of-contracts clause.

In a separate opinion in the same case, Marshall's scholarly colleague Joseph Story (who had been elected to Harvard's board of overseers a year earlier) suggested the means by which states might in the future avoid the restrictive effect of Marshall's holding. Speaking of the state's power over corporations, Story observed that there was "no other control, than what is expressly or implicitly reserved by the charter itself." Indeed, as early as 1805 Virginia had used a **reservation clause** (reserving to the state the power to alter, amend, or repeal a charter) in special incorporation acts. In 1827, following the Dartmouth decision, New York enacted a general law making all charters "hereafter granted . . . subject to alteration, suspension and repeal, in the discretion of the legislature." All states now have such a provision in their constitutions, in general acts, or in both.

By 1830, the doctrine of vested rights was nevertheless accepted in a majority of the states and by leading lawyers and judges as a limit on legislative power. This meant that property rights fixed the contours within which the legislature exercised its powers. These were America's "preferred freedoms"—values so generally recognized and accepted that no such phrase was needed to describe them.

## TWILIGHT OF THE CONTRACT CLAUSE

Meanwhile, political forces of great significance for the development of constitutional law were taking shape. The year 1828 saw the election as president of the democratically inclined Andrew Jackson; in the same decade Massachusetts, New York, and Virginia called conventions to remove certain constitutional safeguards for economic privilege and to broaden the suffrage. Out of all this emerged the doctrine of **popular sovereignty,** the notion that the will of the people is to be discovered at the ballot box, not merely in a document framed in 1787, and that the people's will should at all times prevail. The juristic expression of popular sovereignty is the doctrine of the police power, which was given classic expression and interpretation by Jackson's appointee and Marshall's successor, Roger Brooke Taney.

In the License Cases of 1847, Taney gave the state police power succinct definition: "The power to govern men and things within the limits of its own dominion." A concept of incalculable potential, "police power" came to mean not only legislative authority to remove government-created privilege, but also sanction for state legislation having broad social purpose. Taney's doctrine of the police power did in fact stimulate considerable legislative activity.

The two cases of *Dartmouth College* and **Charles River Bridge v. Warren Bridge** (1837) illustrate two alternate approaches to the police power and to progress. Chief Justice Marshall's thoughts in the first case turned toward security of property and contract rights against government encroachment. Without losing sight of these values, Chief Justice Taney argued in the second case that the community also has rights and it is the object and end of government to promote the prosperity and happiness of all. In holding against the Charles River Bridge Co., Taney maintained that disputes over implied grants of monopolistic privilege should be resolved in favor of the public, not the investors. Echoing Marshall in a 35,000-word dissent, Story argued for the opposite outcome: "I stand upon the old law . . . , in resisting . . . encroachments upon the rights and liberties of citizens, secured by public grants. . . . I can conceive of no surer plan to arrest all public improvements, founded on private capital . . . than to make the outlay of that capital uncertain. . . . The very agitation of a question of this sort, is sufficient to alarm every stockholder. . . ."

After *Charles River Bridge,* which rejected constitutional protection for such **implied contracts,** the contract clause never regained its earlier stature as a barrier against legislative encroachment on property rights. Indeed, in 1934, in one of the first cases foreshadowing the ultimately favorable constitutional fate of the New Deal (**Home Building & Loan Association v. Blaisdell**), the justices, voting 5–4, refused to hold that the contract clause had been breached by a state statute changing the terms of mortgage agreements. The legislation seemed to fly in the face of Article I, Section 10. Distinguishing between the obligation of the contract and the remedy, Chief Justice Hughes tried to demonstrate that the moratorium placed on mortgage foreclosures did not impair the obligation; the statute merely modified the remedy. Justices Cardozo and Stone read the chief justice's first draft with misgivings so serious that each considered writing a concurring opinion. The former actually prepared a draft (reprinted in this chapter) that advocated a contract clause that would adapt with the times.

In *El Paso* v. *Simmons* (1965), this flexible interpretation of the clause won well-nigh unanimous support when eight justices held that not every modification of a contractual promise, even one embodied in a state statute, impairs the obligation of contract. Yet, the flexible approach goes only so far. Twelve years after *El Paso,* the Court invalidated the repeal in 1974 during a national energy crisis of a covenant accepted in 1962 by the Port Authority of New York and New Jersey, limiting subsidization of rail passenger transportation. The repeal amounted to an impairment of the Authority's contract with the bondholders (*United States Trust Co.* v. *New Jersey,* 1977).

## ORIGINS OF DUE PROCESS

No sooner had the contract clause been weakened than a new judicial formula was found for defeating government action under the police power. The 1830s had seen the establishment of the public school system; the 1840s witnessed the first steps toward primitive factory legislation and regulation of the liquor traffic. The character and volume of social legislation created the need for a new constitutional weapon. Special credit for the invention of that weapon must go to the New York Court of Appeals—and to the leading case of *Wynehamer* v. *New York* (1856).

The defendant, Wynehamer, was indicted and convicted by a jury in the Court of Sessions of Erie County for selling liquor in small quantities contrary to the act, passed April 9, 1855, "for the prevention of intemperance, pauperism and crime." It was admitted that the defendant owned the liquors in question before and at the time the law took effect. But on appeal Wynehamer's counsel insisted that he was entitled to an acquittal on the ground, among others, that the statute was unconstitutional and void. The court agreed.

Judge Comstock, who spoke for New York's high court, noted that, although "the legislative power" is vested in the legislature, it is subject to special constitutional limitations, "which are of very great interest and importance" in that they prohibit the deprivation of life, liberty, and property without due process of law. He thus introduced a constitutional injunction of tremendous possibilities—**due process.** What does it mean? To the lay mind this phrase suggests procedural limitations—that is, if it limits legislative power at all, it does so in terms not of *what* can be done but of *how* something must be done. Comstock and the concurring justices made clear that they had something more sweeping in mind. Because the legislature has only limited powers, it cannot encroach, Comstock contended, on the rights of any species of property, even where the action would be of "absolute benefit" to the people of the state. To allow the legislature such a power, even in the public interest, would "subvert the fundamental idea of property." "In a government like ours," he observed, "theories of public good or public necessity may be so plausible, or even so truthful, as to command popular majorities. But whether truthful or plausible merely, and by whatever numbers they are assented to, there are some absolute private rights beyond their reach, and among these the constitution places the right of property." In short, due process placed substantive as well as procedural restraints on legislative power.

Thus, by mid-nineteenth century two great forces were meeting head on: the doctrine of vested rights and the doctrine of the police power. Professor Corwin suggested that on the eve of the Civil War, courts and country were faced with a reincarnation of the old conundrum: What happens when an irresistible force—the doctrine of the police power—meets an immovable object—the doctrine of vested rights? What, moreover, was to be the role of the courts in this situation?

Confronted with cases such as that of *Charles River Bridge,* judges might have done one of two things: surrender the view that rights of property and of contract set absolute barriers against the exercise of public power, or cast about for a new constitutional formula to protect vested rights against regulatory legislative power. Would the phrase *due process* serve this purpose? Could a term suggesting procedural limitations only be fashioned into a limitation on the substance of lawmaking? The significance of *Wynehamer* is that by 1856 an answer was at hand.

## JUDICIAL RESTRAINT AND THE FOURTEENTH AMENDMENT

Before the Civil War, except for the Taney Court's disastrous decision in *Dred Scott* (see Chapter Two), the due process clause in the Fifth Amendment had created no serious limitation on the substance of national legislation. But the clause was no sooner inserted in the Fourteenth Amendment than it became a rallying point for those who resisted the effort of government to regulate the expanding industrial economy. The amendment seemed to add a weapon of untold potentialities to the judicial arsenal; henceforth, the battles to protect property rights against state regulation were destined to revolve around due process. Accordionlike in its contour, it was broad enough to embrace the concept of natural rights.

**TESTING THE NEW AMENDMENT.** Nonetheless, the Supreme Court was at first reluctant to exploit this new source of authority. In the **Slaughterhouse Cases** of 1873, Justice Miller and four colleagues were altogether unreceptive to constitutional objections raised by New Orleans butchers against a Louisiana law that required all slaughtering in the city to be done in a single facility. In Miller's view, the privileges and immunities clause in section 1 of the amendment did not break down the distinction between state and national citizenship. The Fourteenth Amendment conferred on the national government the duty of protecting rights adhering to national, not state, citizenship. National citizenship included the right of coming to the seat of the government, the right to enjoy government offices, and the right to government protection on the high seas. By contrast, state citizenship, predating the Constitution, encompassed the fundamental right to acquire and possess property, among other rights. Because the rights allegedly infringed by the Louisiana statute derived from state citizenship, the butchers could not look beyond the state for protection.

Miller was equally cool to application of the equal protection and due process clauses, also part of Section 1. As for equal protection, he doubted its relevance except in cases involving the rights of the recently freed slaves. As for due process, under no interpretation he had seen could the challenged statute be held lacking in due process. Why did Miller take such a narrow view of judicial power? Essentially it grew out of his conception of the Union—"the structure and spirit of our institutions." The Fourteenth Amendment did not change "the whole theory of the relations of the State and Federal governments to each other and of both these governments to the people." "Such a ruling," Miller said, "would constitute this Court a perpetual censor upon all legislation of the states on the civil rights of their own citizens, with authority to nullify such as it did not approve." The Court felt duty-bound to curb any effort to change the federal balance, even by the amending process.

**A PUBLIC INTEREST.** Judicial hands-off was maintained four years later in ***Munn v. Illinois,*** which upheld a statute fixing rates for grain warehouses. Harking back to principles of common law, Chief Justice Waite reasoned that when people devote their property to a use in which the public has an interest, the property ceases to be private; it becomes "affected with a public interest" and hence subject to a greater degree of regulation. The legislature, not the Court, was to determine how much regulation was permissible, whether it was arbitrary, and whether the business was so affected.

The implications of *Munn* were far-reaching. "Our boasted security in property rights falls away for the lack of a constitutional guaranty against this sovereign power thus discovered in our legislatures," observed commentator George C. Marshall in 1890. "It is apparent that against the whim of a temporary majority, inflamed with class prejudice, envy or revenge, the property of no man is safe. And the danger is even greater in an age teeming with shifting theories of social reform and economic science, which seem to have but one common principle—the subjection of private property to governmental control for the good—or alleged good—of the public." He advised, however, that *Munn* was as sound in constitutional law as it was objectionable in its result. The defect, therefore, could be remedied only by an amendment to the Constitution.

The insecurity revealed by *Munn* was destined to be corrected. But this would be done by interpretation and not by formal amendment, just as a similar breach had been bridged by Chief Justice Marshall years before, when he expanded the scope of the contract clause to overcome *Calder* v. *Bull*. Various forces and factors joined in this movement.

# JUDICIAL ACTIVISM AND THE FOURTEENTH AMENDMENT

In 1878, one year after *Munn,* the American Bar Association was organized. By 1881 it was embarked on a deliberate and persistent campaign of education designed to reverse the Court's broad conception of legislative power. The association stood with John Stuart Mill for individualism, agreed with Charles Darwin's view of the inevitability of the human struggle, and accepted Herbert Spencer's evolutionary theories of politics. Extracts from addresses and papers reveal such thoughts as "The great curse of the world is too much government" and "Forces which make for growth should be left absolutely free to all."[1]

**JUDICIAL REVOLUTION.** A shift from the view that the Court had espoused in *Munn* came swiftly. *Santa Clara Co.* v. *Southern Pacific R.R.* (1886) acknowledged that corporations were "persons" under the due process clause. "It does not at all follow that every statute enacted ostensibly for the promotion of these ends [morals and welfare] is to be accepted as a legitimate exertion of the police powers of the state," commented Justice Harlan for the Court in *Mugler* v. *Kansas* (1887). Legitimacy was to be determined by the Court. "The courts are not bound by mere forms, nor are they to be misled by mere pretenses. They are at liberty—indeed, are under a solemn duty—to look at the substance of things."

At least two factors had been at work to effect this change—the bar association's campaign and powerful dissenting opinions. By the late 1880s, a third element was added—change in judicial personnel. Between 1877 and 1890, seven justices who had participated in the Slaughterhouse and Munn cases retired or died. Field, who had dissented in both, lived on and in 1888 was joined by his nephew David J. Brewer and Chief Justice Melville W. Fuller.

With new justices came a repudiation of *Munn's* hands-off approach. In *Chicago, Milwaukee & St. Paul R.R. Co.* v. *Minnesota* (1890), six justices decided that the question of the reasonableness of rates could not be left by the legislature to a state commission but must be subject to judicial review. This decision completed a judicial revolution. The Court became what Justice Miller had feared in the Slaughterhouse Cases—a "perpetual censor" of state legislation.

The new view was reflected in remarks Justice Brewer made to the New York Bar Association in 1893. Taking account of the state of affairs and of popular and professional protest against the expansion of judicial power, Brewer advocated judicial activism—"Strengthening the judiciary." Brewer believed with Judge John F. Dillon that the Supreme Court was "the only breakwater against the haste and the passions of the people—against the tumultuous ocean of democracy."

The most reasoned response to Brewer's advocacy of judicial activism came from Harvard law professor James Bradley Thayer, who proclaimed a standard of judicial self-restraint. Justice Frankfurter later rated Thayer's article of 1893 "the most important single essay in constitutional law, . . . the great guide for judges, and the great guide for understanding by nonjudges." Excerpts from both Brewer and Thayer appear as an "unstaged debate" in this chapter.

**THE BAKE SHOP CASE.** Until the Court's about-face in 1937 (see Chapter Six), Thayer's sober counsel was to no avail. The Court played a role it had earlier

---

[1] Along with William Graham Sumner, English philosopher Herbert Spencer had a profound impact in the late nineteenth century on American social and economic thought with his emphasis on a minimalist state. The historian Richard Hofstadter credited Spencer with having coined the phrase "survival of the fittest," usually attributed to Charles Darwin.

spurned. Virtually a superlegislature, the Court proceeded to discharge the delicate responsibility of mediating between public power and private rights. Due process was a poor measuring instrument because it varied according to the user. But its very uncertainty as a test of what a legislature might do was useful for judges who wanted to be able to say no, and yet plead inability to say what might be done in the future or precisely what was wrong with that which had been done in the past. It would seem, then, that Justice Iredell's scorn of natural law as a limitation on state legislative power in *Calder* v. *Bull* might be applied equally well to due process. Because this concept provided no "fixed standard," all the Court could properly say in raising it as a constitutional bar was that the legislature had passed an act that, in the opinion of the judges, was inconsistent with abstract principles of justice.

Once the Court abandoned its previous attitude of judicial self-restraint, how could the justices avoid reading their own predilections into the Constitution? The problem was squarely presented in 1905 in the famous Bake Shop Case, ***Lochner v. New York.*** The Court had previously held in an insurance case that **liberty of contract** was implicit in the due process that the Fourteenth Amendment shielded from state interference (*Allgeyer* v. *Louisiana,* 1897). And in 1898, because of the dangerous work involved, it upheld a Utah statute fixing an eight-hour day for miners as a reasonable restriction on liberty of contract (*Holden* v. *Hardy*). Now a bakery owner claimed that New York's maximum hours law for bakers impermissibly intruded into the right of employer and employee to agree on the terms of labor. Justice Peckham's measure of "due process" in delivering the Court's opinion contrasts sharply with Chief Justice Waite's in *Munn.* "To common understanding," wrote Rufus Peckham, "the trade of a baker has never been regarded as an unhealthy one." The statute was unconstitutional because five justices thought it unnecessary.

**THE BRANDEIS BRIEF.** After *Lochner,* reformers realized that saving social legislation from judicial veto called for a different approach. In 1907 the National Consumers League, learning that the Oregon ten-hour law for women was soon to be contested in the Supreme Court, began a search for outstanding counsel to defend the statute. Joseph H. Choate, one of the most distinguished and successful lawyers of his time, the man who had blocked the "march of Communism" in the Income Tax Case of 1895 (see Chapter Seven), refused a retainer, saying that he saw no reason why "a big husky Irish woman should not work more than ten hours in a laundry if she and her employers so desired." The day after Choate's refusal, attorney Louis D. Brandeis of Boston accepted the retainer and began work on his now famous factual brief in *Muller* v. *Oregon* (1908).

"In our judgment," Peckham had said in *Lochner,* "it is not possible *in fact* to discover the connection between the number of hours a baker must work in a bakery and the healthful quality of the bread made by the workman" (emphasis added). Peckham's assumption had been that the bake shop law was not health-based but class (labor) legislation instead and therefore an unacceptable use of the police power. Accepting this challenge, Brandeis took a bold and unprecedented step: He furnished the Court with the requisite social and economic statistics to demonstrate a relationship between working hours and public health and safety. Heretofore lawyers had lacked confidence in their ability to make the judges see a "reasonable" relation, grounded in facts, between the ends and the means. Brandeis had confidence in both himself and the judges.

Instead of the usual array of legal precedents, Brandeis produced facts and statistics on women's health to show that the legislation was within the legal principles already enumerated by the Court. He brought to a bench disposed to make economic and social judgments a method for performing its task more intelligently and more fairly. The **Brandeis brief** contained two pages of conventional legal arguments and over 100 pages of data drawn from reports of government bureaus, legislative committees, commissions on hygiene, and factory inspections—all proving that long hours are, *as a matter of fact,* dangerous to women's health, safety, and morals, and that short hours result in general social and economic benefits.

The Court approved Oregon's ten-hour law, and a more tolerant judicial attitude soon became apparent. In 1917 the Court upheld a ten-hour-day law with an overtime provision for men (*Bunting* v. *Oregon*). But such progressivism was short-lived. Brandeis himself was appointed to the bench in 1916, but his appointment did little more than balance President Woodrow Wilson's earlier elevation of his attorney general, James C. McReynolds, to associate justice. Within a few years Warren G. Harding succeeded Wilson and named William Howard Taft chief justice and George Sutherland associate justice. So skepticism continued to mark the Court's attitudes toward facts. For example, Justice Sutherland, confronted in 1923 with a mass of sociological data in support of a District of Columbia act regulating women's wages, brushed all such extralegal matter aside as "interesting, but only mildly persuasive" (*Adkins* v. *Children's Hospital*). "Freedom of contract is the general rule," Sutherland commented in setting aside the wage law, "restraint the exception."

In contrast, Justice Brandeis considered the Court's function circumscribed whether he approved or disapproved of a particular economic policy. In 1925 the Oklahoma legislature provided that no one could engage in the manufacture of ice for sale without obtaining a license. If a state commission found that the community was adequately served, it might turn down the bid of a would-be competitor, and in this way, perhaps, advance monopoly. On its face, this legislation encouraged precisely the trend Brandeis had tried to prevent as an attorney. "The control here asserted," the Court ruled in a 6–2 opinion setting aside the act, "does not protect against monopoly, but tends to foster it." Yet Brandeis dissented. "Our function," he wrote, echoing Thayer, "is only to determine the reasonableness of the legislature's belief in the existence of evils and in the effectiveness of the remedy. . . ." Viewing the states as social laboratories, Brandeis believed that government should have power "to remould, through experimentation, our economic practices and institutions to meet changing social and economic needs. . . . This Court has the power to prevent an experiment. We may strike down the statute which embodies it on the ground that, in our opinion, the measure is arbitrary, capricious, or unreasonable. . . . But in the exercise of this high power, we must be ever on guard, lest we erect our prejudices into legal principles" (*New State Ice Co.* v. *Liebmann,* 1932).

**THE DECLINE OF DUE PROCESS PROTECTION OF PROPERTY RIGHTS.** In 1934 five justices hinted a return to judicial restraint as ***Nebbia* v. *New York*** sustained a New York statute fixing minimum and maximum milk prices. "With the wisdom of the policy adopted," declared Justice Owen J. Roberts, "the Courts are both incompetent and unauthorized to deal." Yet in 1936 (*Morehead* v. *New York* ex rel. *Tipaldo*), the justices returned to *Adkins* in striking down the state's minimum wage law for women and children, also 5 to 4. Nevertheless, it was soon evident that *Nebbia* had marked the beginning of the end of due process as a substantive limitation on legislation affecting economic rights. The death blow came in 1937 when ***West Coast Hotel Co.* v. *Parrish*** expressly overruled *Adkins,* just as the Court was also relaxing commerce clause constraints on Congress, as described in Chapter Six.

Upholding Washington State's minimum wage for women, Chief Justice Hughes declared, "[T]he liberty safeguarded is liberty in a social organization which requires the protection of law against the evils which menace the health, safety, morals and welfare of the people." Liberty could be infringed by forces other than government, and infringement by those forces required the affirmative action of government for its protection.

The Court relinquished a self-acquired guardianship. Due process would no longer serve as a shield against the substance of commercial regulations. Within a year, without a single change in judicial personnel, self-restraint became the order of the day. Only President Roosevelt's Court-packing threat, reviewed in Chapter Six, had intervened.

It would be extreme to say that the Court has completely abandoned its supervisory role over state economic regulation, but decisions since 1937 reveal a greatly diminished judicial role. As Justice Black emphasized in 1963 (***Ferguson v. Skrupa***), "The doctrine that prevailed in *Lochner* . . . and like cases—that due process authorizes courts to hold laws unconstitutional when they believe the legislature has acted unwisely—has long since been discarded. We have returned to the original constitutional proposition that courts do not substitute their social and economic beliefs for the judgment of legislative bodies, who are elected to pass laws."

***LOCHNER'S* LEGACY.** For Progressive-era and, later, New Deal and post–New Deal reformers, *Lochner* and its progeny stand out as abuses of judicial review. The Court was trying to write laissez-faire economic theory into the Constitution and to protect the entrenched "malefactors of great wealth." More recently others, while conceding that the Lochner majority was misguided, see the decision as opposition to class legislation and as a reflection of ideas of limited government dating from the era of Jacksonian democracy before the Civil War. Regardless, *Lochner* did not pose an insurmountable barrier to all social legislation. During the three decades after *Lochner,* the Court sustained many more reform laws than it struck down. Nonetheless, advocates of social reform had real grounds for concern: The Court had the last word. Any new measure had to jump through the judicial hoops of due process, liberty of contract, and the police power.

While the Supreme Court had abandoned stringent protection of property rights by 1937, *Lochner* nonetheless stands as a harbinger of some of the modern Court's decisions in other contexts in at least four ways: First, it rested on a right—liberty of contract—neither mentioned in the Fourteenth Amendment nor probably intended by those who drafted it. Second, it attributed substantive, not merely procedural, content to the concept of due process of law. Third, it was defense of a right the Court considered fundamental. Fourth, it was the antithesis of judicial deference to lawmaking bodies. For Peckham, the judicial task was essentially legislative: independently to evaluate the need for the regulation, presumably the same task in which the legislature had engaged.

## SEARCH FOR A ROLE: FOOTNOTE FOUR

At the very moment the Court relaxed its supervisory control over social and economic policy, Justice Harlan Stone outlined an affirmative thrust for judicial review. In contrast with his expression of judicial tolerance for regulation of property, he suggested that certain other freedoms deserved heightened constitutional protection. In reviewing state or national action affecting speech, press, or religion, for instance, the Court might employ assumptions and presumptions that differed from those relied on in other cases where the question of constitutionality was raised. The Court began to have a vision of a new hierarchy of constitutionally protected values, with the First Amendment at the apex and property rights placed much further down.

In the otherwise obscure case of *United States* v. *Carolene Products Co.* (1938), Stone tentatively explored the subject. In the body of his opinion upholding a congressional ban on the shipment of "filled milk" (a milk product where palm oil had been substituted for butterfat) against a challenge on due process grounds, he wrote, "Regulatory legislation affecting ordinary commercial transactions is not to be pronounced unconstitutional unless in the light of the facts made known or generally assumed it is of such a character as to preclude the assumption that it rests upon some rational basis within the knowledge and experience of the legislators." He would not go so far as to say that no economic legislation would ever violate constitutional restraints, but he did suggest strictly confining the Court's role. Attached to this proposition was **footnote four:**

> There may be narrower scope for operation of the presumption of constitutionality when legislation appears on its face to be within a specific prohibition of the Constitution, such as those of the first ten amendments, which are deemed equally specific when held to be embraced within the Fourteenth. . . .
>
> It is unnecessary to consider now whether legislation which restricts those political processes which can ordinarily be expected to bring about repeal of undesirable legislation, is to be subjected to more exacting judicial scrutiny under the general prohibitions of the Fourteenth Amendment than are most other types of legislation. . . .
>
> Nor need we enquire whether similar considerations enter into the review of statutes directed at particular religious . . . or national . . . or racial minorities . . . whether prejudice against discrete and insular minorities may be a special condition, which tends seriously to curtail the operation of those political processes ordinarily to be relied upon to protect minorities, and which may call for a correspondingly more searching judicial inquiry. . . .

This footnote of three paragraphs contains a corresponding number of ideas. The first suggests that when legislation, on its face, contravenes the specific constitutional negatives set out in the Bill of Rights, the Court's usual presumption of constitutionality may be curtailed or even waived. The second paragraph indicates that the judiciary has a special responsibility as defender of those liberties to assure the effective functioning of the political process. The Court thus becomes the ultimate guardian against abuses that would poison the primary check on government—the ballot box. It must protect those liberties on which the effectiveness of political action depends. The third paragraph suggests a special role for the Court as protector of minorities and of unpopular groups particularly helpless at the polls in the face of discriminatory or repressive policies.

Under this new banner of self-restraint, the justices would leave protection of property to what Madison called the "primary control," "dependence on the people"—the voters. Judicial activism old-style was dead; judicial activism new-style was just around the corner. Judicial supervision would continue to be an important part of the political system, but new concerns would replace the old. These concerns are largely the topics covered in Chapters Nine through Fifteen.

## TAKINGS, LAND USE, AND THE FIFTH AMENDMENT

With the decline of the due process clause as a barrier to commercial regulation, the **takings clause** of the Fifth Amendment has become a battleground for those who oppose public restrictions on property—especially laws governing land use. The clause states: "nor shall property be taken for public use, without just compensation." As explained in Chapter Nine, the takings clause was the first provision of the Bill of Rights to be applied to the states through the due process clause of the Fourteenth Amendment (*Chicago, B. & Q. R. Co.* v. *Chicago*, 1897).

In its plainest sense the takings clause restricts the power of **eminent domain**—government's authority to acquire control of private property. When that is done, "just compensation" must be paid. The takings clause thus disperses the costs of public policy. A taking without compensation places the burden squarely on the property owner. A taking with compensation distributes the burden or costs among the public.

The clause gives rise to at least three questions: First, what constitutes a "taking"? Second, what is "public use"? And finally, what compensation is "just"?

**TAKINGS.** "[Q]uite simply," confessed Justice Brennan in 1978, the Supreme Court "has been unable to develop any 'set formula' for determining when justice and fairness require that economic injuries caused by public action be compensated by the government. . . ." Whether a Fifth Amendment "taking" has occurred depends instead on the circumstances of individual cases. Several factors seem significant: the economic impact of the regulation, the extent to which the regulation adversely affects "investment-backed" expectations, and the public interest the regulation serves. In the Court's eyes, most zoning laws and other regulations of property are not takings. Neither are taxes, even though they can negatively affect economic values.

Generally, land use regulations do not effect a taking if they promote a legitimate state interest without denying all economically viable use of the land. Moreover, government's power to ban certain uses of land to advance a legitimate interest includes the power to condition such use on some concession by the owner. This relationship between the interest and the concession was apparently crucial to the outcome of ***Nollan* v. *California Coastal Commission*** (1987). Five justices invalidated a state regulation that beachfront property owners had to allow public access across their beach as a condition for obtaining a permit to replace a house with a larger one. Absent in this case, according to Justice Scalia's opinion for the majority, was a close nexus between the restriction and the public interest it was supposed to serve.

In *Dolan* v. *Tigard* (1994), the Court tightened the review exercised in *Nollan*. Five justices concluded that an Oregon town violated the Constitution by conditioning issuance of a building permit on the owner's agreement to dedicate segments of the property for public use. While the majority found a nexus between the restrictions and the government's objectives (preventing flooding and reducing traffic congestion), the former were not "roughly proportional" to the latter. Absent was "some sort of individualized determination that the required dedication is related both in nature and extent to the impact of the proposed development." While rulings such as *Nollan* and *Dolan* hardly tie the hands of local officials, they suggest that the Court now expects localities to tailor land use regulations carefully to a heightened standard of both need and proof.

**PUBLIC USE.** A taking must be for public, not private, use. Although this stipulation has not been nearly so troublesome as the definition of a taking, it has become clear that the Court does not confine **public use** to property maintained by a government agency and accessible to the general public. For example, *Hawaii Housing Authority* v. *Midkiff* (1984) presented a situation in which the state required large landowners to sell their property to others. Against the charge that the law took private property for private use, all eight participating justices decided that Hawaii's plan served a public purpose. "Where the legislature's purpose is legitimate and its means are not irrational," declared Justice O'Connor, "our cases make clear that empirical debates over the wisdom of takings—no less than debates over the wisdom of other kinds of socioeconomic legislation—are not to be carried out in the federal courts."

**JUST COMPENSATION.** If a property owner is not satisfied with the price a government agency is willing to pay, courts ultimately settle the dispute. Owners are "entitled to receive what a willing buyer would pay in cash to a willing seller at the time of the taking," the Court announced in *United States* v. *564.54 Acres of Land* (1979). **Just compensation** is the fair market value of the property taken, not apparently the cost of replacement facilities. Exceptions include situations "where market value has been too difficult to find, or when . . . injustice to owner or public [would result]."

## "NEW PROPERTY" AND DUE PROCESS OF LAW

Expanded economic and social roles for government at all levels are a hallmark of America today. Government has increasingly become a provider, not merely the regulator. As a result, substantial numbers of people are dependent on the government for income support, employment, or services essential to economic well-being. These interests have been labeled the **new property.** To what degree are such government benefits (**entitlements**) constitutionally protected? Put another way, although government may not be constitutionally required to license drivers or to hire college teachers, for example, what constitutional standards, if any, apply when a state suspends a license or fires an instructor? Constitutional protection means that the entitlement, once extended, may not be withdrawn without due process of law.

New property questions differ, therefore, from other issues in this chapter. With *Lochner* v. *New York* or *Ferguson* v. *Skrupa,* the substance of the regulation was at stake. Could a state constitutionally limit the hours of work in a bakery or restrict debt adjustment to lawyers? Raising procedural concerns, new property cases assume the legitimacy of the entitlement or regulatory policy. At issue is procedure—the manner in which entitlements are curtailed and property is restricted.

**A PROTECTED INTEREST.** Having a constitutionally protected entitlement depends on whether the benefit involves a "liberty" or "property" interest within the meaning given the due process clauses of the Fifth and Fourteenth Amendments. In *Goldberg* v. *Kelly* (1970), the Supreme Court concluded that welfare benefits are more "like property than a 'gratuity.' Much of the existing wealth in this country," wrote Justice Brennan, "takes the form of rights that do not fall within traditional common law concepts of property." Thus a state could not stop public assistance payments without affording the recipient "the opportunity for an evidentiary hearing prior to termination."

Public employment may also be "property" if government specifies that a person can be discharged only "for cause" or if an understanding to that effect exists. In *Perry* v. *Sindermann* (1972), the Court held that a fourth-year instructor may have been entitled to a hearing before a junior college decided not to renew his contract.

Even without explicit tenure rules, "there may be an unwritten 'common law' . . . that certain employees shall have the equivalent of tenure." But the majority found no such property interest in *Board of Regents* v. *Roth* (1972), where an instructor was let go after a single year of teaching. According to state law, the "decision whether to rehire a nontenured teacher for another year" was left "to the unfettered discretion of university officials." Unlike *Perry*, there was no other basis such as past practice on which to base the property interest.

Government action implicates a protected "liberty" when a person's good name, reputation, honor, or integrity is at stake. *Goss* v. *Lopez* (1975), for instance, held that the due process clause protected students from suspension from a public school in Columbus, Ohio. A state statute permitting up to a ten-day suspension with neither notice nor a hearing was found constitutionally defective because it infringed on both liberty and property interests.

**WHAT PROCESS IS DUE?** If a court decides that the due process clause applies, it must then determine the process that is due. At one extreme, criminal prosecutions (discussed in Chapter Ten) demand formal proceedings guided by a host of rules designed to ensure fairness. At the other extreme are brief, informal exchanges, which usually occur before a decision is made. In *Goss*, although the majority concluded that the due process clause applied to school suspensions, only the barest process would have sufficed: (1) oral or written notice of the charge against a student, and (2) an opportunity for a student to present his or her side of the story. There need be no delay between the moment of "notice" and the "hearing." The latter could amount to little more than "an informal give-and-take between student and disciplinarian, preferably prior to the suspension. . . ."

*Mathews* v. *Elridge* (1976) attempted to establish guidelines for the process various situations require. At issue was termination of disability insurance payments under the Social Security program. Existing procedures allowed the recipient to submit additional information by mail prior to termination and, within six months of the cutoff, to seek reconsideration in a hearing. Elridge demanded an evidentiary hearing prior to termination. Speaking for the majority, Justice Powell explained that a decision rested on several factors:

> First, the private interest that will be affected by the official action; second, the risk of an erroneous deprivation of such interest through the procedures used, and the probable value, if any, of additional or substitute procedural safeguards; and finally, the Government's interest, including the function involved and the fiscal and administrative burdens that the additional or substitute procedural requirement would entail.

Measured by this formulation, existing procedure satisfied the Constitution. "[T]he prescribed procedures not only provide the claimant with an effective process for asserting his claim prior to any administrative action, but also assure a right to an evidentiary hearing, as well as to subsequent judicial review, before the denial of his claim becomes final."

*Mathews* makes explicit the balancing of interests involved, not in deciding whether a constitutionally protected interest is threatened, but in deciding the process by which it may be withdrawn. The thinking in *Mathews* is economic—the weighing of benefits of added procedure (which would minimize the risks of error) against its costs (which might come out of the resources available for social welfare programs). *Mathews* also leans in favor of a presumption of the adequacy of existing procedure and away from a heightened judicial scrutiny of what the state has offered.

NEW PROPERTY AND THE PRIVILEGES AND IMMUNITIES CLAUSE. In the Slaughterhouse Cases, discussed earlier in this chapter, the justices all but wrote the privileges and immunities clause out of the Fourteenth Amendment. Between 1873 and 1999 the Court relied on the clause but once (*Colgate* v. *Harvey,* 1935), only to overrule that decision five years later (*Madden* v. *Kentucky,* 1940). In **Saenz v. Roe** (1999), however, the Court breathed new life into this provision when it invalidated California's residency requirement (and indirectly the congressional act allowing it) for welfare benefits. Otherwise eligible welfare recipients had to reside in the state for a year in order to receive benefits paid to other eligible Californians; until then, they received an amount equal to what their previous state of residence had paid. Coupling the right to travel with the privileges and immunities clause, seven justices concluded that California's rule denied newer citizens a right of citizenship in their new state of residence. Previously the Court had examined such discriminations under the equal protection clause of the same amendment, as in **Shapiro v. Thompson** (1969), reprinted in Chapter Fourteen. *Saenz* may threaten other state policies that treat people differently and hints that the once moribund privileges and immunities clause may become a repository of new constitutional rights.

PUNITIVE DAMAGES. The award of punitive or exemplary damages in even a single civil suit may amount to millions of dollars. Long a favorite of the tort bar, **punitive damages** further a state's interest in punishing and deterring unlawful conduct. (Punitive damages are in addition to **compensatory damages,** the latter consisting of the concrete loss sustained and nothing more.) Government compels the transfer of money (property) from the defendant (the wrongdoer) to the plaintiff (the one who has been wronged). To what extent does the Constitution set limits on this time-honored practice? The Court confronted this question for the first time in *Pacific Mutual Life Insurance Co.* v. *Haslip* (1991) and turned back a constitutionally based attack. While agreeing that the Fourteenth Amendment imposed at least some limits on the size of a punitive damage award, the majority in *Haslip* left unsaid what those limits were. The case illustrated both the vast sums of money that are placed at risk and the difficulty of formulating precise restraints on state authority. Nonetheless, *TXO Production Corp.* v. *Alliance Resources Corp.* (1993) suggested that those restraints would exist only at the margin; the decision upheld punitive damages that were 525 times the size of the compensatory damages awarded in the case. Not until *BMW* v. *Gore* in 1996 did the Court overturn a punitive award because it was "grossly excessive." In this case an Alabama jury awarded $4 million (a sum subsequently cut in half by the state supreme court) to the purchaser of a new automobile that, unknown to the purchaser, had been repainted because of damage in transit. The repainting reduced the value of the new car by 10 percent ($4,000). The decision effectively established a substantive due process right against grossly excessive judgments; moreover, the Court attempted to mark the limits of acceptability. Reviewing courts were instructed to consider: (1) the degree of reprehensibility of the defendant's misconduct; (2) the disparity between the actual and potential harm suffered by the plaintiff and the punitive award; and (3) the difference between the punitive award and civil penalties that might be imposed for similar conduct. *State Farm Mutual* v. *Campbell* (2003) reemphasized those points from *Gore,* as it set aside a $145 million punitive award where the actual damages were only $1 million. While refusing to set a "bright-line ratio which a punitive damages award cannot exceed," Justice Kennedy admonished "that, in practice, few awards exceeding a single-digit ratio between punitive and compensatory damages, to a significant degree, will satisfy due process."

The procedural standards accorded liberty and property interests make these subjects some of the most encompassing in all constitutional law. Few if any constitutional safeguards touch more citizens directly and on a day-to-day basis. Perhaps in no other subset are more Americans likely at some time in their lives to experience infringement of what may be their constitutionally protected liberty or property.

## KEY TERMS

| | | |
|---|---|---|
| antimony | implied contracts | public use |
| vested rights | due process | just compensation |
| police power | liberty of contract | new property |
| ex post facto laws | Brandeis brief | entitlements |
| contract clause | footnote four | punitive damages |
| reservation clause | takings clause | compensatory damages |
| popular sovereignty | eminent domain | |

## QUERIES

**1.** The decisions in *Dartmouth College* v. *Woodward* and *Charles River Bridge* v. *Warren Bridge* reflect contrasting views on the rigors of the contract clause. Does each also represent contrasting views on the nature of property?

**2.** Use of the due process clause to protect property may have represented an effort to amend the Constitution judicially, to add to the document protections that the framers failed to include. Is there evidence to support this statement in the Slaughterhouse Cases, *Munn* v. *Illinois,* and *Lochner* v. *New York?*

**3.** In 1893, Justice David J. Brewer and Professor James Bradley Thayer spoke out on judicial activism versus judicial restraint. What did they recommend concerning the Court's role?

**4.** Justices on the modern Court have made clear that they reject the judicial philosophy reflected in *Lochner* v. *New York*. Yet, they have by no means turned their backs on intervention in other realms of public policy. Precisely what was wrong with *Lochner?* Does it deserve its bad reputation?

## SELECTED READINGS

CORWIN, EDWARD S. "The Basic Doctrine of American Constitutional Law." 12 *Michigan Law Review* 247 (1914).

DELONG, JAMES. *Property Matters*. New York: Simon & Schuster, 1997.

ELY, JAMES W., JR. *The Guardian of Every Other Right: A Constitutional History of Property Rights*. New York: Oxford University Press, 1992.

FISHEL, WILLIAM A. *Regulatory Takings*. Cambridge, Mass.: Harvard University Press, 1995.

GILLMAN, HOWARD. *The Constitution Besieged: The Rise and Demise of Lochner Era Police Powers Jurisprudence*. Durham, N.C.: Duke University Press, 1993.

KENS, PAUL. *Judicial Power and Reform Politics: The Anatomy of Lochner v. New York*. Lawrence: University Press of Kansas, 1990.

KUTLER, STANLEY I. *Privilege and Creative Destruction: The Charles River Bridge Case*. Philadelphia, Pa.: Lippincott, 1972.

LABBE, RONALD M., and JONATHAN LURIE. *The Slaughterhouse Cases: Regulation, Reconstruction, and the Fourteenth Amendment*. Lawrence: University Press of Kansas, 2003.

NEDELSKY, JENNIFER. *Private Property and the Limits of American Constitutionalism*. Chicago: University of Chicago Press, 1991.

PAUL, ARNOLD M. *Conservative Crisis and Rule of Law: Attitudes of Bar and Bench, 1887–1895*. Ithaca, N.Y.: Cornell University Press, 1960.

PRICE, POLLY J. *Property Rights*. Santa Barbara, Calif.: ABC-CLIO, 2003.

WRIGHT, BENJAMIN F. *The Contract Clause of the Constitution*. Cambridge, Mass.: Harvard University Press, 1938.

# I. VESTED RIGHTS AND THE EX POST FACTO CLAUSE

## *Calder* v. *Bull*
## 3 U.S. (3 Dall.) 386, 1 L.Ed. 648 (1798)
## http://supct.law.cornell.edu/supct/cases/name.htm#Case_Name-C

> The legislature of Connecticut passed a law granting a new hearing to Bull and his wife, after their right to appeal a probate court decree had expired. At the second hearing, Bull was successful, and Calder, the other claimant, after appealing unsuccessfully to the highest Connecticut court, brought his case to the Supreme Court on a writ of error. The opinions of Justices Chase and Iredell are important, not only for their definition of ex post facto laws but also for the views expressed about natural law and judicial review. Majority: Chase, Cushing, Iredell, Paterson. Not participating: Ellsworth, Wilson.

CHASE, JUSTICE. . . .

The counsel for the plaintiffs in error contend, that the . . . law of the legislature of Connecticut, granting a new hearing, in the above case, is an *ex post facto law,* prohibited by the constitution of the United States; that any law of the federal government, or of any of the state governments, contrary to the constitution of the United States, is void; and that this court possess the power to declare such law void. . . .

Whether the legislature of any of the states can revise and correct by law, a decision of any of its courts of justice, although not prohibited by the constitution of the state, is a question of very great importance, and not necessary now to be determined; because the resolution or law in question does not go so far. I cannot subscribe to the omnipotence of a state legislature, or that it is absolute and without control; although its authority should not be expressly restrained by the constitution, or fundamental law of the state. . . . There are acts which the federal or state legislature cannot do, without exceeding their authority. There are certain vital principles in our free republican governments which will determine and overrule an apparent and flagrant abuse of legislative power; as to authorize manifest injustice by positive law; or to take away that security for personal liberty, or private property, for the protection whereof the government was established. An act of the

legislature (for I cannot call it a law), contrary to the great first principles of the social compact, cannot be considered a rightful exercise of legislative authority. The obligation of a law in governments established on express compact, and on republican principles, must be determined by the nature of the power on which it is founded.

A few instances will suffice to explain what I mean. A law that punished a citizen for an innocent action, or, in other words, for an act which, when done, was in violation of no existing law; a law that destroys, or impairs, the lawful private contracts of citizens; a law that makes a man a judge in his own cause; or a law that takes property from A, and gives it to B. It is against all reason and justice for a people to intrust a legislature with such powers; and, therefore, it cannot be presumed that they have done it. The genius, the nature, and the spirit of such acts of legislation; and the general principles of law and reason forbid them. The legislature may enjoin, permit, forbid and punish; they may declare new crimes, and establish rules of conduct for all its citizens in future cases; they may command what is right, and prohibit what is wrong; but they cannot change innocence into guilt, or punish innocence as a crime; or violate the right of an antecedent lawful private contract; or the right of private property. To maintain that our federal or state legislature possesses such powers, if they had not been expressly restrained, would, in my opinion, be a political heresy altogether inadmissible in our free republican governments. . . .

I will state what laws I consider *ex post facto* laws, within the words and the intent of the prohibition. 1st. Every law that makes an action done before the passing of the law, and which was innocent when done, criminal; and punishes such action. 2d. Every law that aggravates a crime, or makes it greater than it was, when committed. 3d. Every law that changes the punishment, and inflicts a greater punishment, than the law annexed to the crime, when committed. 4th. Every law that alters the legal rules of evidence, and receives less, or different testimony, than the law required at the time of the commission of the offense, in order to convict the offender. All these, and similar laws, are manifestly unjust and oppressive. In my opinion, the true distinction is between *ex post facto* laws, and retrospective laws. Every *ex post facto* law must necessarily be retrospective; but every retrospective law is not an *ex post facto* law; the former only are prohibited. Every law that takes away or impairs rights vested, agreeably to existing laws, is retrospective, and is generally unjust, and may be oppressive; and it is a good general rule, that a law should have no retrospect; but there are cases in which laws may justly, and for the benefit of the community, and also of individuals, relate to a time antecedent to their commencement; as statutes of oblivion or of pardon. They are certainly retrospective, and literally both concerning and after the facts committed. But I do not consider any law *ex post facto,* within the prohibition, that mollifies the rigor of the criminal law; but only those that create or aggravate the crime; or increase the punishment, or change the rules of evidence, for the purpose of conviction. Every law that is to have an operation before the making thereof, as to commence at an antecedent time; or to save time from the statute of limitations; or to excuse acts which were unlawful, and before committed, and the like, is retrospective. But such laws may be proper or necessary, as the case may be. There is a great and apparent difference between making an unlawful act

lawful; and the making an innocent action criminal, and punishing it as a crime. . . .

The restraint against making any *ex post facto* laws was not considered, by the framers of the constitution, as extending to prohibit the depriving a citizen even of a vested right to property; or the provision, "that private property should not be taken for public use, without just compensation," was unnecessary.

It seems to me that the right of property, in its origin, could only arise from compact express or implied, and I think it the better opinion, that the right, as well as the mode or manner of acquiring property, and of alienating or transferring, inheriting or transmitting it, is conferred by society, is regulated by civil institution, and is always subject to the rules prescribed by positive law. When I say that a right is vested in a citizen, I mean, that he has the power to do certain actions, or to possess certain things, according to the law of the land. . . .

PATERSON, JUSTICE . . . [omitted].

### IREDELL, JUSTICE. . . .

It is true, that some speculative jurists have held, that a legislative act against natural justice must, in itself, be void; but I cannot think that, under such a government any court of justice would possess a power to declare it so. . . . [I]t has been the policy of all the American states, which have, individually, framed their state constitutions, since the revolution, and of the people of the United States, when they framed the federal constitution, to define with precision the objects of legislative power, and to restrain its exercise within marked and settled boundaries. If any act of congress, or of the legislature of the state, violates those constitutional provisions, it is unquestionably void; though, I admit, that as the authority to declare it void is of a delicate and awful nature, the court will never resort to that authority, but in a clear and urgent case. If, on the other hand, the legislature of the Union, or the legislature of any member of the Union, shall pass a law, within the general scope of their constitutional power, the court cannot pronounce it to be void, merely because it is, in their judgment, contrary to the principles of natural justice. The ideas of natural justice are regulated by no fixed standards: the ablest and the purest men have differed upon the subject; and all that the court could properly say, in such an event, would be, that the legislature (possessed of an equal right of opinion) had passed an act which, in the opinion of the judges, was inconsistent with the abstract principles of natural justice. . . .

Still, however, in the present instance, the act or resolution of the legislature of Connecticut, cannot be regarded as an *ex post facto* law; for the true construction of the prohibition extends to criminal, not to civil issues. . . .

The policy, the reason and humanity of the prohibition, do not . . . extend to civil cases, to cases that merely affect the private property of citizens. Some of the most necessary and important acts of legislation are, on the contrary, founded upon the principle, that private rights must yield to public exigencies. . . . Without the possession of this power, the operations of government would often be obstructed, and society itself would be endangered. It is not sufficient to urge, that the power may be abused, for such is the nature of all power—such is the tendency of every human institution. . . . We must be content to limit power, where we can, and where we cannot, consistently with its use, we must be content to repose a salutary confidence. It is our consolation, that there never existed a government, in ancient or modern times, more free from danger in this respect, than the governments of America. . . .

CUSHING, JUSTICE . . . [omitted].

*Judgment affirmed.*

## II. THE CONTRACT CLAUSE

### *Dartmouth College* v. *Woodward*
### 17 U.S. (4 Wheat.) 518, 4 L.Ed. 629 (1819)
### http://laws.findlaw.com/us/17/518.html

This case involved rival claimants to the records, the seal, and other objects signifying control of Dartmouth College. The college trustees (mainly Federalist in their politics), based their claim on a charter granted in 1769 by King George III, and sought to regain control from a mainly Republican group whose authority had been created by three New Hampshire legislative acts in 1816. These amended the original charter by increasing the number of trustees and vesting the future power of appointment of trustees in the governor and his council. The state Superior Court of Judicature upheld Woodward and the new control group. In 1885 Sir Henry Maine characterized the Marshall Court's decision as "the bulwark of American individualism against democratic impatience and socialistic fantasy." Majority: Marshall, Johnson, Livingston, Story, Washington. Dissenting: Duvall. Not participating: Todd.

**The opinion of the Court was delivered by MARSHALL, CH. J. . . .**

It can require no argument to prove, that the circumstances of this case constitute a contract. An application is made to the crown for a charter to incorporate a religious and literary institution. In the application, it is stated, that large contributions have been made for the object, which will be conferred on the corporation, as soon as it shall be created. The charter is granted, and on its faith the property is conveyed. Surely, in this transaction every ingredient of a complete and legitimate contract is to be found. The points for consideration are, 1. Is this contract protected by the constitution of the United States? 2. Is it impaired by the acts under which the defendant holds? . . .

1. . . . If the act of incorporation be a grant of political power, if it creates a civil institution, to be employed in the administration of the government, or if the funds of the college be public property, or if the state of New Hampshire, as a government, be alone interested in its transactions, the subject is one in which the legislature of the state may act according to its judgment, unrestrained by any limitation of its power imposed by the constitution of the United States.

But if this be a private eleemosynary institution, endowed with a capacity to take property, for objects unconnected with government, whose funds are bestowed by individuals, on the faith of the charter; if the donors have stipulated for the future disposition and management of those funds, in the manner prescribed by themselves; there may be more difficulty in the case, although neither the persons who have made these stipulations, nor those for whose benefit they were made, should be parties to the cause. . . .

A corporation is an artificial being, invisible, intangible, and existing only in contemplation of law. Being the mere creature of law, it possesses only those properties which the charter of its creation confers upon it, either expressly or as incidental to its very existence. These are such as are supposed best calculated to effect the object for which it was created. Among the most important are immortality, and, if the expression may be allowed, individuality; properties by which a perpetual succession of many persons are considered as the same, and may act as a single individual. . . . It is no more a state instrument than a natural person exercising the same powers would be. If, then, a natural person, employed by individuals in the education of youth, or for the government of a seminary in which youth is educated, would not become a public officer, or be considered as a member of the civil government, how is it that this artificial being, created by law for the purpose of being employed by the same individuals for the same purposes, should become a part of the civil government of the country? . . .

. . . Dartmouth College is an eleemosynary institution, incorporated for the purpose of perpetuating the application of the bounty of the donors to the specified objects of the bounty; that its trustees or governors were originally named by the founder, and invested with the power of perpetuating themselves; that they are not public officers, nor is it a civil institution, participating in the administration of government; but a charity school, or a seminary of education, incorporated for the preservation of its property, and the perpetual application of that property to the objects of its creation. Yet a question remains to be considered of more real difficulty, on which more doubt has been entertained than on all that have been discussed. The founders of the college, at least those whose contributions were in money, have parted with the property bestowed upon it, and their representatives have no interest in that property. The donors of land are equally without interest so long as the corporation shall exist. Could they be found, they are unaffected by any alteration in its constitution, and probably regardless of its form or even of its existence. The students are fluctuating, and no individual among our youth has a vested interest in the institution which can be asserted in a court of justice. Neither the founders of the college, nor the youth for whose benefit it was founded, complain of the alteration made in its charter, or think themselves injured by it. The trustees alone complain, and the trustees have no beneficial interest to be protected. Can this be such a contract as the constitution intended to withdraw from the power of state legislation? Contracts, the parties to which have a vested beneficial interest, and those only, it has been said, are the objects about which the constitution is solicitous, and to which its protection is extended.

The court has bestowed on this argument the most deliberate consideration, and the result will be stated. Dr. Wheelock, acting for himself and for those who, at his solicitation, had made contributions to his school, applied for this charter, as the instrument which should enable him and them to perpetuate their beneficent intention. It was granted. An artificial, immortal being was created by the crown, capable of receiving and distributing forever, according to the will of the donors, the donations which should be made to it. On this being, the contributions which had been collected were immediately bestowed. These gifts were made, not indeed to make a profit for the donors or their posterity, but for something, in their opinion, of inestimable value; for something which they deemed a full equivalent for the money with which it was purchased. The consideration for which they stipulated, is the perpetual application of the fund to its objects, in the mode prescribed by themselves. Their descendants may take no interest in the preservation of this consideration. But in this respect their descendants are not their representatives. They are represented by the corporation. The corporation is the assignee of their rights, stands in their place, and distributes their bounty, as they would themselves have distributed it had they been immortal. So with respect to the students who are to derive learning from this source. The corporation is a trustee for them also. Their potential rights, which, taken distributively, are imperceptible, amount collectively to a most important interest. These are, in the aggregate, to be exercised, asserted, and protected by the corporation. They were as completely out of the donors, at the instant of their being vested in the corporation, and as incapable of being asserted by the students, as at present. . . .

This is plainly a contract to which the donors, the trustees, and the crown (to whose rights and obligations New Hampshire succeeds) were the original parties. It is a contract made on a valuable consideration. It is a contract for the security and disposition of property. It is a contract on the faith of which real and personal estate has been conveyed to the corporation. It is then a contract within the letter of the constitution, and within its spirit also, unless the fact that the property is invested by the donors in trustees, for the promotion of religion and education, for the benefit of persons who are perpetually changing, though the objects remain the same, shall create a particular

exception, taking this case out of the prohibition contained in the constitution. . . .

On what safe and intelligible ground can this exception stand? There is no expression in the constitution, no sentiment delivered by its contemporaneous expounders, which would justify us in making it. . . .

. . . These eleemosynary institutions do not fill the place, which would otherwise be occupied by government, but that which would otherwise remain vacant. They are complete acquisitions to literature. They are donations to education; donations, which any government must be disposed rather to encourage than to discountenance. It requires no very critical examination of the human mind, to enable us to determine, that one great inducement to these gifts is the conviction felt by the giver, that the disposition he makes of them is immutable. . . . All such gifts are made in the pleasing, perhaps delusive hope, that the charity will flow forever in the channel which the givers have marked out for it. If every man finds in his own bosom strong evidence of the universality of this sentiment, there can be but little reason to imagine, that the framers of our constitution were strangers to it, and that, feeling the necessity and policy of giving permanence and security to contracts, of withdrawing them from the influence of legislative bodies, whose fluctuating policy, and repeated interferences, produced the most perplexing and injurious embarrassments, they still deemed it necessary to leave these contracts subject to those interferences. The motives for such an exception must be very powerful, to justify the construction which makes it. . . .

2. We next proceed to the inquiry, whether its obligation has been impaired by those acts of the legislature of New Hampshire, to which the special verdict refers? . . .

It has been already stated, that the act "to amend the charter, and enlarge and improve the corporation of Dartmouth College," increases the number of trustees to twenty-one, gives the appointment of the additional members to the executive of the state, and creates a board of overseers, to consist of twenty-five persons, of whom twenty-one are also appointed by the executive of New Hampshire, who have power to inspect and control the most important acts of the trustees.

On the effect of this law [of 1816], two opinions cannot be entertained. Between acting directly, and acting through the agency of trustees and overseers, no essential difference is perceived. The whole power of governing the college is transferred from trustees appointed according to the will of the founder, expressed in the charter, to the executive of New Hampshire. The management and application of the funds of this eleemosynary institution, which are placed by the donors in the hands of trustees named in the charter, and empowered to perpetuate themselves, are placed by this act under the control of the government of the state. The will of the state is substituted for the will of the donors, in every essential operation of the college. This is not an immaterial change. . . .

It results from this opinion, that the acts of the legislature of New Hampshire, which are stated in the special verdict found in this cause, are repugnant to the constitution of the United States; and that the judgment on this special verdict ought to have been for the plaintiffs. The judgment of the State Court must, therefore, be reversed.

MR. JUSTICE WASHINGTON, concurring . . . [omitted].

MR. JUSTICE STORY, concurring . . . [omitted].

MR. JUSTICE DUVALL dissented [without opinion].

## *Charles River Bridge* v. *Warren Bridge*
## 36 U.S. (11 Pet.) 420, 9 L.Ed. 773 (1837)

http://laws.findlaw.com/us/36/420.html

In 1785 the Massachusetts legislature granted to the Charles River Bridge Co. the right to construct a bridge between Charlestown and Boston, with the power to collect tolls for 40 years (later extended to 70 years). This franchise replaced an exclusive ferry right formerly possessed by Harvard College, but which the college yielded in return for annual payments during the life of the bridge charter. In 1828, some Charlestown merchants received a legislative charter for construction of the Warren Bridge, with the power to collect tolls until they had been reimbursed. At that point title to the Warren Bridge would pass to the state and passage would become free. Proprietors of the Charles River Bridge, who would be deprived of their anticipated tolls because the new bridge was to be built close to the old one, unsuccessfully sought an injunction and other relief in state court. The case was first argued in the Supreme Court in 1831, while Marshall was Chief Justice, but absenteeism and a sharp division among the justices delayed decision. The case was reargued in 1837 after Taney succeeded Marshall. A very short excerpt from Justice Story's 65-page dissenting opinion follows Taney's opinion for the Court. Majority: Taney, Baldwin, Barbour, Wayne. Dissenting: McLean, Story, Thompson.

**MR. CHIEF JUSTICE TANEY delivered the opinion of the Court. . . .**

This brings us to the act of the legislature of Massachusetts, of 1785, by which the plaintiffs were incorporated by the name of "The Proprietors of the Charles River Bridge"; and it is here, and in the law of 1792, prolonging their charter, that we must look for the extent and nature of the franchise conferred upon the plaintiffs.

Much has been said in the argument of the principles of construction by which this law is to be expounded, and what undertakings, on the part of the state, may be implied. The court thinks there can be no serious difficulty on that head. It is the grant of certain franchises by the public to a private corporation, and in a matter where the public interest is concerned. The rule of construction in such cases is well settled, both in England and by the decisions of our own tribunals. . . . "This, like many other cases, is a bargain between a company of adventurers and the public, the terms of which are expressed in the statute; and the rule of construction, in all such cases, is now fully established to be this; that any ambiguity in the terms of the contract must operate against the adventurers, and in favor of the public, and the plaintiffs can claim nothing that is not clearly given them by the act." And the doctrine thus laid down is abundantly sustained by the authorities referred to in this decision. . . .

The argument in favour of the proprietors of the Charles River bridge, is . . . that the power claimed by the state, if it exists, may be so used as to destroy the value of the franchise they have granted to the corporation. . . . The existence of the power does not, and cannot depend upon the circumstance of its having been exercised or not. . . .

The object and end of all government is to promote the happiness and prosperity of the community by which it is established, and it can never be assumed, that the government intended to diminish its powers of accomplishing the end for which it was created. And in a country like ours, free, active, and enterprising, continually advancing in numbers and wealth, new channels of communication are daily found necessary, both for travel and trade; and are essential to the comfort, convenience, and prosperity of the people. A state ought never to be presumed to surrender this power, because, like the taxing power, the whole community has an interest in preserving it undiminished. And when a corporation alleges, that a state has surrendered, for seventy years, its power of improvement and public accommodation, in a great and important line of travel, along which a vast number of its citizens must daily pass, the community

has a right to insist, in the language of this court above quoted, "that its abandonment ought not to be presumed in a case in which the deliberate purpose of the state to abandon it does not appear." The continued existence of a government would be of no great value, if by implications and presumptions it was disarmed by the powers necessary to accomplish the ends of its creation; and the functions it was designed to perform, transferred to the hands of privileged corporations. . . . While the rights of private property are sacredly guarded, we must not forget that the community also has rights, and that the happiness and well-being of every citizen depends on their faithful preservation.

Adopting the rule of construction above stated as the settled one, we proceed to apply it to the charter of 1785, to the proprietors of the Charles River bridge. This act of incorporation is in the usual form, and the privileges such as are commonly given to corporations of that kind. It confers on them the ordinary faculties of a corporation, for the purpose of building the bridge; and establishes certain rates of toll, which the company is authorized to take: this is the whole grant. There is no exclusive privilege given to them over the water of Charles River, above or below their bridge; no right to erect another bridge themselves, nor to prevent other persons from erecting one, no engagement from the state, that another shall not be erected; and no undertaking not to sanction competition, not to make improvements that may diminish the amount of its income. Upon all these subjects, the charter is silent; and nothing is said in it about a line of travel, so much insisted on in the argument, in which they are to have exclusive privileges. . . .

In short, all the franchises and rights of property, enumerated in the charter, and there mentioned to have been granted to it, remain unimpaired. But its income is destroyed by the Warren bridge; which, being free, draws off the passengers and property which would have gone over it, and renders their franchise of no value. This is the gist of the complaint. For it is not pretended, that the erection of the Warren bridge would have done them any injury, or in any degree affected their right of property, if it had not diminished the amount of their tolls. In order, then, to entitle themselves to relief, it is necessary to show, that the legislature contracted not to do the act of which they complain; and that they impaired, or in other words, violated, that contract by the erection of the Warren bridge.

The inquiry, then, is, does the charter contain such a contract on the part of the state? Is there any such stipulation to be found in that instrument? It must be admitted on all hands, that there is none; no words that even relate to another bridge, or to the diminution of their tolls, or to the line of travel. If a contract on that subject can be gathered from the charter, it must be by implication; and cannot be found in the words used. Can such an agreement be implied? The rule of construction before stated is an answer to the question; in charters of this description, no rights are taken from the public, or given to the corporation, beyond those which the words of the charter, by their natural and proper construction, purport to convey. There are no words which import such a contract as the plaintiffs in error contend for, and none can be implied. . . .

Indeed, the practice and usage of almost every state in the Union, old enough to have commenced the work of internal improvement, is opposed to the doctrine contended for on the part of the plaintiffs in error. Turnpike roads have been made in succession, on the same line of travel; the later ones interfering materially with the profits of the first. These corporations have, in some instances, been utterly ruined by the introduction of newer and better modes of transportation and traveling. In some cases, railroads have rendered the turnpike roads on the same line of travel so entirely useless, that the franchise of the turnpike corporation is not worth preserving. Yet in none of these cases have the corporations supposed that their privileges were invaded, or any contract violated on the part of the state. . . .

And what would be the fruits of this doctrine of implied contracts, on the part of the states, and of property in a line of travel by a corporation, if it should now be sanctioned by

this court? To what results would it lead us? . . . Let it once be understood, that such charters carry with them these implied contracts, and give this unknown and undefined property in a line of travelling; and you will soon find the old turnpike corporations awakening from their sleep and calling upon this court to put down the improvements which have taken their place. The millions of property which have been invested in railroads and canals, upon lines of travel which had been before occupied by turnpike corporations, will be put in jeopardy. We shall be thrown back to the improvements of the last century, and obliged to stand still, until the claims of the old turnpike corporations shall be satisfied; and they shall consent to permit these states to avail themselves of the lights of modern science, and to partake of the benefit of those improvements which are now adding to the wealth and prosperity, and the convenience and comfort, of every other part of the civilized world. . . . This court is not prepared to sanction principles which must lead to such results. . . .

The judgment of the supreme judicial court of the commonwealth of Massachusetts, dismissing the plaintiff's bill, must therefore, be affirmed with costs.

MR. JUSTICE MCLEAN, dissenting . . . [omitted].

### MR. JUSTICE STORY, dissenting. . . .

I admit, that where the terms of a grant are to impose burdens upon the public, or to create a restraint injurious to the public interests, there is sound reason for interpreting the terms, if ambiguous, in favor of the public. But at the same time, I insist, that there is not the slightest reason for saying, even in such a case, that the grant is not to be construed favourably to the grantee, so as to secure him in the enjoyment of what is actually granted. . . .

For my own part, I can conceive of no surer plan to arrest all public improvements, founded on private capital and enterprise, than to make the outlay of that capital uncertain, and questionable both as to security, and as to productiveness. No man will hazard his capital in any enterprise, in which, if there be a loss, it must be borne exclusively by himself; and if there be success, he has not the slightest security of enjoying the rewards of that success for a single moment. . . .

Upon the whole, my judgment is that the act of the legislature of Massachusetts granting the charter of Warren Bridge, is an act impairing the obligation of the prior contract and grant to the proprietors of Charles River bridge; and, by the Constitution of the United States, it is, therefore, utterly void. . . .

MR. JUSTICE THOMPSON, dissenting . . . [omitted].

## Home Building & Loan Association v. Blaisdell
## 290 U.S. 398, 54 S.Ct. 231, 78 L.Ed. 413 (1934)
### http://laws.findlaw.com/us/290/398.html

> The Minnesota Mortgage Moratorium Law of 1933 was designed to prevent the foreclosure of mortgages during the Depression by extending the redemption period of mortgages under conditions set by a court. The act was to remain in effect "only during the continuance of the emergency and in no event beyond May 1, 1935." Blaisdell had mortgaged a house and lot to the appellant company; when Blaisdell failed to make timely payments, the company foreclosed, and Blaisdell sought an extension. A state court extended the redemption period on condition that certain monthly payments be made, and the Supreme Court of Minnesota affirmed. Majority: Hughes, Brandeis, Cardozo, Roberts, Stone. Dissenting: Sutherland, Butler, McReynolds, Van Devanter.

**MR. CHIEF JUSTICE HUGHES delivered the opinion of the Court. . . .**

The statute does not impair the integrity of the mortgage indebtedness. The obligation for interest remains. The statute does not affect the validity of the sale or the right of a mortgagee-purchaser to title in fee, or his right to obtain a deficiency judgment, if the mortgagor fails to redeem within the prescribed period. Aside from the extension of time, the other conditions of redemption are unaltered. While the mortgagor remains in possession, he must pay the rental value as that value has been determined, upon notice and hearing, by the court. The rental value so paid is devoted to the carrying of the property by the application of the required payments to taxes, insurance, and interest on the mortgage indebtedness. While the mortgagee-purchaser is debarred from actual possession, he has, so far as rental value is concerned, the equivalent of possession during the extended period.

In determining whether the provision for this temporary and conditional relief exceeds the power of the state by reason of the clause in the Federal Constitution prohibiting impairment of the obligations of contracts, we must consider the relation of emergency to constitutional power, the historical setting of the contract clause, the development of the jurisprudence of this Court in the construction of that clause, and the principles of construction which we may consider to be established.

Emergency does not create power. Emergency does not increase granted power or remove or diminish the restrictions imposed upon power granted or reserved. . . .

While emergency does not create power, emergency may furnish the occasion for the exercise of power. . . . The constitutional question presented in the light of an emergency is whether the power possessed embraces the particular exercise of it in response to particular conditions. Thus, the war power of the federal government is not created by the emergency of war, but it is a power given to meet that emergency. It is a power to wage war successfully, and thus it permits the harnessing of the entire energies of the people in a supreme cooperative effort to preserve the nation. But even the war power does not remove constitutional limitations safeguarding essential liberties. When the provisions of the Constitution, in grant or restriction, are specific, so particularized as not to admit of construction, no question is presented. . . . But, where constitutional grants and limitations of power are set forth in general clauses, which afford a broad outline, the process of construction is essential to fill in the details. That is true of the contract clause. . . .

In the construction of the contract clause, the debates in the Constitutional Convention are of little aid. But the reasons which led to the adoption of that clause, and of the other prohibitions of Section 10 of Article I, are not left in doubt, and have frequently been described with eloquent emphasis. The widespread distress following the revolutionary period, and the plight of debtors had called forth in the states an ignoble array of legislative schemes for the defeat of creditors and the invasion of contractual obligations. Legislative interferences had been so numerous and extreme that the confidence essential to prosperous trade had been undermined and the utter destruction of credit was threatened. . . .

It is manifest . . . that there has been a growing appreciation of public needs and of the necessity of finding ground for a rational compromise between individual rights and public welfare. . . .

It is no answer to say that this public need was not apprehended a century ago, or to insist that what the provision of the Constitution meant to the vision of that day it must mean to the vision of our time. If by the statement that what the Constitution meant at the time of its adoption it means today, it is intended to say that the great clauses of the Constitution must be confined to the interpretation which the framers, with the conditions and outlook of their time, would have placed upon them, the statement carries its own refutation. It was to guard against such a narrow conception that Chief Justice Marshall uttered the memorable warning: "We must never forget, that it is a *constitution* we are expounding"; "a constitution intended to endure for ages to come, and consequently, to be adapted to the various crises of human affairs." . . .

The vast body of law which has been developed was unknown to the fathers, but it is believed to have preserved the essential content and the spirit of the Constitution. With a growing recognition of public needs and the relation of individual right to public security, the Court has sought to prevent the perversion of the clause through its use as an instrument to throttle the capacity of the states to protect their fundamental interests. . . .

We are of the opinion that the Minnesota statute as here applied does not violate the contract clause of the Federal Constitution. Whether the legislation is wise or unwise as a matter of policy is a question with which we are not concerned. . . .

The judgment of the Supreme Court of Minnesota is affirmed.

*Judgment affirmed.*

## MR. JUSTICE SUTHERLAND, dissenting. . . .

A provision of the Constitution, it is hardly necessary to say, does not admit of two distinctly opposite interpretations. It does not mean one thing at one time and an entirely different thing at another time. If the contract impairment clause, when framed and adopted, meant that the term of a contract for the payment of money could not be altered *in invitum* [against one not assenting] by a state statute enacted for the relief of hardly pressed debtors to the end and with the effect of postponing payment or enforcement during and because of an economic or financial emergency, it is but to state the obvious to say that it means the same now. . . .

The provisions of the Federal Constitution, undoubtedly, are pliable in the sense that in appropriate cases they have the capacity of bringing within their grasp every new condition which falls within their meaning. But, their *meaning* is changeless; it is only their *application* which is extensible. . . . Constitutional grants of power and restrictions upon the exercise of power are not flexible as the doctrines of the common law are flexible. These doctrines, upon the principles of the common law itself, modify or abrogate themselves whenever they are or whenever they become plainly unsuited to different or changed conditions. . . .

A candid consideration of the history and circumstances which led up to and accompanied the framing and adoption of this clause will demonstrate conclusively that it was framed and adopted with the specific and studied purpose of preventing legislation designed to relieve debtors *especially* in time of financial distress. Indeed, it is not probable that any other purpose was definitely in the minds of those who composed the framers' convention or the ratifying state conventions which followed, although the restriction has been given a wider application upon principles clearly stated by Chief Justice Marshall in the Dartmouth College Case. . . .

The defense of the Minnesota law is made upon grounds which were discountenanced by the makers of the Constitution and have many times been rejected by this court. . . . With due regard for the process of logical thinking, it legitimately cannot be urged that conditions which produced the rule may now be invoked to destroy it.

. . . The opinion concedes that emergency does not create power, or increase granted power, or remove or diminish restrictions upon power granted or reserved. It then proceeds to say, however, that while emergency does not create power, it may furnish the occasion for the exercise of power. I can only interpret what is said on that subject as meaning that while an emergency does not diminish a restriction upon power it furnishes an occa-

sion for diminishing it; and this, as it seems to me, is merely to say the same thing by the use of another set of words, with the effect of affirming that which has just been denied. . . .

The Minnesota statute either impairs the obligation of contracts or it does not. If it does not, the occasion to which it relates becomes immaterial, since then the passage of the statute is the exercise of a normal, unrestricted, state power and requires no special occasion to render it effective. If it does, the emergency no more furnishes a proper occasion for its exercise than if the emergency were nonexistent. And so, while, in form, the suggested distinction seems to put us forward in a straight line, in reality it simply carries us back in a circle, like bewildered travelers lost in a wood, to the point where we parted company with the view of the state court. . . .

I am authorized to say that MR. JUSTICE VAN DEVANTER, MR. JUSTICE McREYNOLDS and MR. JUSTICE BUTLER concur in this opinion.

### MR. JUSTICE CARDOZO, concurring in an *unpublished* opinion.[2] . . .

The economic and social changes wrought by the industrial revolution and by the growth of population have made it necessary for government at this day to [do] a thousand things that were beyond the experience or the thought of a century ago. With the growing recognition of this need, courts have awakened to the truth that the contract clause is perverted from its proper meaning when it throttles the capacity of the states to exert their governmental power in response to crying needs. . . . The early cases dealt with the problem as one affecting the conflicting rights and interests of individuals and classes. This was the attitude of the courts up to the Fourteenth Amendment; and the tendency to some extent persisted even later. . . . The rights and

---

[2] This is part of a draft of an unpublished concurring opinion that Justice Cardozo wrote and sent to Chief Justice Hughes, who incorporated some of Cardozo's ideas into his own majority opinion. Harlan Fiske Stone Papers, Library of Congress.—ED.

interests of the state itself were involved, as it seemed, only indirectly and remotely, if they were thought to be involved at all. We know better in these days, with the passing of the frontier and of the unpeopled spaces of the west. With these and other changes, the welfare of the social organism in any of its parts is bound up more inseparably than ever with the welfare of the whole. . . . The state when it acts today by statutes like the one before us is not furthering the selfish good of individuals or classes as ends of ultimate validity. It is furthering its own good by maintaining the economic structure on which the good of all depends. Such at least is its endeavor, however much it miss the mark. The attainment of that end, so august and impersonal, will not be barred and thwarted by the obstruction of a contract set up along the way.

Looking back over the century, one perceives a process of evolution too strong to be set back. . . . [T]he court in its interpretation of the contract clause has been feeling its way toward a rational compromise between private rights and public welfare. From the beginning it was seen that something must be subtracted from the words of the Constitution in all their literal and stark significance. . . . Contracts were still to be preserved. . . . But a promise exchanged between individuals was not to paralyze the state in its endeavor in times of direful crisis to keep its life-blood flowing.

To hold this may be inconsistent with things that men said in 1787 when expounding to compatriots the newly written constitution. They did not see the changes in the relation between states and nation or in the play of social forces that lay hidden in the womb of time. It may be inconsistent with things that they believed or took for granted. Their beliefs to be significant must be adjusted to the world they knew. It is not in my judgment inconsistent with what they would say today, nor with what today they would believe, if they were called upon to interpret "in the light of our whole experience" the constitution that they framed for the needs of an expanding future.

## III. PROPERTY RIGHTS AND THE FOURTEENTH AMENDMENT

### Slaughterhouse Cases
### (*Butchers' Benevolent Association* v. *Crescent City Livestock Landing & Slaughter-House Co.*)
### 83 U.S. (16 Wall.) 36, 21 L.Ed. 394 (1873)

### http://laws.findlaw.com/us/83/36.html

In 1869 the Louisiana legislature granted a monopoly to a slaughterhouse company for the sheltering and butchering of animals within three parishes, including the city of New Orleans. All other butchers were required to use the slaughterhouse company's facilities, upon payment of a fee. By one account, more than a thousand butchers and their employees were adversely affected by the law. Various butchers then unsuccessfully sought an injunction against the monopoly in the state courts. The three cases which went to the U.S. Supreme Court are collectively known as the Slaughterhouse Cases. The lead suit was brought by the Butchers' Benevolent Association with former justice John A. Campbell as its counsel. Majority: Miller, Clifford, Davis, Hunt, Strong. Dissenting: Field, Bradley, Chase, Swayne.

## Mr. Justice Miller ... delivered the opinion of the Court. ...

The statute is denounced not only as creating a monopoly and conferring odious and exclusive privileges upon a small number of persons at the expense of the great body of the community of New Orleans, but it is asserted that it deprives a large and meritorious class of citizens—the whole of the butchers of the city—of the right to exercise their trade, the business to which they have been trained and on which they depend for the support of themselves and their families; and that the unrestricted exercise of the business of butchering is necessary to the daily subsistence of the population of the city. ...

The wisdom of the monopoly granted by the legislature may be open to question, but it is difficult to see a justification for the assertion that the butchers are deprived of the right to labor in their occupation, or the people of their daily service in preparing food, or how this statute, with the duties and guards imposed upon the company, can be said to destroy the business of the butcher, or seriously interfere with its pursuit. ...

The plaintiffs in error ... allege that the statute is a violation of the Constitution of the United States in these several particulars:

That it creates an involuntary servitude forbidden by the thirteenth article of amendment;
That it abridges the privileges and immunities of citizens of the United States;
That it denies to the plaintiffs the equal protection of the laws; and,
That it deprives them of their property without due process of law; contrary to the provisions of the first section of the fourteenth article of amendment.

This court is thus called upon for the first time to give construction to these articles. ... On the most casual examination of the language of these amendments [the Thirteenth, Fourteenth, and Fifteenth], no one can fail to be impressed with the one pervading purpose found in them all, lying at the foundation of each, and without which none of them would have even been suggested; we mean the freedom of the slave race, the security and firm establishment of that freedom, and the protection of the newly-made freeman and citizen from the oppressions of those who had formerly exercised unlimited dominion over him. It is true that only the fifteenth amendment, in terms, mentions the negro by speaking of his color and his slavery. But it is just as true that each of the other articles was addressed to the grievances of that race, and designed to remedy them as the fifteenth.

We do not say that no one else but the negro can share in this protection. ... But what we do say, and what we wish to be understood is, that in any fair and just construction of any section or phrase of these amendments, it is necessary to look to the purpose which we have said was the pervading spirit of them all, the evil which they were designed to remedy, and the process of continued addition to the Constitution, until that purpose was supposed to be accomplished as far as constitutional law can accomplish it. ...

The next observation is more important in view of the arguments of counsel in the present case. It is, that the distinction between citizenship of the United States and citizenship of a State is clearly recognized and established. Not only may a man be a citizen of the United States without being a citizen of a State, but an important element is necessary to convert the former into the latter. He must reside within the State to make him a citizen of it, but it is only necessary that he should be born or naturalized in the United States to be a citizen of the Union.

It is quite clear, then, that there is a citizenship of the United States, and a citizenship of a State, which are distinct from each other, and which depend upon different characteristics or circumstances in the individual.

We think this distinction and its explicit recognition in this amendment of great weight in this argument, because the next paragraph of this same section, which is the one mainly relied on by the plaintiffs in error, speaks only of privileges and immunities of citizens of the United States, and does not speak of those of citizens of the several States. The argument, however, in favor of the plaintiffs rests wholly on the assumption that the citizenship is the same, and the privileges and immunities guaranteed by the clause are the same.

The language is, "No State shall make or enforce any law which shall abridge the privileges or immunities of citizens *of the United States.*" It is a little remarkable, if this clause was intended as a protection to the citizen of a State against the legislative power of his own State, that the word citizen of the State should be left out when it is so carefully used, and used in contradistinction to citizens of the United States, in the very sentence which precedes it. It is too clear for argument that the change in phraseology was adopted understandingly and with a purpose.

Of the privileges and immunities of the citizen of the United States, and of the privileges and immunities of the citizen of the State, and what they respectively are, we will presently consider; but we wish to state here that it is only the former which are placed by this clause under the protection of the Federal Constitution, and that the latter, whatever they may be, are not intended to have any additional protection by this paragraph of the amendment.

If, then, there is a difference between the privileges and immunities belonging to a citizen of the United States as such, and those belonging to the citizen of the State as such, the latter must rest for their security and protection where they have heretofore rested; for they are not embraced by this paragraph of the amendment. . . .

Fortunately we are not without judicial construction of this clause of the Constitution. The first and the leading case on the subject is that of *Corfield* v. *Coryell* decided by Mr. Justice Washington in the Circuit Court for the District of Pennsylvania in 1823.

"The inquiry," he says, "is, what are the privileges and immunities of citizens of the several States? We feel no hesitation in confining these expressions to those privileges and immunities which are fundamental; which belong of right to the citizens of all free governments, and which have at all times been enjoyed by citizens of the several States which

compose this Union, from the time of their becoming free, independent, and sovereign. What these fundamental principles are, it would be more tedious than difficult to enumerate. They may all, however, be comprehended under the following general heads: protection by the government, with the right to acquire and possess property of every kind, and to pursue and obtain happiness and safety, subject, nevertheless, to such restraints as the government may prescribe for the general good of the whole." . . .

It would be the vainest show of learning to attempt to prove by citations of authority, that up to the adoption of the recent amendments, no claim or pretense was set up that those rights depended on the Federal government for their existence or protection, beyond the very few express limitations which the Federal Constitution imposed upon the States—such, for instance, as the prohibition against ex post facto laws, bills of attainder, and laws impairing the obligation of contracts. But with the exception of these and a few other restrictions, the entire domain of the privileges and immunities of the citizens of the States, as above defined, lay within the constitutional and legislative power of the States, and without that of the Federal government. Was it the purpose of the Fourteenth Amendment, by the simple declaration that no State should make or enforce any law which shall abridge the privileges and immunities of citizens of the United States, to transfer the security and protection of all the civil rights which we have mentioned, from the States to the Federal government? And where it is declared that Congress shall have the power to enforce that article, was it intended to bring within the power of Congress the entire domain of civil rights heretofore belonging exclusively to the States?

All this and more must follow, if the proposition of the plaintiffs in error be sound. For not only are these rights subject to the control of Congress whenever in its discretion any of them are supposed to be abridged by State legislation, but that body may also pass laws in advance, limiting and restricting the exercise of legislative power by the States, in their most ordinary and usual functions, as in its judgment it may think proper on all such subjects. And still further, such a construction followed by the reversal of the judgments of the Supreme Court of Louisiana in these cases, would constitute this court a perpetual censor upon all legislation of the States, on the civil rights of their own citizens, with authority to nullify such as it did not approve as consistent with those rights, as they existed at the time of the adoption of this amendment. The argument we admit is not always the most conclusive which is drawn from the consequences urged against the adoption of a particular construction of an instrument. But when, as in the case before us, these consequences are so serious, so far-reaching and pervading, so great a departure from the structure and spirit of our institutions; when the effect is to fetter and degrade the State governments by subjecting them to the control of Congress, in the exercise of powers heretofore universally conceded to them of the most ordinary and fundamental character; when in fact it radically changes the whole theory of the relations of the State and Federal governments to each other and of both these governments to the people; the argument has a force that is irresistible, in the absence of language which expresses such a purpose too clearly to admit of doubt.

We are convinced that no such results were intended by the Congress which proposed these amendments, nor by the legislatures of the States which ratified them. . . .

[W]e may hold ourselves excused from defining the privileges and immunities of citizens of the United States which no State can abridge, until some case involving those privileges may make it necessary to do so.

But lest it should be said that no such privileges and immunities are to be found if those we have been considering are excluded, we venture to suggest some which owe their existence to the Federal government, its National character, its Constitution, or its laws.

One of these . . . described in . . . *Crandall v. Nevada* . . . is the right of the citizen of this country, protected by implied guarantees of its Constitution, "to come to the seat of government to assert any claim he may have upon that government, to transact any busi-

ness he may have with it, to seek its protection, to share its offices, to engage in administering its functions. He has the right of free access to its seaports, through which all operations of foreign commerce are conducted, to the sub-treasuries, land offices, and courts of justice in the several states." . . .

Another privilege of a citizen of the United States is to demand the care and protection of the Federal government over his life, liberty, and property when on the high seas or within the jurisdiction of a foreign government. Of this there can be no doubt, nor that the right depends upon his character as a citizen of the United States. The right to peaceably assemble and petition for redress of grievances, the privilege of the writ of habeas corpus, are rights of the citizen guaranteed by the Federal Constitution. The right to use the navigable waters of the United States, however they may penetrate the territory of the several States, all rights secured to our citizens by treaties with foreign nations, are dependent upon citizenship of the United States, and not citizenship of a State. . . .

But it is useless to pursue this branch of the inquiry, since we are of opinion that the rights claimed by these plaintiffs in error, if they have any existence, are not privileges and immunities of citizens of the United States within the meaning of the clause of the fourteenth amendment under consideration. . . .

The argument has not been much pressed in these cases that the defendant's charter deprives the plaintiffs of their property without due process of law, or that it denies to them the equal protection of the law. The first of these paragraphs has been in the Constitution since the adoption of the fifth amendment, as a restraint upon the Federal power. . . .

We are not without judicial interpretation, therefore, both State and National, of the meaning of this clause. And it is sufficient to say that under no construction of that provision that we have ever seen, or any that we deem admissible, can the restraint imposed by the State of Louisiana upon the exercise of their trade by the butchers of New Orleans be held to be a deprivation of property within the meaning of that provision.

"Nor shall any State deny to any person within its jurisdiction the equal protection of the laws."

In the light of the history of these amendments, and the pervading purpose of them, which we have already discussed, it is not difficult to give a meaning to this clause. The existence of laws in the States where the newly emancipated negroes resided, which discriminated with gross injustice and hardship against them as a class, was the evil to be remedied by this clause, and by it such laws are forbidden. . . .

We doubt very much whether any action of a State not directed by way of discrimination against the negroes as a class, or on account of their race, will ever be held to come within the purview of this provision. It is so clearly a provision for that race and that emergency, that a strong case would be necessary for its application to any others. . . .

The judgments of the Supreme Court of Louisiana in these cases are

*Affirmed.*

### MR. JUSTICE FIELD, dissenting. . . .

The question presented is . . . one of the gravest importance, not merely to the parties here, but to the whole country. It is nothing less than the question whether the recent amendments to the Federal Constitution protect the citizens of the United States against the deprivation of their common rights by legislation. In my judgment the fourteenth amendment does afford such protection, and was so intended by the Congress which framed and the States which adopted it.

The amendment does not attempt to confer any new privileges or immunities upon citizens, or to enumerate or define those already existing. It assumes that there are such privileges and immunities which belong of right to citizens as such, and ordains that they shall not be abridged by State legislation. If this inhibition has no reference to privileges and immunities of this character, but only refers, as held by the majority of the court in their opinion, to such privileges and immunities as were before its adoption specially designated in the Constitution or necessarily implied as belonging to citizens of the United States, it was a vain and idle enactment, which accomplished nothing, and most unnecessarily excited Congress and the people on its passage. With privileges and immunities thus designated or implied no State could ever have interfered by its laws and no new constitutional provision was required to inhibit such interference. The supremacy of the Constitution and the laws of the United States always controlled any State legislation of that character. But if the amendment refers to the natural and inalienable rights which belong to all citizens, the inhibition has a profound significance and consequence.

What, then, are the privileges and immunities which are secured against abridgment by State legislation? . . .

The terms, "privileges and immunities" are not new in the Amendment; they were in the Constitution before the Amendment was adopted. They are found in the 2d section of the 4th article, which declares that "the citizens of each State shall be entitled to all privileges and immunities of citizens in the several States," and they have been the subject of frequent consideration in judicial decisions. In *Corfield* v. *Coryell* . . . Mr. Justice Washington said he had "no hesitation in confining these expressions to those privileges and immunities which were, in their nature, fundamental; which belong of right to citizens of all free governments, and which have at all times been enjoyed by the citizens of the several States which compose the Union, from the time of their becoming free, independent, and sovereign"; and in considering what those fundamental privileges were, he said that perhaps it would be more tedious than difficult to enumerate them, but that they might be "all comprehended under the following general heads: protection by the government; the enjoyment of life and liberty, with the right to acquire and possess property of every kind, and to pursue and obtain happiness and safety, subject, nevertheless to such restraints as the government may justly prescribe for the general good of the whole." This appears to me to be a sound construction of the clause in question. The privileges and immunities designated are those *which of right belong to the citizens of all free governments.* Clearly among these must be placed the right to pursue a lawful employment in a lawful manner, without other restraint than such as equally affects all persons. . . .

This equality of right, with exemption from all disparaging and partial enactments, in the lawful pursuits of life, throughout the whole country, is the distinguishing privilege of citizens of the United States. To them, everywhere, all pursuits, all professions, all avocations are open without other restrictions than such as are imposed equally upon all others of the same age, sex, and condition. The State may prescribe such regulations for every pursuit and calling of life as will promote the public health, secure the good order and ad-

vance the general prosperity of society, but when once prescribed the pursuit or calling must be free to be followed by every citizen who is within the conditions designated, and will conform to the regulations. This is the fundamental idea upon which our institutions rest, and unless adhered to in the legislation of the country our government will be a republic only in name. . . .

I am authorized by the CHIEF JUSTICE [CHASE], MR. JUSTICE SWAYNE, and MR. JUSTICE BRADLEY, to state that they concur with me in this dissenting opinion.

MR. JUSTICE BRADLEY, dissenting . . . [omitted].

MR. JUSTICE SWAYNE, dissenting . . . [omitted].

## Munn v. Illinois
## 94 U.S. 113, 24 L.Ed. 77 (1877)
## http://laws.findlaw.com/us/94/113.html

Article XIII of the Constitution of Illinois, adopted in 1870, declared grain warehouses to be "public warehouses" and gave to the general assembly the power of passing laws relating to the storage of grain. An act of 1871 fixed the rates warehouse owners might charge, required licenses, and made other regulations governing the conduct of warehouse owners. Munn and his partner Scott were convicted of operating a warehouse without a license and other unlawful practices, and sought review from an adverse judgment in the Illinois Supreme Court. That part of the chief justice's opinion dealing with the commerce clause is omitted. *Munn* and several railroad rate cases also decided on March 1, 1877, are collectively known as the Granger Cases. These cases came down just as the Electoral Commission was completing its task of trying to resolve the disputed presidential election of 1876. That commission consisted of Waite Court justices Clifford, Field, Bradley, Miller, and Strong, plus five members of the House of Representatives and five senators. Majority: Waite, Bradley, Clifford, Davis, Hunt, Miller, Swayne. Dissenting: Field, Strong.

**MR. CHIEF JUSTICE WAITE delivered the opinion of the Court.**

The question to be determined in this case is whether the general assembly of Illinois can, under the limitations upon the legislative powers of the States imposed by the Constitution of the United States, fix by law the maximum of

charges for the storage of grain in warehouses at Chicago and other places in the State having not less than one hundred thousand inhabitants, "in which grain is stored in bulk, and in which the grain of different owners is mixed together, or in which grain is stored in such a manner that the identity of different lots or parcels cannot be accurately preserved." . . .

When one becomes a member of society, he necessarily parts with some rights or privileges which, as an individual not affected by his relations to others, he might retain. "A body politic," as aptly defined in the preamble of the Constitution of Massachusetts, "is a social compact by which the whole people covenants with each citizen, and each citizen with the whole people, that all shall be governed by certain laws for the common good." This does not confer power upon the whole people to control rights which are purely and exclusively private . . . but it does authorize the establishment of laws requiring each citizen to so conduct himself, and so use his own property, as not unnecessarily to injure another. This is the very essence of government, and has found expression in the maxim, *sic utere tuo ut alienum non laedas.* [So use your own as not to injure others.] From this source come the police powers, which, as was said by Mr. Chief Justice Taney in the License Cases, "are nothing more or less than the powers of government inherent in every sovereignty . . . that is to say . . . the power to govern men and things." Under these powers the government regulates the conduct of its citizens one towards another, and the manner in which each shall use his own property, when such regulation becomes necessary for the public good. In their exercise it has been customary in England from time immemorial, and in this country from its first colonization, to regulate ferries, common carriers, hackmen, bakers, millers, wharfingers, innkeepers, &c., and in so doing to fix a maximum of charge to be made for services rendered, accommodations furnished, and articles sold. To this day, statutes are to be found in many of the States upon some or all these subjects; and we think it has never yet been successfully contended that such legislation came within any of the constitutional prohibitions against interference with private property. With the Fifth Amendment in force, Congress in 1820 conferred power upon the city of Washington "to regulate . . . the rates of wharfage at private wharves . . . the sweeping of chimneys, and to fix the rates of fees therefor . . . and the weight and quality of bread" . . . and, in 1848, "to make all necessary regulations respecting hackney carriages and the rates of fare of the same, and the rates of hauling by cartmen, wagoners, carmen, and draymen, and the rates of commission of auctioneers." . . .

From this it is apparent that, down to the time of the adoption of the Fourteenth Amendment, it was not supposed that statutes regulating the use, or even the price of the use, of private property necessarily deprived an owner of his property without due process of law. Under some circumstances they may, but not under all. The amendment does not change the law in this particular: it simply prevents the States from doing that which will operate as such a deprivation.

This brings us to inquire as to the principles upon which this power of regulation rests, in order that we may determine what is within and what is without its operative effect. Looking, then, to the common law, from whence came the right which the Constitution protects, we find that when private property is "affected with a public interest, it ceases to be *juris privati* [of private right] only." This was said by Lord Chief Justice Hale more than two hundred years ago, in his treatise *De Portibus Maris* . . . and has been accepted without objection as an essential element in the law of property ever since. Property does become clothed with a public interest, when used in a manner to make it of public consequence, and affect the community at large. When, therefore, one devotes his property to a use in which the public has an interest, he, in effect, grants to the public an interest in that use, and must submit to be controlled by the public for the common good, to the extent of the interest he has thus created. He may withdraw his grant by discontinuing the use; but, so long as he maintains the use, he must submit to the control. . . .

It is difficult to see why, if the common carrier, or the miller, or the ferryman, or the innkeeper, or the wharfinger, or the baker, or the cartman, or the hackney-coachman, pursues a public employment and exercises "a sort of public office," these plaintiffs in error do not. They stand, to use again the language of their counsel, in the very "gateway of commerce," and take toll from all who pass. . . . Certainly, if any business can be clothed "with a public interest and cease to be *juris privati* only," this has been. It may not be made so by the operation of the Constitution of Illinois or this statute, but it is by the facts.

. . . For our purposes we must assume that, if a state of facts could exist that would justify such legislation, it actually did exist when the statute now under consideration was passed. For us the question is one of power, not of expediency. If no state of circumstances could exist to justify such a statute, then we may declare this one void, because in excess of the legislative power of the State. But if it could, we must presume it did. Of the propriety of legislative interference within the scope of legislative power, the legislature is the exclusive judge. . . .

It is insisted, however, that the owner of property is entitled to a reasonable compensation for its use, even though it be clothed with a public interest, and that what is reasonable is a judicial and not a legislative question.

As has already been shown, the practice had been otherwise. In countries where the common law prevails, it has been customary from time immemorial for the legislature to declare what shall be a reasonable compensation under such circumstances, or, perhaps more properly speaking, to fix a maximum beyond which any charge made would be unreasonable. . . . The controlling fact is the power to regulate at all. If that exists, the right to establish the maximum of charge, as one of the means of regulation, is implied. . . .

We know that this is a power which may be abused; but that is no argument against its existence. For protection against abuses by legislatures the people must resort to the polls, not to the courts. . . .

*Judgment affirmed.*

### MR. JUSTICE FIELD, dissenting. . . .

The declaration of the Constitution of 1870, that private buildings used for private purposes shall be deemed public institutions, does not make them so. The receipt and storage of grain in a building erected by private means for that purpose does not constitute the building a public warehouse. There is no magic in the language, though used by a constitutional convention, which can change a private business into a public one, or alter the character of the building in which the business is transacted. A tailor's or a shoemaker's shop would still retain its private character, even though the assembled wisdom of the State should declare, by organic act or legislative ordinance, that such a place was a public workshop, and that the workmen were public tailors or public shoemakers. One might as well attempt to change the nature of colors, by giving them a new designation. . . .

The doctrine declared is that property "becomes clothed with a public interest when used in a manner to make it of public consequence, and affect the community at large"; and from such clothing the right of the legislature is deduced to control the use of the property, and to determine the compensation which the owner may receive for it. When Sir Matthew Hale, and the sages of the law in his day, spoke of property as affected by a public interest, and ceasing from that cause to be *juris privati* solely, that is ceasing to be held merely in private right, they referred to property dedicated by the owner to public uses, or to property the use of which was granted by the government, or in connection with which special privileges were conferred. Unless the property was thus dedicated or some right bestowed by the government was held with the property, either by specific grant or by prescription of so long a time as to imply a grant originally, the property was not affected by any public interest so as to be taken out of the category of property held in private right. But it is not in any such sense that the terms "clothing property with a public interest" are used in this case. From the nature of the business under consideration—the storage of grain—which, in any sense in which the words can be used, is a private business, in which the public are interested only as they are interested in the storage of other products of the soil, or in articles of manufacture, it is clear that the court intended to declare that, whenever one devotes his property to a business which is useful to the public—

"affects the community at large"—the legislature can regulate the compensation which the owner may receive for its use, and for his own services in connection with it. . . .

If this be sound law, if there be no protection, either in the principles upon which our republican government is founded, or in the prohibitions of the Constitution against such invasion of private rights, all property and all business in the State are held at the mercy of a majority of its legislature. The public has no greater interest in the use of buildings for the storage of grain than it has in the use of buildings for the residence of families, nor, indeed, any thing like so great an interest; and, according to the doctrine announced, the legislature may fix the rent of all tenements used for residences, without reference to the cost of their erection. If the owner does not like the rates prescribed, he may cease renting his houses. He has granted to the public, says the court, an interest in the use of the buildings, and "he may withdraw his grant by discontinuing the use; but, so long as he maintains the use, he must submit to the control." . . .

The same liberal construction which is required for the protection of life and liberty, in all particulars in which life and liberty are of any value, should be applied to the protection of private property. If the legislature of a State, under pretense of providing for the public good, or for any other reason, can determine, against the consent of the owner, the uses to which private property shall be devoted, or the prices which the owner shall receive for its uses, it can deprive him of the property as completely as by a special act for its confiscation or destruction. If, for instance, the owner is prohibited from using his building for the purposes for which it was designed, it is of little consequence that he is permitted to retain the title and possession; or, if he is compelled to take as compensation for its use less than the expenses to which he is subjected by its ownership, he is, for all practical purposes, deprived of the property, as effectually as if the legislature had ordered his forcible dispossession. If it be admitted that the legislature has any control over the compensation, the extent of that compensation becomes a mere matter of legislative discretion. . . .

There is nothing in the character of the business of the defendants as warehousemen which called for the interference complained of in this case. . . . The legislation in question is nothing less than a bold assertion of absolute power by the state to control at its discretion the property and business of the citizen, and fix the compensation he shall receive. . . .

I deny the power of any legislature under our government to fix the price which one shall receive for his property of any kind. If the power can be exercised as to one article, it may as to all articles, and the prices of every thing, from a calico gown to a city mansion, may be the subject of legislative direction. . . .

**MR. JUSTICE STRONG, dissenting . . .** [In a short paragraph Strong indicated agreement with Field's position, and regretted not having had time to prepare his own opinion.—ED.].

## Unstaged Debate of 1893: *Justice Brewer* v. *Professor Thayer*

**DAVID J. BREWER, "THE MOVEMENT OF COERCION," AN ADDRESS BEFORE THE NEW YORK STATE BAR ASSOCIATION, JANUARY 17, 1893**

. . . It is the unvarying law, that the wealth of a community will be in the hands of a few; and the greater the general wealth, the greater the individual accumulations. The large majority of men are unwilling to endure that long self-denial and saving which makes accumulation possible; they have not the business tact and sagacity which bring about large combinations and great financial results; and hence it always has been, and until human nature is remodeled always will be true, that the wealth of a nation is in the hands of a few, while the many subsist upon the proceeds of their daily toil. But security is the chief end of government; and other things being equal, the government is best which protects to the fullest extent each individual, rich or poor, high or low, in the possession of his property and the pursuit of his business. It was the boast of our ancestors in the old country, that they were able to wrest from the power of the king so much security for life, liberty and property. . . .

Here there is no monarch threatening trespass upon the individual. The danger is from the multitudes—the majority, with whom is the power. . . .

This movement expresses itself in two ways: First, in the improper use of labor organizations to destroy the freedom of the laborer, and control the uses of capital. . . .

The other form of this movement assumes the guise of a regulation of the charges for the use of property subjected, or supposed to be, to a public use. This acts in two directions: One by extending the list of those things, charges for whose use the government may prescribe; until now we hear it affirmed that whenever property is devoted to a use in which the public has an interest, charges for that use may be fixed by law. And if there be any property in the use of which the public or some portion of it has no interest, I hardly know what it is or where to find it. And second, in so reducing charges for the use of property, which in fact is subjected to a public use, that no compensation or income is received by those who have so invested their property. By the one it subjects all property and its uses to the will of the majority; by the other it robs property of its value. Statutes and decisions both disclose that this movement, with just these results, has a present and alarming existence. . . .

It may be said that that majority will not be so foolish, selfish and cruel as to strip that property of its earning capacity. I say that so long as constitutional guaranties lift on American soil their buttresses and bulwarks against wrong, and so long as the American judiciary breathes the free air of courage, it cannot. . . .

As might be expected, they who wish to push this movement to the extreme, who would brook no restraint on aught that seems to make for their gain, are unanimous in crying out against judicial interference, and are constantly seeking to minimize the power of the courts. . . . The argument is that judges are not adapted by their education and training to settle such matters as these; that they lack acquaintance with affairs and are tied to precedents; that the procedure in the courts is too slow and that no action could be had therein until long after the need of action has passed. It would be folly to assert that this argument is barren of force. . . . But the great body of judges are as well versed in the affairs of life as any, and they who unravel all the mysteries of accounting between partners, settle the business of the largest corporations and extract all the truth from the mass of scholastic verbiage that falls from the lips of expert witnesses in patent cases, will have no difficulty in determining what is right and wrong between employer and employees, and whether proposed rates of freight and fare are reasonable as between the public and the owners; while as for speed, is there anything quicker than a writ of injunction? . . .

The mischief-makers in this movement ever strive to get away from courts and judges, and to place the power of decision in the hands of those who will the more readily and freely yield to the pressure of numbers, that so-called demand of the majority. . . .

And so it is, that because of the growth of this movement, . . . arises the urgent need of giving to the judiciary the utmost vigor and efficiency. Now, if ever in the history of this country, must there be somewhere and somehow a controlling force which speaks for justice, and for justice only. . . .

What, then, ought to be done? My reply is, strengthen the judiciary. . . .

It may be said that this is practically substituting government by the judges for government by the people, and thus turning back the currents of history. . . . But this involves a total misunderstanding of the relations of judges to government. There is nothing in this power of the judiciary detracting in the least from the idea of government of and by the people. The courts hold neither purse nor sword; they cannot corrupt nor arbitrarily control. They make no laws, they establish no policy, they never enter into the domain of popular action. They do not govern. Their functions in relation to the State are limited to seeing that popular action does not trespass upon right and justice as it exists in written constitutions and natural law. . . .

I am firmly persuaded that the salvation of the Nation, the permanence of government of and by the people, rests upon the independence and vigor of the judiciary. To stay the waves of popular feeling, to restrain the greedy hand of the many from filching from the few that which they have honestly acquired, and to protect in every man's possession and enjoyment, be he rich or poor, that which he hath, demands a tribunal as strong as is consistent with the freedom of human action, and as free from all influences and suggestions other than is compassed in the thought of justice, as can be created out of the infirmities of human nature. To that end the courts exist. . . .

## James Bradley Thayer, "The Origin and Scope of the American Doctrine of Constitutional Law," 7 Harvard Law Review 129 (1893)

How did our American doctrine, which allows to the judiciary the power to declare legislative Acts unconstitutional, and to treat them as null, come about, and what is the true scope of it? . . .

The court's duty, we are told, is the mere and simple office of construing two writings and comparing one with another, as two contracts or two statutes are construed and compared when they are said to conflict; of declaring the true meaning of each, and, if they are opposed to each other, of carrying into effect the constitution as being of superior obligation—an ordinary and humble judicial duty, as the courts sometimes describe it. This way of putting it easily results in the wrong kind of disregard of legislative considerations; not merely in refusing to let them directly operate as grounds of judgment, but in refusing to consider them at all. Instead of taking them into account and allowing for them as furnishing possible grounds of legislative action, there takes place a pedantic and academic treatment of the texts of the constitution and the laws. And so we miss that combination of a lawyer's rigor with a statesman's breadth of view which should be found in dealing with this class of questions in constitutional law. . . .

The courts have perceived with more or less distinctness that this exercise of the judicial function does in truth go far beyond the simple business which judges sometimes describe. If their duty were in truth merely and nakedly to ascertain the meaning of the text of the constitution and of the impeached Act of the legislature, and to determine, as an academic question, whether in the court's judgment the two were in conflict, it would, to be sure, be an elevated and important office, one dealing with great matters, involving large public considerations, but yet a function far simpler than it really is. Having ascertained all this, yet there remains a question—the really momentous question—whether, after all, the court can disregard the Act. It cannot do this as a mere matter of course—merely because it is concluded that upon a just and true construction the law is unconstitutional. That is precisely the significance of the rule of administration that the courts lay down. It can only disregard the Act when those who have the right to make laws have not merely made a mistake, but have made a very clear one—so clear that it is not open to rational question. That is the standard of duty to which the courts bring legislative Acts; that is the test which they apply—not merely their own judgment as to constitutionality, but their conclusion as to what judgment is permissible to another department which the constitution has charged with the duty of making it. This rule recognizes that, having regard to the great, complex, ever-unfolding exigencies of government, much which will seem unconstitutional to one man, or body of men, may reasonably not seem so to another; that the constitution often admits of different interpretations; that there is often a range of choice and judgment; that in such cases the constitution does not impose upon the legislature any one specific opinion, but leaves open this range of choice; and that whatever choice is rational is constitutional. . . . [A legislator] may vote against a measure as being, in his judgment, unconstitutional; and, being subsequently placed on the bench, when this measure, having been passed by the legislature in spite of his opposition, comes before him judicially, may there find it his duty, although he has in no degree changed his opinion, to declare it constitutional. . . .

The legislature in determining what shall be done, what it is reasonable to do, does not divide its duty with the judges, nor must it conform to their conception of what is prudent or reasonable legislation. The judicial function is merely that of fixing the outside border of reasonable legislative action, the boundary beyond which the taxing power, the power of eminent domain, police power, and legislative power in general, cannot go without violating the prohibitions of the constitution or crossing the line of its grants. . . . *[T]he ultimate question is not what is the true meaning of the constitution, but whether legislation is sustainable or not. . . .*

What really took place in adopting our theory of constitutional law was this: we introduced for the first time into the conduct of government through its great departments a judicial sanction, as among these departments, not full and complete, but partial. The judges were allowed, indirectly and in a degree, the power to revise the action of other departments and to pronounce it null. In simple truth, while this is a mere judicial function, it involves, owing to the subject matter with which it deals, taking a part, a secondary part, in the political conduct of government. If that be so, then the judges must apply methods and principles that befit their task. In such a work there can be no permanent or fitting *modus vivendi* [arrangement] between the different departments unless each is sure of the full cooperation of the others, as long as its own action conforms to any reasonable and fairly permissible view of its constitutional power. The ultimate arbiter of what is rational and permissible is indeed always the courts, so far as litigated cases bring the question before them. This leaves to our courts a great and stately jurisdiction. It will only imperil the whole of it if it is sought to give them more. They must not step into the shoes of the lawmaker. . . .

I am not stating a new doctrine, but attempting to restate more exactly and truly an admitted one. If what I have said be sound, it is greatly to be desired that it should be more emphasized by our courts, in its full significance. It has been often remarked that private rights are more respected by the legislatures of some countries which have no written constitution, than by ours. No doubt our doctrine of constitutional law has had a tendency to drive out questions of justice and right, and to fill the mind of legislators with thoughts of mere legality, of what the constitution allows. And, moreover, even in the matter of legality, they have felt little responsibility; if we are wrong, they say, the courts will correct it. If what I have been saying is true, the safe and permanent road towards reform is that of impressing upon our people a far stronger sense than they have of the great range of possible harm and evil that our system leaves open, and must leave open, to the legislatures, and of the clear limits of judicial powers; so that responsibility may be brought sharply home where it belongs. . . . Under no system can the power of courts go far to save a people from ruin; our chief protection lies elsewhere. . . .

## *Lochner* v. *New York*
### 198 U.S. 45, 25 S.Ct. 539, 49 L.Ed 937 (1905)
#### http://laws.findlaw.com/us/198/45.html

Joseph Lochner, a bakery owner in Utica, New York, was convicted of violating a state law that limited the hours of employment in bakeries and confectionery establishments to ten hours a day and sixty hours a week. The New York appellate courts sustained the conviction. A little-known aspect of the litigation concerns Henry

Weismann, formerly a baker who was active in the labor movement in New York. In 1895, as editor of *The Baker's Journal,* he led the drive that resulted in passage of the statute challenged in this case. He later became a master baker, studied law, was admitted to the bar, and came to believe that the law for which he had labored was a mistake. In 1904, he was engaged by the State Association of Master Bakers to advance Lochner's case from the New York Court of Appeals to the United States Supreme Court. The bench of 1905 included one justice (McKenna) who had been reared in a baker's home. Majority: Peckham, Brewer, Brown, Fuller, McKenna. Dissenting: Harlan, Day, Holmes, White.

## MR. JUSTICE PECKHAM . . . delivered the opinion of the Court. . . .

The statute necessarily interferes with the right of contract between the employer and employés, concerning the number of hours in which the latter may labor in the bakery of the employer. The general right to make a contract in relation to his business is part of the liberty of the individual protected by the Fourteenth Amendment of the federal constitution. . . . The right to purchase or to sell labor is part of the liberty protected by this amendment, unless there are circumstances which exclude the right. There are, however, certain powers, existing in the sovereignty of each state in the Union, somewhat vaguely termed police powers, the exact description and limitation of which have not been attempted by the courts. Those powers, broadly stated, and without, at present, any attempt at a more specific limitation, relate to the safety, health, morals and general welfare of the public. Both property and liberty are held on such reasonable conditions as may be imposed by the governing power of the state in the exercise of those powers, and with such conditions the Fourteenth Amendment was not designed to interfere.

It must, of course, be conceded that there is a limit to the valid exercise of the police power by the state. . . . Otherwise the Fourteenth Amendment would have no efficacy and the legislatures of the states would have unbounded power, and it would be enough to say that any piece of legislation was enacted to conserve the morals, the health, or the safety of the people; such legislation would be valid, no matter how absolutely without foundation the

claim might be. The claim of the police power would be a mere pretext—become another and delusive name for the supreme sovereignty of the state to be exercised free from constitutional restraint. . . . In every case that comes before this court, therefore, where legislation of this character is concerned, and where the protection of the federal Constitution is sought, the question necessarily arises: Is this a fair, reasonable, and appropriate exercise of the police power of the state, or is it an unreasonable, unnecessary, and arbitrary interference with the right of the individual to his personal liberty, or to enter into those contracts in relation to labor which may seem to him appropriate or necessary for the support of himself and his family? Of course the liberty of contract relating to labor includes both parties to it. The one has as much right to purchase as the other to sell labor.

This is not a question of substituting the judgment of the court for that of the legislature. If the act be within the power of the state it is valid, although the judgment of the court might be totally opposed to the enactment of such a law. But the question would still remain: Is it within the police power of the state? and that question must be answered by the court.

The question whether this act is valid as a labor law, pure and simple, may be dismissed in a few words. There is no reasonable ground for interfering with the liberty of person or the right of free contract, by determining the hours of labor, in the occupation of a baker. There is no contention that bakers as a class are not equal in intelligence and capacity to men in other trades or manual occupations, or that they are not able to assert their rights and care for themselves without the protecting arm of the state, interfering with their independence of judgment and of action. They are in no sense wards of the state. Viewed in the light of a purely labor law, with no reference whatever to the question of health, we think that a law like the one before us involves neither the safety, the morals, nor the welfare, of the public, and that the interest of the public is not in the slightest degree affected by such an act. The law must be upheld, if at all, as a law pertaining to the health of the individual engaged in the occupation of a baker. It does not affect any other portion of the public than those who are engaged in that occupation. Clean and wholesome bread does not depend upon whether the baker works but ten hours per day or only sixty hours a week. The limitation of the hours of labor does not come within the police power on that ground. . . .

We think that there can be no fair doubt that the trade of a baker, in and of itself, is not an unhealthy one to that degree which would authorize the legislature to interfere with the right to labor, and with the right of free contract on the part of the individual, either as employer or employé. In looking through statistics regarding all trades and occupations, it may be true that the trade of a baker does not appear to be as healthy as some other trades, and is also vastly more healthy than still others. To the common understanding the trade of a baker has never been regarded as an unhealthy one. Very likely physicians would not recommend the exercise of that or of any other trade as a remedy for ill health. Some occupations are more healthy than others, but we think there are none which might not come under the power of the legislature to supervise and control the hours of working therein, if the mere fact that the occupation is not absolutely and perfectly healthy is to confer that right upon the legislative department of the government. It might be safely affirmed that almost all occupations more or less affect the health. . . . But are we all, on that account, at the mercy of legislative majorities? . . .

We do not believe in the soundness of the views which uphold this law. . . . The act is not, within any fair meaning of the term, a health law, but is an illegal interference with the rights of individuals, both employers and employés, to make contracts regarding labor upon such terms as they may think best, or which they may agree upon with the other parties to such contracts. . . .

*Reversed.*

## MR. JUSTICE HARLAN, with whom MR. JUSTICE WHITE and MR. JUSTICE DAY concurred, dissenting. . . .

It is plain that this statute was enacted in order to protect the physical well-being of those who work in bakery and confectionery establishments. . . . [T]he question of the number of hours during which a workman should continuously labor has been . . . a subject of serious consideration among civilized peoples, and by those having special knowledge of the laws of health. . . .

I do not stop to consider whether any particular view of this economic question presents the sounder theory. What the precise facts are it may be difficult to say. It is enough for the determination of this case . . . that the question is one about which there is room for debate and for an honest difference of opinion. There are many reasons . . . in support of the theory that, all things considered, more than ten hours' steady work each day, from week to week, in a bakery or confectionery establishment, may endanger the health and shorten the lives of the workmen. . . .

If some reasons exist that ought to be the end of this case. . . .

## MR. JUSTICE HOLMES, dissenting. . . .

This case is decided upon an economic theory which a large part of the country does not entertain. If it were a question whether I agree with that theory, I should desire to study it further and long before making up my mind. But I do not conceive that to be my duty, because I strongly believe that my agreement or disagreement has nothing to do with the right of a majority to embody their opinions in law. It is settled by various decisions of this court that state Constitutions and state laws may regulate life in many ways which we as legislators might think as injudicious, or if you like as tyrannical as this, and which, equally with this, interfere with the liberty to contract. Sunday laws and usury laws are ancient examples. A more modern one is the prohibition of lotteries. The liberty of the citizen to do as he likes so long as he does not interfere with the liberty of others to do the same, which has been a shibboleth for some well-known writers, is interfered with by school laws, by the post office, by every state or municipal institution which takes his money for purposes thought desirable, whether he likes it or not. The Fourteenth Amendment does not enact Mr. Herbert Spencer's Social Statics. . . . [A] constitution is not intended to embody a particular economic theory, whether of paternalism and the organic relation of the citizen to the state or of *laissez faire*. It is made for people of fundamentally differing views, and the accident of our finding certain opinions natural and familiar, or novel, and even shocking, ought not to conclude our judgment upon the question whether statutes embodying them conflict with the Constitution of the United States.

General propositions do not decide concrete cases. The decisions will depend on a judgment or intuition more subtle than any articulate major premise. But I think that the proposition just stated, if it is accepted, will carry us far toward the end. Every opinion tends to become a law. I think that the word "liberty," in the Fourteenth Amendment, is perverted when it is held to prevent the natural outcome of a dominant opinion, unless it can be said that a rational and fair man necessarily would admit that the statute proposed would infringe fundamental principles as they have been understood by the traditions of our people and our law. It does not need research to show that no such sweeping condemnation can be passed upon the statute before us. . . .

## *Nebbia* v. *New York*
## 291 U.S. 502, 54 S.Ct. 505, 78 L.Ed. 940 (1934)
## http://laws.findlaw.com/us/291/502.html

To combat some of the effects of economic depression on the milk industry, the legislature of New York in 1933 adopted a milk control law under which minimum prices could be set. The board established by the law set a minimum price for the retail sale of milk, which Leo Nebbia, a grocer in Rochester, violated. The New York Court of Appeals affirmed his conviction. Many commentators saw the Court's decision in this case, especially the proposition that "the power to promote the general welfare is inherent in government," as indicating judicial approval of the New Deal. Majority: Roberts, Brandeis, Cardozo, Hughes, Stone. Dissenting: McReynolds, Butler, Sutherland, Van Devanter.

### MR. JUSTICE ROBERTS delivered the opinion of the Court. . . .

Under our form of government the use of property and the making of contracts are normally matters of private and not of public concern. The general rule is that both shall be free of governmental interference. But neither property rights nor contract rights are absolute; for government cannot exist if the citizen may at will use his property to the detriment of his fellows, or exercise his freedom of contract to work them harm. Equally fundamental with the private right is that of the public to regulate it in the common interest. . . .

These correlative rights, that of the citizen to exercise exclusive dominion over property and freely to contract about his affairs, and that of the state to regulate the use of property and the conduct of business, are always in collision. No exercise of the private right can be imagined which will not in some respect, however slight, affect the public; no exercise of the legislative prerogative to regulate the conduct of the citizen which will not to some extent abridge his liberty or affect his property. But subject only to constitutional restraint the private right must yield to the public need.

The Fifth Amendment, in the field of federal activity, and the Fourteenth, as respects state action, do not prohibit governmental regulation for the public welfare. They merely condition the exertion of the admitted power, by securing that the end shall be accomplished by methods consistent with due process. And the guaranty of due process, as has often been held, demands only that the law shall not be unreasonable, arbitrary, or capricious, and that the means selected shall have a real and substantial relation to the object sought to be attained. . . . [T]he reasonableness of each regulation depends upon the relevant facts. . . .

But we are told that because the law essays to control prices it denies due process. . . . The argument runs that the public control of rates or prices is per se unreasonable and unconstitutional, save as applied to businesses affected with a public interest; that a business so affected is one in which property is devoted to an enterprise of a sort which the public itself might appropriately undertake, or one whose owner relies on a public grant or franchise for the right to conduct the business, or in which he is bound to serve all who apply; in short, such as is commonly called a public utility; or a business in its nature a monopoly. The milk industry, it is said, possesses none of these characteristics, and, therefore, not being affected with a public interest, its charges may not be controlled by the state. Upon the soundness of this contention

the appellant's case against the statute depends.

We may as well say at once that the dairy industry is not, in the accepted sense of the phrase, a public utility. . . . But if, as must be conceded, the industry is subject to regulation in the public interest, what constitutional principle bars the state from correcting existing maladjustments by legislation touching prices? We think there is no such principle. The due process clause makes no mention of sales or prices any more than it speaks of business or contracts or buildings or other incidents of property. The thought seems nevertheless to have persisted that there is something peculiarly sacrosanct about the price one may charge for what he makes or sells, and that, however able to regulate other elements of manufacture or trade, with incidental effect upon price, the state is incapable of directly controlling the price itself. This view was negatived many years ago. . . .

The phrase "affected with a public interest" can, in the nature of things, mean no more than that an industry, for adequate reason, is subject to control for the public good. . . .

So far as the requirement of due process is concerned, and in the absence of other constitutional restriction, a state is free to adopt whatever economic policy may reasonably be deemed to promote public welfare, and to enforce that policy by legislation adapted to its purpose. The courts are without authority either to declare such policy, or, when it is declared by the legislative arm, to override it. If the laws passed are seen to have a reasonable relation to a proper legislative purpose and are neither arbitrary nor discriminatory, the requirements of due process are satisfied. . . . With the wisdom of the policy adopted, with the adequacy or practicability of the law enacted to forward it, the courts are both incompetent and unauthorized to deal. . . .

Tested by these considerations we find no basis in the due process clause of the Fourteenth Amendment for condemning the provision of the Agriculture and Markets Law here drawn into question.

The judgment is

*Affirmed.*

## Separate opinion of MR. JUSTICE McREYNOLDS. . . .

If . . . liberty or property may be struck down because of difficult circumstances, we must expect that hereafter every right must yield to the voice of an impatient majority when stirred by distressful exigency. . . . Certain fundamentals have been set beyond experimentation; the Constitution has released them from control by the state. . . .

The exigency is of a kind which inevitably arises when one set of men continue to produce more than all others can buy. The distressing result of the producer followed his ill-advised but voluntary effort. . . .

Of the assailed statute the Court of Appeals says . . . "With the wisdom of the legislation we have naught to do. . . ."

But plainly, I think, this Court must have regard to the wisdom of the enactment.

The Legislature cannot lawfully destroy guaranteed rights of one man with the prime purpose of enriching another, even if for the moment, this may seem advantageous to the public. And the adoption of any "concept of jurisprudence" which permits facile disregard of the Constitution as long interpreted and respected will inevitably lead to its destruction. Then, all rights will be subject to the caprice of the hour; government by stable laws will pass. . . .

Grave concern for embarrassed farmers is everywhere; but this should neither obscure the rights of others nor obstruct judicial appraisement of measures proposed for relief. The ultimate welfare of the producer, like that of every other class, requires dominance of the Constitution. And zealously to uphold this in all its parts is the highest duty intrusted to the courts.

The judgment of the court below should be reversed.

MR. JUSTICE VAN DEVANTER, MR. JUSTICE SUTHERLAND, and MR. JUSTICE BUTLER authorize me to say that they concur in this opinion.

## *West Coast Hotel Co.* v. *Parrish*
## 300 U.S. 379, 57 S.Ct. 578, 81 L.Ed. 703 (1937)

## http://laws.findlaw.com/us/300/379.html

A Washington State act of 1913 authorized the fixing of minimum wages for women and minors by an administrative board. The West Coast Hotel Co. argued unsuccessfully in state court that the statute was invalid on due process grounds because of its similarity to the laws set aside in *Adkins* v. *Children's Hospital* (1923) and in *Morehead* v. *New York* ex rel. *Tipaldo* (1936). *Adkins* in turn had rested on *Lochner* v. *New York.* The decision in *West Coast Hotel,* handed down by the same Supreme Court personnel that had decided the Morehead case in 1936, marked the first stage of the "constitutional revolution" of 1937 (see Chapter Six). Majority: Hughes, Brandeis, Cardozo, Roberts, Stone. Dissenting: Sutherland, Butler, McReynolds, Van Devanter.

## MR. CHIEF JUSTICE HUGHES delivered the opinion of the Court.

This case presents the question of the constitutional validity of the minimum wage law of the state of Washington. . . .

The principle which must control our decision is not in doubt. The constitutional provision invoked is the due process clause of the Fourteenth Amendment governing the states, as the due process clause invoked in the Adkins case governed Congress. In each case the violation alleged by those attacking minimum wage regulation for women is deprivation of freedom of contract. What is this freedom? The Constitution does not speak of freedom of contract. It speaks of liberty and prohibits the deprivation of liberty without due process of law. In prohibiting that deprivation the Constitution does not recognize an absolute and uncontrollable liberty. Liberty in each of its phases has its history and connotation. But the liberty safeguarded is liberty in a social organization which requires the protection of law against the evils which menace the health, safety, morals, and welfare of the people. Liberty under the Constitution is thus necessarily subject to the restraints of due process, and regulation which is reasonable in relation to its subject and is adopted in the interests of the community is due process. . . .

The minimum wage to be paid under the Washington statute is fixed after full consideration by representatives of employers, employees and the public. It may be assumed that the minimum wage is fixed in consideration of the services that are performed in the particular occupations under normal conditions. . . . The statement of Mr. Justice Holmes in the Adkins case is pertinent: "This statute does not compel anybody to pay anything. It simply forbids employment at rates below those fixed as the minimum requirement of health and right living. It is safe to assume that women will not be employed at even the lowest wages allowed unless they earn them, or unless the employer's business can sustain the burden. In short the law in its character and operation is like hundreds of so-called police laws that have been upheld." And Chief Justice Taft forcibly pointed out the consideration which is basic in a statute of this character: "Legislatures which adopt a requirement of maximum hours or minimum wages may be presumed to believe that when sweating employers are prevented from paying unduly low wages by positive law they will continue their business, abating that part of their profits, which were wrung from the necessities of their employees, and will concede the better terms required by the law, and that while in individual cases, hardship may result, the restriction

will enure to the benefit of the general class of employees in whose interest the law is passed and so to that of the community at large." . . .

We think that the views thus expressed are sound and that the decision in the Adkins case was a departure from the true application of the principles governing the regulation by the state of the relation of employer and employed. . . .

The legislature of the state was clearly entitled to consider the situation of women in employment, the fact that they are in the class receiving the least pay, that their bargaining power is relatively weak, and that they are the ready victims of those who would take advantage of their necessitous circumstances. . . . Legislative response to that conviction cannot be regarded as arbitrary or capricious and that is all we have to decide. Even if the wisdom of the policy be regarded as debatable and its effects uncertain, still the legislature is entitled to its judgment. . . .

We may take judicial notice of the unparalleled demands for relief which arose during the recent period of depression and still continue to an alarming extent despite the degree of economic recovery which has been achieved. It is unnecessary to cite official statistics to establish what is of common knowledge through the length and breadth of the land. . . . The community is not bound to provide what is in effect a subsidy for unconscionable employers. The community may direct its law-making power to correct the abuse which springs from their selfish disregard of the public interest. . . .

Our conclusion is that the case of *Adkins* v. *Children's Hospital* should be, and it is, overruled. The judgment of the Supreme Court of the State of Washington is

*Affirmed.*

## MR. JUSTICE SUTHERLAND, dissenting.

MR. JUSTICE VAN DEVANTER, MR. JUSTICE McREYNOLDS, MR. JUSTICE BUTLER and I think the judgment of the court below should be reversed. . . .

Under our form of government, where the written Constitution, by its own terms, is the supreme law, some agency of necessity, must have the power to say the final word as to the validity of a statute assailed as unconstitutional. The Constitution makes it clear that the power has been intrusted to this court when the question arises in a controversy within its jurisdiction; and so long as the power remains there, its exercise cannot be avoided without betrayal of the trust. . . .

The suggestion that the only check upon the exercise of the judicial power, when properly invoked, to declare a constitutional right superior to an unconstitutional statute is the judge's own faculty of self-restraint,[3] is both ill considered and mischievous. Self-restraint belongs in the domain of will and not of judgment. The check upon the judge is that imposed by his oath of office, by the Constitution and by his own conscientious and informed convictions; and since he has the duty to make up his own mind and adjudge accordingly, it is hard to see how there could be any other restraint. . . .

It is urged that the question involved should now receive fresh consideration, among other reasons, because of "the economic conditions which have supervened"; but the meaning of the Constitution does not change with the ebb and flow of economic events. We frequently are told in more general words that the Constitution must be construed in the light of the present. If by that it is meant that the Constitution is made up of living words that apply to every new condition which they include, the statement is quite true. But to say, if that be intended, that the words of the Constitution mean today what they did not mean when written—that is, that they do not apply to a situation now to which they would have applied then—is to rob that instrument of the essential element which continues it in force as the people have made it until they, and not their official agents, have made it otherwise. . . .

The judicial function is that of interpretation; it does not include the power of amendment under the guise of interpretation. To miss the point of difference between the two is to miss all that the phrase "supreme law of the land" stands for and to convert what was intended as inescapable and enduring mandates into mere moral reflections.

If the Constitution, intelligently and reasonably construed in the light of these principles, stands in the way of desirable legislation, the blame must rest upon that instrument, and not upon the court for enforcing it according to its terms. The remedy in that situation—and the only true remedy—is to amend the Constitution. . . .

---

[3] Justice Sutherland refers to the statement by Justice Stone, dissenting in *United States* v. *Butler* (1936), reprinted in Chapter Seven—ED.

## *Ferguson* v. *Skrupa*
## 372 U.S. 726, 83 S.Ct. 1028, 10 L.Ed. 2d 93 (1963)
## http://laws.findlaw.com/us/372/726.html

The relevant facts are included in the opinion. Majority: Black, Brennan, Clark, Douglas, Goldberg, Harlan, Stewart, Warren, White.

**MR. JUSTICE BLACK delivered the opinion of the Court.**

In this case, . . . we are asked to review the judgment of a three-judge District Court enjoining, as being in violation of the Due Process Clause of the Fourteenth Amendment, a Kansas statute making it a misdemeanor for any person to engage "in the business of debt adjusting" except as an incident to "the lawful practice of law in this state." The statute defines "debt adjusting" as "the making of a contract, express, or implied with a particular debtor whereby the debtor agrees to pay a certain amount of money periodically to the person engaged in the debt adjusting business who shall for a consideration distribute the same among certain specified creditors in accordance with a plan agreed upon." . . .

The three-judge court heard evidence by Skrupa tending to show the usefulness and desirability of his business and evidence by the state officials tending to show that "debt adjusting" lends itself to grave abuses against distressed debtors, particularly in the lower income brackets, and that these abuses are of such gravity that a number of States have strictly regulated "debt adjusting" or prohibited it altogether. The court found that Skrupa's business did fall within the Act's proscription and concluded, one judge dissenting, that the Act was prohibitory, not regulatory, but that even if construed in part as regulatory it was an unreasonable regulation of a "lawful business," which the court held amounted to a violation of the Due Process Clause of the Fourteenth Amendment. . . .

Under the system of government created by our Constitution, it is up to legislatures, not courts, to decide on the wisdom and utility of legislation. There was a time when the Due Process Clause was used by this Court to strike down laws which were thought unreasonable, that is, unwise or incompatible with some particular economic or social philosophy. . . .

We have returned to the original constitutional proposition that courts do not substitute their social and economic beliefs for the judgment of legislative bodies, who are elected to pass laws. . . .

We conclude that the Kansas Legislature was free to decide for itself that legislation was needed to deal with the business of debt adjusting. Unquestionably, there are arguments showing that the business of debt adjusting has social utility, but such arguments are properly addressed to the legislature, not to us. We refuse to sit as a "superlegislature to weigh the wisdom of legislation," and we emphatically refuse to go back to the time when courts used the Due Process Clause "to strike down state laws, regulatory of business and industrial conditions, because they may be unwise, improvident, or out of harmony with a particular school of thought." . . . Whether the legislature takes for its textbook Adam Smith, Herbert Spencer, Lord Keynes, or some other is no concern of ours. The Kansas debt adjusting statute may be wise or unwise. But relief, if any be needed, lies not with us but with the body constituted to pass laws for the State of Kansas. . . .

*Reversed.*

MR. JUSTICE HARLAN concurs in the judgment on the ground that this state measure bears a rational relationship to a constitutionally permissible objective.

## IV. FIFTH AMENDMENT TAKINGS AND LAND USE

### *Nollan* v. *California Coastal Commission*
### 483 U.S. 825, 107 S.Ct. 3141, 97 L.Ed. 2d 677 (1987)
### http://laws.findlaw.com/us/483/825.html

In 1982 the California Coastal Commission granted a permit to James and Marilyn Nollan to replace a small bungalow on their beachfront lot in Ventura County with a larger house. With the permit came the condition that the Nollans allow the public an easement to pass across their beach, which was located between two public beaches. The Nollans' property affected by the easement was bounded by the mean high-tide line on one side and their seawall on the other side. The county superior court granted the Nollans a writ of administrative mandamus and directed that the permit condition be removed. In 1986 the state court of appeal reversed, ruling that imposition of the condition did not violate the takings clause of the Fifth Amendment. Majority: Scalia, O'Connor, Powell, Rehnquist, White. Dissenting: Brennan, Blackmun, Marshall, Stevens.

### JUSTICE SCALIA delivered the opinion of the Court. . . .

Had California simply required the Nollans to make an easement across their beachfront available to the public on a permanent basis in order to increase public access to the beach, rather than conditioning their permit to rebuild their house on their agreeing to do so, we have no doubt there would have been a taking. . . .

Given, then, that requiring uncompensated conveyance of the easement outright would violate the Fourteenth Amendment, the question becomes whether requiring it to be conveyed as a condition for issuing a land use permit alters the outcome. We have long recognized that land use regulation does not effect a taking if it "substantially advance[s] legitimate state interests" and does not "den[y] an owner economically viable use of his land." . . . Our cases have not elaborated on the standards for determining what constitutes a "legitimate state interest" or what type of connection between the regulation and the state interest satisfies the requirement that the former "substantially advance" the latter. They have made clear, however, that a broad range of governmental purposes and regulations satisfies these requirements. . . . The Commission argues that among these permissible purposes are protecting the public's ability to see the beach, assisting the public in overcoming the "psychological barrier" to using the beach created by a developed shorefront, and preventing congestion on the public beaches. We assume, without deciding, that this is so—in which case the Commission unquestionably would be able to deny the Nollans their permit outright if their new house (alone, or by reason of the cumulative impact produced in conjunction with other construction) would substantially impede these purposes, unless the denial would interfere so drastically with the Nollans' use of their property as to constitute a taking.

The Commission argues that a permit condition that serves the same legitimate police-power purpose as a refusal to issue the permit should not be found to be a taking if the refusal to issue the permit would not constitute a taking. We agree. Thus, if the Commission attached to the permit some condition that would have protected the public's ability to see the beach notwithstanding construction of the new house—for example, a height limitation, a width restriction, or a ban on fences—so long as the Commission could have exercised its police power (as we have assumed it could) to forbid construction of the house altogether, imposition of the condition would also be constitutional. Moreover (and here we come closer to the facts of the present case), the condition would be constitutional even if it consisted of the requirement that the Nollans provide a viewing spot on their property for passersby with whose sighting of the ocean their new house would interfere. Although such a requirement, constituting a permanent grant of continuous access to the property, would have to be considered a taking if it were not attached to a development permit, the Commission's assumed power to forbid construction of the house in order to protect the public's view of the beach must surely include the power to condition construction upon some concession by the owner, even a concession of property rights, that serves the same end. . . .

The evident constitutional propriety disappears, however, if the condition substituted for the prohibition utterly fails to further the end advanced as the justification for the prohibition. . . . [T]he lack of nexus between the condition and the original purpose of the building restriction converts that purpose to something other than what it was. The purpose then becomes, quite simply, the obtaining of an easement to serve some valid governmental purpose, but without payment of compensation. Whatever may be the outer limits of "legitimate state interests" in the takings and land use context, this is not one of them. In short, unless the permit condition serves the same governmental purpose as the development ban, the building restriction is not a valid regulation of land use but "an out-and-out plan of extortion." . . .

It is quite impossible to understand how a requirement that people already on the public beaches be able to walk across the Nollans' property reduces any obstacles to viewing the beach created by the new house. It is also impossible to understand how it lowers any "psychological barrier" to using the public beaches, or how it helps to remedy any additional congestion on them caused by construction of the Nollans' new house. . . .

We are left, then, with the Commission's justification for the access requirement unrelated to land use regulation:

[T]he Commission notes that there are several existing provisions of pass and repass lateral access benefits already given by past Faria Beach Tract applicants as a result of prior coastal permit decisions. The access required as a condition of this permit is part of a comprehensive program to provide continuous public access along Faria Beach as the lots undergo development or redevelopment.

That is simply an expression of the Commission's belief that the public interest will be served by a continuous strip of publicly accessible beach along the coast. The Commission may well be right that it is a good idea, but that does not establish that the Nollans (and other coastal residents) alone can be compelled to contribute to its realization. Rather, California is free to advance its "comprehensive program," if it wishes, by using its power of eminent domain for this "public purpose"; but if it wants an easement across the Nollans' property, it must pay for it.

*Reversed.*

**JUSTICE BRENNAN, with whom JUSTICE MARSHALL joins, dissenting. . . .**

Even if we accept the Court's unusual demand for a precise match between the condition imposed and the specific type of burden on access created by the appellants, the State's action easily satisfies this requirement. First, the lateral access condition serves to dissipate the impression that the beach that lies behind the wall of homes along the shore is for private use only. It requires no exceptional imaginative powers to find plausible the Commission's point that the average person passing along the road in front of a phalanx of imposing permanent residences, including the appellants' new home, is likely to conclude that this particular portion of the shore is not open to the public. If, however, that person can see that numerous people are passing and repassing along the dry sand, this conveys the message that the beach is in fact open for use by the public. Furthermore, those persons who go down to the public beach a quarter-mile away will be able to look down the coastline and see that persons have continuous access to the tidelands, and will observe signs that proclaim the public's right of access over the dry sand. The burden produced by the diminution in visual access—the impression that the beach is not open to the public—is thus directly alleviated by the provision for public access over the dry sand. The Court therefore has an unrealistically limited conception of what measures could reasonably be chosen to mitigate the burden produced by a diminution of visual access.

The second flaw in the Court's analysis of the fit between burden and exaction is more fundamental. The Court assumes that the only burden with which the Coastal Commission was concerned was blockage of visual access to the beach. This is incorrect. The Commission specifically stated in its report in support of the permit condition that "[t]he Commission finds that the applicants' proposed development would present an increase in view blockage, an increase in private use of the shorefront, and that this impact would burden the public's ability to traverse to and along the shorefront." . . .

As the Commission observed in its report, "The Faria Beach shoreline fluctuates during the year depending on the seasons and accompanying storms, and the public is not always able to traverse the shoreline below the mean high tide line." As a result, the boundary between publicly owned tidelands and privately owned beach is not a stable one, and "[t]he existing seawall is located very near to the mean high water line." When the beach is at its largest, the seawall is about 10 feet from the mean high tide mark; "[d]uring the period of the year when the beach suffers erosion, the mean high water line appears to be located either on or beyond the existing seawall." Expansion of private development on appellants' lot toward the seawall would thus "increase private use immediately adjacent to public tidelands, which has the potential of causing adverse impacts on the public's ability to traverse the shoreline." . . .

The deed restriction on which permit approval was conditioned would directly address this threat to the public's access to the tidelands. It would provide a formal declaration of the public's right of access, thereby ensuring that the shifting character of the tidelands, and the presence of private development immediately adjacent to it, would not jeopardize enjoyment of that right. . . .

In reviewing a Takings Clause claim, we have regarded as particularly significant the nature of the governmental action and the economic impact of regulation, especially the extent to which regulation interferes with investment-backed expectations. The character of the government action in this case is the imposition of a condition on permit approval, which allows the public to continue to have access to the coast. The physical intrusion permitted by the deed restriction is minimal. The public is permitted the right to pass and repass along the coast in an area from the seawall to the mean high tide mark. This area is at its widest 10 feet, which means that even without the permit condition, the public's right of access permits it to pass on average within a few feet of the seawall. Passage closer to the 8-foot high rocky seawall will make the appellants even less visible to the public than passage along the high tide area farther out on the beach. The intrusiveness of such passage is even less than the intrusion resulting from the required dedication of a sidewalk in front of private residences, exactions which are commonplace conditions on approval of development. Furthermore, the high tide line shifts throughout the year, moving up to and beyond the seawall, so that public passage for a portion of the year would either be impossible or would not occur on appellant's property. Finally, although the Commission had the authority to provide for either passive or active recreational use of the property, it chose the least intrusive alternative: a mere right to pass and repass. . . . State agencies . . . require considerable flexibility in responding to private desires for development in a way that guarantees the preservation of public access to the coast. They should be encouraged to regulate development in the context of the overall balance of competing uses of the shoreline. The Court today does precisely the opposite, overruling an eminently reasonable exercise of an expert state agency's judgment, substituting its own narrow view of how this balance should be struck. Its reasoning is hardly suited to the complex reality of natural resource protection in the twentieth century. . . .

JUSTICE BLACKMUN, dissenting . . . [omitted].

JUSTICE STEVENS, with whom JUSTICE BLACKMUN joins, dissenting . . . [omitted].

## V. "NEW PROPERTY"

### Saenz v. Roe
### 526 U.S. 489, 119 S.Ct. 1518, 143 L.Ed. 2d 689 (1999)
http://laws.findlaw.com/us/526/489.html

> In 1997 two welfare recipients challenged California's residency requirement for welfare benefits. Section 11450.03 capped the maximum payment to otherwise eligible recipients who had lived in California for less than one year to the amount paid by the state of the recipient's prior residence. The welfare reform act passed by Congress in 1996 expressly allowed for such differential payments. The U.S. District Court for the Eastern District of California enjoined enforcement of the state rule, and the Ninth Circuit Court of Appeals affirmed. Majority: Stevens, O'Connor, Scalia, Kennedy, Souter, Ginsburg, Breyer. Dissenting: Rehnquist, Thomas.

JUSTICE STEVENS delivered the opinion of the Court. . . .

The word "travel" is not found in the text of the Constitution. Yet the "constitutional right to travel from one State to another" is firmly embedded in our jurisprudence. . . .

In *Shapiro* [v. *Thompson*], we reviewed the constitutionality of three statutory provisions that denied welfare assistance to residents of Connecticut, the District of Columbia, and Pennsylvania, who had resided within those respective jurisdictions less than one year immediately preceding their applications for assistance. . . . We squarely held that it was "constitutionally impermissible" for a State to enact durational residency requirements for the purpose of inhibiting the migration by needy persons into the State. We further held that a classification that had the effect of imposing a penalty on the exercise of the right to travel violated the Equal Protection Clause "unless shown to be necessary to promote a compelling governmental interest," and that no such showing had been made.

In this case California argues that § 11450.03 was not enacted for the impermissible purpose of inhibiting migration by needy persons and that, unlike the legislation reviewed in *Shapiro,* it does not penalize the right to travel because new arrivals are not ineligible for benefits during their first year of residence. California submits that . . . the statute should be up-held if it is supported by a rational basis and that the State's legitimate interest in saving over $10 million a year satisfies that test. . . .

The "right to travel" discussed in our cases embraces at least three different components. It protects the right of a citizen of one State to enter and to leave another State, the right to be treated as a welcome visitor rather than an unfriendly alien when temporarily present in the second State, and, for those travelers who elect to become permanent residents, the right to be treated like other citizens of that State. . . .

Given that § 11450.03 imposed no obstacle to respondents' entry into California, we think the State is correct when it argues that the statute does not directly impair the exercise of the right to free interstate movement. . . .

The second component of the right to travel is . . . expressly protected by the text of the Constitution. The first sentence of Article IV, § 2, provides: "The Citizens of each State shall be entitled to all Privileges and Immunities of Citizens in the several States." Thus, by virtue of a person's state citizenship, a citizen of one State who travels in other States, intending to return home at the end of his journey, is entitled to enjoy the "Privileges and Immunities of Citizens in the several States" that he visits. . . . Those protections are not "absolute," but the Clause "does bar discrimination against citizens of other States where there is no substantial reason for the discrimination beyond the mere fact that they are citizens of other States."

. . . Permissible justifications for discrimination between residents and nonresidents are simply inapplicable to a nonresident's exercise of the right to move into another State and become a resident of that State.

What is at issue in this case, then, is this third aspect of the right to travel—the right of the newly arrived citizen to the same privileges and immunities enjoyed by other citizens of the same State. That right is protected not only by the new arrival's status as a state citizen, but also by her status as a citizen of the United States. That additional source of protection is plainly identified in the opening words of the Fourteenth Amendment: "All persons born or naturalized in the United States, and subject to the jurisdiction thereof, are citizens of the United States and of the State wherein they reside. No State shall make or enforce any law which shall abridge the privileges or immunities of citizens of the United States. . . ."

Despite fundamentally differing views concerning the coverage of the Privileges or Immunities Clause of the Fourteenth Amendment, most notably expressed in the majority and dissenting opinions in the Slaughter-House Cases, it has always been common ground that this Clause protects the third component of the right to travel. Writing for the majority in the Slaughter-House Cases, Justice Miller explained that one of the privileges conferred by this Clause "is that a citizen of the United States can, of his own volition, become a citizen of any State of the Union by a bonâ fide residence therein, with the same rights as other citizens of that State." . . . That newly arrived citizens "have two political capacities, one state and one federal," adds special force to their claim that they have the same rights as others who share their citizenship. Neither mere rationality nor some intermediate standard of review should be used to judge the constitutionality of a state rule that discriminates against some of its citizens because they have been domiciled in the State for less than a year. The appropriate standard may be more categorical than that articulated in *Shapiro,* but it is surely no less strict.

Because this case involves discrimination against citizens who have completed their interstate travel, the State's argument that its welfare scheme affects the right to travel only "incidentally" is beside the point. . . . [S]ince the right to travel embraces the citizen's right to be treated equally in her new State of residence, the discriminatory classification is itself a penalty.

It is undisputed that respondents and the members of the class that they represent are citizens of California and that their need for welfare benefits is unrelated to the length of time that they have resided in California. We thus have no occasion to consider what weight might be given to a citizen's length of residence if the bona fides of her claim to state citizenship were questioned. . . .

Disavowing any desire to fence out the indigent, California has . . . advanced an entirely fiscal justification for its multitiered scheme. The enforcement of § 11450.03 will save the State approximately $10.9 million a year. The question is not whether such saving is a legitimate purpose but whether the State may accomplish that end by the discriminatory means it has chosen. An evenhanded, across-the-board reduction of about 72 cents per month for every beneficiary would produce the same result. But our negative answer to the question does not rest on the weakness of the State's purported fiscal justification. It rests on the fact that the Citizenship Clause of the Fourteenth Amendment expressly equates citizenship with residence: "That Clause does not provide for, and does not allow for, degrees of citizenship based on length of residence." . . . Thus § 11450.03 is doubly vulnerable: Neither the duration of respondents' California residence, nor the identity of their prior States of residence, has any relevance to their need for benefits. . . .

The question that remains is whether congressional approval of durational residency requirements in the 1996 amendment to the Social Security Act somehow resuscitates the constitutionality of § 11450.03. That question is readily answered, for we have consistently held that Congress may not authorize the States to violate the Fourteenth Amendment. Moreover, the protection afforded to the citizen by the Citizenship Clause of that Amendment is a limitation on the powers of the National Government as well as the States. . . .

Congress has no affirmative power to authorize the States to violate the Fourteenth

Amendment and is implicitly prohibited from passing legislation that purports to validate any such violation. "Section 5 of the Fourteenth Amendment gives Congress broad power indeed to enforce the command of the amendment and 'to secure to all persons the enjoyment of perfect equality of civil rights and the equal protection of the laws against State denial or invasion. . . .' Congress' power under § 5, however, 'is limited to adopting measures to enforce the guarantees of the Amendment; § 5 grants Congress no power to restrict, abrogate, or dilute these guarantees.' " . . .

Citizens of the United States, whether rich or poor, have the right to choose to be citizens "of the State wherein they reside." The States, however, do not have any right to select their citizens. The Fourteenth Amendment, like the Constitution itself, was, as Justice Cardozo put it, "framed upon the theory that the peoples of the several states must sink or swim together, and that in the long run prosperity and salvation are in union and not division."

The judgment of the Court of Appeals is affirmed.

*It is so ordered.*

## CHIEF JUSTICE REHNQUIST, with whom JUSTICE THOMAS joins, dissenting.

The Court today breathes new life into the previously dormant Privileges or Immunities Clause of the Fourteenth Amendment. . . . It uses this Clause to strike down what I believe is a reasonable measure falling under the head of a "good-faith residency requirement." Because I do not think any provision of the Constitution—and surely not a provision relied upon for only the second time since its enactment 130 years ago—requires this result, I dissent.

Much of the Court's opinion is unremarkable and sound. . . .

But I cannot see how the right to become a citizen of another State is a necessary "component" of the right to travel, or why the Court tries to marry these separate and distinct rights. A person is no longer "traveling" in any sense of the word when he finishes his journey to a State which he plans to make his home. Indeed, under the Court's logic, the protections of the Privileges or Immunities Clause recognized in this case come into play only when an individual stops traveling with the intent to remain and become a citizen of a new State. The right to travel and the right to become a citizen are distinct, their relationship is not reciprocal, and one is not a "component" of the other. Indeed, the same dicta from the Slaughter-House Cases quoted by the Court actually treats the right to become a citizen and the right to travel as separate and distinct rights under the Privileges or Immunities Clause of the Fourteenth Amendment. At most, restrictions on an individual's right to become a citizen indirectly affect his calculus in deciding whether to exercise his right to travel in the first place, but such an attenuated and uncertain relationship is no ground for folding one right into the other.

No doubt the Court has, in the past 30 years, essentially conflated the right to travel with the right to equal state citizenship in striking down durational residence requirements similar to the one challenged here. . . . These cases marked a sharp departure from the Court's prior right-to-travel cases because in none of them was travel itself prohibited.

Instead, the Court in these cases held that restricting the provision of welfare benefits, votes, or certain medical benefits to new citizens for a limited time impermissibly "penalized" them under the Equal Protection Clause of the Fourteenth Amendment for having exercised their right to travel. . . . In other cases, the Court recognized that laws dividing new and old residents had little to do with the right to travel and merely triggered an inquiry into whether the resulting classification rationally furthered a legitimate government purpose. . . . While [some] reached the wrong result in my view, they at least put the Court on the proper track in identifying exactly what interests it was protecting; namely, the right of individuals not to be subject to unjustifiable classifications as opposed to infringements on the right to travel.

The Court today tries to clear much of the underbrush created by these prior right-to-travel cases, abandoning its effort to define what residence requirements deprive individuals of "important rights and benefits" or "penalize" the right to travel. Under its new analytical framework, a State, outside certain ill-defined circumstances, cannot classify its citizens by the length of their residence in the State without offending the Privileges or Immunities Clause of the Fourteenth Amendment. The Court thus departs from *Shapiro* and its progeny, and, while paying lipservice to the right to travel, the Court does little to explain how the right to travel is involved at all. Instead, . . . this case is only about respondents' right to immediately enjoy all the privileges of being a California citizen in relation to that State's ability to test the good-faith assertion of this right. The Court has thus come full circle by effectively disavowing the analysis of *Shapiro,* segregating the right to travel and the rights secured by Article IV from the right to become a citizen under the Privileges or Immunities Clause, and then testing the residence requirement here against this latter right. For all its misplaced efforts to fold the right to become a citizen into the right to travel, the Court has essentially returned to its original understanding of the right to travel.

In unearthing from its tomb the right to become a state citizen and to be treated equally in the new State of residence, however, the Court ignores a State's need to assure that only persons who establish a bona fide residence receive the benefits provided to current residents of the State. . . . Even when redefining the right to travel in *Shapiro* and its progeny, the Court has "always carefully distinguished between bona fide residence requirements, which seek to differentiate between residents and nonresidents, and residence requirements, such as durational, fixed date, and fixed point residence requirements, which treat established residents differently based on the time they migrated into the State."

Thus, the Court has consistently recognized that while new citizens must have the same opportunity to enjoy the privileges of being a citizen of a State, the States retain the ability to use bona fide residence requirements to ferret out those who intend to take the privileges and run. . . .

While the physical presence element of a bona fide residence is easy to police, the subjective intent element is not. It is simply un-workable and futile to require States to inquire into each new resident's subjective intent to remain. Hence, States employ objective criteria such as durational residence requirements to test a new resident's resolve to remain before these new citizens can enjoy certain in-state benefits. Recognizing the practical appeal of such criteria, this Court has repeatedly sanctioned the State's use of durational residence requirements before new residents receive in-state tuition rates at state universities. . . .

If States can require individuals to reside in-state for a year before exercising the right to educational benefits, . . . then States may surely do the same for welfare benefits. Indeed, there is no material difference between a 1-year residence requirement applied to the level of welfare benefits given out by a State, and the same requirement applied to the level of tuition subsidies at a state university. The welfare payment here and in-state tuition rates are cash subsidies provided to a limited class of people, and California's standard of living and higher education system make both subsidies quite attractive. Durational residence requirements were upheld when used to regulate the provision of higher education subsidies, and the same deference should be given in the case of welfare payments. . . .

The Court today recognizes that States retain the ability to determine the bona fides of an individual's claim to residence, but then tries to avoid the issue. It asserts that because respondents' need for welfare benefits is unrelated to the length of time they have resided in California, it has "no occasion to consider what weight might be given to a citizen's length of residence if the bona fides of her claim to state citizenship were questioned." But I do not understand how the absence of a link between need and length of residency bears on the State's ability to objectively test respondents' resolve to stay in California. There is no link between the need for an education or for a divorce and the length of residence, and yet States may use length of residence as an objective yardstick to channel their benefits to those whose intent to stay is legitimate. . . .

JUSTICE THOMAS, with whom the CHIEF JUSTICE joins, dissenting . . . [omitted].

# CHAPTER NINE

# *Nationalization of the Bill of Rights*

*The very purpose of a Bill of Rights was to withdraw certain subjects from the vicissitudes of political controversy, to place them beyond the reach of majorities and officials and to establish them as legal principles to be applied by the courts. . . . [F]undamental rights may not be submitted to vote; they depend on the outcome of no election.*

—Justice Robert H. Jackson (1943)

Preceding chapters have shown that the Supreme Court's regard for certain strictures in the Constitution dates from the earliest years of the Republic. Aside from property interests, however, judicial attention to the Bill of Rights, though part of the Constitution since 1791, is of more recent origin. Almost all cases that have shaped the meaning of constitutionally protected expression (the First Amendment) and that have defined personal liberty and the rights of persons accused of crimes (the Fourth, Fifth, Sixth, and Eighth Amendments) have been decided since 1920. As late as the 1935–1936 term, only two of the Court's 160 decisions concerned a nonproperty-related **civil liberty** (a guaranty in law against unwarranted governmental intrusion into one's life) or **civil right** (a legally protected freedom to participate in society and in the political system on an equal footing with others). In 1960–1961 the number increased to 54 of the 120 cases decided by full opinion. Disproportionate judicial concern for these matters continues. In 1989–1990, cases involving the Bill of Rights and related provisions accounted for 57 of the term's 146 decisions, and in 2001–2002, 45 of that term's 85 decisions. The data reflect not only an enhanced interest in the Bill of Rights but also the Court's application of the Bill of Rights to the states, a process that has involved due process of law.

## PATHS OF DUE PROCESS OF LAW

The phrase "due process of law" first appeared in an English statute during the reign of King Edward III (1327–1377): "No man of what state or condition he be, shall be put out of his lands or tenements, nor taken, nor imprisoned, nor disinherited, nor put to death, without he be brought to answer by due process of law." The phrase in turn derived from the "law of the land" clause in Magna Carta of 1215. Early American state constitutions carried over parts of both and expanded on them, as illustrated by the Massachusetts Constitution of 1780: "No subject shall be arrested, imprisoned, despoiled, or deprived of his property, immunities, or privileges, put out of the protection of the law, exiled, or deprived of his life, liberty, or estate, but by the judgment of his peers or the law of the land." The thrust across those centuries was procedural. As it acted on the people, government was bound to follow custom or pre-established procedures and protocol. Otherwise individual liberty would be imperiled. So it was hardly surprising that the framers of the Fifth and Fourteenth amendments included provisions forbidding the national and state governments, respectively, from depriving any person of "life, liberty, or property without due process of law."

Chapter Eight chronicled the Supreme Court's transformation of **due process of law** from a procedural limitation on government into a substantive one too. The concept moved beyond being solely a restriction on the manner in which government proceeded against its citizens (*how* something could be done) to a restriction on policy choices themselves (*what* could be done). Between the 1890s and 1937 the Court sat in judgment on economic and social legislation enacted by Congress and state legislatures. Only those regulations the justices deemed "reasonable" passed the constitutional test of due process of law. Even though this use of due process has long since passed into history, due process of law remains very much a lively part of American constitutional law.

At heart, due process is a safeguard against arbitrary government. When government attempts to take away a person's life, liberty, or property, officials must adhere to certain rules that judges view as fair and appropriate. Relaxed and informal procedures might suffice for disciplinary actions in a public school, while far stricter and formal procedures are required in law enforcement when someone is accused of a crime. Generally, as the degree of potential harm that government might do to an individual increases, so does the Court's expectation of what process is due. This would explain the heightened attention to procedure that the Court demands in death penalty cases, as shown in the following chapter. Embodying notions of basic fairness, due process can thus be a bulwark of personal freedom in addition to other more specific guaranties of liberty that the Constitution contains.

Due process is also intimately connected in a substantive way with the right of privacy that is explored in Chapter Thirteen. Although ***Griswold* v. *Connecticut*** (1965) found the right of privacy implied by several provisions of the Bill of Rights, recent decisions concerning privacy or zones of autonomy have tended to rely as well on the language of due process of law. Even more important in terms of its impact on American government, due process has been the vehicle by which the Court has applied the Bill of Rights to the states. Yet, ironically the national Bill of Rights was "an almost forgotten appendage."

# THE BILL OF RIGHTS

Unlike state constitutions adopted in 1776 and in subsequent years, the Constitution as it came from the hands of the framers in 1787 lacked a bill of rights. Alongside a very few explicit prohibitions on national authority, the powers of the national government were enumerated but not defined. Without specification or definition, other powers were reserved to the states or to the people. While the states pondered ratification, Thomas Jefferson urged specific restraints on national authority. Arguing that "a bill of rights is what the people are entitled to against every government on earth," he insisted that natural rights should not be left to "rest on inference."

Alexander Hamilton and James Wilson contended that a bill of rights was not needed. Why make exceptions to power not granted? "In a government of enumerated powers," Wilson declared, "such a measure would not only be unnecessary, but preposterous and dangerous." A list of rights implied that those not included remained unprotected. For Hamilton, bills of rights "would sound much better in a treatise on ethics than in a constitution of government."

Thanks to Jefferson, these arguments did not prevail. Insisting on curbs over and beyond the ballot box and structural checks, he advocated "binding up the several branches of the government by certain laws, which when they transgress their acts become nullities." This would "render unnecessary an appeal to the people, or in other words a rebellion on every infraction of their rights." When a reluctant James Madison yielded to Jefferson's plea for a bill of rights and deduced supporting reasons, Jefferson singled out the argument of "great weight" for him—the legal check it would put in the hands of the judiciary. In presenting bill-of-rights amendments to Congress in 1789, Madison made Jefferson's argument his own. With a bill of rights, "independent tribunals of justice" would be "an impenetrable bulwark against every assumption of power in the legislative or executive." This **Jefferson-Madison correspondence** is reprinted in this chapter.

As a member of the First Congress elected under the new Constitution, Madison drew up 17 amendments. By 1791, ten were ratified, the first eight of which constitute the Bill of Rights. Urged but not ratified on Madison's list was number 14: "*No state* shall infringe the right of trial by jury in criminal cases, nor the right of conscience, nor the freedom of speech or press" (emphasis added). Believing that there was more danger of abuse of power by state governments than by the government of the United States, Madison conceived number 14 to be "the most valuable amendment in the whole list. If there were any reason to restrain the Government of the United States from infringing these essential rights, it was equally necessary that they should be secured against the State governments."

Madison's concern was prophetic. It anticipated the adoption of the Fourteenth Amendment 79 years later. It foreshadowed the drive to apply the specific provisions of the Bill of Rights to state action by way of the Fourteenth Amendment. Without application of the Bill of Rights to the states, the full impact of Justice Stone's Carolene Products Footnote Four, discussed on pages 333–334 in the previous chapter, could not be felt.

The idea of a bill of rights was hardly unique to Americans, however. Bills of rights in the state constitutions and the federal Bill of Rights were themselves offshoots of English constitutional documents such as the Petition of Right of 1628 and the Bill of Rights of 1689. But the onset of democratic government—government by the consent of the governed—changed the nature of bills of rights. Initially, a bill of rights was a device to protect the majority ("the people") from the minority (the Crown), the many from the few. Now, with political power lodged in the hands of a majority of those admitted to the political community, bills of rights came to be devices to protect the few from the many. In Madison's words, "Wherever the real power in a Government lies, there is the danger of oppression."

Fundamental rights gained no greater moral sanctity by being written into the Constitution, but individuals could thereafter resort to courts for protection. Rights formerly natural became civil. Moreover, "tho' written constitutions may be violated in moments of passion or delusion," Jefferson declared, "they furnish a text to which those who are watchful may again rally and recall the people; they fix too for the people principles for their political creed."

## INCORPORATION: APPLYING THE BILL OF RIGHTS TO THE STATES

It was not until 1833 that the Supreme Court answered the question whether the first eight amendments limited state as well as national action. To Chief Justice John Marshall this was a question "of great importance, but not of much difficulty" (*Barron* v. *Baltimore*). The City of Baltimore, under acts of the Maryland legislature, had diverted the flow of several streams. As a result of the changes, silt was deposited around Barron's wharf, making it unfit for shipping and, Barron claimed, depriving him of property without just compensation. Denying the Supreme Court's jurisdiction to declare the state acts repugnant to the Constitution, Marshall observed, "We are of the opinion, that the provision in the Fifth Amendment to the Constitution, declaring that private property shall not be taken for public use without just compensation is intended solely as a limitation of the power of the United States, and is not applicable to the legislation of the states." That was an understandable conclusion. As he explained, "In almost every convention by which the constitution was adopted, amendments to guard against the abuse of power were recommended. These amendments demanded security against the apprehended encroachments of the general [federal] government, not against those of the local [state] governments."

A contrary ruling would have had immense consequences for the jurisdiction of the Court. As a result of *Barron,* most legal disputes between a state government and one of its citizens remained outside the federal judicial system, unless the commerce or contracts clause was at issue. This is important to remember, because until recent decades government action and government policy largely meant the action and policy of state and local governments.

**BEGINNINGS.** Shortly after the end of the Civil War, the question of the applicability of the Bill of Rights to the states reappeared. This time there was a difference. The Fourteenth Amendment had become part of the Constitution in 1868. Did its ratification result in **incorporation**—applying the Bill of Rights to the states—either through the privileges and immunities clause or by virtue of the due process clause? This was a natural question for some people to ask because in June 1866, when Congress sent the Fourteenth Amendment to the states for ratification, many thought that the application of the Bill of Rights to the states was one of the amendment's principal objectives. Yet, after the Slaughterhouse Cases, discussed in Chapter Eight, emasculated the privileges and immunities clause in 1873, only due process remained as a possible medium to make that expectation a reality.

The Court gave its first serious attention to this issue in *Hurtado* v. *California* (1884). (Recall from the last chapter that it was in this same period that litigants were trying to persuade the bench that the due process clause also put limits on the power of states to enact social and economic legislation.) *Hurtado* posed the question whether the due process clause of the Fourteenth Amendment prevented a state from substituting a prosecutor's written accusation for grand jury indictment. The Fifth Amendment called for a grand jury indictment in federal criminal cases, as did most state constitutions for state trials. Did the Fourteenth mandate grand jury indictments for the states? For the majority, Justice Matthews said no. He rejected the view that "any proceeding . . . not . . . sanctioned by usage, or which supersedes and displaces one that is, cannot be regarded as due process of law. . . . [T]o hold that such a characteristic is essential to due process of law, would be to deny every quality of the law but its age, and to render it incapable of progress or improvement. It would be to stamp upon our jurisprudence the unchangeableness attributed to the laws of the Medes and Persians." Besides, the fact that the Fifth Amendment already contained a due process clause meant that "due process" was not intended to include the particular safeguards of the Bill of Rights. If the Fourteenth Amendment required use of grand jury indictments, "it would have embodied, as did the Fifth Amendment, express declarations to that effect."

What, therefore, did "due process" allow? "[A]ny legal proceeding . . . whether sanctioned by age and custom, or newly devised . . . in furtherance of the general public good, which regards and preserves these principles of liberty and justice, must be held to be due process of law." Thus, if a procedure was traditional, that would ordinarily be sufficient ground for finding it compatible with due process. If a procedure was new, that fact alone would be insufficient to invalidate it under the due process clause. The tilt of the opinion was clearly toward welcoming procedural innovation. Nonetheless, the Court placed itself in the position of being the final judge concerning "those fundamental principles of liberty and justice which lie at the base of all our civil and political institutions. . . ." Thus, it was in *Hurtado* that the Court first squarely blended the idea of fundamental fairness into the concept of due process.

Thirteen years later in *Chicago, B. & Q. R. Co.* v. *Chicago* (1897), the Court cast doubt on the Hurtado doctrine by ruling that the Fourteenth Amendment's due process clause limited the taking of property for public use without just compensation. The Fifth Amendment contained the same safeguard. Then *Twining* v. *New Jersey* (1908) took another step beyond *Hurtado*. While rejecting the argument that due process encompassed the Fifth Amendment's protection against self-incrimination, the Court expressly laid to rest the view that the inclusion of a right in the Bill of Rights necessarily excluded that right from the protection offered by the due process clause of the Fourteenth Amendment. "[I]t is possible," acknowledged Justice Moody, "that some of the personal rights safeguarded by the first eight Amendments against national action may also be safeguarded against state action. . . . If this is so, it is not because those rights are enumerated in the first eight Amendments, but because they are of such a nature that they are included in the conception of due process of law." Thus, he asked, did the claim involve "a fundamental principle of liberty and justice which inheres in the very idea of free government and is the inalienable right of a citizen of such a government? If it is, and if it is of a nature that pertains to process of law, this court has declared it to be essential to due process of law."

**ORDERED LIBERTY.** In the 1920s and 1930s, the Supreme Court agreed that the "liberty" protected by the due process clause included some First Amendment freedoms. For example, ***Gitlow*** **v.** ***New York*** (1925) (see Chapter Eleven), "assume[d] that freedom of speech and of the press . . . are among the fundamental personal rights and 'liberties' protected by the due process clause . . . from impairment by the states." Six years later, in *Near* v. *Minnesota,* Chief Justice Hughes insisted that it was "no longer open to doubt that the liberty of the press . . . is within the liberty safeguarded by the due process clause . . . from invasion by state action." And Justice Sutherland in ***Powell*** v. ***Alabama*** (1932) (see Chapter Ten) reasoned that the Sixth Amendment's guaranty of right to counsel was a "necessary requisite of due process of law" and so required states to provide counsel for indigent defendants, at least in capital cases.

Yet because most other provisions of the Bill of Rights had not been absorbed by the Fourteenth Amendment, why were some rights "in" while others remained "out"? Justice Cardozo attempted to answer this question in ***Palko*** v. ***Connecticut*** (1937), which presented the Court with yet another procedural claim—this time, the Fifth Amendment's ban on double jeopardy. Reaffirming the Court's long-held view that the entire Bill of Rights was not incorporated into the Fourteenth Amendment, Cardozo built on *Twining* to spell out and justify a selective process. Due process encompassed those provisions of the Bill of Rights that were essential to a "scheme of **ordered liberty**."

> There emerges the perception of a rationalizing principle which gives to discrete instances a proper order and coherence. The right to trial by jury and the immunity from prosecution except as a result of an indictment may have value and importance. Even so, they are not of the very essence of *a scheme of ordered liberty*. To abolish them is not to violate a "principle of justice so rooted in the traditions and conscience of our people as to be ranked as fundamental. . . ."
>
> We reach a different plane of social and moral values when we pass to the privileges and immunities that have been taken over from the earlier articles of the Federal Bill of Rights and brought within the Fourteenth Amendment by a process of absorption. These in their origin were effective against the federal government. If the Fourteenth Amendment has absorbed them, the process of absorption has had its source in the belief that *neither liberty nor justice would exist if they were sacrificed* [emphasis added].

For Cardozo and most of the rest of the bench, all provisions in the Bill of Rights were not of equal value.

Yet this ordered liberty method of hand-picking rights did not go unchallenged. Consider Justice Black's advocacy of **total incorporation** in ***Adamson*** v. ***California*** (1947).

> My study of the historical events that culminated in the Fourteenth Amendment, and the expressions of those who sponsored and favored, as well as those who opposed its submission and passage, persuades me that one of the chief objects that the provisions of the Amendment's first section, separately, and as a whole were intended to accomplish, was to make the Bill of Rights applicable to the states.

Black's theory never attracted the votes of more than three other justices at any one time, but it pointed in the direction that the Court was moving.

**TRIUMPH OF SELECTIVE INCORPORATION.** As shown in Table 9.1, almost all of the provisions of the Bill of Rights that have contemporary significance have now been applied to the states on a case-by-case basis. The pace of this incorporation accelerated during the 1960s, suggesting that the Court had abandoned or at least modified the ordered liberty test from *Palko*. Justice White's opinion in ***Duncan*** v.

## Table 9.1  Nationalization of the Bill of Rights

| Amendment | Rights Applicable to States | Case Applying Right to States | Rights Not Applicable to the States |
|---|---|---|---|
| I | Establishment of religion | *Everson* v. *Board of Education* (1947) | |
| | Free exercise of religion | *Cantwell* v. *Connecticut* (1940) | |
| | Speech | *Gitlow* v. *New York* (1925) | |
| | Press | *Near* v. *Minnesota* (1931) | |
| | Peaceable assembly | *De Jonge* v. *Oregon* (1937) | |
| | Petition | *De Jonge* v. *Oregon* (1937) | |
| II | | | To keep and bear arms |
| III | | | No quartering of soldiers in homes |
| IV | Protection against unreasonable searches and seizures | *Wolf* v. *Colorado* (1949) | |
| | (With the exclusionary rule) | *Mapp* v. *Ohio* (1961) | |
| V | Protection against double jeopardy | *Benton* v. *Maryland* (1969) | Indictment by grand jury |
| | Protection against compelled self-incrimination | *Malloy* v. *Hogan* (1964) | |
| | Just compensation for public seizure of private property | *Chicago, B. & Q. R. Co.* v. *Chicago* (1897) | |
| VI | Speedy trial | *Klopfer* v. *North Carolina* (1967) | Trial in state and district of offense |
| | Public trial | In re *Oliver* (1948) | |
| | Impartial jury | *Parker* v. *Gladden* (1966) | |
| | Trial by jury in non-petty criminal cases | *Duncan* v. *Louisiana* (1968) | |
| | Nature and cause of accusation | *Cole* v. *Arkansas* (1948) | |
| | Confrontation of accusers | *Pointer* v. *Texas* (1965) | |
| | Compulsory process for appearance of witnesses | *Washington* v. *Texas* (1967) | |
| | Assistance of counsel | *Powell* v. *Alabama* (1932) | |
| | | *Gideon* v. *Wainwright* (1963) | |
| | | *Argersinger* v. *Hamlin* (1972) | |
| | | *Scott* v. *Illinois* (1979) | |
| | | *Strickland* v. *Washington* (1984) | |
| VII | | | Jury trial in specific civil cases |
| VIII | Cruel and unusual punishment | *Robinson* v. *California* (1962) | Ban on excessive bail and fines |

*Louisiana* (1968) reveals what had taken place. The Court was both rethinking the importance of the specific guaranties in the Bill of Rights and recasting the Palko standard. Rather than asking in the abstract whether a particular right was essential for a political system that valued liberty and justice, the Court asked whether a particular right "is fundamental . . . to an Anglo-American regime of ordered liberty."

By 1968 the Court had accomplished almost as much selectively as Black would have done instantly in *Adamson*. Also of significance today are the protections enshrined in due process beyond those strictly enumerated in the Bill of Rights. It is here that Justice Black's total incorporation approach (this much, and no more) stops, and a variation on Justice Cardozo's ordered liberty doctrine begins. If the Fourteenth Amendment's due process clause is not bound to the meaning of the Bill of Rights, it remains a source of inspiration for those who wish to enlarge the list of constitutionally protected liberties.

Today, no one would accept Sir Henry Maine's nineteenth-century characterization of the Bill of Rights as a "certain number of amendments on comparatively unimportant points."

**DUE PROCESS REVOLUTION.** The nationalization of almost all parts of the Bill of Rights has had immense consequences for federalism, personal freedom, and judicial power. Until incorporation became a reality, Americans remained subject to a **double standard** of justice under the Constitution. For a defendant standing trial, the federal constitutional rights one enjoyed depended therefore on whether the trial was in state or federal court. Supreme Court review was far more demanding of the latter than the former. As *Palko* demonstrated, Connecticut was allowed under the Fourteenth Amendment's due process clause to employ a procedure that the Fifth Amendment flatly barred the United States government from using. As long as the totality of circumstances indicated that the defendant had been given a fair trial in state court, the demands of due process were satisfied. This was the **fair trial rule.** "If due process of law requires only fundamental fairness," explained Justice Harlan in his Duncan dissent, "then the inquiry in each case must be whether a state trial process was a fair one."

As Table 9.1 suggests, the Supreme Court devoted more and more time to criminal cases, both state and national, beginning in the 1960s. The result was the **due process revolution.** Never before had an American court brought such rapid and extensive change to virtually all stages of criminal justice. This revolution had at least three elements. The first was the near complete incorporation of the Bill of Rights into the Fourteenth Amendment. By the end of the Warren Court in 1969, there had ceased to be any significant difference under the U.S. Constitution between rights applicable in federal courts and rights applicable in state courts. The venerable double standard had vanished. Criminal cases from state courts now crowded the High Court's docket. Second, decisions reflected a deep appreciation of the liberties enshrined in the Bill of Rights. As explained in detail in Chapter Ten, judicial bombshells demolished or recast many of the old ways of fighting crime, state and federal. Third, and as a result of the first two, this restructuring made the Court for the first time the constitutional overseer of almost every aspect of local law enforcement in each of the 50 states.

## THE NEW JUDICIAL FEDERALISM:
## A NEW DOUBLE STANDARD

During the Warren Court (1953–1969), the bench often found itself pushing state criminal justice systems to provide a longer list of rights for the accused. With less enthusiasm on the Burger (1969–1986) and Rehnquist (1986– ) Courts for some rights of criminal defendants, many state courts have maintained or enlarged these rights as a matter of *state* constitutional law. This phenomenon is sometimes called the **new judicial federalism,** and the result has been the rise of a **new double standard.**

The opportunity for expanded state protection is present because virtually all the states have bills of rights similar to, or even more lengthy than, the federal Bill of Rights. Protection of individual liberties by state courts interpreting state constitutions presents no federal constitutional difficulties, provided the minimum standards of the latter are met. (See the section on judicial federalism in Chapter Four.) Federalism means that a state may grant more freedom under its own constitution than its citizens are granted by the national Constitution.

Ironically, incorporation of the Bill of Rights into the Fourteenth Amendment may have indirectly stimulated the growth of state constitutional rights. Without incorporation, a decision expanding, say, the protections afforded by the Fourth Amendment had only limited effects, directly applying to federal criminal cases alone. Incorporating the Bill of Rights into the Fourteenth Amendment multiplied by thousands the occasions when the commands of the federal Constitution prevailed over state law, affecting every police department, district attorney's office, and courtroom in the land. So a decision contracting a Fourth Amendment right likewise affects all components in both the state and federal systems of criminal justice, unless state judges, using state constitutions, choose otherwise.

## KEY TERMS

| | | |
|---|---|---|
| civil liberty | ordered liberty | due process revolution |
| civil right | total incorporation | new judicial federalism |
| due process of law | double standard | new double standard |
| incorporation | fair trial rule | |

## QUERIES

**1.** Reread the statement by Justice Jackson on the Bill of Rights at the very beginning of this chapter. Should it be qualified in any way?

**2.** Compare the opinions of Justices White and Harlan in *Duncan* v. *Louisiana* (1968). What values were in conflict? What values seemed most important for White? For Harlan?

**3.** If the Supreme Court did not begin to decide substantial numbers of cases involving the Bill of Rights until the 1940s, how were rights and liberties protected prior to that time?

**4.** What would have been the consequences for the American legal system had Justice Black secured one additional vote for his position in *Adamson* v. *California* (1947)?

## SELECTED READINGS

ABRAHAM, HENRY J., and BARBARA A. PERRY. *Freedom and the Court,* 8th ed. Lawrence: University Press of Kansas, 2003.

Brennan, William J., Jr. "The Bill of Rights and the States: The Revival of State Constitutions as Guardians of Individual Rights." 61 *New York University Law Review* 535 (1986).

——. "State Constitutions and the Protection of Individual Rights." 90 *Harvard Law Review* 489 (1977).

Curtis, Michael Kent. *No State Shall Abridge: The Fourteenth Amendment and the Bill of Rights.* Durham, N.C.: Duke University Press, 1986.

Fairman, Charles. "Does the Fourteenth Amendment Incorporate the Bill of Rights? The Original Understanding." 2 *Stanford Law Review* 5 (1949).

Frankfurter, Felix. "Memorandum on 'Incorporation' of the Bill of Rights into the Due Process Clause of the Fourteenth Amendment." 78 *Harvard Law Review* 746 (1965).

Mason, Alpheus T. "The Bill of Rights: An Almost Forgotten Appendage." In Stephen C. Halpern, ed., *The Future of Our Liberties.* Westport, Conn.: Greenwood, 1982.

Rutland, Robert A. *The Birth of the Bill of Rights, 1776–1791.* Chapel Hill: University of North Carolina Press, 1955.

# I. DRIVE FOR A BILL OF RIGHTS

## Jefferson-Madison Correspondence, 1787–1789

The principal author of the Declaration of Independence, Thomas Jefferson was abroad as minister to France during the time the Constitution was written, debated, and ratified. He thus had no direct hand in shaping its contents. From late 1787 into 1789, James Madison, who was a chief mover at the Constitutional Convention, and Jefferson exchanged a series of letters on the Constitution. Recall that trans-Atlantic mail in that day traveled on slow sailing ships and so letters took weeks to reach their destination. Upon receiving a copy of the Constitution from Madison, one of Jefferson's major concerns was the absence of a bill of rights, an omission he found striking, given the threats to liberty posed by the French monarchy, which he observed daily. (Jefferson's diplomatic service in France was to conclude just as the French Revolution began.) Less fearful than others of the tyranny of the majority, Jefferson thought the most important objective of constitutional limitations was to "guard the people against the federal government, as they are already guarded against their state governments in most instances."

### THOMAS JEFFERSON TO JAMES MADISON, 20 DECEMBER 1787

. . . I like much the general idea of framing a government which should go on of itself peaceably, without needing continual recurrence to the state legislatures. I like the organization of the government into Legislative, Judiciary and Executive. . . .

There are other good things of less moment. I will now add what I do not like. First the omission of a bill of rights providing clearly and without the aid of sophisms for freedom of religion, freedom of the press, protection against standing armies, restriction against monopolies, the eternal and unremitting force of the habeas corpus laws, and trials by jury in all matters of fact triable by the laws of the land and not by the law of Nations. To say, as Mr. [James] Wilson does, that a bill of rights was not necessary because all is reserved in the case of the general government which is not given, while in the particular ones all is given which is not reserved might do for the Audience to whom it was addressed, but is surely *gratis dictum,* opposed by strong inferences from the body of the instrument, as well as from the omission of the clause of our present confederation which had declared that in express terms. It was a hard conclusion to say

because there has been no uniformity among the states as to the cases triable by jury, because some have been so incautious as to abandon this mode of trial, therefore the more prudent states shall be reduced to the same level of calamity. It would have been much more just and wise to have concluded the other way that as most of the states had judiciously preserved this palladium, those who had wandered should be brought back to it, and to have established general right instead of general wrong. Let me add that a bill of rights is what the people are entitled to against every government on earth, general or particular, and what no just government should refuse, or rest on inference. . . .

### JAMES MADISON TO THOMAS JEFFERSON, 17 OCTOBER 1788

. . . My own opinion has always been in favor of a bill of rights, provided it be so framed as not to imply powers not meant to be included in the enumeration. At the same time I have never thought the omission a material defect, nor been anxious to supply it even by subsequent amendment, for any other reason than that it is anxiously desired by others. I have favored it because I supposed it might be of use, and if properly executed could not be of disservice. I have not viewed it in an important light. . . .

Experience proves the inefficacy of a bill of rights on those occasions when its control is most needed. Repeated violations of these parchment barriers have been committed by overbearing majorities in every State. In Virginia I have seen the bill of rights violated in every instance where it has been opposed to a popular current. Notwithstanding the explicit provision contained in that instrument for the rights of Conscience, it is well known that a religious establishment would have taken place in that State, if the Legislative majority had found as they expected, a majority of the people in favor of the measure; and I am persuaded that if a majority of the people were not of one sect, the measure would still take place and on narrower ground than was then proposed, notwithstanding the additional obstacle which the law has since created. Wherever the real power in a Government lies, there is the danger of oppression. In our Government, the real power lies in the majority of the Community, and the invasion of private rights is *chiefly* to be apprehended, not from acts of government contrary to the sense of its constituents, but from acts in which the Government is the mere instrument of the major number of the Constituents. This is a truth of great importance, but not yet sufficiently attended to; and is probably more strongly impressed on my mind by facts, and reflections suggested by them, than on yours which has contemplated abuses of power issuing from a very different quarter. Wherever there is an interest and power to do wrong, wrong will generally be done, and not less readily by a powerful & interested party than by a powerful and interested prince. . . .

What use then it may be asked can a bill of rights serve in popular Governments? I answer the two following which, though less essential than in other Governments, sufficiently recommend the precaution: 1. The political truths declared in that solemn manner acquire by degrees the character of fundamental maxims of free Governments, and as they become incorporated with the national sentiment,

counteract the impulses of interest and passion. 2. Altho, it be generally true as above stated that the danger of oppression lies in the interested majorities of the people rather than in usurped acts of the Government, yet there may be occasions on which the evil may spring from the latter source; and on such, a bill of rights will be a good ground for an appeal to the sense of the community. Perhaps too there may be a certain degree of danger, that a succession of artful and ambitious rulers may by gradual & well timed advances, finally erect an independent Government on the subversion of liberty. Should this danger exist at all, it is prudent to guard against it, especially when the precaution can do no injury. . . . It is a melancholy reflection that liberty should be equally exposed to danger whether the Government have too much or too little power, and that the line which divides these extremes should be so inaccurately defined by experience. . . .

## THOMAS JEFFERSON TO JAMES MADISON, 15 MARCH 1789

. . . In the arguments in favor of a declaration of rights, you omit one which has great weight with me, the legal check which it puts into the hands of the judiciary. This is a body, which if rendered independent, and kept strictly to their own department merits great confidence for their learning and integrity. . . .

Experience proves the inefficacy of a bill of rights. True. But tho it is not absolutely efficacious under all circumstances, it is of great potency always, and rarely inefficacious. A brace the more will often keep up the building which would have fallen with that brace the less. There is a remarkable difference between the characters of the inconveniences which attend a Declaration of rights, and those which attend the want of it. The inconveniences of the Declaration are that it may cramp government in its useful exertions. But the evil of this is short-lived, moderate and reparable. The inconveniences of the want of a Declaration are permanent, afflicting and irreparable: they are in constant progression from bad to worse. The executive in our government is not the sole, it is scarcely the principal object of my jealousy. The tyranny of the legislatures is the most formidable dread at present, and will be for long years. That of the executive will come in its turn, but it will be at a remote period. . . .

### JAMES MADISON, SPEECH PLACING THE PROPOSED BILL OF RIGHTS AMENDMENTS BEFORE THE HOUSE OF REPRESENTATIVES, 8 JUNE 1789

Mr. Madison rose, and reminded the House that this was the day that he had heretofore named for bringing forward amendments to the constitution, as contemplated in the fifth article of the constitution. . . .

The first of these amendments relates to what may be called a bill of rights. . . .

It has been said, that it is unnecessary to load the constitution with this provision, because it was not found effectual in the constitution of the particular States. It is true, there are a few particular States in which some of the most valuable articles have not, at one time or other, been violated; but it does not follow but they may have, to a certain degree, a salutary effect against the abuse of power. If they are incorporated into the constitution, independent tribunals of justice will consider themselves in a peculiar manner the guardians of those rights; they will be an impenetrable bulwark against every assumption of power in the legislative or executive; they will be naturally led to resist every encroachment upon rights expressly stipulated for in the constitution by the declaration of rights. Besides this security, there is a great probability that such a declaration in the federal system would be enforced; because the State Legislatures will jealously and closely watch the operations of this Government, and be able to resist with more effect every assumption of power, than any other power on earth can do; and the greatest opponents to a Federal Government admit the State Legislatures to be sure guardians of the people's liberty. I conclude, from this view of the subject, that it will be proper in itself, and highly politic, for the tranquility of the public mind, and the stability of the Government, that we should offer something, in the form I have proposed, to be incorporated in the system of Government, as a declaration of the rights of the people.

I wish also, in revising the constitution, we may throw into that section, which interdicts the abuse of certain powers in the State Legislatures, some other provisions of equal, if not greater importance than those already made. The words, "No State shall pass any bill of attainder, ex post facto law," &c. were wise and proper restrictions in the constitution. I think there is more danger of those powers being abused by the State Governments than by the Government of the United States. The same may be said of other powers which they possess, if not controlled by the general principle, that laws are unconstitutional which infringe the rights of the community. I should therefore wish to extend this interdiction, and add that no State shall violate the equal right of conscience, freedom of the press, or trial by jury in criminal cases; because it is proper that every Government should be disarmed of powers which trench upon those particular rights. I know, in some of the State constitutions, the power of the Government is controlled by such a declaration; but others are not. I cannot see any reason against obtaining even a double security on those points; and nothing can give a more sincere proof of the attachment of those who opposed this constitution to these great and important rights, than to see them join in obtaining the security I have now proposed: because it must be admitted, on all hands, that the State Governments are as liable to attack these invaluable privileges as the General Government is, and therefore ought to be as cautiously guarded against. . . .

[An amendment providing for safeguards against the states was proposed, but it failed of adoption.—ED.]

## II. THE BILL OF RIGHTS AND THE STATES

### *Palko* v. *Connecticut*
### 302 U.S. 319, 58 S.Ct. 149, 82 L.Ed. 288 (1937)
http://laws.findlaw.com/us/302/319.html

> By statute Connecticut permitted the state to appeal from rulings and decisions in its criminal courts on points of law. Convicted of murder in the second degree and given a life sentence, Palko was retried after a successful state appeal. His second trial, held in spite of his objection that he was being twice placed in jeopardy, resulted in a conviction for first-degree murder and a death sentence. Majority: Cardozo, Black, Brandeis, Hughes, Roberts, Sutherland, Stone, Van Devanter. Dissenting: Butler.

**MR. JUSTICE CARDOZO delivered the opinion of the Court. . . .**

The argument for appellant is that whatever is forbidden by the Fifth Amendment is forbidden by the Fourteenth Amendment also. . . . [The] thesis is even broader. Whatever would be a violation of the original bill of rights (Amendments I to VIII) if done by the federal government is now equally unlawful by force of the Fourteenth Amendment if done by a state. There is no such general rule.

The Fifth Amendment provides, among other things, that no person shall be held to answer for a capital or otherwise infamous crime unless on presentment or indictment of a grand jury. This court has held that, in prosecutions by a state, presentment or indictment by a grand jury may give way to informations at the instance of a public officer. . . . The Fifth Amendment provides also that no person shall be compelled in any criminal case to be a witness against himself. This court has said that, in prosecutions by a state, the exemption will fail if the state elects to end it. . . . The Sixth Amendment calls for a jury trial in criminal cases and the Seventh for a jury trial in civil cases of common law where the value in controversy shall exceed twenty dollars. This court has ruled that consistently with those amendments trial by jury may be modified by a state or abolished altogether. . . .

On the other hand, the due process clause of the Fourteenth Amendment may make it unlawful for a state to abridge by its statutes the freedom of speech which the First Amendment safeguards against encroachment by the Congress . . . or the like freedom of the press . . . or the right of peaceable assembly, without which speech would be unduly trammeled. . . .

The line of division may seem to be wavering and broken if there is a hasty catalogue of the cases on the one side and the other. Reflection and analysis will induce a different view. There emerges the perception of a rationalizing principle which gives to discrete instances a proper order and coherence. The right to trial by jury and the immunity from prosecution except as the result of an indictment may have value and importance. Even so, they are not of the very essence of a scheme of ordered liberty. To abolish them is not to violate a "principle of justice so rooted in the traditions and conscience of our people as to be ranked as fundamental." . . . Few would be so narrow or provincial as to maintain that a fair and enlightened system of justice would be impossible without them. What is true of jury trials and indictments is true also, as the cases show, of the immunity from compulsory self-incrimination. . . . This too might be lost, and justice still be done. Indeed, today as in the past there are students of our penal system who look upon the immunity as a mischief rather than a benefit, and who would limit its scope, or destroy it altogether. No doubt there would remain the need to give protection against torture, physical or mental. . . . Justice, however, would not perish if the accused were subject to a duty to respond to orderly inquiry. The exclusion of these immunities and privileges from the privileges and immunities protected against the action of the states has not been arbitrary or casual. It has been dictated by a study and appreciation of the meaning, the essential implications, of liberty itself.

We reach a different plane of social and moral values when we pass to the privileges and immunities that have been taken over from the earlier articles of the Federal Bill of Rights and brought within the Fourteenth Amendment by a process of absorption. These in their origin were effective against the federal government alone. If the Fourteenth Amendment has absorbed them, the process of absorption has had its source in the belief that neither liberty nor justice would exist if they were sacrificed. . . . This is true, for illustration, of freedom of thought and speech. Of that freedom one may say that it is the matrix, the indispensable condition, of nearly every other form of freedom. . . .

Our survey of the cases serves, we think, to justify the statement that the dividing line between them, if not unfaltering throughout its course, has been true for the most part to a unifying principle. On which side of the line the case made out by the appellant has appropriate location must be the next inquiry and the final one. Is that kind of double jeopardy to which the statute has subjected him a hardship so acute and shocking that our polity will not endure it? Does it violate those "fundamental principles of liberty and justice which lie at the base of all our civil and political institutions?" . . . The answer surely must be "no." What the answer would have to be if the state were permitted after a trial free from error to try the accused over again or to bring another case against him, we have no occasion to consider. We deal with the statute before us and no other. The state is not attempting to wear the accused out by a multitude of cases with accumulated trials. It asks no more than this, that the case against him shall go on until there shall be a trial free from the corrosion of substantial legal error. . . .

The judgment is

*Affirmed.*

Mr. Justice Butler dissents [without opinion].

## Adamson v. California
### 332 U.S. 46, 67 S.Ct. 1672, 91 L.Ed. 1903 (1947)
http://laws.findlaw.com/us/332/46.html

Adamson appealed from a judgment of the Supreme Court of California affirming his conviction of murder. The basis of his appeal was the alleged invalidity of a California code provision that permitted the prosecution and the court to comment on the failure of a defendant to take the witness stand to explain or deny evidence against him. In his trial Adamson, who had a record of three previous felony convictions, chose not to take the stand, thus causing adverse comments by the district attorney and court. However, if he had chosen to testify, the district attorney could then have revealed his record of previous convictions to impeach his testimony. It should be noted that the majority of state jurisdictions and the federal courts did not permit comment on a defendant's failure to testify. Majority: Reed, Burton, Frankfurter, Jackson, Vinson. Dissenting: Black, Douglas, Murphy, Rutledge.

**MR. JUSTICE REED delivered the opinion of the Court. . . .**

A right to a fair trial is a right admittedly protected by the due process clause of the Fourteenth Amendment. Therefore, appellant argues, the due process clause of the Fourteenth Amendment protects his privilege against self-incrimination. The due process clause of the Fourteenth Amendment, however, does not draw all the rights of the federal Bill of Rights under its protection. That contention was made and rejected in *Palko* v. *Connecticut*. . . .

Specifically, the due process clause does not protect, by virtue of its mere existence, the accused's freedom from giving testimony by compulsion in state trials that is secured to him against federal interference by the Fifth Amendment. . . . For a state to require testimony from an accused is not necessarily a breach of a state's obligation to give a fair trial. . . .

California . . . is one of a few states that permit limited comment upon a defendant's failure to testify. That permission is narrow. The California law . . . authorizes comment by court and counsel upon the "failure of the defendant to explain or so deny by his testimony any evidence or facts in the case against him." This does not involve any presumption, rebuttable or irrebuttable, either of guilt or of the truth of any fact, that is offered in evidence. It allows inferences to be drawn from proven facts. Because of this clause, the court can direct the jury's attention to whatever evidence there may be that a defendant could deny and the prosecution can argue as to inferences that may be drawn from the accused's failure to testify. . . . It seems quite natural that when a defendant has opportunity to deny or explain facts and determines not to do so, the prosecution should bring out the strength of the evidence by commenting upon defendant's failure to explain or deny it. The prosecution evidence may be of facts that may be beyond the knowledge of the accused. If so, his failure to testify would have little if any weight. But the facts may be such as are necessarily in the knowledge of the accused. In that case a failure to explain would point to an inability to explain. . . .

It is true that if comment were forbidden, an accused in this situation could remain silent and avoid evidence of former crimes and comment upon his failure to testify. We are of the view, however, that a state may control such a situation in accordance with its own ideas of the most efficient administration of criminal justice. The purpose of due process is not to protect an accused against a proper conviction but against an unfair conviction.

*Affirmed.*

**MR. JUSTICE FRANKFURTER, concurring. . . .**

Between the incorporation of the Fourteenth Amendment into the Constitution and the beginning of the present membership of the Court—a period of seventy years—the scope of that Amendment was passed upon by forty-three judges. Of all these judges, only one [the first Justice Harlan], who may respectfully be called an eccentric exception, ever indicated the belief that the . . . Amendment was a shorthand summary of the first eight Amendments. . . . And so they did not find that the Fourteenth Amendment, concerned as it was with matters fundamental to the pursuit of justice, fastened upon the States procedural arrangements which, in the language of Mr. Justice Cardozo, only those who are "narrow and provincial" would deem essential to "a fair and enlightened system of justice." To suggest that it is inconsistent with a truly free society to begin prosecutions without an indictment, to try petty civil cases without the paraphernalia of a common law jury, to take into consideration that one who has full opportunity to make a defense remains silent is, in de Tocqueville's phrase, to confound the familiar with the necessary. . . .

The Amendment neither comprehends the specific provisions by which the founders deemed it appropriate to restrict the federal government nor is it confined to them. The Due Process Clause . . . has an independent potency. . . .

It seems pretty late in the day to suggest that a phrase so laden with historic meaning should be given an improvised content consisting of some but not all of the provisions of the first eight Amendments, selected on an undefined basis. . . .

And so, when . . . a conviction in a State court is here for review under a claim that a right protected by the Due Process Clause . . . has been denied, the issue is not whether an infraction of one of the specific provisions of the first eight Amendments is disclosed by the record. The relevant question is whether the criminal proceedings which resulted in conviction deprived the accused of the due process of law to which the United States Constitution entitled him. Judicial review of that guaranty . . . inescapably imposes on this Court an exercise of judgment upon the whole course of the proceedings in order to ascertain whether they offend those canons of decency and fairness which express the notions of justice of English-speaking peoples. . . . These standards of justice are not authoritatively formulated anywhere as though they were prescriptions in a pharmacopoeia. But neither does the application of the Due Process Clause imply that judges are wholly at large. The judicial judgment . . . must move within the limits of accepted notions of justice and is not to be based upon the idiosyncrasies of a merely personal judgment. The fact that judges among themselves may differ whether in a particular case a trial offends accepted notions of justice is not disproof that general rather than idiosyncratic standards are applied. An important safeguard against such merely individual judgment is an alert deference to the judgment of the State court under review.

### MR. JUSTICE BLACK, with whom MR. JUSTICE DOUGLAS concurs, dissenting. . . .

This decision reasserts a constitutional theory spelled out in *Twining* v. *New Jersey* . . . that this Court is endowed by the Constitution with boundless power under "natural law" periodically to expand and contract constitutional standards to conform to the Court's conception of what at a particular time constitutes "civilized decency" and "fundamental liberty and justice." Invoking this *Twining* rule, the Court concludes that although comment upon testimony in a federal court would violate the Fifth Amendment, identical comment in a state court does not violate today's fashion in civilized decency and fundamentals and is therefore not prohibited by the Federal Constitution as amended. . . .

My study of the historical events that culminated in the Fourteenth Amendment, and the expressions of those who sponsored and favored, as well as those who opposed its submission and passage, persuades me that one of the chief objects that the provisions of the Amendment's first section, separately, and as a whole, were intended to accomplish was to make the Bill of Rights applicable to the states. With full knowledge of the import of the Barron decision, the framers and backers of the Fourteenth Amendment proclaimed its purpose to be to overturn the constitutional rule that case had announced. This historical purpose has never received full consideration or exposition in any opinion of this Court interpreting the Amendment. . . .

In my judgment that history conclusively demonstrates that the language of the first section of the Fourteenth Amendment taken as a whole, was thought by those responsible for its submission to the people, and by those who opposed its submission, sufficiently explicit to guarantee that thereafter no state could deprive its citizens of the privileges and protections of the Bill of Rights. . . .

I cannot consider the Bill of Rights to be an outworn 18th-century "straight jacket." . . . Its provisions may be thought outdated abstractions by some. And it is true that they were designed to meet ancient evils. But they are the same kind of human evils that have emerged from century to century wherever excessive power is sought by the few at the expense of the many. In my judgment the people of no nation can lose their liberty so long as a Bill of Rights like ours survives and its basic purposes are conscientiously interpreted, enforced and respected so as to afford continuous protection against old, as well as new, devices and practices which might thwart those purposes. I fear to see the consequences of the Court's practice of substituting its own concepts of decency and fundamental justice for the language of the Bill of Rights as its point of departure in interpreting and enforcing that Bill of Rights. . . . I would follow what I believe was the original purpose of the Fourteenth Amendment—to extend to all the people of the nation the complete protection of the Bill of Rights. To

hold that this Court can determine what, if any, provisions of the Bill of Rights will be enforced, and if so to what degree, is to frustrate the great design of a written Constitution. . . .

MR. JUSTICE MURPHY, with whom MR. JUSTICE RUTLEDGE concurs, dissenting . . . [omitted].

## Duncan v. Louisiana
## 391 U.S. 145, 88 S.Ct. 1444, 20 L.Ed. 2d 491 (1968)
## http://laws.findlaw.com/us/391/145.html

Gary Duncan was convicted of simple battery, a misdemeanor punishable under Louisiana law by two years' imprisonment and a $300 fine. His request for trial by jury was denied because the state constitution restricted trial by jury to capital offenses and those punishable by hard labor. The Louisiana Supreme Court denied his claim that his right to jury trial under the Sixth and Fourteenth Amendments had been violated. The lengthy footnote in Justice White's opinion is important because it summarizes the changes that transpired in the Court's thinking about the Fourteenth Amendment after *Adamson*. Majority: White, Black, Brennan, Douglas, Fortas, Marshall, Warren. Dissenting: Harlan, Stewart.

### MR. JUSTICE WHITE delivered the opinion of the Court. . . .

The Fourteenth Amendment denies the States the power to "deprive any person of life, liberty, or property, without due process of law." In resolving conflicting claims concerning the meaning of this spacious language, the Court has looked increasingly to the Bill of Rights for guidance; many of the rights guaranteed by the first eight Amendments to the Constitution have been held to be protected against state action by the Due Process Clause of the Fourteenth Amendment. That clause now protects the right to compensation for property taken by the State; the rights of speech, press, and religion covered by the First Amendment; the Fourth Amendment rights to be free from unreasonable searches and seizures and to have excluded from criminal trials any evidence illegally seized; the right guaranteed by the Fifth Amendment to be free of compelled self-incrimination; and the Sixth Amendment rights to counsel, to a speedy and

public trial, to confrontation of opposing witnesses, and a compulsory process for obtaining witnesses.

The test for determining whether a right extended by the Fifth and Sixth Amendments with respect to federal criminal proceedings is also protected against state action by the Fourteenth Amendment has been phrased in a variety of ways in the opinions of this Court. The question has been asked whether a right is among those "fundamental principles of liberty and justice which lie at the base of all our civil and political institutions," whether it is "basic in our system of jurisprudence," and whether it is "a fundamental right, essential to a fair trial." The claim before us is that the right to trial by jury guaranteed by the Sixth Amendment meets these tests. The position of Louisiana, on the other hand, is that the Constitution imposes upon the States no duty to give a jury trial in any criminal case, regardless of the seriousness of the crime or the size of the punishment which may be imposed. Because we believe that trial by jury in criminal cases is fundamental to the American scheme of justice, we hold that the Fourteenth Amendment guarantees a right of jury trial in all criminal cases which—were they to be tried in a federal court—would come within the Sixth Amendment's guarantee.[1] Since we consider the appeal before us to be such a case, we hold that the Constitution was violated when appellant's demand for jury trial was refused.

### MR. JUSTICE BLACK, with whom MR. JUSTICE DOUGLAS joins, concurring.

The Court today holds that the right to trial by jury guaranteed defendants in criminal cases in federal courts by Art. III of the United States Constitution and by the Sixth Amendment is also guaranteed by the Fourteenth Amendment to defendants tried in state courts. With this holding I agree for reasons given by the Court. I also agree because of reasons given in my dissent in *Adamson* v. *California.* . . . And I am very happy to support this selective process through which our Court has since the Adamson case held most of the specific Bill of Rights' protections applicable to the States to the same extent they are applicable to the Federal Government. . . .

While I do not wish at this time to discuss at length my disagreement with Brother Harlan's forthright and frank restatement of the now discredited Twining doctrine, I do want to point out what appears to me to be the basic difference between us. His view, as was indeed the view of *Twining,* is that "due process is an evolving concept" and therefore that it entails a "gradual process of judicial inclusion and exclusion" to ascertain those "immutable principles of free government which no member of the Union may disregard." Thus the Due Process Clause is treated as prescribing no specific and clearly ascertainable constitutional command that judges must obey in interpreting the Constitution, but rather as leaving judges free to decide at any particular time whether a particular rule or judicial formulation embodies an "immutable principle of free government" or "is implicit in the concept of ordered liberty," or whether certain conduct "shocks the judge's conscience" or runs counter to some other similar, undefined and

---

[1] In one sense recent cases applying provisions of the first eight Amendments to the States represent a new approach to the "incorporation" debate. Earlier the Court can be seen as having asked, when inquiring into whether some particular procedural safeguard was required of a state, if a civilized system could be imagined that would not accord the particular protection. . . . The recent cases, on the other hand, have proceeded upon the valid assumption that state criminal processes are not imaginary and theoretical schemes but actual systems bearing virtually every characteristic of the common-law system that has been developing contemporaneously in England and in this country. The question thus is whether given this kind of system a particular procedure is fundamental—whether, that is, a procedure is necessary to an Anglo-American regime of ordered liberty. It is this sort of inquiry that can justify the conclusions that state courts must exclude evidence seized in violation of the Fourth Amendment; that state prosecutors may not comment on a defendant's failure to testify; and that criminal punishment may not be imposed for the status of narcotics addiction. Of immediate relevance for this case are the Court's holdings that the States must comply with certain provisions of the Sixth Amendment, specifically that the States may not refuse a speedy trial, confrontation of witnesses, and the assistance, at state expense if necessary, of counsel. . . . Of each of these determinations that a constitutional provision originally written to bind the Federal Government should bind the States as well it might be said that the limitation in question is not necessarily fundamental to fairness in every criminal system that might be imagined but is fundamental in the context of the criminal processes maintained by the American States.

When the inquiry is approached in this way the question whether the States can impose criminal punishment without granting a jury trial appears quite different from the way it appeared in the older cases opining that States might abolish jury trial. A criminal process which was fair and equitable but used no juries is easy to imagine. It would make use of alternative guarantees and protections which would serve the purposes that the jury serves in the English and American systems. Yet no American State has undertaken to construct such a system. Instead, every American State, including Louisiana, uses the jury extensively, and imposes very serious punishments only after a trial at which the defendant has a right to a jury's verdict. In every state, including Louisiana, the structure and style of the criminal process—the supporting framework and the subsidiary procedures—are of the sort that naturally complement jury trial, and have developed in connection with and in reliance upon jury trial.

undefinable standard. Thus due process, according to my Brother Harlan, is to be a word with no permanent meaning, but one which is found to shift from time to time in accordance with judges' predilections and understandings of what is best for the country. If due process means this, the Fourteenth Amendment, in my opinion, might as well have been written that "no person shall be deprived of life, liberty or property except by laws that the judges of the United States Supreme Court shall find to be consistent with the immutable principles of free government." It is impossible for me to believe that such unconfined power is given to judges in our Constitution that is a written one in order to limit governmental power. . . .

Mr. Justice Fortas, concurring . . . [omitted].

### Mr. Justice Harlan, whom Mr. Justice Stewart joins, dissenting. . . .

The Court's approach to this case is an uneasy and illogical compromise among the views of various Justices on how the Due Process Clause should be interpreted. The Court does not say that those who framed the Fourteenth Amendment intended to make the Sixth Amendment applicable to the States. And the Court concedes that it finds nothing unfair about the procedure by which the present appellant was tried. Nevertheless, the Court reverses his conviction: it holds, for some reason not apparent to me, that the Due Process Clause incorporates the particular clause of the Sixth Amendment that requires trial by jury in federal criminal cases— including, as I read its opinion, the sometimes trivial accompanying baggage of judicial interpretation in federal contexts. . . . With all respect, the Court's approach and its reading of history are altogether topsy-turvy. . . .

Apart from the approach taken by the absolute incorporationists, I can see only one method of analysis that has any internal logic. That is to start with the words "liberty" and "due process of law" and attempt to define them in a way that accords with American traditions and our system of government. This approach, involving a much more discriminating process of adjudication than does "incorporation," is, albeit difficult, the one that was followed throughout the nineteenth and most of the present century. It entails a "gradual process of judicial inclusion and exclusion," seeking, with due recognition of constitutional tolerance for state experimentation and disparity, to ascertain those "immutable principles of free government which no member of the Union may disregard." . . .

Through this gradual process, this Court sought to define "liberty" by isolating freedoms that Americans of the past and of the present considered more important than any suggested countervailing public objective. The Court also, by interpretation of the phrase "due process of law," enforced the Constitution's guarantee that no State may imprison an individual except by fair and impartial procedures.

The relationship of the Bill of Rights to this "gradual process" seems to me to be twofold. In the first place it has long been clear that the Due Process Clause imposes some restrictions on state action that parallel Bill of Rights restrictions on federal action. Second, and more important than this accidental overlap, is the fact that the Bill of Rights is evidence, at various points, of the content Americans find in the term "liberty" and of American standards of fundamental fairness. . . .

The argument that jury trial is not a requisite of due process is quite simple. The central proposition of *Palko* . . . a proposition to which I would adhere, is that "due process of law" requires only that criminal trials be fundamentally fair. As stated above, apart from the theory that it was historically intended as a mere shorthand for the Bill of Rights, I do not see what else "due process of law" can intelligibly be thought to mean. If due process of law requires only fundamental fairness, then the inquiry in each case must be whether a state trial process was a fair one. The Court has held, properly I think, that in an adversary process it is a requisite of fairness, for which there is no adequate substitute, that a criminal defendant be afforded a right to counsel and to cross-examine opposing witnesses. But it simply has not been demonstrated, nor, I think, can it be demonstrated, that trial by jury is the only fair means of resolving issues of fact. . . .

# CHAPTER TEN

# *Criminal Justice*

*The history of American freedom is in no small measure the history of procedure.*
—JUSTICE FELIX FRANKFURTER (1945)

Thanks to Fourteenth Amendment incorporation, as the previous chapter explained, almost all the strictures in the Bill of Rights now apply with equal force to the states, as well as to the national government. Because most of the provisions of the Bill of Rights involve criminal procedure, this fact has had enormous consequences for law enforcement at all levels. While there were some 67,000 criminal cases filed in the 89 U.S. district courts in 2002, more than 5 million serious criminal cases were filed in the 2,501 trial courts of general jurisdiction in the 50 states (minor criminal and traffic offenses generated an additional 9 million proceedings). And in one way or another, every one of these cases intersected the Bill of Rights.

The cases in this chapter illustrate a struggle between two cherished and not necessarily antithetical values. The conflict is between the public's interest in safety and the public's interest in the protection of individual liberty. It is misleading to view the clash as a contest between the safety of law-abiding people and the protection of criminals. Constitutional safeguards belong to everyone, law-abiding and law-breaking alike. The judicial task is one of determining how much protection can be accorded each individual without unduly hampering the effort of government to maintain order, without which there can be no freedom. Small wonder the framers of our national and state constitutions gave special attention to procedural rights. Far from demonstrating fondness for technicalities, this emphasis highlights the belief that without limits to authority, America would be a far different place in which to live. The framers knew firsthand the dangers that the government-as-prosecutor could pose to freedom. Even today, authoritarian regimes in other lands routinely use the tools of law enforcement—arrests, searches, detentions, as well as prosecutions—to squelch political opposition. Limits in the Bill of Rights on government's crime-fighting powers thus help safeguard democracy.

What follows is a brief survey of some of the topics in criminal procedure and a review of the major cases. The field is too vast to include them all. Cases on criminal justice are as myriad as the variety of citizen–police–courtroom encounters themselves.

## SEARCHES AND SEIZURES

"The right of the people," the **Fourth Amendment** grandly declares, "to be secure in their persons, houses, papers, and effects, against unreasonable searches and seizures, shall not be violated, and no Warrants shall issue, but upon probable cause, supported by Oath or affirmation, and particularly describing the place to be searched, and the persons or things to be seized." This amendment differs in at least two important ways from some of the other parts of the Bill of Rights.

First, it has no direct antecedent in English constitutional documents such as Magna Carta of 1215, the Petition of Right of 1628, and the Bill of Rights of 1689. Rather, its origins lie in Great Britain's attempt to collect duties in the American colonies after 1767 on imports such as glass, lead, paint, and tea. To combat smuggling, customs officials were handed **writs of assistance.** These were general search warrants, valid for the life of the sovereign, that allowed virtually unlimited searches of anyone or any place at any time for any reason or for no reason at all. The framers of the Bill of Rights learned a lesson from that experience: when government encroaches on personal liberty, it usually has very good reasons for doing so. The grim experience with writs of assistance also explains the wording of the Fourth Amendment. The emphasis throughout is on *particularity,* not generality. There must be a documented reason—the amendment calls it **probable cause**—to search a particular place or to seize a particular person. The **warrant,** which is the official authorization for the search or the arrest, must also be particular in describing what is to be searched and what is expected to be found. In addition, an assumption of the amendment is that the warrant is to be issued by a judge. This is the principle of separation of powers at work in law enforcement. Before the executive branch, acting through a police officer, may invade a person's physical privacy, the judicial branch must be convinced of the need for *this* search of *this* place before giving its approval.

Second, excepting only the First Amendment, more Americans continually benefit from the protections of the Fourth Amendment than any other part of the Bill of Rights. Provisions of the Fifth, Sixth, and Eighth amendments (to be discussed later in this chapter), while essential, do not normally come into play for an individual until after a criminal investigation has made some headway or until the person has been charged with an offense or has been found guilty. By prohibiting "unreasonable searches and seizures," the Fourth Amendment seeks to guard the physical security of all.

The wording of the Fourth Amendment lends itself generally to two interpretations by the Court. Each involves conclusions about the clauses in the amendment that ban "unreasonable searches and seizures" and specify the conditions for issuance of a warrant. The first approach views the two clauses as inseparably linked. A reasonable, and therefore a permissible, search is one conducted with a warrant. Accordingly, a warrantless search is unreasonable and impermissible, unless it falls into a handful of exceptions. The second approach, more friendly to law enforcement, sees the two clauses as standing alone. From this perspective, searches must be "reasonable" to be lawful, but a warrant is not an essential element of reasonableness. In operation, this reading of the amendment allows police more flexibility, in the absence of a warrant, to make stops and to conduct searches.

**WHOSE RIGHTS?** To say that all Americans benefit from the protection of the Fourth Amendment, however, does not mean that the amendment applies to everyone in all situations. That reality lay at the heart of ***Minnesota* v. *Carter*** (1998). Police arrested two men after an officer, having been tipped by an informer, peeked through an apartment window and observed them and the lessee of the apartment bagging cocaine. The Court side-stepped the intriguing question whether the peek was a search, concluding instead that the men could assert no Fourth Amendment rights in that situation because they were merely short-term guests of the woman who had allowed them to use her apartment for business purposes.

**DEFINING A SEARCH.** The question that the Court never reached in *Carter* is ordinarily an essential threshold issue in every Fourth Amendment case: Has a "search" or "seizure" actually occurred? If it has not, the constraints of the amendment, such as probable cause and a warrant, do not apply. In *California* v. *Ciraolo* (1986), for example, aerial photographic surveillance by police of marijuana plants in the backyard of a house, even though surrounded by two fences, was not deemed a search. Similarly, *Florida* v. *Riley* (1989) held that no search occurred when police in a helicopter hovered at an altitude of 400 feet above a partially covered greenhouse and took photographs of marijuana plants growing inside. Yet, *Bond* v. *United States* (2000) invalidated a warrantless examination of a bus passenger's soft-side luggage after police reached into the overhead bin and felt and squeezed the bag to determine if drugs might be inside. In the Court's view, that tactile inspection amounted to a Fourth Amendment search. Consider these cases alongside ***Kyllo* v. *United States*** (2001), which required the Court to decide if police use of a heat-imaging device constituted a search.

**PROBABLE CAUSE.** With a few exceptions discussed later in this chapter, lawful searches are predicated upon probable cause. The term suggests more than a hunch that someone is engaged in illegal activity, but less than the degree of certainty a prosecutor needs at trial to establish guilt beyond a reasonable doubt. Justice Rutledge once characterized the standard in this manner:

> In dealing with probable cause . . . we deal with probabilities. These are not technical; they are the factual and practical considerations of everyday life on which reasonable and prudent men, not legal technicians, act. . . . Probable cause exists where the facts and circumstances within [the officers'] knowledge, and of which they had reasonably trustworthy information, [are] sufficient in themselves to warrant a man of reasonable caution in the belief that an offense has been or is being committed.

Probable cause, Rutledge said, seeks "to safeguard citizens from rash and unreasonable interferences with privacy and from unfounded charges of crime. [It also seeks] to give fair leeway for enforcing the law in the community's protection." For the Court to require "more would unduly hamper law enforcement. To allow less would be to leave law-abiding citizens at the mercy of the officers' whim or caprice" (*Brinegar* v. *United States,* 1949). Later, the Court emphasized that the standard "is to be applied, not according to a fixed and rigid formula, but rather in the light of the 'totality of the circumstances' made known to the magistrate" who issues the warrant. "[T]he task of a reviewing court," in overseeing the Fourth Amendment, "is not to conduct a de novo determination of probable cause, but only to determine whether there is substantial evidence in the record supporting the magistrate's decision to issue the warrant" (*Massachusetts* v. *Upton,* 1984).

A factor complicating judicial oversight of police practices is the use of anonymous informers in establishing probable cause. Many of the affidavits signed by police officers to establish probable cause recite certain details they learned secondhand from such people, anonymous even to the magistrate issuing the warrant. The constitutional objection to the use of informers on the ground that suspects could not confront their accusers was overcome in *McCray* v. *Illinois* (1967). Key to preventing anonymity from becoming a shield for fictitiousness is the requirement that the officer demonstrate the informant's reliability to the magistrate. Since *Illinois* v. *Gates* (1983), the Court has relied on a totality-of-circumstances approach. Accordingly, the magistrate must make a practical, "commonsense" decision whether, given all the information the officer provides both from and about the informer, a fair probability exists that evidence of a crime will be found in a particular place.

**THE EXCLUSIONARY RULE.** If the Fourth Amendment sets standards for a lawful search, what happens when evidence is seized in violation of the amendment? In English common law, material and relevant evidence has always been held admissible at a trial even though officials may have obtained it through an improper search. Moreover, in the twenty-first century, unlawfully obtained evidence is admissible in the courts of nearly every country in the world. In *Weeks* v. *United States* (1914), however, the Supreme Court fashioned a broad **exclusionary rule** that barred the use at federal trials of evidence obtained illegally by federal agents. In 1949, *Wolf* v. *Colorado* made the Fourth Amendment guaranty against unreasonable search and seizure applicable to the states but refrained from imposing the federal exclusionary rule, asserting with more confidence than accuracy that other remedies were available to state victims of illegal searches and seizures. By 1961, nearly half the states still admitted unlawfully seized evidence in state trials. By then, the Supreme Court had learned what others had long known: civil tort remedies against offending police officers, criminal prosecution, or public outcry had all failed to stop abuses. **Mapp v. Ohio** did what *Wolf* had failed to do and applied the exclusionary rule to the states. Justice Clark's opinion emphasized the twin pillars for suppressing illegally seized evidence: deterrence of unlawful police conduct and the maintenance of judicial integrity. *Mapp* marked the beginning of the Supreme Court's heightened concern with the realities of criminal justice at the state level. As much as any other single decision, *Mapp* put the Court in charge of standards for day-to-day police work.

*Mapp* has remained the linchpin for much of the due process revolution set loose by the Warren Court and discussed in Chapter Nine. Most citizen encounters with law enforcement authorities are with state and local police. Court decisions specifying proper police procedure for stops, searches, and arrests thus have real impact on the criminal justice system when coupled with the exclusionary rule. No wonder Supreme Court decisions interpreting the Fourth Amendment attract such widespread attention, for they define constitutionally correct conduct for all law enforcement officers in the land. *Mapp* gave those rules teeth because a violation of the Fourth Amendment meant a loss of otherwise useful, reliable, and probative evidence. Under *Mapp,* admissibility of evidence depends upon the lawfulness of the search, not on what the search uncovers.

Yet because of the social costs of the rule—a person does not benefit directly from its operation unless incriminating evidence is found—it has long been a center of controversy. Justices antagonistic to the exclusionary rule got results in 1984, as **United States v. Leon** modified the exclusionary rule to permit a limited "good-faith" or "reasonable mistake" exception. Because the ruling applies only to searches with warrants, not warrantless searches, *Leon* does not affect all Fourth Amendment cases.

**WARRANTLESS SEARCHES.** The Court has usually shown a preference for searches authorized by warrants, as opposed to warrantless intrusions. There are times, however, when the requirement for a warrant is so impractical as to pose a serious hindrance to law enforcement.

(1) *Search Incident to a Lawful Arrest.* One of these situations arises at the time of the arrest itself. No warrant is needed to search places under the control of the arrestee so that police can avoid the danger of concealed weapons and prevent destruction of evidence. The permissible extent of this kind of warrantless search, however, has been subject to different interpretations. In *United States* v. *Rabinowitz* (1950), for example, federal agents thoroughly searched an entire office incident to a lawful arrest, and the Court approved the admission at trial of forged stamps discovered during the search. In contrast, the 1969 decision in **Chimel v. California** sharply curtailed the area subject to a warrantless search and, consequently, induced greater use of search warrants.

Under *Chimel,* police making a lawful arrest may search the person and the area within the arrestee's control or reach. The basis of the exception to the warrant requirement is thus the safety of the police and the protection of evidence. Moreover, according to *Maryland* v. *Buie* (1990), where police making an arrest have reason to believe that someone may be present in another part of the house who might pose a threat to them, they may conduct a "protective sweep" for their own safety, even though they have no search warrant. Contraband or other evidence that they see lying about in "plain view" may then be lawfully seized. In situations where there is probable cause to believe that contraband is present in a building, *Illinois* v. *McArthur* (2001) allows police to prevent a suspect from entering his home unaccompanied—in this case for two hours—while a warrant is being procured.

(2) *The Automobile Exception.* The automobile has long been an exception to the general rule that warrants are needed in advance of searches. *Carroll* v. *United States* (1925) allowed the warrantless search of a car when there was probable cause to believe it was carrying contraband or was being used to violate the law. Motor vehicles are not only mobile, and so might quickly depart the jurisdiction while an officer attempted to obtain a warrant, but are already highly regulated by government. Moreover, most justices also see them as involving lesser expectations of privacy than, say, someone's home.

If the automobile itself may be searched without a warrant, what about containers police find in the automobile that may contain contraband? Police who have reason to search a car may coincidentally come across a container, just as police who have reason to search a container may coincidentally find it in a car. The Court has given conflicting answers in such situations. *Arkansas* v. *Sanders* (1979), for example, disallowed the warrantless search of a suitcase—itself the target of the investigation—after police removed it from the trunk of a taxi in which it had just been placed by the suspects. *Robbins* v. *California* (1981) reversed a drug conviction based on a warrantless opening of opaque wrapped bricks of marijuana, which police discovered in the tire well of a station wagon during an otherwise lawful search. Yet on the same day *Robbins* was decided, *New York* v. *Belton* upheld the warrantless search of the passenger compartment (and containers within it) of an automobile as a search incident to arrest. *United States* v. *Ross* (1982) overturned *Robbins* by holding that the warrantless search of an automobile based on probable cause justified "the search of every part of the vehicle and its contents that may conceal the object of the search."

Yet *Ross* also expressly reaffirmed the result in *Sanders,* thus creating what some called the "Ross anomaly." That is, where probable cause existed to search only a container which happened to be in an automobile (as in *Sanders*), a warrant was necessary to open the container. Yet no warrant would be needed to open a container police discovered during a warrantless search of an entire vehicle, provided the vehicle itself was the object of the search.

**California v. Acevedo** (1991) resolved the Ross anomaly in favor of law enforcement interests. In so doing, however, it may have created its own anomaly: A container located in a motor vehicle may now be subject to a warrantless search; the same container carried by a suspect walking along the sidewalk ordinarily is not.

*Wyoming* v. *Houghton* (1999) demonstrates the extent of the automobile exception. Sandra Houghton was a passenger in a car that police stopped for an equipment violation. The officer saw a hypodermic syringe in the driver's shirt pocket, and when asked, the driver acknowledged that he used the syringe to inject illegal drugs. This admission furnished probable cause to search the vehicle for contraband, and everyone was ordered to get out of the car. The police found Houghton's purse on the back seat. A search of the purse turned up drugs and paraphernalia. The state supreme court ruled that the search of the purse violated the Fourth Amendment because the officer knew, or should have known, that it did not belong to the driver and because nothing he had observed suggested that the driver had placed drugs in the purse. The U.S. Supreme Court disagreed. Once probable cause is present, the factor determining the scope of the search is whether a container could hold the object of the search, not the ownership of the container.

(3) *Consent.* A warrant is not required when an individual consents to a search. Nor are police required to inform suspects that they have a right to refuse consent. Rather, reviewing courts are to conclude from the circumstances of a particular situation whether a "reasonable person" would understand that she or he is free to refuse to submit to a search. Consider the facts in *United States* v. *Drayton* (2002) that involved suspicionless searches of two passengers on a bus in Florida. One of three police officers who boarded the bus asked the two to identify their luggage, and they consented to a search of their bag. When the officer asked, "Do you mind if I check your person?" the first passenger replied "Sure" and opened his jacket and positioned himself in a manner that would facilitate the search. Packets of the kind used to transport cocaine were found, and the first passenger was led from the bus. Then the officer asked the second passenger, "Mind if I check you?" He consented, and similar packets were found. For six justices, both searches were reasonable under the Fourth Amendment.

**ELECTRONIC SURVEILLANCE.** Development of electronic means of surveillance in the twentieth century presented the Court with new questions concerning possible violations of the Fourth Amendment. In ***Olmstead*** **v. *United States*** (1928), a sharply divided Court held that wiretapping did not violate the Fourth Amendment guaranty against unreasonable searches and seizures because there was no search: no seizure of papers, tangible material effects, or actual physical invasion of the house. Electronic surveillance by police at all levels continued for nearly 40 years without close federal judicial supervision. Only on the infrequent occasions when defense counsel learned of an official physical trespass on the property subject to the wiretap or eavesdrop was the Court prepared to find a Fourth Amendment violation (*Silverman* v. *United States,* 1961).

For different reasons both civil libertarians and law enforcement agents welcomed ***Katz*** **v. *United States*** (1967), which expressly overruled *Olmstead.* The Court's emphasis now was not on whether a physical trespass had occurred (there was none in *Katz*) but whether the surveillance invaded one's "expectation of privacy." The "Fourth Amendment protects people, not places," declared Justice Stewart. But the individual's expectation must also be one society is prepared to acknowledge as a reasonable expectation. Moreover, for the first time the majority made it plain that Congress could establish constitutionally correct standards governing electronic surveillance with a warrant. The Court was willing to exchange legitimacy for controls.

In the wake of *Katz,* federal communications law today features a three-tiered system that tries to balance law enforcement needs and confidentiality. For some serious offenses, Title III of the 1968 Omnibus Crime Control and Safe Streets Act established an elaborate warrant process for electronic surveillance. (As explained further in Chapter Fifteen, the **Patriot Act** of 2001 added terrorism and some computer crimes to Title III's list of predicate offenses.) For covered offenses, and no others, a Title III warrant, or its state counterpart, may authorize eavesdropping on telephone conversations, face-to-face conversations, or computer and other forms of electronic communication. This is the most stringent level of protection. On a lower tier, with respect to *any* criminal offense, federal law allows warrant-based access to telephone records, email held in third-party storage, and (after the Patriot Act) stored voice mail. Still more relaxed procedures apply to the government's use of trap-and-trace devices and pen registers that capture the source and destination of telephone calls (but not their contents). Those can be put in place on the government's certification alone, rather than the probable cause finding of a court, that the information will be relevant to a criminal investigation.

The 1968 act, however, by no means resolved all constitutional questions. One provision of the law arguably exempted national security electronic surveillance from the warrant requirement, when done on the authority of the president. In a highly significant interpretation of the act in 1972, ***United States*** **v. *United States District Court*** rejected that construction of the law.

The 1968 statute continues to play an important role in crime fighting, especially narcotics and racketeering offenses. As of early 2004, 44 states (seven more than in 1993) and the District of Columbia, in addition to the federal government, had legislatively authorized electronic surveillance. Judges issued 497 federal and 861 state orders in 2002 (the most recent year for which data are available)—the total being 48 percent greater than reported in 1992—approving various kinds of intercepts. Indeed, only one intercept application was refused. Intercepts typically cast big nets: Each surveillance order in 2002 resulted on average in the interception of 1,708 communications (of which 403 were incriminating) by 92 individuals. The average length of each initial period of interception was 29 days, with an average of

29 days for the 889 extensions. Some 96 percent of all intercepts authorized by state judges occurred in New York, New Jersey, California, Pennsylvania, Maryland, Florida, and Illinois. The greater limitation on the use of electronic surveillance may be fiscal, not legal; the average cost to law enforcement budgets of each intercept in 2002 was $54,586.

Congressional action to legitimize electronic surveillance in national security matters came in the **Foreign Intelligence Surveillance Act** of 1978. The statute established two special courts. The **Foreign Intelligence Surveillance Court** consists (since 2001) of eleven sitting U.S. district judges who are chosen for the FISC by the chief justice. It hears requests by the executive branch for warrants to conduct secret physical searches and electronic surveillance of "U.S. persons" believed to be working on behalf of a foreign power, a "foreign power," or an "agent of a foreign power." During 2002, the FISC approved a record 1,228 applications for secret wiretaps and other searches of suspected terrorists and spies, nearly 300 more than in 2001. One explanation for the sharp jump is the Patriot Act, which allows the FBI to conduct FISA searches when foreign intelligence gathering is now only "a significant purpose," not "the purpose," for the surveillance.

The second special court is the **Foreign Intelligence Court of Review,** which consists of three sitting U.S. district or appeals judges who are also appointed by the chief justice. It hears appeals from decisions by the FISC. As of early 2004, there had been only one: a successful appeal by the Justice Department to overturn the FISC's restricted interpretation of the FISA in a terrorism related matter (In re *Sealed Case No. 02–001,* 2002).

**ARRESTS, OTHER DETENTIONS, AND FRISKS.** Police may make felony arrests in public places without warrants where probable cause exists (*United States* v. *Watson,* 1976), but arrest warrants are required when police make felony arrests in a private residence (*Payton* v. *New York,* 1980) in the absence of exigent circumstances. Moreover, in serving an arrest or search warrant, the Fourth Amendment incorporates the common-law requirement that police knock on a dwelling's door and announce their identity and purpose before attempting a **forced entry.** This rule gives way only when the totality of circumstances suggests that there is a threat of physical violence or that evidence will probably be destroyed if advance notice is given (*Richards* v. *Wisconsin,* 1997; *United States* v. *Banks,* 2003). For less serious crimes such as misdemeanors and summary offenses, police ordinarily may arrest without a warrant only when the criminal behavior occurs in their presence. Even then, the Fourth Amendment gives police wide latitude in deciding whether to take an offender into custody, as ***Atwater* v. *City of Lago Vista*** illustrates.

For many years police stopped persons behaving suspiciously and, to protect themselves, patted down (frisked) those who might be armed. Civil libertarians criticized the **frisk** because police normally lacked probable cause for an arrest; the law simply had no provision for a detention less restrictive than arrest. Critics also claimed that stopping, questioning, and frisking for weapons was a police tactic too often directed toward minority groups. ***Terry* v. *Obio*** (1968) presented the Court with a situation in which a police officer confronted suspicious persons and, while frisking one of them, found a weapon. This of course was no search incident to arrest, because no one had been arrested before the frisk. Had the officer acted in accord with the Fourth Amendment? Admitting that probable cause was absent, the Court upheld the search based on a lesser degree of certainty called **reasonable suspicion.**

Not surprisingly, it remains uncertain what combination of facts will satisfy the Court that a legitimate stop and limited search under *Terry* have occurred. For example, the Court ruled admissible the fruits of a frisk that occurred after officers observed an individual in a high-crime area who fled from them without apparent provocation (*Illinois* v. *Wardlow,* 2000). In the same term, however, the Court disallowed evidence seized in a frisk after police received a tip from an anonymous caller that a young black male standing at a particular bus stop and wearing a plaid shirt was carrying a gun. When police arrived at the bus stop, they saw three black males, one of whom was wearing a plaid shirt. Apart from the tip, the officers had no reason to suspect any of the three of illegal conduct. One of the officers frisked the young man in the plaid shirt and seized a gun from his pocket (*Florida* v. *J.L.,* 2000). In the Court's view, the tip failed to provide the reasonable suspicion dictated by *Terry.*

Police may make some stops even when there is no suspicion at all. *Michigan Department of State Police* v. *Sitz* (1990) approved the use of sobriety checkpoints along highways at which police stop and briefly detain all motorists to look for signs of intoxication. However, vehicle checkpoints operated by police who deployed a narcotics-detection dog to sniff the exterior of stopped vehicles violate the Fourth Amendment (*Indianapolis* v. *Edmond,* 2000). In the Courts's view, the sobriety checkpoints upheld in 1990 were closely related to roadway safety, but the narcotics checkpoints were designed primarily to detect evidence of ordinary criminal activity. The latter would require an individualized suspicion that was absent.

**ADMINISTRATIVE SEARCHES.** Searches by public officials for reasons other than enforcing the criminal law, usually termed **administrative searches,** benefit from a relaxed Fourth Amendment standard. Health and safety inspections of homes and most businesses, for example, require an administrative warrant if the occupant refuses entry, not a criminal warrant. The former does not have to have the particularity of the latter, nor does there need to be evidence of a violation. Rather, a reasonable plan of enforcement authorized by statute suffices so long as the state's objective is some **special need** other than enforcement of the criminal law (*Camara* v. *Municipal Court,* 1967). Particularly where the risk to public safety is substantial, even blanket suspicionless searches, such as those that routinely occur in airports and at the entrances of public buildings, may be deemed equally "reasonable."

Such reasoning led the Court to uphold, against Fourth Amendment challenges, tests of blood and urine samples to detect use of illegal drugs among certain classes of employees on the railroads and in the Customs Service (*Skinner* v. *Railway Labor Executives' Association* and *Treasury Employees Union* v. *Von Raab,* 1989). In neither scheme was the testing necessarily triggered by particularized or individualized suspicion, which is normally the requisite for any valid search of the person, even for a frisk. The "special need" served in the first case was public safety; the need served in the second was promotion of public confidence in a drug-free workforce. The vote in the railroad case was 7–2, and in the Customs case 5–4, suggesting that widespread legally mandated drug testing might not be approved.

Nonetheless, six justices approved a school district policy in 1995 that subjected interscholastic athletes to random, suspicionless drug testing. "[S]pecial needs beyond the normal need for law enforcement," noted Justice Scalia, "make the warrant and probable cause requirement impracticable." Along with the addictive effects of drugs among young people generally, drug use by athletes poses a higher risk of harm to the user, and student athletes are frequently "role models" for their peers. Besides, school students have a reduced expectation of privacy, he observed, with student athletes having even less. "School sports are not for the bashful." There is "an element of 'communal undress' inherent in athletic participation" (*Vernonia School District* v. *Acton*). Presumably important in *Acton* were the facts that the school district faced rampant drug use among its students and that drug use by athletes posed health risks to themselves and to others.

That emphasis might explain *Chandler* v. *Miller* two years later, when an all but unanimous bench declared that what was acceptable for student athletes and railroad and customs workers was unacceptable for political candidates. Georgia violated the Fourth Amendment when it stipulated that candidates for designated state offices (including judgeships) test negative for various illegal drugs after submitting to urinalysis. Absent was convincing evidence of a "special need," explained Justice Ginsburg. "However well-meant, the . . . test . . . diminishes personal privacy for a symbol's sake." *Chandler* appears to reject the "symbolism" or "public image" rationale as sole justification for warrantless, suspicionless drug testing. Yet the Court still seems tolerant of suspicionless drug testing in public schools. **Board of Education v. Earls** (2002) upheld random drug testing even when those eligible for testing included participants in *any* competitive extracurricular activity, athletic or not, and in a school district without a serious drug problem.

## RIGHT TO COUNSEL

Legal representation may well be "a right by which virtually all other rights are protected in practice." As William M. Beaney explained, "whenever the judicial process unfolds, whether against the unlicensed orator in a public park, the protagonist of unpopular religious beliefs, or the citizen accused of assault or murder, the trial and its result give us in practice whatever meaning the rule of law possesses." That reality explains the assurance in the **Sixth Amendment** that in "all criminal prosecutions, the accused shall enjoy the right . . . to have the Assistance of Counsel for his defence."

Historically the Sixth Amendment meant that the government could not deny a person the opportunity to retain counsel. But was there also a constitutional obligation to provide counsel for an accused person who could not afford a lawyer? **Powell v. Alabama** (1932) partially answered that question in the affirmative: Where indigent, young, inexperienced, and illiterate defendants were on trial for their lives, states were constitutionally required to furnish counsel for them. Six years later *Johnson* v. *Zerbst* construed the Sixth Amendment so that *every* defendant in federal criminal trials was to be offered counsel, at the government's expense if necessary. Yet the same rule was not mandated for defendants in state courts. In an example of the double standard at work (see Chapter Nine), *Betts* v. *Brady* (1942) dictated appointment of counsel in state courts only where the totality of circumstances made it necessary for a fair trial.

This rule, which resulted in a requirement of counsel in some, but not most, state noncapital cases, was overturned by **Gideon v. Wainwright** (1963), which imposed the prevailing federal rule on state procedures. Accordingly, indigents were entitled to government-provided counsel in all felony prosecutions. Justice Black's opinion sought to give the impression that *Betts* had broken with its own precedents. To one who reexamines *Powell* v. *Alabama* and subsequent decisions, however, Black's reasoning may seem contrived. Yet Black was correct in stating, "The right of one charged with crime to counsel may not be deemed fundamental and essential to fair trials in some countries, but it is in ours."

For counsel at trial, the Burger Court broadened the Gideon rule to include petty offenses, when confinement for any period is part of the sentence. The trial judge's decision to appoint counsel thus affects the sentence imposed later if the defendant is found guilty (*Scott* v. *Illinois,* 1979, clarifying *Argersinger* v. *Hamlin,* 1972). This extension of *Gideon* was significant: In the early 1970s one study found that 75 percent of people accused of these less serious crimes were legally unrepresented. Nevertheless, a defendant has a constitutional right to refuse counsel if the choice is made voluntarily and intelligently (*Faretta* v. *California,* 1975).

Right to counsel is now pervasive throughout the criminal justice process during and following the stage at which formal charges are brought. For instance, counsel must be provided for indigents:

- For the arraignment (*Hamilton* v. *Alabama,* 1961) [Assertion of right to counsel at the **arraignment**—the judicial proceeding at which defendants are formally charged and at which they plead guilty or not guilty—creates an absolute bar to police-initiated questioning without counsel (*Michigan* v. *Jackson,* 1986), but because the right to counsel is "offense specific," that bar does not necessarily extend to offenses that are factually related to those for which the accused has already been arraigned (*Texas* v. *Cobb,* 2001].
- On an appeal by right, not where the appeal is discretionary (*Douglas* v. *California,* 1963; *Pennsylvania* v. *Finley,* 1987).
- While in custody [A defendant's damaging statements overheard by a paid informer are inadmissible at trial (*Massiah* v. *United States,* 1964), as are statements coached by police outside the lawyer's presence (*Brewer* v. *Williams,* 1977)].
- At police lineups, to avoid faulty identification (*United States* v. *Wade,* 1967) [but not including informal identification that occurs prior to initiation of criminal prosecution (*Kirby* v. *Illinois,* 1972)].
- At some probation revocation proceedings (*Gagnon* v. *Scarpelli,* 1973)
- Under sentence of death when they seek federal habeas corpus relief (*McFarland* v. *Scott,* 1994).

Both at trial and on direct appeal, the Court has clarified the Sixth Amendment to require *effective* assistance of counsel (*Strickland* v. *Washington,* 1984). The justices have concluded that a right to assistance of counsel means little if that right does not include effective assistance. But showing ineffective assistance is not easy. What is mandated is not an error-free defense. Rather, one must demonstrate that, but for counsel's mistakes, the result of the proceeding would have been different and that the overall fairness and reliability of the trial were deficient (*Lockhart* v. *Fretwell,* 1993).

## SELF-INCRIMINATION

Assurance in the **Fifth Amendment** that "no person . . . shall be compelled in any criminal case to be a witness against himself" is a right "hard-earned by our forefathers," said Chief Justice Warren. The reasons "for its inclusion in the Constitution—and the necessities for its preservation—are to be found in the lessons of history." The right is a central feature of a system of criminal justice that presumes innocence—that is, which places the burden of proof on the prosecution to establish guilt. No one accused of a crime should have to assist the state in proving its case. Along with other provisions in the Bill of Rights, the protection against self-incrimination stands for the proposition that determining guilt and innocence by fair procedures is as important as punishing the guilty.

The extent of this safeguard has nonetheless presented the Supreme Court with hard questions. How far should the needs of law enforcement be accommodated, and how much freedom should be accorded the individual?

**IMMUNITY.** One may claim Fifth Amendment protection in refusing to testify before a grand jury, trial jury, or legislative committee or in being compelled to produce papers or other evidence (*Counselman* v. *Hitchcock,* 1892; *Quinn* v. *United States,* 1955). Yet the Court has allowed Congress to grant immunity from prosecution to extract testimony from reluctant witnesses, an especially useful technique in investigations of organized crime. "Immunity displaces the danger. Once the reason for the privilege ceases, the privilege ceases," reasoned Justice Frankfurter in *Ullman* v. *United States* (1956). The Immunity Act of 1954 challenged in *Ullman* provided for complete (or "transactional") immunity from both state and federal prosecution in exchange for testimony about various criminal activities. But the Organized Crime Control Act of 1970 permits a federal court, agency, or congressional committee to offer "use and derivative use," as opposed to **transactional immunity** in exchange for compelled testimony. The former is less generous to the witness than the latter because under **use immunity** the witness can still be prosecuted for crimes about which the witness has testified. The limitation on the government is that the prosecutor may not later use this testimony against the witness. Five justices found even this arrangement harmonious with the Fifth Amendment in *Kastigar* v. *United States* (1972).

**INTERROGATIONS.** Police interrogation of suspects raises obvious due process and Fifth Amendment questions. For decades the rule in federal trials was that only voluntary confessions were admissible. The presumption "that one who is innocent will not imperil his safety . . . by an untrue statement," reasoned the first Justice Harlan well over a century ago, ended when hopes or threats deprived the accused "of that freedom of will or self-control essential to make his confessional voluntary" (*Hopt* v. *Utah,* 1884). Moreover, beginning with *Brown* v. *Mississippi* (1936), the Court applied a similar standard against the use of coerced confessions in state courts. In that case, a unanimous bench reversed three murder convictions marked by what Chief Justice Hughes called "compulsion by torture to extort a confession. . . . It would be difficult to conceive of methods more revolting to the sense of justice than those taken to procure the confessions of these petitioners, and the use of the confessions thus obtained as the basis for conviction and sentence was a clear denial of due process."

Some justices later wondered whether interrogations could be anything but threatening and intimidating, even in the absence of threats or use of force, if the accused was denied the right to have a lawyer present. Thus, in *Escobedo* v. *Illinois* (1964), the Court condemned the police practice of preventing a suspect from consulting with a lawyer until the interrogation had ended. This and numerous other cases over the previous three decades had made the Court aware of a variety of law enforcement practices that seemed unfair to accused persons, many of whom were young, ignorant, and members of minority groups. The Court inched toward what Herbert Packer termed the due process model of criminal justice (which stressed fairness and the rights of the accused), in contrast to the older crime control model (which stressed the powers of the prosecution). In ***Miranda* v. *Arizona*** (1966), the Court held 5 to 4 that federal and state officials must give suspects specified warnings or equivalent advice before beginning to interrogate them about alleged crimes. Many police departments have printed the now familiar **Miranda warnings** on cards from which the arresting and/or interrogating officer reads:

> You have the right to remain silent and refuse to answer any questions. Anything you say may be used against you in a court of law.
>
> As we discuss this matter, you have a right to stop answering my questions at any time you desire.
>
> You have a right to a lawyer before speaking to me, to remain silent until you can talk to him/her, and to have him/her present when you are being questioned.
>
> If you want a lawyer but cannot afford one, one will be provided to you at no cost.
>
> Do you understand each of these rights I have explained to you?
>
> Now that I have advised you of your rights, are you willing to answer my questions without an attorney present?

Without such warnings, statements made are inadmissible at trial. The Warren Court's view was that the privilege against self-incrimination could be secured in no other way. Joined were the Sixth Amendment's provisions for right to counsel and the Fifth Amendment's guard against self-incrimination. The belief was that events occurring in the station house greatly influence the outcome of events in the courthouse.

For law enforcement, *Miranda* at first seemed a disaster. But statements made by suspects outside the presence of an attorney may still be introduced as evidence, provided they waived their right to silence "voluntarily, knowingly, and intelligently." Legal challenges to such statements typically turn on whether (1) the suspect has validly waived the Miranda rights, thus agreeing to answer questions, or (2) a Miranda-type "interrogation" has occurred.

The need to answer Miranda-related questions accounted for more than 60 decisions in the Supreme Court between 1966 and 2003. Generally the justices have been hesitant to extend the ruling, and several cases have restricted its scope. For instance,

- Statements, inadmissible as direct testimony because of a Miranda violation, may be used to attack credibility of statements the accused makes on the witness stand (*Harris* v. *New York,* 1971).
- Assertion of right to counsel in the interrogation is an absolute bar to subsequent uncounseled, police-initiated questioning (*Edwards* v. *Arizona,* 1981).
- Questioning that occurs before arrest for a traffic offense does not amount to "custodial interrogation" within *Miranda's* reach (*Berkemer* v. *McCarty,* 1984).
- Off-hand comment by one police offer to another in the presence of a thrice-warned suspect, who had asked to speak to an attorney, that prompts an incriminating statement is not an interrogation (*Rhode Island* v. *Innis,* 1980).
- Public safety allows police to ask a suspect the whereabouts of a gun before administering a Miranda warning (*New York* v. *Quarles,* 1984).
- Incriminating, but unwarned, statements do not necessarily taint later incriminating, and warned, statements (*Oregon* v. *Elstad,* 1985).

**MIRANDA REVISITED.** In 2000, delayed application of a provision in a 32-year-old law reopened matters the Court had presumably settled in *Miranda*.

Anti-Miranda sentiment in Congress led to inclusion of Section 3501 in the Omnibus Crime Control and Safe Streets Act of 1968. This section attempted to overrule *Miranda* by substituting the pre-Miranda standard of voluntariness in place of *Miranda's* specific warnings. In federal prosecutions, confessions that the trial judge deemed voluntary on the basis of the totality of circumstances would be admissible, even if the Miranda warnings had not been administered. At the insistence of a succession of U.S. attorneys general, Section 3501 lay lifeless until 1997, when the Court of Appeals for the Fourth Circuit held that incriminating but unwarned statements by Charles Dickerson in a bank robbery investigation were admissible because they had been voluntarily rendered. If, as the Fourth Circuit held, the Miranda rules were merely judicially crafted rules of evidence, then Congress, as lawmaker in chief, was free to change those rules. On the other hand, if the Miranda rules were constitutionally grounded, as both Dickerson and the U.S. solicitor general insisted, then Congress was without authority to set aside by statute a regimen that the Constitution required. Even in the latter instance, the Court could decide that *Miranda* had been wrongly decided—that adherence to the litany of warnings was not constitutionally mandated. If so, the pre-Miranda voluntariness standard would be constitutionally sufficient. The outcome in **Dickerson v. United States** was ironic. Not only did *Miranda* survive (and Section 3501 succumb) by a 7 to 2 vote (thus exceeding *Miranda's* original majority of five), but it was reaffirmed by a bench more ideologically conservative than the bench that had decided *Miranda* in 1966. Moreover, the majority opinion in *Dickerson* was authored by Chief Justice Rehnquist, initially named to the Court in 1971 by President Richard Nixon, who fashioned his campaign for the White House in 1968 in part by attacking *Miranda*.

## PUNISHMENT

"Excessive bail shall not be required, nor excessive fines imposed, nor cruel and unusual punishments inflicted," declares the **Eighth Amendment.** Similar to language in the English Bill of Rights of 1689, these three clauses are the only express limitations in the Constitution on the severity of punishments in criminal cases, and of these, it has been the ban on "cruel and unusual punishments" that has generated the most litigation in the Supreme Court.

    **CAPITAL PUNISHMENT.** In *Furman* v. *Georgia* (1972), the Supreme Court imposed a moratorium on executions in the United States when it ruled 5 to 4 that the death penalty, as then administered, was cruel and unusual in violation of the Eighth Amendment. Too much discretion in the hands of trial judges and juries made application of the death sentence capricious. Thirty-five states and Congress promptly reinstated capital punishment with more carefully drawn statutes to meet the Court's objections. In **Gregg v. Georgia** (1976), a majority of the bench concluded that the death penalty was not inherently cruel and unusual and upheld a two-step sentencing scheme designed to set strict standards for trial courts. A jury would first decide the question of guilt and then in a separate proceeding impose punishment. Executions could resume, and they did.

    As of January 2004, more than 3,500 convicted felons were under sentence of death, yet since 1976 only 885 persons had been executed (more than a third of them in Texas alone) in the 38 states that now have the death penalty and by the U.S. government. (The U.S. military may also impose the death penalty for crimes committed by persons in the armed forces.) One reason for this discrepancy between the number of prisoners on death row and the number of executions is that the Court, although approving capital punishment in principle, has raised substantial obstacles to carrying it out. Some of the conditions that have led to an invalidation of a death sentence include:

- Complete removal of trial court discretion by making capital punishment mandatory (*Woodson* v. *North Carolina,* 1976).
- Failure to allow the introduction of any mitigating circumstances (*Roberts* v. *Louisiana,* 1977).
- Death penalty imposed for rape (*Coker* v. *Georgia,* 1977).
- Onset of insanity while condemned prisoner is awaiting execution (*Ford* v. *Wainwright,* 1986).
- Death sentence for person younger than 16 where there is no statute explicitly providing for execution of juveniles (*Stanford* v. *Kentucky,* 1989).
- The presence of jurors who would vote for the death penalty regardless of any evidence in mitigation (*Morgan* v. *Illinois,* 1992). This decision mirrors *Witherspoon* v. *Illinois* (1968), which bars imposition of the death penalty by a jury from which persons with scruples against capital punishment are excluded.
- Failure to inform the jury that a life sentence carried no possibility of parole (*Shafter* v. *South Carolina,* 2001).
- A convicted murderer who is mentally retarded (**Atkins v. Virginia,** 2002).
- Where the law requires a judge, not the jury, to assess the factors that result in a death sentence, following a conviction for murder (*Ring* v. *Arizona,* 2002).

Since *Gregg,* a consensus has emerged on the Court that capital sentencing must be both individualized and predictable. This means leaving controlled discretion in the sentencer's hand. Too much discretion opens the door to caprice and discrimination that so worried the Court in *Furman;* too little discretion denies fairness to the defendant by closing off consideration of mitigating factors. The Court would like to believe that the procedures it has approved rationally distinguish between those murderers who should receive life sentences and those who should be put to death. Neither the value of fairness nor the value of rationality, however, can be fully realized without danger to the other, and the justices do not always agree among themselves how the balance between the two should be struck in particular cases.

In contrast to procedural attacks on death sentences that the Court faces every term, *McCleskey* v. *Kemp* (1987) remains the only significant frontal assault on capital punishment since *Gregg.* A statistical study by David Baldus and others showed that in Georgia, during the 1970s, killers of whites were 4.3 times more likely to receive the death penalty than killers of blacks. Although statistics had been sufficient to establish discrimination in jury selection and employment, five justices were unpersuaded by the numbers in this context. The study did not prove that race had been a factor in McCleskey's case. Because each capital jury is unique, explained Justice Powell, and because "discretion is essential to the criminal justice process, we would demand exceptionally clear proof before we would infer that the discretion has been abused."

Looking beyond the role of race in capital sentencing, a study directed by James S. Liebman at Columbia University Law School in 2000 depicted a death penalty system that appears to be replete with error at the trial level. Examining nearly 5,500 judicial decisions between 1973 and 1995, the study made some startling findings: (1) Reversals occurred in 68 percent of capital cases whose appeals were completed during the specified time period. (2) Of those whose death sentences were overturned, 82 percent were given a sentence less than death after the errors were corrected on retrial; 7 percent were found not guilty. (3) High error rates occurred across the country, with 90 percent of states that meted out death sentences having overall error rates of 52 percent or higher.

**FEDERAL HABEAS CORPUS.** Federal courts may review death sentences (as well as convictions for noncapital crimes) imposed by state courts through a congressionally authorized procedure called **habeas corpus** (Latin for "you have the body"). These proceedings ordinarily begin once a prisoner's sentence becomes final—that is, once prisoners have exhausted their direct appeals in state courts and perhaps have been denied review by the U.S. Supreme Court. Under the standard the Court announced in 1963, these collateral attacks on convictions could encompass not only issues already considered by the state courts but "new" issues as well, unless the defendant had "deliberately bypassed" them on direct appeal (*Fay* v. *Noia*). The result has been to keep some cases in the courts for years, not by enlarging the scope of a defendant's constitutional rights but by increasing the defendant's opportunities to convince a judge that a constitutional violation had occurred. Not surprisingly, prisoners on death row have relied heavily on habeas corpus; indeed, as many as two-thirds of all death sentences since 1976 have been set aside in this way.

In the Antiterrorism and Effective Death Penalty Act of 1996, Congress made it more difficult for federal courts to entertain claims from state courts on collateral review. Upheld by the Supreme Court only two months after its enactment (*Felker* v. *Turpin*), the statute erects special hurdles for a state prisoner seeking relief through a second or successive (a claim already rebuffed by one federal court and raised again) petition for habeas corpus in federal court. First, the act directs dismissal of any claim raised in a prior petition by the same petitioner. Second, a claim presented for the first time in a second petition must be dismissed unless the petitioner meets one of two conditions: (a) that the claim relies on a new rule of constitutional law that the Supreme Court has made retroactive to cases on collateral review; or (b) that the factual basis for the claim could not have been discovered previously and that, with the newly acquired information, no reasonable fact finder would have found the petitioner guilty. Third, before seeking relief in a district court, the petitioner must request permission to do so from the proper court of appeals. This court authorizes the petition only if it meets the standards set out above. Finally, the law provides that the appeals court's determination "shall not be and shall not be the subject of . . . a writ of certiorari" to the Supreme Court.

**NONCAPITAL SENTENCING.** Only recently has the Court appeared willing to scrutinize noncapital sentences that might violate the Eighth Amendment because they are excessive. True, the Court in 1910 (*Weems* v. *United States*) struck down as excessive a sentence of a Philippine court which entailed, among other penalties, 12 years of imprisonment at hard labor, while chained day and night at the wrists and ankles. And in 1962 (*Robinson* v. *California*) the Court found "excessive" a 90-day jail term for the crime of being "addicted to the use of narcotics." But a bare majority in *Rummel* v. *Estelle* (1980) refused to become involved in proportionality review of various lengths of prison terms. At issue was application of the Texas recidivist statute under which Rummel was sentenced to life imprisonment after conviction for his third felony for defrauding others. The total amount in question from Rummel's three run-ins with the law was about $230.

In 1983 an equally bare majority in *Solem* v. *Helm* "distinguished" *Rummel*. While stressing that successful challenges to the proportionality of particular sentences would be rare, Justice Powell declared, "[W]e hold as a matter of principle that a criminal sentence must be proportionate to the crime for which the defendant has been convicted. . . . [N]o penalty is per se constitutional. . . . [A] court's proportionality analysis under the Eighth Amendment should be guided by objective criteria, including (i) the gravity of the offense and the harshness of the penalty; (ii) the sentences imposed on other criminals in the same jurisdiction; and (iii) the sentences imposed for commission of the same crime in other jurisdictions."

Successful challenges will be rare indeed. In *Harmelin* v. *Michigan* (1991), five justices rejected a Solem-based attack on the state's drug sentencing statute (the toughest in the nation), which mandated life imprisonment, without possibility of parole, for possession of more than 650 grams of a substance containing cocaine. The law allowed for no mitigating circumstances (such as the potency of the substance or being a first offender), nor did it take drug purity into account. Harmelin had been caught with 672 grams (1 1/2 pounds) during a routine arrest after he ran a red light. The case demonstrates how disagreement flows from the level of generality employed. Some justices asked whether life in prison without parole is cruel and unusual. The dissenters posed a different question: Is life in prison without parole cruel and unusual punishment in *this* case? A similar outcome followed in *Ewing* v. *California* (2003), where five justices found no constitutional objection to a sentence of 25 years to life, under the state's "three strikes" law, for felony theft of three golf clubs valued at $399 each.

Thus, in the Court's view the Eighth Amendment imposes a far greater restraint in capital, in contrast to noncapital, cases. For the latter category and short of the macabre, *Harmelin* and *Ewing* hand legislators apparently boundless discretion.

## KEY TERMS

Fourth Amendment
writs of assistance
probable cause
warrant
exclusionary rule
Patriot Act
Foreign Intelligence
   Surveillance Act
Foreign Intelligence
   Surveillance Court

Foreign Intelligence
   Court of Review
forced entry
frisk
reasonable suspicion
administrative searches
special need
Sixth Amendment

arraignment
Fifth Amendment
transactional immunity
use immunity
Miranda warnings
Eighth Amendment
habeas corpus

## QUERIES

**1.** Why did *Mapp* v. *Ohio* guarantee an increased number of Fourth Amendment cases on the Supreme Court's docket?

**2.** Why should the police have to abide by Marquis of Queensbury rules all the while criminals are acting like thugs?

**3.** In their opposing opinions in *Chimel* v. *California,* Justices Stewart and White agree that the police need probable cause to search the house. They part company, however, over the need for a search warrant. What added protection, if any, does a search warrant provide in such situations for someone suspected of a crime?

**4.** What accounts for the Rehnquist Court's embrace of the Miranda doctrine in *Dickerson* v. *United States?*

## SELECTED READINGS

BALDUS, DAVID C., et al. "Comparative Review of Death Sentences: An Empirical Study of the Georgia Experience," 74 *Journal of Criminal Law and Criminology* 661 (1983).

BEANEY, WILLIAM M. *The Right to Counsel in American Courts.* Ann Arbor: University of Michigan Press, 1955.

BODENHAMER, DAVID J. *Fair Trial: Rights of the Accused in American History.* New York: Oxford University Press, 1992.

HELMHOLZ, R. H., et al. *The Privilege Against Self-Incrimination: Its Origins and Development.* Chicago: University of Chicago Press, 1997.

LIEBMAN, JAMES, et al. "Capital Attrition: Error Rates in Capital Cases, 1973–1995," 78 *Texas Law Review* 1839 (2000).

LAFAVE, WAYNE R. *A Treatise on the Fourth Amendment,* 3d ed., 4 vols. St. Paul, Minn.: West, 1995.

LEWIS, ANTHONY. *Gideon's Trumpet.* New York: Random House. 1964.

MELUSKY, JOSEPH A., and KEITH A. PESTO. *Cruel and Unusual Punishment.* Santa Barbara, Calif.: ABC-CLIO, 2003.

STEPHENSON, D. GRIER, JR., "Justice Blackmun's Eighth Amendment Pilgrimage," 8 *BYU Journal of Public Law* 271 (1994).

# I. SEARCHES AND SEIZURES

## A. WHOSE RIGHTS?

### *Minnesota* v. *Carter*
### 525 U.S. 83, 119 S.Ct. 469, 142 L.Ed. 2d 373 (1998)
### http://laws.findlaw.com/us/525/83.html

After receiving a tip from an informer, a police officer in Eagan, Minnesota, looked in a ground-level apartment window through a gap in the closed blind and observed Wayne Carter and Melvin Johns bagging cocaine with Kimberly Thompson, the lessee of the apartment. Carter and Johns were arrested after they left the apartment. At trial, they moved to suppress the evidence, arguing that the officer's initial observation was an unreasonable search in violation of the Fourth Amendment. The trial court held that since they were not overnight social guests, they were not entitled to Fourth Amendment protection, and that the officer's observation was not a "search." The state court of appeals held that Carter did not have standing to object to the officer's actions because he used the apartment for a business purpose—to package drugs—and, separately, affirmed Johns's conviction without addressing the standing issue. In reversing, the state supreme court held that (1) Carter and Johns could claim Fourth Amendment protection because they had a legitimate expectation of privacy in the invaded place, and (2) the officer's warrantless observation constituted an unreasonable search. (Thompson was not a party to this appeal.) Majority: Rehnquist, O'Connor, Scalia, Kennedy, Thomas, Breyer. Dissenting: Ginsburg, Stevens, Souter.

**CHIEF JUSTICE REHNQUIST delivered the opinion of the Court.**

Respondents and the lessee of an apartment were sitting in one of its rooms, bagging cocaine. While so engaged they were observed by a police officer, who looked through a drawn window blind. The Supreme Court of Minnesota held that the officer's viewing was a search which violated respondents' Fourth Amendment rights. We hold that no such violation occurred. . . .

The Amendment protects persons against unreasonable searches of "their persons [and] houses" and thus indicates that the Fourth Amendment is a personal right that must be invoked by an individual. . . . But the extent to which the Fourth Amendment protects people may depend upon where those people are. We have held that "capacity to claim the protection of the Fourth Amendment depends . . . upon whether the person who claims the protection of the Amendment has a legitimate expectation of privacy in the invaded place."

The text of the Amendment suggests that its protections extend only to people in "their" houses. But we have held that in some circumstances a person may have a legitimate expectation of privacy in the house of someone else. In *Minnesota* v. *Olson* (1990), for example, we decided that an overnight guest in a house had the sort of expectation of privacy that the Fourth Amendment protects. We said:

To hold that an overnight guest has a legitimate expectation of privacy in his host's home merely recognizes the every day expectations of privacy that we all share. Staying overnight in another's home is a long-standing social custom that serves functions recognized as valuable by society. We stay in others' homes when we travel to a strange city for business or pleasure, we visit our parents, children, or more distant relatives out of town, when we are in between jobs, or homes, or when we house-sit for a friend. . . .

From the overnight guest's perspective, he seeks shelter in another's home precisely because it provides him with privacy, a place where he and his possessions will not be disturbed by anyone but his host and those his host allows inside. We are at our most vulnerable when we are asleep because we cannot monitor our own safety or the security of our belongings. It is for this reason that, although we may spend all day in public places, when we cannot sleep in our own home we seek out another private place to sleep, whether it be a hotel room, or the home of a friend.

In *Jones* v. *United States* (1960), the defendant seeking to exclude evidence resulting from a search of an apartment had been given the use of the apartment by a friend. He had clothing in the apartment, had slept there "maybe a night," and at the time was the sole occupant of the apartment. But while the holding of *Jones*—that a search of the apartment violated the defendant's Fourth Amendment rights—is still valid, its statement that "anyone legitimately on the premises where a search occurs may challenge its legality," was expressly repudiated in *Rakas* v. *Illinois* (1978). Thus an overnight guest in a home may claim the protection of the Fourth Amendment, but one who is merely present with the consent of the householder may not.

Respondents here were obviously not overnight guests, but were essentially present for a business transaction and were only in the home a matter of hours. There is no suggestion that they had a previous relationship with Thompson, or that there was any other purpose to their visit. Nor was there anything similar to the overnight guest relationship in *Olson* to suggest a degree of acceptance into the household. While the apartment was a dwelling place for Thompson, it was for these respondents simply a place to do business. . . .

If we regard the overnight guest in *Olson* as typifying those who may claim the protection of the Fourth Amendment in the home of another, and one merely "legitimately on the

premises" as typifying those who may not do so, the present case is obviously somewhere in between. But the purely commercial nature of the transaction engaged in here, the relatively short period of time on the premises, and the lack of any previous connection between respondents and the householder, all lead us to conclude that respondents' situation is closer to that of one simply permitted on the premises. We therefore hold that any search which may have occurred did not violate their Fourth Amendment rights.

Because we conclude that respondents had no legitimate expectation of privacy in the apartment, we need not decide whether the police officer's observation constituted a "search." The judgment of the Supreme Court of Minnesota is accordingly reversed, and the cause is remanded for proceedings not inconsistent with this opinion.

JUSTICE SCALIA, with whom JUSTICE THOMAS joins, concurring . . . [omitted].

JUSTICE KENNEDY, concurring . . . [omitted].

### JUSTICE BREYER, concurring in the judgment. . . .

[Justice Breyer accepted Justice Ginsburg's conclusion that Carter and Johns enjoyed Fourth Amendment protection in the apartment, but concluded that the officer's peek through a gap in the window blinds did not amount to an unreasonable search under the Fourth Amendment.—ED.]

### JUSTICE GINSBURG, with whom JUSTICE STEVENS and JUSTICE SOUTER join, dissenting.

The Court's decision undermines not only the security of short-term guests, but also the security of the home resident herself. In my view, when a homeowner or lessor personally invites a guest into her home to share in a common endeavor, whether it be for conversation, to engage in leisure activities, or for business purposes licit or illicit, that guest should share his host's shelter against unreasonable searches and seizures. . . .

A homedweller places her own privacy at risk, the Court's approach indicates, when she opens her home to others, uncertain whether the duration of their stay, their purpose, and their "acceptance into the household" will earn protection. It remains textbook law that "[s]earches and seizures inside a home without a warrant are presumptively unreasonable absent exigent circumstances." The law in practice is less secure. Human frailty suggests that today's decision will tempt police to pry into private dwellings without warrant, to find evidence incriminating guests who do not rest there through the night. . . . As I see it, people are not genuinely "secure in their . . . houses . . . against unreasonable searches and seizures," if their invitations to others increase the risk of unwarranted governmental peering and prying into their dwelling places.

Through the host's invitation, the guest gains a reasonable expectation of privacy in the home. *Minnesota* v. *Olson* so held with respect to an overnight guest. The logic of that decision extends to shorter term guests as well. . . .

Our leading decision in *Katz* [v. *United States*] is key to my view of this case. There,

we ruled that the Government violated the petitioner's Fourth Amendment rights when it electronically recorded him transmitting wagering information while he was inside a public telephone booth. We were mindful that "the Fourth Amendment protects people, not places," and held that this electronic monitoring of a business call "violated the privacy upon which [the caller] justifiably relied while using the telephone booth." Our obligation to produce coherent results in this often visited area of the law requires us to inform our current expositions by benchmarks already established. . . .

The Court's decision in this case veers sharply from the path marked in *Katz*. I do not agree that we have a more reasonable expectation of privacy when we place a business call to a person's home from a public telephone booth on the side of the street, than when we actually enter that person's premises to engage in a common endeavor.

For the reasons stated, I dissent from the Court's judgment, and would retain judicial surveillance over the warrantless searches today's decision allows.

## B. THE EXCLUSIONARY RULE

### Mapp v. Ohio
### 367 U.S. 643, 81 S.Ct. 1684, 6 L.Ed. 2d 1081 (1961)
### http://laws.findlaw.com/us/367/643.html

Cleveland police officers, acting on information that a bombing-case suspect and betting equipment might be found in Dolores Mapp's house, forced their way in after being refused admission and, without a search warrant, subjected the house and its contents to a thorough search. In a basement trunk they found literature that provided the basis for her conviction for possessing obscene materials. The Ohio Supreme Court upheld the conviction. The brief filed on behalf of Mrs. Mapp in the U.S. Supreme Court argued that the statute criminalizing possession of obscene materials was unconstitutionally vague and that the high-handed behavior by the police amounted to a violation of due process of law but did not ask that the exclusionary rule be applied to state criminal proceedings. That point was raised, seemingly as an afterthought, by the American Civil Liberties Union in its amicus brief when it requested the Court to reexamine *Wolf* v. *Colorado* (1949). Majority: Clark, Black, Brennan, Douglas, Stewart, Warren. Dissenting: Harlan, Frankfurter, Whittaker.

**MR. JUSTICE CLARK delivered the opinion of the Court. . . .**

Today we once again examine *Wolf's* constitutional documentation of the right to privacy free from unreasonable state intrusion, and, after its dozen years on our books, are led by it to close the only courtroom door remaining open to evidence secured by official lawlessness in flagrant abuse of that basic right, reserved to all persons as a specific guarantee against that very same unlawful conduct. We hold that all evidence obtained by searches and seizures in violation of the Constitution is, by that same authority, inadmissible in a state court.

Since the Fourth Amendment's right of privacy has been declared enforceable against the States through the Due Process Clause of the Fourteenth, it is enforceable against them by the same sanction of exclusion as is used against the Federal Government. . . . [T]he admission of the new constitutional right by *Wolf* could not consistently tolerate denial of its most important constitutional privilege, namely, the exclusion of the evidence which an accused had been forced to give by reason of the unlawful seizure. To hold otherwise is to grant the right but in reality to withhold its privilege and enjoyment. . . .

Indeed, we are aware of no restraint, similar to that rejected today, conditioning the enforcement of any other basic constitutional right. The right to privacy, no less important than any other right carefully and particularly reserved to the people, would stand in marked contrast to all other rights declared as "basic to a free society." This Court has not hesitated to enforce as strictly against the States as it does against the Federal Government the rights of free speech and of a free press, the rights to notice and to a fair, public trial, including, as it does, the right not to be convicted by use of a coerced confession, however logically relevant it be, and without regard to its reliability. . . . And nothing could be more certain than that when a coerced confession is involved, "the relevant rules of evidence" are overridden without regard to "the incidence of such conduct by the police," slight or frequent. Why should not the same rule apply to what is tantamount to coerced testimony by way of unconstitutional seizure of goods, papers, effects, documents, etc.? . . .

The ignoble shortcut to conviction left open to the State tends to destroy the entire system of constitutional restraints on which the liberties of the people rest. Having once recognized that the right to privacy embodied in the Fourth Amendment is enforceable against the States and that the right to be secure against rude invasions of privacy by state officers is, therefore, constitutional in origin, we can no longer permit that right to remain an empty promise. Because it is enforceable in the same manner and to like effect as other basic rights secured by the Due Process Clause, we can no longer permit it to be revocable at the whim of any police officer who, in the name of law enforcement itself, chooses to suspend its enjoyment. Our decision, founded on reason and truth, gives to the individual no more than that which the Constitution guarantees him, to the police officer no less than that to which honest law enforcement is entitled, and, to the courts, that judicial integrity so necessary in the true administration of justice. . . .

*Reversed and remanded.*

MR. JUSTICE BLACK, concurring . . . [omitted].

MR. JUSTICE DOUGLAS, concurring . . . [omitted].

MR. JUSTICE STEWART, concurring . . . [omitted].

**MR. JUSTICE HARLAN, whom MR. JUSTICE FRANKFURTER and MR. JUSTICE WHITTAKER join, dissenting. . . .**

At the heart of the majority's opinion in this case is the following syllogism: (1) the rule excluding in federal criminal trials evidence which is the product of an illegal search and seizure is a "part and parcel" of the Fourth Amendment; (2) *Wolf* held that the "privacy" assured against federal action by the Fourth Amendment is also protected against state action by the Fourteenth Amendment; and (3) it is therefore "logically and constitutionally necessary" that the Weeks exclusionary rule should also be enforced against the States.

This reasoning ultimately rests on the unsound premise that because *Wolf* carried into the States, as part of "the concept of ordered liberty" embodied in the Fourteenth Amendment, the principle of "privacy" underlying the Fourth Amendment, it must follow that whatever configurations of the Fourth Amendment have been developed in the particularizing federal precedents are likewise to be deemed a part of "ordered liberty," and as such are enforceable against the States. For me, this does not follow at all. . . .

## *United States* v. *Leon*
### 468 U.S. 897, 104 S.Ct. 3405, 82 L.Ed. 2d 677 (1984)
http://laws.findlaw.com/us/468/897.html

> With information from a confidential informant, police officers in Burbank, California, undertook surveillance of Alberto Leon and others for suspected drug-trafficking activities. Based on an affidavit summarizing police observations, Officer Rombach prepared a warrant application to search three residences and the automobiles of the individuals who lived there. Several deputy district attorneys reviewed Rombach's application, and a state judge issued the warrant. The searches that followed turned up large quantities of illegal drugs and other evidence. Leon and his cohorts were indicted for violating federal drug laws, but the district court suppressed some of the evidence seized in the searches because the affidavit contained insufficient information to establish probable cause to search all of the residences. The Court of Appeals for the Ninth Circuit affirmed. The government's petition for certiorari did not claim that probable cause was present but raised only the question of whether a good-faith exception to the exclusionary rule should be recognized under the Fourth Amendment. Majority: White, Blackmun, Burger, O'Connor, Powell, Rehnquist. Dissenting: Brennan, Marshall, Stevens.

**JUSTICE WHITE delivered the opinion of the Court.**

This case presents the question whether the Fourth Amendment exclusionary rule should be modified so as not to bar the use in the prosecution's case-in-chief of evidence obtained by officers acting in reasonable reliance on a search warrant issued by a detached and neutral magistrate but ultimately found to be unsupported by probable cause. To resolve this question, we must consider once again the tension between the sometimes competing goals of, on the one hand, deterring official misconduct and removing inducements to unreasonable invasions of privacy and, on the other, establishing procedures under which criminal defendants are "acquitted or convicted on the basis of all the evidence which exposes the truth." . . .

The Fourth Amendment contains no provision expressly precluding the use of evidence obtained in violation of its commands, and an examination of its origin and purposes makes clear that the use of fruits of a past unlawful search or seizure "work[s] no new Fourth Amendment wrong." . . . The wrong condemned by the Amendment is "fully accomplished" by the unlawful search or seizure itself . . . and the exclusionary rule is neither intended nor able to "cure the invasion of the defendant's rights which he has already suffered." . . . The rule thus operates as "a judicially created remedy designed to safeguard

Fourth Amendment rights generally through its deterrent effect, rather than a personal constitutional right of the person aggrieved." . . .

Whether the exclusionary sanction is appropriately imposed in a particular case, our decisions make clear, is "an issue separate from the question whether the Fourth Amendment rights of the party seeking to invoke the rule were violated by police conduct." . . . Only the former question is currently before us, and it must be resolved by weighing the costs and benefits of preventing the use in the prosecution's case-in-chief of inherently trustworthy tangible evidence obtained in reliance on a search warrant issued by a detached and neutral magistrate that ultimately is found to be defective.

The substantial social costs exacted by the exclusionary rule for the vindication of Fourth Amendment rights have long been a source of concern. . . .

Particularly when law enforcement officers have acted in objective good faith or their transgressions have been minor, the magnitude of the benefit conferred on such guilty defendants offends basic concepts of the criminal justice system. . . .

To the extent that proponents of exclusion rely on its behavioral effects on judges and magistrates in these areas, their reliance is misplaced. First, the exclusionary rule is designed to deter police misconduct rather than to punish the errors of judges and magistrates. Second, there exists no evidence suggesting that judges and magistrates are inclined to ignore or subvert the Fourth Amendment or that lawlessness among these actors requires application of the extreme sanction of exclusion.

Third, and most important, we discern no basis, and are offered none, for believing that exclusion of evidence seized pursuant to a warrant will have a significant deterrent effect on the issuing judge or magistrate. . . . The threat of exclusion thus cannot be expected significantly to deter them. Imposition of the exclusionary sanction is not necessary meaningfully to inform judicial officers of their errors, and we cannot conclude that admitting evidence obtained pursuant to a warrant while at the same time declaring that the warrant was somehow defective will in any way reduce judicial officers' professional incentives to comply with the Fourth Amendment, encourage them to repeat their mistakes, or lead to the granting of all colorable warrant requests.

If exclusion of evidence obtained pursuant to a subsequently invalidated warrant is to have any deterrent effect, therefore, it must alter the behavior of individual law enforcement officers or the policies of their departments. . . .

[E]ven assuming that the rule effectively deters some police misconduct and provides incentives for the law enforcement profession as a whole to conduct itself in accordance with the Fourth Amendment, it cannot be expected, and should not be applied, to deter objectively reasonable law enforcement activity. . . .

This is particularly true, we believe, when an officer acting with objective good faith has obtained a search warrant from a judge or magistrate and acted within its scope. In most such cases, there is no police illegality and thus nothing to deter. It is the magistrate's responsibility to determine whether the officer's allegations establish probable cause and, if so, to issue a warrant comporting in form with the requirements of the Fourth Amendment. In the ordinary case, an officer cannot be expected to question the magistrate's probable-cause determination or his judgment that the form of the warrant is technically sufficient. . . . Penalizing the officer for the magistrate's error, rather than his own, cannot logically contribute to the deterrence of Fourth Amendment violations.

We conclude that the marginal or nonexistent benefits produced by suppressing evidence obtained in objectively reasonable reliance on a subsequently invalidated search warrant cannot justify the substantial costs of exclusion. We do not suggest, however, that exclusion is always inappropriate in cases where an officer has obtained a warrant and abided by its terms. . . .

Suppression therefore remains an appropriate remedy if the magistrate or judge in issuing a warrant was misled by information in an affidavit that the affiant knew was false or would have known was false except for his reckless disregard of the truth. . . .

When the principles we have enunciated today are applied to the facts of this case, it is apparent that the judgment of the Court of Appeals cannot stand. . . .

Accordingly, the judgment of the Court of Appeals is

*Reversed.*

JUSTICE BLACKMUN, concurring . . . [omitted].

## JUSTICE BRENNAN, with whom JUSTICE MARSHALL joins, dissenting. . . .

The majority ignores the fundamental constitutional importance of what is at stake here. While the machinery of law enforcement and indeed the nature of crime itself have changed dramatically since the Fourth Amendment became part of the Nation's fundamental law in 1791, what the Framers understood then remains true today—that the task of combatting crime and convicting the guilty will in every era seem of such critical and pressing concern that we may be lured by the temptations of expediency into forsaking our commitment to protecting individual liberty and privacy. It was for that very reason that the Framers of the Bill of Rights insisted that law enforcement efforts be permanently and unambiguously restricted in order to preserve personal freedoms. In the constitutional scheme they ordained, the sometimes unpopular task of ensuring that the government's enforcement efforts remain within the strict boundaries fixed by the Fourth Amendment was entrusted to the courts. . . .

At the outset, the Court suggests that society has been asked to pay a high price—in terms either of setting guilty persons free or of impeding the proper functioning of trials—as a result of excluding relevant physical evidence in cases where the police, in conducting searches and seizing evidence, have made only an "objectively reasonable" mistake concerning the constitutionality of their actions. . . . But what evidence is there to support such a claim?

Significantly, the Court points to none, and, indeed, as the Court acknowledges, . . . recent studies have demonstrated that the "costs" of the exclusionary rule—calculated in terms of dropped prosecutions and lost convictions—are quite low. Contrary to the claims of the rule's critics that exclusion leads to "the release of countless guilty criminals" . . . these studies have demonstrated that federal and state prosecutors very rarely drop cases because of potential search and seizure problems. For example, a 1979 study prepared at the request of Congress by the General Accounting Office reported that only 0.4% of all cases actually declined for prosecution by federal prosecutors were declined primarily because of illegal search problems. . . . If the GAO data are restated as a percentage of all arrests, the study shows that only 0.2% of all felony arrests are declined for prosecution because of potential exclusionary rule problems. . . . Of course, these data describe only the costs attributable to the exclusion of evidence in all cases; the costs due to the exclusion of evidence in the narrower category of cases where police have made objectively reasonable mistakes must necessarily be even smaller. The Court, however, ignores this distinction and mistakenly weighs the aggregated costs of exclusion in all cases, irrespective of the circumstances that led to exclusions . . . against the potential benefits associated with only those cases in which evidence is excluded because police reasonably but mistakenly believe that their conduct does not violate the Fourth Amendment. . . .

When such faulty scales are used, it is little wonder that the balance tips in favor of restricting the application of the rule.

What then supports the Court's insistence that this evidence be admitted? Apparently, the Court's only answer is that even though the costs of exclusion are not very substantial, the potential deterrent effect in these circumstances is so marginal that exclusion cannot be justified. The key to the Court's conclusion in this respect is its belief that the prospective deterrent effect of the exclusionary rule operates only in those situations in which police officers, when deciding whether to go forward with some particular search, have reason to know that their planned conduct will violate the requirements of the Fourth Amendment. . . .

The flaw in the Court's argument, however, is that its logic captures only one comparatively minor element of the generally acknowledged deterrent purposes of the exclusionary rule. To be sure, the rule operates to some extent to deter future misconduct by individual officers who have had evidence suppressed in their own cases. But what the Court overlooks is that the deterrence rationale for the rule is not designed to be, nor should it be thought of as, a form of "punishment" of individual police officers for their failures to obey the restraints imposed by the Fourth Amendment. . . . Instead, the chief deterrent function of the rule is its tendency to promote institutional compliance with Fourth Amendment requirements on the part of law enforcement agencies generally. . . .

After today's decision, however, that institutional incentive will be lost. Indeed, the Court's "reasonable mistake" exception to the exclusionary rule will tend to put a premium on police ignorance of the law. Armed with the assurance provided by today's decision that evidence will always be admissible whenever an officer has "reasonably" relied upon a warrant, police departments will be encouraged to train officers that if a warrant has

simply been signed, it is reasonable, without more, to rely on it. Since in close cases there will no longer be any incentive to err on the side of constitutional behavior, police would have every reason to adopt a "let's-wait-until-it's-decided" approach in situations in which there is a question about a warrant's validity or the basis for its issuance. . . .

Although the Court brushes these concerns aside, a host of grave consequences can be expected to result from its decision to carve this new exception out of the exclusionary rule. A chief consequence of today's decision will be to convey a clear and unambiguous message to magistrates that their decisions to issue warrants are now insulated from subsequent judicial review. Creation of this new exception for good faith reliance upon a warrant implicitly tells magistrates that they need not take much care in reviewing warrant applications, since their mistakes will from now on have virtually no consequence: If their decision to issue a warrant was correct, the evidence will be admitted; if their decision was incorrect but the police relied in good faith on the warrant, the evidence will also be admitted. Inevitably, the care and attention devoted to such an inconsequential chore will dwindle. . . .

JUSTICE STEVENS dissenting . . . [omitted].

## C. SEARCH INCIDENT TO ARREST

### *Chimel* v. *California*
### 395 U.S. 752, 89 S.Ct. 2034, 23 L.Ed. 2d 685 (1969)
### http://laws.findlaw.com/us/395/752.html

> After arresting Ted Chimel in his home for burglary of a coin shop, police officers conducted a search of his entire three-bedroom house, including the attic, the garage, a small workshop, and various drawers. Certain items found through the search were admitted into evidence against him and he was convicted. Both the California Court of Appeal and the California Supreme Court affirmed the conviction, holding that although the officers had no search warrant, the search of the defendant's house had been justified on the ground that it had been incident to a valid arrest. Majority: Stewart, Brennan, Douglas, Fortas, Harlan, Marshall, Warren. Dissenting: White, Black.

**Mr. Justice Stewart delivered the opinion of the Court.**

This case raises basic questions concerning the permissible scope under the Fourth Amendment of a search incident to a lawful arrest. . . .

When an arrest is made, it is reasonable for the arresting officer to search the person arrested in order to remove any weapons that the latter might seek to use in order to resist or effect his escape. Otherwise, the officer's safety might well be endangered, and the arrest itself frustrated. In addition, it is entirely reasonable for the arresting officer to search for and seize any evidence on the arrestee's person in order to prevent its concealment or destruction. And the area into which an arrestee might reach in order to grab a weapon or evidentiary items must, of course, be governed by a like rule. A gun on a table or in a drawer in front of one who is arrested can be as dangerous to the arresting officer as one concealed in the clothing of the person arrested. There is ample justification, therefore, for a search of the arrestee's person and the area "within his immediate control"—construing that phrase to mean the area from within which he might gain possession of a weapon or destructible evidence.

There is no comparable justification, however, for routinely searching through all the desk drawers or other closed or concealed areas in that room itself. Such searches, in the absence of well recognized exceptions, may be made only under the authority of a search warrant. The "adherence to judicial processes" mandated by the Fourth Amendment requires no less. . . .

It is argued in the present case that it is "reasonable" to search a man's house when he is arrested in it. But that argument is founded on little more than a subjective view regarding the acceptability of certain sorts of police conduct, and not on considerations relevant to Fourth Amendment interests. Under such an unconfined analysis, Fourth Amendment protection in this area would approach the evaporation point. It is not easy to explain why, for instance, it is less subjectively "reasonable" to search a man's house when he is arrested on his front lawn—or just down the street—than it is when he happens to be in the house at the time of arrest. . . .

Application of sound Fourth Amendment principles to the facts of this case produces a clear result. The search here went far beyond the petitioner's person and the area from within which he might have obtained either a weapon or something that could have been used as evidence against him. There was no constitutional justification, in the absence of a search warrant, for extending the search beyond that area. The scope of the search was, therefore, "unreasonable" under the Fourth and Fourteenth Amendments, and the petitioner's conviction cannot stand.

*Reversed.*

Mr. Justice Harlan, concurring . . . [omitted].

**Mr. Justice White, with whom Mr. Justice Black joins, dissenting. . . .**

The case provides a good illustration of my point that it is unreasonable to require police to leave the scene of an arrest in order to obtain a search warrant when they already have probable cause to search and there is a clear danger that the items for which they may reasonably search will be removed before they return with a warrant. Petitioner was arrested in his home after an arrest whose validity will be explored below, but which I will now assume was valid. There was doubtless probable cause not only to arrest petitioner, but also to search his house. He had obliquely admitted, both to a neighbor and to the owner of the burglarized store, that he had committed the burglary. In light of this, and the fact that the neighbor had seen other admittedly stolen property in petitioner's house, there was surely probable cause on which a warrant could have [been] issued to search the house for the stolen coins. Moreover, had the police simply arrested petitioner, taken him off to the station house, and later returned with a warrant, it seems very likely that petitioner's wife, who in view of petitioner's generally garrulous nature must have known of the robbery, would have removed the coins. For the police to search the house while the evidence they had probable cause to search out and seize was still there cannot be considered unreasonable. . . .

If circumstances so often require the warrantless arrest that the law generally permits it, the typical situation will find the arresting officers lawfully on the premises without arrest or search warrant. Like the majority, I would permit the police to search the person of a suspect and the area under his immediate control either to assure the safety of the officers or to prevent the destruction of evidence. And like the majority, I see nothing in the arrest alone furnishing probable cause for a search of any broader scope. However, where as here the existence of probable cause is independently established and would justify a warrant for a broader search for evidence, I would follow past cases and permit such a search to be carried out without a warrant, since the fact of arrest supplies an exigent circumstance justifying police action before the evidence can be removed, and also alerts the suspect to the fact of the search so that he can immediately seek judicial determination of probable cause in an adversary proceeding, and appropriate redress.

This view, consistent with past cases, would not authorize the general search against which the Fourth Amendment was meant to guard, nor would it broaden or render uncertain in any way whatsoever the scope of searches permitted under the Fourth Amendment. The issue in this case is not the breadth of the search since there was clearly probable cause for the search which was carried out. No broader search than if the officers had a warrant would be permitted. The only issue is whether a search warrant was required as a precondition to that search. It is agreed that such a warrant would be required absent exigent circumstances. I would hold that the fact of arrest supplies such an exigent circumstance, since the police had lawfully gained entry to the premises to effect the arrest and since delaying the search to secure a warrant would have involved the risk of not recovering the fruits of the crime. . . .

## D. Automobile Searches

### California v. Acevedo
### 500 U.S. 565, 111 S.Ct. 1982, 114 L.Ed. 2d 619 (1991)
### http://laws.findlaw.com/us/500/565.html

Police in Santa Ana, California, observed Charles Steven Acevedo leave an apartment carrying a brown paper bag. The bag was the size of one of several wrapped marijuana packages which they knew had been delivered to the apartment earlier in the day. Acevedo placed the bag in the trunk of his car. As he drove away, police stopped the car, opened the trunk and the bag, and found marijuana. Acevedo pleaded guilty to possession of marijuana for sale after his motion to suppress the evidence was denied. However, the California Court of Appeal for the Fourth Appellate District reversed, holding that, while police had probable cause to believe the bag contained marijuana, they lacked probable cause to suspect the car itself. Consequently, a warrant was necessary before police could lawfully open the bag. The Supreme Court of California denied review. Majority: Blackmun, Rehnquist, O'Connor, Scalia, Kennedy, Souter. Dissenting: White, Stevens, Marshall.

## JUSTICE BLACKMUN delivered the opinion of the Court.

This case requires us once again to consider the so-called "automobile exception" to the warrant requirement of the Fourth Amendment and its application to the search of a closed container in the trunk of a car. . . .

In *Carroll* [v. *United States* (1925)], this Court established an exception to the warrant requirement for moving vehicles, for it recognized

> a necessary difference between a search of a store, dwelling house or other structure in respect of which a proper official warrant readily may be obtained, and a search of a ship, motor boat, wagon or automobile, for contraband goods, where it is not practicable to secure a warrant because the vehicle can be quickly moved out of the locality or jurisdiction in which the warrant must be sought.

It therefore held that a warrantless search of an automobile based upon probable cause to believe that the vehicle contained evidence of crime in the light of an exigency arising out of the likely disappearance of the vehicle did not contravene the Warrant Clause of the Fourth Amendment. . . .

In *United States* v. *Ross,* decided in 1982, we held that a warrantless search of an automobile under the Carroll doctrine could include a search of a container or package found inside the car when such a search was supported by probable cause. The warrantless search of Ross' car occurred after an informant told the police that he had seen Ross complete a drug transaction using drugs stored in the trunk of his car. The police stopped the car, searched it, and discovered in the trunk a brown paper bag containing drugs. We decided that the search of Ross's car was not unreasonable under the Fourth Amendment: "The scope of a warrantless search based on probable cause is no narrower—and no broader—than the scope of a search authorized by a warrant supported by probable cause." . . .

In addition to this clarification, *Ross* distinguished the Carroll doctrine from the separate rule that governed the search of closed containers. The Court had announced this separate rule, unique to luggage and other closed packages, bags, and containers, in *United States* v. *Chadwick* (1977). In *Chadwick,* federal narcotics agents had probable cause to believe that a 200-pound double-locked footlocker contained marijuana. The agents tracked the locker as the defendants removed it from a train and carried it through the station to a waiting car. As soon as the defendants lifted the locker into the trunk of the car, the agents arrested them, seized the locker, and searched it. In this Court, the United States did not contend that the locker's brief contact with the automobile's trunk sufficed to make the Carroll doctrine applicable. Rather, the United States urged that the search of movable luggage could be considered analogous to the search of an automobile.

The Court rejected this argument because, it reasoned, a person expects more privacy in his luggage and personal effects than he does in his automobile. Moreover, it concluded that as "may often not be the case when automobiles are seized," secure storage facilities are usually available when the police seize luggage.

In *Arkansas* v. *Sanders* (1979), the Court extended *Chadwick's* rule to apply to a suitcase actually being transported in the trunk of a car. . . .

In *Ross,* the Court endeavored to distinguish between *Carroll,* which governed the Ross automobile search, and *Chadwick,* which governed the Sanders automobile search. It held that the Carroll doctrine covered searches of automobiles when the police had probable cause to search an entire vehicle but that the Chadwick doctrine governed searches of luggage when the officers had probable cause to search only a container within the vehicle. Thus, in a Ross situation, the police could conduct a reasonable search under the Fourth Amendment without obtaining a warrant, whereas in a Sanders situation, the police had to obtain a warrant before they searched. . . . *Ross* took the critical step of saying that closed containers in cars could be searched without a warrant because of their presence within the automobile. Despite the protection that *Sanders* purported to extend to closed containers, the privacy interest in those closed containers yielded to the broad scope of an automobile search. . . .

We now agree that a container found after a general search of the automobile and a container found in a car after a limited search for the container are equally easy for the police to store and for the suspect to hide or destroy. In fact, we see no principled distinction in terms of either the privacy expectation or the exigent circumstances between the paper bag found by the police in *Ross* and the paper bag found by the police here. Furthermore, by attempting to distinguish between a container for which the police are specifically searching and a container which they come across in a car, we have provided only minimal protection for privacy and have impeded effective law enforcement. . . .

At the moment when officers stop an automobile, it may be less than clear whether they suspect with a high degree of certainty that the vehicle contains drugs in a bag or simply contains drugs. If the police know that they may open a bag only if they are actually searching the entire car, they may search more extensively than they otherwise would in order to establish the general probable cause required by *Ross*. . . .

To the extent that the Chadwick-Sanders rule protects privacy, its protection is minimal. Law enforcement officers may seize a container and hold it until they obtain a search warrant. . . . And the police often will be able to search containers without a warrant, despite the Chadwick-Sanders rule, as a search incident to a lawful arrest. In *New York* v. *Belton* (1981), the Court said:

> [W]e hold that when a policeman has made a lawful custodial arrest of the occupant of an automobile, he may, as a contemporaneous incident of that arrest, search the passenger compartment of that automobile.
>
> It follows from this conclusion that the police may also examine the contents of any containers found within the passenger compartment.

Under *Belton,* the same probable cause to believe that a container holds drugs will allow the police to arrest the person transporting the container and search it.

Finally, the search of a paper bag intrudes far less on individual privacy than does the incursion sanctioned long ago in *Carroll*. In that case, prohibition agents slashed the upholstery of the automobile. This Court nonetheless found their search to be reasonable under the Fourth Amendment. If destroying the interior of an automobile is not unreasonable, we cannot conclude that looking inside a closed container is. In light of the minimal protection to privacy afforded by the Chadwick-Sanders rule, and our serious doubt whether that rule substantially serves privacy interests, we now hold that the Fourth Amendment does not compel separate treatment for an automobile search that extends only to a container within the vehicle. . . .

Until today, this Court has drawn a curious line between the search of an automobile that coincidentally turns up a container and the search of a container that coincidentally turns up in an automobile. The protections of the Fourth Amendment must not turn on such coincidences. We therefore interpret *Carroll* as providing one rule to govern all automobile searches. The police may search an automobile and the containers within it where they have probable cause to believe contraband or evidence is contained.

The judgment of the California Court of Appeal is reversed and the case is remanded to that court for further proceedings not inconsistent with this opinion.

*It is so ordered.*

### JUSTICE SCALIA, concurring in the judgment. . . .

Unlike the dissent . . . I do not regard today's holding as some momentous departure, but rather as merely the continuation of an inconsistent jurisprudence that has been with us for years. . . .

Under our precedents (as at common law), a person may be arrested outside the home on the basis of probable cause, without an arrest warrant. Upon arrest, the person, as well as the area within his grasp, may be searched for evidence related to the crime. Under these principles, if a known drug dealer is carrying a briefcase reasonably believed to contain marijuana (the unauthorized possession of which is a crime), the police may arrest him and search his person on the basis of probable cause alone. And, under our precedents, upon arrival at the station house, the police may inventory his possessions, including the briefcase, even if there is no reason to suspect that they contain contraband. According to our current law, however, the police may not, on the basis of the same probable cause, take the less intrusive step of stopping the individual on the street and demanding to see the contents of his briefcase. That makes no sense a priori, and in the absence of any common-law tradition supporting such a distinction, I see no reason to continue it.

JUSTICE WHITE, dissenting . . . [omitted].

## JUSTICE STEVENS, with whom JUSTICE MARSHALL joins, dissenting. . . .

The Fourth Amendment is a restraint on Executive power. The Amendment constitutes the Framers' direct constitutional response to the unreasonable law enforcement practices employed by agents of the British Crown. . . .

Our decisions have always acknowledged that the warrant requirement imposes a burden on law enforcement. And our cases have not questioned that trained professionals normally make reliable assessments of the existence of probable cause to conduct a search. We have repeatedly held, however, that these factors are outweighed by the individual interest in privacy that is protected by advance judicial approval. The Fourth Amendment dictates that the privacy interest is paramount, no matter how marginal the risk of error might be if the legality of warrantless searches were judged only after the fact. . . .

We held in Ross that "the scope of the warrantless search authorized by [the automobile] exception is no broader and no narrower than a magistrate could legitimately authorize by warrant." The inherent mobility of the vehicle justified the immediate search without a war-

rant, but did not affect the scope of the search. Thus, the search could encompass containers, which might or might not conceal the object of the search, as well as the remainder of the vehicle. . . .

We explained that, in such instances, "prohibiting police from opening immediately a container in which the object of the search is most likely to be found and instead forcing them first to comb the entire vehicle would actually exacerbate the intrusion on privacy interests." . . .

These concerns that justified our holding in Ross are not implicated in cases like Chadwick and Sanders in which the police have probable cause to search a particular container rather than the entire vehicle. . . . Chadwick and Sanders had not created a special rule for container searches, but rather had merely applied the cardinal principle that warrantless searches are per se unreasonable unless justified by an exception to the general rule. Ross dealt with the scope of the automobile exception; Chadwick and Sanders were cases in which the exception simply did not apply. . . .

To the extent there was any "anomaly" in our prior jurisprudence, the Court has "cured" it at the expense of creating a more serious paradox. For, surely it is anomalous to prohibit a search of a briefcase while the owner is carrying it exposed on a public street yet to permit a search once the owner has placed the briefcase in the locked trunk of his car. . . .

Under the Court's holding today, the privacy interest that protects the contents of a suitcase or a briefcase from a warrantless search when it is in public view simply vanishes when its owner climbs into a taxicab. Unquestionably the rejection of the Sanders line of cases by today's decision will result in a significant loss of individual privacy. . . .

Even if the warrant requirement does inconvenience the police to some extent, that fact does not distinguish this constitutional requirement from any other procedural protection secured by the Bill of Rights. It is merely a part of the price that our society must pay in order to preserve its freedom. . . .

## E. ELECTRONIC SURVEILLANCE

### Olmstead v. United States
### 277 U.S. 438, 48 S.Ct. 564, 72 L.Ed. 944 (1928)

http://laws.findlaw.com/us/277/438.html

Roy Olmstead and others were charged and convicted of conspiring to violate the national Prohibition Act. Evidence proving the conspiracy had been obtained by four federal agents who tapped the telephone lines of several of the defendants, without, however, committing any trespass on their property. A statute of the state of Washington made it a misdemeanor to "intercept, read or in any way interrupt or delay the sending of a message over any telegraph or telephone line. . . ." Majority: Taft, McReynolds, Sanford, Sutherland, Van Devanter. Dissenting: Brandeis, Butler, Holmes, Stone.

**MR. CHIEF JUSTICE TAFT delivered the opinion of the Court. . . .**

The well-known historical importance of the Fourth Amendment, directed against general warrants and writs of assistance, was to prevent the use of governmental force to search a man's house, his person, his papers and his effects, and to prevent their seizure against his will. . . .

The amendment itself shows that the search is to be of material things—the person, the house, his papers, or his effects. The description of the warrant necessary to make the proceeding lawful is that it must specify the place to be searched and the person or things to be seized. . . . The language of the amendment cannot be extended and expanded to include telephone wires, reaching to the whole world from the defendant's house or office. The intervening wires are not part of his house or office, any more than are the highways along which they are stretched. . . .

Congress may, of course, protect the secrecy of telephone messages by making them, when intercepted, inadmissible in evidence in federal criminal trials, by direct legislation, and thus depart from the common law of evidence. But the courts may not adopt such a policy by attributing an enlarged and unusual meaning to the Fourth Amendment. The reasonable view is that one who installs in his house a telephone instrument with connecting wires intends to project his voice to those quite outside, and that the wires beyond his house, and messages while passing over them, are not within the protection of the Fourth Amendment. Here those who intercepted the projected voices were not in the house of either party to the conversation.

Neither the cases we have cited nor any of the many federal decisions brought to our attention hold the Fourth Amendment to have been violated as against a defendant, unless there has been an official search and seizure of his person or such a seizure of his papers or his tangible material effects or an actual physical invasion of his house "or curtilage" for the purpose of making a seizure.

We think, therefore, that the wire tapping here disclosed did not amount to a search or seizure within the meaning of the Fourth Amendment. . . .

Our general experience shows that much evidence has always been receivable, although not obtained by conformity to the highest ethics. The history of criminal trials shows numerous cases of prosecutions of oathbound conspiracies for murder, robbery, and other crimes, where officers of the law have disguised themselves and joined the organizations, taken the oaths, and given themselves every appearance of active members engaged in the promotion of crime for the purpose of securing evidence. Evidence secured by such means has always been received.

A standard which would forbid the reception of evidence, if obtained by other than nice ethical conduct by government officials, would make society suffer and give criminals greater immunity than has been known heretofore. In the absence of controlling legislation by Congress, those who realize the difficulties in bringing offenders to justice may well deem it wise that the exclusion of evidence should be confined to cases where rights under the Constitution would be violated by admitting it. . . .

*Affirmed.*

MR. JUSTICE HOLMES, dissenting . . . [omitted].

### MR. JUSTICE BRANDEIS, dissenting. . . .

"We must never forget," said Mr. Chief Justice Marshall in *McCulloch* v. *Maryland,* "that it is a *constitution* we are expounding." Since then, this Court has repeatedly sustained the exercise of power by Congress, under various clauses of that instrument, over objects of which the Fathers could not have dreamed. . . . We have likewise held that general limitations on the powers of Government, like those embodied in the due process clauses of the Fifth and Fourteenth Amendments, do not forbid the United States or the States from meeting modern conditions by regulations which "a century ago, or even half a century ago, probably would have been rejected as arbitrary and oppressive." . . . Clauses guaranteeing to the individual protection against specific abuses of power, must have a similar capacity of adaptation to a changing world. . . .

When the Fourth and Fifth Amendments were adopted, . . . [f]orce and violence were then the only means known to man by which a Government could directly effect self-incrimination. It could compel the individual to testify—a compulsion effected, if need be, by torture. It could secure possession of his papers and other articles incident to his private life—a seizure effected, if need be, by breaking and entry. Protection against such invasion of "the sanctities of a man's home and the privacies of life" was provided in the Fourth

and Fifth Amendments, by specific language. But "time works changes, brings into existence new conditions and purposes." Subtler and more far-reaching means of invading privacy have become available to the government. Discovery and invention have made it possible for the government, by means far more effective than stretching upon the rack, to obtain disclosure in court of what is whispered in the closet.

Moreover, "in the application of a constitution, our contemplation cannot be only of what has been, but of what may be." The progress of science in furnishing the government with means of espionage is not likely to stop with wire-tapping. Ways may some day be developed by which the government, without removing papers from secret drawers, can reproduce them in court, and by which it will be enabled to expose to a jury the most intimate occurrences of the home. Advances in the psychic and related sciences may bring means of exploring unexpressed beliefs, thoughts and emotions.

. . . [C]an it be that the Constitution affords no protection against such invasions of individual security? . . .

The makers of our Constitution undertook to secure conditions favorable to the pursuit of happiness. They recognized the significance of man's spiritual nature, of his feelings and of his intellect. They knew that only a part of the pain, pleasure and satisfactions of life are to be found in material things. They sought to protect Americans in their beliefs, their thoughts, their emotions and their sensations. They conferred, as against the Government, the right to be let alone—the most comprehensive of rights and the right most valued by civilized men. To protect that right, every unjustifiable intrusion by the Government upon the privacy of the individual, whatever the means employed, must be deemed a violation of the Fourth Amendment. And the use, as evidence in a criminal proceeding, of facts ascertained by such intrusion must be deemed a violation of the Fifth.

Applying to the Fourth and Fifth Amendments the established rule of construction, the defendant's objections to the evidence obtained by a wire-tapping must, in my opinion, be sustained. It is, of course, immaterial where the physical connection with the telephone wires leading into the defendants' premises was made. And it is also immaterial that the intrusion was in aid of law enforcement. Experience should teach us to be most on our guard to protect liberty when the government's purposes are beneficent. Men born to freedom are naturally alert to repel invasion of their liberty by evil-minded rulers. The greatest dangers to liberty lurk in insidious encroachment by men of zeal, well-meaning, but without understanding. . . .

MR. JUSTICE BUTLER, dissenting . . . [omitted].

MR. JUSTICE STONE, dissenting . . . [omitted].

## *Katz* v. *United States*
## 389 U.S. 347, 88 S.Ct. 507, 19 L.Ed. 2d 576 (1967)

http://laws.findlaw.com/us/389/347.html

> Charles Katz was convicted of transmitting wagering information by telephone from Los Angeles to Miami and Boston in violation of a federal statute. At the trial, the government was permitted to introduce evidence gathered from attaching an electronic listening device to the outside of a public telephone booth from which he placed his calls. The Supreme Court granted certiorari to determine if the recordings had been obtained in violation of the Fourth Amendment. Majority: Stewart, Brennan, Douglas, Fortas, Harlan, Warren, White. Dissenting: Black. Not participating: Marshall.

**MR. JUSTICE STEWART delivered the opinion of the Court.**

The petitioner has strenuously argued that the booth was a "constitutionally protected area." The Government has maintained with equal vigor that it was not. But this effort to decide whether or not a given "area," viewed in the abstract, is "constitutionally protected" deflects attention from the problem presented by this case. For the Fourth Amendment protects people, not places. What a person knowingly exposes to the public, even in his own home or office, is not a subject of Fourth Amendment protection. . . . But what he seeks to preserve as private, even in an area accessible to the public, may be constitutionally protected. . . .

The Government stresses the fact that the telephone booth from which the petitioner made his calls was constructed partly of glass, so that he was as visible after he entered it as he would have been if he had remained outside. But what he sought to exclude when he entered the booth was not the intruding eye—it was the uninvited ear. He did not shed his right to do so simply because he made his calls from a place where he might be seen. No less than an individual in a business office, in a friend's apartment, or in a taxicab, a person in a telephone booth may rely upon the protection of the Fourth Amendment. One who occupies it, shuts the door behind him, and pays the toll that permits him to place a call, is surely entitled to assume that the words he utters into the mouthpiece will not be broadcast to the world. To read the Constitution more narrowly is to ignore the vital role that the public telephone has come to play in private communication.

The Government contends, however, that the activities of its agents in this case should not be tested by Fourth Amendment requirements, for the surveillance technique they employed involved no physical penetration of the telephone booth from which the petitioner placed his calls. It is true that the absence of such penetration was at one time thought to foreclose further Fourth Amendment inquiry. . . . Thus, although a closely divided Court supposed in *Olmstead* that surveillance without any trespass and without the seizure of any material object fell outside the ambit of the Constitution, we have since departed from the narrow view on which that decision rested. . . . Once this much is acknowledged, and once it is recognized that the Fourth Amendment protects people—and not simply "areas"—against unreasonable searches and seizures, it becomes clear that the reach of that Amendment cannot turn upon the presence or absence of a physical intrusion into any given enclosure.

. . . We conclude that the underpinnings of *Olmstead* . . . have been so eroded by our subsequent decisions that the "trespass" doctrine there enunciated can no longer be regarded as controlling. The Government's activities in electronically listening to and recording the petitioner's words violated the privacy upon which he justifiably relied while using the telephone booth and thus constituted a "search and seizure" within the meaning of the Fourth Amendment. The fact that the electronic device employed to achieve that end did not happen to penetrate the wall of the booth can have no constitutional significance.

The question remaining for decision, then, is whether the search and seizure conducted in this case complied with constitutional standards. In that regard, the Government's position is that its agents acted in an entirely defensible manner: They did not begin their electronic surveillance until investigation of the petitioner's activities had established a strong probability that he was using the telephone in question to transmit gambling information to persons in other States, in violation of federal law. Moreover, the surveillance was limited, both in scope and in duration, to the specific purpose of establishing the contents of the petitioner's unlawful telephonic communications. The agents confined their surveillance to the brief periods during which he used the telephone booth, and they took great care to overhear only the conversations of the petitioner himself.

Accepting this account of the Government's actions as accurate, it is clear that this surveillance was so narrowly circumscribed that a duly authorized magistrate, properly notified of the need for such investigation, specifically informed of the basis on which it was to proceed, and clearly apprised of the precise intrusion it would entail, could constitutionally have authorized, with appropriate safeguards, the very limited search and seizure that the Government asserts in fact took place. . . .

It is apparent that the agents in this case acted with restraint. Yet the inescapable fact is that this restraint was imposed by the agents themselves, not by a judicial officer. They were not required, before commencing the search, to present their estimate of probable cause for detached scrutiny by a neutral magistrate. They were not compelled, during the conduct of the search itself, to observe precise limits established in advance by a specific court order. Nor were they directed, after the search had been completed, to notify the authorizing magistrate in detail of all that had been seized. In the absence of such safeguards, this Court has never sustained a search upon the sole ground that officers reasonably expected to find evidence of a particular crime and voluntarily confined their activities to the least intrusive means consistent with that end. Searches conducted without warrants have been held unlawful "notwithstanding facts unquestionably showing probable cause," . . . for the Constitution requires "that the deliberate, impartial judgment of a judicial officer . . . be interposed between the citizen and the police. . . ." . . . [S]earches conducted outside the judicial process, without prior approval by judge or magistrate, are per se unreasonable under the Fourth Amendment—subject only to a few specifically established and well-delineated exceptions.

It is difficult to imagine how any of those exceptions could ever apply to the sort of search and seizure involved in this case. Even electronic surveillance substantially contemporaneous with an individual's arrest could hardly be deemed an "incident" of that arrest. Nor could the use of electronic surveillance without prior authorization be justified on grounds of "hot pursuit." And, of course, the very nature of electronic surveillance precludes its use pursuant to the suspect's consent.

The Government . . . argues that surveillance of a telephone booth should be exempted from the usual requirement of advance authorization by a magistrate upon a showing of probable cause. We cannot agree. Omission of such authorization "bypasses the safeguards provided by an objective predetermination of probable cause, and substitutes instead the far less reliable procedure of an after-the-event justification for the . . . search, too likely to be subtly influenced by the familiar shortcomings of hindsight judgment." . . .

And bypassing a neutral predetermination of the scope of a search leaves individuals secure from Fourth Amendment violations "only in the discretion of the police." . . .

The government agents here ignored "the procedure of antecedent justification . . . that is central to the Fourth Amendment," a procedure that we hold to be a constitutional precondition of the kind of electronic surveillance involved in this case. Because the surveillance here failed to meet that condition, and because it led to the petitioner's conviction, the judgment must be reversed.

*It is so ordered.*

## MR. JUSTICE DOUGLAS, with whom MR. JUSTICE BRENNAN joins, concurring.

While I join the opinion of the Court, I feel compelled to reply to the separate concurring opinion of my Brother White, which I view as a wholly unwarranted green light for the Executive Branch to resort to electronic eavesdropping without a warrant in cases which the Executive Branch itself labels "national security" matters.

Neither the President nor the Attorney General is a magistrate. In matters where they believe national security may be involved they are not detached, disinterested, and neutral as a court or magistrate must be. Under the separation of powers created by the Constitution, the Executive Branch is not supposed to be neutral and disinterested. Rather it should vigorously investigate and prevent breaches of national security and prosecute those who violate the pertinent federal laws. The President and Attorney General are properly interested parties, cast in the role of adversary, in national security cases. They may even be the intended victims of subversive action. Since spies and saboteurs are as entitled to the protection of the Fourth Amendment as suspected gamblers like petitioner, I cannot agree that where spies and saboteurs are involved adequate protection of Fourth Amendment rights is assured when the President and Attorney General assume both the position of adversary-and-prosecutor and disinterested, neutral magistrate. . . .

## MR. JUSTICE HARLAN, concurring. . . .

As the Court's opinion states, "the Fourth Amendment protects people, not places." The question, however, is what protection it affords to those people. Generally, as here, the answer to that question requires reference to a "place." My understanding of the rule that has emerged from prior decisions is that there is a twofold requirement, first that a person have exhibited an actual (subjective) expectation of privacy and second, that the expectation be one that society is prepared to recognize as "reasonable."

## MR. JUSTICE WHITE, concurring.

In joining the Court's opinion, I note the Court's acknowledgment that there are circumstances in which it is reasonable to search without a warrant. In this connection . . . the Court points out that today's decision does not reach national security cases. Wiretapping to protect the security of the Nation has been authorized by successive Presidents. The present Administration would apparently save national security cases from restrictions against wiretapping. . . . We should not require the warrant procedure and the magistrate's judgment if the President of the United States or his chief legal officer, the Attorney General, had considered the requirements of national security and authorized electronic surveillance as reasonable.

### MR. JUSTICE BLACK, dissenting. . . .

My basic objection is twofold: (1) I do not believe that the words of the Amendment will bear the meaning given them by today's decision, and (2) I do not believe that it is the proper role of this Court to rewrite the Amendment in order "to bring it into harmony with the times" and thus reach a result that many people believe to be desirable. . . .

The first clause protects "persons, houses, papers, and effects, against unreasonable searches and seizures. . . ." These words connote the idea of tangible things with size, form, and weight, things capable of being searched, seized, or both. The second clause of the Amendment still further establishes its Framers' purpose to limit its protection to tangible things by providing that no warrants shall issue but those "particularly describing the place to be searched and the person or things to be seized." A conversation overheard by eavesdropping whether by plain snooping or wiretapping, is not tangible and, under the normally accepted meanings of the words, can neither be searched nor seized. In addition the language of the second clause indicates that the Amendment refers to something not only tangible so it can be seized but to something already in existence so it can be described. Yet the Court's interpretation would have the Amendment apply to overhearing future conversations which by their very nature are nonexistent until they take place. How can one "describe" a future conversation, and if not, how can a magistrate issue a warrant to eavesdrop one in the future? It is argued that information showing what is expected to be said is sufficient to limit the boundaries of what later can be admitted into evidence; but does such general information really meet the specific language of the Amendment which says "particularly describing?" Rather than using language in a completely artificial way, I must conclude that the Fourth Amendment simply does not apply to eavesdropping.

Tapping telephone wires, of course, was an unknown possibility at the time the Fourth Amendment was adopted. . . . "In those days the eavesdropper listened by naked ear under the eaves of houses or their windows, or beyond their walls seeking out private discourse." . . . There can be no doubt that the Framers were aware of this practice, and if they had desired to outlaw or restrict the use of evidence obtained by eavesdropping, I believe that they would have used the appropriate language to do so in the Fourth Amendment. They certainly would not have left such a task to the ingenuity of language-stretching judges. . . . It was never meant for this Court to have such power, which in effect would make us a continuously functioning constitutional convention. . . .

## *United States* v. *United States District Court*
### 407 U.S. 297, 92 S.Ct. 2125, 32 L.Ed. 2d 752 (1972)
### http://laws.findlaw.com/us/407/297.html

(This case is reprinted in Chapter Fifteen, beginning on page 694.)

## *Kyllo* v. *United States*
## 533 U.S. 27, 121 S.Ct. 2038, 150 L.Ed. 2d 94 (2001)
http://laws.findlaw.com/us/533/27.html

> Suspicious that marijuana was being grown in Danny Lee Kyllo's home in a triplex, agents in Florence, Oregon, used a thermal imaging device to scan the triplex to determine if the amount of heat emanating from it was consistent with the high-intensity lamps typically used for indoor marijuana growth. The scan showed that Kyllo's garage roof and a side wall were relatively hot compared to the rest of his home and substantially warmer than the neighboring units. Based in part on the thermal imaging, a federal magistrate judge issued a warrant to search Kyllo's home, where the agents found marijuana growing. After Kyllo was indicted on drug charges, he unsuccessfully moved to suppress the evidence and then entered a conditional guilty plea in U.S. district court. The Court of Appeals for the Ninth Circuit eventually affirmed, upholding the thermal imaging on the ground that Kyllo had shown no subjective expectation of privacy because he had made no attempt to conceal the heat escaping from his home. Even if he had, ruled the court, there was no objectively reasonable expectation of privacy because the thermal imager did not expose any intimate details of Kyllo's life, only amorphous hot spots on his home's exterior. Majority: Scalia, Souter, Thomas, Ginsburg, Breyer. Dissenting: Stevens, Rehnquist, O'Connor, Kennedy.

**JUSTICE SCALIA delivered the opinion of the Court.**

This case presents the question whether the use of a thermal-imaging device aimed at a private home from a public street to detect relative amounts of heat within the home constitutes a "search" within the meaning of the Fourth Amendment. . . .

"At the very core" of the Fourth Amendment "stands the right of a man to retreat into his own home and there be free from unreasonable governmental intrusion." With few exceptions, the question whether a warrantless search of a home is reasonable and hence constitutional must be answered no.

On the other hand, the antecedent question of whether or not a Fourth Amendment "search" has occurred is not so simple under our precedent. The permissibility of ordinary visual surveillance of a home used to be clear because, well into the 20th century, our Fourth Amendment jurisprudence was tied to common-law trespass. . . . We have since decoupled violation of a person's Fourth Amendment rights from trespassory violation of his property, but the lawfulness of warrantless visual surveillance of a home has still been preserved. . . .

The present case involves officers on a public street engaged in more than naked-eye surveillance of a home. We have previously reserved judgment as to how much technological enhancement of ordinary perception from such a vantage point, if any, is too much. While we upheld enhanced aerial photography of an industrial complex . . . , we noted that we found "it important that this is *not* an area immediately adjacent to a private home, where privacy expectations are most heightened."

It would be foolish to contend that the degree of privacy secured to citizens by the Fourth Amendment has been entirely unaffected by the advance of technology. . . . The question we confront today is what limits there are upon this power of technology to shrink the realm of guaranteed privacy.

The *Katz* [v. *United States*] test—whether the individual has an expectation of privacy that society is prepared to recognize as reasonable—has often been criticized as circular, and hence subjective and unpredictable. . . . While it may be difficult to refine *Katz* when the search of areas such as telephone booths, automobiles, or even the curtilage and uncovered portions of residences are at issue, in the case of the search of the interior of homes—the prototypical and hence most commonly litigated area of protected privacy—there is a ready criterion, with roots deep in the common law, of the minimal expectation of privacy that exists, and that is acknowledged to be reasonable. To withdraw protection of this minimum expectation would be to permit police technology to erode the privacy guaranteed by the Fourth Amendment. We think that obtaining by sense-enhancing technology any information regarding the interior of the home that could not otherwise have been obtained without physical "intrusion into a constitutionally protected area," constitutes a search—at least where (as here) the technology in question is not in general public use. This assures preservation of that degree of privacy against government that existed when the Fourth Amendment was adopted. On the basis of this criterion, the information obtained by the thermal imager in this case was the product of a search.

The Government maintains, however, that the thermal imaging must be upheld because it detected "only heat radiating from the external surface of the house." The dissent makes this its leading point, contending that there is a fundamental difference between what it calls "off-the-wall" observations and "through-the-wall surveillance." But just as a thermal imager captures only heat emanating from a house, so also a powerful directional microphone picks up only sound emanating from a house—and a satellite capable of scanning from many miles away would pick up only visible light emanating from a house. We rejected such a mechanical interpretation of the Fourth Amendment in *Katz,* where the eavesdropping device picked up only sound waves that reached the exterior of the phone booth. Reversing that approach would leave the homeowner at the mercy of advancing technology—including imaging technology that could discern all human activity in the home. While the technology used in the present case was relatively crude, the rule we adopt must take account of more sophisti-

cated systems that are already in use or in development. The dissent's reliance on the distinction between "off-the-wall" and "through-the-wall" observation is entirely incompatible with the dissent's belief . . . that thermal-imaging observations of the intimate details of a home are impermissible. . . .

The Government also contends that the thermal imaging was constitutional because it did not "detect private activities occurring in private areas." . . .

Limiting the prohibition of thermal imaging to "intimate details" would not only be wrong in principle; it would be impractical in application, failing to provide "a workable accommodation between the needs of law enforcement and the interests protected by the Fourth Amendment." To begin with, there is no necessary connection between the sophistication of the surveillance equipment and the "intimacy" of the details that it observes—which means that one cannot say (and the police cannot be assured) that use of the relatively crude equipment at issue here will always be lawful. The Agema Thermovision 210 might disclose, for example, at what hour each night the lady of the house takes her daily sauna and bath—a detail that many would consider "intimate"; and a much more sophisticated system might detect nothing more intimate than the fact that someone left a closet light on. We could not, in other words, develop a rule approving only that through-the-wall surveillance which identifies objects no smaller than 36 by 36 inches, but would have to develop a jurisprudence specifying which home activities are "intimate" and which are not. And even when (if ever) that jurisprudence were fully developed, no police officer would be able to know in advance whether his through-the-wall surveillance picks up "intimate" details—and thus would be unable to know in advance whether it is constitutional. . . .

Since we hold the Thermovision imaging to have been an unlawful search, it will remain for the District Court to determine whether, without the evidence it provided, the search warrant issued in this case was supported by probable cause—and if not, whether there is any other basis for supporting admission of the evidence that the search pursuant to the warrant produced.

The judgment of the Court of Appeals is reversed; the case is remanded for further proceedings consistent with this opinion.

*It is so ordered.*

### JUSTICE STEVENS, with whom THE CHIEF JUSTICE, JUSTICE O'CONNOR, and JUSTICE KENNEDY join, dissenting.

There is, in my judgment, a distinction of constitutional magnitude between "through-the-wall surveillance" that gives the observer or listener direct access to information in a private area, on the one hand, and the thought processes used to draw inferences from information in the public domain, on the other hand. The Court has crafted a rule that purports to deal with direct observations of the inside of the home, but the case before us merely involves indirect deductions from "off-the-wall" surveillance, that is, observations of the exterior of the home. Those observations were made with a fairly primitive thermal imager that gathered data exposed on the outside of petitioner's home but did not invade any constitutionally protected interest in privacy. Moreover, I believe that the supposedly "bright-line" rule the Court has created in response to its concerns about future technological developments is unnecessary, unwise, and inconsistent with the Fourth Amendment.

There is no need for the Court to craft a new rule to decide this case, as it is controlled by established principles from our Fourth Amendment jurisprudence. One of those core principles, of course, is that "searches and seizures inside a home without a warrant are presumptively unreasonable." . . . That is the principle implicated here.

While the Court "take[s] the long view" and decides this case based largely on the potential of yet-to-be-developed technology that might allow "through-the-wall surveillance," this case involves nothing more than off-the-wall surveillance by law enforcement officers to gather information exposed to the general public from the outside of petitioner's home.

All that the infrared camera did in this case was passively measure heat emitted from the exterior surfaces of petitioner's home; all that those measurements showed were relative differences in emission levels, vaguely indicating that some areas of the roof and outside walls were warmer than others. . . .

Indeed, the ordinary use of the senses might enable a neighbor or passerby to notice the heat emanating from a building, particularly if it is vented, as was the case here. Additionally, any member of the public might notice that one part of a house is warmer than another part or a nearby building if, for example, rainwater evaporates or snow melts at different rates across its surfaces. Such use of the senses would not convert into an unreasonable search if, instead, an adjoining neighbor allowed an officer onto her property to verify her perceptions with a sensitive thermometer. Nor, in my view, does such observation become an unreasonable search if made from a distance with the aid of a device that merely discloses that the exterior of one house, or one area of the house, is much warmer than another. Nothing more occurred in this case.

Thus, the notion that heat emissions from the outside of a dwelling is a private matter implicating the protections of the Fourth Amendment (the text of which guarantees the right of people "to be secure *in* their . . . houses" against unreasonable searches and seizures (emphasis added [by Justice Stevens]) is not only unprecedented but also quite difficult to take seriously. Heat waves, like aromas that are generated in a kitchen, or in a laboratory or opium den, enter the public domain if and when they leave a building. A subjective expectation that they would remain private is not only implausible but also surely not "one that society is prepared to recognize as 'reasonable.'" . . .

Notwithstanding the implications of today's decision, there is a strong public interest in avoiding constitutional litigation over the monitoring of emissions from homes, and over the inferences drawn from such monitoring. Just as "the police cannot reasonably be expected to avert their eyes from evidence of criminal activity that could have been observed by any member of the public," so too public officials should not have to avert their senses or their equipment from detecting emissions in the public domain such as excessive heat, traces of smoke, suspicious odors, odorless gases, airborne particulates, or radioactive emissions, any of which could identify hazards to the community. In my judgment, monitoring such emissions with "sense-enhancing technology," and drawing useful conclusions from such monitoring, is an entirely reasonable public service.

On the other hand, the countervailing privacy interest is at best trivial. After all, homes generally are insulated to keep heat in, rather than to prevent the detection of heat going out, and it does not seem to me that society will suffer from a rule requiring the rare homeowner who both intends to engage in uncommon activities that produce extraordinary amounts of heat, and wishes to conceal that production from outsiders, to make sure that the surrounding area is well insulated. . . .

Since what was involved in this case was nothing more than drawing inferences from off-the-wall surveillance, rather than any "through-the-wall" surveillance, the officers' conduct did not amount to a search and was perfectly reasonable. . . .

Despite the Court's attempt to draw a line that is "not only firm but also bright, the contours of its new rule are uncertain because its protection apparently dissipates as soon as the relevant technology is "in general public use." Yet how much use is general public use is not even hinted at by the Court's opinion, which makes the somewhat doubtful assumption that the thermal imager used in this case does not satisfy that criterion. In any event, putting aside its lack of clarity, this criterion is somewhat perverse because it seems likely that the threat to privacy will grow, rather than recede, as the use of intrusive equipment becomes more readily available. It is clear, however, that the category of "sense-enhancing technology" covered by the new rule, is far too broad.

It would, for example, embrace potential mechanical substitutes for dogs trained to react when they sniff narcotics. But in *United States* v. *Place* (1983), we held that a dog sniff that "discloses only the presence or absence of narcotics" does "not constitute a 'search' within the meaning of the Fourth Amendment," and it must follow that sense-enhancing equipment that identifies nothing but illegal activity is not a search either. Nevertheless, the use of such a device would be unconstitutional under the Court's rule, as would the use of other new devices that might detect the odor of deadly bacteria or chemicals for making a new type of high explosive, even if the devices (like the dog sniffs) are "so limited in both the manner in which" they obtain information and "in the content of the information" they reveal. . . .

Because the new rule applies to information regarding the "interior" of the home, it is too narrow as well as too broad. Clearly, a rule that is designed to protect individuals from the overly intrusive use of sense-enhancing equipment should not be limited to a home. If such equipment did provide its user with the functional equivalent of access to a private place—such as, for example, the telephone booth involved in *Katz,* or an office building—then the rule should apply to such an area as well as to a home. . . .

Although the Court is properly and commendably concerned about the threats to privacy that may flow from advances in the technology available to the law enforcement profession, it has unfortunately failed to heed the tried and true counsel of judicial restraint. Instead of concentrating on the rather mundane issue that is actually presented by the case before it, the Court has endeavored to craft an all-encompassing rule for the future. It would be far wiser to give legislators an unimpeded opportunity to grapple with these emerging issues rather than to shackle them with prematurely devised constitutional constraints. . . .

## F. Arrests, Detentions, and Frisks

### *Atwater* v. *City of Lago Vista*
### 532 U.S. 318, 121 S.Ct. 1536, 149 L.Ed. 2d 549 (2001)
http://laws.findlaw.com/us/532/318.html

Texas law makes it a misdemeanor, punishable only by fine, either for a front-seat passenger in a car equipped with safety belts not to wear one or for the driver to fail to secure any small child riding in front. State law also expressly authorizes the warrantless arrest of anyone violating these provisions, but police, at their discretion, may issue citations in place of arrest. Bart Turek, a police officer in Lago Vista, observed Gail Atwater driving her truck with her small children riding unrestrained in the front seat. Turek pulled Atwater over, berated and handcuffed her, placed her in his squad car, and drove her to the local police station, where she was made to remove her shoes, jewelry, and eyeglasses, and empty her pockets. Officers took her "mug shot" and placed her in a jail cell for an hour, after which she was taken before a magistrate and released on bond. She pleaded no contest to the seatbelt misdemeanors and paid a $50 fine. She and her husband then filed suit alleging that the city had violated her Fourth Amendment right to be free from unreasonable seizure. The U.S. District Court for the Western District of Texas found the Fourth Amendment claim meritless. A panel of the Court of Appeals for the Fifth Circuit reversed, but, sitting en banc, the appeals court affirmed. Majority: Souter, Kennedy, Rehnquist, Scalia, Thomas. Dissenting: O'Connor, Breyer, Ginsburg, Stevens.

**JUSTICE SOUTER delivered the opinion of the Court.**

The question is whether the Fourth Amendment forbids a warrantless arrest for a minor criminal offense, such as a misdemeanor seatbelt violation punishable only by a fine. We hold that it does not. . . .

In reading the Amendment, we are guided by "the traditional protections against unreasonable searches and seizures afforded by the common law at the time of the framing," since "[a]n examination of the common-law understanding of an officer's authority to arrest sheds light on the obviously relevant, if not entirely dispositive, consideration of what the Framers of the Amendment might have thought to be reasonable." Thus, the first step here is to assess Atwater's claim that peace officers' authority to make warrantless arrests for misdemeanors was restricted at common law (whether "common law" is understood strictly as law judicially derived or, instead, as the whole body of law extant at the time of

the framing). Atwater's specific contention is that "founding-era common-law rules" forbade peace officers to make warrantless misdemeanor arrests except in cases of "breach of the peace," a category she claims was then understood narrowly as covering only those nonfelony offenses "involving or tending toward violence." Although her historical argument is by no means insubstantial, it ultimately fails. . . .

The point is that the statutes riddle Atwater's supposed common-law rule with enough exceptions to unsettle any contention that the law of the mother country would have left the Fourth Amendment's Framers of a view that it would necessarily have been unreasonable to arrest without warrant for a misdemeanor unaccompanied by real or threatened violence.

An examination of specifically American evidence is to the same effect. Neither the history of the framing era nor subsequent legal development indicates that the Fourth Amendment was originally understood, or has traditionally been read, to embrace Atwater's position. . . .

What we have here, then, is just the opposite of what we had in *Wilson* v. *Arkansas*. There, we emphasized that during the founding era a number of States had "enacted statutes specifically embracing" the common-law knock-and-announce rule; here, by contrast, those very same States passed laws extending warrantless arrest authority to a host of nonviolent misdemeanors, and in so doing acted very much inconsistently with Atwater's claims about the Fourth Amendment's object. Of course, the Fourth Amendment did not originally apply to the States, but that does not make state practice irrelevant in unearthing the Amendment's original meaning. A number of state constitutional search-and-seizure provisions served as models for the Fourth Amendment, and the fact that many of the original States with such constitutional limitations continued to grant their own peace officers broad warrantless misdemeanor arrest authority undermines Atwater's contention that the founding generation meant to bar federal law enforcement officers from exercising the same authority. . . .

Nor does Atwater's argument from tradition pick up any steam from the historical record as it has unfolded since the framing, there being no indication that her claimed rule has ever become "woven . . . into the fabric" of American law. . . .

The story, on the contrary, is of two centuries of uninterrupted (and largely unchallenged) state and federal practice permitting warrantless arrests for misdemeanors not amounting to or involving breach of the peace. . . .

Small wonder, then, that today statutes in all 50 States and the District of Columbia permit warrantless misdemeanor arrests by at least some (if not all) peace officers without requiring any breach of the peace, as do a host of congressional enactments. . . .

While it is true here that history, if not unequivocal, has expressed a decided, majority view that the police need not obtain an arrest warrant merely because a misdemeanor stopped short of violence or a threat of it, Atwater does not wager all on history. Instead, she asks us to mint a new rule of constitutional law on the understanding that when historical practice fails to speak conclusively to a claim grounded on the Fourth Amendment, courts are left to strike a current balance between individual and societal interests by subjecting particular contemporary circumstances to traditional standards of reasonableness. Atwater accordingly argues for a modern arrest rule, one not necessarily requiring violent breach of the peace, but nonetheless forbidding custodial arrest, even upon probable cause, when conviction could not ultimately carry any jail time and when the government shows no compelling need for immediate detention.

If we were to derive a rule exclusively to address the uncontested facts of this case, Atwater might well prevail. She was a known and established resident of Lago Vista with no place to hide and no incentive to flee, and common sense says she would almost certainly have buckled up as a condition of driving off with a citation. In her case, the physical incidents of arrest were merely gratuitous humiliations imposed by a police officer who was (at best) exercising extremely poor judgment. Atwater's claim to live free of pointless indignity and confinement clearly outweighs anything the City can raise against it specific to her case. But we have traditionally recognized that a responsible Fourth Amendment balance is not well served by standards requiring sensitive, case-by-case determinations of government need, lest every discretionary judgment in the field be converted into an occasion for constitutional review. Often enough, the Fourth Amendment has to be applied on the spur (and in the heat) of the moment, and the object in implementing its command of reasonableness is to draw standards sufficiently clear and simple to be applied with a fair prospect of surviving judicial second-guessing months and years after an arrest or search is made. Courts attempting to strike a reasonable Fourth Amendment balance thus credit the government's side with an essential interest in readily administrable rules. . . .

At first glance, Atwater's argument may seem to respect the values of clarity and simplicity, so far as she claims that the Fourth Amendment generally forbids warrantless arrests for minor crimes not accompanied by violence or some demonstrable threat of it (whether "minor crime" be defined as a fine-only traffic offense, a fine-only offense more generally, or a misdemeanor). But the claim is not ultimately so simple, nor could it be, for complications arise the moment we begin to think about the possible applications of the several criteria Atwater proposes for drawing a line between minor crimes with limited arrest authority and others not so restricted.

One line, she suggests, might be between "jailable" and "fine-only" offenses, between those for which conviction could result in commitment and those for which it could not. The trouble with this distinction, of course, is that an officer on the street might not be able to tell. It is not merely that we cannot expect every police officer to know the details of frequently complex penalty schemes, . . . but that penalties for ostensibly identical conduct can vary on account of facts difficult (if not impossible) to know at the scene of an arrest. Is this the first offense or is the suspect a repeat offender? Is the weight of the marijuana a gram above or a gram below the fine-only line? Where conduct could implicate more than one criminal prohibition, which one will the district attorney ultimately decide to charge? And so on.

But Atwater's refinements would not end there. She represents that if the line were drawn at nonjailable traffic offenses, her proposed limitation should be qualified by a proviso authorizing warrantless arrests where "necessary for enforcement of the traffic laws or when [an] offense would otherwise continue and pose a danger to others on the road." . . . The proviso only compounds the difficulties. Would, for instance, either exception apply to speeding? At oral argument, Atwater's counsel said that "it would not be reasonable to arrest a driver for speeding unless the speeding rose to the level of reckless driving." But is it not fair to expect that the chronic speeder will speed again despite a citation in his pocket, and should that not qualify as showing that the "offense would . . . continue" under Atwater's rule? And why, as a constitutional matter, should we assume that only reckless driving

will "pose a danger to others on the road" while speeding will not? . . .

Just how easily the costs could outweigh the benefits may be shown by asking, as one Member of this Court did at oral argument, "how bad the problem is out there." The very fact that the law has never jelled the way Atwater would have it leads one to wonder whether warrantless misdemeanor arrests need constitutional attention, and there is cause to think the answer is no. . . .

The upshot of all these influences, combined with the good sense (and, failing that, the political accountability) of most local lawmakers and law-enforcement officials, is a dearth of horribles demanding redress. . . .

Accordingly, we confirm today what our prior cases have intimated: the standard of probable cause "applie[s] to all arrests, without the need to 'balance' the interests and circumstances involved in particular situations." If an officer has probable cause to believe that an individual has committed even a very minor criminal offense in his presence, he may, without violating the Fourth Amendment, arrest the offender. . . .

The Court of Appeals's en banc judgment is affirmed.

*It is so ordered.*

## JUSTICE O'CONNOR, with whom JUSTICE STEVENS, JUSTICE GINSBURG, and JUSTICE BREYER join, dissenting. . . .

The Court recognizes that the arrest of Gail Atwater was a "pointless indignity" that served no discernible state interest, and yet holds that her arrest was constitutionally permissible. Because the Court's position is inconsistent with the explicit guarantee of the Fourth Amendment, I dissent.

A full custodial arrest, such as the one to which Ms. Atwater was subjected, is the quintessential seizure. . . . When a full custodial arrest is effected without a warrant, the plain language of the Fourth Amendment requires that the arrest be reasonable. . . .

The majority gives a brief nod to this bedrock principle of our Fourth Amendment jurisprudence, and even acknowledges that "Atwater's claim to live free of pointless indignity and confinement clearly outweighs anything the City can raise against it specific to her case." But instead of remedying this imbalance, the majority allows itself to be swayed by the worry that "every discretionary judgment in the field [will] be converted into an occasion for constitutional review." It therefore mints a new rule that "[i]f an officer has probable cause to believe that an individual has committed even a very minor criminal offense in his presence, he may, without violating the Fourth Amendment, arrest the offender." This rule is not only unsupported by our precedent, but runs contrary to the principles that lie at the core of the Fourth Amendment.

As the majority tacitly acknowledges, we have never considered the precise question presented here, namely, the constitutionality of a warrantless arrest for an offense punishable only by fine. . . .

A custodial arrest exacts an obvious toll on an individual's liberty and privacy, even when the period of custody is relatively brief. The arrestee is subject to a full search of her person and confiscation of her possessions. If the arrestee is the occupant of a car, the entire passenger compartment of the car, including packages therein, is subject to search as well. The arrestee may be detained for up to 48 hours without having a magistrate determine whether there in fact was probable cause for the arrest. Because people arrested for all types of violent and nonviolent offenses may be housed together awaiting such review, this detention period is potentially dangerous. And once the period of custody is over, the fact of the arrest is a permanent part of the public record. . . .

If the State has decided that a fine, and not imprisonment, is the appropriate punishment for an offense, the State's interest in taking a person suspected of committing that offense into custody is surely limited, at best. This is not to say that the State will never have such an interest. A full custodial arrest may on occasion vindicate legitimate state interests, even if the crime is punishable only by fine. Arrest is the surest way to abate criminal conduct. It may also allow the police to verify the offender's identity and, if the offender poses a flight risk, to ensure her appearance at trial. But when such considerations are not present, a citation or summons may serve the State's remaining law enforcement interests every bit as effectively as an arrest. . . .

Because a full custodial arrest is such a severe intrusion on an individual's liberty, its reasonableness hinges on "the degree to which it is needed for the promotion of legitimate governmental interests." In light of the availability of citations to promote a State's interests when a fine-only offense has been committed, I cannot concur in a rule which deems a full custodial arrest to be reasonable in every circumstance. Giving police officers constitutional carte blanche to effect an arrest whenever there is probable cause to believe a fine-only misdemeanor has been committed is irreconcilable with the Fourth Amendment's command that seizures be reasonable. Instead, I would require that when there is probable cause to believe that a fine-only offense has been committed, the police officer should issue a citation unless the officer is "able to point to specific and articulable facts which, taken together with rational inferences from those facts, reasonably warrant [the additional] intrusion" of a full custodial arrest.

The majority insists that a bright-line rule focused on probable cause is necessary to vindicate the State's interest in easily administrable law enforcement rules. . . .

While clarity is certainly a value worthy of consideration in our Fourth Amendment jurisprudence, it by no means trumps the values of liberty and privacy at the heart of the Amendment's protections. . . .

The Court's error, however, does not merely affect the disposition of this case. The per se rule that the Court creates has potentially serious consequences for the everyday lives of Americans. A broad range of conduct falls into the category of fine-only misdemeanors. . . .

To be sure, such laws are valid and wise exercises of the States' power to protect the public health and welfare. My concern lies not with the decision to enact or enforce these laws, but rather with the manner in which they may be enforced. . . .

Such unbounded discretion carries with it grave potential for abuse. The majority takes comfort in the lack of evidence of "an epidemic of unnecessary minor-offense arrests." But the relatively small number of published cases dealing with such arrests proves little and should provide little solace. Indeed, as the recent debate over racial profiling demonstrates all too clearly, a relatively minor traffic infraction may often serve as an excuse for stopping and harassing an individual. After today, the arsenal available to any officer extends to a full arrest and the searches permissible concomitant to that arrest. An officer's subjective motivations for making a traffic stop are not relevant considerations in determining the reasonableness of the stop. But it is precisely because these motivations are beyond our purview that we must vigilantly ensure that officers' poststop actions—which are properly within our reach—comport with the Fourth Amendment's guarantee of reasonableness.

The Court neglects the Fourth Amendment's express command in the name of administrative ease. In so doing, it cloaks the pointless indignity that Gail Atwater suffered with the mantle of reasonableness. . . .

## *Terry* v. *Ohio*
## 392 U.S. 1, 88 S.Ct. 1868, 20 L.Ed. 2d 889 (1968)
### http://laws.findlaw.com/us/392/1.html

This case examined the constitutionality of the "stop and frisk" by police and presented the Warren Court with a Fourth Amendment dilemma. Was the situation Officer Martin McFadden observed sufficient to establish probable cause for arrest? If so, what would such a ruling do to the limits imposed on police behavior by the Constitution? If the Court found McFadden's actions constitutionally unacceptable, could the justices reasonably expect police officers in the future not to do precisely what McFadden had done? The reader should pay particular attention to Chief Justice Warren's emphasis on the facts. The decision came down after several years of increasingly violent street crime. In the courts below, the convictions of John Terry and his companion Richard Chilton for carrying concealed weapons had been upheld. Majority: Warren, Black, Brennan, Fortas, Harlan, Marshall, Stewart, White. Dissenting: Douglas.

**MR. CHIEF JUSTICE WARREN delivered the opinion of the Court. . . .**

Petitioner Terry was convicted of carrying a concealed weapon and sentenced to the statutorily prescribed term of one to three years in the penitentiary. Following the denial of a pretrial motion to suppress, the prosecution introduced in evidence two revolvers and a number of bullets seized from Terry and a codefendant, Richard Chilton, by Cleveland Police Detective Martin McFadden. At the hearing on the motion to suppress this evidence, Officer McFadden testified that while he was patrolling in plain clothes in downtown Cleveland at approximately 2:30 in the afternoon of October 31, 1963, his attention was attracted by two men, Chilton and Terry, standing on the corner of Huron Road and Euclid Avenue. He had never seen the two men before, and he was unable to say precisely what first drew his eye to them. However, he testified that he had been a policeman for 39 years and a detective for 35 and that he had been assigned to patrol this vicinity of downtown Cleveland for shoplifters and pickpockets for 30 years. . . .

His interest aroused, Officer McFadden took up a post of observation in the entrance to a store 300 to 400 feet away from the two men. . . . He saw one of the men leave the other one and walk southwest on Huron Road, past some stores. The man paused for a moment and looked in a store window, then walked on a short distance, turned around and walked back toward the corner, pausing once again to look in the same store window. He rejoined his companion at the corner, and the two conferred briefly. Then the second man went through the same series of motions, strolling down Huron Road, looking in the same window, walking on a short distance, turning back, peering in the store window again, and returning to confer with the first man at the corner. The two men repeated this ritual alternately between five and six times apiece—in all, roughly a dozen trips. At one point, while the two were standing together on the corner, a third man approached them and engaged them briefly in conversation. This man then left the two others and walked west on Euclid Avenue. Chilton and Terry resumed their measured pacing, peering, and conferring. After this had gone on for 10 to 12 minutes, the two men walked off together, heading west on Euclid Avenue, following the path taken earlier by the third man.

By this time Officer McFadden had become thoroughly suspicious. He testified that after observing their elaborately casual and oft-repeated reconnaissance of the store window on Huron Road, he suspected the two men of "casing a job, a stick-up," and that he considered it his duty as a police officer to investigate further. He added that he feared "they may have a gun." Thus, Officer McFadden followed Chilton and Terry and saw them stop in front of Zucker's store to talk to the same man who had conferred with them earlier on the street corner. Deciding that the situation was ripe for direct action, Officer McFadden approached the three men, identified himself as a police officer and asked for their names. At this point his knowledge was confined to

what he had observed. He was not acquainted with any of the three men by name or by sight, and he had received no information concerning them from any other source. When the men "mumbled something" in response to his inquiries, Officer McFadden grabbed petitioner Terry, spun him around so that they were facing the other two, with Terry between McFadden and the others, and patted down the outside of his clothing. In the left breast pocket of Terry's overcoat Officer McFadden felt a pistol. He reached inside the overcoat pocket, but was unable to remove the gun. At this point, keeping Terry between himself and the others, the officer ordered all three men to enter Zucker's store. As they went in, he removed Terry's overcoat completely, removed a .38-caliber revolver from the pocket and ordered all three men to face the wall with their hands raised. Officer McFadden proceeded to pat down the outer clothing of Chilton and the third man, Katz. He discovered another revolver in the outer pocket of Chilton's overcoat, but no weapons were found on Katz. . . .

Our first task is to establish at what point in this encounter the Fourth Amendment becomes relevant. That is, we must decide whether and when Officer McFadden "seized" Terry and whether and when he conducted a "search." . . . It is quite plain that the Fourth Amendment governs "seizures" of the person which do not eventuate in a trip to the station house and prosecution for a crime—"arrests" in traditional terminology. It must be recognized that whenever a police officer accosts an individual and restrains his freedom to walk away, he has "seized" that person. And it is nothing less than sheer torture of the English language to suggest that a careful exploration of the outer surfaces of a person's clothing all over his or her body in an attempt to find weapons is not a "search." . . .

The danger in the logic which proceeds upon distinctions between a "stop" and an "arrest," or "seizure" of the person, and between a "frisk" and a "search" is twofold. It seeks to isolate from constitutional scrutiny the initial stages of the contact between the policeman and the citizen. And by suggesting a rigid all-or-nothing model of justification and regulation under the Amendment, it obscures the utility of limitations upon the scope, as well as the initiation, of police action as a means of constitutional regulation. . . .

We therefore reject the notions that the Fourth Amendment does not come into play at all as a limitation upon police conduct if the officers stop short of something called a "technical arrest" or a "full-blown search." . . .

[W]e cannot blind ourselves to the need for law enforcement officers to protect themselves and other prospective victims of violence in situations where they may lack probable cause for an arrest. When an officer is justified in believing that the individual whose suspicious behavior he is investigating at close range is armed and presently dangerous to the officer or to others, it would appear to be clearly unreasonable to deny the officer the power to take necessary measures to determine whether the person is in fact carrying a weapon and to neutralize the threat of physical harm. . . .

We conclude that the revolver seized from Terry was properly admitted in evidence against him. . . . Each case of this sort will, of course, have to be decided on its own facts. We merely hold today that where a police officer observes unusual conduct which leads him reasonably to conclude in light of his experience that criminal activity may be afoot and that the persons with whom he is dealing may be armed and presently dangerous, where in the course of investigating this behavior he identifies himself as a policeman and makes reasonable inquiries, and where nothing in the initial stages of the encounter serves to dispel his reasonable fear for his own or others' safety, he is entitled for the protection of himself and others in the area to conduct a carefully limited search of the outer clothing of such persons in an attempt to discover weapons which might be used to assault him.

Such a search is a reasonable search under the Fourth Amendment, and any weapons seized may properly be introduced in evidence against the person from whom they were taken.

*Affirmed.*

MR. JUSTICE HARLAN, concurring . . . [omitted].

MR. JUSTICE WHITE, concurring . . . [omitted].

**MR. JUSTICE DOUGLAS, dissenting. . . .**

[I]t is a mystery how that "search" and that "seizure" can be constitutional by Fourth Amendment standards, unless there was "probable cause" to believe that (1) a crime had been committed or (2) a crime was in the process of being committed or (3) a crime was about to be committed. . . .

## G. ADMINISTRATIVE SEARCHES

### *Board of Education of Pottawatomie County* v. *Earls*
### 536 U.S. 822, 122 S.Ct. 2559, 153 L.Ed. 2d 735 (2002)
### http://laws.findlaw.com/us/536/822.html

The Pottawatomie County School Board in the rural community of Tecumseh, Oklahoma, adopted the Student Activities Drug Testing Policy that requires all middle and high school students to consent to urinalysis testing for drugs in order to participate in any extracurricular activity. In practice, the policy has been applied only to competitive extracurricular activities sanctioned by the Oklahoma Secondary Schools Activities Association. Lindsay Earls, a high school student, was a member of the show choir, the marching band, the Academic Team, and the National Honor Society. Daniel James, another student, hoped to participate on the Academic Team. They and their parents challenged the policy as a violation of the Fourth Amendment. Applying *Vernonia School District* v. *Acton* (1995), the U.S. District Court for the Western District of Oklahoma granted the school district summary judgment. The U.S. Court of Appeals for the Tenth Circuit reversed, concluding that the school board had failed to demonstrate (1) the existence of a drug problem among those tested and (2) the efficacy of the policy in addressing whatever drug problem might exist. Majority: Thomas, Breyer, Kennedy, Rehnquist, Scalia. Dissenting: Ginsburg, O'Connor, Souter, Stevens.

## JUSTICE THOMAS delivered the opinion of the Court.

The Student Activities Drug Testing Policy implemented by the Board of Education of Independent School District No. 92 of Pottawatomie County requires all students who participate in competitive extracurricular activities to submit to drug testing. Because this Policy reasonably serves the School District's important interest in detecting and preventing drug use among its students, we hold that it is constitutional. . . .

Searches by public school officials, such as the collection of urine samples, implicate Fourth Amendment interests. We must therefore review the School District's Policy for "reasonableness," which is the touchstone of the constitutionality of a governmental search. . . .

Given that the School District's Policy is not in any way related to the conduct of criminal investigations, respondents do not contend that the School District requires probable cause before testing students for drug use. Respondents instead argue that drug testing must be based at least on some level of individualized suspicion. . . . But we have long held that "the Fourth Amendment imposes no irreducible requirement of [individualized] suspicion." "[I]n certain limited circumstances, the Government's need to discover such latent or hidden conditions, or to prevent their development, is sufficiently compelling to justify the intrusion on privacy entailed by conducting such searches without any measure of individualized suspicion." Therefore, in the context of safety and administrative regulations, a search unsupported by probable cause may

be reasonable "when 'special needs, beyond the normal need for law enforcement, make the warrant and probable-cause requirement impracticable.'" . . .

In *Vernonia,* this Court held that the suspicionless drug testing of athletes was constitutional. The Court, however, did not simply authorize all school drug testing, but rather conducted a fact-specific balancing of the intrusion on the children's Fourth Amendment rights against the promotion of legitimate governmental interests. Applying the principles of *Vernonia* to the somewhat different facts of this case, we conclude that Tecumseh's Policy is also constitutional.

We first consider the nature of the privacy interest allegedly compromised by the drug testing. . . .

A student's privacy interest is limited in a public school environment where the State is responsible for maintaining discipline, health, and safety. Schoolchildren are routinely required to submit to physical examinations and vaccinations against disease. Securing order in the school environment sometimes requires that students be subjected to greater controls than those appropriate for adults.

Respondents argue that because children participating in nonathletic extracurricular activities are not subject to regular physicals and communal undress, they have a stronger expectation of privacy than the athletes tested in *Vernonia.* This distinction, however, was not essential to our decision in *Vernonia,* which depended primarily upon the school's custodial responsibility and authority.

In any event, students who participate in competitive extracurricular activities voluntarily subject themselves to many of the same intrusions on their privacy as do athletes. Some of these clubs and activities require occasional off-campus travel and communal undress. All of them have their own rules and requirements for participating students that do not apply to the student body as a whole. . . . We therefore conclude that the students affected by this Policy have a limited expectation of privacy.

Next, we consider the character of the intrusion imposed by the Policy. Urination is "an excretory function traditionally shielded by great privacy." But the "degree of intrusion" on one's privacy caused by collecting a urine sample "depends upon the manner in which production of the urine sample is monitored."

Under the Policy, a faculty monitor waits outside the closed restroom stall for the student to produce a sample and must "listen for the normal sounds of urination in order to guard against tampered specimens and to insure an accurate chain of custody." The monitor then pours the sample into two bottles that are sealed and placed into a mailing pouch along with a consent form signed by the student. This procedure is virtually identical to that reviewed in *Vernonia,* except that it additionally protects privacy by allowing male students to produce their samples behind a closed stall. Given that we considered the method of collection in *Vernonia* a "negligible" intrusion, the method here is even less problematic.

In addition, the Policy clearly requires that the test results be kept in confidential files separate from a student's other educational records and released to school personnel only on a "need to know" basis. . . .

Moreover, the test results are not turned over to any law enforcement authority. Nor do the test results here lead to the imposition of discipline or have any academic consequences. Rather, the only consequence of a failed drug test is to limit the student's privilege of participating in extracurricular activities. Indeed, a student may test positive for drugs twice and still be allowed to participate in extracurricular activities. . . .

Given the minimally intrusive nature of the sample collection and the limited uses to which the test results are put, we conclude

that the invasion of students' privacy is not significant.

Finally, this Court must consider the nature and immediacy of the government's concerns and the efficacy of the Policy in meeting them. This Court has already articulated in detail the importance of the governmental concern in preventing drug use by schoolchildren. . . .

Additionally, the School District in this case has presented specific evidence of drug use at Tecumseh schools. Teachers testified that they had seen students who appeared to be under the influence of drugs and that they had heard students speaking openly about using drugs. . . .

Respondents consider the proffered evidence insufficient and argue that there is no "real and immediate interest" to justify a policy of drug testing nonathletes. We have recognized, however, that "[a] demonstrated problem of drug abuse . . . [is] not in all cases necessary to the validity of a testing regime," but that some showing does "shore up an assertion of special need for a suspicionless general search program." The School District has provided sufficient evidence to shore up the need for its drug testing program.

Furthermore, this Court has not required a particularized or pervasive drug problem before allowing the government to conduct suspicionless drug testing. For instance, in [*Treasury Employees Union* v.] *Von Raab* the Court upheld the drug testing of customs officials on a purely preventive basis, without any documented history of drug use by such officials. . . . Likewise, the need to prevent and deter the substantial harm of childhood drug use provides the necessary immediacy for a school testing policy. Indeed, it would make little sense to require a school district to wait for a substantial portion of its students to begin using drugs before it was allowed to institute a drug testing program designed to deter drug use.

Given the nationwide epidemic of drug use, and the evidence of increased drug use in Tecumseh schools, it was entirely reasonable for the School District to enact this particular drug testing policy. We reject the Court of Appeals' novel test that "any district seeking to impose a random suspicionless drug testing policy as a condition to participation in a school activity must demonstrate that there is some identifiable drug abuse problem among a sufficient number of those subject to the testing, such that testing that group of students will actually redress its drug problem." Among other problems, it would be difficult to administer such a test. As we cannot articulate a threshold level of drug use that would suffice to justify a drug testing program for schoolchildren, we refuse to fashion what would in effect be a constitutional quantum of drug use necessary to show a "drug problem." . . .

We also reject respondents' argument that drug testing must presumptively be based upon an individualized reasonable suspicion of wrongdoing because such a testing regime would be less intrusive. . . . Moreover, we question whether testing based on individualized suspicion in fact would be less intrusive. Such a regime would place an additional burden on public school teachers who are already tasked with the difficult job of maintaining order and discipline. A program of individualized suspicion might unfairly target members of unpopular groups. The fear of lawsuits resulting from such targeted searches may chill enforcement of the program, rendering it ineffective in combating drug use. . . .

Finally, we find that testing students who participate in extracurricular activities is a reasonably effective means of addressing the School District's legitimate concerns in preventing, deterring, and detecting drug use. . . .

Within the limits of the Fourth Amendment, local school boards must assess the desirability of drug testing schoolchildren. In upholding the constitutionality of the Policy, we express no opinion as to its wisdom. Rather, we hold only that Tecumseh's Policy is a reasonable means of furthering the School District's important interest in preventing and deterring drug use among its schoolchildren. Accordingly, we reverse the judgment of the Court of Appeals.
*It is so ordered.*

JUSTICE BREYER, concurring . . . [omitted].
JUSTICE O'CONNOR, with whom JUSTICE SOUTER joins, dissenting . . . [omitted].

**JUSTICE GINSBURG, with whom JUSTICE STEVENS, JUSTICE O'CONNOR, and JUSTICE SOUTER join, dissenting.**

Seven years ago, in *Vernonia School Dist.* v. *Acton,* this Court determined that a school district's policy of randomly testing the urine of its student athletes for illicit drugs did not violate the Fourth Amendment. In so ruling, the Court emphasized that drug use "increase[d] the risk of sports-related injury" and that Vernonia's athletes were the "leaders" of an aggressive local "drug culture" that had reached "'epidemic proportions.'" Today, the Court relies upon *Vernonia* to permit a school district with a drug problem its superintendent repeatedly described as "not . . . major," to test the urine of an academic team member solely by reason of her participation in a nonathletic, competitive extracurricular activity—participation associated with neither special dangers from, nor particular predilections for, drug use. . . .

The particular testing program upheld today is not reasonable, it is capricious, even perverse: Petitioners' policy targets for testing a student population least likely to be at risk from illicit drugs and their damaging effects. I therefore dissent. . . .

This case presents circumstances dispositively different from those of *Vernonia.* True, as the Court stresses, Tecumseh students participating in competitive extracurricular activities other than athletics share two relevant characteristics with the athletes of *Vernonia.* First, both groups attend public schools. Concern for student health and safety is basic to the school's caretaking, and it is undeniable that "drug use carries a variety of health risks for children, including death from overdose."

Those risks, however, are present for *all* schoolchildren. *Vernonia* cannot be read to endorse invasive and suspicionless drug testing of all students upon any evidence of drug use, solely because drugs jeopardize the life and health of those who use them. . . . If a student has a reasonable subjective expectation of privacy in the personal items she brings to school, surely she has a similar expectation regarding the chemical composition of her urine. Had the *Vernonia* Court agreed that public school attendance, in and of itself, permitted the State to test each student's blood or urine for drugs, the opinion in *Vernonia* could have saved many words.

The second commonality to which the Court points is the voluntary character of both interscholastic athletics and other competitive extracurricular activities. . . .

The comparison is enlightening. While extracurricular activities are "voluntary" in the sense that they are not required for graduation, they are part of the school's educational program; for that reason, the petitioner (hereinafter School District) is justified in expending public resources to make them available. Participation in such activities is a key component of school life, essential in reality for students applying to college, and, for all participants, a significant contributor to the breadth and quality of the educational experience. Students "volunteer" for extracurricular pursuits in the same way they might volunteer for honors classes: They subject themselves to additional requirements, but they do so in order to take full advantage of the education offered them. . . .

Voluntary participation in athletics has a distinctly different dimension: Schools regulate student athletes discretely because competitive school sports by their nature require communal undress and, more important, expose students to physical risks that schools have a duty to mitigate. For the very reason that schools cannot offer a program of competitive athletics without intimately affecting the privacy of students, *Vernonia* reasonably analogized school athletes to "adults who choose to participate in a closely regulated industry." . . . Interscholastic athletics similarly require close safety and health regulation; a school's choir, band, and academic team do not. . . .

*Vernonia* initially considered "the nature of the privacy interest upon which the search [there] at issue intrude[d]." The Court emphasized that student athletes' expectations of privacy are necessarily attenuated. . . .

Competitive extracurricular activities other than athletics, however, serve students of all

manner: the modest and shy along with the bold and uninhibited. Activities of the kind plaintiff-respondent Lindsay Earls pursued—choir, show choir, marching band, and academic team—afford opportunities to gain self-assurance, to "come to know faculty members in a less formal setting than the typical classroom," and to acquire "positive social supports and networks [that] play a critical role in periods of heightened stress."

On "occasional out-of-town trips," students like Lindsay Earls "must sleep together in communal settings and use communal bathrooms." But those situations are hardly equivalent to the routine communal undress associated with athletics; the School District itself admits that when such trips occur, "public-like restroom facilities," which presumably include enclosed stalls, are ordinarily available for changing, and that "more modest students" find other ways to maintain their privacy. . . .

Finally, the "nature and immediacy of the governmental concern" faced by the Vernonia School District dwarfed that confronting Tecumseh administrators. . . .

Not only did the Vernonia and Tecumseh districts confront drug problems of distinctly different magnitudes, they also chose different solutions: Vernonia limited its policy to athletes; Tecumseh indiscriminately subjected to testing all participants in competitive extracurricular activities. Urging that "the safety interest furthered by drug testing is undoubtedly substantial for all children, athletes and nonathletes alike," the Court cuts out an element essential to the *Vernonia* judgment. Citing medical literature on the effects of combining illicit drug use with physical exertion, the *Vernonia* Court emphasized that "the particular drugs screened by [Vernonia's] Policy have been demonstrated to pose substantial physical risks to athletes." . . . Notwithstanding nightmarish images of out-of-control flatware, livestock run amok, and colliding tubas disturbing the peace and quiet of Tecumseh, the great majority of students the School District seeks to test in truth are engaged in activities that are not safety sensitive to an unusual degree. . . .

The Vernonia district, in sum, had two good reasons for testing athletes: Sports team members faced special health risks and they "were the leaders of the drug culture." No similar reason, and no other tenable justification, explains Tecumseh's decision to target for testing all participants in every competitive extracurricular activity. . . .

## II. RIGHT TO COUNSEL

### *Powell* v. *Alabama*
### 287 U.S. 45, 53 S.Ct. 55, 77 L.Ed. 158 (1932)
### http://laws.findlaw.com/us/287/45.html

The 1931 conviction in Scottsboro, Alabama, of seven black men charged with the rape of two white women resulted in a series of legal challenges in the Supreme Court of the United States, of which this case was the first. The chief justice of the Alabama Supreme Court had dissented from that court's affirmance of the convictions, chiefly because of the hostile atmosphere that surrounded the trial and the speed and casualness with which the trial judge had dealt with the question of counsel for the defendants. After the ruling by the Alabama Supreme Court, the Communist-dominated International Labor Defense (ILD) wrested control of the case from the National Association for the Advancement of Colored People (NAACP), which was the first outside group to offer assistance of counsel after the defendants' convictions. The ILD then used the case in a worldwide campaign of mass meetings and picketing of American embassies while it pressed the appeals in the U.S. Supreme Court. Majority: Sutherland, Brandeis, Cardozo, Hughes, Roberts, Stone, Van Devanter. Dissenting: Butler, McReynolds.

**MR. JUSTICE SUTHERLAND delivered the opinion of the Court. . . .**

The record shows that immediately upon the return of the indictment defendants were arraigned and pleaded not guilty. Apparently they were not asked whether they had, or were able to employ, counsel, or wished to have counsel appointed; or whether they had friends or relatives who might assist in that regard if communicated with. That it would not have been an idle ceremony to have given the defendants reasonable opportunity to communicate with their families and endeavor to obtain counsel is demonstrated by the fact that very soon after conviction, able counsel appeared in their behalf. . . .

It is hardly necessary to say that the right to counsel being conceded, a defendant should be afforded a fair opportunity to secure counsel of his own choice. Not only was that not done here, but such designation of counsel as was attempted was either so indefinite or so close upon the trial as to amount to a denial of effective and substantial aid in that regard. This will be amply demonstrated by a brief review of the record.

April 6, six days after indictment, the trials began. When the first case was called, the court inquired whether the parties were ready for trial. The state's attorney replied that he was ready to proceed. No one answered for the defendants or appeared to represent or defend them. Mr. Roddy, a Tennessee lawyer not a member of the local bar, addressed the court, saying that he had not been employed, but that people who were interested had spoken to him about the case. He was asked by the court whether he intended to appear for the defendants, and answered that he would like to appear along with counsel that the court might appoint. . . .

And in this casual fashion the matter of counsel in a capital case was disposed of.

It thus will be seen that until the very morning of the trial no lawyer had been named or definitely designated to represent the defendants. . . .

[D]uring perhaps the most critical period of the proceedings against these defendants, that is to say, from the time of their arraignment until the beginning of their trial, when consultation, thorough-going investigation and preparation were vitally important, the defendants did not have the aid of counsel in any real sense, although they were as much entitled to such aid during that period as at the trial itself.

The Constitution of Alabama provides that in all criminal prosecutions the accused shall enjoy the right to have the assistance of counsel; and a state statute requires the court in a capital case, where the defendant is unable to employ counsel, to appoint counsel for him. The state Supreme Court held that these provisions had not been infringed, and with that holding we are powerless to interfere. The question, however, which it is our duty, and within our power, to decide, is whether the denial of the assistance of counsel contravenes the due process clause of the Fourteenth Amendment to the Federal Constitution. . . .

An affirmation of the right to the aid of counsel in petty offenses, and its denial in the case of crimes of the gravest character, where such aid is most needed, is so outrageous and so obviously a perversion of all sense of proportion that the rule was constantly, vigorously and sometimes passionately assailed by English statesmen and lawyers. . . .

The rule was rejected by the colonies. . . .

The Sixth Amendment, in terms, provides that in all criminal prosecutions the accused shall enjoy the right "to have the Assistance of Counsel for his defence." In the face of the reasoning of the Hurtado case, if it stood alone, it would be difficult to justify the conclusion that the right to counsel, being thus specifically granted by the Sixth Amendment, was also within the intendment of the due process of law clause. But the Hurtado case

does not stand alone. In the later case of *Chicago, Burlington & Q. R. Co.* v. *Chicago,* this court held that a judgment of a state court, even though authorized by statute, by which private property was taken for public use without just compensation, was in violation of the due process of law required by the Fourteenth Amendment, notwithstanding that the Fifth Amendment explicitly declares that private property shall not be taken for public use without just compensation. . . .

The fact that the right involved is of such a character that it cannot be denied without violating those "fundamental principles of liberty and justice which lie at the base of all our civil and political institutions" is obviously one of those compelling considerations which must prevail in determining whether it is embraced within the due process clause of the Fourteenth Amendment, although it be specifically dealt with in another part of the Federal Constitution. . . . While the question has never been categorically determined by this court, a consideration of the nature of the right and a review of the expressions of this and other courts makes it clear that the right to the aid of counsel is of this fundamental character. . . .

What, then, does a hearing include? Historically and in practice, in our own country at least, it has always included the right to the aid of counsel when desired and provided by the party asserting the right. The right to be heard would be, in many cases, of little avail if it did not comprehend the right to be heard by counsel. Even the intelligent and educated layman has small and sometimes no skill in the science of law. If charged with crime, he is incapable, generally, of determining for himself whether the indictment is good or bad. He is unfamiliar with the rules of evidence. Left without the aid of counsel he may be put on trial without a proper charge, and convicted upon incompetent evidence, or evidence irrelevant to the issue or otherwise inadmissible. He lacks both the skill and knowledge adequately to prepare his defense, even though he have a perfect one. He requires the guiding hand of counsel at every step in the proceedings against him. Without it, though he be not guilty, he faces the danger of conviction because he does not know how to establish his innocence. If that be true of men of intelligence, how much more true is it of the ignorant and illiterate, or those of feeble intellect. If in any case, civil or criminal, a state or federal court were arbitrarily to refuse to hear a party by counsel, employed by and appearing for him, it reasonably may not be doubted that such a refusal would be a denial of a hearing, and, therefore, of due process in the constitutional sense. . . .

In the light of the facts outlined in the forepart of this opinion—the ignorance and illiteracy of the defendants, their youth, the circumstances of public hostility, the imprisonment and the close surveillance of the defendants by the military forces, the fact that their friends and families were all in other states and communication with them necessarily difficult, and above all that they stood in deadly peril of their lives—we think the failure of the trial court to give them reasonable time and opportunity to secure counsel was a clear denial of due process.

But passing that, and assuming their inability, even if opportunity had been given, to employ counsel, as the trial court evidently did assume, we are of opinion that, under the circumstances just stated, the necessity of counsel was so vital and imperative that the failure of the trial court to make an effective appointment of counsel was likewise a denial of due process within the meaning of the Fourteenth Amendment. Whether this would be so in other criminal prosecutions, or under other circumstances, we need not determine. All that it is necessary now to decide, as we do decide, is that in a capital case, where the defendant is unable to employ counsel, and is incapable adequately of making his own defense because of ignorance, feeblemindedness, illiteracy, or the like, it is the duty of the court, whether requested or not, to assign counsel for him as a necessary requisite of due process of law; and that duty is not discharged by an assignment at such a time or under such circumstances as to preclude the giving of effective aid in the preparation and trial of the case. . . .

The judgments must be reversed and the causes remanded for further proceedings not inconsistent with this opinion.

MR. JUSTICE BUTLER and MR. JUSTICE MCREYNOLDS dissented without opinion.

---

## Gideon v. Wainwright
### 372 U.S. 335, 83 S.Ct. 792, 9 L.Ed. 2d 799 (1963)
### http://laws.findlaw.com/us/372/335.html

> Clarence Gideon was charged in a Florida state court with breaking and entering a poolroom with the intent to commit a crime. This was a felony under Florida law. He appeared in court without a lawyer, and when he requested that the trial court appoint one for him because he could not afford retained counsel, the judge refused. Florida law at the time provided appointed counsel for indigents only in capital cases. Following conviction, Gideon filed a petition for habeas corpus in the Florida Supreme Court, which denied relief without opinion. Majority: Black, Brennan, Clark, Douglas, Goldberg, Harlan, Stewart, Warren, White.

**MR. JUSTICE BLACK delivered the opinion of the Court. . . .**

Since 1942, when *Betts* v. *Brady* . . . was decided by a divided Court, the problem of a defendant's federal constitutional right to counsel in a state court has been a continuing source of controversy and litigation in both state and federal courts. . . .

The facts upon which Betts claimed that he had been unconstitutionally denied the right to have counsel appointed to assist him are strikingly like the facts upon which Gideon here bases his federal constitutional claim. Betts was indicted for robbery in a Maryland state court. On arraignment, he told the trial judge of his lack of funds to hire a lawyer and asked the court to appoint one for him. Betts was advised that it was not the practice in that county to appoint counsel for indigent defendants except in murder and rape cases. He then pleaded not guilty, had witnesses summoned, crossexamined the State's witnesses, examined his own, and chose not to testify himself. He was found guilty by the judge, sitting without a jury, and sentenced to eight years in prison.

Like Gideon, Betts sought release by habeas corpus, alleging that he had been denied the right to assistance of counsel in violation of the Fourteenth Amendment. Betts was denied any relief, and on review this Court affirmed. It was held that a refusal to appoint counsel for an indigent defendant charged with a felony did not necessarily violate the Due Process Clause of the Fourteenth Amendment, which for reasons given the Court deemed to be the only applicable federal constitutional provision. The Court said,

> Asserted denial [of due process] is to be tested by an appraisal of the totality of facts in a given case. That which may, in one setting, constitute a denial of fundamental fairness, shocking to the universal sense of justice, may, in other circumstances, and in the light of other considerations, fall short of such denial. . . .

Treating due process as "a concept less rigid and more fluid than those envisaged in other specific and particular provisions of the Bill of Rights," the Court held that refusal to appoint counsel under the particular facts and circumstances in the Betts case was not so "offensive to the common and fundamental ideas of fairness" as to amount to a denial of due process. . . .

We accept *Betts* v. *Brady's* assumption, based as it was on our prior cases, that a provision of the Bill of Rights which is "fundamental and essential to a fair trial" is made

obligatory upon the States by the Fourteenth Amendment. We think the Court in *Betts* was wrong, however, in concluding that the Sixth Amendment's guarantee of counsel is not one of these fundamental rights. Ten years before *Betts,* this Court, after full consideration of all the historical data examined in *Betts,* had unequivocally declared that "the right to the aid of counsel is of this fundamental character." While the Court at the close of its Powell opinion did by its language, as this Court frequently does, limit its holding to the particular facts and circumstances of that case, its conclusions about the fundamental nature of the right to counsel are unmistakable. . . .

The fact is that in deciding as it did—that "appointment of counsel is not a fundamental right, essential to a fair trial"—the Court in *Betts* . . . made an abrupt break with its own well-considered precedents. In returning to these old precedents, sounder we believe than the new, we but restore constitutional principles established to achieve a fair system of justice. Not only these precedents but also reason and reflection require us to recognize that in our adversary system of criminal justice, any person haled into court, who is too poor to hire a lawyer, cannot be assured a fair trial unless counsel is provided for him. This seems to us to be an obvious truth. Governments, both state and federal, quite properly spend vast sums of money to establish machinery to try defendants accused of crime. Lawyers to prosecute are everywhere deemed essential to protect the public's interest in an orderly society. Similarly, there are few defendants charged with crime, few indeed, who fail to hire the best lawyers they can get to prepare and present their defenses. That government hires lawyers to prosecute and defendants who have the money hire lawyers to defend are the strongest indications of the widespread belief that lawyers in criminal courts are necessities, not luxuries. The right of one charged with crime to counsel may not be deemed fundamental and essential to fair trials in some countries, but it is in ours. From the very beginning, our state and national constitutions and laws have laid great emphasis on procedural and substantive safe-guards designed to assure fair trials before impartial tribunals in which every defendant stands equal before the law. This noble ideal cannot be realized if the poor man charged with crime has to face his accusers without a lawyer to assist him.

The Court in *Betts* . . . departed from the sound wisdom upon which the Court's holding in *Powell* v. *Alabama* rested. Florida, supported by two other States, has asked that *Betts* . . . be left intact. Twenty-two States, as friends of the Court, argue that *Betts* was "an anachronism when handed down" and that it should now be overruled. We agree.

The judgment is reversed and the cause is remanded to the Supreme Court of Florida for further action not inconsistent with this opinion.

*Reversed.*


MR. JUSTICE DOUGLAS, concurring . . . [omitted].

MR. JUSTICE CLARK, concurring . . . [omitted].

**MR. JUSTICE HARLAN, concurring. . . .**

In noncapital cases, the "special circumstances" rule has continued to exist in form while its substance has been substantially and steadily eroded. In the first decade after *Betts,* there were cases in which the Court found special circumstances to be lacking, but usually by a sharply divided vote. However, no such decision has been cited to us, and I have found none, after *Quicksall* v. *Michigan* . . . decided in 1950. . . . The Court has come to recognize, in other words, that the mere existence of a serious criminal charge constituted in itself special circumstances requiring the services of counsel at trial. In truth the *Betts* . . . rule is no longer a reality.

This evolution, however, appears not to have been fully recognized by many state courts, in this instance charged with the front-line responsibility for the enforcement of constitutional rights. To continue a rule which is honored by this Court only with lip service is not a healthy thing and in the long run will do disservice to the federal system. . . .


## III. SELF-INCRIMINATION

### *Miranda* v. *Arizona*
### 384 U.S. 436, 86 S.Ct. 1602, 16 L.Ed. 2d 694 (1966)
### http://laws.findlaw.com/us/384/436.html

In *Escobedo* v. *Illinois* (1964), five justices overturned a conviction after police interrogated the defendant without first advising him of a right to remain silent and to consult with counsel in circumstances where police also denied his request to consult with counsel waiting outside the interrogation room. Two years later, the Court reviewed four cases that plainly raised the question whether police had an affirmative obligation to advise suspects of certain rights before interrogating them, if the fruits of the interrogation were to be admissible at trial. Although the interrogations in the four cases took place for varying lengths of time, none of the cases contained an allegation of violence or threat of violence to coerce the confession.

In one case, police in Phoenix, Arizona, arrested Ernesto Miranda at his home in 1963 on rape and kidnapping charges. The complaining witness identified him at the police station. Without advising him of a right to have an attorney present, two officers then questioned Miranda for two hours and obtained a signed confession from him. At the top of the statement was a typed paragraph explaining that the confession was made voluntarily, without threats or promises of immunity, and "with full knowledge of my legal rights, understanding any statement I make may be used against me." One of the officers later explained that he read this paragraph to Miranda, but apparently only after Miranda had confessed orally. The prosecution introduced the signed confession at trial, and Miranda was convicted of rape and kidnapping. The Supreme Court of Arizona affirmed. Majority: Warren, Black, Brennan, Douglas, Fortas. Dissenting: Harlan, Clark, Stewart, White.

## MR. CHIEF JUSTICE WARREN delivered the opinion of the Court. . . .

Our holding . . . briefly stated . . . is this: the prosecution may not use statements, whether exculpatory or inculpatory, stemming from custodial interrogation of the defendant unless it demonstrates the use of procedural safeguards effective to secure the privilege against self-incrimination. By custodial interrogation, we mean questioning initiated by law enforcement officers after a person has been taken into custody or otherwise deprived of his freedom of action in any significant way. As for the procedural safeguards to be employed, unless other fully effective means are devised to inform accused persons of their right of silence and to assure a continuous opportunity to exercise it, the following measures are required. Prior to any questioning, the person must be warned that he has a right to remain silent, that any statement he does make may be used as evidence against him, and that he has a right to the presence of an attorney, either retained or appointed. The defendant may waive effectuation of these rights, provided the waiver is made voluntarily, knowingly and intelligently. If, however, he indicates in any manner and at any stage of the process that he wishes to consult with an attorney before speaking there can be no questioning. Likewise, if the individual is alone and indicates in any manner that he does not wish to be interrogated, the police may not question him. The mere fact that he may have answered some questions or volunteered some statements on his own does not deprive him of the right to refrain from answering any further inquiries until he has consulted with an attorney and thereafter consents to be questioned.

The constitutional issue we decide in each of these cases is the admissibility of statements obtained from a defendant questioned while in custody and deprived of his freedom of action. In each, the defendant was questioned by police officers, detectives, or a prosecuting attorney in a room in which he was cut off from the outside world. In none of these cases was the defendant given a full and effective warning of his rights at the outset of the interrogation process. In all the cases, the questioning elicited oral admissions, and in three of them, signed statements as well which were admitted at their trials. They all thus share salient features—incommunicado interrogation of individuals in a police-dominated atmosphere, resulting in self-incriminating statements without full warnings of constitutional rights.

An understanding of the nature and setting of this in-custody interrogation is essential to our decisions today. . . .

[T]he modern practice of in-custody interrogation is psychologically rather than physically oriented. . . . Interrogation still takes place in privacy. Privacy results in secrecy and this in turn results in a gap in our knowledge as to what in fact goes on in the interrogation rooms. A valuable source of information about present police practices, however, may be found in various police manuals and texts which document procedures employed with success in the past, and which recommend various other effective tactics. [The opinion surveys manuals and texts.]

From these representative samples of interrogation techniques, the setting prescribed by the manuals and observed in practice becomes clear. In essence, it is this: To be alone with the subject is essential to prevent distraction and to deprive him of any outside support. The aura of confidence in his guilt undermines his will to resist. He merely confirms the preconceived story the police seek to have him describe. Patience and persistence, at times relentless questioning, are employed. To obtain a confession, the interrogator must "patiently maneuver himself or his quarry into a position from which the desired object may be obtained." When normal procedures fail to produce the needed result, the police may resort to deceptive stratagems such as giving false legal advice. It is important to keep the subject off balance, for example, by trading on his insecurity about himself or his surroundings. The police then persuade, trick, or cajole him out of exercising his constitutional rights.

Even without employing brutality, the "third degree" or the specific stratagems described above, the very fact of custodial interrogation exacts a heavy toll on individual liberty and trades on the weakness of individuals.

In these cases, we might not find the defendants' statements to have been involuntary in traditional terms. Our concern for adequate safeguards to protect precious Fifth Amendment rights is, of course, not lessened in the slightest. To be sure, the records do not evince overt physical coercion or patented psychological ploys. The fact remains that in none of these cases did the officers undertake to afford appropriate safeguards at the outset of the interrogation to insure that the statements were truly the product of free choice. . . .

The circumstances surrounding in-custody interrogation can operate very quickly to overbear the will of one merely made aware of his privilege by his interrogators. Therefore, the right to have counsel present at the interrogation is indispensable to the protection of the Fifth Amendment privilege under the system we delineate today. Our aim is to assure that the individual's right to choose between silence and speech remains unfettered throughout the interrogation process. . . .

Our decision is not intended to hamper the traditional function of police officers in investigating crime. . . . General on-the-scene questioning as to facts surrounding a crime or other general questioning of citizens in the fact-finding process is not affected by our holding. It is an act of responsible citizenship for individuals to give whatever information

they may have to aid in law enforcement. In such situations the compelling atmosphere inherent in the process of in-custody interrogation is not necessarily present.

In dealing with statements obtained through interrogation, we do not purport to find all confessions inadmissible. Confessions remain a proper element in law enforcement. Any statement given freely and voluntarily without any compelling influences is, of course, admissible in evidence. The fundamental import of the privilege while an individual is in custody is not whether he is allowed to talk to the police without the benefit of warnings and counsel, but whether he can be interrogated. There is no requirement that police stop a person who enters a police station and states that he wishes to confess to a crime, or a person who calls the police to offer a confession or any other statement he desires to make. Volunteered statements of any kind are not barred by the Fifth Amendment and their admissibility is not affected by our holding today. . . .

*It is so ordered.*

Mr. Justice Clark, dissenting . . . [omitted].

**Mr. Justice Harlan, whom
Mr. Justice Stewart and
Mr. Justice White join, dissenting.**

I believe the decision of the Court represents poor constitutional law and entails harmful consequences for the country at large. How serious these consequences may prove to be only time can tell. . . . The new rules are not designed to guard against police brutality or other unmistakably banned forms of coercion. Those who use third-degree tactics and deny them in court are equally able and destined to lie as skillfully about warnings and waivers. Rather, the thrust of the new rules is to negate all pressures, to reinforce the nervous or ignorant suspect, and ultimately to discourage any confession at all. The aim in short is toward "voluntariness" in a utopian sense, or to view it from a different angle, voluntariness with a vengeance.

To incorporate this notion into the Constitution requires a strained reading of history and precedent and a disregard of the very pragmatic concerns that alone may on occasion justify such strains. I believe that reasoned examination will show that the Due Process Clause provides an adequate tool for coping with confessions and that, even if the Fifth Amendment privilege against self-incrimination be invoked, its precedents taken as a whole do not sustain the present rules. . . .

The more important premise is that pressure on the suspect must be eliminated though it be only the subtle influence of the atmosphere and surroundings. The Fifth Amendment, however, has never been thought to forbid all pressure to incriminate oneself in the situations covered by it. . . . However, the Court's unspoken assumption that any pressure violates the privilege is not supported by the precedents and it has failed to show why the Fifth Amendment prohibits that relatively mild pressure the Due Process Clause permits. . . .

Examined as an expression of public policy, the Court's new regime proves so dubious that there can be no due compensation for its weakness in constitutional law. . . . [T]he Court has not and cannot make the powerful showing that its new rules are plainly desirable in the context of our society, something which is surely demanded before those rules are engrafted onto the Constitution and imposed on every State and county in the land. . . .

Until today, the role of the constitution has been only to sift out undue pressure, not to assure spontaneous confessions.

**MR. JUSTICE WHITE, with whom MR. JUSTICE HARLAN and MR. JUSTICE STEWART join, dissenting. . . .**

[E]ven if one assumed that there was an adequate factual basis for the conclusion that all confessions obtained during in-custody interrogation are the product of compulsion, the rule propounded by the Court would still be irrational, for, apparently, it is only if the accused is also warned of his right to counsel and waives both that right and the right against self-incrimination that the inherent compulsiveness of interrogation disappears. But if the defendant may not answer without a warning a question such as "Where were you last night?" without having his answer be a compelled one, how can the Court ever accept his negative answer to the question of whether he wants to consult his retained counsel or counsel whom the court will appoint? And why if counsel is present and the accused nevertheless confesses, or counsel tells the accused to tell the truth, and that is what the accused does, is the situation any less coercive insofar as the accused is concerned? The Court apparently realizes its dilemma of foreclosing questioning without the necessary warnings but at the same time permitting the accused, sitting in the same chair in front of the same policemen, to waive his right to consult an attorney. It expects, however, that the accused will not often waive the right; and if it is claimed that he has, the State faces a severe, if not impossible burden of proof. . . .

## Dickerson v. United States
### 530 U.S. 428, 120 S. Ct. 2326, 147 L.Ed. 2d 405 (2000)
#### http://laws.findlaw.com/us/530/428.html

Two years after the Court decided *Miranda* v. *Arizona,* Congress passed the Omnibus Crime Control and Safe Streets Act. Section 3501 attempted to sidestep *Miranda* by allowing use in federal courts of confessions voluntarily given, even if they were not preceded by the precise Miranda warnings. Between 1968 and 1997, a succession of attorneys general made no use of § 3501. In January 1997 Charles Dickerson confessed to an FBI agent and a detective that he had been involved in robbing as many as seven banks in Maryland and Virginia. Following his indictment on federal bank robbery charges, the U.S. District Court for the Northern District of Virginia suppressed the confession because Dickerson had made it before receiving the Miranda warnings. The U.S. attorney asked the district court to reconsider its ruling. Even if the confession ran afoul of *Miranda,* the government contended, it was nonetheless admissible under § 3501 because, by the district court's own holding, the confession was "voluntary." Attorney General Janet Reno's office intervened, directing the U.S. attorney to abandon reliance on § 3501. Accordingly, the government's appeal to the U.S. Court of Appeals for the Fourth Circuit Court maintained, among other things, that Dickerson had confessed only after the Miranda warnings had been administered. In a 2–1 ruling in 1999, the Fourth Circuit agreed with the district court that Dickerson's confession was unwarned (and so was at odds with *Miranda*) but that, because of § 3501, the confession was admissible. In the appeals court's view, Miranda's required warnings were judicially created rules of evidence to guard against involuntary (and hence unconstitutional) confessions. As rules of evidence, not dictates of the Constitution, they were subject to modification by Congress. When the case reached the Supreme Court, both counsel for Dickerson and U.S. Solicitor General Seth Waxman argued against the validity of § 3501. At invitation of the Court, Professor Paul G. Cassell appeared as amicus curiae in support of the statute. Majority: Rehnquist, Stevens, O'Connor, Kennedy, Souter, Ginsburg, Breyer. Dissenting: Scalia, Thomas.

**CHIEF JUSTICE REHNQUIST delivered the opinion of the Court. . . .**

We hold that *Miranda,* being a constitutional decision of this Court, may not be in effect overruled by an Act of Congress, and we decline to overrule *Miranda* ourselves. We therefore hold that *Miranda* and its progeny in this Court govern the admissibility of statements made during custodial interrogation in both state and federal courts. . . .

Prior to *Miranda,* we evaluated the admissibility of a suspect's confession under a voluntariness test. The roots of this test developed in the common law, as the courts of England and then the United States recognized that coerced confessions are inherently untrustworthy. . . . Over time, our cases recognized two constitutional bases for the requirement that a confession be voluntary to be admitted into evidence: the Fifth Amendment right against self-incrimination and the Due Process Clause of the Fourteenth Amendment. . . .

[F]or the middle third of the 20th century our cases based the rule against admitting coerced confessions primarily, if not exclusively, on notions of due process. We applied the due process voluntariness test in "some 30 different cases decided during the era that intervened between *Brown* [v. *Mississippi* (1936)] and *Escobedo* v. *Illinois* (1964). Those cases refined the test into an inquiry that examines "whether a defendant's will was overborne" by the circumstances surrounding the giving of a confession. The due process test takes into consideration "the totality of all the surrounding circumstances—both the characteristics of the accused and the details of the interrogation." . . .

We have never abandoned this due process jurisprudence, and thus continue to exclude confessions that were obtained involuntarily. But our decisions in *Malloy* v. *Hogan* (1964) and *Miranda* changed the focus of much of the inquiry in determining the admissibility of suspects' incriminating statements. In *Malloy,* we held that the Fifth Amendment's Self-Incrimination Clause is incorporated in the Due Process Clause of the Fourteenth Amendment and thus applies to the States. We decided *Miranda* on the heels of *Malloy.*

In *Miranda,* we noted that the advent of modern custodial police interrogation brought with it an increased concern about confessions obtained by coercion. . . . We concluded that the coercion inherent in custodial interrogation blurs the line between voluntary and involuntary statements, and thus heightens the risk that an individual will not be "accorded his privilege under the Fifth Amendment . . . not to be compelled to incriminate himself." Accordingly, we laid down "concrete constitutional guidelines for law enforcement agencies and courts to follow. Those guidelines established that the admissibility in evidence of any statement given during custodial interrogation of a suspect would depend on whether the police provided the suspect with four warnings." . . .

Two years after *Miranda* was decided, Congress enacted § 3501. That section provides, in relevant part:

(a) In any criminal prosecution brought by the United States or by the District of Columbia, a confession . . . shall be admissible in evidence if it is voluntarily given. . . .

(b) The trial judge in determining the issue of voluntariness shall take into consideration all the circumstances surrounding the giving of the confession, including (1) the time elapsing between arrest and arraignment of the defendant making the confession, if it was made after arrest and before arraignment, (2) whether such defendant knew the nature of the offense with which he was charged or of which he was suspected at the time of making the confession, (3) whether or not such defendant was advised or knew that he was not required to make any statement and that any such statement could be used against him, (4) whether or not such defendant had been advised prior to questioning of his right to the assistance of counsel; and (5) whether or not such defendant was without the assistance of counsel when questioned and when giving such confession. . . .

Given § 3501's express designation of voluntariness as the touchstone of admissibility, its omission of any warning requirement, and the instruction for trial courts to consider a nonexclusive list of factors relevant to the circumstances of a confession, we agree with the Court of Appeals that Congress intended by its enactment to overrule *Miranda.* . . . Because of the obvious conflict between our decision in *Miranda* and § 3501, we must address whether Congress has constitutional authority to thus supersede *Miranda*. If Congress has such authority, § 3501's totality-of-the-circumstances approach must prevail over *Miranda's* requirement of warnings; if not, that section must yield to *Miranda's* more specific requirements.

The law in this area is clear. This Court has supervisory authority over the federal courts, and we may use that authority to prescribe rules of evidence and procedure that are binding in those tribunals. However, the power to judicially create and enforce nonconstitutional "rules of procedure and evidence for the federal courts exists only in the absence of a relevant Act of Congress." Congress retains the ultimate authority to modify or set aside any judicially created rules of evidence and procedure that are not required by the Constitution.

But Congress may not legislatively supersede our decisions interpreting and applying the Constitution. This case therefore turns on whether the Miranda Court announced a constitutional rule or merely exercised its supervisory authority to regulate evidence in the absence of congressional direction. Recognizing this point, the Court of Appeals surveyed *Miranda* and its progeny to determine the constitutional status of the Miranda decision. . . . [T]he Court of Appeals concluded that the protections announced in *Miranda* are not constitutionally required.

We disagree with the Court of Appeals' conclusion, although we concede that there is language in some of our opinions that supports the view taken by that court. But first and foremost of the factors on the other side—that *Miranda* is a constitutional decision—is that both *Miranda* and two of its companion cases applied the rule to proceedings in state courts. . . .

In fact, the majority opinion is replete with statements indicating that the majority thought it was announcing a constitutional rule. . . .

Additional support for our conclusion that *Miranda* is constitutionally based is found in the Miranda Court's invitation for legislative action to protect the constitutional right against coerced self-incrimination. . . . [T]he Court emphasized that it could not foresee "the potential alternatives for protecting the privilege which might be devised by Congress or the States," and it accordingly opined that the Constitution would not preclude legislative solutions that differed from the prescribed Miranda warnings but which were "at least as effective in apprising accused persons of their right of silence and in assuring a continuous opportunity to exercise it." . . .

Whether or not we would agree with *Miranda's* reasoning and its resulting rule, were we addressing the issue in the first instance, the principles of stare decisis weigh heavily against overruling it now. . . .

The disadvantage of the Miranda rule is that statements which may be by no means involuntary, made by a defendant who is aware of his "rights," may nonetheless be excluded and a guilty defendant go free as a result. But experience suggests that the totality-of-the-circumstances test which § 3501 seeks to revive is more difficult than *Miranda* for law enforcement officers to conform to, and for courts to apply in a consistent manner. . . .

In sum, we conclude that *Miranda* announced a constitutional rule that Congress may not supersede legislatively. Following the rule of stare decisis, we decline to overrule *Miranda* ourselves. The judgment of the Court of Appeals is therefore

*Reversed.*

**JUSTICE SCALIA, with whom JUSTICE THOMAS joins, dissenting.**

Those to whom judicial decisions are an unconnected series of judgments that produce either favored or disfavored results will doubtless greet today's decision as a paragon of moderation, since it declines to overrule *Miranda* v. *Arizona.* Those who understand the judicial process will appreciate that today's decision is not a reaffirmation of *Miranda,* but a radical revision of the most significant element of *Miranda* (as of all cases): the rationale that gives it a permanent place in our jurisprudence.

*Marbury* v. *Madison* (1803) held that an Act of Congress will not be enforced by the courts if what it prescribes violates the Constitution of the United States. That was the basis on which *Miranda* was decided. One will search today's opinion in vain, however, for a statement (surely simple enough to make) that what 18 U.S.C. § 3501 prescribes—the use at trial of a voluntary confession, even when a Miranda warning or its equivalent has failed to be given—violates the Constitution. The reason the statement does not appear is not only (and perhaps not so much) that it would be absurd, inasmuch as § 3501 excludes from trial precisely what the Constitution excludes from trial, viz., compelled confessions; but also that Justices whose votes are needed to compose today's majority are on record as believing that a violation of *Miranda* is not a violation of the Constitution. . . . [T]he only thing that can possibly mean in the context of this case is that this Court has the power, not merely to apply the Constitution but to expand it, imposing what it regards as useful "prophylactic" restrictions upon Congress and the States. That is an immense and frightening antidemocratic power, and it does not exist.

It takes only a small step to bring today's opinion out of the realm of power-judging and into the mainstream of legal reasoning: The Court need only go beyond its carefully couched iterations that "*Miranda* is a constitutional decision," . . . and come out and say quite clearly: "We reaffirm today that custodial interrogation that is not preceded by Miranda warnings or their equivalent violates the Constitution of the United States." It cannot say that, because a majority of the Court does not believe it. The Court therefore acts in plain violation of the Constitution when it denies effect to this Act of Congress. . . .

It was once possible to characterize the so-called Miranda rule as resting (however implausibly) upon the proposition that what the statute here before us permits—the admission at trial of un-Mirandized confessions—violates the Constitution. That is the fairest reading of the Miranda case itself. The Court began by announcing that the Fifth Amendment privilege against self-incrimination applied in the context of extrajudicial custodial interrogation—itself a doubtful proposition as a matter both of history and precedent. . . . Having extended the privilege into the confines of the station house, the Court liberally sprinkled throughout its sprawling 60-page opinion suggestions that, because of the compulsion inherent in custodial interrogation, the privilege was violated by any statement thus obtained that did not conform to the rules set forth in *Miranda,* or some functional equivalent. . . .

So understood, *Miranda* was objectionable for innumerable reasons, not least the fact that cases spanning more than 70 years had rejected its core premise that, absent the warnings and an effective waiver of the right to remain silent and of the (hitherto unknown) right to have an attorney present, a statement obtained pursuant to custodial interrogation was necessarily the product of compulsion. . . . Moreover, history and precedent aside, the decision in *Miranda,* if read as an explication of what the Constitution requires, is preposterous. There is, for example, simply no basis in reason for concluding that a response to the very first question asked, by a suspect who already knows all of the rights described in the Miranda warning, is anything other than a volitional act. . . . And even if one assumes that the elimination of compulsion absolutely requires informing even the most knowledgeable suspect of his right to remain silent, it cannot conceivably require the right to have counsel present. There is a world of difference, which the Court recognized under the traditional voluntariness test but ignored in *Miranda,* between compelling a suspect to incriminate himself and preventing him from foolishly doing so of his own accord. Only the latter (which is not required by the Constitution) could explain the Court's inclusion of a right to counsel and the requirement that it, too, be knowingly and intelligently waived. Counsel's presence is not required to tell the suspect that he need not speak; the interrogators can do that. The only good reason for having counsel there is that he can be counted on to advise the suspect that he should not speak. . . .

As the Court today acknowledges, since *Miranda* we have explicitly, and repeatedly,

interpreted that decision as having announced, not the circumstances in which custodial interrogation runs afoul of the Fifth or Fourteenth Amendment, but rather only "prophylactic" rules that go beyond the right against compelled self-incrimination. Of course the seeds of this "prophylactic" interpretation of *Miranda* were present in the decision itself. . . . In subsequent cases, the seeds have sprouted and borne fruit: The Court has squarely concluded that it is possible—indeed not uncommon—for the police to violate *Miranda* without also violating the Constitution. . . . [Justice Scalia discusses *Michigan* v. *Tucker* (1974), *Oregon* v. *Hass* (1975), *New York* v. *Quarles* (1984), and *Oregon* v. *Elstad* (1985).]

In light of these cases, . . . it is simply no longer possible for the Court to conclude, even if it wanted to, that a violation of Miranda's rules is a violation of the Constitution. . . .

The Court seeks to avoid this conclusion in two ways: First, by misdescribing these post-Miranda cases as mere dicta. . . . It is not a matter of language; it is a matter of holdings. The proposition that failure to comply with *Miranda's* rules does not establish a constitutional violation was central to the holdings of *Tucker, Hass, Quarles,* and *Elstad.*

The second way the Court seeks to avoid the impact of these cases is simply to disclaim responsibility for reasoned decisionmaking. It says:

> These decisions illustrate the principle—not that *Miranda* is not a constitutional rule—but that no constitutional rule is immutable. No court laying down a general rule can possibly foresee the various circumstances in which counsel will seek to apply it, and the sort of modifications represented by these cases are as much a normal part of constitutional law as the original decision.

The issue, however, is not whether court rules are "mutable"; they assuredly are. It is not whether, in the light of "various circumstances," they can be "modifi[ed]"; they assuredly can. The issue is whether, as mutated and modified, they must make sense. The requirement that they do so is the only thing that prevents this Court from being some sort of nine-headed Caesar, giving thumbs-up or thumbs-down to whatever outcome, case by case, suits or offends its collective fancy. And if confessions procured in violation of *Miranda* are confessions "compelled" in violation of the Constitution, the post-*Miranda* decisions I have discussed do not make sense. The only reasoned basis for their outcome was that a violation of *Miranda* is not a violation of the Constitution. . . .

Finally, the Court asserts that *Miranda* must be a "constitutional decision" announcing a "constitutional rule," and thus immune to congressional modification, because we have since its inception applied it to the States. . . . [T]hough it is true that our cases applying *Miranda* against the States must be reconsidered if *Miranda* is not required by the Constitution, it is likewise true that our cases (discussed above) based on the principle that *Miranda* is not required by the Constitution will have to be reconsidered if it is. So the stare decisis argument is a wash. If, on the other hand, the argument is meant as an appeal to logic rather than stare decisis, it is a classic example of begging the question: Congress's attempt to set aside *Miranda,* since it represents an assertion that violation of *Miranda* is not a violation of the Constitution, also represents an assertion that the Court has no power to impose *Miranda* on the States. To answer this assertion—not by showing why violation of *Miranda* is a violation of the Constitution—but by asserting that *Miranda* does apply against the States, is to assume precisely the point at issue. In my view, our continued application of the Miranda code to the States despite our consistent statements

that running afoul of its dictates does not necessarily—or even usually—result in an actual constitutional violation, represents not the source of *Miranda's* salvation but rather evidence of its ultimate illegitimacy. . . .

Neither am I persuaded by the argument for retaining *Miranda* that touts its supposed workability as compared with the totality-of-the-circumstances test it purported to replace. *Miranda's* proponents cite ad nauseam the fact that the Court was called upon to make difficult and subtle distinctions in applying the "voluntariness" test in some 30-odd due process "coerced confessions" cases in the 30 years between *Brown* . . . and *Miranda*. It is not immediately apparent, however, that the judicial burden has been eased by the "bright-line" rules adopted in *Miranda*. In fact, in the 34 years since *Miranda* was decided, this Court has been called upon to decide nearly 60 cases involving a host of Miranda issues. . . .

Today's judgment converts *Miranda* from a milestone of judicial overreaching into the very Cheops' Pyramid (or perhaps the Sphinx would be a better analogue) of judicial arrogance. In imposing its Court-made code upon the States, the original opinion at least asserted that it was demanded by the Constitution. Today's decision does not pretend that it is—and yet still asserts the right to impose it against the will of the people's representatives in Congress. . . .

I dissent from today's decision, and, until § 3501 is repealed, will continue to apply it in all cases where there has been a sustainable finding that the defendant's confession was voluntary.

# IV. CAPITAL PUNISHMENT

## *Gregg* v. *Georgia*
## 428 U.S. 153, 96 S.Ct. 2909, 49 L.Ed. 2d 859 (1976)
### http://laws.findlaw.com/us/428/153.html

*Furman* v. *Georgia* (1972) held that, as then administered, capital punishment was "cruel and unusual punishment" in violation of the Eighth and Fourteenth Amendments. Of the five-justice majority, only Brennan and Marshall found the death penalty fundamentally at odds with the Constitution. The remaining three justices

(Douglas, Stewart, and White) concluded that capital punishment, as then administered, was invalid: Too much discretion in the hands of juries and too few standards for judges made the death sentence capricious and unpredictable. In addition, Douglas stated that the extreme selectivity of the death penalty created an inequality because those executed were "poor, young, and ignorant." Stewart disallowed retribution alone as a constitutionally acceptable objective of punishment. For White, the death penalty was pointless as well: "the threat of execution is too attenuated to be of substantial service to criminal justice." The positions of Stewart and White were unexpected because they had been part of a six-justice majority in *McGautha* v. *California* (1971), which upheld a death sentence for first-degree murder against arguments similar to those they found persuasive in *Furman.* The four dissenting justices in *Furman* (Burger, Blackmun, Powell, and Rehnquist) were willing to allow the states ample freedom in administration of capital punishment. *Furman* halted executions not only in Georgia but in the 38 other states that allowed the death penalty in 1972.

To meet the Court's objections, the Georgia legislature then enacted a new death penalty law, under which Gregg was sentenced. The new statute provided a bifurcated trial: Only after rendering a verdict of guilty would the jury determine the sentence. A death sentence required a finding beyond a reasonable doubt that at least one of ten specified "aggravating circumstances" was present as well as consideration of "mitigating circumstances" such as the offender's youth, cooperation with police, and emotional state when committing the crime. When the U.S. Supreme Court decided *Gregg,* Douglas had been replaced by Stevens. The justices were unable to agree on a majority opinion, but seven justices concluded that the state's new sentencing scheme was constitutional under the Eighth and Fourteenth Amendments. Majority: Stewart, Blackmun, Burger, Powell, Rehnquist, Stevens, White. Dissenting: Brennan, Marshall.

**Judgment of the Court, and opinion of MR. JUSTICE STEWART, MR. JUSTICE POWELL, and MR. JUSTICE STEVENS, announced by MR. JUSTICE STEWART. . . .**

We address initially the basic contention that the punishment of death for the crime of murder is, under all circumstances, "cruel and unusual" in violation of the Eighth and Fourteenth Amendments of the Constitution. . . .

Although this issue was presented and addressed in *Furman,* it was not resolved by the Court. Four Justices would have held that capital punishment is not unconstitutional per se; two Justices would have reached the opposite conclusion; and three Justices, while agreeing that the statutes then before the Court were invalid as applied, left open the question whether such punishment may ever be imposed. We now hold that the punishment of death does not invariably violate the Constitution. . . .

It is from the foregoing precedents that the Eighth Amendment has not been regarded as a static concept. As Chief Justice Warren said, in an oft-quoted phrase, "[the] amendment must draw its meaning from the evolving standards of decency that mark the progress of a maturing society." . . . Thus, an assessment of contemporary values concerning the infliction of a challenged sanction is relevant to the application of the Eighth Amendment. As we develop below more fully, this assessment does not call for a subjective judgment. It requires, rather, that we look to objective indicia that reflect the public attitude toward a given sanction. . . .

But our cases also make clear that public perceptions of standards of decency with respect to criminal sanctions are not conclusive. A penalty also must accord with "the dignity of man," which is the "basic concept underlying the Eighth Amendment." . . . This means, at least, that the punishment not be "excessive." When a form of punishment in the abstract (in this case, whether capital punishment may ever be imposed as a sanction for murder) rather than in the particular (the propriety of death as a penalty to be applied to a specific defendant for a specific crime) is under consideration, the inquiry into "excessiveness" has two aspects. First, the punishment must not involve the unnecessary and wanton infliction of pain. Second, the punishment must not be grossly out of proportion to the severity of the crime. . . .

The petitioners in the capital case before the Court today renew the "standards of decency" argument, but developments during the four years since *Furman* have undercut substantially the assumptions upon which their argument rested. Despite the continuing debate, dating back to the 19th century, over the morality and utility of capital punishment, it is now evident that a large proportion of American society continues to regard it as an appropriate and necessary sanction.

The most marked indication of society's endorsement of the death penalty for murder is the legislative response to *Furman*. The legislatures of at least 35 states have enacted new statutes that provide for the death penalty for at least some crimes that result in the death of another person. And the Congress of the United States, in 1974, enacted a statute providing the death penalty for aircraft piracy that results in death. . . .

We now consider specifically whether the sentence of death for the crime of murder is a per se violation of the Eighth and Fourteenth Amendments to the Constitution. . . . We note first that history and precedent strongly support a negative answer to this question. . . .

It is apparent from the text of the Constitution itself that the existence of capital punishment was accepted by the framers. At the time the Eighth Amendment was ratified, capital punishment was a common sanction in every state. Indeed, the first Congress of the United States enacted legislation providing death as the penalty for specified crimes. . . .

For nearly two centuries, this Court, repeatedly and often expressly, has recognized that capital punishment is not invalid per se. . . .

Four years ago, the petitioners in *Furman* and its companion cases predicated their argument primarily upon the asserted proposition that standards of decency had evolved to the point where capital punishment no longer could be tolerated. The petitioners in those cases said, in effect, that the evolutionary process had come to an end, and that standards of decency required that the Eighth Amendment be construed finally as prohibiting capital punishment for any crime regardless of its depravity and impact on society. . . .

Although some of the studies suggest that the death penalty may not function as a significantly greater deterrent than lesser penalties, there is no convincing empirical evidence either supporting or refuting this view. We may nevertheless assume safely that there are murderers, such as those who act in passion, for whom the threat of death has little or no deterrent effect. But for many others, the death penalty undoubtedly is a significant deterrent. . . .

In sum, we cannot say that the judgment of the Georgia Legislature that capital punishment may be necessary in some cases is clearly wrong. Considerations of federalism, as well as respect for the ability of a legislature to evaluate, in terms of its particular state the moral consensus concerning the death penalty and its social utility as a sanction, require us to conclude, in the absence of more convincing evidence, that the infliction of death as a punishment for murder is not without justification and thus is not unconstitutionally severe.

Finally, we must consider whether the punishment of death is disproportionate in relation to the crime for which it is imposed. There is no question that death as a punishment is unique in its severity and irrevocability. . . . When a defendant's life is at stake, the Court has been particularly sensitive to insure that every safeguard is observed. . . .

But we are concerned here only with the imposition of capital punishment for the crime of murder, and when a life has been taken deliberately by the offender, we cannot say that the punishment is invariably disproportionate to the crime. It is an extreme sanction, suitable to the most extreme of crimes.

We hold that the death penalty is not a form of punishment that may never be imposed, regardless of the circumstances of the offense, regardless of the character of the offender, and regardless of the procedure followed in reaching the decision to impose it.

We now consider whether Georgia may impose the death penalty on the petitioner. . . .

The basic concern of *Furman* centered on those defendants who were being condemned to death capriciously and arbitrarily. Under the procedures before the Court in that case, sentencing authorities were not directed to give attention to the nature or circumstances of the crime committed or to the character or record of the defendant. Left unguided, juries imposed the death sentence in a way that could only be called freakish. The new Georgia sentencing procedures, by contrast, focus the jury's attention on the particularized nature of the crime and the particularized characteristics of the individual defendant. While the jury is permitted to consider any aggravating or mitigating circumstances, it must find and identify at least one statutory aggravating factor before it may impose a penalty of death. In this way the jury's discretion is channeled. No longer can a jury wantonly and freakishly impose the death sentence; it is always circumscribed by the legislative guidelines. In addition, the review function of the Supreme Court of Georgia affords additional assurance that the concerns that prompted our decision in *Furman* are not present to any significant degree in the Georgia procedure applied here.

For the reasons expressed in this opinion, we hold that the statutory system under which Gregg was sentenced to death does not violate the Constitution. Accordingly, the judgment of the Georgia Supreme Court is affirmed.

*It is so ordered.*

MR. CHIEF JUSTICE BURGER, with whom MR. JUSTICE REHNQUIST joins, concurring . . . [omitted].

MR. JUSTICE WHITE, with whom MR. CHIEF JUSTICE BURGER and MR. JUSTICE REHNQUIST join, concurring . . . [omitted].

MR. JUSTICE BLACKMUN, concurring . . . [omitted].[1]

MR. JUSTICE BRENNAN, dissenting. . . . [omitted].

### MR. JUSTICE MARSHALL, dissenting. . . .

Since the decision in *Furman,* the legislatures of 35 states have enacted new statutes authorizing the imposition of the death sentence for certain crimes, and Congress has enacted a law providing the death penalty for air piracy resulting in death. I would be less than candid if I did not acknowledge that these developments have a significant bearing on a realistic assessment of the moral acceptability of the death penalty to the American people. But if the constitutionality of the death penalty turns, as I have urged, on the opinion of an informed citizenry, then even

[1] Blackmun referenced the dissenting opinions, including his own, in *Furman* v. *Georgia,* where he had written: "Cases such as these provide for me an excruciating agony of the spirit. I yield to no one in the depth of my distaste, antipathy, and, indeed, abhorrence, for the death penalty, with all its aspects of physical distress and fear and of moral judgment exercised by finite minds. That distaste is buttressed by a belief that capital punishment serves no useful purpose that can be demonstrated. For me, it violates childhood's training and life's experiences, and is not compatible with the philosophical convictions I have been able to develop. It is antagonistic to any sense of 'reverence for life.' Were I a legislator, I would vote against the death penalty for the policy reasons argued by counsel for the respective petitioners. . . . I do not sit on these cases, however, as a legislator, responsive, at least in part, to the will of constituents. Our task here, as must so frequently be emphasized and reemphasized, is to pass upon the constitutionality of legislation that has been enacted and that is challenged. This is the sole task for judges. We should not allow our personal preferences as to the wisdom of legislative and congressional action, or our distaste for such action, to guide our judicial decision in cases such as these. . . . I fear the Court has overstepped. It has sought and has achieved an end." In contrast to his positions in *Furman* and *Gregg,* however, Blackmun after 1985 almost always voted against the government in cases involving capital punishment. In March 1994, in his last term on the Supreme Court, Blackmun used a dissent to a denial of certiorari to announce that he was convinced that the death penalty could not be constitutionally administered: "[T]he death penalty remains fraught with arbitrariness, discrimination, caprice and mistake. . . . From this day forward, I no longer shall tinker with the machinery of death" (*Callins* v. *Collins*).—ED.

the enactment of new death statutes cannot be viewed as conclusive. In *Furman,* I observed that the American people are largely unaware of the information critical to a judgment on the morality of the death penalty, and concluded that if they were better informed they would consider it shocking, unjust, and unacceptable. . . .

There remains for consideration, however, what might be termed the purely retributive justification for the death penalty—that the death penalty is appropriate, not because of its beneficial effect on society, but because the taking of the murderer's life is itself morally good. Some of the language of the plurality's opinion appears positively to embrace this notion of retribution for its own sake as a justification for capital punishment. . . .

To be sustained under the Eighth Amendment, the death penalty must "[comport] with the basic concept of human dignity at the core of the amendment"; the objective in imposing it must be "[consistent] with our respect for the dignity of other men." Under these standards, the taking of life "because the wrongdoer deserves it" surely must fall, for such a punishment has as its very basis the total denial of the wrongdoer's dignity and worth. . . .

## *Atkins* v. *Virginia*
## 536 U.S. 304, 122 S. Ct. 2242, 153 L.Ed. 2d 335 (2002)

### http://laws.findlaw.com/us/536/304.html

This case presented an opportunity for the Supreme Court to revisit *Penry* v. *Lynaugh* (1989), which held, among other things, that execution of a mentally retarded person was not categorically prohibited by the Eighth Amendment. In *Penry,* Justices Blackmun, Brennan, Marshall, and Stevens dissented on that point. The facts in *Atkins* follow in Justice Stevens's opinion below. Majority: Stevens, Breyer, Ginsburg, Kennedy, O'Connor, Souter. Dissenting: Rehnquist, Scalia, Thomas.

**JUSTICE STEVENS delivered the opinion of the Court.**

Petitioner, Daryl Renard Atkins, was convicted of abduction, armed robbery, and capital murder, and sentenced to death. At approximately midnight on August 16, 1996, Atkins and William Jones, armed with a semi-automatic handgun, abducted Eric Nesbitt, robbed him of the money on his person, drove him to an automated teller machine in his pickup truck where cameras recorded their withdrawal of additional cash, then took him to an isolated location where he was shot eight times and killed.

Jones and Atkins both testified in the guilt phase of Atkins' trial. Each confirmed most of the details in the other's account of the incident, with the important exception that each stated that the other had actually shot and killed Nesbitt. Jones' testimony, which was both more coherent and credible than Atkins', was obviously credited by the jury and was sufficient to establish Atkins' guilt. At the penalty phase of the trial, the State introduced victim impact evidence and proved two aggravating circumstances: future dangerousness and "vileness of the offense." To prove future dangerousness, the State relied on Atkins' prior felony convictions as well as the testimony of four victims of earlier robberies and assaults. To prove the second aggravator, the prosecution relied upon the trial record, including pictures of the deceased's body and the autopsy report.

In the penalty phase, the defense relied on one witness, Dr. Evan Nelson, a forensic psychologist who had evaluated Atkins before trial and concluded that he was "mildly mentally retarded." . . .

The jury sentenced Atkins to death, but the Virginia Supreme Court ordered a second sentencing hearing because the trial court had used a misleading verdict form. At the resentencing, Dr. Nelson again testified. The State presented an expert rebuttal witness, Dr. Stanton Samenow, who expressed the opinion that Atkins was not mentally retarded, but rather was of "average intelligence, at least," and diagnosable as having antisocial personality disorder. The jury again sentenced Atkins to death.

The Supreme Court of Virginia affirmed. . . .

[W]e granted certiorari to revisit the issue that we first addressed in the *Penry* case.

The Eighth Amendment succinctly prohibits "excessive" sanctions. . . . In *Weems* v. *United States,* (1910), we held that a punishment of 12 years jailed in irons at hard and painful labor for the crime of falsifying records was excessive. We explained "that . . . punishment for crime should be graduated and proportioned to the offense." . . .

A claim that punishment is excessive is judged not by the standards that prevailed in 1685 when Lord Jeffreys presided over the "Bloody Assizes" or when the Bill of Rights was adopted, but rather by those that currently prevail. As Chief Justice Warren explained in his opinion in *Trop* v. *Dulles* (1958): "The basic concept underlying the Eighth Amendment is nothing less than the dignity of man. . . . The Amendment must draw its meaning from the evolving standards of decency that mark the progress of a maturing society." . . .

We have pinpointed that the "clearest and most reliable objective evidence of contemporary values is the legislation enacted by the country's legislatures." . . .

The parties have not called our attention to any state legislative consideration of the suitability of imposing the death penalty on mentally retarded offenders prior to 1986. In that year, the public reaction to the execution of a mentally retarded murderer in Georgia apparently led to the enactment of the first state statute prohibiting such executions. In 1988, when Congress enacted legislation reinstating the federal death penalty, it expressly provided that a "sentence of death shall not be carried out upon a person who is mentally retarded." In 1989, Maryland enacted a similar prohibition. It was in that year that we decided *Penry,* and concluded that those two state enactments, "even when added to the 14 States that have rejected capital punishment completely, do not provide sufficient evidence at present of a national consensus."

Much has changed since then. Responding to the national attention received by . . . our decision in *Penry,* state legislatures across the country began to address the issue. In 1990 Kentucky and Tennessee enacted statutes similar to those in Georgia and Maryland, as did New Mexico in 1991, and Arkansas, Colorado, Washington, Indiana, and Kansas in 1993 and 1994. In 1995, when New York reinstated its death penalty, it emulated the Federal Government by expressly exempting the mentally retarded. Nebraska followed suit in 1998. There appear to have been no similar enactments during the next two years, but in 2000 and 2001 six more States—South Dakota, Arizona, Connecticut, Florida, Missouri, and North Carolina—joined the procession. The Texas Legislature unanimously adopted a similar bill, and bills have passed at least one house in other States, including Virginia and Nevada.

It is not so much the number of these States that is significant, but the consistency of the direction of change. . . . Moreover, even in those States that allow the execution of mentally retarded offenders, the practice is uncommon. . . . The practice, therefore, has become truly unusual, and it is fair to say that a national consensus has developed against it.

. . . [C]linical definitions of mental retardation require not only subaverage intellectual functioning, but also significant limitations in adaptive skills such as communication, self-care, and self-direction that became manifest before age 18. . . .

In light of these deficiencies, our death penalty jurisprudence provides two reasons consistent with the legislative consensus that the mentally retarded should be categorically excluded from execution. First, there is a serious question as to whether either justification that we have recognized as a basis for the death penalty applies to mentally retarded offenders. *Gregg* v. *Georgia* identified "retribution and deterrence of capital crimes by prospective offenders" as the social purposes served by the death penalty. Unless the imposition of the death penalty on a mentally retarded person "measurably contributes to one or both of these goals, it 'is nothing more than the purposeless and needless imposition of pain and suffering,' and hence an unconstitutional punishment."

With respect to retribution—the interest in seeing that the offender gets his "just deserts"—the severity of the appropriate punishment necessarily depends on the culpability of the offender. . . . If the culpability of the average murderer is insufficient to justify the most extreme sanction available to the State, the lesser culpability of the mentally retarded offender surely does not merit that form of retribution. Thus, pursuant to our narrowing jurisprudence, which seeks to ensure that only the most deserving of execution are put to death, an exclusion for the mentally retarded is appropriate.

With respect to deterrence—the interest in preventing capital crimes by prospective offenders—"it seems likely that 'capital punishment can serve as a deterrent only when murder is the result of premeditation and deliberation.'" Exempting the mentally retarded from that punishment will not affect the "cold calculus that precedes the decision" of other potential murderers. Indeed, that sort of calculus is at the opposite end of the spectrum from behavior of mentally retarded offenders. The theory of deterrence in capital sentencing is predicated upon the notion that the increased severity of the punishment will inhibit criminal actors from carrying out murderous conduct. Yet it is the same cognitive and behavioral impairments that make these defendants less morally culpable—for example, the diminished ability to understand and process information, to learn from experience, to engage in logical reasoning, or to control impulses—that also make it less likely that they can process the information of the possibility of execution as a penalty and, as a result, control their conduct based upon that information. . . .

The reduced capacity of mentally retarded offenders provides a second justification for a categorical rule making such offenders ineligible for the death penalty. The risk "that the death penalty will be imposed in spite of factors which may call for a less severe penalty" is enhanced, not only by the possibility of false confessions, but also by the lesser ability of mentally retarded defendants to make a persuasive showing of mitigation in the face of prosecutorial evidence of one or more aggravating factors. Mentally retarded defendants may be less able to give meaningful assistance to their counsel and are typically poor witnesses, and their demeanor may create an unwarranted impression of lack of remorse for their crimes. . . .

Construing and applying the Eighth Amendment in the light of our "evolving standards of decency," we therefore conclude that such punishment is excessive and that the Constitution "places a substantive restriction on the State's power to take the life" of a mentally retarded offender.

The judgment of the Virginia Supreme Court is reversed and the case is remanded for further proceedings not inconsistent with this opinion.

*It is so ordered.*

CHIEF JUSTICE REHNQUIST, with whom JUSTICE SCALIA and JUSTICE THOMAS join, dissenting . . . [omitted].

### JUSTICE SCALIA, with whom the CHIEF JUSTICE and JUSTICE THOMAS join, dissenting.

Today's decision is the pinnacle of our Eighth Amendment death-is-different jurisprudence. Not only does it, like all of that jurisprudence, find no support in the text or history of the Eighth Amendment; it does not even have support in current social attitudes regarding the conditions that render an otherwise just death penalty inappropriate. Seldom has an opinion of this Court rested so obviously upon nothing but the personal views of its members. . . .

Under our Eighth Amendment jurisprudence, a punishment is "cruel and unusual" if it falls within one of two categories: "those modes or acts of punishment that had been considered cruel and unusual at the time that the Bill of Rights was adopted," and modes of punishment that are inconsistent with modern "standards of decency," as evinced by objective indicia, the most important of which is "legislation enacted by the country's legislatures."

The Court makes no pretense that execution of the mildly mentally retarded would have been considered "cruel and unusual" in 1791. Only the *severely* or *profoundly* mentally retarded, commonly known as "idiots," enjoyed any special status under the law at that time. They, like lunatics, suffered a "deficiency in will" rendering them unable to tell right from wrong. Instead, they were often committed to civil confinement or made wards of the State, thereby preventing them from "go[ing] loose, to the terror of the king's subjects." Mentally retarded offenders with less severe impairments—those who were not "idiots"—suffered criminal prosecution and punishment, including capital punishment. . . .

The Court is left to argue, therefore, that execution of the mildly retarded is inconsistent with the "evolving standards of decency that mark the progress of a maturing society." . . .

The Court . . . miraculously extracts a "national consensus" forbidding execution of the mentally retarded from the fact that 18 States—less than *half* (47%) of the 38 States that permit capital punishment (for whom the issue exists)—have very recently enacted legislation barring execution of the mentally retarded. Even that 47% figure is a distorted one. If one is to say, as the Court does today, that *all* executions of the mentally retarded are so morally repugnant as to violate our national "standards of decency," surely the "consensus" it points to must be one that has set its righteous face against *all* such executions. Not 18 States, but only seven—18% of death penalty jurisdictions—have legislation of that scope. Eleven of those that the Court counts enacted statutes prohibiting execution of mentally retarded defendants *convicted after, or convicted of crimes committed after, the effective date* of the legislation; those already on death row, or consigned there before the statute's effective date, or even (in those States using the date of the crime as the criterion of

retroactivity) tried in the future for murders committed many years ago, could be put to death. That is not a statement of absolute moral repugnance, but one of current preference between two tolerable approaches. Two of these States permit execution of the mentally retarded in other situations as well: Kansas apparently permits execution of all except the *severely* mentally retarded; New York permits execution of the mentally retarded who commit murder in a correctional facility. . . .

The Court attempts to bolster its embarrassingly feeble evidence of "consensus" with the following: "It is not so much the number of these States that is significant, but the *consistency* of the direction of change." But in what *other* direction *could we possibly* see change? . . .

But the Prize for the Court's Most Feeble Effort to fabricate "national consensus" must go to its appeal (deservedly relegated to a footnote) to the views of assorted professional and religious organizations, members of the so-called "world community," and respondents to opinion polls. . . . [T]he views of professional and religious organizations and the results of opinion polls are irrelevant. . . .

Beyond the empty talk of a "national consensus," the Court gives us a brief glimpse of what really underlies today's decision: pretension to a power confined *neither* by the moral sentiments originally enshrined in the Eighth Amendment (its original meaning) *nor even* by the current moral sentiments of the American people. " '[T]he Constitution,' " the Court says, "contemplates that in the end *our own judgment* will be brought to bear on the question of the acceptability of the death penalty under the Eighth Amendment.' " (The unexpressed reason for this unexpressed "contemplation" of the Constitution is presumably that really good lawyers have moral sentiments superior to those of the common herd, whether in 1791 or today.) The arrogance of this assumption of power takes one's breath away. . . .

The genuinely operative portion of the opinion, then, is the Court's statement of the reasons why it agrees with the contrived consensus it has found, that the "diminished capacities" of the mentally retarded render the death penalty excessive. The Court's analysis rests on two fundamental assumptions: (1) that the Eighth Amendment prohibits excessive punishments, and (2) that sentencing juries or judges are unable to account properly for the "diminished capacities" of the retarded. The first assumption is wrong. . . . The Eighth Amendment is addressed to always-and-every-where "cruel" punishments, such as the rack and the thumbscrew. But where the punishment is in itself permissible, "[t]he Eighth Amendment is not a ratchet, whereby a temporary consensus on leniency for a particular crime fixes a permanent constitutional maximum, disabling the States from giving effect to altered beliefs and responding to changed social conditions." The second assumption—inability of judges or juries to take proper account of mental retardation—is not only unsubstantiated, but contradicts the immemorial belief, here and in England, that they play an *indispensable* role in such matters. . . .

Proceeding from these faulty assumptions, the Court gives two reasons why the death penalty is an excessive punishment for all mentally retarded offenders. First, the "diminished capacities" of the mentally retarded raise a "serious question" whether their execution contributes to the "social purposes" of the death penalty, viz., retribution and deterrence. . . . Retribution is not advanced, the argument goes, because the mentally retarded are *no more culpable* than the average murderer, whom we have already held lacks sufficient culpability to warrant the death penalty. Who says so? Is there an established correlation between mental acuity and the ability to conform one's conduct to the law in such a rudimentary matter as murder? Are the mentally retarded really more disposed (and hence more likely) to commit willfully cruel and serious crime than others? . . .

Assuming, however, that there is a direct connection between diminished intelligence and the inability to refrain from murder, what scientific analysis can possibly show that a mildly retarded individual who commits an exquisite torture-killing is "no more culpable" than the "average" murderer in a holdup-gone-wrong or a domestic dispute? Or a moderately retarded individual who commits a series of 20 exquisite torture-killings? . . .

As for the other social purpose of the death penalty that the Court discusses, deterrence: That is not advanced, the Court tells us, because the mentally retarded are "less likely" than their non-retarded counterparts to "process the information of the possibility of execution as a penalty and . . . control their conduct based upon that information." Of course this leads to the same conclusion discussed earlier—that the mentally retarded (because they are less deterred) are more likely to kill—which neither I nor the society at large believes. In any event, even the Court does not say that *all* mentally retarded individuals cannot "process the information of the possibility of execution as a penalty and . . . control their conduct based upon that information"; it merely asserts that they are "less likely" to be able to do so. But surely the deterrent effect of a penalty is adequately vindicated if it successfully deters many, but not all, of the target class. . . .

The Court throws one last factor into its grab bag of reasons why execution of the retarded is "excessive" in all cases: Mentally retarded offenders "face a special risk of wrongful execution" because they are less able "to make a persuasive showing of mitigation," "to give meaningful assistance to their counsel," and to be effective witnesses. "Special risk" is pretty flabby language (even flabbier than "less likely")—and I suppose a similar "special risk" could be said to exist for just plain stupid people, inarticulate people, even ugly people. . . .

This newest invention promises to be more effective than any of the others in turning the process of capital trial into a game. One need only read the definitions of mental retardation adopted by the American Association of Mental Retardation and the American Psychiatric Association . . . to realize that the symptoms of this condition can readily be feigned. And whereas the capital defendant who feigns insanity risks commitment to a mental institution until he can be cured (and then tried and executed), the capital defendant who feigns mental retardation risks nothing at all. The mere pendency of the present case has brought us petitions by death row inmates claiming for the first time, after multiple habeas petitions, that they are retarded. . . .

# CHAPTER ELEVEN

# *Freedom of Expression*

*The greater the importance of safeguarding the community from incitements to the overthrow of our institutions by force and violence, the more imperative is the need to preserve inviolate the constitutional rights of free speech, free press and free assembly in order to maintain the opportunity for free political discussion, to the end that government may be responsive to the will of the people and that changes, if desired, may be obtained by peaceful means. Therein lies the security of the Republic, the very foundation of constitutional government.*

—CHIEF JUSTICE CHARLES EVANS HUGHES (1937)

The American political tradition has always been opposed to unlimited government power. In particular, protections of the First Amendment—free speech, free press, and the rights of peaceable assembly and petition—make possible a continuing debate on issues large and small, without which the electoral process becomes an empty ritual and self-expression and the search for truth are stifled. (The religion clauses of the First Amendment are treated separately in the next chapter.)

First Amendment freedoms confront the Court with a difficult task, one that is not present in all cases of judicial review. Where enumerated powers of Congress or the president are subject to interpretation, for example, the Court's function is at an end when the action taken is found to be within the limits of constitutionally granted power. In reaching such a conclusion, the Court is aided by the well-established presumption of constitutionality that accompanies review of most legislative and executive actions.

In cases involving freedom of speech, however, the Court must interpret and apply a grant of power—frequently the "reserved" police power of the states—while, at the same time, it must interpret and apply a constitutional limitation on government power. Such cases thus involve a clash of important objectives: the need for both order and freedom. Government must have authority to "insure domestic Tranquility," just as it must have military power to resist attacks from abroad. Yet excessive emphasis on order negates the freedom the political system is designed to protect. Thus, the easy path to constitutional decision by way of presumption of constitutionality of legislative or administrative action is not readily available in this field.

## TESTS OF FREEDOM

Free-speech cases have been a fixture on the Supreme Court's docket for barely more than 80 years. During this time the justices have developed no single theoretical perspective or framework for resolving them. Instead, when confronted with clashes over free speech, the Court has formulated a series of tests or analytical approaches of varying sophistication. Generally these fall into at least four categories. Whatever measures are used, the Court's answers depend ultimately on the justices' view of correct social policy and their conception of the role of the judiciary in achieving balance between freedom and order.

The first category considers first speech cases in terms of the threat that the speaker poses. As discussed in the following section, by 1925 two such tests had emerged: the **clear-and-present-danger test,** which promised greater judicial protection for speech, and the **bad tendency test,** which was deferential to legislative action. Each emerged from post–World War I cases involving wartime national security legislation. Much later, the clear-and-present-danger test evolved into the **incitement test,** as illustrated by ***Brandenburg* v. *Ohio*** (1969). More permissive for expression than the clear-and-present-danger test, it emphasizes the immediacy of lawless action. A majority has never preferred a fourth and extremely permissive approach advocated by a few justices such as Hugo Black. From this **absolute approach,** once expression is deemed to fall within the purview of the First Amendment (a significant qualification), all government restrictions on what is said are forbidden. The threat posed by the speaker is irrelevant.

The second category looks at free-speech cases not so much from the perspective of the danger the speaker poses but the danger that a law poses to those engaged in legitimate speech. For instance, the **overbreadth doctrine** may be applicable when a law sweeps too broadly, reaching not only speech or speech-related behavior that might constitutionally be proscribed but protected speech as well. Such laws may also be struck down because they have a **chilling effect:** at the margin they may deter people from engaging in expression that the Constitution allows. For similar reasons the Court may declare a law **void for vagueness.** Due process requires that individuals have fair warning of prohibited conduct. A vague statute blurs the line between legal and illegal behavior and therefore may "chill" speech by causing people to censor themselves.

The third category that has developed focuses on the way a regulation affects speech and its impact on speech. Initially, the Court will determine whether government has restricted the *substance* of a speaker's message—that is, whether a regulation discriminates against a certain point of view. If so, the Court applies **strict scrutiny,** its most demanding standard of view. For the statute to survive, government must demonstrate a compelling interest in the restriction and demonstrate that the interest can be achieved in no other way. *Ward* v. *Rock Against Racism* (1989), which challenged a New York City regulation mandating use of the city's sound system and technicians as a means to control volume at the bandstand in Central Park, offered a three-part test to determine whether a regulation is in fact viewpoint-neutral. First, the regulation must concern where or how something is said, not what is said. Second, its adoption must not have been based on disagreement with any particular message. Third, government's interests in having the regulation must be unrelated to the viewpoint of any speaker.

If a law passes the viewpoint-neutrality test, it may nonetheless adversely affect the flow and distribution of a message—the *how*—even though the law is not aimed at a particular message—the *what*. In such situations the Court applies a lower standard of review, balancing the impact on speech against the importance of the regulation. "[A] regulation of the time, place, or manner of protected speech," wrote Justice Kennedy in *Ward,* "must be narrowly tailored to serve the government's legitimate content-neutral interests but . . . it need not be the least-restrictive or least-intrusive means of doing so." The standard "is satisfied 'so long as [the] regulation promotes a substantial government interest that would be achieved less effectively absent the regulation.'" Such regulations are more easily upheld when there are "ample alternative channels of communication" left open to the speaker. The Court adopts a similar approach when regulations impede symbolic or communicative action, as discussed later in this chapter.

In contrast to the third category's focus on *viewpoint* discrimination, a fourth (and still evolving) interpretive approach examines *content* discrimination: situations in which government may proscribe certain types of speech, but not others, within a *class* of expression. For example, the federal government may criminalize threats of violence that are directed to the president of the United States without necessarily being required to criminalize threats of violence that are directed to all other federal officials. "[T]he reason why threats of violence are outside the First Amendment . . . have a special force when applied to the person of the President." When the content discrimination in question rests entirely on "the very reason the entire domain of speech at issue is proscribable, no significant danger of idea or viewpoint discrimination exists" (*R.A.V.* v. *City of St. Paul,* 1995). So, a law criminalizing threats of violence directed to the president is permissible content discrimination, while a law criminalizing such threats made only by Democrats, or only by Republicans, would be impermissible viewpoint discrimination. (A cautionary note on word usage is in order: Supreme Court opinions occasionally create their own internal confusion by using the terms "content" and "viewpoint" interchangeably. And to complicate matters, there is not always agreement on the bench whether a particular discrimination is content or viewpoint in nature.)

## INTERNAL SECURITY

At the end of the first decade of government under the Constitution, the Federalists curbed the speech of their political opponents. With the ink barely dry on the First Amendment, the Sedition Act of 1798 criminalized in sweeping terms any scandalous criticism of the president or Congress made with intent to bring them into disrepute. Before the law expired by its own terms on March 3, 1801, the government obtained indictments against 14 persons and convictions of 10. Considered unconstitutional by many at the time, the law was never tested because Thomas Jefferson and the Democratic-Republicans feared that the Federalist Supreme Court would declare the laws valid, thus establishing an unfortunate precedent. It is noteworthy that the Federalist proponents of these laws, many of whom had played leading roles in the dramatic formulation of the Constitution, used an argument that has become a familiar defense of limitations on speech. Threats to national security, they argued, made restrictions inevitable; preservation of the Constitution was more important than protection of any one right it guaranteed. Obviously, this logic could be used to justify destruction of all constitutional rights.

**CLEAR-AND-PRESENT-DANGER TEST.** Except for President Abraham Lincoln's unofficial suppression of northern critics of his policies during the Civil War, there was no national government action raising free-speech issues until World War I, when Congress passed two laws that focused public attention on basic issues of freedom of speech in wartime. The first, the Espionage Act of 1917, prohibited interferences with recruitment or acts adversely affecting military morale. It was in ***Schenck* v. *United States*** (1919) that Justice Holmes, in upholding the act as applied to antidraft leaflets, first announced the clear-and-present-danger test: "The question in every case is whether the words used are used in such circumstances and are of such a nature as to create a clear and present danger that they will bring about the substantive evils that Congress has a right to prevent." Holmes's test invited more questions than it answered. Enmeshed with highly complex issues of proximity, degree, and content, it nevertheless displayed a preference for a wide latitude of speech.

The second, the Sedition Act of 1918, went far beyond the 1917 law, making punishable speech that now would be deemed mere political comment. It singled out for punishment any "disloyal, profane, scurrilous, or abusive language about the form of government, the Constitution, soldiers and sailors, flag or uniform of the armed forces," and in addition made unlawful any "word or act [favoring] the cause of the German Empire . . . or [opposing] the cause of the United States." This law was upheld in *Abrams* v. *United States* (1919), in which pamphlets opposing the Allied (and American) intervention in Russia after the revolution were held to be within its terms. When this flurry of litigation subsided, cases involving federal action under the First Amendment virtually disappeared until World War II.

**BAD TENDENCY TEST.** In the period between the two world wars, the states were more active in seeking curbs against radical action, principally through efforts to outlaw **criminal syndicalism** and anarchy. Such laws, aimed at left-wing groups, forbade the advocacy of violence to accomplish social reform. This was the basis for Benjamin Gitlow's conviction after he circulated pamphlets urging workers to revolutionary mass action and "dictatorship of the proletariat" (***Gitlow* v. *New York,*** 1925). Application of the bad tendency test in *Gitlow* meant that states had as much authority to stamp out noxious ideas as they did to destroy adulterated meat. Nonetheless, the case did declare that the free-speech clause of the First Amendment was applicable to the states through the Fourteenth Amendment. Similar reasoning prevailed in ***Whitney* v. *California*** (1927) when the Court ruled that even brief membership in the Communist Labor Party and participation in its convention constituted a violation of the state's criminal syndicalism statute. Of lasting interest in *Whitney* is Brandeis's concurring opinion in which he refashioned the merits and justification of the clear-and-present-danger test. Brandeis stressed that Whitney's counsel should have raised that test as a defense, in an effort to distinguish mere membership from the threat of dangerous action.

By World War II, "clear and present danger" had become the accepted test of potential harm. Applied to both state and federal laws, it became the measure of the criminality of unpopular beliefs and potentially dangerous action.

**COLD WAR CASES.** The heightened tension between the United States and the Soviet Union after World War II, with the accompanying fear of Communist subversives, presented new free speech problems. Intended initially to target Nazis, Section 1 of the **Smith Act** of 1940 made it a felony to advocate the violent overthrow of the government of the United States or to conspire to organize a group advocating such violence. In upholding the law as applied to 11 leaders of the American Communist Party, ***Dennis* v. *United States*** (1951) discarded the clear-and-present-danger test in these circumstances and selected instead a test Judge Learned Hand crafted in his opinion when *Dennis* was before the Second Circuit Court of Appeals: "In each case Courts must ask whether the gravity of the 'evil,' discounted by its improbability, justifies such invasion of free speech as is necessary to avoid the danger." In the Supreme Court's view, the clear-and-present-danger test, although applicable to the isolated speech of individuals or small groups, was inappropriate for testing words associated with a large-scale conspiratorial movement. Instead, the majority approved the trial judge's holding that as a matter of law, defendants' alleged activities presented "a sufficient danger of a substantive evil" to justify the application of the statute under the First Amendment. Judge Hand's formula seemed more closely to resemble application of the bad tendency test.

*Dennis* posed the dilemma every democracy faces sooner or later: what to do about antidemocratic forces, which, if they come to power, would surely destroy democratic politics as one of the first orders of business. Should the government wait until subversive elements have committed particular criminal acts (as Justices Black and Douglas advocated in their Dennis dissents), or should the government take steps to protect the nation and its constitutional processes only on the basis of the noxious ideas suspected subversives preach? If the latter option is chosen, how can the nation make the content of speech a crime, given the wording of the First Amendment? Moreover, if the government moves against those who wish the nation ill, how do law enforcement agencies cast the net without placing lawful dissent in danger?

In *Yates* v. *United States* (1957), the Court was again called on to examine the scope of the Smith Act. Its decision took a stricter view of the proof necessary to convict by requiring evidence of the advocacy of *action* and not merely the advocacy of *doctrine* and consequently made it difficult for the government to maintain successful prosecutions. In light of *Yates,* many thought that the membership provisions of the Smith Act would be held invalid. But in *Scales* v. *United States* (1961), the Court rescued the challenged clause by insisting that only active and knowing membership was within the act's coverage. *Scales* and *Yates* thus had the effect of requiring the government to prove more to sustain a conviction under the Smith Act. In exchange for sustaining the constitutionality of the legislation, the justices diminished the circle of people against whom the law could realistically be expected to apply.

*Dennis* turned out to be the high-water mark of judicial tolerance of various state and federal devices to uncover and punish those thought to be engaged in subversive activities. In a succession of cases lasting over a decade, the Court sometimes declared such policies unconstitutional or approved them in principle but required such exacting procedures that implementation of the various policies became more difficult. The justices seemed to be saying that the First Amendment does not prevent the nation from defending itself from internal threats but that, in doing so, the nation must be careful not to tread too heavily on First Amendment values.

**INCITEMENT TEST.** The prevailing view on the Court today is set firmly against virtually all **viewpoint-based restrictions,** as ***Brandenburg* v. *Ohio*** illustrates.

This case involved yet another state criminal syndicalism law, but the defendant this time was no leftist but a member of the Ku Klux Klan. Ohio banned "advocating . . . the duty, necessity, or propriety of crime, sabotage, violence or unlawful methods of terrorism as a means of accomplishing industrial or political reform." Brandenburg notified a Cincinnati reporter of a scheduled Klan rally, and film clips of Brandenburg's remarks were telecast on a local station and on a national network. Recorded for posterity was his speech decrying government repression of the Caucasian race and references to the possibility of revenge. Some people in the crowd carried weapons. With this as evidence, an Ohio court fined him $1,000 and sentenced him to ten years in prison. The Supreme Court reversed, saying that a state may not proscribe "advocacy of the use of force or of law violations except when it is directed to inciting or producing imminent lawless action and is likely to incite or produce such action." *Brandenburg* sets a tough standard for government restrictions aimed at dissident groups. It means that the First Amendment bars practically any conviction based on someone's point of view.

## PUBLIC FORUM

Closely related to regulation of what is said is regulation of where it may be said. This is the problem illustrated by the **public forum**—publicly owned property where people may express their views. A trichotomy has evolved through a series of decisions: the traditional (or open) public forum, the designated (or limited) public forum, and the nonpublic forum. As explained in *Perry Education Association* v. *Perry Local Educators' Association* (1983), the first includes areas such as streets and parks that have long been opened to speech and debate and has the highest free-speech protection. "For the state to enforce a content-based exclusion it must show that its regulation is necessary to serve a compelling state interest and that it is narrowly drawn to achieve that end. The state may also enforce regulations of the time, place, and manner of expression which are content-neutral, are narrowly tailored to serve a significant government interest, and leave open ample alternative channels of communication." One such time-place-manner regulation lay at the heart of the dispute in *Clark* v. *Community for Creative Non-Violence* (1984), where the Court divided over the significance of the government interest at stake.

The second includes places that the government has chosen to open to expressive activity for limited purposes, either for use by certain groups (such as student organizations with access to facilities at a state university) or for discussion of certain subjects (such as a school board meeting for discussion of educational policy). Within those limits, however, government may impose viewpoint-based restrictions only if its regulation meets the rigorous standards of the traditional public forum. Thus, the Court ruled that the University of Virginia violated the First Amendment when it denied funding for the printing of a student-edited Christian journal (*Wide Awake*) while funding other student publications. This was viewpoint discrimination in a designated or limited public forum, five justices declared. The case was complicated by the university's insistence, which the Court found unpersuasive, that to fund the journal would amount to a violation of the same amendment's ban on laws "respecting an establishment of religion" (*Rosenberger* v. *Rector,* 1995). The Virginia case in turn was authority for *Good News Club* v. *Milford Central School* (2001), that upheld a Christian group's free speech right of access to public school facilities that had been open for certain uses by the public after school hours.

The third category—the nonpublic forum—includes public property not by tradition or designation considered an arena for the free exchange of ideas. In addition to time, place, and manner regulations, government may reserve the space for its intended use, communicative or otherwise, so long as the regulation is reasonable and not based on opposition to a speaker's point of view. Thus, no visitor to the U.S. Capitol has a right to make a speech in the gallery of the House of Representatives. Likewise, military bases and grounds around a prison ordinarily may be closed to certain communicative activities entirely (*Adderley* v. *Florida,* 1966; *Greer* v. *Spock,* 1976).

The Court has also tenuously defined the public forum based on a distinction between proprietary and regulatory functions of government (*International Society for Krishna Consciousness* v. *Lee,* 1992). Where government acts as manager of a site's internal operations, such as at a municipally owned airport, no traditional public forum exists. Accordingly, bans on solicitation, for instance, "will not be subject to the heightened review to which [government's] actions as lawmaker may be subject." Regulations of expression are therefore permissible so long as they are reasonable and viewpoint-neutral. This distinction may be easier to state than to apply, however. In the very same case that articulated the distinction, a majority voted to uphold a ban on repetitive solicitation of funds inside New York City area airports but struck down a prohibition on distribution of literature in the same terminals.

## PROTEST AND SYMBOLIC SPEECH

The public forum is frequently the setting for the variety of ways in which Americans express their opinions to other citizens, businesses and organizations, and the government. Those expressions can be subdued or raucous, crude or clever, thoughtful or hate-filled, temperate or vituperative. All implicate the First Amendment.

**FIGHTING WORDS.** Insults and other abusive language present their own First Amendment problem. *Chaplinsky* v. *New Hampshire* (1942) unanimously upheld the conviction of a Jehovah's Witness who in a dispute with a police officer called him a "God damned racketeer" and "a damned Fascist." The Court recognized Chaplinsky's words as "likely to provoke the average person to retaliation." Certain utterances, of which **fighting words** are a part, "are no essential part of any exposition of ideas and are of such slight social value as a step to truth that any benefit that may be derived from them is clearly outweighed by the social interest in order and morality."

Especially here, context is important. *Cohen* v. *California* (1971) reversed the conviction of a young man who, as a method of protest, emblazoned the words "Fuck the draft" on his jacket. He was arrested in a courthouse corridor and charged with "disturbing the peace." "No individual actually or likely to be present could reasonably have regarded the words . . . as a direct personal insult," wrote patrician Justice Harlan. "Nor do we have here an instance of the exercise of the State's police power to prevent a speaker from intentionally provoking a given group to hostile reaction. . . . [W]hile the particular four-letter word being litigated here is perhaps more distasteful than most others of its genre, it is nevertheless often true that one man's vulgarity is another's lyric. Indeed . . . because government officials cannot make principled distinctions in this area . . . the Constitution leaves matters of taste and style so largely to the individual."

**SYMBOLIC SPEECH.** Frequently those protesting government policy resort to tactics that go beyond conventional speech as a way to dramatize a cause and attract media attention. There are also other activities that are obviously expressive even though the feelings and attitudes conveyed are not "political." **Symbolic speech** thus refers to expressive activity—action (or inaction) designed to communicate a message. A constitutional question arises when the actions, stripped of any message, are themselves illegal. Are otherwise illegal actions protected by the First Amendment when they have a speech content? In the Court's view, to be considered "speech" at all, there must be an intent to convey a particular message and a reasonable likelihood that the message will be understood by an audience. Second, as with parades, the justices agree that speech symbolized by conduct is subject to reasonable time, place, and manner rules. Third, symbolic speech may be prohibited or regulated if the conduct itself can constitutionally be regulated. Fourth, the regulation must be narrowly written and must further "a substantial governmental interest." Fifth, that interest must be unrelated to suppressing free speech. Consider how these criteria were applied in ***United States* v. *O'Brien*** (1968) where the Court sustained a protestor's conviction for destroying his draft card in violation of federal law.

May a state or the national government protect the flag of the United States from defacement or destruction? In ***Texas* v. *Johnson*** (1989), the Court overturned a conviction for burning the American flag in violation of a Texas law. In a demonstration at the Dallas City Hall during the Republican National Convention in 1984, protesters chanted, "America, the red, white, and blue, we spit on you," doused the flag with kerosene, and set it ablaze. Short of a protest that sparks a breach of the peace or causes some other kind of serious harm, five justices concluded that government may not criminalize the symbolic act of flag burning. The reasoning is that a flag-protection law is viewpoint-based: Government protects the physical integrity of the flag because the flag is the symbol of the nation. Just as people may verbally speak out against what they believe the nation "stands for," they may also express the same thought by defacing or destroying a national symbol. But the right does not extend to destroying flags or other symbols that are government property.

*Johnson* was not the first time the Court had confronted flag-desecration laws, but it was the first time a majority had spoken forthrightly on their constitutionality under the First Amendment. Johnson's case was also not the last. In the wake of widespread criticism of the Court's ruling, the administration asked Congress for a constitutional amendment to give the states and the national government authority to protect the physical integrity of the American flag. Congress failed to approve the amendment but instead passed the Flag Protection Act, which President George H. W. Bush allowed to become law without his signature. Protestors promptly burned the flag in several cities in defiance of the new law. In *United States* v. *Eichman* the following year, the Court held that the First Amendment also barred Congress from criminalizing flag burning, a decision that sparked a renewed drive, thus far unsuccessful, to amend the Constitution. The legislatures of all states but Vermont have passed resolutions favoring such an amendment.

**HATE SPEECH AND HATE CRIMES.** First Amendment questions also arise when government seeks to protect certain groups or classes of people from offensive or hurtful speech or displays. In two important cases the Supreme Court has signaled the corrective measures it is prepared to reject and accept.

In *R. A. V.* v. *City of St. Paul* (1992), all nine justices voted to invalidate a city ordinance that criminalized the placing of a symbol or graffiti "on public or private property . . . including, but not limited to, a burning cross or Nazi swastika, which one knows or has reasonable grounds to know arouses anger, alarm or resentment in others on the basis of race, color, creed, religion or gender. . . ." Led by Scalia, five justices concluded that the ordinance was viewpoint-based and therefore defective because it banned invectives ("fighting words") aimed only at certain groups, not all. While admitting that government had compelling reason to protect groups that historically have been the target of discrimination, content-neutral alternatives were available to achieve that end. Scalia distinguished decisions that allowed proscription of classes of expression such as libel and obscenity. Those categories could be banned "because of their constitutionally proscribable content." But within a category, government could not ban only libel against the government, for example. For Justice White and three others, Scalia's reasoning was faulty. His approach required a ban on a wider category of speech to reach a smaller category of troublesome speech. Instead, White argued that the ordinance was defective on grounds of overbreadth: Along with expression that could constitutionally be punished, it also criminalized protected expression, such as symbols that merely caused resentment.

Eleven years later, ***Virginia* v. *Black*** struck down Virginia's cross-burning statute. Six justices indicated, however, that they would accept a law that criminalized cross-burning, and perhaps similar acts as well, that were intended to intimidate. The deficiency in the Virginia law was not that it banned cross-burning but that it contained a provision allowing jurors to infer intent from the act of cross-burning itself. Presumably the statute would have escaped censure had the burden been on the prosecution to demonstrates that the act was a threat and not merely symbolic expression.

**PICKETING.** In 1940 peaceful picketing was brought under the protection of freedom of speech (*Thornhill* v. *Alabama*). However, picketing is a special kind of symbolic expression that involves problems of the proper forum as well as the rights of those who are picketed. Picketers convey messages as much through their sheer physical presence as through their placards and spoken words. Nowhere is this clash of rights any more obvious than in the picketing of abortion clinics by anti-abortion activists. On the one hand is the speech interests of abortion opponents. On the other are interests in protecting access to medical services, including termination of a pregnancy, in minimizing the potential for trauma to patients, in assuring public order, and in ensuring the free flow of traffic. Typically, operators of an abortion clinic have obtained injunctions imposing various restrictions on protesters. Because injunctions "carry greater risks of censorship and discriminatory application than do general ordinances," *Madsen* v. *Women's Health Center, Inc*. (1994) held that the usual time-place-manner standard commonly used in picketing cases was not sufficiently rigorous to protect speech interests. Instead, the Court announced that the test in such situations was "whether the challenged provisions of the injunction burden no more speech than necessary to serve a significant government interest." Accordingly, the Court upheld a 36-foot buffer zone around a clinic as well as limits on noise. Bans on posting observable images, approaching patients without their consent within 200 feet of the clinic, and picketing within 300 feet of staff residences, however, went beyond what was deemed necessary to prevent intimidation and to ensure access. In 2000 all parts of Colorado's abortion picketing statute survived Supreme Court review. The state made it unlawful for any person within 100 feet of the entrance to a health care facility to "knowingly approach" within eight feet of another person, without that person's consent, in order to pass "a leaflet or handbill to, displa[y] a sign to, or engag[e] in oral protest, education, or counseling with [that] person." Because the statute regulated places where communication may occur rather than banning particular messages, the Court deemed it viewpoint-neutral. Judged by the less stringent time-place-manner standard, the statute was valid because it was "narrowly tailored" to serve significant government interests and because it left open ample alternative communication channels (*Hill* v. *Colorado,* 2000).

## FREEDOM OF ASSOCIATION

Organizations have long populated American culture. If Americans "want to proclaim a truth or propagate some feeling . . . ," observed Alexis de Tocqueville in the 1830s, "they form an association. In every case, at the head of any new undertaking, . . . you are sure to find an association." Free speech would certainly be less valuable were people unable to act collectively to achieve common objectives. As Chapter Five illustrated with respect to political parties and electoral politics, life in the United States would be vastly different without associations and interest groups of nearly every variety.

*NAACP* v. *Alabama* (1957) first formally recognized a First Amendment right of association as a derivative of the speech and assembly clauses. In that case a unanimous bench barred the state's order that a civil rights organization disclose its membership lists as a condition for continuing to do business in the state. Because of the hostile environment at that time, the justices believed that the directive would threaten the organization's existence and "chill" constitutionally protected liberties. But like other First Amendment freedoms, that of association is not absolute.

State and local governments have restricted the right of association for the purpose of eliminating various forms of discrimination in clubs and other private organizations. (Discrimination by most clubs is forbidden by neither the Constitution nor, at present, federal law.) The view is that such discrimination denies women and racial minorities full participation in the business and professional life of a community. Although continuing to recognize the importance of associational rights staked out in *NAACP,* the Court has nonetheless upheld three state and local antidiscrimination measures aimed at private organizations (*Roberts* v. *Jaycees,* 1984; *Rotary International* v. *Rotary Club of Duarte,* 1987; and *New York State Club Association* v. *New York City,* 1988). In each, the Court found that banning gender discrimination, especially in large membership groups, did not significantly restrict the groups' **expressive association,** that is, the speech that was synonymous with the organization itself. For associational rights to prevail over an antidiscrimination law, there would have to be a nexus between a group's message and its exclusion of women.

This qualification probably explains the outcome in *Hurley* v. *Irish-American Gay, Lesbian and Bisexual Group* (1995). Here, the Court held unanimously that Massachusetts could not apply its public accommodations statute to force a private association of veterans groups—sponsors of Boston's St. Patrick's Day parade—to include among the marchers a gay rights group whose message the sponsors did not wish their parade to convey. A contrary result would have violated a "fundamental rule" of the First Amendment, "that a speaker has the autonomy to choose the content of his own message."

Are the Boy Scouts more analogous to the parade sponsors in *Hurley* or to the New York City clubs, the Jaycees, and the Rotarians? The answer to that question determined whether James Dale would continue as an assistant scoutmaster in New Jersey. The Scouts' Monmouth Council revoked Dale's adult membership, and with it his right to be a scout leader, because of his sexual orientation. The state supreme court held that New Jersey's law banning such discrimination by a "public accommodation" applied to the Scouts and so the revocation was illegal. By the narrowest of margins, the U.S. Supreme Court reversed, finding a sufficient link—which dissenting justices chided as practically nonexistent—between the organization's principles and objectives and its membership policy regarding openly gay people (***Boy Scouts of America and Monmouth Council v. Dale,*** 2000). "Dale's presence in the Boy Scouts would, at the very least," wrote Chief Justice Rehnquist, "force the organization to send a message, both to youth members and the world, that the Boy Scouts accepts homosexual conduct as a legitimate form of behavior."

## FREEDOM OF THE PRESS

"A free press," declared Justice Frankfurter, "is indispensable to the workings of our democratic society." Whether through newspaper, magazine, radio, film, or television, journalism is an industry that "serves one of the most vital of all general interests," surmised Judge Learned Hand—" the dissemination of news from as many different sources, and with as many different facets and colors as is possible." Right conclusions "are more likely to be gathered out of a multitude of tongues, than through any kind of authoritative selection. To many this is, and always will be, folly; but we have staked upon it our all." The First Amendment lays down a claim for a free press, but the involvement of the press with "the workings of our democratic society" guarantees conflict between journalists and public officials.

PRIOR RESTRAINTS. At the very least, the First Amendment was designed to prevent "all such previous restraints upon publications as had been practised by other governments," noted Justice Holmes almost a century ago (*Patterson* v. *Colorado,* 1907). A **prior restraint**—legal action that blocks further publication—is still regarded as the most onerous kind of abridgement of press freedom and is the restriction that the Court is most reluctant to approve.

In the landmark 1931 decision of *Near* v. *Minnesota,* the Court held unconstitutional a Minnesota statute that gave the state power to shut down any "malicious, scandalous and defamatory newspaper, magazine or periodical." Truth published with good motives was available as a defense. Near published *The Saturday Press,* which devoted several issues to virulent attacks on various public officials. The attacks were anti-Semitic in tone and thoroughly tasteless, and the county attorney succeeded in having the law applied to Near. "This is . . . the essence of censorship," concluded Chief Justice Hughes, by a margin of one vote. Five years later, the Court went beyond *Near's* invalidation of outright censorship, when *Grosjean* v. *American Press Co.* struck down tax legislation in Louisiana crafted to apply only to the state's 13 daily newspapers, all but one of which strongly opposed Governor Huey P. (the "Kingfish") Long. Facially, the tax scheme was not censorial, but the justices considered it "to be a deliberate and calculated device . . . to limit the circulation of information."

*Near* itself went on trial in June 1971, when the United States sought to enjoin first the *New York Times* and then the *Washington Post* from publishing the contents of a classified study the *Times* had obtained entitled "History of U.S. Decision-Making Process on Vietnam Policy" (***New York Times Company v. United States***—the Pentagon Papers case). Unlike *Near,* there was no statute giving courts power to block continued publication of a newspaper, even to protect national security. With no time for anyone to write a majority opinion, the Court simply issued a brief per curiam order stating that the government had not met the necessary burden of "showing justification for the enforcement of such a restraint," followed by six concurring and three dissenting opinions.

Such prior restraints on publication may be the hobgoblin of American constitutional interpretation, but this presumption received its severest test eight years later when the federal government sought to prevent publication of an issue of *The Progressive* magazine. Officials were distressed by an article it was to contain: "The H-Bomb Secret; How We Got It, Why We're Telling It." The fear was not that the article would enable anyone to construct a hydrogen bomb in the garage, but that it contained information that would be a significant help to countries attempting to develop a nuclear capability. Unlike the government's position in the Pentagon Papers case, there seemed this time to be statutory authority for a court to issue an injunction. In *United States* v. *Progressive, Inc.* (1979), a U.S. district court in Wisconsin did just that. Before argument in the court of appeals, however, the *Madison* (Wisconsin) *Press Connection* published an 18-page letter recounting much of the information that was to have appeared in *The Progressive*. The issue of prior restraint therefore became moot, and the Justice Department withdrew its suit. Although this case never received full judicial consideration beyond the district court level, it illustrates the practical difficulties in preventing publication of material people want to publish. Moreover, anyone contemplating a prior restraint today must take into account the Internet and all it has done to transform information technology. Short of unplugging the entire national telecommunications system, the physical demands of a prior restraint that works are mind-boggling.

**LIBEL.** Although American judges historically have looked warily on prior restraints, the press has been on notice that it must take responsibility for what it publishes. The press may not be restrained in advance, but it may be punished for what it prints. **Libel** (written defamation of a person's reputation) is one of these subsequent punishments and has long been regarded as an exception to the press freedom protected by the First Amendment. In 1964, however, **New York Times Co. v. Sullivan** virtually abolished the right of public officials to collect damages for libel. Under this decision, the press, and perhaps anyone else, has the right to publish libelous statements about public officials. "Actual malice" must be shown by a plaintiff under the Sullivan rule. The Court's rationale has been summed up this way: "What is added to the field of libel is taken from the arena of debate, and democracy calls for robust, wide-open debate about public issues. Libel, then, that deals with public affairs is not evil; it serves a socially useful function." *Curtis Publishing Co.* v. *Butts* in 1967 extended the Sullivan rule to prominent people outside government. Even parodies that are plainly false and intended to cause emotional distress are protected, the Court held in *Hustler Magazine* v. *Falwell* (1988). Here, a magazine had published a supposed interview with a television evangelist in which he revealed that his "first time" was an intoxicated tryst with his mother in an outhouse.

*Sullivan* has not ended libel suits by public officials and figures. Decisions have allowed more cases to go to trial by making the issue of malice one for the jury to decide. By preserving the possibility of a successful libel action, libel law understandably makes journalists wary. Even if unsuccessful, a suit is costly because of the amount of time a defense requires. A major television network may be able to absorb the costs, but a small newspaper would not and therefore might forgo controversial investigative reporting that might spark a libel suit.

**PORNOGRAPHY.** State and national governments alike continue to be involved in the less dramatic function of protecting the welfare of their citizens. Where these policies attempt to curtail sexually explicit materials, First Amendment problems arise.

*Roth* v. *United States* (1957) was the Court's first formal acceptance under the First Amendment of state and federal action directed against pornography. Justice Brennan wrote for the majority that "obscenity is utterly without redeeming social importance." Therefore, it "is not within the area of constitutionally protected speech or press." The key of course was to define the obscene, and the constitutional standard became "whether to the average person, applying contemporary community standards, the dominant theme of the material taken as a whole appeals to prurient interest."

*Roth* raised as many questions as it answered and only began the Court's long struggle with what Justice Harlan later called "the intractable obscenity problem." In effect, the justices became the censorship board for the nation. With unusual candor, Justice Stewart confessed that his colleagues were trying to define the indefinable. "[U]nder the First and Fourteenth Amendments criminal laws in this area are constitutionally limited to hard-core pornography. I shall not today attempt further to define the kinds of material I understand to be embraced within that shorthand description; and perhaps I could never succeed in intelligibly doing so. But I know it when I see it . . ." (*Jacobellis* v. *Ohio,* 1964).

In 1966, in *Memoirs of a Woman of Pleasure* v. *Massachusetts,* the justices tightened the Roth test and made it more difficult for government to maintain a successful obscenity prosecution. Although formally endorsed only by a plurality, the elements of proof now included a demonstration that the material in question be "patently offensive" and "utterly without redeeming social value." Definitional problems abounded, and as a result so did the number of obscenity cases on the Court's docket. Some of the justices found themselves with no choice but to look at the material in question. The staff then obligingly set up a special viewing room on the ground level of the Supreme Court building. Harlan dutifully attended the video sessions despite cataracts that badly obscured his vision. Justice Stewart sat next to him and described the activity taking place on the screen. As radio journalist Nina Totenberg reported, "And about once every five minutes Harlan would exclaim in his proper way: 'By George, extraordinary.'"

In 1969, *Stanley* v. *Georgia* gave the strong hint that all obscenity laws were living on borrowed time, as the Court held that mere private possession of obscene materials was protected by the First Amendment. But the majority pulled back from the logical implications of *Stanley* in *Miller* v. *California* (1973) and announced new standards. Most significantly, the prosecution now had to show that the material in question lacked only "serious value," not that it was "utterly without" value. Ironically, just as the Court relaxed constitutional protection for sexually explicit matter, society was generally becoming more tolerant of it. The result has been a sharp decline in obscenity prosecutions involving material depicting adults.

Instead, prosecutorial emphasis in recent years has been on child pornography. According to *Ferber* v. *New York* (1982), government may proscribe materials that photographically portray sexual acts or lewd exhibitions of genitalia by children even when the materials are not obscene under *Miller.* The Court's rationale was that such laws were needed to stop sexual exploitation of minors. Yet the battle against child pornography has been complicated by computer technology, allowing the creation of "virtual child pornography." Congress addressed the problem in the Child Pornography Prevention Act of 1996, but its key provisions fell victim to the overbreadth doctrine in **Ashcroft v. Free Speech Coalition** (2002).

**COMMERCIAL SPEECH.** Regulations on advertisements and other commercial messages present a special problem. Not until *Virginia State Board of Pharmacy* v. *Virginia Consumer Council* (1976) did the justices include **commercial speech**

under the shield of the First Amendment, when the Court set aside a law that barred price advertising of prescription drugs. Later cases have extended the freedom to advertise to lawyers (*Bates* v. *State Bar of Arizona,* 1977) and the freedom to solicit in person and by telephone to accountants, but not yet to attorneys (*Edenfield* v. *Fane,* 1993). Nonetheless, governments still have greater latitude in regulating commercial, as compared with other kinds of, speech. *Central Hudson Gas & Electric Corp.* v. *Public Service Commission of New York* (1980) laid down a four-part analysis that the Court continues to use. "At the outset, we must determine whether the expression is protected by the First Amendment. For commercial speech to come within that provision, it at least must concern lawful activity and not be misleading. Next, we ask whether the asserted governmental interest is substantial. If both inquiries yield positive answers, we must determine whether the regulation directly advances the governmental interest asserted, and whether it is not more extensive than is necessary to serve that interest."

Applying *Central Hudson,* the Court has struck down several laws and regulations, including a 1935 federal statute banning disclosure of alcohol content on beer labels and, even in the face of the Twenty-first Amendment, a state ban on retail liquor price advertising (*Rubin* v. *Coors Brewing Co.,* 1995; *44 Liquormart, Inc.* v. *Rhode Island,* 1996).

## RADIO, TELEVISION, AND THE INTERNET

Print and broadcast media do not stand as equals under the First Amendment. While the gap has narrowed in recent years, newspapers and magazines—like the orators and pamphleteers also known to the framers—have been accorded more freedom than radio and television. Perhaps nowhere else has Justice Holmes's observation been more apt: "a page of history is worth a volume of logic."

As commercial radio and television evolved in the 1920s and 1940s, respectively, some regulation by the federal government was of course essential. With a finite broadcast spectrum, chaos would reign on the airwaves without allocation of frequencies and limitations on transmitting locations and power. Coupled with the necessity of licensing, oversight, and license renewal was the premise that access to the broadcast spectrum should be conditional. Stipulations (such as operating "in the public interest," affording "equal time" to political candidates, and telecasting educational programs for children) were imposed that would be constitutionally unacceptable if applied to newspapers. Moreover, because of the pervasiveness of radio and television, the likelihood that listeners and viewers could be exposed to undesirable programming without warning, and the ease with which children could come in contact with such programming, courts may accept carefully drawn regulations to keep offensive material off the air, at least during certain hours of the day.

Thus *Red Lion Broadcasting Co.* v. *FCC* (1969) unanimously upheld rules of the Federal Communications Commission that required broadcasters to grant a right to reply to personal attacks that they transmit and to afford a right of reply to political editorials. (In contrast, the Court rejected Florida's personal attack rule for newspapers five years later in *Miami Herald Publishing Co.* v. *Tornillo.*) While the Court in 1973 denied the authority of the FCC to compel a television network to sell time to a political party for editorial advertising (*CBS* v. *Democratic National Committee*), in 1981 it upheld the validity of a congressional statute guaranteeing "reasonable" access to the airwaves for candidates in federal elections (*CBS* v. *FCC*). And the Court has accepted the FCC's power to set limits on broadcasts containing indecent language (*FCC* v. *Pacifica Foundation,* 1978). Yet one purveyor of sexually explicit (although not necessarily obscene) television programming persuaded five justices to invalidate, as impermissibly content-based, section 505 of the Telecommunications Act of 1996. This statute required cable television operators either to scramble sexually oriented programs fully to prevent both audio and video "signal bleed," or to schedule the programs when children ordinarily would not be watching ("time channeling")—the alternative most cable providers chose. In the majority's view, the government had failed to demonstrate the existence of a pervasive nationwide problem that would justify the ban, nor had it shown the ineffectiveness of other less restrictive measures. One of the latter was embodied within § 504, which directed cable services to block undesired channels at the request of individual households (*United States* v. *Playboy Entertainment Group,* 2000).

Advances in technology seem largely to have undercut the "scarcity" rationale for regulation. Frequencies may remain finite, but almost every home has greater access to radio and television than to newspapers. Commercial and educational stations outnumber daily newspapers by more than seven to one. Thanks to cable and satellite companies that convey outlets (such as ESPN and MSNBC) in addition to those from traditional broadcast stations, most households now receive dozens of video channels. Yet enlarged capacity in the hands of cable monopolies at the community level has itself become a basis for regulation. Against a challenge on First Amendment grounds, *Turner Broadcasting System, Inc.* v. *FCC* (1997) approved a federal "must carry" statute, requiring local cable systems to relay nearby commercial and public broadcast stations even if the cable system preferred to substitute out-of-area stations or cable channels in their place.

The Internet demonstrates that technology continues to generate constitutional questions. An outgrowth of a military program called "ARPANET" (Advanced Research Project Agency Network), created in 1969 to enable computers operated by the military, defense contractors, and universities to communicate with one another on redundant circuits in wartime, the Internet has become both an international network of interconnected computers and a wholly new medium of communication. For a user, the Internet is comparable to both a vast library of readily available and indexed publications and a mall offering goods and services. For the operator of a Web site, the Internet is a platform from which to reach a worldwide audience of readers, voters, researchers, and buyers.

In 1996 Congress passed the Communications Decency Act to protect minors from obscene and indecent materials on the Internet. Several groups immediately challenged the legislation as a violation of freedom of speech. With a history of contrasting approaches in regulating different media, was the Internet to be treated for regulatory purposes like a newspaper or a television station? The Internet, after all, incorporated elements of each. A nearly unanimous answer came in ***Reno* v. *American Civil Liberties Union,*** the first application of the Constitution to cyberspace, which sharply curtailed government's authority to censor content on the Internet.

## POSTSCRIPT

If speech in recent decades has typically prevailed over competing interests, does this mean that the First Amendment is in a favored or preferred position? Justice Stone's footnote four in the Carolene Products case, discussed in Chapter Eight, suggests precisely that. In response Justice Scalia contends that "the First Amendment is not everything." Regardless, constitutional rights are not rights against government so much as rights against the dominant majority represented by government. It would be difficult to label a political system as "democratic" if individuals with points of view in the minority could not freely campaign to become the majority. The Bill of Rights expresses the judgment of the founders that the majority is neither always right nor likely to be tolerant. "The very purpose of a Bill of Rights," Justice Jackson declared in 1943, "was to withdraw certain subjects from the vicissitudes of political controversy, to place them beyond the reach of majorities." Thus the irony of the First Amendment: A guarantee of free speech presupposes a population capable of rational thought and considered judgment; it also assumes a population sometimes eager to squelch unpopular ideas.

## KEY TERMS

clear-and-present-danger
   test
bad tendency test
incitement test
absolute approach
overbreadth doctrine
chilling effect

void for vagueness
strict scrutiny
criminal syndicalism
Smith Act
viewpoint-based
   restrictions
public forum

fighting words
symbolic speech
expressive association
prior restraint
libel
commercial speech

## QUERIES

**1.** Why should freedom of speech be extended to persons who use it to advocate destruction of that freedom for others?

**2.** One university has a rule that bans "discriminatory harassment," which is defined as "conduct (oral, written, graphic, or physical) directed against any person or group . . . that has the purpose or reasonably foreseeable effect of creating an offensive, demeaning, intimidating, or hostile environment." Analyze this rule's impact on free expression using various First Amendment criteria and concepts discussed in this chapter.

**3.** Could a flag-protection law have been written that would have satisfied the majority in *Texas* v. *Johnson?* Consider the language of Congress's Flag Protection Act of 1989, which the Court found unacceptable in *United States* v. *Eichman:* "Whoever knowingly mutilates, defaces, physically defiles, burns, maintains on the floor or ground, or tramples upon any flag of the United States shall be fined . . . or imprisoned. . . ." Is it possible to separate protection of the flag from protection of the values it symbolizes?

**4.** In *Beauharnais* v. *Illinois* (1952), the Supreme Court, voting 5–4, upheld the application to a white supremacist of a group libel law that prohibited publications that portrayed "depravity, criminality, unchastity, or lack of virtue of a class of citizens, of any race, color, creed or religion, [or which] exposes the citizens of any race, color, creed or religion to contempt, derision, or obloquy, or which is productive of breach of the peace or riots." Does *Beauharnais* have relevance to the debate today about efforts to control hate speech? Has *Beauharnais* been eroded by later decisions?

## SELECTED READINGS

CHAFEE, ZECHARIAH, JR. *Free Speech in the United States.* Cambridge, Mass.: Harvard University Press, 1942.

CORWIN, EDWARD S. "Bowing Out 'Clear and Present Danger.'" 27 *Notre Dame Lawyer* 325 (1952).

CURTIS, MICHAEL KENT. *Free Speech, "The People's Darling Privilege."* Durham, N.C.: Duke University Press, 2000.

EMERSON, THOMAS I. *The System of Freedom of Expression.* New York: Random House, 1970.

FISS, OWEN. *Liberalism Divided: Freedom of Speech and the Many Uses of State Power.* Boulder, Colo.: Westview Press, 1996.

HENTOFF, NAT. *Free Speech for Me—But Not for Thee.* New York: HarperCollins, 1992.

KERSCH, KEN I. *Freedom of Speech.* Santa Barbara, Calif.: ABC-CLIO, 2003.

LEVY, LEONARD W. *Emergence of a Free Press.* New York: Oxford University Press, 1985 (a revision of Levy's 1960 work, *Legacy of Suppression*).

LEWIS, ANTHONY. *Make No Law: The Sullivan Case and the First Amendment.* New York: Random House, 1991.

RUDENSTINE, DAVID. *The Day the Presses Stopped: A History of the Pentagon Papers Case.* Berkeley: University of California Press, 1996.

## I. INTERNAL SECURITY

### *Schenck v. United States*
### 249 U.S. 47, 39 S.Ct. 247, 63 L.Ed. 470 (1919)

http://laws.findlaw.com/us/249/47.html

> Charles Schenck and others were convicted of conspiracy to obstruct the draft and other violations of the Espionage Act of 1917. Their specific offense was printing and distributing leaflets that opposed the war effort generally and conscription specifically. Majority: Holmes, Brandeis, Clarke, Day, McKenna, McReynolds, Pitney, Van Devanter, White.

**MR. JUSTICE HOLMES delivered the opinion of the court. . . .**

The document in question upon its first printed side recited the first section of the Thirteenth Amendment, said that the idea embodied in it was violated by the Conscription Act, and that a conscript is little better than a convict. In impassioned language it intimated that conscription was despotism in its worst form and a monstrous wrong against humanity in the interest of Wall Street's chosen few. It said, "Do not submit to intimidation," but in form at least confined itself to peaceful measures such as a petition for the repeal of the act. The other and later printed side of the sheet was headed "Assert Your Rights." It stated reasons for alleging that any one violated the Constitution when he refused to recognize "your right to assert your opposition to the draft," and went on "If you do not assert and support your rights, you are helping to deny or disparage rights which it is the solemn duty of all citizens and residents of the United States to retain." It described the arguments on the other side as coming from cunning politicians and a mercenary capitalist press, and even silent consent to the conscription law as helping to support an infamous conspiracy. It denied the power to send our citizens away to foreign shores to shoot up the people of other lands, and added that words could not express the condemnation such cold-blooded ruthlessness deserves, &c., winding up "You must do your share to maintain, support and uphold the rights of the people of this country." Of course the document would not have been sent unless it had been intended to have some effect, and we do not see what effect it could be expected to have upon persons subject to the draft except to influence them to obstruct the carrying out of it. The defendants do not deny that the jury might find against them on this point.

But it is said, suppose that that was the tendency of this circular, it is protected by the First Amendment to the Constitution. Two of the strongest expressions are said to be quoted respectively from well-known public men. It well may be that the prohibition of laws abridging the freedom of speech is not confined to previous restraints, although to prevent them may have been the main purpose. . . . We admit that in many places and in ordinary times the defendants in saying all that was said in the circular would have been within their constitutional rights. But the character of every act depends upon the circumstances in which it is done. . . . The most stringent protection of free speech would not protect a man in falsely shouting fire in a theatre and causing a panic. It does not even protect a man from an injunction against uttering words that may have all the effect of force. . . . The question in every case is whether the words are used in such circumstances and are of such a nature as to create a clear and present danger that they will bring about the substantive evils that Congress has a right to prevent. It is a question of proximity and degree. When a nation is at war many things that might be said in time of peace are such a hindrance to its effort that their utterance will not be endured so long as men fight and that no Court could regard them as protected by any constitutional right. It seems to be admitted that if an actual obstruction of the recruiting service were proved, liability for words that produced that effect might be enforced. The statute of 1917 in § 4 punishes conspiracies to obstruct as well as actual obstruction. If the act (speaking, or circulating a paper), its tendency and the intent with which it is done are the same, we perceive no ground for saying that success alone warrants making the act a crime.

*Judgments affirmed.*

## *Gitlow* v. *New York*
### 268 U.S. 652, 45 S.Ct. 625, 69 L.Ed. 1138 (1925)
### http://laws.findlaw.com/us/268/652.html

Benjamin Gitlow, a member of the left-wing section of the Socialist Party, was convicted of the New York crime of criminal anarchy. Majority: Sanford, Butler, McReynolds, Sutherland, Taft, Van Devanter. Dissenting: Holmes, Brandeis. Not participating: Stone.

**MR. JUSTICE SANFORD delivered the opinion of the Court. . . .**

The contention here is that the statute, by its terms and as applied in this case, is repugnant to the due process clause of the Fourteenth Amendment. . . .

The indictment was in two counts. The first charged that the defendant had advocated, advised and taught the duty, necessity and propriety of overthrowing and overturning organized government by force, violence and unlawful means, by certain writings therein set forth entitled "The Left Wing Manifesto"; the second that he had printed, published and knowingly circulated and distributed a certain paper called "The Revolutionary Age," containing the writings set forth in the first count, advocating, advising and teaching the doctrine that organized government should be overthrown by force, violence and unlawful means. . . .

The precise question presented, and the only question which we can consider under this writ of error, then is, whether the statute, as construed and applied in this case by the state courts, deprived the defendant of his liberty of expression in violation of the due process clause of the Fourteenth Amendment.

The statute does not penalize the utterance or publication of abstract "doctrine" or academic discussion having no quality of incitement to any concrete action. . . . What it prohibits is language advocating, advising or teaching the overthrow of organized government by unlawful means. . . .

The Manifesto, plainly, is neither the statement of abstract doctrine nor, as suggested by counsel, mere prediction that industrial disturbances and revolutionary mass strikes will result spontaneously in an inevitable process of evolution in the economic system. It advocates and urges in fervent language mass action which shall progressively foment industrial disturbances and through political mass strikes and revolutionary mass action overthrow and destroy organized parliamentary government. It concludes with a call to action in these words: "The proletariat revolution and the Communist reconstruction of society—the struggle for these—is now indispensable. . . . The Communist International calls the proletariat of the world to the final struggle!" This is not the expression of philosophical abstractions, the mere prediction of future events; it is the language of direct incitement. . . .

For present purposes we may add and do assume that freedom of speech and of the press—which are protected by the First Amendment from abridgment by Congress—are among the fundamental personal rights and "liberties" protected by the due process clause of the Fourteenth Amendment from impairment by the states. . . .

It is a fundamental principle, long established, that the freedom of speech and of the press which is secured by the Constitution, does not confer an absolute right to speak or publish, without responsibility, whatever one may choose, or an unrestricted and unbridled license that gives immunity for every possible use of language and prevents the punishment of those who abuse this freedom. . . .

That a State in the exercise of its police power may punish those who abuse this freedom by utterances inimical to the public welfare, tending to corrupt public morals, incite to crime, or disturb the public peace, is not open to question. . . .

By enacting the present statute the State has determined, through its legislative body, that utterances advocating the overthrow of organized government by force, violence and unlawful means, are so inimical to the general welfare and involve such danger of substantive evil that they may be penalized in the exercise of its police power. That determination must be given great weight. Every presumption is to be indulged in favor of the validity of the statute. . . . That utterances inciting to the overthrow of organized government by unlawful means, present a sufficient danger of substantive evil to bring their punishment within the range of legislative discretion, is clear. Such utterances, by their very nature, involve danger to the public peace and to the security of the State. They threaten breaches of the peace and ultimate revolution. And the immediate danger is none the less real and substantial, because the effect of a given utterance cannot be accurately foreseen. The State cannot reasonably be required to measure the danger from every such utterance in the nice balance of a jeweler's scale. A single revolutionary spark may kindle a fire that, smouldering for a time, may burst into a sweeping and destructive conflagration. It cannot be said that the State is acting arbitrarily or unreasonably when in the exercise of its judgment as to the measures necessary to protect the public peace and safety, it seeks to extinguish the spark without waiting until it has enkindled the flame or blazed into the conflagration. . . .

We cannot hold that the present statute is an arbitrary or unreasonable exercise of the police power of the State unwarrantably infringing the freedom of speech or press; and we must and do sustain its constitutionality. . . .

*Affirmed.*

## MR. JUSTICE HOLMES, dissenting:

MR. JUSTICE BRANDEIS and I are of opinion that this judgment should be reversed. . . . I think that the criterion sanctioned by the full court in *Schenck* v. *United States* . . . applies. It is manifest that there was no present danger of an attempt to overthrow the government by force on the part of the admittedly small minority who shared the defendant's views. It is said that this manifesto was more than a theory, that it was an incitement. Every idea is an incitement. It offers itself for belief and if believed it is acted on unless some other belief outweighs it or some failure of energy stifles the movement at its birth. The only difference between the expression of an opinion and an incitement in the narrower sense is the speaker's enthusiasm for the result. Eloquence may set fire to reason. But whatever may be thought of the redundant discourse before us it had no chance of starting a present conflagration. If in the long run the beliefs expressed in proletarian dictatorship are destined to be accepted by the dominant forces of the community, the only meaning of free speech is that they should be given their chance and have their way.

If the publication of this document had been laid out as an attempt to induce an uprising against government at once and not at some indefinite time in the future it would have presented a different question. The object would have been one with which the law might deal, subject to the doubt whether there was any danger that the publication could produce any result, or in other words, whether it was not futile and too remote from possible consequences. But the indictment alleges the publication and nothing more.

## *Whitney v. California*
### 274 U.S. 357, 47 S.Ct. 641, 71 L.Ed. 1095 (1927)
### http://laws.findlaw.com/us/274/357.html

Charlotte Anita Whitney—prominent suffragist, Socialist, and a niece of former Justice Stephen J. Field—was convicted of violating California's criminal syndicalism act of 1919 for having participated in a convention of the Communist Labor Party of California, which was affiliated with the Communist International of Moscow. Evidence showed that she had personally proposed a resolution advocating a strictly political role for the party, which the convention had rejected in favor of a national program advocating various revolutionary measures including national strikes. She remained until the end of the convention and did not withdraw from the party. The case remains significant because of Justice Brandeis's concurring opinion, which soon led the Court to apply the clear-and-present-danger test in many free speech cases. Majority: Sanford, Butler, Brandeis, Holmes, McReynolds, Stone, Sutherland, Taft, Van Devanter.

**MR. JUSTICE SANFORD delivered the opinion of the Court. . . .**

By enacting the provisions of the Syndicalism Act the State has declared, through its legislative body, that to knowingly be or become a member of or assist in organizing an association to advocate, teach or aid and abet the commission of crimes or unlawful acts of force, violence or terrorism as a means of accomplishing industrial or political changes, involves such danger to the public peace and the security of the State, that these acts should be penalized in the exercise of its police power. That determination must be given great weight. Every presumption is to be indulged in favor of the validity of the statute . . . and it may not be declared unconstitutional unless it is an arbitrary or unreasonable attempt to exercise the authority vested in the State in the public interest. . . .

*Affirmed.*

**MR. JUSTICE BRANDEIS, concurring. . . .**

Despite arguments to the contrary which had seemed to me persuasive, it is settled that the due process clause of the Fourteenth Amendment applies to matters of substantive law as well as to matters of procedure. Thus all fundamental rights comprised within the term *liberty* are protected by the Federal Constitution from invasion by the states. . . . But, although the rights of free speech and assembly are fundamental, they are not in their nature absolute. Their exercise is subject to restriction, if the particular restriction proposed is required in order to protect the state from destruction or from serious injury, political, economic or moral. That the necessity which is essential to a valid restriction does not exist unless speech would produce, or is intended to produce, a clear and imminent danger of some substantive evil which the state constitutionally may seek to prevent has been settled. . . .

This court has not yet fixed the standard by which to determine when a danger shall be deemed clear; how remote the danger may be and yet be deemed present; and what degree of evil shall be deemed sufficiently substantial to justify resort to abridgment of free speech and assembly as the means of protection. To reach sound conclusions on these matters, we must bear in mind why a state is, ordinarily, denied the power to prohibit dissemination of social, economic and political doctrine which a vast majority of its citizens believes to be false and fraught with evil consequence.

Those who won our independence believed that the final end of the state was to make men free to develop their faculties, and that in its government the deliberative forces should prevail over the arbitrary. They valued liberty both as an end and as a means. They believed liberty to be the secret of happiness and courage to be the secret of liberty. They believed that freedom to think as you will and to speak as you think are means indispensable to the discovery and spread of political truth; that without free speech and assembly discussion would be futile; that with them, discussion affords ordinarily adequate protection against the dissemination of noxious doctrine; that the greatest menace to freedom is an inert people; that public discussion is a political duty; and that this should be a fundamental principle of the American government. They recognized the risks to which all human institutions are subject. But they knew that order cannot be secured merely through fear of punishment for its infraction; that it is hazardous to discourage thought, hope and imagination; that fear breeds repression; that repression breeds hate; that hate menaces stable government; that the path of safety lies in the opportunity to discuss freely supposed grievances and proposed remedies; and that the fitting remedy for evil counsels is good ones. Believing in the power of reason as applied through public discussion, they eschewed silence coerced by law—the argument of force in its worst form. Recognizing the occasional tyrannies of governing majorities, they amended the Constitution so that free speech and assembly should be guaranteed.

Fear of serious injury cannot alone justify suppression of free speech and assembly.

Men feared witches and burnt women. It is the function of speech to free men from the bondage of irrational fears. To justify suppression of free speech there must be reasonable ground to fear that serious evil will result if free speech is practiced. There must be reasonable ground to believe that the danger apprehended is imminent. There must be reasonable ground to believe that the evil to be prevented is a serious one. . . . The wide difference between advocacy and incitement, between preparation and attempt, between assembling and conspiracy, must be borne in mind. In order to support a finding of clear and present danger it must be shown either that immediate serious violence was to be expected or was advocated, or that the past conduct furnished reason to believe that such advocacy was then contemplated.

Those who won our independence by revolution were not cowards. They did not fear political change. They did not exalt order at the cost of liberty. To courageous, self-reliant men, with confidence in the power of free and fearless reasoning applied through the process of popular government, no danger flowing from speech can be deemed clear and present, unless the incidence of the evil apprehended is so imminent that it may befall before there is opportunity for full discussion. If there be time to expose through discussion the falsehood and fallacies, to avert the evil by the processes of education, the remedy to be applied is more speech, not enforced silence. Only an emergency can justify repression. Such must be the rule if authority is to be reconciled with freedom. Such, in my opinion, is the command of the Constitution. It is therefore always open to Americans to challenge a law abridging free speech and assembly by showing that there was no emergency justifying it.

Moreover, even imminent danger cannot justify resort to prohibition of these functions essential to effective democracy, unless the evil apprehended is relatively serious. Prohibition of free speech and assembly is a measure so stringent that it would be inappropriate as the means for averting a relatively trivial harm to society. A police measure may be unconstitutional merely because the remedy, although effective as means of protection, is unduly harsh or oppressive. . . . The fact that speech is likely to result in some violence or in destruction of property is not enough to justify its suppression. There must be the probability of serious injury to the State. Among free men, the deterrents ordinarily to be applied to prevent crime are education and punishment for violations of the law, not abridgment of the rights of free speech and assembly.

Whether in 1919, when Miss Whitney did the things complained of, there was in California such clear and present danger of serious evil, might have been made the important issue in this case. She might have required that the issue be determined either by the court or by the jury. She claimed below that the statute as applied to her violated the federal Constitution; but she did not claim that it was void because there was no clear and present danger of serious evil, nor did she request that the existence of these conditions of a valid measure thus restricting the rights of free speech and assembly be passed upon by the court or a jury. On the other hand, there was evidence on which the court or jury might have found that such danger existed. . . . Under these circumstances the judgment of the State court cannot be disturbed. . . .

Mr. Justice Holmes joins in this opinion.

## *Dennis* v. *United States*
## 341 U.S. 494, 71 S.Ct. 857, 95 L.Ed. 1137 (1951)
## http://laws.findlaw.com/us/341/494.html

This case represents the last stage of the 1949 trial of the 11 leaders of the Communist Party of the United States for violations of the Smith Act of 1940. The Supreme Court's grant of certiorari to the Second Circuit Court of Appeals was limited to a review of whether Sections 2 or 3 of the Smith Act, inherently or as construed and applied, violated the First or Fifth Amendment. Majority: Vinson, Burton, Frankfurter, Jackson, Minton, Reed. Dissenting: Black, Douglas. Not participating: Clark.

**MR. CHIEF JUSTICE VINSON announced the judgment of the court and an opinion in which MR. JUSTICE REED, MR. JUSTICE BURTON, and MR. JUSTICE MINTON join. . . .**

Sections 2 and 3 of the Smith Act, provide as follows:

Sec. 2

(a) It shall be unlawful for any person—

(1) to knowingly or willfully advocate, abet, advise, or teach the duty, necessity, desirability, or propriety of overthrowing or destroying any government in the United States by force or violence, or by the assassination of any officer of such government;

(2) with the intent to cause the overthrow or destruction of any government in the United States, to print, publish, edit, issue, circulate, sell, distribute, or publicly display any written or printed matter advocating, advising, or teaching the duty, necessity, desirability, or propriety of overthrowing or destroying any government in the United States by force or violence;

(3) to organize or help to organize any society, group, or assembly of persons who teach, advocate, or encourage the overthrow or destruction of any government in the United States by force or violence; or to be or become a member of, or affiliate with, any such society, group, or assembly of persons, knowing the purposes thereof. . . .

Sec. 3. It shall be unlawful for any person to attempt to commit, or to conspire to commit, any of the acts prohibited by the provisions of . . . this title. . . .

The obvious purpose of the statute is to protect existing Government, not from change by peaceable, lawful and constitutional means, but from change by violence, revolution and terrorism. . . . No one could conceive that it is not within the power of Congress to prohibit acts intended to overthrow the Government by force and violence. The question with which we are concerned here is not whether Congress has such power, but whether the *means* which it has employed conflict with the First and Fifth Amendments to the Constitution.

One of the bases for the contention that the means which Congress has employed are invalid takes the form of an attack on the face of the statute on the grounds that by its terms it prohibits academic discussion of the merits of Marxism-Leninism, that it stifles ideas and is contrary to all concepts of a free speech and a free press. . . .

The very language of the Smith Act negates the interpretation which petitioners would have us impose on that Act. It is directed at advocacy, not discussion. Thus, the trial judge properly charged the jury that they could not convict if they found that petitioners did "no more than pursue peaceful studies and discussions or teaching and advocacy in the realm of ideas." He further charged that it was not unlawful "to conduct in an American college or university a course explaining the philosophical theories set forth in the books which have been placed in evidence." Such a charge is in strict accord with the statutory language, and illustrates the meaning to be placed on those words. Congress did not intend to eradicate the free discussion of political theories, to destroy the traditional rights of Americans to discuss and evaluate ideas without fear of governmental sanction. Rather Congress was concerned with the very kind of activity in which the evidence showed these petitioners engaged. . . .

The basis of the First Amendment is the hypothesis that speech can rebut speech, propaganda will answer propaganda, free debate of ideas will result in the wisest governmental policies. It is for this reason that this Court has recognized the inherent value of free discourse. An analysis of the leading cases in this Court which have involved direct limitations on speech, however, will demonstrate that both the majority of the Court and dissenters in particular cases have recognized that this is not an unlimited, unqualified right, but that the societal value of speech must, on occasion, be subordinated to other values and considerations. . . .

The rule we deduce from [past] cases is that where an offense is specified by a statute in nonspeech or nonpress terms, a conviction relying upon speech or press as evidence of violation may be sustained only when the speech or publication created a "clear and present danger" of attempting or accomplishing the prohibited crime, e.g., interference with enlistment. The dissents, we repeat, in emphasizing the value of speech, were addressed to the argument of the sufficiency of the evidence. . . .

Although no case subsequent to *Whitney* and *Gitlow* has expressly overruled the majority opinions in those cases, there is little doubt that subsequent opinions have inclined toward the Holmes-Brandeis rationale. . . . In this case we are squarely presented with the application of the "clear and present danger" test, and must decide what that phrase imports. . . .

Obviously, the words cannot mean that before the Government may act, it must wait until the putsch is about to be executed, the plans have been laid and the signal is awaited. . . . In the instant case the trial judge charged the jury that they could not convict unless they found that petitioners intended to overthrow the Government "as speedily as circumstances would permit." This does not mean, and could not properly mean, that they would not strike

until there was certainty of success. What was meant was that the revolutionists would strike when they thought the time was ripe. We must therefore reject the contention that success or probability of success is the criterion.

The situation with which Justices Holmes and Brandeis were concerned in *Gitlow* was a comparatively isolated event, bearing little relation in their minds to any substantial threat to the safety of the community. . . . They were not confronted with any situation comparable to the instant one—the development of an apparatus designed and dedicated to the overthrow of the Government, in the context of world crisis after crisis.

Chief Judge Learned Hand, writing for the majority below, interpreted the phrase as follows: "In each case [courts] must ask whether the gravity of the 'evil,' discounted by its improbability, justifies such invasion of free speech as is necessary to avoid the danger." . . . We adopt this statement of the rule. As articulated by Chief Judge Hand, it is as succinct and inclusive as any other we might devise at this time. It takes into consideration those factors which we deem relevant, and relates their significances. More we cannot expect from words.

Likewise, we are in accord with the court below, which affirmed the trial court's finding that the requisite danger existed. The mere fact that from the period 1945 to 1948 petitioners' activities did not result in an attempt to overthrow the Government by force and violence is of course no answer to the fact that there was a group that was ready to make the attempt. The formation by petitioners of such a highly organized conspiracy, with rigidly disciplined members subject to call when the leaders, these petitioners, felt that the time had come for action, coupled with the inflammable nature of world conditions, similar uprisings in other countries, and the touch-and-go nature of our relations with countries with whom petitioners were in the very least ideologically attuned, convince us that their convictions were justified on this score. And this analysis disposes of the contention that a conspiracy to advocate, as distinguished from the advocacy itself, cannot be constitutionally restrained, because it comprises only the preparation. It is the existence of the conspiracy which creates the danger. . . . If the ingredients of the reaction are present, we cannot bind the government to wait until the catalyst is added. . . .

We agree that the standard as defined is not a neat, mathematical formulary. Like all verbalizations it is subject to criticism on the score of indefiniteness. But . . . [w]e think it well serves to indicate to those who would advocate constitutionally prohibited conduct that there is a line beyond which they may not go—a line, which they, in full knowledge of what they intend and the circumstances in which their activity takes place, will well appreciate and understand. . . .

*Affirmed.*

### MR. JUSTICE FRANKFURTER, concurring in affirmance of the judgment. . . .

The demands of free speech in a democratic society as well as the interest in national security are better served by candid and informed weighing of the competing interests, within the confines of the judicial process, than by announcing dogmas too inflexible for the non-Euclidian problems to be solved.

But how are competing interests to be assessed? Since they are not subject to quantitative ascertainment, the issue necessarily resolves itself into asking, who is to make the adjustment?—who is to balance the relevant factors and ascertain which interest is in the circumstances to prevail? Full responsibility for the choice cannot be given to the courts. Courts are not representative bodies. They are not designed to be a good reflex of a democratic society. . . .

Primary responsibility for adjusting the interests which compete in the situation before us of necessity belongs to the Congress. The nature of the power to be exercised by this Court has been delineated in decisions not charged with the emotional appeal of situations such as that now before us. . . .

It is not for us to decide how we would adjust the clash of interests which this case presents were the primary responsibility for reconciling it ours. Congress has determined that the danger created by advocacy of overthrow justifies the ensuing restriction on freedom of speech. The determination was made after due deliberation, and the seriousness of the congressional purpose is attested by the volume of legislation passed to effectuate the same ends.

Can we then say that the judgment Congress exercised was denied it by the Constitution? . . . Can we hold that the First Amendment deprives Congress of what it deemed necessary for the Government's protection?

To make validity of legislation depend on judicial reading of events still in the womb of time—a forecast, that is, of the outcome of forces at best appreciated only with knowledge of the topmost secrets of nations—is to charge the judiciary with duties beyond its equipment. We do not expect courts to pronounce historic verdicts on bygone events. Even historians have conflicting views to this day on the origin and conduct of the French Revolution. It is as absurd to be confident that we can measure the present clash of forces and their outcome as to ask us to read history still enveloped in clouds of controversy. . . .

Civil liberties draw at best only limited strength from legal guaranties. Preoccupation by our people with the constitutionality, instead of with the wisdom of legislation or of executive action, is preoccupation with a false value. . . . Focusing attention on constitutionality tends to make constitutionality synonymous with wisdom. When legislation touches freedom of thought and freedom of speech, such a tendency is a formidable enemy of the free spirit. Much that should be rejected as illiberal, because repressive and envenoming, may well be not unconstitutional. The ultimate reliance for the deepest needs of civilization must be found outside their vindication in courts of law; apart from all else, judges, howsoever they may conscientiously seek to discipline themselves against it, unconsciously are too apt to be moved by the deep undercurrents of public feeling. A persistent, positive translation of the liberating faith into the feelings and thoughts and actions of men and women is the real protection against attempts to straitjacket the human mind. . . . Without open minds there can be no open society. And if society be not open the spirit of man is mutilated and becomes enslaved. . . .

MR. JUSTICE JACKSON, concurring . . . [omitted].

### MR. JUSTICE BLACK, dissenting. . . .

At the outset I want to emphasize what the crime involved in this case is, and what it is not. These petitioners were not charged with an attempt to overthrow the Government. They were not charged with overt acts of any kind designed to overthrow the Government. They were not even charged with saying anything or writing anything designed to overthrow the Government. The charge was that they agreed to assemble and to talk and publish certain ideas at a later date: The indictment is that they conspired to organize the Communist Party and to use speech or newspapers and other publications in the future to teach and advocate the forcible overthrow of the Government. No matter how it is worded, this is a virulent form of prior censorship of speech and press, which I believe the First Amendment forbids. I would hold § 3 of the Smith Act authorizing this prior restraint unconstitutional on its face and as applied. . . .

### MR. JUSTICE DOUGLAS, dissenting. . . .

There comes a time when even speech loses its constitutional immunity. Speech in-

nocuous one year may at another time fan such destructive flames that it must be halted in the interests of the safety of the Republic. That is the meaning of the clear and present danger test. . . .

Yet free speech is the rule, not the exception. The restraint to be constitutional must be based on more than fear, on more than passionate opposition against the speech, on more than a revolted dislike for its contents. There must be some immediate injury to society that is likely if speech is allowed. . . .

How it can be said that there is a clear and present danger that this advocacy will succeed is, therefore, a mystery. Some nations less resilient than the United States, where illiteracy is high and where democratic traditions are only budding, might have to take drastic steps and jail these men for merely speaking their creed. But in America they are miserable merchants of unwanted ideas; their wares remain unsold. The fact that their ideas are abhorrent does not make them powerful. . . .

Vishinsky wrote in 1948 in *The Law of the Soviet State,* "In our state, naturally there can be no place for freedom of speech, press, and so on for the foes of socialism."

Our concern should be that we accept no such standard for the United States. Our faith should be that our people will never give support to these advocates of revolution, so long as we remain loyal to the purposes for which our Nation was founded.

*Brandenburg* v. *Ohio*
**395 U.S. 444, 89 S.Ct. 1827, 23 L.Ed. 2d 430 (1969)**
**http://laws.findlaw.com/us/395/444.html**

This case tested the constitutionality of the Ohio criminal syndicalism statute of 1919. The facts are contained in the per curiam opinion that follows. Resort to the per curiam form here may be partly explained by the resignation of Justice Fortas on May 14, three weeks before the case came down. According to Tinsley Yarbrough's *John Marshall Harlan* (1992), the Court's opinion was originally Fortas's. Majority: Warren, Black, Brennan, Douglas, Harlan, Marshall, Stewart, White.

**PER CURIAM.**

The appellant, a leader of a Ku Klux Klan group, was convicted under the Ohio Criminal Syndicalism statute of "advocat[ing] . . . the duty, necessity, or propriety of crime, sabotage, violence, or unlawful methods of terrorism as a means of accomplishing industrial or political reform" and of "voluntarily assembl[ing] with any society, group or assemblage of persons formed to teach or advocate the doctrines of criminal syndicalism." . . . He was fined $1,000 and sentenced to one to 10 years' imprisonment. The appellant challenged the constitutionality of the criminal syndicalism statute under the First and Fourteenth Amendments to the United States Constitution, but the intermediate appellate court of Ohio affirmed his conviction without opinion. The Supreme Court of Ohio dismissed his appeal "for the reason that no substantial constitutional question exists herein." It did not file an opinion or explain its conclusions. Appeal was taken to this Court, and we noted probable jurisdiction. . . . We reverse.

The record shows that a man, identified at trial as the appellant, telephoned an announcer-reporter on the staff of a Cincinnati television station and invited him to come to a Ku Klux Klan "rally" to be held at a farm in Hamilton County. With the cooperation of the organizers, the reporter and a cameraman attended the meeting and filmed the events. Portions of the films were later broadcast on the local station and on a national network.

The prosecution's case rested on the films and on testimony identifying the appellant as the person who communicated with the reporter and who spoke at the rally. . . .

One film showed 12 hooded figures, some of whom carried firearms. They were gathered around a large wooden cross, which they burned. No one was present other than the participants and the newsmen who made the film. Most of the words uttered during the scene were incomprehensible when the film was projected, but scattered phrases could be understood that were derogatory of Negroes and, in one instance, of Jews.[1] Another scene on the same film showed the appellant, in Klan regalia, making a speech. The speech, in full, was as follows:

> This is an organizers' meeting. We have had quite a few members here today which are—we have hundreds, hundreds of members throughout the State of Ohio. I can quote from a newspaper clipping from the Columbus Ohio Dispatch, five weeks ago Sunday morning. The Klan has more members in the State of Ohio than does any other organization. We're not a revengent organization, but if our President, our Congress, our Supreme Court, continues to suppress the white, Caucasian race, it's possible that there might have to be some revengence taken.
>
> We are marching on Congress July the Fourth, four hundred thousand strong. From there we are dividing into two groups, one group to march on St. Augustine, Florida, the other group to march into Mississippi. Thank you.

The second film showed six hooded figures one of whom, later identified as the appellant, repeated a speech very similar to that recorded on the first film. The reference to the possibility of "revengence" was omitted, and one sentence was added: "Personally, I believe the nigger should be returned to Africa, the Jew returned to Israel." Though some of the figures in the films carried weapons, the speaker did not.

The Ohio Criminal Syndicalism Statute was enacted in 1919. From 1917 to 1920, identical

---

[1] The significant phrases that could be understood were:

"How far is the nigger going to—yeah"
"This is what we are going to do to the niggers"
"A dirty nigger"
"Send the Jews back to Israel"
"Let's give them back to the dark garden"
"Save America"
"Let's go back to constitutional betterment"
"Bury the niggers"
"We intend to do our part"
"Give us our state rights"
"Freedom for the whites"
"Nigger will have to fight for every inch he gets from now on."

or quite similar laws were adopted by 20 States and two territories. . . . In 1927, this Court sustained the constitutionality of California's Criminal Syndicalism Act . . . the text of which is quite similar to that of the laws of Ohio. . . . The Court upheld the statute on the ground that, without more, "advocating" violent means to effect political and economic change involves such danger to the security of the State that the State may outlaw it. . . . But *Whitney* has been thoroughly discredited by later decisions. . . . These later decisions have fashioned the principle that the constitutional guarantees of free speech and free press do not permit a State to forbid or proscribe advocacy of the use of force or of law violation except where such advocacy is directed to inciting or producing imminent lawless action and is likely to incite or produce such action. . . . "[T]he mere abstract teaching . . . of the moral propriety or even moral necessity for a resort to force and violence, is not the same as preparing a group for violent action and steeling it to such action." . . . A statute which fails to draw this distinction impermissibly intrudes upon the freedoms guaranteed by the First and Fourteenth Amendments. It sweeps within its condemnation speech which our Constitution has immunized from governmental control. . . .

Measured by this test, Ohio's Criminal Syndicalism Act cannot be sustained. The Act punishes persons who "advocate or teach the

duty, necessity, or propriety" of violence "as a means of accomplishing industrial or political reform"; or who publish or circulate or display any book or paper containing such advocacy; or who "justify" the commission of violent acts "with intent to exemplify, spread or advocate the propriety of the doctrines of criminal syndicalism"; or who ". . . voluntarily assemble" with a group formed "to teach or advocate the doctrines of criminal syndicalism." Neither the indictment nor the trial judge's instructions to the jury in any way refined the statute's bald definition of the crime in terms of mere advocacy not distinguished from incitement to imminent lawless action.

Accordingly, we are here confronted with a statute which, by its own words and as applied, purports to punish mere advocacy and to forbid, on pain of criminal punishment, assembly with others merely to advocate the described type of action. Such a statute falls within the condemnation of the First and Fourteenth Amendments. The contrary teaching of *Whitney* v. *California* . . . cannot be supported, and that decision is therefore overruled.

*Reversed.*

Mr. Justice Black, concurring . . . [omitted].

Mr. Justice Douglas, concurring . . . [omitted].

## II. PUBLIC FORUM

### *Clark* v. *Community for Creative Non-Violence*
### 468 U.S. 288, 104 S.Ct. 3065, 82 L.Ed. 2d 221 (1984)

#### http://laws.findlaw.com/us/468/288.html

In 1982, the National Park Service issued a permit to Community for Creative Non-Violence to erect two symbolic tent cities in Lafayette Park and the Mall in Washington, D.C. Relying on its regulations, the Park Service denied CCNV's request that demonstrators be allowed to sleep in the tents. Alleging a violation of the First Amendment, CCNV filed suit in the U.S. District Court for the District of Columbia. The district court granted summary judgment for the Park Service, but an en banc panel of the Court of Appeals reversed, 6 to 5. Majority: White, Blackmun, Burger, O'Connor, Powell, Rehnquist, Stevens. Dissenting: Marshall, Brennan.

**JUSTICE WHITE delivered the opinion of the Court.**

The issue in this case is whether a National Park Service regulation prohibiting camping in certain parks violates the First Amendment when applied to prohibit demonstrators from sleeping in Lafayette Park and the Mall in connection with a demonstration intended to call attention to the plight of the homeless. We hold that it does not and reverse the contrary judgment of the Court of Appeals. . . .

Expression, whether oral or written or symbolized by conduct, is subject to reasonable time, place, and manner restrictions. We have often noted that restrictions of this kind are valid provided that they are justified without reference to the content of the regulated speech, that they are narrowly tailored to serve a significant governmental interest, and that they leave open ample alternative channels for communication of the information. . . .

The United States submits, as it did in the Court of Appeals, that the regulation forbidding sleeping is defensible either as a time, place, or manner restriction or as a regulation of symbolic conduct. We agree with that assessment. . . .

The requirement that the regulation be content neutral is clearly satisfied. The courts below accepted that view, and it is not disputed here that the prohibition on camping, and on sleeping specifically, is content neutral and is not being applied because of disagreement with the message presented. Neither was the regulation faulted, nor could it be, on the ground that without overnight sleeping the plight of the homeless could not be communicated in other ways. The regulation otherwise left the demonstration intact, with its symbolic city, signs, and the presence of those who were willing to take their turns in a day-and-night vigil. . . .

It is also apparent to us that the regulation narrowly focuses on the Government's substantial interest in maintaining the parks in the heart of our capital in an attractive and intact condition, readily available to the millions of people who wish to see and enjoy them by their presence. To permit camping—using these areas as living accommodations—would be totally inimical to these purposes, as would be readily understood by those who have frequented the National Parks across the country and observed the unfortunate consequences of the activities of those who refuse to confine their camping to designated areas.

It is urged by respondents, and the Court of Appeals was of this view, that if the symbolic city of tents was to be permitted and if the demonstrators did not intend to cook, dig, or engage in aspects of camping other than sleeping, the incremental benefit to the parks could not justify the ban on sleeping, which was here an expressive activity said to enhance the message concerning the plight of the poor and homeless. We cannot agree. In the first place, we seriously doubt that the First Amendment requires the Park Service to permit a demonstration in Lafayette Park and the Mall involving a 24-hour vigil and the erection of tents to accommodate 150 people. Furthermore, although we have assumed for present purposes that the sleeping banned in this case would have an expressive element, it is evident that its major value to this demonstration would be facilitative. Without a permit to sleep, it would be difficult to get the poor and homeless to participate or to be present at all. . . .

Beyond this, however, it is evident from our cases that the validity of this regulation need not be judged solely by reference to the demonstration at hand. . . . Absent the prohibition on sleeping, there would be other groups who would demand permission to deliver an asserted message by camping in Lafayette Park. . . . With the prohibition, however, as is evident in the case before us, at least some around-the-clock demonstrations lasting for days on end will not materialize, others will be limited in size and duration, and the purposes of the regulation will thus be materially served. Perhaps these purposes would be more effectively and not so clumsily achieved by preventing tents and 24-hour vigils entirely in the core areas. But the Park Service's decision to permit non-sleeping demonstrations does not, in our view, impugn the camping prohibition as a valuable, but perhaps imperfect, protection to the parks. If the Government has a legitimate interest in ensuring that the National Parks are adequately protected, which we think it has, and if the parks would be more exposed to harm without the sleeping prohibition than with it, the ban is safe from invalidation under the First Amendment as a reasonable regulation on the manner in which a demonstration may be carried out. . . .

Accordingly, the judgment of the Court of Appeals is

*Reversed.*

CHIEF JUSTICE BURGER, concurring . . . [omitted].

**JUSTICE MARSHALL, with whom JUSTICE BRENNAN joins, dissenting. . . .**

[T]he majority misapplies the test for ascertaining whether a restraint on speech qualifies as a reasonable time, place, and manner regulation. In determining what constitutes a sustainable regulation, the majority fails to subject the alleged interests of the Government to the degree of scrutiny required to ensure that expressive activity protected by the First Amendment remains free of unnecessary limitations. . . .

According to the majority, the significant government interest advanced by denying respondents' request to engage in sleep-speech is the interest in "maintaining the parks in the heart of our capital in an attractive and intact condition, readily available to the millions of people who wish to see and enjoy them by their presence." . . . That interest is indeed significant. However, neither the Government nor the majority adequately explains how prohibiting respondents' planned activity will substantially further that interest.

The majority's attempted explanation begins with the curious statement that it seriously doubts that the First Amendment requires the Park Service to permit a demonstration in Lafayette Park and the Mall involving a 24-hour vigil and the erection of tents to accommodate 150 people. . . . I cannot perceive why the Court should have "serious doubts" regarding this matter and it provides no explanation for its uncertainty. Furthermore, even if the majority's doubts were well-founded, I cannot see how such doubts relate to the problem at hand. The issue posed by this case is not whether the Government is constitutionally compelled to permit the erection of tents and the staging of a continuous 24-hour vigil; rather, the issue is whether any substantial government interest is served by banning sleep that is part of a political demonstration. . . .

The disposition of this case . . . reveals a mistaken assumption regarding the motives and behavior of government officials who create and administer content-neutral regulations. The Court's salutary skepticism of governmental decisionmaking in First Amendment matters suddenly dissipates once it determines that a restriction is not content-based. The Court evidently assumes that the balance struck by officials is deserving of deference so long as it does not appear to be tainted by content discrimination. What the Court fails to recognize is that public officials have strong incentives to overregulate even in the absence of an intent to censor particular views. This incentive stems from the fact that of the two groups whose interests officials must accommodate—on the one hand, the interests of the general public and on the other, the interests of those who seek to use a particular forum for First Amendment activity—the political power of the former is likely to be far greater than that of the latter. . . .

## *Good News Club* v. *Milford Central School*
## 533 U.S. 98, 121 S.Ct. 2093, 150 L.Ed. 2d 151 (2001)
http://laws.findlaw.com/us/533/98.html

Under New York law, Milford Central School enacted a policy authorizing district residents to use its building after school for, among other things, (1) instruction in education, learning, or the arts, and (2) social, civic, recreational, and entertainment uses pertaining to the community welfare. In 1996 Stephen and Darleen Fournier, sponsors of the Good News Club (a Christian organization for children ages 6 to 12), asked school officials for permission to hold the Club's weekly after-school meetings in the school. They denied the request in 1997 on the ground that the proposed use—to sing songs, hear Bible lessons, memorize scripture, and pray—was the equivalent of religious worship prohibited by the community use policy. The Club filed suit in the U.S. District Court for the Northern District of New York, alleging that denial of the Club's application violated its free speech rights. Both sides in the litigation agreed that the school policy had established a limited public forum. In 1998 the District Court found the Club's subject matter to be religious in nature, not merely a discussion of secular matters from a religious perspective that was otherwise permitted, and granted the school summary judgment. In 2000 the U.S. Court of Appeals for the Second Circuit affirmed. In its view the policy was constitutionally acceptable subject-matter (content) discrimination, not unconstitutional viewpoint discrimination. Majority: Thomas, Breyer, Kennedy, O'Connor, Rehnquist, Scalia. Dissenting: Stevens, Souter, Ginsburg.

**JUSTICE THOMAS delivered the opinion of the Court. . . .**

When the State establishes a limited public forum, the State is not required to and does not allow persons to engage in every type of speech. The State may be justified "in reserving [its forum] for certain groups or for the discussion of certain topics." The State's power to restrict speech, however, is not without limits. The restriction must not discriminate against speech on the basis of viewpoint, and the restriction must be "reasonable in light of the purpose served by the forum."

Applying this test, we first address whether the exclusion constituted viewpoint discrimination. We are guided in our analysis by two of our prior opinions, *Lamb's Chapel* [v. *Center Moriches School District* (1993)] and *Rosenberger* [v. *Rector* (1995)]. In *Lamb's Chapel*, we held that a school district violated the Free Speech Clause of the First Amendment when it excluded a private group from presenting films at the school based solely on

the films' discussions of family values from a religious perspective. Likewise, in *Rosenberger*, we held that a university's refusal to fund a student publication because the publication addressed issues from a religious perspective violated the Free Speech Clause. Concluding that Milford's exclusion of the Good News Club based on its religious nature is indistinguishable from the exclusions in these cases, we hold that the exclusion constitutes viewpoint discrimination. Because the restriction is viewpoint discriminatory, we need not decide whether it is unreasonable in light of the purposes served by the forum.

Milford has opened its limited public forum to activities that serve a variety of purposes, including events "pertaining to the welfare of the community." Milford interprets its policy to permit discussions of subjects such as child rearing, and of "the development of character and morals from a religious perspective." For example, this policy would allow someone to use Aesop's Fables to teach children moral values. Additionally, a group could sponsor a debate on whether there should be a constitutional amendment to permit prayer in public schools, and the Boy Scouts could meet "to influence a boy's character, development and spiritual growth." In short, any group that "promote[s] the moral and character development of children" is eligible to use the school building.

Just as there is no question that teaching morals and character development to children is a permissible purpose under Milford's policy, it is clear that the Club teaches morals and character development to children . . . Nonetheless, because Milford found the Club's activities to be religious in nature—"the equivalent of religious instruction itself"—it excluded the Club from use of its facilities.

Applying *Lamb's Chapel,* we find it quite clear that Milford engaged in viewpoint discrimination when it excluded the Club from the afterschool forum. In *Lamb's Chapel,* the local New York school district similarly had adopted § 414's "social, civic or recreational use" category as a permitted use in its limited public forum. The district also prohibited use "by any group for religious purposes." Citing this prohibition, the school district excluded a church that wanted to present films teaching family values from a Christian perspective. . . .

Like the church in *Lamb's Chapel,* the Club seeks to address a subject otherwise permitted under the rule, the teaching of morals and character, from a religious standpoint. . . . The only apparent difference between the activity of Lamb's Chapel and the activities of the Good News Club is that the Club chooses to teach moral lessons from a Christian perspective through live storytelling and prayer, whereas Lamb's Chapel taught lessons through films. This distinction is inconsequential. . . . Thus, the exclusion of the Good News Club's activities, like the exclusion of Lamb's Chapel's films, constitutes unconstitutional viewpoint discrimination.

Our opinion in *Rosenberger* also is dispositive. In *Rosenberger,* a student organization at the University of Virginia was denied funding for printing expenses because its publication, *Wide Awake,* offered a Christian viewpoint. . . . *Wide Awake* "challenge[d] Christians to live, in word and deed, according to the faith they proclaim and . . . encourage[d] students to consider what a personal relationship with Jesus Christ means." Because the university "select[ed] for disfavored treatment those student journalistic efforts with religious editorial viewpoints," we held that the denial of funding was unconstitutional. . . . Given the obvious religious content of *Wide Awake,* we cannot say that the Club's activities are any more "religious" or deserve any less First Amendment protection than did the publication of *Wide Awake* in *Rosenberger.*

Despite our holdings in *Lamb's Chapel* and *Rosenberger,* the Court of Appeals, like Milford, believed that its characterization of the Club's activities as religious in nature warranted treating the Club's activities as different in kind from the other activities permitted by the school. . . . The "Christian viewpoint" is unique, according to the court, because it contains an "additional layer" that other kinds of viewpoints do not. That is, the Club "is focused on teaching children how to cultivate their relationship with God through Jesus Christ," which it characterized as "quintessentially religious." . . .

We disagree that something that is "quintessentially religious" or "decidedly religious in nature" cannot also be characterized properly as the teaching of morals and character development from a particular viewpoint. . . . What matters for purposes of the Free Speech Clause is that we can see no logical difference in kind between the invocation of Christianity by the Club and the invocation of teamwork, loyalty, or patriotism by other associations to provide a foundation for their lessons. . . . According to the Court of Appeals, reliance on Christian principles taints moral and character instruction in a way that other foundations for thought or viewpoints do not. We, however, have never reached such a conclusion. Instead, we reaffirm our holdings in *Lamb's Chapel* and *Rosenberger* that speech discussing otherwise permissible subjects cannot be excluded from a limited public forum on the ground that the subject is discussed from a religious viewpoint. Thus, we conclude that Milford's exclusion of the Club from use of the school, pursuant to its community use policy, constitutes impermissible viewpoint discrimination. . . .

[In the last section of his opinion, Justice Thomas concludes "that permitting the Club to meet on the school's premises would not have violated the Establishment Clause. . . . Because Milford has not raised a valid Establishment Clause claim, we do not address the question whether such a claim could excuse Milford's viewpoint discrimination."]

The judgment of the Court of Appeals is reversed, and the case is remanded for further proceedings consistent with this opinion.

*It is so ordered.*

JUSTICE SCALIA, concurring . . . [omitted].

JUSTICE BREYER, concurring in part . . . [omitted].

### JUSTICE STEVENS, dissenting. . . .

Speech for "religious purposes" may reasonably be understood to encompass three different categories. First, there is religious speech that is simply speech about a particular topic from a religious point of view. . . . Second, there is religious speech that amounts to worship, or its equivalent. . . . Third, there is an intermediate category that is aimed principally at proselytizing or inculcating belief in a particular religious faith.

A public entity may not generally exclude even religious worship from an open public forum. Similarly, a public entity that creates a limited public forum for the discussion of certain specified topics may not exclude a speaker simply because she approaches those topics from a religious point of view. . . .

The novel question that this case presents . . . is whether a school can, consistently with the First Amendment, create a limited public forum that admits the first type of religious speech without allowing the other two.

Distinguishing speech from a religious viewpoint, on the one hand, from religious proselytizing, on the other, is comparable to distinguishing meetings to discuss political issues from meetings whose principal purpose is to recruit new members to join a political organization. If a school decides to authorize after school discussions of current events in its classrooms, it may not exclude people from expressing their views simply because it dislikes their particular political opinions. But must it therefore allow organized political groups—for example, the Democratic Party, the Libertarian Party, or the Ku Klux Klan—to hold meetings, the principal purpose of which is not to discuss the current-events topic from their own unique point of view but rather to recruit others to join their respective groups? I think not. Such recruiting meetings may introduce divisiveness and tend to separate young children into cliques that undermine the school's educational mission. . . .

School officials may reasonably believe that evangelical meetings designed to convert children to a particular religious faith pose the same risk. And, just as a school may allow meetings to discuss current events from a political perspective without also allowing organized political recruitment, so too can a school allow discussion of topics such as moral development from a religious (or nonreligious) perspective without thereby opening its forum to religious proselytizing or worship. . . .

It is clear that, by "religious purposes," the school district did not intend to exclude all speech from a religious point of view. . . . Instead, it sought only to exclude religious speech whose principal goal is to "promote the gospel." . . . As long as this is done in an evenhanded manner, I see no constitutional violation in such an effort. The line between the various categories of religious speech may be difficult to draw, but I think that the distinctions are valid, and that a school, particularly an elementary school, must be permitted to draw them. . . .

JUSTICE SOUTER, dissenting . . . [omitted].

# III. PROTEST AND SYMBOLIC SPEECH

## *United States* v. *O'Brien*
## 391 U.S. 367, 88 S.Ct. 1673, 20 L.Ed. 2d 672 (1968)
http://laws.findlaw.com/us/391/367.html

As a protest against the war in Vietnam, David O'Brien and three companions burned their draft cards on the steps of the South Boston Courthouse in front of an angry crowd on March 31, 1966. FBI agents arrested O'Brien for violating the 1965 amendment to the Universal Military Training and Service Act (UMTSA) of 1948, which provided criminal penalties for anyone who "knowingly destroys [or] knowingly mutilates" a draft card. Following his conviction in the U.S. District Court for the District of Massachusetts, the Court of Appeals for the First Circuit reversed, declaring that the 1965 amendment violated the First Amendment. The Appeals Court nonetheless held that O'Brien could be sentenced because his action violated a regulation of the Selective Service System against nonpossession of one's draft card. Under the UMTSA, violation of a Selective Service regulation was a criminal offense.

According to Bernard Schwartz's *Super Chief* (1983), Chief Justice Warren's first draft of the Court's opinion simply declared O'Brien's act to be nonverbal communication outside the protection of the First Amendment. Harlan and Brennan, however, were sharply critical. Brennan stressed that the conduct did fall under the First Amendment, but that the government's interest in regulating it was "compelling." Warren's revised opinion generally followed Brennan's approach, except that the former rested the outcome on the government's "important or substantial" interest. Majority: Warren, Black, Harlan, Brennan, Stewart, White, Fortas. Dissenting: Douglas. Not participating: Marshall.

**Mr. Chief Justice Warren delivered the opinion of the Court. . . .**

O'Brien first argues that the 1965 Amendment is unconstitutional as applied to him because his act of burning his registration certificate was protected "symbolic speech" within the First Amendment. . . .

. . . This Court has held that when "speech" and "nonspeech" elements are combined in the same course of conduct, a sufficiently important governmental interest in regulating the nonspeech element can justify incidental limitations on First Amendment freedoms. To characterize the quality of the governmental interest which must appear, the Court has employed a variety of descriptive terms: compelling; substantial; subordinating; paramount; cogent; strong. Whatever imprecision inheres in these terms, we think it clear that a government regulation is sufficiently justified if it is within the constitutional power of the Government; if it furthers an important or substantial governmental interest; if the governmental interest is unrelated to the suppression of free expression; and if the incidental restriction on alleged First Amendment freedoms is no greater than is essential to the furtherance of that interest. We find that the 1965 Amendment to § 12(b) (3) of the Universal Military Training and Service Act meets all of these requirements, and consequently that O'Brien can be constitutionally convicted for violating it.

The constitutional power of Congress to raise and support armies and to make all laws necessary and proper to that end is broad and sweeping. The power of Congress to classify and conscript manpower for military service is "beyond question." Pursuant to this power, Congress may establish a system of registration for individuals liable for training and service, and may require such individuals within reason to cooperate in the registration system. The issuance of certificates indicating the registration and eligibility classification of individuals is a legitimate and substantial administrative aid in the functioning of this system. And legislation to insure the continuing availability of issued certificates serves a legitimate and substantial purpose in the system's administration.

O'Brien's argument to the contrary is necessarily premised upon his unrealistic characterization of Selective Service certificates. He essentially adopts the position that such certificates are so many pieces of paper designed to notify registrants of their registration or classification, to be retained or tossed in the wastebasket according to the convenience or taste of the registrant. . . . We agree that the registration certificate contains much information of which the registrant needs no notification. This circumstance, however, does not lead to the conclusion that the certificate serves no purposes but that, like the classification certificate, it serves purposes in addition to initial notification. Many of these purposes would be defeated by the certificates' destruction or mutilation. Among these are:

1. The registration certificate serves as proof that the individual described thereon has registered for the draft. The classification certificate shows the eligibility classification of a named but undescribed individual. Voluntarily displaying the two certificates is an easy and painless way for a young man to dispel a question as to whether he might be delinquent in his Selective Service obligations. . . .
2. The information supplied on the certificates facilitates communication between registrants and local boards, simplifying the system and benefiting all concerned. . . .
3. Both certificates carry continual reminders that the registrant must notify his local board of any change of address, and other specified changes in his status. . . .
4. The regulatory scheme involving Selective Service certificates includes clearly valid prohibitions against the alteration, forgery, or similar deceptive misuse of certificates. The

destruction or mutilation of certificates obviously increases the difficulty of detecting and tracing abuses such as these. Further, a mutilated certificate might itself be used for deceptive purposes. . . .

We think it apparent that the continuing availability to each registrant of his Selective Service certificates substantially furthers the smooth and proper functioning of the system that Congress has established to raise armies. . . . We perceive no alternative means that would more precisely and narrowly assure the continuing availability of issued Selective Service certificates than a law which prohibits their wilful mutilation or destruction. When O'Brien deliberately rendered unavailable his registration certificate, he wilfully frustrated this governmental interest. For this non-communicative impact of his conduct, and for nothing else, he was convicted.

The case at bar is therefore unlike one where the alleged governmental interest in regulating conduct arises in some measure because the communication allegedly integral to the conduct is itself thought to be harmful. . . .

O'Brien finally argues that the 1965 Amendment is unconstitutional as enacted because what he calls the "purpose" of Congress was "to suppress freedom of speech." We reject this argument because under settled principles the purpose of Congress, as O'Brien uses that term, is not a basis for declaring this legislation unconstitutional.

It is a familiar principle of constitutional law that this Court will not strike down an otherwise constitutional statute on the basis of an alleged illicit legislative motive. . . .

Inquiries into congressional motives or purposes are a hazardous matter. When the issue is simply the interpretation of legislation, the Court will look to statements by legislators for guidance as to the purpose of the legislature, because the benefit to sound decision-making in this circumstance is thought sufficient to risk the possibility of misreading Congress' purpose. It is entirely a different matter when we are asked to void a statute that is, under well-settled criteria, constitutional on its face, on the basis of what fewer than a handful of

Congressmen said about it. What motivates one legislator to make a speech about a statute is not necessarily what motivates scores of others to enact it, and the stakes are sufficiently high for us to eschew guesswork. . . .

Since the 1965 Amendment to § 12(b) (3) of the Universal Military Training and Service Act is constitutional as enacted and as applied, the Court of Appeals should have affirmed the judgment of conviction entered by the District Court. Accordingly, we vacate the judgment of the Court of Appeals, and rein-

state the judgment and sentence of the District Court. This disposition makes unnecessary consideration of O'Brien's claim that the Court of Appeals erred in affirming his conviction on the basis of the nonpossession regulation.

*It is so ordered.*

MR. JUSTICE HARLAN, concurring . . . [omitted].

MR. JUSTICE DOUGLAS, dissenting . . . [omitted].

## *Texas* v. *Johnson*
## 491 U.S. 397, 109 S.Ct. 2533, 105 L.Ed. 2d 342 (1989)
### http://laws.findlaw.com/us/491/397.html

Under Texas law, "A person commits an offense if he intentionally or knowingly desecrates: (1) a public monument; (2) a place of worship or burial; or (3) a state or national flag. . . . '[D]esecrate' means deface, damage, or otherwise physically mistreat in a way the actor knows will seriously offend one or more persons likely to observe or discover his action." Gregory Lee Johnson was convicted for violating this statute after an American flag was burned at a demonstration in Dallas during the time of the Republican National Convention in August 1984. A description of the event follows in Justice Brennan's opinion below. The state Court of Appeals for the Fifth District affirmed, but the Texas Court of Criminal Appeals reversed, concluding that Johnson's conduct was protected speech. Majority: Brennan, Marshall, Blackmun, Scalia, Kennedy. Dissenting: Rehnquist, White, Stevens, O'Connor.

**JUSTICE BRENNAN delivered the opinion of the Court. . . .**

Johnson was convicted of flag desecration for burning the flag rather than for uttering insulting words. This fact somewhat complicates our consideration of his conviction under the First Amendment. We must first determine whether Johnson's burning of the flag constituted expressive conduct, permitting him to invoke the First Amendment in challenging his conviction. If his conduct was expressive, we next decide whether the State's regulation is related to the suppression of free expression. If the State's regulation is not related to expression, then the less stringent standard

we announced in *O'Brien* for regulations of noncommunicative conduct controls. If it is, then we are outside of *O'Brien's* test, and we must ask whether this interest justifies Johnson's conviction under a more demanding standard. A third possibility is that the State's asserted interest is simply not implicated on these facts, and in that event the interest drops out of the picture. . . .

The State of Texas conceded for purposes of its oral argument in this case that Johnson's conduct was expressive conduct. . . .

In order to decide whether *O'Brien's* test applies here . . . we must decide whether Texas has asserted an interest in support of Johnson's conviction that is unrelated to the suppression of expression. . . . The State offers two separate interests to justify this conviction: preventing breaches of the peace, and preserving the flag as a symbol of nationhood and national unity. We hold that the first interest is not implicated on this record and that the second is related to the suppression of expression.

Texas claims that its interest in preventing breaches of the peace justifies Johnson's conviction for flag desecration. However, no disturbance of the peace actually occurred or threatened to occur because of Johnson's burning of the flag. . . . The only evidence offered by the State at trial to show the reaction to Johnson's actions was the testimony of several persons who had been seriously offended by the flag-burning.

The State's position, therefore, amounts to a claim that an audience that takes serious offense at particular expression is necessarily likely to disturb the peace and that the expression may be prohibited on this basis. . . . [W]e have not permitted the Government to assume that every expression of a provocative idea will incite a riot, but have instead required careful consideration of the actual circumstances surrounding such expression, asking whether the expression "is directed to inciting or producing imminent lawless action and is likely to incite or produce such action." To accept Texas' arguments that it need only demonstrate "the potential for a breach of the peace," and that every flag-burning necessarily possesses that potential, would be to eviscerate our holding in *Brandenburg*. This we decline to do.

Nor does Johnson's expressive conduct fall within that small class of "fighting words" that are "likely to provoke the average person to retaliation, and thereby cause a breach of the peace." No reasonable onlooker would have regarded Johnson's generalized expression of dissatisfaction with the policies of the Federal Government as a direct personal insult or an invitation to exchange fisticuffs.

We thus conclude that the State's interest in maintaining order is not implicated on these facts. . . .

The State also asserts an interest in preserving the flag as a symbol of nationhood and na-

tional unity. . . . The State, apparently, is concerned that such conduct will lead people to believe either that the flag does not stand for nationhood and national unity, but instead reflects other, less positive concepts, or that the concepts reflected in the flag do not in fact exist, that is, we do not enjoy unity as a Nation. These concerns blossom only when a person's treatment of the flag communicates some message, and thus are related "to the suppression of free expression" within the meaning of *O'Brien*. We are thus outside of *O'Brien*'s test altogether.

It remains to consider whether the State's interest in preserving the flag as a symbol of nationhood and national unity justifies Johnson's conviction. . . . The Texas law is thus not aimed at protecting the physical integrity of the flag in all circumstances, but is designed instead to protect it only against impairments that would cause serious offense to others. Texas concedes as much. . . . "The statute mandates intentional or knowing abuse, that is, the kind of mistreatment that is not innocent, but rather is intentionally designed to seriously offend other individuals."

Whether Johnson's treatment of the flag violated Texas law thus depended on the likely communicative impact of his expressive conduct. . . .

Johnson's political expression was restricted because of the content of the message he conveyed. We must therefore subject the State's asserted interest in preserving the special symbolic character of the flag to "the most exacting scrutiny."

According to Texas, if one physically treats the flag in a way that would tend to cast doubt on either the idea that nationhood and national unity are the flag's referents or that national unity actually exists, the message conveyed thereby is a harmful one and therefore may be prohibited.

If there is a bedrock principle underlying the First Amendment, it is that the Government may not prohibit the expression of an idea simply because society finds the idea itself offensive or disagreeable. We have not recognized an exception to this principle even where our flag has been involved. . . .

We never before have held that the Government may ensure that a symbol be used to express only one view of that symbol or its referents. . . .

To conclude that the Government may permit designated symbols to be used to communicate only a limited set of messages would be to enter territory having no discernible or defensible boundaries. Could the Government, on this theory, prohibit the burning of state flags? Of copies of the Presidential seal? Of the Constitution? In evaluating these choices under the First Amendment, how would we decide which symbols were sufficiently special to warrant this unique status? To do so, we would be forced to consult our own political preferences, and impose them on the citizenry, in the very way that the First Amendment forbids us to do.

There is, moreover, no indication—either in the text of the Constitution or in our cases interpreting it—that a separate juridical category exists for the American flag alone. Indeed, we would not be surprised to learn that the persons who framed our Constitution and wrote the Amendment that we now construe were not known for their reverence for the Union Jack. The First Amendment does not guarantee that other concepts virtually sacred to our Nation as a whole—such as the principle that discrimination on the basis of race is odious and destructive—will go unquestioned in the marketplace of ideas. We decline, therefore, to create for the flag an exception to the joust of principles protected by the First Amendment.

It is not the State's ends, but its means, to which we object. . . .

The way to preserve the flag's special role is not to punish those who feel differently about these matters. It is to persuade them that they are wrong. . . . And, precisely because it is our flag that is involved, one's response to the flag-burner may exploit the uniquely persuasive power of the flag itself. We can imagine no more appropriate response to burning a flag than waving one's own, no better way to counter a flag-burner's message than by saluting the flag that burns, no surer means of preserving the dignity even

of the flag that burned than by—as one witness here did—according its remains a respectful burial. We do not consecrate the flag by punishing its desecration, for in doing so we dilute the freedom that this cherished emblem represents. . . .

The judgment of the Texas Court of Criminal Appeals is therefore

*Affirmed.*

### JUSTICE KENNEDY, concurring. . . .

The hard fact is that sometimes we must make decisions we do not like. We make them because they are right, right in the sense that the law and the Constitution, as we see them, compel the result. And so great is our commitment to the process that, except in the rare case, we do not pause to express distaste for the result, perhaps for fear of undermining a valued principle that dictates the decision. This is one of those rare cases. . . .

I do not believe the Constitution gives us the right to rule as the dissenting Members of the Court urge, however painful this judgment is to announce. Though symbols often are what we ourselves make of them, the flag is constant in expressing beliefs Americans share, beliefs in law and peace and that freedom which sustains the human spirit. The case here today forces recognition of the costs to which those beliefs commit us. It is poignant but fundamental that the flag protects those who hold it in contempt. . . .

### CHIEF JUSTICE REHNQUIST, with whom JUSTICE WHITE and JUSTICE O'CONNOR join, dissenting. . . .

The American flag . . . throughout more than 200 years of our history, has come to be the visible symbol embodying our Nation. It does not represent the views of any particular political party, and it does not represent any particular political philosophy. The flag is not simply another "idea" or "point of view" competing for recognition in the marketplace of ideas. Millions and millions of Americans regard it with an almost mystical reverence regardless of what sort of social, political, or philosophical beliefs they may have. I cannot agree that the First Amendment invalidates the Act of Congress, and the laws of 48 of the 50 States, which make criminal the public burning of the flag. . . .

But the Court insists that the Texas statute prohibiting the public burning of the American flag infringes on respondent Johnson's freedom of expression. Such freedom, of course, is not absolute. . . . [T]he public burning of the American flag by Johnson was no essential part of any exposition of ideas, and at the same time it had a tendency to incite a breach of the peace. Johnson was free to make any verbal denunciation of the flag that he wished; indeed, he was free to burn the flag in private. He could publicly burn other symbols of the Government or effigies of political leaders. He did lead a march through the streets of Dallas, and conducted a rally in front of the Dallas City Hall. He engaged in a "die-in" to protest nuclear weapons. He shouted out various slogans during the march, including: "Reagan, Mondale which will it be? Either one means World War III"; "Ronald Reagan, killer of the hour, Perfect example of U.S. power"; and "red, white and blue, we spit on you, you stand for plunder, you will go under." For none of these acts was he arrested or prosecuted; it was only when he proceeded to burn publicly an American flag stolen from its rightful owner that he violated the Texas statute. . . .

The result of the Texas statute is obviously to deny one in Johnson's frame of mind one of many means of "symbolic speech." Far from being a case of "one picture being worth a thousand words," flag burning is the equivalent of an inarticulate grunt or roar that, it seems fair to say, is most likely to be indulged in not to express any particular idea, but to antagonize others. . . . The Texas statute deprived Johnson of only one rather inarticulate symbolic form of protest—a form of protest that was profoundly offensive to many—and left him with a full panoply of other symbols and every conceivable form of verbal expression to express his deep disapproval of national policy. Thus, in no way can it be said that Texas is punishing him because his hearers—or any other group of people—were profoundly opposed to the message that he sought to convey. . . . It was Johnson's use of this particular symbol, and not the idea that he sought to convey by it or by his many other expressions, for which he was punished. . . .

Uncritical extension of constitutional protection to the burning of the flag risks the frustration of the very purpose for which organized governments are instituted. The Court decides that the American flag is just another symbol, about which not only must opinions pro and con be tolerated, but for which the most minimal public respect may not be enjoined. The government may conscript men into the Armed Forces where they must fight and perhaps die for the flag, but the government may not prohibit the public burning of the banner under which they fight. I would uphold the Texas statute as applied in this case.

JUSTICE STEVENS, dissenting . . . [omitted].

## *Virginia* v. *Black*
**538 U.S. 343, 123 S.Ct. 1536, 155 L.Ed. 2d 535 (2003)**
**http://supct.law.cornell.edu:8080/supct/html/01-1107.ZS.html**

With permission of the owner, Barry Black organized a Ku Klux Klan rally in a field in Carroll County, Virginia, in August 1998. As part of the concluding ritual Klan members set fire to a 25-foot cross that was also visible to nearby residents. In May of the same year, Richard Elliott and Jonathan O'Mara attempted to burn a cross in the yard of James Jubilee, an African-American and Elliott's next-door neighbor in Virginia Beach, Virginia, although Jubilee did not notice the partly burned cross until the next morning. Neither Elliott nor O'Mara belonged to the Klan. They apparently wanted to get even with Jubilee for having complained after Elliott used his backyard as a firing range. In separate proceedings the three men were convicted of violating Virginia's cross-burning statute: "It shall be unlawful for any person or persons, with the intent of intimidating any person or group of persons, to burn, or cause to be burned, a cross on the property of another, a highway or other public place. . . . Any such burning of a cross shall be prima facie evidence of an intent to intimidate a person or group of persons." Against challenges on First Amendment grounds, the state court of appeals affirmed the convictions, but the Supreme Court of Virginia reversed. In the U.S. Supreme Court, the voting alignment was complex. Six justices held that a properly drafted cross-burning statute *could be* constitutional, while seven justices deemed *this* statute unconstitutional. Majority (on the first point): O'Connor, Breyer, Rehnquist, Scalia, Stevens, Thomas. Dissenting: Souter, Ginsburg, Kennedy. Majority (on the second point): O'Connor, Breyer, Ginsburg, Kennedy, Rehnquist, Souter, Stevens. Dissenting: Scalia, Thomas.

**JUSTICE O'CONNOR announced the judgment of the Court and delivered the opinion of the Court with respect to Parts I, II, and III, and an opinion with respect to Parts IV and V, in which THE CHIEF JUSTICE, JUSTICE STEVENS, and JUSTICE BREYER joined.**

In this case we consider whether the Commonwealth of Virginia's statute banning cross burning with "an intent to intimidate a person or group of persons" violates the First Amendment. We conclude that while a State, consistent with the First Amendment, may ban cross burning carried out with the intent to intimidate, the provision in the Virginia statute treating any cross burning as prima facie evidence of intent to intimidate renders the statute unconstitutional in its current form.

I [omitted]

II

. . . Burning a cross in the United States is inextricably intertwined with the history of the Ku Klux Klan. . . .

Often, the Klan used cross burnings as a tool of intimidation and a threat of impending violence. . . . These cross burnings embodied threats to people whom the Klan deemed antithetical to its goals. And these threats had special force given the long history of Klan violence. . . .

And after a cross burning in Suffolk, Virginia, during the late 1940's, the Virginia Governor stated that he would "not allow any of our people of any race to be subjected to terrorism or intimidation in any form by the Klan or any other organization." These incidents of cross burning, among others, helped prompt Virginia to enact its first version of the cross-burning statute in 1950. . . .

To this day, regardless of whether the message is a political one or whether the message is also meant to intimidate, the burning of a cross is a "symbol of hate." . . .

In sum, while a burning cross does not inevitably convey a message of intimidation, often the cross burner intends that the recipients of the message fear for their lives. And when a cross burning is used to intimidate, few if any messages are more powerful.

III

. . . The hallmark of the protection of free speech is to allow "free trade in ideas"—even ideas that the overwhelming majority of people might find distasteful or discomforting. . . . The First Amendment affords protection to symbolic or expressive conduct as well as to actual speech.

The protections afforded by the First Amendment, however, are not absolute, and we have long recognized that the government may regulate certain categories of expression consistent with the Constitution. . . . The First Amendment permits "restrictions upon the content of speech in a few limited areas, which are 'of such slight social value as a step to truth that any benefit that may be derived from them is clearly outweighed by the social interest in order and morality.' "

Thus, for example, a State may punish those words "which by their very utterance inflict injury or tend to incite an immediate breach of the peace." . . . We have consequently held that fighting words—"those personally abusive epithets which, when addressed to the ordinary citizen, are, as a matter of common knowledge, inherently likely to provoke violent reaction"—are generally proscribable under the First Amendment. . . . And the First Amendment also permits a State to ban a "true threat."

"True threats" encompass those statements where the speaker means to communicate a serious expression of an intent to commit an act of unlawful violence to a particular individual or group of individuals. . . . The speaker need not actually intend to carry out the threat. Rather, a prohibition on true threats "protect[s] individuals from the fear of violence" and "from the disruption that fear engenders," in addition to protecting people "from the possibility that the threatened violence will occur." Intimidation in the constitutionally proscribable sense of the word is a type of true threat, where a speaker directs a threat to a person or group of persons with the intent of placing the victim in fear of bodily harm or death. . . .

The Supreme Court of Virginia ruled that in light of *R. A. V.* v. *City of St. Paul,* even if it is constitutional to ban cross burning in a content-neutral manner, the Virginia cross-burning statute is unconstitutional because it discriminates on the basis of content and viewpoint. . . .

In *R. A. V.,* we held that a local ordinance that banned certain symbolic conduct, including cross burning, when done with the knowledge that such conduct would " 'arouse anger, alarm or resentment in others on the basis of race, color, creed, religion or gender' " was unconstitutional. We held that the ordinance did not pass constitutional muster because it discriminated on the basis of content by targeting only those individuals who "provoke violence" on a basis specified in the law. The ordinance did not cover "[t]hose who wish to use 'fighting words' in connection with other ideas—to express hostility, for example, on the basis of political affiliation, union membership, or homosexuality." This content-based discrimination was unconstitutional because it allowed the city "to impose special prohibitions on those speakers who express views on disfavored subjects."

We did not hold in *R. A. V.* that the First Amendment prohibits all forms of content-based discrimination within a proscribable area of speech. Rather, we specifically stated that some types of content discrimination did not violate the First Amendment:

"When the basis for the content discrimination consists entirely of the very reason the entire class of speech at issue is proscribable, no significant danger of idea or viewpoint discrimination exists. Such a reason, having been adjudged neutral enough to support exclusion of the entire class of speech from First Amendment protection, is also neutral enough to form the basis of distinction within the class."

Indeed, we noted that it would be constitutional to ban only a particular type of threat: "[T]he Federal Government can criminalize only those threats of violence that are directed against the President . . . since the reasons why threats of violence are outside the First Amendment . . . have special force when applied to the person of the President." And a State may "choose to prohibit only that obscenity which is the most patently offensive in its prurience—i.e., that which involves the most lascivious displays of sexual activity." Consequently, while the holding of *R. A. V.* does not permit a State to ban only obscenity based on "offensive political messages," or "only those threats against the President that mention his policy on aid to inner cities," the First Amendment permits content discrimination "based on the very reasons why the particular class of speech at issue . . . is proscribable."

Similarly, Virginia's statute does not run afoul of the First Amendment insofar as it bans cross burning with intent to intimidate. Unlike the statute at issue in *R. A. V.,* the Virginia statute does not single out for opprobrium only that speech directed toward "one of the specified disfavored topics." It does not matter whether an individual burns a cross with intent to intimidate because of the victim's race, gender, or religion, or because of the victim's "political affiliation, union membership, or homosexuality." Moreover, as a factual matter it is not true that cross burners direct their intimidating conduct solely to racial or religious minorities. . . . Indeed, in the case of Elliott and O'Mara, it is at least unclear whether the respondents burned a cross due to racial animus. . . .

The First Amendment permits Virginia to outlaw cross burnings done with the intent to intimidate because burning a cross is a particularly virulent form of intimidation. Instead of prohibiting all intimidating messages, Virginia may choose to regulate this subset of intimidating messages in light of cross burning's long and pernicious history as a signal of impending violence. . . . A ban on cross burning carried out with the intent to intimidate is fully consistent with our holding in *R. A. V.* and is proscribable under the First Amendment.

IV

. . . The jury in the case of Richard Elliott did not receive any instruction on the prima facie evidence provision, and the provision was not an issue in the case of Jonathan O'Mara because he pleaded guilty. The court in Barry Black's case, however, instructed the jury that the provision means: "The burning of a cross, by itself, is sufficient evidence from which you may infer the required intent." . . .

The prima facie evidence provision, as interpreted by the jury instruction, renders the statute unconstitutional. . . .

As the history of cross burning indicates, a burning cross is not always intended to intimidate. Rather, sometimes the cross burning is a statement of ideology, a symbol of group solidarity. . . . Indeed, occasionally a person who burns a cross does not intend to express either

a statement of ideology or intimidation. Cross burnings have appeared in movies such as *Mississippi Burning,* and in plays such as the stage adaptation of Sir Walter Scott's *The Lady of the Lake.*

The prima facie provision makes no effort to distinguish among these different types of cross burnings. . . .

It may be true that a cross burning, even at a political rally, arouses a sense of anger or hatred among the vast majority of citizens who see a burning cross. But this sense of anger or hatred is not sufficient to ban all cross burnings. . . . The prima facie evidence provision in this case ignores all of the contextual factors that are necessary to decide whether a particular cross burning is intended to intimidate. The First Amendment does not permit such a shortcut.

For these reasons, the prima facie evidence provision, as interpreted through the jury instruction and as applied in Barry Black's case, is unconstitutional on its face. . . .

V

With respect to Barry Black, we agree with the Supreme Court of Virginia that his conviction cannot stand, and we affirm the judgment of the Supreme Court of Virginia. With respect to Elliott and O'Mara, we vacate the judgment of the Supreme Court of Virginia, and remand the case for further proceedings.

*It is so ordered.*

Justice Stevens, concurring . . . [omitted].

Justice Scalia, with whom Justice Thomas joins in part, concurring in part, concurring in the judgment in part, and dissenting in part . . . [omitted].

**Justice Souter, with whom Justice Kennedy and Justice Ginsburg join, concurring in the judgment in part and dissenting in part.**

I agree with the majority that the Virginia statute makes a content-based distinction within the category of punishable intimidating or threatening expression, the very type of distinction we considered in *R. A. V.* I disagree that any exception should save Virginia's law from unconstitutionality under the holding in *R. A. V.* or any acceptable variation of it.

The issue is whether the statutory prohibition restricted to this symbol falls within one of the exceptions to *R. A. V.*'s general condemnation of limited content-based proscription within a broader category of expression proscribable generally. Because of the burning cross's extraordinary force as a method of intimidation, the *R. A. V.* exception most likely to cover the statute is the first of the three mentioned there, which the *R. A. V.* opinion called an exception for content discrimination on a basis that "consists entirely of the very reason the entire class of speech at issue is proscribable." This is the exception the majority speaks of here as covering statutes prohibiting "particularly virulent" proscribable expression.

I do not think that the Virginia statute qualifies for this virulence exception as *R. A. V.* explained it..., the most obvious hurdle being the statute's prima facie evidence provision. That provision is essential to understanding why the statute's tendency to suppress a message disqualifies it from any rescue by exception from *R. A. V.*'s general rule.

*R. A. V.* defines the special virulence exception to the rule barring content-based subclasses of categorically proscribable expression this way: prohibition by subcategory is nonetheless constitutional if it is made "entirely" on the "basis" of "the very reason" that "the entire class of speech at issue is proscribable" at all. The Court explained that when the subcategory is confined to the most obviously proscribable instances, "no significant danger of idea or viewpoint discrimination exists," and the explanation was rounded out with some illustrative examples. None of them, however, resembles the case before us....

I thus read *R. A. V.*'s examples of the particular virulence exception as covering prohibitions that are not clearly associated with a particular viewpoint, and that are consequently different from the Virginia statute....

[N]o content-based statute should survive even under a pragmatic recasting of *R. A. V.*

without a high probability that no "official suppression of ideas is afoot." I believe the prima facie evidence provision stands in the way of any finding of such a high probability here....

As I see the likely significance of the evidence provision, its primary effect is to skew jury deliberations toward conviction in cases where the evidence of intent to intimidate is relatively weak and arguably consistent with a solely ideological reason for burning....

To the extent the prima facie evidence provision skews prosecutions, then, it skews the statute toward suppressing ideas. Thus, the appropriate way to consider the statute's prima facie evidence term, in my view, is not as if it were an overbroad statutory definition amenable to severance or a narrowing construction. The question here is not the permissible scope of an arguably overbroad statute, but the claim of a clearly content-based statute to an exception from the general prohibition of content-based proscriptions, an exception that is not warranted if the statute's terms show that suppression of ideas may be afoot. Accordingly, the way to look at the prima facie evidence provision is to consider it for any indication of what is afoot. And if we look at the provision for this purpose, it has a very obvious significance as a mechanism for bringing within the statute's prohibition some expression that is doubtfully threatening though certainly distasteful....

I conclude that the statute under which all three of the respondents were prosecuted violates the First Amendment, since the statute's content-based distinction was invalid at the time of the charged activities, regardless of whether the prima facie evidence provision was given any effect in any respondent's individual case....

## JUSTICE THOMAS, dissenting....

Although I agree with the majority's conclusion that it is constitutionally permissible to "ban . . . cross burning carried out with intent to intimidate," I believe that the majority errs in imputing an expressive component to the activity in question....

It strains credulity to suggest that a state legislature that adopted a litany of segregationist laws self-contradictorily intended to squelch the segregationist message [in the 1950s]. Even for segregationists, violent and terroristic conduct, the Siamese twin of cross burning, was intolerable. The ban on cross burning with intent to intimidate demonstrates that even segregationists understood the difference between intimidating and terroristic conduct and racist expression. It is simply beyond belief that, in passing the statute now under review, the Virginia legislature was concerned with anything but penalizing conduct it must have viewed as particularly vicious.

Accordingly, this statute prohibits only conduct, not expression. And, just as one cannot burn down someone's house to make a political point and then seek refuge in the First Amendment, those who hate cannot terrorize and intimidate to make their point. In light of my conclusion that the statute here addresses only conduct, there is no need to analyze it under any of our First Amendment tests. . . .

## IV. FREEDOM OF ASSOCIATION

### *Boy Scouts of America and Monmouth Council* v. *Dale*
### 530 U.S. 640, 120 S.Ct. 2446, 147 L.Ed. 2d 554 (2000)
### http://laws.findlaw.com/us/530/640.html

James Dale became a Boy Scout in New Jersey in 1981 and achieved the rank of Eagle Scout in 1988. In 1989 he applied for adult membership in the Boy Scouts and was named assistant scoutmaster of Troop 73. At about the same time he entered Rutgers University, where he first acknowledged publicly that he was gay and where he became active in the Lesbian/Gay Alliance. In July 1990 a newspaper published his photograph and an interview with him about his advocacy of homosexual teenagers' need for gay role models. Shortly, the Monmouth Executive Council of the Boy Scouts revoked Dale's adult membership on the grounds that the organization "specifically forbid[s] membership to homosexuals." Dale filed a complaint against the Boy Scouts in New Jersey Superior Court, claiming the Boy Scouts had violated the state's public accommodation law by revoking his membership because of his sexual orientation. The court ruled that the statute was inapplicable to the Boy Scouts, but the appellate division concluded in 1998 that the law applied to the Boy Scouts, that the Boy Scouts had violated it, and that no federal constitutional rights of the Boy Scouts had been abridged. In 1999, the New Jersey Supreme Court affirmed. Majority: Rehnquist, O'Connor, Scalia, Kennedy, Thomas. Dissenting: Stevens, Souter, Ginsburg, Breyer.

**CHIEF JUSTICE REHNQUIST delivered the opinion of the Court. . . .**

We granted the Boy Scouts' petition for certiorari to determine whether the application of New Jersey's public accommodations law violated the First Amendment.

In *Roberts* v. *United States Jaycees* (1984), we observed that "implicit in the right to engage in activities protected by the First Amendment" is "a corresponding right to associate with others in pursuit of a wide variety of political, social, economic, educational, religious, and cultural ends." This right is crucial in preventing the majority from imposing its views on groups that would rather express other, perhaps unpopular, ideas. . . .

The forced inclusion of an unwanted person in a group infringes the group's freedom of expressive association if the presence of that person affects in a significant way the group's ability to advocate public or private viewpoints. But the freedom of expressive association, like many freedoms, is not absolute. We have held that the freedom could be overridden "by regulations adopted to serve compelling state interests, unrelated to the suppression of ideas, that cannot be achieved through means significantly less restrictive of associational freedoms."

To determine whether a group is protected by the First Amendment's expressive associational right, we must determine whether the group engages in "expressive association." The First Amendment's protection of expressive association is not reserved for advocacy groups. But to come within its ambit, a group must engage in some form of expression, whether it be public or private. . . .

[T]he general mission of the Boy Scouts is clear: "[T]o instill values in young people." . . . During the time spent with the youth members, the scoutmasters and assistant scoutmasters inculcate them with the Boy Scouts' values—both expressly and by example. It seems indisputable that an association that seeks to transmit such a system of values engages in expressive activity. . . .

Given that the Boy Scouts engages in expressive activity, we must determine whether the forced inclusion of Dale as an assistant scoutmaster would significantly affect the Boy Scouts' ability to advocate public or private viewpoints. This inquiry necessarily requires us first to explore, to a limited extent, the nature of the Boy Scouts' view of homosexuality. . . .

The Boy Scouts explains that the Scout Oath and Law provide "a positive moral code for living; they are a list of 'do's' rather than 'don'ts.'" The Boy Scouts asserts that homosexual conduct is inconsistent with the values embodied in the Scout Oath and Law, particularly with the values represented by the terms "morally straight" and "clean."

Obviously, the Scout Oath and Law do not expressly mention sexuality or sexual orientation. And the terms "morally straight" and "clean" are by no means self-defining. Different people would attribute to those terms very different meanings. . . .

The Boy Scouts asserts that it "teach[es] that homosexual conduct is not morally straight," and that it does "not want to promote homosexual conduct as a legitimate form of behavior." We accept the Boy Scouts' assertion. We need not inquire further to determine the nature of the Boy Scouts' expression with respect to homosexuality. But because the record before us contains written evidence of the Boy Scouts' viewpoint, we look to it as instructive, if only on the question of the sincerity of the professed beliefs. . . . We cannot doubt that the Boy Scouts sincerely holds this view.

We must then determine whether Dale's presence as an assistant scoutmaster would significantly burden the Boy Scouts' desire to not "promote homosexual conduct as a legitimate form of behavior." As we give deference to an association's assertions regarding the nature of its expression, we must also give deference to an association's view of what would impair its expression. . . .

That is not to say that an expressive association can erect a shield against antidiscrimination laws simply by asserting that mere acceptance of a member from a particular group would impair its message. But here Dale, by his own admission, is one of a group of gay Scouts who have "become leaders in their community and are open and honest about their sexual orientation." . . .

*Hurley* [v. *Irish-American GLIB,* 1995] is illustrative on this point. There we considered whether the application of Massachusetts' public accommodations law to require the organizers of a private St. Patrick's Day parade to include among the marchers an Irish-American gay, lesbian, and bisexual group, GLIB, violated the parade organizers' First Amendment rights. We noted that the parade organizers did not wish to exclude the GLIB members because of their sexual orientations, but because they wanted to march behind a GLIB banner. . . .

As the presence of GLIB in Boston's St. Patrick's Day parade would have interfered with the parade organizers' choice not to propound a particular point of view, the presence of Dale as an assistant scoutmaster would just as surely interfere with the Boy Scout's choice not to propound a point of view contrary to its beliefs. . . .

Having determined that the Boy Scouts is an expressive association and that the forced inclusion of Dale would significantly affect its expression, we inquire whether the application of New Jersey's public accommodations law to require that the Boy Scouts accept Dale as an assistant scoutmaster runs afoul of the Scouts' freedom of expressive association. We conclude that it does. . . .

We recognized in cases such as *Roberts* and [*Rotary Int'l.* v. *Rotary Club of*] *Duarte* (1987) that States have a compelling interest in eliminating discrimination against women in public accommodations. But in each of these cases we went on to conclude that the enforcement of these statutes would not materially interfere with the ideas that the organization sought to express. . . .

So in these cases, the associational interest in freedom of expression has been set on one side of the scale, and the State's interest on the other. . . .

We have already concluded that a state requirement that the Boy Scouts retain Dale as an assistant scoutmaster would significantly burden the organization's right to oppose or disfavor homosexual conduct. The state interests embodied in New Jersey's public accommodations law do not justify such a severe intrusion on the Boy Scouts' rights to freedom of expressive association. That being the case, we hold that the First Amendment prohibits the State from imposing such a requirement through the application of its public accommodations law.

JUSTICE STEVENS' dissent makes much of its observation that the public perception of homosexuality in this country has changed. . . . But this is scarcely an argument for denying First Amendment protection to those who refuse to accept these views. The First Amendment protects expression, be it of the popular variety or not. . . . And the fact that an idea may be embraced and advocated by increasing numbers of people is all the more reason to protect the First Amendment rights of those who wish to voice a different view. . . .

We are not, as we must not be, guided by our views of whether the Boy Scouts' teachings with respect to homosexual conduct are right or wrong; public or judicial disapproval of a tenet of an organization's expression does not justify the State's effort to compel the organization to accept members where such acceptance would derogate from the organization's expressive message. . . .

The judgment of the New Jersey Supreme Court is reversed, and the cause remanded for further proceedings not inconsistent with this opinion.

*It is so ordered.*

**JUSTICE STEVENS, with whom JUSTICE SOUTER, JUSTICE GINSBURG and JUSTICE BREYER join, dissenting. . . .**

The majority holds that New Jersey's law violates BSA's right to associate and its right to free speech. But that law does not "impos[e] any serious burdens" on BSA's "collective effort on behalf of [its] shared goals," nor does it force BSA to communicate any message that it does not wish to endorse. New Jersey's law, therefore, abridges no constitutional right of the Boy Scouts. . . .

BSA's claim finds no support in our cases. . . . In fact, until today, we have never once found a claimed right to associate in the selection of members to prevail in the face of a State's antidiscrimination law. To the contrary, we have squarely held that a State's antidiscrimination law does not violate a group's right to associate simply because the law conflicts with that group's exclusionary membership policy. . . .

Several principles are made perfectly clear by *Jaycees* and *Rotary Club*. First, to prevail on a claim of expressive association in the face of a State's antidiscrimination law, it is not enough simply to engage in some kind of expressive activity. Both the Jaycees and the Rotary Club engaged in expressive activity protected by the First Amendment, yet that fact was not dispositive. Second, it is not enough to adopt an openly avowed exclusionary membership policy. Both the Jaycees and the Rotary Club did that as well. Third, it is not sufficient merely to articulate some connection between the group's expressive activities and its exclusionary policy. . . .

The evidence before this Court makes it exceptionally clear that BSA has, at most, simply adopted an exclusionary membership policy and has no shared goal of disapproving of homosexuality. BSA's mission statement and federal charter say nothing on the matter; its official membership policy is silent; its Scout Oath and Law—and accompanying definitions—are devoid of any view on the topic; its guidance for Scouts and Scoutmasters on sexuality declare that such matters are "not construed to be Scouting's proper area," but are the province of a Scout's parents and pastor; and BSA's posture respecting religion tolerates a wide variety of views on the issue of homosexuality. Moreover, there is simply no evidence that BSA otherwise teaches anything in this area, or that it instructs Scouts on matters involving homosexuality in ways not conveyed in the Boy Scout or Scoutmaster Handbooks. In short, Boy Scouts of America is simply silent on homosexuality. There is no shared goal or collective effort to foster a belief about homosexuality at all—let alone one that is significantly burdened by admitting homosexuals.

As in *Jaycees,* there is "no basis in the record for concluding that admission of [homosexuals] will impede the [Boy Scouts'] ability to engage in [its] protected activities or to disseminate its preferred views" and New Jersey's law "requires no change in [BSA's] creed." And like *Rotary Club,* New Jersey's law "does not require [BSA] to abandon or alter any of" its activities. The evidence relied on by the Court is not to the contrary. . . .

Equally important is BSA's failure to adopt any clear position on homosexuality. BSA's temporary, though ultimately abandoned, view that homosexuality is incompatible with being "morally straight" and "clean" is a far cry from the clear, unequivocal statement necessary to prevail on its claim. . . . [T]he group continued to disclaim any single religious or moral position as a general matter and actively eschewed teaching any lesson on sexuality. It also continued to define "morally straight" and "clean" in the Boy Scout and Scoutmaster Handbooks without any reference to homosexuality. As noted earlier, nothing in our cases suggests that a group can prevail on a right to expressive association if it, effectively, speaks out of both sides of its mouth. A State's antidiscrimination law does not impose a "serious burden" or a "substantial restraint" upon the group's "shared goals" if the group itself is unable to identify its own stance with any clarity.

The majority pretermits this entire analysis. It finds that BSA in fact "'teach[es] that homosexual conduct is not morally straight.'" This conclusion, remarkably, rests entirely on statements in BSA's briefs. . . . Moreover, the majority insists that we must "give deference to an association's assertions regarding the nature of its expression" and "we must also give deference to an association's view of what would impair its expression." . . . So long as the record "contains written evidence" to support a group's bare assertion, "[w]e need not inquire further." Once the organization "asserts" that it engages in particular expression, "[w]e cannot doubt" the truth of that assertion.

This is an astounding view of the law. I am unaware of any previous instance in which our analysis of the scope of a constitutional right was determined by looking at what a litigant asserts in his or her brief and inquiring no further. . . . It is an odd form of independent review that consists of deferring entirely to whatever a litigant claims. . . .

Though *Hurley* has a superficial similarity to the present case, a close inspection reveals a wide gulf between that case and the one before us today. . . .

First, it was critical to our analysis that GLIB was actually conveying a message by participating in the parade—otherwise, the parade organizers could hardly claim that they were being forced to include any unwanted message at all. . . .

Second, we found it relevant that GLIB's message "would likely be perceived" as the parade organizers' own speech. . . .

Dale's inclusion in the Boy Scouts is nothing like the case in *Hurley*. His participation sends no cognizable message to the Scouts or to the world. . . . Though participating in the Scouts could itself conceivably send a message on some level, it is not the kind of act that we have recognized as speech. . . .

Under the majority's reasoning, an openly gay male is irreversibly affixed with the label "homosexual." That label, even though unseen, communicates a message that permits his exclusion wherever he goes. His openness is the sole and sufficient justification for his ostracism. Though unintended, reliance on such a justification is tantamount to a constitutionally prescribed symbol of inferiority. . . .

That such prejudices are still prevalent and that they have caused serious and tangible harm to countless members of the class New Jersey seeks to protect are established matters of fact that neither the Boy Scouts nor the Court disputes. That harm can only be aggravated by the creation of a constitutional shield for a policy that is itself the product of a habitual way of thinking about strangers. . . .

JUSTICE SOUTER, with whom JUSTICE GINSBURG and JUSTICE BREYER join, dissenting . . . [omitted].

## V. FREEDOM OF THE PRESS

### *New York Times Co.* v. *Sullivan*
### 376 U.S. 254, 84 S.Ct. 710, 11 L.Ed. 2d 686 (1964)
### http://laws.findlaw.com/us/376/254.html

L. B. Sullivan, an elected city commissioner in Montgomery, Alabama—whose duties included supervision of the police department—brought an action for libel in the Circuit Court of Montgomery County against the *New York Times*. At issue was a paid advertisement that the *Times* had published which described maltreatment in Montgomery of black students protesting racial segregation. Sullivan's suit also named as defendants four individuals whose names, among others, appeared in the advertisement. The jury awarded plaintiff damages of $500,000 against each defendant, and the judgment on the verdict was affirmed by the Supreme Court of Alabama on the grounds that the statements in the advertisement were libelous per se, false, and not privileged, and that the evidence showed malice on the part of the newspaper. The state court rejected the defendants' constitutional objections on the ground that the First Amendment does not protect libelous publications. Majority: Brennan, Black, Clark, Douglas, Goldberg, Harlan, Stewart, Warren, White.

**MR. JUSTICE BRENNAN delivered the opinion of the Court.**

We are required for the first time in this case to determine the extent to which the constitutional protections for speech and press limit a State's power to award damages in a libel action brought by a public official against critics of his official conduct. . . .

Respondent's complaint alleged that he had been libeled by statements in a full-page advertisement that was carried in the *New York Times* on March 29, 1960. Entitled "Heed Their Rising Voices," the advertisement began by stating that "As the whole world knows by now, thousands of Southern Negro students are engaged in widespread non-violent demonstrations in positive affirmation of the right to live in human dignity as guaranteed by the U.S. Constitution and the Bill of Rights." It went on to charge that "in their efforts to uphold these guarantees, they are being met by an unprecedented wave of terror by those who would deny and negate that document which the whole world looks upon as setting the pattern for modern freedom. . . ."

Of the 10 paragraphs of text in the advertisement, the third and a portion of the sixth were the basis of respondent's claim of libel. . . .

Although neither of these statements mentions respondent by name, he contended that the word "police" in the third paragraph referred to him as the Montgomery Commissioner who supervised the Police Department, so that he was being accused of "ringing" the campus with police. He further claimed that the paragraph would be read as imputing to the police, and hence to him, the padlocking of the dining hall in order to starve the students into submission. As to the sixth paragraph, he contended that since arrests are ordinarily made by the police, the statement "They have arrested [Dr. Martin Luther King] seven times" would be read as referring to him; he further contended that the "they" who did the arresting would be equated with the "they" who committed the other described acts and with the "Southern violators." . . .

We hold that the rule of law applied by the Alabama courts is constitutionally deficient for failure to provide the safeguards for freedom of speech and of the press that are required by the First and Fourteenth Amendments in a libel action brought by a public official against critics of his official conduct. We further hold that under the proper safeguards the evidence presented in this case is constitutionally insufficient to support the judgment for respondent. . . .

Respondent relies heavily, as did the Alabama courts, on statements of this Court to the effect that the Constitution does not protect libelous publications. Those statements do not foreclose our inquiry here. None of the cases sustained the use of libel laws to impose sanctions upon expression critical of the official conduct of public officials. . . . In the only

previous case that did present the question of constitutional limitations upon the power to award damages for libel of a public official, the Court was equally divided and the question was not decided. . . .

The general proposition that freedom of expression upon public questions is secured by the First Amendment has long been settled by our decisions. . . .

Thus we consider this case against the background of a profound national commitment to the principle that debate on public issues should be uninhibited, robust, and wide-open, and that it may well include vehement, caustic, and sometimes unpleasantly sharp attacks on government and public officials. . . . The present advertisement, as an expression of grievance and protest on one of the major public issues of our time, would seem clearly to qualify for the constitutional protection. The question is whether it forfeits that protection by the falsity of some of its factual statements and by its alleged defamation of respondent. . . .

Authoritative interpretations of the First Amendment guarantees have consistently refused to recognize an exception for any test of truth, whether administered by judges, juries, or administrative officials—and especially not one that puts the burden of proving truth on the speaker. . . . The constitutional protection does not turn upon "the truth, popularity, or social utility of the ideas and beliefs which are offered." . . . As Madison said, "Some degree of abuse is inseparable from the proper use of every thing; and in no instance is this more true than in that of the press."

[E]rroneous statement is inevitable in free debate. . . .

Injury to official reputation affords no more warrant for repressing speech that would otherwise be free than does factual error. Where judicial officers are involved, this Court has held that concern for the dignity and reputation of the courts does not justify the punishment as criminal contempt of criticism of the judge or his decision. . . . If judges are to be treated as "men of fortitude, able to thrive in a hardy climate," surely the same must be true of other government officials, such as elected city commissioners. Criticism of their official conduct does not lose its constitutional protection merely because it is effective criticism and hence diminishes their official reputations.

If neither factual error nor defamatory content suffices to remove the constitutional shield from criticism of official conduct, the combination of the two elements is no less inadequate. This is the lesson to be drawn from the great controversy over the Sedition Act of 1798, which first crystallized a national awareness of the central meaning of the First Amendment. . . .

Although the Sedition Act was never tested in this Court, the attack upon its validity has carried the day in the court of history. Fines levied in its prosecution were repaid by Act of Congress on the ground that it was unconstitutional. . . . The invalidity of the Act has also been assumed by Justices of this Court. . . . These views reflect a broad consensus that the Act, because of the restraint it imposed upon criticism of government and public officials, was inconsistent with the First Amendment. . . .

A rule compelling the critic of official conduct to guarantee the truth of all his factual assertions—and to do so on pain of libel judgments virtually unlimited in amount—leads to a comparable "self-censorship." Allowance of the defense of truth, with the burden of proving it on the defendant, does not mean that only false speech will be deterred. Even courts accepting this defense as an adequate safeguard have recognized the difficulties of adducing legal proofs that the alleged libel was true in all its factual particulars. . . .

Under such a rule would-be critics of official conduct may be deterred from voicing their criticism, even though it is believed to be true and even though it is in fact true, because of doubt whether it can be proved in court or fear of the expense of having to do so. They tend to make only statements which "steer far wider of the unlawful zone." . . . The rule thus dampens the vigor and limits the variety of public debate. . . .

The constitutional guarantees require, we think, a federal rule that prohibits a public official from recovering damages for a defamatory falsehood relating to his official conduct unless he proves that the statement was made with "actual malice"—that is, with knowledge that it was false or with reckless disregard of whether it was false or not. . . .

Applying these standards, we consider that the proof presented to show actual malice lacks the convincing clarity which the constitutional standard demands, and hence that it would not constitutionally sustain the judgment for respondent under the proper rule of law. The case of the individual petitioners requires little discussion. Even assuming that they could constitutionally be found to have authorized the use of their names on the advertisement, there was no evidence whatever that they were aware of any erroneous statements or were in any way reckless in that regard. The judgment against them is thus without constitutional support.

As to the *Times,* we similarly conclude that the facts do not support a finding of actual malice. . . . We think the evidence against the *Times* supports at most a finding of negligence in failing to discover the misstatements, and is constitutionally insufficient to show the recklessness that is required for a finding of actual malice. . . .

*Reversed and remanded.*

MR. JUSTICE BLACK, with whom MR. JUSTICE DOUGLAS joins, concurring . . . [omitted].

MR. JUSTICE GOLDBERG, with whom MR. JUSTICE DOUGLAS joins, concurring in the result . . . [omitted].

## New York Times Co. v. United States
### 403 U.S. 713, 91 S.Ct. 2140, 29 L.Ed. 2d 822 (1971)

http://laws.findlaw.com/us/403/713.html

This testing of the limits of prior restraint produced one of the fastest start-to-finish bouts of litigation in Supreme Court history. The *New York Times* and the *Washington Post* acquired copies of a 7,000-page classified study (popularized as the "Pentagon Papers") prepared for the Department of Defense on the evolution of U.S. Vietnam policy. On Sunday, June 13, 1971, the *Times* published the first of what would be several installments, which *Times* editors had secretly condensed from the longer study. Serialization began in the *Post* on June 18. On June 15, the Nixon administration went into U.S. District Court in New York, and later in the District of Columbia, to obtain injunctions blocking further publication. The move against the *Post* proved unsuccessful, but the Second Circuit Court of Appeals enjoined further publication in the *Times* pending the outcome of the government's case. On June 25, the Supreme Court granted expedited review, with oral arguments scheduled the next day. The Court rendered its decision four days later on June 30. The format of opinions was unusual—per curiam, with each justice delivering a separate opinion. Opinions by four justices are reprinted here. The opinions of Justices Black and Harlan were their last. Majority: Black, Brennan, Douglas, Marshall, Stewart, White. Dissenting: Burger, Blackmun, Harlan.

PER CURIAM. . . .

"Any system of prior restraints of expression comes to this Court bearing a heavy presumption against its constitutional validity.". . . The Government "thus carries a heavy burden of showing justification for the enforcement of such a restraint." . . . The District Court for the Southern District of New York in the *New York Times* case and the District Court for the District of Columbia and the Court of Appeals for the District of Columbia Circuit in the *Washington Post* case held that the Government had not met that burden. We agree. . . .

MR. JUSTICE BLACK, with whom MR. JUSTICE DOUGLAS joins, concurring.

I adhere to the view that the Government's case against the *Washington Post* should have been dismissed and that the injunction against the *New York Times* should have been vacated without oral argument when the cases were first presented to this Court. I believe that every moment's continuance of the injunc-

tions against these newspapers amounts to a flagrant, indefensible, and continuing violation of the First Amendment. . . . In my view it is unfortunate that some of my Brethren are apparently willing to hold that the publication of news may sometimes be enjoined. Such a holding would make a shambles of the First Amendment.

Our Government was launched in 1789 with the adoption of the Constitution. The Bill of Rights, including the First Amendment, followed in 1791. Now, for the first time in the 182 years since the founding of the Republic, the federal courts are asked to hold that the First Amendment does not mean what it says, but rather means that Government can halt the publication of current news of vital importance to the people of this country.

In seeking injunctions against these newspapers and in its presentation to the Court, the Executive Branch seems to have forgotten the essential purpose and history of the First Amendment. When the Constitution was adopted, many people strongly opposed it because the document contained no Bill of Rights to safeguard certain basic freedoms.

They especially feared that the new powers granted to a central Government might be interpreted to permit the Government to curtail freedom of religion, press, assembly, and speech. In response to an overwhelming public clamor, James Madison offered a series of amendments to satisfy citizens that these great liberties would remain safe and beyond the power of government to abridge. . . . The amendments were offered to curtail and restrict the general powers granted to the Executive, Legislative, and Judicial Branches two years before in the original Constitution. The Bill of Rights changed the original Constitution into a new charter under which no branch of government could abridge the people's freedoms of press, speech, religion, and assembly. Yet the Solicitor General argues and some members of the Court appear to agree that the general powers of the Government adopted in the original Constitution should be interpreted to limit and restrict the specific and emphatic guarantees of the Bill of Rights adopted later. I can imagine no greater perversion of history. . . .

In the First Amendment the Founding Fathers gave the free press the protection it must have to fulfill its essential role in our democracy. The press was to serve the governed, not the governors. The Government's power to censor the press was abolished so that the press would remain forever free to censure the Government. The press was protected so that it could bare the secrets of government and inform the people. Only a free and unrestrained press can effectively expose deception in government. And paramount among the responsibilities of a free press is the duty to prevent any part of the government from deceiving the people and sending them off to distant lands to die of foreign fevers and foreign shot and shell. In my view, far from deserving condemnation for their courageous reporting, the *New York Times,* the *Washington Post,* and other newspapers should be commended for serving the purpose that the Founding Fathers saw so clearly. In revealing the workings of government that led to the Viet Nam war, the newspapers nobly did precisely that which the Founders hoped and trusted they would do. . . .

[W]e are asked to hold that despite the First Amendment's emphatic command, the Executive Branch, the Congress, and the Judiciary can make laws enjoining publication of current news and abridging freedom of the press in the name of "national security." The Government does not even attempt to rely on any act of Congress. Instead it makes the bold and dangerously far-reaching contention that the courts should take it upon themselves to "make" a law abridging freedom of the press in the name of equity, presidential power and national security, even when the representatives of the people in Congress have adhered to the command of the First Amendment and refused to make such a law. . . .

The word "security" is a broad, vague generality whose contours should not be invoked to abrogate the fundamental law embodied in the First Amendment. The guarding of military and diplomatic secrets at the expense of informed representative government provides no real security for our Republic. The Framers of the First Amendment, fully aware of both the need to defend a new nation and the abuses of the English and Colonial governments, sought to give this new society strength and security by providing that freedom of speech, press, religion, and assembly should not be abridged. . . .

MR. JUSTICE DOUGLAS, with whom MR. JUSTICE BLACK joins, concurring . . . [omitted].

MR. JUSTICE BRENNAN, concurring . . . [omitted].

### MR. JUSTICE STEWART, with whom MR. JUSTICE WHITE joins, concurring.

In the governmental structure created by our Constitution, the Executive is endowed with enormous power in the two related areas of national defense and international relations. This power, largely unchecked by the Legislative and Judicial branches, has been pressed to the very hilt since the advent of the nuclear missile age. For better or for worse, the simple fact is that a President of the United States possesses vastly greater constitutional independence in these two vital areas of power than does, say, a prime minister of a country with a parliamentary form of government.

In the absence of the governmental checks and balances present in other areas of our national life, the only effective restraint upon executive policy and power in the areas of national defense and international affairs may lie in an enlightened citizenry—in an informed and critical public opinion which alone can here protect the values of democratic government. For this reason, it is perhaps here that a press that is alert, aware, and free most vitally serves the basic purpose of the First Amendment. For without an informed and free press there cannot be an enlightened people.

Yet it is elementary that the successful conduct of international diplomacy and the maintenance of an effective national defense require both confidentiality and secrecy. Other nations can hardly deal with this Nation in an atmosphere of mutual trust unless they can be assured that their confidences will be kept. And within our own executive departments, the development of considered and intelligent international policies would be impossible if those charged with their formulation could not communicate with each other freely, frankly, and in confidence. In the area of basic national defense the frequent need for absolute secrecy is, of course, self-evident.

I think there can be but one answer to this dilemma, if dilemma it be. The responsibility must be where the power is. If the Constitution gives the Executive a large degree of unshared power in the conduct of foreign affairs and the maintenance of our national defense, then under the Constitution the Executive must have the largely unshared duty to determine and preserve the degree of internal security necessary to exercise that power successfully. . . . [I]t is clear to me that it is the constitutional duty of the Executive—as a matter of sovereign prerogative and not as a matter of law as the courts know law—through the promulgation and enforcement of executive regulations, to protect the confidentiality necessary to carry out its responsibilities in the fields of international relations and national defense.

This is not to say that Congress and the courts have no role to play. Undoubtedly

Congress has the power to enact specific and appropriate criminal laws to protect government property and preserve government secrets. Congress has passed such laws, and several of them are of very colorable relevance to the apparent circumstances of these cases. And if a criminal prosecution is instituted, it will be the responsibility of the courts to decide the applicability of the criminal law under which the charge is brought. Moreover, if Congress should pass a specific law authorizing civil proceedings in this field, the courts would likewise have the duty to decide the constitutionality of such a law as well as its applicability to the facts proved.

But in the cases before us we are asked neither to construe specific regulations nor to apply specific laws. We are asked, instead, to perform a function that the Constitution gave to the Executive, not the Judiciary. We are asked, quite simply, to prevent the publication by two newspapers of material that the Executive Branch insists should not, in the national interest, be published. I am convinced that the Executive is correct with respect to some of the documents involved. But I cannot say that disclosure of any of them will surely result in direct, immediate, and irreparable damage to our Nation or its people. That being so, there can under the First Amendment be but one judicial resolution of the issues before us. I join the judgments of the Court.

MR. JUSTICE WHITE, with whom MR. JUSTICE STEWART joins, concurring . . . [omitted].

MR. JUSTICE MARSHALL, concurring . . . [omitted].

### MR. CHIEF JUSTICE BURGER, dissenting. . . .

The newspapers make a derivative claim under the First Amendment; they denominate this right as the public "right-to-know"; by implication, the *Times* asserts a sole trusteeship of that right by virtue of its journalistic "scoop." The right is asserted as an absolute. Of course, the First Amendment right itself is not an absolute, as Justice Holmes so long ago pointed out in his aphorism concerning the right to shout fire in a crowded theatre. . . . There are no doubt other exceptions no one has had occasion to describe or discuss. Conceivably such exceptions may be lurking in these cases and would have been flushed had they been properly considered in the trial courts, free from unwarranted deadlines and frenetic pressures. A great issue of this kind should be tried in a judicial atmosphere conducive to thoughtful, reflective deliberation, especially when haste, in terms of hours, is unwarranted in light of the long period the *Times,* by its own choice, deferred publication.

It is not disputed that the *Times* has had unauthorized possession of the documents for three to four months, during which it has had its expert analysts studying them, presumably digesting them and preparing the material for publication. During all of this time, the *Times,* presumably in its capacity as trustee of the public's "right to know," has held up publication for purposes it considered proper and thus public knowledge was delayed. No doubt this was for a good reason; the analysis of 7,000 pages of complex material drawn from a vastly greater volume of material would inevitably take time and the writing of good news stories takes time. But why should the United States Government, from whom this information was illegally acquired by someone, along with all the counsel, trial judges, and appellate judges be placed under needless pressure? . . .

We all crave speedier judicial processes but when judges are pressured as in these cases the result is a parody of the judicial process.

**MR. JUSTICE HARLAN, with whom THE CHIEF JUSTICE and MR. JUSTICE BLACKMUN join, dissenting. . . .**

With all respect, I consider that the Court has been almost irresponsibly feverish in dealing with these cases. . . .

Forced as I am to reach the merits of these cases, I dissent from the opinion and judgments of the Court. . . .

It is plain to me that the scope of the judicial function in passing upon the activities of the Executive Branch of the Government in the field of foreign affairs is very narrowly restricted. This view is, I think, dictated by the concept of separation of powers upon which our constitutional system rests. . . .

The power to evaluate the "pernicious influence" of premature disclosure is not, however, lodged in the Executive alone. I agree that, in performance of its duty to protect the values of the First Amendment against political pressures, the judiciary must review the initial Executive determination to the point of satisfying itself that the subject matter of the dispute does lie within the proper compass of the President's foreign relations power. Constitutional considerations forbid "a complete abandonment of judicial control." . . . Moreover, the judiciary may properly insist that the determination that disclosure of the subject matter would irreparably impair the national security be made by the head of the Executive Department concerned—here the Secretary of State or the Secretary of Defense—after actual personal consideration by that officer. This safeguard is required in the analogous area of executive claims of privilege for secrets of state. . . .

Even if there is some room for the judiciary to override the executive determination, it is plain that the scope of review must be exceedingly narrow. I can see no indication in the opinions of either the District Court or the Court of Appeals, in the *Post* litigation that the conclusions of the Executive were given even the deference owing to an administrative agency, much less that owing to a coequal branch of the Government operating within the field of its constitutional prerogative. . . .

MR. JUSTICE BLACKMUN, concurring . . . [omitted].

## Ashcroft v. Free Speech Coalition
## 535 U.S. 234, 122 S.Ct. 1389, 152 L.Ed. 2d 403 (2002)
http://laws.findlaw.com/us/535/234.html

The Child Pornography Prevention Act of 1996 (CPPA) expanded the federal prohibition on child pornography to include not only pornographic images made using actual children, but also [in section 2258(8)(B)] "any visual depiction, including any photograph, film, video, picture, or computer or computer-generated image or picture" that "is, or appears to be, of a minor engaging in sexually explicit conduct," and [in section 2256(8)(D)] any sexually explicit image that is "advertised, promoted, presented, described, or distributed in such a manner that conveys the impression" it depicts "a minor engaging in sexually explicit conduct." Fearing that the CPPA threatened their activities, an adult-entertainment trade association and others organized as the Free Speech Coalition filed suit alleging that the "appears to be" and "conveys the impression" provisions were overbroad and vague, chilling production of works protected by the First Amendment. The U.S. District Court for the Northern District of California granted the Government summary judgment. In 1999 the U.S. Court of Appeals for the Ninth Circuit reversed. Majority: Kennedy, Breyer, Ginsburg, Souter, Stevens, Thomas. Dissenting (on most points): Rehnquist, O'Connor, Scalia.

**JUSTICE KENNEDY delivered the opinion of the Court.**

We consider in this case whether the Child Pornography Prevention Act of 1996 (CPPA) abridges the freedom of speech. The CPPA extends the federal prohibition against child pornography to sexually explicit images that appear to depict minors but were produced without using any real children. The statute prohibits, in specific circumstances, possessing or distributing these images, which may be created by using adults who look like minors or by using computer imaging. The new technology, according to Congress, makes it possible to create realistic images of children who do not exist.

By prohibiting child pornography that does not depict an actual child, the statute goes beyond *New York* v. *Ferber* (1982), which distinguished child pornography from other sexually explicit speech because of the State's interest in protecting the children exploited by the production process. As a general rule, pornography can be banned only if obscene, but under *Ferber,* pornography showing minors can be proscribed whether or not the images are obscene under the definition set forth

in *Miller* v. *California* (1973). *Ferber* recognized that "[t]he *Miller* standard, like all general definitions of what may be banned as obscene, does not reflect the State's particular and more compelling interest in prosecuting those who promote the sexual exploitation of children." . . .

Like the law in *Ferber,* the CPPA seeks to reach beyond obscenity, and it makes no attempt to conform to the *Miller* standard. For instance, the statute would reach visual depictions, such as movies, even if they have redeeming social value.

The principal question to be resolved, then, is whether the CPPA is constitutional where it proscribes a significant universe of speech that is neither obscene under *Miller* nor child pornography under *Ferber.*

Before 1996, Congress defined child pornography as the type of depictions at issue in *Ferber,* images made using actual minors. The CPPA retains that prohibition and adds three other prohibited categories of speech, of which the first, § 2256(8)(B), and the third, § 2256(8)(D), are at issue in this case. . . .

These images do not involve, let alone harm, any children in the production process; but Congress decided the materials threaten children in other, less direct, ways. Pedophiles might use the materials to encourage children to participate in sexual activity. . . . Furthermore, pedophiles might "whet their own sexual appetites" with the pornographic images, "thereby increasing the creation and distribution of child pornography and the sexual abuse and exploitation of actual children." Under these rationales, harm flows from the content of the images, not from the means of their production. In addition, Congress identified another problem created by computer-generated images: Their existence can make it harder to prosecute pornographers who do use real minors. As imaging technology improves, Congress found, it becomes more difficult to prove that a particular picture was produced using actual children. To ensure that defendants possessing child pornography using real minors cannot evade prosecution, Congress extended the ban to virtual child pornography. . . .

Congress may pass valid laws to protect children from abuse, and it has. The prospect of crime, however, by itself does not justify laws suppressing protected speech. It is also well established that speech may not be prohibited because it concerns subjects offending our sensibilities. . . .

As a general principle, the First Amendment bars the government from dictating what we see or read or speak or hear. The freedom of speech has its limits; it does not embrace certain categories of speech, including defamation, incitement, obscenity, and pornography produced with real children. While these categories may be prohibited without violating the First Amendment, none of them includes the speech prohibited by the CPPA. In his dissent from the opinion of the Court of Appeals, Judge Ferguson recognized this to be the law and proposed that virtual child pornography should be regarded as an additional category of unprotected speech. It would be necessary for us to take this step to uphold the statute.

As we have noted, the CPPA is much more than a supplement to the existing federal prohibition on obscenity. Under *Miller* v. *California,* the Government must prove that the work, taken as a whole, appeals to the prurient interest, is patently offensive in light of community standards, and lacks serious literary, artistic, political, or scientific value. The CPPA, however, extends to images that appear to depict a minor engaging in sexually explicit activity without regard to the *Miller* requirements. The materials need not appeal to the prurient interest. Any depiction of sexually explicit activity, no matter how it is presented, is proscribed. The CPPA applies to a picture in a psychology manual, as well as a movie depicting the horrors of sexual abuse. It is not necessary, moreover, that the image be patently offensive. Pictures of what appear to be 17-year-olds engaging in sexually explicit activity do not in every case contravene community standards.

The CPPA prohibits speech despite its serious literary, artistic, political, or scientific value. The statute proscribes the visual depiction of an idea—that of teenagers engaging in sexual activity—that is a fact of modern society and has been a theme in art and literature throughout the ages. Under the CPPA, images are prohibited so long as the persons appear to be under 18 years of age. . . . It is, of course, undeniable that some youths engage in sexual activity before the legal age, either on their own inclination or because they are victims of sexual abuse.

Both themes—teenage sexual activity and the sexual abuse of children—have inspired countless literary works. William Shakespeare created the most famous pair of teenage lovers, one of whom is just 13 years of age. . . . Shakespeare may not have written sexually explicit scenes for the Elizabethan audience, but were modern directors to adopt a less conventional approach, that fact alone would not compel the conclusion that the work was obscene.

Contemporary movies pursue similar themes. Last year's Academy Awards featured the movie, "Traffic," which was nominated for Best Picture. The film portrays a teenager, identified as a 16-year-old, who becomes addicted to drugs. The viewer sees the degradation of her addiction, which in the end leads her to a filthy room to trade sex for drugs.

The year before, "American Beauty" won the Academy Award for Best Picture. In the course of the movie, a teenage girl engages in sexual relations with her teenage boyfriend, and another yields herself to the gratification of a middle-aged man. The film also contains a scene where, although the movie audience understands the act is not taking place, one character believes he is watching a teenage boy performing a sexual act on an older man. . . .

Whether or not the films we mention violate the CPPA, they explore themes within the wide sweep of the statute's prohibitions. If these films, or hundreds of others of lesser note that explore those subjects, contain a single graphic depiction of sexual activity within the statutory definition, the possessor of the film would be subject to severe punishment without inquiry into the work's redeeming value. This is inconsistent with an essential First Amendment rule: The artistic merit of a work does not depend on the presence of a single explicit scene. . . .

The Government . . . argues that the CPPA is necessary because pedophiles may use virtual child pornography to seduce children. There are many things innocent in themselves, however, such as cartoons, video games, and candy, that might be used for immoral purposes, yet we would not expect those to be prohibited because they can be misused. . . . The objective is to prohibit illegal conduct, but this restriction goes well beyond that interest by restricting the speech available to law-abiding adults.

The Government submits further that virtual child pornography whets the appetites of pedophiles and encourages them to engage in illegal conduct. This rationale cannot sustain the provision in question. The mere tendency of speech to encourage unlawful acts is not a sufficient reason for banning it. . . . The right to think is the beginning of freedom, and speech must be protected from the government because speech is the beginning of thought. . . .

The Government next argues that its objective of eliminating the market for pornography produced using real children necessitates a prohibition on virtual images as well. Virtual images, the Government contends, are indistinguishable from real ones; they are part of the same market and are often exchanged. In this way, it is said, virtual images promote the trafficking in works produced through the exploitation of real children. The hypothesis is somewhat implausible. If virtual images were identical to illegal child pornography, the illegal images would be driven from the market by the indistinguishable substitutes. Few pornographers would risk prosecution by abusing real children if fictional, computerized images would suffice. . . .

Finally, the Government says that the possibility of producing images by using computer imaging makes it very difficult for it to prosecute those who produce pornography by using real children. Experts, we are told, may have difficulty in saying whether the pictures were made by using real children or by using computer imaging. The necessary solution, the argument runs, is to prohibit both kinds of images. The argument, in essence, is that protected speech may be banned as a means to ban unprotected speech. This analysis turns the First Amendment upside down. . . .

In sum, § 2256(8)(B) covers materials beyond the categories recognized in *Ferber* and *Miller,* and the reasons the Government offers in support of limiting the freedom of speech have no justification in our precedents or in the law of the First Amendment. The provision abridges the freedom to engage in a substantial amount of lawful speech. For this reason, it is overbroad and unconstitutional.

Respondents challenge § 2256(8)(D) as well. This provision bans depictions of sexually explicit conduct that are "advertised, promoted, presented, described, or distributed in such a manner that conveys the impression that the material is or contains a visual depiction of a minor engaging in sexually explicit conduct." . . . The Government does not offer a serious defense of this provision, and the other arguments it makes in support of the CPPA do not bear on § 2256(8)(D). . . .

The First Amendment requires a more precise restriction. . . . For the reasons we have set forth, the prohibitions of §§ 2256(8)(B) and 2256(8)(D) are overbroad and unconstitutional. Having reached this conclusion, we need not address respondents' further contention that the provisions are unconstitutional because of vague statutory language.

The judgment of the Court of Appeals is affirmed.

*It is so ordered.*

JUSTICE THOMAS, concurring in the judgment . . . [omitted].

**CHIEF JUSTICE REHNQUIST, with whom JUSTICE SCALIA joins in part, dissenting. . . .**

We normally do not strike down a statute on First Amendment grounds "when a limiting instruction has been or could be placed on the challenged statute." . . . This case should be treated no differently.

Other than computer generated images that are virtually indistinguishable from real children engaged in sexually explicitly conduct, the CPPA can be limited so as not to reach any material that was not already unprotected before the CPPA. The CPPA's definition of "sexually explicit conduct" is quite explicit in this regard. It makes clear that the statute only reaches "visual depictions" of: "[A]ctual or simulated . . . sexual intercourse, including genital-genital, oral-genital, anal-genital, or oral-anal, whether between persons of the same or opposite sex; . . . bestiality; . . . masturbation; . . . sadistic or masochistic abuse; . . . or lascivious exhibition of the genitals or pubic area of any person."

The Court and Justice O'Connor suggest that this very graphic definition reaches the depiction of youthful looking adult actors engaged in suggestive sexual activity, presumably because the definition extends to "simulated" intercourse. Read as a whole, however, I think the definition reaches only the sort of "hard core of child pornography" that we found without protection in *Ferber.* So construed, the CPPA bans visual depictions of youthful looking adult actors engaged in *actual* sexual activity; mere *suggestions* of sexual activity, such as youthful

looking adult actors squirming under a blanket, are more akin to written descriptions than visual depictions, and thus fall outside the purview of the statute.

The reference to "simulated" has been part of the definition of "sexually explicit conduct" since the statute was first passed. But the inclusion of "simulated" conduct, alongside "actual" conduct, does not change the "hard core" nature of the image banned. The reference to "simulated" conduct simply brings within the statute's reach depictions of hard core pornography that are "made to look genuine," including the main target of the CPPA, computer-generated images virtually indistinguishable from real children engaged in sexually explicit conduct. Neither actual conduct nor simulated conduct, however, is properly construed to reach depictions such as those in a film portrayal of *Romeo and Juliet,* which are far removed from the hard core pornographic depictions that Congress intended to reach.

Indeed, we should be loath to construe a statute as banning film portrayals of Shakespearian tragedies, without some indication—from text or legislative history—that such a result was intended. In fact, Congress explicitly instructed that such a reading of the CPPA would be wholly unwarranted. . . .

Judge Ferguson similarly observed in his dissent in the Court of Appeals in this case: "From reading the legislative history, it becomes clear that the CPPA merely extends the existing prohibitions on 'real' child pornography to a narrow class of computer-generated pictures easily mistaken for real photographs of real children." . . .

This narrow reading of "sexually explicit conduct" not only accords with the text of the CPPA and the intentions of Congress; it is exactly how the phrase was understood prior to the broadening gloss the Court gives it today. Indeed, had "sexually explicit conduct" been thought to reach the sort of material the Court says it does, then films such as "Traffic" and "American Beauty" would not have been made the way they were. . . . "Traffic" won its Academy Award in 2001. "American Beauty" won its Academy Award in 2000. But the CPPA has been on the books, and has been enforced, since 1996. The chill felt by the Court has apparently never been felt by those who actually make movies. . . .

In sum, while potentially impermissible applications of the CPPA may exist, I doubt that they would be "substantial . . . in relation to the statute's plainly legitimate sweep." The aim of ensuring the enforceability of our Nation's child pornography laws is a compelling one. The CPPA is targeted to this aim by extending the definition of child pornography to reach computer-generated images that are virtually indistinguishable from real chil-dren engaged in sexually explicit conduct. The statute need not be read to do any more than precisely this, which is not offensive to the First Amendment.

For these reasons, I would construe the CPPA in a manner consistent with the First Amendment, reverse the Court of Appeals' judgment, and uphold the statute in its entirety.

JUSTICE O'CONNOR, with whom THE CHIEF JUSTICE and JUSTICE SCALIA join in part, concurring in the judgment in part and dissenting in part . . . [omitted].

## VI. THE INTERNET

### Reno v. American Civil Liberties Union
### 521 U.S. 844, 117 S.Ct. 2329, 138 L.Ed. 2d 874 (1997)
### http://laws.findlaw.com/us/521/844.html

In the Communications Decency Act of 1996, Congress sought to protect minors from harmful material on the Internet. Section 223(a) criminalized the "knowing" transmission of "obscene or indecent" messages to any recipient under 18 years of age. Section 223(d) prohibited the "know[ing]" sending or displaying to a person under 18 of any message "that, in context, depicts or describes, in terms patently offensive as measured by contemporary community standards, sexual or excretory activities or organs." Affirmative defenses were provided for persons who take "good faith, . . . effective . . . actions" to restrict minors' access to the prohibited communications and for persons who restrict such access by requiring certain designated forms of proof of age. The American Civil Liberties Union and other groups promptly challenged the constitutionality of both sections in the U.S. District Court for the Eastern District of Pennsylvania, which enjoined enforcement of the provisions. Majority: Stevens, Scalia, Kennedy, Souter, Thomas, Ginsburg, Breyer. Dissenting (in part): O'Connor, Rehnquist.

**JUSTICE STEVENS delivered the opinion of the Court.**

At issue is the constitutionality of two statutory provisions enacted to protect minors from "indecent" and "patently offensive" communications on the Internet. Notwithstanding the legitimacy and importance of the congressional goal of protecting children from harm-ful materials, we agree with the three-judge District Court that the statute abridges "the freedom of speech" protected by the First Amendment. . . .

In arguing for reversal, the Government contends that the CDA is plainly constitutional under three of our prior decisions: (1) *Ginsberg* v. *New York* (1968); (2) *FCC* v. *Pacifica Foundation* (1978); and (3) *Renton* v.

*Playtime Theatres, Inc.* (1986). A close look at these cases, however, raises—rather than relieves—doubts concerning the constitutionality of the CDA.

In *Ginsberg,* we upheld the constitutionality of a New York statute that prohibited selling to minors under 17 years of age material that was considered obscene as to them even if not obscene as to adults. . . . In four important respects, the statute upheld in *Ginsberg* was narrower than the CDA. First, we noted in *Ginsberg* that "the prohibition against sales to minors does not bar parents who so desire from purchasing the magazines for their children." . . . Second, the New York statute applied only to commercial transactions, whereas the CDA contains no such limitation. Third, the New York statute cabined [sic] its definition of material that is harmful to minors with the requirement that it be "utterly without redeeming social importance for minors." The CDA fails to provide us with any definition of the term "indecent" as used in § 223(a)(1) and, importantly, omits any requirement that the "patently offensive" material covered by § 223(d) lack serious literary, artistic, political, or scientific value. Fourth, the New York statute defined a minor as a person under the age of 17, whereas the CDA, in applying to all those under 18 years, includes an additional year of those nearest majority.

In *Pacifica,* we upheld a declaratory order of the Federal Communications Commission, holding that the broadcast of a recording of a 12-minute monologue entitled "Filthy Words" that had previously been delivered to a live audience "could have been the subject of administrative sanctions." . . . [T]he Court concluded that the ease with which children may obtain access to broadcasts, "coupled with the concerns recognized in *Ginsberg,*" justified special treatment of indecent broadcasting.

As with the New York statute at issue in *Ginsberg,* there are significant differences between the order upheld in *Pacifica* and the CDA. First, the order in *Pacifica,* issued by an agency that had been regulating radio stations for decades, targeted a specific broadcast that represented a rather dramatic departure from traditional program content in order to desig-

nate when—rather than whether—it would be permissible to air such a program in that particular medium. The CDA's broad categorical prohibitions are not limited to particular times and are not dependent on any evaluation by an agency familiar with the unique characteristics of the Internet. Second, unlike the CDA, the Commission's declaratory order was not punitive. . . . Finally, the Commission's order applied to a medium which as a matter of history had "received the most limited First Amendment protection," in large part because warnings could not adequately protect the listener from unexpected program content. The Internet, however, has no comparable history . . . [and] the risk of encountering indecent material by accident is remote because a series of affirmative steps is required to access specific material.

In *Renton,* we upheld a zoning ordinance that kept adult movie theatres out of residential neighborhoods. The ordinance was aimed, not at the content of the films shown in the theatres, but rather at the "secondary effects"— such as crime and deteriorating property values—that these theaters fostered. . . . According to the Government, the CDA is constitutional because it constitutes a sort of "cyberzoning" on the Internet. But the CDA applies broadly to the entire universe of cyberspace. And the purpose of the CDA is to protect children from the primary effects of "indecent" and "patently offensive" speech, rather than any "secondary" effect of such speech. Thus, the CDA is a content-based blanket restriction on speech, and, as such, cannot be "properly analyzed as a form of time, place, and manner regulation." . . .

These precedents, then, surely do not require us to uphold the CDA and are fully consistent with the application of the most stringent review of its provisions. . . .

Moreover, the Internet is not as "invasive" as radio or television. . . .

We distinguished *Pacifica* in *Sable* [*Communications* v. *FCC* (1989)] on just this basis. In *Sable,* a company engaged in the business of offering sexually oriented prerecorded telephone messages (popularly known as "dial-a-porn") challenged the constitutionality of an amendment to the Communications Act that imposed a blanket prohibition on indecent as well as obscene interstate commercial telephone messages. We held that the statute was constitutional insofar as it applied to obscene messages but invalid as applied to indecent messages. . . . We explained that "the dial-it medium requires the listener to take affirmative steps to receive the communication." . . .

Finally, unlike the conditions that prevailed when Congress first authorized regulation of the broadcast spectrum, the Internet can hardly be considered a "scarce" expressive commodity. It provides relatively unlimited, low-cost capacity for communication of all kinds. . . . As the District Court found, "the content on the Internet is as diverse as human thought." We agree with its conclusion that our cases provide no basis for qualifying the level of First Amendment scrutiny that should be applied to this medium. . . .

The vagueness of the CDA is a matter of special concern for two reasons. First, the CDA is a content-based regulation of speech. The vagueness of such a regulation raises special First Amendment concerns because of its obvious chilling effect on free speech. Second, the CDA is a criminal statute. . . . We are persuaded that the CDA lacks the precision that the First Amendment requires when a statute regulates the content of speech. In order to deny minors access to potentially harmful speech, the CDA effectively suppresses a large amount of speech that adults have a constitutional right to receive and to address to one another. . . . [T]he Government may not "reduc[e] the adult population . . . to . . . only what is fit for children." . . .

It is at least clear that the strength of the Government's interest in protecting minors is not equally strong throughout the coverage of this broad statute. Under the CDA, a parent allowing her 17-year-old to use the family computer to obtain information on the Internet that she, in her parental judgment, deems appropriate could face a lengthy prison term. Similarly, a parent who sent his 17-year-old college freshman information on birth control via e-mail could be incarcerated even though neither he, his child, nor anyone in their home

community, found the material "indecent" or "patently offensive," if the college town's community thought otherwise.

The breadth of this content-based restriction of speech imposes an especially heavy burden on the Government to explain why a less restrictive provision would not be as effective as the CDA. It has not done so. . . . Particularly in the light of the absence of any detailed findings by the Congress, or even hearings addressing the special problems of the CDA, we are persuaded that the CDA is not narrowly tailored if that requirement has any meaning at all. . . .

For the foregoing reasons, the judgment of the district court is affirmed.

*It is so ordered.*

### JUSTICE O'CONNOR, with whom THE CHIEF JUSTICE joins, concurring in the judgment in part and dissenting in part.

I write separately to explain why I view the Communications Decency Act of 1996 (CDA) as little more than an attempt by Congress to create "adult zones" on the Internet. . . .

Given the present state of cyberspace, I agree with the Court that the "display" provision cannot pass muster. . . . [T]he only way for a speaker to avoid liability under the CDA is to refrain completely from using indecent speech. . . .

The "indecency transmission" and "specific person" provisions present a closer issue, for they are not unconstitutional in all of their applications. . . . Appellant urges the Court to construe the provision to impose . . . a knowledge requirement, and I would do so. . . .

So construed, both provisions are constitutional as applied to a conversation involving only an adult and one or more minors—e.g., when an adult speaker sends an e-mail knowing the addressee is a minor, or when an adult and minor converse by themselves or with other minors in a chat room. In this context, these provisions are no different from the law we sustained in *Ginsberg*. . . . The relevant universe contains only one adult, and the adult in that universe has the power to refrain from using indecent speech and consequently to keep all such speech within the room in an "adult" zone.

The analogy to *Ginsberg* breaks down, however, when more than one adult is a party to the conversation. . . . The CDA is therefore akin to a law that makes it a crime for a bookstore owner to sell pornographic magazines to anyone once a minor enters his store. . . .

Thus, the constitutionality of the CDA as a zoning law hinges on the extent to which it substantially interferes with the First Amendment rights of adults. Because the rights of adults are infringed only by the "display" provision and by the "indecency transmission" and "specific person" provisions as applied to communications involving more than one adult, I would invalidate the CDA only to that extent. Insofar as the "indecency transmission" and "specific person" provisions prohibit the use of indecent speech in communications between an adult and one or more minors, however, they can and should be sustained. . . .

# CHAPTER TWELVE

# *Religious Liberty*

*Believing . . . that religion is a matter which lies solely between man and his God, that he owes account to none other for his faith or his worship, that the legislative powers of government reach actions only, and not opinions, I contemplate with sovereign reverence that act of the whole American people which declared that their legislature should "make no law respecting an establishment of religion, or prohibiting the free exercise thereof," thus building a wall of separation between church and state.*

—THOMAS JEFFERSON (1802)

"**C**ongress shall make no law respecting an establishment of religion, or prohibiting the free exercise thereof," begins the First Amendment. The **establishment** and **free exercise clauses** embody the American solution to one of the dilemmas of the modern world—the proper relation of state and religion, and of individuals to their God and their government. These clauses are central to the protection of religious beliefs and to the maintenance of civil peace in a religiously diverse culture.

## COMPETING VISIONS

By the time the Bill of Rights became part of the Constitution in 1791, two competing visions or ways of thinking had developed that shaped laws affecting religious liberty: accommodation and separation. Even today, debates about the meaning of the religion clauses in the Constitution are often defined in terms of which of these visions is to prevail.

**Accommodation** is the older of the two visions and stresses freedom *of* religion. Alongside protection for religious practice, it seeks government acknowledgment of, and sometimes support for, religion (Protestant Christianity, in particular, in the eighteenth and nineteenth centuries). Accommodationists believe that government best serves its own purposes when it encourages religion and recognizes religion's contributions to society, all the while it tolerates different faiths. Government is not to meddle in the affairs of particular denominations, but laws should respect, and reflect, dominant religious values. This seems to have been the prevailing view in most of the American states in the late 1700s and for a long time afterward. For example, the Pennsylvania Constitution of 1776 required state legislators, as part of their oath, to affirm belief in the divine inspiration of both the Old and New Testaments in the Bible. Practically on the eve of the Constitutional Convention of 1787, Virginia came close to reinstating a general taxpayer assessment in support of religious congregations. In 1824, the Supreme Court of Pennsylvania affirmed that Christianity was part of the common law of the Commonwealth. Blasphemy was punishable as a crime in many states. Until 1961, Maryland required officeholders to declare belief in the existence of God. As public education took hold in the nineteenth century, religious instruction was part of the curriculum in many states. Brief religious exercises in public schools were widespread as late as the 1960s and remain a subject of contention. People over 50 remember "blue laws" that kept many businesses closed on Sunday, the holy day of rest for most Christians.

A second, more secular, vision that took shape in the United States was closely identified two centuries ago with leaders such as Thomas Jefferson and James Madison. It stresses **separation**—freedom *from* religion. It seeks greater distance between religion and government in a nation that is not only one of the most religious but also one of the most religiously diverse countries on earth. For separationists, both political and religious institutions are more likely to prosper if each involves itself as little as possible in the affairs of the other.

Symbolic of the separationist vision are passages in the national Constitution. In the original text of the Constitution, there is a single, but nonetheless significant, reference to religion. Article VI declares: "no religious Test shall ever be required as a Qualification to any Office or public Trust under the United States." At the outset, by barring **religious tests**—a religious belief requirement—the Constitution disallowed a policy for the nation that was followed by most of the American states and virtually every other country at that time. In its leadership, the federal government could not be sectarian. In the Bill of Rights, the twin provisions of nonestablishment and free exercise have complementary objectives—preserving liberty and order. The free exercise clause preserves a sphere of religious practice free of interference by the government. Most Americans of two centuries ago probably did not crave toleration for beliefs other than their own. Given the presence of so many faiths, however, they had no choice. The violent alternative—as demonstrated in some places in the world even today—was unacceptable.

Even though a few states still maintained some kind of officially supported or designated church in 1791, the establishment clause declared that the nation could not have one. Nonestablishment was thus part of the price of union. The First Amendment sets the government off limits as a prize in a nation of competing faiths. The establishment clause thus protects free exercise by disabling all groups so that none can employ public resources to advance itself and to threaten the others.

The presence of these provisions in the First Amendment, however, raises a question. Why would the states have demanded, and then ratified, a Bill of Rights that in its clauses on religion seemed to contrast sharply with laws and practices in most of the states at that time? In their own eyes, local leaders were being neither foolish nor inconsistent. If religion was to be addressed by government at all, it was a subject for state, not national control. Ironically, the incorporation of the religion clauses into the Fourteenth Amendment in the 1940s—depicted in Table 9.1 in Chapter Nine—meant that the rules that tied the hands of the national government with respect to religion eventually bound the states as well.

Religion's special place in the Constitution also raises an obvious but perplexing problem in interpretation. What is a religion? What is a religious belief? The Supreme Court has given no definitive answer. Indeed, none may be completely acceptable. Generally, the approach in the last half century has been to broaden the meaning of religion to include more than theistic beliefs (*United States* v. *Seeger,* 1965). Religion is usually defined from the believer's perspective (*Thomas* v. *Review Board,* 1981), and while courts may validly inquire into the sincerity of one's beliefs, they may not test their validity (*United States* v. *Ballard,* 1944). Still, "religion" presumably does not encompass every strongly held belief; otherwise, its separate enumeration in the First Amendment would be pointless.

## THE ESTABLISHMENT CLAUSE

The establishment clause limits government support of religious endeavors and, more important, bars it from becoming the tool of one faith against others. Like most other constitutional limitations, however, this one is not self-defining. At the very least, the establishment clause would prohibit a "Church of the United States." But given the many ways in which government may interact with religious institutions, how does one know when a policy "respect[s] an establishment of religion"?

**THE MODERN ERA.** It was not until 1947 and *Everson* v. *Board of Education* that laws began receiving regular scrutiny under the establishment clause. Applying this part of the First Amendment to the states through the Fourteenth Amendment, the Court allowed a state to pay the costs of bus transportation of children attending sectarian as well as public and nonsectarian private schools. Nonetheless, drawing on Thomas Jefferson's reply to the Danbury Baptist Association of Connecticut in 1802, the decision set forth the principle that the religious clauses of the Constitution erected a "wall of separation" between church and state. Dissenting in *Everson,* Justice Rutledge issued a prophetic warning:

> Two great drives are constantly in motion to abridge, in the name of education, the complete division of religion and civil authority which our forefathers made. One is to introduce religious education and observances into the public schools. The other, to obtain public funds for the aid and support of various private religious schools. . . .
>
> In my opinion both avenues were closed by the Constitution. Neither should be opened by this Court. The matter is not one of quantity, to be measured by the amount of money expended. Now as in Madison's day it is one of principle, to keep separate the separate spheres as the First Amendment drew them; to prevent the first experiment upon our liberties; and to keep the question from becoming entangled in corrosive precedents. We should not be less strict to keep strong and untarnished the one side of the shield of religious freedom than we have been of the other.

*Everson* remains significant for several reasons. First, nationalization of the establishment clause means that individual state governments no longer have the final say on church–state matters within their borders. Second, because of the many ways in which state governments may interact with religion, *Everson* was an unmistakable invitation for further litigation. Because the Court upheld the New Jersey law challenged in that case, a reasonable conclusion was that not every policy that arguably supported religion ran afoul of the establishment clause. Later cases would have to discern the location of constitutional limits. Third, the reach of the establishment clause remains broad because, according to *Everson,* it prohibits programs that "aid all religions," not merely those that "aid one religion" or "prefer one over the other."

**TESTING ESTABLISHMENT.** In subsequent cases the justices have devised various "tests" or criteria by which to determine when a government has violated the establishment clause.

1. **Lemon test.** So named because of its use in ***Lemon* v. *Kurtzman*** (1971), this test consists of three elements or "prongs." To pass scrutiny, (a) a policy must have a "secular purpose," (b) its primary effect must be "neutral" (that is, neither advancing nor hindering religion), and (c) it must not promote an "excessive entanglement" between government and religion.
2. **Endorsement test.** Closely identified with Justice O'Connor, this test finds a violation of the establishment clause when government sends a signal that religion is favored or preferred, thus making some people feel as "outsiders" and others as "insiders."
3. **Agostini test.** So named because of ***Agostini* v. *Felton*** (1997), which modified the Lemon test, it is an elaboration of the endorsement test. A challenged policy must have both a secular purpose and a neutral effect. A policy has the impermissible effect of advancing religion if it (a) results in indoctrination of religion by government, (b) defines its recipients or beneficiaries according to religion, *or* (c) creates an excessive entanglement.
4. **Coercion test.** Closely identified with Justice Kennedy, this test allows government to acknowledge or accommodate religion but bars any policy that coerces anyone to support or to participate in any religion or religious exercise.
5. **Child-benefit theory.** Sometimes employed in cases involving state aid to religious schools, this approach focuses on the primary beneficiaries of the challenged plan—the children, rather than the schools themselves—where the aid is a result of decisions made by families about where their children should enroll, and not a result of government decisions to aid religious schools directly.

The fact that the Court has applied different tests to a variety of factual situations at different times has generated uncertainty and sometimes exasperation. One reason may be that no one of the tests appropriately fits all, or even most, of the establishment clause cases that reach the Court. The result is that one case resorts to *Lemon* (or another test), and the next one might not. Sometimes the Court relies on none of the tests by name.

**RELIGION IN THE PUBLIC SCHOOLS.** Of all the establishment clause issues that the Court has faced, those dealing with religious expression in public schools have generated the most controversy and yielded the least inconsistency. In the first of these in 1948, the Court struck down a **released-time** program for religious instruction in Champaign, Illinois (*McCollum* v. *Board of Education*). Students had the option of attending religion classes on site during the school day. Yet factual distinctions only four years later in *Zorach* v. *Clauson* led to the Court's approval of a program in New York, where similar instruction in the school day occurred off school premises. "We are a religious people whose institutions presuppose a Supreme Being," declared Justice Douglas for the majority. "When the state encourages religious instruction or cooperates with religious authorities by adjusting the schedule of public events to sectarian needs, it follows the best of our traditions." The contrast in outcomes prompted Justice Jackson to note in dissent that *Zorach* would "be more interesting to students of psychology and of the judicial processes than to students of constitutional law."

The first of Justice Rutledge's "great drives," however, continued to heat in the crucible of litigation. Any satisfaction to proponents of religion in public schools brought by *Zorach* was short-lived. Prayers and Bible reading in schools next came under fire. *Engel* v. *Vitale* (1962) invalidated the use in New York's public schools of a short prayer, approved by the Board of Regents, to be recited during opening exercises of each school day. In 1963, eight justices went further, declaring in *School District of Abington Township* v. *Schempp* that Bible reading and recitation of the Lord's Prayer in class were also invalid. In deciding whether the "wall of separation" had been breached, Justice Clark explained, "[T]o withstand the strictures of the Establishment Clause, there must be a secular legislative purpose and a primary effect that neither advances nor inhibits religion."

*Engel* and *Schempp* hardly ended the school prayer controversy. Some school districts plainly ignored the decisions. In the early 1980s President Ronald Reagan campaigned for the restoration of prayer in the schools and advocated amending the Constitution to make that possible. "God never should have been expelled from America's classrooms," he declared in his 1983 State of the Union address. So it was not surprising that the justices have continued to face the prayer issue. In 1985 *Wallace* v. *Jaffree* tested Alabama's requirement of a minute of silence "for meditation or voluntary prayer" in the public schools. More than two dozen states had enacted similar laws. Even Justice Brennan's concurring opinion in *Schempp* had suggested that moments of silence might not be unconstitutional. But six justices thought the Alabama law was defective. "[T]he State intends to characterize prayer as a favored practice," announced Justice Stevens. "Such an end is not consistent with the established principle that the Government must pursue a course of complete neutrality toward religion." The Court's decision, with its flurry of separate opinions, seemed Solomonic. Strongly hinted was the constitutionality of a law setting aside a moment of silence "for meditation" where it was not obvious from the record that the state's purpose was one of making an "end run" around *Engel* and *Schempp.*

By only a bare margin, however, did the Court maintain its opposition to public school prayer in 1992. In *Lee* v. *Weisman* a family contested the brief invocation and benediction to be delivered at the principal's invitation by a rabbi at a public middle school commencement ceremony in Providence, Rhode Island. Although inclusive and sensitive to different religious traditions, the prayers were nonetheless addressed to God, asking for blessings and giving thanks. "It is beyond dispute that, at a minimum, the Constitution guarantees that government may not coerce anyone to support or participate in religion or its exercise," declared Justice Kennedy.

Eight years later, the Court confronted another dispute over prayer that varied from *Lee* in several respects (**Santa Fe Independent School District v. Doe,** 2000). Under attack was prayer at a high school football game. Moreover, students—not school officials—through two elections decided whether invocations should be delivered at games, and, if so, selected the person who would pray. Nonetheless, the Court maintained its stance against any official religious expression on school premises, regardless of its source or setting. "The District," wrote Justice Stevens, "asks us to pretend that we do not recognize what every Santa Fe High School student understands clearly—that this policy is about prayer. . . . We refuse to turn a blind eye to the context in which this policy arose, and that context quells any doubt that this policy was implemented with the purpose of endorsing school prayer." *Santa Fe* was significant for another reason as well: Six justices (not five, as in *Lee*) found the policy constitutionally deficient.

**RELIGION IN OTHER OFFICIAL SETTINGS.** Perhaps because of the impressionable nature of schoolchildren and the unique role public schools have long had in the life of the nation, the justices have been quicker to strike down religious influences in the classroom than in other official places. In *Marsh* v. *Chambers* (1983), for example, a majority of the Court found no constitutional objection to the Nebraska practice of having a chaplain for the state legislature paid out of public funds. Nor was a majority prepared to say that the First Amendment banned city officials in Pawtucket, Rhode Island, from annually erecting a municipally owned Christmas display, including a crèche, in a private park (*Lynch* v. *Donnelly,* 1984). In contrast, five justices found unacceptable the display of a privately owned crèche in the county courthouse in Pittsburgh, Pennsylvania, which was adorned by a banner proclaiming "Gloria in excelsis Deo" (*County of Allegheny* v. *American Civil Liberties Union,* 1989). Yet in the same case six justices had no constitutional objection to a display on the steps of the nearby City-County Building, which combined an 18-foot menorah and a 45-foot tree decorated with holiday ornaments. These holdings suggest that publicly sponsored religious displays are permissible only if they have become secularized. Government may "recognize" but not "endorse" religion.

**STATE AID TO RELIGIOUS SCHOOLS.** Litigation involving state assistance to religious schools—the second of Justice Rutledge's "great drives"—is a fixture on the Court's docket. This has been true since the 1960s when state legislatures began to devise various ways to support financially pinched private schools, most of which were operated by the Roman Catholic Church. Some plans made private schools and their students eligible for certain benefits already enjoyed by public schools. Other plans signaled out private schools for special assistance. *Lemon* v. *Kurtzman* (1971) marked the Court's first decision against such programs.

*Lemon* challenged Pennsylvania and Rhode Island laws that, among other things, provided funds for partial support of the salaries of teachers of secular subjects in private schools, including religious schools. Such funding would be acceptable only if the state could demonstrate that the plan had (1) a "secular purpose," (2) a primary effect that was "neutral" (these elements came from *Schempp*), and (3) an absence of "excessive entanglement" between government and religion. This third element of the Lemon test first appeared in *Walz* v. *Tax Commission* in 1970, which upheld state tax exemptions for real property owned by religious and other charitable institutions, even when the property was used for religious purposes.

Judged against *Lemon's* prongs, the Pennsylvania and Rhode Island statutes were constitutionally defective. Although both states could demonstrate a purpose that was secular (supporting education), the plans were snared on a "Catch-22" combination of the second and third prongs. Although the requirement that government and religion not be excessively entangled had been used to save the tax exemption in *Walz,* that same standard proved fatal in *Lemon.* Efforts by the state to ensure a neutral effect were bound to create excessive entanglement. Absent such entanglement, the state could not be sure of a neutral effect.

The Court's rulings in state-aid cases since *Lemon,* however, have not been a model of consistency. A series of decisions demonstrate the complexities. In *Grand Rapids School District* v. *Ball* and *Aguilar* v. *Felton,* decided together in 1985, the

Court, voting 5 to 4, barred the use of state and federal funds, respectively, for **shared-time** programs providing enrichment and remedial instruction by public school teachers on religious school premises. Even though no money changed hands between government and religious schools, the programs were deemed constitutionally defective for at least two reasons: First, public employees might succumb to their surroundings and inject religion into the instruction; second, the program fostered a symbolic union of church and state. As Justice Brennan explained in *Ball,* "Teachers in [a religious] atmosphere may well subtly (or overtly) conform their instruction to the environment in which they teach, while students will perceive the instruction in the context of the dominantly religious message of the institution." Moreover, government "promotes religion as effectively when it fosters a close identification of its powers with those of any—or all—religious denominations as when it attempts to inculcate specific religious doctrines." The result of *Ball* and *Aguilar* was that such programs could continue only by moving instruction into publicly owned and maintained trailers parked off site.

In 1993, an equally narrow majority in *Zobrest* v. *Catalina Foothills School District* moved away from the 1985 rulings in one major respect. James Zobrest, who is deaf, enrolled in a Roman Catholic high school in Tucson, Arizona. He and his parents asked the local school district to provide a sign-language interpreter to attend classes with him. Under the Individuals with Disabilities Education Act and its Arizona counterpart, an interpreter would have been provided had James attended either public school or a nonsectarian private school. Because James attended a church-operated school, however, the school board declined his request. In the board's view, providing an interpreter at public expense for James would violate the establishment clause. The Supreme Court disagreed. Rather than aiding the sectarian school, the district would be assisting only the child. James merely wanted to take advantage of a government program designed to benefit a broad class of disabled persons. As the dissenters were quick to note, for the first time the Court approved a policy that paid a public employee to perform an official function in a sectarian classroom.

Building on *Zobrest, Agostini* v. *Felton* (1997) revisited the precise question addressed, and presumably settled, in *Ball* and *Aguilar.* Again voting 5 to 4, the Court concluded that, with respect to on-site instruction, the 1985 rulings were wrong: The establishment clause tolerates both enrichment and remediation by public employees in sectarian schools—instruction of the sort already provided in the public schools. Dissenters wondered how far the ruling might extend. If enrichment and remediation were acceptable, what about ordinary instruction in between?

*Agostini* made two important modifications in the Lemon-Ball-Aguilar analysis. First, once a secular purpose has been demonstrated, *Lemon's* concern over entanglement is now but one of three independent elements used to assure a neutral effect. A policy does not meet the neutrality criterion if it (1) results in indoctrination of religion by government, (2) defines its recipients or beneficiaries according to religion, *or* (3) creates an excessive entanglement. Second, unlike *Ball* and *Aguilar, Agostini* does not presume that indoctrination or a symbolic union will result in the absence of excessively entangling oversight. Thus *Agostini* removes the Catch-22 that had so often been fatal.

*Mitchell* v. *Helms* (2000) demonstrates the extent of the changes *Agostini* has brought to the establishment clause. The five justices in the Agostini majority plus Justice Breyer upheld the inclusion of religious schools under a provision of the Education Consolidation and Improvement Act of 1981 that provides federal funds to local educational agencies that in turn lend instructional materials and equipment (including library materials and computer hardware and software) to public and private schools for use in "secular, neutral, and nonideological" programs. Just as *Agostini* did not presume that indoctrination would result from the instruction in question, Mitchell did not presume "diversion"—that is, the use of publicly funded equipment for religious purposes. Accordingly, *Lemon*-based *Meek* v. *Pittenger* (1975) and *Wolman* v. *Walter* (1977), insofar as they disallowed the lending of instructional materials to religious schools or to their students, were overruled. The Mitchell majority differed, however, on whether evidence of actual diversion of government aid to religious purposes, after the aid had been distributed according to religiously neutral criteria, should be a factor in assessing effect.

The Court's school voucher decision in ***Zelman* v. *Simmons-Harris*** (2002) yielded the most lenient construction to date of the establishment clause, both in terms of the dollar amount and the number of sectarian schools involved. For the majority, the outcome was only consistent with religion-friendly decisions like *Zobrest*. For the dissenters, approval of vouchers represented a "dramatic departure from basic Establishment Clause principle."

These cases provide strikingly different ways of thinking about aid to religious schools. One might as well have two sets of eyeglasses through which to view the problem. Through one pair, students in church-related schools are merely the beneficiaries of government programs that extend benefits to a broad class of people without reference to religion. Through the other pair, government is an active participant in, and underwriter of, educational programs in religious schools, providing materials and services that the schools otherwise would have to purchase themselves, or do without.

## THE FREE EXERCISE CLAUSE

Cases under the establishment clause typically test public policies that arguably *aid* religion. In contrast, cases under the free exercise clause challenge public policies that seem to *burden* religion.

Religious persecution—that is, penalizing people *because of* their religious beliefs—was undoubtedly the most obvious evil the free exercise clause was intended to prevent. Debate about this part of the First Amendment today, however, usually involves laws of general application that are religiously neutral in their content but in their application work a hardship on members of one faith or another. A law might forbid believers from doing what their faith requires, or it might require them to do something their faith forbids. Does the free exercise clause entitle them to a **faith-based exemption** from an otherwise valid law? The answer given to that question largely follows from how judges perceive the free exercise clause itself. Does it embody merely a nondiscrimination principle that protects believers from hostile legislation, or does it also elevate religious practice to a preferred status? Of course, chaos would result if everyone received an exemption from a law just because it ran counter to the tenets of one's faith. Still, the free exercise clause suggests that the government should not always prevail when the commands of the state and the dictates of faith pull in opposite directions.

This conflict lay at the heart of the first major decision under the free exercise clause. *Reynolds* v. *United States* (1879) upheld application of a law criminalizing polygamy in federal territories to a Mormon whose religion included the practice of polygamy. Chief Justice Waite emphasized the sovereignty of the individual over religious belief but the sovereignty of the state over conduct, a distinction that prevailed for over eight decades. "Congress was deprived of all legislative power over mere opinion," he wrote, "but was left free to reach actions which were in violation of social duties, or subversive of good order."

**THE FLAG-SALUTE CASES.** In one of the first applications of the free exercise clause to the states, the Court sustained a policy requiring all schoolchildren, over the religious objection of Jehovah's Witnesses, to salute the American flag (***Minersville School District* v. *Gobitis***). Justice Frankfurter's opinion even garnered support from liberal Justices Black, Douglas, and Murphy. Only Justice Stone dissented. In an effort to win Stone's support, Frankfurter wrote his colleague at length in a letter reprinted in this chapter, arguing that the case be decided "in the particular setting of our time and circumstances." "It is relevant," he pleaded, "to make the adjustment we have to make within the framework of present circumstances and those that are clearly ahead of us." The year was 1940, soon after Hitler unleashed his diabolical blitzkrieg in Europe and as British forces were being evacuated from the beaches at Dunkirk.

Two years later, Black, Douglas, and Murphy, in a remarkable about-face, recanted:

> Since we joined in the opinion in the Gobitis case, we think this is an appropriate occasion to state that we now believe that it was also wrongly decided. Certainly our democratic form of government functioning under the historical Bill of Rights has a high responsibility to accommodate itself to the religious views of minorities however unpopular and unorthodox those views may be. The First Amendment does not put the right freely to exercise religion in a subordinate position. We fear, however, that the opinion in these and the Gobitis case do exactly that (*Jones* v. *Opelika,* 1942).

Encouraged by the Opelika dissent and the appointment of Justices Jackson and Rutledge, Walter Barnette and several other Jehovah's Witnesses brought suit to enjoin enforcement of the flag salute against their children. Voting 6–3 (***West Virginia State Board of Education* v. *Barnette***), the Court reversed itself in 1943, holding that First Amendment freedoms may be restricted "only to prevent grave and immediate dangers." There are few instances in the Court's history in which the change of views and of judicial personnel were so quickly reflected in judicial decisions. However, *Barnette* turned on the free-speech clause, not the free exercise clause. The flag-salute rule was unconstitutional as applied to anyone, regardless of whether the objection was religiously based, so the *Reynolds* rule remained in force.

**THE CHECKERED CAREER OF RELIGIOUSLY BASED EXEMPTIONS.** The first occasion in which the Supreme Court, resting its decision squarely on the free exercise clause, ordered a faith-based exemption to an otherwise valid policy came in ***Sherbert* v. *Verner*** (1963). (Earlier decisions in addition to *Barnette* had invalidated application of state laws to religiously inspired conduct, but the Court treated these as free-speech cases.) South Carolina law denied unemployment compensation to someone available for work who refused to accept a job. Adell Sherbert, a Seventh-Day Adventist, refused to work on Saturday, lost her job because of her refusal, but was otherwise available for work. No one claimed that South Carolina intended to persecute members of this particular church, but as applied to her, the policy required her to choose between a job and religious disobedience, on the one hand, and no compensation and religious obedience, on the other. A majority of the justices found the law unconstitutional *as applied to Adell Sherbert,* because it unduly burdened her faith. The state had not convinced the justices that it had compelling reasons for denying the unemployment benefits. Faith trumped law.

This decision encouraged adjudication of other free exercise claims. For example, *Sherbert* was authority for *Wisconsin* v. *Yoder* (1972), which exempted Old Order Amish from a state law requiring parents to send their children to school until the age of 16. An all but unanimous bench concluded that the rule compelled the Amish, who are a separatist sect and who do not provide formal education beyond the eighth grade, "to perform acts undeniably at odds with fundamental tenets of their religious beliefs. . . . [C]ompulsory school attendance . . . carries with it a very real threat of undermining the Amish community and religious practice as they exist today; they must either abandon belief and be assimilated into society at large, or be forced to migrate to some other and more tolerant region. . . ." Balanced was the threat to the faith posed by the law against the state's interest in uniform minimum school attendance for all.

Neither *Sherbert* nor *Yoder,* however, should suggest that all free exercise claims during this period prevailed over government regulations. Especially when federal law was challenged, the Court appeared reluctant to apply the free exercise clause with full force, as was seen in *United States* v. *Lee* (1982), which denied Amish an exemption from certain Social Security taxes. In 1988 the Court refused to block a road-building project by the U.S. Forest Service despite the Service's own finding that the road "would cause serious and irreparable damage to the sacred areas which are an integral and necessary part of the belief systems and lifeway of Northwest California Indian peoples" (*Lyng* v. *Northwest Indian Cemetery Protective Association*). Significantly, the claim by the Native American group went beyond most claims based on the free exercise clause. They did not ask for an exemption from application of a law but for the cancellation of the government's project.

Then in 1990, five justices not only refrained from expanding the Sherbert principle but took a step that confined *Sherbert* to its facts. **Employment Division v. Smith** ruled against two drug counselors who were fired from their jobs after they ingested peyote (a hallucinogen) as part of a religious ritual of the Native American Church. Oregon officials had denied them unemployment compensation because their loss of employment resulted from "misconduct." Under state law, peyote was a controlled substance, and its use was forbidden, even for religious purposes. The two ex-counselors cited scientific and anthropological evidence that the sacramental use of peyote was an ancient practice and was not harmful. The Supreme Court, however, concluded that when action based on religious belief runs afoul of a valid law of general application (even when, as in this case, the litigants had not been criminally charged), the latter prevails. Law trumped faith. *Smith* left *Sherbert* dangling by a hair.

*Smith* was widely criticized by religious organizations and civil liberties groups, and Congress responded. Believing that the Court in *Smith* made it too easy for government to infringe on religious liberty, Congress in 1993 passed the **Religious Freedom Restoration Act.** Resting on Congress's enforcement powers under Section 5 of the Fourteenth Amendment, RFRA sought to reverse *Smith* and to restore *Sherbert* v. *Verner* fully in situations where laws of general application conflicted with religious liberty. A test of RFRA did not take long to materialize. A Catholic church in Boerne, Texas, wanted to enlarge its building. Because of a historic preservation ordinance, however, the city refused to issue a permit. Under RFRA, Archbishop Flores argued, the city would need compelling justification to block construction; otherwise the church could proceed, even if a Wal-Mart or a Blockbuster Video could not. In *City of Boerne* v. *Flores* (1997) the Court ruled that Congress's noble intentions exceeded its authority. *Smith* embodied the meaning of the free exercise clause, and according to it the church could claim no faith-based exception under the preservation ordinance. Because RFRA altered that meaning, the act was unconstitutional. (For a recent congressional substitute for RFRA, see the second "Query" at the end of this essay.)

Nonetheless, *Smith* does not mean that the Court has declared open season on religious practice. The free exercise clause still guards against government hostility to religion that is covert as well as overt, as the Court declared unanimously in *Church of the Lukumi Babalu Aye, Inc.* v. *Hialeah* in 1993. The city council of this Florida city had passed a series of ordinances banning animal sacrifice, a central element of worship in Santeria, an Afro-Cuban religion. The ordinances prohibited nothing *except* religious practice and so amounted, in Justice Kennedy's words, to a "religious gerrymander." Because they were hardly religiously neutral, the Court judged them against the "compelling interest" test that the Court had applied in *Sherbert*. This was a standard the city could not meet.

## VALUES IN TENSION

Even though the religion clauses work together to guard religious freedom, they focus on different threats and so at times may be in tension. Rigorous insistence on separationist values may infringe free exercise. Rigorous application of free exercise values may create an establishment of religion. In granting the exemption that Adell Sherbert wanted, for example, the Court not only recognized the religious basis of her claim but aided religion as well. This is no isolated conflict. Reference has already been made to property tax exemptions for nonprofit organizations, including religious institutions, which the Court upheld in *Walz*. No one can deny that such exemptions amount annually to an enormous public subsidy; yet excluding religious institutions from the list of tax-exempt organizations would penalize groups because of their religious nature.

The conflict also arises in public education. Most public schools allow student clubs to meet in the school building during the school day or during a special activity period before or after classes. Because of the Supreme Court's interpretation of the establishment clause banning school-sponsored religious exercises, however, administrators in some schools have not extended the same opportunity to student religious clubs. But denying members of religious clubs a privilege that all other student organizations enjoy is arguably a violation of the free exercise, as well as the free-speech, clauses of the First Amendment. If the Chess Club and the Scuba Diving Club may meet, why not the Bible Club? Congress addressed this issue in 1984 when it passed the Equal Access Act that directs schools receiving federal financial assistance to follow a nondiscriminatory policy. In a case challenging nonrecognition of religious clubs at a high school in Omaha, Nebraska, the Court sided with the students and upheld the act (*Westside Community Schools* v. *Mergens,* 1990). A similar result followed in *Good News Club* v. *Milford Central School* (2001), reprinted in Chapter Eleven. Clearly, neither decision could satisfy fully the values of both the establishment and free exercise clauses.

In the coming years, these and other controversies will continue to probe the fuzzy boundaries of the establishment and free exercise clauses. The framers bequeathed certain values by way of a written Constitution and left it to later generations to apply those values to situations the framers could not foresee. The establishment clause calls for separation, while the free exercise clause leaves Americans free to work for objectives dictated by their faiths. Together, they guarantee that the division mandated by the one will forever be tested because of the freedom ensured by the other.

## KEY TERMS

| | | |
|---|---|---|
| establishment clause | Lemon test | released time |
| free exercise clause | endorsement test | shared time |
| accommodation | Agostini test | faith-based exemption |
| separation | coercion test | Religious Freedom |
| religious test | child-benefit theory | Restoration Act |

## QUERIES

**1.** The First Amendment's free speech clause protects expression of opinions and beliefs, including religious ones. Does the free exercise clause suggest additional protection for religious practice?

**2.** In 2000 Congress passed the Religious Land Use and Institutionalized Persons Act as a partial substitute for the Religious Freedom Restoration Act, which the Court set aside in *City of Bourne* v. *Flores*. A key provision of the new statute declares: "No government shall impose or implement a land use regulation in a manner that imposes a substantial burden on the religious exercise of a person, including a religious assembly or institution, unless the government demonstrates that imposition of the burden on that person, assembly, or institution (A) is in furtherance of a compelling governmental interest; and (B) is the least restrictive means of furthering that compelling governmental interest." The law applies "even if the burden results from a rule of general applicability" and includes regulations by entities receiving federal funds and regulations that affect interstate commerce. Is the new statute on firmer constitutional ground than RFRA?

**3.** After *Santa Fe Independent School District* v. *Doe,* what legitimate role remains for religious expression in public life? Consider that question in light of *Newdow* v. *U.S. Congress* (2002), where the U.S. Court of Appeals for the Ninth Circuit held unconstitutional both a 1954 statute that added "under God" to the Pledge of Allegiance to the Flag and a California school district's policy that included a voluntary recitation of the pledge as part of the school day. In the court's view, the 1954 act was invalid under the endorsement test and first prong of the Lemon test; the policy was invalid under the coercion test and the second prong of the Lemon test.

**4.** *Agostini* v. *Felton* reflects the current Court's toleration for religiously neutral policies that evenhandedly include publicly funded benefits for students in religious schools, especially where financial assistance flows to the religious school as a result of decision by a private individual such as a parent or student. In what respect did *Agostini* portend the outcome in *Zelman* v. *Simmons-Harris?* In what respect did the voucher case break new ground?

## SELECTED READINGS

CARTER, STEPHEN L. *The Culture of Disbelief.* New York: Basic Books, 1993.

FELDMAN, STEPHEN M. *Please Don't Wish Me a Merry Christmas: A Critical History of the Separation of Church and State.* New York: New York University Press, 1997.

HAMBURGER, PHILIP. *Separation of Church and State.* Cambridge, Mass.: Harvard University Press, 2002.

HOWE, MARK DEWOLFE. *The Garden and the Wilderness: Religion and Government in American Constitutional Theory.* Chicago: University of Chicago Press, 1965.

LOCKE, JOHN. *A Letter Concerning Toleration.* Indianapolis, Ind.: Bobbs-Merrill, 1979; originally published in 1689.

MCCONNELL, MICHAEL W. "The Origins and Historical Understanding of Free Exercise of Religion." 103 *Harvard Law Review* 1409 (1990).

MADISON, JAMES. "Memorial and Remonstrance Against Religious Assessments," 1785; reprinted as an appendix to *Everson v. Board of Education,* 330 U.S. 1, 63 (1947).

MANWARING, DAVID R. *Render Unto Caesar: The Flag-Salute Controversy.* Chicago: University of Chicago Press, 1962.

MUÑOZ, VINCENT PHILLIP. "James Madison's Principle of Religious Liberty." 97 *American Political Science Review* 17 (2003).

SMITH, STEVEN D. *Foreordained Failure: The Quest for a Constitutional Principle of Religious Freedom.* New York: Oxford University Press, 1995.

UROFSKY, MELVIN I. *Religious Freedom.* Santa Barbara, Calif.: ABC-CLIO, 2002.

## I. RELIGION IN PUBLIC SCHOOLS

### *Santa Fe Independent School District* v. *Doe*
### 530 U.S. 290, 120 S.Ct. 2266, 147 L.Ed. 2d 295 (2000)

http://laws.findlaw.com/us/530/290.html

Prior to 1995, a student elected as the student council chaplain at Santa Fe High School in Texas delivered a prayer over the public address system before each home varsity football game. Two families—one Mormon and the other Catholic—with students or former students at the school filed suit in the U.S. District Court for the Southern District of Texas challenging this practice under the establishment clause of the First Amendment. The district judge allowed the families (the "Does") to litigate anonymously. While the suit was pending, the school district adopted a different policy that authorized two student elections, the first to determine whether invocations should be delivered at games, and the second to select the person to deliver the invocations. After the students held elections authorizing such prayers and selecting a spokesperson, the district court entered an order modifying the policy to permit only nonsectarian, nonproselytizing prayer. In 1999, the U.S. Court of Appeals for the Fifth Circuit held that, even as modified by the district court, the football prayer policy was constitutionally unacceptable. Previously, the Fifth Circuit had allowed student-led prayer at high school graduation ceremonies that had been approved by a vote of the students and that was "nonsectarian and nonproselytizing" (*Jones* v. *Clear Creek*

*School District,* 1992). The Jones panel distinguished that situation from the facts in *Lee* v. *Weisman* where the Supreme Court, only months before, had declared out of bounds a policy allowing a member of the clergy to deliver the invocation at a middle school commencement in Rhode Island. The Supreme Court denied certiorari. In 1995 a different panel of the Fifth Circuit insisted that *Clear Creek* was inapplicable to sporting events (*Doe* v. *Duncanville School District,* 1995). The Fifth Circuit panel in the Santa Fe case adhered to its holding in *Duncanville.* Majority: Stevens, O'Connor, Kennedy, Souter, Ginsburg, Breyer. Dissenting: Rehnquist, Scalia, Thomas.

## JUSTICE STEVENS delivered the opinion of the Court. . . .

We granted the District's petition for certiorari, limited to the following question: "Whether petitioner's policy permitting student-led, student-initiated prayer at football games violates the Establishment Clause." We conclude, as did the Court of Appeals, that it does. . . .

In *Lee* v. *Weisman* (1992), we held that a prayer delivered by a rabbi at a middle school graduation ceremony violated [the Establishment] Clause. Although this case involves student prayer at a different type of school function, our analysis is properly guided by the principles that we endorsed in Lee.

As we held in that case:

> The principle that government may accommodate the free exercise of religion does not supersede the fundamental limitations imposed by the Establishment Clause. It is beyond dispute that, at a minimum, the Constitution guarantees that government may not coerce anyone to support or participate in religion or its exercise, or otherwise act in a way which "establishes a [state] religion or religious faith, or tends to do so."

In this case the District first argues that this principle is inapplicable . . . because the messages are private student speech, not public speech. It reminds us that "there is a crucial difference between government speech endorsing religion, which the Establishment Clause forbids, and private speech endorsing religion, which the Free Speech and Free Exercise Clauses protect." We certainly agree with that distinction, but we are not persuaded that the pregame invocations should be regarded as "private speech."

These invocations are authorized by a government policy and take place on government property at government-sponsored school-related events. . . .

The District has attempted to disentangle itself from the religious messages by developing the two-step student election process. The text of the . . . policy, however, exposes the extent of the school's entanglement. The elections take place at all only because the school "board *has chosen to permit* students to deliver a brief invocation and/or message" (emphasis added [by Justice Stevens]). The elections thus "shall" be conducted "by the high school student council" and "[u]pon advice and direction of the high school principal." The decision whether to deliver a message is first made by majority vote of the entire student body, followed by a choice of the speaker in a separate, similar majority election. Even though the particular words used by the speaker are not determined by those votes, the policy mandates that the "statement or invocation" be "consistent with the goals and purposes of this policy," which are "to solemnize the event, to promote good sportsmanship and student safety, and to establish the appropriate environment for the competition."

In addition to involving the school in the selection of the speaker, the policy, by its terms, invites and encourages religious messages. The policy itself states that the purpose of the message is "to solemnize the event." A religious message is the most obvious method of solemnizing an event. Moreover, the requirements that the message "promote good citizenship" and "establish the appropriate environment for competition" further narrow the types of message deemed appropriate, suggesting that a solemn, yet nonreligious, message, such as commentary on United States foreign policy, would be prohibited. Indeed, the only type of message that is expressly endorsed in the text is an "invocation"—a term that primarily describes an appeal for divine assistance. . . . Thus, the expressed purposes of the policy encourage the selection of a religious message, and that is precisely how the students understand the policy. . . .

The actual or perceived endorsement of the message, moreover, is established by factors beyond just the text of the policy. Once the student speaker is selected and the message composed, the invocation is then delivered to a large audience assembled as part of a regularly scheduled, school-sponsored function conducted on school property. . . .

In this context the members of the listening audience must perceive the pregame message as a public expression of the views of the majority of the student body delivered with the approval of the school administration. . . . Regardless of the listener's support for, or objection to, the message, an objective Santa Fe High School student will unquestionably perceive the inevitable pregame prayer as stamped with her school's seal of approval. . . .

School sponsorship of a religious message is impermissible because it sends the ancillary message to members of the audience who are nonadherents "that they are outsiders, not full members of the political community, and an accompanying message to adherents that they are insiders, favored members of the political community." The delivery of such a message—over the school's public address system, by a speaker representing the student body, under the supervision of school faculty, and pursuant to a school policy that explicitly and implicitly encourages public prayer—is not properly characterized as "private" speech.

The District next argues that its football policy is distinguishable from the graduation prayer in *Lee* because it does not coerce students to participate in religious observances. Its argument has two parts: first, that there is no impermissible government coercion because the pregame messages are the product of student choices; and second, that there is really no coercion at all because attendance at

an extracurricular event, unlike a graduation ceremony, is voluntary.

The reasons just discussed explaining why the alleged "circuit-breaker" mechanism of the dual elections and student speaker do not turn public speech into private speech also demonstrate why these mechanisms do not insulate the school from the coercive element of the final message. . . .

One of the purposes served by the Establishment Clause is to remove debate over this kind of issue from governmental supervision or control. We explained in *Lee* that the "preservation and transmission of religious beliefs and worship is a responsibility and a choice committed to the private sphere." The two student elections authorized by the policy, coupled with the debates that presumably must precede each, impermissibly invade that private sphere. . . . Although it is true that the ultimate choice of student speaker is "attributable to the students," the District's decision to hold the constitutionally problematic election is clearly "a choice attributable to the State."

The District further argues that attendance at the commencement ceremonies at issue in *Lee* "differs dramatically" from attendance at high school football games, which it contends "are of no more than passing interest to many students" and are "decidedly extracurricular," thus dissipating any coercion. . . . Attendance at a high school football game, unlike showing up for class, is certainly not required in order to receive a diploma. . . .

There are some students, however, such as cheerleaders, members of the band, and, of course, the team members themselves, for whom seasonal commitments mandate their attendance, sometimes for class credit. . . .

Even if we regard every high school student's decision to attend a home football game as purely voluntary, we are nevertheless persuaded that the delivery of a pregame prayer has the improper effect of coercing those present to participate in an act of religious worship.

The Religion Clauses of the First Amendment prevent the government from making any law respecting the establishment of religion or prohibiting the free exercise thereof.

By no means do these commands impose a prohibition on all religious activity in our public schools. Thus, nothing in the Constitution as interpreted by this Court prohibits any public school student from voluntarily praying at any time before, during, or after the schoolday. But the religious liberty protected by the Constitution is abridged when the State affirmatively sponsors the particular religious practice of prayer. . . .

[W]e assess the constitutionality of an enactment by reference to . . . *Lemon* v. *Kurtzman* (1971). . . . Under the Lemon standard, a court must invalidate a statute if it lacks "a secular legislative purpose." . . . [T]he text of the . . . policy alone reveals that it has an unconstitutional purpose. The plain language of the policy clearly spells out the extent of school involvement in both the election of the speaker and the content of the message. Additionally, the text of the . . . policy specifies only one, clearly preferred message—that of Santa Fe's traditional religious "invocation." Finally, the extremely selective access of the policy and other content restrictions confirm that it is not a content-neutral regulation that creates a limited public forum for the expression of student speech. . . .

The District, nevertheless, asks us to pretend that we do not recognize what every Santa Fe High School student understands clearly—that this policy is about prayer. . . . We refuse to turn a blind eye to the context in which this policy arose, and that context quells any doubt that this policy was implemented with the purpose of endorsing school prayer. . . .

Therefore, the simple enactment of this policy, with the purpose and perception of school endorsement of student prayer, was a constitutional violation. We need not wait for the inevitable to confirm and magnify the constitutional injury. . . .

This policy likewise does not survive a facial challenge because it impermissibly imposes upon the student body a majoritarian election on the issue of prayer. Through its election scheme, the District has established a governmental electoral mechanism that turns the school into a forum for religious debate. It further empowers the student body majority with the authority to subject students of minority views to constitutionally improper messages. The award of that power alone, regardless of the students' ultimate use of it, is not acceptable. . . .

Our examination of those circumstances above leads to the conclusion that this policy does not provide the District with the constitutional safe harbor it sought. The policy is invalid on its face because it establishes an improper majoritarian election on religion, and unquestionably has the purpose and creates the perception of encouraging the delivery of prayer at a series of important school events.

The judgment of the Court of Appeals is, accordingly, affirmed.

*It is so ordered.*

**CHIEF JUSTICE REHNQUIST, with whom JUSTICE SCALIA and JUSTICE THOMAS join, dissenting.**

The Court distorts existing precedent to conclude that the school district's student-message program is invalid on its face under the Establishment Clause. But even more disturbing than its holding is the tone of the Court's opinion; it bristles with hostility to all things religious in public life. Neither the holding nor the tone of the opinion is faithful to the meaning of the Establishment Clause, when it is recalled that George Washington himself, at the request of the very Congress which passed the Bill of Rights, proclaimed a day of "public thanksgiving and prayer, to be observed by acknowledging with grateful hearts the many and signal favors of Almighty God." . . .

[R]espondents in this case challenged the district's student-message program at football games before it had been put into practice. As the Court explained in *United States* v. *Salerno* (1987), the fact that a policy might "operate unconstitutionally under some conceivable set of circumstances is insufficient to render it wholly invalid." Therefore, the question is not whether the district's policy may be applied in violation of the Establishment Clause, but whether it inevitably will be. . . .

[T]he district's student-message policy should not be invalidated on its face. The Court applies *Lemon* and holds that the "policy is invalid on its face because it establishes an improper majoritarian election on religion, and unquestionably has the purpose and creates the perception of encouraging the delivery of prayer at a series of important school events." The Court's reliance on each of these conclusions misses the mark.

First, the Court misconstrues the nature of the "majoritarian election" permitted by the policy as being an election on "prayer" and "religion." To the contrary, the election permitted by the policy is a two-fold process whereby students vote first on whether to have a student speaker before football games at all, and second, if the students vote to have such a speaker, on who that speaker will be. It is conceivable that the election could become one in which student candidates campaign on platforms that focus on whether or not they will pray if elected. It is also conceivable that the election could lead to a Christian prayer before 90 percent of the football games. If, upon implementation, the policy operated in this fashion, we would have a record before us to review whether the policy, as applied, violated the Establishment Clause or unduly suppressed minority viewpoints. But it is possible that the students might vote not to have a pregame speaker, in which case there would be no threat of a constitutional violation. It is also possible that the election would not focus on prayer, but on public speaking ability or social popularity. And if student campaigning did begin to focus on prayer, the school might decide to implement reasonable campaign restrictions.

But the Court ignores these possibilities by holding that merely granting the student body the power to elect a speaker that may choose to pray, "regardless of the students' ultimate use of it, is not acceptable." The Court so holds despite that any speech that may occur as a result of the election process here would be private, not government, speech. The elected student, not the government, would choose what to say. Support for the Court's holding cannot be found in any of our cases. And it essentially invalidates all student elections. A newly elected student body president, or even a newly elected prom king or queen, could use opportunities for public speaking to say prayers. Under the Court's view, the mere grant of power to the students to vote for such offices, in light of the fear that those elected might publicly pray, violates the Establishment Clause.

Second, with respect to the policy's purpose, the Court holds that "the simple enactment of this policy, with the purpose and perception of school endorsement of student prayer, was a constitutional violation." But the policy itself has plausible secular purposes: "[T]o solemnize the event, to promote good sportsmanship and student safety, and to establish the appropriate environment for the competition." . . . The Court grants no deference to—and appears openly hostile toward—the policy's stated purposes, and wastes no time in concluding that they are a sham.

For example, the Court dismisses the secular purpose of solemnization by claiming that it "invites and encourages religious messages." . . . But it is easy to think of solemn messages that are not religious in nature, for example urging that a game be fought fairly. And sporting events often begin with a solemn rendition of our national anthem, with its concluding verse "And this be our motto: 'In God is our trust.' " Under the Court's logic, a public school that sponsors the singing of the national anthem before football games violates the Establishment Clause. . . .

The Court also relies on our decision in *Lee* v. *Weisman* to support its conclusion. In *Lee*, we concluded that the content of the speech at issue, a graduation prayer given by a rabbi, was "directed and controlled" by a school official. In other words, at issue in *Lee* was government speech. Here, by contrast, the potential speech at issue, if the policy had been allowed to proceed, would be a message or invocation selected or created by a student. That is, if there were speech at issue here, it would be private speech. The "crucial difference between government speech endorsing religion, which the Establishment Clause forbids, and private speech endorsing religion, which the Free Speech and Free Exercise Clauses protect," applies with particular force to the question of endorsement. . . .

Finally, the Court seems to demand that a government policy be completely neutral as to content or be considered one that endorses religion. This is undoubtedly a new requirement, as our Establishment Clause jurisprudence simply does not mandate "content neutrality." That concept is found in our First Amendment speech cases and is used as a guide for determining when we apply strict scrutiny. For example, we look to "content neutrality" in reviewing loudness restrictions

imposed on speech in public forums, and regulations against picketing. The Court seems to think that the fact that the policy is not content neutral somehow controls the Establishment Clause inquiry.

But even our speech jurisprudence would not require that all public school actions with respect to student speech be content neutral. . . . Schools do not violate the First Amendment every time they restrict student speech to certain categories. . . .

The policy at issue here may be applied in an unconstitutional manner, but it will be time enough to invalidate it if that is found to be the case. I would reverse the judgment of the Court of Appeals.

## II. STATE AID TO RELIGIOUS SCHOOLS

### *Lemon* v. *Kurtzman*
### 403 U.S. 602, 91 S.Ct. 2105, 29 L.Ed. 2d 745 (1971)
### http://laws.findlaw.com/us/403/602.html

This case marked the first time the Supreme Court ruled on the constitutionality of direct state financial support for sectarian schools. Pennsylvania's Nonpublic Elementary and Secondary Education Act of 1968 allowed the state to reimburse private schools directly for costs of teachers' salaries, textbooks, and instructional materials in specified secular subjects. Annual expenses under the law were $5 million, divided among some 1,181 nonpublic schools with an enrollment of 535,000 (more than 20 percent of the total number of students in the state). More than 96 percent of these students attended sectarian schools, most of which were operated by the Roman Catholic Church. The Court combined this case with a challenge to a Rhode Island law enacted in 1969, which authorized state officials to supplement the salaries of teachers of secular subjects in private schools by an amount not exceeding 15 percent of the teachers' annual salary. Rhode Island's nonpublic schools accommodated about 25 percent of the students in the state, of which about 95 percent attended Catholic schools. Some 250 teachers (all from Catholic schools) applied for benefits under the Rhode Island program. In a suit brought in the U.S. District Court for the District of Rhode Island, a three-judge court struck down the salary supplement plan as a violation of the establishment clause. In an action on similar grounds in the U.S. District Court for the Eastern District of Pennsylvania, a three-judge court found no constitutional defect in the Pennsylvania plan and dismissed the complaint. Majority (in the Pennsylvania case): Burger, Douglas, Black, Brennan, Harlan, Stewart, White, Blackmun. Not participating: Marshall. Majority (in the Rhode Island case): Burger, Douglas, Black,

Brennan, Harlan, Stewart, Marshall, Blackmun. Dissenting: White. (Justice White sided with the majority in the Pennsylvania case only because he believed the case should be remanded. However, he rejected the majority's conclusion that the law was unconstitutional on its face.)

**MR. CHIEF JUSTICE BURGER delivered the opinion of the Court. . . .**

The language of the Religion Clauses of the First Amendment is at best opaque, particularly when compared with other portions of the Amendment. Its authors did not simply prohibit the establishment of a state church or a state religion, an area history shows they regarded as very important and fraught with great dangers. Instead they commanded that there should be "no law respecting an establishment of religion." . . . A given law might not establish a state religion but nevertheless be one "respecting" that end in the sense of being a step that could lead to such establishment and hence offend the First Amendment.

Every analysis in this area must begin with consideration of the cumulative criteria developed by the Court over many years. Three such tests may be gleaned from our cases. First, the statute must have a secular legislative purpose; second, its principal or primary effect must be one that neither advances nor inhibits religion . . . ; finally, the statute must not foster "an excessive government entanglement with religion." . . .

Inquiry into the legislative purposes of the Pennsylvania and Rhode Island statutes affords no basis for a conclusion that the legislative intent was to advance religion. On the contrary, the statutes themselves clearly state that they are intended to enhance the quality of the secular education in all schools covered by the compulsory attendance laws. . . .

The two legislatures, however, have . . . recognized that church-related elementary and secondary schools have a significant religious mission and that a substantial portion of their activities is religiously oriented. They have therefore sought to create statutory restrictions designed to guarantee the separation between secular and religious educational functions and to ensure that State financial aid supports only the former. . . . We need not decide whether these legislative precautions restrict the principal or primary effect of the programs to the point where they do not offend the Religion Clauses, for we conclude that the cumulative impact of the entire relationship arising under the statutes in each State involves excessive entanglement between government and religion. . . .

In *Walz* v. *Tax Commission,* the Court upheld state tax exemptions for real property owned by religious organizations and used for religious worship. That holding, however, tended to confine rather than enlarge the area of permissible state involvement with religious institutions by calling for close scrutiny of the degree of entanglement involved in the relationship. The objective is to prevent, as far as possible, the intrusion of either into the precincts of the other.

Our prior holdings do not call for total separation between church and state; total separation is not possible in an absolute sense. Some relationship between government and religious organizations is inevitable. Fire inspections, building and zoning regulations, and state requirements under compulsory school-attendance laws are examples of necessary and permissible contacts. Indeed, under the statutory exemption before us in *Walz,* the State had a continuing burden to ascertain that the exempt property was in fact being used for religious worship. Judicial caveats against entanglement must recognize that the line of separation, far from being a "wall," is a blurred, indistinct, and variable barrier depending on all the circumstances of a particular relationship. . . .

In order to determine whether the government entanglement with religion is excessive, we must examine the character and purposes of the institutions that are benefited, the nature of the aid that the State provides, and the resulting relationship between the government and the religious authority. . . . The District Court [in the Rhode Island case] made extensive findings on the grave potential for excessive entanglement that inheres in the religious character and purpose of the Roman Catholic elementary schools of Rhode Island, to date the sole beneficiaries of the Rhode Island Salary Supplement Act.

The church schools involved in the program are located close to parish churches. This understandably permits convenient access for religious exercises since instruction in faith and morals is part of the total educational process. The school buildings contain identifying religious symbols such as crosses on the exterior and crucifixes, and religious paintings and statues either in the classrooms or hallways. Although only approximately 30 minutes a day are devoted to direct religious instruction, there are religiously oriented extracurricular activities. Approximately two-thirds of the teachers in these schools are nuns of various religious orders. Their dedicated efforts provide an atmosphere in which religious instruction and religious vocations are natural and proper parts of life in such schools.

On the basis of these findings the District Court concluded that the parochial schools constituted "an integral part of the religious mission of the Catholic Church." The dangers and corresponding entanglements are enhanced by the particular form of aid that the Rhode Island Act provides. . . .

To ensure that no trespass occurs, the State has therefore carefully conditioned its aid with pervasive restrictions. An eligible recipient must teach only those courses that are offered in the public schools and use only those texts and materials that are found in the public schools. In addition the teacher must not engage in teaching any course in religion.

A comprehensive, discriminating, and continuing state surveillance will inevitably be required to ensure that these restrictions are obeyed and the First Amendment otherwise respected. Unlike a book, a teacher cannot be inspected once so as to determine the extent and intent of his or her personal beliefs and subjective acceptance of the limitations imposed by

the First Amendment. These prophylactic contacts will involve excessive and enduring entanglement between state and church. . . .

There is another area of entanglement in the Rhode Island program that gives concern. The statute excludes teachers employed by non-public schools whose average per-pupil expenditures on secular education equal or exceed the comparable figures for public schools. In the event that the total expenditures of an otherwise eligible school exceed this norm, the program requires the government to examine the school's records in order to determine how much of the total expenditures is attributable to secular education and how much to religious activity. This kind of state inspection and evaluation of the religious content of a religious organization is fraught with the sort of entanglement that the Constitution forbids. It is a relationship pregnant with dangers of excessive government direction of church schools and hence of churches. . . .

The complaint [in the Pennsylvania case] describes an educational system that is very similar to the one existing in Rhode Island. . . . [T]he very restrictions and surveillance necessary to ensure that teachers play a strictly nonideological role give rise to entanglements between church and state. The Pennsylvania statute, like that of Rhode Island, fosters this kind of relationship. . . .

The Pennsylvania statute, moreover, has the further defect of providing state financial aid directly to the church-related school. . . . The history of government grants of a continuing cash subsidy indicates that such programs have almost always been accompanied by varying measures of control and surveillance. The government cash grants before us now provide no basis for predicting that comprehensive measures of surveillance and controls will not follow. In particular the government's post-audit power to inspect and evaluate a church-related school's financial records and to determine which expenditures are religious and which are secular creates an intimate and continuing relationship between church and state. . . .

A broader base of entanglement of yet a different character is presented by the divisive political potential of these state programs. In a community where such a large number of pupils are served by church-related schools, it can be assumed that state assistance will entail considerable political activity. Partisans of parochial schools, understandably concerned with rising costs and sincerely dedicated to both the religious and secular educational mission of their schools, will inevitably champion this cause and promote political action to achieve their goals. Those who oppose state aid, whether for constitutional, religious, or fiscal reasons, will inevitably respond and employ all of the usual political campaign techniques to prevail. Candidates will be forced to declare and voters to choose. It would be unrealistic to ignore the fact that many people confronted with issues of this kind will find their votes aligned with their faith.

Ordinarily political debate and division, however vigorous or even partisan, are normal and healthy manifestations of our democratic system of government, but political division along religious lines was one of the principal evils against which the First Amendment was intended to protect. . . . The potential divisiveness of such conflict is a threat to the normal political process. . . .

The potential for political divisiveness related to religious belief and practice is aggravated in these two statutory programs by the need for continuing annual appropriations and the likelihood of larger and larger demands as costs and populations grow. . . .

The judgment of the Rhode Island District Court . . . is affirmed. The judgment of the Pennsylvania District Court . . . is reversed, and the case is remanded for further proceedings consistent with this opinion.

MR. JUSTICE DOUGLAS, whom MR. JUSTICE BLACK joins, concurring . . . [omitted].

MR. JUSTICE BRENNAN, concurring . . . [omitted].

**MR. JUSTICE WHITE, dissenting. . . .**

The Court strikes down the Rhode Island statute on its face. No fault is found with the secular purpose of the program; there is no suggestion that the purpose of the program was aid to religion disguised in secular attire. Nor does the Court find that the primary effect of the program is to aid religion rather than to implement secular goals. The Court nevertheless finds that impermissible "entanglement" will result from administration of the program.

The Court thus creates an insoluble paradox for the State and the parochial schools. The State cannot finance secular instruction if it permits religion to be taught in the same classroom; but if it exacts a promise that religion not be so taught—a promise the school and its teachers are quite willing and on this record able to give—and enforces it, it is then entangled in the "no entanglement" aspect of the Court's Establishment Clause jurisprudence. . . .

With respect to Pennsylvania, the Court, accepting as true the factual allegations of the complaint, as it must for purpose of a motion to dismiss, would reverse the dismissal of the complaint and invalidate the legislation. The critical allegations, as paraphrased by the Court, are that "the church-related elementary and secondary schools are controlled by religious organizations, have the purpose of propagating and promoting a particular religious faith, and conduct their operations to fulfill that purpose.". . . From these allegations the Court concludes that forbidden entanglements would follow from enforcing compliance with the secular purpose for which the state money is being paid.

I disagree. There is no specific allegation in the complaint that sectarian teaching does or would invade secular classes supported by state funds. That the schools are operated to promote a particular religion is quite consistent with the view that secular teaching devoid of religious instruction can successfully be maintained. . . .

I do agree, however, that the complaint should have been dismissed for failure to state a cause of action. . . . Hence, I would reverse the judgment of the District Court and remand the case for trial, thereby holding the Pennsylvania legislation valid on its face but leaving open the question of its validity as applied to the particular facts of this case. . . .

## *Agostini* v. *Felton*
## 521 U.S. 203, 117 S.Ct. 1997, 138 L.Ed. 2d 391 (1997)
## http://laws.findlaw.com/us/521/203.html

In *Aguilar* v. *Felton* (1985) the Supreme Court, with Chief Justice Burger and Justices White, Rehnquist, and O'Connor dissenting, held that New York City's program that sent public school teachers into parochial schools to provide remedial education to disadvantaged children pursuant to Title I of the Elementary and Secondary Education Act of 1965 violated the First Amendment's establishment clause. The U.S. District Court for the Eastern District of New York then entered a permanent injunction reflecting that ruling. As a result Title I services were provided to parochial school students in mobile units parked off-site. Some ten years later, petitioners—the parties bound by the injunction—filed motions in the same court seeking relief from the injunction, arguing that *Aguilar* could not be squared with the Court's intervening establishment clause decisions. The District Court denied the motion on the merits, declaring that *Aguilar's* demise had "not yet occurred." The Second Circuit Court of Appeals affirmed. When the case reached the Supreme Court, the Solicitor General asked that *Aguilar* be overruled on a limited basis. This case is unusual not particularly because the Supreme Court changed its mind but because the Court did so on a reconsideration of the original case itself. Majority: O'Connor, Rehnquist, Scalia, Kennedy, Thomas. Dissenting: Stevens, Souter, Ginsburg, Breyer.

**JUSTICE O'CONNOR delivered the opinion of the Court. . . .**

In order to evaluate whether *Aguilar* has been eroded by our subsequent Establishment Clause cases, it is necessary to understand the rationale upon which *Aguilar,* as well as its companion case, *School Dist. of Grand Rapids* v. *Ball* (1985), rested.

In *Ball,* the Court evaluated two programs implemented by the School District of Grand Rapids, Michigan. The district's Shared Time program, the one most analogous to Title I, provided remedial and "enrichment" classes, at public expense, to students attending nonpublic schools. The classes were taught during regular school hours by publicly employed teachers, using materials purchased with public funds, on the premises of nonpublic schools. The Shared Time courses were in subjects designed to supplement the "core curriculum" of the nonpublic schools. Of the 41 nonpublic schools eligible for the program, 40 were "'pervasively sectarian'" in character—that is, "the purpos[e] of [those] schools [was] to advance their particular religions."

The Court conducted its analysis by applying the three-part test set forth in *Lemon* v. *Kurtzman* (1971). . . . The Court acknowledged that the Shared Time program served a purely secular purpose, thereby satisfying the first part of the so-called Lemon test. Nevertheless, it ultimately concluded that the program had the impermissible effect of advancing religion.

The Court found that the program violated the Establishment Clause's prohibition against "government-financed or government-sponsored indoctrination into the beliefs of a particular religious faith" in at least three ways. First, drawing upon the analysis in *Meek* v. *Pittenger* (1975), the Court observed that "the teachers participating in the programs may become involved in intentionally or inadvertently inculcating particular religious tenets or beliefs." *Meek* invalidated a Pennsylvania program in which full-time public employees provided supplemental "auxiliary services"—remedial and accelerated instruction, guidance counseling and testing, and speech and hearing services—to nonpublic school children at their schools. Although the auxiliary services themselves were secular, they were mostly dispensed on the premises of parochial schools, where "an atmosphere dedicated to the advancement of religious belief [was] constantly maintained." Instruction in that atmosphere was sufficient to create "[t]he potential for impermissible fostering of religion." . . .

The Court concluded that Grand Rapids' program shared these defects. As in *Meek,* classes were conducted on the premises of religious schools. Accordingly, a majority found a " 'substantial risk' " that teachers—even those who were not employed by the private schools—might "subtly (or overtly) conform their instruction to the [pervasively sectarian] environment in which they [taught]." The danger of "state-sponsored indoctrination" was only exacerbated by the school district's failure to monitor the courses for religious content. Notably, the Court disregarded the lack of evidence of any specific incidents of religious indoctrination as largely irrelevant, reasoning that potential witnesses to any indoctrination—the parochial school students, their parents, or parochial school officials—might be unable to detect or have little incentive to report the incidents.

The presence of public teachers on parochial school grounds had a second, related impermissible effect: It created a "graphic symbol of the 'concert or union or dependency' of church and state," especially when perceived by "children in their formative years." The Court feared that this perception of a symbolic union between church and state would "convey[] a message of government endorsement . . . of religion" and thereby violate a "core purpose" of the Establishment Clause.

Third, the Court found that the Shared Time program impermissibly financed religious indoctrination by subsidizing "the primary religious mission of the institutions affected." The Court separated its prior decisions evaluating programs that aided the secular activities of religious institutions into two categories: those in which it concluded that the aid resulted in an effect that was "indirect, remote, or incidental" (and upheld the aid); and those in which it concluded that the aid resulted in "a direct and substantial

advancement of the sectarian enterprise" (and invalidated the aid). . . .

The New York City Title I program challenged in *Aguilar* closely resembled the Shared Time program struck down in *Ball,* but the Court found fault with an aspect of the Title I program not present in *Ball:* The Board had "adopted a system for monitoring the religious content of publicly funded Title I classes in the religious schools. Even though this monitoring system might prevent the Title I program from being used to inculcate religion, the Court concluded, as it had in *Lemon* and *Meek,* that the level of monitoring necessary to be "certain" that the program had an exclusively secular effect would "inevitably resul[t] in the excessive entanglement of church and state," thereby running afoul of *Lemon's* third prong. . . .

Distilled to essentials, the Court's conclusion that the Shared Time program in *Ball* had the impermissible effect of advancing religion rested on three assumptions: (i) any public employee who works on the premises of a religious school is presumed to inculcate religion in her work; (ii) the presence of public employees on private school premises creates a symbolic union between church and state; and (iii) any and all public aid that directly aids the educational function of religious schools impermissibly finances religious indoctrination, even if the aid reaches such schools as a consequence of private decision-making. Additionally, in *Aguilar* there was a fourth assumption: that New York City's Title I program necessitated an excessive government entanglement with religion because public employees who teach on the premises of religious schools must be closely monitored to ensure that they do not inculcate religion.

Our more recent cases have undermined the assumptions upon which *Ball* and *Aguilar* relied. To be sure, the general principles we use to evaluate whether government aid violates the Establishment Clause have not changed since *Aguilar* was decided. For example, we continue to ask whether the government acted with the purpose of advancing or inhibiting religion, and the nature of that inquiry has remained largely unchanged. . . . Likewise, we continue to explore whether the aid has the "effect" of advancing or inhibiting religion. What has changed since we decided *Ball* and *Aguilar* is our understanding of the criteria used to assess whether aid to religion has an impermissible effect.

As we have repeatedly recognized, government inculcation of religious beliefs has the impermissible effect of advancing religion. Our cases subsequent to *Aguilar* have, however, modified in two significant respects the approach we use to assess indoctrination. First, we have abandoned the presumption erected in *Meek* and *Ball* that the placement of public employees on parochial school grounds inevitably results in the impermissible effect of state-sponsored indoctrination or constitutes a symbolic union between government and religion. In *Zobrest* v. *Catalina Foothills School Dist.* (1993), we examined whether the IDEA [Individuals with Disabilities Education Act] was constitutional as applied to a deaf student who sought to bring his state-employed sign-language interpreter with him to his Roman Catholic high school. We held that this was permissible, expressly disavowing the notion that "the Establishment Clause [laid] down [an] absolute bar to the placing of a public employee in a sectarian school." . . . Because the only government aid in *Zobrest* was the interpreter, who was herself not inculcating any religious messages, no government indoctrination took place and we were able to conclude that "the provision of such assistance [was] not barred by the Establishment Clause." *Zobrest* therefore expressly rejected the notion—relied on in *Ball* and *Aguilar*—that, solely because of her presence on private school property, a public employee will be presumed to inculcate religion in the students. *Zobrest* also implicitly repudiated another assumption on which *Ball* and *Aguilar* turned: that the presence of a public employee on private school property creates an impermissible "symbolic link" between government and religion. . . .

Second, we have departed from the rule relied on in *Ball* that all government aid that directly aids the educational function of religious schools is invalid. In *Witters* v. *Washington Dept. of Servs. for Blind* (1986), we held that the Establishment Clause did not bar a State

from issuing a vocational tuition grant to a blind person who wished to use the grant to attend a Christian college and become a pastor, missionary, or youth director. Even though the grant recipient clearly would use the money to obtain religious education, we observed that the tuition grants were "'made available generally without regard to the sectarian-nonsectarian, or public-nonpublic nature of the institution benefited.'" The grants were disbursed directly to students, who then used the money to pay for tuition at the educational institution of their choice. In our view, this transaction was no different from a State's issuing a paycheck to one of its employees, knowing that the employee would donate part or all of the check to a religious institution. In both situations, any money that ultimately went to religious institutions did so "only as a result of the genuinely independent and private choices of" individuals. . . .

*Zobrest* and *Witters* make clear that, under current law, the Shared Time program in *Ball* and New York City's Title I program in *Aguilar* will not, as a matter of law, be deemed to have the effect of advancing religion through indoctrination. Indeed, each of the premises upon which we relied in *Ball* to reach a contrary conclusion is no longer valid. First, there is no reason to presume that, simply because she enters a parochial school classroom, a full-time public employee such as a Title I teacher will depart from her assigned duties and instructions and embark on religious indoctrination, any more than there was a reason in *Zobrest* to think an interpreter would inculcate religion by altering her translation of classroom lectures. Certainly, no evidence has ever shown that any New York City Title I instructor teaching on parochial school premises attempted to inculcate religion in students. . . .

As discussed above, *Zobrest* also repudiates *Ball's* assumption that the presence of Title I teachers in parochial school classrooms will, without more, create the impression of a "symbolic union" between church and state. . . .

What is most fatal to the argument that New York City's Title I program directly subsidizes religion is that it applies with equal force when those services are provided off-campus, and *Aguilar* implied that providing the services off-campus is entirely consistent with the Establishment Clause. . . .

We turn now to *Aguilar's* conclusion that New York City's Title I program resulted in an excessive entanglement between church and state. Whether a government aid program results in such an entanglement has consistently been an aspect of our Establishment Clause analysis. . . .

Not all entanglements, of course, have the effect of advancing or inhibiting religion. Interaction between church and state is inevitable, and we have always tolerated some level of involvement between the two. Entanglement must be "excessive" before it runs afoul of the Establishment Clause. . . . The pre-*Aguilar* Title I program does not result in an "excessive" entanglement that advances or inhibits religion. As discussed previously, the Court's finding of "excessive" entanglement in *Aguilar* rested on three grounds: (i) the program would require "pervasive monitoring by public authorities" to ensure that Title I employees did not inculcate religion; (ii) the program required "administrative cooperation" between the Board and parochial schools; and (iii) the program might increase the dangers of "political divisiveness." Under our current understanding of the Establishment Clause, the last two considerations are insufficient by themselves to create an "excessive" entanglement. They are present no matter where Title I services are offered, and no court has held that Title I services cannot be offered off-campus. Further, the assumption underlying the first consideration has been undermined. In *Aguilar,* the Court presumed that full-time public employees on parochial school grounds would be tempted to inculcate religion, despite the ethical standards they were required to uphold. Because of this risk pervasive monitoring would be required. But after *Zobrest* we no longer presume that public employees will inculcate religion simply because they happen to be in a sectarian environment. . . .

To summarize, New York City's Title I program does not run afoul of any of three primary criteria we currently use to evaluate whether government aid has the effect of advancing religion: it does not result in governmental in-doctrination; define its recipients by reference to religion; or create an excessive entanglement. We therefore hold that a federally funded program providing supplemental, remedial instruction to disadvantaged children on a neutral basis is not invalid under the Establishment Clause when such instruction is given on the premises of sectarian schools by government employees pursuant to a program containing safeguards such as those present here. The same considerations that justify this holding require us to conclude that this carefully constrained program also cannot reasonably be viewed as an endorsement of religion. . . . Accordingly, we must acknowledge that *Aguilar,* as well as the portion of *Ball* addressing Grand Rapids' Shared Time program, are no longer good law. . . .

For these reasons, we reverse the judgment of the Court of Appeals and remand to the District Court with instructions to vacate its September 26, 1985, order.

*It is so ordered.*

**JUSTICE SOUTER, with whom JUSTICE STEVENS and JUSTICE GINSBURG join, and with whom JUSTICE BREYER joins in part, dissenting. . . .**

[T]he flat ban on subsidization antedates the Bill of Rights and has been an unwavering rule in Establishment Clause cases. . . . The rule expresses the hard lesson learned over and over again in the American past and in the experiences of the countries from which we have come, that religions supported by governments are compromised just as surely as the religious freedom of dissenters is burdened when the government supports religion. . . . The human tendency, of course, is to forget the hard lessons, and to overlook the history of governmental partnership with religion when a cause is worthy, and bureaucrats have programs. That tendency to forget is the reason for having the Establishment Clause (along with the Constitution's other structural and libertarian guarantees), in the hope of stopping the corrosion before it starts.

These principles were violated by the programs at issue in *Aguilar* and *Ball,* as a consequence of several significant features common to both Title I, as implemented in New York City before *Aguilar,* and the Grand Rapids Shared Time program: each provided classes on the premises of the religious schools, covering a wide range of subjects including some at the core of primary and secondary education, like reading and mathematics; while their services were termed "supplemental," the programs and their instructors necessarily assumed responsibility for teaching subjects that the religious schools would otherwise have been obligated to provide . . . ; the public employees carrying out the programs had broad responsibilities involving the exercise of considerable discretion . . . ; while the programs offered aid to nonpublic school students generally (and Title I went to public school students as well), participation by religious school students in each program was extensive . . . ; and, finally, aid under Title I and Shared Time flowed directly to the schools in the form of classes and programs, as distinct from indirect aid that reaches schools only as a result of independent private choice. . . .

What, therefore, was significant in *Aguilar* and *Ball* about the placement of state-paid teachers into the physical and social settings of the religious schools was not only the consequent temptation of some of those teachers to reflect the schools' religious missions in the rhetoric of their instruction, with a resulting need for monitoring and the certainty of entanglement. . . . What was so remarkable was that the schemes in issue assumed a teaching responsibility indistinguishable from the responsibility of the schools themselves. The obligation of primary and secondary schools to teach reading necessarily extends to teaching those who are having a hard time at it, and the same is true of math. Calling some classes remedial does not distinguish their subjects from the schools' basic subjects, however inadequately the schools may have been addressing them. . . .

There is simply no line that can be drawn between the instruction paid for at taxpayers' expense and the instruction in any subject that is not identified as formally religious. While it would be an obvious sham, say, to channel cash to religious schools to be credited only against the expense of "secular" instruction, the line between "supplemental" and general education is likewise impossible to draw. If a State may constitutionally enter the schools to teach in the manner in question, it must in constitutional principle be free to assume, or assume payment for, the entire cost of instruction provided in any ostensibly secular subject in any religious school. . . .

[I]f a line is to be drawn short of barring all state aid to religious schools for teaching standard subjects, the Aguilar-Ball line was a sensible one capable of principled adherence. It is no less sound, and no less necessary, today. . . . It is accordingly puzzling to find the Court insisting that the aid scheme administered under Title I and considered in *Aguilar* was comparable to the programs in *Witters* and *Zobrest.* Instead of aiding isolated individuals within a school system, New York City's Title I program before *Aguilar* served about 22,000 private school students, all but 52 of whom attended religious schools. . . .

Finally, instead of aid that comes to the religious school indirectly in the sense that its distribution results from private decisionmaking, a public educational agency distributes Title I aid in the form of programs and services directly to the religious schools. . . .

In sum, nothing since *Ball* and *Aguilar* and before this case has eroded the distinction between "direct and substantial" and "indirect and incidental." That principled line is being breached only here and now. . . .

[T]he object of Title I is worthy without doubt, and the cost of compliance is high. In the short run there is much that is genuinely unfortunate about the administration of the scheme under *Aguilar's* rule. But constitutional lines have to be drawn, and on one side of every one of them is an otherwise sympathetic case that provokes impatience with the Constitution and with the line. But constitutional lines are the price of constitutional government.

JUSTICE GINSBURG, with whom JUSTICE STEVENS, JUSTICE SOUTER, and JUSTICE BREYER join, dissenting . . . [omitted].

## *Zelman* v. *Simmons-Harris*
## 536 U.S. 639, 122 S.Ct. 2460, 153 L.Ed. 2d 604 (2002)
http://laws.findlaw.com/us/536/639.html

> Ohio's Pilot Project Scholarship Program provides tuition aid for certain students in
> the Cleveland City School District, the only qualifying district at the time of this liti-
> gation, to attend participating public or private schools of their parent's choosing and
> tutorial aid for students who choose to remain enrolled in public school. Both reli-
> gious and nonreligious schools in the district may participate, as may public schools
> in adjacent school districts. Tuition aid is distributed to parents according to financial
> need, and where the aid is spent depends solely upon where parents choose to en-
> roll their children. The number of tutorial assistance grants provided to students re-
> maining in public school must equal the number of tuition aid scholarships. In the
> 1999–2000 school year, 82% of the participating private schools had a religious af-
> filiation, none of the adjacent public schools participated, and 96% of the students
> participating in the scholarship program were enrolled in religiously affiliated
> schools. Cleveland school children also have the option of enrolling in community
> schools, which are funded under state law but run by their own school boards and
> receive twice the per-student funding as participating private schools, or magnet
> schools, which are public schools emphasizing a particular subject area, teaching
> method, or service, and for which the school district receives the same amount per
> student as it does for a student enrolled at a traditional public school. Simmons-
> Harris and other Ohio taxpayers sought to enjoin the program on the ground that it
> violated the establishment clause. In 1999 the U.S. District Court for the Northern
> District of Ohio granted them summary judgment, and the U.S. Court of Appeals for
> the Sixth Circuit affirmed in 2000. Majority: Rehnquist, Kennedy, O'Connor, Scalia,
> Thomas. Dissenting: Souter, Breyer, Ginsburg, Stevens.

**CHIEF JUSTICE REHNQUIST delivered
the opinion of the Court. . . .**

The question presented is whether [the
Ohio] program offends the Establishment
Clause of the United States Constitution. We
hold that it does not.

There are more than 75,000 children enrolled in the Cleveland City School District.
The majority of these children are from low-
income and minority families. Few of these
families enjoy the means to send their children to any school other than an inner-city
public school. For more than a generation,
however, Cleveland's public schools have
been among the worst performing public
schools in the Nation. . . .

It is against this backdrop that Ohio enacted, among other initiatives, its Pilot Project
Scholarship Program. . . .

The Establishment Clause of the First
Amendment, applied to the States through the
Fourteenth Amendment, prevents a State from
enacting laws that have the "purpose" or
"effect" of advancing or inhibiting religion. . . .
There is no dispute that the program challenged here was enacted for the valid secular
purpose of providing educational assistance
to poor children in a demonstrably failing
public school system. Thus, the question presented is whether the Ohio program nonetheless has the forbidden "effect" of advancing or
inhibiting religion.

To answer that question, our decisions have
drawn a consistent distinction between government programs that provide aid directly to
religious schools, . . . and programs of true private choice, in which government aid reaches
religious schools only as a result of the genuine and independent choices of private

individuals. . . . While our jurisprudence with respect to the constitutionality of direct aid programs has "changed significantly" over the past two decades, our jurisprudence with respect to true private choice programs has remained consistent and unbroken. Three times we have confronted Establishment Clause challenges to neutral government programs that provide aid directly to a broad class of individuals, who, in turn, direct the aid to religious schools or institutions of their own choosing. Three times we have rejected such challenges.

In *Mueller* [v. *Allen*], we rejected an Establishment Clause challenge to a Minnesota program authorizing tax deductions for various educational expenses, including private school tuition costs, even though the great majority of the program's beneficiaries (96%) were parents of children in religious schools. . . .

In *Witters* [v. *Washington*], we used identical reasoning to reject an Establishment Clause challenge to a vocational scholarship program that provided tuition aid to a student studying at a religious institution to become a pastor. Looking at the program as a whole, we observed that "[a]ny aid . . . that ultimately flows to religious institutions does so only as a result of the genuinely independent and private choices of aid recipients." . . .

Finally, in *Zobrest* [v. *Catalina Foothills School District*], we applied *Mueller* and *Witters* to reject an Establishment Clause challenge to a federal program that permitted sign-language interpreters to assist deaf children enrolled in religious schools. Reviewing our earlier decisions, we stated that "government programs that neutrally provide benefits to a broad class of citizens defined without reference to religion are not readily subject to an Establishment Clause challenge." . . . Its "primary beneficiaries," we said, were "disabled children, not sectarian schools." . . .

*Mueller, Witters,* and *Zobrest* thus make clear that where a government aid program is neutral with respect to religion, and provides assistance directly to a broad class of citizens who, in turn, direct government aid to religious schools wholly as a result of their own genuine and independent private choice, the

program is not readily subject to challenge under the Establishment Clause. A program that shares these features permits government aid to reach religious institutions only by way of the deliberate choices of numerous individual recipients. The incidental advancement of a religious mission, or the perceived endorsement of a religious message, is reasonably attributable to the individual recipient, not to the government, whose role ends with the disbursement of benefits. . . .

We believe that the program challenged here is a program of true private choice, consistent with *Mueller, Witters,* and *Zobrest,* and thus constitutional. As was true in those cases, the Ohio program is neutral in all respects toward religion. It is part of a general and multifaceted undertaking by the State of Ohio to provide educational opportunities to the children of a failed school district. It confers educational assistance directly to a broad class of individuals defined without reference to religion, i.e., any parent of a school-age child who resides in the Cleveland City School District. The program permits the participation of *all* schools within the district, religious or nonreligious. Adjacent public schools also may participate and have a financial incentive to do so. Program benefits are available to participating families on neutral terms, with no reference to religion. . . .

Respondents suggest that even without a financial incentive for parents to choose a religious school, the program creates a "public perception that the State is endorsing religious practices and beliefs." But . . . [a]ny objective observer familiar with the full history and context of the Ohio program would reasonably view it as one aspect of a broader undertaking to assist poor children in failed schools, not as an endorsement of religious schooling in general.

There also is no evidence that the program fails to provide genuine opportunities for Cleveland parents to select secular educational options for their school-age children. Cleveland schoolchildren enjoy a range of educational choices: They may remain in public school as before, remain in public school with publicly funded tutoring aid, obtain a scholarship and choose a religious school, obtain a scholarship and choose a nonreligious private school, enroll in a community school, or enroll in a magnet school. That 46 of the 56 private schools now participating in the program are religious schools does not condemn it as a violation of the Establishment Clause. The Establishment Clause question is whether Ohio is coercing parents into sending their children to religious schools, and that question must be answered by evaluating *all* options Ohio provides Cleveland schoolchildren, only one of which is to obtain a program scholarship and then choose a religious school.

. . . Cleveland's preponderance of religiously affiliated private schools certainly did not arise as a result of the program; it is a phenomenon common to many American cities. Indeed, by all accounts the program has captured a remarkable cross-section of private schools, religious and nonreligious. It is true that 82% of Cleveland's participating private schools are religious schools, but it is also true that 81% of private schools in Ohio are religious schools. To attribute constitutional significance to this figure, moreover, would lead to the absurd result that a neutral school-choice program might be permissible in some parts of Ohio, such as Columbus, where a lower percentage of private schools are religious schools, but not in inner-city Cleveland, where Ohio has deemed such programs most sorely needed, but where the preponderance of religious schools happens to be greater. . . .

Respondents and Justice Souter claim that even if we do not focus on the number of participating schools that are religious schools, we should attach constitutional significance to the fact that 96% of scholarship recipients have enrolled in religious schools. They claim that this alone proves parents lack genuine choice, even if no parent has ever said so. We need not consider this argument in detail. . . . The constitutionality of a neutral educational aid program simply does not turn on whether and why, in a particular area, at a particular time, most private schools are run by religious organizations, or most recipients choose to use the aid at a religious school. . . .

This point is aptly illustrated here. The 96% figure upon which respondents and Justice Souter rely discounts entirely (1) the more than 1,900 Cleveland children enrolled in alternative community schools, (2) the more than 13,000 children enrolled in alternative magnet schools, and (3) the more than 1,400 children enrolled in traditional public schools with tutorial assistance. Including some or all of these children in the denominator of children enrolled in nontraditional schools during the 1999–2000 school year drops the percentage enrolled in religious schools from 96% to under 20%. . . .

Respondents finally claim that we should look to *Committee for Public Ed. & Religious Liberty* v. *Nyquist* (1973), to decide these cases. We disagree for two reasons. First, the program in *Nyquist* was quite different from the program challenged here. *Nyquist* involved a New York program that gave a package of benefits exclusively to private schools and the parents of private school enrollees. . . .

Second, were there any doubt that the program challenged in *Nyquist* is far removed from the program challenged here, we expressly reserved judgment with respect to "a case involving some form of public assistance (e.g., scholarships) made available generally without regard to the sectarian-nonsectarian, or public-nonpublic nature of the institution benefited." That, of course, is the very question now before us, and it has since been answered, first in *Mueller,* . . . then in *Witters,* . . . and again in *Zobrest.* . . .

In sum, the Ohio program is entirely neutral with respect to religion. It provides benefits directly to a wide spectrum of individuals, defined only by financial need and residence in a particular school district. It permits such individuals to exercise genuine choice among options public and private, secular and religious. The program is therefore a program of true private choice. In keeping with an unbroken line of decisions rejecting challenges to similar programs, we hold that the program does not offend the Establishment Clause.

The judgment of the Court of Appeals is reversed.

*It is so ordered.*

JUSTICE O'CONNOR, concurring . . . [omitted].

JUSTICE THOMAS, concurring . . . [omitted].

JUSTICE STEVENS, dissenting . . . [omitted].

**JUSTICE SOUTER, with whom JUSTICE STEVENS, JUSTICE GINSBURG, and JUSTICE BREYER join, dissenting. . . .**

If there were an excuse for giving short shrift to the Establishment Clause, it would probably apply here. But there is no excuse. Constitutional limitations are placed on government to preserve constitutional values in hard cases, like these. . . .

The applicability of the Establishment Clause to public funding of benefits to religious schools was settled in *Everson* v. *Board of Ed. of Ewing* (1947), which inaugurated the modern era of establishment doctrine. The Court stated the principle in words from which there was no dissent: "No tax in any amount, large or small, can be levied to support any religious activities or institutions, whatever they may be called, or whatever form they may adopt to teach or practice religion." . . .

How can a Court consistently leave *Everson* on the books and approve the Ohio vouchers? The answer is that it cannot. It is only by ignoring *Everson* that the majority can claim to rest on traditional law in its invocation of neutral aid provisions and private choice to sanction the Ohio law. It is, moreover, only by ignoring the meaning of neutrality and private choice themselves that the majority can even pretend to rest today's decision on those criteria. . . .

Viewed with the necessary generality, [Establishment Clause] cases can be categorized in three groups. In the period from 1947 to 1968, the basic principle of no aid to religion through school benefits was unquestioned. Thereafter for some 15 years, the Court termed its efforts as attempts to draw a line against aid that would be divertible to support the religious, as distinct from the secular, activity of an institutional beneficiary. Then, starting in 1983,

concern with divertibility was gradually lost in favor of approving aid in amounts unlikely to afford substantial benefits to religious schools, when offered evenhandedly without regard to a recipient's religious character, and when channeled to a religious institution only by the genuinely free choice of some private individual. Now, the three stages are succeeded by a fourth, in which the substantial character of government aid is held to have no constitutional significance, and the espoused criteria of neutrality in offering aid, and private choice in directing it, are shown to be nothing but examples of verbal formalism. . . .

Consider first the criterion of neutrality. . . .

In order to apply the neutrality test, then, it makes sense to focus on a category of aid that may be directed to religious as well as secular schools, and ask whether the scheme favors a religious direction. Here, one would ask whether the voucher provisions, allowing for as much as $2,250 toward private school tuition (or a grant to a public school in an adjacent district), were written in a way that skewed the scheme toward benefiting religious schools.

This, however, is not what the majority asks. The majority looks not to the provisions for tuition vouchers, but to every provision for educational opportunity. . . . The majority then finds confirmation that "participation of *all* schools" satisfies neutrality by noting that the better part of total state educational expenditure goes to public schools, thus showing there is no favor of religion.

The illogic is patent. If regular, public schools (which can get no voucher payments) "participate" in a voucher scheme with schools that can, and public expenditure is still predominantly on public schools, then the majority's reasoning would find neutrality in a scheme of vouchers available for private tuition in districts with no secular private schools at all. "Neutrality" as the majority employs the term is, literally, verbal and nothing more. . . . [P]ublic tutors may receive from the State no more than $324 per child to support extra tutoring (that is, the State's 90% of a total amount of $360), whereas the tuition voucher schools (which turn out to be mostly religious) can receive up to $2,250. . . .

The majority addresses the issue of choice the same way it addresses neutrality, by asking whether recipients or potential recipients of voucher aid have a choice of public schools among secular alternatives to religious schools. Again, however, the majority asks the wrong question and misapplies the criterion. The majority has confused choice in spending scholarships with choice from the entire menu of possible educational placements, most of them open to anyone willing to attend a public school. . . . The majority's view that all educational choices are comparable for purposes of choice thus ignores the whole point of the choice test: It is a criterion for deciding whether indirect aid to a religious school is legitimate because it passes through private hands that can spend or use the aid in a secular school. The question is whether the private hand is genuinely free to send the money in either a secular direction or a religious one. The majority now has transformed this question about private choice in channeling aid into a question about selecting from examples of state spending (on education) including direct spending on magnet and community public schools that goes through no private hands and could never reach a religious school under any circumstance. When the choice test is transformed from where to spend the money to where to go to school, it is cut loose from its very purpose.

Defining choice as choice in spending the money or channeling the aid is, moreover, necessary if the choice criterion is to function as a limiting principle at all. If "choice" is present whenever there is any educational alternative to the religious school to which vouchers can be endorsed, then there will always be a choice and the voucher can always be constitutional, even in a system in which there is not a single private secular school as an alternative to the religious school. . . . And because it is unlikely that any participating private religious school will enroll more pupils than the generally available public system, it will be easy to generate numbers suggesting that aid to religion is not the significant intent or effect of the voucher scheme. . . .

It is not, of course, that I think even a genuine choice criterion is up to the task of the

Establishment Clause when substantial state funds go to religious teaching. . . .

I do not dissent merely because the majority has misapplied its own law, for even if I assumed *arguendo* that the majority's formal criteria were satisfied on the facts, today's conclusion would be profoundly at odds with the Constitution. Proof of this is clear on two levels. The first is circumstantial, in the now-discarded symptom of violation, the substantial dimension of the aid. The second is direct, in the defiance of every objective supposed to be served by the bar against establishment.

The scale of the aid to religious schools approved today is unprecedented, both in the number of dollars and in the proportion of systemic school expenditure supported. Each measure has received attention in previous cases. On one hand, the sheer quantity of aid, when delivered to a class of religious primary and secondary schools, was suspect on the theory that the greater the aid, the greater its proportion to a religious school's existing expenditures, and the greater the likelihood that public money was supporting religious as well as secular instruction. . . .

When government aid goes up, so does reliance on it; the only thing likely to go down is independence. . . . A day will come when religious schools will learn what political leverage can do, just as Ohio's politicians are now getting a lesson in the leverage exercised by religion.

Increased voucher spending is not, however, the sole portent of growing regulation of religious practice in the school, for state mandates to moderate religious teaching may well be the most obvious response to the third concern behind the ban on establishment, its inextricable link with social conflict. . . .

[T]he intensity of the expectable friction can be gauged by realizing that the scramble for money will energize not only contending sectarians, but taxpayers who take their liberty of conscience seriously. Religious teaching at taxpayer expense simply cannot be cordoned from taxpayer politics, and every major religion currently espouses social positions that provoke intense opposition. Not all taxpaying

Protestant citizens, for example, will be content to underwrite the teaching of the Roman Catholic Church condemning the death penalty. Nor will all of America's Muslims acquiesce in paying for the endorsement of the religious Zionism taught in many religious Jewish schools, which combines "a nationalistic sentiment" in support of Israel with a "deeply religious" element. . . . Views like these, and innumerable others, have been safe in the sectarian pulpits and classrooms of this Nation not only because the Free Exercise Clause protects them directly, but because the ban on supporting religious establishment has protected free exercise, by keeping it relatively private. With the arrival of vouchers in religious schools, that privacy will go, and

along with it will go confidence that religious disagreement will stay moderate. . . .

*Everson*'s statement is still the touchstone of sound law, even though the reality is that in the matter of educational aid the Establishment Clause has largely been read away. True, the majority has not approved vouchers for religious schools alone, or aid earmarked for religious instruction. But no scheme so clumsy will ever get before us, and in the cases that we may see, like these, the Establishment Clause is largely silenced. I . . . hope that a future Court will reconsider today's dramatic departure from basic Establishment Clause principle.

JUSTICE BREYER, with whom JUSTICE STEVENS and JUSTICE SOUTER join, dissenting . . . [omitted].

## III. FREE EXERCISE OF RELIGION

### The Flag-Salute Cases:

#### *Minersville School District* v. *Gobitis*
#### 310 U.S. 586, 60 S.Ct. 1010, 84 L.Ed. 1375 (1940)
http://laws.findlaw.com/us/310/586.html

#### *West Virginia State Board of Education* v. *Barnette*
#### 319 U.S. 624, 63 S.Ct. 1178, 87 L.Ed. 1628 (1943)
http://laws.findlaw.com/us/319/624.html

One of the most dramatic reversals of a Court decision occurred in 1943 when a precedent of only three years' standing was overruled. Both cases presented the same issue: Could schoolchildren, members of the sect known as Jehovah's Witnesses, be required to salute the flag, a practice forbidden by their religious tenets? In the earlier case, the Court in an 8–1 decision reversed the district court and upheld the action of a Pennsylvania school board expelling two pupils; but in the later case, the Court held a similar action unconstitutional. It should be noted that this about-face was the result partly of personnel changes (which brought Justices Jackson and Rutledge to the bench) and partly of the change of viewpoint of Justices Black, Douglas, and Murphy. Court records misspelled the Gobitas and Barnett family names, hence the landmark decisions continue the error. In both cases, U.S. district courts ruled in favor of the Jehovah's Witnesses. In his *Judging Jehovah's Witnesses* (Lawrence: University Press of Kansas, 2000) Shawn Francis Peters calls the majority opinion in *Gobitis* "Felix's Fall-of-France Opinion" (p. 46). Majority in *Gobitis:* Frankfurter, Black, Douglas, Hughes, McReynolds, Murphy, Reed, Roberts. Dissenting: Stone. Majority in *Barnette:* Jackson, Black, Douglas, Murphy, Rutledge, Stone. Dissenting: Frankfurter, Reed, Roberts.

## *Minersville School District* v. *Gobitis* (1940)

**MR. JUSTICE FRANKFURTER delivered the opinion of the court. . . .**

Lillian Gobitis, aged twelve, and her brother William, aged ten, were expelled from the public schools of Minersville, Pennsylvania, for refusing to salute the national flag as part of a daily school exercise. . . .

The Gobitis children were of an age for which Pennsylvania makes school attendance compulsory. Thus they were denied a free education, and their parents had to put them into private schools. To be relieved of the financial burden thereby entailed, their father, on behalf of the children and in his own behalf, brought this suit. He sought to enjoin the authorities from continuing to exact participation in the flag-salute ceremony as a condition of his children's attendance at the Minersville School. . . .

We must decide whether the requirement of participation in such a ceremony, exacted from a child who refuses upon sincere religious grounds, infringes without due process of law the liberty guaranteed by the Fourteenth Amendment.

Centuries of strife over the erection of particular dogmas as exclusive or all-comprehending faiths led to the inclusion of a guarantee for religious freedom in the Bill of Rights. The First Amendment, and the Fourteenth through its absorption of the First, sought to guard against repetition of those bitter religious struggles by prohibiting the establishment of a state religion and by securing to every sect the free exercise of its faith. So pervasive is the acceptance of this precious right that its scope is brought into question, as here, only when the conscience of individuals collides with the felt necessities of society.

Certainly the affirmative pursuit of one's convictions about the ultimate mystery of the universe and man's relation to it is placed beyond the reach of law. Government may not interfere with organized or individual expression of belief or disbelief. Propagation of belief—or even of disbelief in the supernatural—is protected, whether in church or chapel, mosque or synagogue, tabernacle or meetinghouse. . . .

But the manifold character of man's relations may bring his conception of religious duty into conflict with the secular interests of his fellow-men. When does the constitutional guarantee compel exemption from doing what society thinks necessary for the promotion of some great common end, or from a penalty for conduct which appears dangerous to the general good? To state the problem is to recall the truth that no single principle can answer all of life's complexities. The right to freedom of religious belief, however dissident and however obnoxious to the cherished beliefs of others—even of a majority—is itself the denial of an absolute. But to affirm that the freedom to follow conscience has itself no limits in the life of a society would deny that very plurality of principles which, as a matter of history, underlies protection of religious toleration. . . . Our present task then, as so often the case with courts, is to reconcile two rights in order to prevent either from destroying the other. . . .

The religious liberty which the Constitution protects has never excluded legislation of general scope not directed against doctrinal loyalties of particular sects. Judicial nullification of legislation cannot be justified by attributing to the framers of the Bill of Rights views for which there is no historic warrant. Conscientious scruples have not, in the course of the long struggle for religious toleration, relieved the individual from obedience to a general law not aimed at the promotion or restriction of religious beliefs. The mere possession of religious convictions which contradict the relevant concerns of a political society does not relieve the citizen from the discharge of political responsibilities. The necessity for this adjustment has again and again been recognized.

. . . [T]he question remains whether school children, like the Gobitis children, must be excused from conduct required of all the other children in the promotion of national cohesion. We are dealing with an interest inferior to none in the hierarchy of legal values. National unity is the basis of national security. . . .

Situations like the present are phases of the profoundest problems confronting a democracy—the problem which Lincoln cast in memorable dilemma: "Must a government of necessity be too strong for the liberties of its people, or too weak to maintain its own existence?" No mere textual reading or logical talisman can solve the dilemma. And when the issue demands judicial determination, it is not the personal notion of judges of what wise adjustment requires which must prevail.

. . . [T]he case before us is not concerned with an exertion of legislative power for the promotion of some specific need or interest of secular society—the protection of the family, the promotion of health, the common defense, the raising of public revenues to defray the cost of government. But all these specific activities of government presuppose the existence of an organized political society. The ultimate foundation of a free society is the binding ties of cohesive sentiment. Such a sentiment is fostered by all those agencies of the mind and spirit which may serve to gather up the traditions of a people, transmit them from generation to generation, and thereby create that continuity of a treasured common life which constitutes a civilization. "We live by symbols." The flag is the symbol of our national unity, transcending all internal differences, however large, within the framework of the Constitution. . . .

The precise issue, then, for us to decide is whether the legislatures of the various states and the authorities in a thousand counties and school districts of this country are barred from determining the appropriateness of various means to evoke that unifying sentiment without which there can ultimately be no liberties, civil or religious. To stigmatize legislative judgment in providing for this universal gesture of respect for the symbol of our national life in the setting of the common school as a lawless inroad on that freedom of conscience which the Constitution protects, would amount to no less than the pronouncement of pedagogical and psychological dogma in a field where courts possess no marked and certainly no controlling competence. The influences which help toward a common feeling for the common country are manifold. Some may seem harsh and others no doubt are foolish. Surely, however, the end is legitimate. And the effective means for its attainment are still so uncertain and so unauthenticated by science as to preclude us from putting the widely prevalent belief in flag-saluting beyond the pale of legislative power. It mocks reason and denies our whole history to find in the allowance of a requirement to salute our flag on fitting occasions the seeds of sanction for obeisance to a leader.

The wisdom of training children in patriotic impulses by those compulsions which necessarily pervade so much of the educational process is not for our independent judgment. Even were we convinced of the folly of such a measure, such belief would be no proof of its unconstitutionality. . . . Perhaps it is best, even from the standpoint of those interests which ordinances like the one under review seek to promote, to give to the least popular sect leave from conformities like those here in issue. But the courtroom is not the arena for debating issues of educational policy. It is not our province to choose among competing considerations in the subtle process of securing effective loyalty to the traditional ideals of democracy, while respecting at the same time individual idiosyncracies among a people so diversified in racial origins and religious allegiances. So to hold would in effect make us the school board for the country. That authority has not been given to this Court, nor should we assume it. . . .

Judicial review, itself a limitation on popular government, is a fundamental part of our constitutional scheme. But to the legislature no less than to courts is committed the guardianship of deeply cherished liberties. . . . Where all the effective means of inducing political changes are left free from interference, education in the abandonment of foolish legislation is itself a training in liberty. To fight out the wise use of legislative authority in the forum of public opinion and before legislative assemblies rather than to transfer such a contest to the judicial arena, serves to vindicate the self-confidence of a free people.

*Reversed.*

MR. JUSTICE MCREYNOLDS concurs in the result.

### MR. JUSTICE STONE, dissenting. . . .

The guaranties of civil liberty are but guaranties of freedom of the human mind and spirit and of reasonable freedom and opportunity to express them. They presuppose the right of the individual to hold such opinions as he will and to give them reasonably free expression, and his freedom, and that of the state as well, to teach and persuade others by the communication of ideas. The very essence of the liberty which they guarantee is the freedom of the individual from compulsion as to what he shall think and what he shall say, at least where the compulsion is to bear false witness to his religion. If these guaranties are to have any meaning they must, I think, be deemed to withhold from the state any authority to compel belief or the expression of it where that expression violates religious convictions, whatever may be the legislative view of the desirability of such compulsion.

History teaches us that there have been but few infringements of personal liberty by the state which have not been justified, as they are here, in the name of righteousness and the public good, and few which have not been directed, as they are now, at politically helpless minorities. . . . The Constitution may well elicit expressions of loyalty to it and to the government which it created, but it does not command such expressions or otherwise give any indication that compulsory expressions of loyalty play any such part in our scheme of government as to override the constitutional protection of freedom of speech and religion. And while such expressions of loyalty, when voluntarily given, may promote national unity, it is quite another matter to say that their compulsory expression by children in violation of their own and their parents' religious convictions can be regarded as playing so important a part in our national unity as to leave school boards free to exact it despite the constitutional guarantee of freedom of religion. The very terms of the Bill of Rights preclude,

it seems to me, any reconciliation of such compulsions with the constitutional guaranties by a legislative declaration that they are more important to the public welfare than the Bill of Rights.

But even if this view be rejected and it is considered that there is some scope for the determination by legislatures whether the citizen shall be compelled to give public expression of such sentiments contrary to his religion, I am not persuaded that we should refrain from passing upon the legislative judgment "as long as the remedial channels of the democratic process remain open and unobstructed." This seems to me no more than the surrender of the constitutional protection of the liberty of small minorities to the popular will. We have previously pointed to the importance of a searching judicial inquiry into the legislative judgment in situations where prejudice against discrete and insular minorities may tend to curtail the operation of those political processes ordinarily to be relied on to protect minorities. See *United States* v. *Carolene Products Co.,* note 4 [reprinted in Chapter Eight]. And until now we have not hesitated similarly to scrutinize legislation restricting the civil liberty of racial and religious minorities although no political process was affected. . . .

Here we have such a small minority entertaining in good faith a religious belief, which is such a departure from the usual course of human conduct, that most persons are disposed to regard it with little toleration or concern. In such circumstances careful scrutiny of legislative efforts to secure conformity of belief and opinion by a compulsory affirmation of the desired belief, is especially needful if civil rights are to receive any protection. Tested by this standard, I am not prepared to say that the right of this small and helpless minority, including children having a strong religious conviction, whether they understand its nature or not, to refrain from an expression obnoxious to their religion, is to be overborne by the interest of the state in maintaining discipline in the schools.

The Constitution expresses more than the conviction of the people that democratic processes must be preserved at all costs. It is also an expression of faith and a command that freedom of mind and spirit must be preserved, which government must obey, if it is to adhere to that justice and moderation without which no free government can exist. For this reason it would seem that legislation which operates to repress the religious freedom of small minorities, which is admittedly within the scope of the protection of the Bill of Rights, must at least be subject to the same judicial scrutiny as legislation which we have recently held to infringe the constitutional liberty of religious and racial minorities. . . .

## Justice Frankfurter to Justice Stone, May 27, 1940: A *Qualified* Plea for Judicial Self-Restraint

Students of constitutional interpretation have wondered why it took Black and Douglas, two of the sharpest minds on the Court, both of them ardent liberals, so long to discover their error in joining Frankfurter's well-nigh unanimous opinion in the first Flag-Salute Case. A clue may be found in the letter Frankfurter wrote Stone in trying to win his vote. Hitler's armies were then on the march, threatening to envelop Europe. In this struggle America could not escape involvement.

SUPREME COURT OF THE UNITED STATES
WASHINGTON, D.C.

CHAMBERS
OF JUSTICE FELIX FRANKFURTER

MAY 27, 1940

DEAR STONE:

Were No. 690 an ordinary case, I should let the opinion speak for itself. But that you should entertain doubts has naturally stirred me to an anxious reexamination of my own views, even though I can assure you that nothing has weighed as much on my conscience, since I have come on this Court, as has this case. Your doubts have stirred me to a reconsideration of the whole matter, because I am not happy that you should entertain doubts that I cannot share or meet in a domain where constitutional power is on one side and my private notions of liberty and toleration and good sense are on the other. After all, the vulgar intrusion of law in the domain of conscience is for me a very sensitive area. For various reasons . . . a good part of my mature life has thrown whatever weight it has had against foolish and harsh manifestations of coercion and for the amplest expression of dissident views, however absurd or offensive these may have been to my own notions of rationality and decency. I say this merely to indicate that all my bias and predisposition are in favor in giving the fullest elbow room to every variety of religious, political, and economic view.

But no one has more clearly in his mind than you, that even when it comes to these ultimate civil liberties, insofar as they are protected by the Constitution, we are not in the domain of absolutes. Here, also, we have an illustration of what the

Greeks thousands of years ago recognized as a tragic issue, namely, the clash of rights, not the clash of wrongs. For resolving such clash we have no calculus. But there is for me, and I know also for you, a great makeweight for dealing with this problem, namely, that we are not the primary resolvers of the clash. We are not exercising an independent judgment; we are sitting in judgment upon the judgment of the legislature. I am aware of the important distinction which you so skillfully adumbrated in your footnote 4 (particularly the second paragraph of it) in the Carolene Products Co. case. I agree with that distinction; I regard it as basic. I have taken over that distinction in its central aspect, however inadequately, in the present opinion by insisting on the importance of keeping open all those channels of free expression by which undesirable legislation may be removed, and keeping unobstructed all forms of protest against what are deemed invasions of conscience, however much the invasion may be justified on the score of the deepest interests of national well-being.

What weighs with me strongly in this case is my anxiety that, while we lean in the direction of the libertarian aspect, we do not exercise our judicial power unduly, and as though we ourselves were legislators by holding with too tight a rein the organs of popular government. In other words, I want to avoid the mistake comparable to that made by those whom we criticized when dealing with the control of property. . . . I cannot rid myself of the notion that it is not fantastic, although I think foolish and perhaps worse, for school authorities to believe—as the record in this case explicitly shows the school authorities to have believed—that to allow exemption to some of the children goes far towards disrupting the whole patriotic exercise. And since certainly we must admit the general right of the school authorities to have such flag-saluting exercises, it seems to me that we do not trench on an undebatable territory of libertarian immunity to permit the school authorities a judgment as to the effect of this exemption in the particular setting of our time and circumstances.

For time and circumstances are surely not irrelevant considerations in resolving the conflicts that we do have to resolve in this particular case. . . . [C]ertainly it is relevant to make the adjustment that we have to make within the framework of present circumstances and those that are clearly ahead of us. . . . After all, despite some of the jurisprudential "realists," a decision decides not merely the particular case. . . . [S]o this case would have a tail of implications as to legislative power that is certainly debatable and might easily be invoked far beyond the size of the immediate kite, were it to deny the very minimum exaction, however foolish as to the Gobitis children, of an expression of faith in the heritage and purposes of our country.

For my intention—and I hope my execution did not lag too far behind—was to use this opinion as a vehicle for preaching the true democratic faith of not relying on the Court for the impossible task of assuring a vigorous, mature, self-protecting and tolerant democracy by bringing the responsibility for a combination of firmness and toleration directly home where it belongs—to the people and their representatives themselves. . . .

The duty of compulsion being as minimal as it is for an act, the normal legislative authorization of which certainly cannot be denied, and all channels of affirmative free expression being open to both children and parents, I cannot resist the conviction that we ought to let the legislative judgment stand and put the responsibility for its exercise where it belongs. In any event, I hope you will be good enough to give me the benefit of what you think should be omitted or added to the opinion.

Faithfully yours,
s/Felix Frankfurter

## West Virginia State Board of Education v. Barnette (1943)

**MR. JUSTICE JACKSON delivered the opinion of the Court....**

This case calls upon us to reconsider a precedent decision, as the Court throughout its history often has been required to do. Before turning to the Gobitis case, however, it is desirable to notice certain characteristics by which this controversy is distinguished....

There is no doubt that, in connection with the pledges, the flag salute is a form of utterance. Symbolism is a primitive but effective way of communicating ideas....

It is also to be noted that the compulsory flag salute and pledge requires [sic] affirmation of a belief and an attitude of mind.... To sustain the compulsory flag salute we are required to say that a Bill of Rights which guards the individual's right to speak his own mind, left it open to public authorities to compel him to utter what is not in his mind.

Whether the First Amendment to the Constitution will permit officials to order observance of ritual of this nature does not depend upon whether as a voluntary exercise we would think it to be good, bad or merely innocuous....

Nor does the issue as we see it turn on one's possession of particular religious views or the sincerity with which they are held. While religion supplies appellees' motive for enduring the discomforts of making the issue in this case, many citizens who do not share these religious views hold such a compulsory rite to infringe constitutional liberty of the individual. It is not necessary to inquire whether nonconformist beliefs will exempt from the duty to salute unless we first find power to make the salute a legal duty.

The Gobitis decision, however, *assumed,* as did the argument in that case and in this, that power exists in the State to impose the flag salute discipline upon school children in general. The Court only examined and rejected a claim based on religious beliefs of immunity from an unquestioned general rule. The question which underlies the flag salute controversy is whether such a ceremony so touching matters of opinion and political attitude may be imposed upon the individual by official authority under powers committed to any political organization under our Constitution....

The very purpose of a Bill of Rights was to withdraw certain subjects from the vicissitudes of political controversy, to place them beyond the reach of majorities and officials and to establish them as legal principles to be applied by the courts. One's right to life, liberty, and property, to free speech, a free press, freedom of worship and assembly, and other fundamental rights may not be submitted to vote; they depend on the outcome of no elections.

In weighing arguments of the parties it is important to distinguish between the due process clause of the Fourteenth Amendment as an instrument for transmitting the principles of the First Amendment and those cases in which it is applied for its own sake. The test of legislation which collides with the Fourteenth Amendment because it also collides with the principles of the First, is much more definite than the test when only the Fourteenth is involved. Much of the vagueness of the due process clause disappears when the specific prohibitions of the First become its standard. The right of a State to regulate, for example, a public utility may well include, so far as the due process test is concerned, power to impose all of the restrictions which a legislature may have a "rational basis" for adopting. But freedoms of speech and of press, of assembly, and of worship may not be infringed on such slender grounds. They are susceptible of restriction only to prevent grave and immediate danger to interests which the State may lawfully protect. It is important to note that while it is the Fourteenth Amendment which bears directly upon the State it is the more specific limiting principles of the First Amendment that finally govern this case.

Nor does our duty to apply the Bill of Rights to assertions of official authority depend upon our possession of marked competence in the field where the invasion of rights occurs. True, the task of translating the majestic generalities of the Bill of Rights, conceived as part of the pattern of liberal government in the eighteenth century, into concrete restraints on officials dealing with the problems of the twentieth century, is one to disturb self-confidence. . . . But we act in these matters not by authority of our competence but by force of our commissions. We cannot, because of modest estimates of our competence in such specialties as public education, withhold the judgment that history authenticates as the function of this Court when liberty is infringed. . . .

The case is made difficult not because the principles of its decision are obscure but because the flag involved is our own. Nevertheless, we apply the limitations of the Constitution with no fear that freedom to be intellectually and spiritually diverse or even contrary will disintegrate the social organization. To believe that patriotism will not flourish if patriotic ceremonies are voluntary and spontaneous instead of a compulsory routine is to make an unflattering estimate of the appeal of our institutions to free minds. We can have intellectual individualism and the rich cultural diversities that we owe to exceptional minds only at the price of occasional eccentricity and abnormal attitudes. When they are so harmless to others or to the State as those we deal with here, the price is not too great. But freedom to differ is not limited to things that do not matter much. That would be a mere shadow of freedom. The test of its substance is the right to differ as to things that touch the heart of the existing order.

If there is any fixed star in our constitutional constellation, it is that no official, high or petty, can prescribe what shall be orthodox in politics, nationalism, religion, or other matters of opinion or force citizens to confess by word or act their faith therein. If there are any circumstances which permit an exception, they do not now occur to us. . . .

The decision of this Court in *Minersville School District* v. *Gobitis* . . . [is] overruled, and the judgment enjoining enforcement of the West Virginia Regulation is affirmed.

MR. JUSTICE BLACK, with whom MR. JUSTICE DOUGLAS joins, concurring . . . [omitted].

MR. JUSTICE MURPHY, concurring . . . [omitted].

MR. JUSTICE ROBERTS, with whom MR. JUSTICE REED joins, dissenting . . . [omitted].

**MR. JUSTICE FRANKFURTER, dissenting.**

One who belongs to the most vilified and persecuted minority in history is not likely to be insensible to the freedoms guaranteed by our Constitution. Were my purely personal attitude relevant I should wholeheartedly associate myself with the general libertarian views in the Court's opinion, representing as they do the thought and action of a lifetime. But as judges we are neither Jew nor Gentile, neither Catholic nor agnostic. We owe equal attachment to the Constitution and are equally bound by our judicial obligations whether we derive our citizenship from the earliest or the latest immigrants to these shores. As a member of this Court I am not justified in writing my private notions of policy into the Constitution, no matter how deeply I may cherish them or how mischievous I may deem their disregard. . . . It can never be emphasized too much that one's own opinion about the wisdom or evil of a law should be excluded altogether when one is doing one's duty on the bench. . . .

There is no warrant in the constitutional basis of this Court's authority for attributing different roles to it depending upon the nature of the challenge to the legislation. Our power does not vary according to the particular provision of the Bill of Rights which is invoked. The right not to have property taken without just compensation has, so far as the scope of judicial power is concerned, the same constitutional dignity as the right to be protected against unreasonable searches and seizures, and the latter has no less claim than freedom of the press or freedom of speech or religious freedom. In no instance is this Court the primary protector of the particular liberty that is invoked. . . .

Of course patriotism cannot be enforced by the flag salute. But neither can the liberal spirit be enforced by judicial invalidation of illiberal legislation. Our constant preoccupation with the constitutionality of legislation rather than with its wisdom tends to preoccupation of the American mind with a false value. The tendency of focusing attention on constitutionality is to make constitutionality synonymous with wisdom, to regard a law as all right if it is constitutional. Such an attitude is a great enemy of liberalism. Particularly in legislation affecting freedom of thought and freedom of speech much which should offend a free-spirited society is constitutional. Reliance for the most precious interests of civilization, therefore, must be found outside of their vindication in courts of law. Only a persistent positive translation of the faith of a free society into the convictions and habits and actions of a community is the ultimate reliance against unabated temptations to fetter the human spirit.

## *Sherbert* v. *Verner*
## 374 U.S. 398, 83 S.Ct. 1790, 10 L.Ed. 2d 965 (1963)
## http://laws.findlaw.com/us/374/398.html

Adell Sherbert was a member of the Seventh-Day Adventist Church who lost her job in South Carolina because she would not work on Saturday, the Sabbath of her religion. After looking for other work and finding none because of her strictures against Saturday work, she filed a claim for unemployment compensation under South Carolina law. Her claim was denied because she failed to accept "suitable work when offered . . . by the employment office or the employer. . . ." This ruling of the Employment Security Commission was sustained by the Court of Common Pleas of Spartanburg County. The South Carolina Supreme Court affirmed. Majority: Brennan, Black, Clark, Douglas, Goldberg, Stewart, Warren. Dissenting: Harlan, White.

**MR. JUSTICE BRENNAN delivered the opinion of the Court. . . .**

We turn first to the question whether the disqualification for benefits imposes any burden on the free exercise of appellant's religion. We think it is clear that it does. In a sense the consequences of such a disqualification to religious principles and practices may be only an indirect result of welfare legislation within the State's general competence to enact; it is true that no criminal sanctions directly compel appellant to work a six-day week. But this is only the beginning, not the end, of our inquiry. For "[i]f the purpose or effect of a law is to impede the observance of one or all religions or is to discriminate invidiously between religions, that law is constitutionally invalid even though the burden may be characterized as being only indirect." Here not only is it apparent that appellant's declared ineligibility for benefits derives solely from the practice of her religion, but the pressure upon her to forgo that practice is unmistakable. The ruling forces her to choose between following the precepts of her religion and forfeiting benefits, on the one hand, and abandoning one of the precepts of her religion in order to accept work, on the other hand. Governmental imposition of such a choice puts the same kind of burden upon the free exercise of religion as would a fine imposed against appellant for her Saturday worship. . . .

We must next consider whether some compelling state interest enforced in the eligibility provisions of the South Carolina statute justifies the substantial infringement of appellant's First Amendment right. . . . No such abuse or danger has been advanced in the present case. The appellees suggest no more than a possibility that the filing of fraudulent claims by unscrupulous claimants feigning religious objections to Saturday work might not only dilute the unemployment compensation fund but also hinder the scheduling by employers of necessary Saturday work. But that possibility is not apposite here because no such objection appears to have been made before the South Carolina Supreme Court, and we are unwilling to assess the importance of an asserted state interest without the views of the state court. Nor, if the contention had been made below, would the record appear to sustain it; there is no proof whatever to warrant such fears of malingering or deceit as those which the respondents now advance. . . .

In holding as we do, plainly we are not fostering the "establishment" of the Seventh-day Adventist religion in South Carolina, for the extension of unemployment benefits to Sabbatarians in common with Sunday worshipers reflects nothing more than the governmental obligation of neutrality in the face of religious differences, and does not represent that involvement of religious with secular institutions which it is the object of the Establishment Clause to forestall. . . .

The judgment of the South Carolina Supreme Court is reversed and the case is remanded for further proceedings not inconsistent with this opinion.

*It is so ordered.*

Mr. Justice Douglas, concurring . . . [omitted].

### Mr. Justice Stewart concurring in the result. . . .

I think that the Court's approach to the Establishment Clause has on occasion . . . accorded to the Establishment Clause a meaning which neither the words, the history, nor the intention of the authors of that specific constitutional provision even remotely suggests.

. . . And the result is that there are many situations where legitimate claims under the Free Exercise Clause will run into head-on collision with the Court's insensitive and sterile construction of the Establishment Clause. The controversy now before us is clearly such a case.

Because the appellant refuses to accept available jobs which would require her to work on Saturdays, South Carolina has declined to pay unemployment compensation benefits to her. Her refusal to work on Saturdays is based on the tenets of her religious faith. The Court says that South Carolina cannot under these circumstances declare her to be not "available for work" within the meaning of its statute because to do so would violate her constitutional right to the free exercise of her religion.

Yet what this Court has said about the Establishment Clause must inevitably lead to a diametrically opposite result. If the appellant's refusal to work on Saturdays were based on indolence, or on a compulsive desire to watch the Saturday television programs, no one would say that South Carolina could not hold that she was not "available for work" within the meaning of its statute. That being so, the Establishment Clause as construed by this Court not only permits but affirmatively requires South Carolina equally to deny the appellant's claim for unemployment compensation when her refusal to work on Saturdays is based upon her religious creed. . . .

### Mr. Justice Harlan, whom Mr. Justice White joins, dissenting. . . .

The South Carolina Supreme Court has uniformly applied this law in conformity with its clearly expressed purpose. It has consistently held that one is not "available for work" if his unemployment has resulted not from the inability of industry to provide a job but rather from personal circumstances, no matter how compelling. . . .

Thus in no proper sense can it be said that the State discriminated against the appellant on the basis of her religious beliefs or that she was denied benefits because she was a Seventh-day Adventist. She was denied benefits just as any other claimant would be denied benefits who was not "available for work" for personal reasons. . . .

With this background, this Court's decision comes into clearer focus. What the Court is holding is that if the State chooses to condition unemployment compensation on the applicant's availability for work, it is constitutionally compelled to carve out an exception—and to provide benefits—for those whose unavailability is due to their religious convictions. . . .

My own view is that at least under the circumstances of this case it would be a permissible accommodation of religion for the State, if it chose to do so, to create an exception to its eligibility requirements for persons like the appellant. . . .

## *Employment Division* v. *Smith*
## 494 U.S. 872, 110 S.Ct. 1595, 108 L.Ed. 2d 876 (1990)
### http://laws.findlaw.com/us/494/872.html

In its controlled substance law, Oregon prohibits the knowing possession of a variety of drugs, including peyote, a cactus containing the hallucinogen mescaline. Alfred Smith and Galen Black were fired from their jobs with a private drug rehabilitation clinic because they ingested peyote as part of a ritual of the Native American Church. When they applied for unemployment compensation, the Employment Division of Oregon's Department of Human Resources ruled them ineligible because they had been dismissed for work-related misconduct. The state Court of Appeals reversed, holding that the denial of benefits violated their rights under the free exercise clause of the First Amendment. In 1986 the Supreme Court of Oregon affirmed. The U.S. Supreme Court remanded the case in 1988 for a determination whether the religious use of peyote was a violation of state law. The Oregon Supreme Court ruled that the statute provided no exception for religious use and held that under the free exercise clause the state could not deny unemployment benefits to those who engaged in the practice for religious reasons. Majority: Scalia, Rehnquist, White, Stevens, Kennedy, O'Connor. Dissenting: Blackmun, Brennan, Marshall.

**JUSTICE SCALIA delivered the opinion of the Court.**

This case requires us to decide whether the Free Exercise Clause of the First Amendment permits the State of Oregon to include religiously inspired peyote use within the reach of its general criminal prohibition on use of that drug, and thus permits the State to deny unemployment benefits to persons dismissed from their jobs because of such religiously inspired use. . . .

The free exercise of religion means, first and foremost, the right to believe and profess whatever religious doctrine one desires. Thus, the First Amendment obviously excludes all "governmental regulation of religious beliefs as such." The government may not compel affirmation of religious belief, punish the expression of religious doctrines it believes to be false, impose special disabilities on the basis of religious views or religious status, or lend its power to one or the other side in controversies over religious authority or dogma. . . .

Respondents in the present case, however, seek to carry the meaning of "prohibiting the free exercise [of religion]" one large step further. They contend that their religious motivation for using peyote places them beyond the reach of a criminal law that is not specifically directed at their religious practice, and that is concededly constitutional as applied to those who use the drug for other reasons. They assert, in other words, that "prohibiting the free exercise [of religion]" includes requiring any individual to observe a generally applicable law that requires (or forbids) the performance of an act that his religious belief forbids (or requires). As a textual matter, we do not think the words must be given that meaning. It is no more necessary to regard the collection of a general tax, for example, as "prohibiting the free exercise [of religion]" by those citizens who believe support of organized government to be sinful, than it is to regard the same tax as "abridging the freedom . . . of the press" of those publishing companies that must pay the tax as a condition of staying in business. It is a permissible reading of the text, in the one case as in the other, to say that if prohibiting the exercise of religion (or burdening the activity of printing) is not the object of the tax but merely the incidental effect of a generally applicable and otherwise valid provision, the First Amendment has not been offended. . . .

Our decisions reveal that the latter reading is the correct one. We have never held that an individual's religious beliefs excuse him from compliance with an otherwise valid law prohibiting conduct that the State is free to regulate. . . .

Our most recent decision involving a neutral, generally applicable regulatory law that compelled activity forbidden by an individual's religion was *United States* v. *Lee*. There, an Amish employer, on behalf of himself and his employees, sought exemption from collection and payment of Social Security taxes on the ground that the Amish faith prohibited participation in governmental support programs. We rejected the claim that an exemption was constitutionally required. There would be no way, we observed, to distinguish the Amish believer's objection to Social Security taxes from the religious objections that others might have to the collection or use of other taxes. "If, for example, a religious adherent believes war is a sin, and if a certain percentage of the federal budget can be identified as devoted to war-related activities, such individuals would have a similarly valid claim to be exempt from paying that percentage of the income tax. The tax system could not function if denominations were allowed to challenge the tax system because tax payments were spent in a manner that violates their religious belief." . . .

The only decisions in which we have held that the First Amendment bars application of a neutral, generally applicable law to religiously motivated action have involved not the Free Exercise Clause alone, but the Free Exercise Clause in conjunction with other constitutional protections, such as freedom of speech and of the press. . . .

The present case does not present such a hybrid situation, but a free exercise claim unconnected with any communicative activity or parental right. Respondents urge us to hold, quite simply, that when otherwise prohibitable conduct is accompanied by religious convictions, not only the convictions but the conduct itself must be free from governmental regulation. We have never held that, and decline to do so now. . . .

Respondents argue that even though exemption from generally applicable criminal laws need not automatically be extended to religiously motivated actors, at least the claim

for a religious exemption must be evaluated under the balancing test set forth in *Sherbert* v. *Verner*. Under the Sherbert test, governmental actions that substantially burden a religious practice must be justified by a compelling governmental interest. Applying that test we have, on three occasions, invalidated state unemployment compensation rules that conditioned the availability of benefits upon an applicant's willingness to work under conditions forbidden by his religion. We have never invalidated any governmental action on the basis of the Sherbert test except the denial of unemployment compensation. Although we have sometimes purported to apply the Sherbert test in contexts other than that, we have always found the test satisfied. In recent years we have abstained from applying the Sherbert test (outside the unemployment compensation field) at all. . . .

Even if we were inclined to breathe into *Sherbert* some life beyond the unemployment compensation field, we would not apply it to require exemptions from a generally applicable criminal law. . . .

. . . We conclude today that the sounder approach, and the approach in accord with the vast majority of our precedents, is to hold the test inapplicable to such challenges. . . .

Nor is it possible to limit the impact of respondent's proposal by requiring a "compelling state interest" only when the conduct prohibited is "central" to the individual's religion. It is no more appropriate for judges to determine the "centrality" of religious beliefs before applying a "compelling interest" test in the free exercise field, than it would be for them to determine the "importance" of ideas before applying the "compelling interest" test in the free speech field. What principle of law or logic can be brought to bear to contradict a believer's assertion that a particular act is "central" to his personal faith? Judging the centrality of different religious practices is akin to the unacceptable "business of evaluating the relative merits of differing religious claims." . . .

If the "compelling interest" test is to be applied at all, then, it must be applied across the board, to all actions thought to be religiously commanded. Moreover, if "compelling interest" really means what it says (and watering it down here would subvert its rigor in the other fields where it is applied), many laws will not meet the test. Any society adopting such a system would be courting anarchy, but that danger increases in direct proportion to the society's diversity of religious beliefs, and its determination to coerce or suppress none of them. Precisely because "we are a cosmopolitan nation made up of people of almost every conceivable religious preference," and precisely because we value and protect that religious divergence, we cannot afford the luxury of deeming presumptively invalid, as applied to the religious objector, every regulation of conduct that does not protect an interest of the highest order. The rule respondents favor would open the prospect of constitutionally required religious exemptions from civic obligations of almost every conceivable kind. . . .

Values that are protected against government interference through enshrinement in the Bill of Rights are not thereby banished from the political process. Just as a society that believes in the negative protection accorded to the press by the First Amendment is likely to enact laws that affirmatively foster the dissemination of the printed word, so also a society that believes in the negative protection accorded to religious belief can be expected to be solicitous of that value in its legislation as well. It is therefore not surprising that a number of States have made an exception to their drug laws for sacramental peyote use. But to say that a nondiscriminatory religious-practice exemption is permitted, or even that it is desirable, is not to say that it is constitutionally required, and that the appropriate occasions for its creation can be discerned by the courts. It may fairly be said that leaving accommodation to the political process will place at a relative disadvantage those religious practices that are not widely engaged in; but that unavoidable consequence of democratic government must be preferred to a system in which each conscience is a law unto itself or in which judges weigh the social importance of all laws against the centrality of all religious beliefs.

Because respondents' ingestion of peyote was prohibited under Oregon law, and because that prohibition is constitutional, Oregon may, consistent with the Free Exercise Clause, deny respondents unemployment compensation when their dismissal results from use of the drug. The decision of the Oregon Supreme Court is accordingly reversed.

*It is so ordered.*

JUSTICE O'CONNOR concurring in the judgment. . . . [She rejected the majority's reasoning, believing instead that the same result could be reached using the traditional analysis preferred by the dissenters.]

### JUSTICE BLACKMUN, with whom JUSTICE BRENNAN and JUSTICE MARSHALL join, dissenting.

This Court over the years painstakingly has developed a consistent and exacting standard to test the constitutionality of a state statute that burdens the free exercise of religion. Such a statute may stand only if the law in general, and the State's refusal to allow a religious exemption in particular, are justified by a compelling interest that cannot be served by less restrictive means.

Until today, I thought this was a settled and inviolate principle of this Court's First Amendment jurisprudence. The majority, however, perfunctorily dismisses it as a "constitutional anomaly." . . .

In weighing respondents' clear interest in the free exercise of their religion against Oregon's asserted interest in enforcing its drug laws, it is important to articulate in precise terms the state interest involved. It is not the State's broad interest in fighting the critical "war on drugs" that must be weighed against respondents' claim, but the State's narrow interest in refusing to make an exception for the religious, ceremonial use of peyote. . . .

The State's interest in enforcing its prohibition, in order to be sufficiently compelling to outweigh a free exercise claim, cannot be merely abstract or symbolic. The State cannot plausibly assert that unbending application of a criminal prohibition is essential to fulfill any compelling interest, if it does not, in fact, attempt to enforce that prohibition. In this case, the State actually has not evinced any concrete interest in enforcing its drug laws against religious users of peyote. Oregon has never sought to prosecute respondents, and does not claim that it has made significant enforcement efforts against other religious users of peyote. The State's asserted interest thus amounts only to the symbolic preservation of an unenforced prohibition. . . .

The State proclaims an interest in protecting the health and safety of its citizens from the dangers of unlawful drugs. It offers, however, no evidence that the religious use of peyote has ever harmed anyone. . . .

The fact that peyote is classified as a Schedule I controlled substance does not, by itself, show that any and all uses of peyote, in any circumstance, are inherently harmful and dangerous. The Federal Government, which created the classifications of unlawful drugs from which Oregon's drug laws are derived, apparently does not find peyote so dangerous as to preclude an exemption for religious use. . . .

Finally, the State argues that granting an exception for religious peyote use would erode its interest in the uniform, fair, and certain enforcement of its drug laws. The State fears that, if it grants an exemption for religious peyote use, a flood of other claims to religious exemptions will follow. . . .

The State's apprehension of a flood of other religious claims is purely speculative. Almost half the States, and the Federal Government, have maintained an exemption for religious peyote use for many years, and apparently have not found themselves overwhelmed by claims to other religious exemptions. Allowing an exemption for religious peyote use would not necessarily oblige the State to grant a similar exemption to other religious groups. The unusual circumstances that make the religious use of peyote compatible with the State's interests in health and safety and in preventing drug trafficking would not apply to other religious claims. Some religions, for example, might not restrict drug use to a limited ceremonial context, as does the Native American Church. Some religious claims involve drugs such as marijuana and heroin, in which there is significant illegal traffic, with its attendant greed and violence, so that it would be difficult to grant a religious exemption without seriously compromising law enforcement efforts. That the State might grant an exemption for religious peyote use, but deny other religious claims arising in different circumstances, would not violate the Establishment Clause. . . .

Finally, although I agree . . . that courts should refrain from delving into questions of whether, as a matter of religious doctrine, a particular practice is "central" to the religion, I do not think this means that the courts must turn a blind eye to the severe impact of a State's restrictions on the adherents of a minority religion. . . .

Respondents believe, and their sincerity has never been at issue, that the peyote plant embodies their deity, and eating it is an act of worship and communion. Without peyote, they could not enact the essential ritual of their religion. . . .

For these reasons, I conclude that Oregon's interest in enforcing its drug laws against religious use of peyote is not sufficiently compelling to outweigh respondents' right to the free exercise of their religion. Since the State could not constitutionally enforce its criminal prohibition against respondents, the interests underlying the State's drug laws cannot justify its denial of unemployment benefits. . . .

### City of Boerne v. Flores
**521 U.S. 507, 117 S.Ct. 2157, 138 L.Ed. 2d 624 (1997)**
http://laws.findlaw.com/us/521/507.html

(This case is reprinted in Chapter Two, beginning on page 71.)

# CHAPTER THIRTEEN

# *Privacy*

*The makers of our Constitution . . . conferred, as against the government, the right to be let alone—the most comprehensive of rights and the right most valued by civilized men.*

—Justice Louis D. Brandeis (1928)

The word *privacy* appears not once in the Constitution, yet some aspects of privacy or individual autonomy were recognized by the framers of the Constitution as fundamental—as essential elements of liberty. Today protection of certain privacy interests is integral to American constitutional law. Privacy is also an idea with few apparent limits. Paul Freund once called it a "greedy legal concept." What is privacy? How do questions of privacy involve the Constitution? How are judges supposed to decide what privacy encompasses?

## DIMENSIONS OF PRIVACY

Privacy denotes different things. For some it is a broad right "to be let alone." So put, **privacy** is almost synonymous with freedom. Accordingly, individuals should be allowed to make decisions about their lives without undue interference from others. Carried to an extreme, however, privacy would make organized society impossible. Every day, laws impinge on the liberty of individuals in numerous ways. Being in society means that people are by no means "let alone" to go their own direction entirely in their own way.

More narrowly conceived, privacy may mean physical separation from others. People enter their homes, close the door, and pull the shades for the express purpose of keeping themselves, their activities, and their belongings hidden from public view. Such ordinary actions make it plain that people intend to shield the interior from the prying eyes of neighbors, as well as those of the state.

Protecting one's reputation from defamatory comment is another dimension of privacy. As Chapter Eleven explained, courts must reconcile the privacy interest, recognized by the law of libel, with a competing interest—a free press—recognized by the First Amendment. A third and related dimension is control over information about oneself. Credit and medical records, academic transcripts, bank and credit card statements, and tax returns all contain information that the persons about whom the information is compiled may not intend to become public. **Informational privacy** fosters a dual concern: accuracy and access. Are the data correct, and who is allowed to see and use them? These are questions made more urgent in the age of computers and the Internet.

Privacy may also denote security from intrusion on the intimacies of life, a dimension that is the focus of this chapter. Certain decisions regarding companionship, marriage, and child rearing may not be entirely free of government restrictions, but they should preserve a core of freedom from outside restraint. This suggests a zone of autonomy, which the government may not penetrate without justification.

## PRIVATE LAW AND PUBLIC LAW BEGINNINGS

Not all dimensions of privacy involve the Constitution. Some are regulated by statute alone. From the beginning, American law has offered redress from physical trespass and intrusion, and libel actions have allowed damages when one's reputation has been besmirched. (Both are examples of **private law** at work: legal rules governing relations among individuals. **Public law** involves regulations overseeing the operations of government as well as relations between individuals and their governments. Constitutional law, for example, is a field of public law.) "At common law," Chief Justice Rehnquist has said, "even the touching of one person by another without consent and without legal justification was a battery." As the Supreme Court declared in *Union Pacific R. Co.* v. *Botsford* (1891), "No right is held more sacred, or is more carefully guarded, by the common law, than the right of every individual to the possession and control of his own person, free from all restraint or interference of others, unless by clear and unquestionable authority of law."

Threats to privacy or autonomy are the focus of several provisions of the Constitution. By banning religious tests for public office, Article VI protects the sanctity of personal religious beliefs, and the First Amendment guards rights of individual expression, religious and otherwise. The Third Amendment virtually proscribes the quartering of troops in homes. The Fourth Amendment proclaims "the right of the people to be secure in their persons, houses, papers and effects" and prohibits "unreasonable searches and seizures." The Fifth Amendment protects the integrity of the individual by curtailing the state's power to force people to be witnesses against themselves in criminal proceedings. The Fifth and the Fourteenth remove government's power to take away a person's "life, liberty, or property without due process of law." Spiritual and bodily integrity are important as well in the ban on "cruel and unusual punishments" in the Eighth Amendment. In its own way, each of these provisions addresses some dimension of personality or autonomy.

Yet it was not until after 1890 that "privacy" began to take on life as a subject of its own. In that year Boston attorneys Samuel Warren and Louis Brandeis published a seminal article called "The Right to Privacy." Their immediate concern was nondefamatory, but nonetheless offensive, gossip in the newspapers. Although existing law provided redress for libel and slander, Warren and Brandeis believed that persons should be able to sue for damages when certain kinds of unwanted, unpleasant information appeared in the press. The goal of Warren and Brandeis was law to guard "an inviolate personality," to enforce "the right of the individual to be left alone." The article was partly successful in stemming some of the abuses that troubled its authors. But the article's more lasting impact lay in stimulating thinking about the concept of privacy generally.

Privacy was at least a peripheral concern in several decisions by the U.S. Supreme Court before 1965. In *Meyer* v. *Nebraska* (1923), eight justices overturned a state statute that both prohibited the teaching of subjects in any language other than English and forbade the teaching of foreign languages to any pupil who had not passed the eighth grade. According to Justice McReynolds, liberty "denotes not merely freedom from bodily restraint but also the right of any individual to contract, to engage in any of the common occupations of life, to acquire useful knowledge, to marry, establish a home and bring up children . . . and generally to enjoy those privileges long recognized at common law as essential to the orderly pursuit of happiness by free men." Similarly, *Pierce* v. *Society of Sisters* (1925) invalidated an Oregon law forbidding parents from sending their children to private schools. The "liberty" of the Fourteenth Amendment was construed to include the right of the parents to direct the upbringing of their children.

In *Skinner* v. *Oklahoma* (1942), the Court struck down a compulsory sterilization scheme mandated by Oklahoma for certain classes of habitual criminals. Although the decision rested mainly on equal protection grounds (see the following chapter), Justice Douglas's majority opinion suggested a broader basis: "the Oklahoma legislation . . . involves one of the basic civil rights of man. Marriage and procreation are fundamental to the very existence and survival of the race." The foreign language and private school decisions had arguably been related to the First Amendment, although the Court construed them in traditional terms of "calling" and property. Yet in *Skinner* the right infringed was tied neither to the First Amendment nor to any other express constitutional provision, for that matter. Barely half a decade after discrediting judicial creation of substantive rights in the wake of President Roosevelt's Court-packing plan (see Chapter Six), the justices created another.

Justice Douglas was persistent. When a divided Court in *Public Utilities Commission* v. *Pollack* (1952) refused to recognize a right not to be disturbed by music in public conveyances, his dissent reflected Brandeis's influence: "Liberty in the constitutional sense must mean more than freedom from unlawful governmental restraint; it must include privacy as well, if it is to be a repository of freedom. The right to be left alone is indeed the beginning of all freedom."

The 1961 decision in **Mapp v. Ohio** (see Chapter Ten), in which the Court applied the exclusionary rule to the states as a way of putting "teeth" into the Fourth Amendment, was also proclaimed in the context of protecting privacy. Without the suppression of illegally acquired evidence, said Justice Clark, "the freedom from state invasions of privacy would be so ephemeral and so neatly severed from its conceptual nexus with the freedom from all brutish means of coercing evidence as not to merit this Court's high regard as a freedom 'implicit in the concept of ordered liberty.'" The same term witnessed an unsuccessful challenge in *Poe* v. *Ullman* to Connecticut's law banning the use of birth control devices. Dissenting, Justice

Harlan drew an analogy between the Connecticut law and the protections of the Fourth Amendment.

> Certainly the safeguarding of the home does not follow merely from the sanctity of property rights. The home derives its preeminence as the seat of family life. And the integrity of that life is something so fundamental that it has been found to draw to its protection the principles of more than one explicitly granted Constitutional right. . . . Of this whole "private realm of family life" it is difficult to imagine what is more private or more intimate than a husband and wife's marital relations. . . . [T]he intimacy of husband and wife is necessarily an essential and accepted feature of the institution of marriage, an institution which the State not only must allow, but which always and in every age it has fostered and protected. It is one thing when the State exerts its power either to forbid extra-marital sexuality altogether, or to say who may marry, but it is quite another when, having acknowledged a marriage and the intimacies inherent in it, it undertakes to regulate by means of the criminal law the details of that intimacy. . . .

Thus, by 1961, thinking about privacy had evolved well beyond Warren and Brandeis's article of 1890. The rudiments of a new constitutional right were at hand.

## INVIGORATING A RIGHT OF PRIVACY

The Connecticut anticontraceptive statute came before the Court again in 1965 in **Griswold v. Connecticut.** "Any person who uses any drug, medicinal article or instrument for the purpose of preventing conception," declared the act, "shall be fined not less than fifty dollars or imprisoned not less than sixty days nor more than one year or be both fined and imprisoned." Another statute provided, "Any person who assists, abets, counsels, causes, hires or commands another to commit any offense may be prosecuted and punished as if he were the principal offender." The first law had been on the books since 1879, but this was apparently only the second time anyone had been charged. Arrested and convicted were the state director of Planned Parenthood and a medical professor at Yale. Both had given instruction and advice to married persons.

Though it violated no express provision in the Constitution, the ban foundered on the right of privacy implicit in the Constitution. For the majority, Justice Douglas announced that no fewer than eight amendments (he named the First, Third, Fourth, Fifth, Sixth, Eighth, Ninth, and Fourteenth) "have penumbras, formed by emanations from those guarantees that give them life and substance." In other words, the specific guarantees in the Constitution implied others, equally important though unenumerated. By impinging on "an intimate relation of husband and wife . . ." the statute violated "a right of privacy older than the Bill of Rights. . . ." (Originally an astronomical term, **penumbra** is the partial shadow surrounding a complete shadow in an eclipse.)

If privacy is a penumbral right, how far does it extend? Two years later in *Loving* v. *Virginia,* the Court struck down Virginia's law banning interracial marriages. Relying mainly on the equal protection clause, Chief Justice Warren also drew authority from the constitutionally protected "freedom to marry"—"one of the vital personal rights essential to the orderly pursuit of happiness by free men." Then a 1968 decision, *Stanley* v. *Georgia,* invalidated a state law forbidding private possession of obscene material. Combining privacy as well as First Amendment interests, Justice Marshall reasoned, "Whatever may be the justifications for other statutes regulating obscenity, we do not think they reach into the privacy of one's home."

*Griswold* formed the basis of *Eisenstadt* v. *Baird,* a 1972 challenge to a Massachusetts statute that confined distribution of contraceptive devices to married people. According to Justice Brennan:

> If under *Griswold* the distribution of contraceptives to married persons cannot be prohibited, a ban on distribution to unmarried persons would be equally impermissible. It is true that in *Griswold* the right of privacy in question inhered in the marital relationship. Yet the marital couple is not an independent entity with a mind and heart of its own, but an association of two individuals each with a separate intellect and emotional makeup. If the right of privacy means anything, it is the right of the individual, married or single, to be free from unwarranted governmental intrusion into matters so fundamentally affecting a person as the decision whether to bear or beget a child.

## ABORTION

Abortion laws also affected the decision to bear a child. If a state could not proscribe birth control devices, could it nonetheless ban most abortions?

**NATIONALIZING A RIGHT TO ABORTION.** The landmark 7–2 decision in *Roe* v. *Wade* (1973) came early in the following year with an answer to that question. Stoking the flames of a political conflagration, Justice Blackmun's majority opinion acknowledged abortion as an aspect of the constitutionally protected right of privacy. "[W]hether it be founded in the Fourteenth Amendment's concept of personal liberty and restrictions upon state action, as we feel it is, or . . . in the Ninth Amendment's reservation of rights to the people, [it] is broad enough to encompass a woman's decision whether or not to terminate her pregnancy." Yet the right to abortion was not absolute. According to Blackmun,

> [A] state may properly assert important interests in safeguarding health, in maintaining medical standards, and in protecting potential life. At some point in pregnancy, these respective interests become sufficiently compelling to sustain regulation of the factors that govern the abortion decision. The privacy right involved, therefore, cannot be . . . absolute. . . . These interests are separate and distinct. Each grows in substantiality as the woman approaches term and, at a point during pregnancy, each becomes "compelling."

Roe called into question the abortion laws of nearly every state. In 1973, 21 states had highly restrictive laws similar to the one from Texas invalidated in *Roe* that permitted only those abortions necessary to preserve the woman's life. Typically, these laws dated from the nineteenth century. An additional 25 states also allowed some forms of therapeutic abortions: when continuation of the pregnancy would seriously impair the woman's health, when the fetus would probably be born with a grave and irremediable mental or physical defect, or when the pregnancy resulted from incest or rape. (These less restrictive statutes embodied some or all of the recommendations of the American Law Institute's Model Penal Code of 1962.) The remaining four states (Alaska, Hawaii, New York, and Washington) had repealed all criminal penalties for both elective and therapeutic abortions performed early in the pregnancy. After *Roe,* no outright ban in any state would be allowed before the twenty-fifth week of pregnancy. Even then, a need to protect a woman's life or health would always supersede a ban on later-term abortions.

Furthermore, by finding a protection for abortion in the Constitution, the Court nationalized the abortion debate. No longer would a state's abortion laws be the product of clashing interests within its own legislature. From 1973 forward, much of the battle between those who believed *Roe* was right and those who believed it was wrong would shift to Congress, presidential campaigns, and the federal courts. Moreover, *Roe* reinvigorated debate over the proper role of the Court as expositor of the Constitution.

**TESTING THE LIMITS OF *ROE*.** Those who opposed the new abortion right began almost at once to press for regulations limiting the availability of abortion and discouraging its use. *Planned Parenthood of Central Missouri* v. *Danforth* (1976) knocked down the parts of a statute (1) requiring a married woman to obtain consent of her spouse in most instances before undergoing an abortion; (2) requiring parental consent for an abortion if an unmarried woman was under 18 years of age; (3) banning abortion by saline amniocentesis; and (4) criminalizing a physician's failure to preserve the life and health of a fetus, whatever the stage of pregnancy.

*Bellotti* v. *Baird* (1979) invalidated a Massachusetts parental consent requirement for minors seeking an abortion. The decision was based on the lack of an adequate alternative or "bypass" procedure under which an abortion could be performed without parental consent. The Court's position was essentially a compromise: Neither parents nor minor would necessarily have the final word. Under *Bellotti,* a bypass must meet four criteria. First, the minor must be allowed to demonstrate to a third party (such as a judge) that she possesses the maturity to make the decision. Second, even if she is unable to demonstrate maturity, the minor must be allowed to show that the abortion would be in her best interest. Third, the minor's anonymity must be protected. Fourth, the bypass must be conducted speedily.

Aside from cases on when and how abortion might be performed, litigation also centered on government's discretion to fund some abortions but not others. *Maher* v. *Roe* (1977) upheld Connecticut's policy of granting Medicaid support for therapeutic abortions but not for elective ones. Against the state's argument that it could constitutionally discourage abortions in this fashion because of its rational interest in promoting childbirth, opponents charged that paying for childbirth but not for elective abortions burdened the exercise of a constitutional right, financially forcing poor women to carry a pregnancy full term.

The Court extended the Maher reasoning to Congress in *Harris* v. *McRae* (1980). The **Hyde Amendment** (so named because of its sponsor, Representative Henry Hyde of Illinois) went a step beyond Connecticut's restriction and barred federal Medicaid funds from being spent even on some medically necessary abortions. Only abortions necessary to save the life of the mother qualified. A majority of five concluded that a state was not required to pay for those Medicaid abortions for which federal reimbursement under the Hyde Amendment was unavailable. Neither was the Hyde Amendment itself unconstitutional. It placed no government obstacle, concluded the majority, in the way of an abortion. A poor woman was no worse off than if no Medicaid funds were available for any medical needs.

*Thornburgh* v. *American College of Obstetricians and Gynecologists* (1986) marked the last time that the Court struck down a comprehensive scheme of abortion regulations. At stake was a Pennsylvania statute governing consent, information, record keeping, determination of viability, care of the fetus, and the need for a second physician in postviability abortions. None of the challenged provisions survived. Justice Blackmun was openly impatient with regulations "seemingly designed to prevent a woman, with the advice of her physician, from exercising her freedom of choice." States "are not free, under the guise of protecting maternal health or potential life, to intimidate women into continuing pregnancies."

**IMPACT OF A CHANGING COURT.** The 7–2 majority for *Roe* in 1973 had shrunk to 5–4 by 1986. Retiring immediately after *Thornburgh,* Chief Justice Burger had already let it be known that he thought *Roe* was wrongly decided. The division on the bench in 1987 therefore made Justice Powell's retirement and the designation of a successor all the more critical. More than anything else, the widely held conviction that Judge Robert Bork would undermine the 1973 abortion decision led to his rejection by the Senate when President Reagan nominated him to take Powell's seat. (Bork's confirmation battle is reviewed in the Introduction.) Pro-choice and pro-life activists alike awaited the views of Justice Anthony Kennedy.

His views became partly known in *Webster* v. *Reproductive Health Services* (1989). In dispute was a Missouri statute, which (1) declared in its preamble that life begins at conception, (2) prohibited abortions performed in public facilities or by public employees, (3) prohibited public funding of abortion counseling, and (4) required viability testing prior to an abortion in a pregnancy of 20 weeks or more. Kennedy and four other justices voted to uphold the act. According to Chief Justice Rehnquist's opinion of the Court, the preamble merely expressed a point of view, and the restrictions on use of funds were valid under the Court's own prior decisions. The viability testing provision (the primary focus of both the majority and dissenting opinions) was constitutional because it "permissibly furthers the State's interest in protecting human life." Yet there were not five votes to overturn *Roe* v. *Wade* outright. Writing separately, Justice Scalia would have made that move. In his view the Constitution protected no right to abortion. Chief Justice Rehnquist and Justice White, both dissenters in *Roe,* might have been expected to agree. Justice O'Connor, however, was not prepared to go that far, preferring instead to accept the statute as not "impos[ing] an *undue burden* on a woman's abortion decision" (emphasis added).

*Roe,* however, did not survive unscathed. In addition to upholding a statute which the *Thornburgh* majority of 1986 surely would have struck down, Rehnquist went out of his way to lay aside *Roe's* trimester analysis which had rested on a balancing of the woman's decision to abort, the state's interest in her health, and the state's interest in prenatal life. Moreover, recall that *Roe* had declared the abortion right to be "fundamental," meaning that limits on the right would be approved only for "compelling" reasons. After *Webster,* at least in the view of Rehnquist, White, Kennedy, and Scalia, limits on abortion were now in the category with restrictions on many other forms of behavior and would be constitutional as long as they were "reasonable." O'Connor, who had dissented in *Thornburgh,* would accord the abortion right greater protection but still below the level that the four Webster dissenters (Brennan, Marshall, Blackmun, and Stevens) thought constitutionally required. For O'Connor, regulations were permissible unless they imposed an "**undue burden**" on the woman. As a result, the abortion right, practically speaking, occupied a lower category in the ranking of constitutionally protected liberties.

**THE REMNANTS OF *ROE.*** The retirements of Brennan in 1990 and Marshall in 1991 meant that the views of replacement Justices Souter and Thomas would be decisive. With the number of *Roe's* stalwart defenders reduced to two, both pro-life and pro-choice camps awaited the outcome of ***Planned Parenthood* v. *Casey,*** decided on the eve of the national presidential nominating conventions in 1992. Under review was a Pennsylvania law that imposed several conditions for obtaining an abortion, including informed consent, a 24-hour waiting period, parental consent for minors, spousal consent, and record-keeping requirements for medical personnel. The decision surprised both sides in the abortion controversy. It was neither the complete victory pro-life groups had sought nor the broad defeat pro-choice forces had feared. While the Court upheld all elements of the statute except the spousal consent provision, the fifth vote to overturn *Roe* v. *Wade* again failed to materialize. Confessing "reservations" about the correctness of *Roe* in 1973, Justices Souter, Kennedy, and O'Connor nonetheless reaffirmed what they termed "the central holding" of *Roe,* that abortion involved a constitutionally protected liberty that states were forbidden to burden unduly. Coupled with *Roe's* avowed champions Blackmun and Stevens, the alignment left *Roe's* avowed adversaries (White, Rehnquist, Scalia, and Thomas) in the minority.

Just as *Casey* had done for the race between Arkansas Governor Bill Clinton and President George Bush in the election of 1992, **Stenberg v. Carhart** (2000)— also decided only weeks before the summer nominating conventions—made it certain that the presidential campaigns of Vice President Albert Gore and Texas Governor George W. Bush could not ignore abortion. The case presented the Court with an opportunity to focus solely on a particular abortion procedure. As had 30 other states, Nebraska attempted to ban what it called "partial birth" abortions, those using the technique of "dilation and extraction" (D&X) instead of the more common methods of "vacuum aspiration," used early in pregnancy, and "dilation and evacuation" (D&E), used after the first trimester. But five justices held that "the woman's right to choose" overrode the state's interests in protecting the unborn and "the partially-born," preserving the integrity of the medical profession, and "erecting a barrier to infanticide." Nebraska's law fell for two reasons. First, its wording might have encompassed D&E abortions as well, thus imposing an undue burden by effectively eliminating abortions after the first trimester. Second, the statute lacked the exception for protecting the woman's health, as mandated by *Roe* and *Casey*. However, a legislature could cure both defects by redrafting the law. More fundamentally, some supporters of abortion rights oppose any partial-birth ban because it is based on the gruesomeness and cruelty of the procedure. Were a ban on D&X abortions to be upheld, they fear that gruesomeness could become a back-door attack on abortion rights, with a similar argument being made against the widely used D&E procedure.

On November 6, 2003, President Bush signed into law the first national ban on the same late-term abortion procedure that Nebraska had attempted to prohibit. Like Nebraska's, the statute crafted by Congress contains no exception for a woman's health. Legal challenges were launched immediately, on both privacy and federalism grounds.

*Casey* and *Carhart* point to several conclusions about the constitutional status of abortion. First, abortion no longer has status as a fundamental right but enjoys a kind of intermediate constitutional protection. Second, and as a consequence of the first, total or near-total bans on abortion are almost certainly unconstitutional. Third, the Court will accept restrictions on abortions that would have been rejected prior to 1989. Just how numerous and how burdensome restrictions may be, however, remains to be seen. Finally, more than at any time since 1973, a woman's freedom to terminate a pregnancy now depends largely on what her state legislature, Congress, and the executive branch allow. *Webster* and *Casey* may tolerate more regulations, but they do not require them.

# A DEVELOPING CONCEPT

As the previous sections demonstrate, a right once acknowledged invites application to new situations. The joint opinion in *Casey* recognized as much: "At the heart of liberty is the right to define one's own concept of existence, of meaning, of the universe, and of the mystery of human life." And as the Court has addressed personal autonomy in other contexts in recent years, it has tended to rest it more on the substantive "liberty" that derives from the due process clause, rather than, strictly speaking, on a right of privacy itself.

**FAMILIES.** At least since *Euclid* v. *Ambler Realty Co.* (1926), the Court has recognized the broad powers of states and localities in establishing zoning and other land use regulations. In 1974, against a claim based on privacy and other grounds, seven justices upheld a zoning ordinance in the Village of Belle Terre, New York, near the Stony Brook campus of the State University. Prohibited was occupancy of a dwelling by more than two unrelated persons as a "family." Permitted was occupancy by any number of persons related by blood, marriage, or adoption. The Court was willing to accept the community's judgment that in "families" larger than two, relationship rather than numbers chiefly determined the quality of life in a neighborhood (*Belle Terre* v. *Boraas*).

Such deference to local authorities was not dispositive three years later in *Moore* v. *East Cleveland*. Confronting the Court was an ordinance limiting occupancy of a dwelling unit to members of a family, where a "family" included only some categories of related persons. Specifically, Inez Moore lived with her two grandsons who were cousins, a category not within East Cleveland's definition of "family." In the city's eyes, one of the grandsons was an illegal occupant. In the eyes of five justices, the city's zoning rule impermissibly trod on a constitutional right. "Our decisions establish that the Constitution protects the sanctity of the family . . . ," wrote Justice Powell in a plurality opinion, and "prevents East Cleveland from standardizing its children—and its adults—by forcing all to live in certain narrowly defined family patterns."

As noted, *Meyer* v. *Nebraska* and *Pierce* v. *Society of Sisters* in the 1920s protected the right of parents to make decisions regarding the rearing of their children. Reaffirming that principle, *Troxel* v. *Granville* (2000) struck down a "breathtakingly broad" Washington State statute that permitted a court—subject only to the judge's determination of the child's best interests—to disregard and overturn any decision by a fit custodial parent concerning visitation, where a third party (a grandparent in this instance) affected by the decision filed a visitation petition. For Justice O'Connor's plurality opinion, "the liberty interest at issue in this case—the liberty of parents in the care, custody, and control of their children—is perhaps the oldest of the fundamental liberty interests recognized by this Court."

**THE RIGHT TO DIE.** Another aspect of autonomy concerns the refusal of medical treatment and, more recently, the choice of the manner and timing of one's death. Each is made more complex because medical technology can now sustain life well past the point where natural forces would have once brought death. The complexity is only heightened when a patient is comatose.

The seminal decision is In re *Quinlan* (1976), in which the New Jersey Supreme Court held that the father of Karen Quinlan could approve the removal of the respirator from his daughter, who had suffered severe brain damage in an accident. In the state court's view, Karen Quinlan's right of privacy under the U.S. Constitution included the right to terminate treatment. The court dismissed her previous statements on the subject because they were both casual and equivocal. Instead, it allowed her family (subject to approval by an ethics committee) to make the decision for her. The "only practical way to prevent destruction of the right is to permit the guardian and family of Karen to render their best judgment . . . as to whether she would exercise it in these circumstances."

The general liberty of the Fourteenth Amendment formed the basis of the U.S. Supreme Court's first consideration of the question. In *Cruzan* v. *Director* (1990), the Missouri Supreme Court had turned back the efforts of the parents of Nancy Cruzan to terminate artificial nutrition and hydration for their daughter, who was living in a vegetative condition following an automobile accident. Without nutrition and hydration, Nancy Cruzan would of course die. In the state court's view, because Nancy Cruzan had not complied with Missouri's "living will" statutes and because there was no "clear and convincing, inherently reliable evidence" of the patient's wishes not to continue life under such circumstances, treatment would continue. In other words, short of persuasive evidence that the patient would reject treatment if she only could, the presumption was that she would choose treatment. (**Living wills** set the terms for the withdrawal or withholding of life-sustaining treatment for patients with incurable conditions when the patients are incapable of making decisions regarding their medical treatment.)

On appeal, five justices of the U.S. Supreme Court found the state's standard constitutionally acceptable. According to Chief Justice Rehnquist, a state may require "clear and convincing evidence" (as opposed to the less demanding standard of "preponderance of the evidence") of an incompetent patient's wishes to refuse medical treatment. For the four dissenting justices who regarded the liberty interest at stake as "fundamental," Missouri's requirement of heightened proof was unconstitutionally intrusive into the patient's right to refuse treatment. *Cruzan* was partly responsible for passage of the **Patient Self-Determination Act** in 1991. Under this federal law, hospital employees must ask all patients if they want to plan for their death by making a living will or by designating a health care proxy, to make decisions should they become incapacitated. (In December 1990 Nancy Cruzan died in a Missouri hospital 12 days after a feeding tube was removed under a court order requested by her parents. Following the U.S. Supreme Court's decision, the trial court concluded that the record revealed "clear and convincing evidence" of her wishes not to sustain her life artificially under the circumstances.)

As is sometimes true with a "first step" in constitutional law, *Cruzan* raised as many questions as it answered. Read narrowly, the decision at most acknowledged the right of a conscious and competent person to refuse medical treatment. The Court divided, after all, on the standard of proof that the state could require with respect to the wishes of a comatose patient. Read broadly, the right to refuse medical treatment was an aspect of something far more encompassing: the right to determine the timing of one's own death.

Not surprisingly, terminally ill patients and their doctors challenged laws banning assisted suicide. The courtroom debate thus shifted from the circumstances under which government could require the administration of life-sustaining nutrition and hydration (that is, forcing a person to remain alive) to the state's authority to deny the administration of life-ending medication (that is, forbidding the active intervention of one person in ending another's life). In *Compassion in Dying* v. *Washington,* the Ninth Circuit Court of Appeals ruled in 1995 that Washington State's ban on assisted suicide, at least with respect to physicians and terminally ill patients, violated the liberty protected by the due process clause of the Fourteenth Amendment. While falling short of a "fundamental" liberty, the Ninth Circuit deemed the liberty interest nonetheless "significant," overriding the state's interest in preserving life. In *Quill* v. *Vacco* (1996) the Second Circuit decreed the same fate for a similar statute in New York but did so on different grounds. That court saw no valid difference between competent persons who refuse treatment (thus ending their lives) and competent persons who seek treatment to end their lives. Thus, the state lacked legitimate reasons, as required by the equal protection clause of the Fourteenth Amendment, for treating similarly circumstanced or situated people differently.

In **Washington v. Glucksberg** and *Vacco* v. *Quill* (1997), the Supreme Court reversed both appeals courts. Denying the existence of any constitutional right to commit suicide or to seek the assistance of another in doing so, the High Court preferred to leave the difficult moral and social choices in this area to state legislatures and state courts. Nonetheless, concurring opinions indicated that as many as five justices would reject any state's attempt to block access to pain-relieving medication where its administration would hasten a patient's death.

**SEXUAL ORIENTATION.** A person's sexual orientation and practice also involve a dimension of privacy or autonomy, an issue the Supreme Court squarely confronted in 1986 in *Bowers* v. *Hardwick*. Five justices upheld the constitutionality of Georgia's sodomy statute, which made criminal certain combinations of private parts. The law applied to heterosexual as well as homosexual behavior, but Justice White's opinion of the Court, perhaps deliberately, regarded the act as if it made only the latter criminal.

The 5–4 split revealed that no consensus existed on the Court concerning what privacy encompassed. Since *Griswold,* privacy's "score card" in the Supreme Court had been good. Many observers were surprised that five balked at an extension. Close reading of Justice White's majority opinion and the principal dissent by Justice Blackmun provides insight. To discover what rights, though not expressly mentioned, are constitutionally protected, White looked to two sources: those "implicit in the concept of ordered liberty" and those "deeply rooted in the nation's history and tradition." Framing the investigation in this way, White concluded "that neither of these formulations would extend a fundamental right to homosexuals to engage in acts of consensual sodomy." For Blackmun, the majority asked the wrong question. The case was not "about 'a fundamental right to engage in homosexual sodomy.'. . . Rather, this case is about 'the most comprehensive of rights . . . the right to be let alone.' [W]hat the Court really has refused to recognize is the fundamental interest all individuals have in controlling the nature of their intimate associations with others." White scanned a category of rights. Blackmun focused on a constitutionally protected realm of intimate association.

The Court revisited sexual intimacy in **Lawrence v. Texas** (2003), where the Court, 6–3, not only invalidated a statute that criminalized same-sex sodomy but went out of its way to impugn the intellectual integrity of White's opinion in *Bowers*.

On the basis of *Lawrence* and Scalia's fierce dissent in that case, the Court may soon have to confront laws defining marriage as a union only between a woman and a man. In 1999, the Vermont Supreme Court held that the common benefits clause in the state constitution entitled same-sex couples to the secular benefits and protections offered married couples in Vermont (*Baker* v. *State,* 1999). The decision led the state legislature to authorize "civil unions" that amount to ordinary marriages in everything but name. Also relying on its state constitution, the Supreme Judicial Court of Massachusetts ruled that same-sex couples have a legal right to marry (*Goodridge* v. *Dept. of Public Health,* 2003). Congress had already acted to isolate any such innovations. The **Defense of Marriage Act** (1996) provides that no State shall be required to give effect to a law of any other State with respect to a same-sex marriage, and for purposes of federal law defines "marriage" to mean "only a legal union between one man and one woman and the word 'spouse' to refer only to a person of the opposite sex who is a husband or a wife."

Questions of sexual practice and orientation, like other privacy issues, will continue to arise. Heightened sensitivity throughout the United States to issues of individual privacy virtually guarantee a continued involvement by judges in marking the dimensions of the constitutional right "to be let alone."

## KEY TERMS

privacy
informational privacy
private law
public law

penumbra
Hyde Amendment
undue burden
living wills

Patient Self-
    Determination Act
Defense of Marriage Act

## QUERIES

**1.** In his opinion for the majority in *Griswold* v. *Connecticut,* why might Justice Douglas have felt compelled to rely on "penumbras" from the Bill of Rights rather than the Fourteenth Amendment's due process clause?

**2.** After *Planned Parenthood* v. *Casey,* what is left of *Roe* v. *Wade?*

**3.** In their majority and dissenting opinions, respectively, in *Stenberg* v. *Carhart,* Justices Breyer and Kennedy asserted that their positions were faithful to the Court's holding in *Casey.* Is this possible? Recall that Kennedy coauthored the joint opinion in *Casey.*

**4.** Dissenting in *Lawrence* v. *Texas,* Justice Scalia declared: "Today's opinion dismantles the structure of constitutional law that has permitted a distinction to be made between heterosexual and homosexual unions, insofar as formal recognition in marriage is concerned." Do you agree?

## SELECTED READINGS

BEANEY, WILLIAM M. "The Constitutional Right to Privacy in the Supreme Court." *Supreme Court Review* 212 (1962).

CRAIG, BARBARA, and DAVID O'BRIEN. *Abortion and American Politics.* Chatham, N.J.: Chatham House, 1993.

GARROW, DAVID J. *Liberty and Sexuality: The Right to Privacy and the Making of Roe* v. *Wade.* New York: Macmillan, 1994.

GLENN, RICHARD A. *The Right to Privacy.* Santa Barbara, Calif.: ABC-CLIO, 2003.

O'CONNOR, KAREN. *No Neutral Ground? Abortion Politics in an Age of Absolutes.* Boulder, Colo.: Westview Press, 1996.

PRESIDENT'S COMMISSION FOR THE STUDY OF ETHICAL PROBLEMS IN MEDICINE AND BIOMEDICAL AND BEHAVIORAL RESEARCH. *Deciding to Forego Life-Sustaining Treatment.* Washington, D.C.: Government Printing Office, 1983.

UROFSKY, MELVIN I. *Lethal Judgments: Assisted Suicide and American Law.* Lawrence: University Press of Kansas, 2000.

WARREN, SAMUEL, and LOUIS D. BRANDEIS. "The Right to Privacy." 4 *Harvard Law Review* 220 (1890).

# I. INVIGORATING A RIGHT OF PRIVACY

## *Griswold* v. *Connecticut*
## 381 U.S. 479, 85 S.Ct. 1678, 14 L.Ed. 2d 510 (1965)
http://laws.findlaw.com/us/381/479.html

A Connecticut statute of 1879 made the use of contraceptives a criminal offense. Estelle Griswold, executive director of the Planned Parenthood League of Connecticut, was convicted on a charge of having violated the statute as an accessory by giving information, instruction, and advice to married persons as a means of preventing conception. A professor at the Yale Medical School, serving as medical director for the league, was a codefendant. The Appellate Division of the Circuit Court and the Supreme Court of Errors of Connecticut affirmed the conviction. Majority: Douglas, Brennan, Clark, Goldberg, Harlan, Warren, White. Dissenting: Black, Stewart.

**Mr. Justice Douglas delivered the opinion of the Court....**

Coming to the merits, we are met with a wide range of questions that implicate the Due Process Clause of the Fourteenth Amendment. Overtones of some arguments suggest that *Lochner* v. *New York* ... should be our guide. But we decline that invitation.... We do not sit as a super-legislature to determine the wisdom, need, and propriety of laws that touch economic problems, business affairs, or social conditions. This law, however, operates directly on an intimate relation of husband and wife and their physician's role in one aspect of that relation....

[S]pecific guarantees in the Bill of Rights have penumbras, formed by emanations from those guarantees that help give them life and substance.... Various guarantees create zones of privacy. The right of association contained in the penumbra of the First Amendment is one.... The Third Amendment in its prohibition against the quartering of soldiers "in any house" in time of peace without the consent of the owner is another facet of that privacy. The Fourth Amendment explicitly affirms the "right of the people to be secure in their persons, houses, papers, and effects against unreasonable searches and seizures." The Fifth Amendment in its Self-Incrimination Clause enables the citizen to create a zone of privacy which government may not force him to surrender to his detriment. The Ninth Amendment provides: "The enumeration in the Constitution, of certain rights, shall not be construed to deny or disparage others retained by the people."...

The present case, then, concerns a relationship lying within the zone of privacy created by several fundamental constitutional guarantees. And it concerns a law which, in forbidding the use of contraceptives rather than regulating their manufacture or sale, seeks to achieve its goals by means having a maximum destructive impact upon that relationship. Such a law cannot stand in light of the familiar principle, so often applied by this Court, that a "governmental purpose to control or prevent activities constitutionally subject to state regulation may not be achieved by means which sweep unnecessarily broadly and thereby invade the area of protected freedom." Would we allow the police to search the sacred precincts of marital bedrooms for telltale signs of the use of contraceptives? The very idea is repulsive to the notions of privacy surrounding the marriage relationship.

We deal with a right of privacy older than the Bill of Rights—older than our political parties, older than our school system. Marriage is a coming together for better or for worse, hopefully enduring, and intimate to the degree of being sacred. It is an association that promotes a way of life, not causes; a harmony in living, not political faiths; a bilateral loyalty, not commercial or social projects. Yet it is an association for as noble a purpose as any involved in our prior decisions.

*Reversed.*

### MR. JUSTICE GOLDBERG, whom the CHIEF JUSTICE and MR. JUSTICE BRENNAN join, concurring. . . .

The Ninth Amendment to the Constitution may be regarded by some as a recent discovery and may be forgotten by others, but since 1791 it has been a basic part of the Constitution which we are sworn to uphold. To hold that a right so basic and fundamental and so deep-rooted in our society as the right of privacy in marriage may be infringed because that right is not guaranteed in so many words by the first eight amendments to the Constitution is to ignore the Ninth Amendment and to give it no effect whatsoever. . . .

Nor am I turning somersaults with history in arguing that the Ninth Amendment is relevant in a case dealing with a State's infringement of a fundamental right. While the Ninth Amendment—and indeed the entire Bill of Rights—originally concerned restrictions upon federal power, the subsequently enacted Fourteenth Amendment prohibits the States as well from abridging fundamental personal liberties. And, the Ninth Amendment, in indicating that not all such liberties are specifically mentioned in the first eight amendments, is surely relevant in showing the existence of other fundamental personal rights, now protected from state, as well as federal, infringement. In sum, the Ninth Amendment simply lends strong support to the view that the "liberty" protected by the Fifth and Fourteenth Amendments from infringement by the Federal Government or the States is not restricted to rights specifically mentioned in the first eight amendments. . . .

### MR. JUSTICE HARLAN, concurring in the judgment. . . .

In my view, the proper constitutional inquiry in this case is whether this . . . statute infringes the Due Process Clause of the Fourteenth Amendment because the enactment violates basic values "implicit in the concept of ordered liberty." For reasons stated at length in my dissenting opinion in *Poe* v. *Ullman,* I believe that it does. While the relevant inquiry may be aided by resort to one or more of the provisions of the Bill of Rights, it is not dependent on them or any of their radiations. The Due Process Clause . . . stands . . . on its own bottom. . . .

MR. JUSTICE WHITE, concurring . . . [omitted].

### MR. JUSTICE BLACK, with whom MR. JUSTICE STEWART joins, dissenting. . . .

The Court talks about a constitutional "right of privacy" as though there is some constitutional provision or provisions forbidding any law ever to be passed which might abridge the "privacy" of individuals. But there is not. . . .

. . . I like my privacy as well as the next one, but I am nevertheless compelled to admit that government has a right to invade it unless prohibited by some specific constitutional provision. For these reasons I cannot agree with the Court's judgment and the reasons it gives for holding this Connecticut law unconstitutional. . . .

I think that if properly construed neither the Due Process Clause nor the Ninth Amendment, nor both together, could under any circumstances be a proper basis for invalidating the Connecticut law. I discuss the due process and Ninth Amendment arguments together because on analysis they turn out to be the same thing—merely using different words to claim for this Court and the federal judiciary power to invalidate any legislative act which the judges find irrational, unreasonable or offensive.

The due process argument . . . is based . . . on the premise that this Court is vested with power to invalidate all state laws that it considers to be arbitrary, capricious, unreasonable, or oppressive, or because of this Court's belief that a particular state law under scrutiny has no "rational or justifying purpose," or is offensive to a "sense of fairness and justice." If these formulas based on "natural justice," or others which mean the same thing, are to prevail, they require judges to determine what is or is not constitutional on the basis of their own appraisal of what laws are unwise or unnecessary. The power to make such decisions is of course that of a legislative body. Surely it has to be admitted that no provision of the Constitution specifically gives such blanket power to courts to exercise such a supervisory veto over the wisdom and value of legislative policies and to hold unconstitutional those laws which they believe unwise or dangerous. I readily admit that no legislative body, state or national, should pass laws that can justly be given any of the invidious labels invoked as constitutional excuses to strike down state laws. But perhaps it is not too much to say that no legislative body ever does pass laws without believing that they will accomplish a sane, rational, wise and justifiable purpose. . . . I do not believe that we are granted power by the Due Process Clause or any other constitutional provision or provisions to measure constitutionality by our belief that legislation is arbitrary, capricious or unreasonable, or accomplishes no justifiable purpose, or is offensive to our own notions of "civilized standards of conduct." Such an appraisal of the wisdom of legislation is an attribute of the power to make laws, not of the power to interpret them. The use by federal courts of such a formula or doctrine or whatnot to veto federal or state laws simply takes away from Congress and States the power to make laws based on their own judgment of fairness and wisdom and transfers that power to this Court for ultimate determination—a power which was specifically denied to federal courts by the convention that framed the Constitution. . . .

My Brother Goldberg has adopted the recent discovery that the Ninth Amendment as well as the Due Process Clause can be used by this Court as authority to strike down all state legislation which this Court thinks violates "fundamental principles of liberty and justice," or is contrary to the "traditions and collective conscience of our people." He also states, without proof satisfactory to me, that in making decisions on this basis judges will not consider "their personal and private notions." One may ask how they can avoid considering them. Our Court certainly has no machinery with which to take a Gallup Poll. And the scientific miracles of this age have not yet produced a gadget which the Court can use to determine what traditions are rooted in the "collective conscience of our people." Moreover, one would certainly have to look far beyond the language of the Ninth Amendment to find that the Framers vested in this Court any such awesome veto powers over lawmaking, either by the States or by the Congress. . . . If any broad, unlimited power to hold laws unconstitutional because they offend what this Court conceives to be "the collective conscience of our people" is vested in this Court by the Ninth Amendment, or any other provision of the Constitution, it was not given by the Framers, but rather has been bestowed on the Court by the Court. . . .

### MR. JUSTICE STEWART, with whom MR. JUSTICE BLACK joins, dissenting. . . .

[T]his is an uncommonly silly law. . . .

At the oral argument . . . we were told that the Connecticut law does not "conform to current community standards." But it is not the function of this Court to decide cases on the basis of community standards. . . . If, as I should surely hope, the law before us does not reflect the standards of the people of Connecticut, the people of Connecticut can freely exercise their true Ninth and Tenth Amendment rights to persuade their elected representatives to repeal it. That is the constitutional way to take this law off the books.

## II. ABORTION

### *Roe* v. *Wade*
### 410 U.S. 113, 93 S.Ct. 705, 35 L.Ed. 2d 147 (1973)
http://laws.findlaw.com/us/410/113.html

In 1970, Norma McCorvey of Dallas, Texas, wished to terminate her pregnancy. Because Texas law prohibited abortions except those performed by a physician for the purpose of saving the life of the woman (an exception that did not apply to her), she filed suit against Henry Wade, District Attorney of Dallas County, in the U.S. District Court for the Northern District of Texas, claiming that the Texas law was unconstitutional and seeking an injunction against its enforcement. To protect her anonymity, she used the pseudonym of Jane Roe throughout the litigation. The district court held that the state statute was void on its face because it was unconstitutionally vague and overbroad and violated rights protected by the Ninth Amendment, but declined to enjoin further enforcement of the statute. (An attorney helped to arrange for the newborn's adoption later in 1970.) The Supreme Court twice heard oral arguments in the case—in December of 1971 and October of 1972. Majority: Blackmun, Brennan, Burger, Douglas, Marshall, Powell, Stewart. Dissenting: Rehnquist, White.

**MR. JUSTICE BLACKMUN delivered the opinion of the Court. . . .**

The principal thrust of the appellant's attack on the Texas statutes is that they improperly invade a right, said to be possessed by the pregnant woman, to choose to terminate her pregnancy. Appellant would discover this right in the concept of personal "liberty" embodied in the Fourteenth Amendment's Due Process Clause; or in personal, marital, familial, and sexual privacy said to be protected by the Bill of Rights or its penumbras. . . . Before addressing this claim, we feel it desirable briefly to survey, in several aspects, the history of abortion, for such insight as that history may afford us, and then to examine the state purposes and interests behind the criminal abortion laws.

It perhaps is not generally appreciated that the restrictive criminal abortion laws in effect in a majority of States today are of relatively recent vintage. Those laws, generally proscribing abortion or its attempt at any time during pregnancy except when necessary to preserve the pregnant woman's life, are not of ancient or even of common law origin.

Instead, they derive from statutory changes effected, for the most part, in the latter half of the 19th century. . . .

It is thus apparent that at common law, at the time of the adoption of our Constitution, and throughout the major portion of the 19th century, abortion was viewed with less disfavor than under most American statutes currently in effect. . . .

Three reasons have been advanced to explain historically the enactment of criminal abortion laws in the 19th century and to justify their continued existence.

It has been argued occasionally that these laws were the product of a Victorian social concern to discourage illicit sexual conduct. Texas, however, does not advance this justification in the present case, and it appears that no court or commentator has taken the argument seriously. . . .

A second reason is concerned with abortion as a medical procedure. When most criminal abortion laws were first enacted, the procedure was a hazardous one for the woman. This was particularly true prior to the development of antisepsis. . . . Abortion mortality was high. . . .

Modern medical techniques have altered this situation. . . . Mortality rates for women undergoing early abortions, where the procedure is legal, appear to be as low or lower than the rates for normal childbirth. . . . Of course, important state interests in the area of health and medical standards do remain. The State has a legitimate interest in seeing to it that abortion, like any other medical procedure, is performed under circumstances that insure maximum safety for the patient. . . . Moreover, the risk to the woman increases as her pregnancy continues. Thus the State retains a definite interest in protecting the woman's own health and safety when an abortion is proposed at a late stage of pregnancy.

The third reason is the State's interest—some phrase it in terms of duty—in protecting prenatal life. Some of the argument for this justification rests on the theory that a new human life is present from the moment of conception. The State's interest and general obligation to protect life then extends, it is argued, to prenatal life. Only when the life of the pregnant mother herself is at stake, balanced against the life she carries within her, should the interests of the embryo or fetus not prevail. Logically, of course, a legitimate state interest in this area need not stand or fall on acceptance of the belief that life begins at conception or at some other point prior to live birth. In assessing the State's interest, recognition may be given to the less rigid claim that as long as at least potential life is involved, the State may assert interests beyond the protection of the pregnant woman alone. . . .

It is with these interests, and the weight to be attached to them, that this case is concerned.

The Constitution does not explicitly mention any right of privacy. In a line of decisions, however, going back perhaps as far as *Union Pacific R. Co.* v. *Botsford* (1891), the Court has recognized that a right of personal privacy, or a guarantee of certain areas or zones of privacy, does exist under the Constitution. In varying contexts the Court or individual Justices have indeed found at least the roots of that right in the First Amendment . . . in the Fourth and Fifth Amendments . . . in the penumbras of the Bill of Rights . . . in the Ninth Amendment . . . or in the concept of liberty guaranteed by the first section of the Fourteenth Amendment. . . . These decisions make it clear that only personal rights that can be deemed "fundamental" or "implicit in the concept of ordered liberty" . . . are included in this guarantee of personal privacy. They also make it clear that the right has some extension to activities relating to marriage . . . procreation, contraception, family relationships, and child rearing and education. . . .

We therefore conclude that the right of personal privacy includes the abortion decision, but that this right is not unqualified and must be considered against important state interests in regulation. . . . [A]t some point the state interests as to protection of health, medical standards, and prenatal life, become dominant. . . .

Where certain "fundamental rights" are involved, the Court has held that regulation limiting these rights may be justified only by a "compelling state interest," and that legislative enactments must be narrowly drawn to express only the legitimate state interests at stake. . . .

The appellee and certain amici argue that the fetus is a "person" within the language and meaning of the Fourteenth Amendment. . . .

The Constitution does not define "person" in so many words. Section 1 of the Fourteenth Amendment contains three references to "person." The first, in defining "citizens," speaks of "persons born or naturalized in the United States." The word also appears both in the Due Process Clause and in the Equal Protection Clause. "Person" is used in other places in the Constitution. . . . But in nearly all these instances, the use of the word is such that it has application only postnatally. None indicates, with any assurance, that it has any possible prenatal application. . . .

Texas urges that, apart from the Fourteenth Amendment, life begins at conception and is present throughout pregnancy, and that, therefore, the State has a compelling interest in protecting that life from and after conception. We need not resolve the difficult question of when life begins. When those trained in the respective disciplines of medicine, philosophy, and theology are unable to arrive at any consensus, the judiciary, at this point in the development of man's knowledge, is not in a position to speculate as to the answer. . . .

We do not agree that, by adopting one theory of life, Texas may override the rights of the pregnant woman that are at stake. We repeat, however, that the State does have an important and legitimate interest in preserving and protecting the health of the pregnant woman, whether she be a resident of the State or a nonresident who seeks medical consultation and treatment there, and that it has still another important and legitimate interest in protecting the potentiality of human life. These interests are separate and distinct. Each grows in substantiality as the woman approaches term and, at a point during pregnancy, each becomes "compelling."

With respect to the State's important and legitimate interest in the health of the mother, the "compelling" point, in the light of present medical knowledge, is at approximately the end of the first trimester. This is so because of the now established medical fact . . . that until the end of the first trimester mortality in abortion is less than mortality in normal childbirth. It follows that, from and after this point, a State may regulate the abortion procedure to the extent that the regulation reasonably relates to the preservation and protection of maternal health. Examples of permissible state regulation in this area are requirements as to the qualifications of the person who is to perform the abortion; as to the licensure of that person; as to the facility in which the procedure is to be performed, that is, whether it must be a hospital or may be a clinic or some other place of less-than-hospital status; as to the licensing of the facility; and the like.

This means, on the other hand, that, for the period of pregnancy prior to this "compelling" point, the attending physician, in consultation with his patient, is free to determine, without regulation by the State, that in his medical judgment the patient's pregnancy should be terminated. If that decision is reached, the judgment may be effectuated by an abortion free of interference by the State. . . .

With respect to the State's important and legitimate interest in potential life, the "compelling" point is at viability. This is so because the fetus then presumably has the capability of meaningful life outside the mother's womb. State regulation protective of fetal life after viability thus has both logical and biological justifications. If the State is interested in protecting fetal life after viability, it may go so far as to proscribe abortion during that period except when it is necessary to preserve the life or health of the mother.

Measured against these standards . . . Texas, in restricting legal abortion to those "procured or attempted by medical advice for the purpose of saving the life of the mother," sweeps too broadly. The statute makes no distinction between abortions performed early in pregnancy and those performed later, and it limits to a single reason, "saving" the mother's life, the legal justification for the procedure. The statute, therefore, cannot survive the constitutional attack made upon it here. . . .

To summarize and to repeat: A state criminal abortion statute of the current Texas type, that excepts from criminality only a life-saving procedure on behalf of the mother, without regard to pregnancy stage and without recognition of the other interests involved, is violative of the Due Process Clause of the Fourteenth Amendment.

(a) For the stage prior to approximately the end of the first trimester, the abortion decision and its effectuation must be left to the medical judgment of the pregnant woman's attending physician.

(b) For the stage subsequent to approximately the end of the first trimester, the State, in promoting its interest in the health of the mother, may, if it chooses, regulate the abortion procedure in ways that are reasonably related to maternal health.

(c) For the stage subsequent to viability, the State in promoting its interest in the potentiality of human life may, if it chooses, regulate, and even proscribe, abortion except where it is necessary, in appropriate medical judgment, for the preservation of the life or health of the mother. . . .

The judgment of the District Court . . . is affirmed. . . .

*It is so ordered.*

Mr. Chief Justice Burger, concurring . . . [omitted].

Mr. Justice Douglas, concurring . . . [omitted].

Mr. Justice Stewart, concurring . . . [omitted].

Mr. Justice White, with whom Mr. Justice Rehnquist joins, dissenting . . . [omitted].

## Mr. Justice Rehnquist, dissenting. . . .

I would reach a conclusion opposite to that reached by the Court. . . .

If the Court means by the term "privacy" no more than that the claim of a person to be free from unwanted state regulation of consensual transactions may be a form of "liberty" protected by the Fourteenth Amendment, there is no doubt that similar claims have been upheld in our earlier decisions on the basis of that liberty. I agree with the statement of Mr. Justice Stewart in his concurring opinion that the "liberty," against deprivation of which without due process the Fourteenth Amendment protects, embraces more than the rights found in the Bill of Rights. But that liberty is not guaranteed absolutely against deprivation, but only against deprivation without due process of law. The test traditionally applied in the area of social and economic legislation is whether or not a law such as that challenged has a rational relation to a valid state objective. . . . But the Court's sweeping invalidation of any restrictions on abortion during the first trimester is impossible to justify under that standard, and the conscious weighing of competing factors which the Court's opinion apparently substitutes for the established test is far more appropriate to a legislative judgment than to a judicial one. . . .

While the Court's opinion quotes from the dissent of Mr. Justice Holmes in *Lochner* v. *New York* . . . the result it reaches is more closely attuned to the majority opinion of Mr. Justice Peckham in that case. As in

*Lochner* and similar cases applying substantive due process standards to economic and social welfare legislation, the adoption of the compelling state interest standard will inevitably require this Court to examine the legislative policies and pass on the wisdom of these policies in the very process of deciding whether a particular state interest put forward may or may not be "compelling." The decision here to break the term of pregnancy into three distinct terms and to outline the permissible restrictions the State may impose in each one, for example, partakes more of judicial legislation than it does of a determination of the intent of the drafters of the Fourteenth Amendment.

The fact that a majority of the States, reflecting after all the majority sentiment in those States, have had restrictions on abortions for at least a century seems to me as strong an indication there is that the asserted right to an abortion is not "so rooted in the traditions and conscience of our people as to be ranked as fundamental." . . . Even today, when society's views on abortion are changing, the very existence of the debate is evidence that the "right" to an abortion is not so universally accepted as the appellants would have us believe.

To reach its result the Court necessarily has had to find within the scope of the Fourteenth Amendment a right that was apparently completely unknown to the drafters of the Amendment. As early as 1821, the first state law dealing directly with abortion was enacted by the Connecticut legislature. . . . By the time of the adoption of the Fourteenth Amendment in 1868 there were at least 36 laws enacted by state or territorial legislatures limiting abortion. While many States have amended or updated their laws, 21 of the laws on the books in 1868 remain in effect today. . . .

There apparently was no question concerning the validity of this provision or of any of the other state statutes when the Fourteenth Amendment was adopted. The only conclusion possible from this history is that the drafters did not intend to have the Fourteenth Amendment withdraw from the States the power to legislate with respect to this matter. . . .

## *Planned Parenthood of Southeastern Pennsylvania* v. *Casey*
## 505 U.S. 833, 112 S.Ct. 2791, 120 L.Ed. 2d 674 (1992)
http://laws.findlaw.com/us/505/833.html

Amendments in 1988 and 1989 to Pennsylvania's Abortion Control Act mandated "informed consent" counseling, a 24-hour waiting period, consent of one parent (with a judicial bypass procedure) for minors, and spousal consent; furthermore, the act defined a "medical emergency" that would excuse compliance with these requirements, and imposed certain reporting requirements on facilities providing abortions. The U.S. District Court for the Eastern District of Pennsylvania enjoined enforcement of all the amendments. The Court of Appeals for the Third Circuit reversed except for the husband notification requirement. In deciding the case, the Supreme Court produced five opinions totaling over 125 pages. The voting alignment was complex. Justices White, Scalia, Thomas, and Chief Justice Rehnquist would have upheld all the requirements; Justices O'Connor, Kennedy, and Souter found unconstitutional only the spousal notification requirement; Justice Stevens voted to strike down all but the informed-consent provision; and Justice Blackmun found all the provisions constitutionally deficient. The Court divided 5–4 in support of the position that the Constitution protected, at least to some degree, a woman's decision to abort her pregnancy. Majority: O'Connor, Blackmun, Stevens, Kennedy, Souter. Dissenting: Rehnquist, White, Scalia, Thomas.

**JUSTICE O'CONNOR, JUSTICE KENNEDY, and JUSTICE SOUTER announced the judgment of the Court and delivered an opinion which JUSTICE BLACKMUN and JUSTICE STEVENS joined in part.**

Liberty finds no refuge in a jurisprudence of doubt. Yet 19 years after our holding that the Constitution protects a woman's right to terminate her pregnancy in its early stages, that definition of liberty is still questioned. Joining the respondents as amicus curiae, the United States, as it has done in five other cases in the last decade, again asks us to overrule *Roe*. . . .

After considering the fundamental constitutional questions resolved by *Roe*, principles of institutional integrity, and the rule of stare decisis, we are led to conclude this: the essential holding of *Roe* v. *Wade* should be retained and once again reaffirmed. . . .

Neither the Bill of Rights nor the specific practices of States at the time of the adoption of the Fourteenth Amendment mark the outer limits of the substantive sphere of liberty which the Fourteenth Amendment protects. . . .

The inescapable fact is that adjudication of substantive due process claims may call upon the Court in interpreting the Constitution to exercise that same capacity which by tradition courts always have exercised: reasoned judgment. Its boundaries are not susceptible of expression as a simple rule. That does not mean we are free to invalidate state policy choices with which we disagree; yet neither does it permit us to shrink from the duties of our office. . . .

Our law affords constitutional protection to personal decisions relating to marriage, procreation, contraception, family relationships, child rearing, and education. . . . These matters, involving the most intimate and personal choices a person may make in a lifetime, choices central to personal dignity and autonomy, are central to the liberty protected by the Fourteenth Amendment. At the heart of liberty is the right to define one's own concept of existence, of meaning, of the universe, and of the mystery of human life. Beliefs about these matters could not define the attributes of personhood were they formed under compulsion of the State. . . .

Abortion is a unique act. It is an act fraught with consequences for others; for the woman who must live with the implications of her decision; for the persons who perform and assist in the procedure; for the spouse, family, and society which must confront the knowledge that these procedures exist, procedures some deem nothing short of an act of violence against innocent human life; and, depending on one's beliefs, for the life or potential life that is aborted. Though abortion is conduct, it does not follow that the State is entitled to proscribe it in all instances. That is because the liberty of the woman is at stake in a sense unique to the human condition and so unique to the law. The mother who carries a child to full term is subject to anxieties, to physical constraints, to pain that only she must bear. That these sacrifices have from the beginning of the human race been endured by woman with a pride that ennobles her in the eyes of others and gives to the infant a bond of love cannot alone be grounds for the State to insist she make the sacrifice. Her suffering is too intimate and personal for the State to insist, without more, upon its own vision of the woman's role, however dominant that vision has been in the course of our history and our culture. The destiny of the woman must be shaped to a large extent on her own conception of her spiritual imperatives and her place in society. . . .

It was this dimension of personal liberty that *Roe* sought to protect. . . .

While we appreciate the weight of the arguments made on behalf of the State in the case before us, arguments which in their ultimate formulation conclude that *Roe* should be overruled, the reservations any of us have in reaffirming the central holding of *Roe* are outweighed by the explication of individual liberty we have given combined with the force of stare decisis. . . .

The sum of the . . . inquiry to this point shows *Roe's* underpinnings unweakened in any way affecting its central holding. While it has engendered disapproval, it has not been unworkable. An entire generation has come of age free to assume *Roe's* concept of liberty in defining the capacity of women to act in society, and to make reproductive decisions; no

erosion of principle going to liberty or personal autonomy has left *Roe's* central holding a doctrinal remnant; *Roe* portends no developments at odds with other precedent for the analysis of personal liberty; and no changes of fact have rendered viability more or less appropriate as the point at which the balance of interests tips. Within the bounds of normal stare decisis analysis, then, and subject to the considerations on which it customarily turns, the stronger argument is for affirming *Roe's* central holding, with whatever degree of personal reluctance any of us may have, not for overruling it. . . .

Our analysis would not be complete, however, without explaining why overruling *Roe's* central holding would not only reach an unjustifiable result under principles of stare decisis, but would seriously weaken the Court's capacity to exercise the judicial power and to function as the Supreme Court of a Nation dedicated to the rule of law. To understand why this would be so it is necessary to understand the source of this Court's authority, the conditions necessary for its preservation, and its relationship to the country's understanding of itself as a constitutional Republic.

The root of American governmental power is revealed most clearly in the instance of the power conferred by the Constitution upon the Judiciary of the United States and specifically upon this Court. As Americans of each succeeding generation are rightly told, the Court cannot buy support for its decisions by spending money and, except to a minor degree, it cannot independently coerce obedience to its decrees. The Court's power lies, rather, in its legitimacy, a product of substance and perception that shows itself in the people's acceptance of the Judiciary as fit to determine what the Nation's law means and to declare what it demands.

The underlying substance of this legitimacy is of course the warrant for the Court's decisions in the Constitution and the lesser source of legal principle on which the Court draws. That substance is expressed in the Court's opinions, and our contemporary understanding is such that a decision without principled justification would be no judicial act at all. But even when justification is furnished by apposite legal principle, something more is required. Because not every conscientious claim of principled justification will be accepted as such, the justification claimed must be beyond dispute. The Court must take care to speak and act in ways that allow people to accept its decisions on the terms the Court claims for them, as grounded truly in principle, not as compromises with social and political pressures having, as such, no bearing on the principled choices that the Court is obliged to make. Thus, the Court's legitimacy depends on making legally principled decisions under circumstances in which their principled character is sufficiently plausible to be accepted by the Nation. . . .

In two circumstances, however, the Court would almost certainly fail to receive the benefit of the doubt in overruling prior cases. There is, first, a point beyond which frequent overruling would overtax the country's belief in the Court's good faith. . . .

That first circumstance can be described as hypothetical; the second is to the point here and now. Where, in the performance of its judicial duties, the Court decides a case in such a way as to resolve the sort of intensely divisive controversy reflected in *Roe* and those rare, comparable cases, its decision has a dimension that the resolution of the normal case does not carry. It is the dimension present whenever the Court's interpretation of the Constitution calls the contending sides of a national controversy to end their national division by accepting a common mandate rooted in the Constitution.

The Court is not asked to do this very often. . . . But when the Court does act in this way, its decision requires an equally rare precedential force to counter the inevitable efforts to overturn it and to thwart its implementation. Some of those efforts may be mere unprincipled emotional reactions; others may proceed from principles worthy of profound respect. But whatever the premises of opposition may be, only the most convincing justification under accepted standards of precedent could suffice to demonstrate that a later decision overruling the first was anything but a surrender to political pressure, and an unjustified repudiation of the principle on which the Court staked its authority in the first instance.

So to overrule under fire in the absence of the most compelling reason to reexamine a watershed decision would subvert the Court's legitimacy beyond any serious question. . . .

The Court's duty in the present case is clear. In 1973, it confronted the already-divisive issue of governmental power to limit personal choice to undergo abortion, for which it provided a new resolution based on the due process guaranteed by the Fourteenth Amendment. Whether or not a new social consensus is developing on that issue, its divisiveness is no less today than in 1973, and pressure to overrule the decision, like pressure to retain it, has grown only more intense. A decision to overrule *Roe's* essential holding under the existing circumstances would address error, if error there was, at the cost of both profound and unnecessary damage to the Court's legitimacy, and to the Nation's commitment to the rule of law. It is therefore imperative to adhere to the essence of *Roe's* original decision, and we do so today. . . .

The woman's liberty is not so unlimited, however, that from the outset the State cannot show its concern for the life of the unborn, and at a later point in fetal development the State's interest in life has sufficient force so that the right of the woman to terminate the pregnancy can be restricted. . . .

We conclude the line should be drawn at viability, so that before that time the woman has a right to choose to terminate her pregnancy. . . .

We give this summary:

(a) To protect the central right recognized by *Roe* v. *Wade* while at the same time accommodating the State's profound interest in potential life, we will employ the undue burden analysis as explained in this opinion. An undue burden exists, and therefore a provision of law is invalid, if its purpose or effect is to place a substantial obstacle in the path of a woman seeking an abortion before the fetus attains viability.

(b) We reject the rigid trimester framework of *Roe* v. *Wade*. To promote the State's profound interest in potential life, throughout pregnancy the State may take measures to ensure that the woman's choice is informed, and measures designed to advance this interest will not be invalidated as long as their purpose is to persuade the woman to choose childbirth over abortion. These measures must not be an undue burden on the right.

(c) As with any medical procedure, the State may enact regulations to further the health or safety of a woman seeking an abortion. Unnecessary health regulations that have the purpose or effect of presenting a substantial obstacle to a woman seeking an abortion impose an undue burden on the right.

(d) Our adoption of the undue burden analysis does not disturb the central holding of *Roe* v. *Wade,* and we reaffirm that holding. Regardless of whether exceptions are made for particular circumstances, a State may not prohibit any woman from making the ultimate decision to terminate her pregnancy before viability.

(e) We also reaffirm *Roe's* holding that "subsequent to viability, the State in promoting its interest in the potentiality of human life may, if it chooses, regulate, and even proscribe, abortion except where it is necessary, in appropriate medical judgment, for the preservation of the life or health of the mother."

These principles control our assessment of the Pennsylvania statute, and we now turn to the issue of the validity of its challenged provisions. [Justices O'Connor, Kennedy, and Souter conclude that only the spousal consent rule violates the "undue burden" test.]

[T]he case is remanded for proceedings consistent with this opinion. . . .

*It is so ordered.*

JUSTICE STEVENS, concurring in part and dissenting in part . . . [omitted].

## JUSTICE BLACKMUN, concurring in part and dissenting in part. . . .

In one sense, the Court's approach is worlds apart from that of The Chief Justice and Justice Scalia. And yet, in another sense, the distance between the two approaches is short—the distance is but a single vote.

I am 83 years old. I cannot remain on the Court forever, and when I do step down, the confirmation process for my successor well may focus on the issue before us today. That, I regret, may be exactly where the choice between the two worlds will be made.

## THE CHIEF JUSTICE, with whom JUSTICE WHITE, JUSTICE SCALIA, and JUSTICE THOMAS join, concurring in the judgment in part and dissenting in part.

The joint opinion, following its newly minted variation on stare decisis, retains the outer shell of *Roe* v. *Wade,* but beats a wholesale retreat from the substance of that case. We believe that *Roe* was wrongly decided, and that it can and should be overruled consistently with our traditional approach to stare decisis in constitutional cases. We would adopt the approach of the plurality in *Webster* v. *Reproductive Health Services,* and uphold the challenged provisions of the Pennsylvania statute in their entirety. . . .

The joint opinion . . . cannot bring itself to say that *Roe* was correct as an original matter, but the authors are of the view that "the immediate question is not the soundness of *Roe's* resolution of the issue, but the precedential force that must be accorded to its holding." Instead of claiming that *Roe* was correct as a matter of original constitutional interpretation, the opinion therefore contains an elaborate discussion of stare decisis. This discussion of the principle of stare decisis appears to be almost entirely dicta, because the joint opinion does not apply that principle in dealing with *Roe. Roe* decided that a woman had a fundamental right to an abortion. The joint opinion rejects that view. *Roe* decided that abortion regulations were to be subjected to "strict scrutiny" and could be justified only in the light of "compelling state interests." The joint opinion rejects that view. *Roe* analyzed abortion regulation under a rigid trimester framework, a framework which has guided this Court's decisionmaking for 19 years. The joint opinion rejects that framework. . . .

We have stated above our belief that the Constitution does not subject state abortion regulations to heightened scrutiny. . . . A woman's interest in having an abortion is a form of liberty protected by the Due Process Clause, but States may regulate abortion procedures in ways rationally related to a legitimate state interest. With this rule in mind, we examine each of the challenged provisions. [Chief Justice Rehnquist concludes that each provision of the Pennsylvania statute is rationally related to a legitimate state interest.]

**JUSTICE SCALIA, with whom the CHIEF JUSTICE, JUSTICE WHITE, and JUSTICE THOMAS join, concurring in the judgment in part and dissenting in part. . . .**

The States may, if they wish, permit abortion-on-demand, but the Constitution does not require them to do so. The permissibility of abortion, and the limitations upon it, are to be resolved like most important questions in our democracy: by citizens trying to persuade one another and then voting. As the Court acknowledges, "where reasonable people disagree the government can adopt one position or the other." The Court is correct in adding the qualification that this "assumes a state of affairs in which the choice does not intrude upon a protected liberty,"—but the crucial part of that qualification is the penultimate word. A State's choice between two positions on which reasonable people can disagree is constitutional even when (as is often the case) it intrudes upon a "liberty" in the absolute sense. Laws against bigamy, for example—which entire societies of reasonable people disagree with—intrude upon men and women's liberty to marry and live with one another. But bigamy happens not to be a liberty specially "protected" by the Constitution.

That is, quite simply, the issue in this case: not whether the power of a woman to abort her unborn child is a "liberty" in the absolute sense; or even whether it is a liberty of great importance to many women. Of course it is both. The issue is whether it is a liberty protected by the Constitution of the United States. I am sure it is not. I reach that conclusion not because of anything so exalted as my views concerning the "concept of existence, of meaning, of the universe, and of the mystery of human life." Rather, I reach it for the same reason I reach the conclusion that bigamy is not constitutionally protected—because of two simple facts: (1) the Constitution says absolutely nothing about it, and (2) the longstanding traditions of American society have permitted it to be legally proscribed. . . .

In truth, I am as distressed as the Court, . . . about the "political pressure" directed to the Court: the marches, the mail, the protests aimed at inducing us to change our opinions. How upsetting it is, that so many of our citizens (good people, not lawless ones, on both sides of this abortion issue, and on various sides of other issues as well) think that we Justices should properly take into account their views, as though we were engaged not in ascertaining an objective law but in determining some kind of social consensus. The Court would profit, I think, from giving less attention to the fact of this distressing phenomenon, and more attention to the cause of it. . . .

What makes all this relevant to the bothersome application of "political pressure" against the Court are the twin facts that the American people love democracy and the American people are not fools. As long as this Court thought (and the people thought) that we Justices were doing essentially lawyers' work up here—reading text and discerning our society's traditional understanding of that text—the public pretty much left us alone. Texts and traditions are facts to study, not convictions to demonstrate about. But if in reality our process of constitutional adjudication consists primarily of making value judgments, . . . then a free and intelligent people's attitude towards us can be expected to be (ought to be) quite different. The people know that their value judgments are quite as good as those taught in any law school—maybe better. If, indeed, the "liberties" protected by the Constitution are, as the Court says, undefined and unbounded, then the people should demonstrate, to protest that we do not implement their values instead of ours. Not only that, but confirmation hearings for new Justices should deteriorate into question-and-answer sessions in which Senators go through a list of their constituents' most favored and most disfavored alleged constitutional rights, and seek the nominee's commitment to support or oppose them. Value judgments, after all, should be voted on, not dictated; and if our Constitution has somehow accidentally committed them to the Supreme Court, at least we can have a sort of plebiscite each time a new nominee to that body is put forward. Justice Blackmun not only regards this prospect with equanimity, he solicits it. . . .

## Stenberg v. Carhart
### 530 U.S. 914, 120 S.Ct. 2597, 147 L.Ed. 2d 743 (2000)
### http://laws.findlaw.com/us/530/914.html

At the time of this litigation, Don Stenberg was Attorney General of Nebraska; Leroy Carhart was a physician who performed abortions at a clinic in Nebraska. The remaining facts and constitutional issues are contained in the opinions below.

**JUSTICE BREYER delivered the opinion of the Court. . . .**

Three established principles determine the issue before us. We shall set them forth in the language of the joint opinion in [*Planned Parenthood* v.] *Casey*. First, before "viability . . . the woman has a right to choose to terminate her pregnancy."

Second, "a law designed to further the State's interest in fetal life which imposes an undue burden on the woman's decision before fetal viability" is unconstitutional. An "undue burden is . . . shorthand for the conclusion that a state regulation has the purpose or effect of placing a substantial obstacle in the path of a woman seeking an abortion of a nonviable fetus."

Third, " 'subsequent to viability, the State in promoting its interest in the potentiality of human life may, if it chooses, regulate, and even proscribe, abortion except where it is necessary, in appropriate medical judgment, for the preservation of the life or health of the mother.' "

We apply these principles to a Nebraska law banning "partial birth abortion." The statute reads as follows:

No partial birth abortion shall be performed in this state, unless such procedure is necessary to save the life of the mother whose life is endangered by a physical disorder, physical illness, or physical injury, including a life-endangering physical condition caused by or arising from the pregnancy itself.

The statute defines "partial birth abortion" as:

an abortion procedure in which the person performing the abortion partially delivers vaginally a living unborn child before killing the unborn child and completing the delivery.

It further defines "partially delivers vaginally a living unborn child before killing the unborn child" to mean

deliberately and intentionally delivering into the vagina a living unborn child, or a substantial portion thereof, for the purpose of performing a procedure that the person performing such procedure knows will kill the unborn child and does kill the unborn child.

Dr. Leroy Carhart is a Nebraska physician who performs abortions in a clinical setting. He brought this lawsuit in Federal District Court seeking a declaration that the Nebraska statute violates the Federal Constitution, and asking for an injunction forbidding its enforcement.

After a trial on the merits, during which both sides presented several expert witnesses, the District Court held the statute unconstitutional. On appeal, the Eighth Circuit affirmed. . . .

About 90% of all abortions performed in the United States take place during the first trimester of pregnancy, before 12 weeks of gestational age. During the first trimester, the predominant abortion method is "vacuum aspiration," which involves insertion of a vacuum tube (cannula) into the uterus to evacuate the contents. Such an abortion is typically performed on an outpatient basis under local anesthesia. . . .

Approximately 10% of all abortions are performed during the second trimester of pregnancy (12 to 24 weeks). In the early 1970's, inducing labor through the injection of saline into the uterus was the predominant method of second trimester abortion. Today, however, the medical profession has switched from medical induction of labor to surgical procedures for most second trimester abortions. The most commonly used procedure is called "dilation and evacuation" (D&E). That procedure (together with a modified form of vacuum aspiration used in the early second trimester) accounts for about 95% of all abortions performed from 12 to 20 weeks of gestational age. . . .

At trial, Dr. Carhart . . . described a variation of the D&E procedure, which they referred to as an "intact D&E." Like other versions of the D&E technique, it begins with induced dilation of the cervix. The procedure then involves removing the fetus from the uterus through the cervix "intact," i.e., in one pass, rather than in several passes. It is used after 16 weeks at the earliest, as vacuum aspiration becomes ineffective and the fetal skull becomes too large to pass through the cervix. The intact D&E proceeds in one of two ways, depending on the presentation of the fetus. If the fetus presents head first (a vertex presentation), the doctor collapses the skull; and the doctor then extracts the entire fetus through the cervix. If the fetus presents feet first (a breech presentation), the doctor pulls the fetal body through the cervix, collapses the skull, and extracts the fetus through the cervix. The

breech extraction version of the intact D&E is also known commonly as "dilation and extraction," or D&X. In the late second trimester, vertex, breech, and traverse/compound (sideways) presentations occur in roughly similar proportions. . . .

Despite the technical differences we have just described, intact D&E and D&X are sufficiently similar for us to use the terms interchangeably. . . .

There are no reliable data on the number of D&X abortions performed annually. Estimates have ranged between 640 and 5,000 per year. . . .

The fact that Nebraska's law applies both pre- and postviability aggravates the constitutional problem presented. The State's interest in regulating abortion previability is considerably weaker than postviability. . . .

The question before us is whether Nebraska's statute, making criminal the performance of a "partial birth abortion," violates the Federal Constitution, as interpreted in *Casey* and *Roe* v. *Wade*. We conclude that it does for at least two independent reasons. First, the law lacks any exception " 'for the preservation of the . . . health of the mother.' " Second, it "imposes an undue burden on a woman's ability" to choose a D&E abortion, thereby unduly burdening the right to choose abortion itself. We shall discuss each of these reasons in turn. . . .

[T]he governing standard requires an exception "where it is necessary, in appropriate medical judgment for the preservation of the life or health of the mother," for this Court has made clear that a State may promote but not endanger a woman's health when it regulates the methods of abortion. . . .

Nebraska responds that the law does not require a health exception unless there is a need for such an exception. And here there is no such need, it says. It argues that "safe alternatives remain available" and "a ban on partial-birth abortion/D&X would create no risk to the health of women." . . . The State fails to demonstrate that banning D&X without a health exception may not create significant health risks for women, because the record shows that significant medical authority supports the proposition that in some circumstances, D&X would be the safest procedure. . . .

Nebraska has not convinced us that a health exception is "never necessary to preserve the health of women." Rather, a statute that altogether forbids D&X creates a significant health risk. The statute consequently must contain a health exception. . . . Requiring such an exception in this case is no departure from *Casey,* but simply a straightforward application of its holding. . . .

The Eighth Circuit found the Nebraska statute unconstitutional because, in *Casey's* words, it has the "effect of placing a substantial obstacle in the path of a woman seeking an abortion of a nonviable fetus." It thereby places an "undue burden" upon a woman's right to terminate her pregnancy before viability. Nebraska does not deny that the statute imposes an "undue burden" if it applies to the more commonly used D&E procedure as well as to D&X. And we agree with the Eighth Circuit that it does so apply.

Our earlier discussion of the D&E procedure shows that it falls within the statutory prohibition. . . .

Even if the statute's basic aim is to ban D&X, its language makes clear that it also covers a much broader category of procedures. The language does not track the medical differences between D&E and D&X—though it would have been a simple matter, for example, to provide an exception for the performance of D&E and other abortion procedures. . . .

The Nebraska State Attorney General argues that the statute does differentiate between the two procedures. He says that the statutory words "substantial portion" mean "the child up to the head." He consequently denies the statute's application where the physician introduces into the birth canal a fetal arm or leg or anything less than the entire fetal body. He argues further that we must defer to his views about the meaning of the state statute. We cannot accept the Attorney General's narrowing interpretation of the Nebraska statute. This Court's case law makes clear that we are not to give the Attorney General's interpretative views controlling weight. . . .

We are aware that adopting the Attorney General's interpretation might avoid [this] constitutional problem . . . [but] "such a construction [must be] reasonable and readily apparent." . . . [I]t is not reasonable to replace the term "substantial portion" with the Attorney General's phrase "body up to the head." . . .

[U]sing this law some present prosecutors and future Attorneys General may choose to pursue physicians who use D&E procedures, the most commonly used method for performing previability second trimester abortions. All those who perform abortion procedures using that method must fear prosecution, conviction, and imprisonment. The result is an undue burden upon a woman's right to make an abortion decision. We must consequently find the statute unconstitutional.

The judgment of the Court of Appeals is
*Affirmed.*

JUSTICE STEVENS, with whom JUSTICE GINSBURG joins, concurring . . . [omitted].

JUSTICE O'CONNOR, concurring . . . [omitted].

JUSTICE GINSBURG, with whom JUSTICE STEVENS joins, concurring . . . [omitted].

CHIEF JUSTICE REHNQUIST, dissenting . . . [omitted].

### JUSTICE SCALIA, dissenting.

I am optimistic enough to believe that, one day, *Stenberg* v. *Carhart* will be assigned its rightful place in the history of this Court's jurisprudence beside *Korematsu* and *Dred Scott.* . . . The notion that the Constitution of the United States . . . prohibits the States from simply banning this visibly brutal means of eliminating our half-born posterity is quite simply absurd.

### JUSTICE KENNEDY, with whom THE CHIEF JUSTICE joins, dissenting.

For close to two decades after *Roe* v. *Wade,* the Court gave but slight weight to the interests of the separate States when their legislatures sought to address persisting concerns raised by the existence of a woman's right to elect an abortion in defined circumstances. When the Court reaffirmed the essential holding of *Roe* [in *Casey*], central premise was that the States retain a critical and legitimate role in legislating on the subject of abortion, as limited by the woman's right the Court restated and again guaranteed. The political processes of the State are not to be foreclosed from enacting laws to promote the life of the unborn and to ensure respect for all human life and its potential. The State's constitutional authority is a vital means for citizens to address these grave and serious issues, as they must if we are to progress in knowledge and understanding and in the attainment of some degree of consensus.

The Court's decision today, in my submission, repudiates this understanding by invalidating a statute advancing critical state interests, even though the law denies no woman the right to choose an abortion and places no undue burden upon the right. The legislation is well within the State's competence to enact. . . .

The Court's failure to accord any weight to Nebraska's interest in prohibiting partial-birth abortion is erroneous and undermines its discussion and holding. . . . The majority views the procedures from the perspective of the abortionist, rather than from the perspective of a society shocked when confronted with a new method of ending human life. . . .

As described by Dr. Carhart, the D&E procedure requires the abortionist to use instruments to grasp a portion (such as a foot or hand) of a developed and living fetus and drag the grasped portion out of the uterus into the vagina. Dr. Carhart uses the traction created by the opening between the uterus and vagina to dismember the fetus, tearing the grasped portion away from the remainder of the body. . . . The fetus, in many cases, dies just as a human adult or child would: It bleeds to death as it is torn from limb from limb. The fetus can be alive at the beginning of the dismemberment process and can survive for a time while its limbs are being torn off. . . . At the conclusion of a D&E abortion no intact fetus remains. In Dr. Carhart's

words, the abortionist is left with "a tray full of pieces."

The other procedure implicated today is called "partial-birth abortion" or the D&X. The D&X can be used, as a general matter, after 19 weeks gestation because the fetus has become so developed that it may survive intact partial delivery from the uterus into the vagina. In the D&X, the abortionist initiates the woman's natural delivery process by causing the cervix of the woman to be dilated, sometimes over a sequence of days. The fetus' arms and legs are delivered outside the uterus while the fetus is alive. . . . With only the head of the fetus remaining in utero, the abortionist tears open the skull. . . . The abortionist then inserts a suction tube and vacuums out the developing brain and other matter found within the skull. The process of making the size of the fetus' head smaller is given the clinically neutral term "reduction procedure." . . .

Of the two described procedures, Nebraska seeks only to ban the D&X. In light of the description of the D&X procedure, it should go without saying that Nebraska's ban on partial-birth abortion furthers purposes States are entitled to pursue. . . .

States . . . have an interest in forbidding medical procedures which, in the State's reasonable determination, might cause the medical profession or society as a whole to become insensitive, even disdainful, to life, including life in the human fetus. Abortion, *Casey* held, has consequences beyond the woman and her fetus. . . .

It is argued, however, that a ban on the D&X does not further these interests. This is because, the reasoning continues, the D&E method, which Nebraska claims to be beyond its intent to regulate, can still be used to abort a fetus and is no less dehumanizing than the D&X method. While not adopting the argument in express terms, the Court indicates tacit approval of it by refusing to reject it in a forthright manner. . . . The issue is not whether members of the judiciary can see a difference between the two procedures. It is whether Nebraska can. The Court's refusal to recognize Nebraska's right to declare a moral difference between the procedure is a dispiriting disclosure of the illogic and illegitimacy of the Court's approach to the entire case. . . .

Those who oppose abortion would agree, indeed would insist, that both procedures are subject to the most severe moral condemnation, condemnation reserved for the most repulsive human conduct. This is not inconsistent, however, with the further proposition that as an ethical and moral matter, D&X is distinct from D&E and is a more serious concern for medical ethics and the morality of the larger society the medical profession must serve. Nebraska must obey the legal regime which has declared the right of the woman to have an abortion before viability. Yet it retains its power to adopt regulations which do not impose an undue burden on the woman's right. . . .

Demonstrating a further and basic misunderstanding of *Casey,* the Court holds the ban on the D&X procedure fails because it does not include an exception permitting an abortionist to perform a D&X whenever he believes it will best preserve the health of the woman. . . .

Substantial evidence supports Nebraska's conclusion that its law denies no woman a safe abortion. The most to be said for the D&X is it may present an unquantified lower risk of complication for a particular patient but that other proven safe procedures remain available even for this patient. Under these circumstances, the Court is wrong to limit its inquiry to the relative physical safety of the two procedures, with the slightest potential difference requiring the invalidation of the law. . . .

It is also important to recognize that the D&X is effective only when the fetus is close to viable or, in fact, viable; thus the State is regulating the process at the point where its interest in life is nearing its peak.

Courts are ill-equipped to evaluate the relative worth of particular surgical procedures. The legislatures of the several States have superior factfinding capabilities in this regard. . . .

Justice O'Connor [concurring] assures the people of Nebraska they are free to redraft the law to include an exception permitting the D&X to be performed when "the procedure,

in appropriate medical judgment, is necessary to preserve the health of the mother." The assurance is meaningless. She has joined an opinion which accepts that Dr. Carhart exercises "appropriate medical judgment" in using the D&X for every patient in every procedure, regardless of indications, after 15 weeks' gestation. . . . A ban which depends on the "appropriate medical judgment" of Dr. Carhart is no ban at all. He will be unaffected by any new legislation. This, of course, is the vice of a health exception resting in the physician's discretion. . . .

The Court's next holding is that Nebraska's ban forbids both the D&X procedure and the more common D&E procedure. In so ruling the Court misapplies settled doctrines of statutory construction and contradicts *Casey's* premise that the States have a vital constitutional position in the abortion debate. . . .

The text [of the statute] demonstrates the law applies only to the D&X procedure. Nebraska's intention is demonstrated at three points in the statutory language: references to "partial-birth abortion" and to the "delivery" of a fetus; and the requirement that the delivery occur "before" the performance of the death-causing procedure. . . .

The statute's intended scope is demonstrated by its requirement that the banned procedure include a partial "delivery" of the fetus into the vagina and the completion of a "delivery" at the end of the procedure. Only removal of an intact fetus can be described as a "delivery" of a fetus and only the D&X involves an intact fetus. . . .

Ignoring substantial medical and ethical opinion, the Court substitutes its own judgment for the judgment of Nebraska and some 30 other States and sweeps the law away. . . .

The State chose to forbid a procedure many decent and civilized people find so abhorrent as to be among the most serious of crimes against human life, while the State still protected the woman's autonomous right of choice as reaffirmed in *Casey*. The Court closes its eyes to these profound concerns. . . .

JUSTICE THOMAS, with whom THE CHIEF JUSTICE and JUSTICE SCALIA join, dissenting . . . [omitted].

## III. RIGHT TO DIE

### *Washington* v. *Glucksberg*
### 521 U.S. 702, 117 S.Ct. 2258, 138 L.Ed. 2d 772 (1997)
### http://laws.findlaw.com/us/521/702.html

The state of Washington makes "[p]romoting a suicide attempt" a felony. "A person is guilty of [that crime] when he knowingly causes or aids another person to attempt suicide." In 1994 Harold Glucksberg, three other physicians, Compassion in Dying (a nonprofit organization), and three gravely ill patients (who succumbed before the conclusion of this litigation) brought suit in the U.S. District Court for the Western District of Washington, claiming that the ban was facially unconstitutional. They argued that the liberty protected by the due process clause of the Fourteenth Amendment included a choice by a mentally competent, terminally ill adult to commit suicide with the assistance of a physician. The district court agreed, finding that the statute placed an "undue burden" on the exercise of that constitutionally protected liberty interest. The court also held that the statute violated the requirement of the equal protection clause that similarly situated persons be treated alike. A three-judge panel of the U.S. Court of Appeals for the Ninth Circuit reversed, but on rehearing the en banc Ninth Circuit upheld the district court. Without reaching the equal protection issue, the appeals court balanced the liberty interest, which encompassed a constitutionally recognized "right to die," against the state's interests in prohibiting assisted suicide and concluded that the ban was unconstitutional "as applied to terminally ill competent adults who wish to hasten their deaths with medication prescribed by their physicians. . . ." As of 1997, no state criminalized attempted (or successful) suicide; assisted suicide was illegal in 45 states; its status in the remaining five was unclear. Oregon, one of the five, was the only state which had permitted physician-assisted suicide, but, because of continuing court challenges, the results of that 1994 referendum did not go into effect until after this case was decided. Majority: Rehnquist, Stevens, O'Connor, Scalia, Kennedy, Souter, Thomas, Ginsburg, Breyer.

**CHIEF JUSTICE REHNQUIST delivered the opinion of the Court. . . .**

The question presented in this case is whether Washington's prohibition against "caus[ing]" or "aid[ing]" a suicide offends the Fourteenth Amendment to the United States Constitution. We hold that it does not. . . .

Attitudes toward suicide itself have changed since [it was once an offense at common law], but our laws have consistently condemned, and continue to prohibit, assisting suicide. Despite changes in medical technology and notwithstanding an increased emphasis on the importance of end-of-life decision-making, we have not retreated from this prohibition. Against this backdrop of history, tradition, and practice, we now turn to respondents' constitutional claim.

The Due Process Clause guarantees more than fair process, and the "liberty" it protects includes more than the absence of physical restraint. . . . The Clause also provides heightened protection against government interference with certain fundamental rights and liberty interests. In a long line of cases, we have held that, in addition to the specific freedoms protected by the Bill of Rights, the "liberty" specially protected by the Due Process Clause includes the rights to marry, to have children, to direct the education and upbringing of one's children, to marital privacy, to use contraception, to bodily integrity, and to abortion. We have also assumed, and strongly suggested, that the Due Process Clause protects the traditional right to refuse unwanted lifesaving medical treatment.

But we "ha[ve] always been reluctant to expand the concept of substantive due process because guideposts for responsible decision-making in this unchartered area are scarce and open-ended." By extending constitutional protection to an asserted right or liberty interest, we, to a great extent, place the matter outside the arena of public debate and legislative action. We must therefore "exercise the utmost care whenever we are asked to break new ground in this field," lest the liberty protected by the Due Process Clause be subtly transformed into the policy preferences of the members of this Court.

Our established method of substantive-due-process analysis has two primary features: First, we have regularly observed that the Due Process Clause specially protects those fundamental rights and liberties which are, objectively, "deeply rooted in this Nation's history and tradition," . . . and "implicit in the concept of ordered liberty," such that "neither liberty nor justice would exist if they were sacrificed." Second, we have required in substantive-due-process cases a "careful description" of the asserted fundamental liberty interest. Our Nation's history, legal traditions, and practices thus provide the crucial "guideposts for responsible decisionmaking," that direct and restrain our exposition of the Due Process Clause. . . .

[T]he development of this Court's substantive-due-process jurisprudence . . . has been a process whereby the outlines of the "liberty" specially protected by the Fourteenth Amendment—never fully clarified, to be sure, and perhaps not capable of being fully clarified—have at least been carefully refined by concrete examples involving fundamental rights found to be deeply rooted in our legal tradition. This approach tends to rein in the subjective elements that are necessarily present in due-process judicial review. In addition, by establishing a threshold requirement—that a challenged state action implicate a fundamental right—before requiring more than a reasonable relation to a legitimate state

interest to justify the action, it avoids the need for complex balancing of competing interests in every case.

Turning to the claim at issue here, the Court of Appeals stated that "[p]roperly analyzed, the first issue to be resolved is whether there is a liberty interest in determining the time and manner of one's death," or, in other words, "[i]s there a right to die?" Similarly, respondents assert a "liberty to choose how to die" and a right to "control of one's final days," and describe the asserted liberty as "the right to choose a humane, dignified death," and "the liberty to shape death." . . .

We now inquire whether this asserted right has any place in our Nation's traditions. Here . . . we are confronted with a consistent and almost universal tradition that has long rejected the asserted right, and continues explicitly to reject it today, even for terminally ill, mentally competent adults. To hold for respondents, we would have to reverse centuries of legal doctrine and practice, and strike down the considered policy choice of almost every State. . . .

Respondents contend, however, that the liberty interest they assert is consistent with this Court's substantive-due-process line of cases, if not with this Nation's history and practice. Pointing to [*Planned Parenthood* v.] *Casey* and *Cruzan* [v. *Director*], respondents read our jurisprudence in this area as reflecting a general tradition of "self-sovereignty," and as teaching that the "liberty" protected by the Due Process Clause includes "basic and intimate exercises of personal autonomy." . . . According to respondents, our liberty jurisprudence, and the broad, individualistic principles it reflects, protects the "liberty of competent, terminally ill adults to make end-of-life decisions free of undue government interference." The question presented in this case, however, is whether the protections of the Due Process Clause include a right to commit suicide with another's assistance. With this "careful description" of respondents' claim in mind, we turn to *Casey* and *Cruzan*.

In *Cruzan*, we considered whether Nancy Beth Cruzan, who had been severely injured in an automobile accident and was in a persistive vegetative state, "ha[d] a right under the United States Constitution which would require the hospital to withdraw life-sustaining treatment" at her parents' request. We . . . stated that "[t]he principle that a competent person has a constitutionally protected liberty interest in refusing unwanted medical treatment may be inferred from our prior decisions." Therefore, "for purposes of [that] case, we assume[d] that the United States Constitution would grant a competent person a constitutionally protected right to refuse lifesaving hydration and nutrition." We concluded that, notwithstanding this right, the Constitution permitted Missouri to require clear and convincing evidence of an incompetent patient's wishes concerning the withdrawal of life-sustaining treatment. . . .

The right assumed in *Cruzan,* however, was not simply deduced from abstract concepts of personal autonomy. Given the common-law rule that forced medication was a battery, and the long legal tradition protecting the decision to refuse unwanted medical treatment, our assumption was entirely consistent with this Nation's history and constitutional traditions. The decision to commit suicide with the assistance of another may be just as personal and profound as the decision to refuse unwanted medical treatment, but it has never enjoyed similar legal protection. . . .

Respondents also rely on *Casey.* . . .

The Court of Appeals, like the District Court, found *Casey* "highly instructive" and "almost prescriptive" for determining "what liberty interest may inhere in a terminally ill person's choice to commit suicide." . . . [T]he Court's opinion in *Casey* described, in a general way and in light of our prior cases, those personal activities and decisions that this Court has identified as so deeply rooted in our history and traditions, or so fundamental to our concept of constitutionally ordered liberty, that they are protected by the Fourteenth Amendment. . . . That many of the rights and liberties protected by the Due Process Clause [involve] personal autonomy does not warrant the sweeping conclusion that any and all important, intimate, and personal decisions are so protected, and *Casey* did not suggest otherwise.

The history of the law's treatment of assisted suicide in this country has been and continues to be one of the rejection of nearly all efforts to permit it. That being the case, our decisions lead us to conclude that the asserted "right" to assistance in committing suicide is not a fundamental liberty interest protected by the Due Process Clause. The Constitution also requires, however, that Washington's assisted-suicide ban be rationally related to legitimate government interests. This requirement is unquestionably met here. As the court below recognized, Washington's assisted-suicide ban implicates a number of state interests.

First, Washington has an "unqualified interest in the preservation of human life." . . . This remains true, as *Cruzan* makes clear, even for those who are near death.

Relatedly, all admit that suicide is a serious public-health problem, especially among persons in otherwise vulnerable groups. . . .

Those who attempt suicide—terminally ill or not—often suffer from depression or other mental disorders. . . . Thus, legal physician-assisted suicide could make it more difficult for the State to protect depressed or mentally ill persons, or those who are suffering from untreated pain, from suicidal impulses.

The State also has an interest in protecting the integrity and ethics of the medical profession. . . . [P]hysician-assisted suicide could, it is argued, undermine the trust that is essential to the doctor-patient relationship by blurring the time-honored line between healing and harming. . . .

Next, the State has an interest in protecting vulnerable groups—including the poor, the elderly, and disabled persons—from abuse, neglect, and mistakes. . . .

The State's interest here goes beyond protecting the vulnerable from coercion; it extends to protecting disabled and terminally ill people from prejudice, negative and inaccurate stereotypes, and "societal indifference." The State's assisted-suicide ban reflects and reinforces its policy that the lives of terminally ill, disabled, and elderly people must be no less valued than the lives of the young and healthy, and that a seriously disabled person's suicidal impulses should be interpreted and treated the same way as anyone else's. . . .

Finally, the State may fear that permitting assisted suicide will start it down the path to voluntary and perhaps even involuntary euthanasia. The Court of Appeals struck down Washington's assisted-suicide ban only "as applied to competent, terminally ill adults who wish to hasten their deaths by obtaining medication prescribed by their doctors." Washington insists, however, that the impact of the court's decision will not and cannot be so limited. If suicide is protected as a matter of constitutional right, it is argued, "every man and woman in the United States must enjoy it." The Court of Appeals' decision, and its expansive reasoning, provide ample support for the State's concerns. . . .

This concern is further supported by evidence about the practice of euthanasia in the Netherlands. The Dutch government's own study revealed that in 1990, there were 2,300 cases of voluntary euthanasia (defined as "the deliberate termination of another's life at his request"), 400 cases of assisted suicide, and more than 1,000 cases of euthanasia without an explicit request. In addition to these latter 1,000 cases, the study found an additional 4,941 cases where physicians administered lethal morphine overdoses without the patients' explicit consent. . . . This study suggests that, despite the existence of various reporting procedures, euthanasia in the Netherlands has not been limited to competent, terminally ill adults who are enduring physical suffering, and that regulation of the practice may not have prevented abuses in cases involving vulnerable persons, including severely disabled neonates and elderly persons suffering from dementia. . . .

We need not weigh exactingly the relative strengths of these various interests. They are unquestionably important and legitimate, and Washington's ban on assisted suicide is at least reasonably related to their promotion and protection. We therefore hold that [the Washington law] does not violate the Fourteenth Amendment, either on its face or "as applied to competent, terminally ill adults who wish to hasten their deaths by obtaining medication prescribed by their doctors."

Throughout the Nation, Americans are engaged in an earnest and profound debate about the morality, legality, and practicality of physician-assisted suicide. Our holding permits this debate to continue, as it should in a democratic society. The decision of the en banc Court of Appeals is reversed, and the case is remanded for further proceedings consistent with this opinion.

*It is so ordered.*

JUSTICE O'CONNOR, with whom JUSTICES GINSBURG and BREYER joined in part, concurring . . . [omitted].

JUSTICE STEVENS, concurring in the judgment . . . [omitted].

JUSTICE SOUTER, concurring in the judgment . . . [omitted].

JUSTICE GINSBURG, concurring in the judgment . . . [omitted].

JUSTICE BREYER, concurring in the judgment . . . [omitted].

[The concurring opinions generally emphasized that physicians may take aggressive steps, such as prescribing more potent drugs to relieve the pain of terminal patients, even if the treatment hastens death. Justice O'Connor suggested that this "palliative care" may be a constitutional right, and Justice Breyer counseled that a law that exposed dying patients to "serious and otherwise unavoidable physical pain" would be constitutionally suspect.—ED.]

## IV. SEXUAL ORIENTATION

### *Lawrence* v. *Texas*
### 539 U.S. 558, 123 S.Ct. 2472, 156 L.Ed. 2d 508 (2003)
### http://supct.law.cornell.edu/supct/html/02-102.ZS.html

Because of a reported weapons disturbance, police in Houston, Texas, entered the apartment of John Lawrence where they observed Lawrence and Tyron Garner, both adults, engaging in consensual anal intercourse. Both Lawrence and Garner were arrested and convicted under a Texas law that criminalized "deviate sexual intercourse with another individual of the same sex." Deviate sexual intercourse was in turn defined as: "(a) any contact between any part of the genitals of one person and the mouth or anus of another person; or (b) the penetration of the genitals or the anus of another person with an object." Against objections that the statute violated the due process and equal protection clauses of the Fourteenth Amendment, the Texas Court of Appeals for the Fourteenth District in 2001 affirmed their convictions, citing the U.S. Supreme Court's decision in *Bowers* v. *Hardwick* (1986) as dispositive of their due process claim. Justice Kennedy's opinion of the Court is noteworthy because it was the first to cite a decision by the European Court of Human Rights. Majority: Kennedy, Breyer, Ginsburg, O'Connor, Souter, Stevens. Dissenting: Scalia, Rehnquist, Thomas.

**JUSTICE KENNEDY delivered the opinion of the Court.**

Liberty protects the person from unwarranted government intrusions into a dwelling or other private places. In our tradition the State is not omnipresent in the home. And there are other spheres of our lives and existence, outside the home, where the State should not be a dominant presence. Freedom extends beyond spatial bounds. Liberty presumes an autonomy of self that includes freedom of thought, belief, expression, and certain intimate conduct. The instant case involves liberty of the person both in its spatial and more transcendent dimensions.

The question before the Court is the validity of a Texas statute making it a crime for two persons of the same sex to engage in certain intimate sexual conduct. . . .

We conclude the case should be resolved by determining whether the petitioners were free as adults to engage in the private conduct in the exercise of their liberty under the Due Process Clause of the Fourteenth Amendment to the Constitution. For this inquiry we deem

it necessary to reconsider the Court's holding in *Bowers*. . . .

The facts in *Bowers* had some similarities to the instant case. A police officer, whose right to enter seems not to have been in question, observed Hardwick, in his own bedroom, engaging in intimate sexual conduct with another adult male. The conduct was in violation of a Georgia statute making it a criminal offense to engage in sodomy. One difference between the two cases is that the Georgia statute prohibited the conduct whether or not the participants were of the same sex, while the Texas statute, as we have seen, applies only to participants of the same sex. Hardwick was not prosecuted, but he brought an action in federal court to declare the state statute invalid. He alleged he was a practicing homosexual and that the criminal prohibition violated rights guaranteed to him by the Constitution. The Court, in an opinion by Justice White, sustained the Georgia law. . . . Four Justices dissented.

The Court began its substantive discussion in *Bowers* as follows: "The issue presented is whether the Federal Constitution confers a

fundamental right upon homosexuals to engage in sodomy and hence invalidates the
laws of the many States that still make such
conduct illegal and have done so for a very
long time." That statement, we now conclude,
discloses the Court's own failure to appreciate
the extent of the liberty at stake. To say that
the issue in *Bowers* was simply the right to
engage in certain sexual conduct demeans the
claim the individual put forward, just as it
would demean a married couple were it to be
said marriage is simply about the right to have
sexual intercourse. The laws involved in
*Bowers* and here are, to be sure, statutes that
purport to do no more than prohibit a particular sexual act. Their penalties and purposes,
though, have more far-reaching consequences,
touching upon the most private human conduct, sexual behavior, and in the most private
of places, the home. The statutes do seek to
control a personal relationship that, whether or
not entitled to formal recognition in the law, is
within the liberty of persons to choose without
being punished as criminals.

This, as a general rule, should counsel
against attempts by the State, or a court, to define the meaning of the relationship or to set
its boundaries absent injury to a person or
abuse of an institution the law protects. It suffices for us to acknowledge that adults may
choose to enter upon this relationship in the
confines of their homes and their own private
lives and still retain their dignity as free persons. When sexuality finds overt expression
in intimate conduct with another person, the
conduct can be but one element in a personal
bond that is more enduring. The liberty protected by the Constitution allows homosexual
persons the right to make this choice.

Having misapprehended the claim of liberty there presented to it, and thus stating the
claim to be whether there is a fundamental
right to engage in consensual sodomy, the
Bowers Court said: "Proscriptions against that
conduct have ancient roots." In academic writings, and in many of the scholarly amicus
briefs filed to assist the Court in this case,
there are fundamental criticisms of the historical premises relied upon by the majority and
concurring opinions in *Bowers*. We need not

enter this debate in the attempt to reach a definitive historical judgment, but the following
considerations counsel against adopting the
definitive conclusions upon which *Bowers*
placed such reliance.

At the outset it should be noted that there is
no longstanding history in this country of laws
directed at homosexual conduct as a distinct
matter. Beginning in colonial times there were
prohibitions of sodomy derived from the
English criminal laws passed in the first instance by the Reformation Parliament of 1533.
The English prohibition was understood to
include relations between men and women
as well as relations between men and men.
Nineteenth-century commentators similarly
read American sodomy, buggery, and crime-
against-nature statutes as criminalizing certain
relations between men and women and between men and men. The absence of legal
prohibitions focusing on homosexual conduct
may be explained in part by noting that according to some scholars the concept of the
homosexual as a distinct category of person
did not emerge until the late 19th century. . . .
Thus early American sodomy laws were not
directed at homosexuals as such but instead
sought to prohibit nonprocreative sexual activity more generally. This does not suggest
approval of homosexual conduct. It does tend
to show that this particular form of conduct
was not thought of as a separate category from
like conduct between heterosexual persons.

Laws prohibiting sodomy do not seem to
have been enforced against consenting adults
acting in private. A substantial number of
sodomy prosecutions and convictions for
which there are surviving records were for
predatory acts against those who could not
or did not consent, as in the case of a minor or
the victim of an assault. As to these, one purpose for the prohibitions was to ensure there
would be no lack of coverage if a predator
committed a sexual assault that did not constitute rape as defined by the criminal law. . . .

It was not until the 1970's that any State singled out same-sex relations for criminal prosecution, and only nine States have done so. . . .

It must be acknowledged, of course, that
the Court in *Bowers* was making the broader

point that for centuries there have been powerful voices to condemn homosexual conduct as immoral. . . . For many persons these are not trivial concerns but profound and deep convictions accepted as ethical and moral principles to which they aspire and which thus determine the course of their lives. These considerations do not answer the question before us, however. The issue is whether the majority may use the power of the State to enforce these views on the whole society through operation of the criminal law. . . .

In all events we think that our laws and traditions in the past half century are of most relevance here. These references show an emerging awareness that liberty gives substantial protection to adult persons in deciding how to conduct their private lives in matters pertaining to sex. "[H]istory and tradition are the starting point but not in all cases the ending point of the substantive due process inquiry."

This emerging recognition should have been apparent when *Bowers* was decided. In 1955 the American Law Institute promulgated the Model Penal Code and made clear that it did not recommend or provide for "criminal penalties for consensual sexual relations conducted in private." . . .

[A]lmost five years before *Bowers* was decided the European Court of Human Rights considered a case with parallels to *Bowers* and to today's case. An adult male resident in Northern Ireland alleged he was a practicing homosexual who desired to engage in consensual homosexual conduct. The laws of Northern Ireland forbade him that right. He alleged that he had been questioned, his home had been searched, and he feared criminal prosecution. The court held that the laws proscribing the conduct were invalid under the European Convention on Human Rights. Authoritative in all countries that are members of the Council of Europe (21 nations then, 45 nations now), the decision is at odds with the premise in *Bowers* that the claim put forward was insubstantial in our Western civilization.

In our own constitutional system the deficiencies in *Bowers* became even more apparent in the years following its announcement. The 25 States with laws prohibiting the rele-

vant conduct referenced in the Bowers decision are reduced now to 13, of which 4 enforce their laws only against homosexual conduct. In those States where sodomy is still proscribed, whether for same-sex or heterosexual conduct, there is a pattern of nonenforcement with respect to consenting adults acting in private. . . .

*Planned Parenthood of Southeastern Pa.* v. *Casey* reaffirmed the substantive force of the liberty protected by the Due Process Clause. The Casey decision again confirmed that our laws and tradition afford constitutional protection to personal decisions relating to marriage, procreation, contraception, family relationships, child rearing, and education. . . . Persons in a homosexual relationship may seek autonomy for these purposes, just as heterosexual persons do. The decision in *Bowers* would deny them this right. . . .

*Bowers* was not correct when it was decided, and it is not correct today. It ought not to remain binding precedent. *Bowers* v. *Hardwick* should be and now is overruled.

The present case does not involve minors. It does not involve persons who might be injured or coerced or who are situated in relationships where consent might not easily be refused. It does not involve public conduct or prostitution. It does not involve whether the government must give formal recognition to any relationship that homosexual persons seek to enter. The case does involve two adults who, with full and mutual consent from each other, engaged in sexual practices common to a homosexual lifestyle. The petitioners are entitled to respect for their private lives. The State cannot demean their existence or control their destiny by making their private sexual conduct a crime. Their right to liberty under the Due Process Clause gives them the full right to engage in their conduct without intervention of the government. The Texas statute furthers no legitimate state interest which can justify its intrusion into the personal and private life of the individual.

Had those who drew and ratified the Due Process Clauses of the Fifth Amendment or the Fourteenth Amendment known the components of liberty in its manifold possibilities, they might have been more specific. They did not presume to have this insight. They knew times can blind us to certain truths and later generations can see that laws once thought necessary and proper in fact serve only to oppress. As the Constitution endures, persons in every generation can invoke its principles in their own search for greater freedom.

The judgment of the Court of Appeals for the Texas Fourteenth District is reversed, and the case is remanded for further proceedings not inconsistent with this opinion.

*It is so ordered.*

### JUSTICE O'CONNOR, concurring in the judgment. . . .

I joined *Bowers,* and do not join the Court in overruling it. Nevertheless, I agree with the Court that Texas' statute banning same-sex sodomy is unconstitutional. Rather than relying on the substantive component of the Fourteenth Amendment's Due Process Clause, as the Court does, I base my conclusion on the Fourteenth Amendment's Equal Protection Clause. . . .

### JUSTICE SCALIA, with whom THE CHIEF JUSTICE and JUSTICE THOMAS join, dissenting.

"Liberty finds no refuge in a jurisprudence of doubt." That was the Court's sententious response [in *Planned Parenthood* v. *Casey*], barely more than a decade ago, to those seeking to overrule *Roe* v. *Wade.* The Court's response today, to those who have engaged in a 17-year crusade to overrule *Bowers* v. *Hardwick* is very different. The need for stability and certainty presents no barrier. . . .

Our opinions applying the doctrine known as "substantive due process" hold that the Due Process Clause prohibits States from infringing fundamental liberty interests, unless the infringement is narrowly tailored to serve a compelling state interest. . . . All other liberty interests may be abridged or abrogated pursuant to a validly enacted state law if that law is rationally related to a legitimate state interest.

*Bowers* held, first, that criminal prohibitions of homosexual sodomy are not subject to heightened scrutiny because they do not implicate a "fundamental right" under the Due Process Clause. . . .

The Court today does not overrule this holding. Not once does it describe homosexual sodomy as a "fundamental right" or a "fundamental liberty interest," nor does it subject the Texas statute to strict scrutiny. Instead, having failed to establish that the right to homosexual sodomy is " 'deeply rooted in this Nation's history and tradition,' " the Court concludes that the application of Texas's statute to petitioners' conduct fails the rational-basis test, and overrules *Bowers*' holding to the contrary. . . .

I shall address that rational-basis holding presently. First, however, I address some aspersions that the Court casts upon *Bowers*' conclusion that homosexual sodomy is not a "fundamental right"—even though, as I have said, the Court does not have the boldness to reverse that conclusion. . . .

It is (as *Bowers* recognized) entirely irrelevant whether the laws in our long national tradition criminalizing homosexual sodomy were "directed at homosexual conduct as a distinct matter." Whether homosexual sodomy was prohibited by a law targeted at same-sex sexual relations or by a more general law prohibiting both homosexual and heterosexual sodomy, the only relevant point is that it was criminalized—which suffices to establish that homosexual sodomy is not a right "deeply rooted in our Nation's history and tradition." The Court today agrees that homosexual sodomy was criminalized and thus does not dispute the facts on which *Bowers* actually relied.

Next the Court makes the claim, again unsupported by any citations, that "[l]aws prohibiting sodomy do not seem to have been enforced against consenting adults acting in private." The key qualifier here is "acting in private"—since the Court admits that sodomy laws were enforced against consenting adults (although the Court contends that prosecutions were "infrequent"). I do not know what "acting in private" means; surely consensual sodomy, like heterosexual intercourse, is rarely performed on stage. If all the Court means by "acting in private" is "on private premises, with the doors closed and windows covered," it is entirely unsurprising that evidence of enforcement would be hard to come by. (Imagine the circumstances that would enable a search warrant to be obtained for a residence on the ground that there was probable cause to believe that consensual sodomy was then and there occurring.) . . . There are 203 prosecutions for consensual, adult homosexual sodomy reported in the West Reporting system and official state reporters from the years 1880–1995. . . . *Bowers'* conclusion that homosexual sodomy is not a fundamental right "deeply rooted in this Nation's history and tradition" is utterly unassailable.

Realizing that fact, the Court instead says: "[W]e think that our laws and traditions in the past half century are of most relevance here. These references show an emerging awareness that liberty gives substantial protection to adult persons in deciding how to conduct their private lives in matters pertaining to sex." Apart from the fact that such an "emerging awareness" does not establish a "fundamental right," the statement is factually false. States continue to prosecute all sorts of crimes by adults "in matters pertaining to sex": prostitution, adult incest, adultery, obscenity, and child pornography. . . .

Constitutional entitlements do not spring into existence because some States choose to lessen or eliminate criminal sanctions on certain behavior. Much less do they spring into existence, as the Court seems to believe, because foreign nations decriminalize conduct. . . . The Court's discussion of these foreign views (ignoring, of course, the many countries that have retained criminal prohibitions on sodomy) is therefore meaningless dicta. Dangerous dicta, however, since "this Court . . . should not impose foreign moods, fads, or fashions on Americans."

I turn now to the ground on which the Court squarely rests its holding: the contention that there is no rational basis for the law here under attack. This proposition is so out of accord with our jurisprudence—indeed, with the jurisprudence of any society we know—that it requires little discussion.

The Texas statute undeniably seeks to further the belief of its citizens that certain forms of sexual behavior are "immoral and unacceptable"—the same interest furthered by criminal laws against fornication, bigamy, adultery, adult incest, bestiality, and obscenity. *Bowers* held that this was a legitimate state interest. The Court today reaches the opposite conclusion. The Texas statute, it says, "furthers no legitimate state interest which can justify its intrusion into the personal and private life of the individual." The Court embraces instead Justice Stevens' declaration in his *Bowers* dissent, that "the fact that the governing majority in a State has traditionally viewed a particular practice as immoral is not a sufficient reason for upholding a law prohibiting the practice." This effectively decrees the end of all morals legislation. If, as the Court asserts, the promotion of majoritarian sexual morality is not even a legitimate state interest, none of the above-mentioned laws can survive rational-basis review.

Today's opinion is the product of a Court, which is the product of a law-profession culture, that has largely signed on to the so-called homosexual agenda, by which I mean the agenda promoted by some homosexual activists directed at eliminating the moral opprobrium that has traditionally attached to homosexual conduct. . . .

One of the most revealing statements in today's opinion is the Court's grim warning that the criminalization of homosexual conduct is "an invitation to subject homosexual persons to discrimination both in the public and in the private spheres." It is clear from this that the Court has taken sides in the culture war, departing from its role of assuring, as neutral observer, that the democratic rules of engagement are observed. Many Americans do not want persons who openly engage in homosexual conduct as partners in their business, as scoutmasters for their children, as teachers in their children's schools, or as boarders in their home. They view this as protecting themselves and their families from a lifestyle that they believe to be immoral and destructive. The Court views it as "discrimination" which it is the function of our judgments to deter. So imbued is the Court with the law profession's anti-anti-homosexual culture, that it is seemingly unaware that the attitudes of that culture are not obviously "mainstream"; that in most States what the Court calls "discrimination" against those who engage in homosexual acts is perfectly legal; that proposals to ban such "discrimination" under Title VII have repeatedly been rejected by Congress, that in some cases such "discrimination" is mandated by federal statute, (. . . discharge from the armed forces of any service member who engages in or intends to engage in homosexual acts); and that in some cases such "discrimination" is a constitutional right . . . (*Boy Scouts of America* v. *Dale*).

Let me be clear that I have nothing against homosexuals, or any other group, promoting their agenda through normal democratic means. Social perceptions of sexual and other morality change over time, and every group has the right to persuade its fellow citizens that its view of such matters is the best. That homosexuals have achieved some success in that enterprise is attested to by the fact that Texas is one of the few remaining States that criminalize private, consensual homosexual acts. But persuading one's fellow citizens is one thing, and imposing one's views in absence of democratic majority will is something else. . . . What Texas has chosen to do is well within the range of traditional democratic action, and its hand should not be stayed through the invention of a brand-new "constitutional right" by a Court that is impatient of democratic change. It is . . . the premise of our system that those judgments are to be made by the people, and not imposed by a governing caste that knows best.

One of the benefits of leaving regulation of this matter to the people rather than to the courts is that the people, unlike judges, need not carry things to their logical conclusion. The people may feel that their disapprobation of homosexual conduct is strong enough to disallow homosexual marriage, but not strong enough to criminalize private homosexual acts—and may legislate accordingly. The Court today pretends that it possesses a similar freedom of action, so that we need not fear judicial imposition of homosexual marriage, as has recently occurred in Canada. . . . At the end of its opinion—after having laid waste the foundations of our rational-basis jurisprudence—the Court says that the present case "does not involve whether the government must give formal recognition to any relationship that homosexual persons seek to enter." Do not believe it. More illuminating than this bald, unreasoned disclaimer is the progression of thought displayed by an earlier passage in the Court's opinion, which notes the constitutional protections afforded to "personal decisions relating to marriage, procreation, contraception, family relationships, child rearing, and education," and then declares that "[p]ersons in a homosexual relationship may seek autonomy for these purposes, just as heterosexual persons do." Today's opinion dismantles the structure of constitutional law that has permitted a distinction to be made between heterosexual and homosexual unions, insofar as formal recognition in marriage is concerned. If moral disapprobation of homosexual conduct is "no legitimate state interest" for purposes of proscribing that conduct, . . . what justification could there possibly be for denying the benefits of marriage to homosexual couples exercising "[t]he liberty protected by the Constitution?" Surely not the encouragement of procreation, since the sterile and the elderly are allowed to marry. This case "does not involve" the issue of homosexual marriage only if one entertains the belief that principle and logic have nothing to do with the decisions of this Court. Many will hope that, as the Court comfortingly assures us, this is so. . . .

JUSTICE THOMAS, dissenting . . . [omitted].

# CHAPTER FOURTEEN

# *Equal Protection of the Laws*

*[T]here is no more effective practical guaranty against arbitrary and unreasonable government than to require that the principles of law which officials would impose upon a minority must be imposed generally. Conversely, nothing opens the door to arbitrary action so effectively as to allow those officials to pick and choose only a few to whom they will apply legislation and thus to escape the political retribution that might be visited upon them if larger numbers were affected.*

—JUSTICE ROBERT H. JACKSON (1949)

The founders, James Madison in particular, were wedded to the notion that unequal distribution of wealth is the natural result in a society where individuals of differing capacities are free. Accordingly, any affirmative government action on behalf of those less fortunate, ignoring merit, was suspect. Americans today might glibly tell a pollster that they favor of both "liberty" and "equality," but that response obscures an unmistakable tension between those cherished values. As the founders recognized, emphasis on individual liberty promotes inequality among individuals; measures to promote equality constrict individual liberty.

For whatever reason, a conspicuous omission from the Constitution of 1787, as well as the Bill of Rights, is a guaranty guarding against unequal treatment under the law. This provision now so conspicuous in a wide range of Supreme Court decisions dates only from 1868, when it was made part of the Fourteenth Amendment. Along with the privileges and immunities clause and the due process clause designed to safeguard individual rights against encroachment by the states, Section 1 declares: "No State shall . . . deny to any person within its jurisdiction the equal protection of the laws." The **equal protection clause** applies when states make distinctions among similarly situated people and treat them differently. The meaning the Supreme Court gives the clause largely determines what differences among people will be allowed to matter in public policy.

The command of equal protection may sound simple enough, but its meaning continues to spark intense debate both within the Court and throughout the nation. This is partly because the word *equality* itself signifies different things to different people. For some, it stands for **equality of opportunity.** Accordingly, government's duty is to remove discriminatory barriers so that all can participate. Others favor **equality of condition** and so advocate policies such as Head Start or need-based college scholarships that reduce or even eliminate handicaps that many people encounter. Still others find even those measures inadequate. The crippling effects of existing inequalities, whether of wealth, race, or gender, are too strong and pervasive, and so call for policies that promote **equality of result.** Such competing visions of equality play out in contemporary political and legal dramas.

## IDENTIFYING FORBIDDEN DISCRIMINATION

Virtually all legislation *classifies*—that is, discriminates. The challenge presented by the equal protection clause, therefore, is identifying which classifications are permitted and which ones are not. When the Court first considered the clause in the **Slaughterhouse Cases** (1873) (see Chapter Eight) less than a decade after the Civil War and the end of slavery, Justice Miller doubted whether "this sweeping injunction would ever be invoked against any state action" not directed by way of discrimination against blacks as a class. "It is," he wrote, "so clearly a provision for that race and that emergency, that a strong case would be necessary for its application to any other." Indeed, until recent decades, the Supreme Court was inhospitable to litigants who sought protection under the clause to any meaningful degree, outside the contexts (and then only occasionally) of racial discrimination and state regulation of business. Decisions like *Strauder* v. *West Virginia* (1880), invalidating a law that barred blacks from jury service, and *Gulf, C. & S. R.* v. *Ellis* (1897), striking down a requirement that railroads (but not other defendants) pay attorneys' fees in certain cases, were very much the exception. Reliance on the equal protection clause, Justice Holmes observed in 1927, was the "last resort of constitutional arguments" (*Buck* v. *Bell*). Claims of denial of equal protection were "frequently asserted" but "rarely sustained," agreed Justice Jackson in 1949. As will be seen in the sections below, however, the Court in the past half century has put teeth into this part of the Fourteenth Amendment, thus suggesting a "new" equal protection. This dramatic change—from constitutional omission to constitutional nullity to constitutional prominence—carries within itself a fascinating story.

An invigorated guaranty of equal protection persists largely because, in another example of judicial power, the Court has grafted a three-tier interpretive model onto the clause. On the bottom tier is the **rational basis test.** It is the least demanding and has long been used for most classifications. The justices ask only whether the classification in question has a *rational* (or reasonable) relation to a *legitimate* state interest. In other words, is there a nexus between a lawful objective and the means chosen to achieve it? On the top tier and the most demanding is the **strict scrutiny test** that is employed for classifications such as race that the Court deems "suspect," or (as later explained) for classifications that impinge on rights the Court considers fundamental. Ironically, the Court articulated the strict scrutiny test for the first time in **Korematsu v. United States** (1944) in upholding the wartime removal of Japanese-Americans from the West Coast (see Chapter Fifteen). The test of strict scrutiny asks whether the classification is *necessarily related* to a *compelling* government interest. Moreover, such classifications must be *narrowly tailored* to accomplish their purpose.

Laws judged against strict scrutiny are almost certain to fail: "'strict' in theory and fatal in fact." In contrast, laws measured by the rationality test are almost certain to pass. Occasionally, however, as in ***Romer v. Evans*** (1996), a case involving discrimination based on sexual orientation, even this most lenient standard appears to have teeth. Especially for gender-based classifications and those involving illegitimate children, the Court draws from a middle tier to apply **intermediate scrutiny,** or near-strict scrutiny. In such situations, the question is whether the challenged statute is *substantially related* to an *important* state interest. Sometimes the level of scrutiny applied is a function of which government has made the classification: State laws discriminating against aliens, for example, are usually judged by strict scrutiny; congressional acts are not. At other times the Court divides over the appropriate level of scrutiny to apply, as ***Cleburne v. Cleburne Living Center*** (1985) illustrates with respect to mental retardation.

## RACIAL DISCRIMINATION

After abolition of slavery by the Thirteenth Amendment and ratification of the Fourteenth Amendment, whites in some states faced a dilemma. If they wished to keep blacks in an inferior status, they would need an acceptable legal principle. The answer was found in laws requiring segregation of whites and blacks under the formula "**separate but equal.**"

**LEGALIZING THIRD-CLASS CITIZENSHIP.** When the Fourteenth Amendment was invoked in ***Plessy v. Ferguson*** (1896) on behalf of blacks against Louisiana's law requiring racial segregation on trains, the Court refused to allow the equal protection clause to serve even the limited purpose that Justice Miller had earlier acknowledged. Justice Brown's majority opinion in *Plessy* drew an important distinction between political and social equality. The Fourteenth Amendment demanded only the former, and the state law merely reflected prevailing social inequality. Racially segregated facilities were reasonable (and therefore permissible) so long as they were otherwise "equal." In dissent, the Court's only ex-slave owner, Justice Harlan, deplored this emasculation: "Our Constitution is color-blind, and neither knows nor tolerates classes among citizens. In respect to civil rights all citizens are equal before the law." Denouncing the majority's separate-but-equal formula, Harlan predicted that "the judgment this day rendered will in time prove to be quite as pernicious as the decision made by this tribunal in the Dred Scott case" (see Chapter Two).

In the wake of *Plessy,* three kinds of policies developed which denied African Americans their rights well into the twentieth century. First, virtually every aspect of life in the South became racially segregated by law. This fact alone is significant when one remembers that as late as 1930, 79 percent of all American blacks lived in the states of the old Confederacy. Second, laws in southern states systematically excluded blacks from the political process. Third, without the vote, blacks were shortchanged across the board in the delivery of public services such as education. Favors are rarely extended to entire groups that are permanently disfranchised. The spirit of *Plessy* was therefore honored only in part. Though separate, services and facilities (when provided at all) were only occasionally "equal" for blacks.

Although racism backed by law was most visible in the South, where most blacks lived, other regions of the country were hardly immune, as custom and private discrimination combined to perpetuate racist attitudes, segregated neighborhoods, and racially motivated violence, including riots and lynchings. True, the Court struck down an ordinance requiring racially segregated neighborhoods in 1917 (*Buchanan v. Warley*), yet later refused to condemn judicial enforcement of **racially restrictive covenants** in deeds that accomplished the same thing (*Corrigan* v. *Buckley*, 1926).

COUNTERATTACK: THE ROAD TO *BROWN.* In one of the first cases in which the Court began to give serious attention to the equality requirement, the justices invalidated a law under which Gaines, a black applicant, was refused admission to the School of Law of the University of Missouri (*Missouri* ex rel. *Gaines* v. *Canada,* 1938). Missouri made funds available to Gaines and other black applicants to finance their legal education in schools of adjacent states that offered unsegregated educational facilities and argued that by this action it was meeting the separate-but-equal requirement. Chief Justice Hughes, for the majority of seven, disposed of the state's contention emphatically. "By the operation of the laws of Missouri a privilege has been created for white law students which is denied to negroes by reason of their race. The white resident is afforded legal education within the State; the negro resident having the same qualifications is refused it there and must go outside the State to obtain it. That is a denial of equality of legal right. . . ."

A cluster of cases between 1948 and 1950 indicated that the separate-but-equal doctrine would in the future be more difficult to apply in practice. *Sipuel* v. *University of Oklahoma* (1948) held that blacks must be admitted to a state law school or be furnished equivalent professional education within the state. *McLaurin* v. *Oklahoma State Regents* (1950) nullified state efforts to segregate the scholastic activities *on campus* of a black student who had been admitted to the graduate school of the University of Oklahoma pursuant to a federal court order. Finally, a direct challenge to segregated education was presented in *Sweatt* v. *Painter* (1950), where an applicant who had been denied admission to the University of Texas Law School solely on the basis of color claimed that the instruction available in the newly established state law school for blacks was markedly inferior to the instruction at the university and that equal protection of laws was thus denied. In a unanimous decision the Supreme Court ordered his admission to the white school, indicating that it was virtually impossible in practice, at least in professional education, for a state to comply with the separate-but-equal doctrine. Taking into account professional and psychological considerations, thus anticipating the thrust of Chief Justice Warren's opinion in **Brown v. Board of Education** (1954), Chief Justice Vinson of Kentucky left that judicial creation hanging by a hair.

Following the decision in *Sweatt* the National Association for the Advancement of Colored People and other organizations pressed the fight against segregation in public elementary and secondary schools. One of the prominent black attorneys in this drive was Thurgood Marshall, later a justice on the Supreme Court from 1967 to 1991. Would the Court retract the principle of separate but equal, or alternatively, would it construe the requirement of equality so strictly that segregation in practice would be either constitutionally impossible or prohibitively expensive? After hearing arguments in a group of public school segregation cases presented at the 1952 term, the justices were unable to reach a decision. In setting the cases for reargument during the 1953 term, the Court took the unusual step of requesting counsel to provide answers to several questions, some seeking information concerning the intention of the Congress that proposed, and the states that ratified, the Fourteenth Amendment and others requesting advice concerning the kind of orders that the Court should issue were it to find segregated school arrangements unconstitutional.

The Court's caution, though unusual, was understandable. Its decision would affect more than 8 million white children and $2\frac{1}{2}$ million black children in the school systems of 17 states and the District of Columbia, where segregation was required by law, and those of 4 states where segregation was permitted by local option. Even greater issues were involved: If segregation in public schools was deemed a denial of equal protection of the laws, it would be difficult, if not impossible, to defend segregation in other sectors of public life. The legal underpinnings of the social structure of a great part of the nation were under attack.

On May 17, 1954, the Court handed down its decision in *Brown* v. *Board of Education*. Speaking for a unanimous bench, Chief Justice Earl Warren declared that "in the field of public education the doctrine of 'separate but equal' has no place. Separate educational facilities are inherently unequal." The opinion was remarkable not only for its brevity but also for its references to sociological and psychological factors. Reduced to a footnote, these were gratuitous. Earlier decisions had eroded the constitutional foundations of the separate-but-equal formula to the vanishing point. Nor did the historical evidence, furnished at the Court's request and available to it in briefs of counsel, influence the decision. "In approaching this problem," said the chief justice, "we cannot turn the clock back to 1868, when the Amendment was adopted, or even to 1896, when *Plessy* v. *Ferguson* was written. We must consider public education in the light of its full development and its present place in American life throughout the nation."

With *Brown* from Kansas, the Court had combined cases from South Carolina, Virginia, and Delaware. **Bolling v. Sharpe** was the companion case from the District of Columbia and was decided separately on the same day. In the District of Columbia case, the Court came to a similar conclusion, finding an equal protection component in the due process clause of the Fifth Amendment. Having achieved unanimity on this difficult issue, the Court postponed formulation of a decree until the 1954–1955 term and called for additional argument.

**THE LAW AND POLITICS OF RACIAL INTEGRATION.** In the following term the Court handed down its decree in the second Brown case, expressing the conclusion that desegregation in public education would necessarily take place at varying speeds and in different ways, depending on local conditions. U. S. district court judges, employing the flexible principles of equity, were given the task of determining when and how desegregation should take place. In a historic pronouncement, the Court said, "The judgments below . . . are remanded to the district courts to take such proceedings and enter such orders and decrees consistent with this opinion as are necessary and proper to admit to public schools on a racially nondiscriminatory basis *with all deliberate speed*" the parties to these cases (italics added).

Although border states showed a disposition to comply with the Supreme Court's mandate, states in the Deep South began a campaign of active and passive resistance, adopting various legal tactics and devices that delayed the implementation of *Brown*. Several legislatures passed resolutions declaring the desegregation decisions "unlawful." Almost all southern senators and representatives joined in 1956 in issuing a "Declaration of Constitutional Principles" and advocated resistance to compelled desegregation by "all lawful means."

When litigation developed, the Supreme Court staunchly upheld lower federal court decisions ordering steps toward desegregated schools, either by denying certiorari or handing down per curiam rulings. The Eisenhower administration, initially lukewarm in support of *Brown,* took strong steps (including the dispatch of troops) in 1958 to support the orders of a federal court in Arkansas, actions that were upheld by a powerful decision of the Supreme Court in *Cooper* v. *Aaron* (see Chapter Two). The Court did not issue its next significant decision on school integration until 1964 when it ordered the reopening of a public school system in Virginia that had been closed to avoid compliance with *Brown* (*Griffin* v. *School Board of Prince Edward County*). Such defiance was possible partly because most African Americans in southern states were still denied the right to vote. Not until the late 1960s, after rigorous enforcement of the Voting Rights Act (see Chapter Five) had begun, would southern representatives in Congress and local elected officials become more responsive to the needs of black citizens.

The pace of integration also quickened after 1965 because of the combination of two congressional enactments that brought both administrative and financial pressure to bear on school districts. The mid-1960s witnessed the first mass infusion of federal funds into local school coffers, and the Civil Rights Act of 1964 in several ways made continued receipt of Washington's largess conditional on integrated education. Whereas litigation often took years to effect even small changes in the schools, bureaucrats with their hands on the federal faucet could accomplish substantial changes in months. Their efforts were reinforced by the Court.

In 1968 the Court confronted a "freedom-of-choice" integration plan from New Kent County, Virginia (*Green* v. *School Board*). Here, there was no longer an official "white" or "black" label for schools, but all the white children in this rural district elected to remain in the school they had previously attended, and 85 percent of the black children chose to stay at the school they had previously attended. Labels aside, the school populations were "racially identifiable." What the Constitution required, said Justice Brennan, was a plan that produced compliance with *Brown*— a **unitary** as opposed to a **dual school system.** "The burden on a school board today is to come forward with a plan that promises realistically to work, and promises realistically to work now."

Implications of *Green* became apparent in *Swann* v. *Charlotte-Mecklenburg Board of Education* (1971) when the Court upheld an integration plan involving widespread busing within a single metropolitan school district in North Carolina. A previous desegregation plan had left large numbers of predominantly one-race schools. Not surprisingly, this residual segregation in the schools was caused partly by racially segregated neighborhoods, themselves shaped over the years by a system of legally enforced school segregation. "The objective today," declared Chief Justice Burger, "remains to eliminate from the public schools all vestiges of state-imposed segregation."

**CONTINUING EFFECTS OF *BROWN*.** The target of judicial efforts to apply *Brown* was **de jure segregation**—separation of the races that existed because of law and public policy. The most obvious place to find de jure segregation was in the school systems of the southern states, and through 1971, segregation cases in the Supreme Court had a southern focus. Not reached by the Constitution and not at issue in those cases was **de facto segregation**—racial separation that was a product of nongovernmental actions and practices.

In 1973 the Court's attention was drawn to the problem of school segregation outside the South. *Keyes* v. *School District* (1973) involved not statutes or other obvious official actions to create segregated schools but instead various administrative decisions in the 1960s that confined black students to schools in a section of Denver, Colorado. The Supreme Court ruled that where one part of a school system was segregated, the remedy could include busing of students from one part of the district to another to reduce the number of **racially identifiable** (that is, mainly one-race) **schools.** Attendance zones drawn by school boards that resulted in racial imbalances in the classroom could be a constitutional violation just as if old-style southern segregation laws had been in effect.

Although continuing to insist that a distinction be made between de facto and de jure segregation—the former being lawful, the latter unconstitutional—*Keyes* signaled northern communities that federal courts would give close scrutiny to all official decisions affecting the racial composition of schools and that absence of statutory provisions requiring segregation would not prevent judicial action. In other words, *Keyes* enlarged the concept of de jure segregation and correspondingly shrank the concept of de facto segregation.

By this time, a much larger percentage of black pupils attended integrated schools in the South than in the North. As the flight of whites to the suburbs accelerated and blacks and other racial minorities became the dominant population in cities, the question of how to achieve racially integrated schools in multidistrict metropolitan areas became acute. More and more the argument was made that the state governments should bear ultimate responsibility for achieving desegregation: If school district lines perpetuated segregation, a failure by state governments to intercede violated the Fourteenth Amendment. Thus, **Milliken v. Bradley** (1974) posed the question whether the judiciary could impose a multidistrict remedy to correct racial imbalances between districts.

Recall that the remedies the Court upheld in both *Keyes* and *Swann* did not extend beyond the bounds of the single school district involved. *Milliken* began in Detroit as litigation similar to *Keyes*. After attempting to remove racial imbalances within the city school district, the federal district judge recognized the obvious: a school district with a large black majority would still have mainly black schools, even with extensive busing within Detroit. Suburban areas, in contrast, had heavily white school populations. Because the segregation was metropolitan in scope, his remedy encompassed 53 separate suburban school districts covering an area approximately the size of the state of Delaware. By a vote of 5–4, however, the Supreme Court found the remedy excessive. It would be acceptable only on a showing that government was responsible for the racial imbalances between the school districts.

Building on the logic in the 1973 Denver single-district decision, the Court in 1979 approved judicially ordered integration on a massive scale in the public school systems of Columbus and Dayton, Ohio (*Columbus Board of Education* v. *Penick; Dayton Board of Education* v. *Brinkman*). Where schools in a district were largely segregated by race in 1954—not necessarily by law or even by school board policy, such as in the way attendance zones were drawn—and where racially segregated schools persisted, the presumption then became that the schools remained segregated intentionally. The burden of proof shifted to the school board to explain that it was not responsible for the existing segregation. For single school districts, therefore, *Penick* and *Brinkman* almost entirely erased the distinction between de jure and de facto.

Where courts have ordered remedial measures to eliminate de jure segregation, the question of duration sooner or later arises. In *Board of Education* v. *Dowell* (1991), six justices agreed that "federal supervision of local school systems was intended as a temporary measure." If a school board has taken action in good faith to eliminate the vestiges of segregation, the district court may release the board from the integration decree, even if some **resegregation** occurs. Resegregation may have several causes, one being demographic changes within a school district. Reviewing the status of school integration in DeKalb County, Georgia, in 1992, the Court declared that officials were under no obligation to employ "heroic" measures to attain or retain racial balance when the imbalance results neither from the former de jure segregation nor from a later violation by the district, but is attributable only to independent demographic forces. Public schools, however, bear the "burden of showing that any current imbalance is not traceable, in a proximate way, to the prior violation" (*Freeman* v. *Pitts*). The effects, nationwide, of demographic changes on school integration patterns have been profound. Data released in 2003 by the Civil Rights Project at Harvard University revealed that the public schools attended by more than half of black and Latino children had mainly nonwhite enrollments.

**HIGHER EDUCATION.** Integration has been a special problem in states that formerly maintained racially segregated colleges and universities. Before 1954, for instance, Mississippi operated five institutions for whites and three for blacks. Even though the state adopted a race-neutral admission policy after 1964, the campuses remained largely segregated. By the 1990s, 99 percent of the state's white students attending in-state public institutions were enrolled on the five historically white campuses, and 71 percent of the state's black students attending state-run colleges attended the three historically black institutions, where the racial makeup ranged from 92 to 99 percent black. As a result of litigation begun against the state in 1975, the Supreme Court acknowledged an important difference between higher education and primary and secondary education: the role that student choice plays in the former. Even so, race-neutral admission policies may not be enough to satisfy the Constitution's requirement that dual systems be eliminated. Rather, "[i]f the State perpetuates policies and practices traceable to its prior system that continue to have segregative effects—whether by influencing student enrollment decisions or by fostering segregation in other facets of the university system—and such policies are without sound educational justification and can be practicably eliminated," Justice White announced, "the State has not satisfied its burden of proving that it has dismantled its prior system" (*United States* v. *Fordice,* 1992). Lower courts must now determine when previously dual systems must take measures to reduce racial disparities among students and faculty, possibly affecting the existence of degree programs and even of some institutions.

## STATE ACTION

As the distinction between de jure and de facto segregation illustrates, the role of *government* in promoting segregation is crucial to a violation of the equal protection clause. Indeed, the Supreme Court made it clear well over a century ago in the **Civil Rights Cases** that the Fourteenth Amendment does not forbid racial discrimination by everyone, but only by states and their political subdivisions. This is the concept of **state action**—conduct by government, not by a private entity. Confronted in 1883 with congressional legislation guaranteeing equal access to hotels and similar places of public accommodation, the Court balked at giving the equal protection clause positive meaning. By reading the first and fifth sections of the Fourteenth Amendment to mean merely that Congress could pass legislation to supersede discriminatory state legislation and official acts (a power similar to that of judicial review), it preserved the existing federal system at the expense of implementing equal treatment. Bradley's opinion for the Court naively assumed that state laws already required innkeepers and public carriers to serve all unobjectionable persons, and that anyone refused service had an adequate remedy under state law.

Private discrimination is therefore not touched by the Constitution. The line between public and private discrimination, however, is sometimes blurred. How much state involvement must there be in particular situations before the strictures of the equal protection clause apply? During the last 65 years, the Court has expanded the state action principle so that if a state becomes so "entwined" with private affairs that the action of private citizens becomes tantamount to "state action," the Fourteenth Amendment then applies. Thus, in 1972 *Moose Lodge* **v.** *Irvis* posed the question whether the Loyal Order of Moose forfeited its liquor license when it refused to admit Leroy Irvis, black majority leader of the Pennsylvania House of Representatives, as a guest of one of its members. Irvis conceded that Moose members had a constitutional right of association, permitting them to exclude him from their club. But, he argued, their club could not hold a liquor license if they did. Allowing the club to do so would amount to state licensing of racial discrimination. Six justices led by Rehnquist rejected the sweeping argument, instead resolving the case by severing the most objectionable link between the state and the lodge: the Pennsylvania Liquor Control Board's rule that private clubs adhere to their membership rules as a condition for holding a liquor license.

Three years before ratification of the Fourteenth Amendment, the **Thirteenth Amendment** outlawed slavery and involuntary servitude and continues to have a potency of its own. Unlike the Fourteenth, the Thirteenth does not present a state action problem, as the Supreme Court demonstrated in 1968 when it construed the Civil Rights Act of 1866, enacted on the authority of the Thirteenth, to bar private discrimination in housing. **Section 1982** of that act reads, "All citizens of the United States shall have the same right, in every State and Territory, as is enjoyed by white citizens thereof to inherit, purchase, lease, sell, hold and convey real and personal property." *Jones* v. *Mayer* upheld the right of a black complainant to sue a white housing development company for refusing to sell him a house. Lower federal courts had assumed that the statute outlawed only state-required or -authorized discrimination, but the Supreme Court found it applicable to all forms of discrimination in housing, public or private. Ironically, Congress originally proposed the Fourteenth Amendment partly to ensure the constitutionality of the 1866 act, doubting whether the Thirteenth Amendment provided a sure footing for the statute.

*Jones* was the basis for *Runyon* v. *McCrary* (1976), which applied **Section 1981** of the 1866 act to commercially operated, nonsectarian private schools that refused admission to black applicants solely on grounds of race. Section 1981 guarantees all persons "the same right [to] make and enforce contracts, to sue, be parties, give evidence, and to the full extent and equal benefits of all laws and proceedings for the security of persons and property as is enjoyed by white citizens." *Patterson* v. *McLean Credit Union* (1989), however, refused to extend the law's coverage to include acts of racial harassment committed in connection with employment, a conclusion Congress rejected in the Civil Rights Act of 1991 when the lawmakers broadened Section 1981 expressly to encompass all forms of racial discrimination in contractual relationships.

## GENDER DISCRIMINATION

Because the Constitution has been the battleground for so many years in the struggle for racial equality, one might suppose that sexual equality has occupied the attention of Congress and the courts for just as long. It has not. Until the late twentieth century, the legal (and constitutional) status of women in the United States remained one of substantial inequality.

Making the nation free of discrimination based on gender has been a national priority for barely four decades. There have been some citizens fighting gender-based discriminations since the earliest years of the Republic, but for a long time justices of the Supreme Court were not among them. As late as 1961 (seven years after *Brown* and the first year of President John Kennedy's "New Frontier"), the Court unanimously upheld a Florida law that excluded women from jury duty unless they affirmatively requested to be added to the list of potential jurors. Justice Harlan did not think such laws were unreasonable. "Despite the enlightened emancipation of women from the restrictions and protections of bygone years, and their entry into many parts of community life formerly considered to be reserved to men, woman is still regarded as the center of home and family life" (*Hoyt* v. *Florida,* 1961). Public policies of both state and federal governments routinely took gender into account. As of 1973, some 900 sex-based federal laws were still on the books.

It was not until *Reed* v. *Reed* (1971) that the Supreme Court invalidated a gender-based statute as violative of the equal protection clause. An Idaho law directed that males be preferred to equally qualified females in the appointment of administrators for estates. The Court acknowledged that "the objective of reducing the work load on probate courts by eliminating one class of contests is not without some legitimacy." Then, purporting to apply the traditional rationality standard, a unanimous bench held that "a mandatory preference to members of either sex over members of the other, merely to accomplish the elimination of hearings on the merits, is to work the very kind of arbitrary legislative choice forbidden by" the Fourteenth Amendment.

In 1973, in ***Frontiero* v. *Richardson*** (one of several important gender discrimination cases argued by Ruth Bader Ginsburg), as many as four justices were willing to consider gender a suspect classification, a position urged on the Court in *Reed*. Challenged under the equal protection component of the Fifth Amendment was a Defense Department policy that treated male and female personnel differently when obtaining support for dependent spouses. Even without the tough standard of strict scrutiny, however, four other justices probed the "rationality" of the statute and reached the same result.

Compromise between the rational basis and strict scrutiny tests accounts for Justice Brennan's opinion in ***Craig* v. *Boren*** (1976) that spelled out an intermediate level of scrutiny that emerged for gender-based distinctions. In this case, an Oklahoma statute prohibiting the sale of 3.2 percent beer to males under 21 and to females under 18 was found to fall short constitutionally. "[T]o withstand constitutional challenge, previous cases establish that classifications by gender must serve important governmental objectives and must be substantially related to achievement of those objectives." In other words, the purpose of the statute must be valid, and the justices must be convinced that another law treating the sexes equally would not do as well. As *Craig* demonstrates, gender-based distinctions today are constitutionally at high risk.

That assessment has turned out to be especially true with respect to single-sex education in state-supported institutions of higher education, a matter the Court first confronted in ***Mississippi University for Women* v. *Hogan*** (1982). Joe Hogan could have enrolled in two state-supported coeducational nursing schools in Mississippi but not the nursing school at MUW, said the state, because he was male. "Our decisions . . . establish that the party seeking to uphold a statute that classifies individuals on the basis of their gender must carry the burden of showing an 'exceedingly persuasive justification' for the classification," wrote Justice O'Connor for the majority, apparently tightening the standard in *Craig* v. *Boren*. The justices found unpersuasive the state's argument that a female-only nursing school served a substantial government interest by compensating for discrimination against women. Instead, they concluded that the Mississippi policy only tended to perpetuate the stereotyped view of nursing as exclusively a woman's job. Furthermore, even though Title IX of the Education Amendments of 1972 expressly authorized traditionally single-sex state universities to continue admitting only men or women, O'Connor explained that Congress could not permit by statute something the Fourteenth Amendment forbids. *Hogan* later determined the outcome of the six-year courtroom battle fought by Virginia Military Institute to retain its all-male status. In 1996, with only a single dissent, the Court ordered an end to single-sex education at VMI when it invalidated an arrangement by which women seeking specialized military education could instead enroll in the state-financed Virginia Women's Institute for Leadership at nearby Mary Baldwin, an independent college for women (*United States* v. *Virginia*).

## FUNDAMENTAL RIGHTS ANALYSIS

The equal protection clause can also be a far-reaching tool for judicial protection of fundamental rights specified or implicit in the Constitution, as the Court first hinted in *Skinner* v. *Oklahoma* (1942). This decision struck down a compulsory sterilization scheme mandated by Oklahoma for certain, but not all, habitual criminals. The classification threatened "marriage and procreation," wrote Justice Douglas, which "are fundamental to the very existence and survival of the race." Today classifications that infringe on rights the Court deems fundamental are judged by the strict scrutiny test.

    ***Shapiro* v. *Thompson*** (1969) illustrates how **fundamental rights analysis** (also called **substantive equal protection**) can be used to shield particular rights. Held invalid were one-year residence requirements states imposed on all persons seeking welfare assistance. Justice Brennan for the majority spoke of the "right" of freedom to travel throughout the states: "Thus, the purpose of deterring the inmigration of indigents cannot serve as justification for the classification created by the one-year waiting period, since that purpose is constitutionally impermissible. Because the classification here touches on the fundamental right of interstate movement, its constitutionality must be judged by the stricter standard—whether it promotes a compelling state interest. Under this standard, the waiting period requirement clearly violates the Equal Protection Clause." And as Chapter Eight explained, ***Saenz* v. *Roe*** suggests another way of dealing with such discriminations.

    Is education a "fundamental right"? If so, financing of public schools by a property tax stands in constitutional jeopardy because of the substantial inequalities present between property-rich and property-poor districts. But in ***San Antonio Independent School District* v. *Rodriguez*** (1973), five justices declared that education was "not among the rights afforded explicit protection under our Constitution" and did not fall within any of the categories calling for strict judicial scrutiny. Accordingly, the Texas local property tax funding law for public schools did not deny equal protection to children residing in districts with a low property tax base. The majority agreed that the tax system needed reform, but this "must come from the law makers and from the pressures of those who elect them." The Court might have held that education is a fundamental right and poverty a suspect classification. Either finding would have placed a burden on the state to show a compelling interest. Instead, the Court rejected both possible grounds in upholding the Texas scheme for financing public schools, which admittedly permitted substantial disparities in expenditures per pupil between districts.

## CONGRESSIONAL PROTECTION OF CIVIL RIGHTS

Legislation has become as important as the Constitution in fighting discrimination. Indeed, because of the concept of state action, some forms of discrimination can be reached only by statute. Since the 1960s Congress has enacted a variety of laws to combat discrimination based not only on race and gender but on age, religion, and disability as well. Many have also urged Congress to add sexual orientation to the list of protected categories. Most of this legislation falls outside the scope of this book, but a few of the most important provisions merit mention here.

Probably the most comprehensive civil rights law ever passed by Congress is the **Civil Rights Act of 1964.** Title II outlawed discrimination in hotels, restaurants, theaters, gas stations, and other public facilities affecting interstate commerce. The statutory coverage was intended to be pervasive because "affect commerce" was defined to include both establishments serving interstate travelers and those serving or selling products that had "moved" in interstate commerce. Contrary to the Court's position in the Civil Rights Cases of 1883, Congress also claimed authority under the Fourteenth Amendment for this provision of the 1964 act. In **Heart of Atlanta Motel v. United States,** the Court chose to rely only on the power to regulate interstate commerce in upholding application of the new statute to motels that catered to interstate travelers. **Katzenbach v. McClung** allowed congressional power to reach a restaurant in Birmingham which annually used about $70,000 worth of food that had moved in interstate commerce. (Both cases are reprinted in Chapter Six.) Title II was also held to apply to a 232-acre recreational facility (*Daniel* v. *Paul,* 1969) and to a community swimming pool (*Tillman* v. *Wheaton-Haven Association,* 1973). Such generous interpretation means that no facility, otherwise open to the public, may any longer discriminate on the basis of race or any of the other protected classifications.

**Title VII** of the same law remains the principal weapon against racial as well as gender-based and religious discrimination in employment, salary matters, promotions, and the like. Cases brought under Title VII differ from those brought under the Fourteenth Amendment in at least two major ways: First, the Fourteenth Amendment constrains only state governments and their political subdivisions, whereas Title VII includes the private sector too. Second, discriminatory *intent* is a necessary element of a violation of the Fourteenth Amendment; for Title VII, discriminatory *effect* is sufficient to establish a prima facie case of discrimination. According to *Griggs* v. *Duke Power Co.* (1971), Title VII "proscribes not only overt discrimination but also practices that are fair in form, but discriminatory in operation. . . . Good intent or absence of discriminatory intent does not redeem employment procedures or testing mechanisms that operate as 'built-in headwinds' for minority groups and are unrelated to measuring job capability." Under the Griggs rule, employers had the burden of showing that the questionable device was "a reasonable measure of job performance." In *Wards Cove Packing Co.* v. *Atonio* (1989), however, five justices modified *Griggs*. Statistical disparities remained important, but the plaintiff had to establish that the employer had no "legitimate business justification" for the allegedly discriminatory practice. *Wards Cove* thus made it easier for the employer to win a discrimination case. The decision also sparked a drive in Congress for corrective legislation.

The Civil Rights Act of 1991 restored the Griggs rule. If a particular practice has a discriminatory effect on women or racial minorities, the employer must show that the practice is "job-related for the position in question and consistent with business necessity." The act also removed one of the major differences between suits brought under Title VII, which bans several forms of discrimination, and suits brought under Section 1981 (discussed above), which deals exclusively with racial discrimination. Punitive damages, albeit capped, are now allowed under Title VII. (There is no cap on punitive damages in actions brought under Section 1981.) Prior to 1991, Title VII litigants could seek compensatory damages such as back pay as well as legal fees, but the absence of punitive damages discouraged attorneys from accepting Title VII cases on a contingency fee basis.

Another significant statutory provision, especially for universities, their students, and their athletic programs, is **Title IX** of the Education Amendments of 1972, prohibiting sex discrimination in "any education program or activity receiving Federal financial assistance." (Title VI of the 1964 Civil Rights Act had already proscribed racial discrimination in such programs.) In *Grove City College* v. *Bell* (1984), the Court determined that Title IX applies to an institution with students who receive direct federal financial aid even though the institution itself accepts no funds from the government. Under the statute, institutions not in compliance with regulations written by the Department of Education implementing Title IX would be denied federal aid. The cutoff of funds would also apply, the Court said, to an institution's students receiving direct support, such as Basic Educational Opportunity Grants. Although that interpretation left virtually no American campus outside the reach of Title IX, the Court then held that federal assistance to one part of a college's program did not trigger institution-wide coverage, thus limiting the impact of institutional sanctions under Title IX. In the Civil Rights Restoration Act of 1988, Congress overturned the Court's narrow reading of Title IX, leaving no doubt that it intended the cutoff of aid to be institution-wide.

## AFFIRMATIVE ACTION

If much litigation under the equal protection clause and the civil rights acts has been aimed at halting practices deemed harmful to certain minorities, what is the legal status of **affirmative action**—policies designed to help those same minorities? As the makeup of the bench has changed since the 1970s, the Supreme Court's position on such race-conscious measures has shifted from general tolerance to deep suspicion to something in between.

**UNIVERSITY ADMISSIONS.** The Supreme Court first squarely confronted affirmative action in *Regents of the University of California* v. *Bakke* (1978). The medical school at the University of California at Davis operated a special admissions program in which 16 of the 100 seats in the entering class were set aside for qualifying minority students. No white had ever been admitted through the special admissions program, and the Davis medical school had no prior history of racial discrimination in its admissions policy. After his rejection in 1974, Allan Bakke, a white male, challenged the program on equal protection grounds, and the California Supreme Court ordered his admission. For those hoping for a clear, forthright, thunderbolt pronouncement by the High Court, the decision in *Bakke* was a disappointment. Bakke won (and so gained admission to medical school) but so did advocates of affirmative action. These seemingly conflicting results came about because the justices were divided into three camps.

Justices Brennan, White, Marshall, and Blackmun found no constitutional violation in the admissions program at Davis. Race-based admissions for ameliorative purposes should be judged by, at most, intermediate scrutiny, a standard that, in their view, Davis easily met. Neither did they see it as being in conflict with **Title VI** of the Civil Rights Act of 1964 that banned racial and certain other kinds of discrimination in programs receiving federal financial assistance. Four others (Stevens, Burger, Stewart, and Rehnquist) considered the Davis plan a violation of Title VI and so did not reach the constitutional question. Left was Justice Powell. The Davis plan was flawed, he thought, because the presence of the quota meant that race was used as an exclusionary factor. Race, however, could be taken into account as an illuminating factor in evaluating an applicant and to achieve racial diversity in the student body for educational reasons. Indeed, for Powell, diversity was sufficiently compelling to pass the strict scrutiny test.

Thus, *Bakke* pointed in two distinctly different directions. Combining Powell's concession with the Brennan group, *Bakke* suggested that one could constitutionally use race to some extent in deciding whom to admit. Combining Powell's view with the position put forth by the Stevens group, *Bakke* not only invalidated the Davis plan but cast doubt on any admissions policy that relied on race-based quotas or percentages.

After *Bakke,* the Court did not fully revisit affirmative action in higher education until it decided two cases involving the University of Michigan in 2003: ***Grutter* v. *Bollinger*** and ***Gratz* v. *Bollinger.*** The first involved the admissions policy at the law school, where race was used as a factor to obtain a "critical mass" of minority students; the second tested the undergraduate admissions policy in the college of literature, science, and the arts, where a point system gave a boost to minority applicants. In both, litigants challenged the policies as a violation of equal protection and Title VI. In both, the university argued that the plans were designed to promote racial diversity and, drawing on Justice Powell's opinion in *Bakke,* that diversity was a compelling interest—a position a majority of the bench now accepted.

The contrasting outcomes of the Michigan cases in the Supreme Court may now point the way more clearly than *Bakke* did to the ways in which race may constitutionally be used in college and university settings. The Court made clear that race may now be used as one tool to achieve a diverse student body. Academic institutions, however, may not employ quotas or separate admission tracks for certain racial groups, nor apparently may they define diversity solely in terms of race. What is permissible is "truly individualized consideration" in which race is one of many factors taken into account. This permissible, but limited, use of race would probably account for the Court's approval of the Michigan law school's admission policy but its rejection of the more mechanical system deployed at the undergraduate level.

**JOBS.** In employment, Title VII of the Civil Rights Act of 1964 authorizes "make whole" remedies for victims of discrimination, but may employers voluntarily give preferential treatment to minorities? *United Steelworkers of America* v. *Weber* (1979) upheld the legality of an affirmative action plan agreed to by a union and a corporation, showing that even if the Supreme Court someday were to lose its power of judicial review, statutory interpretation would nonetheless allow the justices considerable influence over public policy. In this case, the union and a Kaiser Aluminum & Chemical Corporation plant in Gramercy, Louisiana, entered into a collective bargaining agreement, part of which was designed to increase the number of blacks in craft jobs. Although no solid evidence of intentional discrimination in hiring or in admission to craft apprenticeships was part of the record, the Office of Federal Contract Compliance, acting under executive order, had encouraged the union and the company to develop a plan. At stake were federal contracts and therefore jobs and profits. In operation, the plan meant choosing blacks with less seniority over white workers with more. One of the latter was Brian Weber, who thought the plan violated Title VII. In part the statute declares, "It shall be an unlawful employment practice for any employer [or] labor organization . . . to discriminate against any individual because of his race, color, religion, sex, or national origin in admission to, or employment in, any program established to provide apprenticeship or other training."

For the majority of five, Justice Brennan found that the legislative history of the act did not speak precisely to this question. Discrimination against blacks and other minorities was uppermost in the minds of members of Congress when the law had been passed 15 years before. Because the statute was enacted for the purpose of helping minorities, "the natural inference is that Congress chose not to forbid all voluntary race-conscious affirmative action," Brennan concluded.

*Weber* was then reaffirmed by six justices in upholding a gender-based affirmative action plan in *Johnson* v. *Transportation Agency* (1987). Officials in Santa Clara County, California, had a long-range goal of building a workforce that reflected the proportion of women and racial minorities in the area. Seven people qualified for a road dispatcher's job, and the agency selected a female even though a male candidate had scored higher on the promotion test.

This pattern of acceptance of most forms of affirmative action in employment appears to end when layoffs result. In *Wygant* v. *Jackson Board of Education* (1986), five justices overturned a collective bargaining agreement that provided for retention of the most senior teachers during layoffs "except that at no time will there be a greater percentage of minority personnel laid off than the current percentage of minority personnel employed at the time of the layoff." The board and the union wanted to retain the more recently hired minority teachers. But the Court ruled that race-based layoffs would be acceptable only to correct prior discrimination, a factor not present in this case. This view prevailed even though voluntary race-based hiring was constitutionally permissible even in the absence of proven discrimination.

**CONGRESS AND RACE-CONSCIOUS MEASURES.** With cooperation of the executive branch Congress has promoted affirmative action through a variety of programs. In *Fullilove* v. *Klutznick* (1980), six justices upheld a **set-aside:** a congressional stipulation that "absent an administrative waiver, 10 percent of the federal funds granted for local public works projects must be used by the state or local grantee to procure services or supplies from businesses owned and controlled by members of statutorily identified minority groups." Only three justices (Brennan, Marshall, and Blackmun) gave the mandate their unqualified approval. The remaining three justices in the majority (Burger, White, and Powell) went out of their way to demonstrate a very qualified approval. Their first qualification consisted of the findings by Congress and the Civil Rights Commission that the continuing effects of discrimination in the construction industry had kept minority participation to a minimum. Second was the limited nature of the set-aside itself. The figure of 10 percent fell roughly halfway between the percentage of minority contractors and the percentage of minority-group members in the nation. Moreover, the set-aside applied to less than 1 percent of all funds expended yearly in the United States on construction. The third qualification rested on Congress's unique role under the Fourteenth Amendment. No fewer than 10 times did Chief Justice Burger's plurality opinion refer specifically to Congress's authority under the enforcement clause in Section 5 of the amendment. Yet even with this unique role, the Burger three hinted that the set-aside came close to the line: The "program press[ed] the outer limits of congressional authority. . . ." The set-aside may have survived its 1980 review by a whisker.

In 1989, six justices in *Richmond* v. *J. A. Croson Co.* declared that states lacked the remedial powers enjoyed by Congress. Invalidated was a city's 30 percent minority set-aside quota for contractors. "Under Richmond's scheme," wrote O'Connor for the majority, "a successful black, Hispanic or Oriental entrepreneur from anywhere in the country enjoys an absolute preference over other citizens based solely on their race." Because the city had not established a convincing record of purposeful municipal discrimination, the Court evaluated Richmond's policy under the formidable strict scrutiny test. The ruling called into question similar policies in 36 states and at least 190 cities.

One year later, however, five justices in *Metro Broadcasting, Inc.* v. *FCC* not only reaffirmed congressional power in this area but, going beyond *Fullilove,* seemed to divorce the justification for a national affirmative action program from the need for official findings of the persistent effects of discrimination. In contrast to state and local programs, congressionally mandated affirmative action programs were subject not to strict scrutiny, but to the less demanding test of intermediate scrutiny that Justice Brennan had urged in the context of state university admissions in *Bakke.* Upholding two minority-preference policies of the Federal Communications Commission for minority-owned enterprises, the Court declared that race-conscious ameliorative programs were therefore acceptable if they served important governmental objectives and were substantially related to achieving those objectives, even if they were not intended to compensate victims of past public or private discrimination.

*Adarand Constructors Co.* v. *Peña* (1995) then reversed *Metro Broadcasting* outright. In a major defeat for advocates of affirmative action, federal programs containing racial classifications, like those of state and local governments, are subject to strict scrutiny, regardless of whether the classifications or preferences are invidious or benign. In dispute was a clause in a prime contractor's contract with the Department of Transportation, challenged by the low bidder, that awarded a bonus to the prime contractor for choosing as subcontractors small businesses controlled by "socially and economically disadvantaged individuals." The clause required the contractor to presume that those individuals include "Black Americans, Hispanic Americans, Native Americans, Asian Pacific Americans, and other minorities."

Affirmative action will undoubtedly continue to vex the Court. As the record demonstrates, the justices have not spoken unequivocally. Indeed, one need look no further than its most recent pronouncements on affirmative action—*Grutter* and *Gratz* in 2003. They reflect a Solomonic reluctance among the justices in the majority either fully to embrace or to shun race-based policies in all situations. This may be expected in view of the divisiveness and complexity of the issue. Changes in the personnel of the Court will surely keep these questions in flux.

## KEY TERMS

equal protection clause
equality of opportunity
equality of condition
equality of result
rational basis test
strict scrutiny test
intermediate scrutiny
separate but equal
racially restrictive
    covenants
unitary school system

dual school system
de jure segregation
de facto segregation
racially identifiable
    schools
resegregation
state action
Thirteenth Amendment
Section 1982
Section 1981

fundamental rights
    analysis
substantive equal
    protection
Civil Rights Act of 1964
Title VII
Title IX
affirmative action
Title VI
set-aside

## QUERIES

**1.** In *Strauder* v. *West Virginia* (1880), Justice William Strong stated that the purpose of the Fourteenth Amendment was to grant blacks "the right to exemption from un-friendly legislation against them as distinctively colored." Measured by this standard, was the outcome in *Plessy* v. *Ferguson* correct? Are there elements of the Strauder understanding of the Fourteenth Amendment in Chief Justice Warren's opinion in *Brown* v. *Board of Education?*

**2.** More than a half century has past since the Court's historic decision in *Brown* v. *Board of Education*. Assessments vary considerably regarding the Court's impact on civil rights since *Brown*. At one extreme is the accolade by federal appeals judge J. Harvie Wilkinson III that *Brown* was essential to the civil rights revolution and its achievements: "Very little could have been accomplished in mid-century America without the Supreme Court. . . . *Brown* may be the most important political, social, and legal event in America's twentieth-century history." At the other is the nearly tragic despondency reflected by the 1993 statement of Kenneth Clark (whose re-search in psychology loomed large in the Brown litigation) that *Brown* and related cases accomplished little: "I am forced to face the likely possibility that the United States will never rid itself of racism and reach true integration. I look back and shud-der at how naive we all were in our belief in the steady progress racial minorities would make through programs of litigation and education." What have been the effects of that decision, as well as of subsequent decisions involving school integra-tion, on public education, on broader matters of race in American society, and on the Court and constitutional law generally?

**3.** What does *Romer* v. *Evans* suggest about the status of any law or government policy that discriminates on the basis of sexual orientation?

**4.** What are the implications of *Grutter* v. *Bollinger* and *Gratz* v. *Bollinger* for col-lege and university scholarships for which only members of certain racial groups are eligible, or other programs such as job fairs and special orientations in which only such persons may participate? What are the implications of that same pair of deci-sions outside the context of higher education?

## SELECTED READINGS

BARDOLF, RICHARD, ed. *The Civil Rights Record: Black Americans and the Law, 1849–1970*. New York: Crowell, 1970.

GERSTMANN, EVAN. *The Constitutional Underclass: Gays, Lesbians, and the Failure of Class-Based Equal Protection*. Chicago: University of Chicago Press, 1999.

KLUGER, RICHARD F. *Simple Justice: The History of Brown v. Board of Education and Black America's Struggle for Equality*. New York: Knopf, 1976.

LEE, FRANCIS GRAHAM. *Equal Protection*. Santa Barbara, CA: ABC–CLIO, 2003.

LOFGREN, CHARLES A. *The Plessy Case*. New York: Oxford University Press, 1987.

PATTERSON, JAMES T. *Brown v. Board of Education: A Civil Rights Milestone and Its Troubled Legacy*. New York: Oxford University Press, 2001.

RHODE, DEBORAH L. *Justice and Gender*. Cambridge, Mass.: Harvard University Press, 1989.

SCHWARTZ, BERNARD. *Behind Bakke: Affirmative Action and the Supreme Court*. New York: New York University Press, 1988.

STRUM, PHILIPPA. *Women in the Barracks: The VMI Case and Equal Rights*. Lawrence: University Press of Kansas, 2002.

UROFSKY, MELVIN I. *Affirmative Action on Trial*. Lawrence: University Press of Kansas, 1997.

VOSE, CLEMENT. *Caucasians Only: The Supreme Court, the NAACP, and the Restrictive Covenant Cases*. Berkeley: University of California Press, 1959.

## I. IDENTIFYING FORBIDDEN DISCRIMINATON

### *Korematsu* v. *United States*
### 323 U.S. 214, 65 S.Ct. 193, 89 L.Ed. 194 (1944)
http://laws.findlaw.com/us/323/214.html

(This case is reprinted in Chapter Fifteen, beginning on page 691.)

### *Cleburne* v. *Cleburne Living Center*
### 473 U.S. 432, 105 S.Ct. 3249, 87 L.Ed. 2d 313 (1985)
http://laws.findlaw.com/us/473/432.html

The facts of this case are contained in Justice White's opinion of the Court. While all justices agreed that the city council's denial of the permit amounted to a violation of the equal protection clause, they differed over the appropriate level of scrutiny to apply. Majority: White, Blackmun, Brennan, Burger, Marshall, O'Connor, Powell, Rehnquist, Stevens.

**JUSTICE WHITE delivered the opinion of the Court.**

A Texas city denied a special use permit for the operation of a group home for the mentally retarded, acting pursuant to a municipal zoning ordinance requiring permits for such homes. The Court of Appeals for the Fifth Circuit held that mental retardation is a "quasi-suspect" classification and that the ordinance violated the Equal Protection Clause because it did not substantially further an important governmental purpose. We hold that a lesser standard of scrutiny is appropriate, but conclude that under that standard the ordinance is invalid as applied in this case. . . .

[W]e conclude for several reasons that the Court of Appeals erred in holding mental retardation a quasi-suspect classification calling for a more exacting standard of judicial review than is normally accorded economic and social legislation. First, it is undeniable, and it is not argued otherwise here, that those who are mentally retarded have a reduced ability to cope with and function in the everyday world. Nor are they all cut from the same pattern: as the testimony in this record indicates, they range from those whose disability is not immediately evident to those who must be constantly cared for. They are thus different, immutably so, in relevant respects, and the states' interest in dealing with and providing for them is plainly a legitimate one. How this large and diversified group is to be treated under the law is a difficult and often a technical matter, very much a task for legislators guided by qualified professionals and not by the perhaps ill-informed opinions of the judiciary. Heightened scrutiny inevitably involves substantive judgments about legislative decisions, and we doubt that the predicate for such judicial oversight is present where the classification deals with mental retardation.

Second, the distinctive legislative response, both national and state, to the plight of those who are mentally retarded demonstrates not only that they have unique problems, but also that the lawmakers have been addressing their difficulties in a manner that belies a continuing antipathy or prejudice and a corresponding need for more intrusive oversight by the judiciary. . . .

Such legislation thus singling out the retarded for special treatment reflects the real and undeniable differences between the retarded and others. That a civilized and decent society expects and approves such legislation indicates that governmental consideration of those differences in the vast majority of situations is not only legitimate but desirable. It may be, as CLC contends, that legislation designed to benefit, rather than disadvantage, the retarded would generally withstand examination under a test of heightened scrutiny. . . . The relevant inquiry, however, is whether heightened scrutiny is constitutionally mandated in the first instance. Even assuming that many of these laws could be shown to be substantially related to an important governmental purpose, merely requiring the legislature to justify its efforts in these terms may lead it to refrain from acting at all. . . .

Third, the legislative response, which could hardly have occurred and survived without public support, negates any claim that the mentally retarded are politically powerless in the sense that they have no ability to attract the attention of the lawmakers. Any minority can be said to be powerless to assert direct control over the legislature, but if that were a criterion for higher level scrutiny by the courts, much economic and social legislation would now be suspect.

Fourth, if the large and amorphous class of the mentally retarded were deemed quasi-suspect for the reasons given by the Court of Appeals, it would be difficult to find a principled way to distinguish a variety of other groups who have perhaps immutable disabilities setting them off from others, who cannot themselves mandate the desired legislative responses, and who can claim some degree of prejudice from at least part of the public at large. One need mention in this respect only the aging, the disabled, the mentally ill, and the infirm. We are reluctant to set out on that course, and we decline to do so. . . .

Our refusal to recognize the retarded as a quasi-suspect class does not leave them entirely unprotected from invidious discrimination. To withstand equal protection review, legislation that distinguishes between the mentally retarded and others must be rationally related to a legitimate governmental purpose. This standard, we believe, affords government the latitude necessary both to pursue policies designed to assist the retarded in realizing their full potential, and to freely and efficiently engage in activities that burden the retarded in what is essentially an incidental manner. The State may not rely on a classification whose relationship to an asserted goal is so attenuated as to render the distinction arbitrary or irrational. . . .

We turn to the issue of the validity of the zoning ordinance insofar as it requires a special use permit for homes for the mentally retarded. We inquire first whether requiring a special use permit for the Featherston home in the circumstances here deprives respondents of the equal protection of the laws. If it does, there will be no occasion to decide whether the special use permit provision is facially invalid where the mentally retarded are involved, or to put it another way, whether the city may never insist on a special use permit for a home for the mentally retarded in an R-3 zone. This is the preferred course of adjudication since it enables courts to avoid making unnecessarily broad constitutional judgments.

The constitutional issue is clearly posed. The City does not require a special use permit in an R-3 zone for apartment houses, multiple dwellings, boarding and lodging houses, fraternity or sorority houses, dormitories, apartment hotels, hospitals, sanitariums, nursing homes for convalescents or the aged (other than for the insane or feeble-minded or alcoholics or drug addicts), private clubs or fraternal orders, and other specified uses. It does, however, insist on a special permit for the Featherston home, and it does so, as the District Court found, because it would be a facility for the mentally retarded. May the city require the permit for this facility when other care and multiple dwelling facilities are freely permitted?

It is true . . . that the mentally retarded as a group are indeed different from others not sharing their misfortune, and in this respect

they may be different from those who would occupy other facilities that would be permitted in an R-3 zone without a special permit. But this difference is largely irrelevant unless the Featherston home and those who would occupy it would threaten legitimate interests of the city in a way that other permitted uses such as boarding houses and hospitals would not. Because in our view the record does not reveal any rational basis for believing that the Featherston home would pose any special threat to the city's legitimate interests, we affirm the judgment below insofar as it holds the ordinance invalid as applied in this case. . . .

The short of it is that requiring the permit in this case appears to us to rest on an irrational prejudice against the mentally retarded, including those who would occupy the Featherston facility and who would live under the closely supervised and highly regulated conditions expressly provided for by state and federal law.

The judgment of the Court of Appeals is affirmed insofar as it invalidates the zoning ordinance as applied to the Featherston home. The judgment is otherwise vacated.

*It is so ordered.*

**JUSTICE STEVENS, with whom THE CHIEF JUSTICE joins, concurring.**

The Court of Appeals disposed of this case as if a critical question to be decided were which of three clearly defined standards of equal protection review should be applied to a legislative classification discriminating against the mentally retarded. In fact, our cases have not delineated three—or even one or two—such well defined standards. Rather, our cases reflect a continuum of judgmental responses to differing classifications which have been explained in opinions by terms ranging from "strict scrutiny" at one extreme to "rational basis" at the other. I have never been persuaded that these so called "standards" adequately explain the decisional process. Cases involving classifications based on alienage, illegal residency, illegitimacy, gender, age, or—as in this case—mental retardation, do not fit well into sharply defined classifications. . . .

In my own approach to these cases, I have always asked myself whether I could find a "rational basis" for the classification at issue. The term "rational," of course, includes a requirement that an impartial lawmaker could logically believe that the classification would serve a legitimate public purpose that transcends the harm to the members of the disadvantaged class. Thus, the word "rational"—for me at least—includes elements of legitimacy and neutrality that must always characterize the performance of the sovereign's duty to govern impartially.

The rational basis test, properly understood, adequately explains why a law that deprives a person of the right to vote because his skin has a different pigmentation than that of other voters violates the Equal Protection Clause. It would be utterly irrational to limit the franchise on the basis of height or weight; it is equally invalid to limit it on the basis of skin color. None of these attributes has any bearing at all on the citizen's willingness or ability to exercise that civil right. We do not need to apply a special standard, or to apply "strict scrutiny," or even "heightened scrutiny," to decide such cases.

In every equal protection case, we have to ask certain basic questions. What class is harmed by the legislation, and has it been subjected to a "tradition of disfavor" by our laws? What is the public purpose that is being served by the law? What is the characteristic of the disadvantaged class that justifies the disparate treatment? In most cases the answer to these questions will tell us whether the statute has a "rational basis." The answers will result in the virtually automatic invalidation of racial classifications and in the validation of most economic classifications, but they will provide differing results in cases involving classifications based on alienage, gender, or illegitimacy. But that is not because we apply an "intermediate standard of review" in these cases; rather it is because the characteristics of these groups are sometimes relevant and sometimes irrelevant to a valid public purpose, or, more specifically, to the purpose that the challenged laws purportedly intended to serve.

Every law that places the mentally retarded in a special class is not presumptively irrational. . . .

The discrimination against the mentally retarded that is at issue in this case is the city's decision to require an annual special use permit before property in an apartment house district may be used as a group home for persons who are mildly retarded. The record convinces me that this permit was required because of the irrational fears of neighboring property owners, rather than for the protection of the mentally retarded persons who would reside in respondent's home. . . .

**JUSTICE MARSHALL, with whom JUSTICE BRENNAN and JUSTICE BLACKMUN join, concurring in the judgment in part and dissenting in part. . . .**

The Court holds the ordinance invalid on rational-basis grounds and disclaims that anything special, in the form of heightened scrutiny, is taking place. Yet Cleburne's ordinance surely would be valid under the traditional rational-basis test applicable to economic and commercial regulation. . . .

I have long believed the level of scrutiny employed in an equal protection case should vary with "the constitutional and societal importance of the interest adversely affected and the recognized invidiousness of the basis upon which the particular classification is drawn." When a zoning ordinance works to exclude the retarded from all residential districts in a community, these two considerations require that the ordinance be convincingly justified as substantially furthering legitimate and important purposes. . . .

## Romer v. Evans
### 517 U.S. 620, 116 S.Ct. 1620, 134 L.Ed. 2d 855 (1996)
### http://laws.findlaw.com/us/517/620.html

> The facts of the case appear in Justice Kennedy's opinion below. The Colorado Supreme Court had subjected the constitutional amendment in question to strict scrutiny because it infringed the fundamental right of gays and lesbians to participate in the political process, and affirmed the trial court's decision enjoining its enforcement. Majority: Kennedy, Stevens, O'Connor, Souter, Ginsburg, Breyer. Dissenting: Scalia, Rehnquist, Thomas.

**JUSTICE KENNEDY delivered the opinion of the Court.**

One century ago, the first Justice Harlan admonished this Court that the Constitution "neither knows nor tolerates classes among citizens." Unheeded then, those words now are understood to state a commitment to the law's neutrality where the rights of persons are at stake. The Equal Protection Clause enforces this principle and today requires us to hold invalid a provision of Colorado's Constitution.

The enactment challenged in this case is [Amendment 2] to the Constitution of the State of Colorado, adopted in a 1992 statewide referendum. . . . The impetus for the amendment . . . came in large part from ordinances that had been passed in various Colorado municipalities . . . which banned discrimination in many transactions and activities, including housing, employment, education, public accommodations, and health and welfare services . . . by reason of . . . sexual orientation. . . .

Amendment 2 . . . does more than repeal or rescind these provisions. It prohibits all legislative, executive or judicial action at any level of state or local government designed to protect the named class, a class we shall refer to as homosexual persons or gays and lesbians. The amendment reads:

No Protected Status Based on Homosexual, Lesbian, or Bisexual Orientation. Neither the State of Colorado, through any of its branches or departments, nor any of its agencies, political subdivisions, municipalities or school districts, shall enact, adopt or enforce any statute, regulation, ordinance or policy whereby homosexual, lesbian or bisexual orientation, conduct, practices or relationships shall constitute or otherwise be the basis of or entitle any person or class of persons to have or claim any minority status, quota preferences, protected status or claim of discrimination. . . .

. . . We . . . now affirm the judgment [of Colorado Supreme Court], but on a rationale different from that adopted by [that] Court.

The State's principal argument in defense of Amendment 2 is that it puts gays and lesbians in the same position as all other persons. So, the State says, the measure does no more than deny homosexuals special rights. This reading of the amendment's language is implausible. . . .

Homosexuals, by state decree, are put in a solitary class with respect to transactions and relations in both the private and governmental spheres. The amendment withdraws from homosexuals, but no others, specific legal protection from the injuries caused by discrimination, and it forbids reinstatement of these laws and policies. . . .

[T]he amendment imposes a special disability upon those persons alone. Homosexuals are forbidden the safeguards that others enjoy or may seek without constraint. They can obtain specific protection against discrimination only by enlisting the citizenry of Colorado to amend the state constitution or perhaps, on the State's view, by trying to pass helpful laws of general applicability. . . . These are protections taken for granted by most people either because they already have them or do not need them; these are protections against exclusion from an almost limitless number of transactions and endeavors that constitute ordinary civic life in a free society.

The Fourteenth Amendment's promise that no person shall be denied the equal protection of the laws must co-exist with the practical necessity that most legislation classifies for one purpose or another, with resulting disadvantage to various groups or persons. We have attempted to reconcile the principle with the reality by stating that, if a law neither burdens a fundamental right nor targets a suspect class, we will uphold the legislative classification so long as it bears a rational relation to some legitimate end.

Amendment 2 fails, indeed defies, even this conventional inquiry. First, the amendment has the peculiar property of imposing a broad and undifferentiated disability on a single named group, an exceptional and, as we shall explain, invalid form of legislation. Second, its sheer breadth is so discontinuous with the reasons offered for it that the amendment seems inexplicable by anything but animus toward the class that it affects; it lacks a rational relationship to legitimate state interests.

Taking the first point, even in the ordinary equal protection case calling for the most deferential of standards, we insist on knowing the relation between the classification adopted and the object to be attained. . . .

Amendment 2 confounds this normal process of judicial review. It is at once too narrow and too broad. It identifies persons by a single trait and then denies them protection across the board. The resulting disqualification of a class of persons from the right to seek specific protection from the law is unprecedented in our jurisprudence. . . .

It is not within our constitutional tradition to enact laws of this sort. Central both to the idea of the rule of law and to our own Constitution's guarantee of equal protection is the principle that government and each of its parts remain open on impartial terms to all who seek its assistance. "Equal protection of the laws is not achieved through indiscriminate imposition of inequalities.". . . A law declaring that in general

it shall be more difficult for one group of citizens than for all others to seek aid from the government is itself a denial of equal protection of the laws in the most literal sense. . . .

A second and related point is that laws of the kind now before us raise the inevitable inference that the disadvantage imposed is born of animosity toward the class of persons affected. . . .

The primary rationale the State offers for Amendment 2 is respect for other citizens' freedom of association, and in particular the liberties of landlords or employers who have personal or religious objections to homosexuality. Colorado also cites its interest in conserving resources to fight discrimination against other groups. The breadth of the Amendment is so far removed from these particular justifications that we find it impossible to credit them. . . .

We must conclude that Amendment 2 classifies homosexuals not to further a proper legislative end but to make them unequal to everyone else. This Colorado cannot do. A State cannot so deem a class of persons a stranger to its laws. Amendment 2 violates the Equal Protection Clause, and the judgment of the Supreme Court of Colorado is affirmed.

*It is so ordered.*

### JUSTICE SCALIA, with whom THE CHIEF JUSTICE and JUSTICE THOMAS join, dissenting.

The Court has mistaken a Kulturkampf for a fit of spite. . . .

In holding that homosexuality cannot be singled out for disfavorable treatment, the Court . . . places the prestige of this institution behind the proposition that opposition to homosexuality is as reprehensible as racial or religious bias. Whether it is or not is *precisely* the cultural debate that gave rise to the Colorado constitutional amendment (and to the preferential laws against which the amendment was directed). Since the Constitution of the United States says nothing about this subject, it is left to be resolved by normal democratic means, including the democratic adoption of provisions in state constitutions. This Court has no business imposing upon all Americans the resolution favored by the elite class from which the Members of this institution are selected, pronouncing that "animosity" toward homosexuality, is evil. I vigorously dissent. . . .

The only denial of equal treatment [the Court] contends homosexuals have suffered is this: They may not obtain *preferential* treatment without amending the state constitution. That is to say, the principle underlying the Court's opinion is that one who is accorded equal treatment under the laws, but cannot as readily as others obtain *preferential* treatment under the laws, has been denied equal protection of the laws. If merely stating this alleged "equal protection" violation does not suffice to refute it, our constitutional jurisprudence has achieved terminal silliness.

The central thesis of the Court's reasoning is that any group is denied equal protection when, to obtain advantage (or, presumably, to avoid disadvantage), it must have recourse to a more general and hence more difficult level of political decisionmaking than others. The world has never heard of such a principle, which is why the Court's opinion is so long on emotive utterance and so short on relevant legal citation. And it seems to me most unlikely that any multilevel democracy can function under such a principle. For *whenever* a disadvantage is imposed, or conferral of a benefit is prohibited, at one of the higher levels of democratic decisionmaking (i.e., by the state legislature rather than local government, or by the people at large in the state constitution rather than the legislature), the affected group has (under this theory) been denied equal protection. To take the simplest of examples, consider a state law prohibiting the award of municipal contracts to relatives of mayors or city councilmen. Once such a law is passed, the group composed of such relatives must, in order to get the benefit of city contracts, persuade the state legislature—unlike all other citizens, who need only persuade the municipality. It is ridiculous to consider this a denial of equal protection, which is why the Court's theory is unheard-of. . . .

I turn next to whether there was a legitimate rational basis for the substance of the constitutional amendment—for the prohibition of special protection for homosexuals. . . .

. . . No principle set forth in the Constitution, nor even any imagined by this Court in the past 200 years, prohibits what Colorado has done here. But the case for Colorado is much stronger than that. What it has done is not only unprohibited, but eminently reasonable, with close, congressionally approved precedent in earlier constitutional practice.

First, as to its eminent reasonableness. The Court's opinion contains grim, disapproving hints that Coloradans have been guilty of "animus" or "animosity" toward homosexuality, as though that has been established as Unamerican. Of course it is our moral heritage that one should not hate any human being or class of human beings. But I had thought that one could consider certain conduct reprehensible—murder, for example, or polygamy, or cruelty to animals—and could exhibit even "animus" toward such conduct. Surely that is the only sort of "animus" at issue here: moral disapproval of homosexual conduct, the same sort of moral disapproval that produced the centuries-old criminal laws that we held constitutional in *Bowers* [v. *Hardwick*]. The Colorado amendment does not, to speak entirely precisely, prohibit giving favored status to people who are *homosexuals*; they can be favored for many reasons—for example, because they are senior citizens or members of racial minorities. But it prohibits giving them favored status *because of their homosexual conduct*—that is, it prohibits favored status *for homosexuality.*

But though Coloradans are, as I say, entitled to be hostile toward homosexual conduct, the fact is that the degree of hostility reflected by Amendment 2 is the smallest conceivable. The Court's portrayal of Coloradans as a society fallen victim to pointless, hate-filled "gay-bashing" is so false as to be comical. Colorado not only is one of the 25 States that have repealed their antisodomy laws, but was among the first to do so. . . .

There is a problem, however, which arises when criminal sanction of homosexuality is eliminated but moral and social disapprobation of homosexuality is meant to be retained. . . . The problem (a problem, that is, for those who wish to retain social disapprobation of homosexuality) is that, because those who engage in homosexual conduct tend to reside in disproportionate numbers in certain communities, . . . and of course care about homosexual-rights issues much more ardently than the public at large, they possess political power much greater than their numbers, both locally and statewide. Quite understandably, they devote this political power to achieving not merely a grudging social toleration, but full social acceptance, of homosexuality. . . .

That is where Amendment 2 came in. It sought to counter both the geographic concentration and the disproportionate political power of homosexuals by (1) resolving the controversy at the statewide level, and (2) making the election a single-issue contest for both sides. . . . [The Court's theory] is proved false every time a state law prohibiting or disfavoring certain conduct is passed, because such a law prevents the adversely affected group—whether drug addicts, or smokers, or gun owners, or motorcyclists—from changing the policy thus established in "each of [the] parts" of the State. . . .

But there is a much closer analogy, one that involves precisely the effort by the majority of citizens to preserve its view of sexual morality statewide, against the efforts of a geographically concentrated and politically powerful minority to undermine it. The constitutions of the States of Arizona, Idaho, New Mexico, Oklahoma, and Utah to this day contain provisions stating that polygamy is "forever prohibited." . . . [T]he proposition that polygamy can be criminalized, and those engaging in that crime deprived of the vote, remains good law. . . . Has the Court concluded that the perceived social harm of polygamy is a "legitimate concern of government," and the perceived social harm of homosexuality is not?

I strongly suspect that the answer to the last question is yes. . . .

The people of Colorado have adopted an entirely reasonable provision which does not even disfavor homosexuals in any substantive sense, but merely denies them preferential treatment. Amendment 2 is designed to prevent piecemeal deterioration of the sexual morality favored by a majority of Coloradans, and is not only an appropriate means to that legitimate end, but a means that Americans have employed before. Striking it down is an act, not of judicial judgment, but of political will. I dissent.

## II. RACIAL DISCRIMINATION

### *Plessy* v. *Ferguson*
### 163 U.S. 537, 16 S.Ct. 1138, 41 L.Ed. 256 (1896)
### http://laws.findlaw.com/us/163/537.html

A Louisiana statute of 1890 required railroad companies carrying passengers within the state to provide "equal but separate" accommodations for white and "colored" persons, empowered train officials to enforce the law, and provided penalties for those who refused to obey segregation orders. Blacks in New Orleans promptly formed a committee to challenge the constitutionality of the separate car law through a test case. On June 7, 1892, a 34-year-old black man named Homer A. Plessy bought an intrastate ticket for a ride between New Orleans and Covington on the East Louisiana Railway. Apparently by prearrangement with railroad officials, who also opposed the law, Plessy was arrested for violating the law and arraigned in district court. Because Louisiana procedure did not provide for a direct appeal for minor convictions of this sort, Plessy's attorney petitioned the state Supreme Court to halt the trial proceedings before they began. On November 22, Chief Justice Francis T. Nicholls (who as governor in 1890 had signed the separate car bill into law) ordered the trial judge to show cause why the prohibition should not be made permanent. The following month, the full court found that there was no constitutional conflict between the law and the Thirteenth and Fourteenth Amendments. Plessy's attorney was then in a position to appeal the case to the Supreme Court of the United States. It was not until January 1897, after the U.S. Supreme Court's decision in Plessy's case, that Homer Plessy entered a plea of guilty for boarding the car reserved for white passengers and paid a fine of $25. Majority: Brown, Field, Fuller, Gray, Peckham, Shiras, White. Dissenting: Harlan. Not participating: Brewer.

**MR. JUSTICE BROWN . . . delivered the opinion of the Court. . . .**

The constitutionality of this act is attacked upon the ground that it conflicts both with the Thirteenth Amendment of the Constitution, abolishing slavery, and the Fourteenth Amendment, which prohibits certain restrictive legislation on the part of the States.

That it does not conflict with the Thirteenth Amendment, which abolished slavery and involuntary servitude, except as a punishment for crime, is too clear for argument. . . .

The object of the [Fourteenth] amendment was undoubtedly to enforce the absolute equality of the two races before the law, but in the nature of things it could not have been intended to abolish distinctions based upon color, or to enforce social, as distinguished from political equality, or a commingling of the two races upon terms unsatisfactory to either. Laws permitting, and even requiring, their separation in places where they are liable to be brought into contact do not necessarily imply the inferiority of either race to the other, and have been generally, if not universally, recognized as within the competency of the state legislatures in the exercise of their police power. The most common instance of this is connected with the establishment of separate schools for white and colored children, which has been held to be a valid exercise of the legislative power even by courts of States where the political rights of the colored race have been longest and most earnestly enforced.

One of the earliest of these cases is that of *Roberts* v. *City of Boston* [1849], in which the Supreme Judicial Court of Massachusetts held that the general school committee of Boston had power to make provisions for the instruction of colored children in separate schools established exclusively for them, and to prohibit their attendance upon the other schools. . . .

The distinction between laws interfering with the political equality of the negro and those requiring the separation of the two races in schools, theatres, and railway carriages has been frequently drawn by this court. . . .

So far, then, as a conflict with the Fourteenth Amendment is concerned the case reduces itself to the question whether the statute of Louisiana is a reasonable regulation, and with respect to this there must necessarily be a large discretion on the part of the legislature. In determining the question of reasonableness it is at liberty to act with reference to the established usages, customs and traditions of the people, and with a view to the promotion of their comfort, and the preservation of the public peace and good order. Gauged by this standard, we cannot say that a law which authorizes or even requires the separation of the two races in public conveyances is unreasonable, or more obnoxious to the Fourteenth Amendment than the acts of Congress requiring separate schools for colored children in the District of Columbia, the constitutionality of which does not seem to have been questioned, or the corresponding acts of state legislatures.

We consider the underlying fallacy of the plaintiff's argument to consist in the assumption that the enforced separation of the two races stamps the colored race with a badge of inferiority. If this be so, it is not by reason of anything found in the act, but solely because the colored race chooses to put that construction upon it. The argument necessarily assumes that if, as has been more than once the case, and is not unlikely to be so again, the colored race should become the dominant power in the state legislature, and should enact a law in precisely similar terms, it would thereby relegate the white race to an inferior position. We imagine that the white race, at least, would not acquiesce in this assumption. The argument also assumes, that social prejudices may be overcome by legislation, and that equal rights cannot be secured to the negro except by an enforced commingling of the two races. We cannot accept this proposition. If the two races are to meet upon terms of social equality, it must be the result of natural affinities, a mutual appreciation of each other's merits and a voluntary consent of individuals. . . . Legislation is powerless to eradicate racial instincts or to abolish distinctions based upon physical differences, and the attempt to do so can only result in accentuating the difficulties of the present situation. If the civil and political rights of both races be equal, one cannot be inferior to the other civilly or politically. If one race be inferior to the other socially, the Constitution of the United States cannot put them upon the same plane. . . .

The judgment of the court below is, therefore,

*Affirmed.*

### MR. JUSTICE HARLAN, dissenting. . . .

It was said in argument that the statute of Louisiana does not discriminate against either race, but prescribes a rule applicable alike to white and colored citizens. But this argument does not meet the difficulty. Everyone knows that the statute . . . had its origins in the purpose, not so much to exclude white persons from railroad cars occupied by blacks, as to exclude colored people from coaches occupied by . . . white persons. . . .

[I]n view of the Constitution, in the eye of the law, there is in this country no superior, dominant, ruling class of citizens. There is no caste here. Our Constitution is color-blind, and neither knows nor tolerates classes among citizens. In respect of civil rights, all citizens are

equal before the law. The humblest is the peer of the most powerful. The law regards man as man, and takes no account of his surroundings or of his color when his civil rights as guaranteed by the supreme law of the land are involved. It is, therefore, to be regretted that this high tribunal, the final expositor of the fundamental law of the land, has reached the conclusion that it is competent for a state to regulate the enjoyment by citizens of their civil rights solely upon the basis of race. . . .

In my opinion, the judgment this day rendered will, in time, prove to be quite as pernicious as the decision made by this tribunal in the Dred Scott case. . . . The present decision, it may well be apprehended, will not only stimulate aggressions, more or less brutal and irritating, upon the admitted rights of colored citizens, but will encourage the belief that it is possible, by means of state enactments, to defeat the beneficent purposes which the people of the United States had in view when they adopted the recent amendments of the Constitution, by one of which the blacks of this country were made citizens of the United States and of the States in which they respectively reside, and whose privileges and immunities, as citizens, the States are forbidden to abridge. Sixty millions of whites are in no danger from the presence here of eight millions of blacks. The destinies of the two races, in this country, are indissolubly linked together, and the interests of both require that the common government of all shall not permit the seeds of race hate to be planted under the sanction of law. . . .

If evils will result from the commingling of the two races upon public highways established for the benefit of all, they will be infinitely less than those that will surely come from state legislation regulating the enjoyment of civil rights upon the basis of race. We boast of the freedom enjoyed by our people above all other people. But it is difficult to reconcile that boast with a state of the law which, practically, puts the brand of servitude and degradation upon a large class of our fellow-citizens, our equals before the law. The thin disguise of "equal" accommodations for passengers in railroad coaches will not mislead any one, nor atone for the wrong this day done. . . .

[T]he statute of Louisiana is inconsistent with the personal liberty of citizens, white and black, in that state, and hostile to both the spirit and letter of the Constitution of the United States. If laws of like character should be enacted in the several states of the Union, the effect would be in the highest degree mischievous. Slavery as an institution . . . would, it is true, have disappeared from our country, but there would remain a power in the states, by sinister legislation, to interfere with the full enjoyment of the blessings of freedom; to regulate civil rights, common to all citizens, upon the basis of race; and to place in a condition of legal inferiority a large body of American citizens, now constituting a part of the political community, called the people of the United States, for whom and by whom, through representatives, our government is administered. Such a system is inconsistent with the guarantee given by the Constitution to each state of a republican form of government. . . .

## *Brown* v. *Board of Education* (First Case)
## 347 U.S. 483, 74 S.Ct. 686, 98 L.Ed. 873 (1954)
## http://laws.findlaw.com/us/347/483.html

On May 17, 1954, the Supreme Court handed down its long-awaited decision in the public school segregation cases. Although the cases directly involved only South Carolina, Virginia, Delaware, Kansas, and the District of Columbia, the answer to the question whether segregation of races was permissible under the Constitution affected a total of 17 states and the District of Columbia, which required segregation in public schools, and four states that permitted segregation at the option of local communities. The Court postponed issuing a decree until the next term. Majority: Warren, Black, Burton, Clark, Douglas, Frankfurter, Jackson, Minton, Reed.

**MR. CHIEF JUSTICE WARREN delivered the opinion of the court.**

These cases come to us from the States of Kansas, South Carolina, Virginia, and Delaware. They are premised on different facts and different local conditions, but a common legal question justifies their consideration together in this consolidated opinion.

In each of the cases, minors of the Negro race, through their legal representatives, seek the aid of the courts in obtaining admission to the public schools of their community on a nonsegregated basis. In each instance, they had been denied admission to schools attended by white children under laws requiring or permitting segregation according to race.

This segregation was alleged to deprive the plaintiffs of the equal protection of the laws under the Fourteenth Amendment. In each of the cases other than the Delaware case, a three-judge Federal District Court denied relief to the plaintiffs on the so-called "separate but equal" doctrine, announced by this court in *Plessy* v. *Ferguson.* . . .

The plaintiffs contend that segregated public schools are not "equal" and cannot be made "equal," and that, hence, they are deprived of the equal protection of the laws. Because of the obvious importance of the question presented, the Court took jurisdiction. Argument was heard in the 1952 term, and reargument was heard this term on certain questions propounded by the Court.

Reargument was largely devoted to the circumstances surrounding the adoption of the Fourteenth Amendment in 1868. It covered, exhaustively, consideration of the Amendment in Congress, ratification by the states, then existing practices in racial segregation, and the views of proponents and opponents of the Amendment.

This discussion and our own investigation convince us that, although these sources cast some light, it is not enough to resolve the problem with which we are faced.

At best, they are inconclusive. The most avid proponents of the postwar Amendments undoubtedly intended them to remove all legal distinctions among "all persons born or naturalized in the United States."

Their opponents, just as certainly, were antagonistic to both the letter and the spirit of the Amendments and wished them to have the most limited effect. What others in Congress and the State legislatures had in mind cannot be determined with any degree of certainty.

An additional reason for the illusive nature of the Amendment's history, with respect to segregated schools, is the status of public education at that time. In the South, the movement toward free common schools, supported by general taxation, had not yet taken hold. Education of white children was largely in the hands of private groups. Education of Negroes was almost nonexistent, and practically all of the race was illiterate. In fact, any education of Negroes was forbidden by law in some states. . . .

As a consequence, it is not surprising that there should be so little in the history of the Fourteenth Amendment relating to its intended effect on public education. . . .

In approaching this problem, we cannot turn the clock back to 1868, when the Amendment was adopted, or even to 1896, when *Plessy* v. *Ferguson* was written. We must consider public education in the light of its full development and its present place in American life throughout the nation. Only in this way can it be determined if segregation in public schools deprives these plaintiffs of the equal protection of the laws.

Today, education is perhaps the most important function of state and local governments. Compulsory school attendance laws and the great expenditures for education both demonstrate our recognition of the importance of education to our democratic society. It is required in the performance of our most basic public responsibilities, even service in the armed forces. It is the very foundation of good citizenship.

Today, it is a principal instrument in awakening the child to cultural values, in preparing him for later professional training, and in helping him to adjust normally to his environment.

In these days, it is doubtful that any child may reasonably be expected to succeed in life if he is denied the opportunity of an education. Such an opportunity, where the state has undertaken to provide it, is a right which must be made available to all on equal terms.

We come then to the question presented: Does segregation of children in public schools solely on the basis of race, even though the physical facilities and other "tangible" factors may be equal, deprive the children of the minority group of equal educational opportunities? We believe that it does. . . .

To separate them from others of similar age and qualifications solely because of their race generates a feeling of inferiority as to their status in the community that may affect their hearts and minds in a way unlikely ever to be undone. . . .

Whatever may have been the extent of psychological knowledge at the time of *Plessy* v. *Ferguson,* this finding is amply supported by modern authority. . . . Any language in *Plessy* v. *Ferguson* contrary to this finding is rejected.

We conclude that in the field of public education the doctrine of "separate but equal" has no place. Separate educational facilities are inherently unequal. Therefore, we hold that the plaintiffs and others similarly situated for whom the actions have been brought are, by reason of the segregation complained of, deprived of the equal protection of the laws guaranteed by the Fourteenth Amendment. . . .

We have now announced that such segregation is a denial of the equal protection of the laws. In order that we may have the full assistance of the parties in formulating decrees the cases will be restored to the docket, and the parties are requested to present further argument on Questions 4 and 5 previously propounded by the court for the reargument this Term. [These pertained to the form of decree to be issued if segregated schools were outlawed.] . . .

*It is so ordered.*

## Bolling v. Sharpe
## 347 U.S. 497, 74 S.Ct. 693, 98 L.Ed. 884 (1954)

### http://laws.findlaw.com/us/347/497.html

This was the companion case to *Brown* v. *Board of Education,* decided the same day. In *Brown,* the Court held that the equal protection clause prohibited the states from maintaining racially segregated public schools. In *Bolling* v. *Sharpe,* the question was whether the due process clause of the Fifth Amendment prohibited racial segregation in the public schools of the District of Columbia. Majority: Warren, Black, Burton, Clark, Douglas, Frankfurter, Jackson, Minton, Reed.

**MR. CHIEF JUSTICE WARREN delivered the opinion of the Court.**

This case challenges the validity of segregation in the public schools of the District of Columbia. The petitioners, minors of the Negro race, allege that such segregation deprives them of due process of law under the Fifth Amendment. . . .

We have this day held that the equal protection clause of the Fourteenth Amendment prohibits the states from maintaining racially segregated public schools.

The legal problem in the District of Columbia is somewhat different, however. The Fifth Amendment, which is applicable in the District of Columbia, does not contain an equal protection clause as does the Fourteenth Amendment, which applies only to the states.

But the concepts of equal protection and due process, both stemming from our American ideal of fairness, are not mutually exclusive. The "equal protection of the laws" is a more explicit safeguard of prohibited unfairness than "due process of law," and,

therefore, we do not imply that the two are always interchangeable phrases.

But, as this court has recognized, discrimination may be so unjustifiable as to be violative of due process. Classifications based solely upon race must be scrutinized with particular care, since they are contrary to our traditions and hence constitutionally suspect. . . .

Segregation in public education is not reasonably related to any proper governmental objective, and thus it imposes on Negro children of the District of Columbia a burden that constitutes an arbitrary deprivation of their liberty in violation of the Due Process Clause.

In view of our decision that the Constitution prohibits the states from maintaining racially segregated public schools, it would be unthinkable that the same Constitution would impose a lesser duty on the Federal Government. We hold that racial segregation in the public schools of the District of Columbia is a denial of the Due Process of Law guaranteed by the Fifth Amendment to the Constitution. . . .

*It is so ordered.*

## Brown v. *Board of Education* (Second Case)
## 349 U.S. 294, 75 S.Ct. 753, 99 L.Ed. 1083 (1955)

### http://laws.findlaw.com/us/349/294.html

In the term following the first Brown decision, the Court handed down its decree to guide lower courts in litigation involving desegregation. Majority: Warren, Black, Burton, Clark, Douglas, Frankfurter, Harlan, Minton, Reed.

**MR. CHIEF JUSTICE WARREN delivered the opinion of the Court.**

These cases were decided on May 17, 1954. The opinions of that date, declaring the fundamental principle that racial discrimination in public education is unconstitutional, are incorporated herein by reference. All provisions of federal, state, or local law requiring or permitting such discrimination must yield to this principle. There remains for consideration the manner in which relief is to be accorded. . . .

In fashioning and effectuating the decrees, the courts will be guided by equitable principles. Traditionally, equity has been characterized by a practical flexibility in shaping its remedies and by a facility for adjusting and reconciling public and private needs. These cases call for the exercise of these traditional attributes of equity power. At stake is the personal interest of the plaintiffs in admission to public schools as soon as practicable on a nondiscriminatory basis. To effectuate this interest may call for elimination of a variety of obstacles in making the transition to school systems operated in accordance with the constitutional principles set forth in our May 17, 1954, decision. Courts of equity may properly take into account the public interest in the elimination of such obstacles in a systematic and effective manner. But it should go without saying that the vitality of these constitutional principles cannot be allowed to yield simply because of disagreement with them.

While giving weight to these public and private considerations, the courts will require that the defendants make a prompt and reasonable start toward full compliance with our May 17, 1954, ruling. Once such a start has been made, the courts may find that additional time is necessary to carry out the ruling in an effective manner. The burden rests upon the defendants to establish that such time is necessary in the public interest and is consistent with good faith compliance at the earliest practicable date. To that end, the courts may consider problems related to administration, arising from the physical condition of the school plant, the school transportation system, personnel, revision of school districts and attendance areas into compact units to achieve a system of determining admission to the public schools on a nonracial basis, and revision of local laws and regulations which may be necessary in solving the foregoing problems. They will also consider the adequacy of any plans the defendants may propose to meet these problems and to effectuate a transition to a racially nondiscriminatory school system. During this period of transition, the courts will retain jurisdiction of these cases. The judgments below . . . are accordingly reversed and the cases are remanded to the District Courts to take such proceedings and enter such orders and decrees consistent with this opinion as are necessary and proper to admit to public schools on a racially nondiscriminatory basis with all deliberate speed the parties to these cases. . . .

*It is so ordered.*

## *Milliken* v. *Bradley*
## 418 U.S. 717, 94 S.Ct. 3112, 41 L.Ed. 2d 1069 (1974)
### http://laws.findlaw.com/us/418/717.html

This case began as a suit against the Detroit Board of Education seeking desegregation of the city's public schools. The district court ordered submission of desegregation plans for the city proper, as well as for the three-county metropolitan area, even though the 53 suburban school districts were not parties to the action and there was no finding that they had committed any constitutional violations. The U.S. Court of Appeals, Sixth Circuit, affirmed. Majority: Burger, Blackmun, Powell, Rehnquist, Stewart. Dissenting: Marshall, Brennan, Douglas, White.

**MR. CHIEF JUSTICE BURGER delivered the opinion of the Court.**

We granted certiorari in these consolidated cases to determine whether a federal court may impose a multi-district, areawide remedy to a single district de jure segregation problem absent any finding that the other included school districts have failed to operate unitary school systems within their districts, absent any claim or finding that the boundary lines of any affected school district were established with the purpose of fostering racial segregation in public schools, absent any finding that the included districts committed acts which effected segregation within the other districts, and absent a meaningful opportunity for the included neighboring school districts to present evidence or be heard on the propriety of a multi-district remedy or on the question of constitutional violations by those neighboring districts. . . .

Viewing the record as a whole, it seems clear that the District Court and the Court of Appeals shifted the primary focus from a Detroit remedy to the metropolitan area only because of their conclusion that total desegregation of Detroit would not produce the racial balance which they perceived as desirable. Both courts proceeded on an assumption that the Detroit schools could not be truly desegregated—in their view of what constituted desegregation—unless the racial composition of the student body of each school substantially reflected the racial composition of the population of the metropolitan area as a whole. The metropolitan area was then defined as Detroit plus 53 of the outlying school districts. . . .

The Michigan educational structure involved in this case, in common with most States, provides for a large measure of local control and a review of the scope and character of these local powers indicates the extent to which the interdistrict remedy approved by the two courts could disrupt and alter the structure of public education in Michigan. The metropolitan remedy would require, in effect, consolidation of 54 independent school districts historically administered as separate units into a vast new super school district. . . . Entirely apart from the logistical and other serious problems attending large-scale transportation of students, the consolidation would give rise to an array of other problems in financing and operating this new school system. . . .

Of course, no state law is above the Constitution. School district lines and the present laws with respect to local control, are not sacrosanct and if they conflict with the Fourteenth Amendment, federal courts have a duty to prescribe appropriate remedies. . . .

The controlling principle consistently expounded in our holdings is that the scope of the remedy is determined by the nature and extent of the constitutional violation. . . . Before the boundaries of separate and autonomous school districts may be set aside by consolidating the separate units for remedial purposes or by imposing a cross-district remedy, it must first be shown that there has been a constitutional violation within one district that produces a significant segregative effect in another district. Specifically it must be shown that racially discriminatory acts of the state or local school districts, or of a single school district have been a substantial cause of inter-district segregation. Thus an inter-district remedy might be in order where the racially discriminatory acts of one or more school districts caused racial segregation in an adjacent district, or where district lines have been deliberately drawn on the basis of race. In such circumstances an inter-district remedy would be appropriate to eliminate the inter-district segregation directly caused by the constitutional violation. Conversely, without an inter-district violation and inter-district effect, there is no constitutional wrong calling for an inter-district remedy. . . .

We conclude that the relief ordered by the District Court and affirmed by the Court of Appeals was based upon an erroneous standard and was unsupported by record evidence that acts of the outlying districts affected the discrimination found to exist in the schools of Detroit. Accordingly, the judgment of the Court of Appeals is reversed and the case is remanded for further proceedings consistent with this opinion leading to prompt formulation of a decree directed to eliminating the segregation found to exist in Detroit city schools, a remedy which has been delayed since 1970.

*Reversed and remanded.*

MR. JUSTICE STEWART, concurring . . . [omitted].

MR. JUSTICE DOUGLAS, dissenting . . . [omitted].

MR. JUSTICE WHITE, with whom MR. JUSTICE DOUGLAS, MR. JUSTICE BRENNAN, and MR. JUSTICE MARSHALL join, dissenting . . . [omitted].

**MR. JUSTICE MARSHALL, with whom MR. JUSTICE DOUGLAS, MR. JUSTICE BRENNAN, and MR. JUSTICE WHITE join, dissenting. . . .**

After 20 years of small, often difficult steps toward that great end, the Court today takes a giant step backwards. . . . Ironically purporting to base its result on the principle that the scope of the remedy in a desegregation case should be determined by the nature and the extent of the constitutional violation, the Court's answer is to provide no remedy at all. . . .

Our precedents, in my view, firmly establish that where, as here, state-imposed segregation has been demonstrated, it becomes the duty of the State to eliminate root and branch all vestiges of racial discrimination and to achieve the greatest possible degree of actual desegregation. . . . [T]his duty cannot be fulfilled unless the State of Michigan involves

outlying metropolitan area school districts in its desegregation remedy. . . .

We deal here with the right of all our children, whatever their race, to an equal start in life and to an equal opportunity to reach their full potential as citizens. Those children who have been denied that right in the past deserve better than to see fences thrown up to deny them that right in the future. Our Nation, I fear, will be ill served by the Court's refusal to remedy separate and unequal education, for unless our children begin to learn together, there is little hope that our people will ever learn to live together.

The great irony of the Court's opinion and, in my view, its most serious analytical flaw may be gleaned from its concluding sentence, in which the Court remands for "prompt formulation of a decree directed to eliminating the segregation found to exist in Detroit city schools, a remedy which has been delayed since 1970.". . . The majority, however, seems to have forgotten the District Court's explicit finding that a Detroit-only decree, the only remedy permitted under today's decision, "would not accomplish desegregation.". . .

Today's holding, I fear, is more a reflection of a perceived public mood that we have gone far enough in enforcing the Constitution's guarantee of equal justice than it is the product of neutral principles of law. In the short run, it may seem to be the easier course to allow our great metropolitan areas to be divided up each into two cities—one white, the other black—but it is a course, I predict, our people will ultimately regret. I dissent.

## III. STATE ACTION

## Civil Rights Cases (*United States* v. *Stanley*)
## 109 U.S. 3, 3 S.Ct. 18, 27 L.Ed. 835 (1883)
## http://laws.findlaw.com/us/109/3.html

Five cases from Kansas, California, Missouri, New York, and Tennessee, collectively known as the Civil Rights Cases and with *United States* v. *Stanley* docketed first, involved the constitutionality of the Civil Rights Act of 1875. Resting on the Thirteenth and Fourteenth Amendments, the act made it a misdemeanor to deny any person equal rights and privileges in inns, theaters and amusement places, and transportation facilities on the basis of color or previous condition of servitude. After the Supreme Court's decision, *Harper's Weekly* editorialized that since the "long and terrible Civil War sprang from the dogma of State sovereignty, invoked to protect and perpetuate slavery, it was natural that, at its close, the tendency to magnify the National authority should have been very strong, and especially to defend the victims of slavery. . . . In a calmer time, the laws passed under the humane impulse are reviewed, and when found to be incompatible with strict constitutional authority, they are set aside." Majority: Bradley, Blatchford, Field, Gray, Matthews, Miller, Waite, Woods. Dissenting: Harlan.

## MR. JUSTICE BRADLEY delivered the opinion of the Court. . . .

The essence of the law is, not to declare broadly that all persons shall be entitled to the full and equal enjoyment of the accommodations, advantages, facilities, and privileges of inns, public conveyances, and theatres; but that such enjoyment shall not be subject to any conditions applicable only to citizens of a particular race or color, or who had been in a previous condition of servitude. . . .

Has congress constitutional power to make such a law? Of course, no one will contend that the power to pass it was contained in the Constitution before the adoption of the last three amendments. The power is sought, first, in the Fourteenth Amendment. . . .

It is State action of a particular character that is prohibited [by that amendment]. Individual invasion of individual rights is not the subject matter of the amendment. It has a deeper and broader scope. It nullifies and makes void all State legislation, and State action of every kind, which impairs the privileges and immunities of citizens of the United States, or which injures them in life, liberty or property without due process of law, or which denies to any of them the equal protection of the laws. It not only does this, but, in order that the national will, thus declared, may not be a mere *brutum fulmen* [empty threat], the last section of the amendment invests Congress with power to enforce it by appropriate legislation. To enforce what? To enforce the prohibition. To adopt appropriate legislation for correcting the effects of such prohibited State laws and State acts, and thus to render them effectually null, void, and innocuous. This is the legislative power conferred upon Congress, and this is the whole of it. It does not invest Congress with power to legislate upon subjects which are within the domain of State legislation; but to provide modes of relief against State legislation, or State action, of the kind referred to. It does not authorize Congress to create a code of municipal law for the regulation of private rights; but to provide modes of redress against the operation of State laws, and the action of State officers, executive or judicial, when these are subversive of the fundamental rights specified in the amendment.

. . . Until some State law has been passed, or some State action through its officers or agents had been taken, adverse to the rights of citizens sought to be protected by the Fourteenth Amendment, no legislation of the United States under said amendment nor any proceeding under such legislation, can be called into activity: for the prohibitions of the amendment are against State laws and acts done under State authority. . . . Such legislation cannot properly cover the whole domain of rights appertaining to life, liberty and property, defining them and providing for their vindication. That would be to establish a code of municipal law regulative of all private rights between man and man in society. It would be to make Congress take the place of the State legislatures and to supersede them. . . .

If this legislation is appropriate for enforcing the prohibitions of the amendment, it is difficult to see where it is to stop. Why may not Congress with equal show of authority enact a code of laws for the enforcement and vindication of all rights of life, liberty, and property? . . . The truth is, that the implication of a power to legislate in this manner is based upon the assumption that if the States are forbidden to legislate or act in a particular way on a particular subject, and power is conferred upon Congress to enforce the prohibition, this gives Congress power to legislate generally upon that subject, and not merely power to provide modes of redress against such State legislation or action. The assumption is certainly unsound. It is repugnant to the Tenth Amendment of the Constitution, which declares that powers not delegated to the United States by the Constitution, nor prohibited by it to the States, are reserved to the States respectively or to the people. . . .

In this connection it is proper to state that civil rights, such as are guaranteed by the constitution against state aggression, cannot be impaired by the wrongful acts of individuals, unsupported by state authority in the shape of laws, customs, or judicial or executive proceedings. The wrongful act of an individual, unsupported by any such authority, is simply a private wrong, or a crime of that individual; an invasion of the rights of the injured party, it is true, whether they affect his person, his property, or his reputation; but if not sanctioned in some way by the state, or not done under state authority, his rights remain in full force, and may presumably be vindicated by resort to the laws of the state for redress. . . .

But the power of Congress to adopt direct and primary, as distinguished from corrective legislation, on the subject in hand, is sought, in the second place, from the Thirteenth Amendment, which abolishes slavery. This amendment declares "that neither slavery, nor involuntary servitude, except as a punishment for crime, whereof the party shall have been duly convicted, shall exist within the United States, or any place subject to their jurisdiction"; and it gives Congress power to enforce the amendment by appropriate legislation. . . .

There were thousands of free colored people in this country before the abolition of slavery, enjoying all the essential rights of life, liberty and property the same as white citizens; yet no one, at that time, thought that it was any invasion of his personal status as a freeman because he was not admitted to all the privileges enjoyed by white citizens, or because he was subjected to discriminations in the enjoyment of accommodations in inns, public conveyances and places of amusement. Mere discriminations on account of race or color were not regarded as badges of slavery. If, since that time, the enjoyment of equal rights in all these respects has become established by constitutional enactment, it is not by force of the Thirteenth Amendment (which merely abolishes slavery), but by force of the Fourteenth and Fifteenth Amendments. . . .

On the whole, we are of opinion that no countenance of authority for the passage of the law in question can be found in either the Thirteenth or Fourteenth amendment of the constitution; and . . . it must necessarily be declared void. . . . And it is so ordered.

### MR. JUSTICE HARLAN dissenting. . . .

I am of the opinion that such discrimination practiced by corporations and individuals in the exercise of their public or quasi public functions is a badge of servitude the imposition of which Congress may prevent under its power, by appropriate legislation, to enforce the Thirteenth Amendment; and, consequently, without reference to its enlarged power under the Fourteenth Amendment, the act of March 1, 1875, is not, in my judgment, repugnant to the Constitution. . . . The assumption that this amendment [the Fourteenth] consists wholly of prohibitions upon State laws and State proceedings in hostility to its provisions, is unauthorized by its language. [Its] first clause. . . . "All persons born or naturalized in the United States, and subject to the jurisdiction thereof, are citizens of the United States, and of the state wherein they reside"— is of a distinctly affirmative character. In its application to the colored race . . . it created and granted, as well as citizenship of the United States, citizenship of the State in which they respectively resided. It introduced all of that race, whose ancestors had been imported and sold as slaves, at once, into the political community known as the "People of the United States." They became, instantly, citizens of the United States, and of their respective States. Further, they were brought, by this supreme act of the nation, within the direct operation of that provision of the Constitution which declares that "the citizens of each State shall be entitled to all privileges and immunities of citizens in the several States."

The citizenship thus acquired by that race, in virtue of an affirmative grant from the nation, may be protected, not alone by the judicial branch of the government, but by congressional legislation of a primary direct character; this, because the power of Congress is not restricted to the enforcement of prohibitions upon State laws or State action. It is, in terms distinct and positive, to enforce *"the provisions of this article"* of amendment; not simply those of a prohibitive character, but the provisions—all of the provisions—affirmative and prohibitive, of the amendment. . . .

It is said that any interpretation of the Fourteenth Amendment different from that adopted by the majority of the court, would imply that Congress had authority to enact a municipal code for all the States, covering every matter affecting the life, liberty, and property of the citizens of the several States. Not so. . . . The personal rights and immuni-

ties recognized in the prohibitive clauses of the amendment were, prior to its adoption, under the protection, primarily, of the States, while rights, created by or derived from the United States, have always been, and, in the nature of things, should always be, primarily, under the protection of the general government. Exemption from race discrimination in respect of the civil rights which are fundamental in *citizenship* in a republican government, is, as we have seen, a new right, created by the nation, with express power in Congress, by legislation, to enforce the constitutional provision from which it is derived. If, in some sense, such race discrimination is, within the letter of the last clause of the first section, a denial of that equal protection of the laws which is secured against State denial to all persons, whether citizens or not, it cannot be possible that a mere prohibition upon such State denial, or a prohibition upon State laws abridging the privileges and immunities of citizens of the United States, takes from the nation the power which it has uniformly exercised of protecting, by direct primary legislation, those privileges and immunities which existed under the Constitution before the adoption of the Fourteenth Amendment, or have been created by that amendment in behalf of those thereby made *citizens* of their respective States. . . .

## *Moose Lodge* v. *Irvis*
## 407 U.S. 163, 92 S.Ct. 1965, 32 L.Ed. 2d 627 (1972)
### http://laws.findlaw.com/us/407/163.html

A white member of the national organization of Moose took Pennsylvania legislator Leroy Irvis as his guest to the dining room of the Harrisburg lodge and requested food and beverage. Irvis was refused service solely because he was black. The lodge is a private club, which permits only members and their guests to frequent the clubhouse. Irvis claimed that refusal of service to him was "state action" in violation of the Fourteenth Amendment's equal protection clause. Significantly, the Pennsylvania Liquor Control Board had granted the lodge a license with the requirement that it "adhere to the provisions of its own constitution and bylaws." The United States District Court required the state liquor board to revoke the lodge's license as long as it continued its discriminatory practices. Majority: Rehnquist, Blackmun, Burger, Powell, Stewart, White. Dissenting: Brennan, Douglas, Marshall.

**MR. JUSTICE REHNQUIST delivered the opinion of the Court. . . .**

Appellee, while conceding the right of private clubs to choose members upon a discriminatory basis, asserts that the licensing of Moose Lodge to serve liquor by the Pennsylvania Liquor Control Board amounts to such State involvement with the club's activities as to make its discriminatory practices forbidden by the Equal Protection Clause of the Fourteenth Amendment. The relief sought and obtained by appellee in the District Court was an injunction forbidding the licensing by the liquor authority of Moose Lodge until it ceased its discriminatory practices. We conclude that Moose Lodge's refusal to serve food and beverages to a guest by reason of the fact that he was a Negro does not, under the circumstances here presented, violate the Fourteenth Amendment.

In 1883, this Court in The Civil Rights Cases . . . set forth the essential dichotomy between discriminatory action by the State, which is prohibited by the Equal Protection Clause, and private conduct, "however discriminatory or wrongful," against which that clause "erects no shield." . . .

While the principle is easily stated, the question of whether particular discriminatory conduct is private, on the one hand, or amounts to "State action," on the other hand, frequently admits of no easy answer. . . .

Our cases make clear that the impetus for the forbidden discrimination need not originate with the State if it is state action that enforces privately originated discrimination. . . . The Court held in *Burton* v. *Wilmington Parking Authority* . . . that a private restaurant owner who refused service because of a customer's race violated the Fourteenth Amendment, where the restaurant was located in a building owned by a state-created parking authority and leased from the authority. . . .

Here there is nothing approaching the symbiotic relationship between lessor and lessee that was present in *Burton,* where the private lessee obtained the benefit of locating in a building owned by the state-created parking authority, and the parking authority was enabled to carry out its primary public purpose of furnishing parking space by advantageously leasing portions of the building constructed for that purpose to commercial lessees such as the owner of the Eagle Restaurant. Unlike *Burton,* the Moose Lodge building is located on land owned by it, not by any public authority. Far from apparently holding itself out as a place of public accommodation, Moose Lodge quite ostentatiously proclaims the fact that it is not open to the public at large. Nor is it located and operated in such surroundings that although private in name, it discharges a function or performs a service that would otherwise in all likelihood be performed by the State. In short, while Eagle was a public restaurant in a public building, Moose Lodge is a private social club in a private building.

. . . The only effect that the state licensing of Moose Lodge to serve liquor can be said to have on the right of any other Pennsylvanian to buy or be served liquor on premises other than those of Moose Lodge is that for some purposes club licenses are counted in the maximum number of licenses which may be issued in a given municipality. Basically each municipality has a quota of one retail license for each 1,500 inhabitants. Licenses issued to hotels, municipal golf courses and airport restaurants are not counted in this quota, nor are club licenses, until the maximum number of retail licenses is reached. Beyond that point, neither additional retail licenses nor additional club licenses may be issued so long as the number of issued and outstanding retail licenses remains above the statutory maximum. . . .

However detailed this type of regulation may be in some particulars, it cannot be said to in any way foster or encourage racial discrimination. . . . We therefore hold that, with the exception hereafter noted, the operation of the regulatory scheme enforced by the Pennsylvania Liquor Control Board does not sufficiently implicate the State in the discriminatory guest policies of Moose Lodge so as to make the latter "State action" within the ambit of the Equal Protection Clause of the Fourteenth Amendment.

The District Court found that the regulations of the Liquor Control Board adopted pursuant to the statute affirmatively require that "every club licensee shall adhere to all the provisions of its constitution and bylaws." . . .

Even though the Liquor Control Board regulation in question is neutral in its terms, the result of its application in a case where the constitution and bylaws of a club required racial discrimination would be to invoke the sanctions of the State to enforce a concededly discriminatory private rule. State action, for purposes of the Equal Protection Clause, may emanate from rulings of administrative and regulatory agencies as well as from legislative or judicial action. . . . [T]he application of state sanctions to enforce such a rule would violate the Fourteenth Amendment. . . .

Appellee was entitled to a decree enjoining the enforcement of . . . the regulations promulgated by the Pennsylvania Liquor Control Board insofar as that regulation requires compliance by Moose Lodge with provisions of its constitution and bylaws containing racially discriminatory provisions. He was entitled to no more. The judgment of the District Court is reversed, and the cause remanded with instructions to enter a decree in conformity with this opinion.

*Reversed and remanded.*

## Mr. Justice Douglas, with whom Mr. Justice Marshall joins, dissenting.

My view of the First Amendment and the related guarantees of the Bill of Rights is that they create a zone of privacy which precludes government from interfering with private clubs or groups. The associational rights which our system honors permit all white, all black, all brown, and all yellow clubs to be formed. They also permit all Catholic, all Jewish, or all agnostic clubs to be established. . . . So the fact that the Moose Lodge allows only Caucasians to join or come as guests is constitutionally irrelevant. . . .

Pennsylvania has a state store system of alcohol distribution. Resale is permitted by hotels, restaurants, and private clubs which all must obtain licenses from the Liquor Control Board. The scheme of regulation is complete and pervasive. . . . Among these requirements is regulation No. 113.09 which says "Every club licensee shall adhere to all the provisions of its Constitution and Bylaws." . . .

Were this regulation the only infirmity in Pennsylvania's licensing scheme, I would perhaps agree with the majority that the appropriate relief would be a decree enjoining its enforcement. But there is another flaw in the scheme not so easily cured. Liquor licenses in Pennsylvania, unlike driver's licenses, or marriage licenses, are not freely available to those who meet racially neutral qualifications. . . . What the majority neglects to say is that the Harrisburg quota, where Moose Lodge No. 107 is located, has been full for many years. No more club licenses may be issued in that city.

This state-enforced scarcity of licenses restricts the ability of blacks to obtain liquor, for liquor is commercially available only at private clubs for a significant portion of each week. . . .

Thus, the State of Pennsylvania is putting the weight of its liquor license, concededly a valued and important adjunct to a private club, behind racial discrimination. . . .

Mr. Justice Brennan, with whom Mr. Justice Marshall joins, dissenting . . . [omitted].

## IV. GENDER DISCRIMINATION

### *Frontiero* v. *Richardson*
### 411 U.S. 677, 93 S.Ct. 1764, 36 L.Ed. 2d 583 (1973)
http://laws.findlaw.com/us/411/677.html

> A servicewoman's application for increased quarters allowances and medical and dental benefits for her husband was disallowed because she failed, as required by law, to demonstrate that her husband was dependent on her for more than one-half of his support. The servicewoman instituted action, contending that the statutes that allowed a serviceman to claim his wife as a dependent for such benefits, without regard to whether she was in fact dependent on him for any part of her support, were discriminatory on the basis of sex and in violation of the Fifth Amendment's due process clause. A three-judge district court upheld the constitutionality of the statutes. Majority: Brennan, Blackmun, Burger, Douglas, Marshall, Powell, Stewart, White. Dissenting: Rehnquist.

**MR. JUSTICE BRENNAN announced the judgment of the Court in an opinion in which MR. JUSTICES DOUGLAS, MARSHALL, and WHITE joined.**

At the outset, appellants contend that classifications based upon sex, like classifications based upon race, alienage, and national origin, are inherently suspect and must therefore be subjected to close judicial scrutiny. We agree and, indeed, find at least implicit support for such an approach in our unanimous decision only last term in *Reed* v. *Reed*. . . .

In *Reed,* the Court considered the constitutionality of an Idaho statute providing that, when two individuals are otherwise equally entitled to appointment as administrator of an estate, the male applicant must be preferred to the female. . . .

[T]he Court held the statutory preference for male applicants unconstitutional. In reaching this result, the Court implicitly rejected appellee's apparently rational explanation of the statutory scheme, and concluded that, by ignoring the individual qualifications of particular applicants, the challenged statute provided "dissimilar treatment for men and women who are . . . similarly situated." The Court therefore held that, even though the State's interest in achieving administrative efficiency "is not without some legitimacy," "[t]o give a mandatory preference to members of

either sex over members of the other, merely to accomplish the elimination of hearings on the merits, is to make the very kind of arbitrary legislative choice forbidden by the [Constitution]. . . ." This departure from "traditional" rational basis analysis with respect to sex-based classification is clearly justified.

There can be no doubt that our Nation has had a long and unfortunate history of sex discrimination. Traditionally, such discrimination was rationalized by an attitude of "romantic paternalism" which, in practical effect, put women not on a pedestal, but in a cage. . . .

As a result of notions such as these, our statute books gradually became laden with gross, stereotypical distinctions between the sexes and, indeed, throughout much of the 19th century the position of women in our society was, in many respects, comparable to that of blacks under the pre-Civil War slave codes. Neither slaves nor women could hold office, serve on juries, or bring suit in their own names, and married women traditionally were denied the legal capacity to hold or convey property or to serve as legal guardians of their own children. . . . And although blacks were guaranteed the right to vote in 1870, women were denied even that right—which is itself "preservative of other basic and civil and political rights"—until adoption of the Nineteenth Amendment half a century later.

It is true, of course, that the position of women in America has improved markedly in recent decades. Nevertheless, it can hardly be doubted that, in part because of the high visibility of the sex characteristic, women still face pervasive, although at times more subtle, discrimination in our educational institutions, on the job market and, perhaps most conspicuously, in the political arena. . . .

Moreover, since sex, like race and national origin, is an immutable characteristic determined solely by the accident of birth, the imposition of special disabilities upon the members of a particular sex because of their sex would seem to violate "the basic concept of our system that legal burdens should bear some relationship to individual responsibility. . . ." And what differentiates sex from such nonsuspect statuses as intelligence or physical disability, and aligns it with the recognized suspect criteria, is that the sex characteristic frequently bears no relation to ability to perform or contribute to society. As a result, statutory distinctions between the sexes often have the effect of invidiously relegating the entire class of females to inferior legal status without regard to the actual capabilities of its individual members. . . .

With those considerations in mind, we can only conclude that classifications based upon sex, like classifications based upon race, alienage, or national origin, are inherently suspect, and must therefore be subjected to strict judicial scrutiny. Applying the analysis mandated by that stricter standard of review, it is clear that the statutory scheme now before us is constitutionally invalid.

The sole basis of the classification established in the challenged statutes is the sex of the individuals involved. . . . Thus . . . a female member of the uniformed services seeking to obtain housing and medical benefits for her spouse must prove his dependency in fact, whereas no such burden is imposed upon male members. In addition, the statutes operate so as to deny benefits to a female member, such as appellant Sharron Frontiero, who provides less than one-half of her spouse's support, while at the same time granting such benefits to a male member who likewise provides less than one-half of his spouse's support. Thus, to this extent at least, it may fairly be said that these statutes command "dissimilar" treatment for men and women who are . . . "similarly situated." . . .

Moreover, the Government concedes that the differential treatment accorded men and women under these statutes serves no purpose other than mere "administrative convenience." In essence, the Government maintains that, as an empirical matter, wives in our society frequently are dependent upon their husbands, while husbands rarely are dependent upon their wives. Thus, the Government argues that Congress might reasonably have concluded that it would be both cheaper and easier simply conclusively to presume that wives of male members are financially dependent upon their husbands, while burdening female members with the task of establishing dependency in fact. . . .

[A]ny statutory scheme which draws a sharp line between the sexes, solely for the purpose of achieving administrative convenience, necessarily commands "dissimilar treatment for men and women who are . . . similarly situated," and therefore involves the "very kind of arbitrary legislative choice forbidden by the [Constitution]. . . ." We therefore conclude that, by according differential treatment to male and female members of the uniformed services for the sole purpose of achieving administrative convenience, the challenged statutes violate the Due Process Clause of the Fifth Amendment insofar as they require a female member to prove the dependency of her husband.

*Reversed.*

MR. JUSTICE STEWART, concurring in the judgment . . . [omitted].

**MR. JUSTICE POWELL, with whom the CHIEF JUSTICE and MR. JUSTICE BLACKMUN join, concurring in the judgment. . . .**

It is unnecessary for the Court in this case to characterize sex as a suspect classification, with all of the far-reaching implications of such a holding. . . . In my view, we can and should decide this case on the authority of

*Reed* and reserve for the future any expansion of its rationale.

There is another, and I find compelling, reason for deferring a general categorizing of sex classifications as invoking the strictest test of judicial scrutiny. The Equal Rights Amendment, which if adopted will resolve the substance of this precise question, has been approved by the Congress and submitted for ratification by the States. . . .

MR. JUSTICE REHNQUIST dissents [without opinion].

## Craig v. Boren
## 429 U.S. 190, 97 S.Ct. 451, 50 L.Ed. 2d 397 (1976)
### http://laws.findlaw.com/us/429/190.html

Two sections (241 and 245) of an Oklahoma statute combined to prohibit the sale of 3.2 percent beer to males under the age of 21 and to females under the age of 18. Craig (a male between 18 and 21 years of age) and Whitener (a licensed vendor of 3.2 percent beer who operated the Honk 'n' Holler convenience store) sought injunctive relief against the statute in the U.S. District Court for the Western District of Oklahoma. They contended that the gender-based differential constituted an invidious discrimination against males 18–20 years old, in violation of the equal protection clause. The three-judge panel upheld the classification and dismissed the action. In this case, unlike *Frontiero* v. *Richardson,* Justice Brennan was able to amass a majority behind his opinion, but only by settling for a slightly lower standard of review. Majority: Brennan, Blackmun, Marshall, Powell, Stevens, Stewart, White. Dissenting: Rehnquist, Burger.

**MR. JUSTICE BRENNAN delivered the opinion of the Court. . . .**

To withstand constitutional challenge, previous cases establish that classifications by gender must serve important governmental objectives and must be substantially related to achievement of those objectives. . . .

We accept for purposes of discussion the District Court's identification of the objective underlying § 241 and 245 as the enhancement of traffic safety. Clearly, the protection of public health and safety represents an important function of state and local governments. However, appellees' statistics in our view cannot support the conclusion that the gender-based distinction closely serves to achieve that objective and therefore the distinction cannot . . . withstand equal protection challenge.

The appellees introduced a variety of statistical surveys. . . .

Even were this statistical evidence accepted as accurate, it nevertheless offers only a weak answer to the equal protection question presented here. The most focused and relevant of the statistical surveys, arrests of 18–20-year-olds for alcohol-related driving offenses, exemplifies the ultimate unpersuasiveness of this evidentiary record. Viewed in terms of the correlation between sex and the actual activity that Oklahoma seeks to regulate—driving while under the influence of alcohol—the statistics broadly establish that .18 percent of females and 2 percent of males in that age group were arrested for that offense. While such a disparity is not trivial in a statistical sense, it can hardly form the basis for employment of a gender line as a classifying device. Certainly if maleness is to serve as a proxy for drinking and driving, a correlation of 2 percent must be considered an unduly tenuous "fit." . . .

There is no reason to belabor this line of analysis. It is unrealistic to expect either members of the judiciary or state officials to be well versed in the rigors of experimental or statistical technique. But this merely illustrates that proving broad sociological propositions by statistics is a dubious business, and one that inevitably is in tension with the normative philosophy that underlies the Equal Protection Clause. Suffice to say that the showing offered by the appellees does not satisfy us that sex represents a legitimate, accurate proxy for the regulation of drinking and driving. In fact, when it is further recognized that Oklahoma's statute prohibits only the selling of 3.2% beer to young males and not their drinking the beverage once acquired (even after purchase by their 18–20-year-old female companions), the relationship between gender and traffic safety becomes far too tenuous to satisfy *Reed's* requirement that the gender-based difference be substantially related to achievement of the statutory objective. . . .

We conclude that the gender-based differential . . . constitutes a denial of the equal protection of the laws to males aged 18–20 and reverse the judgment of the District Court.

*It is so ordered.*

MR. JUSTICE STEWART, concurring . . . [omitted].

MR. JUSTICE BLACKMUN, concurring . . . [omitted].

MR. JUSTICE POWELL, concurring . . . [omitted].

MR. JUSTICE STEVENS, concurring . . . [omitted].

MR. CHIEF JUSTICE BURGER, dissenting . . . [omitted].

## MR. JUSTICE REHNQUIST, dissenting.

The Court's disposition of this case is objectionable on two grounds. First is its conclusion that men challenging a gender-based statute which treats them less favorably than women may invoke a more stringent standard of judicial review than pertains to most other types of classifications. Second is the Court's enunciation of this standard, without citation to any source, as being that "classifications by gender must serve important governmental objectives and must be substantially related to achievement of those objectives. . . . The only redeeming feature of the Court's opinion, to my mind, is that it apparently signals a retreat by those who joined the plurality opinion in *Frontiero* . . . from their view that sex is a "suspect" classification for purposes of equal protection analysis. I think the Oklahoma statute challenged here need pass only the "rational basis" equal protection analysis . . . and I believe that it is constitutional under that analysis. . . .

The Court's conclusion that a law which treats males less favorably than females "must serve important governmental objectives and must be substantially related to achievement of those objectives" apparently comes out of thin air. The Equal Protection Clause contains no such language, and none of our previous cases adopt that standard. I would think we have had enough difficulty with the two standards of review which our cases have recognized—the norm of "rational basis," and the "compelling state interest" required where a "suspect classification" is involved—so as to counsel weightily against the insertion of still another "standard" between those two. How is this Court to divine what objectives are important? How is it to determine whether a particular law is "substantially" related to the achievement of such objective, rather than related in some other way to its achievement? Both of the phrases used are so diaphanous and elastic as to invite subjective judicial preferences or prejudices relating to particular types of legislation, masquerading as judgments whether such legislation is directed at "important" objectives or, whether the relationship to those objectives is "substantial" enough.

I would have thought that if this Court were to leave anything to decision by the popularly elected branches of the Government, where no constitutional claim other than that of equal protection is invoked, it would be the decision as to what governmental objectives to be achieved by law are "important," and which are not. . . .

## *Mississippi University for Women* v. *Hogan*
## 458 U.S. 718, 102 S.Ct. 331, 73 L.Ed. 2d 1090 (1982)
http://laws.findlaw.com/us/458/718.html

When this litigation began in 1979, the state of Mississippi operated 8 universities and 16 junior colleges. All except Mississippi University for Women in Columbus were coeducational. Joe Hogan applied for admission to the MUW School of Nursing, but was denied entrance solely because of his gender. While he could have applied to the two state coed schools of nursing in Mississippi, he preferred MUW's because it was nearest his home. He then filed an action in the U.S. District Court for the Northern District of Mississippi, claiming that MUW's single-sex admissions policy violated the equal protection clause. Applying the rational basis test, the court ruled in favor of the university. The Court of Appeals for the Fifth Circuit reversed. In its view the state had the heavier burden, which it had not met, of showing that the gender-based classification was substantially related to an important government objective. Majority: O'-Connor, Brennan, White, Marshall, Stevens. Dissenting: Burger, Blackmun, Powell, Rehnquist.

JUSTICE O'CONNOR delivered the opinion of the Court. . . .

We begin our analysis aided by several firmly established principles. Because the challenged policy expressly discriminates among applicants on the basis of gender, it is subject to scrutiny under the Equal Protection Clause of the Fourteenth Amendment. That this statutory policy discriminates against males rather than against females does not exempt it from scrutiny or reduce the standard of review. Our decisions also establish that the party seeking to uphold a statute that classifies individuals on the basis of their gender must carry the burden of showing an "exceedingly persuasive justification" for the classification. The burden is met only by showing at least that the classification serves "important governmental objectives and that the discriminatory means employed" are "substantially related to the achievement of those objectives." . . .

The State's primary justification for maintaining the single-sex admissions policy of MUW's School of Nursing is that it compensates for discrimination against women and, therefore, constitutes educational affirmative action. As applied to the School of Nursing, we find the State's argument unpersuasive. . . .

It is readily apparent that a State can evoke a compensatory purpose to justify an otherwise discriminatory classification only if members of the gender benefited by the classification actually suffer a disadvantage related to the classification. We considered such a situation in *Califano* v. *Webster* (1977), which involved a challenge to a statutory classification that allowed women to eliminate more low-earning years than men for purposes of computing Social Security Retirement benefits. Although the effect of the classification was to allow women higher monthly benefits than were available to men with the same earning history, we upheld the statutory scheme, noting that it took into account that women "as such have been unfairly hindered from earning as much as men" and "work[ed] directly to remedy" the resulting economic disparity. . . .

In sharp contrast, Mississippi has made no showing that women lacked opportunities to obtain training in the field of nursing or to attain positions of leadership in that field when the MUW School of Nursing opened its door or that women currently are deprived of such opportunities. In fact, in 1970, the year before the School of Nursing's first class enrolled, women earned 94 percent of the nursing baccalaureate degrees conferred in Mississippi and 98.6 percent of the degrees earned nationwide. . . .

Rather than compensate for discriminatory barriers faced by women, MUW's policy of excluding males from admission to the School of Nursing tends to perpetuate the stereotyped view of nursing as an exclusively woman's job. . . . Thus, we conclude that, although the State recited a "benign, compensatory purpose," it failed to establish that the alleged objective is the actual purpose underlying the discriminatory classification.

The policy is invalid also because it fails the second part of the equal protection test, for the State has made no showing that the gender-based classification is substantially and directly related to its proposed compensatory objective. To the contrary, MUW's policy of permitting men to attend classes as auditors fatally undermines its claim that women, at least those in the School of Nursing, are adversely affected by the presence of men. . . .

In an additional attempt to justify its exclusion of men from MUW's School of Nursing, the State contends that MUW is the direct beneficiary "of specific congressional legislation which, on its face, permits the institution to exist as it has in the past." The argument is based upon the language of § 901(a) in Title IX of the Education Amendments of 1972. Although § 901(a) prohibits gender discrimination in education programs that receive federal financial assistance, subsection 5 exempts the admissions policies of undergraduate institutions "that traditionally and continually from [their] establishment [have] had a policy of admitting only students of one sex" from the general prohibition. Arguing that Congress enacted Title IX in furtherance of its power to enforce the Fourteenth Amendment, a power granted by § 5 of that Amendment, the State would have us conclude that § 901(a)(5) is but "a congressional limitation upon the broad prohibitions of the Equal Protection Clause of the Fourteenth Amendment."

The argument requires little comment. Initially, it is far from clear that Congress intended, through § 901(a)(5), to exempt MUW from any constitutional obligation. Rather, Congress apparently intended, at most, to exempt MUW from the requirements of Title IX.

Even if Congress envisioned a constitutional exemption, the State's argument would fail. Section 5 of the Fourteenth Amendment gives Congress broad power indeed to enforce the command of the Amendment and "to secure to all persons the enjoyment of perfect equality of civil rights and the equal protection of the laws against State denial or invasion. . . ." Congress' power under § 5, however, "is limited to adopting measures to enforce the guarantees of the Amendment; § 5 grants Congress no power to restrict, abrogate, or dilute these guarantees." Although we give deference to congressional decisions and classifications, neither Congress nor a State can validate a law that denies the rights guaranteed by the Fourteenth Amendment. . . .

Because we conclude that the State's policy of excluding males from MUW's School of Nursing violates the Equal Protection Clause of the Fourteenth Amendment, we affirm the judgment of the Court of Appeals.

*It is so ordered.*

CHIEF JUSTICE BURGER, dissenting . . . [omitted].

JUSTICE BLACKMUN, dissenting . . . [omitted].

### JUSTICE POWELL, with whom JUSTICE REHNQUIST joins, dissenting.

The Court's opinion bows deeply to conformity. Left without honor—indeed, held unconstitutional—is an element of diversity that has characterized much of American education and enriched much of American life. The Court in effect holds today that no State now may provide even a single institution of higher learning open only to women students. It gives no heed to the efforts of the State of Mississippi to provide abundant opportunities for young men and young women to attend coeducational institutions, and none to the preferences of the more than 40,000 young women who over the years have evidenced their approval of an all-women's college by choosing Mississippi University for Women over seven coeducational universities within the State. . . .

Coeducation, historically, is a novel educational theory. From grade school through high school, college, and graduate and professional training, much of the nation's population during much of our history has been educated in sexually segregated classrooms. At the college level, for instance, until recently some of the most prestigious colleges and universities— including most of the Ivy League—had long histories of single-sex education. As Harvard, Yale, and Princeton remained all-male colleges well into the second half of this century, the "Seven Sister" institutions established a parallel standard of excellence for women's colleges. . . .

The arguable benefits of single-sex colleges also continue to be recognized by students of higher education. The Carnegie Commission on Higher Education has reported that it "favor[s] the continuation of colleges for women. They provide an element of diversity . . . and [an environment in which women] generally . . . speak up more in their classes, . . . hold more positions of leadership on campus, . . . and have more role models and mentors among women teachers and administrators." . . .

Despite the continuing expressions that single-sex institutions may offer singular advantages to their students, there is no doubt that coeducational institutions are far more numerous. But their numerical predominance does not establish—in any sense properly cognizable by a court—that individual preferences for single-sex education are misguided or illegitimate, or that a State may not provide its citizens with a choice. . . .

By applying heightened equal protection analysis to this case, the Court frustrates the liberating spirit of the Equal Protection Clause. It forbids the States from providing women with an opportunity to choose the type of university they prefer. And yet it is these women whom the Court regards as the victims of an illegal, stereotyped perception of the role of women in our society. The Court reasons this way in a case in which no woman has complained, and the only complainant is a man who advances no claims on behalf of anyone else. His claim, it should be recalled, is not that he is being denied a substantive educational opportunity, or even the right to attend an all-male or a coeducational college. It is only that the colleges open to him are located at inconvenient distances.

The Court views this case as presenting a serious equal protection claim of sex discrimination. I do not and I would sustain Mississippi's right to continue MUW on a rational basis analysis. But I need not apply this "lowest tier" of scrutiny. I can accept for present purposes the standard applied by the Court: that there is a gender-based distinction that must serve an important governmental objective by means that are substantially related to its achievement. The record in this case reflects that MUW has a historic position in the State's educational system dating back to 1884. More than 2,000 women presently evidence their preference for MUW by having enrolled there. The choice is one that discriminates invidiously against no one. And the State's purpose in preserving that choice is legitimate and substantial. Generations of our finest minds, both among educators and students, have believed that single-sex college-level institutions afford distinctive benefits. . . .

A distinctive feature of America's tradition has been respect for diversity. This has been characteristic of the peoples from numerous lands who have built our country. It is the essence of our democratic system. At stake in this case as I see it is the preservation of a small aspect of this diversity. . . .

# V. FUNDAMENTAL RIGHTS ANALYSIS

## *Shapiro* v. *Thompson*
## 394 U.S. 618, 89 S.Ct. 1322, 22 L.Ed. 2d 600 (1969)
http://laws.findlaw.com/us/394/618.html

Welfare laws in Connecticut, Pennsylvania, and the District of Columbia required applicants for benefits to show one-year residence. The rules were authorized but not required by the Social Security Act of 1935. Three-judge federal district courts held the residency provision unconstitutional. Majority: Brennan, Douglas, Fortas, Marshall, Stewart, White. Dissenting: Harlan, Black, Warren.

**MR. JUSTICE BRENNAN delivered the opinion of the Court. . . .**

[T]he Connecticut Welfare Department invoked § 17-2d of the Connecticut General Statutes to deny the application of appellee Vivian Marie Thompson for assistance under the program for Aid to Families with Dependent Children (AFDC). She was a 19-year-old unwed mother of one child and pregnant with her second child when she changed her residence in June 1966 from Dorchester, Massachusetts, to Hartford, Connecticut, to live with her mother, a Hartford resident. She moved to her own apartment in Hartford in August 1966, when her mother was no longer able to support her and her infant son. Because of her pregnancy, she was unable to work or enter a work training program. Her application for AFDC assistance, filed in August, was denied in November solely on the ground that . . . she had not lived in the State for a year before her application was filed. . . .

There is no dispute that the effect of the waiting-period requirement in each case is to create two classes of needy resident families indistinguishable from each other except that one is composed of residents who have resided a year or more, and the second of residents who have resided less than a year, in the jurisdiction. On the basis of this sole difference the first class is granted and the second class is denied welfare aid upon which may depend the ability of the families to obtain the very means to subsist—food, shelter, and other necessities of life. . . .

There is weighty evidence that exclusion from the jurisdiction of the poor who need or may need relief was the specific objective of these provisions. In the Congress, sponsors of federal legislation to eliminate all residence requirements have been consistently opposed by representatives of state and local welfare agencies who have stressed the fears of the States that elimination of the requirements would result in a heavy influx of individuals into States providing the most generous benefits. . . .

We do not doubt that the one-year waiting period device is well suited to discourage the influx of poor families in need of assistance. An indigent who desires to migrate, resettle, find a new job, start a new life will doubtless hesitate if he knows that he must risk making the move without the possibility of falling back on state welfare assistance during his first year of residence when his need may be most acute. But the purpose of inhibiting migration by needy persons into the State is constitutionally impermissible.

This Court long ago recognized that the nature of our Federal Union and our constitutional concepts of personal liberty unite to require that all citizens be free to travel throughout the length and breadth of our land uninhibited by statutes, rules, or regulations which unreasonably burden or restrict this movement. . . .

We have no occasion to ascribe the source of this right to travel interstate to a particular constitutional provision. . . . "It is a right that has been firmly established and repeatedly recognized. . . ."

Appellants next advance as justification certain administrative and related governmental objectives allegedly served by the waiting-period requirement. They argue that the requirement (1) facilitates the planning of the welfare budget; (2) provides an objective test of residency; (3) minimizes the opportunity for recipients fraudulently to receive payments from more than one jurisdiction; and (4) encourages early entry of new residents into the labor force. . . .

The argument that the waiting-period requirement facilitates budget predictability is wholly unfounded. . . .

The argument that the waiting period serves as an administratively efficient rule of thumb for determining residency similarly will not withstand scrutiny. . . .

Similarly, there is no need for a State to use the one-year waiting period as a safeguard against fraudulent receipt of benefits; far less drastic means are available, and are employed, to minimize that hazard. . . .

We conclude therefore that appellants in these cases do not use and have no need to use the one-year requirement for the governmental purposes suggested. Thus, even under traditional equal protection tests a classification of welfare applicants according to whether they have lived in the State for one year would seem irrational and unconstitutional. But, of course, the traditional criteria do not apply in these cases. Since the classification here touches on the fundamental right of interstate movement, its constitutionality must be judged by the stricter standard of whether it promotes a compelling state interest. Under this standard, the waiting period requirement clearly violates the Equal Protection Clause. . . .

*Affirmed.*

Mr. Justice Stewart, concurring . . . [omitted].

Mr. Chief Justice Warren, with whom Mr. Justice Black joins, dissenting . . . [omitted].

### Mr. Justice Harlan, dissenting. . . .

In upholding the equal protection argument, the Court has applied an equal protec-

tion doctrine of relatively recent vintage: the rule that statutory classifications which either are based upon certain "suspect" criteria or affect "fundamental rights" will be held to deny equal protection unless justified by a "compelling" governmental interest. . . .

The "compelling interest" doctrine has two branches. The branch which requires that classifications based upon "suspect" criteria be supported by a compelling interest apparently had its genesis in cases involving racial classifications, which have . . . been regarded as inherently "suspect." . . .

I think that this branch of the "compelling interest" doctrine is sound when applied to racial classifications, for historically the Equal Protection Clause was largely a product of the desire to eradicate legal distinctions founded upon race. However, I believe that the more recent extensions have been unwise. . . .

The second branch of the "compelling interest" principle is even more troublesome. For it has been held that a statutory classification is subject to the "compelling interest" test if the result of the classification may be to affect a "fundamental right," regardless of the basis of the classification. . . .

I think this branch of the "compelling interest" doctrine particularly unfortunate and unnecessary. It is unfortunate because it creates an exception which threatens to swallow the standard equal protection rule. Virtually every state statute affects important rights. This Court has repeatedly held, for example, that the traditional equal protection standard is applicable to statutory classifications affecting such fundamental matters as the right to pursue a particular occupation, the right to receive greater or smaller wages or to work more or less hours, and the right to inherit property. Rights such as these are in principle indistinguishable from those involved here, and to extend the "compelling interest" rule to all cases in which such rights are affected would go far toward making this Court a "super-legislature." This branch of the doctrine is also unnecessary. When the right affected is one assured by the federal Constitution, any infringement can be dealt with under the Due Process Clause. But when a statute affects only matters not mentioned in the federal Constitution and is not arbitrary or irrational, I must reiterate that I know of nothing which entitles this Court to pick out particular human activities, characterize them as "fundamental," and give them added protection under an unusually stringent equal protection test. . . .

## San Antonio Independent School District v. Rodriguez
## 411 U.S. 1, 93 S.Ct. 1278, 36 L.Ed. 2d 16 (1973)
http://laws.findlaw.com/us/411/1.html

Public elementary and secondary education in the United States has been traditionally financed through taxes imposed by local school boards on property within the school district. Other funds come from the state and federal governments. In 1968, Demetrio Rodriguez and other parents living in Texas's Edgewood School District filed suit in the U.S. District Court for the Western District of Texas, claiming that reliance on local property taxes for the support of public education violated the equal protection clause. Edgewood had an average assessed property value of $5,960 for each of its 22,000 students. With a tax of $1.05 per $100 of assessed value (the highest in the San Antonio area), the district received less per pupil from property taxes than did the affluent Alamo Heights district, which taxed at a rate of only $0.85 but which contained assessed property worth more than $49,000 for each of its 5,000 students. With state, federal, and other support included, Edgewood spent $356, and Alamo Heights $594, per pupil. These situations reflected a pattern: Property-poor districts typically taxed more and spent less for each enrolled child than did property-rich districts. Ruling that education was a fundamental constitutional right and that wealth-based distinctions in the state's system of school financing were constitutionally suspect, a three-judge panel instructed the state to adopt a system of school financing so that the amount spent per pupil would not be a function of the wealth of the district in which a child lived. Majority: Powell, Blackmun, Burger, Rehnquist, Stewart. Minority: White, Brennan, Marshall, Douglas.

**MR. JUSTICE POWELL delivered the opinion of the Court. . . .**

The District Court's opinion does not reflect the novelty and complexity of the constitutional questions posed by appellees' challenge to Texas' system of school financing. In concluding that strict judicial scrutiny was required, that court relied on decisions dealing with the rights of indigents to equal treatment in the criminal trial and appellate processes, and on cases disapproving wealth restrictions on the right to vote. Those cases, the District Court concluded, established wealth as a suspect classification. Finding that the local property tax system discriminated on the basis of wealth, it regarded those precedents as controlling. It then reasoned, based on decisions of this Court affirming the undeniable importance of education, that there is a fundamental right to education and that, absent some compelling state justification, the Texas system could not stand.

We are unable to agree that this case, which in significant aspects is *sui generis* [unique], may be so nearly fitted into the conventional mosaic of constitutional analysis under the Equal Protection Clause. Indeed, for the several reasons that follow, we find neither the suspect-classification nor the fundamental-interest analysis persuasive.

The wealth discrimination discovered by the District Court in this case, and by several other courts that have recently struck down school-financing laws in other States, is quite unlike any of the forms of wealth discrimination heretofore reviewed by this Court. Rather than focusing on the unique features of the alleged discrimination, the courts in these cases have virtually assumed their findings of a suspect classification through a simplistic process of analysis: since, under the traditional systems of financing public schools, some poorer people receive less expensive educations than other more affluent people, these systems discriminate on the basis of wealth. This approach largely ignores the hard threshold questions, including whether it makes a difference for purposes of consideration under the Constitution that the class of disadvantaged "poor" cannot be identified or defined in customary equal protection terms, and whether the relative— rather than absolute—nature of the asserted deprivation is of significant consequence. Before a State's laws and the justifications for the classifications they create are subjected to strict judicial scrutiny, we think these threshold considerations must be analyzed more closely than they were in the court below. . . .

First, in support of their charge that the system discriminates against the "poor," appellees have made no effort to demonstrate that it operates to the peculiar disadvantage of any class fairly definable as indigent, or as composed of persons whose incomes are beneath any designated poverty level. Indeed, there is reason to believe that the poorest families are not necessarily clustered in the poorest property districts. . . .

Second, neither appellees nor the District Court addressed the fact that . . . lack of personal resources has not occasioned an absolute deprivation of the desired benefit. The argument here is not that the children in districts having relatively low assessable property values are receiving no public education; rather, it is that they are receiving a poorer quality education than that available to children in districts having more assessable wealth. Apart from the unsettled and disputed question whether the quality of education may be determined by the amount of money expended for it, a sufficient answer to appellees' argument is that, at least where wealth is involved, the Equal Protection Clause does not require absolute equality or precisely equal advantages. . . .

For these two reasons . . . the disadvantaged class is not susceptible of identification in traditional terms. . . .

[I]t is clear that appellees' suit asks this Court to extend its most exacting scrutiny to review a system that allegedly discriminates against a large, diverse, and amorphous class, unified only by the common factor of residence in districts that happen to have less taxable wealth than other districts. The system of alleged discrimination and the class it defines have none of the traditional indicia of suspectness: the class is not saddled with such disabilities, or subjected to such a history of purposeful unequal treatment, or relegated to such a position of political powerlessness as to command extraordinary protection from the majoritarian political process.

We thus conclude that the Texas system does not operate to the peculiar disadvantage of any suspect class. . . .

Nothing this Court holds today in any way detracts from our historic dedication to public education. . . . But the importance of a service performed by the State does not determine whether it must be regarded as fundamental for purposes of examination under the Equal Protection Clause. . . . It is not the province of this Court to create substantive constitutional rights in the name of guaranteeing equal protection of the laws. . . .

Education, of course, is not among the rights afforded explicit protection under our Federal Constitution. Nor do we find any basis for saying it is implicitly so protected. . . .

Even if it were conceded that some identifiable quantum of education is a constitutionally protected prerequisite to the meaningful exercise of . . . [both the First Amendment rights and the right to vote] we have no indication that the present levels of educational expenditures in Texas provide an education that falls short. Whatever merit appellees' argument might have if a State's financing system occasioned an absolute denial of educational opportunities to any of its children, that argument provides no basis for finding any interference with fundamental rights where only relative differences in spending levels are involved and where—as is true in the present case—no charge fairly could be made that the system fails to provide each child with an opportunity to acquire the basic minimal skills necessary for the enjoyment of the rights of speech and of full participation in the political process. . . .

In sum, to the extent that the Texas system of school financing results in unequal expenditures between children who happen to reside in different districts, we cannot say that such disparities are the product of a system that is so irrational as to be invidiously discriminatory. . . . We are unwilling to assume for ourselves a level of wisdom superior to that of legislators, scholars, and educational authorities in 50 States, especially where the alternatives proposed are only recently conceived and nowhere yet tested. The constitutional standard under the Equal Protection Clause is whether the challenged state action rationally furthers a legitimate state purpose or interest. We hold that the Texas plan abundantly satisfies this standard. . . .

*Reversed.*

MR. JUSTICE STEWART, concurring . . . [omitted].

MR. JUSTICE BRENNAN, dissenting . . . [omitted].

**MR. JUSTICE WHITE, with whom MR. JUSTICE DOUGLAS and MR. JUSTICE BRENNAN join, dissenting. . . .**

Requiring the State to establish only that unequal treatment is in furtherance of a permissible goal, without also requiring the State to show that the means chosen to effectuate that goal are rationally related to its achievement, makes equal protection analysis no more than an empty gesture. In my view, the parents and children in Edgewood, and in like districts, suffer from an invidious discrimination violative of the Equal Protection Clause. . . .

There is no difficulty in identifying the class that is subject to the alleged discrimination and that is entitled to the benefits of the Equal Protection Clause. I need go no further than the parents and children in the Edgewood district, who are plaintiffs here and who assert that they are entitled to the same choice as Alamo Heights to augment local expenditures for schools but are denied that choice by state law. This group constitutes a class sufficiently definite to invoke the protection of the Constitution. They are as entitled to the protection of the Equal Protection Clause as were the voters in allegedly underrepresented counties in the reapportionment cases. . . .

**MR. JUSTICE MARSHALL, with whom MR. JUSTICE DOUGLAS concurs, dissenting.**

The Court today decides, in effect, that a State may constitutionally vary the quality of education which it offers its children in accordance with the amount of taxable wealth located in the school districts within which they reside. The majority's decision represents an abrupt departure from the mainstream of recent state and federal court decisions concerning the unconstitutionality of state educational financing schemes dependent upon taxable local wealth. More unfortunately, though, the majority's holding can only be seen as a retreat from our historic commitment to equality of educational opportunity and as unsupportable acquiescence in a system which deprives children in their earliest years of the chance to reach their full potential as citizens. The Court does this despite the absence of any substantial justification for a scheme which arbitrarily channels educational resources in accordance with the fortuity of the amount of taxable wealth within each district. . . .

The only justification offered by appellants to sustain the discrimination in educational opportunity caused by the Texas financing scheme is local educational control. Presented with this justification, the District Court concluded that "[n]ot only are defendants unable to demonstrate compelling state interests for their classifications based upon wealth, they fail even to establish a reasonable basis for these classifications." I must agree with this conclusion. . . .

[E]ven if we accept Texas' general dedication to local control in educational matters, it is difficult to find any evidence of such dedication with respect to fiscal matters. It ignores reality to suggest—as the Court does, that the local property tax element of the Texas financing scheme reflects a conscious legislative effort to provide school districts with local fiscal control. . . . In fact, [under] the Texas scheme . . . [l]ocal school districts cannot choose to have the best education in the State by imposing the highest tax rate. Instead, the quality of the educational opportunity offered by any particular district is largely determined by the amount of taxable property located in the district—a factor over which local voters can exercise no control. . . .

In my judgment, any substantial degree of scrutiny of the operation of the Texas financing scheme reveals that the State has selected means wholly inappropriate to secure its purported interest in assuring its school districts local fiscal control. . . .[1]

[1]In 1984 the Mexican American Legal Defense and Education Fund challenged funding inequalities in Texas state court on behalf of the Rodriguez family and others. In *Edgewood* v. *Kirby* (1989), the Supreme Court of Texas held that the funding arrangement violated the state constitution's requirement of "an efficient system of public free schools" and directed the state legislature to redesign the financing of public education. By this time, the courts of nine other states had also relied on their state constitutions to invalidate similar property-based systems.—ED.

## VI. AFFIRMATIVE ACTION

### *Grutter* v. *Bollinger*
### 539 U.S. 306, 123 S.Ct. 2325, 156 L.Ed. 2d 304 (2003)
### http://supct.law.cornell.edu/supct/html/02-241.ZS.html

An admission policy approved in 1992 at the University of Michigan Law School has aspired to "achieve that diversity which has the potential to enrich everyone's education and thus make a law school class stronger than the sum of its parts." The policy also reaffirmed the law school's commitment to "one particular type of diversity," that is, "racial and ethnic diversity with special reference to the inclusion of students from groups which have been historically discriminated against, like African-Americans, Hispanics and Native Americans, who without this commitment might not be represented in our student body in meaningful numbers." Under the policy, the law school seeks to enroll a "critical mass" of underrepresented minority students to ensure "their ability to make unique contributions to the character of the Law School."

Barbara Grutter was an unsuccessful applicant for the University of Michigan Law School's entering class in the fall of 1997. At the time of her application in December 1996, she was 43 years of age, had achieved an undergraduate grade point average of 3.8 (on a 4.0 scale), and had scored 161 (the 86th percentile) on the Law School Admission Test. She filed suit in the United States District Court for the Eastern District of Michigan, claiming that the law school's use of race as a "predominant factor" in admissions, under which some minority applicants with weaker numerical credentials than hers were admitted, violated her rights under the Fourteenth Amendment and Title VI of the 1964 Civil Rights Act. After a 15-day trial, the district court ruled in favor of Ms. Grutter in 2001, rejecting the law school's argument that a racially diverse student body was a compelling state interest that would excuse an otherwise unlawful reliance on race. In 2002, sitting en banc, the U. S. Court of Appeals for the Sixth Circuit reversed the district court 5 to 4. The appeals court majority construed *Regents* v. *Bakke* (1978) as sanctioning educational diversity as a compelling government interest and found that the admission policy was narrowly tailored to accomplish that end. Majority: O'Connor, Breyer, Ginsburg, Souter, Stevens. Dissenting: Rehnquist, Kennedy, Scalia, Thomas.

## JUSTICE O'CONNOR delivered the opinion of the Court. . . .

We last addressed the use of race in public higher education over 25 years ago. In the landmark Bakke case, we reviewed a racial set-aside program that reserved 16 out of 100 seats in a medical school class for members of certain minority groups. The decision produced six separate opinions, none of which commanded a majority of the Court. Four Justices would have upheld the program against all attack on the ground that the government can use race to "remedy disadvantages cast on minorities by past racial prejudice." Four other Justices avoided the constitutional question altogether and struck down the program on [Title VI] statutory grounds. Justice Powell provided a fifth vote not only for invalidating the set-aside program, but also for reversing the state court's injunction against any use of race whatsoever. The only holding for the Court in *Bakke* was that a "State has a substantial interest that legitimately may be served by a properly devised admissions program involving the competitive consideration of race and ethnic origin." Thus, we reversed that part of the lower court's judgment that enjoined the university "from any consideration of the race of any applicant."

Since this Court's splintered decision in *Bakke*, Justice Powell's opinion announcing the judgment of the Court has served as the touchstone for constitutional analysis of race-conscious admissions policies. . . . We therefore discuss Justice Powell's opinion in some detail. . . .

In Justice Powell's view, when governmental decisions "touch upon an individual's race or ethnic background, he is entitled to a judicial determination that the burden he is asked to bear on that basis is precisely tailored to serve a compelling governmental interest." Under this exacting standard, only one of the interests asserted by the university survived Justice Powell's scrutiny.

First, Justice Powell rejected an interest in "'reducing the historic deficit of traditionally disfavored minorities in medical schools and in the medical profession'" as an unlawful interest in racial balancing. Second, Justice Powell rejected an interest in remedying societal discrimination because such measures would risk placing unnecessary burdens on innocent third parties "who bear no responsibility for whatever harm the beneficiaries of the special admissions program are thought to have suffered." Third, Justice Powell rejected an interest in "increasing the number of physicians who will practice in communities currently underserved," concluding that even if such an interest could be compelling in some circumstances, the program under review was not "geared to promote that goal."

Justice Powell approved the university's use of race to further only one interest: "the attainment of a diverse student body."

Justice Powell was, however, careful to emphasize that in his view race "is only one element in a range of factors a university properly may consider in attaining the goal of a heterogeneous student body." . . .

[F]or the reasons set out below, today we endorse Justice Powell's view that student body diversity is a compelling state interest that can justify the use of race in university admissions.

The Equal Protection Clause provides that no State shall "deny to any person within its jurisdiction the equal protection of the laws." Because the Fourteenth Amendment "protect[s] *persons,* not *groups,*" all "governmental action based on race—a *group* classification long recognized as in most circumstances irrelevant and therefore prohibited—should be subjected to detailed judicial inquiry to ensure that the *personal* right to equal protection of the laws has not been infringed." . . . It follows from that principle that "government may treat people differently because of their race only for the most compelling reasons."

We have held that all racial classifications imposed by government "must be analyzed by a reviewing court under strict scrutiny." This means that such classifications are constitutional only if they are narrowly tailored to further compelling governmental interests. . . .

Although all governmental uses of race are subject to strict scrutiny, not all are invalidated by it. . . . Context matters when reviewing race-based governmental action under the Equal Protection Clause. . . . Not every decision influenced by race is equally objectionable, and strict scrutiny is designed to provide a framework for carefully examining the importance and the sincerity of the reasons advanced by the governmental decisionmaker for the use of race in that particular context.

With these principles in mind, we turn to the question whether the Law School's use of race is justified by a compelling state interest. . . . [T]he Law School asks us to recognize, in the context of higher education, a compelling state interest in student body diversity. . . . Today, we hold that the Law School has a compelling interest in attaining a diverse student body.

The Law School's educational judgment that such diversity is essential to its educational mission is one to which we defer. . . . Our scrutiny of the interest asserted by the Law School is no less strict for taking into account complex educational judgments in an area that lies primarily within the expertise of the university. . . .

As part of its goal of "assembling a class that is both exceptionally academically qualified and broadly diverse," the Law School seeks to "enroll a 'critical mass' of minority students." The Law School's interest is not simply "to assure within its student body some specified percentage of a particular group merely because of its race or ethnic origin." . . . Rather, the Law School's concept of critical mass is defined by reference to the educa-

tional benefits that diversity is designed to produce.

These benefits are substantial. . . . [T]he Law School's admissions policy promotes "cross-racial understanding," helps to break down racial stereotypes, and "enables [students] to better understand persons of different races." . . . [N]umerous studies show that student body diversity promotes learning outcomes, and "better prepares students for an increasingly diverse workforce and society, and better prepares them as professionals." . . .

These benefits are not theoretical but real, as major American businesses have made clear that the skills needed in today's increasingly global marketplace can only be developed through exposure to widely diverse people, cultures, ideas, and viewpoints. What is more, high-ranking retired officers and civilian leaders of the United States military assert that, "[b]ased on [their] decades of experience," a "highly qualified, racially diverse officer corps . . . is essential to the military's ability to fulfill its principle mission to provide national security." . . .

Even in the limited circumstance when drawing racial distinctions is permissible to further a compelling state interest, government is still "constrained in how it may pursue that end: [T]he means chosen to accomplish the [government's] asserted purpose must be specifically and narrowly framed to accomplish that purpose." . . .

We find that the Law School's admissions program bears the hallmarks of a narrowly tailored plan. As Justice Powell made clear in *Bakke,* truly individualized consideration demands that race be used in a flexible, nonmechanical way. It follows from this mandate that universities cannot establish quotas for members of certain racial groups or put members of those groups on separate admissions tracks. Nor can universities insulate applicants who belong to certain racial or ethnic groups from the competition for admission. Universities can, however, consider race or ethnicity more flexibly as a "plus" factor in the context of individualized consideration of each and every applicant. . . .

The Law School's goal of attaining a critical mass of underrepresented minority students does not transform its program into a quota. . . .

Here, the Law School engages in a highly individualized, holistic review of each applicant's file, giving serious consideration to all the ways an applicant might contribute to a diverse educational environment. The Law School affords this individualized consideration to applicants of all races. There is no policy, either *de jure* or *de facto,* of automatic acceptance or rejection based on any single "soft" variable. . . . All applicants have the opportunity to highlight their own potential diversity contributions through the submission of a personal statement, letters of recommendation, and an essay describing the ways in which the applicant will contribute to the life and diversity of the Law School.

Petitioner and the United States argue that the Law School's plan is not narrowly tailored because race-neutral means exist to obtain the educational benefits of student body diversity that the Law School seeks. We disagree. Narrow tailoring does not require exhaustion of every conceivable race-neutral alternative. Nor does it require a university to choose between maintaining a reputation for excellence or fulfilling a commitment to provide educational opportunities to members of all racial groups. . . .

We agree with the Court of Appeals that the Law School sufficiently considered workable race-neutral alternatives. The District Court took the Law School to task for failing to consider race-neutral alternatives such as "using a lottery system" or "decreasing the emphasis for all applicants on undergraduate GPA and LSAT scores." But these alternatives would require a dramatic sacrifice of diversity, the academic quality of all admitted students, or both.

We acknowledge that "there are serious problems of justice connected with the idea of preference itself." Narrow tailoring, therefore, requires that a race-conscious admissions program not unduly harm members of any racial group. . . . To be narrowly tailored, a race-conscious admissions program must not "unduly burden individuals who are not members of the favored racial and ethnic groups." We are satisfied that the Law School's admissions program does not. . . .

We are mindful, however, that "[a] core purpose of the Fourteenth Amendment was to do away with all governmentally imposed discrimination based on race." . . . We see no reason to exempt race-conscious admissions programs from the requirement that all governmental use of race must have a logical end point. . . .

In the context of higher education, the durational requirement can be met by sunset provisions in race-conscious admissions policies and periodic reviews to determine whether racial preferences are still necessary to achieve student body diversity. . . .

It has been 25 years since Justice Powell first approved the use of race to further an interest in student body diversity in the context of public higher education. Since that time, the number of minority applicants with high grades and test scores has indeed increased. We expect that 25 years from now, the use of racial preferences will no longer be necessary to further the interest approved today.

In summary, the Equal Protection Clause does not prohibit the Law School's narrowly tailored use of race in admissions decisions to further a compelling interest in obtaining the educational benefits that flow from a diverse student body. Consequently, petitioner's statutory claims based on Title VI also fail. . . . The judgment of the Court of Appeals for the Sixth Circuit, accordingly, is affirmed.

*It is so ordered.*

JUSTICE GINSBURG, with whom JUSTICE BREYER joins, concurring . . . [omitted].

**CHIEF JUSTICE REHNQUIST, with whom JUSTICE SCALIA, JUSTICE KENNEDY, and JUSTICE THOMAS join, dissenting.**

I agree with the Court that, "in the limited circumstance when drawing racial distinctions is permissible," the government must ensure that its means are narrowly tailored to achieve a compelling state interest. . . . I do not believe, however, that the University of Michigan Law School's means are narrowly tailored to the interest it asserts. The Law School claims it must take the steps it does to achieve a "'critical mass'" of underrepresented minority students. But its actual program bears no relation to this asserted goal. Stripped of its "critical mass" veil, the Law School's program is revealed as a naked effort to achieve racial balancing. . . .

Before the Court's decision today, we consistently applied the same strict scrutiny analysis regardless of the government's purported reason for using race and regardless of the setting in which race was being used. . . .

Although the Court recites the language of our strict scrutiny analysis, its application of that review is unprecedented in its deference. . . .

In practice, the Law School's program bears little or no relation to its asserted goal of achieving "critical mass." . . .

From 1995 through 2000, the Law School admitted between 1,130 and 1,310 students. Of those, between 13 and 19 were Native American, between 91 and 108 were African-Americans, and between 47 and 56 were Hispanic. If the Law School is admitting between 91 and 108 African-Americans in order to achieve "critical mass," thereby preventing African-American students from feeling "isolated or like spokespersons for their race," one would think that a number of the same order of magnitude would be necessary to accomplish the same purpose for Hispanics and Native Americans. Similarly, even if all of the Native American applicants admitted in a given year matriculate, which the record demonstrates is not at all the case, how can this possibly constitute a "critical mass" of Native Americans in a class of over 350 students? In order for this pattern of admission to be consistent with the Law School's explanation of "critical mass," one would have to believe that the objectives of "critical mass" offered by respondents are achieved with only half the number of Hispanics and one-sixth the number of Native Americans as compared to African-Americans. But respondents offer no race-specific reasons for such disparities.

Instead, they simply emphasize the importance of achieving "critical mass," without any explanation of why that concept is applied differently among the three underrepresented minority groups.

These different numbers, moreover, come only as a result of substantially different treatment among the three underrepresented minority groups. . . . Specifically, the Law School states that "[s]ixty-nine minority applicants were rejected between 1995 and 2000 with at least a 3.5 [Grade Point Average (GPA)] and a [score of] 159 or higher on the [Law School Admissions Test (LSAT)]" while a number of Caucasian and Asian-American applicants with similar or lower scores were admitted.

Review of the record reveals only 67 such individuals. Of these 67 individuals, 56 were Hispanic, while only 6 were African-American, and only 5 were Native American. This discrepancy reflects a consistent practice. For example, in 2000, 12 Hispanics who scored between a 159–160 on the LSAT and earned a GPA of 3.00 or higher applied for admission and only 2 were admitted. Meanwhile, 12 African-Americans in the same range of qualifications applied for admission and all 12 were admitted. Likewise, that same year, 16 Hispanics who scored between a 151–153 on the LSAT and earned a 3.00 or higher applied for admission and only 1 of those applicants was admitted. Twenty-three similarly qualified African-Americans applied for admission and 14 were admitted.

These statistics have a significant bearing on petitioner's case. Respondents have never offered any race-specific arguments explaining why significantly more individuals from one underrepresented minority group are needed in order to achieve "critical mass" or further student body diversity. They certainly have not explained why Hispanics, who they have said are among "the groups most isolated by racial barriers in our country," should have their admission capped out in this manner. True, petitioner is neither Hispanic nor Native American. But the Law School's disparate admissions practices with respect to these minority groups demonstrate that its alleged goal of "critical mass" is simply a sham. Petitioner may use these statistics to expose this sham, which is the basis for the Law School's admission of less qualified underrepresented minorities in preference to her. Surely strict scrutiny cannot permit these sort of disparities without at least some explanation.

Only when the "critical mass" label is discarded does a likely explanation for these numbers emerge. The Court states that the Law School's goal of attaining a "critical mass" of underrepresented minority students is not an interest in merely " 'assur[ing] within its student body some specified percentage of a particular group merely because of its race or ethnic origin.' " The Court recognizes that such an interest "would amount to outright racial balancing, which is patently unconstitutional." The Court concludes, however, that the Law School's use of race in admissions, consistent with Justice Powell's opinion in *Bakke,* only pays " '[s]ome attention to numbers.' "

But the correlation between the percentage of the Law School's pool of applicants who are members of the three minority groups and the percentage of the admitted applicants who are members of these same groups is far too precise to be dismissed as merely the result of the school paying "some attention to [the] numbers." . . . [F]rom 1995 through 2000 the percentage of admitted applicants who were members of these minority groups closely tracked the percentage of individuals in the school's applicant pool who were from the same groups. . . .

For example, in 1995, when 9.7% of the applicant pool was African-American, 9.4% of the admitted class was African-American. By 2000, only 7.5% of the applicant pool was African-American, and 7.3% of the admitted class was African-American. This correlation is striking. . . . The tight correlation between the percentage of applicants and admittees of a given race, therefore, must result from careful race-based planning by the Law School. It suggests a formula for admission based on the aspirational assumption that all applicants are equally qualified academically, and therefore that the proportion of each group admitted should be the same as the proportion of that group in the applicant pool. (See Brief for Respondent Bollinger . . . discussing

admissions officers' use of "periodic reports" to track "the racial composition of the developing class.") . . .

But the divergence between the percentages of underrepresented minorities in the applicant pool and in the enrolled classes is not the only relevant comparison. In fact, it may not be the most relevant comparison. The Law School cannot precisely control which of its admitted applicants decide to attend the university. But it can and, as the numbers demonstrate, clearly does employ racial preferences in extending offers of admission. Indeed, the ostensibly flexible nature of the Law School's admissions program that the Court finds appealing, appears to be, in practice, a carefully managed program designed to ensure proportionate representation of applicants from selected minority groups.

I do not believe that the Constitution gives the Law School such free rein in the use of race. The Law School has offered no explanation for its actual admissions practices and, unexplained, we are bound to conclude that the Law School has managed its admissions program, not to achieve a "critical mass," but to extend offers of admission to members of selected minority groups in proportion to their statistical representation in the applicant pool. But this is precisely the type of racial balancing that the Court itself calls "patently unconstitutional." . . .

The Court, in an unprecedented display of deference under our strict scrutiny analysis, upholds the Law School's program despite its obvious flaws. We have said that when it comes to the use of race, the connection between the ends and the means used to attain them must be precise. But here the flaw is deeper than that; it is not merely a question of "fit" between ends and means. Here the means actually used are forbidden by the Equal Protection Clause of the Constitution.

JUSTICE SCALIA, with whom JUSTICE THOMAS joins, concurring in part and dissenting in part . . . [omitted].

JUSTICE KENNEDY, dissenting . . . [omitted].

JUSTICE THOMAS, with whom JUSTICE SCALIA joins, concurring in part and dissenting in part . . . [omitted].

## *Gratz* v. *Bollinger*
### 539 U.S. 244, 123 S.Ct. 2411, 156 L.Ed. 2d 257 (2003)
http://supct.law.cornell.edu/supct/html/02-516.ZS.html

Jennifer Gratz and Patrick Hamacher, both Caucasian and Michigan residents, applied for admission to the University of Michigan's College of Literature, Science, and the Arts (LSA), in 1995 and 1997, respectively. Both were denied admission. The undergraduate admission policy when Gratz applied evaluated applicants using tables; applicants with similar credentials fared differently based on their race. When Hamacher applied, the policy had been modified to give minority applicants additional points in the selection process. After 1998 the University dispensed with the tables in favor of a selection index, on which an applicant could score a maximum of 150 points. Under the new guidelines each applicant received points based on high school grade point average, standardized test scores, academic quality of an applicant's high school, strength or weakness of high school curriculum, in-state residency, alumni relationship, personal essay, and personal achievement or leadership. Under a "miscellaneous" category, applicants were entitled to 20 points if they were part of an underrepresented racial or ethnic minority group. Applicants with 100 points or more were admitted. Admission counselors, however, could "flag" an applicant in the 75–100 point range for special consideration by the Admission Review Committee (ARC), which could then admit, defer, or reject the applicant even if the index score fell below 100.

Gratz and Hamacher filed suit in 1997 in the U. S. District Court for the Eastern District of Michigan, challenging the admission policy under the Fourteenth Amendment and Title VI of the 1964 Civil Rights Act. The district court concluded that the earlier policies under which Gratz and Hamacher had been rejected functioned as a racial quota and so were prohibited by *Regents* v. *Bakke,* but upheld the later index policy as a narrowly tailored method to achieve a racially diverse student body. Both sides appealed to the U. S. Court of Appeals for the Sixth Circuit. When the appeals court issued its ruling in *Grutter* v. *Bollinger* involving the University of Michigan Law School, Gratz and Hamacher successfully petitioned the Supreme Court for certiorari in advance of a ruling by the Sixth Circuit in their case. The excerpts that follow omit discussion of the petitioners' standing to sue. Majority: Rehnquist, Breyer, Kennedy, O'Connor, Scalia, Thomas. Dissenting: Ginsburg, Souter, Stevens.

**CHIEF JUSTICE REHNQUIST delivered the opinion of the Court.**

We granted certiorari in this case to decide whether "the University of Michigan's use of racial preferences in undergraduate admissions violate[s] the Equal Protection Clause of the Fourteenth Amendment [and] Title VI of the Civil Rights Act of 1964. Because we find that the manner in which the University considers the race of applicants in its undergraduate admissions guidelines violates these constitutional and statutory provisions, we reverse that portion of the District Court's decision upholding the guidelines. . . .

Petitioners argue, first and foremost, that the University's use of race in undergraduate admissions violates the Fourteenth Amendment. Specifically, they contend that this Court has only sanctioned the use of racial classifications to remedy identified discrimination, a justification on which respondents have never relied. Petitioners further argue that "diversity as a basis for employing racial preferences is simply too open-ended, ill-defined, and indefinite to constitute a compelling interest capable of supporting narrowly-tailored means." But for the reasons set forth today in *Grutter* v. *Bollinger*, the Court has rejected these arguments of petitioners.

Petitioners alternatively argue that even if the University's interest in diversity can constitute a compelling state interest, the District Court erroneously concluded that the University's use of race in its current freshman admissions policy is narrowly tailored to achieve such an interest. Petitioners argue that the guidelines the University began using in 1999 do not "remotely resemble the kind of consideration of race and ethnicity that Justice Powell endorsed in *Bakke*." Respondents reply that the University's current admissions program is narrowly tailored and avoids the problems of the Medical School of the University of California at Davis program (U. C. Davis) rejected by Justice Powell.... Specifically, respondents contend that the LSA's policy provides the individualized consideration that "Justice Powell considered a hallmark of a constitutionally appropriate admissions program." For the reasons set out below, we do not agree.

It is by now well established that "all racial classifications reviewable under the Equal Protection Clause must be strictly scrutinized." This " 'standard of review . . . is not dependent on the race of those burdened or benefited by a particular classification.' " Thus, "any person, of whatever race, has the right to demand that any governmental actor subject to the Constitution justify any racial classification subjecting that person to unequal treatment under the strictest of judicial scrutiny."

To withstand our strict scrutiny analysis, respondents must demonstrate that the University's use of race in its current admission program employs "narrowly tailored measures that further compelling governmental interests." . . . We find that the University's policy, which automatically distributes 20 points, or one-fifth of the points needed to guarantee admission, to every single "underrepresented minority" applicant solely because of race, is not narrowly tailored to achieve the interest in educational diversity that respondents claim justifies their program.

In *Bakke*, Justice Powell reiterated that "[p]referring members of any one group for no reason other than race or ethnic origin is discrimination for its own sake." He then explained, however, that in his view it would be permissible for a university to employ an admissions program in which "race or ethnic background may be deemed a 'plus' in a particular applicant's file." He explained that such a program might allow for "[t]he file of a particular black applicant [to] be examined for his potential contribution to diversity without the factor of race being decisive when compared, for example, with that of an applicant identified as an Italian-American if the latter is thought to exhibit qualities more likely to promote beneficial educational pluralism." Such a system, in Justice Powell's view, would be "flexible enough to consider all pertinent elements of diversity in light of the particular qualifications of each applicant."

Justice Powell's opinion in *Bakke* emphasized the importance of considering each particular applicant as an individual, assessing all of the qualities that individual possesses, and in turn, evaluating that individual's ability to contribute to the unique setting of higher education. . . .

The current LSA policy does not provide such individualized consideration. The LSA's policy automatically distributes 20 points to every single applicant from an "underrepresented minority" group, as defined by the University. The only consideration that accompanies this distribution of points is a factual review of an application to determine whether an individual is a member of one of these minority groups. Moreover, unlike Justice Powell's example, where the race of a "particular black applicant" could be considered without being decisive, the LSA's automatic distribution of 20 points has the effect of making "the factor of race . . . decisive" for virtually every minimally qualified underrepresented minority applicant.

Also instructive in our consideration of the LSA's system is the example provided in the description of the Harvard College Admissions Program, which Justice Powell both discussed in, and attached to, his opinion in *Bakke*. . . . It provided as follows:

> The Admissions Committee, with only a few places left to fill, might find itself forced to choose between A, the child of a successful black physician in an academic community with promise of superior academic performance, and B, a black who grew up in an inner-city ghetto of semi-literate parents whose academic achievement was lower but who had demonstrated energy and leadership as well as an apparently abiding interest in black power. If a good number of black students much like A but few like B had already been admitted, the Committee might prefer B; and vice versa. If C, a white student with extraordinary artistic talent, were also seeking one of the remaining places, his unique quality might give him an edge over both A and B. Thus, the critical criteria are often individual qualities or experience not dependent upon race but sometimes associated with it.

This example further demonstrates the problematic nature of the LSA's admissions system. Even if student C's "extraordinary artistic talent" rivaled that of Monet or Picasso, the applicant would receive, at most, five points under the LSA's system. At the same time, every single underrepresented minority applicant, including students A and B, would automatically receive 20 points for submitting an application. Clearly, the LSA's system does not offer applicants the individualized selection process described in Harvard's example. Instead of considering how the differing backgrounds, experiences, and characteristics of students A, B, and C might benefit the University, admissions counselors reviewing LSA applications would simply award both A and B 20 points because their applications indicate that they are African-American, and student C would receive up to 5 points for his "extraordinary talent."

Respondents emphasize the fact that the LSA has created the possibility of an applicant's file being flagged for individualized consideration by the ARC. We think that the flagging program only emphasizes the flaws of the University's system as a whole when compared to that described by Justice Powell. Again, students A, B, and C illustrate the point. First, student A would never be flagged. This is because, as the University has conceded, the effect of automatically awarding 20 points is that virtually every qualified underrepresented minority applicant is admitted. Student A, an applicant "with promise of superior academic performance," would certainly fit this description. Thus, the result of the automatic distribution of 20 points is that the University would never consider student A's individual background, experiences, and characteristics to assess his individual "potential contribution to diversity." Instead, every applicant like student A would simply be admitted.

It is possible that students B and C would be flagged and considered as individuals. This assumes that student B was not already admitted because of the automatic 20-point distribution, and that student C could muster at least 70 additional points. But the fact that the "review committee can look at the applications individually and ignore the points," once an application is flagged, is of little comfort under our strict scrutiny analysis. The record does not reveal precisely how many applications are flagged for this individualized consideration, but it is undisputed that such consideration is the exception and not the rule in the operation of the LSA's admissions program. . . . Additionally, this individualized review is only provided after admissions counselors automatically distribute the University's version of a "plus" that makes race a decisive factor for virtually every minimally qualified underrepresented minority applicant.

Respondents contend that "[t]he volume of applications and the presentation of applicant information make it impractical for [LSA] to use the . . . admissions system" upheld by the Court today in *Grutter*. But the fact that the implementation of a program capable of providing individualized consideration might present administrative challenges does not render constitutional an otherwise problematic system. . . .

We conclude, therefore, that because the University's use of race in its current freshman admissions policy is not narrowly tailored to achieve respondents' asserted compelling interest in diversity, the admissions policy violates the Equal Protection Clause of the Fourteenth Amendment. We further find that the admissions policy also violates Title VI. . . . Accordingly, we reverse that portion of the District Court's decision granting respondents summary judgment with respect to liability and remand the case for proceedings consistent with this opinion.

*It is so ordered.*

JUSTICE O'CONNOR, concurring . . . [omitted].

JUSTICE THOMAS, concurring . . . [omitted].

JUSTICE BREYER, concurring in the judgment . . . [omitted].

JUSTICE STEVENS, with whom JUSTICE SOUTER joins, dissenting . . . [omitted].

JUSTICE SOUTER, with whom JUSTICE GINSBURG joins in part, dissenting . . . [omitted].

**JUSTICE GINSBURG, with whom JUSTICE SOUTER joins, and with whom JUSTICE BREYER joints in part, dissenting.**

Educational institutions, the Court acknowledges, are not barred from any and all consideration of race when making admissions decisions. But the Court once again maintains that the same standard of review controls judicial inspection of all official race classifications. This insistence on "consistency" would be fitting were our Nation free of the vestiges of rank discrimination long reinforced by law. But we are not far distant from an overtly discriminatory past, and the effects of centuries of law-sanctioned inequality remain painfully evident in our communities and schools.

In the wake "of a system of racial caste only recently ended," large disparities endure. Unemployment, poverty, and access to health care vary disproportionately by race. Neighborhoods and schools remain racially divided. African-American and Hispanic children are all too often educated in poverty-stricken and underperforming institutions. Adult African-Americans and Hispanics generally earn less

than whites with equivalent levels of education. Equally credentialed job applicants receive different receptions depending on their race. Irrational prejudice is still encountered in real estate markets and consumer transactions. "Bias both conscious and unconscious, reflecting traditional and unexamined habits of thought, keeps up barriers that must come down if equal opportunity and nondiscrimination are ever genuinely to become this country's law and practice."

The Constitution instructs all who act for the government that they may not "deny to any person . . . the equal protection of the laws." In implementing this equality instruction, as I see it, government decisionmakers may properly distinguish between policies of exclusion and inclusion. Actions designed to burden groups long denied full citizenship stature are not sensibly ranked with measures taken to hasten the day when entrenched discrimination and its aftereffects have been extirpated. "[T]o say that two centuries of struggle for the most basic of civil rights have been mostly about freedom from racial categorization rather than freedom from racial oppressio[n] is to trivialize the lives and deaths of those who have suffered under racism. To pretend . . . that the issue presented in [*Bakke*] was the same as the issue in [*Brown* v. *Board of Education*] is to pretend that history never happened and that the present doesn't exist." . . .

Our jurisprudence ranks race a "suspect" category, "not because [race] is inevitably an impermissible classification, but because it is one which usually, to our national shame, has been drawn for the purpose of maintaining racial inequality." But where race is considered "for the purpose of achieving equality," no automatic proscription is in order. For, as insightfully explained, "[t]he Constitution is both color blind and color conscious. To avoid conflict with the equal protection clause, a classification that denies a benefit, causes harm, or imposes a burden must not be based on race. In that sense, the Constitution is color blind. But the Constitution is color conscious to prevent discrimination being perpetuated and to undo the effects of past discrimination." . . .

Examining in this light the admissions policy employed by the University of Michigan's College of Literature, Science, and the Arts, . . . I see no constitutional infirmity. . . . The racial and ethnic groups to which the College accords special consideration (African-Americans, Hispanics, and Native-Americans) historically have been relegated to inferior status by law and social practice; their members continue to experience class-based discrimination to this day. There is no suggestion that the College adopted its current policy in order to limit or decrease enrollment by any particular racial or ethnic group, and no seats are reserved on the basis of race. . . . Nor has there been any demonstration that the College's program unduly constricts admissions opportunities for students who do not receive special consideration based on race.

The stain of generations of racial oppression is still visible in our society, and the determination to hasten its removal remains vital. One can reasonably anticipate, therefore, that colleges and universities will seek to maintain their minority enrollment—and the networks and opportunities thereby opened to minority graduates—whether or not they can do so in full candor through adoption of affirmative action plans of the kind here at issue. Without recourse to such plans, institutions of higher education may resort to camouflage. For example, schools may encourage applicants to write of their cultural traditions in the essays they submit, or to indicate whether English is their second language. Seeking to improve their chances for admission, applicants may highlight the minority group associations to which they belong, or the Hispanic surnames of their mothers or grandparents. In turn, teachers' recommendations may emphasize who a student is as much as what he or she has accomplished. . . . If honesty is the best policy, surely Michigan's accurately described, fully disclosed College affirmative action program is preferable to achieving similar numbers through winks, nods, and disguises.

For the reasons stated, I would affirm the judgment of the District Court.

# CHAPTER FIFTEEN

# *Epilogue: Security and Freedom in Wartime*

*It seems to have been reserved for the people of this country, by their conduct and example, to decide the important question, whether societies of men are really capable or not of establishing good government from reflection and choice, or whether they are forever destined to depend for their political constitutions on accident and force.*

—ALEXANDER HAMILTON (1787)

On the morning of September 11, 2001, members of the al Qaeda terrorist network commandeered four airliners to launch assaults on the United States. Two planes flew into and destroyed the twin towers of the World Trade Center in New York City. A third plane crashed into the west face of the Pentagon, headquarters of the Department of Defense, across the Potomac River from Washington, D.C. Yet another attack by the fourth plane on a third target was foiled when passengers and crew attempted to regain control of the aircraft. It crashed in Somerset County, in southwestern Pennsylvania. Together, in the bloodiest attacks on American soil since the Civil War, the 19 hijackers killed more than 3,000 persons within the span of two hours. The effects of that morning's destruction on families, society, the economy—and the Constitution—continue to be felt.

## THE FRAGILITY OF CIVIL LIBERTIES

Those horrific events and the policy responses to them have thrust to the forefront a tension that is older than the Constitution: security versus freedom. Measures designed to increase security often entail a constriction of liberty. Too much insistence on maintaining liberties may jeopardize security. American constitutional history is partly an attempt to find an appropriate balance between the two, although a perfect and final adjustment will probably forever remain out of reach. The record suggests that we are eager to embrace liberty when danger seems remote but that we lean in the other direction when the nation seems imperiled. There is thus a recurring pattern of under- and over-reaction. Underestimating threats to security, whether in 1860, 1941, 1946, or 2000 (to pick but four crisis-laden years), may lead to needless contractions of freedom in response. Sometimes lost amidst shifting policies is recognition that the nation's strength derives as much from the ideas and values it reflects as from the armies and munitions it deploys. "Constitutional law," wrote Edward Corwin decades ago, "has for its primary purpose not the convenience of the state but the preservation of individual rights."

Charters of individual liberties, like a bill of rights, are commonplace today in the constitutions of many governments in the world. Yet even a casual observer of world affairs knows that civil liberties are more likely to be preserved (or suspended) in some countries than in others. Moreover, as cases in this book illustrate, American freedoms have at times expanded and contracted in accordion-like fashion. Exactly why civil liberties thrive in one place or time and not another is a complex phenomenon, but this much is certain: civil liberties are fragile.

Civil liberties rest on at least two kinds of supports: First are rules and institutions. Federal and state statutes and constitutions carve out certain rights for protection, and courts and other bodies exist to enforce them. Second are the attitudes and values of the people generally and of opinion leaders and those entrusted with making, enforcing, and interpreting the laws. As events since September 11 have demonstrated, the interplay between these two sets of supports takes place within a context where, from one month to the next, the felt needs for freedom and security compete in shaping policy. As Justice Brandeis observed more than 75 years ago, the most frequent and often the most serious threats to civil liberties in American history have come not from people intent on throwing the Bill of Rights away but from well-meaning, though overzealous, people who find the Bill of Rights an inconvenience, standing in the way of objectives deemed more urgent and important. Thus, constitutional protections ironically are sometimes worth the least when they are needed the most.

## THE USA PATRIOT ACT

On October 26, 2001, President Bush signed the **USA Patriot Act** (115 Stat. 272) into law. An acronym drawn from **U**niting and **S**trengthening **A**merica by **P**roviding **A**ppropriate **T**ools **R**equired to **I**ntercept and **O**bstruct **T**errorism, the act significantly broadened the law-enforcement powers of the federal government. Indeed, probably no single piece of legislation in recent decades has done more to enhance the government's crime-fighting powers. That expansion, however, has come with a price: a curtailment of some freedoms.

Yet this response to the terrorist attacks of September 11 demonstrated once more that the scheme of separation of powers and checks and balances embedded in the Constitution can also work to protect civil liberties. An unusual alliance of conservative Republicans and liberal Democrats in Congress in 2001 succeeded in moderating some of the terms of the Patriot Act that the administration had proposed and in inserting a "sunset" stipulation of December 31, 2005, for others. As the executive branch attempted to expand its authority on many fronts, legislators insisted on a more reasonable balance between security and liberty. Thus as the bill emerged from Congress, the president had secured less than he wanted, although more than many civil libertarians were prepared to give. "The Constitution is an instrument of government," once wrote the second Justice Harlan, "fundamental to which is the premise that in a diffusion of governmental authority lies the greatest promise that this Nation will realize liberty for all it citizens."

Along with provisions dealing with money laundering and forfeitures, the Patriot Act:

- Creates new federal crimes for various terrorist acts.
- Clarifies and strengthens provisions of the Antiterrorism and Effective Death Penalty Act of 1996 that bar "material support" to terrorists and terrorist organizations. The 1996 act requires only that the supplier of the material support have knowledge of its intended use; it does not require that the supplier also have the specific intent of the perpetrator of the actual terrorist act.
- Authorizes **"sneak and peek" search warrants** that allow agents to conduct a search without notifying the owner and to delay notification indefinitely that a search has taken place.
- Adds terrorist and computer crimes to the list of predicate offenses subject to warrant-authorized and Justice Department-approved electronic surveillance under Title III of the 1968 Omnibus Crime Control and Safe Streets Act (see Chapter Ten).
- Adds electronic communications (such as e-mail) to those communications already subject to "trap and trace" devices and pen registers. These identify the source and destination of a communication, but not its contents.
- Treats stored voicemail like e-mail in third-party storage or communications records. Under the 1968 Crime Control Act, warrants for such material may be issued without prior Justice Department approval and in connection with *any* criminal investigation, and so are not limited to Title III's predicate offenses.
- Allows officials to intercept communications to and from a trespasser within a computer system, with approval of the owner of the system.
- Permits "roving" electronic surveillance that is not confined to a particular telephone or e-mail account but covers any electronic communications device that a suspect might use in any location.
- Encourages cooperation and information-sharing between law enforcement and foreign intelligence investigators.
- Amends the **Foreign Intelligence Surveillance Act** (FISA) (see Chapter Ten) by eliminating the need for the FBI to show probable cause before conducting secret searches or surveillance, unless the evidence sought is to be used in a criminal proceeding.
- Amends the FISA so that foreign intelligence gathering may now be "a significant purpose," not "*the* purpose," for conducting the electronic surveillance or other search.
- Extends the FISA permitting judges to issue an order allowing FBI access to tangible items, such as records from bookstores and libraries, upon FBI certification that the items are sought "to protect against international terrorism or clandestine intelligence activities."
- Authorizes the FBI to monitor and observe religious and political groups even in the absence of evidence of wrongdoing.
- Gives the attorney general authority to certify legal aliens as risks and to detain and deport them.

As important as these measures are, few have been tested in the courts; as of January 2004, none had been the subject of a decision by the United States Supreme Court. For these and other matters discussed below, no doubt that time is approaching. "We know that terrorism is a problem," acknowledged Justice Breyer on April 4, 2003. "We also know we live in a country that wants to protect basic civil liberties." Courts "are fully aware of mistakes that have been made in American history," he added. "You want to know how it's going to come out? So do I."

## OTHER ANTI-TERRORIST ACTIONS AND POLICIES

Administrative actions, either by executive order or other presidential directive, as well as prosecutions, have also begun to test or to define the legal and constitutional limits within which the war on terrorism will be fought.

**PRISONERS OF WAR OR SOMETHING ELSE?** Seven days after the attacks on September 11, Congress approved Senate Joint Resolution 23 (115 Stat. 2241) on Authorization for Use of Military Force (see Chapter Three). This led to a U.S. invasion of Afghanistan to topple the Taliban government that had provided a base of operations to members of **al Qaeda.** Within a few weeks, many Taliban and al Qaeda fighters were captured, and some 600 were later transferred for detention and questioning to the U.S. naval base at Guantanamo Bay, Cuba. On November 13, 2001, President Bush in an executive order declared that members of al Qaeda and other terrorists, who were not U.S. citizens, were subject to trial by military tribunals. In February 2002, Bush announced that none of the captives merited the legal status of prisoners of war (POWs). They would not possess what is perhaps the most valuable right of POWs: the right not to be tried for having made war on their captors.

According to the Geneva Convention of 1949, POW status for captured combatants depends upon whether they: (1) report to a superior officer within a command-and-control structure; (2) wear a fixed insignia or uniform, visible from some distance away, that defines their identity; (3) openly bear arms; and (4) conduct their military operations according to the laws and customs of war. Al Qaeda fighters assuredly did not meet those qualifications, but blanket denial of POW status to certain Taliban soldiers appeared more questionable.

Whatever their status, could the Guantanamo detainees be held indefinitely? In a lawsuit initiated by the "best friends" of 12 Kuwaitis and four other Guantanamo detainees who insisted they had done nothing wrong, the U.S. Court of Appeals for the District of Columbia Circuit ruled on March 11, 2003, that noncitizens held in such circumstances lack the rights of Americans. "The Constitution does not entitle the detainees to due process," the three-judge panel held without dissent. "They cannot invoke the jurisdiction of our courts to test the constitutionality or the legality of restraints on their liberty." Given the fact that the naval base is not on American soil but on land leased from Cuba in 1903, decisions about detention and interrogation should be "left to the exclusive discretion of the executive branch . . ." (*Odah* v. *United States*).

An appeal from this decision led to a grant of certiorari by the Supreme Court in November 2003 (*Rasul* v. *Bush*). The fundamental jurisdictional question posed by the Guantanamo detainees requires the justices to revisit *Johnson* v. *Eisentrager* (1950). This case involved German nationals who were taken into custody in China by American forces after the Japanese surrender in 1945 and who were then convicted by a U.S. military commission in China for violations of the laws of war. A majority in *Eisentrager* held that the prisoners, as nonresident alien enemies not present on American soil, had no right to initiate habeas corpus proceedings in a federal court. If *Eisentrager* is deemed to have been correctly decided, the question thus becomes whether the leased military base at Guantanamo Bay is more analogous to a foreign country or to American territory.

**MILITARY OR CIVILIAN JUSTICE?** Article I, Section 9, of the Constitution seemingly limits Congress's power to suspend the **writ of habeas corpus** to "cases of rebellion or invasion." (This writ, routinely available to civilians, is a judicial order to inquire into the legality of one's detention and, as such, is a safeguard against unlawful confinement.) Yet during the Civil War President Lincoln suspended the writ without congressional authorization and ordered his officers to refuse service of a writ issued by Chief Justice Taney in his capacity as circuit judge (Ex parte *Merryman,* 1861). Subsequently, Congress authorized suspension in certain instances; the Supreme Court, however, refused to pass on the validity of the president's action (Ex parte *Vallandigham,* 1864), concluding that it had no jurisdiction to review directly the judgment of a military tribunal.

In another Civil War action, Lincoln imposed **martial law** on portions of the northern states and substituted trial by military commission for the judicial process in dealing with traitors and others charged with violations of wartime statutes. (Such commissions or tribunals, then as now, operate under their own rules. They are comprised of military officers and are separate from courts martial that today are governed by the Uniform Code of Military Justice and adjudicate offenses involving military personnel.) **Ex parte *Milligan*** (1866) held that Lincoln had exceeded his authority. The regular courts of Indiana, where the military commission had convicted and sentenced Milligan to the gallows, were open and prepared to handle the charges against him. Five members of the Court went further and stated that martial law could never exist where civilian courts were open. Four members thought that Congress could have sanctioned what the executive could not. In World War II a similar result followed when the governor-general of Hawaii, pursuant to presidential authorization, invoked martial law, which gave military commissions jurisdiction over all criminal offenses. "I do not worry about the constitutional question. . . ," said President Franklin Roosevelt. "The whole matter is one of immediate and present war emergency." In 1946, the Court held such action invalid on the basis of *Milligan* (*Duncan* v. *Kahanamoku*). In both cases, final judicial decisions came after the shooting had stopped. However, **Ex parte *Quirin*** (1942), decided in the early months of World War II, upheld the trial by military commission—without the panoply of constitutional rights—of German saboteurs, including one who was probably an American citizen, who had been captured on American soil. And civilian courts were functioning.

What will be the pattern of events in the war on terrorism? Within a few months of the attacks on September 11, the Bush administration announced that a committee composed of the attorney general, secretary of defense, and director of central intelligence was empowered to designate suspected terrorists, U.S. citizens and non-citizens alike, as "**enemy combatants,**" and to hold them in military custody indefinitely, without bringing charges and without access to judicial review. However, this policy does not seem to have been consistently applied. Indeed, in terms of access to the courts and to constitutional protections such as right to counsel and notice of charges, some non-citizens have fared better than citizens.

- California-born John Walker Lindh, captured among **Taliban** forces in Afghanistan, was brought to trial in federal court. He pled guilty and was convicted on October 4, 2002.
- Richard Reid, a British subject, was brought to trial in federal court after he attempted to explode a "shoe bomb" on board a trans-Atlantic aircraft. He pled guilty and was convicted on October 4, 2002, as well.
- Louisiana-born Yassar Esam Hamdi was captured among Taliban forces in the same location as Lindh. In April 2002, he was transferred to the Norfolk Naval Station Brig where he has remained as an enemy combatant. In early 2003, the U.S. Court of Appeals for the Fourth Circuit upheld his indefinite detention, at least in circumstances where American citizens are apprehended on a foreign battlefield (***Hamdi v. Rumsfeld***).
- Zacarias Moussaoui, a French citizen of Moroccan descent, had been arrested in Minnesota in August 2001, but was later charged as the so-called "20th hijacker" in the attacks on September 11. He was scheduled for trial in federal court.
- New York-born Jose Padilla was arrested by the FBI at Chicago's O'Hare Airport on May 8, 2002, as a suspect in a plot to explode a "dirty bomb" in the United States. He was designated an enemy combatant and was held in a naval brig in South Carolina without charges being filed.

In December 2003, the U.S. Court of Appeals for the Second Circuit ruled that Padilla's detention was unlawful because (1) it was not authorized by Congress and (2) the president had no independent Article II authority "to detain as an enemy combatant an American citizen seized on American soil outside a zone of combat. . . . Under any scenario, Padilla will be entitled to the constitutional protections extended to other citizens." Dispositive for the appeals panel was the Non-Detention Act [18 U.S.C. § 4001(a)]—passed to preclude anything similar to the mass incarceration of Japanese-Americans during World War II—that prohibits such detentions absent congressional authorization. Contrary to the Defense Department's insistence, two judges deemed Congress's Joint Resolution of September 18, 2001 (see Chapter Three) "not such an authorization, and no exception to section 4001(a) otherwise exists" (*Padilla* v. *Rumsfeld*).

## "INTER ARMA SILENT LEGES"

This Latin maxim, that in time of war the laws are silent, has never been applied broadly in the United States. War has never been thought to justify a wholesale suspension of constitutional rights. "We do not lose our right to condemn either measures or men because the country is at war," remarked Justice Holmes in 1919 (after World War I, in *Frohwerk* v. *United States*).

Yet, although the laws are not silent in wartime, they sometimes speak with a different voice, as Chief Justice Rehnquist has observed. Indeed, when Congress's legislative powers are combined with the president's already expansive powers as commander-in-chief, constitutional limitations have occasionally seemed virtually to vanish. This was certainly true in the World War II relocation case of ***Korematsu v. United States*** (1944), where the civil rights of thousands of persons of Japanese ancestry, including many American citizens, were abridged on an unprecedented scale. The government's policy was justified by supposed threats to national security on the west coast. In 1987, toward the end of his long judicial career, Justice Brennan acknowledged in a lecture in Israel what most by then had conceded. The national security claims were "so baseless that they would be comical if not for the serious hardships they caused."

More encouraging were the Supreme Court's decisions in **New York Times Company v. United States** (1971) and **United States v. United States District Court** (1972). During a time of widespread domestic unrest toward the end of the Vietnam War, the Nixon administration insisted in the first case on national security grounds that the federal judiciary possessed inherent authority to block publication of classified documents (the "Pentagon Papers") that had been given to a newspaper by a third party. By a vote of 6 to 3, the Court upheld the newspaper's right under the First Amendment to continue publication. The second case tested the authority of the president, acting through the attorney general, to "constitutionally authorize the [warrantless] use of electronic surveillance in cases where he ha[s] determined that, in order the preserve the national security the use of such surveillance is reasonable." Asserting countervailing Fourth Amendment values, the Supreme Court rejected the claim, 8 to 0, at least in the context of electronic snooping on domestic groups (as opposed to agents of foreign powers) plotting sabotage and other illegal acts.

Nonetheless, the Fourth Circuit's opinion in *Hamdi* v. *Rumsfeld* is a recent reminder that in time of war judges often defer to the executive in matters of military necessity, at least up to a point. "In time of . . . national crisis," Geoffrey Stone reminds Americans, "we respond too harshly in our restriction of civil liberties, and then regret our behavior." More than four decades ago, Chief Justice Warren—hardly bashful himself about wielding judicial power—candidly acknowledged that courts are unreliable bulwarks during emergencies. Other parts of the government, he said, "must bear the primary responsibility for determining whether specific actions they are taking are consonant with our Constitution." It is "the Legislature and the elected executive who have the primary responsibility for fashioning and executing policy consistent with the Constitution." Beyond them, he added, "the day-to-day job of upholding the Constitution really lies elsewhere. It rests, realistically, on the shoulders of every citizen." Warren's assessment remains a sobering reminder that the Constitution in practice is much more than what the judges say it is.

## KEY TERMS

USA Patriot Act
"sneak and peek" search
    warrants
Foreign Intelligence
    Surveillance Act

al Qaeda
writ of habeas corpus
martial law

enemy combatants
Taliban

## QUERIES

**1.** On the day that the Court released its opinion in Ex parte *Quirin*, Attorney General Francis Biddle wrote a memo to President Roosevelt summarizing the main points of the decision. Noting that the Court had distinguished Ex parte *Milligan*, Biddle declared, "Practically then, the Milligan case is out of the way and should not again plague us." Did *Quirin* truly set *Milligan* "out of the way?"

**2.** In *Korematsu* v. *United States,* how do the opinions of Justices Black and Murphy differ in terms of the standard that must be met in order to justify an abridgement of constitutionally protected liberties?

**3.** In what respects do provisions in the USA Patriot Act relax some safeguards for civil liberties?

**4.** As Chapter Three explained, the framers believed that structural features such separation of powers and checks and balances were essential because, together, they would protect personal liberty. What use does Judge Wilkinson make of separation of powers in *Hamdi* v. *Rumsfeld* in outlining a role for the judiciary when national security clashes with individual rights?

## SELECTED READINGS

BELKNAP, MICHAEL R. "The Supreme Court Goes to War: The Meaning and Implications of the Nazi Saboteur Case." 89 *Military Law Review* 59 (1980).

FISHER, LOUIS. *Nazi Saboteurs on Trial: A Military Tribunal and American Law.* Lawrence: University Press of Kansas, 2003.

NG, WENDY. *Japanese American Internment during World War II: A History and Reference Guide.* Westport, Conn.: Greenwood, 2002.

NEVINS, ALLAN. "The Case of the Cooperhead Conspirator." In John A. Garraty, ed. *Quarrels That Have Shaped the Constitution*, rev. ed. New York: Harper & Row, 1987.

REHNQUIST, WILLIAM H. *All the Laws but One: Civil Liberties in Wartime.* New York: Knopf, 1998.

ROSTOW, EUGENE V. "The Japanese American Cases—A Disaster." 54 *Yale Law Journal* 489 (1945).

SCHEIBER, HARRY N., and JANE L. SCHEIBER. "Taking Liberties." 2 *Legal Affairs* 46 (May/June 2003).

STONE, GEOFFREY R. "Civil Liberties in Wartime." 28 *Journal of Supreme Court History* 215 (2003).

## Ex Parte *Milligan*
## 71 U.S. (4 Wall.) 2, 18 L.Ed. 281 (1866)
### http://laws.findlaw.com/us/71/2.html

In 1864, Lambdin P. Milligan, a southern sympathizer living in Indiana, was seized and tried on charges of disloyalty by a military commission in the military district of Indiana and sentenced to be hanged. A citizen of Indiana, but not in the military forces, Milligan objected to the jurisdiction of the military commission and sought a writ of habeas corpus in the U. S. circuit court. In 1863 Congress had authorized suspension of the writ, but Milligan insisted that the commission had no jurisdiction of his case. Sitting as circuit judges, Justice Davis and the district judge agreed to a division in order to certify the constitutional question to the Supreme Court. Meanwhile, Davis and others convinced President Andrew Johnson to stay Milligan's execution until the Supreme Court could decide the case. Majority: Davis, Chase, Clifford, Field, Grier, Miller, Nelson, Swayne, Wayne. Note that concurring justices Chase, Swayne, Miller, and Wayne did not accept Davis's sweeping restriction on Congress.

### MR. JUSTICE DAVIS delivered the opinion of the Court. . . .

During the late wicked Rebellion, the temper of the times did not allow that calmness and deliberation in discussion so necessary to a correct conclusion of a purely judicial question. *Then*, considerations of safety were mingled with the exercise of power, and feelings and interests prevailed which are happily terminated. *Now* that the public safety is assured, this question, as well as all others, can be discussed and decided without passion or the admixture of any element not required to form the legal judgment. We approach the investigation of this case, fully sensible of the magnitude of the inquiry and of the necessity of full and cautious deliberation.

The controlling question in the case is this: Upon the facts stated in Milligan's petition, and the exhibits filed, had the military commission mentioned in it jurisdiction, legally, to try and sentence him? Milligan, not a resident of one of the rebellious States, or a prisoner of war, but a citizen of Indiana for twenty years past, and never in the military or naval service, is while at his home, arrested by the military power of the United States, imprisoned, and, on certain criminal charges preferred against him, tried, convicted, and sentenced to be hanged by a military commission, organized under the direction of the military commander of the military district of Indiana. Had this tribunal the legal power and authority to try and punish this man?

No graver question was ever considered by this court, nor one which more nearly concerns the rights of the whole people, for it is the birthright of every American citizen when charged with crime to be tried and punished according to law. . . .

The Constitution of the United States is a law for rulers and people, equally in war and in peace, and covers with the shield of its protection all classes of men, at all times, and under all circumstances. No doctrine involving more pernicious consequences was ever intended by the wit of man than that any of its provisions can be suspended during any of the great exigencies of government. Such a doctrine leads directly to anarchy or despotism, but the theory of necessity on which it is based is false; for the government, within the Constitution, has all the powers granted to it which are necessary to preserve its existence; as has been happily proved by the result of the great effort to throw off its just authority.

Have any of the rights guaranteed by the Constitution been violated in the case of Milligan? and if so, what are they?

Every trial involves the exercise of judicial power; and from what source did the military commission that tried him derive their authority? Certainly no part of the judicial power of the country was conferred on them; because the Constitution expressly vests it "in one supreme court and such inferior courts as the Congress may from time to time ordain and establish," and it is not pretended that the commission was a court ordained and established by Congress. They cannot justify on the mandate of the President, because he is controlled by law, and has his appropriate sphere of duty, which is to execute, not to make, the laws; and there is "no unwritten criminal code to which resort can be had as a source of jurisdiction." . . .

Why was he not delivered to the Circuit Court of Indiana to be proceeded against according to law? No reason of necessity could be urged against it; because Congress had declared penalties against the offenses charged, provided for their punishment, and directed that court to hear and determine them. And soon after this military tribunal was ended, the Circuit Court met, peacefully transacted its business, and adjourned. It needed no bayonets to protect it, and required no military aid to execute its judgments. It was held in a State, eminently distinguished for patriotism, by judges commissioned during the

Rebellion, who were provided with juries, upright, intelligent, and selected by a marshal appointed by the President. The government had no right to conclude that Milligan, if guilty, would not receive in that court merited punishment. . . .

The discipline necessary to the efficiency of the army and navy required other and swifter modes of trial than are furnished by the common-law courts; and, in pursuance of the power conferred by the Constitution, Congress has declared the kinds of trial, and the manner in which they shall be conducted, for offenses committed while the party is in the military or naval service. Every one connected with these branches of the public service is amenable to the jurisdiction which Congress has created for their government, and, while thus serving, surrenders his right to be tried by the civil courts. All other persons, citizens of States where the courts are open, if charged with crime, are guaranteed the inestimable privilege of trial by jury. . . .

It is claimed that martial law covers with its broad mantle the proceedings of this military commission. The proposition is this: that in a time of war the commander of an armed force (if, in his opinion, the exigencies of the country demand it, and of which he is the judge) has the power, within the lines of his military district, to suspend all civil rights and their remedies, and subject citizens as well as soldiers to the rule of his will; and in the exercise of this lawful authority cannot be restrained, except by his superior officer or the President of the United States.

If this position is sound to the extent claimed, then when war exists, foreign or domestic, and the country is subdivided into military departments for mere convenience, the commander of one of them can, if he chooses, within his limits, on the plea of necessity, with the approval of the Executive, substitute military force for, and to the exclusion of, the laws, and punish all persons, as he thinks right and proper, without fixed or certain rules.

The statement of this proposition shows its importance; for, if true, republican government is a failure, and there is an end of liberty regulated by law. . . .

This nation, as experience has proved, cannot always remain at peace, and has no right to expect that it will always have wise and humane rulers, sincerely attached to the principles of the Constitution. Wicked men, ambitious of power, with hatred of liberty and contempt of law, may fill the place once occupied by Washington and Lincoln; and if this right is conceded, and the calamities of war again befall us, the dangers to human liberty are frightful to contemplate. . . .

The two remaining questions in this case must be answered in the affirmative. The suspension of the privilege of the writ of *habeas corpus* does not suspend the writ itself. The writ issues as a matter of course; and on the return made to it the court decides whether the party applying is denied the right of proceeding any further with it.

If the military trial of Milligan was contrary to law, then he was entitled, on the facts stated in his petition, to be discharged from custody by the terms of the act of Congress of March 3, 1863. . . .

### THE CHIEF JUSTICE [CHASE] delivered the following opinion. . . .

We think . . . that the power of Congress, in the government of the land and naval forces and of the militia, is not at all affected by the Fifth or any other amendment. . . .

We cannot doubt that, in such a time of public danger, Congress had power, under the Constitution, to provide for the organization of a military commission, and for trial by that commission of persons engaged in this conspiracy. The fact that the Federal courts were open was regarded by Congress as a sufficient reason for not exercising the power; but that fact could not deprive Congress of the right to exercise it. Those courts might be open and undisturbed in the execution of their functions, and yet wholly incompetent to avert threatened danger, or to punish, with adequate promptitude and certainty, the guilty conspirators. . . .

MR. JUSTICE WAYNE, MR. JUSTICE SWAYNE, and MR. JUSTICE MILLER concur with me in these views.

# Ex parte *Quirin*
## 317 U.S. 1, 63 S.Ct. 2, 97 L.Ed. 3 (1942)
### http://laws.findlaw.com/us/317/1.html

On June 13, 1942, a German submarine landed four saboteurs on Long Island, New York. Four days later, another German submarine landed four more saboteurs at Ponte Vedra Beach, Florida. Once ashore, all discarded their German Marine uniforms and assumed civilian dress. All had been born in Germany, but each had lived for several years in the United States. One (Haupt) was arguably an American citizen by virtue of the naturalization of his parents. After their capture in Chicago and New York City, President Franklin Roosevelt ordered that the captured saboteurs be tried by military commission, even though during 1942 the state and federal courts in all 48 states were functioning normally. Seven of the prisoners petitioned the U.S. District Court for the District of Columbia for a writ of habeas corpus. On appeal, the Supreme Court announced its judgment on July 31. Six of the prisoners were executed a few days later. The Chief Justice's opinion for the Court was issued on October 29. (More lengthy excerpts from the opinion may be found at www.prenhall.com/mason.) Majority: Stone, Black, Byrnes, Douglas, Frankfurter, Jackson, Reed, Roberts. Not participating: Murphy.

**MR. CHIEF JUSTICE STONE delivered the opinion of the Court. . . .**

The question for decision is whether the detention of petitioners by respondent for trial by Military Commission, appointed by Order of the President of July 2, 1942, on charges preferred against them purporting to set out their violations of the law of war and of the Articles of War, is in conformity to the laws and Constitution of the United States. . . .

Petitioners' main contention is that the President is without any statutory or constitutional authority to order the petitioners to be tried by military tribunal for offenses with which they are charged; that in consequence they are entitled to be tried in the civil courts with the safeguards, including trial by jury, which the Fifth and Sixth Amendments guarantee to all persons charged in such courts with criminal offenses. . . .

The Government . . . insists that petitioners must be denied access to the courts, both because they are enemy aliens or have entered our territory as enemy belligerents, and because the President's Proclamation undertakes in terms to deny such access to the class of persons defined by the Proclamation, which aptly describes the character and conduct of petitioners. It is urged that if they are enemy aliens or if the Proclamation has force, no court may afford the petitioners a hearing. But there is certainly nothing in the Proclamation to preclude access to the courts for determining its applicability to the particular case. . . .

Congress and the President, like the courts, possess no power not derived from the Constitution. . . . The Constitution . . . invests the President as Commander in Chief with the power to wage war which Congress has declared, and to carry into effect all laws passed by Congress for the conduct of war and for the government and regulation of the Armed Forces, and all laws defining and punishing offences against the law of nations, including those which pertain to the conduct of war.

By the Articles of War, Congress has provided rules for the government of the Army. It has provided for the trial and punishment, by courts martial, of violations of the Articles by members of the armed forces and by specified classes of persons associated or serving with the Army. But the Articles also recognize the "military commission" appointed by military command as an appropriate tribunal for the trial and punishment of offenses against the law of war not ordinarily tried by court martial. Articles 38 and 46 authorize the President, with certain limitations, to prescribe the procedure for military commissions. . . .

It is unnecessary for present purposes to determine to what extent the President as Commander in Chief has constitutional power to create military commissions without the support of Congressional legislation. For here Congress has authorized trial of offenses against the law of war before such commissions. We are concerned only with the question whether it is within the constitutional power of the national government to place petitioners upon trial before a military commission for the offenses with which they are charged. We must therefore first inquire whether any of the acts charged is an offense against the law of war cognizable before a military tribunal, and if so whether the Constitution prohibits the trial. . . . [A]s we shall show, these petitioners were charged with an offense against the law of war which the Constitution does not require to be tried by jury. . . .

By universal agreement and practice the law of war draws a distinction between the armed forces and the peaceful populations of belligerent nations and also between those who are lawful and unlawful combatants. Lawful combatants are subject to capture and detention as prisoners of war by opposing military forces. Unlawful combatants are likewise subject to capture and detention, but in addition they are subject to trial and punishment by military tribunals for acts which render their belligerency unlawful. The spy who secretly and without uniform passes the military lines of a belligerent in time of war, . . . or an enemy combatant who without uniform comes secretly through the lines for the purpose of waging war by destruction of life or property, are familiar examples of belligerents who are generally deemed not to be entitled to the status of prisoners of war, but to be offenders against the law of war subject to trial and punishment by military tribunals. . . .

Our Government, by thus defining lawful belligerents entitled to be treated as prisoners of war, has recognized that there is a class of unlawful belligerents not entitled to that privilege, including those who though combatants do not wear "fixed and distinctive emblems." And by Article 15 of the Articles of War Congress has made provision for their trial and punishment by military commission, according to "the law of war."

Citizenship in the United States of an enemy belligerent does not relieve him from the consequences of a belligerency which is unlawful because in violation of the law of war. Citizens who associate themselves with the military arm of the enemy government, and with its aid, guidance and direction enter this country bent on hostile acts are enemy belligerents within the meaning of the Hague Convention and the law of war. It is as an enemy belligerent that petitioner Haupt is charged with entering the United States, and unlawful belligerency is the gravamen of the offense of which he is accused. . . .

[P]etitioners insist that even if the offenses with which they are charged are offenses against the law of war, their trial is subject to the requirement of the Fifth Amendment that no person shall be held to answer for a capital or otherwise infamous crime unless on a presentment or indictment of a grand jury, and that such trials by Article III, § 2, and the Sixth Amendment must be by jury in a civil court. Before the Amendments, § 2 of Article III, the Judiciary Article, had provided: "The Trial of all Crimes, except in Cases of Impeachment, shall be by Jury," and had directed that "such Trial shall be held in the State where the said Crimes shall have been committed." . . .

In the light of . . . long-continued and consistent interpretation we must conclude that § 2 of Article III and the Fifth and Sixth Amendments cannot be taken to have extended the right to demand a jury to trials by military commission, or to have required that offenses against the law of war not triable by jury at common law be tried only in the civil courts. . . .

The exception from the Amendments of "cases arising in the land or naval forces" was not aimed at trials by military tribunals, without a jury, of such offenses against the law of war. Its objective was quite different—to authorize the trial by court martial of the members of our Armed Forces for all that class of crimes which under the Fifth and Sixth Amendments might otherwise have been deemed triable in the civil courts. . . .

We cannot say that Congress in preparing the Fifth and Sixth Amendments intended to extend trial by jury to the cases of alien or citizen offenders against the law of war otherwise triable by military commission, while withholding it from members of our own armed forces charged with infractions of the Articles of War punishable by death. . . . We conclude that the Fifth and Sixth Amendments did not restrict whatever authority was conferred by the Constitution to try offenses against the law of war by military commission, and that petitioners, charged with such an offense not required to be tried by jury at common law, were lawfully placed on trial by the Commission without a jury.

Petitioners, and especially petitioner Haupt, stress the pronouncement of this Court in the Milligan case, that the law of war "can never be applied to citizens in states which have upheld the authority of the government, and where the courts are open and their process

unobstructed." Elsewhere in its opinion, the Court was at pains to point out that Milligan, a citizen twenty years resident in Indiana, who had never been a resident of any of the states in rebellion, was not an enemy belligerent either entitled to the status of a prisoner of war or subject to the penalties imposed upon unlawful belligerents. We construe the Court's statement as to the inapplicability of the law of war to Milligan's case as having particular reference to the facts before it. From them the Court concluded that Milligan, not being a part of or associated with the armed forces of the enemy, was a non-belligerent, not subject to the law of war save as—in circumstances found not there to be present and not involved here—martial law might be constitutionally established.

The Court's opinion is inapplicable to the case presented by the present record. . . . Accordingly, we conclude that [the president's] Order convening the Commission was a lawful order. . . . It follows that the orders of the District Court should be affirmed, and that leave to file petitions for habeas corpus in this Court should be denied.

## *Korematsu* v. *United States*
## 323 U.S. 214, 65 S.Ct. 193, 89 L.Ed. 194 (1944)
## http://laws.findlaw.com/us/323/214.html

Shortly after America entered World War II in December 1941, President Roosevelt issued an executive order authorizing creation of military areas from which persons suspected of sabotage and espionage might be excluded. This order authorized military commanders to prescribe regulations controlling the right of persons to enter, leave, or remain in the areas. In 1942 Congress provided penalties for violation of these regulations. Acting under these executive and congressional authorizations, the Western Defense Command divided the Pacific Coast into two military areas and imposed restrictions on persons living in them, including a curfew that applied only to aliens and persons of Japanese ancestry. In *Hirabayashi* v. *United States* (1943), the Court unanimously upheld the curfew as a legitimate wartime measure. Soon after the curfew went into effect, the commanding general removed all Japanese, including many American citizens, to war relocation centers. Toyosaburo Korematsu, an American citizen who refused to leave his home in Alameda County, California, was convicted in U.S. district court for violation of the exclusion order. The Ninth Circuit Court of Appeals affirmed. Majority: Black, Douglas, Frankfurter, Reed, Rutledge, Stone. Dissenting: Jackson, Murphy, Roberts.

**MR. JUSTICE BLACK delivered the opinion of the Court. . . .**

It should be noted, to begin with, that all legal restrictions which curtail the civil rights of a single racial group are immediately suspect. That is not to say that all such restrictions are unconstitutional. It is to say that courts must subject them to the most rigid scrutiny. Pressing public necessity may sometimes justify the existence of such restrictions; racial antagonism never can. . . .

In the light of the principles we announced in the Hirabayashi Case, we are unable to conclude that it was beyond the war power of Congress and the Executive to exclude those of Japanese ancestry from the West Coast war area at the time they did. . . . [E]xclusion from a threatened area, no less than curfew, has a definite and close relationship to the prevention of espionage and sabotage. The military authorities, charged with the primary responsibility of defending our shores, concluded that curfew provided inadequate protection and ordered exclusion. They did so, as pointed out in our Hirabayashi opinion, in accordance with congressional authority to the military to say who should, and who should not, remain in the threatened areas. . . .

Like curfew, exclusion of those of Japanese origin was deemed necessary because of the presence of an unascertained number of disloyal members of the group, most of whom we have no doubt were loyal to this country. It was because we could not reject the finding of the military authorities that it was impossible to bring about an immediate segregation of the disloyal from the loyal that we sustained the validity of the curfew order as applying to the whole group. In the instant case, temporary exclusion of the entire group was rested by the military on the same ground. The judgment that exclusion of the whole group was for the same reason a military imperative answers the contention that the exclusion was in the nature of group punishment based on antagonism to those of Japanese origin. That there were members of the group who retained loyalties to Japan has been confirmed by investigations made subsequent to the exclusion. . . .

We uphold the exclusion order as of the time it was made and when the petitioner violated it. . . . In doing so, we are not unmindful of the hardships imposed by it upon a large group of American citizens . . . Compulsory exclusion of large groups of citizens from their homes, except under circumstances of direst emergency and peril, is inconsistent with our basic governmental institutions. But when under conditions of modern warfare our shores are threatened by hostile forces, the power to protect must be commensurate with the threatened danger. . . .

Our task would be simple, our duty clear, were this a case involving the imprisonment of a loyal citizen in a concentration camp because of racial prejudice. Regardless of the true nature of the assembly and relocation centers—and we deem it unjustifiable to call them concentration camps with all the ugly connotations that term implies—we are dealing specifically with nothing but an exclusion order. To cast this case into outlines of racial prejudice, without reference to the real military dangers which were presented, merely confuses the issue. Korematsu was not excluded from the Military Area because of hostility to him or his race. He was excluded because we are at war with the Japanese Empire, because the properly constituted military authorities feared an invasion of our West Coast and felt constrained to take proper security measures, because they decided that the military urgency of the situation demanded that all citizens of Japanese ancestry be segregated from the West Coast temporarily, and finally, because Congress, reposing its confidence in this time of war in our military leaders—as inevitably it must—determined that they should have the power to do just this. . . . We cannot—by availing ourselves of the calm perspective of hindsight—now say that at the time these actions were unjustified.

*Affirmed.*

MR. JUSTICE FRANKFURTER, concurring . . . [omitted].

MR. JUSTICE ROBERTS, dissenting . . . [omitted].

**MR. JUSTICE MURPHY, dissenting. . . .**

This exclusion of "all persons of Japanese ancestry, both alien and non-alien," from the Pacific Coast area on a plea of military necessity in the absence of martial law ought not to be approved. Such exclusion goes over "the very brink of constitutional power" and falls into the ugly abyss of racism. . . .

The judicial test of whether the Government, on a plea of military necessity, can validly deprive an individual of any of his constitutional rights is whether the deprivation is reasonably related to a public danger that is so "immediate, imminent, and impending" as not to admit of delay and not to permit the intervention of ordinary constitutional processes to alleviate the danger." . . .

[T]hat relation is lacking because the exclusion order necessarily must rely for its reasonableness upon the assumption that all persons of Japanese ancestry may have a dangerous tendency to commit sabotage and espionage and to aid our Japanese enemy in other ways. It is difficult to believe that reason, logic or experience could be marshalled in support of such an assumption. . . .

The main reasons relied upon by those responsible for the forced evacuation, therefore, do not prove a reasonable relation between the group characteristics of Japanese Americans and the dangers of invasion, sabotage and espionage. The reasons appear, instead, to be largely an accumulation of much of the misinformation, half-truths and insinuations that for years have been directed against Japanese Americans by people with racial and economic prejudices—the same people who have been among the foremost advocates of the evacuation. A military judgment based upon such racial and sociological considerations is not entitled to the great weight ordinarily given the judgments based upon strictly military considerations. . . .

I dissent, therefore, from this legalization of racism. . . .

**MR. JUSTICE JACKSON, dissenting. . . .**

Much is said of the danger to liberty from the Army program for deporting and detaining these citizens of Japanese extraction. But a judicial construction of the due process clause that will sustain this order is a far more subtle blow to liberty than the promulgation of the order itself. A military order, however unconstitutional, is not apt to last longer than the military emergency. Even during that period a succeeding commander may revoke it all. But once a judicial opinion rationalizes such an order to show that it conforms to the Constitution, or rather rationalizes the Constitution to show that the Constitution sanctions such an order, the Court for all time has validated the principle of racial discrimination in criminal procedure and of transplanting American citizens. The principle then lies about like a loaded weapon ready for the hand of any authority that can bring forward a plausible claim of an urgent need. Every repetition imbeds that principle more deeply in our law and thinking and expands it to new purposes. All who observe the work of the courts are familiar with what Judge Cardozo described as "the tendency of a principle to expand itself to the limit of its logic." . . . Nothing better illustrates this danger than does the Court's opinion in this case.

It argues that we are bound to uphold the conviction of Korematsu because we upheld one in *Hirabayashi* v. *United States* . . . when we sustained these orders in so far as they applied a curfew requirement to a citizen of Japanese ancestry. I think we would learn something from that experience.

In that case we were urged to consider only the curfew feature, that being all that technically was involved, because it was the only count necessary to sustain Hirabayashi's conviction and sentence. We yielded, and the Chief Justice guarded the opinion as carefully as language will do. He said: "Our investigation here does not go beyond the inquiry whether, in the light of all the relevant circumstances preceding and attending their promulgation, the challenged orders and statute *afforded a reasonable basis for the action taken in imposing the curfew.*" . . . "We decide only the issue as we have defined it— we decide only that the *curfew order* as applied, and at the time it was applied, was within the boundaries of the war power." . . . And again: "It is unnecessary to consider whether or to what extent *such findings would support orders differing from the curfew order.*" . . . [Italics supplied by Justice Jackson.] Now the principle of racial discrimination is pushed from support of mild measures to very harsh ones, and from temporary deprivations to indeterminate ones. And the precedent which it is said requires us to do so is *Hirabayashi*. The Court is now saying that in *Hirabayashi* we did decide the very things we there said we were not deciding. Because we said that these citizens could be made to stay in their homes during the hours of dark, it is said we must require them to leave home entirely; and if that, we are told they may also be taken into custody for deportation; and if that, it is argued they may also be held for some undetermined time in detention camps. How far the principle of this case would be extended before plausible reasons would play out, I do not know. . . .

I do not suggest that the courts should have attempted to interfere with the Army in carrying out its task. But I do not think they may be asked to execute a military expedient that has no place in law under the Constitution. I would reverse the judgment and discharge the prisoner.[1]

[1] Calling the internment "part of an unfortunate episode in our nation's history," the Justice Department in 1983 successfully petitioned the U.S. district court in San Francisco to set aside Korematsu's conviction. Claiming the government exaggerated the wartime security risks on the West Coast, Korematsu and other Japanese Americans then filed a suit for damages against the government. In 1984, the District Court for the District of Columbia ruled that the Korematsu litigation was barred by a six-year statute of limitations, for suits against the government. Reversing the district court, the court of appeals held 2–1 in 1986 that previously uncompensated internees could press their suit for damages. Important in the ruling was evidence that the government had concealed information that those interned did not pose a danger to national security during World War II. In *United States v. Hohri* (1987), the Supreme Court vacated the appeals court decision because the appeal should have been heard by the Court of Appeals for the Federal Circuit. During oral argument in *Hohri*, Solicitor General Charles Fried described the 1944 Korematsu ruling as the "greatest departure from the values for which we were fighting" during World War II. He accepted Justice Murphy's contention that the decision was based on "amateur socioanthropology" with a "racist cast." In 1988 the Supreme Court denied certiorari in *Hohri v. United States*, in which the Court of Appeals for the Federal Circuit had held that the statute of limitations barred the claims under the takings clause of the Fifth Amendment pressed by the interned citizens and their descendants. Congress then authorized token payments of $20,000 to surviving internees.—ED.

## *New York Times Company* v. *United States*
### 403 U.S. 713, 91 S.Ct. 2140, 29 L.Ed. 2d 822 (1971)

http://laws.findlaw.com/us/403/713.html

(This case is reprinted in Chapter Eleven, beginning on page 522.)

## *United States* v. *United States District Court*
### 407 U.S. 297, 92 S.Ct. 2125, 32 L.Ed. 2d 752 (1972)

http://laws.findlaw.com/us/407/297.html

During pretrial proceedings in a prosecution in the U.S. District Court for the Eastern District of Michigan for conspiracy to destroy government property, the court ordered the government to make full disclosure to one of the defendants of his conversations overheard by electronic surveillance instituted without a search warrant. The U.S. Court of Appeals for the Sixth Circuit denied the government's petition for a writ of mandamus to compel the district judge to vacate the disclosure order. Majority: Powell, Blackmun, Brennan, Burger, Douglas, Marshall, Stewart, White. Not participating: Rehnquist.

## MR. JUSTICE POWELL delivered the opinion of the Court.

The issue before us is an important one for the people of our country and their Government. It involves the delicate question of the President's power, acting through the Attorney General, to authorize electronic surveillance in internal security matters without prior judicial approval. Successive Presidents for more than one quarter of a century have authorized such surveillance in varying degrees, without guidance from the Congress or a definitive decision of this Court. This case brings the issue here for the first time. Its resolution is a matter of national concern, requiring sensitivity both to the Government's right to protect itself from unlawful subversion and attack and to the citizen's right to be secure in his privacy against unreasonable Government intrusion. . . .

Title III of the Omnibus Crime Control and Safe Streets Act . . . authorizes the use of electronic surveillance for classes of crimes carefully specified. . . . The Act represents a comprehensive attempt by Congress to promote more effective control of crime while protecting the privacy of individual thought and expression. . . .

Together with the elaborate surveillance requirements in Title III, there is the following proviso, 18 USC § 2511 (3):

Nothing contained in this chapter or in section 605 of the Communications Act of 1934 shall limit the constitutional power of the President to take such measures as he deems necessary to protect the Nation against actual or potential attack or other hostile acts of a foreign power, to obtain foreign intelligence information deemed essential to the security of the United States, or to protect national security information against foreign intelligence activities. *Nor shall anything contained in this chapter be deemed to limit the constitutional power of the President to take such measures as he deems necessary to protect the United States against the overthrow of the Government by force or other unlawful means, or against any other clear and present danger to the structure or existence of the Government.* The contents of any wire or oral communication intercepted by authority of the President in the exercise of the foregoing powers may be received in evidence in any trial hearing or other proceeding only where such interception was reasonable, and shall not be otherwise used or disclosed except as is necessary to implement that power. (Emphasis supplied [by Justice Powell]).

The Government relies on § 2511 (3). It argues that "in excepting national security surveillances from the Act's warrant requirement Congress recognized the President's authority to conduct such surveillances without prior judicial approval." . . . The section thus is viewed as a recognition or affirmance of a constitutional authority in the President to conduct warrantless domestic security surveillance such as that involved in this case.

We think the language of § 2511 (3), as well as the legislative history of the statute, refutes this interpretation. . . . At most, this is an implicit recognition that the President does have certain powers in the specified areas. Few would doubt this, as the section refers—among other things—to protection "against actual or potential attack or other hostile acts of a foreign power." But so far as the use of the president's electronic surveillance power is concerned, the language is essentially neutral.

Section 2511 (3) certainly confers no power, as the language is wholly inappropriate for such a purpose. It merely provides that the Act shall not be interpreted to limit or disturb such power as the President may have under the Constitution. In short, Congress simply left presidential powers where it found them. . . .

[N]othing in § 2511 (3) was intended to *expand* or to *contract* or to *define* whatever presidential surveillance powers existed in matters affecting the national security. If we could accept the Government's characterization of § 2511 (3) as a congressionally prescribed exception to the general requirement of a warrant, it would be necessary to consider the question of whether the surveillance in this case came within the exception and, if so, whether the statutory exception was itself constitutionally valid. But viewing § 2511 (3) as a congressional disclaimer and expression of neutrality, we hold that the statute is not the measure of the executive authority asserted in this case. Rather, we must look to the constitutional powers of the President.

It is important at the outset to emphasize the limited nature of the question before the Court. This case . . . requires no judgment on the scope of the President's surveillance power with respect to the activities of foreign powers, within or without this country. . . . There is no evidence of any involvement, directly or indirectly, of a foreign power.

Our present inquiry, though important, is therefore a narrow one. . . .

Though the Government and respondents debate their seriousness and magnitude, threats and acts of sabotage against the Government exist in sufficient number to justify investigative powers with respect to them. . . . It would be contrary to the public interest for Government to deny to itself the prudent and lawful employment of those very techniques which are employed against the Government and its law-abiding citizens. . . .

But a recognition of these elementary truths does not make the employment by Government of electronic surveillance a welcome development—even when employed with restraint and under judicial supervision. There is, understandably, a deepseated uneasiness and apprehension that this capability will be used to intrude upon cherished privacy of law-abiding citizens. . . .

History abundantly documents the tendency of Government—however benevolent and benign its motives—to view with suspicion those who most fervently dispute its policies. Fourth Amendment protections become the more necessary when the targets of official surveillance may be those suspected of unorthodoxy in their political beliefs. The danger to political dissent is acute where the Government attempts to act under so vague a concept as the power to protect "domestic security." Given the difficulty of defining the domestic security interest, the danger of abuse in acting to protect that interest becomes apparent. . . . The price of lawful public dissent must not be a dread of subjection to an unchecked surveillance power. Nor must the fear of unauthorized official eavesdropping deter vigorous citizen dissent and discussion of Government action in private conversation. For private dissent, no less than open public discourse, is essential to our free society.

As the Fourth Amendment is not absolute in its terms, our task is to examine and balance the basic values at stake in this case: the duty of Government to protect the domestic security, and the potential danger posed by unreasonable surveillance to individual privacy and free expression. If the legitimate need of Government to safeguard domestic security requires the use of electronic surveillance, the question is whether the needs of citizens for privacy and free expression may not be better protected by requiring a warrant before such surveillance is undertaken. We must also ask whether a warrant requirement would unduly frustrate the efforts of Government to protect itself from acts of subversion and overthrow directed against it. . . .

Fourth Amendment freedoms cannot properly be guaranteed if domestic security surveillances may be conducted solely within the discretion of the executive branch. The Fourth Amendment does not contemplate the executive officers of Government as neutral and disinterested magistrates. Their duty and responsibility is to enforce the laws, to investigate and to prosecute. . . .

The Fourth Amendment contemplates a prior judicial judgment, not the risk that executive discretion may be reasonably exercised. This judicial role accords with our basic constitutional doctrine that individual freedoms will best be preserved through a separation of powers and division of functions among the different branches and levels of Government. . . . The independent check upon executive discretion is not satisfied, as the Government argues, by "extremely limited" post-surveillance judicial review. Indeed, post-surveillance review would never reach the surveillances which failed to result in prosecutions. Prior review by a neutral and detached magistrate is the time-tested means of effectuating Fourth Amendment rights. . . .

The Government argues that the special circumstances applicable to domestic security surveillances necessitate a further exception to the warrant requirement. It is urged that the requirement of prior judicial review would obstruct the President in the discharge of his constitutional duty to protect domestic security. We are told further that these surveillances are directed primarily to the collecting and maintaining of intelligence with respect to subversive forces and are not an attempt to gather evidence for specific criminal prosecutions. It is said that this type of surveillance should not be subject to traditional warrant requirements which were established to govern investigation of criminal activity, not on-going intelligence gathering. . . .

The Government further insists that courts "as a practical matter would have neither the knowledge nor the techniques necessary to determine whether there was probable cause to believe that surveillance was necessary to protect national security." These security problems, the Government contends, involve "a large number of complex and subtle factors" beyond the competence of courts to evaluate. . . .

But we do not think a case has been made for the requested departure from Fourth Amendment standards. The circumstances described do not justify complete exemption of domestic security surveillance from prior judicial scrutiny. . . .

We cannot accept the Government's argument that internal security matters are too subtle and complex for judicial evaluation. Courts regularly deal with the most difficult issues of our society. There is no reason to believe that federal judges will be insensitive to or uncomprehending of the issues involved in domestic security cases. Certainly courts can recognize that domestic security surveillance involves different considerations from the surveillance of ordinary crime. If the threat is too subtle or complex for our senior law enforcement officers to convey its significance to a court, one may question whether there is probable cause for surveillance. . . .

Thus, we conclude that the Government's concerns do not justify departure in this case from the customary Fourth Amendment requirement of judicial approval prior to initiation of a search or surveillance. Although some added burden will be imposed upon the Attorney General, this inconvenience is justified in a free society to protect constitutional values. Nor do we think the Government's domestic surveillance powers will be impaired to any significant degree. A prior warrant establishes presumptive validity of the surveillance and will minimize the burden of justification in post-surveillance judicial review. By no means of least importance, will be the reassurance of the public generally that indiscriminate wiretapping and bugging of law-abiding citizens cannot occur. . . .

The judgment of the Court of Appeals is hereby

*Affirmed.*

MR. CHIEF JUSTICE BURGER, concurring . . . [omitted].

MR. JUSTICE WHITE, concurring . . . [omitted].

MR. JUSTICE DOUGLAS, concurring . . . [omitted].

## Hamdi v. Rumsfeld
### 316 F. 3d 450 (4th Cir. 2003)

http://laws.findlaw.com/4th/027338pv2.html

Yaser Esam Hamdi was born in Louisiana to Saudi parents but moved with them to Saudi Arabia when he was a child. In the fall of 2001 he was captured in Afghanistan when United States forces removed the Taliban government from power. Later detained at Guantanamo Bay, Cuba, he was designated an "enemy combatant" and transferred to the Norfolk Naval Station Brig in April 2002. His father challenged the lawfulness of his confinement without charges, access to a judicial tribunal, and the right to counsel, by initiating habeas corpus proceedings in the U.S. District Court for the Eastern District of Virginia. In August 2002, following some initial litigation, the district court held that the Defense Department's reliance on a declaration by Michael Mobbs (special adviser to the under secretary of defense for policy) that Hamdi was a combatant fell "far short" of justifying his detention. It ordered the government to produce, among other things, copies of Hamdi's statements and notes taken during interrogations, the names and addresses of all of his interrogators, and statements by members of the Northern Alliance concerning the circumstances of his capture. The Court of Appeals for the Fourth Circuit granted the government's petition for interlocutory review (an immediate appeal prior to the outcome of the case in the trial court). Following the decision by the appeals court, reprinted below, the Supreme Court granted Hamdi's petition for a writ of certiorari on January 9, 2004.

WILKINSON, CHIEF JUDGE, AND WILKINS AND TRAXLER, CIRCUIT JUDGES. . . .

[T]he United States challenges the district court's order requiring the production of various materials regarding Hamdi's status as an alleged enemy combatant. The district court certified for appeal the question of whether a declaration by a Special Advisor to the Under Secretary of Defense for Policy setting forth what the government contends were the circumstances of Hamdi's capture was sufficient by itself to justify his detention. Because it is undisputed that Hamdi was captured in a zone of active combat in a foreign theater of conflict, we hold that the submitted declaration is a sufficient basis upon which to conclude that the Commander in Chief has constitutionally detained Hamdi pursuant to the war powers entrusted to him by the United States Constitution. No further factual inquiry is necessary or proper, and we remand the case with directions to dismiss the petition. . . .

Yaser Esam Hamdi is apparently an American citizen. He was also captured by allied forces in Afghanistan, a zone of active military operations. This dual status—that of American citizen and that of alleged enemy combatant—raises important questions about the role of the courts in times of war. The importance of limitations on judicial activities during wartime may be inferred from the allocation of powers under our constitutional scheme. . . .

The war powers . . . invest "the President, as Commander in Chief with the power to wage war which Congress has declared, and to carry into effect all laws passed by Congress for the conduct of war and for the government and regulation of the Armed Forces, and allows defining and punishing offences against the law of nations, including those which pertain to the conduct of war." These powers include the authority to detain those captured in armed struggle. . . . Article III contains nothing analogous to the specific powers of war so carefully enumerated in Articles I and II. . . .

The reasons for this deference are not difficult to discern. Through their departments and committees, the executive and legislative branches are organized to supervise the conduct of overseas conflict in a way that the judiciary simply is not. The Constitution's allocation of the warmaking powers reflects not only the expertise and experience lodged within the executive, but also the more fundamental truth that those branches most accountable to the people should be the ones to undertake the ultimate protection and to ask the ultimate sacrifice from them. Thus the Supreme Court has lauded "[t]he operation of a healthy deference to legislative and executive judgments in the area of military affairs." The deference that flows from the explicit enumeration of powers protects liberty as much as the explicit enumeration of rights. The Supreme Court has underscored this founding principle: "The ultimate purpose of this separation of powers is to protect the liberty and security of the governed." Thus, the textual allocation of responsibilities and the textual enumeration of rights are not dichotomous, because the textual separation of powers promotes a more profound understanding of our rights. For the judicial branch to trespass upon the exercise of the warmaking powers would be an infringement of the right to self-determination and self-governance at a time when the care of the common defense is most critical. This right of the people is no less a right because it is possessed collectively. These interests do not carry less weight because the conflict in which Hamdi was captured is waged less against nation-states than against scattered and unpatriated forces. We have emphasized that the "unconventional aspects of the present struggle do not make its stakes any less grave." . . .

Despite the clear allocation of war powers to the political branches, judicial deference to executive decisions made in the name of war is not unlimited. . . .

The duty of the judicial branch to protect our individual freedoms does not simply cease whenever our military forces are committed by the political branches to armed conflict. . . . The detention of United States citizens must be subject to judicial review. . . .

The safeguards that all Americans have come to expect in criminal prosecutions do not translate neatly to the arena of armed conflict. In fact, if deference to the executive is not exercised with respect to military judgments in the field, it is difficult to see where deference would ever obtain. . . .

If anything, separation of powers bears renewed relevance to a struggle whose unforeseeable dangers may demand significant actions to protect untold thousands of American lives. The designation of Hamdi as an enemy combatant thus bears the closest imaginable connection to the President's constitutional responsibilities during the actual conduct of hostilities. . . .

On this appeal, it is argued that Hamdi's detention is invalid even if the government's assertions were entirely accurate. If that were clearly the case, there would be no need for further discovery such as that detailed in the August 16 production order, because Hamdi's detention would be invalid for reasons beyond the scope of any factual dispute. . . .

We also note that the order, if enforced, would present formidable practical difficulties. The district court indicated that its production request might well be only an initial step in testing the factual basis of Hamdi's enemy combatant status. The court plainly did not preclude making further production demands upon the government, even suggesting that it might "bring Hamdi before [the court] to inquire about [his] statements." . . .

The cost of such an inquiry in terms of the efficiency and morale of American forces cannot be disregarded. . . .

For the foregoing reasons, the court's August 16 production request cannot stand. . . .

Hamdi contends that, although international law and the laws of this country might generally allow for the detention of an individual captured on the battlefield, these laws must vary in his case because he is an American citizen now detained on American soil. As an American citizen, Hamdi would be entitled to the due process protections normally found in the criminal justice system, including the right to meet with counsel, if he had been charged with a crime. But as we have previously pointed out, Hamdi has not been charged with any crime. He is being held as an enemy combatant pursuant to the well-established laws and customs of war. Hamdi's citizenship rightfully entitles him to file this petition to challenge his detention, but the fact that he is a citizen does not affect the legality of his detention as an enemy combatant. Indeed, this same issue arose in [Ex parte] *Quirin*.

The Quirin principle applies here. One who takes up arms against the United States in a foreign theater of war, regardless of his citizenship, may properly be designated an enemy combatant and treated as such. The privilege of citizenship entitles Hamdi to a limited judicial inquiry into his detention, but only to determine its legality under the war powers of the political branches. At least where it is undisputed that he was present in a zone of active combat operations, we are satisfied that the Constitution does not entitle him to a searching review of the factual determinations underlying his seizure there. Similarly, we reject Hamdi's argument that even if his initial detention in Afghanistan was lawful, his continuing detention on American soil is not. Specifically, Hamdi contends that his petition does not implicate military concerns because "the underlying claims in this case are designed to test the legality of Hamdi's imprisonment in a naval brig in Norfolk, Virginia, not a military determination made overseas on the basis of caution rather than accuracy." But the fact that Hamdi is presently being detained in the United States—as opposed to somewhere overseas—does not affect the legal implications of his status as an enemy combatant. For the same reason that courts are ill-positioned to review the military's distinction between those who should or should not be detained in an arena of combat, courts are not in the position to overturn the military's decision to detain those persons in one location or another. . . .

To conclude, we hold that, despite his status as an American citizen currently detained on American soil, Hamdi is not entitled to challenge the facts presented in the Mobbs declaration. Where, as here, a habeas petitioner has been designated an enemy combatant and it is undisputed that he was captured in a zone of active combat operations abroad, further judicial inquiry is unwarranted when the government has responded to the petition by setting forth factual assertions which would establish a legally valid basis for the petitioner's detention. Because these circumstances are present here, Hamdi is not entitled to habeas relief on this basis.

Finally, we address Hamdi's contention that even if his detention was at one time lawful, it is no longer so because the relevant hostilities have reached an end. . . .

The executive branch is . . . in the best position to appraise the status of a conflict, and the cessation of hostilities would seem no less a matter of political competence than the initiation of them. . . .

The government notes that American troops are still on the ground in Afghanistan, dismantling the terrorist infrastructure in the very country where Hamdi was captured and engaging in reconstruction efforts which may prove dangerous in their own right. Because under the most circumscribed definition of conflict hostilities have not yet reached their end, this argument is without merit.

It is important to emphasize that we are not placing our imprimatur upon a new day of executive detentions. We earlier rejected the summary embrace of "a sweeping proposition—namely that, with no meaningful judicial review, any American citizen alleged to be an enemy combatant could be detained indefinitely without charges or counsel on the government's say-so." . . .

Hamdi's status as a citizen, as important as that is, cannot displace our constitutional order or the place of the courts within the Framer's scheme. Judicial review does not disappear during wartime, but the review of battlefield captures in overseas conflicts is a highly deferential one. That is why, for reasons stated, the judgment must be reversed and the petition dismissed.

*It is so ordered.*

# APPENDIX

# *The Constitution of the United States of America*

We the people of the United States, in order to form a more perfect Union, establish Justice, insure domestic Tranquility, provide for the common defence, promote the general Welfare, and secure the Blessings of Liberty to ourselves and our Posterity, do ordain and establish this CONSTITUTION for the United States of America.

## Article I

### SECTION 1

All legislative Powers herein granted shall be vested in a Congress of the United States, which shall consist of a Senate and House of Representatives.

### SECTION 2

The House of Representatives shall be composed of Members chosen every second Year by the People of the several States, and the Electors in each State shall have the Qualifications requisite for Electors of the most numerous Branch of the State Legislature.

No Person shall be a Representative who shall not have attained to the Age of twenty-five Years, and been seven Years a Citizen of the United States, and who shall not, when elected, be an Inhabitant of that State in which he shall be chosen.

[Representatives and direct Taxes shall be apportioned among the several States which may be included within this Union, according to their respective Numbers, which shall be determined by adding to the whole Number of Free Persons, including those bound to Service for a Term of Years, and excluding Indians not taxed, three fifths of all other persons.][1] The actual Enumeration shall be made within three Years after the first Meeting of the Congress of the United States, and within every subsequent Term of ten Years, in such Manner as they shall by Law direct. The Number of Representatives shall not exceed one for every thirty thousand, but each State shall have at least one Representative; and until such enumeration shall be made, the State of New Hampshire shall be entitled to chuse three, Massachusetts eight, Rhode Island and Providence Plantations one, Connecticut five, New York six, New Jersey four, Pennsylvania eight, Delaware one, Maryland six, Virginia ten, North Carolina five, South Carolina five, and Georgia three.

When vacancies happen in the Representation from any State, the Executive Authority thereof shall issue Writs of Election to fill such Vacancies.

The House of Representatives shall chuse their Speaker and other Officers; and shall have the sole Power of Impeachment.

### SECTION 3

The Senate of the United States shall be composed of two Senators from each State, chosen by

---

[1] This provision was modified by the Sixteenth Amendment. The three-fifths reference to slaves was rendered obsolete by the Thirteenth and Fourteenth Amendments.

the Legislature thereof,[2] for six Years; and each Senator shall have one Vote.

Immediately after they shall be assembled in Consequence of the first Election, they shall be divided as equally as may be into three Classes. The Seats of the Senators of the first Class shall be vacated at the Expiration of the second Year, of the Second Class at the Expiration of the fourth Year, and of the third Class at the Expiration of the sixth Year, so that one-third may be chosen every second Year; and if Vacancies happen by Resignation, or otherwise, during the Recess of the Legislature of any State, the Executive therefore may make temporary Appointments until the next Meeting of the Legislature, which shall then fill such Vacancies.

No Person shall be a Senator who shall not have attained to the Age of thirty Years, and been nine Years a Citizen of the United States, and who shall not, when elected, be an Inhabitant of that State in which he shall be chosen.

The Vice President of the United States shall be President of the Senate, but shall have no vote, unless they be equally divided.

The Senate shall chuse their other Officers, and also a President pro tempore, in the absence of the Vice President, or when he shall exercise the Office of President of the United States.

The Senate shall have the sole Power to try all Impeachments. When sitting for that Purpose, they shall be on Oath or Affirmation. When the President of the United States is tried, the Chief Justice shall preside; And no Person shall be convicted without the Concurrence of two thirds of the Members present.

Judgment in Cases of Impeachment shall not extend further than to removal from Office, and disqualification to hold and enjoy any Office of honor, Trust or Profit under the United States; but the Party convicted shall nevertheless be liable and subject to Indictment, Trial, Judgment, and Punishment, according to Law.

## SECTION 4

The Times, Places and Manner of holding Elections for Senators and Representatives, shall be prescribed in each State by the Legislature thereof; but the Congress may at any time by Law make or alter such Regulations, except as to the Places of chusing Senators.

The Congress shall assemble at least once in every Year, and such Meeting shall be on the first Monday in December, unless they shall by Law appoint a different Day.[3]

## SECTION 5

Each House shall be the Judge of the Elections, Returns and Qualifications of its own Members, and a Majority of each shall constitute a Quorum to do Business; but a smaller Number may adjourn from day to day, and may be authorized to compel the Attendance of absent Members, in such Manner, and under such Penalties, as each House may provide.

Each House may determine the Rules of its Proceedings, punish its Members for disorderly Behavior, and, with the Concurrence of two thirds, expel a Member.

Each House shall keep a Journal of its Proceedings and from time to time publish the same, excepting such Parts as may in their Judgment require Secrecy; and the Yeas and Nays of the Members of either House on any question shall, at the Desire of one fifth of those Present, be entered on the Journal.

Neither House, during the Session of Congress, shall without the Consent of the other, adjourn for more than three days, nor to any other Place than that in which the two Houses shall be sitting.

## SECTION 6

The Senators and Representatives shall receive a Compensation for their Services, to be ascertained by Law, and paid out of the Treasury of the United States. They shall in all Cases, except Treason, Felony, and Breach of the peace, be privileged from Arrest during their Attendance at the Session of their respective Houses, and in going to and returning from the same; and for any Speech or Debate in either House, they shall not be questioned in any other Place.

No Senator or Representative shall, during the Time for which he was elected, be appointed to any civil Office under the Authority of the United States, which shall have been created, or the Emoluments whereof shall have been encreased during such time; and no Person holding any Office under the United States shall be a Member of either House during his continuance in Office.

## SECTION 7

All Bills for raising Revenue shall originate in the House of Representatives; but the Senate may propose or concur with Amendments as on other Bills.

Every Bill which shall have passed the House of Representatives and the Senate, shall, before it

---

[2] This provision was modified by the Seventeenth Amendment.

[3] See the Twentieth Amendment.

become a Law, be presented to the President of the United States; if he approve he shall sign it, but if not he shall return it, with his Objections to that House in which it shall have originated, who shall enter the Objections at large on their Journal, and proceed to reconsider it. If after such Reconsideration two thirds of that House shall agree to pass the Bill it shall be sent, together with the Objections, to the other House, by which it shall likewise be reconsidered, and if approved by two thirds of that House, it shall become a Law. But in all such Cases the Votes of both Houses shall be determined by Yeas and Nays, and the Names of the Persons voting for and against the Bill shall be entered on the Journal of each House respectively. If any Bill shall not be returned by the President within ten Days (Sundays excepted) after it shall have been presented to him, the Same shall be a Law, in like Manner as if he had signed it, unless the Congress by their Adjournment prevent its Return, in which Case it shall not be a Law.

Every Order, Resolution, or Vote to which the Concurrence of the Senate and House of Representatives may be necessary (except on a question of Adjournment) shall be presented to the President of the United States; and before the Same shall take Effect, shall be approved by him, or being disapproved by him, shall be repassed by two thirds of the Senate and House of Representatives, according to the Rules and Limitations prescribed in the Case of a Bill.

## SECTION 8

The Congress shall have Power To lay and collect Taxes, Duties, Imposts and Excises, to pay the Debts and provide for the common Defence and general Welfare of the United States; but all Duties, Imposts and Excises shall be uniform throughout the United States;

To borrow money on the Credit of the United States;

To regulate Commerce with foreign Nations, and among the several States, and with the Indian Tribes;

To establish an uniform Rule of Naturalization, and uniform Laws on the subject of Bankruptcies throughout the United States;

To coin Money, regulate the Value thereof, and of foreign Coin, and fix the Standard of Weights and Measures;

To provide for the Punishment of counterfeiting the Securities and current Coin of the United States;

To Establish Post Offices and Post Roads;

To promote the Progress of Science and useful Arts, by securing for limited Times to Authors and Inventors the exclusive Right to their respective Writings and Discoveries;

To constitute Tribunals inferior to the supreme Court;

To define and punish Piracies and Felonies committed on the high Seas, and Offenses against the Law of Nations;

To declare War, grant Letters of Marque and Reprisal, and make Rules concerning Captures on Land and Water;

To raise and support Armies, but no Appropriation of Money to that Use shall be for a longer Term than two Years;

To provide and maintain a Navy;

To make Rules for the Government and Regulation of the land and naval Forces;

To provide for calling forth the Militia to execute the Laws of the Union, suppress Insurrections and repel Invasions;

To provide for organizing, arming, and disciplining the Militia, and for governing such Part of them as may be employed in the Service of the United States, reserving to the States respectively, the Appointment of the Officers, and the Authority of training the Militia according to the discipline prescribed by Congress;

To exercise exclusive Legislation in all Cases whatsoever, over such District (not exceeding ten Miles square) as may, by Cession of particular States, and the acceptance of Congress, become the Seat of the Government of the United States, and to exercise like Authority over all Places purchased by the Consent of the Legislature of the State in which the Same shall be, for the Erection of Forts, Magazines, Arsenals, dock-Yards, and other needful Buildings;—And

To make all Laws which shall be necessary and proper for carrying into Execution the foregoing Powers, and all other Powers vested by this Constitution in the Government of the United States, or in any Department or Officer thereof.

## SECTION 9

The Migration or Importation of such Persons as any of the States now existing shall think proper to admit, shall not be prohibited by the Congress prior to the Year, one thousand eight hundred and eight, but a tax or duty may be imposed on such Importation, not exceeding ten dollars for each person.

The privilege of the Writ of Habeas Corpus shall not be suspended, unless when in Cases of Rebellion or Invasion the public Safety may require it.

No Bill of Attainder or ex post facto Law shall be passed.

No capitation, or other direct Tax shall be laid, unless in Proportion to the Census or Enumeration herein before directed to be taken.[4]

No Tax or Duty shall be laid on Articles exported from any State.

No Preference shall be given by any Regulation of Commerce or Revenue to the Ports of one State over those of another: nor shall Vessels bound to, or from one State, be obliged to enter, clear, or pay Duties in another.

No Money shall be drawn from the Treasury, but in Consequence of Appropriations made by Law; and a regular Statement and Account of the Receipts and Expenditures of all public Money shall be published from time to time.

No Title of Nobility shall be granted by the United States:—And no Person holding any Office of Profit or Trust under them, shall, without the Consent of the Congress, accept of any present, Emolument, Office, or Title, of any kind whatever, from any King, Prince or foreign State.

## SECTION 10

No State shall enter into any Treaty, Alliance, or Confederation; grant Letters of Marque and Reprisal; coin Money; emit Bills of Credit; make any Thing but gold and silver Coin a Tender in Payment of Debts; pass any Bill of Attainder, ex post facto Law, or Law impairing the Obligation of Contracts, or grant any Title of Nobility.

No State shall, without the Consent of the Congress, lay any Imposts or Duties on Imports or Exports, except what may be absolutely necessary for executing its inspection Laws: and the net Produce of all Duties and Imposts, laid by any State on Imports or Exports, shall be for the Use of the Treasury of the United States and all such Laws shall be subject to the Revision and Controul of the Congress.

No State shall, without the Consent of Congress, lay any duty of Tonnage, keep Troops, or Ships of War in time of Peace, enter into any Agreement or Compact with another State, or with a foreign Power, or engage in War, unless actually invaded, or in such imminent Danger as will not admit of delay.

## Article II

### SECTION 1

The executive Power shall be vested in a President of the United States of America. He shall hold his Office during the Term of four Years, and,

together with the Vice-President, chosen for the same term, be elected, as follows.

Each State shall appoint, in such Manner as the Legislature thereof may direct, a number of Electors, equal to the whole number of Senators and Representatives to which the State may be entitled in the Congress; but no Senator or Representative, or Person holding an Office of Trust or Profit under the United States, shall be appointed an Elector.

The Electors shall meet in their respective States, and vote by Ballot for two persons, of whom one at least shall not be an Inhabitant of the same State with themselves. And they shall make a List of all the Persons voted for, and of the Number of Votes for each; which List they shall sign and certify, and transmit sealed to the Seat of the Government of the United States, directed to the President of the Senate. The President of the Senate shall, in the Presence of the Senate and House of Representatives, open all the Certificates, and the Votes shall then be counted. The Person having the greatest Number of Votes shall be the President, if such Number be a Majority of the whole Number of Electors appointed; and if there be more than one who have such Majority, and have an Equal Number of Votes, then the House of Representatives shall immediately chuse by Ballot one of them for President; and if no Person have a Majority, then from the five highest on the List the said House shall in like Manner chuse the President, but in chusing the President, the Votes shall be taken by States, the Representation from each State having one Vote; a quorum for this Purpose shall consist of a Member or Members from two-thirds of the States, and a Majority of all the States shall be necessary to a Choice. In every Case, after the Choice of the President, the Person having the greatest Number of Votes of the Electors shall be the Vice-President. But if there should remain two or more who have equal Votes, the Senate shall chuse from them by Ballot the Vice-President.[5]

The Congress may determine the Time of chusing the Electors, and the Day on which they shall give their Vote; which Day shall be the same throughout the United States.

No person except a natural born Citizen, or a Citizen of the United States, at the time of the Adoption of this Constitution, shall be eligible to the Office of President; neither shall any Person be eligible to that Office who shall not have attained to the Age of thirty-five Years, and been fourteen Years a Resident within the United States.

[4] See the Sixteenth Amendment.

[5] This paragraph was superseded by the Twelfth Amendment.

In Case of the Removal of the President from Office, or of his Death, Resignation, or Inability to discharge the Powers and Duties of the said Office, the same shall devolve on the Vice-President, and the Congress may by Law provide for the Case of Removal, Death, Resignation, or Inability, both of the President and Vice-President, declaring what Officer shall then act as President, and such Officer shall act accordingly, until the Disability be removed, or a President shall be elected.

The President shall, at stated Times, receive for his Services, a Compensation, which shall neither be encreased nor diminished during the Period for which he shall have been elected, and he shall not receive within that Period any other Emolument from the United States, or any of them.

Before he enters on the Execution of his Office, he shall take the following Oath or Affirmation: "I do solemnly swear (or affirm) that I will faithfully execute the Office of President of the United States, and will to the best of my Ability, preserve, protect and defend the Constitution of the United States."

### SECTION 2

The President shall be Commander in Chief of the Army and Navy of the United States, and of the Militia of the several States, when called into the actual Service of the United States; he may require the Opinion in writing, of the principal Officer in each of the executive Departments, upon any subject relating to the Duties of their respective Offices, and he shall have Power to grant Reprieves and Pardons for Offenses against the United States, except in Cases of Impeachment.

He shall have Power, by and with the Advice and Consent of the Senate, to make Treaties, provided two-thirds of the Senators present concur; and he shall nominate, and by and with the Advice and Consent of the Senate, shall appoint Ambassadors, other public Ministers and Consuls, Judges of the supreme Court, and all other Officers of the United States, whose Appointments are not herein otherwise provided for, and which shall be established by Law: but the Congress may by Law vest the Appointment of such inferior Officers, as they think proper, in the President alone, in the Courts of Law, or in the Heads of Departments.

The President shall have Power to fill up all Vacancies that may happen during the Recess of the Senate, by granting Commissions which shall expire at the End of their next Session.

### SECTION 3

He shall from time to time give to the Congress Information of the State of the Union, and recommend to their Consideration such Measures as he shall judge necessary and expedient; he may, on extraordinary Occasions, convene both Houses, or either of them, and in Cases of Disagreement between them, with Respect to the Time of Adjournment, he may adjourn them to such Time as he shall think proper; he shall receive Ambassadors and other public Ministers; he shall take Care that the Laws be faithfully executed, and shall Commission all the Officers of the United States.

### SECTION 4

The President, Vice-President and all civil Officers of the United States, shall be removed from Office on Impeachment for, and Conviction of, Treason, Bribery, or other high Crimes and Misdemeanors.

## Article III

### SECTION 1

The judicial Power of the United States, shall be vested in one supreme Court, and in such inferior Courts as the Congress may from time to time ordain and establish. The Judges, both of the supreme and inferior Courts, shall hold their offices during good Behaviour, and shall, at stated Times, receive for their Services a Compensation, which shall not be diminished during their Continuance in Office.

### SECTION 2

The judicial Power shall extend to all Cases, in Law and Equity, arising under this Constitution, the Laws of the United States and Treaties made, or which shall be made, under their Authority;—to all Cases affecting Ambassadors, other public Ministers and Consuls;—to all Cases of admiralty and maritime Jurisdiction;—to Controversies to which the United States shall be a Party;—to Controversies between two or more States;—between a State and Citizens of another State;[6]—Between Citizens of different States;—between Citizens of the same State claiming Lands under Grants of different States, and between a State, or the Citizens thereof, and foreign States, Citizens or Subjects.

In all Cases affecting Ambassadors, other public Ministers and Consuls, and those in which a State shall be a Party, the supreme Court shall have original Jurisdiction. In all the other Cases before mentioned, the supreme Court shall have appellate Jurisdiction, both as to Law and Fact, with such Exceptions, and under such Regulations as the Congress shall make.

[6]See the Eleventh Amendment.

The trial of all Crimes, except in Cases of Impeachment, shall be by Jury, and such Trial shall be held in the State where the said Crimes shall have been committed; but when not committed within any State, the Trial shall be at such Place or Places as the Congress may by Law have directed.

### SECTION 3

Treason against the United States, shall consist only in levying War against them, or, in adhering to their Enemies, giving them Aid and Comfort. No Person shall be convicted of Treason unless on the Testimony of two Witnesses to the same overt Act, or on Confession in open Court.

The Congress shall have Power to declare the Punishment of Treason, but no Attainder of Treason shall work Corruption of Blood, or Forfeiture except during the Life of the Person attainted.

## Article IV

### SECTION 1

Full Faith and Credit shall be given in each State to the public acts, Records, and judicial Proceedings of every other State. And the Congress may by general Laws prescribe the Manner in which such Acts, Records and Proceedings shall be proved, and the Effect thereof.

### SECTION 2

The Citizens of each State shall be entitled to all Privileges and Immunities of Citizens in the several States.

A person charged in any State with Treason, Felony, or other Crime, who shall flee from Justice, and be found in another State, shall on demand of the executive Authority of the State from which he fled, be delivered up, to be removed to the State having Jurisdiction of the Crime.

No Person held to Service or Labour in one State, under the Laws thereof, escaping into another, shall, in Consequence of any Law or Regulation therein, be discharged from such Service or Labour, but shall be delivered up on Claim of the Party to whom such Service or Labour may be due.[7]

### SECTION 3

New States may be admitted by the Congress into this Union; but no new States shall be formed or erected within the Jurisdiction of any other State;

---

[7]Obsolete. See the Thirteenth Amendment.

---

nor any State be formed by the Junction of two or more States, or parts of States, without the Consent of the Legislatures of the States concerned as well as of the Congress.

The Congress shall have Power to dispose of and make all needful Rules and Regulations respecting the Territory or other Property belonging to the United States; and nothing in this Constitution shall be so constructed as to Prejudice any Claims of the United States, or of any particular State.

### SECTION 4

The United States shall guarantee to every State in this Union a Republican Form of Government, and shall protect each of them against Invasion; and on Application of the Legislature, or of the Executive (when the Legislature cannot be convened) against domestic Violence.

## Article V

The Congress, whenever two-thirds of both Houses shall deem it necessary, shall propose Amendments to this Constitution, or, on the Application of the Legislatures of two-thirds of the several States, shall call a Convention for proposing Amendments, which, in either Case, shall be valid to all Intents and Purposes, as part of this Constitution, when ratified by the Legislatures of three-fourths of the several States, or by Conventions in three-fourths thereof, as the one or the other Mode of Ratification may be proposed by the Congress; Provided that no Amendment which may be made prior to the Year One thousand eight hundred and eight shall in any Manner affect the first and fourth Clauses in the Ninth Section of the first Article; and that no State, without its Consent, shall be deprived of its equal Suffrage in the Senate.

## Article VI

All Debts contracted and Engagements entered into, before the Adoption of this Constitution, shall be as valid against the United States under this Constitution, as under the Confederation.

This Constitution, and the Laws of the United States which shall be made in Pursuance thereof; and all Treaties made, or which shall be made, under the Authority of the United States, shall be the supreme Law of the Land; and the Judges in every State shall be bound thereby, any Thing in the Constitution or Laws of any State to the Contrary notwithstanding.

The Senators and Representatives before mentioned, and the Members of the several State Legislatures, and all executive and judicial Officers, both of the United States and of the several States, shall be bound by Oath or Affirmation, to support this Constitution; but no religious Test shall ever be required as a Qualification to any Office or public Trust under the United States.

## Article VII

The Ratification of the Conventions of nine States shall be sufficient for the Establishment of this Constitution between the States so ratifying the Same.

Done in Convention by the Unanimous Consent of the States Present the Seventeenth Day of September in the Year of our Lord one thousand seven hundred and eighty-seven and of the Independence of the United States of America the Twelfth. In Witness whereof We have hereunto subscribed our Names. [Names of signatories omitted.—ED.]

## AMENDMENTS[8]

## Amendment I

Congress shall make no law respecting an establishment of religion, or prohibiting the free exercise thereof; or abridging the freedom of speech, or of the press; or the right of the people peaceably to assemble, and to petition the Government for a redress of grievances.

## Amendment II

A well regulated Militia, being necessary to the security of a free State, the right of the people to keep and bear Arms, shall not be infringed.

## Amendment III

No Soldier shall, in time of peace be quartered in any house, without the consent of the Owner, nor in time of war, but in a manner to be prescribed by law.

## Amendment IV

The right of the people to be secure in their persons, houses, papers, and effects, against unreasonable searches and seizures, shall not be violated, and no Warrants shall issue, but upon probable cause, supported by Oath or affirmation, and

particularly describing the place to be searched, and the persons or things to be seized.

## Amendment V

No person shall be held to answer for a capital, or otherwise infamous crime, unless on a presentment or indictment of a Grand Jury, except in cases arising in the land or naval forces, or in the Militia, when in actual service in time of War or public danger; nor shall any person be subject for the same offense to be twice put in jeopardy of life or limb, nor shall be compelled in any criminal case to be a witness against himself, nor be deprived of life, liberty, or property, without due process of law; nor shall private property be taken for public use, without just compensation.

## Amendment VI

In all criminal prosecutions, the accused shall enjoy the right to a speedy and public trial, by an impartial jury of the State and district wherein the crime shall have been committed, which district shall have been previously ascertained by law, and to be informed of the nature and cause of the accusation; to be confronted with the witnesses against him; to have compulsory process for obtaining witnesses in his favor, and to have the Assistance of Counsel for his defence.

## Amendment VII

In suits at common law, where the value in controversy shall exceed twenty dollars, the right of trial by jury shall be preserved, and no fact tried by jury, shall be otherwise reexamined in any Court of the United States, than according to the rules of the common law.

## Amendment VIII

Excessive bail shall not be required, nor excessive fines imposed, nor cruel and unusual punishments inflicted.

## Amendment IX

The enumeration in the Constitution, of certain rights, shall not be construed to deny or disparage others retained by the people.

## Amendment X

The powers not delegated to the United States by the Constitution, nor prohibited by it to the States, are reserved to the States respectively, or to the people.

[8] The first ten amendments were adopted in 1791 as the Bill of Rights.

## Amendment XI (1798)

The Judicial power of the United States shall not be construed to extend to any suit in law or equity, commenced or prosecuted against one of the United States by Citizens of another State, or by Citizens or Subjects of any Foreign States.

## Amendment XII (1804)

The Electors shall meet in their respective states and vote by ballot for President and Vice-President, one of whom, at least, shall not be an inhabitant of the same state with themselves; they shall name in their ballots the person voted for as President, and in distinct ballots the person voted for as Vice-President, and they shall make distinct lists of all persons voted for as president, and all persons voted for as Vice-President, and of the number of votes for each, which lists they shall sign and certify, and transmit sealed to the seat of the government of the United States, directed to the President of the Senate;—The President of the Senate shall, in the presence of the Senate and House of Representatives, open all the certificates and the votes shall then be counted;—The person having the greatest number of votes for President, shall be the President, if such number be a majority of the whole number of Electors appointed; and if no person have such majority, then from the persons having the highest numbers not exceeding three on the list of those voted for as President, the House of Representatives shall choose immediately, by ballot, the President. But in choosing the President, the votes shall be taken by states, the representation from each state having one vote; a quorum for this purpose shall consist of a member or members from two-thirds of the states, and a majority of all the states shall be necessary to a choice. And if the House of Representatives shall not choose a President whenever the right of choice shall devolve upon them, before the fourth day of March next following, then the Vice-President shall act as President, as in the case of the death or other constitutional disability of the President.—The person having the greatest number of votes as Vice-President, shall be the Vice-President, if such number be a majority of the whole number of Electors appointed, and if no person have a majority, then from the two highest numbers on the list, the Senate shall choose the Vice-President; a quorum for the purpose shall consist of two-thirds of the whole number of Senators, and a majority of the whole number shall be necessary to a choice. But no person constitutionally ineligible to the office of the President shall be eligible to that of Vice-President of the United States.

## Amendment XIII (1865)

### SECTION 1

Neither slavery nor involuntary servitude, except as a punishment for crime whereof the party shall have been duly convicted, shall exist within the United States, or any place subject to their jurisdiction.

### SECTION 2

Congress shall have power to enforce this article by appropriate legislation.

## Amendment XIV (1868)

### SECTION 1

All persons born or naturalized in the United States and subject to the jurisdiction thereof, are citizens of the United States and of the State wherein they reside. No State shall make or enforce any law which shall abridge the privileges or immunities of citizens of the United States; nor shall any State deprive any person of life, liberty, or property, without due process of law; nor deny to any person within its jurisdiction the equal protection of the laws.

### SECTION 2

Representatives shall be apportioned among the several States according to their respective numbers, counting the whole number of persons in each State, excluding Indians not taxed. But when the right to vote at any election for the choice of electors for President and Vice-President of the United States, Representatives in Congress, the Executive and Judicial Officers of a State, or the members of the Legislature thereof, is denied to any of the male inhabitants of such State, being twenty-one years of age, and citizens of the United States, or in any way abridged, except for participation in rebellion, or other crime, the basis of representation therein shall be reduced in the proportion which the number of such male citizens shall bear to the whole number of male citizens twenty-one years of age in such State.

### SECTION 3

No person shall be a Senator or Representative in Congress, or elector of President and Vice-President, or hold any office, civil or military, under the United States, or under any State, who, having previously taken an oath, as a member of Congress, or as an officer of the United States, or as a member of any State legislature, or as an executive or judicial officer of any State, to support the Constitution of the United States, shall have engaged in insurrection or rebellion against the same, or given aid or comfort to the enemies thereof. But Congress may by a vote of two-thirds of each House, remove such disability.

## SECTION 4

The validity of the public debt of the United States, authorized by law, including debts incurred for payment of pensions and bounties for services in suppressing insurrection or rebellion, shall not be questioned. But neither the United States nor any State shall assume or pay any debt or obligation incurred in aid of insurrection or rebellion against the United States, or any claim for the loss or emancipation of any slave; but all such debts, obligations, and claims shall be held illegal and void.

## SECTION 5

The Congress shall have power to enforce, by appropriate legislation, the provisions of this article.

## Amendment XV (1870)

### SECTION 1

The right of citizens of the United States to vote shall not be denied or abridged by the United States or by any State on account of race, color, or previous condition of servitude.

### SECTION 2

The Congress shall have the power to enforce this article by appropriate legislation.

## Amendment XVI (1913)

The Congress shall have power to lay and collect taxes on incomes, from whatever source derived, without apportionment among the several States, and without regard to any census or enumeration.

## Amendment XVII (1913)

The Senate of the United States shall be composed of two Senators from each State, elected by the people thereof, for six years, and each Senator shall have one vote. The electors in each State shall have the qualifications requisite for electors of the most numerous branch of the State legislatures.

When vacancies happen in the representation of any State in the Senate, the executive authority of such State shall issue writs of election to fill such vacancies: Provided, That the legislature of any State may empower the executive thereof to make temporary appointments until the people fill the vacancies by election as the legislature may direct.

This amendment shall not be so construed as to affect the election or term of any Senator chosen before it becomes valid as part of the Constitution.

## Amendment XVIII (1919)[9]

### SECTION 1

After one year from the ratification of this article the manufacture, sale, or transportation of intoxicating liquors within, the importation thereof into, or the exportation thereof from the United States and all territory subject to the jurisdiction thereof for beverage purposes is hereby prohibited.

### SECTION 2

The Congress and the several States shall have concurrent power to enforce this article by appropriate legislation.

### SECTION 3

This article shall be inoperative unless it shall have been ratified as an amendment to the Constitution by the legislatures of the several States, as provided in the Constitution, within seven years from the date of the submission hereof to the States by the Congress.

## Amendment XIX (1920)

The right of citizens of the United States to vote shall not be denied or abridged by the United States or by any State on account of sex.

Congress shall have power to enforce this article by appropriate legislation.

## Amendment XX (1933)

### SECTION 1

The terms of the President and Vice-President shall end at noon on the 20th day of January, and the terms of Senators and Representatives at noon on the 3rd day of January, of the years in which such terms would have ended if this article had not been ratified; and the terms of their successors shall then begin.

### SECTION 2

The Congress shall assemble at least once in every year, and such meeting shall begin at noon

---

[9] Repealed by the Twenty-first Amendment.

on the 3rd day of January, unless they shall by law appoint a different day.

### SECTION 3

If, at the time fixed for the beginning of the term of the President, the President elect shall have died, the Vice-President elect shall become President. If a President shall not have been chosen before the time fixed for the beginning of his term, or if the President elect shall have failed to qualify, then the Vice-President elect shall act as President until a President shall have qualified; and the Congress may by law provide for the case wherein neither a President elect nor a Vice-President elect shall have qualified, declaring who shall then act as President, or the manner in which one who is to act shall be selected, and such person shall act accordingly until a President or Vice-President shall have qualified.

### SECTION 4

The Congress may by law provide for the case of the death of any of the persons from whom the House of Representatives may choose a President whenever the right of choice shall have devolved upon them, and for the case of the death of any of the persons from whom the Senate may choose a Vice-President whenever the right of choice shall have devolved upon them.

### SECTION 5

Sections 1 and 2 shall take effect on the 15th day of October following the ratification of this article.

### SECTION 6

This article shall be inoperative unless it shall have been ratified as an amendment to the Constitution by the legislatures of three-fourths of the several States within seven years from the date of its submission.

## Amendment XXI (1933)[10]

### SECTION 1

The eighteenth article of amendment to the Constitution of the United States is hereby repealed.

### SECTION 2

The transportation or importation into any State, Territory, or possession of the United States for

---

[10] This is the only amendment to date to have been ratified not by state legislatures but by specially called conventions in the states.

delivery or use of intoxicating liquors, in violation of the laws thereof, is hereby prohibited.

### SECTION 3

This article shall be inoperative unless it shall have been ratified as an amendment to the Constitution by conventions in the several States, as provided in the Constitution, within seven years from the date of the submission hereof to the states by the Congress.

## Amendment XXII (1951)

### SECTION 1

No person shall be elected to the office of the President more than twice, and no person who has held the office of President, or acted as President, for more than two years of a term to which some other person was elected President shall be elected to the office of President more than once. But this Article shall not apply to any person holding the office of President when this Article was proposed by the Congress, and shall not prevent any person who may be holding the office of President, or acting as President, during the term within which this Article becomes operative from holding the office of President, or acting as President during the remainder of such term.

### SECTION 2

This article shall be inoperative unless it shall have been ratified as an amendment to the Constitution by the legislatures of three-fourths of the several States within seven years from the date of its submission to the States by the Congress.

## Amendment XXIII (1961)

### SECTION 1

The District constituting the seat of Government of the United States shall appoint in such manner as the Congress may direct:

A number of electors of President and Vice-President equal to the whole number of Senators and Representatives in Congress to which the District would be entitled if it were a State, but in no event more than the least populous State; they shall be in addition to those appointed by the States, but they shall be considered, for the purposes of the election of President and Vice-President, to be electors appointed by a state; and they shall meet in the District and perform such duties as provided by the twelfth article of amendment.

## SECTION 2

The Congress shall have power to enforce this article by appropriate legislation.

### Amendment XXIV (1964)

#### SECTION 1

The right of citizens of the United States to vote in any primary or other election for President or Vice-President, for electors for President or Vice-President, or for Senator or Representative in Congress, shall not be denied or abridged by the United States or any State by reason of failure to pay any poll tax or other tax.

#### SECTION 2

The Congress shall have power to enforce this article by appropriate legislation.

### Amendment XXV (1967)

#### SECTION 1

In case of the removal of the President from office or his death or resignation, the Vice-President shall become President.

#### SECTION 2

Whenever there is a vacancy in the office of the Vice-President, the President shall nominate a Vice-President who shall take the office upon confirmation by a majority vote of both houses of Congress.

#### SECTION 3

Whenever the President transmits to the President pro tempore of the Senate and the Speaker of the House of Representatives his written declaration that he is unable to discharge the powers and duties of his office, and until he transmits to them a written declaration to the contrary, such powers and duties shall be discharged by the Vice-President as Acting President.

#### SECTION 4

Whenever the Vice-President and a majority of either the principal officers of the executive departments or of such other body as Congress may by law provide, transmit to the President pro tempore of the Senate and the Speaker of the House of Representatives their written declaration that the President is unable to discharge the powers and duties

of his office, the Vice-President shall immediately assume the powers and duties of the office as Acting President.

Thereafter, when the President transmits to the President pro tempore of the Senate and the Speaker of the House of Representatives his written declaration that no inability exists, he shall resume the powers and duties of his office unless the Vice-President and a majority of either the principal officers of the executive department or of such other body as Congress may by law provide, transmit within four days to the President pro tempore of the Senate and the Speaker of the House of Representatives their written declaration that the President is unable to discharge the powers and duties of his office. Thereupon Congress shall decide the issue, assembling within 48 hours for that purpose if not in session. If the Congress, within 21 days after receipt of the latter written declaration, or, if Congress is not in session, within 21 days after Congress is required to assemble, determines by two-thirds vote of both houses that the President is unable to discharge the powers and duties of his office, the Vice-President shall continue to discharge the same as Acting President; otherwise, the President shall resume the powers and duties of his office.

### Amendment XXVI (1971)

#### SECTION 1

The Right of Citizens of the United States, who are eighteen years of age or older, to vote shall not be denied or abridged by the United States or any State on account of age.

#### SECTION 2

The Congress shall have the power to enforce this article by appropriate legislation.

### Amendment XXVII (1992)

No law varying the compensation for the services of the Senators and Representatives shall take effect, until an election of Representatives shall have intervened.[11]

---

[11]This is the so-called Lost Amendment, proposed in 1789 along with 11 others submitted to the states. One of the 11 was never ratified; the other ten were ratified in 1791 as the Bill of Rights. With no limitation imposed on the time allowed for ratification, the remaining amendment was finally adopted more than two centuries later.

**Table 1: Justices of the Supreme Court (arranged by natural court)***

| Year | | | | | | | | | | |
|---|---|---|---|---|---|---|---|---|---|---|
| 1789 | Jay | Rutledge, J. | Cushing | Wilson | Blair | | | | | |
| 1790–1791 | Jay | Rutledge, J. | Cushing | Wilson | Blair | Iredell | | | | |
| 1792 | Jay | Johnson, T. | Cushing | Wilson | Blair | Iredell | | | | |
| 1792–1794 | Jay | Paterson | Cushing | Wilson | Blair | Iredell | | | | |
| 1795 | Rutledge, J. | Paterson | Cushing | Wilson | Blair | Iredell | | | | |
| 1796–1797 | Ellsworth | Paterson | Cushing | Wilson | Chase, S. | Iredell | | | | |
| 1798–1799 | Ellsworth | Paterson | Cushing | Washington | Chase, S. | Iredell | | | | |
| 1800 | Ellsworth | Paterson | Cushing | Washington | Chase, S. | Moore | | | | |
| 1801–1803 | Marshall, J. | Paterson | Cushing | Washington | Chase, S. | Moore | | | | |
| 1804–1805 | Marshall, J. | Paterson | Cushing | Washington | Chase, S. | Johnson, W. | | | | |
| 1806 | Marshall, J. | Livingston | Cushing | Washington | Chase, S. | Johnson, W. | | | | |
| 1807–1810 | Marshall, J. | Livingston | Cushing | Washington | Chase, S. | Johnson, W. | Todd | | | |
| 1811–1822 | Marshall, J. | Livingston | Story | Washington | Duvall | Johnson, W. | Todd | | | |
| 1823–1825 | Marshall, J. | Thompson | Story | Washington | Duvall | Johnson, W. | Todd | | | |
| 1826–1828 | Marshall, J. | Thompson | Story | Washington | Duvall | Johnson, W. | Trimble | | | |
| 1829 | Marshall, J. | Thompson | Story | Washington | Duvall | Johnson, W. | McLean | | | |
| 1830–1834 | Marshall, J. | Thompson | Story | Baldwin | Duvall | Johnson, W. | McLean | | | |
| 1835 | Marshall, J. | Thompson | Story | Baldwin | Duvall | Wayne | McLean | | | |
| 1836 | Taney | Thompson | Story | Baldwin | Barbour | Wayne | McLean | | | |
| 1837–1840 | Taney | Thompson | Story | Baldwin | Barbour | Wayne | McLean | Catron | McKinley | |
| 1841–1844 | Taney | Thompson | Story | Baldwin | Daniel | Wayne | McLean | Catron | McKinley | |
| 1845 | Taney | Nelson | Woodbury | | Daniel | Wayne | McLean | Catron | McKinley | |
| 1846–1850 | Taney | Nelson | Woodbury | Grier | Daniel | Wayne | McLean | Catron | McKinley | |
| 1850–1852 | Taney | Nelson | Curtis | Grier | Daniel | Wayne | McLean | Catron | McKinley | |
| 1853–1857 | Taney | Nelson | Curtis | Grier | Daniel | Wayne | McLean | Catron | Campbell | |
| 1858–1860 | Taney | Nelson | Clifford | Grier | Daniel | Wayne | McLean | Catron | Campbell | |
| 1861 | Taney | Nelson | Clifford | Grier | | Wayne | McLean | Catron | Campbell | |
| 1862 | Taney | Nelson | Clifford | Grier | Miller | Wayne | Swayne | Catron | Davis | |
| 1863 | Taney | Nelson | Clifford | Grier | Miller | Wayne | Swayne | Catron | Davis | Field |
| 1864–1865 | Chase, S. P. | Nelson | Clifford | Grier | Miller | Wayne | Swayne | Catron | Davis | Field |
| 1866–1867 | Chase, S. P. | Nelson | Clifford | Grier | Miller | Wayne | Swayne | | Davis | Field |
| 1868–1869 | Chase, S. P. | Nelson | Clifford | Grier | Miller | | Swayne | | Davis | Field |
| 1870–1871 | Chase, S. P. | Nelson | Clifford | Strong | Miller | Bradley | Swayne | | Davis | Field |
| 1872–1873 | Chase, S. P. | Hunt | Clifford | Strong | Miller | Bradley | Swayne | | Davis | Field |
| 1874–1876 | Waite | Hunt | Clifford | Strong | Miller | Bradley | Swayne | | Davis | Field |
| 1877–1879 | Waite | Hunt | Clifford | Strong | Miller | Bradley | Swayne | | Harlan (I) | Field |

| Year | | | | | | | | | |
|---|---|---|---|---|---|---|---|---|---|
| 1880 | Waite | Hunt | Clifford | Woods | Miller | Bradley | Swayne | Harlan (I) | Field |
| 1881 | Waite | Hunt | Clifford | Woods | Miller | Bradley | Matthews | Harlan (I) | Field |
| 1882–1887 | Waite | Blatchford | Gray | Woods | Miller | Bradley | Matthews | Harlan (I) | Field |
| 1888 | Fuller | Blatchford | Gray | Lamar, L. | Miller | Bradley | Matthews | Harlan (I) | Field |
| 1889 | Fuller | Blatchford | Gray | Lamar, L. | Miller | Bradley | Brewer | Harlan (I) | Field |
| 1890–1891 | Fuller | Blatchford | Gray | Lamar, L. | Brown | Bradley | Brewer | Harlan (I) | Field |
| 1892 | Fuller | Blatchford | Gray | Lamar, L. | Brown | Shiras | Brewer | Harlan (I) | Field |
| 1893 | Fuller | Blatchford | Gray | Jackson, H. | Brown | Shiras | Brewer | Harlan (I) | Field |
| 1894 | Fuller | White, E. | Gray | Jackson, H. | Brown | Shiras | Brewer | Harlan (I) | Field |
| 1895–1897 | Fuller | White, E. | Gray | Peckham | Brown | Shiras | Brewer | Harlan (I) | Field |
| 1898–1901 | Fuller | White, E. | Gray | Peckham | Brown | Shiras | Brewer | Harlan (I) | McKenna |
| 1902 | Fuller | White, E. | Holmes | Peckham | Brown | Shiras | Brewer | Harlan (I) | McKenna |
| 1903–1905 | Fuller | White, E. | Holmes | Peckham | Brown | Day | Brewer | Harlan (I) | McKenna |
| 1906–1908 | Fuller | White, E. | Holmes | Peckham | Moody | Day | Brewer | Harlan (I) | McKenna |
| 1909 | Fuller | White, E. | Holmes | Peckham | Moody | Day | Brewer | Harlan (I) | McKenna |
| 1910–1911 | White, E. | Van Devanter | Holmes | Lurton | Lamar, J. | Day | Hughes | Harlan (I) | McKenna |
| 1912–1913 | White, E. | Van Devanter | Holmes | Lurton | Lamar, J. | Day | Hughes | Pitney | McKenna |
| 1914–1915 | White, E. | Van Devanter | Holmes | McReynolds | Lamar, J. | Day | Hughes | Pitney | McKenna |
| 1916–1920 | White, E. | Van Devanter | Holmes | McReynolds | Brandeis | Day | Clarke | Pitney | McKenna |
| 1921 | Taft | Van Devanter | Holmes | McReynolds | Brandeis | Day | Clarke | Pitney | McKenna |
| 1922 | Taft | Van Devanter | Holmes | McReynolds | Brandeis | Day | Sutherland | Pitney | McKenna |
| 1923–1924 | Taft | Van Devanter | Holmes | McReynolds | Brandeis | Butler | Sutherland | Sanford | McKenna |
| 1925–1929 | Taft | Van Devanter | Holmes | McReynolds | Brandeis | Butler | Sutherland | Sanford | Stone |
| 1930–1931 | Hughes | Van Devanter | Holmes | McReynolds | Brandeis | Butler | Sutherland | Roberts | Stone |
| 1932–1936 | Hughes | Van Devanter | Cardozo | McReynolds | Brandeis | Butler | Sutherland | Roberts | Stone |
| 1937 | Hughes | Black | Cardozo | McReynolds | Brandeis | Butler | Sutherland | Roberts | Stone |
| 1938 | Hughes | Black | Cardozo | McReynolds | Brandeis | Butler | Reed | Roberts | Stone |
| 1939 | Hughes | Black | Frankfurter | McReynolds | Douglas | Butler | Reed | Roberts | Stone |
| 1940 | Hughes | Black | Frankfurter | McReynolds | Douglas | Murphy | Reed | Roberts | Stone |
| 1941–1942 | Stone | Black | Frankfurter | Byrnes | Douglas | Murphy | Reed | Roberts | Jackson, R. |
| 1943–1944 | Stone | Black | Frankfurter | Rutledge, W. | Douglas | Murphy | Reed | Roberts | Jackson, R. |
| 1945 | Stone | Black | Frankfurter | Rutledge, W. | Douglas | Murphy | Reed | Burton | Jackson, R. |
| 1946–1948 | Vinson | Black | Frankfurter | Rutledge, W. | Douglas | Murphy | Reed | Burton | Jackson, R. |
| 1949–1952 | Vinson | Black | Frankfurter | Minton | Douglas | Clark | Reed | Burton | Jackson, R. |
| 1953–1954 | Warren | Black | Frankfurter | Minton | Douglas | Clark | Reed | Burton | Jackson, R. |
| 1955 | Warren | Black | Frankfurter | Minton | Douglas | Clark | Reed | Burton | Harlan (II) |

**Table 1: Justices of the Supreme Court (arranged by natural court)\* (Continued)**

| | | | | | | | | | |
|---|---|---|---|---|---|---|---|---|---|
| 1956 | Warren | Black | Frankfurter | Brennan | Douglas | Clark | Reed | Burton | Harlan (II) |
| 1957 | Warren | Black | Frankfurter | Brennan | Douglas | Clark | Whittaker | Burton | Harlan (II) |
| 1958–1961 | Warren | Black | Frankfurter | Brennan | Douglas | Clark | Whittaker | Stewart | Harlan (II) |
| 1962–1965 | Warren | Black | Goldberg | Brennan | Douglas | Clark | White, B. | Stewart | Harlan (II) |
| 1965–1967 | Warren | Black | Fortas | Brennan | Douglas | Clark | White, B. | Stewart | Harlan (II) |
| 1967–1969 | Warren | Black | Fortas | Brennan | Douglas | Marshall, T. | White, B. | Stewart | Harlan (II) |
| 1969 | Warren | Black | Fortas | Brennan | Douglas | Marshall, T. | White, B. | Stewart | Harlan (II) |
| 1969–1970 | Burger | Black | | Brennan | Douglas | Marshall, T. | White, B. | Stewart | Harlan (II) |
| 1970–1971 | Burger | Black | Blackmun | Brennan | Douglas | Marshall, T. | White, B. | Stewart | Harlan (II) |
| 1971–1975 | Burger | Powell | Blackmun | Brennan | Douglas | Marshall, T. | White, B. | Stewart | Rehnquist |
| 1975–1981 | Burger | Powell | Blackmun | Brennan | Stevens | Marshall, T. | White, B. | Stewart | Rehnquist |
| 1981–1986 | Burger | Powell | Blackmun | Brennan | Stevens | Marshall, T. | White, B. | O'Connor | Rehnquist |
| 1986–1987 | Rehnquist | Powell | Blackmun | Brennan | Stevens | Marshall, T. | White, B. | O'Connor | Scalia |
| 1987 | Rehnquist | | Blackmun | Brennan | Stevens | Marshall, T. | White, B. | O'Connor | Scalia |
| 1988–1990 | Rehnquist | Kennedy | Blackmun | Brennan | Stevens | Marshall, T. | White, B. | O'Connor | Scalia |
| 1990–1991 | Rehnquist | Kennedy | Blackmun | Souter | Stevens | Marshall, T. | White, B. | O'Connor | Scalia |
| 1991–1993 | Rehnquist | Kennedy | Blackmun | Souter | Stevens | Thomas | White, B. | O'Connor | Scalia |
| 1993–1994 | Rehnquist | Kennedy | Blackmun | Souter | Stevens | Thomas | Ginsburg | O'Connor | Scalia |
| 1994– | Rehnquist | Kennedy | Breyer | Souter | Stevens | Thomas | Ginsburg | O'Connor | Scalia |

\*A "natural court" or "discrete court" refers to the period of time in which the Supreme Court's membership is stable.

# Table 2: Presidents and Justices*

| President | Justices Appointed | Years of Service | Age at Start of Term |
|---|---|---|---|
| Washington (F) | | 1789–1797 | 52 |
| | Jay (F)** | 1789–1795 | 43 |
| | J. Rutledge (F)@ | 1789–1791 | 50 |
| | Cushing (F) | 1789–1810 | 57 |
| | Wilson (F) | 1789–1798 | 47 |
| | Blair (F) | 1789–1796 | 57 |
| | Iredell (F) | 1790–1799 | 38 |
| | Johnson (F) | 1791–1793 | 58 |
| | Paterson (F) | 1793–1806 | 47 |
| | J. Rutledge (F)**§ | 1795 | 55 |
| | S. Chase (F) | 1796–1811 | 54 |
| | Ellsworth (F)** | 1796–1800 | 50 |
| Adams, J. (F) | | 1797–1801 | 61 |
| | Washington (F) | 1798–1829 | 36 |
| | Moore (F) | 1799–1804 | 44 |
| | J. Marshall (F)** | 1801–1835 | 45 |
| Jefferson (DR) | | 1801–1809 | 57 |
| | Johnson (DR) | 1804–1834 | 32 |
| | Livingston (DR) | 1806–1823 | 49 |
| | Todd (DR) | 1807–1826 | 42 |
| Madison (DR) | | 1809–1817 | 57 |
| | Duval (DR) | 1812–1835 | 58 |
| | Story (DR) | 1812–1845 | 32 |
| Monroe (DR) | | 1817–1825 | 58 |
| | Thompson (DR) | 1823–1843 | 55 |
| Adams, J. Q. (DR) | | 1825–1829 | 57 |
| | Trimble (DR) | 1826–1828 | 49 |
| Jackson (D) | | 1829–1837 | 61 |
| | McLean (D) | 1829–1861 | 43 |
| | Baldwin (D) | 1830–1844 | 49 |
| | Wayne (D) | 1835–1867 | 45 |
| | Taney (D)** | 1836–1864 | 58 |
| | Barbour (D) | 1836–1841 | 52 |
| | Catron (D) | 1837–1865 | 51 |
| Van Buren (D) | | 1837–1841 | 54 |
| | McKinley (D) | 1837–1852 | 57 |
| | Daniel (D) | 1841–1860 | 56 |
| Harrison, W. (W)# | | 1841 | 68 |
| Tyler (W) | | 1841–1845 | 50 |
| | Nelson (W) | 1845–1872 | 52 |
| Polk (D) | | 1845–1849 | 49 |
| | Woodbury (D) | 1845–1851 | 56 |
| | Grier (D) | 1846–1870 | 52 |
| Taylor (W)# | | 1849–1850 | 65 |
| Fillmore (W) | | 1850–1853 | 50 |
| | Curtis (W) | 1851–1857 | 42 |
| Pierce (D) | | 1853–1857 | 48 |
| | Campbell (D) | 1853–1861 | 41 |
| Buchanan (D) | | 1857–1861 | 65 |
| | Clifford (D) | 1858–1881 | 54 |
| Lincoln (R) | | 1861–1865 | 52 |
| | Swayne (R) | 1862–1881 | 57 |
| | Miller (R) | 1862–1890 | 46 |
| | Davis (R) | 1862–1877 | 47 |
| | Field (D) | 1863–1897 | 46 |
| | S. P. Chase (R)** | 1864–1873 | 56 |
| Johnson, A. (D)# | | 1865–1869 | 56 |

# Table 2: Presidents and Justices* (*Continued*)

| President | Justices Appointed | Years of Service | Age at Start of Term |
|---|---|---|---|
| Grant (R) | | 1869–1877 | 46 |
| | Strong (R) | 1870–1880 | 61 |
| | Bradley (R) | 1870–1892 | 56 |
| | Hunt (R) | 1872–1882 | 62 |
| | Waite (R)** | 1874–1888 | 57 |
| Hayes (R) | | 1877–1881 | 54 |
| | Harlan, I (A)& | 1877–1911 | 44 |
| | Woods (R) | 1880–1887 | 56 |
| Garfield (R) | | 1881 | 49 |
| | Matthews (R) | 1881–1889 | 56 |
| Arthur (R) | | 1881–1885 | 50 |
| | Gray (R) | 1881–1902 | 53 |
| | Blatchford (R) | 1882–1893 | 62 |
| Cleveland (D) | | 1885–1889 | 47 |
| | Lamar (D) | 1888–1893 | 62 |
| | Fuller (D)** | 1888–1910 | 55 |
| Harrison, B (R) | | 1889–1893 | 55 |
| | Brewer (R) | 1889–1910 | 52 |
| | Brown (R) | 1891–1906 | 54 |
| | Shiras (R) | 1892–1903 | 60 |
| | H. Jackson (D) | 1893–1895 | 60 |
| Cleveland (D) | | 1893–1897 | 55 |
| | E. White (D)@ | 1894–1910 | 48 |
| | Peckham (D) | 1896–1909 | 57 |
| McKinley (R) | | 1897–1901 | 54 |
| | McKenna (R) | 1898–1925 | 54 |
| Roosevelt, T. (R) | | 1901–1909 | 42 |
| | Holmes | 1902–1932 | 61 |
| | Day (R) | 1903–1922 | 53 |
| | Moody (R) | 1906–1910 | 52 |
| Taft (R) | | 1909–1913 | 51 |
| | Lurton (D) | 1909–1914 | 65 |
| | Hughes (R)@ | 1910–1916 | 48 |
| | E. White† (D)** | 1910–1921 | 65 |
| | Van Devanter (R) | 1910–1937 | 51 |
| | Lamar (D) | 1910–1916 | 53 |
| | Pitney (R) | 1912–1922 | 54 |
| Wilson (D) | | 1913–1921 | 56 |
| | McReynolds (D) | 1914–1941 | 52 |
| | Brandeis (R) | 1916–1939 | 59 |
| | Clarke (D) | 1916–1922 | 59 |
| Harding (R) | | 1921–1923 | 55 |
| | Taft (R)** | 1921–1930 | 63 |
| | Sutherland (R) | 1922–1938 | 60 |
| | Butler (D) | 1922–1939 | 56 |
| | Sanford (R) | 1923–1930 | 57 |
| Coolidge (A) | | 1923–1929 | 50 |
| | Stone (R)@ | 1925–1941 | 52 |
| Hoover (R) | | 1929–1933 | 54 |
| | Hughes (R)** | 1930–1941 | 68 |
| | Roberts (R) | 1930–1945 | 55 |
| | Cardozo (D) | 1932–1938 | 61 |
| Roosevelt, F. (D) | | 1933–1945 | 51 |
| | Black (D) | 1937–1971 | 51 |
| | Reed (D) | 1938–1957 | 53 |
| | Frankfurter (Ind) | 1939–1962 | 56 |
| | Douglas (D) | 1939–1975 | 40 |

## Table 2: Presidents and Justices* (*Continued*)

| President | Justices Appointed | Years of Service | Age at Start of Term |
|---|---|---|---|
| | Murphy (D) | 1940–1949 | 49 |
| | Byrnes (D) | 1941–1942 | 62 |
| | Stone⁺ (R)** | 1941–1946 | 68 |
| | R. Jackson (D) | 1941–1954 | 49 |
| | W. Rutledge (D) | 1943–1949 | 48 |
| Truman (D) | | 1945–1953 | 60 |
| | Burton (R) | 1945–1958 | 57 |
| | Vinson (D)** | 1946–1953 | 56 |
| | Clark (D) | 1949–1967 | 49 |
| | Minton (D) | 1949–1956 | 58 |
| Eisenhower (R) | | 1953–1961 | 62 |
| | Warren (R)** | 1953–1969 | 62 |
| | Harlan, II (R)ᐞ | 1955–1971 | 55 |
| | Brennan (D) | 1956–1990 | 50 |
| | Whittaker (R) | 1957–1962 | 56 |
| | Stewart (R) | 1958–1981 | 43 |
| Kennedy (D) | | 1961–1963 | 43 |
| | B. White (D) | 1962–1993 | 44 |
| | Goldberg (D) | 1962–1965 | 54 |
| Johnson, L. (D) | | 1963–1969 | 55 |
| | Fortas (D) | 1965–1969 | 55 |
| | T. Marshall (D) | 1967–1991 | 58 |
| Nixon (R) | | 1969–1974 | 56 |
| | Burger (R)** | 1969–1986 | 61 |
| | Blackmun (R) | 1970–1994 | 61 |
| | Powell (D) | 1971–1987 | 64 |
| | Rehnquist (R)@ | 1971–1986 | 47 |
| Ford (R) | | 1974–1977 | 61 |
| | Stevens (R) | 1975– | 55 |
| Carter (D)# | | 1977–1981 | 52 |
| Reagan (R) | | 1981–1989 | 70 |
| | O'Connor (R) | 1981– | 51 |
| | Rehnquist⁺ (R)** | 1986– | 61 |
| | Scalia (R) | 1986– | 50 |
| | Kennedy (R) | 1988– | 51 |
| Bush, G. (R) | | 1989–1993 | 64 |
| | Souter (R) | 1990– | 51 |
| | Thomas (R) | 1991– | 43 |
| Clinton (D) | | 1993–2001 | 46 |
| | Ginsburg (D) | 1993– | 60 |
| | Breyer (D) | 1994– | 55 |
| Bush, G. W. (R) | | 2001– | 54 |

*Letter following name indicates political party affiliation.

(F)—Federalist

(DR)—Democratic-Republican

(D)—Democrat

(W)—Whig

(R)—Republican

(Ind)—Independent

**Denotes appointment as chief justice.

@Later appointed as chief justice.

⁺Indicates appointment from associate to chief justice.

#Indicates no appointments to Supreme Court.

§Holding a recess appointment, John Rutledge presided over the Supreme Court at the August Term, 1795, but was denied confirmation by the Senate in December 1795.

ᐞJohn Marshall Harlan (I) was a grandfather of John Marshall Harlan (II) and is thus far the only justice to have had a lineal descendant who also became a justice.

# Index of Cases[1]

[1]**Boldface type** indicates opinions reprinted in this volume and the pages at which they may be found. *Lightface italic type* denotes cases cited in the essays, case headnotes, and case footnotes inserted by the author. See pages 34–35 for information on the reporting of judicial decisions.

# Index of Subjects and Names[1]

[1]**Boldface type** indicates the pages at which excerpted opinions and other writings can be found.